Canada
a Lonely Planet travel survival kit

Mark Lightbody
Dorinda Talbot
Jim DuFresne
Tom Smallman

Canada

6th edition

Published by
Lonely Planet Publications
Head Office: PO Box 617, Hawthorn, Vic 3122, Australia
Branches: 155 Filbert St, Suite 251, Oakland, CA 94607, USA
10 Barley Mow Passage, Chiswick, London W4 4PH, UK
71 bis rue du Cardinal Lemoine, 75005 Paris, France

Printed by
Colorcraft Ltd, Hong Kong

Photographs by

W Barrett	JR Graham	James Lyon	Nick Robinson
M Beedell	Colleen Kennedy	W Oliver	Tom Smallman
Jim DuFresne	Mark Lightbody	Parks Canada	Deanna Swaney
Richard Everist	W Lynch	Province of BC	Dorinda Talbot

Front cover: 'Castles of the New World' – Grain elevators in southern Alberta (Mark Lightbody)

First Published
March 1983

This Edition
February 1997

Although the authors and publisher have tried to make the information as accurate as possible, they accept no responsibility for any loss, injury or inconvenience sustained by any person using this book.

National Library of Australia Cataloguing in Publication Data

Lightbody, Mark
  Canada – a travel survival kit

  6th ed.
  Includes index.
  ISBN 0 86442 409 4

  1.Canada – Guidebooks. I. Talbot, Dorinda. II. DuFresne, Jim. III. Title. (Series: Lonely Planet travel survival kit)

917.104647

text & maps © Lonely Planet 1997
photos © photographers as indicated 1997

Mark Lightbody

As well as being the coordinating author on this edition, Mark also updated Quebec, Alberta, British Columbia and the Yukon and Northwest Territories. He was born and grew up in Montreal and was educated there and in London, Ontario. He holds an honours degree in journalism. Among a variety of occupations, he's worked in radio news and in the specialty graphics industry. Mark has travelled in nearly 50 countries, visiting every continent but Antarctica. He made his first foray across Canada at the age of four. Since then he has repeated the trip numerous times using plane, train, car and thumb.

Besides writing and updating the Lonely Planet guide to Canada, Mark has worked on former editions of LP's *Papua New Guinea, Australia, Malaysia, Singapore & Brunei* and *South-East Asia. He now lives in Toronto.*

Dorinda Talbot

Dorinda updated the Ontario, Manitoba and Saskatchewan chapters. Born in Melbourne, Australia, she began travelling at the age of 18 months – to visit her grandparents in Blighty – and has since taken in a fair slice of the world, including Papua New Guinea, South-East Asia, the United States, Britain and Europe.

After studying journalism at Deakin University in Geelong, Dorinda began work as a reporter in Alice Springs. She went on to work as a sub-editor in Melbourne before embarking on the traditional Aussie sojourn to London, England. She has worked as a freelance sub-editor in Cambridge, for numerous magazine titles in London, as a banana vendor in Brixton Market, a sandwich maker in Pall Mall and now has visions of becoming a travel writer.

Jim DuFresne

Jim updated the Newfoundland, Nova Scotia, Prince Edward Island and New Brunswick chapters. He is a former sports and outdoors editor of the *Juneau Empire* and the first Alaskan sportswriter to win a national award from Associated Press. He is presently a freelance writer, specialising in outdoor and travel writing. His other books for Lonely Planet include *Alaska* and *Tramping in New Zealand*. He has also written guides to Isle Royale, Voyageurs and Glacier Bay national parks.

Tom Smallman

Tom was born and raised in the UK where he was educated. He now lives in Melbourne, Australia. He had a number of jobs before joining Lonely Planet as an editor in 1988 and is now working full time as an author. As well as working as a co-author on previous editions of *Canada* and updating a substantial amount of the previous (5th) edition of this book, he coordinated the 2nd edition of the *Ireland* guide, helped to update the 2nd edition of the *Dublin* city guide and worked on *New York, New Jersey & Pennsylvania.*

From the Authors

Mark Lightbody It's very gratifying to have a book reach its sixth edition, to see that it has successfully met the test of time and the critical eyes of real travellers. But along with the satisfaction comes the increased challenge to improve, distil and concentrate further. In my research I'm always looking for the hole, the gap, for what is essential and may have been missed. These now, I trust, are few but I'm convinced the more you travel around Canada, the bigger it gets.

For this edition for the first time there were three of us out and about in places near and far, small and large. The research has never been more thorough or more complete and we hope this will be evident. In 17,000 km on the roads I know I've never talked so much to so many people.

Special thanks go to Colleen Kennedy for research assistance, editorial help, a range of suggestions and countless phone calls. Diane Carpentier supplied much help with the Montreal chapter. Nina Chung of Hostelling International – Canada in Ottawa and Lloyd Jones of Backpackers' Canada both offered generous support. Special thanks also go to Dave Burgess in Victoria for the time he freely spent revealing his knowledge. Also in Victoria, thanks to Beth Wilcox and Dave Pollock for advice and hospitality. Ditto for Brad Piekkola in Nanaimo who supplied hot tea and conversation while bouncing along miles of logging roads. In Yellowknife, Melissa Daoust at the Visitor Centre offered a lot of useful informal information as well as admirably answering scores of questions in her official capacity. Thanks also to Konrad Sechley for technical assistance day or night.

Again, warm thanks to those who sent letters, many of whom will see that their information was not only interesting but helpful and useful. Lastly, thanks to the travellers around the country who supplied personally the kinds of tips you only come across out on the road.

Dorinda Talbot I would especially like to thank fellow author Mark Lightbody, his wife Colleen, and Jonathan Gilbert for their assistance, support and encouragement. Many thanks also to the helpful tourist-office staff across Ontario, Manitoba and Saskatchewan. Thanks to Keith Thorsteinson and Vicki McMillan for their Saskatchewan hospitality; to Sean Collins for revealing all in Regina; to André Guindon of Parks Canada; to Michael Brady, Joyce Coupland, Cloudia Rohrbach, and Carol Waters; to the LP staff in both London and Melbourne – in particular to Dan Levin for much-needed computer expertise; and to all the other travellers along the way.

Jim DuFresne I'm an American but I live north of Canada. Honestly! That's because Detroit is one of those geographic oddities in actually being situated north of Windsor. All my life I could see Canada and over time learned that there are no friendlier people than Canadians. My extensive trip into the Maritime provinces to research a portion of this book only confirmed that notion.

I deeply appreciate the assistance of every travel official, park ranger and local innkeeper that gave me a bit of information, a little insight or pointed me in the right direction. But I am especially indebted to Donald and Kathy McKay of St John's, Newfoundland when a blood clot forced me into a longer than expected stay at their home. Like any Canadian would, they lent me a spare bedroom, arranged for me to see doctors, and assisted with all my needs until I was ready to move on.

Americans are awfully lucky to have neighbours like the Canadians to the north of us ... or in my case, just to the south.

This Book

The first three editions were researched and updated by Mark Lightbody, the fourth and fifth editions were updated by Mark Lightbody and Tom Smallman. For this edition Mark was joined by Dorinda Talbot and Jim DuFresne.

From the Publisher

This edition was coordinated by Chris Wyness in the Melbourne office. Additional editing was done by Lindsay Brown, with help from Cathy Oliver, Kirsten John, Paul Harding, Adrienne Costanzo, Mary Neighbour and Brigitte Barta. Andrew Tudor coordinated the design and mapping, and took the book through layout with the help of Jane Hart. Michael Weldon drew the chapter ends while other illustrations were done by Richard Stewart, Tamsin Wilson, Rose Keevins and Tracey O'Mara. David Kemp and Michael Signal designed the cover. The coordinating editor would also like to thank Bruce Baird and Sean Collins for the help they gave the authors while Vancouver and Regina were being researched.

Warning & Request

Things change – prices go up, schedules change, good places go bad and bad places go bankrupt – nothing stays the same. So, if you find things better or worse, recently opened or long since closed, please tell us and help make the next edition even more accurate and useful.

We value all of the feedback we receive from travellers. Julie Young coordinates a small team who read and acknowledge every letter, postcard and email, and ensure that every morsel of information finds its way to the appropriate authors, editors and publishers.

Everyone who writes to us will find their name in the next edition of the appropriate guide and will also receive a free subscription to our quarterly newsletter, *Planet Talk*. The very best contributions will be rewarded with a free Lonely Planet guide.

Excerpts from your correspondence may appear in updates (which we add to the end pages of reprints); new editions of this guide; in our newsletter, *Planet Talk*; or in the Postcards section of our Web site – so please let us know if you don't want your letter published or your name acknowledged.

Thanks

Many thanks to the travellers who used the last edition and wrote to us with helpful hints, useful advice and interesting anecdotes. Your names follow.

Piet Bels, Florence Blanchard, Frank Bonneville, Howard Brown, Jonathon Buchanan, R Bulich, Joice & Edmund Butterworth, M Callaghan, Helene Chagny, David Christopher, Leonard Clarke, David Cole, Roger Cook, Yvette Creighton, Helen Cretan, Norma & William Cross, Martina D'Ascola, Pam & Nick Davidson, Penny Dufty, Chiara Fantani, Lior S Feldman, Kerin Flengl, Michael Fletcher, Selena Sung Li Foong, Ingo Friese, Laura Frost, Joan Gilliatt, Joy Goertzen, Jose Alberto M Gonzalez, Caroline Goodel, Kristen Green, Marcia Green, Joanne Grindlay, Gejza Halasz, Sarah Hughes, Mrs J Hope, Henrik Jessen, Duncan Joisley, Andrew Jones, Christopher Knapp, Peg Knight, Belinda Lees, Peter Lehrke, Mike Leussink, S K Loomes, Peter Lunt, Chow Kai Ming, Geert Maas, B Manser, Yvonne Manville, Shannan McDonald, Judith McRostie, Heather Montgomery, Gordon Moodie, My Mullen, Dawn & Stephen Munday, Bridget Nay, Andrew Noblet, John O'Brien, Jane Organ, Franzisha Ott, Fred & Daisy Paulley, Richard Pedder, Carol Pederson, Tilly & Iain Perkins, Uli Pfeiffer, Chris Phillips, Richard Phillips, Ann Pilley, Jean-Francois Pin, Karen Roberts, Susan Roberts, Glen L Ross, Barbara Ruzicka, Bruce Schultz, Andy Serra, S W Shekvadod, Kerren Sherry, Victor Sloan, David Spaven, Julian Tang, Eve Tate, Janice Tausig, Lorna Terry, Frank Theissen, John Titterington, Larissa Tomlinson, V Torche, Ron Wallace, Andrew Willers, Andrew Wright, David Yau, Mary Yearsley, Mrs G K Yeoh

Contents

QUEBEC 288

NEWFOUNDLAND & LABRADOR 397

NOVA SCOTIA 463

PRINCE EDWARD ISLAND 539

THE YUKON & NORTHWEST TERRITORIES 898

GLOSSARY 948

INDEX 951

Map Legend

BOUNDARIES

······················ International Boundary
························· Regional Boundary

ROUTES

································· Freeway
································· Highway
······························ Major Road
············ Unsealed Road or Track
·································· City Road
·································· City Street
··································· Railway
················· Underground Railway
··································· Tram
······························ Walking Track
································ Walking Tour
································· Ferry Route
··················· Cable Car or Chairlift

AREA FEATURES

······························ Parks
························· Built-Up Area
······················ Pedestrian Mall
···························· Market
····························· Cemetery
······························· Reef
························ Beach or Desert
····························· Rocks

HYDROGRAPHIC FEATURES

······························ Coastline
···························· River, Creek
··········· Intermittent River or Creek
···················· Rapids, Waterfalls
·············· Lake, Intermittent Lake
······························· Canal
······························ Swamp

SYMBOLS

✪ CAPITAL	···················· National Capital	
◉ Capital	···················· Regional Capital	
▨ CITY	···················· Major City	
● City	···························· City	
● Town	···························· Town	
● Village	···························· Village	
■ ▼	········· Place to Stay, Place to Eat	
☎ ▌	··················· Cafe, Pub or Bar	
✉ ☎	·············· Post Office, Telephone	
❶ ❸	·········· Tourist Information, Bank	
◔ ℗	···················· Transport, Parking	
⌂ ✿	············· Museum, Youth Hostel	
◫ ⚑	Caravan Park, Camping Ground	
✛ ➡	···················· Church, Cathedral	
☪ ✡	·············· Mosque, Synagogue	
⌺ ⚑	Buddhist Temple, Hindu Temple	
✚ ★	·············· Hospital, Police Station	

◔ ⛽	·········· Embassy, Petrol Station	
✈ ✝	················· Airport, Airfield	
▬ ✿	········ Swimming Pool, Gardens	
❖ 🐘	·········· Shopping Centre, Zoo	
⚲ ⛱	···Winery or Vineyard, Picnic Site	
← A25	One Way Street, Route Number	
⌂ ▲	········ Stately Home, Monument	
⛫ ▣	···················· Castle, Tomb	
⌒ ⛩	··············· Cave, Hut or Chalet	
▲ ✳	·········· Mountain or Hill, Lookout	
⛨ ⟋	·············· Lighthouse, Shipwreck	
)(◎	···················· Pass, Spring	
⚓ ⚐	···················· Beach, Surf Beach	
∴	······ Archaeological Site or Ruins	
	·············· Ancient or City Wall	
	········ Cliff or Escarpment, Tunnel	
	···················· Railway Station	

Note: not all symbols displayed above appear in this book

Map Legend

AREA FEATURES

Park
Built-Up Area
Pedestrian Mall
Market
Cemetery
Pool
Place of Interest
Rocks

HYDROGRAPHIC FEATURES

Coastline
River, Creek
Intermittent River or Creek
Flooded Water Site
Salt Lake, Intermittent Lake
Canal
Swamp

BOUNDARIES

International Boundary
Regional Boundary

ROUTES

Freeway
Highway
Major Road
Unsealed Road or Track
City Road
City Street
Railway
Underground Railway
Tram
Walking Track
Walking Tour
Ferry Route
Cable Car or Chairlift

SYMBOLS

◎	CAPITAL	National Capital	
●	Capital	Regional Capital	
●	MAJOR CITY	Major City	
●	City	City	
●	Town	Town	
●	Village	Village	

Place to Stay, Place to Eat		Embassy, Rapid Transit	
Cafe, Pub or Bar		Airport, Airfield	
Post Office, Telephone		Swimming Pool, Gardens	
Tourist Information, Bank		Shopping Centre, Zoo	
Transport, Parking		Winery or Vineyard, Picnic Site	
Museum, Youth Hostel		One Way Street, Route Number	
Caravan Park, Camping Ground		Stately Home, Monument	
Church, Cathedral		Castle, Tomb	
Mosque, Synagogue		Cave, Hut or Chalet	
Buddhist Temple, Hindu Temple		Mountain or Hill, Lookout	
Hospital, Police Station		Lighthouse, Shipwreck	
		Pass, Spring	
		Beach, Surf Beach	
		Archaeological Site or Ruins	
		Ancient or City Wall	
		Cliff or Escarpment, Tunnel	
		Railway Station	

Note: not all symbols appear in the legend

Introduction

Canada is big, spacious, rugged, uncluttered and tremendously varied. You can stand in places where perhaps nobody else has ever stood and yet the cities are large and modern.

From the Atlantic Ocean it's over 7000 km to the Pacific coast. In between you can have a coffee and a croissant at a sidewalk cafe or canoe on a silent northern lake. You can peer down from the world's tallest building or over the walls of a centuries-old fort. You can spy moose and bears in the forests or seals and whales in the oceans. You can hike amid snowcapped peaks or watch the sunset where it's an unobstructed 30 km to the horizon.

The four very different seasons can bring the cold, harsh winters Canada is known for, but also sweltering hot summer days. Short explosive springs and intensely brilliant yellow-red autumns mean dramatic transitions.

It's said that the national personality has been shaped by the harsh realities of life in the northern frontier. Because the country is so young, a modern identity is still forming. But it's there, distinctly different from that of Canada's neighbour to the south.

The cultural mix of Canada is often described as a mosaic, not the melting pot of the USA. This patchwork of peoples is made up of British, French and many others, ranging from Europeans to those from Asia as well as the original Native peoples.

The Canadian dollar remains low compared with the US greenback, making exchange rates excellent for US citizens and many Europeans while holding steady for many other currencies.

With its history, people, land and nature, Canada has a lot to offer the traveller.

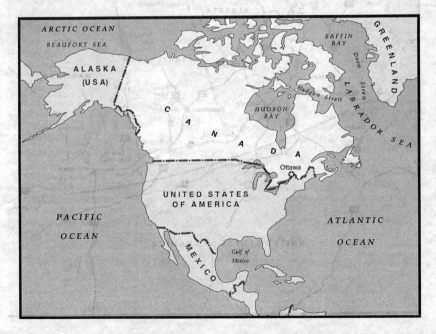

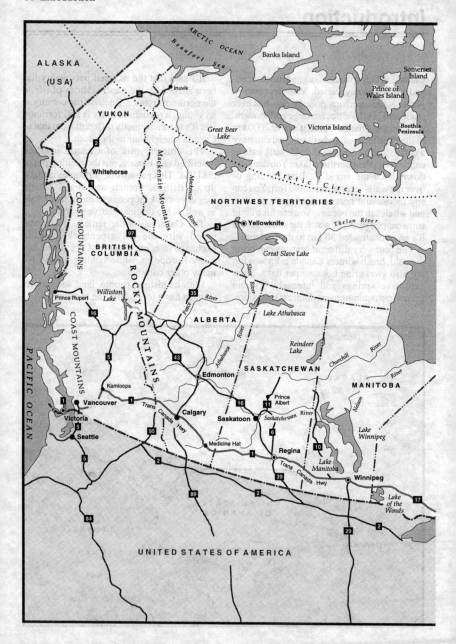

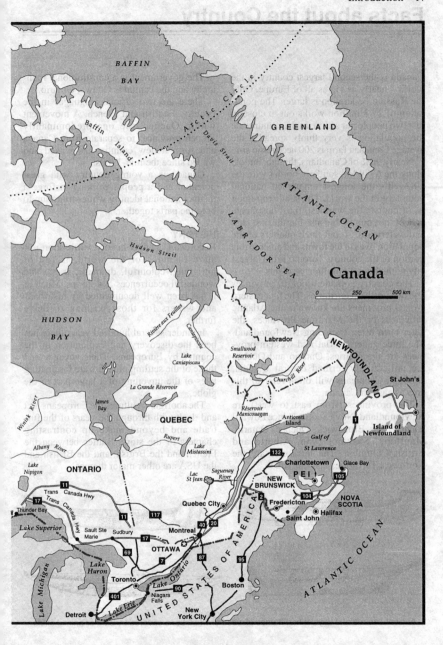

Facts about the Country

Canada is the second largest country in the world – nearly as big as all of Europe. Only the Russian Federation is larger. The population of 27.3 million works out to close to just two people per sq km. In the countryside the population is very thinly spread – the average Canadian farm is 200 hectares in size.

Nearly 90% of Canadians, though, huddle along the 6379-km southern border with the USA. It's the longest unguarded national boundary in the world. The southern region is, of course, the warmest, most hospitable area of the country and also has the best land and waterways. About three-quarters of the population lives in the towns and cities in this portion of the country. Toronto is the largest city with about 2.5 million residents.

The country is made up of 10 provinces and two northern territories. The four eastern coastal provinces are known as the Atlantic Provinces or the Maritime Provinces, the latter term often excluding Newfoundland. The three generally flat mid-western provinces are the prairies. Ontario and Quebec are collectively termed central Canada, although Canadians will often refer to this area as eastern Canada.

The provinces (from east to west) are Newfoundland, Nova Scotia, Prince Edward Island, New Brunswick, Quebec, Ontario, Manitoba, Saskatchewan, Alberta and British Columbia. The territories are the Northwest Territories and the Yukon.

The government is a constitutional monarchy and the capital is Ottawa, Ontario.

There are two official languages in the country, English and French. A movement within Quebec, the one predominantly French province, to separate from Canada and form a new country has waxed and waned since the mid-1960s.

Canada is a young country with great potential and a people working to forge a distinct national identity while struggling to hold the parts together.

HISTORY

Recorded Canadian history, while short relative to much of the world, is full of intriguing, colourful, dramatic, tragic and wonderful occurrences and stories. Much of it has been well documented by historians and writers for those wishing to delve further.

In under several hundred years there has been the discovery and exploration of the country by Europeans. Their voyages and those of the settling pioneers are fascinating tales of the unveiling of a large part of the globe.

The aboriginal cultures the Europeans met and dealt with through the years of the fur-trade and beyond make up contrasting chapters of the story. Battles between the French and the British, and the British and the USA are other major themes.

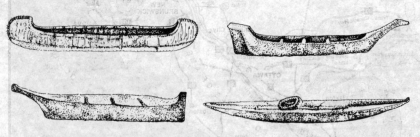

Ancient canoes and kayaks had frames of wood or whalebone covered by bark or animal skins

Canadians have recently come to appreciate and admire their nation's history. National Historic Sites and buildings of every description can be found across the country and are well worth discovering.

Original Inhabitants

When Columbus 'discovered' America in 1492, thinking he had hit the lands south of China, vaguely called 'the Indies', he sensibly called the people he found 'Indians'.

Ironically, he was nearly correct, for the Native Indians had come from Asia, across the Bering Strait, after the last great Ice Age – about 15,000 years ago. The earliest known occupation site in Canada is the Bluefish Caves of the Yukon.

By the time Columbus arrived the descendants of these people had spread throughout the Americas, from Canada's frozen north to Tierra del Fuego at the southern tip of Argentina and Chile.

The major American Indian cultures – Mayan, Aztecan and Incan – developed in Central and South America. Although no comparably sophisticated Indian societies sprang up in Canada, partially due to the climate, the Canadian Indian tribes had evolved dramatically through prehistory. When the Europeans arrived Native people across the country had developed a multitude of languages, customs, religious beliefs, trading patterns, arts & crafts, highly specialised skills, laws and government.

At this time, around the early 1500s, six distinct groupings of people could be discerned each with its own language and customs. These six major groups are classified by their geographic location.

The Arctic peoples lived in the far north. The subarctic group were found across the country from Newfoundland to British Columbia. The eastern woodlands tribes lived across the top of the Great Lakes, along the St Lawrence River and in what was to become Nova Scotia, New Brunswick and Prince Edward Island. The plains people roamed across the prairies from Lake Winnipeg to the foothills of the Rocky Mountains. The plateau area covers those groups in

History at a Glance

13,000 BC

Earliest occupation site in Canada (the Bluefish Caves of the Yukon)

1000 AD

Vikings from Iceland and Greenland briefly settled in Newfoundland

1497

The first fish is pulled from the Grand Banks by Italian navigator John Cabot who, while working for the British, went on to make landfall in Newfoundland

1534

The founding of New France. Jacques Cartier reaches the gulf of the St Lawrence River and claims the surrounding area for France

1608

Samuel de Champlain sets up a fur-trading post at the site of Quebec

1609

Samuel de Champlain commits New France to side with the Algonquin and Hurons against the Iriquoi (including the Mohawk)

1642

Montreal is founded as a missionary outpost

1663

New France becomes a province of France

continued on page 21

central southern British Columbia and the north-west group ranges from Vancouver to Alaska along the Pacific coast and includes all the ocean islands of British Columbia.

Most of these peoples depended on hunting, fishing and gathering. The more complex societies lived either on the mild west coast or around the fertile southern Ontario and St Lawrence Valley region in the east. The Eastern Woodland Indians had developed agriculture and lived in more-or-less permanent settlements. The tribes of the north and midwest lived a more hand-to-mouth existence. The Inuit (meaning 'people', and once called the Eskimos) eked out an existence in a world virtually unchanged until the 1950s.

Within each grouping were numerous tribes which, in turn, comprised numbers of smaller bands who came together to winter or in times of celebration or hardship and when marriage partners were sought. Even today, 53 distinct indigenous languages are spoken and many of these have various dialects. Other languages are now extinct. The existing languages fall into 11 broader families, most of which are independent from all the others. North America is generally considered to be one of the most complex linguistic regions in the world. Today, about half of Canada's Native people can speak their original language.

The Inuit, who arrived from Asia after the forefathers of all other American Indians, are a separate people. There are about 100,000 Inuit in the Arctic areas of the USA, Russia, Greenland (Denmark) and Canada. Canada is home to roughly 25% of the total population.

The peaceful Inuit had little to do with the more southerly Indian groups and, other than meetings with European explorers around the north-east coast, remained in relative isolation. They were the last group of Native Canadians to give up the traditional, nomadic way of life, although, despite more modern housing many remain primarily hunters. Despite having to face brutal weather conditions and frequent starvation, the Inuit were a remarkably healthy lot and the pristine conditions helped protect them from disease and sickness. The arrival of European infectious diseases reduced their numbers dramatically to the point where their very survival was in question.

Today they have increased to close to 30,000 which is more than when the Europeans first showed up. The Beothuks of Newfoundland did not fare so well. They ceased to exist as a people when the last two women died in the early 1800s.

Across the rest of Canada, the explorers and pioneers, both intentionally and by accident, brought to an end the way of life of all Native people. The eastern tribes, such as those of the Iroquois Confederacy, had to side against each other with the French or English in their seemingly never-ending battles and ended up losing all their land. The plains people, such as the Cree and Blackfoot, with their teepees, horses, bows and arrows and spectacular feathered headdresses, perhaps the archetypal North American Indian, were forced into the Europeans' world by the virtual extinction of the buffalo.

The west coast tribes such as the Haida, were more fortunate, their isolation, strong tradition of independence and long, stable history affording some protection.

Overall, the European discovery and settlement of the country reduced Native Indians from about 350,000 to 100,000. Through treaty arrangements, the formation of reservations (now called reserves) and strong policing, notably by the Royal Canadian Mounted Police (RCMP), the remaining groups were provided some measure of protection. Canada never had the all out wars and massacres that marred the clash of cultures in the USA.

European Exploration
The first European visitors to Canada were the Vikings from Iceland and Greenland. There is evidence that they settled in northern Newfoundland at the eastern edge of Canada around 1000 AD. How long they stayed, how much they explored and what happened to them is unknown.

It was around 1500 AD that the action around the Americas started to heat up. The Spanish, French, British and Italians all wanted in.

In Canada, it was the French who got first licks. After a few earlier exploratory visits by the Europeans in 1534, Jacques Cartier of France, a subject of Francis I, reached the gulf of the St Lawrence River and claimed all the surrounding area for France. It was probably from Cartier that Canada got its name. Originally *Kanata*, a Huron-Iroquois word for 'village' or 'small community', its derivative showed up in Cartier's journal. The name was used for the St Lawrence area and eventually became the official name of the new country.

The French didn't bother much with this new colony throughout the 1500s, but the pattern of economic development which began then has continued through to the present. This is, put bluntly and simply, the selling of its resources to whoever is buying, thus enabling the country to pay for everything else it needs. The first commodities prized by the French were the fish of the east coast and furs for the fashion-conscious of France.

Samuel de Champlain, another Frenchman, began further explorations in the early 1600s. He settled Quebec City, and Montreal was founded soon after in 1642 as a missionary outpost. Throughout the 17th century fur-trading companies dominated this new world. In 1663 Canada became a province of France. There were about 60,000 French settlers by then – the ancestors of a good percentage of today's French Canadians.

Throughout the 1600s the French fought the Native Indians, who soon realised that they were getting a raw deal in the fur trade and through development of their lands. The French kept busy, too, with further explorations. They built a long chain of forts down to Louisiana – another major settlement – in what is now the southern USA. In the 1730s another of the major explorers, Pierre Gaultier de Varennes, Sieur de la Vérendrye, was responsible for another series of forts. This one stretched across the south of what are

History at a Glance

1670
Hudson's Bay Company set up in London

1702-13
British-French hostilities culminate in Queen Anne's War

1754
British and French rivalry for North America escalates into war

1759
The British defeat the French at Quebec City

1763
The Seven Years' War between British and French forces culminates in the Treaty of Paris under which France cedes its territory to Britain

1774
The Quebec Act allows the Roman Catholic French majority of citizens the right to vote

1812
Outbreak of war between Canada and the USA - declared a draw in 1814

1867
British North America Act establishes the Dominion of Canada which includes the provinces of Ontario, Quebec, Nova Scotia and New Brunswick

1869
Louis Riel leads the Métis in an armed resistance of the westward expansion of the new dominion

continued on page 23

now the provinces of Ontario, Manitoba and Saskatchewan.

The Struggle for Power

Of course, the British weren't just sipping pints through all this. Though concentrating on the lands of America's east coast, the Hudson's Bay Company (still one of Canada's main department-store chains but now known simply as The Bay) had moved into the Hudson Bay area in northern Ontario around 1670.

The British soon muscled into settlements on the Canadian east coast. By 1713 they had control over much of Nova Scotia and New-foundland. And then, for a while, there was peace.

In 1745 a British army from New England, in what is now the USA, moved north and captured a French fort in Nova Scotia. The struggle for control of the new land was on. What is known as the French and Indian War began in 1754 and the war in Europe known as the Seven Years' War began in 1756. The French held the upper hand for the first four years. In one of Canada's most famous battles, the British defeated the French at Quebec City in 1759. Both General Wolfe, leader of the British, and the Marquis de Montcalm, who led the French, were killed in battle. After this major victory, the British turned the tide. At the Treaty of Paris in 1763, France handed Canada over to Britain.

The British, however, didn't quite know how to manage the newly acquired territory. The population was nearly exclusively French and at that time in Britain, Roman Catholics had very few rights – they couldn't vote or hold office. In 1774 the Quebec Act gave the French Canadians the right to their religion, the use of French civil law in court and the possibility of assuming political office. The British, however, maintained positions of power and influence in politics and business. It was during this period that the seeds of the Quebec separatist movement were sown.

During the American Revolution (1775-83) against Britain, about 50,000 settlers –

termed 'Loyalists' due to their loyalty to Britain – shifted north to Canada. They settled mainly in the Atlantic Provinces and Ontario.

This migration helped to balance the number of French and British in Canada. Soon after, Quebec and Ontario were formed with their own governors. Throughout the late 1700s and into the 1800s Canada's frontiers were pushed further and further afield. Sir Arthur Mackenzie explored the north (Mackenzie River) and much of British Columbia. Simon Fraser followed the river which was named after him to the Pacific Ocean. David Thompson travelled the Columbia River, also in British Columbia. In 1812, Lord Selkirk formed a settlement of Scottish immigrants around the Red River Valley near Winnipeg, Manitoba.

Also in 1812, the last war between Canada and the USA, the War of 1812, began. Its causes were numerous, but the US attempt to take over its northern neighbour was only part of the campaign against Britain. Each side won a few battles, and in 1814 a draw was declared.

The Dominion Period

With the end of the US threat and the resulting confidence in themselves, many of the colonists became fed up with some aspects of British rule. Some spoke out for independence. In both Upper (Ontario) and Lower (Quebec) Canada, brief rebellions broke out. In 1840 both areas united under one government. But by this stage, the population in Upper (British, mainly) outnumbered that in Lower Canada (French) and wanted more than a half-say. The government became bogged down, with Britain attempting to work out something new. Again you can see the historical disputes between the British and French.

Britain, of course, didn't want to lose Canada, as it had the USA, so it stepped lightly and decided on a confederation giving a central government some powers and the individual colonies others.

In 1867 the British North America Act (BNA Act) was passed by the British government. This established the Dominion of Canada and included Ontario, Quebec, Nova Scotia and New Brunswick. The BNA Act became Canada's equivalent to a constitution, though it was far less detailed and all-inclusive than that of the USA.

John Alexander Macdonald (known as Sir John A) became Canada's first prime minister. The total population was 3.5 million, nearly all living in the east and mostly on farms. It had been decided at the Act's signing in 1867 that other parts of the country should be included in the Dominion whenever possible.

The completion of the Canadian Pacific Railway – one of Canada's great historical sagas – joined the west coast with the east, linking those areas with the Dominion. By 1912 all provinces had become part of the central government except Newfoundland, which finally joined in 1949.

In the last few years of the 19th century Canada received large numbers of immigrants, mainly from Europe.

The government continued to grapple with French and British differences. These reached a peak during WWI, which Canada had entered immediately on Britain's behalf. In 1917, despite bitter French opposition in Quebec, the Canadian government began a military draft.

The Modern Era

After WWI Canada slowly grew in stature and prosperity, and in 1931 became a voluntary member of the Commonwealth.

With the onset of WWII, Canada once again supported Britain, but this time also began defence agreements with the USA, and after the attack on Pearl Harbor, declared war on Japan.

In the years after WWII Canada experienced another huge wave of European immigration. The postwar period saw economic expansion and prosperity right across North America. The 1950s were a time of unprecedented wealth. The middle class mushroomed.

The 1960s brought social upheaval and social-welfare programmes with their ideals

History at a Glance

1870

As part of a settlement between the Métis and the new dominion, the fledgling province of Manitoba is created

1871

British Columbia joins Canada

1873

Prince Edward Island joins Canada

1880

The Indian Act places Native people under the jurisdiction of the Minister of Indian Affairs who has near dictatorial control over their rights and activities

1885

The Canadian Pacific Railway linking the Atlantic and Pacific coasts is completed

1896-8

The Klondike gold rush and the settlement of the Northwest Territories

1905

Alberta and Saskatchewan are created as provinces

1917

Halifax, Nova Scotia experiences the biggest man-made explosion prior to atomic bombs when a French ship carrying TNT collides with another ship in the harbour

1949

Newfoundland becomes the last province to join Canada

continued on page 25

and liberalism. Canada's first Bill of Rights was signed in 1960. Nuclear-power generators and US nuclear warheads became major issues in Canada.

The Quebec separatist movement attracted more attention. A small group used terrorism to press its point for an independent Quebec.

In 1967 the country celebrated its 100th anniversary with the World's Fair in Montreal – Expo – as one of the highlights.

Well-known Pierre Elliot Trudeau, a Liberal, became Canada's prime minister in 1968 and, except for a brief period in 1979, held power until his retirement in 1984. Despite great initial support and international recognition, Trudeau was, to be kind, not a popular man at the end of his stay. In 1976 the Parti Québecois (PQ), advocating separatism, won the provincial election. Trudeau campaigned hard for a united Canada. In 1980 a Quebec referendum found that 60% of Quebeckers were against independence and the topic was more or less dropped.

Trudeau's leadership was also largely responsible for the formation of a Canadian Constitution, one of the last steps in full independence from Britain. It came into being in 1982 along with a Charter of Rights and Freedoms. Quebec, however, never ratified the agreement and it was passed without their participation. They wanted to be recognised as a 'distinct society' with special rights. Later talks to bring them into the fold and thus make the agreement more national have failed. Constitutional matters have now been put aside for what many see as more practical, less divisive topics. The issue didn't go away, however, and played a part in the next startling election.

The 1984 election saw the Progressive Conservatives, led by Brian Mulroney, sweep into power with a tremendous nationwide majority, slamming the door on the Trudeau era. The 1988 World Economic Summit of the seven major industrial nations was held in Toronto and the winter Olympics were hosted in Calgary, each bringing increased prestige and favourable attention to Canada's somewhat fragile international self-image. The government was re-elected to another five-year term in 1988.

Following the customary pattern this government, too, fell from grace with a loud thump. Among the major issues through the later Mulroney years were the very controversial free-trade alliance with the USA and the attempt to reach a consensus, known as the Meech Lake Accord, on overhauling the distinctions between provincial and federal powers, rights and jurisdictions. Another live wire was the introduction of a Goods & Services Tax (GST). Mounting concern over the colossal national debt and the massive annual federal deficit also plagued the government. Further difficulties were encountered in attempting to deal with the Native peoples of the country, their land claims and search for more power.

In the early 1990s Canadians were fed up with politicians in general, the poor economy, high unemployment and perhaps more than anything else their own pessimism. Mulroney stepped down as prime minister and Kim Campbell was chosen as the new leader at a Conservative convention in the spring of 1993. Her term as Canada's first female prime minister was to be very short-lived. The federal election in October saw the most dramatic change in government in Canada's history as the country sought a way out of the tangle of so many serious problems.

The Liberals, led by Quebecker Jean Chrétien, routed the Conservatives. Chrétien, a one time associate of Trudeau, has been around a long time, knows the ropes and appeals with his lack of artifice and posturing.

The USA pushed for, and got, an extension to the Free Trade Agreement (FTA) which included Mexico in the North American Free Trade Agreement (NAFTA). Big business likes the agreement but many Canadians see it as killing jobs rather than creating them. Canada, after asking for some modifications, ratified the agreement. Chrétien's main focus has been to create jobs and to reshape the economy.

The social programmes including the 'free' universal Medicare system, unemployment insurance and welfare for the needy, of which Canadians are justifiably proud and protective, are coming under ever-increasing threat from a cash-strapped country. Other major areas being looked at by the government are defence and immigration. Nobody really seems to know what to do with the military and its high costs in light of the end of the Cold War. Equally contentious is the issue of immigration and the thorny allegations of racism which surround it.

The Liberals are also facing a new-look parliament with the traditional opposition parties, the Conservatives and the New Democrats, virtually absent. They both suffered resounding defeats in the election and were replaced with two fractious regional parties, the Reform Party from the west and the separatist Bloc Québecois (federal party) from Quebec (see under Political Parties later for more details). The latter is now the official opposition.

Under the guidance of Lucien Bouchard (now the PQ leader and premier of Quebec) Quebec independence sprang up again in the early 1990s and another referendum was held in Quebec. In late 1995 the 'No Side' once again won but you could barely wedge a ballot through the margin of victory. The 1% difference in the vote means that the issue will remain in the forefront for the foreseeable future. It seems at the moment that most Canadians would prefer Quebec to stay, while about half of Quebeckers feel the formation of a separate, distinct political entity is preferable and even inevitable.

Internationally, Canada maintains its position in NATO and as one of the so-called G-7 countries. (The G-7 group of Germany, France, the US, the UK, Japan, Italy and Canada meet regularly to develop major economic policies.) In 1995 Canada won world headlines (and friends) over its hard line with Spain in the so-called fish wars. The disastrous depletion of Canada's once boundless fish stalks on both the Atlantic coast (cod) and more recently Pacific coast (salmon) is a combined political, economic, environmental and emotional issue. In late 1995 Canada enacted some of the world's toughest

History at a Glance

1963
The push-up bra is created by Canadelle in Montreal

1965
The maple leaf is adopted as the national flag

1970
Greenpeace is founded in Vancouver

1980
In a referendum on Quebec separatism, 60% of Quebecers vote to stay with Canada

1982
Britain proclaims the Canada Act giving Canada political autonomy and a Charter of Rights and Freedoms

1989
Canada and the USA ratify the Free Trade Agreement, which later includes Mexico

1995
In a referendum on Quebec separatism, only 51% of Quebecers vote to stay with Canada

anti-gun legislation. For most of 1996 the prime minister kept his head down and spent a lot of time abroad. Skirmishes continue between Canada and the USA regarding trade, especially in the realm of culture (books, television, radio).

Canadian troops continue to be among the world's foremost peacekeepers, working not only in the Middle East, Cyprus and traditional trouble spots but also playing leading roles in Somalia, Kuwait and currently the provinces of former Yugoslavia.

GEOGRAPHY

Canada is about 7730 km from east to west. Its only neighbour is the USA, which includes Alaska in the north-west. With such size the country can boast a tremendous variety of topography.

Though much of the land is lake and river-filled forest, there are mountains, plains and even a small desert. Canada has (or shares with the USA) seven of the world's largest lakes and also contains three of the globe's longest 20 rivers. The country is blessed with the most freshwater of any country. About 25% of the country is covered in forest. Canada's highest mountain, Mt Logan at 5951 metres, is found in the south-west Yukon.

Despite being bordered on three sides by oceans Canada is not generally viewed as a maritime country. This is in part due to the large, central regions which contain the bulk of the population and dominate in so many ways. Also the Rocky Mountains and Niagara Falls, the country's two best known and most visited geographic features, are found inland.

From eastern Quebec to the eastern edge of the country, the Atlantic Ocean plays a major part in the population's day-to-day life and offers the visitor much to discover and explore. The same can be said of the Pacific Ocean and British Columbia to the west.

Canada can be divided into seven geographic regions each with its own characteristic scenery and landforms.

The far eastern area, the Appalachian Region, includes Newfoundland, Prince Edward Island, New Brunswick, Nova Scotia and the part of Quebec south of the St Lawrence River. The land is mainly hilly and wooded.

The St Lawrence-Great Lakes Lowland is roughly the area between Quebec City and Windsor, Ontario, and includes most of the country's large towns, cities and industry. In all, about half of Canada's people live here. The land, originally forested, later nearly all used for farming, is generally flat.

Centrally, south of vast Hudson Bay, the most dominant characteristics of the Cana-dian map, are the Hudson Bay and Arctic Lowlands. This region is mainly flat, bog or muskeg – little-inhabited or visited with the notable exception of Churchill, Manitoba.

Most of the north is taken up by the Canadian Shield, also known as the Precambrian Shield, formed 2.5 billion years ago. This geographic area covers all of northern Manitoba, Ontario and Quebec and stretches further east across Labrador and west to the northern edge of Alberta. It's an enormous ancient, rocky, glacially sanded region of typical Canadian river and lake-filled timberland. It is also very rugged, cool and little-developed, with mining and logging the two primary ingredients in human settlement. This semi-remote area is best explored by visiting and/or camping in the government parks throughout the region.

The fifth region, the Great Plains, runs through Manitoba, Saskatchewan and parts of Alberta. The plains, formerly grasslands, make up a huge, flat region now responsible for Canada's abundant wheat crop.

The sixth geographic area is the Mountain or Western Cordillera Region covering British Columbia, the Yukon and parts of Alberta. Mountains dominate this region. The Rocky Mountains form the eastern edge of the area rising from 2000 to 4000 metres. Between them and the coastal peaks lie a series of lesser mountain ranges and valleys. Among the latter is the long, narrow valley called the Rocky Mountain Trench.

The interior of British Columbia consists of countless troughs, plateaus, hills, gorges, basins and river deltas. The province is by far the most scenically varied and spectacular in the country. Further north, the twenty highest mountains in the country are found in the Yukon.

Lastly, there is the far north, the Arctic region. The northernmost section of the north is made up of islands frozen together for much of the year.

CLIMATE

Canada has four distinct seasons all of which occur right across the country although their arrival times vary. The single most significant factor in climate, and even day-to-day weather, is latitude. In just a few hours travelling north by road, a drop (sometimes a considerable one) in temperature can often be felt.

The warmest area of Canada is along the US border. It's no accident that nearly everybody lives in this southernmost region. The overall warmest areas of the country are British Columbia's south and central coast and southern Ontario particularly around the Niagara Peninsula. These districts have the longest summers and the shortest winters.

July and August are the warmest months across the country and generally they are reasonably dry. Along the US border, summer temperatures are usually in the mid and upper 20°Cs. Each year there are a few

days in the 30°Cs. Manitoba through to central British Columbia gets the hottest summer temperatures as well as the most sunshine. The west and east coasts are very wet with 2500 mm of precipitation a year but much of that is through the winter months. The prairies are fairly dry all year but southeastern Canada including Montreal, Ottawa

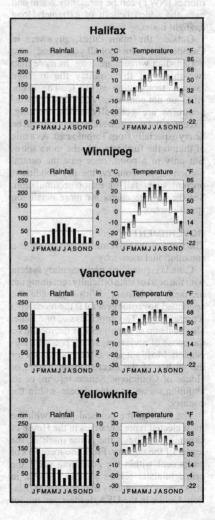

and Toronto can be quite humid in summer and damp in winter.

Ontario and Quebec have warm summers without a lot of rain. Southern Ontario can be hot in midsummer. The east coast is generally cooler than the rest of the country and can have more summer rain as well.

Summers in the Yukon and Northwest Territories (NWT) can be pleasantly warm and have the added benefit of extremely long daylight hours.

Outside the main cities, anywhere in Canada, nights are cool all year round.

Canadian winters are long. In more than two-thirds of the country the average January temperature is -18°C. The major cities are not consistently this cold but temperatures are generally below freezing. Except in the warmest areas, snowfall can be heavy especially from Toronto east. As a rule of thumb the further north, the more snow. But only to a point, once past the central portion of the country, the dry conditions prevent snow fall of major accumulation. See the climate charts for more details on specific areas.

GOVERNMENT

The form of the government of Canada is a constitutional monarchy.

Canada is ruled by a parliamentary system with the head of state officially remaining the monarch of Britain. Within Canada the appointed governor general is the monarch's representative. The upper house, or Senate, also made up of appointees, is deemed to be the house of review regarding potential legislation. Mostly it acts as a rubber stamp for the wishes of the elected lower house, or House of Commons. Senate reform, or its abolition, is an ongoing debate within the country.

The head of the political party with the most elected representatives in the House of Commons becomes the prime minister, the leader of the country. From the members of parliament within the governing party, the prime minister selects a cabinet which, in effect, runs the country and initiates legislation. Unlike in the USA, leaders can run for

as long as they maintain popular support within their party. Governments are elected for five years, but elections can be called earlier.

The 10 provinces are largely self-governing and are presided over by premiers, elected provincially. Each province has a lieutenant governor appointed by the federal government. The two northern territories are for the most part the domain of the federal government, although more independence is being sought and some has been granted to the eastern part of the Northwest Territories.

The constitution consists of both written proclamations under the Constitution Acts (1867 and 1932) and unwritten conventions. Updating, changing and clarifying constitutional matters and the balance of powers between the provinces and between them and the federal government are on-going contentious issues.

Political Parties

Canadian voters were 'cranky' upon entering the 90s, as one losing politician lamented. This general widespread dissatisfaction has meant major changes in voting patterns.

The last federal election changed the scene in Ottawa more than anyone could have foretold. The lambasting that the Progressive Conservatives and their leader Kim Campbell took has resulted in fundamental alterations in parliament.

That the Liberals (Grits) won a landslide majority is not so unusual, even the Conservatives (Tories) under Brian Mulroney did that. It was more who else won and who lost. Now forming the official opposition, after garnering the second highest number of seats in the country, is the Bloc Québecois party of Quebec. They have no members in any other part of Canada and their stated goal is to work toward the separation of Quebec from Canada. They rose dramatically and nearly swept the province of Quebec which, due to its large size and population, can supply enough seats to out-elect more widespread parties.

In third place and a mere two seats behind, another regional party called the Reform

Party of Canada, which is based in Alberta, came out of nowhere. Their platform of fiscal restraint, deficit reduction and less government/more responsibility attracted voters across the country but especially in Alberta and British Columbia.

Between the overwhelming number of votes for the Liberals and the support given the two regional upstarts, the Conservatives and New Democratic Party (NDP) have found themselves without enough backing to even maintain official party status and the privileges that brings.

Until this upheaval, the party structure was somewhere between stable and staid. The three principal political parties were the Liberals (who for much of the country's history have virtually owned the reins of power), the Progressive Conservatives (not a lot unlike the Liberals but without the success) and the NDP (known as the 'socialist menace').

The Conservatives have been voted in every once in a while, apparently as an effort to keep the Liberals somewhat humble and honest. The NDP has never formed a federal government and always came up third. They have, however, ruled provincially in several provinces and generally accept their opposition status, considering themselves the 'conscience of the nation' keeping socialist-type initiatives on the burners.

Provincially, the three main parties are again the Liberals, the Progressive Conservatives and the NDP. In British Columbia the Social Credit Party periodically forms a government. The provincial parties generally keep their distance from their federal cousins and act independently from them. The voters, too, treat them differently and have elected the NDP in four provinces since the mid 1980s. The Parti Québecois (PQ), a Quebec provincial party, stresses Quebec rights and fuels the dream of separation.

ECONOMY

Canadians enjoy the high standard of living that major Western countries are accustomed to and tend to take for granted. Income and employment has fallen over the past 10 years so maintaining the wealth experienced by the previous generation is becoming ever more difficult, even elusive. Today nearly half the work force is women and by far the majority of households have two incomes, often by necessity.

The Canadian economy is based, as it always has been, on abundant natural resources. These natural renewable and non-renewable riches include fish, timber and wood products, minerals, natural gas, oil and hydroelectricity. Although only 5% of the land is arable, the agricultural sector, primarily in wheat and barley, accounts for much of the Canadian export total.

Manufacturing has long been a weak component of the economy and today employs just 14% of the country's workers. The most important manufactured product is motor vehicles. Hi-tech industries and developers in the space and computer fields are recent additions to this area but remain small.

꩜꩜꩜꩜꩜꩜꩜꩜꩜꩜꩜꩜꩜꩜꩜꩜꩜

Flag & Anthem

Canada's current flag was proclaimed in 1965 after 2000 public design entries were hotly debated in parliament. The side bars represent the ocean boundaries and are not blue because an important reason for the entire procedure was to show independence from Britain and France. Before the new flag, between 1924 and 1965, the Red Ensign, which included a Union Jack, rippled over the country.

Each province also has its own flag many of which I dare say would not be recognised by most Canadians. The white and blue 'fleur de lys' of Quebec is probably an exception.

The national anthem, 'O Canada', was composed by Calixa Lavalée in 1880. ■

꩜꩜꩜꩜꩜꩜꩜꩜꩜꩜꩜꩜꩜꩜꩜꩜꩜

By far the largest part of the economy at a whopping 75% is in services which includes an enormous civil service. Banking, insurance, education, communication and consulting bring in foreign exchange. The rest of the service sector does not.

The country's major trading partner is the USA although business people are increasingly strengthening ties to Japan, China and all of the Pacific Rim. Mexico, too, is poised to become a major trading partner.

The high degree of foreign ownership of Canadian business has also been problematic, drawing profits away from the country. Overall, about 40% of the country's industry is owned by non-Canadians, led by US interests.

Currently unemployment hovers around 10% with regional variations, and the inflation rate is about 2.5%.

Canada has an immense 'underground economy'. This does not refer simply to various, more or less traditional, criminal activities but the hidden transactions of legitimate businesses done in order to avoid paying tax. Estimates of the extent of this underground economy range to over 20% of the country's internal economic output. This is a staggering amount of taxes going unpaid which means rates have to go up. This means people feel hard done by and so redouble their efforts to avoid paying. The car mechanic offers a tune-up, you offer to fix his plumbing; you stay at my B&B, I'll design you a brochure. The variations are infinite. There are even 'contra' or service-exchange clubs to join. All by word of mouth, of course.

Many transactions are done 'under the table', meaning paid for in cash with no bills, receipts, written guarantees or paperwork generated. Offering to pay cash usually results in a lower price as well as the tax saving. On top of this there is cross-border shopping done in the USA with goods brought back hidden in the trunk or under the sleeping baby with no duty paid. And then there is the lucrative smuggling of US liquor and cigarettes. Obviously, the government has a bit of a problem but solutions are difficult to find.

POPULATION & PEOPLE

Canada's population is now over 27 million. About 40% of Canadians are of British stock. French descendants of the original pioneers long made up about 30% of the population but this has dropped to about 25% and continues to fall. By far the majority of people of French descent live in Quebec but there are large numbers in New Brunswick, Ontario and Manitoba.

The English-speaking population has grown mainly by immigration from Britain and the USA. Over 3.5 million Canadians are of Scottish or Irish ancestry.

Generally speaking, the French are Catholic, the British Protestant, but religion does not play a large part in Canadian life.

Early Central and Eastern European settlers went to the prairies but can now be found everywhere, particularly in the large cities. Canada's third-largest ethnic group is German. Other major groups are Italian, Ukrainian, Dutch, Greek, Polish and Scandinavian. More recently Asians, particularly Chinese from Hong Kong, and to a lesser degree Latin Americans and Blacks from the Caribbean have been immigrating in larger numbers. Canada receives refugees from around the world. Unlike the early days of rapid expansion and settlement, today's arrivals head for the large cities. Toronto, the centre for international immigration, is one of the most cosmopolitan cities in the world.

Aboriginal Peoples

These now number about 330,000 Native Indians and 27,000 Inuit, roughly a third more than when Europeans first arrived. There are also approximately 400,000 Métis, the name used to denote those of mixed aboriginal and European blood. All together the three groups make up about 4% of Canada's total population. The majority are found in the Yukon, Northwest Territories and Ontario but every province has some aboriginal communities.

Inuit is the general name for the Eskimo peoples in Canada. This is their preferred name, as it distinguishes them from the

Eskimo of Asia or the Aleuts of the Aleutian Islands.

Collectively the Indians, Inuit and Métis are also called Native Canadians. Another term which has gained currency is 'First Nations' which recognises the one-time independent status of individual aboriginal groups.

Since the early pioneering days the Native Indians' lot has been marked by sadness and tragedy. At first their numbers dropped dramatically with the influx of European diseases. Then they lost not only their power and traditions but also their land and eventually, in many cases, their self-respect.

There are about 2250 reserves scattered across Canada and 600 government registered Native Indian 'bands' which has become a political and organisational term. Every Native Indian is officially affiliated with a band. Some bands can own more than one reserve.

About 72% of Native Indians now live on these government reserves, most in poverty and on some form of government assistance. In the cities, with little education and few modern skills, many end up on the streets without a job or a place to live. Infant mortality, life expectancy, literacy, income and incarceration rates all compare unfavourably with those of other Canadians.

Native Indian leaders have, since the early 1980s, become more political, making stands on constitutional matters, land claims and mineral rights. A range of national organisations such as the Assembly of First Nations keep Native Indian interests from being pushed aside. It is through these channels, however slow-moving, that the Native Indian voice will make the changes they feel necessary. Most Canadians now feel the aboriginal peoples have had a raw deal and sympathise with many of their complaints.

This, however, has not so far resulted in the introduction of many concrete attempts to improve the situation. Increasingly, ugly, highly-publicised and potentially deadly confrontations have arisen across the country. Each summer Native Indian roadblocks and armed camps have erupted and

disrupted the status quo. Accordingly, both provincial and federal governments are finding it less and less possible to ignore the state of affairs, and many issues regarding Native Indian rights and claims are currently before the courts. Among the many issues to be dealt with is some form of self-government for aboriginal peoples. Native Indian schools to provide control over religious and language instruction and a Native Indian justice system are being discussed and slowly implemented on a district by district basis. Fishing and hunting rights and taxation are other debated subjects. Native Indians have also become more active in revitalisation movements which encourage original spirituality, culture, language and a respect for their history. Celebratory powwows, to which non-Native Indians are welcome, are now a regular cultural occurrence.

Note In North America, Indians from the Asian subcontinent are often called East Indians to distinguish them from the indigenous peoples. People from the Caribbean countries are sometimes referred to as West Indians.

EDUCATION

Under the jurisdiction of the provinces, Canada provides free education from elementary through to secondary school. Beyond that tuition must be paid in what are known as community colleges (CÉGEPS in Quebec) and universities, although the true cost is subsidised through taxes. Community colleges present one to three-year programmes in a range of fields from graphic design to jewellery-making to nursing. These are taught under the broad categories of Arts, Business, Science & Technology and Health Services. Universities provide higher academic and professional training.

At the early levels, there are two basic school systems, known as the public and the separate. Both are free and essentially the same but the latter is designed for Catholics and offers more religious education along with the three 'R's. Anyone can attend either one but the two systems do split pretty much along religious denomination.

French-immersion programmes, in which English children are taught all their courses in French, are quite popular across Canada.

There are also a number of private schools but no real private system. Schools in this category include alternative educational methods such as Waldorf and Montessori.

The education system has been under constant scrutiny in recent years. Students leaving high school have fared poorly in international testing, have been called essentially illiterate by universities and, according to business leaders, are poorly prepared for jobs in industry.

A national survey in 1989 found that 62% of Canadians had enough reading skills to get through an average Canadian day reasonably competently. Numeracy came out to about the same percentages. Since then there has been an effort to tighten up on the teaching and testing of the fundamentals.

Not quite half of all Canadians finish high school. About 10% have a university degree. Students from around the world attend Canadian universities.

ARTS

Literature

Canada has produced an impressive body of writing. Most of it has appeared since the 1940s.

Among the best known, most-read poets are EJ Pratt, Earle Birney, Gwendolyn McEwen, Irving Layton, Leonard Cohen (who also wrote the less-known novels, *Beautiful Losers* and *The Favourite Game*), BP Nichol for concrete poetry, Milton Acorn and Al Purdy. One of the world's favourite poems, the straight forward but poignant *In Flanders Fields* was written by Canadian soldier John McCrae in 1915.

Perhaps more familiar internationally are short-story and novel writers such as Margaret Atwood (equally famous as a poet),

Native Indian Literature

One of the most exciting developments in Canadian literature is the increasing voice of Native Indian writers. Born from a need to tell the bloody colonial truth (it's not all log cabins and costumed workers) and a desire to share and celebrate the wealth of their own cultures, the work of the past decade or so includes some powerful and challenging novels, stories, plays and poetry. It's literature that breaks new ground and old rules, much of it drawing from the rich Native Indian tradition of oral storytelling.

Some particularly strong work is being produced by women. Written initially as a letter to herself, Maria Campbell's autobiography *Halfbreed* was published in 1973 and became a bestseller. Like other Native Indian writers, Campbell emphasises the need for authors to reclaim their own language. Many writers are angered at the appropriation of Native Indian stories by European authors. After having their land taken and their culture undermined, the 'stealing' of their own stories was seen by many as the last straw. The irony being, perhaps, that it is non-Native Indians who need those stories and the values they speak of the most.

The struggle for Native Indian self determination was explored by Jeannette Armstrong in her internationally acclaimed novel *Slash*, published in 1985. Also successful was Beatrice Culleton's 1983 novel *In Search of April Raintree* about the lives of two Métis girls. Another recommended novel is Ruby Slipperjack's *Honour the Sun*. Published in 1987, it charts the development of a young girl growing up in an isolated, fractured community.

Thompson Highway has also been internationally recognised for his two very successful plays *The Rez Sisters* and *Dry Lips Oughta Move to Kapuskasing*. Though Highway, who sees theatre as a natural extension of the storytelling medium, is perhaps the most widely known Native Indian playwright, he is just one of many working across the country.

Recent years have seen the publication of a number of excellent poetry and short story anthologies, too. *Achimoona*, published in 1985, contains short fiction by younger Native Indian writers. *All My Relations*, published in 1990, is a large collection of short stories edited by the writer Thomas King. The anthology *Seventh Generation*, edited by Heather Hodgson and published in 1989, contains a collection of contemporary Native Indian poetry. ■

Morley Callaghan, Robertson Davies, Marion Engel, Timothy Findley, Margaret Laurence, WO Mitchell, Alice Munro, Michael Ondaatje, Mordecai Richler and Rudy Wiebe.

Who has Seen the Wind, WO Mitchell's best-known book, is about a boy growing up in Weyburn, Saskatchewan, the birthplace of the author.

Humorist Stephen Leacock's *Sketches of a Little Town*, based on Orillia (a town at the north end of Lake Simcoe in Ontario), has been called the most Canadian book ever written.

Douglas Coupland in *Generation X, Shampoo Planet* and *Life After God* writes about the world of those in their 20s and 30s. William Gibson in work such *Neuromancer* and *Count Zero* has a futuristic 'cyberpunk' perspective. His story, *Johnny Mnemonic* was made into a Canadian film in 1995. WP Kinsella writes of contemporary Native Indian life as well as baseball and is best known for *Shoeless Joe*, which was made into the film *Field of Dreams* with Kevin Costner. *Dance Me Outside* was made into a feature length film with a Native Indian cast. Brian Moore's *Black Robe* is about Native Indian-European relations in the 17th century and has been filmed too. Rohinton Mistry has been heaped with international praise for his novel *Such a Long Journey* written in the early 1990s. His latest offering is called *A Fine Balance*. Carol Shields' *The Stone Diaries* of the same period was another prize winner. Elizabeth Smart's *By Grand Central Station I Sat Down and Wept* is slight in size, powerful in impact.

Canada seems to produce writers who excel in the short story so an anthology of these would make a good introduction to Canadian fiction. For a short-story collection, try one of the anthologies published annually by Oberon Press or by Penguin.

English writer Malcolm Lowry spent most of his productive writing years in British Columbia, many of them in a basic shack on the beach near Vancouver.

French Quebec writers who are widely read in English include Anne Hebert, Marie-Claire Blais, Roch Carrier, Gabrielle Roy and Mavis Gallant. Very reclusive novelist Réjean Ducharme of Montreal is considered one of the major French language writers. His latest book is *Va Savoir*.

Two Native Indian writers are George Clutesi and Markoosie.

Most good bookstores have a Canadiana section with both fiction and nonfiction works. Two publishers specialising in Canadian fiction are Oberon and House of Anansi. McClelland & Stewart is an important, large Canadian publishing house.

Music

Canadian musicians have become increasingly and deservedly well known in the past few decades with many achieving international stature. The country has always tended to produce individualistic musicians who emphasise lyrics and personal sentiments. Many of the most established names have found it necessary to temporarily or permanently establish residency in the USA.

Canadians have perhaps been best known in the field of folk and folk rock. Among the top names are Leonard Cohen, Bruce Cockburn, Gordon Lightfoot, Joni Mitchell, Stompin' Tom and Neil Young. In more of a country vein there are Patricia Conroy, George Fox, kd lang, Anne Murray, Prairie Oyster, Rita McNeil, Ian and/or Sylvia Tyson and Shania Twain. Sort of between the two categories and current are Jann Arden, the Barenaked Ladies, Blue Rodeo, the Cowboy Junkies, Kate & Anna McGarrigle and Sarah McLachlan. Buffy Sainte Marie was the first in an increasing line-up of Native Indian musicians which now includes Inuit singer Susan Aglukark. First Nations is a record label producing Native Indian musicians. Two contemporary acts are Kastin and Lawrence Martin.

Jeff Healy and Collin James both play scintillating blues guitar. In rock, big names include Bryan Adams, Tom Cochrane, Allanah Miles and Kim Mitchell. Among newcomers are the Tragically Hip and Alanis Morissette, who blew everyone away at the 1996 Grammy Awards. Quebec's Celine

Dion is also approaching megastardom. Among Quebec singers who are rarely heard outside that province, except perhaps in France, Gilles Vigneault could be the biggest name. Others are Michel Rivard and Daniel Lavois but there are many more. The province has its own successful pop, rock and semi-traditional folk bands and artists.

The traditional Celtic-based music of the Atlantic Provinces remains very popular in that region and efforts to hear some are recommended. The Barra MacNeils, the Rankin Family and the Irish Descendants are bringing this music to wider audiences.

In the classical field, three of Canada's best known artists are guitarist Liona Boyd, the eccentric pianist Glenn Gould and composer R Murray Schafer.

Pianist Oscar Peterson is the country's highest profile jazz musician.

Painting

Artists began painting Canada as early as the 1700s and their work has grown to encompass a wide variety of styles and international influences. One of the earliest distinctive Canadian painters was Cornelius Krieghoff who used the St Lawrence River area of Quebec as his subject matter. Out west Paul Kane was equally captivated by the Native Indians and their way of life. Landscape painters travelled and explored the country often following the laying of railway lines.

Tom Thompson and the Group of Seven beginning just before WWI established the style and landscape subject matter which was to dominate Canadian art for about 30 years. The Group of Seven are: Franklin Carmichael, AJ Casson, Lawren Harris, AY Jackson, Arthur Lismer, JEH MacDonald and Frederick Varley. Their work, drawn from the geography of the eastern Canadian lakelands, is still the country's best known both inside and outside Canada. Emily Carr in a similar tradition painted the west coast, its forests and Native Indian villages and totems.

In the 1950s, another group of painters, which included Jack Bush, Tom Hodgson and Harold Town helped bring new abstract influences into Canadian painting. Joyce Wieland and Michael Snow, two of the best known among more contemporary visual artists, grew out of this period. Well-known realists include Ken Danby, Alex Colville, Christopher and Mary Pratt and, for nature studies, Robert Bateman.

As with the previous music and literature sections, this is but a very brief overview of some of the country's artists.

Film

Canadian film is well respected abroad primarily through the work of the National Film Board (NFB) whose productions are, perhaps surprisingly, little-viewed and scarcely known at home. Each year the film board, formed in 1939, releases a combination of animation, documentary and dramatic films. The film board is considered to have created the documentary genre. National Film Board offices can be found in many of the country's large cities. Films are often screened at the centres and, increasingly, videos of the vast collection can be rented.

Canada also has a commercial feature-length film industry. Its output is relatively small and the quality varies in the same way as Hollywood productions. In the past few years Quebec has been the most prolific and artistically successful in film. The better-known movies are subtitled or dubbed into English. Denys Arcand's *Decline of the American Empire* and *Jesus of Montreal* were major critical successes. Other examples from Quebec include *Wind from Wyoming* by Andre Forcier, gritty *Night Zoo* directed by Jean Claude Lauzon and riotous *Perfectly Normal* by Yves Simoneau. *Black Robe*, directed by Australian Bruce Beresford tells a story set in 17th-century Quebec.

Norman Jewison who directed *Moonstruck* could be considered the father of English Canadian directors. Among established English directors is David Cronenberg known for *The Fly*, *Dead Ringers* and *Naked Lunch*. Another is Atom Egoyan with a series of off-beat, challenging films including the highly-praised *Exotica*. Bruce Macdonald has done *Highway 61* and *Road Kill*, two rock & roll movies and *Dance Me Outside* about contemporary Native Indian life. Ron Mann makes full length entertaining documentaries such as *Comic Book Confidential* and *Twist. I've Heard the Mermaids Singing* by Patricia Rozema is a good comedy-drama. Lesser known films and their makers can be seen at the major annual film festivals in Toronto, Montreal and Vancouver. Better video stores have a Canadian section.

Native Indian Art

Among the country's most distinctive art is that of the Inuit of the north, particularly their sculptures and carvings. These also represent some of the more affordable pieces, although many of their prices too can range into the stratosphere for larger works by some well-established artists.

Materials used for Inuit carvings include bone, ivory, antler and occasionally horn or wood. By far the most common, though, is a group of rock types known generically as soapstone. They include the soft steatite and harder serpentine, argillite, dolomite and others. Quarried across the far north, the stone material can vary from black to grey to green and may be dull or highly polished.

Carving styles vary from one isolated community to the other across the far north, with some better known than others. Almost all work is done completely by hand with low-tech tools. Northern Quebec tends to produce realistic, naturalistic work such as birds or hunting scenes. Baffin Island sculpture is more detailed and finer often with varying depictions of people. The central Arctic area art embraces spiritual themes, and whalebone is often employed.

As a result of interest and appreciation in Inuit carvings there are now mass-produced imitations which are widely seen and sold. Genuine works are always marked with a tag or sticker with an igloo symbol on it. Many are also signed by the artist. The type of retail outlet is also an indicator. A reputable store and not a souvenir kiosk will likely be stocking the real thing. Aside from the maker and the quality, imitations are not often even made of the true raw material and really are of no value or interest.

Inuit artists also produce prints which are highly regarded. Subject matter often is taken from mythology but other works depict traditional day-to-day activities, events and chores. Prices are best in the Northwest Territories and the Yukon.

The best of Native Indian art is also expressed in printmaking although there is some fine carving and basketry. The country's best-known Indian paintings are those by artist Norval Morrisseau. The carvings and totems of Bill Reid and Roy Henry Vickers from the west coast have established them as major international figures. Across the country much of what is sold as Native Indian art & craft is pretty cheap and tacky and a poor likeness to the work which was done at one time and to what can still be found with some effort.

Some of the most interesting and best quality items from either Inuit or Native Indian artisans are the clothes: moccasins (*mukluks*), knitted sweaters (from Vancouver Island, known as Cowichan sweaters) and parkas (warm winter coats). Some interesting jewellery and beadwork can also be found.

RELIGION

Canada was settled by Christians, primarily the Roman Catholics of France and Ireland and the Protestants of England and Scotland. Even today the largest single religious group is the Catholic but it has been bolstered by the immigration of other Catholic Europeans.

Within the Protestant group, the Anglicans form the largest denomination, followed by the United Church. Montreal, Toronto and Winnipeg have considerable Jewish populations. More recent immigration has brought Hinduism and Islam to Canada. The Sikhs in Vancouver have a sizeable community, and is in fact the largest Sikh population outside India's Punjab province. The Chinese populations of Vancouver and Toronto maintain the Buddhist tradition. Canada also has small but determined pockets of rural, traditional religious sects such as those of the Mennonites, Hutterites and Doukhobors.

Regardless, formal religion plays an ever-diminishing role in Canadian life. Attendance at the established churches has declined steadily since WWII. Following in their peers' footsteps, the lack of interest in the religion by the children of immigrants seems cause for some family strife.

Among the Native Indian population, most list their religion as Catholic, an indication of the efficiency of the early Jesuits. There is, however, a small but growing movement back to the original spiritual belief systems based on the natural world and the words of the ancestors.

LANGUAGE

English and French are the two official languages of Canada. You will notice both on highway signs, maps, tourist brochures and all types of packaging. In the west, the use of French is less visible. In Quebec, English can be at a premium. There, roadside signs and visitor information is often seen in French only. Outside Montreal and Quebec City some French, or your own version of sign language, will be necessary at least some of the time.

Many immigrants use their mother tongues, as do some groups of Native Indians and Inuit. In some Native Indian communities though, it is now only the older members who know the original indigenous language. Few non-Native Indian Canadians speak any Native Indian or Inuit language but some words such as igloo, parka, muskeg and kayak are commonly used.

The Inuit languages are interesting for their specialisation and use of many words for what appears to be the same thing; eg the word for 'seal' depends on whether it's old or young, in or out of the water. There are up to 20 or so words for 'snow' depending on its consistency and texture.

Canadian English

Canada inherited English primarily from the British settlers of the early and mid-1800s. This form of British English remains the basis of Canadian English. There are some pronunciation differences; Britons say 'clark' for clerk, Canadians say 'clurk'. Grammatical differences are few. The Canadian vocabulary has been added to considerably by the need for new words in a new land and the influence of the Native Indian languages as well as the pioneering French.

Canada has never developed a series of easily detectable dialects such as those of England, Germany, or even the USA. There are, though, some regional variations in idiom and pronunciation. In Newfoundland, for example, some people speak with an accent reminiscent of the west country of England (Devon and Cornwall) or Ireland and some use words such as 'screech' (rum) and 'shooneen' (coward).

The spoken English of the Atlantic Provinces, too, has inflections not heard in the west. The Ottawa Valley has a slightly different sound due mainly to the large numbers of Irish who settled there in the mid 1800s. In British Columbia some expressions reflect that province's history: a word like 'leaverite' meaning a worthless mineral is a prospecting word derived from the phrase 'Leave 'er right there'.

Canadian English has been strongly influenced by the USA, particularly in recent years via the mass media and the use of US textbooks and dictionaries in schools. Most spellings follow British English such as centre, harbour, cheque etc but there are some exceptions like tire (tyre) and aluminum (aluminium). US spelling is becoming more common, to the consternation of some. Perhaps the best known difference between US and Canadian English is in the pronunciation of the last letter of the alphabet. In the USA it's pronounced 'zee', while in Canada it's pronounced 'zed'.

Canadian English as a whole has also developed a few of its own distinctive idioms and expression. The most recognisable is the interrogative 'eh?' which sometimes seems to appear at the end of almost every spoken sentence. Although to many non-North Americans, Canadians and Americans may sound the same, there are real differences. Canadian pronunciation of 'ou' is the most notable of these: words like 'out' and 'bout' sound more like 'oat' and 'boat' when spoken by Canadians.

English Canadians have added to the richness of the global English language too with words like kerosene (paraffin), puck (from ice hockey), bushed (exhausted) and moose and muskeg from anglicised Native Indian words.

Canadian French

The French spoken in Canada is not, for the most part, the language of France. At times it can be nearly unintelligible to a Parisian. The local tongue of Quebec, where the vast majority of the population is French, is known as Québecois or *joual*, but variations on it occur around the province. Many English students in Quebec and even many or most French students are still, however, taught the French of France. This notwithstanding, where many around the world schooled in Parisian French would say *Quelle heure est-il?* for 'What time is it?', on the streets of Quebec you're likely to hear *Y'est quelle heure?* Most Quebeckers will understand a more formal French, it will just strike them as a little peculiar. Remember, too, that broken French can sound as charming as the French speaker's broken English if said with a warm attitude.

Other differences between European French and the Quebec version worth remembering (because you don't want to go hungry) are the terms for breakfast, lunch and dinner. Rather than *petit déjeuner*, *déjeuner* and *diner* you're likely to see *déjeuner*, *diner* and *souper*.

If you have any car trouble, you'll be happy to know that generally, English terms are used for parts. Indeed the word *char* for car may be heard. Hitchhiking is known not as *auto stop* but as *le pousse* (the thumb).

Announcers and broadcasters on Quebec TV and radio tend to speak a more refined, European style of French. Visitors to the country and students without much real-use experience will have the most luck understanding them. Despite all this, the preservation of French in Quebec is a primary concern and fuels the separatist movement.

New Brunswick is, perhaps surprisingly, the only officially bilingual province. French is widely spoken, particularly in the north and east. Again, it is somewhat different from the French of Quebec. Nova Scotia and Manitoba also have significant French populations but there are pockets in most provinces.

The following is a short guide to some French words and phrases which may be useful for the traveller. The combinations 'ohn/ehn/ahn/' in the phonetic transcriptions are nasal sounds – the 'n' is not pronounced. 'zh' is pronounced as the 's' in 'measure'. Quebec French employs a lot of English words so this may make understanding and speaking easier.

Basics

Yes.
wee — Oui.
No.
nohn — Non.
Please.
seel voo pleh — S'il vous plaît.
Thank you.
mehr-see — Merci.
Welcome.
bee-ahn ven-ew — Bienvenu.
Excuse me.
par-dohn — Pardon.
Pardon/What?
commonh? — Comment?
kwah? — Quoi? (slang)
You're welcome.
zhe voo-zohn pri (bee-ahn ven-oo) — Je vous en prie. (often Bienvenu)
How much?
kom-bee-ahn? — Combien?

Greetings & Civilities

Hello. (day)
bohn-joor — Bonjour.
Hello. (evening)
bohn-swar — Bonsoir.

Hello. (commonly)
sa-lew — Salut.
How are you?
commohn sa vah? — Comment ça va? (often just Ça va)
I'm fine.
sa vah bee-ahn — Ça va bien.

Language Difficulties

I understand.
zhe com-prohn — Je comprends.
I don't understand.
zhe ne com-prohn pah — Je ne comprends pas.
Do you speak English?
parlay vooz anglay? — Parlez-vous anglais?
I don't speak French.
zhe neh parl pah fronh-say — Je ne parle pas francais.

Getting Around

Where is ...?
oo eh ...? — Où est ...?
What time does the ... leave/arrive?
a kel err pahr/ ahreeve le ...? — A quelle heure part/arrive le ...?

bus
auto-boos — autobus
train
trahn — train
plane
a-vee-ohn — avion
train station
gahr — gare
platform
kay — quai
bus station
stas-ion d'auto-boos — station d'autobus
one-way ticket
beeyay sarmple — billet simple
return ticket
beeyay alay eh reh-tour — billet aller et retour

Signs	
ENTRANCE	*ENTRÉE*
EXIT	*SORTIE*
NO ENTRY	*ENTRÉE INTERDITE*
OPEN	*OUVERT*
CLOSED	*FERMÉ*
INFORMATION	*RENSEIGNE-MENT*
PROHIBITED	*INTERDIT*
NO SMOKING	*DÉFENSE DE FUMER*
NO CAMPING	*INTERDICTION DE CAMPER*
NO PARKING	*STATIONNE-MENT INTERDIT*
RESERVED	*RÉSERVÉ*

petrol/gas
gaz — gaz
lead-free (petrol)
sohn plom — sans plomb
self-serve
sairvees lee-br — service libre

Directions

I want to go to ...
zhe ver ahlay a ... — Je veux aller à ...

left
a go-shh — à gauche
right
a drwat — à droit
straight ahead
too drwat — tout droit
near
prosh — proche
far
lwahn — loin
here
ee-see — ici
there
lah — là

Accommodation

Do you have any
rooms available?
  ehs-ker voo zah-   Est-ce que vous
  vay day shombr   avez des chambres
  leebr?   libres?
hotel
  o-tell   hôtel
YHA
  o-bairzh de   auberge de jeunesse
  zheuness
a room
  oon shombr   une chambre
a double room
  oon shombr   une chambre
  doobl   double
with a bathroom
  ahvek sahl de   avec salle de bain
  bahn

Around Town

bank
  bohnk   banque
travellers' cheque
  shek vwoy-yazh   cheque voyage
the bill
  la-dis-yohn/   l'addition/le reçu
  le reh soo
post office
  bew-roh de   bureau de poste
  post
store
  mag-a-zahn   magasin
museum
  mew-zay   musée
the police
  la polees   la police
toilet
  twah-leh   toilet
tourist office
  bew-ro dew   bureau du tourisme
  too-rism

Food

restaurant
  rest-a-ronh   restaurant
snack bar
  kass krewt   casse croûte

I am a vegetarian.
  zhe swee vayzhay-   Je suis
  tahr-yahn/yen   végétarien(m)/
                         végétarienne (f)
bread
  pahn   pain
cheese
  fro-mahj   fromage
vegetables
  lay-goom   légumes
fruit
  frwee   fruit

Drinks

water
  owe   eau
milk
  leh   lait
beer
  bee-y air   bière
wine
  vahn   vin
red wine
  vahn roozh   vin rouge
white wine
  vahn blohn   vin blanc

Useful Words

big
  grond   grand
small
  peh-tee   petit
much/many
  boh-coo   beaucoup
cheap
  bohn mar-shay/   bon marché/pas
  pa sher/ceh cheep   chère/c'est cheap
expensive
  share   cher
before
  ah-vonh   avant
after
  ah-preh   après
tomorrow
  de-mahn   demain
yesterday
  yeah   hier

Numbers

1	*uhn*	un	21	*vahn-teh-un*	vingt et un
2	*der*	deux	25	*vahn sank*	vingt-cinq
3	*twah*	trois	30	*tronht*	trente
4	*cat*	quatre	40	*car-ohnt*	quarante
5	*sank*	cinq	50	*sank-ohnt*	cinquante
6	*cease*	six	60	*swa-sohnt*	soixante
7	*set*	sept	70	*swa-sohnt dees*	soixante-dix
8	*weet*	huit	80	*cat-tr'vahn*	quatre-vingt
9	*neuf*	neuf	90	*cat-tr'vahn dees*	quatre-vingt-dix
10	*dees*	dix	100	*sohn*	cent
20	*vahn*	vingt	500	*sank sohn*	cinq cents
			1000	*meel*	mille

Canadian Firsts, Inventions & Discoveries

Canadians can lay claim to quite an assortment of the products of human ingenuity. The Native Indians have given the world snowshoes and the birch-bark canoe; the Inuit developed the winter parka and accompanying boots known as mukluks, and the kayak. More recent Canadian inventions include the electron microscope and the manipulable space arm used on the US space shuttle.

Canadians have been active in the food arena, too. Important research developed strains of wheat suitable to a variety of world climates. Pablum, a baby cereal, was created in Canada and perhaps even more significant, was the development of instant mashed potatoes. The country's most important, best-known fruit, the MacIntosh apple, comes from a wild apple tree found in Ontario which was reproduced through grafting. The chocolate bar was created by Ganong Brothers Ltd which still produces bars and chocolates in St Stephen, New Brunswick. Canada Dry Ginger Ale is found throughout the world.

Other firsts include the paint roller (a simple yet great little device), the telephone, the wireless photograph transmitter, the friction match, the chainsaw and the snowmobile. To clear snow, the rotating snowplough was created in 1911, and 10 years later the snowblower was devised.

Canadians have pioneered the development of short take-off and landing (STOL) aircraft. For trains the observation car, known as the dome car, was designed in Canada.

The use of calcium carbide-acetylene gas for light was discovered by Canadian Thomas Wilson. It replaced kerosene, another Canadian invention, and led to the formation of the giant Union Carbide Company. Standard Time adopted around the world was devised in Canada.

In the world of fashion Canada can lay claim to both the push-up bra, created by Canadelle in Montreal in 1963, and the clothes zipper.

Insulin was discovered by Banting and Best in 1921. The radiation source stronger than X-rays, cobalt, used to treat cancer around the world was developed in Canada.

The first battery-less radio was invented in Canada in 1925 and the first all-electric, battery-less radio station followed two years later. It was called CFRB and to this day the station in Toronto is the most listened to in the country. The IMAX large format films and technology were developed by a Canadian company.

Greenpeace, one of the world's predominant environmental groups, was founded in Vancouver. On the other hand, the green, plastic garbage bag was also created in Canada.

Two Canadians created Trivial Pursuit, a board game which swept the world even outselling Monopoly. About 50 million games have been sold.

The inexpensive Laser sailboat, popular around the world, was designed by Canadians. Ice hockey was developed in the mid-1800s. And, to the chagrin of the country's US friends, it should be noted that the game of basketball was created by a Canadian. ■

CANADA'S FLORA, FAUNA
AND
NATIONAL PARKS

W LYNCH

JR GRAHAM

W LYNCH

W LYNCH

Top: Cougar, Yoho National Park, BC
Middle: Scarlet tanger, Point Pelee National Park, Ont
Bottom: Sockeye salmon, South Moresby Gwaii Haanas National Park, BC
Right: Bald eagle, South Moresby Gwaii Haanas National Park, BC

W LYNCH

W LYNCH

W LYNCH

W LYNCH

COLLEEN KENNEDY

A	D
B	E
C	

A: Grizzly bear, Glacier NP, BC
B: Beaver, Nahanni NP, NWT
C: Dall sheep, Kluane NP, Yuk
D: Prairie rattlesnake, Grasslands NP, Sas
E: Wildflower, Peyto Lake Lookout, Alb

FLORA & FAUNA

Flora

Canada's vegetation is considered young. Except for the west coast, the entire country was under ice 15,000 years ago making the forests across the country relatively new. Canada comprises eight vegetation zones.

In the far north is the **Arctic tundra**. This area, north of the tree-line, contains essentially no trees or shrubs. In this mostly flat, barren, rocky region the most common plants are lichens and briefly blooming small wildflowers.

South of the tundra is the **boreal (northern) forest**, the largest vegetative zone, and perhaps the most typical, best known physical representation of Canada. By far the dominant vegetation of the country is forest and the boreal forest makes up th majority of all the woodlands. Within the vast, largely undeveloped boreal forest whi stretches across the country the dominant tree species are the white and black spru In the east, balsam fir and jack pine are also common, in the west, alpine fir lodgepole pine.

In the east, the **Great Lakes-St Lawrence River forest zone** is found south boreal forest. This forest is a mix of the more northerly coniferous (evergreen, soft trees and the deciduous (broadleaf, hardwood) trees more common in the so portions of the country. In this region are the pines including the majestic wh and spruces but also the maples, oaks, birches and others which supply the colours of Canadian autumns.

The sugar maple is one of Canada's best known symbols and the leaf a the country's flag. The sugar maples also produce edible maple syrup, speciality worth sampling. In the southernmost areas there are walnut, beech trees as well as fruit trees.

The fourth region, the **Acadian forest** of New Brunswick, Prince Edwa Nova Scotia, is made up of red spruce, balsam fir, maple, yellow birch a It is not unlike the Great Lakes forest.

The **parkland zone** is the area between the eastern forests and the which begin in Manitoba. Trembling aspen is the dominant tree in th

Manitoba, Saskatchewan and Alberta are best known for their f **lands**, the sixth zone, now mostly covered in cultivated grains. Th contained short, mixed and tall grass regions but these have all but are now protected pockets of native grasslands which can be vis are listed in the provincial chapters. Within these areas willow a

British Columbia contains a richer variety of vegetation tha some of the country's most impressive flora. The **Rocky Moun** sub-alpine species such as Engelman spruce, alpine fir and lar elevation there are lodgepole pine and aspen. Scattered aroun also contain some of the species found at the coast but h dramatic size seen further west.

It is around the coastal areas though, in the **Pacific C** awesome trees of the country may be seen. This last veg by the ancient, gigantic western red cedar, Douglas fir spruce. These are the forests which inspire the major e the logging industry. These west-coast forests are the c individual trees over 1000 years old.

Among the country's countless **wildflowers**, just seen ones are mentioned. For those with a keen int

Throughout the east, canoeists will appreciate th flower with yellow centre surrounded by rounded f

The trillium, the provincial flower of Ontario, is o Trilliums bloom in the spring in shaded areas of t large white or pink flowers often nearly carpeti They grow about 20 cm high and have three di

The pitcher plant seen from Saskatchewan is carnivorous, that is, it feeds on insects. T attracted to the plant by its purplish-red colo leaves into the water where they drown and the protein the pitcher plant does not grow hand.

41

The pickerel weed, with its deep-blue, purplish spiked flower and narrow, long, green leaves, grows around ponds and shallow streams from Ontario to Nova Scotia.

Loosestrife is a beautiful waist-high bright pinky purple plant seen along roadsides and in ditches and marshes across the country. Now considered a nuisance weed because of its rapid growth and spread which crowds out other native aquatic plants, it was once sold as a garden ornamental. Across the Maritimes the lupine (blue, pink or somewhere in between) grows wild in fields and by the roadsides.

Sea blush cast a pink glow over the rocks along the southern west coast in spring. Even the early explorers wrote about their beauty as they travelled the Strait of Juan de Fuca.

The bright-red, common Indian paintbrush supplies wonderful contrast to the blues and greys of the Rocky Mountains.

Those with a keen eye who enjoy the less travelled forest paths anywhere in the country may glimpse the Indian pipe or ghostly pipe. This uncommon plant forces its way up through the debris of the forest floor in shady moist areas. It is a ghostly, silvery white with no greenery and no coloured flowers. They grow about as long as a finger, with the top part nodding over (as in the shape of a pipe) when in bloom.

A delicious assortment of wild berries can be picked across the country. Blueberries are the most common and abundant. The blessed may happen upon a patch of wild raspberries, one of life's exalted moments. The forests, meadows and marsh areas all have plenty of other edible plants and mushrooms. They also have plenty of poisonous plants and mushrooms. Telling the difference is difficult at times even with years of experience and a good book. If in any doubt at all, don't take a chance. Some species can be fatal.

Less deadly but more irritating is the three-leaved but difficult to identify poison ivy found in wooded southern regions of the country. A brush against this small, nondescript plant will result in a skin reaction causing blisters and a very maddening itch.

Fauna

Canada, with so much land and much of it relatively remote, has abundant wildlife yet conservation is an ongoing necessity. Campers and hikers can see a number of different animals in the wild. The following are some of the most interesting and/or most common.

Bears

These are Canada's largest and most dangerous animals. They are widely dispersed, and as there are four major types, most of the country is populated with at least one kind. For detailed information on the hazards of bears, see the Dangers & Annoyances section in the Facts for the Visitor chapter.

Grizzly Bear This is the most notorious bear and is found on the higher slopes of the Rocky and Selkirk mountains of British Columbia, Alberta and the Yukon. The grizzly is big – standing up to 275 cm high. It can be recognised by the white ends of its brownish hair and the hump on the back behind its neck. It can't see well but makes up for that with its excellent senses of smell and hearing. To make matters worse, it's a very fast animal. The best thing about a grizzly is that it can't climb trees. Like other bears, it is normally afraid of people but can be unpredictable and is easily provoked.

Brown Bear Actually a black bear but brown in colour, the mostly nocturnal brown bear is found mainly in British Columbia, Alberta and the Yukon. Not to be confused with the brown bear of Europe and Asia which is closely related to the grizzly.

Black Bear The most common of bears, the black is found all across Canada and is the one you'll most likely spot. The black bear often mooches around campgrounds, villages and garbage dumps. It is usually less than 150 cm high at the shoulders and 135 kg in weight. It's active during the day and can climb trees.

Polar Bear The polar bear is very large – up to 680 kg – with thick, white-ish fur. It is found only in the extreme north but can be viewed in Churchill, Manitoba and in zoos. A majestic animal, it is graceful in the water despite its size and apparent awkwardness. Once hunting, it is now a protected animal.

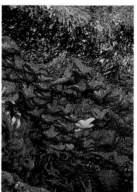

NICK ROBINSON   W LYNCH   NICK ROBINSON

JR GRAHAM

W BARRETT

A	B	C
D		
E		

A: Starfish, North Vancouver, BC
B: Polar bear, Churchill, Man
C: Flower, Yoho National Park, BC
D: Monarch butterflies, Pt Pelee NP, Ont
E: Namekus Lake, Prince Albert NP, Sas

Beaver

One of Canada's symbols, the beaver is an animal known for its industriousness, hence the expression 'busy as a beaver'. Found all across Canada, it is usually seen in the early morning or early evening paddling across a stream or lake with its head just above water. It chews down trees for food and for material with which to build its home. This home, a lodge, looks like a rounded pile of mud and sticks and is located in streams and ponds dammed off by the beaver.

Buffalo/Bison

The buffalo now exists only in government parks. It is a huge, heavy-shouldered, shaggy herbivore that once roamed the prairies in vast herds. Its near-extinction has become symbolic of the Europeans' effect on North American Indians and their environment. Technically, Canadian buffalo are bison, and there are two races, woodland and plains. Recently there have been sporadic attempts to raise buffalo for their meat and it does occasionally show up on menus.

Wolf

The wolf looks like a large, silver-grey dog. Its ferocious reputation is more misconception than fact. Hunting has pretty well banished this animal from the southern populated regions, but you may hear the wolf's howl late at night if you're in the bush. It usually hunts in packs and rarely harms humans.

Coyote

More widespread than the wolf, the coyote is smaller and more timid, with an eerie howl or series of yaps used for communicating. It is more scavenger than hunter and is sometimes the victim of massive poison-bait campaigns by western ranchers and farmers.

Deer

Various types of deer are plentiful in the woodlands of Canada, ranging across the entire width of the country. They are quiet and timid and the object of much hunting.

Moose This is one of the largest animals and again, a popular target for hunters. The moose is found in woods and forests all across Canada, particularly around swamps. Moose are, for the most part, a more northerly ranging animal than deer. They have large, thick antlers and are brown.

The moose is reclusive, generally solitary, and may be seen swimming to escape biting bugs. The male bellows in October and November in its search for a mate. At that time, their behaviour can be erratic and the normally timid moose can become aggressive. Both deer and moose can be road hazards, especially at night. Watch for them and the roadside signs warning of their presence.

Caribou The barren-ground caribou live in herds in the far north and are still used by some Inuit for food and for their hides. Their numbers are now carefully monitored, as over-hunting and radioactive fallout from Chernobyl have affected them.

A full herd on its seasonal migration is said to be a wondrous sight. There are some small groups of woodland caribou in more southern areas such as the Gaspé Peninsula of Quebec and the Lake Superior region of Ontario. A close relative of the North American caribou is the reindeer found in Europe and Asia.

Elk The elk, a cousin of the European red deer, is also called the wapiti. They can be seen around the Rocky Mountains. They are striking animals and can appear quite tame often allowing visitors to approach for picture taking. This is not recommended as people have been attacked in either the rutting or calving seasons.

Rocky Mountain Goat

This goat is as close as you can get to an all-Canadian animal. Found in British Columbia and the Yukon, it is white and hairy, has horns and looks like an old man. Around populated areas it is quite tame. Generally though, it prefers the higher, more remote mountain regions. Part of its dietary intake is clay which aides its digestive system, and you may see one pawing at the ground and gobbling up clumps of earth.

Lynx

Another nearly exclusively Canadian animal, the lynx is a grey cat about 90 cm long and is found all across the undeveloped Canadian woodlands. It has a furry trim around its face and sharp pointed ears. The mainly nocturnal cat eats small animals. Although rarely seen, humans are its main enemy, largely by destroying its habitat.

Cougar

Larger, rarer and even less often seen than the lynx is the majestic cougar. Found in the forests of the west coast, it is a mostly nocturnal hunter and its favoured prey is the Columbian blacktail deer. Its numbers are increasing on Vancouver Island.

Skunk

The skunk resembles a large black cat but has a white stripe down its back and a big, bushy tail. It is seen everywhere – in woods, in larger city parks, even in residential suburbs and their household garbage. It's dangerous only in that its defence mechanism is the spraying-out of the foulest, longest lasting, clothes-clingingest smell you can imagine. The cure is a bath in tomato juice. Watch out!

Porcupine

A curious animal about 90 cm long, the porcupine weighs 18 kg. It is grey, lives in the woods across Canada and feeds mainly on bark and tree buds. Its protection from abuse are its hollow, barbed quills projecting from its body like long hair, which are easily dislodged, as many a dog will remember.

Birds

Five hundred species have been spotted in Canada but many of them are quite rare. One of the most notable among the feathered residents is the loon, a water bird with a mournful yet beautiful call which is often heard on the quieter lakes across the country in early morning or evening. It is most abundant in northern Ontario.

The great blue heron, one of the country's largest birds, is a wonder to see when it takes off. Seen in quiet marsh areas it is very timid, taking to flight at the least provocation.

Canada geese are seen across the country, especially during their spring and fall migration when the large V-shaped formations are not an unusual sight in the sky. Big, black and grey, these so-called honkers can be aggressive.

There are many species of duck, the mallard being the most common, the wood duck the most attractive and colourful. The whisky jack or grey jay, found mainly in the Rockies, is a fluffy, friendly and commonly seen bird that will eat out of your hand. Bald eagles and ospreys are large, impressive birds of prey. Owls may be seen or heard in wooded areas across the country. Sparrows are the most common garden songbirds. Finches, blue jays, chickadees and cardinals are also readily viewed and/or heard.

Around the coasts there is a very interesting array of marine birdlife including puffins and razorbills.

Whales & Seals

Whale watching has become so popular it is now a successful commercial enterprise. A number of different species can be seen off the coast in British Columbia, in the St Lawrence River in Quebec, and in the Atlantic Ocean off the country's east coast. More details can be found in the text.

In the Atlantic Provinces the bloody, annual seal hunt (for pelts, boots, coats, etc) diminished following the European Union's ban on imports. Indeed, tourists with the money can now fly out to the east-coast ice floes to see, touch and photograph the new-born calves.

Fish

Northern pike, bass and various trout varieties are the most common freshwater fish. There are several species of Pacific salmon which are prolific on the west coast. In the Atlantic Provinces and Quebec the Atlantic salmon is a highly sought after species. Arctic char, found only in the far north (and on some southern menus), is also fine eating. Fishing is a popular Canadian pastime and also attracts visitors in large numbers.

Off the coasts there is deep-sea fishing for both sport and table species.

NATIONAL PARKS

Canada has 37 **national parks**, which have been developed to protect, preserve and make accessible a unique, special or otherwise interesting and significant environment. All of them are well worth visiting. Plans are to complete the system with 15 more by the year 2001 but this may be overly optimistic. They are managed under a federal ministry department called Canadian Heritage-Parks Canada. Its office (☎ (819) 997-0055) is at Room 10H2, 25 Eddy St, Hull, Quebec K1A 0M5. It doesn't provide much public information but does produce a free map brochure indicating where the parks are and giving their mailing addresses. This can be obtained by contacting the office. Further information can then be had by contacting the specific parks of interest. In 1996 the government suggested it might start using private businesses to run the parks. What effect this controversial proposal may have is unknown.

Most parks have camping facilities. Several are close to major population centres and are heavily used, others are more remote and offer good wilderness opportunities. Many manage to combine both characteristics. Among the most popular are the Cape Breton Highlands in Nova Scotia, Prince Edward Island in PEI, Riding Mountain in Manitoba, Pacific Rim on Vancouver Island and all of the parks in the western Rocky Mountains.

Some parks rent canoes and/or rowing boats. In parks with numerous lakes and rivers, a canoe is ideal; you can portage to different lakes. Doing this a few times may be hard work but you'll be rewarded with peace and solitude. At other parks, bicycles may be rented. Many have established walking or longer hiking trails. The towns of Banff and Jasper are within the boundaries of the mountain parks of the same names.

Entrance fees to national parks vary from park to park and from nil to several dollars. Some offer free day-use but charge, as they all do, for overnight camping. Some such as Cape Breton and the Rocky Mountain Parks have daily, multi-day and yearly permits. The latter type is good for any park in the system.

In addition to national parks, the system contains 129 **National Historic Sites**. These are for 'day use only' and present various aspects of Canadian history including forts, pioneer homesteads and battle sites. Most include interpretation centres, some with costumed workers, which offer an accurate glimpse of life during an earlier era. Many have picnic areas. There are also seven nationally designated **Heritage Canals** and about two dozen **Heritage Rivers**.

For information on all the above contact Canadian Heritage-Parks Canada as listed. It also has offices in some cities such as Toronto.

For more information on the national and provincial parks, see Camping under Accommodation in the Facts for the Visitor chapter.

Provincial Parks

Each province runs its own system of parks and reserves. These can vary dramatically in size, accessibility, characteristics and main purpose. Some are developed for recreation, others to preserve something of historical interest, still others to protect wildlife or natural geographic features of particular beauty or uniqueness.

Some provincial parks provide camping and other conveniences. In many provinces day-use is free and admission is charged only for those staying overnight. Most parks have knowledgeable staff who will answer questions and offer lectures, walks and other presentations. Some parks have a biologist or a naturalist on duty.

Provincial tourist boards and offices have free material available which provides some information on the parks under their jurisdiction. These outline camping facilities and basic features of the parks.

There is also a series of provincial historic sites across the country. These tend to be small and are meant, for the most part, to be visited for anywhere from an half an hour up to half a day. They usually deal with one significant event or period of the province's history.

Crown Land, Reserves & Other Recreation Areas

Undeveloped crown land (government-owned land) can be used for hiking, canoeing and camping at no cost. Some national or provincial parks are adjacent to crown lands. Other crown lands are scattered over much of the northern areas of the provinces and in more inaccessible remote parts of the country. Some crown land areas do have basic campsites carved out of the woods or lake edges and/or portage routes and hiking paths.

Provincial nature reserves and designated wilderness areas can also generally be used by those seeking wilderness experiences. A careful scanning of provincial maps will often reveal some of these areas.

The BC Ministry of Forests produces a Recreation Guide and an excellent series of Forest District maps covering much of the province not part of any park system. Visitors are welcome to use these undeveloped areas. Information can be obtained at regional tourist offices. In the west in particular, land designated for timber harvesting and licensed to lumber companies can still be used for recreational pursuits, but inquire about logging activity and what is permitted and where.

Local people will be able to help with advice and access information. Be well equipped and be especially careful with fire when enjoying these undeveloped areas.

United Nations World Heritage Sites

In a world of ever-increasing population and development, the permanent setting aside of specific areas around the world for international protection and appreciation by mankind is particularly timely and politically noble. In 1972 the UN's United Nations Educational, Scientific and Cultural Organisation (UNESCO) adopted The Convention Concerning the Protection of the World Cultural and Natural Heritage. Its mandate, signed by over 130 countries, is to identify and then help preserve the world's most valuable, unique and special cultural and natural wonders. Given growing threats of pollution, commercialisation, even tourism, UNESCO's intention is to help maintain the original characteristics and integrity of the designated areas through educational, technical and financial assistance.

Its work, it is hoped, will never end. To date, it has selected over 400 sites in more than 80 countries. They include America's Grand Canyon, Australia's Uluru (Ayers Rock), Ecuador's Galapagos Islands, England's Stonehenge and India's Taj Mahal. Canada is one of the 21 member representatives on the World Heritage Committee.

Canada has 12 sites designated by the World Heritage Convention. Of the eight of these that are natural, all are either national or provincial parks. They are: Gros Morne National Park, Wood Buffalo National Park, Dinosaur Provincial Park, Head-Smashed-In Buffalo Jump, Waterton Lakes National Park, Rocky Mountain National Parks, Kluane National Park and Nahanni National Park.

Four sites involve human endeavour: Quebec City, a European-style gem; L'Anse aux Meadows in Newfoundland, a 1000-year-old Viking camp; the seaside colonial town of Lunenburg, Nova Scotia; and Anthony Island with the historic Haida Indian settlement of Ninstints. This last is part of Gwaii Haanas National Park, on the Queen Charlotte Islands in British Columbia, which also has outstanding natural features. All are definitely worth visiting.

The entire central downtown core of **Quebec City** has been made a Heritage Site. The old part of town is the only walled city in North America. Within the stone ramparts, fortifications, churches, houses and countless original buildings preserve the development of the city from the 17th century. The future of Canada was decided here during the English-French colonial period. It's essentially a vibrant, living museum attractively situated overlooking the St Lawrence River.

L'Anse aux Meadows at the tip of Newfoundland's Northern Peninsula is a 1000-year-old Viking settlement. This is the oldest European habitation site in North America. There is evidence that they weren't newcomers though, that the site was occupied 4000 years before that by Archaic People. It's a wonderfully low-key national park set at the edge of the Strait of Belle Isle across from Labrador in a rough, rocky northern environment. It doesn't look much different than when the Norse sailors first arrived. Some reconstruction brings the site alive.

Further south but along the same road is **Gros Morne National Park**. It is scenically majestic with mountains and fjords but qualifies for its outstanding scientifically valuable geographic characteristics. These include major evidence of plate tectonics and glaciation – the creation of the surface of the earth, in other words. There are barren lands, sandy beaches, wildlife and ancient human history to discover within its borders.

Lunenburg's hilly historic streets edge back from a protective harbour on Nova Scotia's jagged south shore. The old, central district was designated primarily for its largely unchanged character typifying an 18th-century British colonial town. Lunenburg's tradition of wood-construction architecture has been maintained since the 1750s. In addition to the rows of fine homes, there are five central churches of note including Canada's oldest Presbyterian, dating from 1754, and the country's second-oldest Anglican.

Aside from its well-preserved architectural heritage, Lunenburg is the base for Atlantic Canada's largest deep-sea trawler fleet and home to the biggest fish-processing plant. It has also kept intact its ship-building reputation confirmed with the launching of the famous racing schooner *Bluenose* in 1921 and bolstered with its successor, *Bluenose II*, from the same yards in 1963.

In Alberta, way up north along the border with the Northwest Territories, is immense **Wood Buffalo National Park**, one of the world's largest parks. This wild, 45,000 sq km reserve is a critical wildlife habitat. It contains about 4000 bison – the world's largest, free-roaming herd. It is also the planet's only nesting site for the rare, endangered whooping crane. The subarctic mix of bog, forest, caves, and salt plains is home to thousands of waterfowl and a range of northern mammals and birds. The delta of the Peace and Athabaska rivers is among the world's largest inland deltas. This is a park on the grandest of scales.

Set on the floor of an ancient, tropical ocean, **Dinosaur Provincial Park** in eastern Alberta is virtually unrecognisable as part of Canada. The bizarre, convoluted, eroded terrain in dusty shades of ochre, sienna and brown contain secrets sunken and lost 75 million years past. Here in the glacially-sculpted badlands of the Red Deer River Valley is an unparalleled source of dinosaur fossils. Dozens of major museums around the world display specimens unearthed in this park region. Guided interpretation and walking trails make accessible this fascinating area.

In the foothills of south-west Alberta, in the traditional lands of the Blackfoot Indian, is the intriguing **Head-Smashed-In Buffalo Jump**. It protects North America's oldest, largest and best preserved Native bison jump. Where the rocky ledges of the Porcupine Hills meet the plains, generations of Native People ingeniously hunted the revered herds of bison. An excellent interpretation centre and trails around the undisturbed site make this story of early Canada captivating.

The joint Canada-USA **Waterton-Glacier International Peace Park** straddles the Alberta-Montana border at the narrowest section of the Rocky Mountains. In Canada, it runs westward to the British Columbia border.

The joining of Canada's Waterton National Park with Montana's Glacier National Park in 1932 created the world's first international park. As a symbol for international cooperation in preserving places of global significance it has helped inspire the creation of other such parks.

The parks uniquely combine prairie landscape with lofty snow-capped peaks. Within a distance of just one km, the dry, rolling hills of the southern Alberta plains rise dramatically to 3000 metres.

The lowlands support antelope and coyotes, the alpine meadows and slopes, mountain goats and grizzly bears. Deer are often seen in Crandall Mountain campground.

The scenic three Waterton Lakes wedged between mountains permit boat access to much of the park including excellent walking trails covering three vegetative zones. The park was originally the home of the Blackfoot people and Waterton has two National Historic Sites, western Canada's first commercial oil well and the Prince of Wales Hotel, a marvellous example of early mountain resort lodging featuring a timber-framed interior.

Glacier contains 50 smallish glaciers and is one of the USA's largest national parks.

Best known among Canada's Heritage Sites is the **Rocky Mountain Parks** straddling the Alberta-British Columbia border. Deservedly attention-getting and internationally famous, Banff and Jasper national parks are the main focus of the site. But there are other significant components as smaller, towering Mt Assiniboine Provincial Park, diverse Yoho National Park with the renowned Burgess Shale fossil beds, and BC's Mt Robson, at 3954 metres, the highest peak in the Rockies. To the south, Kootenay National Park is also included. Alpine meadows, glaciers, hot springs, rushing rivers – the list of outstanding features and the outdoor possibilities they present is stunning.

Tiny **Anthony Island**, part of the park, is the most westerly of Canada's Heritage Sites. Ninstints, a former Haida village on the island, is regarded as the most significant of all Pacific Northwest Indian sites. It contains still standing totems and mortuary poles as well as longhouse vestiges and is believed to have been an inhabited area for 2000 years.

Featuring clean, uncluttered, unspoiled northern qualities is the south-western Yukon's **Kluane National Park**. Together with the adjacent Wrangell-St Elias Park of Alaska and the Tatshenshini-Alsek rivers of northern British Columbia, Kluane makes up one of the world's largest protected areas. It is also among the most untamed regions on earth. Another site of magnitudes, Kluane contains the world's largest non-polar icefields with glaciers from the time when Canada was uninhabited. In one of the two mountain chains sits secluded, aloof Mt Logan at 5951 metres, Canada's highest peak. Wildlife includes grizzly bears, moose, mountain goats, Dall sheep and sometimes caribou.

Off the coast of British Columbia sit the Queen Charlotte Islands, sometimes referred to as the Canadian Galapagos for the rich variety of life in and amongst the west-coast rainforest. The southern half of Moresby Island has become **South Moresby Gwaii Hanaas National Park**, managed in part by the native Haida Nation.

Tucked exclusively in the south-western corner of the Northwest Territories is remote mountainous **Nahanni National Park**, inaccessible by road. This Heritage Site of pristine, unbridled far northern wilds is dominated by the turbulent South Nahanni River, also classed a Canadian Heritage River. It cuts through awe-inspiring canyons from the tundra zones of rocky peaks to the forested valleys at its mouth on the Liard River. At Virginia Falls, it plunges over 90 metres, twice the height of Niagara. With hot springs along the way as well as abundant wildlife, a once-in-a-lifetime river trip here is a dream for many.

W OLIVER

Grey Owl, a naturalist who wrote and lectured on conservation in the 1930s, lived with his wife, Anahereo, in Saskatchewan's Prince Albert National Park where much of his research was done. For more information on Grey Owl and the park see the Prince Albert National Park section in the Saskatchewan chapter.

Top: Wildflowers, Dinosaur Provincial Park, Alb
Middle: Hattie Cove, Pukaskwa National Park, Ont
Bottom: Mt Logan, Kluane National Park, Yuk

W LYNCH

W LYNCH

W LYNCH

W LYNCH

Top Left: Grizzly bear, Kluane National Park, Yuk
Top Right: Bald eagle, Riding Mountain National Park, Man
Middle: Tundra Lake, Churchill, Man
Bottom: Stellor sea lion, South Moresby Gwaii Haanas National Park, BC

Visa Extensions

An application for a visa extension must be submitted one month before the current visa expires. The fee for an extension is $65. For more information and to obtain an application call or visit a Canadian Immigration centre. These can be found in major cities. Requirements for receiving an extension include having a valid passport, an onward ticket and adequate finances.

Foreign Embassies & Consulates

The principal diplomatic representations to Canada are in Ottawa and these are listed here. Other offices can be found in major cities and some of these are listed in the relevant sections of the text. Those addresses not listed in the text can be found by looking in the Yellow Pages phone book.

Australia
High Commission, 50 O'Connor St, Ottawa, Ont K1P 6L2 (☎ (613) 236-0841)

Austria
Embassy, 445 Wilbrod St, Ottawa, Ont K1N 6M7 (☎ (613) 789-1444)

Belgium
Embassy, 80 Elgin St, Ottawa, Ont K1P 1B7 (☎ (613) 236-7267)

Denmark
Embassy, 47 Clarence St, Ottawa, Ont K1N 9K1 (☎ (613) 562-1811)

Finland
Embassy, 850-55 Metcalfe St, Ottawa, Ont K1P 6L5 (☎ (613) 236-2389)

France
Embassy, 42 Sussex Drive, Ottawa, Ont K1M 9 (☎ (613) 789-1795)

Germany
Embassy, 1 Waverley St, Ottawa, Ont K2P 0T7 (☎ (613) 232-1101)

Ireland
Embassy, 76-80 Maclaren St, Ottawa, Ont K2P (☎ (613) 238-6271)

Italy
Embassy, 130 Albert St, Ottawa, Ont K1A 0L6 (☎ (613) 233-6281)

Japan
Embassy, 275 Slater St, 21st Floor, Ottawa, Ont 5H9 (☎ (613) 232-2401)

Netherlands?
Embassy, 255 Sussex Drive, Ottawa, Ont K1N (☎ (613) 241-8541)

Korea
Embassy, 151 Slater St, Ottawa, Ont K1P 5H3 (☎ (613) 232-1715)

Netherlands
Embassy, 350 Albert St, Ste 2020 Ottawa, Ont K1R 1A4 (☎ (613) 237-5030)

New Zealand
High Commission, 727-99 Bank St, Ottawa, Ont K1P 6G3 (☎ (613) 238-5991)

Norway
Embassy, 90 Sparks St, Ottawa, Ont K1P 5B4 (☎ (613) 238-6571)

Russia
Embassy, 285 Charlotte St, Ottawa, Ont K1N 8L5 (☎ (613) 235-4341)

South Africa
High Commission, 15 Sussex Drive, Ottawa, Ont K1M 1M8 (☎ (613) 744-0330)

Spain
Embassy, 350 Sparks St, Suite 802, Ottawa, Ont, K1R 7S8 (☎ (613) 237-2193)

Sweden
Embassy, 377 Dalhousie St, Ottawa, Ont K1N 9N8 (☎ (613) 241-8553)

Switzerland
Embassy, 5 Marlborough Ave, Ottawa, Ont, K1N 8E6 (☎ (613) 235-1837)

UK
High Commission, 80 Elgin St, Ottawa, Ont K1P 5K7 (☎ (613) 237-1530)

USA
Embassy, 100 Wellington St, PO Box 866, Station B, Ottawa, Ont K1P 5T1 (☎ (613) 238-5335)

Side Trips to the USA

Visitors to Canada who are planning to spend some time in the USA should be aware of a few things to avoid being met with disappointment. First, admission requirements to the USA when arriving by land can be significantly different than when arriving by air or sea from your country of origin. These regulations are also subject to rapid change; it's best never to assume. The duration of the visit, whether one afternoon or three months, is inconsequential; the same rules apply. Visitors to the USA from nearly all Western countries do not need visas but there are exceptions. These include Australians and the Portuguese.

Residents of countries for whom US visas are necessary should get them at home. Australians, for example, can apply for US visas in Canada but it is generally easier and

W LYNCH

W LYNCH

W LYNCH

W LYNCH

A	B
	C
D	

A: Rough-legged hawk, Churchill, Man
B: Bighorn sheep, Jasper National Park, Alb
C: Arctic tern, Aulavik National Park, NWT
D: Elk, Jasper National Park, Alb

W OLIVER

W LYNCH

NICK ROBINSON

M BEEDELL

W LYNCH

A	B
C	D
E	

A: Grey Owl feeds young beaver, Prince Albert NP, Sas
B: Moose, Terra Nova NP, Nf
C: Red squirrel, Banff NP, Alb
D: Virginia Falls, Nahanni NP, NWT
E: Frenchman Valley, Grasslands NP, Sas

Facts for the Visitor

VISAS & EMBASSIES

Visitors from nearly all Western countries don't need visas. Exceptions are citizens of Portugal and South Africa. Tourists from Hong Kong, Korea and Taiwan also need visas as do visitors from developing or Third World countries and residents of some Eastern European countries. Those from Communist nations definitely need one too.

Visitor visas, which are free, are granted for a period of six months and are extendable for a fee. Extensions must be applied for at a Canadian Immigration Centre. Visa requirements change frequently and since visas must be obtained before arrival in Canada, check before you leave – Europeans included. A separate visa is required for visitors intending to work or to go to school in Canada.

A passport and/or visa does not guarantee entry. Admission and duration of permitted stay is at the discretion of the immigration officer at the border. The decision is based on a number of factors, some of which you control, including: being of good health; being law abiding; having sufficient money; and possibly being in possession of a return ticket out of the country. This latter requirement will not often be asked of any legitimate traveller, especially from a Western country.

If you are refused entry but have a visa you have the right of appeal at the Immigration Appeal Board at the port of entry. Those under 18 years of age should have a letter from a parent or guardian.

Canadian Embassies, High Commissions & Consulates Abroad

Australia
High Commission, Commonwealth Ave, Canberra ACT 2600 (☎ 06-273-3844)
Canadian Consulate General, 111 Harrington St, Level 5, Quay West, Sydney, New South Wales 2000 (☎ 02-9364-3000); Visa Immigration Office (☎ 02-9364-3050)

Consulate of Canada, 11th Flo
Mutual Centre, 111 St George's
Western Australia 6000 (☎ 09-932
Denmark
Embassy, Kr Bernikowsgade 1,
gen K (☎ 33-12-22-99)
France
Embassy, 35 Avenue Montaign
(☎ 01-44-43-29-00)
Germany
Canadian Embassy, Godesber
53175 Bonn, Germany (☎ 0228
Ireland
Embassy, 65-68 St Stephen's
(☎ 01-478-1988) (Note: the im
of this office has closed.)
Italy
Embassy, Via G B de Rossi
(☎ 06-44-59-81)
Japan
Embassy, 3-38 Akasaka 7-c
Tokyo 107 (☎ 3408-2101)
Netherlands
Embassy, Sophialaan 7, 250
(☎ 070-311-1600)
New Zealand
High Commission, 61 Moles
Wellington (☎ 4-473-957
immigration inquiries are ha
ate General of Canada in Sy
Spain
Embassy, Edificio Goya, C
35, Madrid (☎ 1-431-4300
Sweden
Embassy, Tegelbacken 4 (
(☎ 8-613-9900)
Switzerland
Embassy, Kirchenfeldstra
(☎ 31-352-63-81)
UK
High Commission, M
Grosvenor Square, Lond
(☎ 0171-258-6600)
USA
Consulate General, 125
cas, New York City,
(☎ 212-596-1600) (No
ate Generals in Buffalo
can provide visa inform
Generals in Atlanta, B
Dallas, Detroit, Los A
York, Seattle and Was
information. The only
DC.)

quicker to apply at home and your chances of being refused are reduced. Visas can not be obtained upon arrival in the USA. When getting a visa, ask for a multiple entry one as this may be useful.

Most visitors to the USA (by air or sea) are required to have either a return or onward ticket in their possession. These tickets may be 'open', that is undated. Visitors entering the USA by land from Canada are not required to have any ticket but some show of finances may be required as well as some indication of a residence abroad, ie some document that shows you have a permanent address.

As mentioned, the border between Canada and the USA has tightened up even for citizens of either of these countries. Anyone travelling with young children should be aware of the extra need for good documentation. This is true whether on plane, bus, train or driving a vehicle. Because of the heightened fear of child abductions parents can find themselves in the unenviable position of having to prove that the baby in their arms is in fact their own.

This is particularly the case for male single parents but may affect anyone crossing the border without their spouse. In the latter case, a letter of consent, preferably notarised, from the missing partner should be considered. You may be asked to legally document custody of the child.

Commercial carriers such as Amtrak and Greyhound are facing threats of heavy fines for carrying passengers without sufficient documentation and so have been forced to be more strict in requiring proper identification for crossing the border in either direction. Any potential trouble can also be minimised by having valid passports for all members of the family.

Check that your entry permit to Canada, whatever it may be, includes multiple entry. For people holding passports from Western countries multiple entry is generally given. But check, because if not, you may find your afternoon side trip across the border to the USA involuntarily extended when Canadian officials won't let you back in to Canada.

Also, the time spent on a side trip to the USA will be included as time spent in Canada for the purpose of your time allotment upon arrival. For example, if you have been given a six-month stay in Canada and after three months you spend one month in California, upon your return to Canada you will only be permitted to stay the remaining two months.

For those wishing to visit duty-free shops and perhaps take advantage of the prices, you must be in the USA for a minimum of 48 hours to be entitled to use them. The selection and prices at these shops has never been all that impressive anyway and the concept is a bit overrated. Smokers may find the cigarettes aren't a bad buy.

DOCUMENTS

Visitors from all countries but the USA need a passport. Two minor exceptions include people from Greenland (Denmark) and Saint Pierre & Miquelon (France) who do not need passports if they are entering from their areas of residence. All the above do need to have good identification, however, when visiting Canada.

For US and Canadian citizens, a driver's licence has traditionally been all that was required to prove residency but often this is no longer sufficient. A birth certificate or a certificate of citizenship or naturalisation, if not a passport, is recommended and may indeed be required in some cases before admission is granted.

US citizens arriving in Canada from somewhere other than the USA should have a passport. US citizens travelling in Canada may want to investigate the Canadian Non-resident Interprovince Motor Vehicle Liability Insurance Card which is only available in the USA.

If you've rented a car, trailer or any other vehicle in the USA and you are driving it into Canada, bring a copy of the rental agreement to save any possible aggravation by border officials. The rental agreement should stipulate that taking the vehicle to Canada is permitted.

CUSTOMS

How thoroughly customs will check you out upon arrival at a Canadian entry point depends on a number of things. First among them are point of departure, nationality and appearance. Arriving from countries known as drug sources or with a history of illegal immigration or refugees will add to the scrutiny. Always make sure the necessary papers are in order.

Don't get caught bringing drugs into Canada: this includes marijuana and hashish, as they are termed narcotics in Canada. The sentence is seven years minimum and it doesn't matter if you're a nice person – the judge has little choice by law.

Adults (age varies by province but is generally 19 years) can bring in 1.1 litres (40 oz) of liquor or a case of 24 beers as well as 200 cigarettes, 50 cigars and 400 grams of tobacco (all cheaper in the USA). You can bring in gifts up to $60 in value.

Sporting goods, including 200 rounds of ammunition, cameras and film and two days' worth of food can also be brought in without trouble. Registering excessive or expensive sporting goods, cameras, etc might save you some hassle when you leave, especially if you'll be crossing the Canadian-US border a number of times.

If you have a dog or cat you will need proof that it's had a rabies shot in the past 36 months. For US citizens this is usually easy enough; for residents of other countries there may well be more involved procedures. If you must bring a pet from abroad, to save a lot of potential headaches, check with the Canadian government or a representative before arriving at the border.

For boaters, pleasure craft may enter Canada either on the trailer or in the water and stay for up to one year. An entry permit is required and is obtainable from the customs office at or near the point of entry. All boats powered by motors over 10 hp must be licensed.

Pistols, fully automatic weapons and any firearms less than 66 cm (26 inches) in length are not permitted into the country. Most rifles and shotguns will be admitted without a permit.

MONEY

Currency

Canadian currency is much like that of the USA with some noteworthy variations. Coins come in one-cent (penny), five-cent (nickel), 10-cent (dime), 25-cent (quarter), $1 (loonie) and $2 (twoonie) pieces. The loonie is an 11-sided, gold-coloured coin known for the common loon (a species of waterbird) featured swimming on it. In 1996 the twoonie was introduced. It's a two-toned coin with a nickel outer ring and aluminum-bronze core featuring a polar bear. This means the phasing out of the $2 bill like the $1 bill before it. There is also a 50-cent coin but this is not regularly seen.

With the demise of the $2 bill, paper currency is found in $5, $10 and $20 denominations. The $50, $100 and larger bills are less common and could prove difficult to cash, especially in smaller businesses or at night. Service stations, for example, are sometimes reluctant to deal with larger bills. Canadian bills are all the same size but vary in their colours and images. Some denominations have two styles as older versions in good condition continue to circulate.

All prices quoted in this book are in Canadian dollars, unless stated otherwise.

Exchange Rates

Australia	A$1	=	C$1.08
France	1FF	=	C$0.26
Germany	DM1	=	C$0.89
Japan	¥100	=	C$1.22
New Zealand	NZ$1	=	C$0.95
UK	UK£1	=	C$2.13
USA	US$1	=	C$1.36

Changing money is best done at companies such as Thomas Cook or American Express which specialise in international transactions. In some of the larger cities these companies operate small exchange offices and booths along main streets. The second option for changing money are the banks and trust companies. Lastly there are hotels (always open at least), stores, attractions and service stations. The rates at the latter group are not likely to be in your favour.

American Express and Thomas Cook are the best travellers' cheques to use in either US or Canadian dollars. Some smaller places don't know exchange rates, so you'll have to pay for a call to find the rate as well as the mailing charges. Some banks charge a couple of dollars to cash travellers' cheques, so ask first. If a charge is levied be sure to cash several cheques as generally the charge remains the same no matter how many cheques are being cashed. Despite this service charge, banks usually offer better rates than places such as hotels, restaurants and visitor attractions. Personal cheques are rarely accepted at any commercial enterprise.

Banking hours are generally shorter than regular retail hours. Some banks have evening hours while others, more likely trust companies, are open on Saturday morning. For more information see the Business Hours section later in this chapter.

Credit Cards

Carrying a credit card is a good idea in Canada. Their use is widespread and they can serve a number of purposes. They are good identification (ID) and are more or less essential for use as security deposits for such things as renting a car or even a bicycle. They are perfect for using as a deposit when making reservations for accommodation, and even the Hostelling International (HI) hostels will take credit-card reservations and payments. They can be used to book and purchase ferry tickets, airplane tickets or theatre tickets. Lastly, they can be used at banks to withdraw cash, termed cash advances.

Visa, MasterCard and American Express credit cards are honoured in most places in larger centres and many in the smaller cities and towns. American Express has the advantage of offering a free mail pick-up service at their offices. In tiny, out-of-the-way communities, the use of travellers' cheques or cash is advisable.

Automated Teller Machines

Automated teller machines (ATMs) with Interac are now common throughout

Canada. As well as being located at banks, they can be found in some grocery stores, service stations, variety stores, shopping centres, bus and train stations and elsewhere. Known in Canada as banking machines, these can be used day or night, any day of the week. Cards must be applied for at home through your own bank. Ask if the cards are good for use in the Canadian banking networks.

Be sure to obtain a list of addresses where banking machines can be found or the 800 toll-free telephone number which can be called to help locate one. Often tourist offices or any bank will be able to direct you to the nearest machine. Use of the Interac card has increased dramatically by travellers and is often the most convenient, quickest way to replenish your cash. Bank cards are often used now instead of cash. With 'direct payment' the card is swiped through the retailer's scanner and your account is instantly debited.

Costs

Finding a place to sleep and eat is not a lot different here than in Europe or other Western countries. The Canadian lifestyle, like the Canadian personality, has been influenced by Britain and the USA but is somehow different from both. There are no formal social classes, but there are widely different incomes, and therefore a range in housing, eating and entertainment prices.

For many visitors, the biggest expense will be accommodation. There are, however, alternatives to the standard hotels which can make paying for a bed nothing to lose sleep over. The larger cities generally have the more expensive lodging prices, while those in country towns can be quite reasonable. In the far north, accommodation rates are a little more than in the south, only sometimes outlandishly so.

The heavily touristed areas such as Niagara Falls and Quebec City tend not to have really inflated prices because the volume of places to stay means plenty of competition, particularly when it's not peak season. An exception is Banff in the Rocky

Mountains which is costly. As a rule, accommodation prices are a little higher in the summer months. After this period, asking about a discount if one is not forthcoming is well worthwhile.

Food prices are lower than those in much of Western Europe but are higher than those in the USA and about parallel to those in Australia.

Gasoline prices vary from province to province but are always more than US rates, sometimes shockingly so, so remember to fill up before crossing the border if you are coming from the USA. Canada's gasoline prices are, however, lower than those in most of Europe. Within Canada the eastern provinces and the far north have the highest prices. Also, as a rule, the more isolated the service station, the higher the prices. Alberta has traditionally had the lowest prices. Of course, these prices reflect on all transportation costs.

Buses are almost always the least expensive form of public transport. Train fares, except when using one of the various special price rates, are moderate. Again, they are more expensive than US fares, less than European ones and comparable to those in Australia.

Inter-provincial airfares are high. Distances are great and the competition minimal. Again, always inquire about specials, excursion fares or last minute deals.

Most prices that you see posted (and most found in the text) do not include taxes, which can add significantly to your costs. It's a good idea to ask if the price of something includes tax. See the Consumer Taxes section later in this chapter.

Note In the text, train and plane fares given are the standard, one-way, no advance booking price. With advance booking, by even as little as a week, prices drop considerably. Planning ahead can save a *lot* of money. When flying, often return tickets are less than one-way fares, even if the return portion is not used, and booking two weeks in advance can mean additional savings.

Tipping
Normal tipping is 10% to 15% of the bill. Tips are usually given to cabbies, waiting staff, hairdressers, barbers, hotel attendants and bellhops. Tipping helps for service in a bar, too, especially if a fat tip is given on the first order. After that you won't go thirsty all night.

A few restaurants have the gall to include a service charge on the bill. No tip should be added in these cases.

Consumer Taxes & Visitor Refunds
Provincial Tax In most of Canada, provincial sales tax must be paid on all things purchased. Alberta has a sales tax only on accommodation in hotels and motels, but the other provinces also have sales taxes on most items bought in shops and on food bought at restaurants and cafes. The Yukon and Northwest Territories have no consumer sales tax.

Quebec and Manitoba allow partial rebates on accommodation tax and sales tax on goods being taken out of Canada. Check with a provincial tourist office for information and to obtain the necessary forms for reimbursement – it's worth the trouble on a tent, camera or similarly large purchase. Tax information is published in the provincial tourist information booklets.

Note, that you need to send the original receipts to obtain the tax refund. The originals are also required to receive the GST refunds. Get around this by applying first for the GST refund as the original receipts will be returned. Receipts are not returned from provincial refund offices. Some conditions apply and the form must be posted to the provincial tax office after you return home. For information on Manitoba and Quebec refunds see the following section on GST.

Goods & Services Tax Known as the Gouge & Screw Tax, the GST adds 7% to just about every product, service and transaction. Unfortunately for tourists, it hits the travel industry hard. And the GST tax is applied on top of the usual provincial sales tax. In Ontario, for example, this total can mean an additional 15% on a bill, so remember to calculate it in before reaching the checkout cash register. Under political pressure, some provinces have now combined their provincial tax with the GST to make one general sales tax of about 15%.

For visitors or travellers who prepare their own food, there is no tax applied to groceries.

Some tourist homes (the small ones), guesthouses, B&Bs etc don't charge GST for rooms, and foreign visitors should try asking for an exemption from the GST on their hotel bill when making payment. If paid, the GST added to all other accommodation except camp sites is refundable.

A rebate or refund is available for visitors on accommodation and nonconsumable goods bought for use outside Canada, provided the goods are removed from the country within 60 days. Tax paid on services or transportation is not refundable. The value of the goods taxed must be over $100 and you must have original receipts. Credit-card slips and photocopies are not sufficient. Most 'tourist' or duty-free shops have a GST rebate booklet and mailing form or you can contact Revenue Canada, Custom, Excise & Taxation, Visitors' Rebate Program, Ottawa, Ontario K1A 1J5. The forms are also available at tourist information offices. The forms can also be used to apply for sales tax rebates on tax paid in the provinces of Quebec and Manitoba.

WHEN TO GO

Spring, summer and autumn are all ideal for touring. The far north is best in summer as the roads are open, ferries can cross rivers and daylight hours are long. Many of the country's festivals are held over the summer, one notable exception being the Quebec Winter Carnival. If you're skiing and visiting the cities, a winter visit won't present any major hurdles. Also Canada's ballet, opera and symphony season runs through the winter months. You will, of course, need a different set of clothes.

Note that outside the main summer season which runs roughly from mid-June to mid-September, many visitor-oriented facilities, attractions, sights and even accommodation

may be closed. This is especially true in the Atlantic Provinces. Advantages are the slower pace, lack of crowds, lower prices and perhaps more time for the people serving you. Spring and autumn make a good compromise between the peak season and the cold of winter. For campers, though, July and August are the only reliably hot months. For more detail see the climate charts in the Facts about the Country chapter.

WHAT TO BRING

Travellers to Canada have no real need for any special articles. Those with allergies or any particular medical ailments or conditions should bring their customary medicines and supplies. Extra prescription glasses and/or contact lenses are always a good idea. A small travel alarm clock is useful.

Those planning trips out of the summer season should bring a number of things to protect against cold. Layering of clothes is the most effective and the most practical way to keep warm. One thin and one thick sweater and something more or less windproof is recommended. On particularly cool days a T-shirt worn under a long sleeved-shirt and then a combination of the above is quite effective. Gloves, scarf and hat should be considered and are mandatory in winter.

Even in winter a bathing suit, which weighs next to nothing, is always good to throw in the pack. Aside from possible ocean and lake summer swimming there are city, hotel and motel pools of which some are heated and others are indoors, and some hotels have saunas. A collapsible umbrella is a very useful, practical accessory. A good, sturdy pair of walking shoes or boots is a good idea for all but the business traveller with no spare time.

For English-language speakers planning on spending some time in Quebec, a French/English dictionary or phrase book should be considered although these are available in Montreal.

Drivers travelling long distances should have a few basic tools, a spare tyre that has been checked for pressure, a first-aid kit and a torch (flashlight). A few favourite tapes may help pass the hours driving in remote areas where there's nothing on the radio but static.

TOURIST OFFICES
Local Tourist Offices
Each province in Canada has a governmental ministry or affiliate responsible for tourism and the major cities generally have an office for distributing provincial information. In addition, most cities and towns have at least a seasonal local information office. Many of these are mentioned in the text. The small, local tourist offices are the best place for obtaining specialised information on a specific area. As a rule they will have little knowledge or information on other parts of the country.

Provincial/Territory Tourist Offices Each province has one or more major provincial tourist offices located within its borders. These may be in the major city, at provincial boundaries or at a major provincial attraction.

The provincial tourist offices can supply, at no charge, the basic information requirements including maps and guides on accommodation, camp sites and attractions. They can also provide information on events scheduled for the current or upcoming year. On request, they will furnish more specialised information on, for example, a particular activity or an organised wilderness tour, however, they do not have detailed information on any given area of their province or territory. For this information, a city tourist office in your area of choice must be contacted by phone, mail or in person.

Ontario
  Ontario Travel, Queen's Park, Toronto, Ontario M7A 2E5 (☎ 1-800-668-2746, free from Canada, continental USA and Hawaii; ☎ 1-800-268-3736, in French – free from anywhere in Canada)
Quebec
  Tourism Quebec, PO Box 979, Montreal, Quebec H3C 2W3 (☎ 1-800-363-7777, free from anywhere in continental North America)

Newfoundland & Labrador
  Newfoundland Department of Tourism, Culture & Recreation, PO Box 8730, St John's, Newfoundland A1B 4K2 (☎ 1-800-563-6353, free from continental North America)
Nova Scotia
  Tourism Nova Scotia, PO Box 130, Halifax, Nova Scotia B3J 2M7 (☎ 1-800-565-0000, free from anywhere in Canada; ☎ 1-800-341-6096, free from anywhere in the USA)
Prince Edward Island
  Prince Edward Island Visitor Services, PO Box 940, Charlottetown, Prince Edward Island C1A 7M5 (☎ 1-800-463-4734, free from continental North America)
New Brunswick
  New Brunswick Tourism, Department of Economic Development & Tourism, PO Box 12345, Fredericton, New Brunswick E3B 5C3 (☎ 1-800-561-0123, free from anywhere in continental North America)
Manitoba
  Travel Manitoba, Department SM5, 7th Floor, 155 Carlton St, Winnipeg, Manitoba R3C 3H8 (☎ 1-800-665-0040, free from anywhere in continental North America)
Saskatchewan
  Tourism Saskatchewan, 500-1900 Albert St, Regina, Saskatchewan S4P 4L7 (☎ 1-800-667-7191, free from anywhere in continental North America)
Alberta
  Alberta Economic Development & Tourism, 3rd Floor, 10155-102nd St, Edmonton, Alberta T5J 4L6 (☎ 1-800-661-8888, free from anywhere in continental North America)
British Columbia
  Tourism British Columbia, Parliament Buildings, Victoria, British Columbia V8V 1X4 (☎ 1-800-663-6000, free from continental North America, Hawaii & parts of Alaska)
Yukon
  Tourism Yukon, PO Box 2703, Whitehorse, Yukon Territories Y1A 2C6 (☎ (403) 667-5340)
Northwest Territories
  Northwest Territories Economic Development & Tourism, PO Box 1320, Yellowknife, Northwest Territories X1A 2L9 (☎ 1-800-661-0788, free from anywhere in continental North America)

Federal Tourist Offices
Due to government restructuring and cutbacks, there is no longer a federal tourism department which supplies information to the public. All tourism information is handled by the individual provinces.

For basic help in planning a visit to

Canada, see your closest Canadian embassy, consulate or high commission, listed earlier in this chapter under Visas & Embassies. They can furnish details on entry requirements, the weather, duty regulations, and where to get travel information. Travel agents can also be consulted.

BUSINESS HOURS
Banks
Most banks are open Monday to Thursday from 10 am to 4.30 pm, and on Friday to 5 or 6 pm. Some banks are open Saturday morning. Trust companies open for longer hours, perhaps to 6 pm Monday to Friday and are often open Saturday from 10 am to 1 pm. Banks and trust companies are closed on Sunday and on holidays. Many banks now have ATMs, known as banking machines in Canada, which are accessible 24 hours a day.

Stores
Cities and their suburbs generally have the longest retail store hours. Opening time is usually from about 9 am with closing time around 6 pm. On Friday, and sometimes Thursday, shops are open until 9 pm. Shopping malls, plazas, large department stores and some downtown stores may remain open until 9 pm every day.

Larger centres have a limited number of stores which remain open 24 hours. The vast majority of these are convenience shops which sell basic groceries, cigarettes and newspapers. Also, some supermarkets remain open 24 hours as do some chemists (drug stores).

Shops in smaller centres generally have shorter hours with little evening shopping and nothing much available on Sunday except for basic groceries and movies.

The issue of Sunday opening has been hotly debated for years but no consensus has been reached. In general, from British Columbia to Quebec there is limited Sunday shopping while in Eastern Canada shops are basically closed up tight.

On major highways 24-hour service stations sell gasoline and food.

Restaurants
Many restaurants generally close at about midnight as Canadians do not dine particularly late, rarely eating out later than 10 pm. Many of the better places open for lunch and dinner only. Smaller cafes and coffee shops open as early as 6 am. All cities and many towns have restaurants that are open 24 hours.

Bars & Liquor Sales
Hours vary according to the province. Most bars, pubs and lounges open at noon and close at 1 or 2 am. In Ontario last call is 2 am. In Quebec laws are more liberal allowing bars to stay open until 3 or 4 am. The larger cities usually have after-hours bars which remain open for music or dancing but stop serving alcohol. West of Ontario there is 'off-sales' meaning bars and hotels are permitted to sell takeaway beer. In Alberta all alcohol is sold through private retailers, and in Quebec wine and beer can be bought at grocery stores and corner shops. In all other cases, alcohol must be bought through government retail stores.

The drinking age varies from province to province but the norm is 19 years old.

HOLIDAYS
The school summer holidays in Canada are from the end of June to Labour Day in early September. This is also the period when most people take their vacations. University students have a longer summer break running from some time in May to the beginning or middle of September. Labour Day is an important holiday as this long weekend is unofficially seen as the end of summer. It marks the closing of many businesses, attractions and services, and the beginning of a change of hours of operation for many others.

Although not officially a holiday, Halloween, 31 October, is a significant and fun celebration. Based on a Celtic pagan tradition, Halloween is a time of ghosts, goblins and witches. Children dress in costume and in the evening go door to door 'trick-or-treating' where they receive candy treats.

Houses are decorated with candle-lit hollowed-out pumpkins. Adults, too, often have costume parties. Traditionally costumes have been based on the supernatural but nowadays anything goes. In larger cities, the gay community has adopted Halloween as a major event and nightclubs are often the scene of wild costume parties.

March Break is a week-long intermission in studies for elementary and high school students across the country. The time taken each year varies with each province and school board but is sometime in the month of March. Many people take this as an opportune time for a holiday and all trains, planes and buses are generally very busy.

National Holidays

The following is a list of the main national public holidays:

January
  New Year's Day (1 January)
April-May
  Easter (Good Friday, also Easter Monday for government & schools)
  Victoria Day (Monday preceding May 24 except in the Atlantic Provinces)
July
  Canada Day, called Memorial Day in Newfoundland (1 July)
September-October
  Labour Day (first Monday in September)
  Thanksgiving (second Monday in October)
November-December
  Remembrance Day (11 November – banks & government)
  Christmas Day (25 December)
  Boxing Day (26 December – many retailers open, other businesses closed)

Provincial Holidays

The following is a list of the provincial public holidays:

February-March
  Alberta – Family Day, third Monday in February
  Newfoundland – St Patrick's Day (Monday nearest 17 March), St George's Day (Monday nearest 23 April)

June-July
  Quebec – Fête Nationale, formerly known as Saint Jean Baptiste Day (24 June)
  Newfoundland – Discovery Day (Monday nearest 24 June)
  Orangeman's Day (Monday nearest 13 July)
August
  Yukon – Discovery Day (third Monday in August)
  All other provinces Civic Holiday (1 August or first Monday in August)

CULTURAL EVENTS

Major events are listed in the text under the city or town where they occur. There are many others.

The provincial governments publish annual lists of events and special attractions as part of their tourism promotion packages. Each give dates, locations and often brief descriptions. Local tourist departments may print up more detailed and extensive lists of their own, which include cultural and sporting exhibitions and happenings of all kinds. Military and historic celebrations, ethnic festivals and music shows are all included. Some provinces produce separate booklets for summer and winter events.

Major provincial and national holidays are usually cause for some celebration, especially in summer when events often wrap up with a fireworks display. The 1 July Canada Day festivities are particularly noted for this with the skies lit up from coast to coast.

POST & COMMUNICATIONS
Post

The mail service is neither quick nor cheap but it's reliable. Canadian post offices will keep poste-restante mail marked 'c/o General Delivery' for two weeks and then return it to sender.

Standard 1st-class air-mail letter is limited to 50 grams to North American destinations but as much as 500 grams to other international destinations. To the US, heavier mail can go either by surface or, more expensively, by air in small packet mail. Anything over one kg goes by surface parcel post.

To other international destinations, letter packages, to a maximum of two kg, can be sent by air. Small packet mail up to the same weight can go by either surface or air. Packages over two kg are sent by parcel post and different rates apply. For full details go to a post office; full-page pamphlets which explain all the various options, categories, requirements and prices are available. Suffice it to say there are numerous methods for posting something, depending on the sender's time and money limitations: air, surface or a combination of these. Rates vary according to destination. Mail over 10 kg goes surface only. For added security, speed or other requirements there is registered mail and special delivery, and both surface and air mail for packages. Canada Post also offers an international courier-style service.

Some countries require a customs declaration on incoming parcels. Check at the post office.

Aside from the post offices themselves, stamps and postal services are often available at other outlets such as chemists (drug stores) and some small variety stores. Finding them is a matter of asking around. Hotel concessions also often stock stamps.

Postal Rates

1st-class letter or postcard within Canada: 45 cents (up to 30 grams; includes GST)

1st-class letter or postcard to US: 52 cents (up to 30 grams)

1st-class letter or postcard to other destinations: 90 cents (up to 20 grams)

Aerogrammes (which are not common) cost the same.

Telephone

Canada has an excellent telephone system. Rates tend to be low for local use and rather costly for long distances. Overall, the rates are about the same as in the USA but probably more expensive (at least for long distances) than in Europe. Public telephones are generally quite readily available and can be found in hotel lobbies, bars, restaurants, large department stores and many public buildings. Telephone booths can be found on street corners in cities and towns.

The basic rate of a call varies but is generally 25 cents for a local connection. If you wish to speak to an operator (dial ☎ 0) you will be connected free of charge. There is also no charge from a public phone for dialling ☎ 411, the telephone information number or for ☎ 911, the emergency number. For inquiries on long-distance calls, dial ☎ 1 (area code) 555-1212. This is also a free call.

Long-distance calls to anywhere in the world can be made from any phone but the rate varies depending on how it is done and when. A call made without the assistance of an operator is not only cheapest but quickest. This can be done if you know the area code as well as the number of the party to be reached. With operator assistance, calls in increasing order of cost are, station to station (no particular person to speak to required), collect (reverse charge) and person to person.

In Canada, long-distance rates are cheapest from 11 pm to 8 am daily. The second most economical time slot is from 6 pm to 11 pm daily except Sunday when this rate runs from 8 am to 11 pm.

The most expensive time to call is from 8 am to 6 pm Monday to Friday.

Reductions can also apply to calls to the USA or overseas. All international rates and codes are listed in the front pages of the telephone book.

Telephone Area Codes	
South-eastern Ontario	613
Toronto City	416
Greater Toronto	905
South-western Ontario	519
Western Ontario	807
Central Ontario	705
Montreal	514
Quebec	819
Eastern Quebec	418
Newfoundland & Labrador	709
Nova Scotia	902
Prince Edward Island	902
New Brunswick	506
Manitoba	204
Saskatchewan	306
Alberta	403
Vancouver Region	604
British Columbia	250
Yukon	403
Northwest Territories (West)	403
Northwest Territories (East)	819-709

The 1-800 and 1-888 numbers which many businesses, ferries, hotels and tourist offices operate are toll free; no long-distance charges apply. Note that some of these numbers are good for anywhere in North America, others may be within Canada only and still others may cover just one province. You don't know until you try the number.

All Canadian business and residential phones are paid for on a flat monthly rate system, the number of calls made is immaterial. So don't feel guilty about the cost of using a friend's telephone to make local calls.

For those who will be using the telephone in hotels, motels, guesthouses, and other such places, note that most places charge a service fee for the use of the phone on a per call basis even for local calls. At maybe 50 cents per call, this can add up resulting in a bit of a shock on the final room bill, especially if you aren't expecting it.

Many Canadian businesses, tourist attractions and information offices use the touch-tone menu information system. After dialling, the caller is given a range of options and recorded messages. This can be useful in learning the hours of operation of a museum, for example, but also frustrating because it's difficult to reach someone to whom you can direct specific questions.

Telephone calling cards allow callers to make long-distance calls and have them charged to their home number thus eliminating the need to feed the phone a pocketful of change.

Something else to look for are the pre-paid calling cards sold by a number of different companies. These plastic cards are available in various values from $10 to $100 and allow the holder to make long-distance calls from any phone quickly until the value of the card has been used up in charges. Calling the supplied number provides dialling instructions in various languages. Calls can be made from any touch-tone telephone. These cards are for sale at some convenience stores and some hostels. One company offering them is CardCaller Canada in Toronto (☎ (416) 733-2163).

Bell Canada has its own card which can be purchased from Bell Canada Phone Centres or at Shopper's Drug Mart stores.

Before purchasing any one of the passes be sure to check on how long it is good for and whether it can be used for calls in Canada only, across North America or internationally as well.

Fax, Telegraph & E-mail

Fax machines accessible to the public are available at major hotels, city post offices and at a range of small businesses in major centres. To locate one of the latter, check under facsimile, stationers or mail box services in the Yellow Pages.

To send a telegram anywhere in Canada or overseas, contact CN-CP Telecommunications listed in the telephone directory. Other than in some private businesses, telex is not readily available.

E-mail access is available at most large, corporate hotels. In addition, most cities and some smaller centres now have Internet cafes which offer on-line computer use at low rates.

TIME

Canada spans six of the world's 24 time zones. As shown on the map, the eastern zone in Newfoundland is unusual in that it's only a half-hour different from the adjacent zone. The time difference from coast to coast is 4½ hours.

Canada uses Daylight Saving Time during summer. It begins on the last Sunday in April and ends on the last Sunday in October. It is one hour later than Standard Time, meaning a seemingly longer summer day. Saskatchewan is the exception, using Standard Time all year round.

For details of each provincial time zone see the Information section at the beginning of each province chapter.

Some examples for time comparisons are: if it's noon in Toronto (UST/GMT), it is 9 am in Vancouver or Los Angeles, 1 pm in Halifax, 5 pm in London, 2 am (the following day) in Tokyo, and 3 am (the following day) in Sydney.

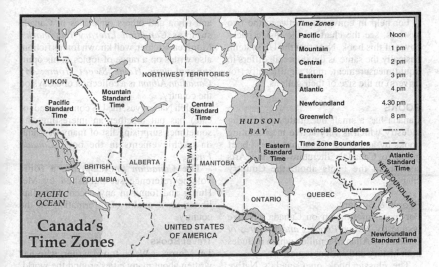

Time Zones	
Pacific	Noon
Mountain	1 pm
Central	2 pm
Eastern	3 pm
Atlantic	4 pm
Newfoundland	4.30 pm
Greenwich	8 pm
Provincial Boundaries	————
Time Zone Boundaries	— — —

Canada's Time Zones

ELECTRICITY

Canada, like the USA, operates on 110-V, 60-cycle electric power. Non-North American visitors should bring a plug adapter if they wish to use their own small appliances such as razors, hairdryers etc. Canadian electrical goods come with either a two-pronged plug (the same as a US one) or sometimes a three-pronger with the added ground. Most sockets can accommodate both types of plugs.

LAUNDRY

All cities and major towns have central storefronts known as laundromats with rows of coin-operated washing machines and dryers. These tend to be open every day until about 11·pm. There is rarely an attendant on the premises. Many laundromats have machines which will dispense change and ones for dispensing soap. It is less trouble, more reliable, more convenient and cheaper to bring both. It's fine to go out for a coffee while the wash goes through its cycle, but if you leave a load too long it may be dumped on top of a machine when somebody takes it over for their clothes. A wash and dry costs a couple of dollars, most often in one dollar or 25-cent coins.

Also common are dry cleaners, known simply as 'the cleaners', where clothes can be cleaned and pressed in about a day, sometimes two or three.

The better hotels will likely have an in-house service but rates will be higher than going to the cleaners on your own.

Many campgrounds and some B&Bs have a washer and dryer that guests may use, generally at an extra fee.

WEIGHTS & MEASURES

Canada officially changed from imperial measurement to the metric system in the 1970s. Most citizens accepted this change only begrudgingly and even today both systems remain for many day-to-day uses.

All speed-limit signs are in metric – so do not go 100 mph! Gasoline is sold in litres but items such as hamburger meat and potatoes are still often sold by the pound. Radio stations will often give temperatures in both Celsius and Fahrenheit degrees.

The expensive changeover has really resulted in a bit of a mess. The old system can never be eliminated completely as long as the USA, Canada's largest trading partner, still uses their version of imperial measure.

For help in converting between the two systems, see the chart on the inside back-cover of this book. Note that the US system, basically the same as the imperial, differs in liquid measurement, most significantly (for drivers) in the size of their gallons.

BOOKS

Canada has a small but quality publishing industry which is very active in promoting books by and about Canadians. For a brief guide to Canada's literature see the Arts section in the Facts about the Country chapter.

People & Society

For more information on Canada's Native people try *Native Peoples and Cultures of Canada* by Allan Macmillan which includes both history and current issues.

The classic book on Canada's Native people, *The Indians of Canada* was written in 1932 by Diamond Jenness. Originally from New Zealand, the author's life is an amazing story in its own right as he spent years living with various indigenous people across the country. The book has been reprinted many times.

History

Pierre Berton is Canada's prime chronicler of the country's history. He has written on a wide range of subjects such as the gold rush, the railways and the Depression in an entertaining and informative way. Peter C Newman writes on Canadian business but has also produced an intriguing history of the Hudson's Bay Company, *Caesar's of the Wilderness*, beginning with the early fur-trading days.

A basic primer on the country's history is *The Penguin History of Canada* by Kenneth McNaught.

General Reference

Among academic writers, two who stand out are Northrop Frye for literary criticism and Marshall McLuhan for media observations.

John Robert Colombo has written a number of books of Canadian facts, figures

and trivia and others on places in Canada such as *Canadian Literary Landmarks*. Mordecai Richler, well known for his fiction, also writes on a range of topics in his opinionated way. *Home Sweet Home: My Canadian Album* is a collection of essays on the country.

Ralph Nader (yes, the US consumer advocate) has put together an interesting and sometimes surprising list of many of Canada's achievements in the book *Canada Firsts*.

The *Canadian Encyclopedia*, a four-volume reference set published by Mel Hurtig and found in any decent Canadian library, is a wealth of information on the country.

Travel Books

Jan Morris, a Welsh travel writer, who has written about many cities around the world, published *City to City* in 1990. Written after travelling Canada coast to coast it is a highly readable collection of essays of fact and opinion about 10 Canadian cities and their people. Note that this book was also published under the name *O Canada: Travels in an Unknown Country*.

Maple Leaf Rag is a quirky collection of travel essays by Stephen Brook. Stuart McLean in *Welcome Home: travels in small town Canada* reveals much about the character of small-town life and describes in a very approachable style some of the changes taking place within them.

Kildare Dobbs wrote of a bus trip across the country in *Ribbon of Highway: The Trans Canada Hwy Coast to Coast*. John and Martha Stradiotta describe the many, accessible varied national and provincial parks across the country in *The Road to Canada's Wild's: parks along the Trans Canada Hwy*. *Canada's National Parks – A Visitor's Guide* by Marylee Stephenson is the most complete guide to the country's national parks and provides all the essential information.

Gary and Joanie McGuffin have written *Where Rivers Run: a 6000-mile exploration of Canada by canoe*. Also for adventurers is *Freshwater Saga: memoirs of a lifetime of wilderness canoeing* by Eric Morse. *Lords of the Arctic: A journey among the polar bears* by Richard Davids is based in Churchill which many travellers may visit.

Farley Mowat, with such books as *Never Cry Wolf*, writes about the north, wildlife, nature and speaks for their conservation.

Wild is Always There: Canada through the eyes of foreign writers is a collection of pieces by a variety of writers who have spent some time in the country. It is edited by Greg Gatenby of Toronto who puts together writer festivals and readings featuring writers from around the world.

Bookshops

Any store of reasonable size will have a Canadiana section covering both fiction and nonfiction titles. Other stores of note are mentioned in the text in the city sections. The country's two largest book store chains are SmithBooks and Coles which merged in 1995 and have giant outlets called Chapters. Outside of Quebec and New Brunswick, books written in French are generally available only at specialised shops which are found in most major cities.

MAPS

Good provincial road maps are available from the respective provincial tourist offices. Bookstores generally sell both provincial and city maps. Service stations often have road maps as well.

For a list and order form for topographic maps of anywhere in the country contact the Canada Map Office (☎ (613) 952-7000), 615 Booth St, Ottawa, Ont K1A 0E9. Through this address any map can be ordered by mail. Although there is a retail outlet on the premises, it is small and deals only with Ottawa area maps. The main retail store with all the maps is well out of the centre south in Nepean at 130 Bentley St.

World of Maps & Travel Books (☎ (613) 724-6776), 118 Holland Ave, Ottawa, Ont K1Y 0X6 stocks thousands of road maps and topographic maps of Canada and the world. The store accepts orders by electronic mail (maps@magi.com) and has a world-wide

web site where new maps and publications are reviewed.

Canada Map Company (☎ (416) 362-9297), 211 Yonge St, Toronto, Ont M5B 1M4, has a wide selection of maps of all kinds. Standard highway maps, city maps, fishing maps, nautical and aviation charts and topographic maps are all available. They will fill phone and mail orders.

Others are listed in the text.

MEDIA
Newspapers & Magazines
The *Globe & Mail* newspaper, sometimes termed Canada's newspaper, is published in Toronto but is available across the country daily and provides a well-written record of national affairs from politics to the arts. Other principal newspapers are the *Montreal Gazette*, *Ottawa Citizen*, *Toronto Star*, and *Vancouver Sun*.

In Quebec, readers of French should have a look at both the federalist *La Presse*, the largest circulation French daily and the separatist-leaning *Le Devoir*, although there are other French dailies as well. *Maclean's* is Canada's weekly news magazine.

Shops specialising in magazines and newspapers from around the world can be found in many cities across the country. Staff of major hotels should be able to direct you to these central outlets although some hotels also stock a selection of foreign papers. A selection of international periodicals may also be available at airport kiosks.

Radio & TV
The Canadian Broadcasting Corporation (CBC) with both national and regional broadcasts in both radio (on AM and FM bands) and TV can be seen or heard almost anywhere in the country including some of the more remote areas. It carries more Canadian content in music and information than any of the private broadcast companies. CBC Radio, in particular, is a fine service which unites listeners across the country with some of its programmes.

Highly recommended is the Morningside show heard between 9 am and noon during weekdays. It's entertaining, educational and offers listeners a well-rounded view of the nation's opinions.

The CBC also has a French radio and TV network, both going under the name Radio-Canada. These can also be tuned into anywhere across the country.

The other major national TV network is the Canadian Television Network (CTV). It is the main commercial channel broadcasting a mix of Canadian, US and national programmes. Its nightly national news show is seen across the country.

Many Canadians can readily tune into TV and radio stations from the USA and often do.

PHOTOGRAPHY & VIDEO

Camera shops in the major centres are good, well-informed and stock a range of products. All films are available at these outlets. Stores in larger centres also provide the freshest film (always check the expiry date) and the best prices.

Once widely and easily available, transparency film (slides) has now become increasingly difficult to get without going to a camera shop. Chemists, department stores and corner convenience shops generally no longer carry anything other than basic Kodak and Fuji print film.

Most film in Canada is bought with processing not included. An exception is Kodachrome which can be purchased with processing included (the cheapest option) or finishing extra. The Kodachrome processing plant is in the USA and film can be mailed directly to them, or you can leave the film at a camera store where, for a modest fee, the delivery will handled. Black's is a good retail outlet found across the country except in Quebec. It sells a good selection of film and offers quick processing, too.

Carrying an extra battery for your built-in light metre is a good idea because you know it will die at the most inopportune time.

Canadian airports use new X-ray scanning machines for security which should pose no problems (but can) to most films. Any given roll should not be scanned more than half a dozen times to be on the safe side. Also with specialised film, for example film with an ASA (ISO) of 400 or higher, X-ray damage is a real threat. For those who do not want to take a chance with any film, good camera shops now offer lead-lined pouches which can hold several canisters of film and which provide total protection. And, no, they are not unduly heavy.

Many people around the world are now using video camcorders and Canada is no exception. There are four-size formats in use in the country; VHS, VHS C size, Beta and 8 mm. For best service and selection visit a camera store. Tapes are also available at Radio Shack, a cross-country electronic retailer.

HEALTH

Canada is a pretty safe place to visit and little is necessary in the way of preparation. Travel health depends on your predeparture preparations, your day-to-day health care while travelling and how you handle any medical problem or emergency that does develop.

While the list of potential dangers can seem quite frightening, with a little luck, some basic precautions and adequate information few travellers experience more than upset stomachs.

Travel Health Guide
Travel with Children, Maureen Wheeler, Lonely Planet Publications, includes basic advice on travel health for younger children.

Predeparture Preparations
Health Insurance A travel insurance policy to cover theft, loss and medical problems is a wise idea. There is a wide variety of policies and your travel agent will have recommendations. The international student travel policies handled by STA Travel or other student travel organisations are usually good value. Some policies offer lower and higher medical expenses options but the higher one is chiefly for countries like the USA which have extremely high medical costs. Check the small print:

- Some policies specifically exclude 'dangerous activities' which can include scuba diving, motorcycling, even trekking. If such activities are on your agenda, you don't want that sort of policy. A locally acquired motor-cycle licence may not be valid under your policy.
- You may prefer a policy which pays doctors or hospitals direct rather than you having to pay on the spot and claim later. If you have to claim later make sure you keep all documentation. Some policies ask you to call back (reverse charges) to a centre in your home country where an immediate assessment of your problem is made.
- Check if the policy covers ambulances or an emergency flight home. If you have to stretch out you will need two seats and somebody has to pay for them.

Check to see if your health insurance covers you during a visit to Canada and the precise details, limitations and exclusions of that coverage. Medical, hospital and dental care is excellent but very expensive in Canada. The standard rate for a bed in a city hospital is at least $500 a day and up to $2000 a day in the major centres for nonresidents.

The largest seller of hospital and medical insurance to visitors to Canada is John Ingle Insurance. They offer hospital medical care (HMC) policies from a minimum of seven days to a maximum of one year with a possible renewal of one additional year. The 30-day basic coverage costs $88 for an adult under the age of 55, $115 for ages 55 to 64 and $136 above that. Family rates are available. Coverage includes the hospital rate, doctors' fees, extended health care and other features. Visitors to Canada are not covered for conditions which they had prior to arrival.

Be sure to inquire about coverage details if you intend to make side trips to the USA, Mexico, the Caribbean countries or others.

Ingle also offers insurance policies for foreign students (at reduced rates) and to those visiting Canada on working visas. Its policies may be very beneficial in filling in coverage gaps before either a government policy kicks in, in the case of students, or the employers' paid benefits begin, in the case of foreign workers. Again, the policies may vary depending where in the country you settle.

Ingle has offices in major cities across the country and representatives in the northern territories. The head office is (☎ (416) 340-0100, 1-800-387-4770) 438 University Ave, Suite 1200, Toronto, Ont, M7Y 2Z1. It can supply information pamphlets in over 15 languages and staff in the office in Toronto even speak most of them. The pamphlet includes an application form and payment can be made before or after arrival in Canada. It can often be found at post offices, banks, chemists, doctors' offices and some shopping centres. Read the information carefully. There are exclusions, conditions etc which should be clearly understood. Also check the maximum amounts payable, different policies allow for greater payments.

There are many other companies offering travellers' insurance, consult the telephone Yellow Pages.

Medical Kit It's wise to carry a small, straightforward medical kit. The kit should include:

- Aspirin or paracetamol (acetaminophen in the US) – for pain or fever.
- Antihistamine (such as Benadryl) – useful as a decongestant for colds and allergies, to ease the itch from insect bites or stings, and to help prevent motion sickness. There are several antihistamines on the market, all with different pros and cons (eg a tendency to cause drowsiness), so it's worth discussing your requirements with a pharmacist or doctor. Antihistamines may cause sedation and interact with alcohol so care should be taken when using them.
- Antibiotics – useful if you're travelling well off the beaten track, but they must be prescribed and you should carry the prescription with you. Some individuals are allergic to commonly prescribed antibiotics such as penicillin or sulpha drugs. It would be sensible to always carry this information when travelling.
- Loperamide (eg Imodium) or Lomotil for diarrhoea; prochlorperazine (eg Stemetil) or metaclopramide (eg Maxalon) for nausea and vomiting. Antidiarrhoea medication should not be given to children under the age of 12.
- Rehydration mixture – for treatment of severe diarrhoea. This is particularly important if travelling with children, but is recommended for everyone.

- Antiseptic such as povidone-iodine (eg Betadine), which comes as a solution, ointment, powder and impregnated swabs – for cuts and grazes.
- Calamine lotion or Stingose spray – to ease irritation from bites or stings.
- Bandages and Band-aids – for minor injuries.
- Scissors, tweezers and a thermometer (note that mercury thermometers are prohibited by airlines).
- Cold and flu tablets and throat lozenges
- Insect repellent, sunscreen, chap stick and water purification tablets.

Ideally, antibiotics should be administered only under medical supervision and should never be taken indiscriminately. Take only the recommended dose at the prescribed intervals and continue using the antibiotic for the prescribed period, even if the illness seems to be cured earlier. Antibiotics are quite specific to the infections they can treat. Stop immediately if there are any serious reactions and don't use them at all if you are unsure if you have the correct one.

Health Preparations Make sure you're healthy before you start travelling. If you are embarking on a long trip make sure your teeth are OK.

If you wear glasses take a spare pair and your prescription. Losing your glasses can be a real problem, although in many places you can get new spectacles made up quickly, cheaply and competently.

If you require a particular medication take an adequate supply, as it may not be available locally. Take the prescription or, better still, part of the packaging showing the generic rather than the brand name (which may not be locally available), as it will make getting replacements easier. It's a wise idea to have a legible prescription with you to show that you legally use the medication – it's surprising how often over-the-counter drugs from one place are illegal without a prescription or even banned in another.

Immunisations Normally no vaccinations are required and there's nothing to recommend for protection here. You need shots for cholera and yellow fever if you're coming

from an endemic area or have been in contact with these diseases.

Basic Rules
Water Purification Canadian tap water from coast to coast is safe to drink. The following information is for those who intend to be out in the woods or in the wilds on outdoor excursions using lake and river water. Since most extended adventure trips are taken in government parks, ask the ranger about local water quality. The simplest way of purifying water is to boil it thoroughly. Vigorously boiling for five minutes should be satisfactory even at high altitude. Remember that at high altitude water boils at a lower temperature, so germs are less likely to be killed.

Simple filtering will not remove all dangerous organisms, so if you cannot boil water it should be treated chemically. Chlorine tablets (Puritabs, Steritabs or other brand names) will kill many pathogens, but not giardia and amoebic cysts. Iodine is very effective in purifying water and is available in tablet form (such as Potable Aqua), but follow the directions carefully and remember that too much iodine can be harmful.

If you can't find tablets, tincture of iodine (2%) or iodine crystals can be used. Two drops of tincture of iodine per litre or quart of clear water is the recommended dosage; the treated water should be left to stand for 20 to 30 minutes before drinking. Iodine crystals can also be used to purify water but this is a more complicated process, as you have to first prepare a saturated iodine solution. Iodine loses its effectiveness if exposed to air or damp so keep it in a tightly sealed container. Flavoured powder will disguise the taste of treated water and is a good idea if you are travelling with children.

Nutrition If you're travelling hard and fast and therefore missing meals, or if you simply lose your appetite, you can soon start to lose weight and place your health at risk. Make sure your diet is well balanced, if not, it's a good idea to take vitamin and iron pills.

Everyday Health A normal body temperature is 37°C (98.6°F); more than 2°C (4°F) higher is a 'high' fever. A normal adult pulse rate is 60 to 80 per minute (children 80 to 100, babies 100 to 140). You should know how to take a temperature and a pulse rate. As a general rule the pulse increases about 20 beats per minute for each °C (2°F) rise in fever.

Respiration (breathing) rate is also an indicator of illness. Count the number of breaths per minute: between 12 and 20 is normal for adults and older children (up to 30 for younger children, 40 for babies). People with a high fever or serious respiratory illness (like pneumonia) breathe more quickly than normal. More than 40 shallow breaths a minute usually means pneumonia.

Medical Problems & Treatment
Potential medical problems can be broken down into several areas. First there are the climatic and geographical considerations problems caused by extremes of temperature, altitude or motion. Then there are diseases and illnesses caused by insect bites or stings and animal or human contact.

Self-diagnosis and treatment can be risky, so wherever possible seek qualified help. This is when that medical insurance really comes in handy. Help can be found at the emergency department of any hospital although a lengthy wait may be necessary for non-critical attention. During regular hours, it's worth calling a hospital or doctor and asking the location of the nearest clinic. The wait is unlikely to be as long as at big city emergency wards.

Climatic & Geographical Considerations
Sunburn & Windburn Sunburn and windburn should be primary concerns for anyone planning to spend time trekking or travelling over snow and ice. The sun will burn you even if you feel cold and the wind will cause dehydration and chafing of skin. Use a good sunscreen and a moisture cream on exposed skin, even on cloudy days. A hat provides added protection and zinc cream or some other barrier cream for your nose and lips is recommended if you're spending any time on ice or snow.

Reflection and glare from ice and snow can cause snow blindness so high-protection sunglasses should be considered essential for any sort of glacier visit or ski trip. Calamine lotion is good for mild sunburn.

Cold Despite the perception by some that Canada is a perpetually ice-bound wasteland, health problems due to extreme cold are not likely to be suffered by many people. On winter days when frost bite is a possibility (due almost always to a combination of low temperature and high wind, the result of which is a reading known as the wind-chill factor) you will be aware of it. Everybody will be discussing it, the radio will broadcast warnings about how many minutes of exposed skin is acceptable and ... it will be bloody cold.

If you are in the mountains or the north, you should always be prepared for cold, wet or windy conditions even if you're just out walking or hitching.

Hypothermia occurs when the body loses heat faster than it can produce it and the core temperature of the body falls. It is surprisingly easy to progress from very cold to dangerously cold due to a combination of wind, wet clothing, fatigue and hunger, even if the air temperature is above freezing. It is best to dress in layers; silk, wool and some of the new artificial fibres are all good insulating materials. A hat is important, as a lot of heat is lost through the head. A strong, waterproof outer layer is essential, as keeping dry is vital. Carry basic supplies, including food containing simple sugars to generate heat quickly and take lots of fluid to drink.

Symptoms of hypothermia are exhaustion, numb skin (particularly toes and fingers), shivering, slurred speech, irrational or violent behaviour, lethargy, stumbling, dizzy spells, muscle cramps and violent bursts of energy. Irrationality may take the form of sufferers claiming they are warm and trying to take off their clothes.

To treat hypothermia, first get the person

out of the wind and/or rain, remove their clothing if its wet and replace it with dry, warm clothing. Give them hot liquids – not alcohol – and some high-kilojoule, easily digestible food. Do not rub victims, instead allow them to slowly warm themselves. This should be enough for the early stages of hypothermia. If it has gone further it may be necessary to place victims in warm sleeping bags and get in with them.

Altitude Sickness Acute Mountain Sickness or AMS occurs at high altitude and can be fatal. The lack of oxygen at high altitudes affects most people to some extent.

A number of measures can be adopted to prevent acute mountain sickness:

- Ascend slowly – have frequent rest days, spending two to three nights at each rise of 1000 metres. If you reach a high altitude by trekking, acclimatisation takes place gradually and you are less likely to be affected than if you fly direct.
- Drink extra fluids. The mountain air is dry and cold and moisture is lost as you breathe.
- Eat light, high-carbohydrate meals for more energy.
- Avoid alcohol as it may increase the risk of dehydration.
- Avoid sedatives.

Even with acclimatisation you may still have trouble adjusting. Headaches, nausea, dizziness, a dry cough, insomnia, breathlessness and loss of appetite are all signs to heed. Mild altitude problems will generally abate after a day or so but if the symptoms persist or become worse the only treatment is to descend even 500 metres can help. Increasing tiredness, confusion, and lack of coordination and balance are real danger signs. Any of these symptoms individually, even just a persistent headache, can be a warning.

There is no hard and fast rule as to how high is too high: AMS has been fatal at altitudes of 3000 metres, although 3500 to 4500 metres is the usual range. It is always wise to sleep at a lower altitude than the greatest height reached during the day.

Motion Sickness Eating lightly before and during a trip will reduce the chances of motion sickness. If you are prone to motion sickness try to find a place that minimises disturbance – near the wing on aircraft, close to midships on boats, near the centre on buses. Fresh air usually helps, reading or cigarette smoke doesn't. Commercial anti-motion-sickness preparations, which can cause drowsiness, have to be taken before the trip commences; when you're feeling sick it's too late. Ginger (available in capsule form) and peppermint (including mint-flavoured sweets) are natural preventatives.

Diseases Spread by Animals & People

Giardiasis If you're going to backcountry camp, you should take precautions against an intestinal parasite *(Giardia lamblia)* which causes giardiasis, known colloquially as 'beaver fever'. This intestinal parasite is present in contaminated water.

The symptoms are stomach cramps, nausea, a bloated stomach, watery, foul-smelling diarrhoea and frequent gas. Giardiasis can appear several weeks after you have been exposed to the parasite. The symptoms may disappear for a few days and then return; this can go on for several weeks. Tinidazole, known as Fasigyn, or metronidazole (Flagyl) are the recommended drugs for treatment. Either can be used in a single treatment dose. Antibiotics are of no use. At the beginning of the 1980s, the condition was considered rare and nobody had ever heard of it but it is now widespread and has caused many hikers and canoeists a lot of discomfort.

Rabies This isn't a major problem, but rabies is something to be aware of when spending any time in the woods or undeveloped areas. Animals most likely affected are the squirrel, skunk, racoon, bat and particularly, the fox. Paradoxically, all of the above animals have learned to adapt quite well to populated regions, and may be seen in city parks and recreation areas, wooded areas around rivers and streams and even along residential streets after dark. Especially on garbage nights!

Rabies is caused by a bite or scratch by an infected animal. Any bite, scratch or even lick from a mammal should be cleaned immediately and thoroughly. Scrub with soap and running water, and then clean with an alcohol or iodine solution. If there is any possibility that the animal is infected, medical help should be sought immediately. Even if the animal is not rabid, all bites should be treated seriously as they can become infected or can result in tetanus. A rabies vaccination is now available and should be considered if you are in a high-risk category – eg, if you intend to explore caves (bat bites could be dangerous) or work with animals.

Lyme Disease Less of a threat but still something to be aware of is the relatively recent threat of Lyme disease (doesn't it seem as though there's always something new out there to get you?).

Since the late 1980s each summer sees more of this disease although the vast majority of North American cases have occurred in the USA. The disease is really more of a condition transmitted by a certain species of deer tick, similar to a tick found on a dog but smaller. The tick infects the skin with the spirochaete bacterium which causes the disease.

The disease was first identified on the continent in 1975 in Lyme, Connecticut, hence the name. Most cases still go undetected, misdiagnosed or unreported. It is a difficult disease to diagnose because symptoms vary widely. Consult a doctor if you experience the following:

Sometime within 30 days after being bitten a small red bump appears surrounded by a rash often but not always accompanied by flu-like symptoms.

Treatment with antibiotics – often tetracycline, 250 mg four times a day for at least 10 days – is simple and effective, if the disease is caught at this early stage. Later symptoms

can be quite severe and include a form of arthritis which affects the knees.

The best way to avoid the whole business is to take precautions in areas where it has been reported such as Turkey Point, Ontario.

If walking in the woods, cover the body as much as possible, use an insect repellent containing diethylmetatoluamide (DEET) and at the end of the day check yourself, children or pets for the ticks. DEET is not recommended for children, so a milder substitute will have to do. Chances are that you will not feel it if bitten. Of course, most ticks are not the right sort to pass on the disease and even most of the nasties do not carry the harmful bacteria.

Sexually Transmitted Diseases (STDs) In common with other Western countries, Canada has its share of sexually transmitted diseases. As might be expected, the rates for such conditions are highest in the large cities. Sexual contact with an infected sexual partner spreads these diseases. While abstinence is the only 100% preventative, using condoms is also effective.

Gonorrhoea and syphilis are the most common of these diseases; sores, blisters or rashes around the genitals, discharges or pain when urinating are common symptoms. Symptoms may be less marked or not observed at all in women. Syphilis symptoms eventually disappear completely but the disease continues and can cause severe problems in later years. The treatment of gonorrhoea and syphilis is by antibiotics.

There are numerous other sexually transmitted diseases, for most of which effective treatment is available. However, there is no cure for herpes and there is also currently no cure for AIDS. Using condoms is the most effective preventative. Canadian government advertising, promoting the use of condoms, encourages young women to lay down the law: 'no glove, no love'.

HIV/AIDS HIV, the Human Immunodeficiency Virus, may develop into AIDS, Acquired Immune Deficiency Syndrome. HIV is a major problem in many countries.

Any exposure to blood, blood products or bodily fluids may put the individual at risk. In many developing countries transmission is predominantly through heterosexual sexual activity. This is quite different from industrialised countries where transmission is mostly through contact between homosexual or bisexual males or contaminated needles in IV drug users. Apart from abstinence, the most effective preventative is always to practise safe sex using condoms. It is impossible to detect the HIVpositive status of an otherwise healthy-looking person without a blood test.

HIV/AIDS can also be spread through infected blood transfusions; most developing countries cannot afford to screen blood for transfusions. It can also be spread by dirty needles – vaccinations, acupuncture, tattooing and body piercing can potentially be as dangerous as intravenous drug use if the equipment is not clean.

Women's Health

Gynaecological Problems Poor diet, lowered resistance due to the use of antibiotics for stomach upsets and even contraceptive pills can lead to vaginal infections when travelling in hot climates. Wearing skirts or loose-fitting trousers and cotton underwear will help to prevent infections.

Yeast infections, characterised by a rash, itch and discharge, can be treated with a vinegar or even lemon-juice douche or with yoghurt. Nystatin, miconazole or clotrimazole suppositories are the usual medical prescription. Trichomonas and gardnerella are more serious infections; symptoms are a discharge and a burning sensation when urinating. Male sexual partners must also be treated, and if a vinegar-water douche is not effective medical attention should be sought. Metronidazole (Flagyl) is the prescribed drug.

Pregnancy Most miscarriages occur during the first three months of pregnancy, so this is the most risky time to travel as far as your own health is concerned. Miscarriage is not uncommon, and can occasionally lead to severe bleeding. The last three months should also be spent within reasonable distance of good medical care. A baby born as early as 24 weeks stands a chance of survival, but only in a good modern hospital. Pregnant women should avoid all unnecessary medication, but vaccinations and malarial prophylactics should still be taken where possible. Additional care should be taken to prevent illness and particular attention should be paid to diet and nutrition. Alcohol and nicotine, for example, should be avoided.

Women travellers often find that their periods become irregular or even cease while they're on the road. Remember that a missed period in these circumstances doesn't necessarily indicate pregnancy. There are Family Planning clinics in many small and large urban centres where you can seek advice and have a urine test to determine whether you are pregnant or not.

WOMEN TRAVELLERS

More and more, women are travelling alone in Canada. This goes for vacationers, visitors and women on business.

There are no overriding differences for men and women travelling in Canada and as a Western country there are no particular cultural or traditional pitfalls of which females need to be aware.

As in so much of the world, though, women may face some sexism and the threat of violence is certainly felt more by women than by men. The following tips to consider have been suggested by women.

When travelling alone, try to arrive at your destination before dark. If arriving at a bus or train station (bus stations in particular are often not in the best parts of town) take a taxi to the place where you're spending the night. In some of the larger cities, the bus and/or train station is connected to the subway system. Subways in Canada are clean and safe. Once close to your destination, catch a taxi from the subway stop.

Some parts of the downtown areas of major cities should be avoided at night especially on a Friday or Saturday. Where applicable these areas are noted in the text.

If driving, keep your vehicle well maintained and don't get low on gasoline. If you do break down on the highway, especially at night, a large pre-made sign placed in the window reading 'Call Police' is not a bad idea. Once driving I saw such a sign, stopped to call police and was told they already had a dozen calls and a cruiser was on the way, so motorists do respond to this. Away from busy areas, it is not advisable for women alone to get out of their car and wait beside it, especially at night. Wait inside with the doors locked. In cities avoid underground parking lots, these are uniformly creepy.

Care should be taken when hitchhiking, especially if you're travelling alone – use common sense and don't be afraid to say no to lifts. It is rare indeed to see women alone hitching and it can't be recommended. Mixed sex couples are the better way for women to hitch a ride if they are determined to travel this way. For more information see the Hitching section in the Getting Around chapter.

Women alone may be more comfortable if their room is booked before they arrive in a new town. Many women prefer to simply use an initial with their surname and not to use a title when making reservations or appointments. Many of the chain hotels and motels have toll-free numbers which allow for reservations to be made in advance.

Hostels and B&Bs are good, safe choices. Many Canadian B&Bs are run by couples or women. In B&Bs and guesthouses, ask whether the rooms have locks – some do not.

When checking into a motel, ask to see the room first and make sure the doors and windows can be secured. Most motel rooms come with a telephone.

A few of the cheaper inner-city hotels listed in the text are not suitable for women alone. Where these places are mentioned it is suggested that accommodation should be sought elsewhere.

Unaccompanied women in nightclubs or bars will often find they get a lot of attention (and possibly drinks) whether they want it or not.

For women who enjoy the outdoors, the smell of perfumes and fragrant cosmetics attracts bears so, if you're likely to be in an area where they're around, it's best not to wear any. Insects, too, are said to find perfume a pleasant lure.

GAY & LESBIAN TRAVELLERS

As a generally tolerant country, Canada doesn't present any particular problems for homosexuals. Laws in Canada protect against discrimination on the basis of sexual orientation.

Montreal, Toronto and Vancouver have sizeable gay communities with support groups, associations and any number of clubs and bars. Specialised bookstores and entertainment & news weeklies may also be found. In Toronto, *Xtra* magazine is a biweekly with a full range of information including advertisements for lodgings and other businesses which cater primarily to gays. It also publishes *Xtra West* in Vancouver and *Capitol Xtra* in Ottawa. Halifax has *Wayves* and Montreal *Fugues* which are similar. These magazines may be able to help with contacts in other parts of the country. All major cities have at least a dance club or two. Toronto and Vancouver have celebratory Gay Pride Days which attract big crowds including straights.

DISABLED TRAVELLERS

Canada has come a long way in making day-to-day life less burdensome to the physically disabled, most notably the wheelchair bound. In general, Canada has gone further in this regard than the vast majority of the world's countries and this process continues. Most public buildings are wheelchair accessible, including major tourist offices. Ditto for major museums, art galleries and principal attractions. All the above and many restaurants also have washroom facilities suitable for wheelchairs. Major hotels are often equipped to deal with wheelchairs and some less-expensive motel chains such as the countrywide Comfort Inn (frequently mentioned through the text) has wheelchair access through ramps.

Many of the national and provincial parks have accessible interpretive centres and even some of the shorter nature trails and/or boardwalks have been developed with wheelchairs or self-propelled mobility aids in mind.

The VIA Rail system is prepared to accommodate the wheelchair bound but advance notice of 48 hours should be given. All bus lines will help passengers and take chairs or any other aids providing they collapse and will fit in the usual luggage compartments. Canadian airlines are accustomed to dealing with disabled passengers and provide early boarding and disembarking as standard practice.

In major cities, parking lots all have designated parking spots for the physically disabled, usually marked with a painted wheelchair. These spots, located closest to the door or access point of the place being visited can not be used by others under threat of serious fine.

Car-rental agencies can provide special accessories such as handcontrols but again, advance notice is required. Toronto's public transportation system, the TTC, has a special bus service around town with lifts for wheelchairs.

SENIOR TRAVELLERS

Visitors over the age of 65, and sometimes 60, should take advantage of the many cost reductions they are offered in Canada. Canadians of this age are classed as 'seniors' and it is this term that is seen frequently. Seniors' discounts are offered on all means of transportation and can mean substantial savings. Many of the government parks have reduced rates as do most of the country's attractions, museums, historic sites, even movie houses. Some hotels and motels may provide a price reduction – it's always worth asking.

Elderhostel with branches in many countries is also found in Canada. It specialises in inexpensive, educational packages for those over 60 years of age. The standard type of programme consists of mornings of talks and lectures followed by afternoon field trips and visits to related sights. Participants are accommodated in university dorms or the like. There is generally a full-package price which includes meals, lodging and some transportation. The courses are of varying lengths but may be several weeks long. Subject matter is drawn from a variety of interests including history, nature, geography and art. For more information contact Elderhostel Canada (☎ (613) 530-2222), 308 Wellington St, Kingston, Ontario K7K 7A7.

DANGERS & ANNOYANCES

Check the Health section earlier in this chapter for possible health risks. See also the Road Rules & Safety section in the Getting Around chapter for tips about driving.

Fire

When camping outside legitimate campgrounds do not start a fire. This is extremely dangerous and could cause untold amounts of devastation during the dry summer months.

In designated campgrounds make sure that anything that was burning is put out completely when you've finished with it, including cigarettes.

Bears

A serious problem encountered when you're camping in the woods is the animals – most importantly bears – who are always looking for an easy snack. Keep your food in nylon bags; a sleeping-bag sack is good. Tie the sack to a rope and sling it over a branch away from your tent and away from the trunk of the tree as some bears can climb. Hoist it up high enough, about three metres, so a standing bear can't reach it. Don't leave food scraps around the site and never, ever keep food in the tent.

Don't try to get close-up photographs of bears and never come between a bear and its cubs. If you see any cubs, quietly and quickly disappear. If you do see a bear, try to get upwind so it can smell you and you won't startle it. While hiking through woods or in the mountains in bear country, some people wear a noise-maker, like a bell. Talking or

Grizzly Bear

singing is just as good. Whatever you do, don't feed bears – they lose their fear of people and eventually their lives to park wardens.

Blackflies & Mosquitoes

In the woods of Canada, particularly in the north, the blackflies and mosquitoes can be murder – they seems to get worse the further north you get. There are tales of lost hikers going insane from the bugs. This is no joke – they can make you miserable. The effect of a bite (or sting, technically, by the mosquito) is a small itchy bump. The moment of attack is itself a very minor, passing pain. Some people are allergic to blackfly bites and will develop a fair bit of swelling. But other than the unsightly welt, there is no real danger. The potential trouble is in the cumulative effects of scores of them and even this hazard is mainly psychological.

As a rule, darker clothes are said to attract biting insects more than lighter ones. Perfume, too, evidently attracts the wrong kind of attention. Take 'bug juice' liquid or spray repellents. Two recommended names are Muskol and Off; the latter also has an extra strength version known as Deep Woods Off. An ingredient often used in repellents

known as DEET should not be used on children. There are brands without it. Try to minimise the amount of skin exposed by wearing a long-sleeved shirt, long pants and a close-fitting hat or cap.

June is generally the worst month, and as the summer wears on the bugs disappear. The bugs are at their worst deep in the woods. In clearings, along shorelines or anywhere there's a breeze you'll be safe, except for the buzzing horseflies, which are basically teeth with wings.

Mosquitoes come out around sunset; building a fire will help keep them away. For campers, a tent with a zippered screen is pretty much a necessity.

If you do get lost and are being eaten alive, submerge your body in water if you are by a lake or river. This will enable you to think clearly about where you are and what to do. Lemon or orange peel rubbed on your skin will help if you're out of repellent.

Other Stings & Bites

Canada is relatively problem-free regarding stings and bites. There are no poisonous spiders or insects. Rattlesnakes do live in parts of Ontario, Alberta and British Columbia but are rarely seen – even by serious hikers – and actually are generally timid. Still the bite is a matter of concern and immediate medical attention is essential. The normal run of bees, wasps and hornets is found across the country. Those with allergies should carry kits outside of urban areas.

In some areas, sand gnats and 'no-see-ums', bugs so called because you never see them but rather just feel their bites, may be encountered. There is not much to be done about it; fortunately neither are overly common. Campers should have very finely meshed tents to prevent a possible night invasion of noseeums. All this insect-generated horror really isn't so bad but it's better to hear the worst than to be caught off guard. Millions spend time in the bush each year and actually live to tell about it. And besides, this is the only kind of terrorism you have to concern yourself with in Canada – bugs are better than bombs.

Camp-Site Pests

Campers are unlikely to encounter bears but squirrels, chipmunks, mice and raccoons are common. And they all love human food. They will spend a lot of time tearing through any bags of food or garbage you leave about and even smack pots and pans around making a heck of a clatter in the middle of the night. The best defence is not to feed them, no matter how cute, and store all food securely.

EMERGENCY

In most of the country, particularly urban areas, telephone ☎ 911 for all police, fire, accident and medical emergencies. See under the province introductions for details. In all other areas or when in doubt, call ☎ 0 and ask the operator for assistance. You will then be put through to the appropriate service. Dialling ☎ 911 results in a faster response. For non-emergency police matters, consult the local telephone book for the number of the station.

Should your passport get lost or stolen, contact your nearest consulate. They will be able to issue a temporary replacement and inform you when and how to go about getting another. You may not need another depending on your travel plans. For lost or stolen travellers' cheques, contact the issuer or their representative. Upon purchase of the cheques you should have received a list of telephone numbers to call in case of loss. To make matters as easily as possible do record which cheques you cash as is suggested. If you supply a list of which cheques are gone, a refund should be forthcoming with minimal inconvenience.

If you plan to make an insurance claim be sure to contact the police and have them make a record of the theft. Ask for the reference number on the police report as the insurance company will want it.

STUDY & WORK

Student and work authorisations must be obtained outside Canada and may take six months. A work permit is valid for one specific job and one specific time, for one specific employer. If you want to study get the information and apply in your country of residence.

It is difficult to get a work permit: opportunities go first to Canadians. However, employers hiring casual, temporary, service workers (hotel, bar, restaurant) construction, farm or forestry workers often don't ask for the permit. Visitors working here legally have Social Insurance numbers beginning with '9'. If you don't have this, and get caught, you will be told to leave the country.

Many young European women come to Canada as nannies. Japan has a programme called Contact Canada which includes one-year work permits with pre-arranged work generally on farms. Many countries have agencies where details on these programmes can be obtained.

Student Work Abroad Programme (SWAP)

Of particular interest to Australian students may be the SWAP. Organised by the National Union of Students (NUS) and the Canadian Federation of Students (CFS), the programme allows Australians between the ages of 18 and 25 to spend a year in Canada on a working holiday. This programme only has space for 200 people a year and applicants must be enroled in a post-secondary educational institution.

After an orientation programme in Vancouver you find your own job with help from the CFS. Most jobs are in the service area – as waiters, bar attendants, cleaners and maids – particularly in the snowfields over winter, although SWAP participants have worked in other kinds of jobs ranging from farmhands to hotel porters. You are issued with a one-year, nonextendable visa which allows you to work anywhere in the country. 'Swappers' must be Australian citizens and pass a medical check-up.

NUS, in conjunction with STA Travel, arranges group departures at reduced fares leaving from Sydney, Melbourne and Brisbane in November and December. Independent departures leave throughout the rest of the year. Participants are given orientation information and a copy of this Lonely Planet book prior to departure.

For full details contact the NUS (☎ 03-9348-1777), PO Box 1130, Carlton, Victoria, 3053.

Working Holiday Programme

This is another programme, which is open to all Australians between the ages of 18 and 25 and they need not be enroled in a post-secondary educational institution. This programme has a quota of 3000 annually. Application forms can be obtained by contacting the Canadian Consulate General in Sydney, Australia. See the Visas & Embassies section earlier in this chapter for the address. Applications for this programme take up to two months to process.

ACTIVITIES

Canada's greatest attribute is its natural environment. This, for the most part, is what it has to offer visitors and what makes it unique. Much of Canada's appeal lies in the range of physical activities such as hiking, canoeing, fishing, skiing and observing and photographing flora & fauna.

There are wilderness trips of all types, organised or self-directed. Provincial tourist offices have information on activities in their region and also details on the hundreds of private businesses, operators and outfitters offering adventure tours and trips. Many provinces have booklets and maps on canoeing and hiking. All have information on national and provincial parks, many of which can be highlights of a trip to Canada. Many of the national and provincial parks are detailed in the text (see the special section on Canada's Flora, Fauna and National Parks, or the province chapters for more detail).

Activities of most interest to visitors are detailed below. In addition to these, the popularity of cycling, including long-distance cycle touring increases each year. Once obscure, climbing has become one of the country's fastest growing sports.

Although the season is short, boating is very popular across the country. It has been said there are more boats per capita in Canada than anywhere except Sweden. Kayaking, both whitewater and in the sea has increased markedly in recent years as has bird-watching (birding). Hang gliding has its steadfast converts. People even surf off the west coast. And if you want to try your luck, you can pan for gold.

Skating on frozen rivers and ponds and outdoor rinks is a Canadian tradition and a pleasant way to exercise. Joggers are a familiar sight and roller blades have caught on in the past few years, too. Tennis and golf are popular activities. Curling is popular across the country as a winter sport for both men and women.

The clean, safe and vital cities are also enticing with myriad arts and cultural activities if the outdoors starts to wear you down.

Entering the various lotteries is a less rigorous but favourite Canadian pastime as is staking out a spot at one of the increasing numbers of full-fledged casinos. Bingo is another favourite form of small-time gambling. A whimsical variation is cow-pie bingo played in some rural areas often as a fundraiser for charity.

This involves dividing, marking and numbering a pasture into equal-sized sections. Each participant then selects one of these squares to bet on. A cow is let into the field. The 'owner' of the square upon which the cow relieves itself is the winner; good wholesome, if not necessarily clean, fun.

Hiking

Canada offers a range of walks and hikes that are long or short, rugged or gentle, mountain or coastal. Almost all of the country's trails, and certainly most of the best, are found in either the provincial or national parks.

The majority of parks have some type of walking path although some may be no more than a short nature trail. The larger the park, as a rule, the longer the trail. Some require one or more nights camping to complete. Conservation areas, wildlife reserves and sanctuaries often have marked trails. Throughout the text, parks with trails are discussed and some individual trails are outlined.

In Ontario, Killarney Provincial Park has a long-distance trail around the tops of its rounded mountains. Other mountainous regions with good trails include Gaspésie Park and Mont Tremblant Park in Quebec, Gros Morne National Park in Newfoundland, and Cape Breton National Park in Nova Scotia. In Manitoba, Riding Mountain Park also has a series of trails. Prime hiking is found throughout the Rockies in all of the several national parks in Alberta and British Columbia.

Among the toughest of trails is the multi-day lakeside trail in Pukaskwa National Park on Lake Superior in Ontario, and the coastal hike on the west coast of Vancouver Island in Pacific Rim National Park.

Outside the federal and provincial park systems there are also some extended trails running through a mix of public and private lands. A few to consider, which are described in the text, are the following: in Ontario the Bruce Trail which runs from Lake Ontario 700 km north to Georgian Bay (see the Bruce Peninsula section for details), and the Voyageur Trail in Sault Ste Marie (see the Gros Cap section for details); in New Brunswick the Dobson Trail (see the Moncton section for details), and the trail between St Martins and Fundy National Park (see the St Martins section for details); and in the Yukon the historic gold-rush Chilkoot Trail which goes near Skagway in Alaska (see the Klondike Highway section for details).

Work is continuing on the Trans Canada Trail, a 15,000-km-long crushed stone path winding from coast to coast with an offshoot from Calgary to Tuktoyaktuk on the Arctic Ocean. It is hoped much of it will be completed by year 2000. It will take 300 days to cycle, 500 days to ride on horseback and 750 days to walk. For the current status and information on completed sections call the trail foundation at ☎ 1-800-465-3636.

Canoeing

The possibilities for canoeing are almost limitless from an easy half-day paddle to some of the most challenging white waters. Again, the government parks are a good place to start and many of them are quite accessible. Some parks provide outfitters able to supply all equipment, at other parks private operators do much the same thing from just outside the park boundaries.

In major cities operators can be found who can help organise trips and you'll find excellent sporting-equipment stores. Provincial tourist boards will be able to help with information on canoeing areas and outfitters. Better bookstores and outdoor stores sell good guides to canoeing in Canada.

Some of the country's main canoeing areas follow. Details for many can be found through the text. In Nova Scotia try Kejimkujik National Park or inquire about the numerous inland nature reserves. In Quebec there are a series of canoe routes in La Mauricie National Park, La Verendrye Provincial Park and excellent coastal canoeing or kayaking at Mingan Archipelago National Park.

Ontario offers terrific canoeing at accessible Algonquin Provincial Park, Killarney Provincial Park and at Temagami and its adjoining wilderness areas.

Across the prairies, the northern sections are vast, undeveloped lake-filled forest. Prince Albert National Park in Saskatchewan is one area to consider.

British Columbia has a well-known week-long canoe circuit around Bowron Lake Provincial Park near Barkerville. Wells Gray Provincial Park also has fine flat water canoeing. The coastal areas around the Gulf Islands offer sea canoeing and kayaking.

Many of the country's rivers and the far north regions offer the experienced challenging, white-water opportunities. One of the most spectacular of these trips is in Nahanni National Park of the Northwest Territories. The Yukon has numerous excellent flat-water river canoe routes.

Fishing

Freshwater fishing is abundant and popular across the country with both residents and visitors. Casting a line is one of the country's basic outdoor activities. In winter many northern areas set up and rent 'huts', small wooden shacks, out on frozen lakes. Inside there is a bench, sometimes a heater, a hole in the ice and often more than a few bottles of beer.

Anglers must purchase fishing licences which vary in duration and price from province to province. Any tourist office can help with information and advice on where to buy one. At the same time pick up a guide to the various 'open' seasons for each species and also a guide to the eating of fish. In southern regions there are recommended consumption guidelines due to natural contaminants and pollution such as mercury which are important especially for pregnant women and young children. Also be sure to check on daily limits and if there are any bait restrictions. In some areas live minnows or other bait is prohibited.

Swimming

Although Canada is surrounded on three sides by ocean, by far the majority of the swimming is done inland, in the much warmer freshwater lakes and rivers. Still, Canadians do swim in the oceans during July and August and it is along the coastal areas where some of the country's finest beaches can be enjoyed. Beaches are popular summer gathering and relaxing places even when the water is too cold for the vast majority to venture into the water. With very few exceptions (mainly gay-oriented places) Canada does not have nude or topless beaches. Below are some of Canada's best strips of sand.

At the eastern end of Canada, Ingonish Beach just out of Cape Breton National Park, Nova Scotia is a fine arch of sand surrounded by green hills where, in the middle of a good summer, the swimming can be quite pleasant. For warmer waters, Melmerby and Caribou beaches near Pictou and New Glasgow are long, wide and reap the spin-offs of the Gulf Stream, meaning the waters reach 19°C.

Rissers Beach south of Halifax is easy paced, relatively quiet, close to town and is edged with some dunes, too.

The north coast of Prince Edward Island

is lined with good beaches notably best-known Cavendish which may get slightly warmer than those of Nova Scotia.

In New Brunswick, Parlee Beach, east of Moncton, draws people from around the province for the relatively warm waters and party atmosphere.

Ontario has some of the finest beaches. Wasaga north of Toronto on Georgian Bay is the big city's closest real beach and gets jam packed on summer weekends. Longer, wider and quieter is beautiful Sauble Beach on Lake Huron with warm, shallow waters and superb sunsets. Immense sandy beaches can also be found at popular Sandbanks and Presqu'ile provincial parks near Belleville on Lake Ontario. Sandbanks also boasts some of the country's largest sand dunes.

North of Winnipeg in Manitoba, Grand Beach on Lake Winnipeg is also one of the country's best and attracts people all summer long. The interior of British Columbia has a fine central, urban beach in Kelowna where the surroundings and warm temperatures and blue skies make a day at the beach well worthwhile. Osoyoos beaches have the country's warmest waters.

Kitsilano Beach in Vancouver is a classic strut-and-preen beach and can attract thousands on any given hot, summer day. The water is not as clean as elsewhere but who is here to swim? Nearby nude, anti-conformist, infamous Wreck Beach carries the counter-culture torch. Rough, wild Long Beach in Pacific Rim National Park on Vancouver Island is at the other end of the spectrum – natural as opposed to cultural.

Way up in the Yukon, the small beach at Kookatsoon Lake offers very fine scenery, warm summer temperatures and sun nearly all day and night in July and August.

Skiing

Good cross-country skiing is found all across Canada and the downhill skiing is justly internationally renowned. There are four main alpine ski centres located in Ontario, Quebec, Alberta and B.C.

In Ontario, north of Toronto toward Georgian Bay between the towns of Barrie and

Collingwood, there are good downhill runs although hills are not found in the same number or at the same elevations as those in the prime Laurentian districts of Quebec. There is also downhill skiing in the Thunder Bay region.

In Quebec the slopes of the Laurentian Mountains are about a two-hour drive north of Montreal and Quebec City. South of Montreal there are also ski centres which are part of the Appalachian Mountains, and these are well known to skiers in Vermont and New Hampshire.

In Alberta the Rocky Mountains has truly international status with skiing in Banff and Lake Louise, which have runs higher than any in the European Alps. Calgary is a two-hour drive to the east.

In BC the Whistler ski area north of Vancouver is a major resort which has hosted international competitions. There is also good skiing in the Okanagan and the Kootenay regions of the province.

The provincial tourist boards produce guides to skiing, and travel agents can arrange full-package tours which include transportation and accommodation. As the country's major ski resorts are all close to cities, it is quite straightforward to travel on your own to the slopes for a day's skiing and head back to the city that same night.

Each of these areas and many more offer cross-country skiing as well.

Ecotourism

With Canada's remote undeveloped areas and abundant wildlife, opportunities for nature appreciation and outdoor recreation are nearly limitless. Long before the environmental movement came to the forefront, Canada was into what is now referred to as ecotourism. Wilderness trips and lodges, outdoor resorts and remote escapes have long been a part of the travel possibilities on offer in Canada.

Since the mid 1980s though, respect for the country's natural wonders has grown markedly not only by Canadians but by international travellers. There have been changes, innovations and growth in the ecotourism movement resulting in a much wider range of possibilities.

Perhaps the perfect example of the new ecotourism (and one of the first) are the trips operated to the Magdalen Islands of Quebec to see and photograph baby seals. It was publicity surrounding the bloody slaughter of the seal pups (activist Brigitte Bardot was seen on the icefloes with the seals and their hunters) which diminished the controversial hunt which had long been part of the fur fashion business. Run by Nortour, the trips from Montreal can be arranged through travel agents, or call Tourism Quebec.

Rather than hunting with guns, many tour operators specialising in wildlife are now geared to shooting with cameras. There are trips specialising in the culture of Native people. Others offer hiking in the west coast rainforest or whale-watching. Guided camping trips provide instruction on plant ecology, geology and low-impact wilderness travel. Wild rivers can be run in kayaks and canoes. Seeing the polar bears in Churchill, Manitoba is popular with travellers from around the world and is relatively accessible.

Ecotours have until recently been notoriously costly (as elsewhere around the world) but this is no longer the case in Canada and a number of good, small, inexpensive operators are discussed in the text. Also see the special section on Canada's Flora, Fauna, and National Parks.

HIGHLIGHTS
Ontario

Ottawa, the country's capital, has nearly a dozen museums and galleries including some of Canada's most important. Added to these are the edifices of power including the Parliament Buildings and the Supreme Court. Ottawa, Montreal, Quebec City make a short circuit which manages to cover both British and French centres as well as some of the country's oldest and most important history.

From Ottawa, a short tour of Ontario can take in handsome Kingston, an old military town and sight of a major university. In Toronto, Canada's largest city and easily the country's most ethnically varied, distinct 'neighbourhoods' provide sights, sounds and foods from around the world. A recent United Nations report stated Toronto was the most culturally diverse city in the world. A major league baseball game can be seen at the Skydome or the entire city can be seen from the top of the world's tallest structure, the CN Tower. A short ferry ride leads to the quiet Toronto Islands where a skyline view of the city and a harbour cruise can be enjoyed at the same time.

Two hours to the south-west is one of Canada's top attractions, Niagara Falls. Walk along the undeveloped gorge for an inkling of how this world-renowned site appeared to the Native peoples of the region. A short tour of South-Western Ontario can take in the Niagara wine district, German and Mennonite Kitchener, Shakespearean Stratford and the rural tourist centre of Elora. A side trip from Toronto going north could include Midland with its Huron Indian sites and Georgian Bay with its classic rocky, pine-edged shorelines. From here it is not far to another of the country's best-known nature areas, Algonquin Provincial Park with excellent camping, canoeing and wildlife viewing possibilities. From Algonquin, Ottawa is about as far as Toronto, so it can be included in a circular tour of southern Ontario.

Quebec

Montreal is a blend of French and British sophistication. Chuck the budget and splurge on a meal, wander the cobblestone streets of Old Montreal on a warm night or have a drink somewhere along Rue Saint Denis. A hockey game at the Forum is something many Canadians would cherish. From Montreal it's only three hours to Quebec City, the only walled city in North America and an historic gem designated as such by the United Nations. This is the centre of French culture in Canada. The country's largest winter festival, the Quebec Winter Carnival is held each February. For breakfast have a bowl of café au lait and a croissant and spend the day on the battlefield that might well have determined the history of the country.

From Quebec travel down the St Lawrence River to Tadoussac and the fjord of the Saguenay River. There is great walking in the area and whale-watching tours where the two rivers meet. Drivers could take the ferry across the river, visit Rivière-du-Loup and return to Quebec or Montreal along the south side of the river.

If more time is available, the Gaspé Peninsula at the eastern extremity of southern Quebec is recommended for fine coastal and mountain topography, small typically Quebecois communities and the excellent, uncrowded provincial and national parks

The largest original group of totem poles is found on the Queen Charlotte Islands in BC

which are good for camping, hiking and flora & fauna. Impressive Percé Rock is one of the country's best known geographic features.

For those going to or from New Brunswick, the road through Quebec's Matapédia Valley is suggested as a route. It can be used as the western portion of a circular tour around the Gaspé Peninsula.

Travellers heading to Quebec from anywhere in New England can easily spend a couple of days around the Eastern Townships south of Montreal en route. This is one of the province's top ski regions as well as a summer holiday area.

Newfoundland & Labrador

Hilly, chilly St John's with a fabulous, storied harbour tucked beside rocky Signal Hill is the headquarters of the distinctive Newfoundland culture. A night out for music or satirical theatre has to be included here.

Twillingate and the islands of Notre Dame Bay provide some of the best of Newfoundland's coastal features including drifting icebergs.

Gros Morne National Park offers fjords, mountain hiking and other geographic and historic features. Beyond it, at the northern tip of the island, is a 1000-year-old former Viking settlement. The isolated fishing villages of the south coast are unique in North America.

Remote but increasingly road and ferry accessible Labrador presents the determined visitor with the grandeur and solitude of the Canadian north. Outdoor adventures and isolated villages are attractions which take some pre-planning in this corner of the country. For suggestions on travel routes here see the Newfoundland introduction.

Nova Scotia

Nova Scotia is best known, and rightly so, for its rugged Cape Breton Island reminiscent of the Scottish Highlands. Traditional Scottish arts can be seen at Ste Anne's and Gaelic can still be heard in various smaller communities. The best of the region is protected within Cape Breton National Park. The Cabot Trail around a magnificent coastal

stretch of the mountainous park is one of the most scenic stretches of roadway in Canada. The park also contains some excellent hiking trails. Also on Cape Breton is Louisbourg National Historic Site, an early French fort and now home to one of the best re-creations of Canadian history.

Historic Halifax, the capital, is green, attractive, compact and well preserved with fine lodging, dining and a lively music scene. The Citadel, a massive 18th-century British fort, dominates the central area of the city.

Digby Neck, stretching out into the Bay of Fundy, is a good place to hop aboard whale-watching boat tours. In Digby, a meal caught by the local scallop fleet should be considered.

The Annapolis Valley, site of the first European settlement, offers some fascinating history particularly that involving the Acadians. The apple-growing valley is at its best in spring when the apple blossoms are in bloom and visitor numbers are below the peaks of midsummer.

Prince Edward Island

Among the island's low-key charms are the north-coast beaches and the pastoral Anne of Green Gables house and property, the setting for the internationally known stories. Also not to be missed are the casual, fun, exceptional-value lobster suppers held around the province. In Charlottetown, known as the birthplace of Confederation, visit Province House where the representatives of the British colonies began working out the details for the formation of the country. Try to catch one of the costumed re-enactments.

A short tour could begin at Summerside near one of the ferry landings to the national park beaches and then on to Charlottetown. From there another ferry can be caught to Nova Scotia.

New Brunswick

This is Canada's only truly bilingual province. Mt Carlton in the north is a huge, undeveloped park with some excellent hiking and fine wildlife viewing possibilities. The Trans Canada Hwy extends from the north-west corner of the province down along the green, fertile Saint John River Valley which the British Empire Loyalists settled after the American Revolution. Historic sights which make an educational comparison are two re-created pioneer villages; Loyalist King's Landing near Fredericton and Acadian Historic Village near Caraquet on the French Acadian Peninsula. The river ends at the Bay of Fundy where the world's highest tides can be seen. Out in the bay, the Fundy Isles are a peaceful ocean retreat.

Manitoba

The Museum of Man in Winnipeg is a major Canadian museum worth a couple of hours. On the outskirts of Winnipeg, Canada's largest folk festival is held each summer. South of town, fields of three-metre-high sunflowers as far as the eye can see are both unique and unusual. In the far north at Churchill, at the edge of Canada's tree-line, nature in a variety of guises can be experienced. The aurora borealis, seals, whales and the big draw – polar bears. There is also plenty of the country's early history to discover here as well.

Saskatchewan

The flat wheatfields and skyscapes of the central prairies are the dominant feature of the open space of southern Saskatchewan. The Wanuskewin Heritage Park north of Saskatoon is a must for its blend of geography, history and Native peoples' culture. From here a side trip to Prince Albert National Park, with its western Canadian Shield topography and features can be added. A walking trail or canoe route leads to the former home of Grey Owl, one of the country's most intriguing adventurers and one of the first international conservationists.

Alberta

Alberta with the famous resort towns of Banff and Jasper is best known for its Rocky Mountain western border region. Busy Lake Louise and less-known Peyto Lake are two of the undeniable beauty spots in the mountains. The drive or cycle along the Icefields Parkway takes in some supreme alpine scenery and is one of the best remembered strips of pavement in Canada.

The south-central badlands and former dinosaur stomping grounds around Drumheller should not be missed either. The Royal Tyrell Museum of Palaeontology, north-west of Drumheller, has some magnificent exhibits and is a must.

The Calgary Stampede is one of the country's best-known events and continues the province's western traditions. Calgary's Glenbow Museum is a primer to understanding some of the Canadian history and culture.

British Columbia

Vancouver is Canada's third and fastest growing city and has been booming along while the rest of the country has suffered through the international recession. It's blessed with the best setting of Canada's main population centres having the ocean at its side and mountains hovering nearby. Victoria prides itself on its British roots and acts as a base for any explorations of Vancouver Island and environs, which should include seeing the ancient trees of Canada's original growth forests.

The western region of the province is dominated by the Columbia and Rocky Mountain chains which can be explored in a number of government parks. A soak in one of the regional hot springs early in the morning when the air is cool and fellow travellers are not yet out and about is a highlight, as is a walk in the bugaboos although picking a site for hiking here is a fool's game; there are hundreds of memorable trails.

The interior of the province around the Okanagan region is geographically similar to the south of France with its appealing scrubby, dry rounded hills, orchards and vineyards.

Yukon & Northwest Territories

In the Yukon you can hike amid some of the highest mountains in Canada in Kluane National Park, or along the Chilkoot Trail once followed by gold seekers, or stroll around Dawson City which still has many of the original buildings from the gold-rush days.

In the Northwest Territories you can visit the pristine wilderness of Nahanni National Park, see the wildlife of the Mackenzie Delta or take a boat out on the Arctic Ocean to see beluga whales and other marine life.

In summer the hours of daylight are long, and in spring and autumn the aurora borealis puts on a magnificent display at night.

ACCOMMODATION
Camping

There are campgrounds all over Canada – federal, provincial and privately owned. Government sites are nearly always better and cheaper and, not surprisingly, fill up the quickest. Government parks are well laid out, green and well-treed. They are usually quiet, situated to take advantage of the local landscape, and offer a programme of events and talks. The private campgrounds are generally geared to trailers (caravans) and recreational vehicles (RVs) and often have more services available as well as swimming pools and other entertainment facilities.

In national parks, camping fees range from $9 to $16 for an unserviced site, and to as high as $20 for sites with services like electricity. There is usually a park entrance fee as well. See under Tourist Offices earlier for more information.

Provincial-park camping rates vary with each province but range from $10 to $22. Interior camping in the wilderness parks is always less, about $4 or $5. Commercial campgrounds are generally several dollars more expensive than those in either provincial or national parks.

Government parks start closing in early September for the winter. Dates vary according to the location. Some remain open for maintenance even when camping is finished and they might let you camp at a reduced rate. Other places, late in autumn or early in spring, are free. The gate is open and there is not a soul around. Still others block the road and you just can't enter the campgrounds although the park itself can still be visited.

So, out of the main summer season, you have to investigate but using the parks after official closing can save the hardy a fair bit of money.

There are also campgrounds every 150 km or so along the Trans Canada Hwy.

Many people travel around the country camping and never pay a dime. For those with cars or vans, using roadside rest areas and picnic spots is recommended. I've done this many times. If there are signs indicating no overnight camping, don't do something like set up a tent. If you're asleep in the car and a cop happens to wake you, just say you were driving, got tired, pulled over for a quick rest and fell asleep. For less chance of interruption, little side roads and logging roads off the highway are quiet and private.

Hostels

There are some excellent traveller's hostels in Canada much like those found in countries around the world. The term hostel in Canada, however, has some unfortunate connotations for travellers as well as those running them and working in them. The term has long been and continues to be used in reference to both government and private shelters for the underprivileged, sick and abused. There are, for example, hostels for battered women who have been victimised by their mates and hostels for recovering drug addicts. So, if you get a sideways glance when you smilingly say you are on the way to spend the night at the hostel, now you know why. Indicating traveller's hostel or international hostel should help.

There are two hostelling groups operating in Canada geared to low-budget visitors. They represent the cheapest places to stay in the country and are where you'll probably meet the most travellers.

Visitors to Quebec are sometimes surprised to find the mixed-sex dorms common in Europe but not often seen elsewhere in Canada.

Hostelling International The oldest, best known and most established hostelling association is Hostelling International (HI) Canada. This national organisation is part of the internationally-known hostelling association. It was formerly known as the Canadian Hostelling Association which operated in conjunction with the then International Youth Hostels Federation (IYHF). The hostels are no longer called youth hostels, although they are sometimes still referred to in this way, but rather are known simply as hostels. Through the text of this book these hostels are referred to as HI Hostel. Their symbol is an evergreen tree and stylised house within a blue triangle.

HI Canada has about 60 hostels with members in all parts of the country. Nightly costs range from $10 to $22.50 with most around $15. At many, nonmembers can stay for an additional $2 to $5. A membership can quickly pay for itself and has now been built into the system so that after a few stays you automatically become a member.

In July and August space may be a problem at some Canadian hostels, particularly in the large cities and in some of the resort areas such as Banff, so calling ahead to make a reservation is a good idea. Reservations must be made more than 24 hours in advance and you need a credit card to pre-pay.

Reservations for North American hostels can be booked through hostels in Europe, Australia, New Zealand and Japan using computer systems and faxes. This can be convenient for those flying into 'gateway' cities who don't want to hassle for a bed upon arrival. Outside July and August, traffic thins and getting a bed should not be difficult. Many of the hostels are closed in winter.

In addition to the lower nightly rates, members can often take advantage of discounts offered by various businesses. Local hostels should have a list of where discounts are available. Guidebooks, sleeping sheets and other travel accessories can also be purchased at one of half a dozen hostel shops across the country. Some of the regional offices and hostels organise outdoor activities such as canoeing, climbing, skiing, hiking and city walks.

A yearly international membership costs $26.75 for an adult. Children under 17 stay free with a parent. Many hostels now have family rooms set aside.

For more information contact Hostelling International (HI) Canada, (☎ (613) 237-7884; fax (613) 237-7868), National Office, 400-205 Catherine St, Ottawa, Ontario K2P 1C3.

Backpackers' Hostels The second group is a network of independent hostels collectively known as Backpackers' Hostels Canada. Currently there are over 100 hostels in the network and a membership is not required to use the facilities. Their symbol is a circled howling wolf with a map of Canada in the background. For information, including a list of hostels, contact the Longhouse Village Hostel (☎ (807) 983-2042, 1-800 705-3666; fax (807) 983-2914), RR 13, Thunder Bay, Ontario, Canada, P7B 5E4. A self-addressed envelope and two international postal-reply coupons should be included with your request for information.

Aside from typical hostels, they also have campgrounds, campus and church facilities, organic farms, motels, retreats, and tourist homes which provide budget travellers with inexpensive accommodation. Several places offer an interesting work-for-stay system in which your labour means free room and board. A major benefit of Backpackers' is that while they have the main cities covered, they also offer accommodation in a range of smaller, out of the way locations where nothing else of the sort is available.

Many of the hostels are in regular contact with one another so a stay at one will turn up leads on others. The average price is about $15, and rooms for couples and families are often available.

A sort of sub-network of Backpackers' is the Pacific Rim Network (☎ 1-800-861-1366) which focuses on hostels of the Pacific Coast region.

Other Hostels In addition to these two organisations, totally independent hostels are found around the country, but their numbers are small. Most of these are found by word of mouth. The province of British Columbia has an informal network of privately run hostels which charge about the same rates as the 'official' ones. Quebec, too, is most likely to have some of the unofficial variety.

YM-YWCA The familiar YM-YWCAs are for the most part slowly getting out of the accommodation end of their operations in Canada. They are tending to concentrate more on fitness, recreation and various other community-oriented programmes. That said, many still offer good lodging in a style between that of a hostel and a hotel, but prices have been creeping up. In YM-YWCAs where complete renovations have occurred, costs can be as high as those of a mid-range hotel. In Vancouver, a brand new hotel-like Y has just opened.

YM-YWCAs are clean and quiet and often have swimming pools and cheap cafeterias. They are also as a rule very central which is a big plus and they are open all year. Some offer hostel-style dormitory accommodation throughout the summer. Many are mentioned through the text under hostels in the accommodation sections.

The average price for men is from $24 to $36 a single, and usually a bit more for women. Sharing a double can bring the price down to quite a reasonable level. Also, some places permit couples and these doubles are fair value.

For information contact YMCA Canada, (☎ (416) 485-9447), 2160 Yonge St, Toronto, Ontario M4S 2A9. A printed sheet on the country's Y's offering accommodation will be mailed out but the information is always outdated.

Universities Many Canadian universities rent out beds in their residence dormitories during the summer months. The 'season' runs roughly from May to some time in August with possible closures for such things as large academic conferences. Prices average $30 a day and, at many places, students are offered a further reduction. Campus residences are open to all including families and seniors.

Reservations are accepted but aren't necessary. Breakfasts are sometimes included in the price but if not, there is generally a cafeteria which offers low-priced meals. The other campus facilities, such as the swimming pool, are sometimes available to guests.

Directories of the various residences are sometimes published and may be available on the campus through the residence manager, the alumni association or general information.

Campus accommodation is listed in the text under hostels. This form of budget accommodation seems to be somewhat unknown in Canada and at most places finding a room even in peak season should not be a problem.

Efficiency Units

Efficiencies are also called housekeeping units or serviced apartments and are rooms with cooking facilities and light housekeeping. This type of room is often geared to business clients but can be especially helpful for travelling families.

Efficiencies are usually found at motels where some of the rooms have been converted or enlarged for this purpose and for which the owners can ask a few more dollars. A few guesthouse or B&Bs have a room or two with cooking facilities. Some hotels also offer such rooms usually calling them suites, although this broad term may not mean there is a kitchen.

In the country's larger cities some apartment complexes have also been set up to offer this type of lodging. Again, these suites are primarily aimed at the business traveller or those in town for a week or longer.

Guesthouses & Tourist Homes

Another alternative is the simple guesthouse or tourist home. These may be an extra room in someone's home but are more commonly commercial lodging houses. They are found mainly in places with a large tourist trade such as Niagara, Banff, Victoria, Quebec City and Montreal. In Quebec's principal centres they are popular and plentiful, and usually the best places to stay.

Rooms range in size and have varying amenities. Some include private bathrooms, many do not. The standard cost is about $40 to $65 a double.

Some so-called tourist homes are really rooming houses rented more often by the week or month, and usually have shared kitchens.

B&Bs

B&Bs are an established part of the accommodation picture and continue to grow in number. They offer a more personal alternative to the standard traditional motel/hotel and are found throughout the country.

In many of the larger cities associations manage B&Bs, while in other places they are listed directly with tourist offices. Some operate as full-time businesses, others just provide their operators with part-time income for a few months in the summer.

Prices of B&Bs vary quite a bit, ranging roughly from $30 for a single to $100 a double with the average being from $55 to $70 for two people.

The more expensive ones generally provide more impressive furnishings and decor. Many are found in classic heritage houses. Rooms are almost always in the owner's home and are clean and well kept. Note that smoking is almost always prohibited. Some places will take children and the odd one will allow a pet. Breakfast can vary from light or continental to a full breakfast of eggs, bacon, toast and coffee. It's worth inquiring about the breakfast before booking.

Several guidebooks dealing exclusively with B&Bs across the country are widely available in Canadian bookstores.

Hotels

Good, inexpensive hotels are not a Canadian strong point. Though there is a wide range of hotel types, the word usually means one of two things to a Canadian – a rather expensive place to stay or a cheap place to drink. Most new hotels are part of international chains and are designed for either the luxury market or for businesspeople.

Canadian liquor laws have historically been linked to renting beds, so the older, cheap hotels are often principally bars, and quite often low-class bars at that. Examples

are found in number all over the country. For the impecunious, who don't mind some noise and a somewhat worn room, these hotels can come in handy.

Prices usually range from $25 to $35 a single, but rooms are often taken by more permanent guests on a monthly basis. There are some places in this category which are fine and which are mentioned in this book. They are not suitable for families or females travelling alone but couples and single males may find these basic hotels more than adequate, at least on occasion.

Between the very new and the very old hotels, there are places to be found in between. In the larger cities in particular you can still find good older, small hotels which mainly rent rooms. Prices vary with the amenities and location and range from about $30 to $75 for singles or doubles.

Motels

In Canada, like the USA (both lands of the automobile), motels are ubiquitous, and until the early-1980s represented the only uniformly acceptable type of moderately priced accommodation. Mostly they are simple and clean, if somewhat nondescript. Many can be found dotting the highways and clustered in groups on the outskirts of larger towns and cities. They usually range from $40 to $75 for singles or doubles.

Outside the cities motel prices drop so they can be a bargain, especially if there are two or more of you. Before entering a large city it's a good idea to get off the main route and onto one of the secondary roads. This is where you'll find motels as cheaply as they come. The less-travelled parts of the country tend to have lower prices, too.

Prices tend to go up in summer or when a special event is on. Off-season bargaining is definitely worthwhile and acceptable. This need not be haggling as in a Moroccan market; just a simple counter-offer will sometimes work. Unlike many hotels, motels are still pretty much 'mom and pop' operations and so retain more flexibility and often reflect more of the character of the owners.

One motel chain which is seen from coast to coast is Comfort Inn (☎ 1-800-424-64230). They are moderately priced, not the cheapest, not the most expensive but always reliable and good value. The rooms are plain and simple but spotless and always well maintained. The benefit of the chain system is that it allows for reserving a room anywhere through their toll-free telephone number. Other links in the chain include Econo Lodge, Quality Hotel, Quality Inn and Friendship Inn.

Some motels offer 'suites'. This usually means there is a separate second bedroom (good for those with children) but may mean there is a sitting room with TV and chesterfield set apart from the bedroom. It may also mean there are some cooking facilities.

Farm Vacations

Each province has a farm or ranch vacation programme enabling visitors to stay on working farms for a day, a week or even longer. The size and type of farm varies considerably, as do the activities you can take part in. There are usually chores to do and animals to tend. Rates range from roughly $35 to $40 for singles, $45 to $65 for doubles depending on meals taken. There are also family rates and reductions for children. Details of these programmes are available from provincial tourist boards.

FOOD

Gastronomy in English Canada was, in general and with exceptions, long based on the British 'bland is beautiful' tradition. While there are still no distinctive national dishes or unique culinary delights, good food is certainly plentiful. The large numbers of varying ethnic groups spread across the country continue to contribute to the epicurean improvements.

In most cities it's not difficult to find a Greek, Italian, Mexican or Chinese restaurant. Small bistro-type places are found across the country with menus emphasising freshness, spices and the latest trends. They tend to fill the gap between the low-end 'greasy spoons' and the priciest restaurants.

Many of these, as well as numerous soup, salad and sandwich bars, provide good-value lunches as they compete for office workers' appetites. In the country's largest cities, vegetarian restaurants, although not abundant, can be found. Such places may be known as natural food or health-food restaurants. East Indian restaurants also offer a selection of vegetarian dishes.

On the east coast of Canada, through all the Atlantic Provinces, deep-fried food is common; all too common for many. It does not hurt to ask for an alternative cooking method or pick from menus carefully.

The common 'spoons', the equivalent of the USA diners, are found throughout Canada with names like 'George's' or 'Linda's Place'. Little changed since the 1930s, these small, basic places are the blue-collar workers' restaurants. Some are excellent, some bad news, but they're always cheap. There's usually a breakfast special until 11 am for about $4, followed by a couple of lunch specials. A fairly balanced, if functional, meal costs around $6.

Fruit is a bargain in summer and locally grown varieties such as apples, peaches and cherries are superb. In June watch for strawberries; in August, blueberries. Farmers' stands are often seen along highways and secondary roads.

Canada produces excellent cheeses, in particular, cheddars – mild, medium and old. Oka from Quebec is a more expensive, subtler and very tasty cheese developed by Trappist monks.

On both coasts, there is abundant seafood that is delicious and affordable. On the west coast the salmon, fresh or smoked, is a real treat, and crab is plentiful. The east coast has the less-known but highly esteemed freshwater Atlantic salmon. The Atlantic region is also famous for lobster and scallops. In the far north, Arctic char is a speciality. The king of inland fish is the walleye, often called pickerel.

One truly Canadian creation must be mentioned: the butter tart. This delectable little sweet can best be described as...well, just get on the outside of one and you'll see.

French Food

Most of the country's few semi-original repasts come from the French of Quebec. French pea soup is thick, filling and delicious. The *tourtières* (meat pies) are worth sampling. Quebec is also the world's largest producer of maple syrup, made in the spring when the sap is running, and it's great on pancakes or ice cream.

French fries in Quebec, where they are known simply as *frites* or *patates*, are unbeatable, especially those bought at the small roadside chip wagons. *Poutine* is a variation with gravy and cheese curds.

Further east into the Atlantic Provinces the Acadian French carry on some of their centuries-old culinary traditions in such dishes as rapie pie *(paté à la rapure)* – a type of meat pie (maybe beef, chicken or clam) topped with grated paste-like potato from which all the starch has been drawn.

Native Indian Food

Native Indian foods based on wild game such as deer (venison) and pheasant are something to sample if the opportunity presents itself. Buffalo meat, beginning to be sold commercially in a few places, turns up on menus occasionally. It's lean and has more protein and less cholesterol than beef.

The fiddlehead is a distinctive green, only edible in springtime. It's primarily picked from the woodlands of the Maritime Provinces.

Wild rice, with its black husks and almost nutty flavour is very tasty and often accompanies Native Indian-style meals. Most of it is picked by hand around the Ontario and Manitoba borders but it's widely available in natural-food shops.

Markets

Many cities have farmers' markets where fresh produce can be bought at good prices. Roadside stands offering the crops of the season can be found in all rural areas. Corn is something to look for and is easy to prepare. On the coasts, seafood can often be purchased at the docks.

Prices

As with most things, food is costlier than in the USA. If you're from Europe, though, or are travelling with a strong currency, you'll find prices are reasonable.

Generally, for dinner, under $8 is a bargain and $15 to $25 is moderate. Lunches are a lot less, almost always under $10. Most of the places mentioned in this book fit into these categories but some costlier places are listed for treats and splurges.

DRINKS

Alcohol

Beer Canadian beer, in general, is good, not great. It's more flavourful and stronger than US brands and is always served cold. Lagers are by far the most popular beers but ales, light beers, porters and stouts are all available. The two big companies are Molson and Labatt, with the most popular beers being Molson Export and Canadian, and Labatt 50 and Blue.

A welcome trend is the continuing success of small breweries producing real or natural beers and pubs brewing their own for consumption on the premises. Both these breaks from tradition are developing rapidly across the country but are most evident in the large cities.

In a bar, a draught beer ranges from about $2.25 for a 340-ml glass to $4.50 for a pint. Draught beer by the glass or pitcher is the cheapest way to drink. In places featuring live music, prices usually go up after the night's entertainment arrives. At retail outlets beer bought in cases works out to be about $1.35 for a bottle or a can.

Wine Canadian wine once had a deservedly poor reputation. Since the 1980s, though, the product has improved steadily, in some cases considerably. Unfairly, the stigma often remains. True, the bottom-end wines are the domestics and they taste as cheap as the price. But most of the Canadian wineries now also take great care with at least some of their labels.

The country has two main wine-producing regions, Ontario's Niagara Peninsula, with by far the largest share, and British Columbia's Okanagan Valley. Wineries can also be found in southern Quebec, elsewhere in Ontario (the Lake Erie Shoreline, and Pelee Island which is out in Lake Erie) and in Nova Scotia.

Most of these areas now have their own Vintners Quality Alliance (VQA) grading and classification system, meant to establish and maintain standards for the better wines in much the same way as is done in Europe. Wines sporting the VQA label are among the ones recommended to sample. A similar grading system is found in British Columbia.

Red, white, dry and sweet are all produced as are some sparkling wines, but the dry whites and the very expensive ice wines are Canada's best. Import duties keep foreign wine prices up to protect the Canadian wine industry but you can still get a pretty low-priced bottle of French or Californian wine.

Spirits Canada produces its own gins, vodkas, rums, liqueurs, brandies and coolers. But Canadian whisky, generally known in the country as rye, is the best-known liquor and the one with the biggest reputation. Canadian Club and VO rye whisky are Canada's most famous drinks – good stuff. Rye is generally taken with ginger ale or soda but some like it straight with ice. Canadian whisky has been distilled since the mid-1800s and has been popular in the USA as well as Canada from the early days of production. Most of the high price of spirits in Canada is attributable to tax.

Nonalcoholic Drinks

The fruit-growing areas of Ontario, Quebec and British Columbia produce excellent apple and cherry ciders, some with alcohol, most without. In Quebec and the Atlantic Provinces, visitors may want to sample a local nonalcoholic brew called spruce beer. It's produced in small batches by individuals and doesn't have a large commercial base but is sold in some local stores. It varies quite a bit and you can never be too sure what will happen when the cap comes off, but some people love the stuff.

Canadian mineral and spring waters are popular and readily available. Bottle waters from Europe, especially France, are also stocked.

A cup of standard coffee in Canada is not memorable but it isn't expensive either. If fresh it can be fairly decent. Restaurant coffee is almost always a filtered brew. In the western provinces it is not uncommon to be offered free refills (sometimes multiple) with every purchased cup. This is not the case in the rest of the country. Some cafes and restaurants offer varieties such as espresso and cappuccino. Speciality coffee bars such as those operated by The Second Cup are becoming increasingly popular across the country and offer a selection of good coffees. A respectable cup of coffee can also be found at the ubiquitous doughnut shops found everywhere across Canada.

Tea is also common and is served hot, unlike in the USA where tea often means iced lemon tea. In restaurants it is always made with bags. It is often served in a small, steel pot which is impossible to pour without spilling.

ENTERTAINMENT

Entertainment in major Canadian cities is top rate. Theatre, ballet, opera and symphony orchestras can be enjoyed across the country. The main 'cultural' season is from November to May, however, first-rate productions are performed through the summer as well.

Toronto and Vancouver (the largest English-speaking cities) have particularly noteworthy theatre and dinner-theatre scenes.

Montreal is the capital of French theatre and performance arts. Nightclubs and bars present nightly jazz, blues, and rock of widely varying calibre. National and international names perform regularly in the main centres. Most large cities and towns now have at least one comedy club. There are two widespread trends in city bars. The first is sports bars with numerous televisions for watching an array of live sporting events. The second is clubs featuring pool tables coupled with recorded music.

Casinos are increasingly numerous as governments seek new ways of raising revenue.

For more information on Canadian arts see the Arts section in the Facts about the Country chapter.

SPECTATOR SPORTS

Technically, Canada's official national sport is lacrosse, a Native Indian game similar to soccer but played with a small ball and sticks. Each stick has a woven leather basket in which the ball is caught and carried.

The sport that really creates passion, and is the de facto national game, is ice hockey. This is especially true in Quebec, home of the Montreal Canadiens, a hockey legend and one of the most consistently successful professional sports teams anywhere. If you're in Canada in winter, a National Hockey League (NHL) game is recommended. The season runs from October to

Hockey Night in Canada

For close to 100 years ice hockey has brought out the passion in Canadians. No sport comes close to 'the world's fastest game' for a spot in a Canadian's heart. Now played in 20 countries, it is easily Canada's most important contribution to the world of sports.

The first game with rules (borrowed from field hockey, lacrosse and rugby) was played in Montreal in 1879 by McGill University students. Before that a version of the game had been played as early as the 1850s by British soldiers stationed in eastern Canada. In the 1880s several leagues were formed but the game really gained national attention in 1892 when the Canadian governor general, Frederick Arthur, Lord Stanley of Preston, donated a trophy to be given annually to the top Canadian team. The pursuit of the Stanley Cup by teams of the National Hockey League (NHL), which came into existance in 1917, has ever since become an annual quest.

Although almost all the players were Canadian, cities in the USA became home to several teams, with the Boston Bruins being the first to join the NHL in 1924. Eventually the league consisted of teams in Montreal, Toronto, Boston, New York, Detroit and Chicago. This six-team league existed until 1967 when it expanded to 12 teams, and today consists of 26 teams.

In the 1950s and 60s, hockey announcer Foster Hewitt could be heard across the country every Saturday night on the radio, and later on TV, as he called the game live from Maple Leaf Gardens in Toronto. Hewitt's 'play-by-play' of Hockey Night in Canada helped to secure hockey as the national game.

From this period on hockey stars became not just household names, but Canadian legends. People still speak of the 'Rocket Richard riot', a time in the 1950s when the city of Montreal went berserk at having their Hall of Fame player, Maurice 'Rocket' Richard, suspended by league president Clarence Campbell. Some even say that this was the catalyst for the Quebec separatist movement!

Through the 1980s superstar Wayne Gretzky became known around the world as he shattered every offensive record in the books. When he was traded from Edmonton to Los Angeles in 1988, not only was it front page news across the country for days but one politician brought it up in parliament saying the trade should be prevented. It was said that Gretzky was as much a symbol of Canada as the beaver or the maple leaf. In 1996 Gretzky, as a free agent, signed a two-year $10.2-million contract to play with the New York Rangers.

Now with excellent players and teams in such countries as Sweden, Finland, the Czech and Slovak republics and Russia, as well as semi-professional and college teams in the USA, international matchups are always close and many European players are drafted by NHL teams. Still, despite this influx of players from Europe and increased US influence and expansion, the majority of players in the NHL remain Canadian.

While 'He shoots, he scores' is perhaps the most Canadian of phrases, hockey is also a game for girls and women. Women have played the game since its formative stages but in a much less organised fashion. In 1992, Manon Rhéaume from Quebec City, a goalie, became the first woman ever invited to a NHL training camp when the Tampa Bay Lightning offered her a try-out. She didn't make the team but was offered a contract to play in their minor-league team. While amateur leagues were plentiful, there is still no professional women's league. The first Women's World Championship was held in 1990 and, incidentally, was won by Canada. In 1998, there will be a women's hockey tournament in the Winter Olympics – it's the same game but without body checking.

The Hockey Hall of Fame can be visited in Toronto and professional hockey games can be seen in many major Canadian cities. At any outdoor rink through the winter you will likely find a pick-up game in progress. If you've got skates and a stick you're in the game, and a part of a Canadian tradition. ■

April. There are teams in six Canadian cities and 26 teams altogether with the rest being located in US cities although most of the players are from Canada, with other players coming from places such as Russia, Sweden, Finland and the Czech Republic. In Canada, NHL teams are found in Ottawa, Toronto, Montreal, Edmonton, Calgary and Vancouver. Many other cities have minor league teams.

US-style football, with some modifications, is played in the Canadian Football League (CFL). There are teams in Ottawa, Toronto, Hamilton, Montreal, Winnipeg, Regina, Edmonton, Calgary and Vancouver. Although the Canadian game is faster and more interesting, fans seem to be deserting the game for the US version. The championship game, known as the Grey Cup, is played in late November.

Baseball is popular in Canada and there are two teams in the predominately US-based major leagues – the Montreal Expos in the National League, and the Toronto Blue Jays in the American League. Toronto won the World Series Championship (in which the winning team of the National League plays the winning team of the American League) in 1992 and 1993. Minor league teams play in many cities across the country.

In 1995 Canada gained entry into the American professional basketball league, known as the National Basketball Association (NBA). The new Vancouver Grizzlies and Toronto Raptors have become part of the sport's increasing popularity.

Soccer and rugby have never really caught on and are strictly small-time in Canada. Soccer, being one of the few remaining inexpensive sports to play, is part of many school curriculums, and park pick-up games are common. Rugby has a following in British Columbia and despite its low profile in the rest of the country, Canada has done well in international competition and the World Rugby Cup. With both sports, there are amateur and semi-professional teams and leagues found in some Canadian cities.

More details on spectator sports can be found in the city sections in the book. For information on participating in sports and all outdoor activities see the Activities section in this chapter.

THINGS TO BUY

Despite being a Western consumer society largely filled with the goods of the international market place, Canada does offer the discriminating a number of interesting or unique things to buy.

Outdoor or camping specialists may turn up something you haven't seen before and some of the outdoor clothing is particularly good. One Canadian name to look for is Tilley. These clothing products are not cheap but their longevity pays off.

For edibles, the British Columbia smoked salmon is a real treat and from west coast outlets fresh salmon can be packed to take on flights home. In Quebec there is maple syrup and maple sugar which make different, inexpensive gifts. The wines of the Niagara region can be very good, advice is available at liquor outlets in southern Ontario. Rye whisky is a Canadian speciality.

Most good bookstores have a Canadiana section for books on Canada or Canadian literature. Likewise, record shops offer tapes of Canadian music. Traditional folk music is especially abundant in Eastern Canada.

At art-gallery gift shops prints of the work of Canadian painters can be found. Wood carving has a long tradition in Quebec notably at the town of Saint Jean Port Joli. Another area for this, but to a lesser degree, is along the French Shore of Nova Scotia. Also in Nova Scotia at Cheticamp you'll find some fine handmade rugs.

In the west, British Columbia jade can be bought in a number of ways including jewellery. Saskatchewan and Alberta have a Western tradition which reveals itself in leatherwork – belts, vests, jackets, cowboy boots and hats can be good value.

Traditional Hudson's Bay blankets and coats of 100% wool can be bought at The Bay department stores run by Canada's oldest company. For both these items look for the tell-tale green, red, yellow and black stripes on a white background. Classic cloth lumberjack jackets in either red or blue checks are cheap and distinctive, if not elegant.

Crafts shows, flea markets and speciality shops showcase the work of Canadian artisans. Craftspeople such as potters, weavers, and jewellers turn out some fine work.

For information on the worthwhile Native arts & crafts to consider as purchases see Native Art in the Arts section in the Facts about the Country chapter. These represent some of the best value, most 'Canadian' souvenirs.

Shops designed to serve tourists at the country's attractions such as Niagara Falls are not the place to look for a meaningful keepsake. Canadiana kitsch in the form of plastic Mounties, cheap pseudo-Native Indian dolls, miniature beavers and tasteless T-shirts are good for a smirk and nothing more.

Getting There & Away

AIR

The most common way to enter Canada is via the USA. Many overseas flights to North America go to the USA, with New York, San Francisco and Los Angeles being the major destinations. You can then either fly to a major Canadian city, such as Montreal or Vancouver, or catch a bus or train. Often though, flying directly into Canadian gateway cities such as Halifax, Montreal, Toronto and Vancouver can be more or less the same price as first arriving in US cities.

Also, from Europe anyway, getting a reasonably priced ticket has become increasingly straightforward. The budget airlines and the lesser-known, smaller airlines out of countries such as Iceland or Belgium have given way to the competitive prices of airlines such as Air Canada and British Airways.

The lowest priced tickets are often found in cities that have the largest number of airlines passing through them such as New York, London, Athens, Bangkok, Hong

---

Air Travel Glossary

Apex Apex, or 'advance purchase excursion' is a discounted ticket which must be paid for in advance. There are penalties if you wish to change it.

Baggage Allowance This will be written on your ticket: usually one 20 kg item to go in the hold, plus one item of hand luggage.

Bucket Shop An unbonded travel agency specialising in discounted airline tickets.

Bumped Just because you have a confirmed seat doesn't mean you're going to get on the plane — see Overbooking.

Cancellation Penalties If you have to cancel or change an Apex ticket there are often heavy penalties involved, insurance can sometimes be taken out against these penalties. Some airlines impose penalties on regular tickets as well, particularly against 'no show' passengers.

Check In Airlines ask you to check in a certain time ahead of the flight departure (usually 1½ hours on international flights). If you fail to check in on time and the flight is overbooked the airline can cancel your booking and give your seat to somebody else.

Confirmation Having a ticket written out with the flight and date you want doesn't mean you have a seat until the agent has checked with the airline that your status is 'OK' or confirmed. Meanwhile you could just be 'on request'.

Discounted Tickets There are two types of discounted fares - officially discounted (see Promotional Fares) and unofficially discounted. The lowest prices often impose drawbacks like flying with unpopular airlines, inconvenient schedules, or unpleasant routes and connections. A discounted ticket can save you other things than money — you may be able to pay Apex prices without the associated Apex advance booking and other requirements. Discounted tickets only exist where there is fierce competition.

Full Fares Airlines traditionally offer first class (coded F), business class (coded J) and economy class (coded Y) tickets. These days there are so many promotional and discounted fares available from the regular economy class that few passengers pay full economy fare.

Lost Tickets If you lose your airline ticket an airline will usually treat it like a travellers' cheque and, after inquiries, issue you with another one. Legally, however, an airline is entitled to treat it like cash and if you lose it then it's gone forever. Take good care of your tickets.

No Shows No shows are passengers who fail to show up for their flight, sometimes due to unexpected delays or disasters, sometimes due to simply forgetting, sometimes because they made more than one booking and didn't bother to cancel the one they didn't want. Full fare passengers who fail to turn up are sometimes entitled to travel on a later flight. The rest of us are penalised (see Cancellation Penalties).

On Request An unconfirmed booking for a flight, see Confirmation.

Open Jaws A return ticket where you fly out to one place but return from another. If available this can save you backtracking to your arrival point.

Kong and Manila. If these departure points are not feasible, shop around the travel agents at home. There are often travel agencies which specialise in trips to North America and which will know of organised charters or good deals.

One of the basics in air travel is that most airlines, particularly the larger ones (including the Canadian companies flying internationally), provide the greatest discount on return tickets rather than on one-way fares. Generally, one-way fares are no bargain and if they are less than a return, it is not by much. With both overseas flights and domestic airlines, it is not uncommon for one-way tickets to cost more than returns.

The USA

Flights between US and Canadian cities are abundant and frequent. Between larger cities there are generally direct flights. Montreal, Toronto and Vancouver are the busiest Canadian destinations but all major cities are plugged into the extensive North American system.

Canadian Airlines flies from Los Angeles, California, to Vancouver for US$308 plus taxes, one way.

Air Canada flies in and out of New York City to Montreal and Toronto. A one-way New York City to Toronto ticket costs US$165. American Airlines also serves this route.

Overbooking Airlines hate to fly empty seats and since every flight has some passengers who fail to show up (see No Shows) airlines often book more passengers than they have seats. Usually the excess passengers balance those who fail to show up but occasionally somebody gets bumped. If this happens guess who it is most likely to be? The passengers who check in late.

Promotional Fares Officially discounted fares like Apex fares which are available from travel agents or direct from the airline.

Reconfirmation At least 72 hours prior to departure time of an onward or return flight you must contact the airline and 'reconfirm' that you intend to be on the flight. If you don't do this the airline can delete your name from the passenger list and you could lose your seat. You don't have to reconfirm the first flight on your itinerary or if your stopover is less than 72 hours. It doesn't hurt to reconfirm more than once.

Restrictions Discounted tickets often have various restrictions on them - advance purchase is the most usual one (see Apex). Others are restrictions on the minimum and maximum period you must be away, such as a minimum of 14 days or a maximum of one year. See Cancellation Penalties.

Standby A discounted ticket where you only fly if there is a seat free at the last moment. Standby fares are usually only available on domestic routes.

Tickets Out An entry requirement for many countries is that you have an onward or return ticket, in other words, a ticket out of the country. If you're not sure what you intend to do next, the easiest solution is to buy the cheapest onward ticket to a neighbouring country or a ticket from a reliable airline which can later be refunded if you do not use it.

Transferred Tickets Airline tickets cannot be transferred from one person to another. Travellers sometimes try to sell the return half of their ticket, but officials can ask you to prove that you are the person named on the ticket. This is unlikely to happen on domestic flights, on an international flight tickets may be compared with passports.

Travel Agencies Travel agencies vary widely and you should ensure you use one that suits your needs. Some simply handle tours while full-service agencies handle everything from tours and tickets to car rental and hotel bookings. A good one will do all these things and can save you a lot of money but if all you want is a ticket at the lowest possible price, then you really need an agency specialising in discounted tickets. A discounted ticket agency, however, may not be useful for other things, like hotel bookings.

Travel Periods Some officially discounted fares, Apex fares in particular, vary with the time of year. There is often a low (off-peak) season and a high (peak) season. Sometimes there's an intermediate or shoulder season as well. At peak times, when everyone wants to fly, not only will the officially discounted fares be higher but so will unofficially discounted fares or there may simply be no discounted tickets available. Usually the fare depends on your outward flight – if you depart in the high season and return in the low season, you pay the high-season fare. ■

The *New York Times*, the *Chicago Tribune*, the *San Francisco Chronicle Examiner* and the *LA Times* produce weekly travel sections containing lots of ads with current airfares. You could also try the student travel service STA Travel, which has offices in all the major cities, or its Canadian counterpart CUTS (see the Getting Around chapter for details).

The UK & Continental Europe

The key to cross-Atlantic flights is timing. In either direction, the season is the price guide. That said, how high and low seasons are defined varies with particular airlines, the day of the week, the duration of the stay and other factors. Usually, the longer the stay, the higher the cost.

Many of Europe's major centres are served by either Canadian Airlines or Air Canada. They arrange return fares starting on either side of the Atlantic.

For example, Air Canada flies from London, Paris and Frankfurt (among many others) to Toronto. Fares vary a lot depending on the time of year, with the summer months and Christmas being the most expensive seasons. In any case an advance booking of 21 days is required for the best prices. From London, return fares can vary from as low as UK£319 in low season.

Air Canada flies one way London to St John's, Newfoundland twice a week for UK£377 or UK£754 return on a regular economy, no advance notice fare. With a 21-day advance booking this return fare drops to high season UK£509 and low season UK£349.

This is a flight to consider for a couple of reasons. It's one of the so-called open jaw return tickets which allow for landing in one city and departing from another, sometimes at no extra charge, sometimes with a small additional payment required. The fare to Toronto is the same price so you can fly into St John's make your way across eastern Canada and head home from Toronto. Another benefit to this particular flight is that transportation from mainland Canada to Newfoundland, for example, is costly and time-consuming. This way you start there and move to the rest of Canada without having to backtrack.

Canadian Airlines has London, Amsterdam and Frankfurt as major cities although they serve many other European cities, too. From Frankfurt midweek, midsummer the return ticket costs DM1399. The low-season rate for the above fare is about 30% less. Prices are highest between 15 June and 15 August.

Both Canadian companies offer youth fares to Canada from Europe.

The British Airways direct one-way flight London to Montreal is UK£350 regular economy fare or double that for return. The advance booking return excursion fare is UK£479 midweek, midsummer. Youth and standby fares may be offered. Alternatively, British Airways offers a return to John F Kennedy Airport, New York City, for UK£368 (low season). From New York City, it's about an eight-hour bus ride or a 10-hour train ride to Montreal.

Stopover privileges in Canada for tickets such as London-Montreal-Toronto-Vancouver-London are offered on some tickets.

Charters If you are travelling between Europe and Canada you might investigate these. Most charter trips with a Canadian connection are between Canada and Europe. Other Canadian charters connect to US destinations, mostly Florida or Hawaii (the sunspots), or to the Caribbean.

Private Canadian charter companies operate flights to various European countries. Often a good place to look in Canada is at the travel agencies in an ethnic part of a major city where immigrants are often seeking cheap trips back to the homeland.

Some of the bigger, better established charter companies and tour wholesalers in Canada work in conjunction with one of the two principal Canadian airlines. An example is Air Canada Vacations which puts packages together in Europe for visitors to Canada. Canadian charter companies don't seem to have either an easy or a long life so the names change frequently. In Canada or abroad, travel agencies and university student offices should have some information on potential charter trips.

There are probably good charters from France to the province of Quebec.

Budget Airlines The halcyon days of budget airlines created by flamboyant owners seem to be a thing of the past. Rumours come and go but the tight profit margins have restrained small upstart airlines that undercut everybody else on the cross-Atlantic route. Such airlines usually fly into and out of New York from a Western European city so keep your ears open. If you're very lucky, a new airline will spring up just before you leave.

Asia
From Asia it's often cheaper to fly first to the USA rather than directly to Canada. Singapore Airlines and Korean Airlines run cheap flights around the Pacific, ending on the USA's west coast.

Check in Singapore and in travel agencies in Bangkok and Kuala Lumpur. For example, from Bangkok to the USA's west coast, Thai Airways charges US$540 one-way and US$1012 return, while Korean Airlines charges US$520 one-way and US$992 return.

From Hong Kong, one-way fares to Los Angeles, San Francisco or Vancouver are also reasonable and usually cheaper than going the other way. The cheapest one-way fare to Los Angeles is around US$460, to Vancouver US$420.

Australia & NZ
Continental Airlines, Canadian Airlines, United Airlines, Qantas and Air New Zealand offer regular flights to Vancouver from Australia and New Zealand.

Qantas offers standard economy airfares from Australia to Canada: a return ticket to Vancouver is a whopping A$4966 all year. However, there are much cheaper advance-purchase tickets available with varying conditions attached. These fares range from A$1752 in the low season to a high of $2145.

From Auckland the regular return economy fare with Air New Zealand is also huge at NZ$5468, but like Qantas it offers discounted advance-purchase airfares. These start from NZ$2019 in the low season, for a minimum stay of five days and must be purchased seven days in advance.

Coming from Australia, New Zealand or Asia, it's also possible to travel to Canada via the USA. After arriving in Los Angeles, San Francisco, or possibly Seattle on the west coast, a train or bus will take you to Vancouver.

In addition, Qantas and Air New Zealand flights from Australia to US cities (in California), often include many stopovers in the Pacific – Fiji, Rarotonga, Hawaii and even Tahiti.

The fares given are only the airlines' official fares. You will find the best deals by shopping around the travel agencies.

Round-the-World Tickets
If you are covering a lot of distance, a Round-the-World (RTW) ticket could be worthwhile. A good ticket can include a lot of stops in places all over the world, with a maximum ticket validity of 12 months. Check out the huge variety of RTW tickets available.

Out of Canada, Air Canada in conjunction with other airlines offers such tickets but they're only good for six months. Air Canada uses just one other airline per ticket, but which airline that is varies. Depending on which you select, the price of the fare will change. Three that are regularly part of such a deal are Cathay Pacific, Qantas and Singapore Airlines.

Air Canada and Singapore Airlines offer a RTW fare of C$3131 for unlimited stopovers (their destinations only), going in one direction. Side trips can be arranged in Europe at a reasonable cost. Similar fares are offered out of many countries but you should investigate in the country of first departure.

LAND
Bus
The Greyhound bus network connects the major continental US cities with most major

destinations in Canada but with a bus transfer at the border or nearest town to it. Note, however, that the multi-day passes available in the USA cannot be used in Canada. If you're using a US pass, enquire as to how close you can get to your Canadian destination before having to buy a separate ticket.

There is one exception to this. Only one city in Canada is served by a US Greyhound bus and that is Montreal, Quebec. The last trip taken on a US Greyhound pass can be used to travel from New York City to Montreal. Other US bus lines do run directly to Canadian cities with no stop or need for a bus change.

Alaska's Gray Line Alaskon buses connect Fairbanks, Anchorage, Skagway and Haines in Alaska with Whitehorse in the Yukon. Alaska Direct Busline does the same routes.

Train

Amtrak has three main routes between the USA and Canada: these are New York City to Montreal (10 hours), New York City to Toronto (12 hours; via Niagara Falls) and Chicago to Toronto (11½ hours). On the west coast, Seattle is as far north as Amtrak reaches. Buses run from Seattle to Vancouver. For information about fares and schedules contact Amtrak (☎ 1-800-872-7245), 60 Massachusetts Ave NE, Washington, DC 20002, USA.

Car

The highway system of the continental USA connects directly with the Canadian highway system along the border at numerous points, which then meet up with the Trans Canada Highway further north.

During the summer months, Friday and Sunday can be very busy at major international border crossings with shoppers, vacationers and visitors all travelling at the same time. Delays can be especially bad on the holiday weekends in summer. Waits at these times can be hours, so avoid them if possible. Crossings that are particularly prone to lengthy queues are: Windsor, Ont

and Detroit, Mich; Fort Erie, Ont and Buffalo, NY; Niagara Falls, Ont and Niagara Falls, NY; Quebec and Rouse's Point, NY; and White Rock, BC and Blaine, Wash. The small, secondary border points elsewhere are always quiet, sometimes so quiet the officers have nothing to do except tear your luggage apart.

Between the Yukon Territory and Alaska the main routes are the Alaska and Klondike highways and the Haines Road.

Visitors with US or British passports are allowed to bring their vehicles in for six months.

SEA
Ferry

On the east coast, Canada is connected with the USA by several ferries. Yarmouth, Nova Scotia, is linked to both Bar Harbor, Maine, and to Portland, Maine, in the USA with two different ferry routes. See the Yarmouth section in the Nova Scotia chapter for more details. From the south end of Deer Island, New Brunswick in the Bay of Fundy, another ferry runs to Eastport, Maine. A ferry at the north end of Deer Island connects it to the New Brunswick mainland.

On the west coast there are ferries between Washington state and Victoria on Vancouver Island. From Port Hardy, on northern Vancouver Island, ferries also head north along the Inside Passage to Alaska. See the Getting There & Away sections for Port Hardy and Victoria in the British Columbia chapter.

Yacht

Many flights from Australasia stop off in Hawaii. With a bit of persistence and luck it might be possible to find someone with a yacht who needs a hand. Hawaii is a favourite vacation spot with Western Canadians, but don't count on hitting the jackpot.

If you're coming from the Caribbean you might also find a yacht there (it's been done). Most head for Florida and from there, some edge up the east coast. Experienced sailors and females have the best chance at getting a place on board.

Passenger Ship

Regular, long-distance passenger ships disappeared with the advent of cheap air travel, to be replaced by a small number of luxury cruise ships. The standard reference for passenger ships is the OAG Cruise and Ferry Guide published by the Reed Travel Group (☎ 01582-600-111), Church St, Dunstable, Bedfordshire LU5 4HB, UK. Cunard's *Queen Elizabeth II*, sails 20 times a year between Southampton in the UK and New York; the trip takes six nights one way.

Travel agents are the best source of information as some cruise lines do not sell directly to the public. Princess Cruises is one company with sailings from New England to east coast Canada and the St Lawrence River. Cunard Lines is another.

Seabourn Cruise Line (☎ 415-391-7444), 55 San Francisco St, San Francisco, California 94133, USA, offers cruises to and around Eastern Canada from Boston and New York. Both seven and 14-day trips are offered with stops in many Canadian ports ending up in Montreal. These trips are in the $1000 a day range.

American Canadian Caribbean Lines (☎ 1-800-556-7450) has a trip from New England up the Hudson River to Montreal and Quebec City. Many of the major lines cruise the Inside Passage and Alaska and these generally mean stops at either Vancouver or Victoria.

Adventure Canada (☎ 1-800-363-7566), 14 Front St, Mississauga, Ontario L5H 2C4, have east and west-coast cruises stressing wildlife, history and the environment and include lectures and input by various guests on board.

Freighter

A more adventurous, though not necessarily cheaper, alternative is as a paying passenger on a freighter. Freighters are more numerous than cruise ships and there are more routes from which to choose. Passenger freighters typically carry six to 12 passengers (more than 12 would require a doctor on board) and, though less luxurious than dedicated cruise ships, give you a real taste of life at sea.

The previously mentioned *ABC Passenger Shipping Guide* is a good source of information. Also contact the Cruise & Freighter Travel Association (☎ 1-800-872-8584), Box 580218-D1, Flushing, NY 11358, USA.

LEAVING CANADA
Departure Tax

There is a departure/airport tax of $55 levied on all international flights out of Canada, other than those to US destinations. To US destinations the tax is 7% of the ticket value plus $6 to a maximum of $55.

Most tickets purchased in Canada for international flights out of Canada include this tax; but tickets out of Canada, purchased in another country, usually don't include it. If you did buy your ticket in another country and it didn't include departure tax, you will be asked for this tax after you pass through customs and immigration. When you're changing money, consider saving enough to cover it.

Also, sales taxes and the GST may or may not be included in any quoted airline ticket in Canada, so ask. In Vancouver there is an additional tax known as the airport improvement tax. A flight leaving Canada for a US destination is taxed at $10, every other international flight is taxed at $15. This tax is not included with the ticket price and must be paid at the airport. Montreal's Dorval Airport is also considering an improvement tax.

Remember, too, that if you intend to apply for any GST rebate this is your last chance to get a form (see the Consumer Taxes section in the Facts for the Visitor chapter for more details).

WARNING

This chapter is particularly vulnerable to change. Prices for international travel are volatile, routes are introduced and cancelled, schedules change, rules are amended and special deals come and go.

Airlines and governments seem to take a perverse pleasure in making price structures and regulations as complicated as possible and you should check directly with the airline or a travel agency to make sure you understand how a fare (and ticket you may buy) works.

The upshot of all this is that you should get opinions, quotes and advice from as many airlines and travel agencies as possible before you part with your hard-earned cash. The details given in this chapter should be regarded as pointers and are not a substitute for your own up-to-the-minute research.

Getting Around

Within Canada, land travel is much cheaper and much more interesting than flying. The bus network is the most extensive public transportation system and is generally less expensive than the more limited train service. VIA Rail, the national passenger train service does, however, offer multi-day passes as well as discount prices for travelling on specific days, for example during midweek. Train travel can also be quicker than riding the buses.

Although quite a bit higher than in the USA, driving costs are reasonable with gasoline prices considerably lower than those in Europe. Still, it's a big country and if you really want to get around quickly your wallet will be thinned.

Whether using the train or bus network or a combination of both, visitors should remember that despite Canada's size the population is small. In many ways this is an asset and part of the country's appeal but can also mean that transportation is not always frequent, convenient or even available. Hopping on a bus or train on a whim, as may be possible in much of Europe, is not realistic here unless you're in one of the main population areas. However, as any traveller knows, the greater the hassle to get there, the less likely the place will be inundated by tourists.

Air fares are expensive, but for those with a little extra money and not much time, the odd flight may be useful. You may even be able to take advantage of one of the 'seat sales' (last-minute ticket price reductions) often offered by the airlines.

AIR

The country has two major airlines both privately operated, Air Canada and Canadian Airlines International, usually referred to simply as Canadian. Both work in conjunction with a number of regional carriers known as partners to form widespread domestic networks. Canadian Airlines is also linked financially and managerially with American Airlines of the USA. Air Canada has financial ties and agreements with Continental and United of the USA. These mean close working relationships and better connecting flights.

In 1995 an 'open skies' policy – a sort of a free-trade of the air system – was signed between Canada and the USA. This means that more airlines on both sides of the border can fly to more destinations in both countries. In theory this should mean better prices. Critics say Canadian airline companies will have difficulty matching prices and competing.

Air Canada partners in Canada include Air BC, Air Creebec (northern Ontario & northern Quebec), Air Nova, Air Ontario, Bearskin Airways, First Air (NWT) and NWT Air.

Many of the Canadian Airlines partners have been amalgamated into Canadian Regional Airlines. Within this group are Air Atlantic, Calm Air, Canadian North and Inter-Canadienne. These names may still be heard although the airlines do not formally exist – just their routes do.

In early summer 1996 Canadian air passengers greeted the arrival of Greyhound Air (yes, the bus people but using Kelowna Flightcraft Air) which promises a new choice and hence better fares for internal flights. All their flights can be booked through one telephone number, ☎ 1-800-661-8747. No tickets are given, just a reference number and restrictions are few including no advance booking requirements. They fly from Ottawa and Toronto to five major western cities including Vancouver. There are also some independent regional and local airlines which tend to focus on small specialised regions, particularly in the north.

Together all these airlines cover most small cities and towns across the country. On smaller airlines it's worth inquiring about student rates but you will need an International Student Identity Card (ISIC).

Domestic flights tend to be costly. The prices and schedules of flights change and fluctuate often. Phone an airline for information one week, and the next week they'll tell you something quite different. The best thing to do is shop around – directly with the airline or through a travel agent – and be flexible. Waiting a day or two or avoiding a weekend flight could save you a lot. If you have the time, advance-booking flights are usually the most economical.

Air Canada may be cheap for one flight, Canadian Airlines for another, although each keeps pretty well abreast of what the other is up to.

In order to keep down the price of air travel there are a few general rules to follow. First, plan in advance because the best bargains are excursion fares, pre-booked return flights with minimum and maximum stays. Flights booked at least seven days in advance are lower than spur-of-the-moment prices. Booking either 14 or 30 days in advance may well result in further reductions. Secondly, don't fly at peak times, that is between 7 am and 7 pm. Thirdly, be prepared to make stops; direct flights may cost more.

Both airlines offer year-round youth fares on domestic flights. On Air Canada and Canadian, those 24 years of age and younger are offered standby fares which mean reductions of about 30%. Photo ID is required. If you call in the morning the airline should be able to give you a good idea of what flight to try for.

Occasionally, there are short-term specials for promotion of a certain flight; these can be cheap but are irregular. Both Canadian airlines occasionally offer 'seat sales'.

Another thing to consider is getting a ticket from point A to B and stopping off in the middle. This can often be done for little more than the straight-through fare.

Canadian Airlines and Air Canada sometimes offer fly-drive packages which cover the air fare and car rental. The packages, only available on return flights, sometimes include accommodation. Other possibilities include reductions on cars, hotels and bus tours. The hotels used, however, are expensive. You just have to ask about the latest gimmicks and offers. Greyhound's new approach may shake things up and make the other two airlines reduce both prices and restrictions.

Travel agencies offer economical charters and package tours to various Canadian cities as well as to US destinations. These turn up throughout the year but especially over Christmas and through the summer holiday season. Book well in advance to take advantage of these specials. There's a varying minimum and maximum stay on charter flights. No student or youth fares are offered on these types of tickets.

Cheap tickets can be found in the classified ads of newspapers under Travel or Business Personals. These tickets are the unused half of a return ticket. Because return tickets are often the same price, or even cheaper, than one-way tickets, travellers will sell the unused half of a return ticket. These offers are also advertised on university and hostel noticeboards. It isn't strictly legal, as tickets are officially nontransferable, but it's done a lot.

Air fares in Canada are generally quoted as the base fare only and all taxes, including the GST, are an additional cost. Ticket agents will quickly total these for you, but you do need to ask. This is worth doing as taxes can add quite a bit to the bill, perhaps resulting in a rather nasty surprise. In Vancouver, passengers must pay an additional tax to help finance airport expansion. This is billed at $5 to fly within the province and $10 within the rest of the country. This tax is not added on to the ticket price and must be paid at the airport. It can be paid with a credit card if you don't have the cash.

The standard no-notice one-way fares listed in this book should be used as a rough guide since prices fluctuate regularly and taxes change with new governments – both provincial and federal. Prices of regular economy flights go up for the high seasons of Christmas and summer.

Always confirm your bookings and ask for a specific seat number as this will guarantee you a seat on the plane.

BUS

Buses supply the most extensive transportation routes across the country. They go nearly everywhere and are normally cheaper than trains. Buses are usually clean, safe and comfortable. They are also generally efficient and run on time.

The largest carrier is Greyhound with routes from Toronto westwards. Other major companies include Voyageur in Ontario and Quebec, Greyhound-Gray Coach Lines in Ontario, Orleans Express in eastern Quebec, SMT in New Brunswick, Acadian Lines in Nova Scotia and Roadcruiser in Newfoundland. There are other provincial, regional and local lines. Bus services are covered in the text.

Services are not exhaustive nor always convenient. Routes between any two given destinations may not be frequent and in some cases may not run daily, perhaps only two or three times a week. In more out of the way places there may be no service at all.

Some bus lines offer specials such as reduced return fares some of the time. Always ask, the policies often change.

On long trips the journey can usually be broken with stopovers but inquire if this is so and how many stops are permitted. A one-way ticket is usually good for 60 days and a return ticket is valid for a year.

If a destination is beyond one company's territory and involves switching bus lines at some point, the connection is generally free. Through tickets are sold for many routes in central and eastern Canada but generally not westward into Greyhound territory.

Some bus lines offer student fares on some routes, so ask. For example, Voyageur Colonial provides student rates (ID required) for trips from Toronto to either Montreal or Ottawa. There's a deal on some routes for students where two free tickets are given with every four purchased. There is no student age limit.

Highway Distances between Major Cities (km)

	Calgary	Charlottetown	Edmonton	Fredericton	Halifax	Montreal	Ottawa	Quebec	Regina	St John's	Saskatoon	Thunder Bay	Toronto	Vancouver	Victoria	Whitehorse	Winnipeg
Charlottetown	4917																
Edmonton	299	4949															
Fredericton	4558	359	4598														
Halifax	5042	232	5082	346													
Montreal	3743	1184	3764	834	1318												
Ottawa	3553	1374	3574	1024	1508	190											
Quebec	4014	945	4035	586	912	270	460										
Regina	764	4163	785	3813	4297	2979	2789	3249									
St John's	6183	1294	6212	1622	1349	2448	2638	2208	5427								
Saskatoon	620	4421	528	4070	4554	3236	3046	3507	257	5684							
Thunder Bay	2050	2878	2071	2527	3011	1693	1503	1963	1286	4141	1543						
Toronto	3434	1724	3455	1373	1857	539	399	810	2670	2987	2927	1384					
Vancouver	1057	5985	1244	5634	6119	4801	4611	5071	1822	7248	1677	3108	4492				
Victoria	1123	6051	1310	5700	6185	4867	4677	5137	1888	7314	1743	3174	4558	66			
Whitehorse	2385	7034	2086	6684	7168	5850	5660	6120	2871	8298	2614	4157	5528	2697	2763		
Winnipeg	1336	3592	1357	3241	3726	2408	2218	2678	571	4855	829	715	2099	2232	2298	3524	
Yellowknife	1811	6460	1511	6109	6593	5275	5086	5546	2297	7723	2039	3582	4966	2411	2477	2704	2868

Some bus companies in larger towns offer sightseeing tours ranging from one day to several weeks in length. Some include accommodation, meals and admission fees to attractions. You need to make reservations for these types of trips.

Bus Passes & Deals

There are some bus passes available in Canada which work much like the famous Eurail pass.

Greyhound has the Canada Travel Pass which allows for unlimited travel. This pass comes in seven ($213), 15 ($278), 30 ($374) and 60-day ($481) variations. Tax is included. Students and seniors can get 10% off. These are available all year except during major holiday times such as Christmas and Easter. The pass cannot be used on other bus lines with the exception of a connection to Montreal on Voyageur. You must buy the ticket at least a week before the first trip.

There are several other specials to consider. Any one-way ticket can include four stopovers along the way but you must specify them when buying the ticket and it must be used within 60 days. A return ticket good for one year permits 12 stopovers.

The Companion Fare Pass is very good if there are two people travelling together. One person pays full fare and the second person pays 50% of that. This applies to both one-way and return fares but must be purchased at least seven days prior to departure.

Lastly, there is the Family Fare with which each adult paying full fare can take one child to 15 years old free. Extra children are billed at half fare from age three to seven, full fare from age eight and up. Children under age two are free. Again this requires a seven-day advance purchase.

There is also a pass offered by Voyageur Colonial called Tourpass Voyageur which is good for 15 consecutive days of unlimited travel in Quebec and Ontario from May to September. The cost is $215, taxes included, with extra days possible at a daily rate. Many other bus lines in Quebec and Ontario honour this pass so free connections can be made out of Voyageur territory. Note that Greyhound does not accept the pass.

Travel agents in Europe may have Canadian bus passes for sale. Compare them carefully to those listed here. Representatives in Europe say the bus passes are likely to be not as good as what is available in Canada.

Tips

All bus lines (except in rare cases) use the same central bus station in any given Canadian city so you can change bus lines or make connections at the same place. Buses are also convenient because reservations are not necessary. Indeed, reservations are not offered. When one bus fills up, another is added so waiting hours for the next one is avoided. Always check this, however, as it may not be the case for all routes all the time. This does not apply unless you are getting on at the point of origin. For this reason, in a big city, if you have a choice of using the downtown station or a suburban stop, pick the downtown station. The bus may be full by the time it reaches the outskirts and you will be left waving good-bye. Seating is on a first-come, first-served basis. Smoking is not permitted.

Arrive at the station about an hour before the departure to purchase a ticket. Tickets can also be purchased up to several days in advance if this is convenient. Beware that advance tickets do not apply to any specific bus and do not guarantee a seat. You still must arrive early and line up for your bus.

On holiday weekends, especially Friday night or around major holidays such as Easter, the bus stations can get pretty crowded and chaotic. At these times arriving early or having bought a ticket beforehand is recommended as the ticket counters become very busy.

On longer trips always ask if there is a direct or express bus. On some routes some buses go straight through while others stop seemingly everywhere and these trips can be interminable. The price is generally the same and you may save hours.

In summer, the air-conditioners on buses can be far too effective. Take a sweater on board.

Take your own picnic whenever possible. Long-distance buses stop at highway service-station restaurants where you pay an awful lot for plastic food.

Most of the larger bus stations have coin-operated luggage lockers. Many have small, simple cafeterias or restaurants for break-fasts and other basic, inexpensive meals. Some bus stations are not in the best areas of a city so some care should be taken after late-night arrivals.

TRAIN

The railway was part of the formation of Canada and has played a major role in the country's history. It was the promise of a rail connection that brought the west into the Dominion of Canada and it was the same line which transported the first European settlers across the country. Because of the history of the Canadian Pacific Railway (CPR) and because so many have worked for the huge company at one time, Canadians feel a special nationalistic attachment to the 'ribbons of steel' from coast to coast. Unfortunately, this does not mean they take the train very often. Both Canadian Pacific (CP) and the government-run Canadian National (CN) are now out of the passenger business and operate only the freight trains in Canada. Privately owned CP is into just about everything including trucking, shipping, hotels and mining, and used to run Canadian Airlines. It is one of Canada's biggest, most pervasive companies. CN is currently for sale to private interests.

VIA Rail

Despite lack of support and slow dismemberment of the network, Canada still has a passenger train system extensive enough to be useful as well as appealing. Except as noted in this section (and some urban commuter trains), VIA Rail, which is a federal government agency, operates all the passenger trains in Canada. The word VIA has become synonymous with train travel and the stations and their road-side direction signs are labelled in this way. VIA uses CP

and CN trains and lines but is responsible for the service.

Most of the country's major cities are connected by rail, however, there are no passenger trains in Newfoundland (on the island) nor in Prince Edward Island. Some routes provide the only overland travel option allowing passengers a glimpse of otherwise unseeable countryside.

Train service is best in the so-called Quebec City to Windsor, Ontario corridor. In this densely populated area of the country, which includes Montreal, Ottawa, Kingston, Toronto and Niagara Falls, trains are frequent and the service is quick. Meals are available at extra cost but free snacks and drinks are brought to your seat. A first-class option available in the 'corridor' includes plush waiting areas, pre-boarding, deluxe seating and complete meals. On some routes there is food and bar service to your seat – this food is quite good but not cheap. The snack-bar food is usually lousy but the bar car, when there is one, can be fun.

Generally, long-distance train travel is more expensive than taking the bus, and reservations are important especially on weekends and holidays.

For train schedules and routes, you can pick up the *National Timetable* booklet at any VIA Rail station.

In smaller towns the station may only be open at arrival and departure times and this may not be every day. Also when telephoning the station you may be speaking to someone in a central location in another part of the country who handles all questions and reservations.

The pricing policy at VIA Rail is essentially that every trip is considered to be a one-way fare. A return trip between points A and B is billed as a one-way fare A to B, and a one-way fare B to A. There are no return or excursion fares. There are, however, ways to reduce your costs considerably.

In the Quebec City to Windsor corridor tickets are 40% off with five days notice but you can't travel on Friday or Sunday.

Everywhere else in Ontario and eastwards, travel on any day is discounted

40% if the trip is booked seven or more days in advance. The discount does not apply to trains linking the Maritimes to Quebec during the summer months, but does include trains within each of these areas all year. Note that there may be sales which do offer good discounts between Quebec and the Maritimes during the summer.

In the provinces west of Ontario, ticket reductions of at least 25% are available from the beginning of October to the end of May with seven days or more advance notice. More than the minimum advance notice is recommended.

The reason for booking well ahead is that a limited number of seats are offered at the discount rates. Once they are gone, you're back into the full fare. Also note there are no discounts on holidays or on days around the major holidays such as Christmas. Children, seniors (over 60) and students with international cards are entitled to discounts any time. People with children should inquire about family fares which are offered at various times and can mean substantial savings.

Long-Distance Travel A transcontinental train tour right across much of Canada passing through nearly all the provinces is possible by linking routes together. Taking approximately five days the journey rolls through vastly different scenery, some of it spectacular.

This can be a very pleasant, relaxing way to go, particularly if you have your own room. During the summer months this trip should be booked well in advance.

The longest continuous route in the country is from Toronto to Vancouver. VIA Rail calls this train the *Canadian*, in memory of CP's original. The train looks like the 1950s stainless steel classic complete with the two-storey windowed 'dome' car for sightseeing. The route it takes passes through Sudbury, Sioux Lookout, Winnipeg, Saskatoon, Edmonton, Jasper and the Rocky Mountains. There are three of these four-day trips weekly.

The fare varies with the season. During high season from 1 June to 30 September the coach-seat fare is $522 including tax. In May and October it drops 25%. The rest of the year a 40% reduction is in place with seven day's notice.

If you want to begin further east and go across the country, the train can be boarded in Halifax but you will have to change trains in Montreal and Toronto. The fare from Halifax to Vancouver is $213 plus the $522.

For all long-distance travel, VIA offers several types of cars and different sleeping arrangements. They range from semi-reclining seats, to upper and lower pull-out berths, to self-contained private roomettes of varying sizes. The price of any sleeping arrangement is added to the basic coach seat fare or Canrailpass. Discounts are available on beds, too, with advance purchase.

If you're going long distances you may want to take some of your own food. Train meals can be expensive and, as mentioned, the snack food is not particularly good. In the west, booking any sleeping arrangement other than the basic seat means getting all meals included. In the east it means getting breakfast.

Canrailpass For those who intend to travel a lot, or far, or both, VIA Rail offers the Canrailpass. The *National Timetable* booklet will help you plan your travels. The pass is available to anybody and is good for 12 days of coach-class travel within a 30-consecutive day period beginning on the day of the first trip.

The pass is good for any number of trips and stopovers from coast to coast. Reserving early is recommended, though, as the number of seats on the train set aside for pass holders is limited. You can buy the Canrailpass in Canada or in Europe (ask a travel agent or a VIA Rail outlet) but there's no difference in cost.

The Canrailpass comes in two price versions – low season and high season. Low season is from roughly 6 January to 31 May and from 1 October to 15 December. The cost with tax is $381 or $352 for those aged 24 and under, students or those 60 and over.

High season is roughly 1 June to 30 September, when the pass with tax is $573 full fare or $516 for those in the specified age categories. For all passes, extra days can be purchased at additional cost.

Canrailpass holders may be entitled to discounts at a car-rental agency, at Gray Line for bus tours and at some hotels; inquire if these options are in effect.

Other Train Lines

Canada has a few, small, local train companies which may be of interest to the traveller and which are mentioned in the text. An example includes the Algoma Central Railway in Sault Ste Marie, Ontario which provides access to a northern wilderness area. Another is Ontario Northland which operates northwards from Toronto and includes the Polar Bear Express up to Moosonee on Hudson Bay.

The Quebec North Shore & Labrador Railway runs from Sept-Îles, Quebec north to Labrador.

British Columbia Rail runs from Vancouver north to Prince George.

The Rocky Mountaineer

The privately run Mountaineer is a tourist train operating through some of the country's finest western scenery including one route along the old CPR line through the southern Rockies connecting Banff, perhaps Canada's most spectacular stretch of track.

All trips run between Vancouver and Kamloops with variations to Jasper, Banff and Calgary. A range of side trips and tours is offered. Trips are offered from the beginning of May to the middle of October. Reservations should be made well in advance but seats can be available at any time. Prices are discounted for brief periods at the beginning and the end of the season.

The train is operated by Rocky Mountain Railtours (☎ (604) 606-7200), 1-800-665-7245), Suite 130, 1150 Station St, Vancouver, British Columbia V6A 2X7. See the Vancouver section in the British Columbia chapter for more details.

Amtrak

Amtrak is the US equivalent of VIA Rail. Good-value passes and information on Amtrak's services are available at many Canadian train stations. See the Train section in the Getting There & Away chapter for more details.

CAR

In many ways, driving is the best way to travel. You can go where and when you want, use secondary highways and roads and get off the beaten track. It's particularly good in summer when you can camp or even sleep in the car. Cars with reclining seats are great for this and surprisingly comfortable with a sleeping bag.

Canada's roads are good and well-marked. In Quebec, non-French-speaking visitors may have some difficulty with the French-only signs. Getting hold of a decent provincial highway map is advisable. Provincial tourist offices have both provincial and national road maps – usually free. Service stations and variety stores sell similar maps.

There are few toll roads in the country although crossing some bridges requires a small payment.

The Trans Canada Hwy runs from St John's, Newfoundland across 7000-plus km to Victoria, British Columbia. There are campgrounds and picnic stops all along the route, often within 100 km to 150 km of each other. Rural routes are among the smallest road categories: they're found in rural Canada and are marked RR1, RR7, etc.

Drivers expecting to travel long distances or to more out-of-the-way areas may wish to bring along some audio tapes. The CBC radio network does cover much of the country but radio station options may be limited and in some areas nonexistent.

City rush hours – especially around 5 pm and on Friday – can be bad, particularly in Montreal, Toronto and Vancouver. Toronto's main access routes are busy night and day and everybody is impatient. In Montreal, drivers possessing nerves of steel, abundant confidence and a devil-may-care attitude will fare best. To compound the fun there are no lines painted on the roads in some places and driving becomes a type of high speed free-for-all. Guess what? The province of Quebec has the highest accident rate in the country. All told, avoiding city driving anywhere as much as possible is recommended, regardless of the time. Walking or taking the bus is generally cheaper than paying the costly parking fees, and it's a lot less wearing on your nerves.

Road Rules & Safety Precautions
Canadians drive on the right, as in the USA, but use the metric system for measuring distance: 90 to 100 km/h = 60 mph, 50 km/h = 30 mph. The speed limit on highways is usually 100 km/h; in towns, it's 50 km/h or less.

The use of seat belts is compulsory throughout Canada and the fines for not wearing them are heavy. All traffic violations in money short Quebec will cost you plenty, so take it easy there. All provinces require motorcyclists and passengers to wear helmets and to drive with the lights on.

Traffic in both directions must stop when stationary school buses have their red lights flashing: this means children are getting off and on. In cities with pedestrian crosswalks, cars must stop to allow pedestrians to cross. Provided it is safe to do so, turning right at red lights (after first coming to a complete stop) is permitted in some provinces. Just watch what everybody else is doing, or listen for the impatient blast of the horn behind you to figure things out.

Sleeping at roadside parks, picnic spots or other areas on the highways is OK, just don't set up a tent.

A valid driver's licence from any country is good in Canada for three months while an International Driving Permit, available in your home country, is cheap and good for one year almost anywhere in the world. You can't drive in Canada without auto insurance.

Driving in areas where there is heavy snow is best avoided but if you do, it may mean having to buy snow tyres. Many Cana-

dian cars have four-season radial tyres. If you get stuck, don't stay in the car with the engine going; every year people die of carbon monoxide suffocation by doing this during big storms. A single candle burning in the car will keep it reasonably warm.

When driving in the north of the provinces, the Yukon Territory and the Northwest Territories there can be long distances between service stations – try not to let your tank get much below half and always carry extra gasoline. Make sure the vehicle you're driving is in good condition and take along some tools, spare parts, water and food.

On the gravel roads the biggest problems are dust and flying stones from other vehicles: keep a good distance from the vehicle in front of you and when you see an oncoming vehicle, slow down and keep well to the right (this also applies to ones overtaking you). A bug and gravel screen is recommended, as are a spare tyre, fan belt and hose. Some people also protect their gasoline tank and lights.

In much of the country, wildlife on the road such as deer and moose are a potential hazard. Most run-ins occur at night when animals are active and visibility is poor. In areas with road-side signs alerting drivers to possible animal crossings keep your eyes scanning both sides of the road and be prepared to stop or swerve. Often a vehicle's headlights will mesmerise the animal leaving it frozen in the middle of the road. Try flashing the lights or turning them off, as well as using the horn.

Rental
Car-rental agencies are abundant across the country. The main companies are Avis, Budget, Hertz and Tilden but there are many more. The biggies can all book cars for you at any outlet for any outlet. They also have rental desks and cars at almost all of the country's airports. To be certain of finding one and to save time, it is worthwhile making a reservation before your arrival.

Budget generally has the best rates among the new-car agencies and also provides good service. Rent-A-Wreck is a well-known used-car rental agency and its prices are somewhat less. Note that rates are not consistent within any company and each outlet is run independently. Rates vary from city to city, location to location. Downtown is usually cheaper than the airport.

Most companies have a daily rate of about $35 to $50 plus a km fee. Others offer a flat rate which is nearly always better if you're travelling far.

Weekend rates are often the cheapest and can include extra days so building a schedule around this can save a lot of money. Weekends in car renting can mean three or even four days. For example, if you pick-up a car Friday morning and return it before midnight Monday it may be billed as just three days.

Once a car has been rented you may be able to extend your rental at the given rate. Negotiation is possible. Also if renting for extended periods of time, say weeks, ask for a discount beyond the weekly rate. Weekly rates are generally 10% less than daily rates.

Depending on the locations, it is possible to drop a car off at a different office than where it was picked-up. In some places a fee, sometimes very high, is charged for this privilege.

Book early, especially for weekend use, and request a small, more economical car.

Beware that prices can be deceptive. The daily rate may be an enticing $29 but by the time you finish with insurance, gasoline (fill it up before taking it back or you pay their prices plus a fee for doing it), the number of km, provincial sales tax, GST and any other bits and pieces, you can be handed a pretty surprising bill. So make sure you know all the extra costs.

Some companies offer vans and, with a number of people sharing, this can work out to be quite economical. These should be booked well in advance.

Count on needing a credit card to rent a car in Canada. Cash is not considered good enough. There may be some companies here and there who will rent to those without plastic but even after the hassle of finding one, expect more problems. First the company will need a few days (at least) to

check you out. If you're not working, things can be sticky: bring a letter from an employer or banker if you can, and lots of good identification. You may also need to leave a deposit, sometimes as much as several hundred dollars a day. And after all that you may still have to sign away your first child, too. It's not worth the headache.

Some companies require you to be over 21 years of age, others over 26. You may be asked to buy extra insurance depending on your age, but the required premiums are not high. Insurance is generally optional. Check to see if your car insurance at home includes rentals or offers a rental clause. Doing it this way is cheaper than buying the insurance from the rental agency.

Parents note, children under 18 kg (40 lbs) are required to be in a safety car seat which must be secured by a seatbelt. The big-name rental companies can supply seats at a small daily rental fee. Out of the major cities it may take a couple of days for the outlet to come up with one but the cost is the same.

Recreational Vehicle Rental Renting recreational vehicles (RVs) or campers, or various trailers (caravans) is another option. The RV market is big in the west with specialised agencies in Calgary, Edmonton and Whitehorse. Vancouver is the main centre but RVs can also be rented in Toronto and other central and eastern cities. They are very popular with Europeans and should be booked before May for the summer. High season is most expensive with mid to large-size vehicles costing $180 to $200 a day. These are good for five to seven people and include six appliances. Make sure to ask for a diesel engine as this will save considerably on running costs. Cheaper camper vans are also available but these should be booked even earlier. Two companies to try are Go Vacations (☎ (604) 276-8710), 5400 Airport Rd South, Richmond, BC (also in Toronto) and Go West Campers International (☎ (604) 987-5288), 1577 Lloyd St, North Vancouver.

Buying a Car
Older cars can be bought quite cheaply in

Canada. Look in the local newspaper or, in larger centres, the weekly *Buy & Sell Bargain Hunter Press*, *Auto Trader* or an equivalent, all of which can be bought at corner variety stores. Private deals are nearly always the most economical way to buy a car. Many used-car businesses must mark up the prices in order to make a profit. Generally, North American cars are lower priced than Japanese and European cars.

For those who prefer a semi-scientific approach to car buying take a look at Phil Edmunston's excellent *Lemon-Aid*, an annual book published by the Canadian Automobile Protection Association. It is available in stores and libraries and details all the used cars on the market, rates them and gives rough price guidelines. Haggling over car prices, whether at a dealership or at someone's home, is the norm. Expect to knock off hundreds or even a thousand dollars depending on the value of the car.

For a few months driving, a used car can be an excellent investment, especially if there are two of you. You can usually sell the car for nearly what you paid for it. An old bomb can probably be had for around $1000. A fairly decent older car should be available for under $4000. West coast cars last longer because salt doesn't have to be used on the roads in winter which means the cars rust less quickly.

The potential problem for visitors is getting insurance at a reasonable rate. Most companies will offer a six-month term but costs vary widely and can change dramatically from province to province. Regardless of where you buy, it is useful to have proof of insurance from your homeland. In addition to making a transaction easier, this might well entitle you to some discount as it makes you a more credible risk. As a rule, the rates for women are noticeably less than for a man of comparable age and driving record. If you're planning a side trip to the USA, make sure the insurance you negotiate is valid over the border, too. Also remember that rates are linked to the age and type of car. A newer car may cost more to insure but may also be easier to sell.

Drive-Aways

One of the best driving deals is the uniquely North American Drive-Away system. The basic concept is that you drive someone's car for them to a specific destination. Usually the car belongs to someone who has been transferred for work and has had to fly, or doesn't have the time, patience or ability to drive a long distance. Arrangements are made through a Drive-Away agency which are found in the major cities.

After the agency matches you up with a suitable car, you put down a deposit of $300 to $500 and are given a certain number of days to deliver the car. If you don't show up with the car in the allotted time, the police are notified. Most outlets suggest a route to take and may give you a very rough km guideline.

You are not paid to deliver the car (but may be if you really hit the jackpot and someone's in a rush) and generally you pay for gasoline, although sometimes a portion or all of the gasoline costs are paid by the owner. With two or more people, this can be an especially great deal. The company will want to know who will be driving.

You'll require good identification, the deposit and a couple of photos. Look for Drive-Away companies under transportation or business personal ads in the newspaper classifieds or in the Yellow Pages under Drive-Away Automobiles. Some trips can take you across the border – from Montreal to Florida is a common route. About eight days is normal for a trip from the east to west coast. Try to get a smaller, newer car. They're less comfortable but cheaper on gasoline.

In summer when demand is highest, cars may be more difficult to obtain and you could be asked for a nonrefundable administrative payment, perhaps $100.

One thing to ask about is what happens if the car breaks down. Get this information in writing if possible. Generally minor car repairs of say $100 or less are paid by you. Keep the receipt and you will be re-imbursed upon delivery. If bad luck strikes and a major repair is required there may be hassles. The agency might get in touch with the owner and ask how to proceed. This might take time and could involve some inconvenience.

Usually the cars offered with drive-aways are fairly new and in good working order. If not, the owner wouldn't be going to the bother and expense and would have just dumped the car. Occasionally you hear of a Jaguar or something similar available – class on a shoestring.

Car Sharing

Allo Stop, started in Quebec, is a company which acts as an agency for car sharing. It unites people looking for rides with people who have cars and are looking for company and someone to share gasoline expenses. It is a good service which has been around a number of years.

There are now offices in Montreal, Quebec City, Toronto, Ottawa and many of the smaller towns around the province of Quebec. More information is given in the various chapters under the Getting There & Away section. Prices are good and destinations include Quebec, Ontario, further afield in Canada and even down to New York City.

Call them a couple of days before your planned trip and they will try to link you up with someone. Costs of the service are low.

A new service operating out of Montreal, Toronto and Ottawa takes passengers in vans between the cities. These van shuttle services ply the routes between these major cities on a regular, scheduled basis taking six to a dozen passengers at far below bus rates. Check hostel noticeboards and the classified-ad section in weekly newspapers for more information.

They work unofficially because only registered carriers have the right to take passengers for money. Also, insurance coverage may not be sufficient in cases of accident or emergency. Nonetheless, these van trips are a popular, fun, casual way to get between some major cities. Some trips go to New York City as well. Call ahead a few days before your departure to book and get the full details.

Canadian Automobile Association

Known as the CAA this organisation, like its counterpart the American Automobile Association (AAA), provides assistance to member motorists. The services provided include 24-hour emergency roadside assistance, trip planning and advice, and they can supply travellers' cheques.

If you have a decent car the association's help may not be necessary, but if you have bought an older car to tour the country the fee may well be invaluable, and after one or two breakdowns will have paid for itself as towing charges are high.

For information contact the central Ontario office (☎ 1-800-268-3750), 60 Commerce Valley Drive East, Thornhill, Ontario, Canada L3T 7P9. Each province has its own regional office and branches can be found in most major cities and towns. An annual membership costs $68.50.

Gasoline

Gasoline (petrol) or simply gas (gaz in Quebec), varies in price across the country with the highest prices in the far north and on the east coast. In the east, prices are highest in Quebec, Newfoundland and Labrador. Drivers approaching Quebec from Ontario should top up the tank before the border. Those arriving from the USA should always have a full tank as the low US prices will never be seen in Canada. Alberta's prices, with less tax, are relatively low. Fill up there before hitting British Columbia.

In general, the big cities have the best prices so fill up in town. The more remote a place, the higher the price. Major highway service stations offer no bargains and often jack up the price on long weekends and at holiday time in order to fleece the captive victims. Gasoline is always sold by the litre. On average a litre of gasoline costs about 60 cents, or about $2.70 per imperial gallon. The Canadian (imperial) gallon is one-fifth larger than the US gallon.

Credit cards are accepted at service stations, many of which are now self-service and will not accept large bills at night. The large cities have some service stations that are open 24 hours but you may have to search around. On the highways, truck stops stay open the longest hours and some have showers you can use.

BICYCLE

This method of travelling long distances is becoming more and more popular in Canada. Obviously you need a lot of time to cover much of Canada. Most people can't really consider traversing vast regions, so it's best to concentrate on one area. Some of the most popular are around the Gaspé Peninsula in Quebec and all around the Atlantic Provinces, excluding Newfoundland. The Gaspé Peninsula is very hilly, Prince Edward Island is flat, and New Brunswick and Nova Scotia offer a fair bit of variety and are relatively small, with towns close together. You get a good mix of country and city. All these areas have good scenery.

The other major cycling area is around the Rocky Mountains and through British Columbia. The weather there in summer is fairly reliable and again there's grand and varied scenery.

Between these eastern and western sections of the country, cycling would be more of a chore than anything else and the landscape, generally, is similar for very long stretches. Still, each year cyclists peddle over the north of the Great Lakes across northern Ontario. Also in Ontario, the Bruce Peninsula is good for cycling as is the Thousand Islands Parkway area around Kingston.

VIA Rail allows passengers to take bicycles for free on trains that have baggage cars. This would mean pretty well any train going a fair distance. Local and commuter trains wouldn't be included. You don't have to pack the bike up or disassemble it, but then it may not be covered by insurance. For full protection bicycles must be boxed.

The provincial highway maps have more detail and secondary roads than the usual service-station maps. You can pick them up at tourist offices. Bookshops may also have cycling guides, and cycling magazines might contain useful information.

Some cities such as Edmonton, Montreal, Ottawa, Toronto and Vancouver have routes marked around town for bikes only. The extent of these routes varies considerably. Toronto's is minimal, Ottawa's is good.

Most cyclists, at least for touring, now wear helmets although this is not mandatory.

Canada has a number of cycling associations but these are mainly geared to competitive riders. For more casual cyclists or travellers, general information on cycling within a province is available through the provincial tourist office. In several of the large cities, the local city tourist office will have a cycling map and information on cycling within the city. Bicycle rentals, some routes and events are discussed in the text.

Bicycle shops are also good sources of information. Major cities have specialised stores where all manner of supplies and cycling gear can be purchased.

Bicycle couriers, practically their own sub-culture with radios, day-glo clothes, and individualistic headgear and jewellery, are a familiar sight speeding around inner cities delivering packages to businesses.

Provincial tourism offices and travel agencies can also help with finding companies which specialise in organising overnight and long-distance cycling trips. These have become increasingly popular in recent years. Accommodation, guidance and automobile support are usually part of the package.

HITCHING

Readers' letters indicate there have been no problems hitching in Canada, however, hitching is never entirely safe in any country in the world, and we don't recommend it. Travellers who decide to hitch should understand that they are taking a small but potentially serious risk.

That said, hitching is good in Canada. It's not the UK, which is a hitchhiker's dream, but thumbing a ride is still a worthwhile option. Many travellers depend on hitching at least for a portion of their trip. Transportation can be expensive but more often lack of buses or trains means the thumb can fill in a gap in the most convenient way. And of course you meet people you would otherwise never speak to. Two people, one of each gender, is ideal. If you're three or more, or a single woman, forget it.

If you feel you've waited a long time to be picked up, remember that the ride you get may take you over 1500 km.

Out of the big cities, stay on the main highways. Traffic can be very light on the smaller roads. Always get off where there's a service station or restaurant and not at a side road or farmer's gate.

Around towns and cities, pick your spots carefully. Stand where you can be seen and where a car can easily stop. A foreign T-shirt, like one with 'University of Stockholm' on it, might be useful. Some people find a cardboard sign with large clear letters naming their destination can be a help.

If you're going into a large city, make sure the ride is going all the way. If it's not, get dropped where you can catch a city bus, especially after dark. When leaving a city, it's best to take a bus out a little way.

You must stay off inter-city expressways, though the feeder ramps are OK. In Toronto and Vancouver particularly, the police will stop you on the expressway.

Hitching in town is not recommended. A lot of prostitutes employ this technique and it's generally considered that the inner-city hitcher is a less desirable breed than those out on the open roads, so most people ignore them.

It's illegal to hitch within some city limits; fines can be steep. Generally, the scruffier you look, the more ID and documents you should have to prove your identity should the police decide to question you.

Around the large cities there will be heavy traffic leaving on Friday and returning on Sunday. Despite the volume, hitching is difficult then because most cars are full with families. Weekdays are best, when you get salespeople and truckers on the road. Many companies forbid truck drivers to pick up people, though some do anyway.

If you're in a hurry, from Toronto to Vancouver shouldn't take longer than five days and has been done in three.

As early as the end of summer, nights can be very cold, depending where you are, and snow can fall in October in much of the country. Do not overestimate your luck.

One last tip: if you don't want to spend time in Northern Ontario, get a ride straight through from Sault Ste Marie to Thunder Bay. The same in reverse.

Wawa, a small town between the two, is a notorious waiting spot. Its reputation as a tough, anti-hitchhiker, mining and drinking town is outdated, but it's still a small, cold, nothing-to-do place to try to hitch from. I once heard of a guy who waited so long he finally got a job then married and settled in Wawa! Southern Saskatchewan is also a place with a reputation for long waits.

Mark Lightbody

BOAT

With oceans at both ends of the country and a lake and river filled interior some boat travel is often called for.

On the east coast, major ferries link provinces and islands to the mainland. New Brunswick and Nova Scotia are connected to Prince Edward Island. From Prince Edward Island, ferries connect with the Magdalen Islands of Quebec out in the Gulf of the St Lawrence. Nova Scotia is connected to Maine, USA, by two ferry routes and to New Brunswick across the Bay of Fundy by another. Newfoundland is connected to Nova Scotia.

Other ferries run around the edges of Newfoundland and up to Labrador. The major operator is Marine Atlantic (☎ (902) 794-5700) in Canada. For information and reservations write to Marine Atlantic Reservations Bureau, PO Box 250, North Sydney, Nova Scotia B2A 3M3. Details are found in the Getting There & Away sections of the port towns.

Along the St Lawrence River the north and south shore of central Quebec is connected at several points by ferry.

Across the country various boat tours and ferry services, both long and short, are discussed in the text.

On Canada's west coast, ferries connect mainland British Columbia with Vancouver Island, the Gulf Islands and the Queen Charlotte Islands. For schedules and fares contact BC Ferries (☎ (604) 386-3431; (604) 669-1211 in Vancouver), 1112 Fort St, Victoria, British Columbia V8V 4V2.

ORGANISED TOURS

Organised group tours are best arranged through bus companies, travel agencies or tour companies themselves. Many of the private specialised tour companies are listed in the tourist brochures available from provincial and territorial governments.

The larger transportation companies are reliable and they're your best bet if you want a general type of organised tour. Many of the larger regional bus companies offer trips of varying lengths, including transportation and accommodation. Some offer sightseeing as well.

Small companies offering low-cost, often nature-based, tours are discussed in the text. These can be found across the country offering a variety of adventure trips of different lengths and difficulty. Good camping stores often carry pamphlets put out by such companies. You can also pick them up at hostels and tourist offices.

AmeriCan Adventures is a private company which runs tours throughout the Americas for 18 to 35-year-olds. Most of the trips are two to five-weeks long and are 'city & sights' oriented. Included are tours which cross Canada one way and return through the USA. Others are more slanted towards outdoor activities, with everything included but sleeping bags. These are expedition and camping-type trips. Participants must help with the chores and cooking. An example is an eight-day canoe trip in Ontario's Algonquin Park. For information contact Goway Travel (☎ (416) 322-1034), 3284 Yonge St, Toronto, Ontario M4N 3M7.

The Canadian Outward Bound Wilderness School, with offices in Vancouver and Toronto, runs good, rigorous outdoor adventure trips which are more like courses than holidays. Ranging from seven to 24 days, they take place in various rugged parts of the country; many programmes include a solo portion. In Toronto the school can be contacted at, (☎ (416) 421-8111), 302-150 Laird Drive, M7Y 5R1 and will send out a pamphlet outlining its programmes.

The Canadian Universities Travel Service Ltd (see the following section), runs various trips and outings that include activities like hiking, cycling and canoeing. It can also arrange ski and sun-destination holidays. It has offices in every major city in Canada. In Toronto the office is at (☎ (416) 979-2406), 187 College St, M5T 1P7.

Hostelling International (HI) Canada also runs some tours and special-event trips featuring hiking, cross-country (nordic) skiing, etc. Check at hostels for organised activities.

Major museums and art galleries also sometimes run specialised educational/recreational tours, for example to the Canadian Arctic and the Inuit carvers. These trips, when available and with lectures included, are interesting but can also be very costly. If you have a particular interest a phone call may turn up the perfect opportunity.

Always make sure you know exactly what sort of tour you're getting and how much it will cost. If you have any doubts about the agency or the company it may be dealing with, pay your money into what is called the 'tour operators escrow account'. The law requires that this account number appear on tourist brochures (you may have to look for a while). Doing this protects you and your money should the trip fall through for any reason. It's a good idea to pay by cheque because cash is always harder to get back; write the details of the tour, with destination and dates, on the front of the cheque. On the back write 'for deposit only'.

Canadian University Travel Service

For budget, young or student travellers, this service known as Travel CUTS offers a wealth of information. This is Canada's student travel bureau and they have offices in Halifax, Ottawa, Toronto, Saskatoon, Edmonton and Vancouver. In Montreal it is called Voyages Campus. Some offices are on university campuses, others have central downtown storefronts.

To obtain student discounts you must have

an International Student Identity Card (ISIC) available at these outlets. You must have proper ID though – this isn't Athens or Bangkok.

CUTS deal mostly in ways to get you out of Canada cheaply. They also sell European train passes, arrange working holidays and set up language courses. They can, however, provide tickets and advice for getting around Canada.

Within Canada, CUTS can arrange tours and canoe trips and help with domestic flights. They have a *Discount Handbook* which lists over 1000 stores and service establishments offering bargains to ISIC card holders.

Ontario

The name 'Ontario' is derived from an Iroquois Indian word meaning 'rocks standing high near the water', probably referring to Niagara Falls.

Located smack in the middle of the country, Ontario is the centre of Canadian politics and economics, and much of the arts as well.

The country's largest city, Toronto, is here, as are Niagara Falls and Ottawa, Canada's capital. These three places alone make this region one of the most heavily visited in the country. Historic Kingston, located between Ottawa and Toronto, and some of the middle-sized towns to the west of Toronto, with their country flavour and varying attractions (such as the Shakespeare Theatre of Stratford and the German Oktoberfest of Kitchener), are also busy tourist centres.

Less visited, but equally representative of the province, are the beaches of Lake Huron and Georgian Bay – a shoreline made archetypally Canadian by the country's best known painters. Further north again, accessible wilderness parks offer respite from the densely populated southern regions and provide opportunities to see the northern transitional and Boreal forests. The resource-based cities of Sudbury, Sault Ste Marie and Thunder Bay, each with their own attractions, are also good starting points for trips around the more rugged areas of Ontario, from the Lake Superior shoreline to as far north as James Bay, where you'll find one of the province's oldest settlements, Moosonee.

Ontario is traditionally conservative, politically and socially, despite a recent flirtation with the left-wing policies of the provincial New Democratic Party (NDP). In the summer of 1995 Ontarians overwhelmingly rejected the NDP in favour of the hard-headed Progressive Conservatives and their pledge to tackle the province's $98 billion debt.

HIGHLIGHTS

Entered Confederation: 1 July 1867
Area: 1,068,587 sq km
Population: 10,084,885
Provincial Capital: Toronto

- Visit Canada's capital, Ottawa, with its numerous museums and art galleries and markets
- Spend time in cosmopolitan Toronto, the country's largest city, where the CN Tower and a Blue Jays baseball game are 'must sees'
- Be overwhelmed by Niagara Falls
- Enjoy Shakespearean theatre at Stratford or the works of GB Shaw at Niagara-on-the-Lake
- Celebrate Oktoberfest in Kitchener
- Search out Georgian Bay's Native Indian sites and rocky, pine-edged shorelines
- Canoe the lakes and rivers in Algonquin Provincial Park
- Explore the undeveloped timberlands above Lake Superior

History

When Europeans arrived in the region, they found it settled and occupied by numerous Indian Nations. The Algonquin and Huron first dominated the southern portion of the province, but by the time of European exploration and trade in the 1700s, the Iroquois Confederacy, also known as the Five Nations, dominated the area south of Georgian Bay and east to Quebec. In the north and west, the Ojibway covered the lands north of the Great Lakes and west to the Cree territory of the prairies.

French explorers and traders in the 1600s were the first Europeans to see much of Ontario as they set up forts to link with the Mississippi. It wasn't until around 1775 with the arrival of the British Loyalists that large-scale settlement began. After the War of 1812 with the USA, British immigrants began to arrive in still larger numbers. By the end of the century specialised farming, industry and cities were growing markedly. At the end of each of the World Wars immigration rose with people coming from many countries of continental Europe.

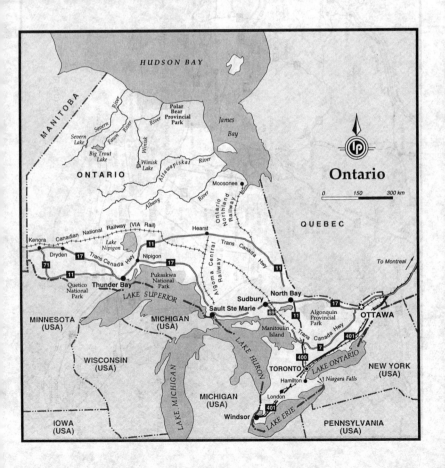

ONTARIO

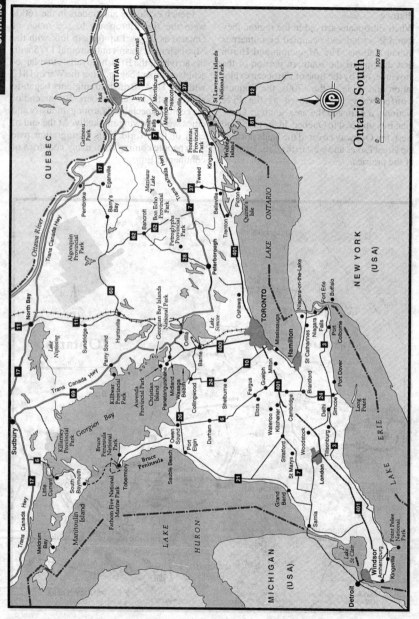

Ontario South

Climate

Within Ontario is the country's most southerly region, important when considering climatic factors. Southern Ontario, particularly around Niagara has long summers and mild winters. From Ottawa to Windsor, July and August can be hot and muggy. Temperatures drop progressively (and considerably) the further north you go.

Economy

Ontario is by far the richest province, although the recession of the early 1990s hit harder here than elsewhere and its effects linger. There is as much manufacturing in Ontario as in all the other provinces combined and most of it is found in the area around the western shore of Lake Ontario. Hamilton is Canada's iron and steel centre, while nearby cities such as Oshawa and Windsor make Ontario the national leader in car production.

Odd as it may seem, Ontario is also tops in farm income, although the area of excellent farmland (around the Great Lakes) shrinks each year as fields are lost to asphalt. The Niagara Peninsula is a significant fruit and wine-producing region.

Further north are tremendous resources. Sudbury produces a quarter of the world's nickel; Elliot Lake sits on the largest uranium deposits known – and, of course, there are the forests. I guess you can see why Ontario is called one of the 'have' provinces.

Population & People

The province is Canada's most populous and ethnically diverse, with about a third of all Canadians living within its borders. Over 80% of Ontarians are urban dwellers, most living between Kingston and Windsor along the great waterways that make up the southern boundary.

Information

Provincial Symbols The provincial flower is the trillium, the provincial tree is the eastern white pine, and the as yet unofficial bird is the loon.

Tourist Offices Ontario Travel is the provincial tourism arm. It operates 10 year-round offices and several seasonal ones. Permanent offices can be found in Toronto, Niagara Falls, Windsor and at other major border crossings. The year-round general information number is ☎ 1-800-668-2746 from anywhere in North America. Ontario Travel produces a range of free publications from accommodations to events. Their mailing address is Queen's Park, Toronto M7A 2E5. City and regional tourist offices acting independently can be found around the province.

Telephone The area code for Toronto and immediate vicinity is 416. The area surrounding Toronto is 905. This district includes Colborne to the east, Lake Simcoe to the north, Hamilton and Niagara to the south-east.

South-western Ontario and the Bruce Peninsula are covered by area code 519. Eastern Ontario (including Ottawa) is area code 613. Northern Ontario (including Manitoulin Island and Sault Ste Marie) is area code 705. The north-western section of the province from Thunder Bay west to the Manitoba border is area code 807.

For emergency service dial ☎ 911 anywhere in the province.

Time Ontario is on Eastern Standard Time, except for the far western area which is on Central Time (matching neighbouring Manitoba). Thunder Bay is on Eastern Time, Kenora is on Central Time.

Tax Ontario's provincial sales tax is 8%.

Activities

Despite urbanisation and development there remains much uncluttered, wooded lakeland and many quiet country towns surrounded by small market gardens. The northern regions contain vast areas of wilderness. The province offers fine camping, canoeing, hiking and whitewater rafting among other outdoor possibilities. A good place to start is one of the many excellent government parks. Details are outlined in the text.

Accommodation

Lodgings vary from the poshest hotels to the most primitive of camp sites. Ontario Travel publishes booklets on country inns, B&Bs and farm vacations. Their general guides also list some campgrounds. The provincial road map shows provincial campgrounds.

Ottawa

Ottawa, the capital of the country, arouses in all Canadians the mixed emotions worthy of a nation's capital. It sits attractively on the south bank of the Ottawa River at its confluence with the Rideau River. The gently rolling Gatineau Hills of Quebec are visible to the north.

The government is the largest employer, and the stately Gothic-style parliament buildings act as landmarks.

The city attracts five million tourists a year, many to see just what the heck the capital is like. The abundance of museums and cultural activities is another enticement. And then, of course, in summer you can see the traditionally garbed Royal Canadian Mounted Police (RCMP), also known as the Mounties.

You may be surprised by the amount of French you hear around town. Quebec is just a stone's throw away, but probably just as important is the fact that most federal government workers are required to be bilingual.

Ottawa is not an exciting city but its streets, if not lively, are wide and clean; the air is not fouled by heavy industry. Everywhere people are jogging and cycling.

Hull (in Quebec), easily reached across the river, is smaller but is noted for good restaurants and late nightlife.

Note that many of Ottawa's sights are closed on Monday.

History

In 1826 British troops founded the first settlement in order to build the Rideau Canal (linking the Ottawa River to Lake Ontario). First called Bytown, the name was changed in 1855, and Queen Victoria made it the capital in 1857.

After WWII, the Paris city planner Jacques Greber was put in charge of plans to beautify Ottawa. This pleasant city of 314,000 residents is now dotted with parks, and most of the land along the waterways is for recreational use.

Orientation

Ottawa's central core is quite compact, containing many of the places of interest, making walking a feasible method of getting about. Downtown Ottawa is divided into eastern and western sections by the Rideau Canal.

On the western side, Wellington St is the principal east-west street and has Parliament Hill and many government buildings. The Ottawa River lies just to the north. One block south of Wellington St is Sparks St, a pedestrian mall with shops and fast-food outlets.

Bank St runs south and is the main shopping street, with many restaurants and several theatres.

Just to the west of the canal is Elgin St, and large Confederation Square with the National War Memorial in its centre. The tourist office is here, in the National Arts Centre. The large, French-looking palace is the Château Laurier Hotel.

The Rideau Canal flows south through town, with walking and cycling paths at its edge. In winter the frozen canal is used for skating.

Gladstone Ave roughly marks the southern boundary of the downtown area. About eight km from the Château Laurier, the canal joins Dows Lake.

On the other side of the canal is Ottawa East, with Rideau St as the main street. The huge Rideau Centre is here, a three-level enclosed shopping mall with an overhead walkway across the street. North, between George and York Sts, is Byward Market. Opened in the 1840s, it's an interesting renovated area where activity peaks on Saturday, market day. Farmers from west Quebec and the Ottawa Valley sell vegetables, fruit and flowers while specialty shops offer gourmet meats, seafood, baked goods and cheeses. Crafts are sold in the market building, and there are plenty of restaurants nearby.

Along Wellington St and up Sussex Drive are many 19th-century buildings. Along Sussex Drive between George and St Patrick Sts, walking through the archways or alleys leads to a series of old connected courtyards, where you may find an outdoor cafe.

North up Sussex Drive and to the left (west) is Nepean Point. The view is well worth the short walk.

There are four bridges across to Hull. The Pont du Portage, which leads into Wellington St on the Ottawa side, is the one to take in order to end up in downtown Hull. The others are to the east or west of Hull's centre, but not by much.

Information

Tourist Offices The tourist office (☎ 237-5158) is in the National Arts Centre, at 65 Elgin St, opposite the corner of Queen St. It's open from 9 am to 9 pm daily from the beginning of May to the beginning of September. At other times it is open from 9 am to 5 pm Monday to Saturday, and from 10 am to 4 pm on Sunday. There is free parking (for half an hour) under the NAC building.

There is a larger office, called Canada's Capital Information Centre (☎ 239-5000 or 1-800-465-1867), at 14 Metcalfe St. It's near Sparks St, opposite the parliament buildings, and is open every day. The centre is run by the National Capital Commission (NCC), a federal agency which helps beautify and promote Ottawa-Hull. Their main operations office (☎ 239-5555) is at 40 Elgin St.

The Visitors & Convention Bureau (☎ 237-5150) is in suite 1800 at 130 Albert St.

Hull has its own information office, on Rue Laurier at the corner of Boulevard Saint Laurent, near the Alexandra Bridge. There is another in City Hall, in downtown Hull.

The museums and attractions of Ottawa are often in a state of flux and are frequently closed, either being renovated, repaired, upgraded or moved. If there is something you really wish to see, it is not a bad idea to

call first to find out its current status. Also note that admission at many of them is free on Thursday.

Money Several banks can be found along Sparks St. Accu-Rate Foreign Exchange at 153 Sparks has longer hours and sells travellers' cheques.

Post There is a post office at 59 Sparks St.

Foreign Consulates See the Facts for the Visitor chapter for listings.

Travel Agencies The Hostel Shop (☎ 569-1400) at 75 Nicholas St can help with budget travel. Travel CUTS (☎ 238-5493) has a branch at Carleton University, south of the canal along Bronson Avenue.

Bookshops & Maps The World of Maps and Travel Books, (☎ 724-6776), 118 Holland Ave at Wellington St, has an excellent selection of maps (including topos) and guidebooks. Also good is The Map Store (☎ 233-6277), open daily at 113 O'Connor St. Books Canada at 71 Sparks St has a good Canadiana section.

Medical Services Ottawa General Hospital (☎ 737-7777) is at 501 Smyth Rd.

Dangers & Annoyances Nearly all day and night, the market area of Ottawa is busy. Late at night, however, it does get a bit of an edge to it, with some drug and prostitution traffic. Walking alone in the quieter areas in the wee hours should probably be avoided.

On weekend nights the Promenade du Portage in Hull can be pretty wild on occasion, with nasty fights, rowdy drunkenness and worse. The city has put in video surveillance cameras to keep a lid on the bar strip, so exercise common sense if it looks as though the troublemakers are getting cranked up.

Ottawa-Hull

To Casino

RIVER

HULL

0   250   500 m

Rue Papineau
Rue Laval
Rue Papineau
Rue Kent
Boulevard
Rue
Champlain
Maisonneuve
Rue Notre Dame
Rue Laurier
Rue Hôtel de Ville
Promenade du Portage
Boulevard Alexandre Taché
Pont du Portage

Macdonald Cartier Bridge
Rideau River

Sussex Drive

Boteler Street
Bolton St
Cathcart St
Bruyer   Street
St Andrew   Street
Guigues   Ave
St Patrick   Street
Murray   Street
Clarence   Street
York Street
George   Street
Rideau Street
Dalhousie   Ave
Cumberland St
Daly Ave
King Edward Avenue
Waller Street

Nepean
Point

Alexandra Bridge

OTTAWA

Ottawa
Locks

OTTAWA

Majors
Hill
Park

Parliament
Buildings

Ottawa
River
Parkway

Mackenzie Ave

Rideau
Centre

Wellington Street
Sparks St
Queen St
Albert St
Slater St
Gloucester St
Lisgar St
Cooper St
Somerset St
Maclaren St
Gilmour St
James St
Florence St
Gladstone Ave
McLeod St
Flora St
Arlington Ave
Catherine St

Sparks St Mall

DOWNTOWN

Laurier Avenue West

OTTAWA

CHINATOWN

Bronson Avenue
Percy St
Bay St
Lyon St
Kent St
Bank Street
O'Connor St
Metcalfe St
Elgin Street
Cartier Street
Macdonald St
Robert St

Nepean St

Mackenzie King Bridge

Laurier Bridge

Laurier Ave East

University
of
Ottawa

Nicholas Street

Queen Elizabeth Driveway

Colonel By Drive

Rideau Canal

Argyle   Ave

Trans Canada Hwy   417
Chamberlain Ave
Queensway
Isabella Street

Main St

To Camp
LeBreton

To Airport &
Carleton University

To VIA Rail Station
& Ottawa General
Hospital

PLACES TO STAY		15	Bagel Bagel	9	National Gallery
		21	Cyber Perk Café	11	Canadian Ski Museum
5	Couette et Croissants	25	Oregano's	13	Rainbow Bistro
10	Foisy House	30	Suisha Gardens	16	Zaphod Beeblebrox
19	Château Laurier	32	Mekong Restaurant	17	National Archives
27	Quality Hotel by	33	The Royal Oak	18	Bytown Museum
	Journey's End	34	Charlie's Party Palace	20	Byward Market
28	Gasthaus Switzerland	35	The Ritz	22	Tourist Information
	Inn			23	Post Office
29	HI Ottawa Hostel	**OTHER**		24	Confederation Square,
31	Lord Elgin Hotel				National Arts Centre
39	YM-YWCA	2	Maison du Citoyen		& Tourist Information
		3	La Maison du Tourisme	26	Take Five Jazz Café
PLACES TO EAT		4	Canadian Museum of	36	Penguin Rock Bar &
1	Le Bistro		Civilisation		Club
12	Crêpe de France	6	City Hall	37	Bus Terminal
	Restaurant	7	Royal Canadian Mint	38	Canadian Museum of
14	Café Bohemian	8	Canadian War		Nature
			Museum		

Views & Walks

For a good, free view of the Ottawa River area where it's met by the Rideau River, and across to Hull, go to the cafeteria on the 8th floor of Ottawa City Hall, 111 Sussex Drive (☎ 244 5464). It sits on Green Island overlooking Rideau Falls, which are east of the Macdonald Cartier Bridge. It's open Monday to Friday from 8.30 am to 4 pm. There is also a pleasant park along the river beside City Hall.

Parliament Hill

Federal government buildings dominate downtown Ottawa, especially those on Parliament Hill off Wellington St, near the canal.

The Parliament Building itself, with its Peace Tower and clock, is most striking. The tower, however, has recently been closed for renovation so be prepared to see it swathed in scaffolding. Beside it are East and West blocks, with their sharp, green, oxidised copper-topped roofing.

Inside the Parliament Building, the Commons and Senate sit and can be viewed in session. The interior is all hand-carved limestone and sandstone. See the beautiful library with its wood and wrought iron. Free tours (☎ 239-5000), about 20 minutes long, run frequently, but reservations are required, and be prepared for tight security including metal detectors. In summer book the tour in

the white tent out on the lawn; in winter there is a desk inside for making the reservation.

When parliament is in session, Question Period in the House of Commons is a major attraction. It occurs early every afternoon and at 11 am on Friday. For information and tickets (no cost) call ☎ 992-4793.

At 10 am daily in summer, see the Changing of the Guard on the lawns – very colourful.

Pick up a free copy of the *Walking Tour of Parliament Hill*, which lists various details in and around the buildings. Free tours are also given in the External Affairs Building, 125 Sussex Drive.

At night during the summer, there is a free sound & light show on Parliament Hill – one version is in English and the other in French.

National Gallery

The National Gallery (☎ 990-1985) is a must. As Canada's premier art gallery, it has a vast collection of North American and European works in various media, all housed in an impressive building in the centre of town, on Sussex Drive. It's just 15 minutes' walk from the Parliament Buildings.

Opened in 1988, the striking glass and pink granite gallery overlooking the Ottawa River was designed by Moshe Safdie, who also created Montreal's Habitat (a unique apartment complex) and Quebec City's

Musée de la Civilisation. He also renovated City Hall. The numerous galleries, some arched and effectively coloured, display both classic and contemporary pieces, with the emphasis in general on Canadian artists. The US and European collections do, however, contain examples from nearly all the heavy-weights. The gallery also presents changing exhibits and special shows.

The excellent, chronological display of Canadian painting and sculpture not only gives a history of Canadian art but also, in a real sense, provides an outline of the development of the country itself, beginning with the depictions of Native Indian life at the time the Europeans arrived.

For a recharging break, two pleasant courtyards offer the eyes a rest. Between them sits one of the gallery's most unusual and most appealing components, the beautifully restored 1888 **Rideau St Chapel**, which was saved from destruction a few blocks away.

On level 2, along with the contemporary and international work, is the **Inuit Gallery**, and one room for the display of some of the extensive and fine photography collection.

The complex is large; you'll need a few hours and still you will tire before seeing all the exhibits, let alone the changing film and video presentations, lectures and concerts. There is a pleasant cafe and a restaurant as well as a very good gift and bookshop. Underneath the gallery are two levels of parking. Admission is free to all the permanent collections. An entry fee of around $5 is charged for special exhibitions. The gallery is open from 10 am to 6 pm daily in summer, except on Thursday, when it's open until 8 pm. The rest of the year, it's open Wednesday to Sunday from 10 am to 5 pm. It's closed on public holidays in the winter.

Canadian Museum of Nature

The Museum of Nature (☎ 996-3102) is housed in the attractive old Victorian building on the corner of McLeod and Metcalf Sts. The four-storey building fostering an appreciation and understanding of nature includes a good section on the dinosaurs once found in Alberta. Also excellent are the realistic mammal and bird dioramas depicting Canadian wildlife. Major temporary exhibits on specific mammal, mineral or ecological subjects are a feature.

The Viola MacMillan Mineral Gallery is excellent, with some of the largest gems and minerals you're ever likely to see. The reproduction mine comes complete with shaky elevator. The east-coast tidal zone re-creation is also very realistic.

A separate section of the museum is geared to children.

The museum is open until 5 pm every day of the year, opening at 9.30 am in summer and at 10 am the rest of the year. On Thursday, hours are extended until 8 pm. Check for more extended hours during the summer. Admission is $4, with special rates for seniors, kids and families. On Thursday, it is half-price from opening time to 5 pm and then free from 5 to 8 pm. It's free on 1 July, Canada Day.

There is a restaurant and a cafeteria on the premises. From Confederation Square, take buses Nos 5, 6 or 14 down Elgin St. Walking from the Parliament Buildings takes about 20 minutes.

Supreme Court of Canada

This rather intimidating structure (☎ 995-4330) is partially open to nonlitigants. Visitors can stroll around the grounds and lobby from 9 am to 5 pm. Construction of the home for the highest court of the land was begun in 1939 but not completed until 1946. The grand entrance hall, 12 metres high, is certainly impressive. During the summer a visit can include a free tour given by a law student. Call for the schedule. The court's on the corner of Wellington and Kent Sts.

Bytown Museum & The Ottawa Locks

Focusing on city history, Bytown Museum (☎ 234-4570) is in the oldest stone building in Ottawa. It's east of Parliament Hill, beside the canal – go down the stairs from Wellington St and back to the locks at the river. Used during construction of the canal for storing military equipment and money, it now contains artefacts and documents pertaining to local history.

On the ground floor, Parks Canada runs an exhibit about the building of the canal. The museum is open from the end of April to the middle of May. The hours are 10 am to 5 pm Monday to Saturday, and 1 pm to 5 pm Sunday. The series of locks at the edge of the Ottawa River in the Colonel By Valley, between the Château Laurier and the Parliament Buildings, marks the north end of the 198-km Rideau Canal, which runs to Kingston and the St Lawrence River. Colonel By, who was put in charge of constructing the canal, set up his headquarters here in 1826. Though never fulfilling any military purpose, the canal was used commercially for a while and then fell into disuse. The locks are now maintained by the government as heritage parks.

Canadian War Museum

At 330 Sussex Drive, this museum (☎ 776-8600), with the country's largest war-related collection, contains all manner of things military and traces Canadian military history. The life-sized replica of a WWI trench is good. You'll also see large displays, with sound and the museum also contains the country's largest collection of war art.

The museum is open from 9.30 am to 5 pm daily (until 8 pm on Thursday) in the summer, and from Tuesday to Sunday in the winter. Admission is $2.50 for adults, $1.25 for students and seniors and free for veterans. It's free for everyone on Thursday.

Royal Canadian Mint

Next door to the War Museum is the mint (☎ 993-8990). No longer producing day-to-day coinage, it now strikes special-edition coins, commemorative pieces, bullion investment coins and the like. Founded in 1908 and renovated in the mid-1980s, this imposing stone building has always been Canada's major refiner of gold. Tours are given by appointment; call to arrange one and see the process – from sheets of metal to bags of coins. It's open (in summer only)

from 10.15 am to noon and 12.30 to 4.30 pm Monday to Friday. Admission is $2. Sorry, no free samples.

The main circulation-coin mint is now in Winnipeg, Manitoba.

Currency Museum

For those who like to look at money, you can see lots more of it at the Currency Museum (☎ 782-8914) in the Bank of Canada at 245 Sparks St. In summer, it's open Monday to Saturday and on Sunday afternoon. From September to May, it is closed on Monday. Various displays tell the story of money through the ages, from whales' teeth to collectors' banknotes. Admission is $2 (free on Tuesday).

National Aviation Museum

This collection of over 100 aircraft is housed in a huge triangular building (about the size of four football fields) at Rockcliffe Airport (☎ 993-2010), north-east of the downtown area, near the river and the Canadian Forces base. See planes ranging from the Silver Dart of 1909 or the first turbo-powered Viscount passenger carrier right through to more recent jets. Peace and wartime planes are equally represented; included is the renowned Spitfire. The Cessna Crane is the very one your author's father (Alexander Lightbody) trained in for the RCAF.

Other exhibits include aviation-related video games and audiovisual presentations.

Admission is $5, less for seniors and kids, and it's free after 5 pm on Thursday. From May to September the museum is open daily from 9 am to 5 pm (until 9 pm on Thursday). In winter it's closed on Monday (unless it is a holiday). Call to check on opening hours, though, as they tend to vary according to attendance levels and the time of year.

National Museum of Science & Technology

At 1867 Saint Laurent Blvd, on the corner of Russell Rd, this museum (☎ 991-3044) has all kinds of participatory scientific learning exhibits. Try things out, test yourself, watch physical laws in action, see optical illusions. Also on display are farm machines, trains, model ships and stagecoaches. The bicycle and motorcycle collections are good. Higher-tech exhibits include computers and communication technologies. And don't miss the incubator, where you can see live chicks in various stages of hatching.

The large display on space technology is interesting, with an assortment of Canadian space artefacts. An astronomy section has films and slides about the universe; on clear nights, take a peep through the large refracting telescope. Telephone reservations should be made for stargazing.

While popular with all age groups, this place is great for kids. Those without children may wish to avoid weekends and the increased numbers of young ones.

Admission is $5 for adults, less for students, seniors and children, and is free on Thursday from 5 pm to 9 pm. In summer, opening hours are 9 am to 6 pm daily (until 9 pm on Thursday). After September it is closed on Monday. In winter it also closes earlier in the day. Free parking is supplied.

Canadian Ski Museum

The ski museum (☎ 233-5832) has a small, specialised exhibit at 457A Sussex Drive, near the market, with a collection of equipment and memorabilia outlining the 5000-year history of skiing. The museum is open Tuesday to Saturday, from 11 am to 4 pm in summer, from noon to 4 pm throughout the winter. The entry fee is $1.

Canadian Centre for Caricature

At 136 St Patrick St, by the corner of Sussex Drive at the edge of the market, this unusual collection (☎ 995-3145) from the National Archives consists of 20,000 drawn cartoons and caricatures concerning Canadian history and people, culled from periodicals from the past two centuries, though the vast majority of the collection is from the 1960s onwards. If you like political cartoons and social satire, this is the place – otherwise it's a real yawner. It's free and is open every day.

Canadian Museum of Contemporary Photography

Wedged in between the Château Laurier and the canal, in a reconstructed railway tunnel at 1 Rideau Canal, CMCP (☎ 990-8257) is the photo museum. Originally part of the still photography division of the National Film Board, this is where the still photography division houses its photographic research departments and the country's vast photographic archives. Unfortunately, gallery space is limited, so you may want to check what's on before visiting. Exhibits are not always of Canadians' work and may not be of very much interest to the casual viewer unacquainted with esoteric approaches to the photographic medium. Shows change quarterly.

The gallery is open from May to October from 11 am to 5 pm daily (until 8 pm on Thursday), except Wednesday, when hours are just 4 to 8 pm. The rest of the year it is closed on Monday and Tuesday. Admission is free.

Cathedral Basilica of Notre Dame

Built in 1839, this is one of the city's most impressive houses of worship. A pamphlet available at the door outlines the many features, including carvings, windows, the organ and the Gothic-style ceiling. It is on Guigues Ave, across from the National Gallery, in the Byward Market area.

Central Experimental Farm

This Agriculture Canada government farm (☎ 759-1000) at 930 Carling Ave is about 500 hectares of flowers, trees, shrubs and gardens. The site is used for research on all aspects of farming and horticulture. There are tours, or you can go on your own walking tour. The farm also has livestock and showcase herds of cattle, an observatory, a tropical greenhouse and arboretum. The latter is good for walking or having a picnic and is great in winter for tobogganing. The farm is linked to the rest of Ottawa's cycling routes. Admission is $2 and the farm is open every day. Call regarding shows and special displays.

Laurier House
This Victorian home at 335 Laurier Ave (☎ 992-8142), built in 1878, was the residence of two prime ministers: Wilfrid Laurier and the eccentric Mackenzie King. It's beautifully furnished throughout – don't miss the study on the top floor. Each of the two prime ministers is represented by mementoes and various possessions. Admission is $2.50, and it's open Tuesday to Saturday and on Sunday afternoon.

From 1 April to 30 September it's open Tuesday to Saturday from 9 am to 5 pm (the rest of the year it opens at 10 am), and Sunday from 2 to 5 pm. An early morning visit is suggested (that is, before the tour buses arrive) so you'll have the knowledgeable guides all to yourself.

Prime Minister's & Governor General's Houses
You can view the outside of the present prime minister's house, at 24 Sussex Drive, as well as Rideau Hall, the governor general's pad, around the corner and up from the river, at 1 Sussex Drive. Both houses are north-east of the market area. Rideau Hall is off Princess Drive, the eastern extension of Sussex Drive.

For security reasons, there is no strolling around the grounds of either place, but at the latter residence 45-minute walking tours are given, with stories of some of the goings-on over the years. Tours are offered through the day, in summer only.

The governor general's house was built in the early 1900s. At the main gate there's the small Changing of the Guard ceremony, which happens on the hour throughout the day, from the end of June to the end of August.

Rockcliffe Village
East along Sussex Drive, this is one of the poshest, most prestigious areas in the country. Behind the mansion doors live some very prominent Canadian citizens and many foreign diplomats.

Prince of Wales Falls
Where the Rideau River meets the canal south of town (at the junction of Colonel By St and Hog's Back Rd), there are falls, walking and cycling paths, and some historical plaques.

RCMP Stables & Practice Ground
Even the Mounties have to practise, and the RCMP Stables & Practice Ground (☎ 993-3751) is where the musical ride pageant is perfected. The public is welcome to watch the practice sessions and the other equestrian displays held from time to time.

Every evening for the week prior to Canada Day, there is a full musical ride with band. Otherwise the daily evening practices are without the band and colourful uniforms. Also note that the ride is sometimes away on tour. Call for details. Tours are given of the stables Monday to Friday from 8.30 to 11 am and 1.30 to 3.30 pm.

The grounds are out of the centre. If travelling by car, take Sussex Drive east to the Rockcliffe Parkway. At Birch St, turn right to the grounds. No admission fee is charged.

Log Farm
A re-creation of a 19th-century farm (☎ 825-4352), complete with costumed workers, this site is 20 km south-west of Parliament Hill. It is located off Cedarview Rd in Nepean. There are historical exhibits and activities, some of which you can participate in. Sporadically through the year, special events are put on. The farm is open daily in summer but on Sunday only for the rest of the year. Admission is $4.50 per adult, less for seniors, and there is a family rate.

Organised Tours
Gray Line (☎ 725-1441) offers a 50-km, 2½-hour tour of the city. They operate daily from May to October. Tickets are $16 and are available from a kiosk in Confederation Square. They also do longer tours of the region.

A double-decker bus makes a similar, though shorter, trip. It operates during summer only and is run by Piccadilly Tours (☎ 820-6745).

Capital Trolley Tours (☎ 1-800-823-6147) uses a bus decorated to look like a trolley (?!) to run tours of the city, allowing passengers to get on and off at any of 20 stops along the way. A ticket is $16 and rides begin at Confederation Square.

Paul's Boat Lines (☎ 235-8409) runs cruises on the Ottawa River and the Rideau Canal. Each takes about 1½ hours and costs $12, less for kids. For tickets and information there is a dock at the Rideau Canal, across from the National Arts Centre

The Ottawa Riverboat Company (☎ 562-4888), at 30 Murray St, does much the same thing but along the river only. Some trips include dinner and/or dancing.

Choo Choo (☎ 778-7246) runs a two-hour trip by steam engine up the Gatineau River area to Wakefield, daily from the end of May to the end of September and then less frequently through October. The Gatineau is a major north-south tributary of the Ottawa River. Call about ticket prices, as they vary a lot but weekdays are cheaper. The lunches in the *Railway Station Restaurant* in Wakefield are very good. The train station is in Hull not far from the casino at 165 Boulevard Deveault.

Ottawa Valley Tours (☎ 725-3045) runs several day trips to attractions in Eastern Ontario, including the Thousand Islands, Upper Canada Village and Kingston.

Activities

In summer you can rent a boat for trips along the canal. Canoe and rowing-boat rentals are at Dows Lake Marina (☎ 232-5278), or at the marina on Hog's Back Rd (☎ 736-9894). Both are located south of the city centre. Hourly to weekly rentals are available.

Surrounding the city on the east, south and west and connecting with the Ottawa River on each side is a broad strip of connected parkland known as the Greenbelt. Within this area of woodlands, marsh and fields are nature trails, bicycle paths, boardwalks and picnic areas. In the western Greenbelt, 20 minutes by vehicle from the downtown area off Richmond Rd, the Stony Swamp Interpretive Centre has a staff naturalist, trails and

displays about the area. It's open from Friday to Sunday. On the eastern side of the Greenbelt is another conservation area, Mer Bleue.

There are several outfits not far from Ottawa which run one or two-day whitewater rafting trips. No experience is needed and the locations are less than two hours from town. Recommended Esprit Rafting (☎ 1-800-596-7238) takes out small groups in state-of-the-art self-bailing rafts and offers free pick-up and delivery from the Ottawa International Hostel. Esprit also runs four-day canoe trips on the Petawawa River in Algonquin Provincial Park as well as kayaking courses. Cheap accommodation is available at their rustic river lodge just over the Quebec border near Fort Colonge. A one-day rafting trips costs $85.

Two other organisations, both in Foresters Falls, are Wilderness Tours (☎ 646-2241 in Quebec or ☎ 1-800-267-9166) and OWL Rafting (☎ 1-800-461-7238). The Ottawa and the Magnetawan are two rivers that are used. Book ahead for weekends, as the trips fill up. Considerable savings can be enjoyed by going on a weekday.

In winter there's skiing as close as 20 km from town, in the Gatineau Hills. Two resorts with variously graded hills are Camp Fortune and Mont Cascades. Tow passes are more expensive on weekends. Gatineau Park has excellent cross-country ski trails with lodges along the way. In warm weather, the park is good for walking and picnicking.

Again in winter, the Rideau Canal is famous for the skating along five km of maintained ice. Rest spots on the way serve great doughnuts (known as beavertails) to go with the hot chocolate, although the beaver must be getting scarce to judge by the prices. Ask at the tourist office about skate rentals.

The city has an excellent parks system with a lot of inner-city green space. There are many walking, jogging and cycling trails as well as picnic areas. You'll even find some fishing. The tourist office has a sheet, with map, of all the parks and a description of each. Bicycle paths wind all over town; get a map of them. For rentals see the Getting Around section.

Festivals

Some of the major events held here are:

February

Winterlude – This good and popular festival is held in early February. The three consecutive weekends of festivities centre mainly on or around frozen Dows Lake and the canal. The ice sculptures are really worth seeing.

May

Canadian Tulip Festival – This big annual event is held in late May, when the city is decorated with 200 types of tulips, mainly from Holland. Festivities include parades, regattas, car rallies, dances, concerts and fireworks.

June

Le Franco Festival – Held in June, this festival is good fun and an opportunity to see some of the country's French culture through music, crafts and more.

July-August

International Jazz Festival – This event lasts for 10 days at the end of July, with venues in Ottawa and Hull.

Cultures Canada – In July and August the outdoor stage in Major's Hill Park, known as Astrolabe, is used for concerts, dance, mime and other performances. It's open nightly and is free.

Central Canada Exhibition – An annual event held towards the end of August, it involves 10 days of displays, a carnival and entertainment. The exhibition is held at Lansdowne Park.

Places to Stay

Camping There is an excellent campground practically right in the centre of town for $7.50 per night per person, with a stay limited to five nights. You'll find room for 200 tents on the corner of Fleet and Booth Sts. The site is called *Camp Le Breton* (☎ 943-0467), west along Wellington St past the Parliament Buildings. The camp, designed primarily for cyclists and hikers, has no electric or water hook-ups and is for tents only. It's open from mid-May to Labour Day. The city bus from the downtown area goes right to the campground, which is near the Ottawa River. Close to the campground are some rapids known as Chaudière Falls.

Camp Hither Hills (☎ 822-0509), 10 km south of the city limits on Hwy 31 (Bank St), charges $13 for a tent.

There are other places to camp both east and west of town on Hwy 17. The tourist office has lists of places in the Ottawa area, and there is camping in Gatineau Park, across the river in Quebec.

Hostels The HI *Ottawa Hostel* (☎ 235-2595), at 75 Nicholas St, in the old Ottawa jail – see the gallows at the back – is one of the best known hostels in the country. It has a very good, central location near the Parliament Buildings. Nicholas St is just east of the Rideau Canal, off Rideau St. There are 130 beds in the restored building, most of them in old cells – wake up behind bars.

Prices are $15 for members, $19 for non-members and there is 24-hour check-in. Facilities include kitchen and laundry and a summer cafe. Reservations are recommended in midsummer and in February when the Winterlude festival is on.

The No 4 bus from the bus station at the corner of Arlington and Kent Sts goes within two blocks of the hostel. From the train station, the No 95 bus does the same thing.

The *YM-YWCA* (☎ 237-1320) is at 180 Argyle Ave on the corner of O'Connor St, in the southern downtown area. Singles for either sex are $42 with a shared bathroom; better value are doubles for $49. More expensive rooms with private bath are available. There's a cafeteria and a pool which guests can use.

The *University of Ottawa* (☎ 564-5400) has some of the cheapest dormitory space in Canada. The dorms are open for visitors from May to August. Rates for singles/doubles are $20/35 for students, $32/40 for non-students. It has laundry facilities, a swimming pool, parking, and a cafeteria with cheap meals. Reception is in the Residence Commons at 100 University St. The university is an easy walk south-east of the Parliament Buildings. It also offers accommodation at Little White Fish Camp, in Gracefield, Quebec, where there are extensive sports facilities. For enquiries call Sports Services on ☎ 562-5789.

Carleton University (☎ 788-5609), pretty central but south of the downtown core, has a residence offering summer rooms at 1233 Colonel By Drive. The price is $30 per person with breakfast included. Athletic facilities and full meal service are available. Check at the Tour & Conference Centre in the Commons Building at the university. Families are welcome.

B&Bs Spending nights in this town can make a mess of a budget. While not necessarily the cheapest form of accommodation in Ottawa (motels and some hotels are about the same price), this category generally has the advantage of a central location, a bit of personality and breakfast.

Ottawa B&B (☎ 563-0161) is an organisation listing, promoting and booking such places. There are city, suburban and country locations and prices begin at $45/55 for singles/doubles. Another such service is Capital B&B Reservation Service (☎ 737-4129), again with a variety of places and locations. Prices vary. Some locations offer perks such as fireplaces or swimming pools and nearly all have free parking.

Generally, whether independent or under an agency, the places closer to the centre of town are more expensive than those further out. Most included here are central because of their added convenience to the city's sites and because they do not require a car for easy access. Almost all prices include either a continental or full breakfast.

In the downtown area, just east over the canal and south of Rideau St, is a small pocket where many of the central guesthouses are found. Convenient Daly St has some good places but they are not among the cheapest. Smaller places with just a few rooms do not have to charge tax.

The Swiss-style *Gasthaus Switzerland Inn* (☎ 237-0335) has one of the best locations in town, at 89 Daly St, two blocks south of Rideau St and the market. Go south along Cumberland St to Daly St and it's near the north-east corner. The No 4 bus runs along Rideau St from the downtown area. The guesthouse has been created out of a large, old stone house and now has 22 rooms, all with private bathroom. Single rooms go for $68 with a breakfast of muesli, bread, cheese and coffee. Doubles are $78. Prices go down

a few dollars through the winter. The managers, from Switzerland, speak an impressive array of languages, including German and French.

At 201 Daly St is the heritage *Maison-McFarlane House* (☎ 241-0095), with doubles from $75. There are only three rooms but they include full bathroom and air-conditioning, and there is parking. The pricier suite has its own jacuzzi.

Also on Daly St, at No 185, *McGee's Inn* (☎ 237-6089) has 14 rooms in a restored Victorian mansion. Prices here begin at $52/68 and increase with the number of features. Some rooms have private bathrooms and a full breakfast is included.

Guesthouses of varying size and price seem to constantly open and close along Stewart St, one block south of Daly St. A stroll along the street may also turn up someone who has just opened a few rooms for the summer. There are certainly some fine houses in the neighbourhood. Recommended is *Ottawa House* (☎ 789-4433), at 264 Stewart St, run by the friendly Connie McElman. Three rooms with shared bath are available in this Victorian house, at $50/70 a single/double. A good breakfast is included.

Another street to check is Marlborough St, south-east of Daly and Stewart Sts, south from Laurier Ave, west of the Rideau River. It is still quite central but a bit of a walk to the downtown area – it takes about half an hour to get to the Parliament Buildings. Prices here are quite a bit lower.

The comfy *Australis Guesthouse* (☎ 235-8461), at 35 Marlborough St, is also recommended for excellent breakfasts and helpful hosts Carol & Brian Waters. There are four rooms; singles/doubles with shared bathroom are $48/58, a room with a private bath is $69. The Waters offer a pick-up service from the train or bus station if arranged in advance.

There are a couple of places to check in the convenient Byward Market area north of Rideau St. *Henrietta Walker's* (☎ 789-3286), at 203 York Street, is very close to the market. It has six rooms, with shared bathroom, at $50/65 a single/double. A full breakfast is included. The inviting, rural-looking *Foisy House* (☎ 562-1287), at 188 St Andrew St, has three rooms and charges $45 a single or double with breakfast. It has a pool, which can be a real plus. St Andrew St runs east-west through the market area a couple of blocks north of most of the action.

Another central place to try is *L'Auberge du Marché* (☎ 241-6610), at 87 Guigues Ave. It's a renovated older house with three rooms at $45/55 and there is parking.

Closer to the downtown area but on the other side of the canal is *Albert House* (☎ 236-4479), 478 Albert St, but this is more a real inn, with 17 rooms. It is more expensive than the small, modest guesthouses, with rooms starting at $62/72, but it has a good location, is a heritage home and offers all the comforts.

For Château Laurier luxury on a B&B scale there's *Paterson House* (☎ 565-2030), a recently restored Queen Anne style mansion at 500 Wilbrod Street, north of Laurier Avenue and west of King Edward Avenue. The three exquisitely furnished rooms are $120 a night.

If Ottawa seems booked up or you want to try staying across the river in Quebec, there are a few guesthouses in Hull.

Hotels – bottom end One of the very few older no-star hotels left in town is the *Somerset House Hotel* (☎ 233-7762), at 352 Somerset St West. It has 35 rooms starting at $45 with shared bath, $62 with private facilities. Somerset St runs perpendicular to Bank St about 10 blocks south from the Parliament Buildings.

The *Town House Motor Hotel* (☎ 789-5555), at 319 Rideau St, charges $55/60. The *Butler Motor Hotel* ☎ 746-4641) is comparable, at $50/58. The 38 rooms are large and it's just a five-minute drive to downtown. The hotel is at 112 Montreal Rd, an extension of Rideau Street east of the Rideau River.

Hotels – middle & top end In the middle range is the straightforward *Quality Hotel by Journey's End* (☎ 789-7511), at 290 Rideau St. Singles/doubles are from $85.

The *Days Inn* (☎ 237-9300), 123 Metcalfe St, is good value with rooms starting from $65.

The classic *Château Laurier* (☎ 241-1414), the castle-like place at 1 Rideau St, by the canal, is the city's best known hotel and a landmark in its own right. Rates are $129 to $169 and there is a large indoor swimming pool.

During the summer, when Parliament is in recess and business traffic is light, many of the corporate-oriented downtown hotels offer very good daily and weekend specials. Even the Château Laurier offers discounts. The *Aristocrat Hotel* (☎ 232-9471), at 131 Cooper St, rents its rooms at $80 for two people. The stately old *Lord Elgin* (☎ 235-3333), at 100 Elgin St (with free parking), has summer prices starting at $79.

Efficiencies The central *Doral Inn* (☎ 230-8055), at 486 Albert St, is good value; there are 40 rooms at $65/75 a single/double, plus a few housekeeping units (kitchenettes). The inn has a coffee shop and a swimming pool.

The *Capital Hill Motel & Suites* (☎ 235-1413), at 88 Albert St, is much larger, has kitchen facilities and can be a relative bargain. A room with two double beds, suitable for four people, goes for $72.

Motels There are two main motel strips, one on each side of the downtown area. On the east side, look along Montreal Rd, an extension of Rideau St, which leads east out of town. The motels are about six km from the centre.

The *Travellers Inn* (☎ 745-1531), 2098 Montreal Rd, charges $45/55 a single/double and has a pool. The *Concorde Motel* (☎ 745-2112), at 333 Montreal Rd in Vanier, is simpler and less expensive, with rooms from $40.

The *Parkway Motel* (☎ 789-3781), at 475 Rideau St, has little character but isn't bad value and is close to downtown. Doubles are from $65, including breakfast in the inexpensive coffee shop.

On the west side of town, check along Carling Ave, where there are numerous places to choose from about 10 km from

ONTARIO

downtown. The *Stardust* (☎ 828-2748), at 2965 Carling Ave, charges $45/48 for each of its 25 rooms. There are others closer to the centre but they tend to be more costly. *Webb's Motel* (☎ 728-1881), at 1705 Carling Ave, for example, is $65 but has its own restaurant.

Places to Eat

Byward Market Area The market is central, very popular and offers a good selection. During the warm months many of the eateries in the area have outdoor tables.

For breakfast try *Zak's Diner*, a 1950s-style eatery at 14 Byward St, which opens early and stays open late. It's usually busy and prices are reasonable. For something a little quieter, the *Domus Café*, at 87 Murray St is recommended. It's open every day from 9 am (11 am on Sunday) for breakfast and lunch and the food is becoming well known.

The *Café Bohemian*, at 89 Clarence St, is good for lunch or dinner. It's a busy European-style place with meals like quiche, fish and the latest trendy foods for $6 to $10. Their weekend brunch is good value, with desserts and coffee. You can get a good, large café au lait here served in a bowl.

Across the street, the inexpensive *Bagel Bagel* has all sorts of bagel toppings and sandwiches, as well as salads and other light meals and deli items. It's open daily and is also a good spot for breakfast.

For those needing more than just food, the *Cyber Perk Cafe*, at 347 Dalhousie St, offers access to the Internet ($4 for half an hour) as well as gourmet coffees, sandwiches, desserts and a selection of beer and wine. The cafe is open from 10 am to 10 pm daily – later on weekends.

Crêpe de France is at 76 Murray St, at the corner of Parent Ave. It specialises in crêpes from $5 and has a patio bar and glassed-in terrace.

For inexpensive pasta dishes there is *Oregano's*, on the corner of William and George Sts There is a good-value, all-you-can-eat lunch ($5.95) or, for another dollar, an early-bird dinner (from 4.30 to 8 pm) of pasta, salad and soup. On Sunday the menu changes slightly and there is a brunch.

Another international choice is *Las Palmas*, at 111 Parent Ave, which has been recommended for its Mexican food. The fajitas especially are not to be missed.

Excellent Indian food is dished up at the *Haveli*, 87 George St. The tandoori chicken is highly recommended. Also in the market building, at the York St end, look for the stand selling 'beavertails' – hot, flat doughnuts which first became popular when sold to skaters along the canal in winter. There is a food fair in the Rideau Centre.

Downtown Along Bank St and its side streets are numerous restaurants. *Suisha Gardens*, on Slater St near the corner of Bank St, is a highly recommended Japanese place. The food is excellent (though somewhat Westernised), the environment authentic and the service perfect. The best room is downstairs and to the left. It's inexpensive at lunch time; prices are higher after 6 pm.

There are several British-style pubs around; try the *Royal Oak*, 318 Bank St, for British beer and food. It's friendly and you can play darts.

Kamal's, at 683 Bank St, has good inexpensive Lebanese food and is licensed. *Flippers*, upstairs on the corner of Bank St and Fourth Ave, is a reliable fish restaurant with main courses (entrées) from $10 to $16.

Further south, the *Glebe Café*, at 840 Bank St, is good. It offers a few Middle Eastern dishes, some vegetarian food and burgers. Try the lentil soup. Prices are $6 to $12. It's a casual place, with newspapers to read and an information noticeboard.

At 895 Bank St, *Mexicali Rosa's* is pleasantly decorated and has tasty, moderately priced Mexican food. There are three other locations around town.

Good, cheap, mainly vegetarian Indian food can be found at the unlikely named *Roses Café*, at 523 Gladstone Ave, between Bay and Lyon Sts. It's closed on Sunday.

All through the downtown area and around the market, look for one of the numerous chip wagons, with names like *Chipsy Rose*. They're excellent for French fries and hamburgers.

Chinatown & Little Italy Ottawa has a small Chinatown with numerous restaurants within walking distance west of the centre. It's based around the corner of Bronson Ave and Somerset St West. *Ben Ben*, at 697 Somerset St, has Sichuan and Cantonese food. The *Mekong*, at 637 Somerset St, is good for Vietnamese as well as Chinese dishes. Main meals are from $7 to $12.

For a splurge, *Chez Jean Pierre*, at 210 Somerset St West, is said to be good for French food. If you're out this way, why not go a little further to 200 Preston St (Preston St runs north-south), a few blocks west of Bronson St, and try the *Paticceria-Gelateria Italiana* for a dessert and coffee. Preston St has been designated Ottawa's Little Italy so you'll find plenty of Italian restaurants along this busy street.

Rideau St Across the canal from Wellington St, this area also has a number of eateries. *Sam's Falafel Tabouleh Garden*, at 464 Rideau St, is bright, cheery and offers excellent Lebanese food at very reasonable prices.

The difficult-to-find *Sitar*, at 417A Rideau St, is in the bottom of a high-rise building not far east from the canal. It's not cheap ($22 to $34 for two) but the Indian food is good.

Nate's, at No 316, is something of a local institution. This Jewish delicatessen is known far and wide for its low prices on basic food. The popular breakfast special is the cheapest in the country ($1.75 for the works). Ask for the Rideau Rye – good bread for toast. The service is incredibly fast. They also serve things like blintzes and cream-cheese bagels. It's open and busy on Sunday.

Elgin St A stroll along Elgin St always turns up a couple of places to eat; it's popular for nightspots too. The *Ritz*, at 274 Elgin St, is very good for Italian food; in fact, there's usually a line of people waiting to get in. Prices range from $6 to $13. *Charlie's Party Palace*, known simply as the Party Palace, is at 252 Elgin St (with the neon sign jutting out over the sidewalk). This locally famous place has been around forever. It serves the usual low-cost Canadian standards and is another place that's good for breakfast.

Entertainment

Music Check Friday's *Ottawa Citizen* for complete club and entertainment listings.

Zaphod Beeblebrox, at 27 York St, is a popular eclectic place for everything from new-age rock to African music and rhythm and blues. Live bands play every Tuesday, Thursday, Friday and Saturday nights. They also have a good selection of small-brewery beers.

You can catch live blues every night of the week at the popular *Rainbow Bistro*, upstairs at 76 Murray St. *Take-Five*, at 412 Dalhousie St, offers live jazz nightly.

Barrymores, on Bank St, has live rock and blues and is a busy spot. The *Penguin Rock and Bar Club*, at 292 Elgin St, brings in a very good assortment of jazz, blues and folk acts. There is a cover charge (which varies). Comfortable *Irene's Pub Restaurant*, at 885 Bank St, often has live Celtic and folk music to go with the great variety of imported beers.

Patty's Place is a cosy Irish pub with music from Thursday to Saturday and an outdoor patio in summer. It's on the corner of Bank and Euclid Sts. *Yuk Yuk's*, in the Beacon Arms Hotel, 88 Albert St, has live standup comedy from Wednesday to Saturday, admission is not cheap, however. The *Hotel Lafayette*, in Byward Market on York St, is good for its cheap draught beer day or night. It's your old basic hotel beer-parlour, but its character attracts a wide cross-section of people.

For more entertainment, see the Hull section.

Performing Arts The *National Arts Centre*, known as the NAC, has theatres for drama and opera and is home to the symphony orchestra. It also presents a range of concerts and films. It's on the banks of the canal, in Confederation Square.

Cinema There are several repertory theatres around Ottawa, showing two films a night.

The *Mayfair* (☎ 730-3403), at 1074 Bank St, charges $7 for nonmembers but has less expensive matinees. The *Bytown Cinema* (☎ 789-3456), at 325 Rideau St, between King Edward and Nelson Sts, is about the same price.

Cinémathèque Canada (☎ 232-6727), run by the Canadian Film Institute, also presents non-commercial alternative, classic and foreign films on a regular basis. The screenings take place in the National Archives building on Wellington St West of Parliament Hill.

Spectator Sports The capital's Canadian Football League team, the Ottawa Rough Riders, play home games during the summer at the Frank Clair Stadium in Lansdowne Park, several blocks south of Isabella St between Bank St and Queen Elizabeth Dr. Call ☎ 235-2200 for dates and ticket information. In winter the Ottawa Senators play NHL hockey in the Corel Centre. For game and schedule information call ☎ 721-4300.

Getting There & Away

Air The airport is 20 minutes south of the city and is surprisingly small. The main airlines serving the city are Canadian Airlines (☎ 237-1380) and Air Canada (☎ 247-5000). Canadian Airlines destinations include Toronto ($239), Halifax ($395) and Winnipeg ($539). Excursion fares (return) are much cheaper.

Bus The bus station is at 265 Catherine St, near Bank St, about a dozen blocks south of the downtown area. The main bus lines are Voyageur which runs to Montreal, and Greyhound which runs to Toronto. Both lines can be contacted on ☎ 238-5900. One-way fares include Toronto $55, Kingston $28, Montreal $25 and Sudbury $72. Students can get a third off the price for a book of tickets.

There are about seven buses daily to Montreal and Toronto, some of which are express. There are frequent departures for Kingston, Belleville, Sudbury and other towns.

Train The VIA Rail station (☎ 244-8289) is a long way south-east of the downtown area. It's at 200 Tremblay Rd, near the junction of Alta Vista Rd and Hwy 417, just east of the Rideau Canal.

There are four trains a day to Toronto and to Montreal. One-way fares include Toronto $83, Kingston $36 and Montreal $39. Booking at least five days in advance can sometimes save up to 40% if you avoid peak days, eg Friday.

For trips west, say to Sudbury, there is no direct line and connections must be made in Toronto, so it's a long trip.

Car Tilden (☎ 232-3536) is at 199 Slater St and also at the airport. Their small-car rate is $51 per day (with 200 free km, and 12 cents per km after that) or $229 a week (with 1550 free km). Budget and Hertz are not as central as Tilden.

Ride Sharing Allo Stop (☎ 562-8248), a popular service in Montreal, Quebec City and Toronto which gets drivers together with passengers, has an office at 238 Dalhousie St. It shouldn't be difficult to get low-priced share rides to the cities mentioned above, or to Kingston.

Carleton University's radio station, CKCU (☎ 788-2898), also has a ride-sharing bulletin board – people call in with rides wanted/offered.

Hitching Hitching is easy between Montreal and Ottawa but is convoluted if you're heading for Toronto. Going to Montreal, take the eastbound Montreal-Ogilvy bus on Rideau St; this leads to Hwy 17 East, where you can begin. For Toronto take Hwy 31 south to Hwy 401 near the town of Morrisburg. The busy Hwy 401 (probably the most travelled route in Canada) connects Toronto with Montreal and hitching is fairly common along the way. For a more rural trip, take Hwy 7 and 37 to Tweed and then to Belleville, then Hwy 401 from there.

Getting Around

The Airport The cheapest way to get to the airport is by city bus. Take bus No 5 on Elgin

St going south (away from the river) to Billings Bridge Mall and then transfer to the No 96 to the airport. Or simply catch the No 96 as it runs along Slater downtown.

There is also an airport bus, which leaves every half hour on the half hour from in front of the Château Laurier Hotel from 6.30 am to midnight. It costs around $7 and takes about 25 minutes. The bus is not as frequent on weekends; ask about scheduling.

Bus Both Ottawa and Hull operate separate bus systems. A transfer is valid from one system to the other but may require an extra partial payment. The city bus system here is volatile, with frequent changes in routes and fares. There is a two-tier fare structure: during peak hours (6.30 to 8.30 am and 3 to 5.30 pm Monday to Friday), a ticket is $2.10; at any other time, the fare drops to $1.60. Using tickets is cheaper than cash, and these can be purchased at many convenience or corner milk stores.

For Ottawa information call ☎ 741-4390 – they're very helpful. All Ottawa buses quit by around midnight, most quit earlier. The office of OC Transport (which runs the city buses) is at 112 Kent St. You can take the following buses from downtown to:

Bus terminal – No 4 south on Bank St or, more frequently, either the No 1 or No 7 stop within a block of the terminal
Train station – Transitway No 95 east on Slater St or the No 99 along Chamberlain
Museum of Nature – No 14 on Elgin St is good but Nos 99, 1, 4 and 7 all go within a block or so
Hull – No 8 west on Albert St, but only during the day; the Outaouais bus service runs to Rideau St from Hull and continues at night.

Car Visitors to the city can park free at many locations; get the details at any tourist information office.

Bicycle Ottawa is the best city in Canada for cyclists, with an extensive system of paths in and around town and through the parks. Get a bicycle route map from a tourist office.

For rentals try Cycle Tour Rent-A-Bike (☎ 241-4140), at the Château Laurier.

They're open every day from May to September and rent three, five and 10-speed bikes for $18 per day. ID is required. They run tours, with discounts for HI hostel members, and have a repair shop as well. It's at the side of the hotel, near the entrance to the parking garage.

HULL

Across the river, in Quebec, Hull (population 61,000) is as much the other half of Ottawa as it is a separate city (that's why it's included in the Ontario chapter of this book). It warrants a visit for more than the Canadian Museum of Civilisation. Hull has its share of government offices, and workers cross the river in both directions each day, but the Hull side remains home to most of the area's French population. The architecture (at least the older stuff) is different, and you'll find the top restaurants here, as well as livelier, later nightlife.

Promenade du Portage, easily found from either Pont du Portage or Alexandra Bridge, is the main downtown street. Between the two bridges are numerous and varied eating spots, bars and discos, Place Aubry (a square), as well as a few places where people have to work.

The City Hall, known as Maison du Citoyen, is an attention-getting, dominating modern building with a 20-metre-high glass tower in the centre of town, at 25 Rue Laurier. It also contains an art gallery and a meditation centre. (What English-speaking bureaucracy would do that?)

The tourist office for Hull, La Maison du Tourisme (☎ 1-800-265-7822), is at the corner of Boulevard Saint Laurent and Rue Laurier, just over the Alexandra Bridge. There is also a tourist information desk in the Maison du Citoyen (☎ 595-7175), which covers the Outaouais region of western Quebec. The desk is open every day in summer, on weekdays only for the rest of the year. Look out for Hull's tourist information bicycle squad around Ottawa's Parliament Hill and the National Gallery.

From May to October you can take a 1½-hour trolleybus tour around the city, hopping on and off as you like. Another trolleybus trundles through the 36,000 hectares of Gatineau Park, just to the north-west of town. Call ☎ 241-0658 for information.

In July, Hull is home to the Gatineau Clog, a weekend-long bluegrass festival. The tourist office has a list of other events based on this side of the river.

Hull is also the main city of the region of Quebec known as Outaouais (which is pronounced basically as though you were saying Ottawa with a French accent). The Quebec government has a booklet outlining the region's attractions and activities, mostly of the outdoor variety. Within a few hours' drive, there are some huge parks and reserves.

The telephone code for Hull is 819

Canadian Museum of Civilisation

The Canadian Museum of Civilisation (☎ 776-7000) is Ottawa/Hull's feature museum. It's in the large, striking complex with the copper domes at 100 Rue Laurier, on the river bank opposite the Parliament Buildings. Allow the best part of a day to seriously explore the place.

The museum is principally concerned with the history of Canada. The **Grand Hall** of the lower level, with its simulated forest and seashore, explores Native Indian cultures and offers explanations of the huge totems and other coastal Native Indian structures. The upper-level **History Hall** presents displays and realistic re-creations tracing the story of the European founding, voyages of the country's explorers, settlement and historical developments through to the 1880s. The Basque ship section, complete with the sound of creaking wood in the living quarters, brings to life the voyages undertaken to reach the New World. Also particularly good are the Acadian farm model and the replica of the early Quebec town square.

The entertaining and educational **Children's Museum** section includes some excellent interactive exhibits.

The main level consists of three halls containing temporary exhibits on varying aspects of human history, culture and art. The

Native Indian & Inuit Art Gallery usually, but not always, offers various shows by Native Indian artists – painting, dance, crafts and more. Don't miss the chance to see the art of British Columbian Native Indians, especially that of the Haida.

Cineplus is a film theatre for IMAX and OMNIMAX, realistic large-format film presentations. The ever-changing shows are extremely popular, with waits of two to three shows not uncommon, so arrive early for a ticket.

There is a good cafeteria which offers, among other things, sandwiches and a salad bar or economical full meals all served within view of the river and Parliament Hill. The museum bookstore and gift shop are worth a browse.

Native Indian vase

From May to October the museum is open every day; for the rest of the year it is closed on Monday. On Thursday it stays open until 9 pm, otherwise it closes at 6 pm during the summer and an hour earlier the rest of the year. Admission is $5, less for seniors and kids and free on Sunday morning. A Cineplus ticket is extra; prices vary depending on the show but tend to be rather high. Again, it's less for kids and seniors. Admission is free from 9 am to noon on Sunday. Parking is found under the museum.

Places to Stay

If you want to stay on this side of the river, there are a number of accommodation choices.

The *Couette et Croissants* (☎ 771-2200), at 330 Champlain St, is a B&B in central Hull. Although a bit of a walk from Promenade du Portage, it's close to the Canadian Museum of Civilisation.

There are others, and prices tend to be a bit lower here than the Ottawa average. The tourist office has information on B&Bs in the surrounding area. Motels can be found along Boulevard Alexandre Taché, which runs beside the river to the west of downtown Hull after coming across the bridge from Ottawa.

There are also some large, typical business-oriented hotels in the central area.

Places to Eat

For a bite, head for *Café Le Coquetier*, at 145 Promenade du Portage, an unpretentious, casual bistro with very good yet cheap food. *Le Bistro*, on Rue Aubry just off Promenade du Portage, is a bar/cafe serving light lunches for under $10. There's a variety of restaurants nearby along Rue Laval.

The central *Brasserie Le Vieux Hull*, at 50 Rue Victoria, in the Place du Portage office complex, is an inexpensive tavern for a beer or two or a cheap meal, and there is a low-priced cafeteria geared to staff in the building, too.

Rues Papineau and Montcalm have several restaurants, including some of the expensive French ones for which the city has a reputation.

Entertainment

After 2 am, when the Ontario bars close, partygoers head across the river from Ottawa to Hull, where things are open until 3 am and later. Promenade du Portage, in the middle of the downtown area, has numerous nightspots, some with live music, some dressy, some quiet and dark – there's a good range.

Chez Henri, on Promenade du Portage, is an upmarket music club. *Le Bistro* attracts a more casual and younger crowd for loud dance music. It's on Rue Aubry, at the top of the hill, on the brick pedestrian mall off the Promenade.

To the west of the centre, Boulevard Saint Joseph has several popular, dressy clubs. Alternatively, *Les Raftsmen*, at 60 Rue Saint Raymond, which runs east of Boulevard Saint Joseph, has live music in a large, friendly, typically Québécois brasserie. They also have a menu of standard beer-hall fare at good prices, served until 9 pm.

The brand new casino (☎ 282-8080) is at 1 Boulevard de Casino in Hull, off the third exit going over Macdonald Cartier Bridge from Ottawa.

Getting There & Away

Bus The Outaouais Bus System (☎ 770-3242) has buses which run along Rideau and Wellington Sts in Ottawa. From downtown Ottawa, bus Nos 33, 35 and 42 all go to Promenade du Portage. Within Hull, bus Nos 37, 39 or 60 go up to and along Boulevard Saint Joseph.

Bicycle A bicycle route over the Alexandra Bridge from Ottawa connects with a trail system which goes around much of the Hull centre and to Ruisseau de la Brasserie (Brewery Creek), a park area east of downtown Hull.

AROUND OTTAWA-HULL
Gatineau Park

Gatineau Park is a deservedly popular 36,000-hectare area of woods and lakes in the Gatineau Hills of Quebec, north-west of downtown Hull.

It's only a 20-minute drive from the Parliament Buildings in Ottawa. On weekends some roads may be closed to cars, and note that parking must be paid for at the more popular destinations such as Lac Meech and the King Estate.

The park has plenty of wildlife, including about 100 species of birds, as well as some 150 km of hiking trails. **Lac Meech, Lac Phillipe** and **Lac Lapêche** have beaches for swimming and so are the most popular. Many of the camping facilities are around Lapêche and are accessible by canoe only. (Canoes can be rented.) You can fish in the lakes and streams, and the hiking trails are good for cross-country (nordic) skiing in winter. Small **Pink Lake** is pretty but is off limits for swimming. A boardwalk rims the lake for strolling. The lake is best during the week, when there are fewer people around. Lac Meech has a nude gay beach.

Also in the park is Kingsmere, the summer estate of William Lyon Mackenzie King, prime minister in the 1920s, late 1930s and early 1940s. Here he indulged his hobby of collecting ruins, both genuine and fake. In 1941, King had bits of London's House of Commons brought over after the German blitz. His home, **Moorside**, is now a museum. An astute politician, King was much interested in the occult and apparently talked to both his dead dog and deceased mother. There's a pleasant tea room at Moorside, with items such as cucumber sandwiches or blackforest ham on pumpernickel bread.

Festivals Occurring in September or October, **Fall Rhapsody** celebrates the brief but colourful season when the leaves change colour – a time when the maples and birches of the Gatineau Hills are having their last fling before winter. An arts festival is part of the affair, as are hot-air ballooning and various concerts and competitions. Events are held in the park, with a few around town as well. During Fall Rhapsody, there are cheap buses from Ottawa-Hull to various spots in Gatineau Park.

Eastern Ontario

West from Ottawa there are two main routes through Ontario. Hwy 17, the Trans Canada Hwy, leads north-west to Pembroke, then continues to North Bay and on to Sudbury. This is the quickest way to western Canada.

From Pembroke, Hwy 60/62 leads west through the southern portion of Algonquin Park to Huntsville, where Hwy 11 runs north to North Bay and south to Toronto.

The southern route from Ottawa goes to the more populated southern region of Ontario, the St Lawrence River, the Great Lakes and Toronto. From Ottawa, Hwys 31 and 16 lead directly down to the 401, the expressway to Toronto. A prettier, though slower drive is to take Hwy 7 west out of Ottawa going through Perth and as far as Hwy 37. From here Hwy 37 leads south through Tweed before dropping down to Hwy 401. This route is a standard itinerary and is a compromise between speed and aesthetics. Taking Hwy 7 any further west really starts to add on the hours. Ottawa to Toronto on the Hwys 7 and 37 route takes about five hours.

EGANVILLE

If you are in the region, this small town north-west of Ottawa is worth a stop for the nearby **Bonnechere Caves**. The caves and passages, eight km south-east, were the bottom of a tropical sea about 500 million years ago and contain fossils of animals from long before the dinosaur age. Pathways lead through parts of the extensive system, past fossil banks and stalactites. Tours are offered through the summer months at this privately developed and operated site.

MERRICKVILLE

South-west of Ottawa, Merrickville is a small, pleasant late 18th-century town along the Rideau River/Canal route from Ottawa to Kingston. There are a couple of B&Bs in town, as well as some places to eat and a bakery along St Lawrence St. A few craft and antique shops can also be found.

Historic sites include the **locks** (dating from 1830) and the **blockhouse**, its metre-thick walls built by the British in 1832 to protect the canal in case of attack. The blockhouse is now a small museum.

SMITHS FALLS
Midway along the Rideau Canal system, Smiths Falls is a small centre for the many recreational boats that use the system. Unfortunately, there are no commercial ventures here for trips along the canal.

Smiths Falls has become known as much for the **Hershey Chocolate Factory** here as for its history or its canal location. A tour of the Canadian branch plant of this famous US chocolate company based in Hershey, Pennsylvania is recommended. Find out all about how chocolate bars are created and then start eating. It's open from Monday to Saturday and is on Hershey Drive off Hwy 43 East – just follow your nose. No tours are given on Saturday.

Best of the three small historical museums is the **Rideau Canal Museum**, in a 19th-century mill at 34 Beckworth St South. Exhibits detail the history of the canal.

CORNWALL
Cornwall is the first city of any size in Ontario along the St Lawrence Valley and has the Seaway International Bridge to the USA. It was here in the 1870s that Thomas Edison, creator of the light bulb, helped set up the first factory lit by electricity.

Despite this corner of Ontario having Scottish and Loyalist ancestry, there is a good-sized French population in Cornwall.

The Pitt St Mall, in the centre of town, is a pedestrian-only two-block section of stores and gardens.

There are a couple of **museums** in town, and the **RH Saunders Energy Information Centre** has displays on the big, important hydroelectric facility here. It's open daily in July and August, on weekdays only in June. Tours of the power facilities at the dam are available. The **Inverarden Regency**

Cottage Museum represents Ontario's finest example of Regency Cottage architecture. Built in 1816 by a retiring fur trader who had evidently done quite well, it's on the corner of Hwy 2 and Boundary Rd and is open from April to November.

Just out of town, at the college on the Native Indian reserve on Cornwall Island, there is a **log cabin museum** focusing on the Cree, Iroquois and Ojibway Indians. It's not open on weekends. The big Native Indian powwow held at the reserve in July or August is worth catching, as it's one of the biggest in the province. Traditional crafts and souvenirs can be purchased.

The bridge over to Massena, New York makes Cornwall another busy port of entry for US visitors.

In **Maxville**, to the north, Scottish Highland Games held at the beginning of August commemorate the region's Scottish heritage. **St Raphaels** has some interesting church ruins dating from 1815.

West of Cornwall, the **Long Sault Parkway** connects a series of parks and beaches along the river.

MORRISBURG & UPPER CANADA VILLAGE
This small town lies west of Cornwall on the St Lawrence River. Despite its small size, it's known far and wide for its good historic site – Upper Canada Village (☎ 543-3704), the detailed re-creation of a country town of a century ago. About 40 buildings and costumed workers bring the past to life. There's a blacksmith's shop, inn and sawmill as well as a working farm, all set by the river.

You'll need at least several hours to fully explore the site, which is open from 20 May to 9 October. Hours are 9.30 am to 5 pm. Admission is $9.50, less for kids.

Without transport, the village can be reached aboard buses running between Ottawa and Cornwall and on some buses which follow the Montreal to Toronto route. Many are direct, while others putt along, stopping at the smaller towns en route. Nearby **Crysler Battlefield Park** is a memorial to those who died fighting the USA in 1812.

Parks of the St Lawrence (☎ 543-3704), a government agency based in Morrisburg, runs Upper Canada Village, the **Upper Canada Migratory Bird Sanctuary** and **Fort Henry**, as well as many of the campgrounds and parks along the river between Cornwall and Kingston.

Hwy 2 along the river is slower to travel on but provides a more scenic trip than Hwy 401. It's used by many cyclists, including long-distance riders between Montreal and Toronto. There are numerous provincial parks along the way, especially east of town along the Long Sault Parkway. Going west there is a seaway-viewing platform at **Iroquois** and a good campground for cyclists.

There are about half-a-dozen motels in Morrisburg and four campgrounds. Among the latter is the *Upper Canada Migratory Bird Sanctuary Nature Awareness Campsite* (☎ 543-3704). It's a little different from the average campground and is educational, too. Find it 14 km east of town along Hwy 2. They have about 50 tent sites but few creature comforts.

PRESCOTT

Another 19th-century town, Prescott is the site of the International Bridge to Ogdensburg, New York. The harbour area has been overhauled and has a busy marina, but there isn't anything of note for the traveller passing through.

Just to the east of the downtown area and walkable from the centre is the **Fort Wellington National Historic Site** (☎ 925-2896). The original fort was built during the War of 1812. It was rebuilt in 1838 and served militarily until the 1920s. Some original fortifications remain, as does a blockhouse and the officer's quarters from the 1830s. During the summer, guides in costume supplement the interpretive displays. In the third week of July, the fort hosts the country's largest military pageant, which includes mock battles in full regalia.

The fort is open daily from the end of May to 30 September. Also here, outside the grounds, are a few picnic tables with views of the river.

BROCKVILLE

A small community along the river, Brockville is a particularly attractive town, with its many old stone buildings and the classic-looking main street. The courthouse and jail in the centre of town date from 1842. During the summer, many of the finest buildings are lit up, accentuating the slight resort flavour of this casual river port by the Thousand Islands.

The historic museum in **Beecher House** provides a look at the area's history but there really is no reason to linger. The other principal attraction, the oldest train tunnel in the country, isn't worth the trouble.

For the Thousand Island Parkway area west of Brockville, see the Around Kingston section following the Kingston description.

KINGSTON

Kingston (population 137,000) is a handsome town that retains much of its past through preservation of many historic buildings and defence structures. Built strategically where Lake Ontario flows into the St Lawrence River, it is a convenient stopping-off point almost exactly halfway between Montreal and Toronto, and it's not difficult to spend an interesting and enjoyable day or three in and around town.

Once a fur-trading depot, Kingston later became the principal British military post west of Quebec, and was the national capital for a while. The many 19th-century buildings of local grey limestone and the streets of Victorian red-brick houses give the downtown area a certain distinctive charm. The attractive waterfront is also pleasant.

There is a major university here, Queen's, and the city is also known across the country for its several prisons.

On Tuesday, Thursday, Saturday and Sunday a small open-air market takes place downtown, behind City Hall on King St.

Orientation

The town lies a few km south of Hwy 401. Princess St, the main street, runs right down to the St Lawrence River, along which are many fine old buildings. The whole city is

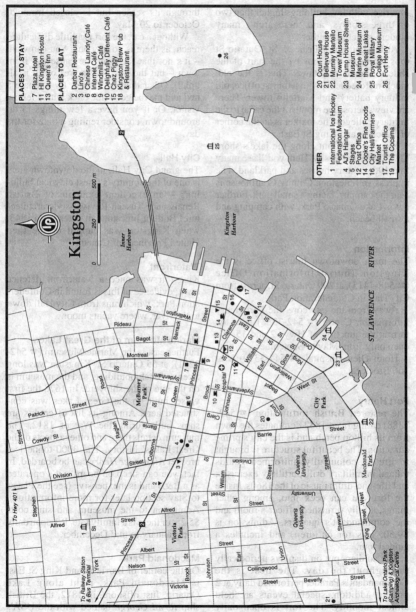

Kingston

PLACES TO STAY
7 Plaza Hotel
11 HI Kingston Hostel
13 Queen's Inn

PLACES TO EAT
2 Darbar Restaurant
3 Lino's
6 Chinese Laundry Café
8 Internet Café
9 Windmills Café
10 Delightfully Different Café
15 Chez Piggy
18 Kingston Brew Pub
      & Restaurant

OTHER
1 International Ice Hockey
    Federation Museum
4 Murney Martello
    Tower Museum
5 A J's Hangar
12 Post Office
14 Cooke's Fine Foods
16 City Hall/Farmers'
      Market
17 Tourist Office
19 The Cocama
20 Court House
21 Bellevue House
22 Murney Martello
      Tower Museum
23 Pump House Steam
      Museum
24 Marine Museum of
      the Great Lakes
25 Royal Military
      College Museum
26 Fort Henry

0   250   500 m

Inner Harbour

Kingston Harbour

ST LAWRENCE RIVER

To Railway Station
& Bus Terminal

To Hwy 401

To Lake Ontario Park
(Camping) & Kingston
Archaeological Centre

low-rise, with few buildings higher than two or three storeys, and there aren't many modern structures either.

At the bottom of Princess St, Ontario St runs along the harbour by the start of the Rideau Canal to Ottawa. This is the old, much-restored area, with a tourist office, old military battery and Martello tower. There are views across the mouth of the canal to the military college. The market is on the corner of Brock St and King St East.

King St leads out along the lake's shore towards the university. Here you'll see many fine 19th-century houses and parkland. The impressive limestone County Courthouse is near the campus, facing a small park. Further out is Lake Ontario Park, with camping and a small beach.

Information

The main downtown tourist office is the Kingston Tourist Information Office (☎ 548-4415), at 209 Ontario St, across from City Hall in Confederation Park.

Away from the city core, the Fort Henry Information Centre (☎ 542-7388) is at the fort, at the junction of Hwys 2 and 15. It's open only from May to September.

Hotel Dieu Hospital (☎ 544-3310) is at 166 Brock St.

Fort Henry

The restored British fortification (☎ 542-7388) dating from 1832 dominates the town from its hilltop perch and is the city's prime attraction. The beautiful structure is brought to life by colourfully uniformed guards trained in military drills, artillery exercises, and fife-and-drum music of the 1860s. Inside the fort you can peek into, among other things, a fully furnished officer's room and the commandant's quarters. Admission is $9.50, less for children, and includes a guided tour.

The soldiers put on displays periodically throughout the day. The best is the Commandant's Parade, performed daily at 2 pm. In addition, special events are held almost monthly. The fort is open daily through its season but is closed from 20 October to 20 May.

Without a car, the fort is a little difficult to reach, as there is no city bus. You can walk – it's not that far, over the causeway from town – but the last 500 metres or so is all uphill. Other than hoofing it, try to share a taxi and maybe get a ride back with a fellow visitor. Or if you have a few things to do around town, consider renting a bike for the day.

City Hall

The grand City Hall, in the downtown area, is one of the country's finest classical buildings – an excellent example of British Renaissance Tuscan Revival-style architecture! Built of limestone, it dates from 1843, when Kingston was capital of the then United Provinces of Canada.

Waterfront

Kingston was once a waterfront defence town; evidence of this is found in Confederation Park, which runs from City Hall down to the river, where yachts moor.

Marine Museum of the Great Lakes

Further east is the Marine Museum (☎ 542-2261), at 55 Ontario St. Kingston was long a centre for shipbuilding, and the museum is on the site of the shipyard. In 1678 the first vessel built on the Great Lakes was constructed here. Among its list of credits are ships built during the War of 1812. The museum details these and other aspects of the Great Lakes' history. The 3000-tonne icebreaker *Alexander Henry* can be boarded. In fact, you can sleep on board – it's operated as a B&B and is inexpensive (see the Places to Stay section later for more information). Admission to the museum and ship costs $5.25, or there is a family rate. It's open daily from January to mid December.

Macdonald Park

On the corner of Barrie St and King St East is Macdonald Park, right along Lake Ontario. Just offshore, in 1812, the British ship *Royal George* battled with the USA's

USS *Oneida*. At the western end of the park is the **Murney Martello Tower**, dating from 1846. This round defence structure was part of the early riverside fortifications and is now a museum housing local military and historical tidbits. Admission is $2. The museum is open daily from the end of May to the beginning of September. There are walking and bicycle paths along here and good swimming by the jetty.

On the corner of King St East and West St is City Park featuring a statue of Canada's first prime minister, Sir John Alexander Macdonald.

Bellevue House

This National Historic Site (☎ 545-8666) is an immaculately maintained Tuscan-style mansion, which apparently means a very odd-shaped, balconied, brightly painted architect's field day. It works, though, and in the garden setting this is an impressive and interesting house. It was once the home of Sir John Alexander Macdonald. The mansion, at 35 Centre St, houses many good antiques. It's open daily during the summer from 9 am to 6 pm and in winter from 10 am to 5 pm. Admission is $2.50.

Brock St

Brock St was the middle of town in the 1800s, and many of the original shops still stand along it. It's worth a walk around. Take a look in Cooke's Fine Foods, at 61 Brock St, a gourmet shop with old, wooden counters and a century-old, pressed-tin ceiling. There are lovely aromas and a curious assortment of goods and shoppers, including local professors drinking the fresh coffee at the back of the store.

Correctional Service of Canada Museum

Correctional Service is what Canadian bureaucrats call jails, and here is about as close as you'll get to finding out what they're like without doing something nasty. Located at 555 King St West, in the administration building across from the main prison, the museum (☎ 530-3122) has a collection of articles ranging from confiscated weapons to tools used in escapes. It's open from May to September, Wednesday to Friday from 9 am to 4 pm and Saturday and Sunday from 10 am to 4 pm.

Pump House Steam Museum

Here we have a one-of-a-kind, completely restored, steam-run pump station (☎ 542-2261). First used in 1849, it now contains several engines and some scale models, all run on steam. The address is 23 Ontario St. It's open daily from the start of May to Labour Day. Admission is $3.75.

Train buffs will also want to see the 20 model trains from around the world displayed in a special exhibit room.

Royal Military College Museum

In the Fort Frederick Martello Tower on the grounds of the college (☎ 541-5010) is the Royal Military College Museum. This is the largest of the city's historic towers and has a collection on the history of the century-old military college. You have to wonder how or why, but also here lies the small arms collection of General Porfirio Diaz, president of Mexico from 1886 to 1912. The museum is just east of town, off Hwy 2, and is open daily in summer.

International Ice Hockey Federation Museum

On the corner of Alfred and York Sts, this collection (☎ 544-2355) honours the history and stars of Canada's most-loved sport. The displays include lots of memorabilia, photos and equipment. The museum is open daily from mid-June to mid-September, but on weekend afternoons only for the rest of the year. Admission is $2.

Kingston Archaeological Centre

If you've been out along Hwy 401, you probably noticed the sedimentary rock outcrops, one of the few interesting things along that highway's entire length from Montreal to Toronto. The Kingston Archaeological Centre, at 370 King St West, in the Tett Centre, has displays on the 8000-year human history of the area, featuring items dug from the surrounding landscape or found along the shoreline. It's open on weekdays and there is no charge.

Kingston Mills Lockstation Blockhouse
Away from the centre, up Kingston Mills Rd just north of Hwy 401, this restored blockhouse (☎ 359-5377) dates from 1839. The purpose of the lock station and what it was like to run it are part of the explanatory exhibits. The blockhouse is open daily through the summer and is free.

Other Museums
There are several other specialised museums in or near Kingston (see the Around Kingston section), including one on county schools, one at the military base detailing the history of military communications and electronics, and others on such things as geology and mineralogy and art. The tourist office has details.

Wolfe Island
It's possible to have a free mini-cruise by taking the car ferry from Kingston to Wolfe Island. The 20-minute trip affords views of the city, the fort and a few of the Thousand Islands. Wolfe Island, the largest in the chain, lies halfway to the USA and is basically flat farmland, although many of its inhabitants now work in town.

There is not a lot to see on the island, but there is the *General Wolfe Hotel*, a short walk from the dock, with its three busy and highly regarded dining rooms. Prices are moderate to slightly expensive. There are also some moderately priced cabins on the island, and a campground. On the Kingston side, the ferry terminal is at the intersection of Ontario and Barrack Sts. The ferry runs continuously every hour or so from 6.15 am to 2 am daily, taking about 50 vehicles at a time. From Wolfe Island, another ferry links Cape Vincent, New York, but a toll is charged on this segment if you have a car.

Organised Tours
The tourist office has a pamphlet with map for a self-guided walking tour of the older part of town.

Historic Kingston Bike Tours (☎ 531-8609) offer one and two-hour cycle tours of the city for $12 and $20 respectively.

During the summer a Haunted Walk, featuring stories of hangings and grave robbers, leaves from the tourist information office every Tuesday to Saturday at 8 pm. The tour takes about two hours and costs $6.

On summer days, a trackless mini-train departs regularly from the tourist office area for a tour of the central Kingston area.

St Lawrence Cruise Lines (☎ 1-800-267-7868), 253 Ontario St, runs cruises out of Kingston to Ottawa, Montreal and Quebec City aboard the *Canadian Empress*. Trips last four, five or six nights and fares include all meals, entertainment and activities.

Several other local boat tours from Kingston go around the Thousand Islands; see the Around Kingston section for details of these.

Places to Stay
Kingston doesn't have a lot of hotels. Most accommodation is in B&Bs and motels.

Camping There are quite a few places to camp in the area. *Hi-Lo Hickory* (☎ 385-2430), on Wolfe Island, is reached by ferry from Kingston. There's a beach, and a bridge on the other side connects the island with New York state. The campground is about 12 km east of the Kingston ferry terminal.

In town, only four km from the centre, you can camp at *Lake Ontario Park* (☎ 542-6574), which is operated by the city's parks department. It's west out along King St, and there's a beach too. A city bus runs from downtown right to the campground, from Monday to Saturday until 7.30 pm and on Friday until 10.30 pm.

KOA (Kampgrounds of America, seen all over North America) has a branch 1.6 km north of Hwy 401 off Hwy 38 (☎ 546-6140). These places can be very plastic, having as little to do with camping as possible, and are also expensive, big and generally pretty busy. They cater mainly for trailers but have some tent sites.

Hostels The HI *Kingston Hostel* (☎ 546-7203), at 210 Bagot St, is conveniently central – buses (No 1 from the train, No 2 from the bus) will get you within a block or two. It has 30 beds in summer (about half that many in winter), a room for couples and some rooms for families. Continental breakfasts are available and there's also a complete kitchen. Rates are $12/17 for members/non-members. The hostel is closed from 15 December to 15 January.

Rooms are available in residences at *Queen's University* (☎ 545-2529) from mid-May to mid-August. Rooms cost $38 (less for students) and continental breakfast is included. The campus is on the corner of University and Union Sts.

The *YM-YWCA* (☎ 546-2647), west of downtown at 100 Wright Crescent, has beds for women only at $26 per night. There are kitchen facilities and a pool.

B&Bs Kingston & Area B&B Association (☎ 542-0214) runs a booking agency. There are about 40 participating homes in and around town. Tell them where you want to be and what your interests are and you'll be matched up suitably. Rates start at $40/50 for singles/doubles with full breakfast included, plus $10 to $15 extra for children. Cheaper rates are available for extended stays.

In summer, you can stay at a unique B&B on a moored, retired 64-metre icebreaker, the *Alexander Henry* (☎ 542-2261), which is part of the downtown Marine Museum of the Great Lakes. Beds are in the former crew's quarters and a continental breakfast is served from the galley. You can wander all over the ship. It hasn't been gentrified at all – the vessel is plain, simple and functional and the 19 rooms are pretty much like those on a working ship. This partially explains the good prices, which start at $38 a double and go up to $65 if you want the captain's cabin.

O'Brien House (☎ 542-8660), at 39 Glenaire Mews, up near the train station and north-west of the downtown area, is a little less costly than the city norm. It's a B&B whose owner seems to particularly like overseas visitors. Singles/doubles cost $37/48, including a full breakfast and coffee or tea at any time. There are reduced rates for children.

Hotels A couple of the older downtown hotels have been overhauled and make pleasant, if a bit pricey, central places to stay.

Among the old cheapies, only the *Plaza Hotel*, 46 Montreal St, on the corner of Queen St, remains. It exists basically for the downstairs bar but is not badly kept. It's no family place and is not recommended for single women, but it is cheap – $25/35 a single/double with private bathroom.

Also inexpensive, but better, the *Donald Gordon Centre* (☎ 545-2221), at 421 Union St, is affiliated with (and very near) Queen's University. The centre rents their quiet, air-conditioned rooms for $40/45.

Moving up and offering more amenities, style and services is the *Queen's Inn* (☎ 546-0429), 125 Brock St, dating from 1839. It now offers modern facilities in 17 rooms in a central setting. It's one of the oldest hotels in the country. Rooms vary from $65 to $95 in high season (April to November) and from $45 to $75 for the rest of the year.

Motels At 1454 Princess St is *Comfort Inn by Journey's End* (☎ 549-5550), a two-storey place. Rooms are a couple of dollars cheaper upstairs and cost $61 to $79 for singles or doubles.

A little cheaper is the *Hilltop* (☎ 542-3846), at 2287 Princess St, where singles/doubles are $48/56. There are many other motels on Princess St, and some along Hwy 2 on each side of town.

Places to Eat
Windmills Café, 184 Princess St, serves very good vegetarian food in pleasant surroundings. Lunch prices range from $5 to $8 and might include Thai Shrimp Salad or Warm Goat Cheese Torte. Dinner costs between $6 and $12. It's also open for breakfast and offers weekend brunch. Around the corner,

at 19 Montreal St, Windmills To Go offers a good variety of take-out food.

The *Delightfully Different Café*, at 118 Sydenham St, is an unlikely looking place which turns out excellent fresh sandwiches, salads, bagels etc for lunch, and muffins and the like for breakfast. It's only open from 7 am to 4 pm Monday to Friday but is worth getting to for a light meal and is very inexpensive. It's between Brock and Johnson Sts.

At 34 Clarence St, the *Kingston Brew Pub & Restaurant* brews its own ales and lagers – try their Dragon's Breath Ale – and also has a good selection of non-house brands. There are inexpensive tavern-style things to munch on and, interestingly, a daily curry.

For a light lunch, snack, dessert or just a coffee, try the friendly *Chinese Laundry Café*, at 291 Princess St. It has an outdoor courtyard patio and is open late.

At 479 Princess St, you can get a good Indian meal at the *Darbar*. It serves the usual northern dishes, including tandoori, and is open daily for lunch (with five specials each day) or dinner.

For a real splurge there's *Chez Piggy*, probably the city's best known restaurant, in a renovated early 19th-century building at 68 Princess St but really down a small alley off King St between Brock and Princess Sts. At lunch, from 11.30 am to 2 pm, soup and a sandwich or the good salads are not expensive. Dinners, starting at 6 pm, cost $9 to $17 for a main course, so the final bill can be quite high. There is also a Sunday brunch, with some items you don't see on a standard brunch menu (but again, it is not for the budget-conscious). The restaurant is owned by a member of a successful (and tuneful) 1960s US pop band. No clues, but he likes it that way. It's open daily.

Division St, towards Hwy 401, has a good cross-section of places representing the standard restaurant chains. *Lino's*, on the corner of Division and Princess Sts, is open 24 hours a day.

For coffee, cake and an information fix, check out Kingston's very own *Internet Café* at 303 Bagot Street in the LaSalle Mews complex.

Entertainment

Bars & Nightspots The *Cocama*, at 178 Ontario St, is a huge dance bar down near the water. It's styled after the Limelight in New York City. *AJ's Hangar*, at 393 Princess St, is a place to check out for live rock and blues bands on weekends (or for a drink the rest of the week). *Stages*, at 390 Princess St, just across the road from AJ's, is a popular dance club.

Kingston has quite a few British-style pubs. The *Toucan*, at 76 Princess St, near King St, often has live music. On the corner of King St East and Brock St, near City Hall, the *Duke of Kingston Pub* serves British beers in British-style decor.

Cinema The *Princess Court Cinema* (☎ 546-3456), at 394 Princess St, is a good repertory movie house.

Things to Buy

The Canadian Shop, at 219 Princess St, near Montreal St, sells handicrafts, including Cowichan sweaters from Vancouver Island for about the same price they are there. The shop also sells Inuit carvings and all kinds of books about Canada.

The Book Bin, at 225 Princess St, sells second-hand books.

Getting There & Away

Bus The Voyageur bus station (☎ 547-4916) is at 175 Counter St, a couple of km south of Hwy 401. Services going to Toronto are frequent throughout the day (at least eight trips); to Montreal, buses are slightly less frequent. To Ottawa, there are buses each morning, afternoon and evening. Services also go to some of the smaller centres, such as Pembroke and Cornwall. One-way fares include Montreal $38, Ottawa $27 and Toronto $37.

Train The VIA Rail station (☎ 544-5600) is a long way north-west from the downtown area, but city bus No 1 stops at the corner of Princess and Counter Sts, just a short walk from the station. There are five train services to Montreal daily, costing $50. To Ottawa

($32) there are four trains a day. To Toronto ($50) there are eight services daily. Discounts are offered on tickets purchased five days or more in advance.

Car Tilden (☎ 546-1145), at 2232 Princess St, offers daily, weekly and longer car rentals.

Getting Around
Bus For information on buses, call Kingston Transit (☎ 544-5289). The city bus office is at 181 Counter St.

For getting into town, there is a city bus stop across the street from the bus station. Buses depart at a quarter to and a quarter past the hour.

Bicycle Bicycle rentals are available at Source For Sports, 121 Princess St. A second place to try is La Salle Sports (☎ 544-4252), at 574 Princess St. The area is generally flat and both Hwys 2 and 5 have paved shoulders.

AROUND KINGSTON
Thousand Islands Parkway
East of Kingston between Gananoque (which is pronounced 'gan-an-ok-way') and Mallorytown Landing, a small road – the Thousand Islands Parkway – dips south of Hwy 401, runs along the river and then rejoins the highway. This can make for a scenic and recommended side trip when travelling Hwy 401 in either direction. The route offers picnic areas and good views out to many of the islands from the pastoral strip of shoreline. There is also a **bicycle path** over the fibre-optic telephone lines. Bicycles can be rented at the 1000 Islands Camping Resort (☎ 659-3058), eight km east of Gananoque. The St Lawrence Parks System maintains a series of recreational and historic places along this route and on Hwy 2 from Adolphustown to beyond Upper Canada Village at Morrisburg and all the way to Lancaster, near the Quebec border.

Boat cruises around the islands depart from Rockport and Gananoque.

Sixteen km east of Kingston, in a log house in Grass Creek Park, you'll find the **MacLachlan Woodworking Museum**. The museum uses an extensive collection of tools to outline the development of working in wood.

Close to the town of **Lansdowne** between Gananoque and Rockport is the busy bridge to New York State. The **Skydeck**, a 125-metre-high observation tower, is open every day from May to October. Its three decks provide great views over the river area. Admission is reasonable and there is a restaurant on the premises.

At **Mallorytown Landing** is the headquarters for the **Thousand Islands National Park**, Canada's smallest national park, consisting of 17 islands together with the mainland location.

Along the parkway are privately run campgrounds, numerous motels, and some cottages to rent for longer stays. In Gananoque, at 279 King St West, the *Victoria & Rose Inn* (☎ 382-3368) is a fabulous-looking place dating from around 1870. The interior has been totally updated and guests will not lack for comforts. Prices reflect this and start at $75 a double.

There is a bit of an art colony in the area, and in the fall many of the local studios are open to the public. Ask the tourist office in Kingston for a list of the painters, sculptors, woodworkers, glass workers, weavers, etc.

The Thousand Islands This scenic area just east of Kingston actually has more than 1000 islands which dot the river between the two national mainlands. In spring the islands undulate with the white blooms of the trillium, the provincial flower.

Boat tours from Kingston will take you around some of the islands; a couple of companies run daily trips in summer. The short and straightforward one is aboard the *Island Belle* (☎ 549-5544), a 1½-hour trip around the interesting Kingston shoreline with a commentary on some of the noteworthy sites. Departing from the same place is the *Island Queen* showboat, providing live family entertainment or a three-hour evening cruise with a buffet dinner. Through the summer they offer two or three trips a day, leaving from the *Island Queen* dock, on Ontario St at the foot of Brock St.

Other tours leave from Rockport and Gananoque, two small towns east down the river a bit. Most tours last about 3½ hours, cost $15 per adult and include glimpses of such island curiosities as **Boldt Castle**. The Rockport Boat Line (☎ 659-3402) has two-hour trips out among the international islands for $10. Trips depart hourly in peak season, less frequently in spring and autumn, from the dock three km east of the Thousand Islands International Bridge.

The Gananoque Boat Line (☎ 382-2144) does much the same thing but offers a 90-minute trip that goes through the Admiralty and Fleet groups of islands. They also have sunset cruises. At impressive looking Boldt Castle, you can get off for a closer look and return to Gananoque on a later boat.

A new angle is to do it all yourself on a rented houseboat. This is gaining in popularity all over Ontario and can be a lot of fun, but tends to be a little pricey unless you get a few people together. If you want to look into it, check out Thousand Islands Houseboats (☎ 634-3979) in Kingston. They rent by the day, week or part of a week. Prices depend on when you go – at weekends it costs considerably more than midweek. The boats come with all kitchen necessities and sleep eight people.

Kingston is also home to the St Lawrence Cruise Lines (☎ 1-800-267-7868), which runs four, five and six-night luxury cruises on replica steamboats down the St Lawrence River to Ottawa, Montreal and Quebec City.

St Lawrence Islands National Park Within the gentle, green archipelago, this park covers 17 islands scattered along 80 km of the river. At Mallorytown Landing, as well as the park interpretive and information centre, you'll find a 60-site campground but no campervan or trailer hook-ups. There are some trails and a beach.

Many of the islands have picnicking and camping, with minimal facilities, and 13 islands offer primitive camp sites accessible only by boat. Water-taxis and boat rentals are available from the park headquarters (☎ 923-5261) and from many of the small towns along the parkway. Tourist offices or park headquarters will have information on what's available. National Park islands stretch from just off Mallorytown all the way down to Gananoque.

West of Kingston
West of town along the coast, Hwy 33 has been designated the Loyalist Parkway. It retraces the steps of the Loyalists who settled this area some 200 years ago after fleeing the American Revolution. The parkway runs for 94 km from Kingston to Trenton, passing over Quinte's Isle.

Just west of Kingston, in Amherstview, **Fairfield Historical Park** runs along the shoreline. It includes **Fairfield House**, one of the province's oldest, built in 1793 by Loyalists from New England. North about 10 km, in Odessa, the historic **Babcock Mill** is a working water-powered mill which again produces the baskets originally made here in the mid-19th century.

At **Adulphustown**, catch the continuously running short, free ferry over to Glenora (on Quinte's Isle) and continue on to Picton.

North of Kingston
North of Kingston is the **Rideau Lakes** region, an area of small towns, cottages, lodges and marinas with opportunities for fishing and camping. In a day's drive you can explore some of the smaller, rural Ontario villages.

Wilton has one of the many southern Ontario regional cheese factories with a retail outlet. In the little town of **Yarker**, straight up Hwy 6 from Hwy 401, the *Waterfall Tea Room* is right on the river, by a waterfall, and has been highly recommended.

Camden East, home of *Harrowsmith Magazine*, has an excellent bookstore specialising in gardening, country living and all things natural.

The region has attracted 'back-to-the-landers' and countercultural people. Their

The Loyalists

The issue of American independence from Britain divided the American colonies into two camps: the Patriots and the Loyalists. During the American Revolution of 1775-83, the Loyalists maintained their allegiance to the British Crown. About a third of the 13 Colonies' population remained loyal to Britain. Severe laws were passed against them, forcing some 200,000 to leave during and after the Revolution. Of those, between 50,000 and 60,000 fled to Canada, settling in the Maritimes, the Eastern Townships of Lower Canada (Quebec) and the St Lawrence-Lake Ontario region of Upper Canada (Ontario). Unknown to many today, not all were of British descent – they represented a mix of ethnic backgrounds. Regardless, their arrival strengthened Great Britain's hold on this part of the Empire. In Nova Scotia, for example, the migration meant that the French no longer made up the majority of the population.

In this region, the Loyalists' arrival essentially meant the formation of the province of Ontario. Both the British and local governments were generous in their support, offering clothing, rations, and various aid and land grants.

Soon the Loyalists in Canada were not only self-sustaining but prosperous and powerful. Today their descendants make up a significant and influential segment of the Canadian population.

Loyalist sites can be seen in southern Quebec, the Gaspé and, in particular, Saint John, New Brunswick and Shelburne, Nova Scotia. ∎

influences show up in the number of health-food stores, craft outlets and bakeries. In **Tamsworth**, where there is a big arts & crafts outlet, try the *Devon Tea House*. In nearby **Marlbank** there is *Phioloxia's Zoo, Bakery, B&B and Vegetarian Restaurant*.

Frontenac Provincial Park (☎ 376-3489) straddles both the lowlands of southern Ontario and the more northern Canadian Shield, so the flora, fauna and geology of the park are mixed. The park is designed for overnight hikers and canoeists. There is no formal campground – rather, there are interior camp sites scattered through the park, accessible only on foot or by water. Trails and canoe routes have been mapped out. Though the park is large, there aren't many designated camp sites; this is not yet a big problem, as the park remains relatively unknown.

The entrance and the information centre are at **Otter Lake**, off Hwy 5A north of Sydenham. The swimming is excellent, the bass fishing is pretty good and there are no bears to worry about.

North-west from Kingston up Hwy 41 is **Bon Echo Provincial Park** (☎ 336-2228). One of the largest parks in eastern Ontario, it's another good spot for canoeing. Some of the lakes are quite shallow and get very warm. There are walk-in and canoe-in camp

sites or roadside campgrounds with facilities. At **Mazinaw Lake** there are Native Indian rock paintings on granite cliffs.

Rideau Canal The 150-year-old, 200-km-long canal/river/lake system connects Kingston with Ottawa. The historical route is good for boating or canoeing trips, with parks, small towns, lakes and many places to stop en route. When travelling from one end to the other, boats must pass through 47 lock systems. The old defence buildings along the way have been restored.

After the War of 1812 there was a fear that there could be yet another war with the Americans. The Duke of Wellington decided to link Ottawa and Kingston with a canal in order to have a reliable communications and supply route between the two military centres. Although the canal is just 200 km in length, its construction was a brutal affair, involving as many as 4000 men, battling malaria and the Canadian Shield, with some of the world's hardest rock. It climbs 84 metres from Ottawa over the Shield, then drops 49 metres to Lake Ontario. And guess what? Right! It never saw any military service.

It did prove useful later in the century for shipping goods around, but is now used mainly for recreation. Houseboat Holidays (☎ 382-2842), based in Gananoque, rent houseboats for meandering along the canal.

The boats sleep six and prices start at $450 for a weekend. Roads run parallel to much of the canal, so walking or cycling is also possible.

Rideau Trail The Rideau Trail is a 400-km hiking-trail system which links Kingston with Ottawa. It passes through Westport, Smiths Falls and many conservation areas, traversing forests, fields and marshes as well as some stretches of road along the way. There are some historic sites on the route, and you'll see the Rideau Canal. There are also 64 km of side loops. Most people use the route only for day trips, but longer trips and overnighting are possible. The main trail is marked by orange triangles, side trails are marked by blue triangles. The Rideau Trail Association, which has an office in Kingston, prints a map kit for the entire route. Between Kingston and Smiths Falls are numerous camping spots. The rest of the way, there is not as much provision for camping but there is commercial accommodation. Camping on private land is possible; get the owner's permission first.

BELLEVILLE & AROUND

There's not much for the visitor in Belleville, a town with 35,000 residents – it's more a departure point for Quinte's Isle to the south. In July, the Waterfront & Folklorama Festival is three days of events, music and shows.

Twenty-nine km east of town, in Deseronto, Native Renaissance II has a sizeable collection of Native Indian arts & crafts and a section where new ones are created. It's open every day and can be found on Hwy 49.

At Shannonville, in the same direction but just 12 km from Belleville, the Mosport Speedway is the site of motorcycle and drag racing periodically through the summer.

Mapledale Cheese sells excellent cheddar. It's north of Belleville up Hwy 37, roughly 10 km north of Hwy 401.

Hwy 37 continues north through old Tweed to Hwy 7, which is the main route to Toronto from Ottawa. It's a bit slow, with only two lanes, but the scenery is good. There are a couple of parks along the way and several places to eat.

QUINTE'S ISLE

Irregularly shaped Quinte's Isle provides a quiet and scenic retreat from the bustle of much of southern Ontario. The rolling farmland is reminiscent of Prince Edward Island, and in fact Quinte's Isle is also known as Prince Edward County. Many of the little towns were settled in the 18th and 19th centuries. The cemeteries adjacent to the village churches reveal clues to these earlier times.

It's only been in the past few years that the island has been somewhat discovered and developed for visitors, but it still hasn't changed very much.

Things to See & Do

Traffic is light on most of the island's roads, which lead past large old farmhouses and cultivated fields. The **St Lawrence River** is never far away and many routes offer good views. Fishing is quite good in the **Bay of Quinte** and the locals use the waters for sailing. The island is popular with cyclists – it's generally flat and some of the smaller roads are well shaded.

The excellent strawberry picking in late June draws many outsiders.

There are three provincial parks, including **North Beach** and the fine **Sandbanks.** Sandbanks (☎ 393-3319), the only one offering camping, is one of the most popular parks in the province. Book ahead – reservations are definitely required for weekends, when a fair bit of partying goes on. The park is divided into two sections: the Outlet (with an excellent strip of sandy beach) and Sandbanks itself (containing most of the area's sand dunes, some over three-storeys high). There's a large undeveloped section at the end of the beach – good for walking and for exploring the dunes and backwaters.

On the other side of the island, **Lake on the Mountain**, the third park, is really nothing more than a picnic site but is worth a visit to see the unusual lake. It sits on one side of the road at a level actually higher than that of the road, while just across the street is a terrific view over Lake Ontario and some islands hundreds of metres below. Geologists are still speculating as to the lake's origins. The local Mohawk Indians have their own legends about the lake, which appears to have no source.

Picton This small town is the only town of any size on the island and has one of the six district museums. The tourist office has detailed maps of the island and some information on current accommodation. Pick up the walking-tour guide of Picton which leads you past some of the fine historic buildings in town. Another guide lists various island attractions, including **Bird House City**, with dozens of painted birdhouses (including a fire station and courthouse).

Tyendinaga Indian Reserve This is just off Quinte's Isle and is also mainly farmland. In mid-May the original coming of the Mohawks is re-enacted in full tribal dress.

Places to Stay
The area is best known for its camping. There are several commercial campgrounds nearby which, if you can't get in at Sandbanks, aren't quite as busy. The large one opposite the Outlet is geared mainly for recreational vehicles. There's also quite a nice one, good for tenting as well, out at the tip of Salmon Arm; it offers minimal facilities but great sunsets.

There are numerous resorts, cottages, motels and B&Bs covering a range of prices. For a day or two you're best off at a B&B, but for longer stays check into one of the simpler cabins or cottages. Some of the less costly places seem to be in the Cherry Valley area. For B&B information contact Belleville Tourism (☎ 966-1333).

Isiah Tubbs Resort (☎ 393-2090), the most expensive place on the island, is costly even by Toronto or Muskoka standards but the luxury facilities and very fine design keep visitors coming back for more.

If all the accommodation options are booked out, try the motels around Belleville's perimeter – it's not far to return to the island the following day.

TRENTON
Small Trenton is known as the starting point of the Trent-Severn Waterway, which runs 386 km through 44 locks to Georgian Bay in Lake Huron. Yachties and sailors of every description follow this old Native Indian route each summer. **Presqu'ile Provincial Park** (☎ 475-2204) is west of town and south of Brighton. A popular feature is the immense beach, but bird watchers make up a sizeable portion of the campers. The park has a large adjacent marsh, which is home to many species and represents a migration pit stop to many more in spring and autumn. Boardwalks allow access to portions of the wetlands. The camping is good, too, with large, treed sites. At Beach 3, you can rent boats, sailboarding equipment and bicycles.

The Loyalist Parkway road route leads down onto Quinte's Isle and heads east.

Trent-Severn Waterway
The Trent-Severn Waterway cuts diagonally across southern Ontario cottage country, following rivers and lakes for 386 km from Trenton (on Lake Ontario) to Georgian Bay at the mouth of the Severn River (near Port Severn and Honey Harbour). It travels past, through or near many of the region's best known resort towns and areas, including **Kawartha Lakes, Bobcaygeon, Fenelon Falls** and **Lake Simcoe**.

Used a century ago for commerce, the system is now strictly recreational and is operated by Parks Canada. The waterflow is regulated by a series of 125 dams along the route. The canal is opened for use in mid-May and closes in mid-October. A cruise ship plies the route, taking seven days. Shorter, four-day trips are also available. These are not cheap, but ask in Peterborough for details.

Several companies along the route rent houseboats by the weekend, by the week or for longer periods. The boats come more or less fully equipped, some even have barbecues, and can accommodate up to eight people (six adults), which makes for not only a good party but also a reasonably priced one. The trips are good for families, too, with separate sleeping rooms for the kids.

One organisation to try is well-established Egan Houseboat Rentals (☎ (705) 799-5745), located at Egan Marine, RR4 in the village of Omemee, west of Peterborough on Route 7. Being right by the Kawartha Lakes, gives you the option of hanging around the lakes or going all the way to Lake Simcoe.

Rates vary quite a bit, depending on timing, but start at about $500 for a weekend. On average, you will use about $100 worth of gasoline in a week.

Lake Ontario Waterfront Trail

Three years of work by provincial and local governments, community groups and conservation authorities has recently come to fruition with the opening of the 325-km Lake Ontario Waterfront Trail, which stretches from Trenton through Toronto to Hamilton on the far western edge of Lake Ontario.

Suitable for walking, cycling and even roller-skating, the trail links 160 natural areas, 126 parks and dozens of museums, galleries and historic sites. Hundreds of organised activities, from sidewalk sales to jazz festivals, take place along the trail during the summer. The Waterfront Regeneration Trust (☎ (416) 314-8572) can provide maps and information on trail events, or ask at the Trenton tourist office.

KAWARTHA LAKES

Many of the pretty towns in the Kawartha Lakes vacation region have a good restaurant or two and, usually, a couple of antique dealers – **Bobcaygeon** and **Fenelon Falls** are two that are worth dropping into if you're up this way. (The former also hosts a big fiddle contest each July.)

Nearby **Balsam Lake** is popular for swimming and fishing. In **Lindsay**, a more ordinary small town, don't miss the *Dutch Treat*, on Kent St, for excellent, cheap food – good homemade muffins and various treats. There's also a summer theatre programme.

At **Burleigh Falls**, who could resist a place called the *Lovesick Café*? It's a typical country shop with food, souvenirs, fishing tackle, etc. The date squares are recommended.

The district has some interesting parks as well. **Petroglyphs Provincial Park** has probably the best collection of prehistoric rock carvings in the country. Rediscovered in 1954, there are reportedly 900 figures and shapes carved into the park's limestone ridges. The portions of the collection which are easy to view are much smaller than the figure 900 might suggest, and though interesting, it is not an overwhelming site. The most visible have been enclosed to protect the rock from acid rain, a serious problem over much of Ontario. The area and small lake within the park remain important spiritual sites for the local Native Indians.

Serpent Mounds Provincial Park (☎ 295-6879) is the site of an ancient Native Indian burial ground. The **Warsaw Caves Conservation Area** contains tunnels eroded into limestone and walking trails.

Peterborough

Peterborough is a middle-sized town more or less at the centre of the Kawartha Lakes region. The older downtown area has some fine buildings; it's all very green, although the city seems in some danger of becoming a Toronto suburb. Trent University is another feature of the town's character.

The Trent-Severn Waterway passes through the large hydraulic-lift lock, a major landmark in town. A visitor centre shows how the locks along the system operate, and there is a working model. You can go on a trip through the locks into the Otonabee River or, if you're hooked, on a three or five-day cruise through the locks and along part of the system.

Canoeing is a popular activity. Possibilities include easy trips on the canal or, in spring, tougher whitewater trips on rivers in the area. From Peterborough, you can get to Serpent Mounds Provincial Park. Ask at the tourist office. The Ministry of Natural Resources publishes a map called *North Kawartha Canoe Routes*, which shows some possible trips and their portage distances.

Around Peterborough

South-east of Peterborough is **Century Village**, a pioneer village with costumed workers, demonstrations, and 20 buildings dating from 1820 to 1899.

A few km north is **Lakefield**, a small town with a co-educational school (formerly a boys' only school to which Queen Elizabeth II sent Prince Andrew).

About 900 Ojibway people live on 400-hectare **Curve Lake Indian Reserve**, roughly 34 km north of Peterborough. A trip to the reserve's Whetung Ojibway Arts & Crafts Gallery is worthwhile. The log building contains both new and old examples of Native Indian art and the museum section has traditional pieces and valuable works from such artists as Norval Morrisseau.

In the gallery area, newer articles created by Native Indian craftspeople from across the country are displayed. Many articles can be bought, including handmade jackets and baskets.

Lunch is available and you can sample a number of traditional Native Indian foods or try a buffalo burger. The reserve, established in 1825, is off Curve Lake Rd, which runs out of Hwy 507.

NORTH OF KAWARTHA LAKES

Continuing north you come to a less busy, less populated, hilly region known as the Haliburton Highlands. Hwy 507, leading up from Bobcaygeon through Catchacoma and Gooderham (which has a small waterfall), is perhaps the narrowest, oldest-looking highway in the province. It often looks more like a country lane.

Bancroft

A district centre, Bancroft is well known for its minerals and for the big gem festival held each August. Examples of 80% of the minerals found in Canada can be dug up in this area.

Combermere

On Hwy 62 north from Bancroft is the **Madonna House Pioneer Museum** (☎ 756-3713), 18 km south of Combermere.

Run by a lay religious group operating a cooperative farm, the museum has displays on the area's early settlers. An adjoining gift shop sells a range of items, with the profits going to charity.

Barry's Bay

The old lumber town is now a supply centre for the cottagers in the area around **Lake Kaminiskeg**. It's also pretty close to **Algonquin Park** and is on the main highway to Ottawa. Odd as it may seem, this is the centre for a sizeable Polish population, attracted to the hilly, green topography, which is much like that along the Baltic Sea in northern Poland. The town of **Wilno** in this area was the first Polish settlement in Canada. Nearby Killaloe, towards Ottawa, is a small centre for craftspeople and artisans.

The entire region has cottages for rent and lakeside resorts, but advance reservations are a very good idea. **Pembroke**, east at the Quebec border, is the nearest town of any size.

Toronto

Metropolitan Toronto (population 2.6 million) is the country's largest 'city', and it continues to grow, due mainly to its popularity with new immigrants who arrive from an ever-increasing number of disparate homelands.

The City of Toronto and its surrounding suburbs joined together to form the Municipality of Metropolitan Toronto, usually referred to as Metro. The City of Toronto forms the central part of Metro which consists of the cities of Etobicoke, Scarborough, North York, York and the Borough of East York.

The economic boom of the late 1980s saw Toronto become well entrenched as the nation's financial, communications and business capital as well as being a primary focus for English Canadian arts and culture. The recession of the early 1990s was (and continues to be) felt deeply but the city is not about to lose its prominence.

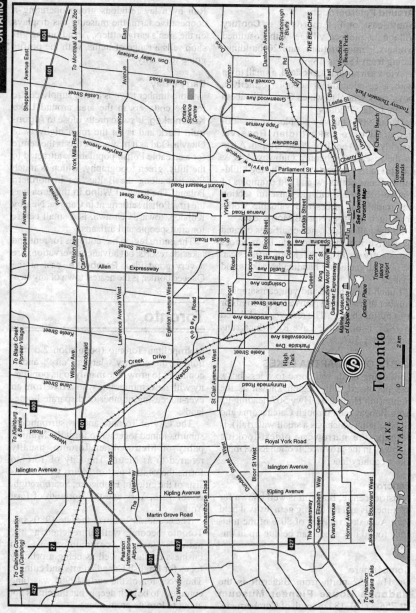

Two of the first things you'll notice about Toronto are the vibrancy and the cleanliness of the downtown area. These factors alone separate it from the bulk of large North American cities, but another great thing is that Toronto is safe. The streets are busy at night, with restaurants and entertainment places open and the downtown streetcars and subways generally used without hesitation. Of course, some prudence is always wise and women alone should take care after dark. There are some rougher parts of town, but these tend to be away from the centre and not where most visitors are likely to be.

There is a lot of central housing, part of an urban planning scheme which has kept a healthy balance between businesses and residences, making it a more livable city than many. Despite high costs, there are no areas of concentrated poverty. Toronto is one of the most expensive cities in North America in which to live, but fortunately this is not overly evident to visitors, for much of the cost is in real estate.

Throughout the city, various ethnic and immigrant groups have collected in fairly tight communities to form bustling, prosperous districts. These various neighbourhoods are one of the best and most distinctive aspects of the city and have helped to warm up what has been the rather stand-offish character of Toronto.

Toronto celebrated 150 years as a city in 1984 but has only recently attained its prominent stature and international attention. About 1970, the city scored points in its traditional rivalry with Montreal by surpassing it in size. Since this largely symbolic achievement, Toronto has grown in every way. It is the busiest Canadian port on the Great Lakes and is a major centre for banking, manufacturing and publishing. The Toronto Stock Exchange is one of North America's most important and the city is the provincial capital.

Tobacco lovers should know that Toronto has passed strict anti-smoking bylaws. Lighting up in virtually any indoor public place has been banned. Enforcement may prove to be more relaxed.

History

In the 17th century the Seneca Indians lived in this area. Étienne Brule, on a trip with Samuel de Champlain in 1615, was the first European to see the site. The Native Indians did not particularly relish the visit, and it wasn't until around 1720 that the French established a fur-trading post and mission in what's now the west end of the city.

After years of hostility with the French, the British took over. John Simcoe, lieutenant-governor of the new Upper Canada, chose Toronto as the capital in 1793 and it became known as York. Previously, Niagara-on-the-Lake had served as the capital.

During the War of 1812, the USA held York and burnt the Legislature. In retaliation, British forces headed towards Washington and burnt the US political headquarters. Apparently the burn marks were painted over in white, leading to the name the 'White House'.

In 1814, when the war ended, York began to expand. Stagecoach services began on Yonge St in 1828. In 1834, with William Lyon Mackenzie as the first mayor, York was renamed Toronto, a Native Indian name meaning 'meeting place'. During this time under conservative politicians, the city became known as 'Toronto the Good', a tag which only began to fade in the 1970s. Religious restraints and strong anti-vice laws (it was illegal to hire a horse on Sunday) were largely responsible for this. Not all that long ago, curtains were drawn in department-store windows on Sunday because window shopping was considered sinful, and movie theatres were also closed on the holy day.

Like many big cities, Toronto has had its great fire. In 1904 over five hectares of the inner city burned, levelling 122 buildings. Amazingly, no one was killed. The 1920s saw the first population boom, but in 1941 80% of the population was still Anglo-Celtic.

It was after WWII that the city began to change. Well over half-a-million immigrants have arrived since then, mainly Europeans. Italians make up the largest non-British ethnic group. The influx of new tongues, customs and food has livened up a place once thought to be a hopeless case.

With its staid background and some excellent urban planning, Toronto has developed cautiously. At least until the 1980s, when anyone with a shovel could break ground, construction has been regulated, with parks, housing and retail places generally being built alongside offices. Progressive and reactionary forces continue to do battle, the pendulum swinging first to one side and then the other. In general, for a city of its size and importance, Toronto remains conservative, particularly on moral issues, but perhaps this is the price to be paid for the benefits.

Orientation

The land around Toronto is flat and the city tends to sprawl over a large area. Despite its size, the city's grid-style layout, with nearly all the streets running north-south and east-west, means it's easy to get oriented.

Yonge St (pronounced Young), the main north-south artery, is called the longest street in the world – it runs about 18 km from Lake Ontario north to the city boundary, Steeles Ave, and beyond. The central downtown area is bounded by Front St to the south, Bloor St to the north, Spadina Ave to the west and Jarvis St to the east. Yonge St runs parallel to and in between Spadina Ave and Jarvis St, a few blocks from each of these. Street names change from 'East' to 'West' at Yonge St, and the street numbers begin there. Bloor St and College St (called Carlton St east of Yonge St), which is about halfway between Bloor St and the lake, are the two main east-west streets.

At the foot of Yonge St and nearby York St is the lake and the redeveloped waterfront area called Harbourfront. The old docks have given way to restaurants, theatres, galleries, artists' workshops, stores, condominiums and some parkland all along Queen's Quay. The ferries for the Toronto Islands moor here, as do many private vessels.

A few blocks north is Front St, where you'll find Union Station (the VIA Rail terminal), the classic old Royal York Hotel, and the Hummingbird Centre, a theatre for the performing arts. Two blocks west of Union Station is the CN Tower and, next door, Skydome, the vast sports stadium. East of the tower, the massive railway lands redevelopment project has begun with a park featuring the old railway roundhouse to open in 1997. About three or four blocks north of the Skydome, around Adelaide St West, Peter St and John St, there's a new and vibrant collection of small restaurants and nightclubs.

Heading north from Union Station on Bay St to Queen St, you'll hit Nathan Phillips Square, site of rallies and concerts and the unique City Hall buildings. To the east, the Victorian building dating from 1899 is the old City Hall, now used mainly for law courts. Check out the gargoyles.

One block east is Yonge St, lined with stores, bars, restaurants and theatres catering mainly to the young. North of the centre, along Yonge St and Eglinton Ave, is an enclave of upmarket stores and busy restaurants.

On Yonge St, between Dundas and Queen Sts, is the enormous modern shopping complex known as the Eaton Centre. The main tourist office is here, downstairs on level 1 by Eaton's the department store. Further east is an area known as Cabbagetown, a formerly run-down neighbourhood now renovated and trendy in sections but still retaining some of its earlier character. Go further east, along Danforth Ave west of Pape Ave, to explore the Greek area of town and some of Toronto's best restaurants.

On the west side of City Hall is Osgood Hall, home of the Law Society. Queen St West between University Ave and Spadina Ave and beyond to Bathurst St is busy with many restaurants and antique, book, record and distinctive clothing shops. A lot of young people involved in and on the fringes of the arts live in the area.

University Ave, lined with offices and trees, is Toronto's widest street and the location of most major parades. The lit beacon atop the stately Canada Life Building on the corner of University Ave and Queen St is a guide to the weather. The light at the top is colour-coded: green means clear, red means cloudy, flashing red means rain and flashing white means snow. If the tower lights are ascending, the temperature will rise; if they're descending it will cool. Temperatures are stable if the lights are on and static.

Toronto's busy Chinatown starts along Dundas St, west of Beverley St, and then runs both north and south along Spadina Ave. Interesting old Spadina Ave, once a strictly Jewish area, shares its remaining delis and textile shops with the burgeoning Oriental businesses. Dundas St and College St West are mainly Italian. Little Italy, west of Euclid along College St, has lots of outdoor cafes and is fast becoming one of Toronto's most popular spots for eating and being seen. The more established Italian district, Corso Italia, runs along St Clair Ave West between Dufferin St and Lansdowne Ave.

University Ave leads north to Queen's Park at College St. Here you'll find the provincial Parliament Buildings. To the west is the University of Toronto. North of the park the street is called Queen's Park Ave; it leads to Bloor St, where you'll find the city's principal museum, the Royal Ontario Museum.

Just north of Bloor St, between Avenue Rd (Queen's Park Ave) and Yonge St, fashionable, upmarket Yorkville Ave (and vicinity) was once the scene of the 1960s folk music and drug vanguard.

The city has been called Hollywood North and you may well come across one of a number of on-going movie shoots around town.

Toronto is served by expressways on all four sides. Along the lake, the Gardiner Expressway runs west into the Queen Elizabeth Way (QEW). The QEW goes to Niagara Falls. Just at the city's western border is Hwy 427, which runs north to the airport, and Hwy 401. Hwy 401 runs east-west above the downtown area, east to Montreal and west to Windsor, Ontario, which is opposite Detroit, USA. The often bumper to bumper segment of the 401 between Hwy 427 and Yonge St has been called the busiest stretch of road in North America after California's Santa Monica Freeway. On the eastern side of the city, the Don Valley Parkway connects Hwy 401 to the Gardiner Expressway at the southern edge of the city.

Information

Tourist Offices The Toronto Visitor Information Centre (☎ 203-2500 or 1-800-363-1990) has an office in the Queen's Quay terminal, down by the lake at Harbourfront between Yonge and York Sts. It's open all year from 9 am to 5 pm Monday to Friday. On weekends and holidays, someone will answer telephone questions. To get to the office, take the elevator (midway down the mall) up to the Galleria offices on level 5.

For information on other areas of Ontario as well as Toronto, the Ontario Travel Centre (☎ 314-0944, or 314-0956 for French speakers) is located on level 1 (two below street level) of the Eaton Centre (which is at 220 Yonge St, on the corner of Dundas St). It's open the same hours as the shopping centre, 10 am to 9 pm on weekdays, 9.30 am to 6 pm on Saturday and noon to 5 pm on Sunday. From outside Toronto call ☎ 1-800-668-2746 (English) or 1-800-268-3736 (French).

Money Currencies International (☎ 368-7945), at 120 Adelaide St West near Yonge St changes money and sells travellers' cheques. Branches of the Bank of Montreal and the Canadian Bank of Commerce can be found at the corner of Yonge and Queen Sts.

Post Mail can be picked up at General Delivery, 25 The Esplanade, Toronto M5W 1A0, Monday to Friday from 8 am to 5.45 pm. There's a good post office at 31 Adelaide St East and numerous postal outlets in chemists and stores around town.

The telephone area code for Toronto is 416.

Travel Agencies For the purchase of tickets around the country and out of Canada, Travel Cuts (Canadian University Travel Services) is recommended. It has six offices in town, the main one being central at 187 College St (☎ 979-2406). The staff will shop around for the best deal, and offer even better rates for young people (under age 26) and students. For the latter two groups, identification cards can be issued.

Alternatively, agencies such as the Last Minute Club (☎ 441-2582), which specialise in late sell-offs and the filling of flights and charters, may be worth a call. For flights to destinations such as Mexico or Florida, particularly during the Canadian winter, you could turn up a bargain.

Seeking out travel agencies in ethnic neighbourhoods can often turn up bargains back to the respective homelands.

The newspapers' classifieds, especially the weekly *Now Magazine,* also list tickets for sale.

Bookshops & Maps The World's Largest Bookstore at 20 Edward St, one block north of the Eaton Centre, is a browser's delight.

For travel books, guides, maps and a range of books on nature, camping and outdoor activities, see Open Air (☎ 363-0719), 25 Toronto St, near the corner of Adelaide St East and Yonge St; the door is downstairs off Toronto St.

Also selling maps, including a wide selection of topos, is Canada Map (☎ 362-9297), just around the corner from Open Air at 63 Adelaide St East.

The Great Canadian News Co in BCE Place at the corner of Yonge and Front Sts has newspapers from around the world and a vast periodical selection. Librarie champlain at 468 Queen St East is a good French bookstore.

Library The excellent Metropolitan Toronto Reference Library (☎ 393-7000) is at 789 Yonge St, about a block north of Bloor St on the east side.

Medical Services Central Toronto Hospital (☎ 340-4611), is at 22 Elizabeth St near University Ave.

CN Tower
The highest free-standing structure in the world, the CN Tower (☎ 360-8500) has become a symbol and landmark of Toronto. The tower is in the southern end of the city, near the lake, south of Front St West at John St. The top antenna was put in place by helicopter, making the tower 533 metres high. Its primary function is communica-

tions – radio and TV signals – but up at the top there is a restaurant, a disco and two observation decks. The one outside is windy, naturally, and not for those easily subject to vertigo. On a good, clear day you can see for about 160 km. On a hazy day, however, you won't be able to see a thing. If you want to go up keep an eye on the weather, or go up at night for a spectacular view of the city lights. It's also worth bearing in mind that during the height of summer you may have to queue for up to two hours – going up and down.

A glass elevator whisks you up the outside of the tower. And for extra thrills there is now a new glass floor section on the main observation deck – stand on it and sweat! Also new on the observation deck is EcoDek, a series of interactive video displays about the environment and our wilful destruction of it (the glass floor is more fun).

The cost of a trip up plus entry to the main observation deck is $12 for adults (you need to pay a further $3 to get to the top deck). If you're eating either lunch or dinner at the recently transformed 360 Revolving Restaurant (☎ 362-5411), the elevator ticket price is waived. Lunch prices start at $15, dinner prices at around $25. Sunday brunch is also offered. If you just want a drink in the bar (minimum $5) the elevator must be paid for.

The tower is open daily until 10 pm, an hour later on Saturday. The time and weather display at ground level is worth a look.

At the base of the tower are two separate attractions: Mindwarp, a flight simulator showing various surround-sound films and Q-Zar, a state-of-the-art laser game. Admission to each costs $8 for adults, $6.50 for children aged five to 12. A combination ticket for the tower, Mindwarp and Q-Zar costs $19.75 for adults. Both attractions are open from 10 am to 10 pm daily.

Other Views
For a pleasant and free view of the city, head to the rooftop bar of the Park Plaza Hotel. It's on the corner of Bloor St West and University Ave. You can sit under the sun at white wrought-iron tables and chairs and sip a cool

one 18 floors above the masses. It's open daily from 2.30 pm until 1 am.

The Aquarius Lounge, on the 51st floor of the Manulife Centre at 55 Bloor St West (on the corner of Bay St), is popular with a generally younger but mixed crowd. A beer costs around $4 up here. The lounge is open Monday to Saturday from noon to 1 am. The upmarket Canoe Bar & Restaurant, 54 floors up atop the Toronto Dominion Bank Tower at 66 Wellington St West (corner of Bay St), offers fine views from Monday to Friday.

Skydome

Beside the CN Tower, at 1 Blue Jay Way, this dome-roofed sports stadium (☎ 341-3663) was opened in 1989 and is best known for its fully retractable roof, the world's first such facility. The stadium, often referred to as simply the 'Dome', is used primarily for professional baseball and football but also stages concerts, trade shows and various other presentations.

Although not particularly eye-catching from the outside, the interior is strikingly impressive. It can be seen on the tours which are offered every day, on the hour, until 5 pm, events permitting. The tour is not cheap ($9). It's a bit rushed but quite thorough, offering a look at one of the box suites, the view from the stands and press section, a locker room (without athletes), a walk on the field and all sorts of informative statistics and tidbits of information. Did you know that eight 747s would fit on the playing field and that the stadium uses enough electricity to light the province of Prince Edward Island?

Another way to see the place (and a game) is via one of the three restaurants at the stadium (see the Places to Eat section). For those with money (lots of it), rooms can be rented in the adjacent Skydome Hotel, with rooms overlooking the playing field.

The hotel became instantly notorious when, during one of the first baseball games, a couple in one of the upper-field side rooms either forgetfully or rakishly became engaged in some sporting activity of their own with the lights on, much to the amusement of the crowd. Since then the hotel insists on signed waivers stipulating there will be no such free performances; party poopers.

A cheap-seat ticket ($6) to a Blue Jays baseball game is easily the least expensive way to see the Skydome. See the Spectator Sports section later for more information.

Royal Ontario Museum (ROM)

The multidiscipline museum (☎ 586-5551), on the corner of Queen's Park Ave and Bloor St West, is Canada's largest and has exhibits covering the natural sciences, the animal world, art and archaeology and, broadly, the history of humankind. The museum covers five floors, so a visit takes some time.

The collection of Chinese crafts, textiles and assorted arts is considered one of the best anywhere. The Egyptian, Greek, Roman and Etruscan civilisations are also represented. The newly designed dinosaur and mammalogy rooms are fascinating, with the latter containing a replica of part of an immense bat cave found in Jamaica. Another section outlines the history of trade between the East and West, from the ancient caravan routes through to more modern times. The bird gallery, with a huge stuffed albatross and numerous display cabinets with pull-out drawers to explore, is very good.

The SR Perron Gem & Gold Room (actually four octagonal rooms), displays a dazzling collection of riches, including the 193-carat Star of Lanka Sapphire, a 776-carat behemoth opal from Australia and handfuls of rubies, diamonds and gold nuggets. They are made all the more appealing by the unique fibre-optic lighting system. In addition to these permanent exhibits there are often in-depth touring exhibits – these are generally excellent but a surcharge is added to the admission fee.

The museum is open Monday to Saturday from 10 am to 6 pm, until 8 pm on Tuesday, and on Sunday from 11 am to 6 pm. Admission is $8 for adults, $4 for seniors and students, and is free on Tuesday from 4.30 pm until closing time. Family rates are also offered. The subway is close by (Museum stop), but if you're driving there is parking on Bedford Rd, west of Avenue Rd north of Bloor St.

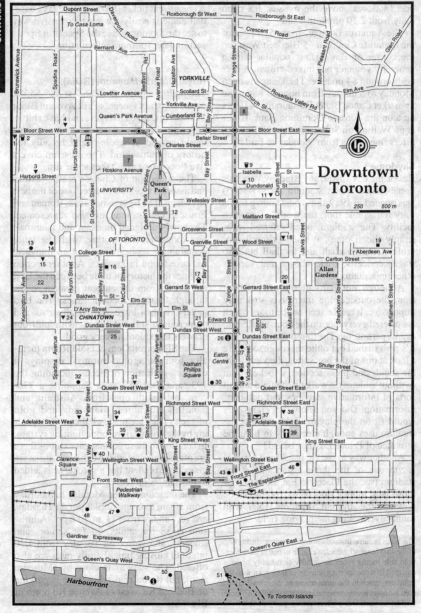

Downtown Toronto

YORKVILLE

UNIVERSITY

OF TORONTO

CHINATOWN

Nathan Phillips Square

Eaton Centre

Clarence Square

Pedestrian Walkway

Gardiner Expressway

Harbourfront

To Casa Loma

Allan Gardens

Queen's Park

To Toronto Islands

0   250   500 m

PLACES TO STAY

16 Beverley Place
17 HI Hostel
19 Aberdeen Guest House
20 Neill Wycik College Hotel
41 Royal York Hotel

PLACES TO EAT

1   Future Bakery
3   Kensington Kitchen
4   Master's Buffeteria
9   Artful Dodger
10 Health Haven
11 The Mango
15 Peter's Chung King
18 Le Baron Steak House
23 Pho Hung
24 Swatow
31 Queen Mother
33 Zupa's Deli
34 Zocalo
35 Old Ed's
38 Young Thailand
40 Wayne Gretzky's

OTHER

2   Brunswick Tavern
5   Bata Shoe Museum
6   Royal Ontario Museum
7   McLaughlin
    Planetarium
8   Metropolitan Toronto
    Reference Library
12 Parliament Buildings
13 Free Times Café
14 Silver Dollar Room
21 Bus Station
22 Kensington Market
25 Art Gallery of Ontario
26 Tourist Office
27 Pantages Theatre
28 Massey Hall
29 Elgin & Wintergarden Theatres
30 Old City Hall
32 Bamboo Club
36 Royal Alexandra Theatre
37 Post Office
39 St James Cathedral
42 VIA Rail Station
43 Hockey Hall of Fame
44 O'Keefe Centre
45 General Delivery PO
46 St Lawrence Market
47 CN Tower
48 Skydome
49 Queen's Quay Terminal,
    Tourist Office &
    Premiere Dance Theatre
50 York Quay Centre
51 Island Ferry Terminal

An annex to the museum is the **Canadian Decorative Arts Department**, down the street in the Sigmund Samuel Building, at 14 Queen's Park Crescent West. The focus is on Canada's early artists and craftspeople. It's open Monday to Saturday from 10 am to 5 pm and from 1 to 5 pm on Sunday. Admission is free.

A ticket to the ROM also permits free entry to the Gardiner Museum.

George R Gardiner Museum of Ceramic Art

At 111 Queen's Park Ave, this museum is part of the ROM just across the street. The collection is divided into four periods of ceramic history: pre-Columbian, Italian majolica from the 15th and 16th centuries, English delftware of the 17th century and English porcelain of the 18th century. The pottery from Mexico and Peru done before the arrival of Europeans is wonderful. It's quite an extensive collection spread over two floors. Admission costs $8 (which includes entry to the Royal Ontario Museum) and opening hours are 10 am to 5 pm Tuesday to Saturday and 11 am to 5 pm Sunday.

Art Gallery of Ontario (AGO)

This is one of the top three art galleries in the country (☎ 977-0414), the others being in Ottawa and Montreal. Though not the Louvre, it is excellent, and unless you have a lot of stamina, you'll need more than one trip to see it all. The gallery houses works (mainly paintings) from the 14th century to the present. There is also a Canadian section and rooms for changing exhibitions, which can sometimes be the highlight of a visit. The gallery is best known for its vast Henry Moore sculpture collection – one room holds about 20 of his major sculptures of the human form.

The gallery is at 317 Dundas St West, two blocks west of University Ave. There is a restaurant if you need a break and an excellent shop selling books, posters, crafts and jewellery. At the door, pick up a schedule of the films, lectures, performances and concerts that go on in the gallery.

ONTARIO

From May to October the gallery is open from 10 am to 5.30 pm Tuesday to Sunday (until 10 pm on Wednesday). From October to May it's closed Monday and Tuesday. It's open on holiday Mondays throughout the year.

Admission is a rather steep $7.50, students and seniors $4, but entry is free to all on Wednesday evening from 5 pm. Seniors get in free on Friday too.

Cinémathèque Ontario (☎ 923-3456) regularly screens quality cinema from around the world in the gallery's Jackman Hall.

The Grange The Grange (☎ 977-0414) is a restored Georgian house adjoining the AGO (from the Art Gallery, there is a door down in the basement, beside the cafeteria). Admission is included with the gallery ticket. Authentic 19th-century furniture and workers in period dress represent life in a 'gentleman's residence' of the time. Hours are noon to 4 pm Tuesday to Sunday and until 9 pm on Wednesday. The Grange looks onto a pleasant city park where Chinese people do their early morning Tai Chi.

Bata Shoe Museum
Designed to resemble a large and very stylish lidded shoebox, Toronto's brand new Bata Shoe Museum (☎ 979-7799) has more to offer than you might imagine. Beginning with a set of footprints almost four million years old, and incorporating some neat interactive displays, the general All About Shoes exhibit provides a fascinating look at human history and culture. From the gruesome to the gorgeous, every type of footwear imaginable is there (Imelda Marcos eat your heart out). Upstairs there's a detailed look at 19th century women's shoes and an excellent exhibit devoted to the central role of bootmaking in Inuit culture.

Located at 327 Bloor St West, opposite the St George subway, the museum is open from 10 am to 5 pm Tuesday to Saturday (until 8 pm Thursday) and from noon to 5 pm Sunday. Admission is $6 and it's free on the first Tuesday of every month.

Casa Loma
This is a 98-room medieval-style castle-cum-mansion built between 1911 and 1914 by Sir Henry Pellat, a very wealthy and evidently eccentric man. The mansion (☎ 923-1171) has been a tourist site since 1937, when the cost of upkeep became too much for its owner. The interior is sumptuous, built with the finest materials imported from around the world. Note especially the conservatory. Pellat even brought in stonemasons from Scotland to build the walls around the estate.

In summer, the 2.5 hectares of restored gardens behind the castle are worth a visit in themselves. This area is open to the public (without the need to buy a ticket to the castle) on the first Monday of each month and every Tuesday from 4 pm to dusk.

At Christmas time, elaborate thematic indoor exhibits are put on, geared mainly to children.

Casa Loma is open every day from 10 am to 4 pm. A ticket costs $8 and parking at the site is pricey. If you're lucky, you may find a spot in the surrounding neighbourhood; alternatively, consider using the subway; the Dupont subway station is within walking distance. The address is 1 Austin Terrace, off Spadina Ave. From the corner of Dupont and Bathurst Sts, it can be clearly seen, perched impressively above its surroundings.

Provincial Parliament Buildings
The attractive pinkish sandstone Legislature (☎ 325-7500) sits in Queen's Park, just north of College St on University Ave. The stately building was completed in 1892 and is kept in superb condition. Free tours are given frequently throughout the day, Monday to Friday until 3.30 pm. For some home-grown entertainment, head for the visitors' gallery when parliament is in session (roughly from October to December and February to June).

City Hall
In Nathan Phillips Square, on the corner of Queen and Bay Sts, this distinctive three-part building (☎ 392-7341) represented the beginning of Toronto's becoming a grown-

up city. It was completed in 1965 to Finnish architect Viljo Revell's award-winning design. The twin clamshell towers, with a flying saucer-style structure between them at the bottom, are unmistakable. Free tours are given throughout the day. The square out the front is a meeting place and the location for concerts, demonstrations and office-worker lunches.

In winter the attractive fountain pool becomes a popular artificial skating rink. Rental skates are available until 10 pm daily. It's a lot of fun; don't feel intimidated if you are a novice – you won't be alone. Immigrants from around the world are out there gingerly making strides towards assimilation.

Ontario Science Centre

The science centre (☎ 696-3127) has an interesting assortment of scientific and technological exhibits and demonstrations, most of which you can take part in. It's a museum where you can touch everything. You might even learn something, although it's best for children (but be warned, on weekends there are hundreds of them).

The approachable yet detail-conscious Living Earth exhibit includes a simulated rainforest, a limestone cave and an ocean ecosystem designed to encourage respect, knowledge and awe for the real thing.

The Information Highway, the centre's latest exhibit, allows you to explore the Internet and take a look at virtual reality. There is also a new theatre for the large-format OMNIMAX films.

To get to the science centre, which is located in a small ravine on the corner of Eglinton Ave East and Don Mills Rd, take the subway to Eglinton, transfer to the Eglinton East bus and get off at Don Mills Rd. The centre is open from 10 am to 6 pm daily. Admission is $7.50 for adults, $3 for children aged five to 10, and parking is $4. Family, youth and senior rates are available. On Wednesday night it remains open to 8 pm and is free from 4 pm until closing time, parking included.

City Neighbourhoods

Toronto has a wide variety of ethnic groups, some concentrated in neighbourhoods which offer outsiders glimpses of foreign cultures. Such areas are good for restaurants, and several are mentioned in the Places to Eat section. Other neighbourhoods are mixed areas that preserve a distinctive character. Descriptions of a few of the most prominent districts follow.

Chinatown Toronto has by far the largest (and growing) Chinese population in the country, and the principal Chinatown area is right in the centre of town. The original old area runs along Dundas St from Bay St, by the bus station, west to University Ave. There are many restaurants here, but this area has become rather touristy and isn't really where the local Chinese shop.

The bigger and more interesting segment of Chinatown is further west. Also on Dundas St West, it runs from Beverley St, near the Art Gallery, to Spadina Ave and a little beyond. Most of Spadina Ave, from south of Dundas St all the way north to College St and then east and west for a bit along College St, is now primarily Chinese.

Again there are lots of restaurants, but also variety and grocery stores, jobbers, herbalists, bakeries and places selling things recognisable only to the initiated. In addition to all the businesses, vendors often set up along the sidewalks. The area gets packed on weekends, when it's sharp with sounds and smells and the restaurants do good business. There are a few Japanese and more and more Vietnamese places in the neighbourhood.

There's a smaller, but equally busy, pocket of Chinese merchants and restaurants around Gerrard St and Broadview Ave in the city's east end.

Rosedale One of the city's wealthiest areas is just north-east of the corner of Yonge and Bloor Sts. Driving or walking up Sherbourne St, north of Bloor St, leads to Elm Ave where nearly every house on the north side is listed by the Historical Board as being of architectural or historical note. All the streets

ONTARIO

branching from Elm Ave contain some
impressive domains, however. East along
Elm Ave, Craigleigh Gardens is a small and
elegant old park.

Cabbagetown This district, east of Parliament St, was settled by Irish immigrants
fleeing the potato famine of 1841 and
became known as Cabbagetown because the
sandy soil of the area provided ideal growing
conditions for cabbages. It's now both a residential district (ranging from poor to
comfortable) and a commercial district. As
well as the differences between its denizens,
the area is distinguished primarily by its
19th-century Victorian terrace houses: possibly the richest concentration of fine
Victorian architecture in North America.

The last couple of decades has seen considerable gentrification of the once run-
down area. It's worth a stroll to peek at some
of the beautifully renovated houses and their
carefully tended gardens.

Cabbagetown is bounded roughly by
Gerrard St East to the south, Wellesley St to
the north, Parliament St to the west (which
is the main business centre) and Sumach St
to the east.

The necropolis off Sumach St at Winches-
ter St is one of the city's oldest and most
interesting cemeteries. Across the street is
Riverdale Farm, a popular place for families
and kids. It's run as a real working farm, with
two barns to wander through and a selection
of waterfowl and animals, some of which
may permit a pat or two. It's a good place to
start a walking tour of the area.

The Danforth In the east end of town along
Danforth Ave, roughly between Pape and
Woodbine Aves, is a large Greek community.
Often called The Danforth, this has become
one of the city's most popular dining areas,
and warm summer nights in particular bring
out serious crowds. There are many restaurants, a few smoky men's cafes, and also
some big, busy, colourful fruit, vegetable and
flower stores which stay open into the night.

Little India Also out this way is Little India,

with numerous speciality stores, women in
saris and the scent of spices in the air. There
is also a handful of restaurants here, some
with very cheap prices. It's along Gerrard St
East, one block west of Coxwell Ave.

Corso Italia Italians, in number, are found in
many parts of the city, but if there is one
centre of the community it's probably on St
Clair Ave West, east and west of the Dufferin
St intersection. Here you'll find Italian
movies, espresso cafes and pool halls. A
secondary Italian area known as Little Italy,
on College St west of Euclid Ave, is a good
and trendier spot filling up fast with outdoor
cafes and small restaurants.

Nearby is a Portuguese neighbourhood,
based along Dundas St West between
Ossington and Dufferin Sts.

Yorkville Once Toronto's small version of
Greenwich Village or Haight-Ashbury, this
old counter-cultural bastion has become the
city's expensive boutique area. The district
is central, just above Bloor St between Yonge
St and Avenue Rd. It's centred around Cumberland St, Yorkville Ave and Hazelton Ave.
Along the narrow, busy streets are many art
galleries, cafes, restaurants, nightspots and
glamorous shops. The boutiques of the
enclosed Hazelton Lanes Shopping Centre
are some of the most exclusive in the
country.

The whole swish area can be pleasant in
summer for its outdoor cafes and people-
watching. It's worth a stroll but the pretension and snobbery can grate.

Still, there are some intriguing shops and
the galleries present a range of work, several
displaying or selling Inuit pieces (for big
dollars). The Inuit Gallery on Prince Arthur
Ave specialises in Inuit art.

To linger, the Bellair Café has long maintained its position as the place to go (but at
$7.50 for a glass of wine, you might want to
linger elsewhere).

Markham Village As you approach the
corner of Bloor and Markham Sts (one block
west of Bathurst St), you'll see Toronto's

most colourful, gaudy store: the zany Honest Ed's. Giant signs say things like 'Don't just stand there, buy something'. Hardly subtle but you won't believe the queues outside the door before opening time. Most patrons are from the nearby Italian and Portuguese districts. There are some good buys – cheap running shoes, T-shirts and various household necessities. With the money Eddie Mirvish has made, he's established quite a reputation and become a major patron of the arts. Markham St south from Bloor St, with its galleries, boutiques and bookshops, is mostly his or his son's doing.

There are some interesting little specialised import shops to browse in. The Mirvish bookshop has good sales on Sunday. Bloor St around this area is fun to stroll along, with numerous restaurants and bars, patronised mostly by a mix of students and immigrants.

Harbourfront

Harbourfront is a strip of lakefront land running from the foot of Bay St westward to roughly Bathurst St. Once a run-down district of old warehouses, factories and under used docklands, the area was originally slated for redevelopment, primarily as parkland but with people and arts-oriented halls, theatres, galleries and workshops, etc included. Although this has happened to some degree, it is now generally acknowledged that construction was allowed to run amok and too much of the waterfront has been blighted by ugly condos.

For visitors, the centre of activity is the attractive York Quay, at 235 Queen's Quay, where there's a tourist information office. Nearby is the du Maurier Theatre and Molson Place, a covered outdoor concert venue. There's a performance of some sort happening nearly every night and some presentations are free. For information on Harbourfront events call ☎ 973-3000. There are also a couple of nearby restaurants and a place or two for a drink. Boat tours depart from the shore here and many private boaters moor around the area.

Just to the east is the impressive looking Queen's Quay terminal, with the green glass top. It's a refurbished 1927 warehouse containing some interesting speciality and gift shops, restaurants, the Premier Dance Theatre and, up above, offices and apartments.

Contemporary art is displayed in the Power Plant, an old power station near Queen's Quay.

On weekends the area is popular for a walk along the pier or a browse in the antique and junk market. Try the French fries from one of the many chip wagons. The Canoe School rents canoes, which can be used for an enjoyable paddle out around the harbour.

To visit Harbourfront, first get to Union Station, the train station on Front St, a few blocks north of the lake. The subway will take you this far south. From here, either walk south on Yonge St or take the LRT streetcar which goes south, running along the Harbourfront area on Queen's Quay to Spadina Ave and then returning the same way. Service is continuous through the day and evening. Parking in the area can be a headache and/or costly, so seriously consider public transport.

Toronto Islands

From the foot of Bay St near the Harbour Castle Hotel, you can take a 10-minute ferry ride out to the three Toronto Islands: Ward, Centre and Hanlan's Point. Once mainly residential, the islands are now largely public park and are very pleasant – particularly since there are no cars! Centre Island has the most facilities, many summer events and the most people. Boats can be rented, and there is a small animal farm and an amusement area for kids. Beaches line the southern and western shores, and there are two licensed restaurants and some snack bars.

Hanlan's, to the west, is the best beach. You may see some nude sunbathing at Hanlan's south-western end – it's popular with homosexuals – but this is illegal, even though the law is only sporadically enforced. Inland from the beach are picnic tables and some barbecue pits. Towards the city, on Hanlan's Point, is a small airport.

Ward Island, the one on the east side, still has quite a few houses inhabited all year. There is a small restaurant here for snacks and light lunches out on the lawn.

A ferry ride is as good as a harbour tour and offers good views of the city. Ferries (☎ 392-8193) to the islands run frequently in summer and cost $3 return, less for children and seniors. You can walk around the islands in under two hours. The cool breezes are great on a hot, sticky day, and it's pretty quiet during the week. Cycling along the islands' boardwalk on the southern shores isn't a bad way to spend some time. You can take bicycles on some of the ferries or rent them on Centre Island.

Because there is a year-round community living on Ward Island, the ferries run through the winter (though less frequently) and between September and May service only Ward. The other islands can be reached on foot, but note that pretty much everything else on the islands is shut tight. Good thing, too, because the winter wind over here is none too hospitable.

Ontario Place

This 40-hectare recreation complex (☎ 314-9900) is built on three artificial islands offshore from the CNE grounds, 955 Lake Shore Blvd West. Entrance to the site is free but almost all activities and attractions must be paid for separately. The futuristic buildings and parkland contain about a dozen restaurants, beer gardens, the new Molson Amphitheatre and an IMAX cinema (the Cinesphere), where 70-mm films are shown on a six-storey-high curved screen. Check what film is showing; the effects can be amazing. There is also a large, free, popular play area for kids where you can just let them go nuts. A water park with slides, a wading pool and other water activities has an admission fee. Or, for those at a loose end, there is a bungee jump.

In summer there are nightly concerts at the amphitheatre, with everything from ballet to rock. At the western end is another stage with a waterfall as a curtain, where amateurs or lesser names perform free shows. Nearby is

the 700-metre-long flume water slide with simulated rapids and tunnels.

Moored off one of the islands is the *Haida*, a destroyer, which is open to visitors.

The park is open from mid-May to October from 10.30 am to 1 am (until midnight on Sunday). If there is a concert you really want to see or the act is a big name, arrive early (or even better, very early with a picnic dinner). The price of the concerts varies from $5 to $15. The IMAX prices are $6 to $9. If you are driving, parking is a whopping $9. Take a subway or streetcar to Bathurst St and then the streetcar south down Bathurst St to the CNE exhibition grounds. Over the summer months a shuttle bus runs from Union Station to the gate of Ontario Place and back frequently through the day. Take a sweater, even on a hot day it gets cold at night down by the water.

High Park

The city's biggest park is popular for picnics, walking, cycling and jogging. There is a small children's zoo, a lake where people fish in the summer and skate in the winter and a pool for swimming (which is free). Some parts of the park are manicured; other bits are left as natural woods. No cars are allowed on summer weekends.

Also in the park is **Colborne Lodge**, built by one of Toronto's first architects and now run as an historical site with costumed workers. It's open daily.

Not far from the swimming pool, on the main road through the park, is a restaurant which serves a vast selection of quite good homemade meals at low prices. The park is off Bloor St West at Parkside Drive and runs south down to Lake Shore Blvd, west of the CNE. The subway stop is either Keele or High Park.

Tommy Thompson Park & the Port

Formerly called and often still known as the Leslie St Spit, this artificial landfill site is presided over by the Metro Toronto Conservation Authority (☎ 661-6600). It extends out into the lake and has unexpectedly become a phenomenal wildlife success. It was designed to improve and develop shipping facilities but within a few years became the second largest ring-billed seagull nesting place in the world. Terns and other bird species nest here too, and you may spot many more types which drop by.

The area, a narrow five-km-long strip, is open to the public on weekends and holidays. Some construction work is still going on and marinas have been built on portions of it. The park is south of the corner of Queen St East and Leslie St, on the corner of Unwin Ave and Leslie St.

From April to October a free shuttle bus runs from the nearest bus stop, on Leslie St at Commissioners Rd (about three long blocks from the main gate), through the gate at the spit and down about half way. It runs every half-hour from 9 am to 5 pm. At the far end (named Vicki Keith Point after a local long-distance swimmer), out by the eastern edges of the Toronto Islands, there is a lighthouse and views to the city. The park closes at 6 pm. No vehicles are permitted, but many people use bicycles – the Martin Goodman Recreational Trail runs by in both directions.

At the gate there is a map and a bird checklist. Occasional portable toilets can be found along the main path. Although some small sections are wooded, note that there is very little shade, so be prepared in midsummer. Check the schedule at the gate for the free guided walks, which often have an ornithological (birding) or photography angle.

At the foot of industrial Cherry St, connected to Leslie St by Unwin St, the sandy, relatively quiet, poseur-free beach is popular with windsurfers and those seeking a cool breeze on hot days. There's a snack bar, a few barbecues among the trees and some walking paths along the shoreline.

The Port of Toronto is further north along Cherry St towards Lake Shore Blvd. Freighters can be seen moored along the docks, but you can't get very close and there is no public access or viewing station. Off Cherry St, there is a small park at the end of Poulson St from where there is a fine view of the harbour, the islands and the city skyline.

The Beaches & the Bluffs

The Beaches is a rather wealthy, mainly professional neighbourhood along Queen St East at Woodbine Ave, down by the lakeshore. For those who are not local residents, The Beaches means the beach itself and the parkland along the lake. The sandy beaches are good for sunbathing and picnicking, and for strolling, a three-km boardwalk edges the sand. There's also a paved path for cycling and roller-skating. Water quality inhibits swimmers. You can rent sailboards, with or without lessons, and Sports Rent (☎ 694-7368), at 2210 Queen St East, has bicycles, canoes and roller-skates for hire. At the west end, in Woodbine Beach Park, there's an excellent Olympic-size public swimming pool. There are quite a few places to eat nearby along Queen St East. For some tasty halibut try *Nova Fish and Chips* at No 2209. To get to The Beaches jump on a Queen St streetcar.

About five km further east are the Scarborough Bluffs, limestone cliffs set in parkland at the lake edge. Erosion has created some odd shapes and has revealed layers of sediment that indicate five different glacial periods. There are paths here with good views over the lake. Below, in the lake itself, landfill has been used to form parkland, Bluffers Park, and boat-mooring space. To access Bluffers Park turn south off Kingston Rd at Brimley Rd.

If you want to be atop the cliffs (and you do), there are several parks which afford excellent views of the bluffs and panoramas of Lake Ontario. To reach one area worth visiting, for those with vehicles, turn south of Kingston Rd onto Scarboro Crescent and then Drake Crescent. Park here; the bluffs are within walking distance. Another excellent vantage point at the highest section of the bluffs (about 98 metres high) is at Cathedral Bluffs Park. Still further east along Kingston Rd, turn south at Cathedral Bluffs Drive.

Not far (by vehicle) east of the park is the Guild Inn, with its large lakefront grounds and good views along the shoreline. In the garden is a collection of sculptures, columns and gargoyles rescued from condemned

ONTARIO

buildings. Tea is served on the patio in the afternoon. The Guild Inn is on Guildwood Parkway, south from Kingston Rd at Livingstone Rd.

Other Parks

Allan Gardens is an often-mentioned park that's rather over-rated. Bounded by Carlton, Jarvis and Gerrard Sts, most of it is nothing more than a city block of grass interspersed with a few trees and benches. The highlight is the large, old, round-domed greenhouse filled with huge palms and flowering trees from around the world. It's open daily from 10 am to 5 pm and is free. After dark, the entire place is unsavoury enough not to be recommended and that includes even taking a short cut through the park.

Just around the corner from Yonge St, west a few doors on Adelaide St West is a tiny **inner city park** that provides a sanctuary in the downtown centre. Built vertically as a 'modernist ruin' this park was to be part of the 57-storey Adelaide-Bay Centre. Ironically, the recession put the project on hold in 1992 and only the garden, with its exposed steel, creeping vines, waterfall and mural to construction workers, was completed.

Though short on city parks, Toronto does have some substantial, largely natural parks in numerous ravines formed by rivers and streams running down to the lake. Start in **Edwards Gardens**, on the corner of Lawrence Ave East and Leslie St. It's a big, cultivated park with flower gardens, a pond and picnic sites. You can take a ravine walk from the gardens via **Wilket Creek Park**. The Science Centre backs onto the park here. Along Wilket Creek you can walk for hours all the way down to Victoria Park Ave, just north of Danforth Ave. Much of the way is through woodland.

From the corner of Yonge St and St Clair Ave, walk east to the bridge and the sign for the nature trail. This leads down into the **Don River Valley**, another good walk.

Markets

The city's prime one, **Kensington Market** is a colourful and lively multicultural, old-style

market squeezed along Baldwin St and Augusta Ave off Spadina Ave, just south of College St and east of Bathurst St. It's open daily but is busiest on Saturday morning. The cheese shops are good, and there's all manner of fresh fruit and vegetables. You can bargain over prices. This was the heart of the city's Jewish area, but as you'll see, people from many countries have changed that. There are some excellent restaurants in the area, too. On Saturday, don't even think of driving down here.

The **St Lawrence Market** is at 92 Front St East (at Jarvis St) in what was Toronto's first City Hall, dating from 1844. Here nearly all the shoppers are of British ancestry and the atmosphere is closer to sedate – there may even be classical musicians playing. Although it's best on Saturday, it is open every day but Monday. The range and quality of produce – from fish to more rice varieties than you knew existed – is superb. On Sunday there is an antique and flea market here.

Just north of the old City Hall building is **St Lawrence Hall**, topped with its clock tower. It is one of the city's finest old buildings; used as a public meeting hall in the last century, it is now, among other things, the venue for National Ballet rehearsals.

The **Market Gallery** on the 2nd floor of the market building, is the city's exhibition hall and displays good, rotating shows (paintings, photographs, documents, artefacts) on Toronto's history. It's free, but is closed on Monday, Tuesday and holidays.

The Harbourfront **Antique Market**, at 390 Queen's Quay West, features 100 shops selling collectibles. It's open Tuesday to Sunday with an additional outdoor section on Sunday.

Two major health-food stores are the Big Carrot Natural Food Market, 348 Danforth Ave, and the more central Baldwin Natural Foods, at 20 1/2 Baldwin St.

Historic Sites

There isn't a lot for history buffs, as the city is so new, but the few small sites are well presented and the tourist office has a guide to the historic homes and sites. Many of these remaining old buildings stand where the old town of York was situated – in the southern portion of the city. Descriptions of some of the best sites follow. See also The Grange, listed after the Art Gallery of Ontario earlier.

Fort York The fort (☎ 392-6907) was established by the British in 1793 to protect the town, which was then called York. It was largely destroyed at the end of the 1812 War but was quickly rebuilt. Now restored, it has eight original log, stone and brick buildings. In summer, men decked out in 19th-century British military uniforms carry out marches and drills, and fire musket volleys. The fort is open every day, all year, from 9.30 am to 5 pm. Admission is $5 for adults, less for kids and seniors. Free tours are given on the hour, to 4 pm. It's on Garrison Rd, which runs off Fleet St West (which in turn is near the corner of Bathurst and Front Sts). Take the streetcar south on Bathurst St.

Mackenzie House Owned by William Lyon Mackenzie, the city's first mayor and the leader of a failed rebellion against the government, this mid-Victorian home (☎ 392-6915) is furnished with 19th-century antiques. In the basement is an old print shop where (it's said) the machines can be heard mysteriously working some nights. The house is at 82 Bond St, a couple of blocks east of Yonge St, near Dundas St East. It's open daily (afternoon only on Sunday) and admission is $3.50.

Spadina House This was the gracious mansion (☎ 392-6910) of local businessman James Austin. Built in 1866, the impressive interior contains fine furnishings and art collected over three generations. About 10 of its 35 rooms are open to the public. The family gave the house to the historical board in 1982. The address is 285 Spadina Ave, just east of Casa Loma, and it's open daily (but only in the afternoon on Sunday and holidays). Admission is $5.

Campbell House Downtown on the corner of Queen St and University Ave, this house

(☎ 597-0227) was once the residence of the chief justice of Upper Canada. It is a colonial-style brick mansion furnished in early 19th century fashion. The house is open daily (afternoons only on weekends) and admission is $3.

Colborne Lodge Situated in High Park, the lodge (☎ 392-6916), built in 1836, is a Regency-style cottage and contains many original furnishings, including possibly the first indoor flush toilet in the province. Informative tours are offered by the costumed staff and may include baking or craft demonstrations. In summer it's open Monday to Saturday from 9.30 am to 5 pm, and on Sunday from noon to 5 pm. Admission is $3.50.

Gibson House This Georgian-style house (☎ 395-7432) which belonged to a successful surveyor and politician offers a glimpse of daily life in the 1850s. Costumed workers demonstrate crafts and cooking and offer a tour around the house daily except Monday. Special activities are planned regularly through the year. On weekends it's only open in the afternoons. It's not far from the Sheppard subway stop in the far northern part of the city, at 5172 Yonge St north of Sheppard Ave. Admission is $2.50.

Churches The Anglican **Church of the Holy Trinity** (☎ 598-4521), hidden right downtown in behind the Eaton Centre on Trinity Square, is one of a kind. It's a funky, welcoming cross between a house of worship and a drop-in centre – everything a community oriented inner-city church should be. Opened in 1847, it was the first church in the city not to charge parishioners for pews. And it's been going its own way ever since. Don't miss the wonderful Christmas pageant tradition if you're in town in December. There is no charge (a donation is suggested) but tickets are required – call for information.

On the corner of King and Church Sts, the town's first church was built, in 1807. **St James' Cathedral**, built in 1853, now stands here, and is the country's tallest church. Nearby, on the corner of Queen and Parliament Sts, the first Catholic church was constructed in 1822. On this site, a second **St Paul's Anglican Church** now stands, one of Toronto's most impressive Renaissance-style buildings.

Montgomery's Inn Built in 1832 by an Irish military captain of the same name, Montgomery's Inn (☎ 394-8113) is a fine example of Loyalist architecture and has been restored to the period from 1830 to 1855. Afternoon tea is served, and costumed staff answer questions, bake bread and demonstrate crafts. Open daily (afternoons only on weekends and holidays), it's at 4709 Dundas St West, near Islington Ave, in the city's far western end. Admission is $2.50.

Enoch Turner Schoolhouse The school (☎ 863-0010) dates from 1848. It's a restored, simple, one-room schoolhouse where kids are shown what the good old days were like. It was opened as the first free school so that the children of poorer citizens could learn the three Rs. You can visit it, free, when classes or other special events are not being held – call ahead and check the schedule. The address is 106 Trinity St, which is near the corner of King and Parliament Sts.

Post Office Toronto's first post office, dating from the 1830s, is at 260 Adelaide St East. One of only two original city buildings remaining in its original location (the other is the Bank of Upper Canada), it has been designated a National Historic Site. Letters can still be sealed with wax by costumed employees and sent from here. It's open seven days a week.

University of Toronto The principal campus of the large, prestigious university is just west of the Queen's Park Parliament Buildings, off College St at University Ave. The attractive grounds feature a range of architectural styles, from the University College building of 1859 to the present. Free walking tours of the campus are given on

weekdays through the summer months, departing from Hart House three times daily (weather permitting).

Other Historic Sites Todmorden Mills Historic Site, near the location of an important 1794 sawmill and gristmill on the Don River, preserves two houses, complete with period furnishings, and a brewery dating from around 1825. Also on the site is a train station (now a small railway museum) and a former paper mill (now used as a playhouse). The park is at 67 Pottery Rd and is open daily (except Monday) from May to December. A small admission fee is charged.

The large, red-brick houses found all over downtown Toronto were built around the 1920s. The taller, narrower ones, often with more ornately decorative features, are Victorian and mostly date from 1890 to 1900 – a few are older.

Black Creek Pioneer Village

A replica of an Ontario village a century ago, Black Creek Pioneer Village (☎ 736-1733) is the city's top historic attraction. It's about a half-hour drive from the downtown area, on the corner of Steeles Ave and Jane St in the north-west section of town, and is accessible by public transport.

Restored buildings and workers in authentic dress give a feeling of what rural life was like in the 19th century. Crafts and skills of the times are demonstrated, using the old tools and methods. One reader raved about the herb garden. You can buy the results of the cooking and baking. In one of the barns is a large toy museum and a woodcarving collection. It's open daily from May to December. Adult admission is $7.50. Special events are offered regularly through the season. There is parking, which is free – a rarity in Toronto, as you know by now.

Toronto Zoo

This huge zoo (☎ 392-5900), with an excellent reputation, is one of the country's largest and best and continues to expand. There are around 5000 animals on the 283 hectares, some in natural-setting pens the size of football fields. Of course, with enclosures so large, it takes a lot of leg work to see it. There is a small train that goes around the site, but walking is best. You need a full day to see it all.

The animals are in five areas, each covering a major world geographical zone. There are outdoor sections, as well as simulated climates in indoor pavilions. A good idea is the black-light area that enables you to observe nocturnal animals. Other good exhibits include those which allow for underwater viewing of beavers, polar bears and seals. One area has displays especially geared to children, with some animals to touch and ponies to ride.

The zoo is on Meadowvale Rd, north of Hwy 401, at the eastern edge of the city. To get there using public transport, take the subway on the Bloor St line east to Kennedy, the last stop. From there get the No 86A Scarborough bus to the zoo. It's quite a trip – about 20 minutes on the subway from the centre of town and then about 40 minutes on the bus, plus waiting time.

Admission is $9.95, less for kids. Parking is $5. It's open daily in summer from 9 am to 7.30 pm, and in winter from 9.30 am to 4.30 pm. Call for the current schedule.

You may want to take your lunch, as McDonald's has an exclusive food contract for the grounds.

Paramount Canada's Wonderland

Wonderland (☎ 905-832-7000) is a sort of Canadian Disneyland. The large-scale $120 million theme park has over 50 rides, including some killer roller coasters (the latest is a looping inverted jet coaster which travels at 90 km/h). There are also live shows, a five-hectare water park and loads of Hanna Barbera characters wandering around.

Covering 150 hectares, the park can't all be seen in one day. Get a guidebook at the entrance and decide what you want to see the most. Prices vary but are not low. A one-day pass, good for all attractions and rides, is $31. ($15.45 for seniors and children under seven). Straight admission to the grounds is $18. Parking is another $6. Top-name enter-

tainers appear in summer at the Kingswood Theatre; tickets for these shows cost extra. The park is open from approximately early June to early September, and on weekends a month before and after these dates. Opening hours are 10 am to 10 pm in peak season.

Wonderland is away from the centre of town, on Hwy 400, 10 minutes' drive north of Hwy 401. Exit at Rutherford Rd if you're travelling north, at Major Mackenzie Drive if you're going south. There are buses from Yorkdale and York Mills subway stations.

Wildwater Kingdom

Open daily from June to September, this huge water park (☎ 369-9453) offers about half a dozen twisting water slides and a couple of steep, high, straight speed slides, along with a wave pool and massive whirlpools. There are picnic grounds and food concessions. An all-day ticket is $15.88, less for kids. The park is 1.6 km west of Hwy 427 on Finch Ave, north-west of the centre of Toronto. On the grounds is a sports complex, with activities available on a pay-as-you-play basis.

Museum for Textiles

Obscurely situated with no walk-in traffic at all, this excellent museum (☎ 599-5321) is highly recommended for anyone with the slightest interest in textiles. It's the only museum in the country to exclusively collect and display handmade textiles and tapestries from around the world. There are pieces from Latin America, Africa, Europe, South-East Asia and India.

The Tibetan collection is particularly fine, as is the one from Indonesia. In addition, there are changing shows of contemporary textiles.

The museum can be found (look hard, the door is tucked back from the street) at 55 Centre Ave (running south off Dundas St West in Chinatown between Bay St and University Ave), behind the Toronto City Hall. It's open Tuesday to Friday from 11 am to 5 pm, and from noon to 5 pm on weekends. Admission is $5.

Marine Museum of Upper Canada & Historic Restaurant

In the officers' quarters of an 1841 army barracks at Exhibition Place, this museum (☎ 392-1765) shows the history of the city as a port. On exhibit are models and old ship relics, and in summer, there's a restored steam tugboat moored outside. Admission is $3.50, less for children. It's open Tuesday to Friday from 9.30 am to 5 pm, and on weekends from noon to 5 pm.

In the basement of the museum is the *Officer's 1893 Restaurant* (☎ 597-1893), which every Thursday to Saturday night recreates a dinner party held in 1893 to celebrate the naming of Stanley Barracks. Original recipes are used for the menu. The cost for the 12-course meal, including alcohol, is around $75 per person, and it's usually sold out.

Hockey Hall of Fame

Housed in the beautiful old Bank of Montreal building (dating from 1885) at the north-west corner of Front and Yonge Sts, the Hockey Hall of Fame (☎ 360-7765) gives young and old fans all they could ask for, and more. And for visitors unfamiliar with the game, enough background and history is presented to perhaps help explain Canadians' passion for this, the fastest of sports. Included is hockey's biggest prize – the Stanley Cup (or a replica), a re-creation of the Montreal Canadiens' dressing room and all manner of interactive exhibits and activities. Admission is $8.75 for adults, less for seniors and kids. It's open every day, with extended evening hours on Thursday and Friday.

Police Museum

The police museum (☎ 324-6201), housed in the impressive headquarters building at 40 College St, displays a small collection of equipment, uniforms etc from 1834 to the present. The confiscated weapons display certainly gives pause. There are some interactive displays, details of some noteworthy cases, a police car and motorbike and an old jail cell. It's open daily and admission is free.

Redpath Sugar Museum

Along the waterfront, at 95 Queen's Quay West, a free museum (☎ 366-3561) is part of the large sugar mill. There is a film on the production of the sweet stuff, as well as exhibits of equipment. The museum is open Monday to Friday from 10 am to 3.30 pm.

Toronto Dominion Gallery of Inuit Art

Housed on the mezzanine floor of the AETNA Tower of the Toronto Dominion Centre, on Wellington St between Bay and York Sts, this gallery (☎ 982-8473) displays a top-rate collection of far-northern art dating mainly from WWII to the present. It consists primarily of sculpture in stone and bone, which is the foremost form of Inuit art.

The gallery is free and is open daily. Hours are 8 am to 6 pm Monday to Friday, 10 am to 4 pm on weekends. Occasionally, you may find a rope across the door of the gallery. Just take it down and go in; the gallery is still open though there may well be no attendant. Free tours are given once a day on Tuesday and Thursday but can be arranged for any day – call and ask.

Toronto Stock Exchange

The city's stock exchange (☎ 947-4676) is Canada's largest and one of the most modern anywhere. Stock worth $100 million is bought and sold each day, so it's a fairly hectic place. A leap in trading volumes in 1994 put the TSE into the top 10 stock exchanges of the world – the only other North American exchange on the list being New York. A free 45-minute presentation on the exchange's history and operation is offered Tuesday to Friday at 2 pm sharp. The public viewing gallery is open on weekdays from 9 am to 4.30 pm. The stock exchange is at 130 King St West, on the north-east corner of King and York Sts, right in the centre of the city's financial district.

Chess Games Corner

Right in the heart of the city, at the corner of Yonge and Gould Sts, is the unofficial chess centre. Here through all kinds of weather, night and day, chess players and aficionados of every description gather to duel and bet. It all began with the late 'open highway' Joe Smolij in 1977, who can be found in the Guinness Book of Records as the world's fastest chess player.

Activities

Cycling For cyclists (and roller-bladers), the Martin Goodman Trail is a bicycle route along the waterfront which stretches from The Beaches in the east end, past Harbourfront and the downtown area, to the Humber River in the west end. From here, it connects with paths in parkland running northwards along the Humber. This section is a really fine ride. You can go at least as far as Eglinton, and that's quite a few km.

If you fancy a longer trek, the Martin Goodman Trail now links into the recently completed Lake Ontario Waterfront Trail which stretches 325 km from Hamilton to Trenton. Visit the tourist office for maps and pamphlets detailing sights along the way.

The Toronto Bicycling Network (☎ 766-1985) organises short, medium and long weekend trips (some overnight) throughout the summer. A Taste of the World (☎ 463-9233) runs a series of summer bicycle tours around neighbourhood nooks and crannies; one visits the hidden ice-cream parlours of the city.

Water Sports Free swimming in public pools can be found in High Park, the Gus Ryder Pool (formerly known as the Sunnyside Natatorium) south of the park at the lake on Lakeshore Drive, and in Woodbine Park at The Beaches in east-end Toronto, at the foot of Woodbine Ave. Many other city parks include pools but the three above are selected for their good locations, large size and popularity.

Sandy beaches, shady parks, a boardwalk and, on any hot summer day (especially on weekends), lots of people can also be found around The Beaches. Kew Beach is the most popular section and the boardwalk goes through here. The same thing on a smaller scale can be enjoyed at Sunnyside Beach in

the west end, south of High Park. Both are fun, relaxed and relaxing. Work continues to make the water fit to swim in.

There is windsurfing at The Beaches too, rentals are available in the Ashbridges Bay area at the western end of the beach.

Other Activities In winter there are good, free places to skate at City Hall and at Harbourfront, both with artificial ice. If it's been quite cold, there is also large Grenadier Pond in High Park. Skates can be rented at the City Hall rink.

The Balloonery (☎ 1-800-561-4435) provides the opportunity to go hot-air ballooning. It's big bucks – about $140 an hour or more. Flights go on summer weekends outside of the city, with champagne included.

For out-of-town outdoor activities, two of the city's best-known camping stores – Trail Head, at 40 Wellington St East, and Mountain Equipment Co-op, nearby at 41 Front St East – have information on adventure trips such as whitewater canoeing and wilderness hiking.

Organised Tours

The reliable Gray Line (☎ 594-3310) runs a basic, two-hour, inner-city tour for $25, less for seniors and children. Various other, more specialised tours lasting from 2½ hours and up are offered, with stops at sites included. Another, an all-day affair, runs west to Niagara Falls and costs $89. Passengers are picked up from downtown hotels and at the main bus terminal (610 Bay St). Tickets can be bought on the bus, or at the Gray Line desk in the Royal York Hotel, on York St across from the train station.

Civitas Cultural Resources (☎ 966-1550) offer three walking tours of the city. One looks at early colonial architecture, the second takes in Victorian Toronto and the third explores the Yorkville neighbourhood. Tours run on weekends only. They last about two hours and cost $10. Call to reserve a place and to check meeting times and places.

Another very interesting walking tour is

Chinatown Cuisine, a three to 3½-hour intensive look at Chinatown, with visits to shops, a herbalist and much more, plus a dim sum lunch. It's put on by David Ko (☎ 618-8238) and is offered every day, all year. The price ($50) includes pick-up from and return to your lodgings, and the meal.

A whole host of free city walks are organised by volunteers from the Royal Ontario Museum through the summer. Walks take place, rain or shine, on Sunday afternoon and Wednesday evening. Call ☎ 586-5797 for details or pick up a brochure at the tourist office or ROM.

The University of Toronto (☎ 978-5000) runs free guided tours of the campus through the summer, three times daily. This is the country's largest university and the campus has some fine buildings. Tours start from the map room in Hart House.

Several companies run boat tours in and around the harbour and the islands. Most depart from Harbourfront around Queen's Quay, John Quay and, especially, York Quay. For general information on boat tours call ☎ 973-4094.

The main operator is Mariposa Cruise Lines (☎ 203-0178). The *Chippewa*, a retired *Maid of the Mist* from Niagara, is used for the one-hour, basic, narrated tour. A ticket is $12. Mariposa also offers more leisurely (and expensive) evening trips aboard the *Northern Spirit*, with buffet, cash bar and dancing. For all of the above, purchase tickets in advance at Queen's Quay Terminal, Pier Six.

Some privately owned sailing ships and schooners offer trips of varying duration as far as Niagara-on-the-Lake. The *Challenge* (☎ 260-6355), a three-masted schooner, goes out beyond the islands on its cruises. Other boats are geared for fishing. Look around the dock area; you'll see signs advertising these and various charters, some of which offer good deals.

The island ferry has good views of the city and is very cheap. If you're visiting the islands, remember to check the time of the last return trip. In summer the ferries run about every half-hour but not very late at night. See under Toronto Islands for more details.

There are now quite a few Toronto-based companies offering out-of-town activities and wilderness tours. The Canadian Experience, operating through Hostelling International (☎ 971-4440 or 1-800-668-4487), has been highly recommended by several LP readers. It's a very full 2½-day trip which includes a visit to the reconstructed French mission Sainte-Marie among the Hurons near Georgian Bay, a hike along the spectacular Bruce Trail, a drive through some of Ontario's Mennonite towns and a look at Niagara Falls. Tours leave from the Toronto hostel once a week and cost around $200; for an extra $65 you can camp overnight and spend a full day hiking the Bruce Trail.

Niagara Falls Sightseeing Alternative (☎ 778-9686) offers a day trip to Niagara Falls and Niagara-on-the-Lake, wine tasting included, for $39.95. Students get a $10 discount.

Canadian Woodlands (☎ 469-4356) provides direct transport into Algonquin Provincial Park from downtown Toronto through June to the end of September. Departing Toronto at 7.30 am Monday, Wednesday and Friday, the trip costs $35 each way. Passengers can be dropped off at any access point along the Hwy 60 corridor which runs through the southern portion of the park. A same-day return (which allows for around five hours in the park) costs $50 and includes the option of guided trips along some of the shorter trails.

Festivals
Some of the major events held here are:

May

Toronto International Powwow – The two day event celebrates Native Indian culture with dancers, costumes and crafts. It's held at the Skydome in the middle of May.

June

Caravan – This is a nine-day event of cultural exchange during which ethnic groups offer music, dance and food native to their homelands. A passport ($14) entitles you to visit the 50 or so different ethnic pavilions set up around the city. Buses travel between the pavilions. The event takes place during the middle or end of June. Ask at the tourist office for a complete list of events and things to see and do. The Japanese pavilion is always rated highly and has frequently taken first prize in recent years.

Queen's Plate – The year's major horse race and one of North America's oldest (held since 1859), it is run at the Woodbine Track (☎ 675-6110) around the end of June.

Gay Pride Day Parade – Now well into its second decade and continuing to get larger and more flamboyant, Gay Pride Day culminates in an outrageous downtown out-of-the-closet parade towards the end of June. People of all persuasions come to watch floats and the participants and to generally party, with recent crowds estimated as high as 100,000. Toronto has a large gay and lesbian community based around Church St between Carlton and Bloor Sts, and this is where the parade takes place.

Du Maurier Downtown Jazz Festival – The excellent and ever-growing annual festival is held throughout the central city in June and early July, with a week of concerts day and night. The jazz is varied, featuring local, US and European players. More gospel, blues and world beat influences have been creeping into the mix. In recent years, about a thousand musicians have performed annually. Workshops, films and even jazz cruises are part of the event. Shows range from freebies on the streets, to nightclub performances, to concert hall recitals. Prices vary considerably but for the most part are pretty reasonable.

July

Soul & Blues Festival – This festival is held on weekends at Harbourfront.

International Picnic – At the beginning of July each year, to welcome summer, the huge picnic is held at the CNE grounds. Admission is free and there's music, dancing, contests and lots of food. It's very popular with the Italian community.

The Molson Indy – Toronto's only major car race, this has now become an annual tradition, held in early or mid-July. Well-known names from the international circuit compete in front of large crowds during the two days of practice and qualifying trials, with the big race on the last day of the three-day event. It's held in and around Exhibition Place and Lake Shore Blvd, in the south-central portion of the city.

Fringe Theatre Festival – With over 400 performances in six venues over 10 days, generally in July, the festival (☎ 534-5919) has become a major theatrical hit. The participants are chosen by lottery, so the performances vary widely in style, format and quality. Expect the unexpected.

Drama, comedy, musicals and cabaret-style shows are all part of the event. Ask at the tourist office for a programme guide.

Mariposa Folk Festival – Begun in the early 1960's, Mariposa is a festival of mainly folk music but also includes bluegrass and American Indian music. Finances have been a problem recently and the location and format vary annually. For current information call the Mariposa Folk Foundation (☎ 924-4839). Jam sessions and workshops are generally part of the multi-day event which takes place in July or August.

August

Caribana – An ever-growing annual West Indian festival (☎ 465-4884), it celebrated its 30th year in 1996. Held along Lake Shore Blvd West around the beginning of August, it is primarily a weekend of reggae, steel drum, and calypso music and dance. The main attraction, however, is the huge parade featuring outrageous costumes à la carnival in Rio. This parade can have perhaps 6000 people in it and can take five hours or more to pass by. Other events and concerts are spread over the two weeks leading up to the island weekend.

Canadian National Exhibition (CNE) – The CNE claims to be the oldest (about 100 years old) and the largest annual exhibition in the world. It includes agricultural and technical exhibits, concerts, displays, crafts, parades, an air show, a horse show, all manner of games and rides, and fireworks. The exhibition is held during the two weeks prior to, and including, the Labour Day holiday. The location is Exhibition Place, which is by the old CNE football stadium on Lake Shore Blvd West.

September

Festival of Festivals – The annual film festival is now a prestigious and major international cinematic event. Usually held in September, it lasts about a week and a half and features films of all lengths and styles, as well as gala events and well-known stars. Call ☎ 968-3456 for more information and check the papers for special guides and reviews. You can obtain tickets for individual screenings or buy expensive, all-inclusive packages. Tickets do, however, sell out very quickly.

October

International Festival of Authors – Held in autumn (usually October) at Harbourfront, this is the largest literary event of its kind in the world. Dozens of well-known novelists, poets and short-story writers gather to read and discuss their work. Each evening three or four writers are presented. Readings are also held through the year on a weekly basis, generally featuring less prominent authors.

Places to Stay

Camping There are several camping/trailer grounds within 40 km of the city. The tourist office has a complete list. One of the closest is *Indian Line Campground*, part of Clairville Conservation Area (☎ (905) 678-1233). It's north up Indian Line Rd, which runs north-south on the east side of the airport. The campground, with 224 sites, is near Steeles Ave, which marks the northern edge of the city limits. This is probably the best place for tenters. The nightly rate is $15.

Also close to the city is *Glen Rouge Park* (☎ 392-8092), on Kingston Rd (Hwy 2) at Altona Rd, near Sheppard Ave East. It's on the lakefront, at the border of Scarborough – part of Metropolitan Toronto – and the town of Pickering at the eastern edge of the city. There are about 120 sites. Tent sites are $16 per night.

Hostels The HI *Toronto Hostel* (☎ 971-4440 or 1-800-668-4487) has taken over several floors of the large Hospital Residence building at 90 Gerrard St West. It's very central, just two blocks north of the bus station and within walking distance of some of the city's main attractions. The nearest subway is Queens Park.

The hostel has space for 200 guests. Most rooms have just two beds and all have private washbasins. The building is air conditioned and facilities include a large kitchen, laundry, swimming pool, squash courts and gymnasium. The hostel is open 24 hours, year round, with reservations advised between May and September. Rates are $23/27 for members/non members, including continental breakfast. The Great Lakes regional hostel office is also based here.

A good alternative is the independent *Leslieville Hostel* (☎ 461-7258 or 1-800-280-3965), which consists of three houses, all close to each other in an east-end residential neighbourhood four km from downtown. The main hostel is at 185 Leslie St. To get there take a 20-minute streetcar ride along Queen St to Leslie St and walk north along Leslie. The streetcar operates 24 hours. The family-run hostel can accommodate up to 70

people. Most beds are in dormitories, but there are eight private rooms as well. Dorm beds are $13; private rooms are $32/39 a single/double. A $2 breakfast is available. There are kitchen and laundry facilities and free parking.

The *Marigold International Hostel* (☎ 536-8824), affiliated with Backpackers, is in the west end of town, at 2011 Dundas St West. It, too, is right on the streetcar line. Take either the College St or Dundas St cars from downtown for the 20-minute or so ride. On weekends the Dundas car is slow (and colourful) as it rolls through the heart of busy Chinatown. An alternative is the subway to the Dundas West stop, from where the Dundas streetcar begins its route eastbound, going right by the hostel.

The dormitory beds are $22. There are no cooking facilities but complimentary coffee and doughnuts are supplied each morning. There are around 40 beds and two rooms for couples. The door is generally locked until the 3 pm check-in but if you have spent the night you do not need to leave by any particular time – the door locks behind you. It's open all year.

The *YWCA* (☎ 923-8454), for women only, is central at 80 Woodlawn Ave, near Yonge St. The price for a single room is $44, less if you share a double, and a dormitory bed costs $18. A continental breakfast is included and there's an inexpensive cafeteria. Winter discounts for stays of a week or longer are offered.

Colleges *Neill-Wycik College Hotel* (☎ 977-2320 or 1-800-268-4358) is a well-located, apartment-style student residence at 96 Gerrard St East, by Ryerson Polytechnic University. During the summer (early May to late August) the residence's rooms are rented out to short and long-term guests. Rooms are $32/38 a single/double; a family room costs $47. There are laundry facilities and a student-run cafeteria for breakfasts. The building isn't air-conditioned so the small rooms can get very hot in mid-summer. During a recent visit standards of cleanliness weren't great.

The central *University of Toronto* (☎ 978-8735) rents rooms in a couple of college residences. The campus is by the corner of University Ave and College St. Rooms are available from the middle of May until late August. Rooms cost from a hefty $44 per person and include breakfast and maid service. There are very good weekly rates (but without the daily-rate perks).

York University (☎ 736-5020) at 4700 Keele St, near Steeles Ave, has a similar deal, renting rooms from May to the end of August. The trouble with accommodation here is that it's a long way from the downtown area, at the northern boundary of the city. Singles/doubles are $37/55, less for students, and reservations are preferred.

B&Bs & Tourist Homes These have become an increasingly popular segment of the accommodation scene and most establishments seem to be extremely busy. Though all B&Bs and the vast majority of guesthouses include breakfast in their room prices some, mainly those still classed as tourist homes, don't. Double check before you book.

There are several B&B associations in town which check, list and book rooms in the participating homes. Indicate where you'd like to be and any other preferences and attempts will be made to find a particularly suitable host. Prices are fairly standardised, at $45/65 a single/double, with some variation (mostly upward). Places in suburban areas cost about $5 less than those downtown. There is generally no need to go to the agency – a telephone call should get things sorted.

The Downtown Toronto Association of B&B Guesthouses (☎ 368-1420; fax 368-1653) specialises in rooms downtown, mainly in renovated Victorian houses. Prices range from $40 to $60 for singles and $50 to $90 for doubles. The mailing address is PO Box 190, Station B, Toronto, M5T 2W1.

Metropolitan B&B Registry (☎ 964-2566) is the largest outfit, with members in and out of town. The office is at 615 Mount Pleasant Rd, Suite 269, Toronto M4S 3C5.

Single and double rooms start at $40 and $50. Foreign languages are spoken at some places and, as is the norm generally, smoking is not permitted in the homes.

Toronto B&B Inc (☎ 588-8800) has about 25 members. Single rooms are $50 to $60; doubles $60 to $85. There's no office to visit; if you're in town, just call. The mailing address is Box 269, 253 College St, Toronto M5T 1R5.

Each of these associations produces a booklet listing the participating hosts and the type of places and features they offer. Send a stamped self-addressed envelope to receive one of the listing guides.

One recommended B&B is *Beverley Place* (☎ 977-0077), at 235 Beverley St, a small north-south street running south from College St to Queen St West between University and Spadina Aves. It's excellently situated near the corner of College St, very close to the university. Chinatown, Queen St West and even the CN Tower are all within walking distance.

The house is a well-restored, three-storey Victorian place dating from 1877, with lots of original features and wonderfully high ceilings. The entire place is furnished and decorated with interesting antiques and collectibles. An excellent breakfast is served at the large kitchen table overlooking a secluded garden patio.

The owner, Bill Ricciuto, also runs a similar house across the street. Guests staying here go to No 235 for breakfast.

The prices are quite reasonable and vary depending on the room. Singles/doubles begin at $45/65. The 'Queen Room' (with an impressive bed) costs more, as does the 3rd-floor, self-contained apartment with its own balcony and city view. Between June and November reservations are not a bad idea (the same goes for all the places listed in this section).

Karabanow Guesthouse (☎ 923-4004) has a good location, at 9 Spadina Rd, just north of Bloor St West. The tariff includes parking, daily cleaning and cable TV. There are nine rooms. Singles start at $46 and doubles range from $56 to $62.

Very convenient, just north of College St at 322 Palmerston Blvd, a quiet tree-lined avenue, is the *Palmerston Inn B&B* (☎ 920-7842). It's a well-kept, large older house with eight guest rooms and a pleasant 2nd-storey balcony. Prices are a little higher than at the others – from $50/70 for singles/doubles. All rooms are air conditioned and some have their own fireplaces. Some free parking is available.

Aberdeen Guesthouse (☎ 920-8968), at 52 Aberdeen Ave (which runs west off Parliament St just north of Carlton St), is a small renovated Victorian home in the east-end area of Cabbagetown. There are three beautifully decorated rooms, with shared bathroom, all at $50/70 a single/double. Breakfast is fabulous, the house is air-conditioned and there's a shady back garden.

At 1233 King St West is the simple *Candy Haven Tourist Home* (☎ 532-0651), right on the King St streetcar line; look for the bright paint job and sign. It's central and there are sinks in the rooms. Prices start at around $45.

Still further west, at 1546 King St, near Roncesvalles Ave, is the *Grayona Tourist Home* (☎ 535-5443). It's a renovated old house run by Marie Taylor, a friendly, enthusiastic Australian. Singles range from $40 to $50 and doubles are $50 to $65. Every room has a fridge and all but one a TV. Marginally more expensive rooms, which are good for families (there's even a cot), have cooking facilities. A large family room with bathroom and kitchen goes for around $90 a night.

The Grayona is about seven km from the centre of town, and although some of the visitors walk, there is a streetcar along King St which stops practically at the door. There are two other guesthouses within a few doors to the west towards Roncesvalles Ave.

Hotels – bottom end Toronto doesn't have much in the way of good, low-cost inner city hotels. Many of the cheaper hotels are in the Church, Jarvis and Sherbourne Sts area east of Yonge St. Sections of this part of town can be a little rough, with some hotel rooms used for more than sleeping. Women walking alone at night are likely to be hassled by kerb-crawlers. This is particularly the case around Church and Jarvis Sts near Isabella St and around Dundas St. The southern section of Jarvis St, between Carlton and Queen Sts, and the streets nearby, should be avoided late at night.

Despite these considerations, the area needn't be avoided altogether. Best in the low-budget category, and good value, the perfectly safe *Selby* (☎ 921-3142) is at 592 Sherbourne St, north of Wellesley St. The turreted Victorian mansion, dating from 1882 and designated as a heritage site, has an interesting history. At one time it was a girls' school. Later, Ernest Hemingway lived here when he worked for the *Toronto Star* in his younger days, before heading to Paris.

Much of the hotel has been upgraded. Rooms cost $70 to $80 for either singles or doubles, depending on size and features. This makes the less-expensive rooms quite a bargain for two people sharing. There is a $20 discount through the slower winter months and a weekly rate is always in effect. A continental breakfast is included in the price. Reservations are recommended from May to October.

The bar here is popular with men from the local gay community but straights make up a good portion of the hotel clientele.

Further south is the *St Leonard* (☎ 924-4902), at 418 Sherbourne St. It's worn and perhaps a little less judicious in screening guests but is clean and friendly. There are 22 simple rooms, some with private bath and TV, with singles starting at $39 and rising to $45. Doubles range from $45 to $55.

For connoisseurs of classic dives there's the *Gladstone*, at 1214 Queen St West. It's a beautiful old building long past its hey day (although sandblasted), with plenty of 'rubbies' throwing 'em back in the bar downstairs. Rates are cheap – under $30 – but this place is not recommended for women.

Hotels – middle The mid-range *Strathcona* (☎ 363-3321) is also an older place that has been overhauled and upgraded. It now has all the usual amenities and yet is, for the downtown area, moderately priced (rooms start at $75). The Strathcona has an excellent location, at 60 York St, very near the train station. There's a dining room, a coffee shop and a bar.

One of the best of the small, old downtown hotels is the *Victoria* (☎ 363-1666), at 56 Yonge St, near its southern end. Refurbished throughout, it maintains such older features as the fine lobby. Prices start at $75 for a single or double. Also in the more European mode is the *Comfort Hotel* (☎ 924-7381), at 15 Charles St. Prices start at $82.

The more standard high-rise *Bond Place* (☎ 362-6061) has a great location near the Eaton Centre, at 65 Dundas St East, and is often busy with vacationers. Prices start at $89.

More like a motel, but perfectly good, cheaper and with parking, is the *Executive Motor Hotel* (☎ 504-7441), at 621 King St West. The 75 rooms are priced at about $76 a double. It's central and the King St streetcar goes right by.

Hotels – top end Toronto has an abundance of large, new, modern hotels. There are many downtown, plenty around the city's edges and a good number around the airport. Many offer discount weekend packages. The costliest rooms in town are found at the *Four Seasons* (☎ 964-0411) in Yorkville, at 21 Avenue Rd, where prices start at around $295 a night (less on weekends). Also well appointed, with a good reputation and a fine lobby area, the *Hilton International* (☎ 869-3456) is right in the centre, at 145 Richmond St West. Singles/doubles cost from $250.

The *Harbour Castle Westin* (☎ 869-1600) has a fine location right at the edge of the lake, opposite the Toronto Islands. The address is 1 Harbour Square, near the bottom of Yonge St. The revolving restaurant offers good views over the city and lake. Rooms cost from $145.

The venerable *Royal York* (☎ 368-2511), at 100 Front St, opposite the train station, deserves mention. Among the top-class hotels, it's the oldest and has served people from rock stars to royalty. There are several bars and places to get a bite to eat on the

premises. Singles or doubles start at $169 and rise depending on vacancy levels. During peak times singles/doubles go for $260.

The airport strip features a number of upper-end hotels convenient for those who need to be near the runways. At the low end is the plain *Quality Inn by Journey's End* (☎ 240-9090), at 2180 Islington Ave.

Apartment Hotels Although they can be reasonable value, most places of this type are in the top-end category and tend to be geared to the corporate client and business executive. Many have a minimum stay, which ranges from three days to a month.

Very central is the *Town Inn Hotel* (☎ 964-3311), at 620 Church St, two blocks south of Bloor St. For the price of a hotel room, you can get a suite here with kitchen. There is also a pool and sauna. A double starts at $95 a day, including a small breakfast.

Executive Travel Suites (☎ (905) 273-9641) has four such properties in the downtown area, with prices starting at about $100 a day (with a three-day minimum stay). Each unit has a separate bedroom and living room and each building offers one or more extras, such as a pool, balconies, roof deck or restaurant.

Another place is the *Cromwell* (☎ 962-5604), at 55 Isabella St. The minimum rental is for three days and rates average $55 a day. This location is central but is also in one of the downtown prostitution districts. It is not really a tough or dangerous area but women alone at night may well be mistaken for being 'on the game'.

The tourist office will know of other apartments for short-term rent.

Motels For such a large city, Toronto is rather short on motels, so in summer they are often full. There are two main districts for motels in the city and others scattered throughout and around the perimeter.

On the west side of town, a shrinking motel strip (due to redevelopment) can be found along the lake on Lake Shore Blvd West, informally known as 'the lakeshore'.

Those remaining are mostly between the Humber River and Park Lawn Ave, just west of High Park. This district isn't too far from the downtown area, about 12 km from Yonge St, and the streetcar lines run the whole way. To get there, take the Queen St or King St streetcar from downtown to Roncesvalles Ave and continue on the Queen St streetcar to the Humber River. Switch (for no charge) to the Humber streetcar, which goes along the lakeshore. The motels edge the shoreline, and several nearby parks on the waterfront offer cool breezes in summer and good views of the city and islands.

Furthest west, with the yellow sign, the *Beach Motel*, at 2183 Lake Shore Blvd West (☎ 259-3296), is good. It has 40 rooms (from $60) and is beside the entrance to a park. The large, modern, well-maintained *Seahorse* (☎ 255-4433), at 2095 Lakeshore, is probably the most prosperous of the lot. It features rooms for the amorous, with waterbeds, lots of mirrors etc. And there is a swimming pool. Double rooms start at $62.

Back closer to town, before the start of the motel strip itself, the *Inn on the Lake* (☎ 766-4392) is at 1926 Lake Shore Blvd West. Room prices start at around $89. The adjacent Golden Griddle pancake house is a good place for a buffet breakfast and packs them in for brunch at weekends.

Not all that far away, but west on the Queensway, try the *Queensway Motel* (☎ 252-5821), at No 638. It's sort of away from the traffic, may have rooms when others are booked out and has considerably lower prices ($49 for a double).

Motels dot Lake Shore Blvd sporadically all the way along its course to Hamilton but there is no real concentration like the one by the Humber River.

Several motels can be found along Dundas St West, west of Hwy 427 (which is in the suburb of Mississauga rather than Toronto proper). From Lake Shore Blvd, go north up Hwy 427 and turn left.

The other main motel district is on the east side of town, further from the centre, on Kingston Rd which branches off Queen St East, east of Coxwell Ave, and later turns into the old Hwy 2 to Montreal. Motels start just east of Brimley Rd. Access to it is slower. The Guildwood station of the GO train, a commuter service, is just east of the motel strip. It has parking, and trains run frequently into downtown. Alternatively, public transit can get you into town but is slower still. Many of these motels are now used by the government as overflow welfare accommodation. Those listed here rely on visitors for some or most of their clients.

The *Avon* (☎ 267-0339), at 2800 Kingston Rd, just past Bluffers Park, is quite an attractive looking place. Rooms here cost $35 to $60 with TV and radio, and there is a heated pool. It's near Brimley Rd. Up Brimley Rd one block north at St Clair Ave, buses can be caught going to the subway system.

At 3126 Kingston Rd is the *Park* (☎ 261-7241) with summer rates of $55 for one double bed.

Further out, east of Eglinton, the appealing *Idlewood Inn* (☎ 286-6861) is a large, modern motel with a well-treed property and a pool. It's often used by businesspeople. The address is 4212 Kingston Rd. Rates here are higher, ranging from $60 to $90.

Places to Eat

Toronto has a good selection of restaurants in all price categories and a wide variety to choose from, thanks to the many nationalities represented in the city. The following places are mostly central and accessible by public transport. They are listed according to area and cuisine categories.

Yonge St & Around Yonge St itself, although busy night and day, is not one of the prime restaurant districts of the city. In the downtown centre, Yonge St has, in general, become swamped with fast-food franchises and cheap takeout counters. There are exceptions on and near Toronto's main street but some places tend to be geared more to lunch than to dinner.

South of the Eaton Centre, Yonge St has always been a bit of a backwater, so we'll start with the centre itself and work north to Bloor St. Among the many places to eat in the huge shopping mall are a couple of busy pubs. *Café Michel* (there are at least two of them on level 1) offers a tasty array of baked goods as well as salads, sandwiches and good coffee. *Aida's* (on the lower level) cranks out quite decent and cheap felafels, tabouli and a limited number of other Lebanese basics.

At 362 Yonge St, *Swiss Chalet* is an outlet of the popular Canadian roast chicken & chips chain. The meals are economical and tasty.

The large, crowded, noisy cafeteria at *Ryerson Polytechnic University* serves up reasonable meals at student prices. Food is served (at meal times only) in the cafeteria in Jorgenson Hall, which is on the corner of Gerrard St East and Victoria St.

Most of the better places to munch at are between College and Bloor Sts. Between the Eaton Centre area and College St there isn't much, but north of there things pick up again and it's busy all the way to Bloor St and beyond. At the hole-in-the-wall *Papaya Hut*, at 513A Yonge St, the homemade vegetable soup, a good sandwich and one of the vast array of fruit drinks or smoothies provide an alternative to the nearby junk food. There's a second outlet at 228 Yonge St.

British-style pub grub and a variety of beers can be found at the *Artful Dodger*, which has a pleasant outdoor patio. It's on Isabella St, a few doors east from Yonge St.

The cafeteria-style vegetarian *Health Haven*, at 4 Dundonald St, just a few doors from Yonge St, is one of the few of its kind in the city and is recommended. The tasty and inexpensive fare includes daily specials, create-your-own sandwiches, good desserts and an all-you-can-eat buffet on Tuesday night. It's a very quiet, low-key place, open every day but closed on Sunday until late in the afternoon.

Church St Church St, around Wellesley St, has quite a few cafes and restaurants and a range of nightspots. The area is the centre for Toronto's gay community and is particularly lively on a Saturday night.

The *Mango*, at 580 Church St, near Wellesley, has the best patio of the lot and serves simple food very well. A club sandwich of chicken and bacon on foccacio with a large salad and homemade dressing costs around $9.

For a splurge on a good steak, try *Le Baron*, further south at 425 Church St, an established place in an area with many new restaurants. They've been doing it since the 60s and steaks are the only main courses on the menu. The restaurant offers soft lights and attentive service but dress is casual.

Recommended for convivial atmosphere and classic Thai cuisine at reasonable prices is *Young Thailand*, at 81 Church St. There's a second restaurant at 111 Gerrard St East. Both are open until late.

Eastward into Cabbagetown you'll find Toronto's first Internet cafe *Eek-A-Geek* at 460 Parliament St. Here you can munch on organic salads and blow the froth off a decent cappuccino. An Internet session costs $5 per hour.

Theatre/Entertainment District A clutch of exciting new restaurants and nightclubs (some ferociously hip) has joined the established places north of the Skydome in the area containing the Mirvish theatres and Roy Thompson Hall.

Zocalo, at 109 John St, is a small place serving simple Mexican food with a twist. How about strips of Atlantic salmon marinated in lime juice served with plain tortilla chips and a glass of dry white wine? The food is excellent and the prices very reasonable; about $15 for a meal with wine.

Down at 287 King St West at John St is the *Groaning Board*, a mainstay for many years among Toronto restaurants. As well as the good soups and salads there are some vegetarian dishes available. It has long been known for its nightly showing of reels of international advertisements and commercials which can be food for thought or just plain funny. It's open every day from 8 am to midnight.

Wayne Gretzky's (as in the hockey legend) is the place to go for good ol' burgers and fries. It's at 99 Blue Jay Way.

There are several places in the Skydome itself. Among them is the rock'n'roll *Hard Rock Café* catering to the young. When no game is on, it runs as the regular sports bar that it is; you can simply go in for a hamburger and a beer and have a look at the playing field. It's open every day from lunch until late.

Pricier is *Windows* serving dinners on game nights. It's open sided with great views of the field. A meal and ticket is in the $50 range. For restaurant information and reservations call ☎ 341-2424.

The *Rotterdam Bar & Bistro*, at 600 King St West (at Portland St), brews its own fine beer but can also sell you pints from around the world. All main courses are under $10.

For those in need of a smoked-meat sandwich in a small, busy, Jewish-style deli check out *Zupa's Deli* at 342½ Adelaide St West, east of Spadina. You'd have to be an alligator to get your mouth around one of these megasandwiches. It's closed on Sunday.

Down on the corner of King and Simcoe Sts is Ed Mirvish's one-man development complex. Across from Roy Thompson Hall and centred around the Royal Alexander Theatre are his unmistakable restaurants more famous for their garish exteriors and sumptuous interiors of antiques and oddities lit by dozens of Tiffany lamps than for the food. Simple meals consist of quality meats accompanied by forgettable instant potato and frozen vegetables.

Old Ed's is a fairly casual place, with dinners costing $10 to $18 and lunches a few dollars less. Selections include lasagna, chicken, fish, ribs and veal. *Ed's Warehouse* is a bit more upmarket. Prices are $14 to $18 at dinner, a few dollars less at lunch. The menu offers a couple of selections of roast beef and steak only. The CN Tower is one block south.

St Lawrence Market Further east, past the Hummingbird Centre which is on Front St at Yonge, is this other busy eating, entertainment and nightclub area popular with both visitors and residents. Toronto, like many Canadian cities of any size, has its *Spaghetti*

Factory. This one is at 54 The Esplanade. The restaurant offers good value; meals start at $8 and are served in an interesting eclectic, colourful atmosphere popular with everybody, including families and teenagers. The lunch menu is even cheaper.

At 12 Market St, across from the market building, the *Old Fish Market* is perhaps the city's favourite place for seafood (main dishes $10 to $15) at dinner. Two meals for the price of one are offered on Tuesday.

Bloor St If you're near Spadina and looking for a cheap place, there's *Master's Buffeteria* at 310 Bloor St West. It's in the University Faculty of Education Building. Mostly for students, it's open from 8 am to 6 pm Monday to Friday. Cafeteria-style meals like lamb, sole and shepherd's pie are served at rock-bottom prices. Complete breakfasts are also available.

Bloor St West around Bathurst St is a lively student area, with many good cheap restaurants, a few cafes, the *Brunswick Tavern* – an institution – and the popular Bloor St Cinema.

At the cosy *Continental*, a Hungarian place at 521 Bloor St West, about five meal choices are offered each day, including rice dishes and schnitzels, for an average of $10. It's open seven days a week from 11 am to 10 pm.

The name says it all for the *Kensington Natural Bakery & Vegetarian Café*, at 460 Bloor St West. It's not jumping, but it is wholesome.

If it's comfort food you need, head straight for the *Future Bakery* at 483 Bloor St West. It's a very popular spot for cheese crêpes with sour cream, or perogies and sauerkraut, followed by fabulous cakes and bowls of café au lait. Just across the road, the *By the Way Café*, is an equally busy sitting and meeting place which serves pretty decent Middle Eastern or vegetarian food and excellent desserts.

Queen St West Queen St West between Spadina and University is one of the lively central districts. Some places cater more to trend than to quality, but it's an interesting and varied area with some good and reasonably priced restaurants. One of the better and more stable eateries is the comfortable *Queen Mother*, at 208 Queen St West. It offers a varied menu with a Thai slant for full meals and serves coffee and snacks all day.

Many of the area's younger residents and more impecunious artists have now moved further west to between Spadina Ave and Bathurst St and beyond. The local Goths and vampires/Edwardians also stroll the area. Along here you'll find a range of new, small restaurants, clubs and speciality stores. For a light meal, snack or coffee at any time of day (or night) there's another *Future Bakery*, at 735 Queen St West. *Dufflet's*, who create Toronto's best known desserts, have a small retail outlet with a couple of tables at 787 Queen St West. The chocolate cakes are unreal.

Small, cosy *Cities* at 859 Queen West serves up good-value, mainly traditional dishes making them seem totally modern with the tasteful use of fresh ingredients and understated flair. Main courses such as scallops are about $15.

Also recommended is the tiny *Babur Restaurant* at 273 Queen St West, near City TV. It's informal but the food is top rate. It's open seven days a week. Dinner without wine for two ranges from $30 to $50.

Little Italy Based along College St west of Bathurst, Little Italy is a very popular spot for eating, meeting and hanging out. *Kalendar Koffee House*, at 546 College St, is an intimate restaurant offering delicious things wrapped in pastry, as well as salads, soups, pasta dishes and big desserts. Main courses start at around $8. They also have a good selection of imported beer. Always crowded, *Bar Italia*, at 584 College St, has lots of atmosphere, excellent Italian sandwiches at good prices and pool tables upstairs. Complete dinners with a glass of wine start at $16.

Café Diplomatico, at 594 College St, is a busy restaurant and pizzeria with a large patio and particularly good cappuccino. It's open from 8 am till late seven days a week. For the best tartufo and Sicilian ice cream in town, head further west to the *Sicilian Ice Cream Co* at 712 College St.

Chinatown & Around The city's large Chinatown is based around the corner of Spadina Ave and Dundas St West and is home to scores of restaurants. Cantonese, Sichuan, Hunan and Mandarin food is all served. The district extends along Dundas St West, especially to the east of Spadina Ave and north up Spadina Ave to College St.

For tasty, inexpensive Chinese food in a variety of styles, including some fine spicy dishes, *Peter's Chung King Restaurant*, at 281 College St, is recommended. As well as the superior food, the decor is a cut above the usual fluorescent and plastic, yet prices are no higher – around $25 to $35 for two. Longstanding *Lee Garden*, at No 331 Spadina Ave, offers a consistently good and unusually varied Cantonese menu and is not expensive.

Vietnamese places can also be found as some Chinese leave the central core for more suburban areas. A good, quick, little noodle shop is the *Swatow*, at 309 Spadina Ave. Excellent meals of soups and noodles cost $5 to $15. It's open for lunch and until late daily. Also for Vietnamese, the simple *Pho Hung*, at 374 Spadina Ave, is recommended.

An interesting street on the edge of Chinatown, which not too many out-of-towners get to, is Baldwin St running east off Spadina Ave about two blocks north of Dundas St. About three blocks from Spadina Ave towards the east end of Baldwin St is a small, low-key commercial and restaurant enclave. Long a blend of Chinese and Western counterculture, it's especially pleasant on summer evenings when many of the varied restaurants have outdoor patios.

One place to consider is *Café La Gaffe*, at 24 Baldwin St, offering simple pastas, seafood dishes and interesting salads. There's an intimate patio in front, a larger one out the back and a bar inside. Prices are

ONTARIO

moderate. Next door, the *Yung Sing Pastry Shop* specialises in Chinese tarts and dumplings. Help yourself to Chinese tea for 35 cents. It's strictly take-away but there's a shady picnic table in front of the shop.

To the west of Spadina Ave, the market area on Kensington Ave and particularly on Augusta Ave is busy during the day and has some small cheap cafes. Further north, the *Kensington Kitchen*, at 124 Harbord St, is a fine and comfortable Middle Eastern restaurant. They serve generous portions; try the soup with a felafel and I'll bet you'll have found a favourite little lunch spot in Toronto.

Little India Little India, based on Gerrard St East just west of Coxwell Ave, has numerous inexpensive restaurants. The *Moti Mahal*, at No 1422, is plain (and bright!) but the food is good and ridiculously cheap. The *Madras Durbar* at 1435 Gerrard St East is a tiny, exclusively vegetarian place that serves South Indian dishes. The thali plate is good and makes a complete meal for only $4.50. The peculiarly named *Bar-Be-Que Hut*, at No 1455, is plusher than most; again, the food is good, though the portions are pretty small. The Sunday lunch buffet ($7) is great value. On Friday and Sunday evenings there's live music. The quiet *Haandi*, at 1401 Gerrard St East, serves very good dishes from the extensive menu or offers very cheap ($7 at dinner) complete buffets. After dinner, take a walk around the area and pop into one of the shops to ask for a paan made to order. With or without tobacco, this is a cheap, exotic taste experience.

Danforth Ave The Greek area along Danforth Ave, east of the city centre between Pope and Woodbine Aves, is also a good place to get a meal. Most of the restaurants along here get very busy on summer weekend nights, when there's quite a festive air to the street. Casual, cheap kebab houses with a noisy, informal atmosphere suitable for children are abundant. Eating early or after 8.30 or 9 pm is recommended if you want to avoid the crowds.

A busy, low-cost place – just look for the queue – is *Omonia*, at 426 Danforth Ave. The outside tables are a little less hectic. Similar is the *Astoria*, at 390 Danforth Ave, with several barbecue-style dishes to try. It's near the Chester subway stop.

Quieter *Ellas*, at 702 Pape Ave, carries on the tradition of presenting most of the Greek standards, many on view as you enter.

The popular *Ouzeri*, at 500A Danforth Ave, presents a range of slightly more sophisticated main courses amid colourfully trendy surroundings and fellow diners. Fresh sardines in mustard sauce with a Greek salad and a cold beer will cost around $14.

The comfortably upmarket *Pan*, at 516 Danforth, is recommended for very well-prepared meals featuring traditional Greek ingredients and flavourings. Open every day for dinner ($55 for two) only.

Myth, nearby at 417 Danforth, is a wonderfully decorated mezze bar with an outdoor patio and five pool tables good for an after-dinner drink.

Entertainment

Toronto is busy after dark, with countless nightspots, concerts, films, lectures and the country's largest theatre scene.

All three daily newspapers provide weekly entertainment listings. Check either the Thursday *Star* or the Friday *Sun* for full listings or the *Saturday Globe & Mail* for film and theatre. The city's most complete entertainment guide is provided by *Now Magazine*, a good weekly tabloid-style paper available free around town. Find it at cinemas, restaurants, cafes, record stores and some street-corner newsboxes (where it must be paid for).

Bar hours are 11 am to 2 am, as they are all over Ontario. Numerous clubs stay open until 3 or 4 am without serving any more alcohol, and who knows how many illegal mercurial boozecans there are where pricey drinks can be had at all hours. Beer can be bought retail at Brewers Retail Stores, now often marked as the Beer Store, and liquor and wine at Liquor Control Board of Ontario (LCBO) outlets.

Live Music The *Bamboo* (☎ 593-5771), at 312 Queen St, is very popular, with lots of African and reggae sounds. It's always busy, with a 30-ish crowd. There's a rooftop patio to catch a breath and a kitchen serving tasty, spicy meals. Admission costs $5 to $10. *Chicago's Diner*, at 335 Queen St West, offers live blues. The kitchen is open daily until 1 am and often there's no cover charge. Nearby is the *Horseshoe* (☎ 598-4753), at 370 Queen St West, which presents a mixture of rock, country, blues and R&B. Again, there's mostly no cover charge.

The *St Louis*, at 2050 Yonge St, often has good R&B or blues bands with dancing and there's no cover.

The small, crowded *El Mocambo* (☎ 928 3393), at 464 Spadina Ave, just south of College St, is a local institution and the city's best known (if no longer so popular) bar. It's had a long, celebrated history, and the Rolling Stones once played here. Shows feature live rock and blues. Admission varies with the band upstairs and can be a bit high; downstairs admission is free and there's cheaper drinking with a local band.

Just down the street, at 379 Spadina Ave, *Grossman's* is grubby but one of the cheapest places in town. Very good bands sometimes play here and there's usually an interesting, mixed crowd. Sunday afternoons and evenings are reserved for blues jams. Admission is free.

The *Brunswick* (☎ 964-2242), at 481 Bloor St West, is a funky student hang-out, a bit like a pub and a bit like a fraternity house and often eats a lot of fun. There's live folk music at the *Free Times Café*, at 320 College St.

For jazz, *C'est What*, at 67 Front St East, has a new act nearly every night. Another is the *Café des Copains*, at 48 Wellington St. For more experimental music, the *Music Gallery* (no liquor served) is at 1087 Queen St West. *Meyer's Deli*, at 69 Yorkville St, has more conventional jazz.

Allen's Restaurant, at 143 Danforth Ave, has live Celtic music on Tuesday and Saturday nights. Sometimes there's a cover charge if the band is big.

The free *Island Club*, at the western end of Ontario Place, has great live Latin American music on Saturday night during the summer. If this stuff doesn't get your feet tapping, you're probably dead.

Dance Clubs & Other Bars A range of nightclubs can be found around town but by far the most happening place is the booming entertainment district near the Skydome. Between Queen and Front Sts, Richmond St West and Adelaide St West and the small streets of Duncan, John and Peter are packed with dance clubs. The area is jammed on weekends; the best way to find a place to your taste is to take a wander and check-out the people queuing to get in. Other busy streets are Blue Jay Way and from there King St West to John. For variety, some places in the area offer pool and more of a hip-pub atmosphere. Try *Montana's* at the corner of John and Richmond Sts, or *Milano's* at 325 King St West.

Another busy, popular place with a twenties crowd is the *Big Bop* at 651 Queen St West on the corner of Bathurst St. *Sneaky Dee's* at the corner of College and Bathurst Sts is cheap and popular. For the older, better-heeled party goers, Yorkville has numerous places.

Those from Down Under may be interested to drop in at the TRANZAC (Toronto Australia New Zealand Club), at 292 Brunswick Ave, where there is a bar open to all.

For a real gas, experimentalists will want to inhale the atmosphere of Canada's first oxygen bar. Modelled after the I-need-a-boost stations of Japan, the *O2 Spa Bar* 2044 Yonge St, hooks you up to a pure oxygen hose for 20 minutes for $16.

Cinema There are several repertory film houses around town. The *Bloor Cinema* (☎ 532-6677), at 506 Bloor St West, is popular with the many students in the area. A wide variety of films is shown – US, European, old and new. The *Revue* (☎ 531-9959), at 400 Roncesvalles Ave, in the west end, also features different films nearly every night.

ONTARIO

Prices are a couple of dollars less than those at first-run theatres and are much lower for those with an inexpensive annual membership card. There are three or four similar theatres around town, and the AGO and *Cinémathèque Ontario* also screen noncommercial films. IMAX movies can be seen at *Ontario Place*.

For first-run movies, the *Eglinton* (☎ 487-4721) has the best screen and sound. It's north of downtown at 400 Eglinton Ave West. *Carlton Cinemas* (☎ 598-2309), at 20 Carlton St, screens non-mainstream new releases.

Theatre There is plenty of good theatre in Toronto, in fact only London and New York sell more theatre tickets. Productions range from Broadway-type spectacles and musicals to Canadian contemporary dramas. Also big is dinner theatre. The classified sections of the *Sun* and *Star* newspapers list tickets available for every sold-out event in town, from opera to Rolling Stones, hockey to baseball. For a price, any seat is yours.

Theatre costs vary widely. A dinner show costs $40 to $60 per person for a meal and show. The city's longest-running play is Agatha Christie's *The Mousetrap*, which has played at the *Toronto Truck Theatre* for 19 years. A ticket is about $20.

One of the more physically impressive theatres is the traditional *Royal Alex*, on King St West, which presents established plays and performers. Next door is the new, lavish *Princess of Wales Theatre*, with one of the largest stages in North America. The theatre was built to accommodate the musical *Miss Saigon*. *Pantages* (with the long-running *Phantom of the Opera*), is a classic 1920s theatre worth visiting just for its gorgeous lobby. It's right downtown near the Eaton Centre. There are daily tours of the theatre for $4. The restored historic *Elgin* and *Wintergarden* theatres, both at 189 Yonge St, are worth checking for their high profile productions. Tours are offered on Thursday and Saturday.

The *Dream* in High Park is a great summer theatre presentation in which one Shake-

spearean play is put on each night through July and August with a donation requested. The Toronto Free Theatre's production and acting is top rate. For details, call their downtown theatre (☎ 367-8243). Shows begin at 8 pm, but go very early with a blanket and picnic or you'll require binoculars.

TO Tix (☎ 596-8211) sells half-price leftover theatre and dance tickets for shows the same day. They have a booth at 208 Yonge St (you can't place telephone orders). It's open from noon to 7.30 pm Tuesday to Saturday, and on Sunday from 11 am to 3 pm.

Other Entertainment Toronto has several places for comics, called *Yuk Yuks*. A central club (☎ 967-6425) is at 1280 Bay St. Presentations are sometimes funny, sometimes gross, sometimes a joke. Admission ranges from $4 on some weekdays to $15 on weekend nights, when there are two of the two-hour shows. Dinner packages are also available. Second City (☎ 863-1111), at 110 Lombard St, has an excellent reputation for both its comedy shows and the people it develops.

The Toronto Symphony (☎ 598-3375) plays at *Roy Thompson Hall*, 60 Simcoe St, not far from the CN Tower. A range of other, mainly classical concerts are presented here. In early autumn, the Canadian Opera Company performs at the *Hummingbird Centre* (☎ 393-7469), on Front St. The National Ballet of Canada, based in town, shares this facility.

The world renowned Tafelmusik orchestra performs baroque and classical music on period instruments in Trinity-St Paul's United Church at 427 Bloor St West.

The marvellous Recital Hall of the *Ford Centre for the Performing Arts* (☎ 733-9388), at 5040 Yonge St, presents classical concerts by the world's top musicians and vocalists. The North York Centre subway station is nearby.

The city's oldest concert hall, *Massey Hall*, 178 Victoria St, has excellent acoustics and is a wonderfully intimate and warm place to see a show.

For dance, look into what's happening at

Harbourfront's *Premiere Dance Theatre*, 207 Queen's Quay West in the Queen's Quay Terminal. The dance, symphony and opera seasons start in October or November and run through the winter.

Spectator Sports The Toronto Blue Jays play major-league baseball at the *Skydome* against US teams of the American League. The Jays won the World Series in 1992 and 1993 – the only times that baseball's top prize has been won by a non-US team.

If you'd like to take in a game, book early by calling (☎ 341-1234) and use a credit card. Tickets are also available at the box office at gate 9 at the stadium or from a ticket outlet in the CIBC building on the corner of Bay and King Sts. There are four price brackets. The cheap tickets are a mere $6 but are a long way away and are high above the field. Recommended are the $18 seats at the 500 level behind home plate. Try for somewhere between the 517s and the 530s, through gates 7, 8 or 9. The priciest seats go for $23 and rim the infield. Behind the home plate at this low level, beware of the protective net, which must be peered through. Those aged 14 and under are entitled to half-price tickets (except on the top-price seats) for Saturday games and all games with a 12.35 pm start.

Tickets are always available from scalpers at the stadium just prior to the game. After the game has started it is often possible to get tickets for less than face value.

Note that food and drink, especially beer, is expensive and that bottles or cans cannot be taken into the dome. Take a jacket as things cool off down here at night if the roof is open.

The Toronto Argonauts, of the professional Canadian Football League (CFL), also play in the Skydome.

The brand new Toronto Raptors (☎ 214-2255) of the National

Basketball Association began playing at the Skydome for the 1995-96 season. A new 22,000-seat basketball stadium, the Air Canada Centre, at the corner of Bay St and Lake Shore Blvd (not far from the Skydome) is scheduled to open in 1997.

In winter, National League hockey is played at Maple Leaf Gardens (☎ 977-1641), downtown on the corner of Carlton and Church Sts, a couple of blocks from Yonge St. Tickets are hard to get at the box office, as every game is pretty well sold out, but they can be bought without difficulty from scalpers outside the door just before the game. Hockey tickets are costly, with the 'cheap' seats and standing room at $23.

For horse racing, *Woodbine Racetrack* (☎ 675-6110) features thoroughbreds and standard-breds (harness racing) and is home to the prestigious Queen's Plate. It's northwest of the centre, at 555 Rexdale Blvd. By public transport, take the subway to Islington and then catch the direct 'Race' bus. Admission to the track is $3.50 and bets start at $2.

Things to Buy

You'll find an excellent range of camping gear and outdoor equipment in Toronto, most of it reasonably priced. Mountain Equipment Co-op, at 41 Front St East, and Trailhead, at 61 Front St East, are good for camping gear, tents, sleeping bags, packs, footwear and more.

Europe Bound, at 49 Front St East and with three other locations, sells books as well as hiking clothes and camping gear. They'll even rent you a tent or take a passport photo.

For the best in outdoor clothing, visit Tilley Endurables, a small Canadian company which turns out some of the finest, toughest, low-maintenance threads imaginable. The shorts ($95) are guaranteed for life and the well-known hats cost around $45. The main store, which also sells pants, shirts and skirts, is at 900 Don Mills Rd, and there is an outlet at the Queen's Quay terminal at Harbourfront.

Getting There & Away

Air The airport, Pearson International, is about 24 km north-west of the downtown area in a part of the city known as Malton. This is actually a separate city, but you wouldn't know it from the continuous urban landscape. The major Canadian airlines fly in and out of Toronto, as do many of the international companies. Pearson is by far the busiest airport in the country.

The third terminal, known as Trillium Terminal, was the first in Canada to be developed, owned and operated by private interests rather than by the government. Distinguishing features include a Harrod's outlet. Food, drink and parking are costly, particularly at the Trillium Terminal.

When departing from the airport or picking someone up at arrivals, be sure to ask the terminal number. Signs on the roads into the airport direct you to each terminal and indicate which airlines they serve. Trillium is the main terminal for Canadian Airlines, American Airlines, British Airways, KLM, Lufthansa and Air France. Within the Trillium Terminal, Pier A handles domestic flights and Pier B handles international ones. Terminal 2 is home to Air Canada.

Some one-way fares on Air Canada (☎ 925-2311) are: Montreal $222, Halifax $397, and Calgary $675. Canadian Airlines (☎ 675-7587) has virtually the same prices, but they do vary during the numerous special promotions.

Small Toronto Islands Airport, on the lake at the foot of Bathurst St, is used by commuter-style airlines and private planes.

Air Ontario (☎ 925-2311) regularly flies from here. The smaller aircraft get you to where you're going a lot quicker than the major carriers because you don't have to drag yourself all the way out to the airport, which costs time and money. Air Ontario serves mainly the business market, with flights to and from Montreal, Ottawa and London (Ontario).

A shuttle bus (free for flight ticket-holders) runs from the Royal York Hotel down to the two-minute ferry across to the airport. The Union subway stop is across the street from the Royal York Hotel. Otherwise there is TTC service close to the airport ferry – take the streetcar south on Bathurst St to Lake Shore Blvd (generally known as Lake Shore Road or The Lakeshore). From there the ferry is a two-block walk.

A bridge connecting the Toronto Islands Airport to the mainland has been approved but won't be completed for a couple of years.

It is not uncommon for Canadians (and visitors) to skip over to Buffalo to take advantage of the periodically much cheaper US airfares. For example, a flight from Buffalo to Seattle could cost hundreds of dollars less than the fare from, say, Toronto to Vancouver. At either end, a short bus ride links the Canadian cities. Recently, the US fares have not been the bargains they were a few years ago, and with the expense of getting to Buffalo and the difference in the exchange rate, flights out of Canada have been comparably priced.

Bus The coach terminal for out-of-town destinations is central on the corner of Bay and Dundas Sts, at the edge of Chinatown, one long block west of Yonge St. It's the station for the numerous bus lines which cover Ontario from Toronto. For destinations in Eastern Ontario and north of Toronto call ☎ 393-7911. This number covers Voyageur, PMCL (Penetang-Midland Coach Lines), Canar, Ontario Northland and Trentway Wager bus companies. Collectively these lines serve Niagara Falls, Barrie, Orillia, Huntsville, Parry Sound, North Bay, Montreal and their districts as well as some US destinations, including New York.

Gray Coach (run by Greyhound) and Greyhound (☎ 367-8747) pretty much cover Ontario west of Toronto, including the Niagara region, Guelph, Kitchener, London, Windsor, Owen Sound, Sudbury and beyond, on to western Canadian cities such as Winnipeg and Vancouver. They also run to Detroit, New York and Boston. Greyhound also operates the route to Ottawa and Peterborough. Smaller, local bus lines around Ontario connect to towns served by one or more of the above major carriers. Always ask about express buses.

Some routes have slow, milk-run trips (which stop frequently) and other express, direct trips (which can be hours quicker). Ask about return tickets – some bus lines offer these at reduced rates.

There are departures for Ottawa at 9.30 and 11.30 am and 2.30 and 4.30 pm. The five-hour trip costs $55 one way.

To Montreal, there are five or six buses a day, depending on the day of the week. One of them is an overnighter, which leaves at 12.15 am. Tickets for Montreal cost $64.

Greyhound goes to Niagara Falls but Trentway Wager does the route at less cost ($22 one way, about two hours). A discounted, same-day return ticket is offered too. Each company has several services daily.

To Thunder Bay, buses depart at 1 and 5 pm and 1 am ($127 one way, about 20 hours). There are regular buses for Buffalo, New York and Detroit.

The station is also the depot for Gray Line (☎ 594-3310) sightseeing buses.

Lockers can be found on the lower level, and the upper floor has a restaurant. There's a bakery and cafe on the other side of Bay St. On the evening prior to a holiday or long weekend, expect crowds and arrive early to ensure getting a ticket before departure time.

Adjacent to the terminal, on the western side, is the bus station for (among other runs) the GO buses (☎ 869-3200), a government line which services many of the nearby surrounding towns, stopping frequently along the way. It's mainly used by commuters but goes a relatively long way (to Hamilton, for example) to the west of Toronto.

GO buses also go to the satellite communities of Barrie (to the north) and Oshawa (to the east), supplementing the regular bus service. Trips in these directions are not as frequent as the westbound ones and the downtown bus terminal is not used as the departure point. For Barrie, catch the GO bus at the Finch subway station during evening rush hour. For Oshawa, catch it at the York Mills subway, also during the end-of-day rush hour. In the morning the buses come into town.

Train Grand old Union Station, for VIA Rail (☎ 366-8411) trains, is conveniently situated. It's on Front St (which runs east-west) at the south end of the city, at the bottom of University Ave, York and Bay Sts. The subway goes right into the station; the stop is called Union.

Trains leave for Ottawa daily at 11 am and 5.30 pm; at 9 am Monday to Saturday and 3 pm on Monday, Wednesday and Thursday ($87 tax included, about six hours). There are frequent services to Kingston. To Montreal, there are daily trains at noon, 3.45 pm and 6 pm ($96).

To Sudbury, there are three trips weekly, departing on Tuesday, Thursday and Saturday at 12.45 pm ($79, 7½ hours). Note that for Sudbury, the train actually goes to Sudbury Junction, a station about 10 km from the centre of town. Remember five days' notice drops the fares considerably.

Other cities which can be reached by train include Niagara Falls and London. Ontario Northland (☎ 314-3750) runs trains to northern Ontario destinations, including the Polar Bear Express to Moosonee.

Amtrak (☎ 800-872-7245) trains link Toronto with New York City, Buffalo or Chicago, with stops or other possible connections along the way. Amtrak offers good-value return fares. Reservations are needed for all trains.

The station has several restaurants, some fast-food outlets and a bar. Sometimes on the arrival level, just as you come out the gate from the train, a travellers' aid booth is in operation to help with basic directions and to answer questions.

GO trains also use the station; see the Getting Around section later.

Car If you're renting a car, be aware that many places require that you be at least 21 years old; for some places the minimum age is 23. There are countless rental agencies in the city. Surprisingly, it can be difficult to get a car on holiday weekends, so plan ahead.

The cheapest place to try is Rent-A-Wreck (☎ 961-7500), at 374 Dupont St, between Spadina Ave and Bathurst St; used cars cost $35 a day (plus 14 cents per km after the first 200 km) for a middle-sized vehicle, less for compacts. There are weekly and monthly rates, too. Insurance is extra, as it is at all places, and goes up as the driver's age decreases. If you're going for a used car, check it out before proceeding too far – reliability can be a problem. A place with a choice of new or used cars and with a good central location is Downtown Car & Truck Rental (☎ 585-7782), at 77 Nassau St, in Kensington Market off Spadina Ave. The used ones (best for using in or near the city) start at $29 a day, plus nine cents per km over the first 100 km. The new vehicles (for trips further afield) are priced competitively.

Tilden (☎ 364-4191), with an office in Union Station as well as several other downtown locations and one at the airport, is a more standard rental company and offers new cars. Their average rates start at $40 per day for the smallest economy cars, plus 15 cents per km after the first 200 km. They offer weekend specials; book early. Also available are child seats and ski racks.

Avis (☎ 964-2051 or 1-800-879-2847) is on the concourse level of the Hudson Bay Centre, on the corner of Yonge and Bloor Sts. Again, reservations are often required.

Car Sharing & Drive-Aways Easy Ride (☎ 977-4572) at 421A Queen St, 2nd Floor has a van service taking passengers between Toronto, Montreal ($28) and Ottawa ($25). You can arrange to get off at Kingston. These low-cost trips are frequent and friendly but perhaps not entirely legal. There are also trips to New York.

Allo-Stop (☎ 531-7668) is a service based on a great idea – getting drivers and cars together with passengers. Their central Toronto office is at 609 Bloor St West. They mainly deal with trips to Montreal and Ottawa, but other things come up too, including rides to New York City and even to Florida. Give them a call a couple of days before you want to go and they may be able to line up a ride. Rates are very good.

For long-distance trips, there are drive-away cars – about half a dozen places are listed in the Yellow Pages. One company is Toronto Drive-Away Service (☎ 225-7754), with cars for Canadian and US destinations. Also check the business personal columns in either the *Toronto Sun* or the *Star* and the ads in the weekly *Now Magazine* entertainment tabloid. (See the notes in the introductory

Getting Around chapter for more information on drive-aways.)

Hitching Thumbing is illegal on the expressways in the city. On city streets there's no problem but it's not commonly done, except by women offering their company for a price. You can hitch on Hwy 401 out of town or on the lead-in ramps in town.

If you're heading east for Montreal, the best bet is to take the city transit to roughly the corner of Port Union Rd and Hwy 401 in Scarborough, near the Metro Zoo. To get there from downtown is a bit complicated and the fastest way takes about 1½ hours. Take the subway east to Kennedy stop. From there catch the Scarborough LRT (light rail transit) to the Lawrence East station. Transfer to the Lawrence East 54E bus. Go east to East Drive at Lawrence East. Transfer (free again) to the Rouge Hill No 13 bus to Hwy 401.

If you're going west, take the subway to Kipling. Transfer to the West Mall bus, Nos 112 or 112B, and go to the corner of Carlingview Drive and International Blvd almost at Hwy 401. This is just at the city limits, so you are OK on the highway, but it could be busy and difficult for cars to stop at rush hour. Public transit to this point takes about one hour from downtown.

If you're northbound, you're stuck. The best bet is to take the bus to Barrie and then hitch the rest of the way on Hwy 400 or Hwy 11, depending on your destination. The Trans Canada Hwy westbound can be picked up at Sudbury.

Getting Around
The Airport In Toronto, there are several ways to get to the airport. The cheapest is to take the subway to Kipling on the east-west line. From there, take the Kipling or Martingrove bus (Nos 45 or 46) north up to Dixon Rd. Transfer to the Malton No 58A bus, which goes west to the airport. Keep your transfer from the subway, but the second bus will cost $2 extra. Reverse the same route to get downtown from the airport.

Alternatively, take the subway to the Lawrence West stop on the north-south Spadina-University line and from there catch the Malton No 58A bus. Again, the bus costs an additional $2.

The next method is a little easier, a little quicker and a little more costly. Between the airport and the Islington subway stop (one before Kipling), at the far western end of the Bloor Line, there is a direct bus run by Pacific Western (☎ (905) 672-0293). It leaves every 20 minutes or so, every day, takes half an hour and costs $6.40 one way. Another bus runs between the airport and the Yorkdale and York Mills subway stations. Each of these stops costs a bit more.

Pacific Western also operates buses every 20 minutes to and from the airport and half-a-dozen major hotels, such as the Royal York, the Sheraton, the Hilton Harbour Castle and the Holiday Inn, which is very near the bus terminal. The one-way fare is $11.45 and the trip takes about 80 minutes. These buses operate roughly between the hours of 4 am and 10.30 pm.

The buses leave the airport terminals from outside the arrival levels.

Of course, there are taxis and, for a couple more bucks, limousines. The taxi fare from Yonge and Bloor Sts to the airport is $34.

Toronto Transit Commission (TTC) The city has a good subway, bus and streetcar system (see the following Toronto Subway map), called the TTC (☎ 393-4636). There is a 24-hour, recorded, route and fare information line, (☎ 393-8663). Regular adult fare is $2 cash, or 10 tickets, or tokens for $16. Day passes are also available. Tickets or tokens (small dime-like coins) are available in the subway or at some convenience and corner variety stores. Once one fare is paid, you can transfer to any other bus, subway or streetcar within one hour at no extra charge. One ticket can get you anywhere the system goes. Get a transfer from the driver, or in the subway from the machine inside the turnstiles where you pay the fare.

The subway system is clean and fast. There is one east-west line, which goes along Bloor St and Danforth Ave, and two north-south lines, one up Yonge St and one along Spadina Ave, where some of the stops are decorated with the work of Canadian artists. The above-ground Scarborough RT train line connects the subway with the north-east part of the city, from the Victoria Park stop to the Scarborough Town Centre. The Harbourfront LRT (Light Rail Transit) car runs above and below ground from Union Station (on Front St) to Harbourfront, along Queens's Quay West to Spadina Ave and back again.

The subway runs until about 1.30 am and begins at 6 am (except on Sunday, when it starts at 9 am). Bus hours vary; some run late but are infrequent.

The Toronto system connects with bus routes in surrounding suburban cities such as Mississauga, Markham and Vaughan.

GO Train GO trains, (☎ 869-3200), leaving from Union Station from 7 am to 11.30 pm daily, service the suburbs of Toronto east to Whitby and west to Hamilton. Ticket inspection is random and basically on an honour system. Service is fast and steady through the day and frequent during weekday rush hours.

Streetcar Toronto is one of the few North American cities still using streetcars. They roll on St Clair Ave and on College, Dundas, Queen and King Sts, all of which run east-west.

Car All over Ontario, you can turn right on a red light after first having made a full stop. All vehicles must stop for streetcars, behind the rear doors, while the streetcar is loading or unloading passengers. Pedestrians use the painted crosswalks across the street and traffic must stop for them. If you're driving, keep an eye out for these.

In Toronto, parking is expensive – usually about $2 to $3.50 for the first half-hour, then slightly less. Most places have a flat rate after 6 pm. Look for the city of Toronto municipal lots, which are scattered around the downtown area and are marked by green signs. These are cheaper than the privately run lots.

Rush hours are impossible, so avoid them.

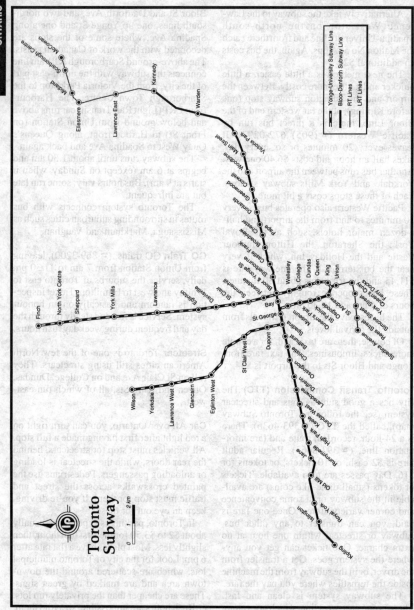

Toronto
Subway

0   1   2 km

And watch where you park during rush hours because the tow trucks show no mercy and getting your vehicle back will cost a bundle in cash and aggravation.

Bicycle The most central place to rent bicycles is McBride Cycle (☎ 763-5651), found at 180 Queen's Quay West, at Harbourfront. There are also rentals on Centre Island at Toronto Island Bicycle Rental (☎ 203-0009), on the south shore more or less straight back from the ferry landing.

Further out but cheaper is Brown's Sports & Cycle (☎ 763-4176), at 2447 Bloor St West, near Jane St and on the subway route. They rent 10-speed bikes for the day and also offer good weekly rates. It's not really that far from High Park, Lake Shore Blvd (along the lakeshore), and the Martin Goodman Trail for walkers and cyclists.

High Park Cycle (☎ 532-7300), at 1168 Bloor St West, will also rent you wheels.

When cycling, be careful on the streetcar rails; cross at right angles or you'll land on your ear.

Pedicab Pedicabs, deluxe bicycle rickshaws peddled by sweating young men and women, can be hired in summer along Yonge St, around the theatre district, and in Yorkville. Prices are around $2 to $3 per person per block.

AROUND TORONTO

Within approximately 1½ hours' drive of the city are a large number of small, old towns that were, until fairly recently, centres for the local farming communities. Some of the country's best land is here, but working farms are giving way to urban sprawl and many of the old downtown areas are now surrounded by modern housing developments. Day trips around the district, especially on a Sunday, are popular. There is still some nice rolling landscape and a few conservation areas, which are basically parks used for walking or picnicking. Quite a few of the towns attract antique hunters, and craft and gift shops are plentiful.

North-west of Toronto, **Caledon** is one of the larger and closer examples and is set in the Caledon Hills. Not far south-west of Caledon, in **Terra Cotta**, is an inn (☎ 905-873-2223) of the same name. It makes a good place to stop later in the day for afternoon tea of scones, cream and jam. Call the inn to check hours and dates of operation. Terra Cotta is also one of the closest points to Toronto for access to an afternoon's walk along part of the **Bruce Trail**, which runs for 780 km north-south. The **Hockley Valley** area near Orangeville provides more of the same. The **Credit River** has trout fishing, and in winter the area is not bad for cross-country skiing, although the hills aren't high enough for downhill skiing.

Kleinburg

The **McMichael Collection** is an excellent art gallery (☎ (905) 893-1121), just north of the city, in the village of Kleinburg. The gallery, consisting of handmade wooden buildings in a pleasant rural setting, displays an extensive and impressive collection of Canadian paintings. Well represented are Canada's best known painters, collectively termed the Group of Seven. If you're going to see northern Ontario, where much of the group's work was done, a visit to the McMichael Collection is all the more worthwhile.

Other exhibits include Inuit and west coast Native Indian art. On display are sculptures, prints and paintings. Special changing exhibitions may feature photography or one particular artist or school of work. The surrounding wooded property is crossed with walking trails, where deer may be seen. The gallery has a book/gift shop and a restaurant.

Admission is $6, less for children, seniors and families. Schoolchildren often visit on weekday mornings. The gallery is open daily in summer, but is closed on Monday from mid October to May. Opening hours are 10 am to 5 pm in the summer season, 10 am to 4 pm the rest of the year.

In Kleinburg itself, a rather pricey retreat from Toronto, there are numerous antique shops, small galleries, craft shops and places for a nosh.

The Group of Seven

The Group of Seven is the name of a group of painters who came together in 1920 to celebrate the Canadian landscape in a new and vital way. Sounding suspiciously like the title of an Enid Blyton adventure story, the group was in fact a bit of a boy's club. Fired by an almost adolescent enthusiasm, the group (all male) was very much about exploring and capturing the rugged wilderness of Canada, land of the lumberjack, the free and the brave. But the energy and enthusiasm they felt then can be seen today in some really stunning paintings – vibrant, light-filled canvases of Canada's mountains, lakes, forests and townships.

Influenced by the Impressionists, the post-impressionists and Britain's Bloomsbury Group, the Group of Seven spent a lot of time in the wilds of Northern Ontario capturing the landscape through the seasons and under all weather conditions. Favourite places included Algonquin Park, Georgian Bay, Lake Superior and Algoma. The Algoma Central Railway even converted an old box-car into living quarters for the painters – a freight train would deposit them on a siding for a week or more and the intrepid painters would set off from there, on foot or by canoe, to paint from morning till night.

The original seven members (the group later expanded to become the Canadian Group of Painters) were Franklin Carmichael, Lawren Harris, AY Jackson, Frank Johnston, Arthur Lismer, JEH MacDonald and FH Varley. Although he died before the group was officially formed, the painter Tom Thompson was considered by the other members as the group's leading light.

An experienced outdoorsman, Thompson drowned in 1917 just as he was producing some of his most powerful work. His deep connection to the land can be clearly seen in his vivid paintings. When the group took studios in Toronto (they sketched outside but produced finished work indoors) Thompson preferred working and living in his small rustic shack out the back. And as soon as the winter ice broke he'd be off to the great north.

Good places to see work by the Group of Seven include the McMichael Collection in the village of Kleinburg, north of Toronto, the Art Gallery of Ontario in Toronto, and the National Gallery of Canada in Ottawa. ■

Getting There & Away Kleinburg is 18 km north from the corner of Islington Ave and Hwy 401 in Toronto. To get there by car, go north up Hwy 427 to Hwy 27 and continue north. Turn right at Nashville Rd.

PMCL bus lines has an early morning bus and gallery package from the main Toronto bus terminal. Call the station for details. Otherwise, public transportation is limited and a little awkward, but can be used. There is no service, though, on weekends or holidays. First, take the Toronto subway west to Islington on the east-west line. From there, catch the bus No 37 north for around 35 minutes to Steeles Ave. At the intersection of Steeles and Islington Aves, transfer to the No 3 Vaughan bus. The only one of these of any use for those wishing to visit the gallery is at 8.15 am, so you must make this connection. The bus will take you to the gallery gate in about 20 minutes, from where it is a 10-minute walk in. On the way back, the bus No 3 leaves at 5 and 6 pm. To check details, call Vaughan Transit (☎ (905) 832-2281).

Dunlap Observatory

Just north of the Toronto city limits, the Dunlap Observatory (☎ (905) 884-2112) has what was once the world's second-largest telescope; it remains the biggest in Canada. From April to October, it is open to the public on Saturday evening at 9.30 pm. A brief introductory talk is given to accompany a slide show, which is then followed by a bit of stargazing through the scope.

The programmes are free, but you must call ahead on a weekday for reservations. Every Tuesday at 10 am, tours of the grounds and buildings are offered. To reach the observatory, drive up Hwy 11 (the continuation of Yonge St) towards Richmond Hill; you'll see the white dome on the right. For public transportation, check with the TTC and their Vaughan Transit connections.

Cathedral of the Transfiguration

It seems nobody builds churches any more, especially on the grand old scale. But north of Toronto, straight up Hwy 404 from the city, at 10350 Woodbine Ave in the village of Gormley (near the town of Markham), there is one heck of an exception. Opened in 1987, this Byzantine Catholic cathedral (☎ (905) 887-5706) is one of the country's largest, standing 62.7 metres high to the tip of its copper-topped spire. Based on a smaller version found in the Czech Republic, this is a 1000-seater church. One of the impressive features is the French-made main bell, ringing in at 16,650 kg, second in size only to the one in Sacré Coeur in Paris. Also, it is the first cathedral in the Western hemisphere to be blessed by a pope – John Paul II did the honours in 1984.

Pickering Nuclear Plant
About 40 km east of Toronto on the Lake Ontario shoreline is this nuclear power station (☎ (905) 839-0465), which has portions open to the public. Whether you're pro or con nuclear plants, you could find out something you didn't know. Free films, displays and a drive around the site explain the operation. It's open from 9 am to 4 pm daily. Look for the signs on Hwy 401 – the plant is at the foot of Liverpool Rd. If your kids are born glowing in the dark, don't blame me.

Cullen Gardens & Miniature Village
About a 45-minute drive east from Toronto on Hwy 401, in the town of Whitby, is a 10-hectare site of carefully tended gardens interspersed with miniature models (☎ (905) 668-6606). A path, which will take two or three hours to walk if you're looking at all the impressive detail, winds through the gardens past a village, modern suburban subdivision, farm and a scene from cottage country. The buildings, people and activities portrayed offer, in a sense, a glimpse of life in southern Ontario. The floral aspect of the gardens, although colourful and quite extensive, should not be confused with botanical gardens but, rather, should be viewed as the setting for the various scenes. The park appeals to a variety of people but is particularly fascinating to children.

The gardens are on Taunton Rd West, off Hwy 12 about five km north along Hwy 401.

They're open daily from the middle of April to the beginning of January. Admission is $9.95, less for children and seniors. When hunger strikes, there is a pleasant picnic and snack bar area (bring your own food) or a fairly pricey sit-down restaurant.

Canadian Automotive Museum
Further east, near Oshawa (a centre for car assembly), this museum (☎ 905-576-1222 from Toronto) has a collection of over 60 cars. Included are a Redpath Runabout from 1890, a Model T (of course) and various automotive memorabilia. It's at 99 Simcoe St South and is open daily all year. Admission is $5.

Parkwood
Also in Oshawa, at 270 Simcoe St North, Parkwood (☎ 905-579-1311 from Toronto) is the estate of RS McLaughlin, who once ran the Canadian division of General Motors. The property consists of a 55-room mansion with antique furnishings, set amidst large gardens. Admission is $5. It's closed on Monday (unless it's a holiday, when it remains open). Afternoon tea is served outside during summer and in the conservatory during winter.

Local Conservation Areas
South-western Ontario is urban. To offset this somewhat, the government has designated many conservation areas – small nature parks for walking, picnicking and (sometimes) fishing, swimming and cross-country skiing. The quality and characteristics vary markedly. Some protect noteworthy geographic areas, others are more historic in emphasis. Generally, they are not wild areas by any means, and some are not even pretty, but they are close to major centres and do offer some relief from concrete. The tourist office has a list of those around Toronto and within a 160-km radius of town. The Metro Toronto Conservation Authority (☎ 661-6600) is responsible for their development and operation. Most areas are difficult to reach without a vehicle.

One place which makes a good, quick escape on a nice summer day is the large **Albion Hills Conservation Area**. It's primarily a quiet, wooded area with walking trails. In winter it allows for decent cross-country skiing. On the west side of town, take Indian Line (by the airport) north. It becomes Hwy 50, which then leads to the park.

Also in this region, near Kleinburg, is the **Kortright Centre for Conservation**. There are trails here, too, but it's more of a museum, with displays and demonstrations on resources, wildlife, ecology, etc. It's open daily to 4 pm.

West of Toronto, near Milton, there are two conservation areas to consider visiting. **Crawford Lake** (☎ 905-854-0234) is one of the most interesting in the entire system. The deep, cool and pretty glacial lake set in the woods is surrounded by walking trails. Details on its formation and unique qualities are given in the well laid-out interpretive centre. Also on the site is a reconstructed 15th-century Iroquoian longhouse village.

Crawford Lake is open on weekends all year, and daily from May to October. It is five km south of Hwy 401 down a road called Guelph Line. There is a snack bar and some picnic tables at the site. The Bruce Trail, described elsewhere (see Tobermory in the Georgian Bay & Lakelands section for details), also runs through the park. Admission is $2.75.

In about the same general area is the **Mountsberg Conservation Area** (☎ 905-854-2276). To reach it, exit south off Hwy 401 at Guelph Line and continue to the No 9 Sideroad. Travel west to Town Line and turn north for 3.2 km. It's 19 km west of the town of Milton. The centre provides a series of country related educational programmes throughout the year. One of the best is the maple syrup/sugaring-off demonstration put on each spring; it explains in detail the history, collection and production of this Canadian speciality (for more information about maple syrup see the Lanaudière section in the Quebec chapter).

South-Western Ontario

This designation covers everything south and west of Toronto to Lake Huron and Lake Erie, which border the USA. For the most part, the area is flat farmland – the only area in Ontario with little forest – and population density is high. With the warm climate and long growing season, this southern tip of Canada was settled early.

Arching around Lake Ontario is a continuous strip of urbanisation. This 'Golden Horseshoe' helps make the region one of the most industrialised and wealthy in the country.

Hamilton, the largest city in the area, is a major steel town. Niagara, with its famous falls, is an important fruit-growing and wine-producing district.

Further west, the soil becomes sandier and the main crop is tobacco, although this is changing as the Canadian cigarette market shrinks. Around Kitchener and London, the small towns are centres for the mixed farming of the region. Lake Erie and, especially, Lake Huron have sandy beaches. In some of the older country towns, crafts and antiques are available.

Windsor – like Detroit, Michigan, its counterpart across the river – is a centre for auto manufacturing.

Because the area is heavily populated and the USA is close by, attractions and parks do get busy in summer. In general, this is an area for people-related activities and pastimes, not for nature or rugged landscapes.

The telephone area code for south-western Ontario is 519.

HAMILTON

Hamilton, sometimes referred to as Steeltown, is a heavily industrialised city with about 319,000 residents. It's halfway between Toronto and Niagara Falls. This is the centre of Canada's iron and steel industry, with two major companies here: Stelco and Dofasco. Because of this, the city has a bit of a reputation as a pollution centre.

Action has been taken to clean it up and work in this direction continues. Although the air cannot be compared to that of the far north (what can?), these days some of what one sees billowing from the many smoke-stacks is actually steam. While Hamilton is obviously not a tourist centre, there are nonetheless a few good things to see in and around town. As accommodation is reasonable here, it may be worth considering spending the night if you're planning a look around Niagara-on-the-Lake, which has high prices.

Orientation
King St (a one-way street going west) and Main St (one way going east, parallel to and one block south of King St) are the two main streets. King St has most of the downtown shops and restaurants. King and John Sts are the core of the downtown area. Jackson Square, on King St between Bay and James Sts, is a large, shopping complex that includes restaurants, cinemas and even an indoor skating rink. The Convention Centre (with an art gallery) is on the corner of King and McNab Sts. Just south across Main St is City Hall. The bus terminal is at the corner of James and Hunter Sts about three blocks south of the centre of town.

Information
The downtown central tourist office (☎ 546-2666) is at 127 King St East and operates seven days a week during the summer. Other summer-only information centres are in busy visitor centres around the city, such as the Royal Botanical Gardens or the African Lion Safari.

Royal Botanical Gardens
The Royal Botanical Gardens – nearly 1000 hectares of flowers, natural park and wildlife sanctuary – is probably the big attraction in the area. It is one of the largest of its kind in the country and only one of five in the world to be designated 'Royal'. The grounds are split into sections, with trails connecting some areas.

During spring the Rock Garden is a high-light with its three hectares of rare trees and shrubs, waterfalls, ponds and 125,000 spring-flowering bulbs. From June to October thousands of roses, including many antique varieties, bloom in the Centennial Rose Garden. The arboretum has the world's largest lilac collection (what an olfactory treat), which is best in May.

The sanctuary takes up nearly half of the grounds and consists of trails winding through marsh and wooded ravines – a paradise for bird watchers and home to deer, fox, muskrat and coyotes. There is also an interpretive centre and two restaurants at the gardens.

The site is between Hamilton and the suburban community of Burlington, on Plains Rd near the junction of Hwys 2 and 6, and is open daily all year. General admission is $4.25.

Art Gallery of Hamilton
The art gallery (☎ 527-6610), the province's third largest, is spacious and has a good selection of Canadian and international paintings. They also run an interesting film series, with screenings mainly on weekends.

The gallery, at 123 King St West, is open Wednesday to Saturday from 10 am to 5 pm (until 9 pm on Thursday) and on Sunday from 1 to 5 pm. There's no set charge, but donations are welcome.

Hamilton Place
In the same complex as the art gallery, this theatre-auditorium for the performing arts features shows of various types almost nightly, including regular performances by the Philharmonic and the Opera Company. Tours are available.

Dundurn Castle
One man's castle, Dundurn (☎ 546-2872) is actually a 36-room mansion once belonging to Sir Allan Napier McNab, prime minister from 1854 to 1856 of what was then the United Provinces of Canada. It's furnished in mid-19th century style. The mansion is on York Blvd just out of town, about a 15-minute walk (or you can grab the York city bus). It's open daily all year, in the afternoon only from June to September. Admission is $5.

ONTARIO

Concerts are held on the grounds through the summer. Also at the site is a military museum, with weapons and uniforms dating from the War of 1812.

Whitehern
At 41 Jackson St West, this elegant mansion (☎ 546-2018), lived in by the prominent McQuesten family from 1852 to 1968, contains original furnishings and art works and is surrounded by well-tended gardens. It offers a peek into both the Victorian era and the life of the well-to-do. Admission is charged.

Canadian Warplane Heritage Museum
The spacious new museum (☎ 679-4183) is at 9280 Airport Rd just east of the airport. Its impressive collection contains about 20 vintage planes, including a restored Lancaster bomber from WWII. All are in flying condition. It's open daily and there is a cafeteria and a gift shop. Many of the planes, together with newer ones from a variety of sources, are part of an excellent two-day air show held in mid-June.

Museum of Steam & Technology
The old pumphouse (☎ 546-4797), dating from 1860, was built to supply clean water when cholera and typhus menaced the city. Now restored, these steam engines are among the largest in North America. Trimmed with mahogany and brass, they are rather attractive objects. Also featured are photographs and engine exhibits. Admission costs $2.50 and the museum, at 900 Woodward Ave, is open daily (but in the afternoon only from October to May).

Confederation Park
Not too far north of town on Centennial Parkway, this park contains Wild Waterworks, featuring a waterslide and a swimming pool with waves. There is also a beach along Lake Ontario, and picnic and camping facilities.

African Lion Safari
About 1000 animals and birds roam this vast,

cageless park (☎ 623-2620). You drive through, sometimes getting very close to lions, tigers and other animals. Monkeys and others climb and grope all over the car, and for this reason those with particular pride in their vehicle are advised to use the park tour bus instead.

The park is not cheap ($14.50 for adults, $10.50 for children), but seeing the whole thing can take a full afternoon and most people feel it's worth the money, especially if you have children with you. Try to make time for the live demonstrations such as the one on birds of prey.

African Lion Safari is open from April to October. The longest hours are in July and August, but even at that time of year it closes at 5.30 pm. The park is between Hamilton and Cambridge, on Hwy 8. For the daring, there is a campground at the site.

Lake Ontario Waterfront Trail
This recently completed trail follows the shoreline of Lake Ontario for 325 km from Trenton to Hamilton. It's good for walking, cycling and roller-blading and in summer there are dozens of organised outdoor activities and festivals along its length. Ask at the tourist office for a map and calendar of events.

Festivals
The Festival of Friends happens each August in Gage Park and features music, crafts and foods from many countries.

Each June, in the town of Stoney Creek (south of Hamilton), an interesting spectacle is the re-enactment of a War of 1812 battle between British and US soldiers. It's held at Stoney Creek Battlefield Park.

Places to Stay
Camping There are numerous local campgrounds, including one in Confederation Park, just north of town on Centennial Parkway.

Hostels For low-budget lodgings, the *YMCA* (☎ 529-7102), at 79 James St, has 172 rooms, for men only, at $28 a single. The

YWCA (☎ 522-9922), at 75 McNab St, is comparable, although much smaller, with rooms at $30/44 for singles/doubles. Both have pools and inexpensive cafeterias.

B&Bs *Haddo House* (☎ 524-0071), one km from downtown, at 107 Aberdeen Ave, is a turn-of-the-century home offering two rooms complete with private bathroom. Singles/doubles are $45/55 and include a full breakfast. It's a no smoking and no children house. *Inchbury Street Bed & Breakfast* (☎ 522-3520), at 87 Inchbury St, is a 15-minute walk from the Botanical Gardens. There are two rooms with shared bathroom. Rates are also $45/55.

Hotels Though many of the downtown hotels are new and large, there are some choices that are not too expensive. Accommodation is generally more reasonable here than in either Toronto or around the heavily touristed region of Niagara-on-the-Lake.

At 737 King St East, the *Budget Motor Inn* (☎ 527-2708) has singles/doubles at $45/56. Also central, the *Visitors Inn* (☎ 529-6979), at 649 Main St West, is more expensive but quite good value. Singles/doubles are $62/68.

Further out, close to McMaster University, the *Mountainview Motel* (☎ 528-7521), at 1870 Main St West, costs $40/50 for singles/doubles.

On the outskirts, either east or west, motels abound, and for the most part they are in the budget to moderate price categories, with rates much lower than those around Niagara-on-the-Lake.

Places to Eat
The downtown area around King St has numerous restaurants, including various ethnic places. Many others suiting a range of budgets can be found along Main and William Sts.

At Ferguson and King Sts, the *Black Forest Inn*, with a German and Austrian slant, is pleasant and reasonable for soups and sandwiches. The more expensive and extensive dinner menu features a variety of schnitzels.

Le Ganges, at 234 King St, is not really cheap but serves good Indian food.

In Hess Village, two blocks west of the Convention Centre, the *Gown & Gavel*, a British-style pub at 24 Hess St, serves light meals and beer under the umbrellas.

There are many low-priced places to eat in the Jackson Square shopping mall.

Spectator Sports
The Hamilton Tiger Cats play CFL football at the Ivor Wynn Stadium. Call the stadium on ☎ 544-7978 for ticket information.

ST CATHARINES
Between Hamilton and the Niagara River, St Catharines is the major town of the Niagara fruit and wine-growing district. To each side are farms and small towns with vineyards and wineries.

Port Dalhousie (pronounced 'dal-oo-zey') is an old harbour area where the early canals opened into Lake Ontario. It is now a blend of the new and historic, with a reconstructed wooden lock, the oldest and smallest jail in the province and a lighthouse set alongside contemporary bars and restaurants.

In late September, the Niagara Grape & Wine Festival is held, with concerts, wine-and-cheese parties and a parade.

WELLAND CANAL
The most noteworthy feature of the area is the historic Welland Canal, a bypass of Niagara Falls which connects Lake Ontario with Lake Erie. A series of locks along the 42-km-long canal overcomes the difference of about 100 metres in the lakes' water levels.

The canal was initiated in 1829 by local businessmen to promote trade and commerce. Now in its fourth incarnation and part of the St Lawrence Seaway, it is a vital link in international freight service, allowing shipping into the industrial heart of North America from the Atlantic Ocean.

The three principal cargoes going through the canal are wheat, iron ore and coal. The

ONTARIO

average trip through the canal and its eight locks takes 12 hours.

Remnants of the first three canals (built in 1829, 1845 and 1887) can be seen at various points. The fourth version, still in use but with some modifications and additions, was built between 1914 and 1932.

At Lakeside Park, along the waterfront in Port Dalhousie, the early canals met Lake Ontario. Old locks, lighthouses and various structures from the last century can be viewed. At **Mountain View Park,** on the corner of Mountain and Bradley Sts, there are locks at the escarpment from the second canal, along with some other 19th-century buildings.

For a more up-to-date look, visit the **Welland Canal Viewing & Information Centre,** on Canal Rd also in St Catharines. It's at lock 3 of the currently used canal, and includes a museum with exhibits on the canal and its construction, a viewing platform and audiovisual displays on many aspects of the waterway. Ships from around the world may be seen on their way to and from the centre of North America and the Atlantic Ocean. Fifty million tonnes of cargo are transported through the canal annually. Open daily all year, the centre is on Canal Rd, off Glendale Ave (which exits from the Queen Elizabeth Hwy). Follow the signs to the locks. You can also get a bite to eat and something to drink here while you watch the ships. A daily shipping schedule is posted.

The last lock, number eight, is at Port Colbourne (on Lake Erie).

Chaudiere Navigation (☎ 834-1536) offers one hour cruises along the canal for $7. Getting to the dock area is a little tricky. It's near Lakeside Park in Port Dalhousie. If driving, take the Ontario St exit off the Queen Elizabeth Way (QEW) and continue north to Lakeport Rd, where a left turn should be made. From there just keep going over the bridges and you should see a sign.

For hikers, there is the Merritt Trail, a walk

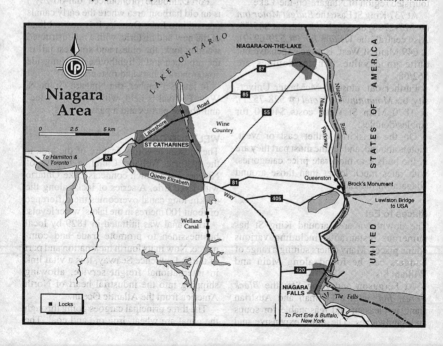

which stretches from Port Dalhousie in St Catharines to Port Colbourne, mainly following the Welland Canal. It is detailed in the Bruce Trail guidebook; see Tobermory later in this chapter. Local tourist offices will also have information about this trail.

WELLAND

Despite the predominance of agriculture in the region, Welland is primarily a steel town. A portion of the canal cuts right through town, with a larger bypass channel two km from the downtown area; from there, international freighters can be viewed.

The city has become known for its two dozen or so painted murals depicting scenes from the history of the area and the canal. They can be seen around town on the sides of buildings with the heaviest concentration along East Main St and the streets connecting it to parallel Division St, one block away. There are others along King and Niagara Sts. A pamphlet on the paintings can be picked up at one of the local tourist offices. The Chamber of Commerce is at 32 Main St East.

The museum at 65 Hooker St offers more details on the canals.

In the Seaway Mall, a shopping centre at 800 Niagara St, the Seaway Serpentarium has a fairly extensive reptile collection of 250 species, including some endangered ones which are studied and bred here.

In early June, the two-week Rose Festival celebrates the queen of flowers. There are displays, contests, a parade and other events.

PORT COLBORNE

Situated on Lake Erie at the southern end of the Welland Canal, Port Colborne has one of the largest water locks in the world. This lock (lock 8) can be seen from Fountain View Park. The summer tourist information booth is here, too. The quiet town doesn't really offer much to see or do. At 280 King St is a small pioneer heritage village. There are some beaches in the area, and a number of cottage communities along the shoreline.

NIAGARA-ON-THE-LAKE

This small, attractive village (population 12,900) is about 20 km downstream from the falls, and with its upmarket shops and restaurants, well-known George Bernard Shaw Festival and curbs on development, it acts as a sort of foil to the hype and flash of Niagara Falls. The surrounding vineyards and history filled parkland add to its appeal. Originally a Native Indian site, it was settled by Loyalists from New York State after the American Revolution. In the 1790s it was made the first capital of Ontario, and it is considered one of the best preserved, 19th-century towns in North America.

The main street, Queen St, has many well-maintained shops from the early 19th century. The lakeside location, tree-lined streets and old houses make Niagara-on-the-Lake a nice place to see before or after the falls. The village does get busy on good summer days, though generally only on the main street. Stroll down the side streets and

The Niagara Escarpment

An escarpment is a steep rock face, or cliff of great length. The Niagara Escarpment, so often referred to in southern Ontario, runs for 725 km, with a maximum height of 335 metres. Once the shore of an ancient sea centred in what is now Michigan, USA, the escarpment begins in Ontario, at the town of Queenston on the Niagara River. On its way north to Tobermory and Manitoulin Island, it passes through or beside Hamilton, Collingwood and Owen Sound. A major outcropping of the escarpment can clearly be seen from Hwy 401 west of Oakville, at Kelso Conservation Area.

The Niagara Escarpment Commission, through a series of parks and conservation areas, seeks to preserve the escarpment's natural beauty, flora & fauna. Now largely a recreation area, the escarpment is used for activities such as skiing and bird-watching but is best known for the hiking along the Bruce Trail. For more details on the trail, see Tobermory. ■

ONTARIO

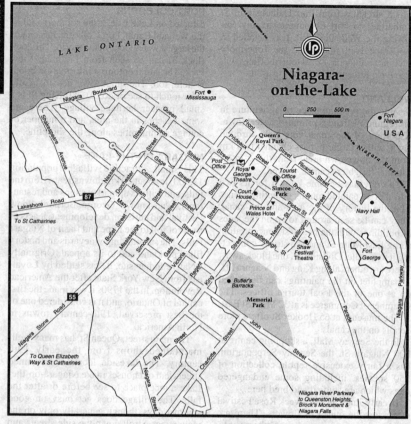

Niagara-
on-the-Lake

LAKE ONTARIO

Fort Mississauga

Fort Niagara

USA

Niagara River

0   250   500 m

Niagara Boulevard

Shakespeare Avenue

Nassau Street

Dorchester Street

Centre Street

William Street

Mary Street

Mississauga Street

Simcoe Street

Gate Street

Victoria Street

Regent Street

King Street

Rye Street

Charlotte Street

Niagara Street

Johnson Street

Gage Street

Queen Street

Prideaux Street

Front Street

Castlereagh St

Nelles St

Wellington St

Picton St

Byron St

Ricardo Street

Queens Parade

Niagara Parkway

Queen's Royal Park

Post Office

Royal George Theatre

Court House

Prince of Wales Hotel

Simcoe Park

Tourist Office

Shaw Festival Theatre

Navy Hall

Fort George

Butler's Barracks

Memorial Park

John Street

Lakeshore Road

87

To St Catharines

Niagara Stone Road

55

To Queen Elizabeth Way & St Catharines

Niagara River Parkway to Queenston Heights, Brock's Monument & Niagara Falls

you'll get a quiet taste of former times in a small, prosperous Ontario town. Decidedly atypical (sort of rural Japan in Canada) and worth a look is the house at the corner of Wellington and Byron Sts, not far from the tourist office.

Information
The tourist office (☎ 468-4263) in the Chamber of Commerce, on the corner of King St and Prideaux/Byron Sts, is good, friendly and helpful and will book accommodation for you. From March to December the office is open every day; later in the year,

the hours are shortened and it's closed on Sunday. On the eastern side of the downtown area towards Niagara Falls, King St crosses Queen St at large Simcoe Park, on the east side of Queen St.

Ask for the *Historic Guide*, a free pamphlet outlining in brief the town's history and a self-guided walking tour. It lists many of the noteworthy structures around town and indicates them on a map.

Also ask about the Garden Tour (usually on the third weekend in June) put on by the Conservancy, which allows visitors a peek around some of the splendid gardens in town.

In October, the annual B&B tour gives you another chance to see behind the fences and doors of town.

Queen St

The town's main street, Queen St, is the prime attraction. Restored and well-preserved wooden buildings and shops now contain antiques, bakeries, various specialities, Scottish souvenirs and restaurants. Note particularly the apothecary dating from 1866, now a museum, fitted with great old cabinets, remedies and jars. Also recommended is a jam sample from the Greaves store; the people here are fourth-generation jam-makers. There are a couple of fudge shops, too.

The renovated courthouse, on Queen St, is another impressive building.

Towards the falls but still in town, Queen St becomes Picton St.

Museums

The **Historical Museum** at 43 Castlereagh St is the oldest local museum in the province. It opened in 1907 and has a vast collection of early 20th-century items relating to the town's past, ranging from some Native Indian artefacts to Loyalist and War-of-1812 collectibles. Admission is $2.50. From March to December, it is open daily from 10 am to 6 pm. During January and February, it opens only on weekend afternoons.

McFarland House is a handsome Georgian-style place built around 1800 by John McFarland, a carpenter from Scotland. Restored in 1959, it is now furnished with pre-1840 articles. During the War of 1812 it was used as a hospital. The house is in McFarland Park, two km south of town on the Niagara Parkway, and is open daily during summer from 11 am to 5 pm. Tea is served.

Also in town is the **Fire Museum**, with firefighting equipment that dates from 1816.

Historic Military Sites

Just out of Niagara-on-the-Lake towards the falls, **Fort George**, dating from 1797, is one of several local historic military sites. It's

open daily and admission is $4 for adults. The fort was the site of important battles during the War of 1812 and changed hands between the British and US forces a couple of times. Within the walls are the officers' quarters, a working kitchen, the powder magazine and storage houses. There isn't a lot to see, but the various costumed workers, particularly the soldiers performing different exercises, provide some atmosphere.

Tucked behind the fort is **Navy Hall**, at the water's edge. Only one building remains of what was a sizeable supply depot for British forts on the Great Lakes during the 18th century. It was destroyed during the War of 1812. The US Fort Niagara is across the river.

In a fine location on the west side of town, at the opposite end of Ricardo/Front St, are the minimal remains of **Fort Mississauga**. There are some plaques but no organised tours or facilities.

Also in town are **Butler's Barracks**, off John St at King St. Pedestrians can reach it either from Mary St or along a trail leading from Fort George. First used by the British at the end of the War of 1812 as a storage and barracks site, the location has since been used for a variety of purposes by the Canadian military. Troops trained here for both World Wars and for the Korean War. Some buildings remain from the various periods of use, and markers lead visitors around on a mini-Canadian military history tour.

Whirlpool Jet

The only Niagara Falls-like attraction in town, the Whirlpool Jet (☎ 468-4800) is a boat which takes passengers on an hour-long trip through the rapids of the lower Niagara River. Reservations are required. Trips depart from 61 Melville St and passengers are advised to take a change of clothing. Tickets cost, brace yourself, $47.

Organised Tours

Short $5 walking tours of town leave from opposite the tourist office every hour from 11 am to 5 pm on Saturday and Sunday.

Niagara Bicycle Tours (☎ 468-1300) offer

two daily tours of the area ($35) which take in wine tastings and visits to three of the major local wineries. It also does a trip along the Niagara Escarpment and offers accommodation packages for one or two-day bicycle tours.

Sentineal Carriages (☎ 468-4943) has leisurely 20-minute or half-hour tours around town in a horse-drawn buggy.

Festivals

The Shaw Festival is an internationally respected theatre festival held annually (April to October). It features the plays of George Bernard Shaw and his contemporaries, played by top actors. There are three different theatres, within walking distance of the town centre, and the location has a bearing on ticket prices. Cheapest are the weekday matinees.

Tickets range from $21 up to $53 for the best seats in the house on Saturday night at Festival Theatre. Cheaper rush seats go on sale at 9 am on the day of performance but are not available for Saturday shows. There are brief lunch-time plays for $10.

The box office (☎ 468-2172) is open from 9 am to 8 pm every day from 12 April to 16 January. If you're planning to take in a play call ☎ 1-800-267-4759 from anywhere in Canada or the USA, well in advance, and ask for the Shaw Festival guide. It will give you all the details, the year's performances and other useful information, as well as ticket order forms.

Places to Stay

Accommodation is expensive. For many people, a few hours spent browsing around town will suffice before finding cheaper lodging elsewhere. When the Shaw Festival is on the town can get booked out on weekends, so plan accordingly.

The town has some fine inns and several good hotels. By far the majority of the accommodation, though, is in the many

---

The Shaw Festival

The only festival in the world devoted exclusively to producing the plays of George Bernard Shaw and his contemporaries takes place in the picturesque town of Niagara-on-the-Lake every year from April to October.

The Shaw Festival was founded in 1962 by a group of local residents led by Brian Doherty, a lawyer and dramatist who had a passion for theatre. The very first season consisted of eight perfomances of Shaw's *Candida* and *Don Juan in Hell* from *Man and Superman*. The following year Doherty recruited Andrew Allan, a well-known producer of Canadian Broadcasting Corporation radio dramas, as the festival's first artisitic director.

Doherty chose Shaw because he was 'a great prophet of the 20th century' and also because Shaw 'was the only outstanding playwright writing in English, with the obvious exception of Shakespeare, who produced a sufficient number of plays to support a festival'.

Ten plays are performed every season in three theatres around town – the Court House Theatre, the Festival Theatre and the Royal George Theatre, a one-time vaudeville house and cinema. As well as producing Shaw's work the festival aims to give space to a variety of plays not widely performed nowadays. These include Victorian drama, plays of continental Europe, classic US drama, musicals, and mystery and suspense plays.

The 1995 Shaw Festival season included *You Never Can Tell* by Shaw, *The Petrified Forest*, a melodrama written by the US playwright Robert E Sherwood in 1934, Nole Coward's *Cavalcade*, Oscar Wilde's *An Ideal Husband*, and *The Zoo* a musical written by Arthur Sullivan and Bolton Rowe in 1875.

The festival Academy was established in 1985 primarily as a vehicle for the exchange of skills among the festival's ensemble of actors. Since then it has expanded to include various educational programmes. There are specialised seminars held through the season and, on selected Saturdays, informal Lunchtime Conversations where the public can join in discussions with members of the Shaw Festival company.

The Shaw Festival has ticket outlets throughout Canada. Prices range from $10 to $60 and tend to sell like hot cakes. The Box Office opens on 16 January and can be contacted on ☎1-800-267-4759 or (905) 468-2172. ■

cheaper B&Bs. This does not mean cheap, however, with rates of about $75 and up for a double. The tourist office has a free accommodation reservation service.

One of the least expensive B&Bs is the central *Endicott's B&B* (☎ 468-3671), at 331 William St. Prices are $50 to $55 and bicycles are available.

Similarly priced is *Rose Cottage*, also in the downtown area, at 308 Victoria St. There's just one room and it comes with a private bath. Book through the Chamber of Commerce (☎ 468-4263).

Also with reasonable rates is *Amberlea Guest House* (☎ 468-3749), found at 285 John St. There are two double rooms, both with private bathroom, at $75, and one twin with shared bathroom at $55. A single is $50. All include a full breakfast.

Another possibility is the central *Saltbox* (☎ 468-5423), in an old house at 223 Gate St. Again, a full breakfast is provided and smoking is not permitted. It's open all year and charges around $75 for doubles.

Mrs Lynda Kay Knapp (☎ 468-4398) offers a separate, private unit (almost like a little apartment, with some cooking facilities and a fridge) at $80 for two people. It's close to the centre of town at 390 Simcoe St but not open in winter.

Among the pricier options (from $99) is the *Angel Inn* (☎ 468-3411), dating from 1823, one block south from Queen St on Regent St. The slightly older *Kiely House Inn* (☎ 468-4588) is a 13-room B&B at 209 Queen St. The *Moffat Inn* (☎ 468-4116), an attractive white-and-green place at 60 Picton St, offers all the amenities for reasonable rates starting from $90.

Places to Eat

There are a number of good places to eat in town. At 45 Queen St, the *Stagecoach* is cheap and always busy. You can get a good-value breakfast before 11 am.

For a pub meal, try the *Buttery*, at 19 Queen St, with a pleasant patio. Lunch starts at around $7. On Saturday night a Henry VIII-style feast is put on with entertainment, drink and victuals aplenty.

Fans Court, around the back at 135 Queen St, provides some fine ethnic diversion in this most Anglo of towns. It serves Chinese and Asian dishes, such as Singapore noodles with curry. Apart from the pleasant dining room, there are also a few tables outside in a small courtyard. Prices are moderate at lunch but the dinner menu has become a little pricey.

The *Prince of Wales Hotel* has a good dining room for finer, more costly eating. Most of the inns and hotels have their own dining rooms. At the *Kiely House Inn*, 209 Queen St, you can enjoy afternoon cream teas on the porch overlooking the golf course.

For a good cup of coffee try *Monika's*, at 126 Queen St.

A few blocks from Queen St, Queen's Royal Park makes a good place for a picnic along the water.

Entertainment

In Simcoe Park, right in town, there are often free classical-music concerts on Saturday during the summer.

Getting There & Away

Bus There is one bus daily each way between here and Toronto from May to September. The fare is $21.50 for the two-hour trip. Charterways Bus Lines runs between St Catharines and Niagara-on-the-Lake three times a week. In town, the buses to and from St Catharines stop at Simcoe Park.

From May to September a shuttle bus runs three times daily between Niagara-on-the-Lake and Niagara Falls. Check the times at the tourist office. There's one run a day during the winter.

Taxi Taxis to Niagara Falls charge $23.

Getting Around

Bicycle Cycling is a fine way to explore the area, and bicycles can be rented by the hour, half day or full day at 92A Picton St (☎ 468-0044), past the Moffat Inn. They also hire out roller skates and protection pads.

ONTARIO

AROUND NIAGARA-ON-THE-LAKE
Vineyards & Wine Tours

The triangle between St Catharines, Niagara-on-the-Lake and Niagara Falls is an important wine-producing area. The Ontario region, produces about 80% of the grapes used in Canada's wine production. The moderate microclimate that is created by the escarpment and Lake Ontario is a big part of the area's success.

The ever-increasing number of wineries – there are now 23 – are producing some pretty fine wine. The better wines have a Vinter's Quality Alliance (VQA) designation.

Since the end of the 1980s, the wine producers have grown from operating an essentially small cottage industry to being internationally recognised vintners capable of turning out calibre vintages. Many offer visitors a look around and a taste. A full day could be enjoyed touring the countryside and emptying glasses. Three of the principal wines are riesling, chardonnay and gewurztraminer. Whites tend to dominate but reds are also produced. The expensive icewines have gained a lot of favourable attention. Many of the wineries are open year round. Some of the commercial tour operators include a winery or two on their bus excursions. Most of these operate out of Niagara Falls.

The eight premier wineries are known collectively as the Group of Seven Plus One. The following are taken from this group. They tend to be clustered south of Niagara-on-the-Lake.

The Reif Estate Winery (☎ 468-7738) is south of Niagara-on-the-Lake, between Line 2 and Line 3 on the Niagara Parkway. The winery, with tastings, is open every day of the year, as is the shop. Call for tour times.

Inniskillin (☎ 468-3554) is practically next door, at Line 3. It's open year round. Inniskillin has developed a good reputation and is the leading award winner of the region. A display outlines the process and history of wine making in Niagara.

Château des Charmes (☎ 262-4219) is in St David's, between the falls and Niagara-on-the-Lake. It's on Line 7 off Four Mile Creek Rd, not far from Hwy 55, and is open all day, every day. Again, although the store with tastings is virtually always open, call for tour times for a more in-depth look around the estate.

Others of the Group of Seven Plus One are Marynissen, Konzelmann, Stonechurch, Hillebrand and Pillitteri.

Another vintner is Brights (☎ 357-2400), Canada's oldest winery. It's at 4887 Dorchester Rd, Niagara Falls, north off Hwy 420. Call for tour times and for specific directions; the best route depends on where you're starting from.

Area tourist offices will have complete lists of the wineries and their locations.

NIAGARA PARKWAY & RECREATIONAL TRAIL

A slow, 20-km trip along the two-lane **Niagara Parkway** to Niagara Falls is most enjoyable. Along the way are parks, picnic areas, good views over the river and a couple of campgrounds, all of which make up part of the Niagara Parks Commission park system. It runs pretty well the entire length of the Niagara River, for 56 km, from Niagara-on-the-Lake past the falls to Fort Erie. A three-metre-wide paved recreational trail for cycling, jogging, walking or roller-skating runs the entire way, paralleling the parkway. It's excellent for either a short or long cycling excursion. The terrain is flat and the riverside scenery pleasant, and it's rarely very busy.

The trail can be easily divided into four sections, each of which would take around one to two hours of leisurely pedalling. Historic and natural points of interest are marked with plaques. Perhaps best of all, in season, are the fresh-fruit stands with cold cherry ciders and juices. Ask at the tourist office for the Parks Commission's excellent Recreation Trail Map.

In the small village of Queenston, just before the Lewiston Bridge to the USA, is the **Laura Secord Homestead**. Laura, one of Canada's best known heroines (partly because of the chocolate company which bears her name), lived here, on the corner of

Queenston and Partition Sts, during the War of 1812. At one point during the war, she hiked nearly 30 km to warn the British soldiers of impending attack by the USA. The house can be visited for a small fee, which includes a chocolate sample. There is also a small candy shop on the premises. The rose garden out front is said to have been planted by Laura herself.

At the juncture of the Niagara Parkway and Queenston St (the main street in Queenston), by the War Memorial, is the **Samuel Weir Collection & Library of Art**. Mr Weir had the house built as a live-in gallery and library in 1916 to house his remarkably extensive art, book and antique collection. He formed a foundation to administer the estate for public access, provided that he was buried on the front lawn. He was. It's free and is open from May to October, from Wednesday to Saturday and on Sunday afternoon.

In Mackenzie House, also in town, the **Mackenzie House Printery** has a collection highlighting printing and printing equipment as history. Displays detail historic newspapers, such as the *Colonial Advocate* edited by William Lyon Mackenzie, who later led the Upper Canada Rebellion.

Also in Queenston is the southern end of the Bruce Trail, which extends 780 km to Tobermory on Georgian Bay. There are numerous access points in the Niagara and Hamilton area. For more details on the trail, see the Tobermory section in this chapter.

A little further along the parkway is **Queenston Heights Park**, known for its large monument of Major General Brock. The winding inside stairwell will take you up 60 metres to a fabulous view. Also here is the Queenston Heights Restaurant, which itself has fine views of the river. Enjoy a summer beer on the balcony. This is not a bad place for a meal, either, although it's not in the low-budget category.

Near the restaurant is a monument to Laura Secord, and from here begins a 45-minute self-guided walking tour of the hillside, detailing the Battle of Queenston Heights. Pick up a copy of the good walking-

tour booklet at any of the information offices. It explains some of the historical background, outlines the War of 1812 and describes how the British victory here was significant in Canada's not becoming part of the USA. Interpreters are on hand at the huge **Brock Monument**, and the guidebook should be available there.

The Niagara Parkway continues through Niagara Falls and beyond, southbound. Attractions between Queenston and Niagara Falls, all of which can be reached on the Niagara Falls People Mover buses during the summer season, are covered in the Niagara Falls section; there is an Around Niagara Falls section to cover the southern part of the route to Fort Erie.

NIAGARA FALLS

The roaring falls make this town one of Canada's top tourist destinations. It's a busy spot – about 12 million people visit annually and you'll hear and see people from all over the world.

The falls themselves, spanning the Niagara River between Ontario and upper New York State, are impressive, particularly the Canadian Horseshoe Falls. They look good by day and by night, when colourful spotlights flicker across the misty foam. Even in winter, when the flow is partially hidden and the edges are frozen solid – like a stopped film – it's quite a spectacle. (But as one reader warned – the mist freezes on contact!) Very occasionally the falls stop altogether. The first recorded instance of this occurred on the morning of Easter Sunday 1848, and it caused some to speculate that the end of the world was nigh. An ice jam had completely cut off the flow of water. Some residents, obviously braver than we, took the opportunity to scavenge the river bed beneath the falls!

It is said that Napoleon's brother rode from New Orleans in a stagecoach with his new bride to view the falls and that it has been a honeymoon attraction ever since. In fact, the town is sometimes humorously but disparagingly called a spot for newlyweds and nearly deads. Supplementing the falls,

ONTARIO

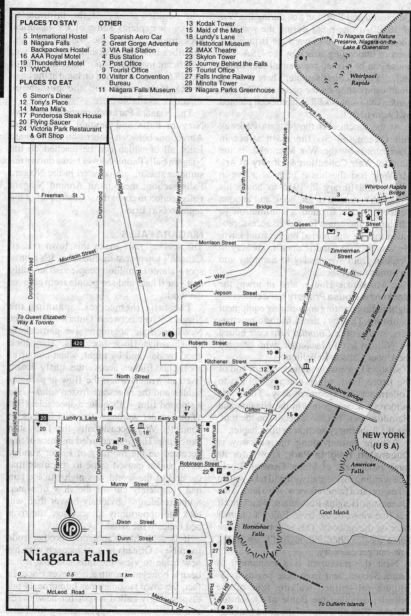

PLACES TO STAY

5 International Hostel
8 Niagara Falls
   Backpackers Hostel
16 AAA Royal Motel
19 Thunderbird Motel
21 YWCA

PLACES TO EAT

6 Simon's Diner
12 Tony's Place
14 Mama Mia's
17 Ponderosa Steak House
20 Flying Saucer
24 Victoria Park Restaurant
   & Gift Shop

OTHER

1 Spanish Aero Car
2 Great Gorge Adventure
3 VIA Rail Station
4 Bus Station
7 Post Office
9 Tourist Office
10 Visitor & Convention
   Bureau
11 Niagara Falls Museum
13 Kodak Tower
15 Maid of the Mist
18 Lundy's Lane
   Historical Museum
22 IMAX Theatre
23 Skylon Tower
25 Journey Behind the Falls
26 Tourist Office
27 Falls Incline Railway
28 Minolta Tower
29 Niagara Parks Greenhouse

To Niagara Glen Nature
Preserve, Niagara-on-the-
Lake & Queenston

Whirlpool
Rapids

Whirlpool Rapids
Bridge

Niagara Parkway

Freeman St

Portage Road

Drummond Road

Stanley Avenue

Fourth Ave

Victoria Avenue

Bridge   Street

Queen

Erie Ave

Ave

Street

Morrison Street

Dorchester Road

Morrison Street

Road

Valley   Way

Zimmerman
Street

Bampfield St

Jepson   Street

Palmer Ave

River Road

Niagara River

To Queen Elizabeth
Way & Toronto

Stamford   Street

Roberts   Street

420

Kitchener Street

North   Street

Centre St

Ellen Ave

Victoria Avenue

Rainbow Bridge

Brookfield Avenue

Franklin Avenue

Drummond Road

Main St

Clifton Hill

Ferry St

20

Lundy's Lane

Culp St

Buchanan Avenue

Clark Avenue

Niagara Parkway

**NEW YORK
(USA)**

American
Falls

Robinson Street

Murray   Street

Stanley   Avenue

Goat Island

Dixon   Street

Dunn   Street

Niagara Falls

Horseshoe
Falls

0   0.5   1 km

McLeod   Road

Marineland Dr

Portage Road

Fraser Hill

To Dufferin Islands

the city now has an incredible array of artificial attractions (such as the Elvis Presley Museum and the new JFK Assassination Exhibit & Research Centre) which, together with the hotels, restaurants and flashing lights, produce a sort of Canadian Las Vegas. It's a sight in itself and the comparison has been made more complete with the opening of a casino.

Niagara Falls is about a two-hour drive from Toronto by the Queen Elizabeth Way (QEW), past Hamilton and St Catharines. Public transport between Toronto and Niagara Falls is frequent and quick.

Orientation

The town of Niagara Falls is split into two main sections: the older commercial area, where the locals go about their business, and the other part around the falls, which has been developed for visitors. In the 'normal' part of town, known as downtown, Queen St and Victoria Ave are the main streets. The area around Bridge St, near the corner of Erie St, has both the train and bus stations and a couple of cheap hotels. The international hostels are not far from the train station. Generally, however, there is little to see or do in this part of town.

About three km south along the river are the falls and all the trappings of the tourist trade – restaurants, motels, shops and attractions. In the vicinity of the falls, the main streets are the busy Clifton Hill, Falls Ave, Centre St and Victoria Ave. The latter has many places to stay, and some of the numerous restaurants which can be found on all the main streets. Going north along the river is scenic parkland, which runs from the falls downstream about 20 km to Niagara-on-the-Lake. Many of the local B&Bs are also between the two sections of town.

Information

Tourist Offices The most central place for tourist information is at Horseshoe Falls, in the building known as Table Rock Centre. The Niagara Parks Commission runs the good but busy desk here (☎ 356-7944). It's open daily from 9 am to 6 pm (until 10 pm

in summer). The area's main tourist office, though, is the Ontario Travel Information Centre (☎ 358-3221), which is out of the centre west on Hwy 420 from the Rainbow Bridge toward the Queen Elizabeth Way, at 5355 Stanley Ave. It's about half way between the bridge and the highway. Ontario maps and information on destinations across the province can be picked up here. It's open until 8 pm through the summer. There are also a couple of information offices around town run by the Visitors & Convention Bureau, which use the same central phone (☎ 356-6061). One of these offices is at 5433 Victoria Ave.

Parking A good, free parking lot about 15 minutes' walk from the falls is by the IMAX movie theatre, south of Murray St towards Robinson St, near the Skylon. After leaving your car, walk to the concrete bridge on the north side of the parking lot. Go across the bridge to the top of the stairs, which lead down through some woods to the gardens and the river. Another parking place is the huge Rapids View Parking Lot, 3.2 km south of the falls. It's off River Rd where the bus loop depot is situated. From here, a pleasant walk leads to the falls.

Medical Services The Greater Niagara General Hospital (☎ 358-0171) is at 5546 Portage Rd.

The Falls

Some wags have said the falls are the brides' second disappointment, but the roaring water tumbling 56 metres is a grand sight – close up, just where the water begins to plunge down, is the most intense spot. Also good, and free, is the observation deck of the souvenir shop by the falls.

After checking out all the angles at all times of day, you can try several services offering yet different approaches. The *Maid of the Mist* boat takes passengers up to the falls for a view from the bottom – it's loud and wet and costs $9.55. Board the boat at the bottom of the incline railway at the foot of Clifton Hill. From the Table Rock Centre right at the falls, you can pay $5.50, don a plastic poncho and walk down through rock-cut tunnels for a close-up (wet) look from behind the falls and halfway down the cliff. If I was going to bother with any of these extras, the latter, called Journey Behind the Falls, is the one most worth paying for, with the *Maid of the Mist* second choice. It's one way to cool off on a hot day, although the tunnels do get crowded and you should be prepared to wait in line in them for a turn beside the spray. The wall of water is thick enough to pretty well block out the light of day. A million people a year see the falls from this vantage point – as close as you can get without getting in a barrel.

Further north along the river is the Great Gorge Adventure, an elevator to some rapids and whirlpools. Don't bother. They also have a collection of pictures of the barrels and vessels that many of the wackos attempting to shoot the falls have used.

Surprisingly, a good proportion of those who have gone over purposely, suicides aside, do live to tell about it. But only one who took the trip accidentally has had the same good fortune. He was a seven-year-old boy from Tennessee who surged over from a tipped boat upstream and did it without even breaking a bone.

The 1980s was a particularly busy period, with five stunt people taking the plunge, all successfully. One of them said he did it to show teenagers there were thrills available without drugs (yeah, right). The first attempt of the 1990s, witnessed and photographed by startled visitors, was original. No conventional barrel here – it was over the edge in a kayak. He's now paddling the great white water in the sky.

In September 1993, a local daredevil went over for the second time. For this outing he used a modified round diving bell, and became, apparently, the first person to do it twice and come up breathing. He said it was a bad one, though, and that he had hit hard. In October 1995, a US citizen at-tempted to jet ski over the falls with the help of a para-chute. He might have made it if his parachute had opened. Ride Niagara, located under Rainbow Bridge, allows everyone to try the plunge via electronic simulation.

A little further downstream, about six or seven km from Horseshoe Falls, is the Niagara Spanish Aero Car, a sort of gondola stretched 550 metres between two outcrops, both on the Canadian side, above a whirlpool created by the falls. It offers a pretty good angle of the falls for a picture as it glides above the logs, tyres and various debris spinning in the eddies below. Tickets can be bought separately for each of the above three land-based views, or buy the Explorer's Passport, a ticket for all three, which costs less than the total of the three individual tickets. It's not necessary to visit all three in the same day. The Explorer's Passport Plus also includes the People Mover Bus Pass.

At night, the falls are illuminated with constantly changing colours.

Other Views

The Skylon Tower (☎ 356-2651), at 5200 Robinson St, is the large, grey tower with yellow elevators running up the outside. There is an observation deck at about 250 metres, with both indoor and outdoor viewing. Aside from great views of the falls, both Toronto and Buffalo can be seen on clear days. The cost is $6.50. There are also a couple of dining rooms at the top, the more expensive of which revolves once per hour. The other one offers buffet-style breakfasts, lunches and dinners at more moderate (but not inexpensive) prices. In the revolving restaurant, the early-bird dinner special (4 to 5.30 pm) saves some money.

The Minolta Tower (☎ 356-1501), at 6732 Oakes Drive, is close to the falls and virtually overlooks the lip. The trip up is $5.95. It has a restaurant with spectacular views and observation galleries. The food served here is not just an afterthought, and meals are well prepared, if straightforward. An incline railway leads from the base of the tower down the hillside close to the falls.

Views can also be had from the tower at Maple Leaf Village, a shopping and eating complex near Rainbow Bridge. The new casino is also here.

Bridges

Two bridges run over the river to New York State: the Whirlpool Rapids Bridge and, closer to the falls, Rainbow Bridge, which celebrated its 50th year in 1991. You can walk or drive across to explore the falls from the US side, but have your papers in order. Both pedestrians and drivers have to pay a bridge toll. It's 25 cents each way for walkers, $2 for cars.

Niagara Falls Museum

Established in 1827, this is the original of the many 'daredevil collections' of objects in which people have gone over the falls. As well as telling the stunt stories, there are displays of curios and artefacts from around the world, including Egyptian mummies and a dinosaur exhibit. The address is 5651 River Rd and the museum is open all year.

Lundy's Lane Historical Museum

Sitting on the site of the 1814 Battle of Lundy's Lane, the museum catalogues local pioneer and military history, notably the War of 1812. It's at 5180 Ferry St.

Clifton Hill

Clifton Hill is a street name but also refers more generally to the commercial part of the downtown area near the falls given over in sense-bombarding intensity to artificial attractions in Disney-like concentration. You name it – museums, galleries, displays such as Ripley's Believe It or Not, Tussaud's Wax Museum, Houdini's Museum, Criminal's Hall of Fame (you get the drift) – they're all here. Looking is fun, but in most cases paying the entrance fee will leave you feeling like a sucker. Most don't live up to their own hype. Also in this bright, busy section are dozens of souvenir shops and restaurants.

Marineland

Of the many commercial attractions, this is probably one of the best. Marineland (☎ 356-9565) is an aquarium with special family shows by dolphins, sea lions and killer whales. Admission includes entry to a wildlife park containing bison, bears, deer and elk. There are also rides (including the world's largest steel roller coaster), all covered in the cost of admission. You may, however, want to take a picnic lunch with you – the restaurants here are expensive and offer a limited selection. Marineland is open daily from April to October from 9 am to 6 pm. Entry is $21 for adults. It's roughly two km from the falls, south on Portage Rd. There is camping nearby.

IMAX Theatre

The large-format (the screen is six storeys high) IMAX cinema (☎ 374-4629), at 6170 Buchanan Ave, near the Skylon Tower, presents a 45-minute show about the falls, its history and some of the stunts that have been pulled in and over them. Shows run continually and cost $7.50. In the same complex is a museum, with artefacts from some of those who have run the falls.

Niagara Parks Greenhouse

Flowers and gardens are plentiful in and around Niagara Falls, which has moderate temperatures. The greenhouse and conservatory less than one km south of the Horseshoe Falls provide a year-round floral display and are free. A bonus is the tropical birds.

The Old Scow

Across the street, rusting away in the river, the Old Scow is a steel barge which has been lodged on rocks waiting to be washed over the falls since 1918. So were the three men aboard when it broke free of the tug pulling it and drifted to within 750 metres of the brink (or is that drink?). Without speed boats or helicopters, rescuing the men was some feat. Red Hill Senior, a local daredevil, climbed out hand over hand along a line that had been shot out from the roof of the waterside power-plant building. He was able to untangle the lines, allowing an attached buoy to reach the men, who climbed on and were pulled ashore.

Botanical Gardens & School of Horticulture Gardens

Also free for browsing around are these fastidiously maintained 40 hectares. The school and gardens, which are open all year, are north along the Parkway towards Queenston, about nine km from Horseshoe Falls. A further 2.5 km north is the **floral clock**, which is over 12 metres in diameter. Beside the floral clock, don't miss the Centennial Lilac Gardens, which are at their fragrant best in late May.

Other flower gardens are at Queen Victoria Park (right beside the Canadian falls) and at Oakes Garden Theatre (opposite the Maid of the Mist Plaza, near the falls). Opposite the US falls, Victoria Park also has varied and colourful floral displays through most of the year.

Green Areas

Niagara Falls can be a fairly congested, urban experience, but there are some worthwhile quiet places to explore apart from the well-tended areas of plant life listed above.

Niagara Glen Nature Preserve Top of the list and highly recommended, this is the only place where you can gain a sense of what the area was like before the arrival of Europeans. There are seven different walking trails here covering four km, where the falls were situated 8000 years ago. The preserve is maintained by the Parks Commission (☎ 356-2241), who offer free guided walks four times a day through the summer (July to early September). But the trails are always open to public use at no charge. The paths wind down the gorge, past huge boulders, icy cold caves, wildflowers and woods. Some people fish at the bottom from the shore. The river trail runs north to Pebbly Beach and south to the whirlpool, site of the Spanish Aero Car attraction. The whirlpool is an impressive sight from the Aero Car terminal, but the size of the gorge itself isn't fully appreciated until seen from the shoreline. As noted above, there seems to be a lot of garbage trapped in the currents, mainly wood and tyres, often from cottage docks and boathouses, but remember that everything which leaves Lake Erie has to pass into the whirlpool. Officially, the excellent trails end here. Some people do clamber over the rocks along the water's edge – to be safe, a good dozen or more metres back from the water – upstream toward the falls. The area where the river flows (or rather shoots) into the whirlpool can be reached and is very dramatic. This is not easy walking: the rocks can be slippery and the river is dangerous. A local resident has said that from here, a further arduous 30 minutes leads to another set of even more overwhelming (and more dangerous) rapids. Twenty minutes beyond is the boardwalk for the Great Gorge Adventure. At this stage you can turn around, carry on for another five hours to a point close to the falls, or hop the Great Gorge elevator up to street level. Tickets evidently are not checked at the bottom, only at the top, because there are so few misfits who would take the time and effort to get down there on their own. Walkers should take a snack and something to drink, for despite all the water, the Niagara is one river from which you do not want to drink – this region is one of the industrial centres of North America. The Niagara Glen Nature Preserve is one km north of the Whirlpool Golf Course entrance on the Niagara Parkway (towards Niagara-on-the-Lake). The People Mover stops at the site, or in spring and autumn at the Spanish Auto Car, from where the glen is walkable (about three km).

Dufferin Islands This series of small, interconnected, artificial islands was created during the development of the hydro system. The area is green parkland, with walking paths and a short nature trail around the islands and through the woods. There are picnic tables, and a small area for swimming which is best for children (though anyone can be a kid if it's hot enough). The islands are less than two km south of the falls, on the west side of the road. Entry is free. Another 250 metres south is King's Bridge Park with more picnic facilities and another small beach.

Organised Tours

Double Deck (☎ 374-7423) offers bus tours on British red double-decker buses. For $34.50, one of the tours includes admission to three of the city's major attractions and stops at other free sites. You can stay on or get off at will, even taking two days to complete the tour. A second, 50-km trip takes in many more of the things to see and travels further, taking about six hours. A third goes to Niagara-on-the-Lake and a winery. Honeymoon City Scenic Lines (☎ 356-5487) offers a 3½-hour tour for $21 that includes no less than 75 sites. A second tour, which costs $25, includes all of the first plus a visit to one of Niagara's wineries. More extravagant are the helicopter tours over the falls offered by Niagara Helicopters (☎ 357-5672), at 3731 Victoria Ave.

Festivals

The Blossom Festival is held in early or mid-May, when spring flowers bloom. Featured are parades and ethnic dances. The annual Niagara Grape & Wine Festival is held in late September. There are many events, including parades and tours of five major wineries. In addition, activities are planned throughout the region. For winter visitors, the annual Festival of Lights is a season of day and night events stretching from the end of November to the middle of February. The highlight is a series of spectacular night lighting displays set up along a 36-km route.

Places to Stay

Accommodation is plentiful and, overall, prices aren't too bad, what with all the competition from both sides of the border. Outside the peak summer season, costs drop, and through the winter there are some good bargains. At this time many of the hotels and motels offer two or three-day packages, often including meals, discounts on attractions and maybe even a bottle of wine. Checking the travel section of weekend newspapers in town or in Toronto will turn up some deals. Since a room is a room, many

places offer enticements such as waterbeds, saunas, heart-shaped jacuzzis, FM stereos, movies etc for a 'dirty weekend' escape.

Camping There are campgrounds all around town. Three are on Lundy's Lane, leading out of Niagara Falls, and two are on Montrose Ave south-west of downtown. They are decidedly not primitive. *Niagara Glen View Campground* (☎ 358-8689), with tent and electrical sites, is closest to the falls at Victoria Ave and River Rd, north of town toward Queenston. There are others along the Niagara Parkway further north.

Hostels The HI *Niagara Falls International Hostel* (☎ 357-0770), has taken new digs in a former commercial building at 4529 Cataract St in the old town close to the train and bus stations. Small Cataract St runs west off Bridge St near River Rd not far from the Whirlpool Rapids Bridge. The hostel has room for about 70 people and a bed costs $16.80. There's a good-sized kitchen, laundry facilities, lockers and a large lounge. They offer bicycle rentals, and discounts for some of the museums and the *Maid of the Mist*.

An alternative is the nearby *Niagara Falls Backpackers Hostel* (☎ 357-4266 or 1-800-891-7022), a section of the huge, impressive *Doc's Inn* B&B at 4711 Zimmerman St. The hostel entrance is around the corner at 4219 Huron St. There are dorms for $15 and two rooms for couples. The price includes bed sheets, and a morning coffee and muffin. Guests have use of kitchen facilities and good-value dinners may be offered. It's open all year.

B&Bs The best value in commercial accommodation will often be found in B&Bs and guesthouses (no breakfast). They are often cheaper (but not always) than either motels or hotels and are usually more interesting. Many are central. The Visitors & Convention Bureau (☎ 356-6061) is the best of the tourist offices to try for accommodation assistance. A look around some of the streets mentioned here will definitely turn up something. Prices range from about $35 to $75, with the average being $45 for singles and $60 for doubles. River Rd links the falls area with old Niagara Falls downtown, three km downriver. There are quite a few B&Bs along this convenient location with good views of the river.

Butterfly Manor (☎ 358-8988), at 4917 River Rd, operates a B&B programme with homes all around town; some include extras such as swimming pools or air-conditioning. When booking a room, double check the breakfast situation. (For these sort of prices you really should get more than a coffee and a doughnut.) Butterfly Manor has rooms from $55 a double. Breakfast included.

Glen Mhor Guesthouse (☎ 354-2600), at 5381 River Rd, has five rooms from $45/65 a single/double. A full breakfast is included. You can walk to the falls or bicycles are offered. Also in the same price range is *Gretna Green* (☎ 357-2081), just a little further north at 5077 River Rd, and the equally welcoming *Bedham Hall* (☎ 374-8515) at 4835 River Rd. Both have four rooms, provide full breakfasts and offer bicycles. Most rooms have private bathrooms. The *Eastwood Tourist Lodge* (☎ 354-8686) at 5359 River Rd, is in a fine old home with balconies overlooking the river. Each room is large with ensuite bath so prices are a little higher. English, German and Spanish are spoken.

Lodging can usually be found on Robert St or Victoria Ave. The other main area for guesthouses is along Lundy's Lane.

Hotels There are few hotels in town; most accommodation is in motels. True hotels tend to be new and expensive. A couple of basic, budget alternative hotels can be found away from the falls, near the train and bus stations. The better of the two is the *Europa* (☎ 374-3231), on the corner of Bridge St and Erie Ave, where a room can cost less than $30. Nearby, across from the train station, is the slightly tattered *Empire* (☎ 357-2550), on Erie Ave. Neither are recommended for single women.

Motels There are millions of them. The cheapest ones seem to be along Lundy's Lane, which leads west out from the falls and later becomes Hwy 20. There are many other motels on Murray and Ferry Sts. The wide price ranges are partially because many places have honeymoon rooms with double bathtubs, waterbeds and other price-bumping features. Rates vary dramatically by season but are most costly in July and August. Later, it's a buyer's market. You may be able to strike a deal if you're staying two, three or more nights.

Very near the lights of Clifton Hill and the restaurants, and under 30 minutes' walk to the falls, is the central *AAA Royal Motel* (☎ 354-2632), at 5284 Ferry St. The rooms are plain but fine and there is a small pool. Meal vouchers are offered to guests for discounts at several nearby eateries. Rates range from $30 to $65, with a double just $35 in June, before the big crowds arrive. The *Thunderbird Motel* (☎ 356-0541), at 6019 Lundy's Lane, has rooms from $35 all the way up to $90.

At 7742 Lundy's Lane is the small *Alpine Motel* (☎ 356-7016). Their rates are $40 to $75 and they also have a pool. The *Melody Motel* (☎ 227-1023), at 13065 Lundy's Lane, charges $38 to $78 and has a pool. This street has literally dozens of other motels. The modestly priced *USA Motel* (☎ 374-2621) is at 6541 Main St, near George's Parkway.

Places to Eat
Finding food in Niagara Falls is no problem, and while the dining isn't great, it isn't bad either; most places provide pretty good value. Down by the falls, around Clifton Hill and along Victoria or Stanley Aves, there are scores of restaurants. Japanese, German, Hungarian and, especially, ever-popular Italian eateries can all be found. Some offer breakfast and/or lunch specials – just look around. Taking a leaflet from one of the hustlers on the street can lead to a good bargain.

Mama Mia's, at 5719 Victoria Ave, has been serving up standard Italian fare at moderate prices for many years. Inexpensive meals can also be found at the *Victoria Park Cafeteria*, opposite the US falls, in the building complex in the park of the same name, run by the Parks Commission. On the 2nd floor is a more expensive restaurant and an outdoor beer garden where you can get smoked-meat sandwiches and hamburgers for around $6. *Ponderosa* is a budget steak house where all meals ($10 to $15) are accompanied by a huge help-yourself salad bar. Chicken and pasta are also available. It's at 5329 Ferry St. For good fast food at any time of the day, try the unmistakably shaped *Flying Saucer* at 6768 Lundy's Lane. There are breakfast specials from 6 am for 99 cents. It's open daily until 3 am during the week and until 4 am Friday and Saturday. There are plenty of other restaurants along Lundy's Lane.

Tony's Place, a large, popular spot at 5467 Victoria Ave, specialises in ribs and chicken. Until 6.30 pm they offer an early-bird special ($10). Regular à la carte dishes range from $7 to $16 and there is a lower-priced children's menu. For an unbeatable breakfast, pull up a stool in *Simon's Diner*, the oldest restaurant in Niagara Falls. It's in the slow part of town, on Bridge St near the corner of River Rd.

There are also restaurants in both the Skylon and Minolta Towers (see under Other Views earlier).

Getting There & Away

Bus The bus station (☎ 357-2133) is in the older part of town and away from the falls area, across the street from the train station, on the corner of Bridge St and Erie Ave. This is the station for buses to other cities, but a shuttle to the falls and even bus tours also depart from here.

For Toronto, service is frequent with a bus leaving about once an hour from early morning (around 5.30 am during the week) to about 11 pm, although on weekends there are fewer runs. Both Trentway Wager and Greyhound cover this route. Trentway at $23 one-way is a couple of dollars cheaper and

offers good one-day return fares. The trip takes about two hours.

Shuttle buses run to Niagara-on-the-Lake three times daily during the summer and once a day through the winter. Buses also depart from here for Buffalo, New York, and for Detroit, Michigan.

Train The station (☎ 1-800-361-1235 for reservations; 357-1644 for timetable information) is in the older part of town on Bridge St, close to this area's downtown section. There are two runs a day to Toronto – from Monday to Friday trains leave at 6.35 am and 5.15 pm; on Saturday and Sunday trains depart at 8.30 am and 5.15 pm. The trip takes about two hours and the one-way fare is $22. There is a special reduced fare if you go and return between Toronto and Niagara on the same day, but you must book this five days in advance. There are two daily trains west to London and one to New York City.

Getting Around

Walking is best; most things to see are concentrated in a small area.

Bus For getting further afield, there is the economical and efficient Niagara Parks People Mover bus system, which operates from 29 April to mid-October. It runs in a straight line from upstream beyond the falls, past the Greenhouse and Horseshoe Falls, along River Rd past both the Rainbow and Whirlpool bridges, north to the Niagara Spanish Aero Car attraction and, depending on the time of the year, beyond to Queenston Heights Park. From there, it turns around and follows the same path nine km back. From the falls, it gets you close to either the bus or train station. One ticket is good for the whole day and you can get on and off as much as you like at any of the stops. For a low extra charge, transfers can be made to the regular city bus system. Such a connection will get you right to the door of the train or bus station. The People Mover ticket is good value at $4 and can be purchased at most of the stops. Throughout the summer, the bus runs daily from 9 am to 11 pm, but after 9 pm does not go further out than the Rainbow Bridge. In spring and autumn the schedule is somewhat reduced, and in winter the system does not run at all.

Niagara Transit (☎ 356-1179) runs two similar shuttle services around town. One route, the Red Line Shuttle, goes around the bus and train stations then downtown and up Lundy's Lane. The other, the Blue Line Shuttle, runs from the Rapids View depot (at the southern end of the People Mover route, by the falls) along Portage Rd and around the downtown area. Both run half-hourly from 8.30 am to midnight. Free transfers can be made from these shuttles to any city bus. All-day shuttle passes are available and can be bought from the driver. Both these routes cover many of the more popular sites and may be worth considering.

Car Driving in and around the centre is nothing but a headache. Follow the signs to one of the several parking districts and stash the car for the day.

AROUND NIAGARA FALLS

See Around Niagara-on-the-Lake for details about the area between Niagara Falls and Niagara-on-the-Lake.

South from Niagara Falls, the Niagara Parkway, which begins at Niagara-on-the-Lake continues to Fort Erie, edged by parkland. The land along this strip is much flatter, the river clearly in view as the falls have not yet cut a gorge out of the river bed. But they are coming this way. Come back again in a few thousand years. There isn't much of interest here, as the road runs through residential districts, but there are certainly plenty of places to stop for a picnic or to rest in a shady spot by the water.

Fort Erie

The town of Fort Erie, situated where the Niagara River meets Lake Erie, across from Buffalo, New York, is connected to the USA by the Peace Bridge. This is a major border-crossing point and buses from Toronto connecting with many eastern US cities use it. On summer weekends, expect queues.

Some air travellers find it worthwhile to go by bus to Buffalo from Toronto and its vicinity to take advantage of sometimes cheaper US airfares. At times (when the discrepancy in fares warrants the traffic), there are buses from Toronto direct to the Buffalo airport, and some connecting with specific flights. This situation varies with airlines opening and folding and fares increasing and decreasing, but is worth remembering.

The town is best visited for the reconstruction of **Fort Erie**, first built in 1764 and which the USA seized in 1814 before retreating. At the fort, a museum, military drills and uniformed soldiers can be seen. Admission is $3.50.

On Central Ave is the **Historical Railroad Museum**, with articles and a locomotive relating to the steam era of train travel. Fort Erie is also well known for its old, attractive horse-racing track. Races are held from May to October. The track is off the Queen Elizabeth Way at Bertie St. Slightly south of town is **Crystal Beach**, a small, rather run-down beach-cottage resort which is too bad because this is one of the warmest areas of the country, and the one with the longest summer.

BRANTFORD

West of Hamilton and surrounded for the most part by farmland, Brantford is known for several things. It has long been associated with Native Indians – Chief Joseph Brant was based here. He led the Six Nation Indians, who lived in an area stretching from the district to parts of upper New York. The **Brant County Museum**, at 57 Charlotte St, has information and artefacts on Brant and his people. **Her Majesty's Chapel of the Mohawks**, three km from the centre of town on Mohawk St, is the oldest Protestant church in Ontario and the world's only Royal Indian Chapel. It's open every day from 1 July to Labour Day, and from Wednesday to Sunday the rest of the year.

The **Woodland Cultural Centre Museum**, at 84 Mohawk St, has displays on the various aboriginal peoples of eastern Canada and offers some history of the Six Nations

Confederacy. The confederacy, made up of the Mohawk, Seneca, Cayuga, Oneida, Onendaga and Tuscarora tribes, was a unifying cultural and political association which helped settle disputes between bands.

Brantford was the home of Alexander Graham Bell, inventor of the telephone. The **Bell Homestead**, at 94 Tutela Heights, displays some of his other inventions and is furnished the way it was when he lived in it. It's closed on Monday.

The town is also known for local son Wayne Gretzky, the greatest ice-hockey player the world has yet produced. There are some additional attractions, such as **Myrtleville House**, dating from 1837, and the interesting **Octagon House**, now a restaurant.

SIX NATIONS INDIAN RESERVE

To the east of Brantford, in Ohsweken, this Iroquois reserve is one of the best known in the country. Established in the late 18th century, it provides interested visitors with a glimpse of Native Indian culture. Through the week (and on weekends by appointment), tours are given of the reserve and its Band Council House, the seat of decision-making. Various events are held through the year, including the major Grand River Powwow, a summer theatre programme, and a handicrafts sale in November.

ONTARIO AGRICULTURAL MUSEUM

With 30 buildings on 32 hectares of land, the museum brings to life the farming history of the area through demonstrations, displays, and costumed workers in historical settings. It's near Milton, 52 km south-west of Toronto, about a 45-minute drive. Leave Hwy 401 at exit 320 and follow the signs. The museum is on Townline (also called Tremaine Rd), and is open daily from the middle of May to late September.

GUELPH

West on Hwy 401 from Toronto, Guelph is an old, attractive, middle-sized university town that makes a nice place to live (and a great word to say) but doesn't have a lot to offer visitors. There are some fine houses along tree-lined streets, and the Speed River and downtown area is overseen by the dominant **Church of Our Lady**. The local **Farmers' Market** takes place by the historic square in the heart of town on Wednesday and Saturday mornings (Saturday only in the winter). Almost 100 vendors come in from the surrounding countryside to sell their produce. You'll also find an assortment of local craftspeople, artists and booksellers here.

The **Macdonald Stewart Art Centre**, at 358 Gordon St, often has good shows in its galleries, which specialise in Inuit and other Canadian art. It's open every afternoon except Monday, and is free.

McCrae House is the birthplace of John McCrae, the author of the antiwar poem *In Flanders Fields*, written during WWI, which every Canadian reads as a kid in school. The museum, at 108 Water St, is open every afternoon.

Through the summer, cheap accommodation can be found at the *University of Guelph* (☎ 824-4128). The campus is on Old Brock Rd (Hwy 6) at College Rd.

Near the main intersection of town (Wyndham and Quebec Sts), at 41 Quebec St, is the *Bookshelf Café*. The front area contains a good bookshop, while the back portion is an excellent restaurant, although not in the low-budget category. There is also an outdoor patio, a bar and, upstairs, a repertory cinema. Less expensive for a good meal is *Latino's*, at 51 Cork St East, which features Latin American food. Most menu items are in the $8 range.

KORTRIGHT WATERFOWL PARK

This is a wildlife area and waterfowl research centre with 3000 birds representing close to 100 species. There is an observation tower, an interpretive centre and some nature trails. The park is open daily from March to October and admission is $2.15. The park is on the Speed River near Guelph, on Kortright Rd, two km west of the Hanlon Expressway.

ROCKWOOD CONSERVATION AREA

About 10 km east of Rockwood along Hwy 7, Rockwood Conservation Area makes a good destination for an afternoon outdoors. It's definitely one of the best conservation areas within the Toronto area. Admission is $5. The park offers swimming, canoeing and picnicking, but of most interest is the landscape itself. There are woods, cliffs, caves and glacial potholes, all of which can be explored on foot. Trails wind all through the park and canoes can be rented. There is also overnight camping available.

In the village of Rockwood, an hour or so can easily be spent strolling along the main street, with its antique and junk shops, craft boutiques and eateries of various types.

Saunders Bakery has been turning out baked goods for 75 years. Good, inexpensive food can be had at the *Out-to-Lunch* restaurant, open every day but Monday. The afternoon tea with fresh scones is good value. You'll find a B&B or two in town as well.

Nearby **Acton**, a larger town, is known for its leather-goods warehouse and its *Tannery* restaurant.

KITCHENER-WATERLOO

These twin cities – amalgamated to form one – are about an hour west of Toronto, in the heart of rural southern Ontario. About 55% of the 210,000 inhabitants are of German origin (which probably explains why Kitchener was originally named Berlin). The city

---

The Mennonites

The Mennonites are one of Canada's best-known yet least understood religious minorities – everybody knows of them but few know about them. Most people will tell you that Mennonites wear black, ride in horse-drawn carriages and, eschewing modern life, work farms in a traditional manner. And while basically true, these characteristics are, of course, only part of the story.

The Mennonites originated in Switzerland in the early 1500s as a Protestant sect among the Anabaptists. Forced from country to country due to their religious disagreements with the state, they arrived in Holland and took their name from one of their early Dutch leaders, Menno Simons. To escape persecution in Europe and to develop communities in rural settings, they took up William Penn's promise of religious freedom and began arriving in North America around 1640, settling in southeastern Pennsylvania, where they are still a significant group. Most of North America's 250,000 Mennonites still live in that state. In the early 1800s, lured by the undeveloped and cheaper land of southern Ontario, some moved northwards.

There are about a dozen Mennonite groups or branches in Ontario, each with slightly different approaches, practices and principles. The Mennonite Church is the middle ground, with the numerous other branches either more or less liberal. The majority of Mennonites are moderates. Most visible are the stricter or 'plain' groups, known for their simple clothes. The women wear bonnets and a long, plain dress; the men tend to wear black and grow beards. Automobiles, much machinery and other trappings of modern life are shunned. The Old Order Mennonites are the strictest in their adherence to the traditions.

The Amish, who took their name from Jacob Ammon, a native of Switzerland, are another Mennonite branch. They split from the main body, believing Mennonites to be too worldly. Traditional Amish are the plainest of the plain; they won't even wear buttons on their clothes, considering them a vanity. They don't worship in a church, but hold rotating services in houses in the community. Homes are very spartan, with no carpets, curtains or wall pictures.

Despite their day-to-day differences, all the groups agree on a number of fundamentals, which include the freedom of conscience, separation of church and state, adult baptism, refusal to take oaths, practical piety and education stressing the moral and practical. Science is rejected by many. The simple life is esteemed. Mennonite and Amish communities are largely self-sufficient and they do no proselytising. Less than 10% of their followers are not born into Mennonite families.

Mennonite sites can be visited in Kitchener-Waterloo, St Jacob's and Elmira. It is not uncommon to see their carriages rolling along local roads or, on Sunday, parked by their country churches.

Many local stores and farmers' markets feature Mennonite goods. Perhaps the best-known, most sought after of crafts are the beautiful, but pricey, bed quilts. The simple, well-made furniture is also highly regarded. More recently, their organic produce and meat has become of interest, and the very good baked goods and jams are inexpensive and readily available. ■

also acts as a centre for the surrounding Amish and Mennonite religious farming communities. It is these two factors that attract visitors and make the towns stand out from their neighbours. There is not a lot to see, and at a glance things here are much the same as in any other large town. However, it's worth a short visit, particularly if your timing is right and you arrive for Oktoberfest. The towns share two universities and therefore have a fair number of young people.

Orientation

Kitchener is the southern portion of the twin cities and is nearly three times the size of Waterloo, but you can't really tell where one ends and the other begins. The downtown area refers to central Kitchener. King St is the main street and runs roughly north-south (even though it's called King St West and East); at the northern end it runs to the two universities and beyond.

The farmers' market on the corner of King and Frederick Sts marks the centre of downtown. This area of town has the train and bus stations, hotels and restaurants. King St runs south to Hwy 8, which continues to Hwy 401, west for Windsor and east for Toronto. Hwy 8 West, at the junction of King St, heads to Stratford.

Information

Maps and information are available at the Kitchener-Waterloo Visitors & Convention Bureau (☎ 748-0800), south of the centre, at 2848 King St East. From June to the end of August, it's open from 9 am to 5 pm Monday to Wednesday, from 9 am to 7 pm on Thursday and Friday and from 10 am to 4 pm on weekends. The rest of the year, hours are 9 am to 5 pm Monday to Friday.

Farmers' Market

The central market is held downtown, on the corner of King St East and Frederick St. The market began in 1839 and features the products of the Amish and Mennonites – breads, jams, many cheeses and sausages, and handicrafts such as quilts, rugs, clothes and handmade toys. Whether they like it or not, it is the farmers themselves who are often the main attraction. Some of these religious people, whose ancestors were originally from Switzerland via Pennsylvania, live much as their grandparents did in the 19th century. There are also many merchants, including bakers, craftspeople and farmers, who aren't Mennonite. The market is held on Saturday from 5 am to 2 pm.

Across the street, on the corner of King and Benton Sts, a 23-bell glockenspiel rings at noon and at 5 pm.

Woodside National Historic Park

This park contains the 100-year-old mansion where former prime minister William Lyon Mackenzie King (Canada's 10th prime minister) once lived. It has been restored and refurnished in upper-class 1890s style. The basement houses displays on the life of Mackenzie King. On weekends you can witness demonstrations of period crafts, music and cooking by guides in costume. The park is at 528 Wellington St North in Kitchener. It is open daily and admission is $2.

Universities of Waterloo & Wilfrid Laurier

In Waterloo, west off King St North on University Ave, these two universities sit right beside each other, and both have attractive, green campuses. The former is well regarded for its engineering; the latter specialises in economics. Waterloo has an art gallery, and the **Museum & Archive of Games** (☎ 888-4424), which depicts the history of games around the world. Hours vary depending on exhibits.

Doon Heritage Crossroads

The Doon Heritage Crossroads (☎ 748-1914), south of Kitchener (20 minutes by vehicle or call for transit information), is a re-creation of a pioneer settlement circa 1914. The 23 buildings include a general store, workshops and a sawmill. There is also a model of an original Russian Mennonite village and a replica of an 1856 railway. To get to the site, go down King St, turn right

ONTARIO

on Fairway, left at Manitou St and left again at Homer Watson Blvd. Admission is $5, less for students, seniors and families. It's open daily from May to August and on weekdays during the winter. Special events are often held on weekends.

Joseph Schneider Haus

At 466 Queen St South, not far from the market, this Heritage Canada site (☎ 742-7752) is the restored house of a prosperous German Mennonite. It's a museum depicting life in the mid-1850s, with demonstrations of day-to-day chores and skills. Through the summer, it is open every day; the rest of the year it is closed on Monday. Note that it is shut completely for the last week in December and for the first six weeks of the new year. There is a nominal admission fee.

Seagram Museum

Set in a section of the original Seagram distillery in Waterloo, this neatly laid-out museum (☎ 885-1857) shows the history and technology of booze production. On display are 2000 artefacts from around the world and many different time periods, including some beautiful tools and equipment. Explanatory films are shown. Also on the premises are an elegant restaurant, gift shop and speciality liquor store. The address is 57 Erb St. The museum is open daily from May to December but is closed on Monday during the rest of the year.

The Centre in the Square

On the corner of Queen and Ellen Sts is this performing-arts complex, with an art gallery and a theatre.

Homer Watson House & Gallery

One of Canada's first notable landscape painters is the subject of this quite small, specialised museum. Watson (1855-1936) once lived here, and there are various pieces relating to his life and work. The museum, at 1754 Old Mill Rd, is open every afternoon from April to December (but is closed on Monday).

Festivals

Some of the major events held here are:

May
Mennonite Relief Sale – It is a large sale of homemade foods and crafts and also includes a quilt auction. It's held on the last Saturday in May in New Hamburg, 19 km west of Kitchener-Waterloo.

June
Summer Music Festival – This festival is four days of free or low-cost outdoor music concerts held at the end of June at venues around the downtown area.

August
Busker Carnival – An annual festival of street entertainers which takes place in late August. Some of these performers are very good and the whole thing is free.

October
Oktoberfest – The event of the year, Octoberfest, the biggest of its kind in North America and said to be the largest outside of Germany, attracts 500,000 people annually. The nine-day festival starts in early to mid-October and includes 20 beer halls, German music and foods, and dancing. A huge parade wraps up the festivities on the last day. For more information, ring K-W Oktoberfest Inc (☎ 570-4267). Upon arrival, visit one of the reception areas for a map, tickets, information and all the details on how to tie on your stein so you don't lose it. Reservations for accommodation during the festival should be made well in advance. For getting around, there is a free bus in addition to the usual city buses.

Places to Stay

Hostels Backpackers' has a hostel here, the *Waterloo International Home Hostel* (☎ 725-5202), at 102B Albert St. Room rates are $14 for all. The *YWCA* (☎ 744-0120) (for women only) is at Frederick and Weber Sts in Kitchener. It charges $35 per night, including breakfast, and offers weekly rates.

The *University of Waterloo* (☎ 884-5400) has summer accommodation. The cost for singles/doubles is $30/48. Meals are available on the campus at several outlets. Free parking and use of the swimming pool are included. Buses run frequently to the campus. At *Wilfrid Laurier University* (☎ 884-1970), contact the housing officer at 75 University Ave West. Singles/doubles are $20/37. Rooms are available from 1 May to 15 August but are generally used by those attending conferences. The dining room is open in the summer, too.

B&Bs Out of Millbank, a village to the west of Kitchener, a local B&B association (☎ 595-4604) has the latest on guesthouses in Kitchener. The rates aren't bad, starting at $35/45 for singles/doubles. During Oktoberfest, many more local residents offer rooms.

Hotels For the dollar-conscious, a central hotel is not in the cards. For those holding a different hand, the *Walper Terrace Hotel* (☎ 745-4321) is central, at 1 King St West. It's an old place that has been restored and has won a heritage award. It has over 100 rooms, starting at $80, which is good value compared to the other top-end places in town. The *Guest Inn* (☎ 893-7011), at 2933 King St East, has rooms from $42.

During Oktoberfest, many people rent out rooms. For information, call K-W Oktoberfest Inc (☎ 570-4267).

Motels Motels are numerous, good and clean. Most of them are on Victoria St, which runs east-west off King St, just north of downtown Kitchener. Two of the cheapest are the *Mayflower* (☎ 745-9493), at 1189 Victoria St, which costs $35/46 for singles/doubles, and the *Shamrock* (☎ 743-4361), situated at 1235 Victoria St, with singles/doubles at $25/40.

Places to Eat
There are many restaurants on or near King St in Kitchener. *Williams Coffee Pub*, at 198 King St West next to City Hall, serves good coffee, cheap pasta, bagels and sandwiches and has an outdoor patio. For solid German fare try the *Concordia Club*, at 429 Ottawa St South, for lunch or dinner. Live entertainment is included on Friday and Saturday nights and the restaurant is closed on Sunday. There are quite a few European delis in Kitchener. *Fiedlers*, at 197 King St East, is stacked full of cheeses, rye breads, sausages and salamis.

After the nose gets a whiff of the *Café Mozart*, at 53 Queen St South, the mouth will soon be munching on pastries, cakes or something covered with chocolate. It's not far from the bus station and is open until 10 pm (except Friday and Saturday nights, when it serves late-night snacks until midnight).

At 130 King St in Waterloo, the *Ali Baba* is a steak house which has been in business since the 1960s.

Entertainment
Nightclubs Known far and wide, *Lulu's* is an immense, popular dance club located on Hwy 8 in Kitchener, with what is said to be the world's longest bar. On a weekend evening, buses arrive from as far away as Toronto. The *Circus Room* (☎ 571-1456), at 729 King St East, has live music every night and often features jazz and blues.

Entertainment Parks Sportsworld (☎ 653-4442) is an entertainment park containing, among other diversions, a water slide, wave pool, go-kart track and snack bars and restaurants. Bingeman Park, (☎ 744-1555) at 1380 Victoria St North, on the Grand River, is bigger than Sportsworld and offers much the same thing and 600 camp sites.

Getting There & Away
Bus The station (☎ 741-2600) is at 15 Charles St West in Kitchener, a five-minute walk from the centre. Gray Coach run frequent services to Guelph and Toronto. There are around five buses a day to London.

Train There are two VIA Rail (☎ 1-800-361-1235) trains a day to Toronto and two to London. The station is on the corner of Victoria and Weber Sts, an easy walk north of downtown Kitchener.

AROUND KITCHENER-WATERLOO
St Jacobs
Just north of town is St Jacobs, a small historic village with the **Meeting Place**, a little museum and interpretive centre on the Mennonites and their history, and numerous arts & crafts shops housed in original buildings dating from the 19th century. The

museum, at 33 King St, is open daily through the summer (afternoons only on Sunday). Through the winter it is closed on weekdays. Admission is by donation. The MCC Craft Shop sells Mennonite goods.

Also in town is the **Maple Syrup Museum** with exhibits on the production of this Canadian speciality. The museum is at 8 Spring Rd and is open daily all year, except for Monday in January and February.

The **St Jacobs Farmers' Market** is another, more authentic version of the Kitchener farmers' market, with horse-and-buggy sheds still in place. It's two km south of the village and is open Thursday from 7 am to 4 pm and Saturday from 7 am to 3 pm year round. There's also a flea market here and on Tuesday and Thursday cattle are auctioned next door at the Livestock Exchange. For cheap brand-name goods check out the nearby St Jacobs factory outlet mall.

If you want to stay, the town has an inn, *Benjamin's*, and a guesthouse, *Jakobstettel*, neither of which are particularly cheap, as well as a couple of restaurants. The St Jacobs B&B Association (☎ 664-2622) can fix you up with a less costly bed in the area. Singles/doubles average $50/65. Whether you spend the night or not, drop in to the bakery. The main street also has numerous craft shops to browse through.

A Local Drive

Take Hwy 401 past Kitchener (going west) to the Doon exit and go to New Dundee. From there, travel north-west to Petersburg, where you'll find the Blue Moon Pub. Then on to St Agatha, with the church steeple, followed by St Clements and Lindwood – both are Mennonite towns with some interesting stores. Drive back east to Hawkersville, where there is a blacksmith's shop, and take a gravel road with fine scenery to St Jacobs. Continue north up to Elmira and over to West Montrose, where there is a covered bridge – one of the few left in Ontario.

The Pub Crawl

Just west of Kitchener-Waterloo, four fine historic, country taverns can be found in four neighbouring villages. Each one is at least 120 years old and offers atmosphere, good food and something to wash it down with. Begin in Petersburg, at the *Blue Moon* (☎ 634-8405), a Georgian-style inn dating from 1848. It's off Hwy 7 and 8 at Regional Rd 6 and 12.

Next stop to the west is *EJ's* (☎ 634-5711), in Baden, again with some intriguing original decor, including hand-painted ceiling tiles. In fine weather there is a patio as well. Beer from around the world is offered on tap.

Kennedy's Country Tavern (☎ 747-1313) is back east and north (not far from stop one – remember to designate a nondrinking driver, it's getting confusing). Kennedy's, in the village of St Agatha, has a bit of an Irish slant, although much of the food shows a German influence.

Last stop is the *Heidelberg Restaurant & Brew Pub* (☎ 699-4413) in Heidelberg, north from St Agatha, at the junction of Hwys 15 and 16. Here, in the middle of Mennonite country, a German country style meal can be enjoyed with Bavarian beer brewed on the premises. The Heidelberg was built in 1838. Stops one and two are closed on Sunday. Call any one of them and ask about the bus tours which sometimes do the circuit.

The Grand River

Beginning near Georgian Bay, the Grand River winds its way south just to the east of Kitchener-Waterloo, eventually emptying into Lake Erie. The Grand River watershed is the largest inland river system in the southern portion of the province. Numerous parks and conservation areas are located along the river – the tourist office should have a guide to them. Canoeing is possible in some sections; at others there are swimming facilities and walking trails.

CAMBRIDGE

South of Kitchener, Cambridge is an old mill town now grown large, set alongside the Speed and Grand rivers. There isn't much to see, but the redeveloped waterfront area known as Riverbank, with its many factories, is pleasant and attracts shoppers. Many of the businesses once drawn by the power from the mill now have factory outlets. Cambridge has a Scottish background, and this is celebrated with the annual summer Highland Games.

ELMIRA

Not far north of Kitchener-Waterloo and slightly west is Elmira, another Mennonite centre. In spring, there is a Maple Syrup Festival, with street activities and pancake breakfasts. The Sap Bucket is a store specialising in local crafts, including fine quilts, but these are not cheap. Brox's Old Towne Village is a shopping centre designed to look like it belongs to an earlier era. Brubacher's Country Store, in the complex, is a 19th-century general store. You'll also find antiques and restaurants in the centre.

You can visit the Elmira Mennonite Church, at 58 Church St West, and see a film on the congregation. The MCC Thrift Shop sells Mennonite products.

There are quite a few B&Bs in the area, many on farms and with owners who speak Pennsylvania Dutch or German. For information on local B&Bs call the Elmira Chamber of Commerce (☎ 669-2605). Rates start at $45/65 for singles/doubles. One farm B&B is *Washa Farms* (☎ 846-9788), seven km north of town, with rooms from $55 for two (with breakfast). It's on an 88-hectare working farm where the house dates from 1877.

ELORA

Not far from Kitchener-Waterloo, northwest up Hwy 6 from Guelph, is this small, heavily touristed town. Named after Elora in India, with its famous cave temples, this was once a mill town using the falls on the Grand River, which runs through town. The falls, the old mill, the pleasant setting and the nearby gorge and park make the town a popular day trip for both out-of-province visitors and Ontarians.

The main streets are Metcalfe, Mill and Geddes Sts, all right by the mill and river.

There is a tourist office in the Village Common, a small shopping mall on Metcalfe St up the hill from Mill St.

Things to See & Do

Not far from town, at the **Elora Gorge Conservation Area**, the river flows through a deep limestone canyon. Much of the area is park, and trails lead to cliff views and caves at the water's edge. Riding the water in a tyre tube is a fun way to spend a warm afternoon. There are also picnic areas in the park.

About a dozen blocks east of town along Mill St East is the Elora Quarry – worth a look and, better, a swim.

The Grand River is good for canoeing, and overnight trips are possible. You can paddle along the river all the way to Lake Erie. More information is available at the park.

Festivals

The Elora Festival (☎ 846-0331), an annual music festival, is held during the last weeks of July and into the first two weeks of August. The music is primarily classical (with an emphasis on choral works) or folk. Some of the concerts are held at the quarry, with performers playing in the middle of the water on a floating stage. On a warm summer night with the stage lit up, it really is an impressive experience.

Other events include the annual summer Antique Show & Sale and, in May, the Open House Tour, when many of the older local houses are open to the public.

Places to Stay

There is a large campground at the *Elora Gorge Conservation Area* (☎ 846-9742) which, though usually full on holiday weekends, has a number of sites that can be reserved one week in advance.

There are quite a few B&Bs in and around town. For information, ring ☎ 846-9841 or call at 1 MacDonald Sq. Average price is $50 for two with breakfast. One to try that's central and costs a little less than the rest is *Speers Home* (☎ 846-9744), at 256 Geddes St, just off the main street. Rooms are $40/45 for singles/doubles. *Hornsby Home* (☎ 846-9763), at 231 Queens St, is also close to the centre and has single/doubles from just $30/40.

The *Gingerbread House* (☎ 846-0521), at 22 Metcalfe St, has rooms, but the deluxe features, special breakfasts, fine furnishings and decor put it into a considerably higher price bracket.

The *Elora Mill Inn* (☎ 846-5356) is the prestige place to stay in town; it offers a convenient location, views of the river, fireplaces and a dining room but you may have to look in both pockets to pay the bill. Rooms start at $95.

Places to Eat

Elora Confectioner's Delicatessen, at 54 Metcalfe St, has fresh sandwiches and baked goods. *Tiffany's* is a fish & chips place at 146 Metcalfe St. At the back of *Leyanders*, a store at 40 Mill St, is a quiet tearoom, good for afternoon cream tea with a view of the river.

Other places along Mill St, and the dining room of the *Mill Inn*, offer more expensive menus. The *Metcalfe Inn*, at the corner of Mill and Metcalfe Sts, has an outdoor patio where beer is served.

Things to Buy

Plenty of small stores in Elora offer crafts, jewellery, paintings and pottery, much of it produced by the numerous local artisans.

FERGUS

Fergus is Elora's neighbour and a quiet, farming town. As the name suggests, the heritage here is Scottish, and this is best appreciated at the annual Highland Games, held during the second week of August. Included are Scottish dancing, pipe bands, foods, and sports events such as the caber toss. It is one of the largest Scottish festivals and Highland Games held in North America.

The main street is St Andrew St. Many of the attractive buildings are made of limestone and a town oddity are the painted fire hydrants. The **Templin Gardens** are in the centre of town, along the Grand River. A farmers' market is held on weekends.

Between Fergus and Elora Sts is the **Wellington County Museum**, with artefacts relating to the history of the county.

Canoes can be rented in town at Templin

Gardens for a paddle down the gorge to Elora. The annual Old Time Fiddle & Step Dance Contest is held on the second weekend in July.

Like Elora, Fergus is quite busy, and accommodation is not overly abundant. For B&Bs, call or drop around to the *4 Eleven* (☎ 843-5107), at 411 St Andre St East, within walking distance of the downtown area. You can get a room here or they'll fix you up with someone else. Prices are from $40/50 for singles/doubles (in general, a little lower than in Elora).

For food try the *Honeycomb Café*, at 135 St David St North, which has homemade soups, breads and desserts.

STRATFORD

With a population of 28,000, this commercial centre surrounded by farmland is a fairly typical slow-paced, rural Ontario town except that it's consciously prettier than most and is home to the world-famous Shakespearean Festival. Many of the numerous older buildings in the attractive, architecturally interesting central area have been restored, and the layout along the river adds to the charm. Stratford's Avon River, with its swans and green lawns, together with the theatres help the town deliberately and successfully resemble Stratford-upon-Avon in England.

London is about 60 km or 45 minutes' drive south-west, and Toronto is about two hours' drive east.

Orientation

Ontario St is the main street and everything is close to it. At the foot of Huron St is the Perth County Courthouse, one of the town's most distinctive and dominant landmarks.

Information

There is a friendly, helpful and well-informed tourist office (☎ 273-3352) on the corner of York and Erie Sts, in the heart of town. You can see pictures of guesthouses and peruse menus from many of the town's restaurants.

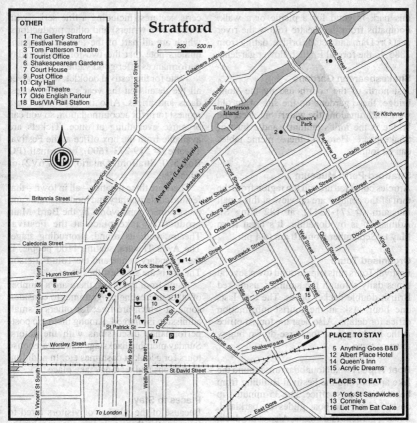

Stratford

OTHER
1 The Gallery Stratford
2 Festival Theatre
3 Tom Patterson Theatre
4 Tourist Office
6 Shakespearean Gardens
7 Court House
9 Post Office
10 City Hall
14 Avon Theatre
17 Olde English Parlour
18 Bus/VIA Rail Station

0 250 500 m

Delamere Avenue

Romeo Street

William Street

Mornington Street

Tom Patterson Island

Queen's Park

To Kitchener

Parkview Dr

Ontario Street

Avon River (Lake Victoria)

Lakeside Drive

Front Street

Albert Street

Brunswick Street

Britannia Street

Elizabeth Street

William Street

Water Street

Coburg Street

Ontario Street

Douro Street

King Street

Well Street

Queen Street

Caledonia Street

14

York Street

4

13

Waterloo Street

Albert Street

Brunswick Street

Nile Street

Douro Street

Bay Street

15

Front Street

St Vincent St North

Huron Street

5

8

12

11

9

10

George St

16

St Patrick St

6

7

Erie Street

Wellington Street

Worsley Street

17

P

Downie Street

Shakespeare Street

18

St Vincent St South

St David Street

East Gore

To London

PLACE TO STAY
5 Anything Goes B&B
12 Albert Place Hotel
14 Queen's Inn
15 Acrylic Dreams

PLACES TO EAT
8 York St Sandwiches
13 Connie's
16 Let Them Eat Cake

On fine days, heritage walks depart from the tourist office at 9.30 am Monday to Saturday from 1 July to Labour Day. With one of the descriptive maps available, you could do your own walking tour. One map, put out by the Local Architectural Conservation Advisory Committee, details some of the history and architecture of the downtown area. Don't miss out on a walk along the river where the park, lawns and theatres have been laid out in a charming and attractive manner.

Between November and May, information can be obtained from Tourism Stratford at 88 Wellington St.

The Gallery/Stratford

This is a good art gallery (☎ 271-5271) in a fine old building near Confederation Park, at 54 Romeo St North. Featured are changing international shows of modern painting, with the emphasis on Canadian works. Three shows are presented at any given time. The gallery is closed on Monday. *Gallery Indigena*, at 151 Downie St, specialises in work by Inuit, Iroquois and north Pacific-coast Native Indian artists.

Queen's Park

Down by the river, near the Festival Theatre,

this park is good for a picnic or a walk. Footpaths from the theatre follow the river past Orr Dam and a stone bridge, dating from 1885, to the formal English flower garden.

Shakespearean Gardens

Just north of the courthouse by the stone bridge, these gardens on the site of an old wool mill run along the waterfront. Near the bridge is the mill's chimney and a bust of Shakespeare. Here and there, picnic tables can be found.

Stratford-Perth Museum

Articles collected around the region from the turn of the century are on view at this small museum (☎ 271-5311), at 182 King St. Admission is by donation. It's open from May to September from 10 am to 4 pm.

Organised Tours

Festival Tours runs trips around town several times daily through the summer, using red British double-decker buses. The tour lasts one hour. Ask at the tourist information office for details. Also near the tourist office is the hitching post for horse-drawn buggy tours of town.

Boat Trips A small tour boat runs around the lake and beyond the Festival Building from behind the tourist office. The 35-minute trip costs $6 and the boat glides by parkland, houses, gardens and swans. Also at the dock, canoes and paddle boats can be rented.

Shakespearean Festival

Begun humbly in a tent in 1953, the theatre now attracts international attention. The productions are first rate, as are the costumes, and respected actors are featured. The season runs from May to October each year. Tickets for plays cost between $18 and $59, depending on the day, seat and theatre, and go on sale from 25 February. By show time, nearly every performance is sold out. A limited number of rush seats are available at good reductions, and for some performances, students and seniors are entitled to discounts. Less-costly tickets are available to the con-

certs, lectures (including a fine series with well-known writers) and other productions, which are all part of the festival. Bargain-hunters note that the two-for-one Tuesday performances offer good value.

Write for the festival booklet, which gives all the details on the year's performances, dates and prices. Also in the booklet is a request form for accommodation, so you can organise everything at once. Tickets are available from the box office at the Festival Theatre (☎ 519-273-1600), or by mail (PO Box 520, Stratford, Ontario, N5A 6V2) or telephone.

There are three theatres – all in town – that feature contemporary and modern drama and music, operas and works by the Bard. Main productions take place at the Festival Theatre, with its round, protruding stage. The Avon Theatre, seating 1100 people, is the secondary venue and the Tom Patterson Theatre is the smallest theatre.

Aside from the plays, there are a number of other interesting programmes to consider, some of which are free; for others a small admission is charged. Among them are post-performance discussions with the actors, Sunday morning backstage tours, warehouse tours for a look at costumes etc. In addition, workshops and readings take place.

Places to Stay

Because of the number of visitors lured to town by the theatre, lodging is, thankfully, abundant. By far the majority of rooms are in B&Bs and the homes of residents with a spare room or two. In addition, in the higher price brackets, there are several well-appointed, traditional-style inns in refurbished, century-old hotels.

Camping There is camping at the *Stratford Fairgrounds* (☎ 271-5130), at 20 Glastonbury Drive. The farmers' market and a number of other events take place here on the grounds, which are quite central, about seven blocks from the tourist office. There is also camping in St Marys (see under that town later).

Hostels A possibility worth considering is a room at the *General Hospital Residence* (☎ 271-5084), and no, you don't have to get hit by a car to qualify. Similar to university dorms, the small, neat rooms come with single or twin beds, a fridge and a sink. A single/twin is $37/42 and there are excellent weekly rates. There are laundry and cooking facilities, a cafeteria and an outdoor swimming pool – all in all, a pretty fair bargain. The address is 130 Youngs St.

See also the Burnside Guest Home, listed in the following section.

B&Bs A good way to find an economical bed is to book through the Stratford Festival Accommodation Department (☎ 519-273-1600), at 55 Queen St. They will find a room in someone's home from as low as $31/33 a single/double if you have a ticket to a play. For a couple more dollars, breakfast can be included. Payment must be made in full when booking.

The Stratford & Area B&B Association (☎ 273-2052) does much the same thing, but not being part of the festival, their prices are higher and their members are trying to run viable businesses. Rates are around $35 to $45 for singles and from $55 to $65 and upwards for doubles.

The *Burnside Guest Home* (☎ 271-7076) is at 139 William St, which runs along the river, across from the downtown core. A 15-minute walk will get you to any of the theatres or the downtown area. Singles start at just $35 and doubles range to $65. There are also cheaper hostel-style rooms for $25.

At 107 Huron St, within walking distance of the centre of town, *Anything Goes* (☎ 273-6557) is open all year, with a range of rooms, from twins with shared bathroom to rooms with ensuite bath and kitchenette. The breakfasts are good and bicycles are available. It is open all year.

Also central, at 220 Church St, the *Maples of Stratford* (☎ 273-0810) is in a large Victorian house. Rooms start at $50 with a good continental breakfast included.

At 66 Bay St is *Acrylic Dreams* (☎ 271-7874), an updated cottage from 1879 which has some pleasant little touches for guests to set it apart. Moving up in price, one to try is *Stratford Knights* (☎ 273-6089), at 66 Britannia St. It's away from the centre a bit, on the other side of the river, off Mornington St. This fine old house has a pool in the yard, which guests can use. Doubles start at $58, including a continental breakfast.

Hotels The refurbished *Queen's Inn* (☎ 271-1400), 161 Ontario St (near Waterloo St), dating from the mid-1800s, is the oldest hotel in town. In summer prices range from $75 double. The popular standard room with full bath goes for $120.

Motels Motels are generally expensive. Try the *Noretta* (☎ 271-6110), on Hwy 7 towards Kitchener. Rooms cost from $54 a double. *Majers Motel* (☎ 271-2010), a little further out, has rooms for about the same price. There are other motels along here, including the *Rosecourt*, which is attractive but more costly.

Places to Eat

At 11 York St, near the tourist office, is a small sandwich shop, which is literally a hole in the wall doing takeout orders only. They make good sandwiches, and picnic plates which might include a bit of smoked salmon or corn on the cob. The park by the river (right across the street) makes a good eating spot. The shop is closed on Monday.

Let Them Eat Cake is a dessert and coffee bar at 82 Wellington St. There are a few fast-food joints and a Chinese place on Ontario St heading out of town.

Connie's, at 159 Ontario St (near Waterloo St), covers the basics and has pizza and spaghetti. Away from the centre, over the bridge and down Huron St about two km, *Madelyn's Diner* is a friendly little place to have any meal. Breakfasts are served all day (from 7 am) and are good, as are the homemade pies. It's at 377 Huron St, and is closed on Sunday evening and all day Monday.

As befits an English-style town, there are quite a few pubs about. *Stratford's Olde English Parlour*, at 101 Wellington St, has

ONTARIO

an outdoor patio. The *Queen's Inn*, at 161 Ontario St, with several different eating rooms, brews its own beer and the pub has an inexpensive and standard menu including a ploughman's lunch. Good value are the Queen's Sunday and Wednesday evening buffets in the dining room. Dining rooms in some of the other inns also cater to the theatre crowd with more costly fare. Expensive *Rundles*, at 9 Coburg St, has a good reputation.

Getting There & Away

Bus Several small bus lines servicing the region operate out of the VIA Rail station, which is quite central at 101 Shakespeare St, off Downie St about eight blocks from Ontario St. Cha-Co Trails (☎ 271-7870) buses connect Stratford with Kitchener, from where you can go to Toronto. They also run buses to Goderich, London and Owen Sound, among other southern Ontario towns.

Train There are two daily trains to Toronto from the VIA Rail station (☎ 273-3234). Trains also go west to London or Sarnia, with connections for Windsor.

SHAKESPEARE

Twelve km east of Stratford along Hwy 8, this village is geared to visitors, and the main street has numerous antique, furniture and craft shops. The *Shakespeare Inn* is a large, upmarket hotel.

ST MARYS

To the west of Stratford, St Marys is a small Victorian crossroads with a former opera house and some fine stone homes as reminders of its good times last century.

The *Westover Inn*, tucked down Thomas St, and surrounded by lawns and trees, is a quiet, five-star hotel with a dining room.

Several km from town, off Hwy 7 and back towards Stratford, is the **Wildwood Conservation Area**. It isn't particularly attractive but you can camp or go for a quick swim. For better swimming, try the spring-fed limestone quarry just outside St Marys. It costs a couple of dollars and there are change rooms and a snack bar.

TILLSONBURG & DELHI

These two small towns are in the centre of a flat, sandy, tobacco-growing region. The number of smokers has been declining more rapidly in Canada than in other Western countries, so various crop alternatives are being sought to keep the area productive.

On Hwy 3 west of Delhi there is a **Tobacco Museum**, with displays on the history and production of tobacco. It's open daily through the summer, and on weekdays only the rest of the year.

For males, casual work picking tobacco starts in mid-August. Ask at the Canada Manpower offices in these towns. Jobs last roughly a month. It's hard work, but room and board are often thrown in with the wage and you can have a good time. Watch your valuables in the bunkhouse.

LAKE ERIE SHORELINE WEST

As the shallowest of the five Great Lakes, Erie long suffered the most with pollution. Continuing environmental work has brought the waters back from the brink. Scattered along the lake's Canadian northern shoreline, from Windsor to Fort Erie, there are government parks, some with camping, some for day use only. Most are busy on summer weekends.

Turkey Point and, even more so, **Long Point** are good and popular. However, for swimming, the parks along the Lake Huron shoreline are superior. Apart from these Lake Erie recreational areas, the region is mainly summer cottages, small towns and farmland.

Port Dover is a centre for commercial lake fishing, although some people (your author among them) are leery of eating any of the lower Great Lakes catch due to possible chemical contamination. There is a fishing museum in town and cruises along the lake's edge are available.

At **Port Stanley**, a small resort village, a five-km portion of the old London and Port Stanley railroad still operates, running north to the village of Union. The trip takes about 45 minutes and there are three afternoon trips through the summer months. A ticket costs $6.50.

Further west is **Point Pelee National Park** (☎ 322-2365), on the southernmost point of mainland Canada. It's known primarily for the thousands of birds that show up in spring and autumn on their migrations. Up to 342 species have been observed here – about 60% of all the species known in Canada. The region also contains some plants found nowhere else in the country, such as the prickly pear cactus. There are numerous nature trails, a 1.5-km boardwalk through the marsh, forest areas and sandy beaches within the park. Bicycles and canoes can be rented.

Hillman Marsh on the shoreline north of Point Pelee, offers good bird watching as well and provides an observation tower and a boardwalk. Nearby, in the town of Wheatley, *Burton House* (☎ 825-4956) is a moderately priced B&B. *Marsh View* (☎ 326-9746), also in Wheatley, has rooms for $45/60 a single/double. Note that during bird migration periods, this is a relatively busy area. For other possibilities call the local B&B association (☎ 326-7169).

Quite close to Windsor, about 40 km driving straight overland rather than around the lakeshore, are the lakeside towns of Leamington and Kingsville, from which ferries run to the largest island in the lake, **Pelee Island**. Pelee (pronounced 'pee-lee') is halfway across to Ohio, and ferries run over to the US side as well. Ferries run from March to the beginning of December. Tickets cost $5 each way for adults; vehicles from $11. For reservations call ☎ 1-800-661-2200.

The island is known for its good beaches and small vineyards. Visit the ruins of Vin Villa Winery and the old lighthouse. There are tours, with tastings, of Pelee Island Winery (☎ 733-6551). Quite a variety of wines are produced here, including Canadian champagne. There are a few restaurants on the island, an inn and one B&B.

LONDON
London (population 316,000) is the most important town in the Lake Erie area and blends a fair bit of industry and manufacturing with its insurance company head offices and one of the country's largest universities. The overall ambience is quiet, clean and conservative.

Even though the town has its own Thames River, Hyde Park and Oxford St, London bears no resemblance whatsoever to London, England. There are a few things to see in and around town, and it might prove a convenient stopover, as it lies roughly halfway between the US-Canadian border at Detroit-Windsor and Toronto.

Orientation
The main east-west street is Dundas St; Richmond St is the main north-south street. The central area is bounded by York St to the south, Talbot St to the west, Oxford St to the north and Waterloo St to the east. There are some pleasant tree-lined streets and elegant Victorian houses around the edges of the downtown area.

Information
There is a downtown tourist office (☎ 661-5000), on the main floor of City Hall, on Dufferin Ave at the corner of Wellington St. It's open from 8.30 am to 4.30 pm Monday to Friday.

A second office is on Wellington Rd between Hwy 401 and Commissioners Rd heading north into town from the highway. It's open daily from 8 am to 8 pm and also has provincial information.

London Museum of Archaeology & Lawson Indian Village
Both an educational and a research facility affiliated with the university, the museum (☎ 473-1360) displays materials and artefacts spanning 11,000 years of Native peoples' history in Ontario. Adjacent to the museum building is an active dig of a Neutral Indian village of about 500 years ago. Parts of the village, including a longhouse, have been reconstructed.

Special events are scheduled through the year and some displays in the museum are changed regularly. A gift shop offers crafts such as baskets, quill boxes and pottery.

ONTARIO

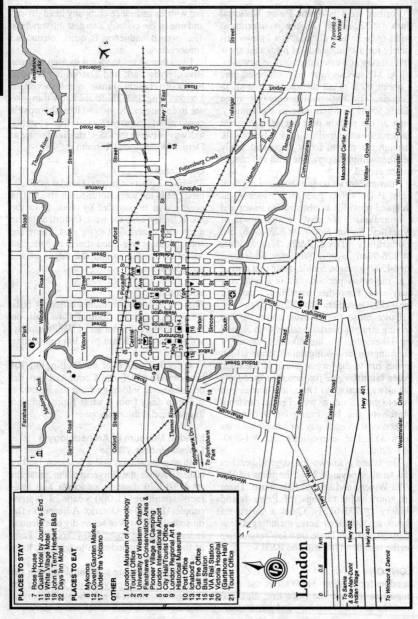

PLACES TO STAY
7 Rose House
11 Quality Hotel by Journey's End
18 White Village Motel
19 John & Terry Herbert B&B
22 Days Inn Motel

PLACES TO EAT
8 Mykonos
12 Covent Garden Market
17 Under the Volcano

OTHER
1 London Museum of Archeology
2 Tourist Office
3 University of Western Ontario
4 Fanshawe Conservation Area &
  Pioneer Village & Camping
5 London International Airport
6 City Hall
9 London Regional Art &
  Historical Museums
10 Post Office
13 Ichabod's
14 Call the Office
15 Bus Station
16 VIA Rail Station
20 Victoria Hospital
   (Gartshore Hall)
21 Tourist Office

London

0   0.5   1 km

To Sarnia
& Ska-Nah-Doht
Indian Village

To Windsor & Detroit

Well worth a visit, the museum is open daily from 10 am to 5 pm. The Indian village is open daily from May to August. An adult ticket is $3.50 and there are senior, student and family rates. The address is 1600 Attawandaron Rd, north-west of the university.

Fanshawe Pioneer Village

On the eastern edge of the city, at the 22-building Pioneer Village (☎ 457-1296), staff in costume reveal skills and crafts and give a sense of pioneer village life in the 19th-century. There is a tea room at the site, or you can bring your own picnic (tables supplied).

Tickets are $5 for adults, less for students and kids, and there is a family rate, too. The site is open daily from May to October from 10 am to 4.30 pm. The entrance is off Fanshawe Park Rd just east of Clark Rd.

The adjoining Fanshawe Park is a conservation and recreation area with swimming, walking and picnicking areas.

Royal Canadian Regiment Museum

Known as the RCR (☎ 660-5102), this is the oldest infantry regiment in Canada. The museum has displays on its involvement in the North-West Rebellion of 1885 right through both World Wars and the Korea War. As well as the various displays, exhibits and dioramas, there is a gift shop with a range of military items.

The museum is at Wolseley Hall National Historic Site, on the Canadian Forces Base on Oxford St East (at the corner of Elizabeth St). Admission is free. It's closed on Monday.

The University of Western Ontario

North of the downtown area, the beautiful university campus is pleasant to stroll around. Western is one of the country's larger universities and is known particularly for its business, medical and engineering faculties. The tourist office has a self-guided walking-tour pamphlet outlining some history.

Eldon House

At 481 Rideout St North and dating from 1834, Eldon House is the city's oldest house and is now an historical museum, with period furnishings from the Victorian era. It's open afternoons only, from Tuesday to Sunday. On Tuesday it's free; otherwise there is an admission charge of $3.

Guy Lombardo Museum

At 205 Wonderland Rd South in Springbank Park, this museum (☎ 473-9003) honours the musician and native son Guy Lombardo, well known across the continent for his New Year's Eve concerts. The collection of articles and memorabilia outlines his career. Admission is $2. Note that the museum is open daily from May to September only, from 11 am to 5 pm.

Springbank Park

Located by the Thames on the western side of the city, Springbank is a huge, well-tended park of lawns and gardens. Within the park is Storybook Gardens, a children's play area with figures from fairy tales and a small zoo. This area has a small admission charge but the park itself is free.

Banting Museum

This museum is situated in the house where Sir Frederick Banting, Nobel Prize winner and the co-discover of insulin, once lived and worked. The museum (☎ 673-1752) outlines the history of diabetes and displays include a doctor's office from the 1920s. The museum is at 442 Adelaide St North and is open Tuesday to Saturday from noon to 4.30 pm. A ticket costs $3 for an adult, less for students and seniors.

Children's Museum

Walkable from downtown, the London Regional Children's Museum (☎ 434-5726), at 21 Wharncliffe Rd South, provides a variety of hands-on exhibits for kids to play and learn with. It's open every day from 10 am to 5 pm and admission is $3 per child, $3.50 per adult.

Ska-Nah-Doht Indian Village

Thirty-two km west of the city, Ska-Nah-Doht (☎ 264-2420) is a re-creation of a small Iroquois longhouse community of about

ONTARIO

1000 years ago. Guided tours are available or you can wander about yourself. It's in the Longwoods Road Conservation Area off Hwy 2 and is open daily through the summer and in January and February. For the rest of the year, it is closed on weekends. Admission is $6.50 per car.

Sifton Bog

This site is a little different – in fact, it's unique in southern Ontario. It's an acid bog which is home to a range of unusual plants and animals, including lemmings, shrews, the carnivorous sundew plant and nine varieties of orchids. Access to the bog can be gained off Oxford St between Hyde Park Rd and Sanatorium Rd. There is also a pedestrian gate into the bog from the Oakridge Shopping Mall parking lot.

Westminster Ponds

Also for nature-seekers, this area of woods, bogs and ponds supports a variety of wildlife, including foxes and herons. There is a viewing tower, and a boardwalk around some sections of the large undeveloped area. Two thousand years ago, indigenous people used to camp here. There is a trail into the area, heading east out of the tourist office on Wellington Rd South.

Organised Tours

Bus Tour Two-hour tours (☎ 661-5000) of the city aboard British double-decker buses depart from City Hall, 300 Dufferin Ave, daily from the end of June to the beginning of September. A ticket is $7.

Wine Tour London Winery (☎ 686-8431) offers tours of the winery (with tastings) and, at a different location, of its vineyard and research centre. Call for details.

Boat Cruise Departing from a landing in Springbank Park, the *London Princess* (☎ 473-0363) does a number of different cruises along the river. The basic trip lasts about 45 minutes and costs $7, with discounts for seniors, students and children. There are also Sunday brunch trips and evening dinner cruises. Reservations are a good idea. The season runs from the end of May to October.

Festivals

In the first week in June there is an International Air Show, and in mid-September the Western Fair, a 10-day agricultural and amusement event, is held. In mid-July, watch for the Home County Folk Festival. It's held in the centre of town, in Victoria Park. There are some pretty big names on stage over the course of the four-day event, and it's free. Dance, crafts and a range of inexpensive food are also featured.

Places to Stay

Camping Within the city limits, there is convenient camping at Fanshawe Conservation Area (☎ 451-2800). It's in the northeastern section of town, off Fanshawe Park Rd, and is open from 28 April to 9 October.

Hostels During summer *Alumni House* (☎ 661-3814) at the University of Western Ontario rents rooms. It's at the Richmond Gates, the entrance into the campus from Richmond St. It costs $30 a single ($24 for students), and the rates include a continental breakfast.

There are some comfortable rooms at Victoria Hospital's *Victoria Gartshore Hall* (☎ 667-6556), at 370 South St, for $29/38 a single/double. In the lounges you'll find a TV, a fridge, a microwave oven and a coffee pot. There are also laundry facilities.

B&Bs The London & Area B&B Association (☎ 641-0467), at 2 Normandy Gardens, has a list of places to stay, with prices ranging from $25 to $45 a single, $40 to $55 a double.

Betty & Doug Rose offer three rooms in their 19th-century home, *Rose House* (☎ 433-9978). It's central, at 526 Dufferin Ave, and costs from $35/55 a single/double with breakfast. *John & Terry Herbert* (☎ 673-4598), at 87 Askin St, off Wharncliffe Rd, are also fairly central and they have two rooms in their house (built in 1871). Rates are $35/40 and there is room for kids.

Hotels The small, older downtown hotels tend to be alcoholic city. If you don't mind the ambience, there are a couple on Dundas St which are cheap.

Most economical in the central core is the plain, no-frills *National Traveller Hotel* (☎ 433-8161), at 636 York St. Rooms cost from $35.

The *Quality Hotel by Journey's End* (☎ 661-0233), at 374 Dundas St, is central and has its own restaurant. Rooms here are in the $65 to $80 range.

Motels For many visitors, the most convenient area to look will be along Wellington Rd, which leads north up from Hwy 401 to the centre of town. Of course, prices are higher here. Both *Days Inn* (☎ 681-1240), at 1100 Wellington Rd South, and *Econo Lodge* (☎ 681-1550), at No 1170, are clean, decent and reasonably priced. Prices at the former start at $50/60, a bit less than at the latter.

On the west side of town, the *Rainbow Motel* (☎ 685-3772), at 1100 Wharncliffe Rd South (Hwy 2 toward Windsor), is cheap – and you get what you pay for. It's seen better days but the beds are good and the location makes it quiet. Oh yeah, there may not be any hot water. Rooms start at $22, depending on the day and season, but bargaining is worthwhile if the quote is a lot higher. The nearby *Rossholme Motel* rents rooms by the hour; give it a miss.

If you're sleepy on the east side of town, Dundas St East, a commercial strip, has a number of motels between the 1500 and 2300 street-number addresses. Dundas St East becomes Hwy 2 East away from the centre of the city. Quality and prices here are somewhere in between the other two motel districts. One to try is the *White Village* (☎ 451-5840), at 1739 Dundas St East.

Places to Eat
A good place to whet and satisfy the appetite is the excellent market known as *Covent Garden*, which is in the centre of downtown, behind the Bay department store at the corner of Richmond and Dundas Sts. There's plenty of fresh produce, as well as cheeses and breads. A number of small counters also prepare food. The adjacent Covent Garden restaurant is fine for basic meals, especially breakfasts. While in the market, check out Mac the macaw, in the pet shop. He's been there forever. Sometimes he talks, sometimes he bites, sometimes he just sits.

Say Cheese, at 246 Dundas St (near Clarence St), is both a speciality shop with fine breads and cheeses and a restaurant with good fresh food which can be washed down with featured wines. Lunch will set you back about $10.

On Dundas St at Wellington St is *Scots Corner*, a British-style pub. For excellent Greek food and atmosphere try *Mykonos* on the east side of town at 572 Adelaide St North. Main courses (including a range of vegetarian dishes and lots of seafood) start at around $8. There's an outdoor patio and Greek music in the evenings.

Under the Volcano, named after Malcolm Lowry's great novel, is worth getting to for its Mexican food. Main dishes are about $10. It's open every day (but not for lunch on Sunday) and the location is 300 Colborne St.

Expensive, fine dining in a well-appointed, oak-lined room overlooking the Thames River can be found at *Michael's on the Thames* (☎ 672-0111), at 1 York St. Specialities are seafood and Chateaubriand.

On Richmond St, north of Dufferin, there are plenty of cafes and some interesting shops to browse in.

Entertainment
London has always been a bit of a blues town, and though bars come and go, there is usually at least one place to hear some bar classics. Try the *Old Chicago Speak Easy & Grill*, at 153 Carling St, which runs off Richmond St between Dundas St and Queens Ave. *Ichabod's*, at 335 Richmond St, has dance music. *Call the Office*, at 216 York St, features alternative bands three nights a week and stays open till 3 am. The *CEEPS* at 671 Richmond St (at Mill St), is a drinking spot for university students.

Getting There & Away

Bus The Greyhound bus station (☎ 434-3991) is at 101 York St, at the corner of Talbot St, in central downtown. Buses run to Toronto ($25) every couple of hours and to Windsor about half-a-dozen times daily.

Train The VIA Rail station (☎ 672-5722) is nearby, on York St at the foot of Richmond St. It serves Toronto at least four times a day, two trips going via Stratford. In the other direction, the train goes to Chicago via Sarnia. The standard Toronto train fare is $38.

Getting Around

For fares and route information, the London Transit Commission (☎ 451-1347), the city bus service, has an office at 167 Dundas St a couple of doors east of Richmond St.

ST THOMAS

South of London, St Thomas is a small farm community made a little more interesting by the fine Victorian and other period architecture. In the downtown area, City Hall, the Court House and St Thomas Church are all worth a look. Also for history buffs are the two small museums, one on pioneer life, the other on the military past in the vicinity. The Guildhouse Building (dating from 1912), at 180 Talbot St, houses a number of arts & crafts stores and galleries.

St Thomas has another, not-so-agreeable claim to fame: it was here in 1885 that Jumbo, that famous circus elephant, was hit and killed by a train. The life-sized statue at the west end of town pays tribute to him.

Eleven km west and three km south of St Thomas, near the village of Iona, are the earthwork remains of a double-walled Neutral Indian fort.

WINDSOR

Windsor, with a population of 194,000, sits at the south-western tip of the province, across the Detroit River from Detroit, Michigan. Like its US counterpart, Windsor is primarily a car-making city. The inner cities, however, differ markedly. Recent reports from across the river suggest that the core has just about been given up for dead. In contrast, the downtown area of Windsor is neat and clean, with an abundance of parks and gardens, especially along the river.

And now Windsor has another up on Detroit. In 1994 the city became home to the first casino in the province. Casino Windsor took $100 million in its first three months of operation and has been attracting a daily attendance of about 20,000 ever since. No wonder Detroit wants one too.

Apart from the delights of the casino, Windsor doesn't have a great deal to offer the visitor but it is a major international border crossing. From here it is about two hours' drive to London, 4½ hours to Toronto. From Detroit, there are routes to Chicago.

The central area can be found around the junction of Riverside and Ouellette Sts. There are good views of the Detroit skyline, especially from Dieppe Gardens, which run right along the waterfront from the junction of these streets. Pitt and Chatham Sts are also important.

For information, there is a very helpful Ontario Travel Information Centre (☎ 973-1338) at 110 Park St East, just a few minutes walk from the bus station. It's open daily all year from 8.30 am to 4.30 pm; until 6 pm on Friday and Saturday during the summer.

The International Freedom Festival combines Canada's 1 July national holiday with the 4 July celebrations in the USA for an event of parades, concerts and dances, with one of the continent's largest fireworks displays to end the affair.

Casino Windsor

The casino (☎ 258-7878) is temporarily housed in what was (and will be again) the city art gallery on Riverside Dr. There are 62 gaming tables, including blackjack and roulette, and 1,700 slot machines which take anything from 25 cents to $500. There are no dice games as these are illegal in Ontario. The minimum age of entry is 19 years. The casino is open all year, 24 hours a day. The permanent casino, also on Riverside Dr, between Aylmer and Glengarry Sts, is to open in the spring of 1997.

ONTARIO

Places to Stay

B&Bs The *Nisbet Inn* (☎ 256-0465), at 131 Elliott St West, is quite central and offers B&B at $55/65 a single/double. *Diotte Bed & Breakfast* (☎ 256-3937, at 427 Elm Ave, about five blocks west of the casino, has rooms from $45. A full breakfast is included. The tourist office has a complete list of B&Bs but most tend to be away from the centre.

Motels Most accommodation is in motels, and the place to look for moderately priced ones is in South Windsor, on Dougall Ave. For example, the *ABC* (☎ 969-5090), at 3048 Dougall Ave, charges $45 to $50 for either a single or double. Another to try is the *Star Economy* (☎ 969-8200), at about the same price. A little more expensive and with a better rating is the *Cadillac Motel* (☎ 969-9340), at 2498 Dougall St. Rooms here start at $50.

Another area rich in motels is Huron Church Rd. Division Rd, out by the airport,

also has a number of places, such as the *Casa Don* (☎ 969-2475), at No 2130, where rooms are from $45.

Places to Eat

Has Beans Caffé, one block east of the casino at 128 Ferry St, offers light meals (from $3), desserts and specialty coffees and is open until midnight. There's no shortage of eateries along Ouellette St, which runs down to Riverside Dr. *Howl at the Moon* is a popular sports bar, at 670 Ouellette St, serving the usual finger foods. The *Wooden Spoon*, at 309 Chatham St, which runs across Ouellette, serves Canadian homestyle cooking and does breakfast specials until 1 pm daily. For seafood, try the *Old Fish Market* at 156 Chatham St West, two blocks east of the casino. Dishes start at around $9 and go up to $30.

Getting There & Away

The bus station (☎ 254-7575) is central, on

Black Settlement in Ontario

To the story of the Native peoples, the French and the English, who created so much of Canada's early history, this region of southern Ontario can add new plots and themes. Together Essex and Kent counties around Windsor and Chatham make up one of the two regions of early Black settlement in Canada. (The other is around Halifax, Nova Scotia.)

Windsor, as a terminal on the so-called Underground Railroad, was a gateway to freedom for thousands of former Black slaves in pre-Civil War (1861-65) USA. The railway was really just a network of people ('conductors') who aided, directed and fed the fleeing slaves as, each night, they followed the north star to the next 'station'.

Aside from the museum in Amherstburg, there are several sites in the region relating directly to this saga.

The John Freeman Walls Historic Site is located 1.6 km north off Hwy 401 at exit 28 out of Windsor heading west. The site includes the log cabin built in 1876 by Walls, a fugitive slave from North Carolina. The Underground Railroad Museum is here.

Further west, visit the Raleigh Township Centennial Museum near Chatham, on County Rd 6 south of Hwy 401 after exiting at Bloomfield Rd. This museum concentrates on the lives of the Black settlers who turned the Elgin Settlement into a new home and welcoming centre for others following in their footsteps.

In the town of Dresden is Uncle Tom's Cabin Historic Site. Uncle Tom was a fictional character in the controversial novel of the same name written by Harriet Beecher Stowe in 1852. It was based on the life of Josiah Henson, another southern Black man. The site displays articles relating to the story and salient history.

Just how much the tales of the Underground Railway are engrained in the hearts of Black Americans was suggested a few years ago when the Toronto Argonaut football team outbid some American teams for the services of a new hot rookie, Raghib 'Rocket' Ismail, just out of college. A few days after he toured Toronto and sensed the racial tolerance, the deal was struck. After Rocket signed for some obscene amount of money, reporters at the obligatory news conference asked his mother what she thought of the agreement. Her reply was that they were going to ride that train north to freedom. ■

Chatham St slightly east of Ouellette St. The VIA Rail station (☎ 256-5511) is about three km east of the downtown core, at the corner of Walker and Wyandotte Sts. There are frequent trains to Toronto via London.

AMHERSTBURG

Located south of Windsor, where the Detroit River flowing from Lake St Clair runs into Lake Erie, Amherstburg is a small, historic town.

Much of this history is outlined at the **Fort Malden National Historic Park**, along the river, at 100 Laird Ave. There are some remains of the British fort of 1840. Beginning with the arrival of the fur traders, the area was the focal point for a lot of tension between the Native Indians, French and English and, later, the USA. Here during the War of 1812, General Brock (together with ally Shawnee Chief Tecumseh) discussed plans to take Detroit.

The **North American Black Historical Museum** has displays on both Black history in North America in general and Black settlement of the Windsor area in particular. It's at 277 King St West and is open Wednesday to Sunday.

Park House Museum, the oldest house in town, wasn't built here but rather it was ferried across the river in 1799 and is now furnished in 1850s style. Located at 214 Dalhousie St, it's open daily in summer but is closed on Monday and Saturday the rest of the year. Also from here, ferries run to Canadian **Boblo Island**, where there is a huge amusement park which has been here for about 100 years. Boats also connect the island to Detroit. Moonlit night cruises run in midsummer.

LAKE HURON SHORELINE & AREA

North of Windsor, on the southern tip of Lake Huron, **Sarnia** is an industrial and oil-refining centre. Sarnia is the hub of Chemical Valley, a large, modern oil-and-chemical production complex. Across the Bluewater Bridge over the St Clair River is Port Huron, Michigan.

South-east of Sarnia on Hwy 21 is the **Oil Museum of Canada**, a National Historic Site and the location of the first commercial oil well on the continent. Producing wells can be seen in the area, and the search for more oil continues.

Along Lake Huron as far up as Tobermory on the Bruce Peninsula are numerous and popular parks, good sandy beaches, cottages and summer resort towns. The water is warm and clean, the beaches broad and sandy.

At **Kettle Point**, about 40 km north-east of Sarnia, is a 350-million-year-old attraction. Along the shoreline are a series of spherical rocks called kettles (to geologists, concretions). Some of these calcite formations, which sit on beds of softer shale, are nearly one metre in diameter. The rare kettles are found in other countries but are often underground, and this collection is considered top rate. A little further up the coast, both **Ipperwash Provincial Park** and the **Pinery Provincial Park**, south of Grand Bend, have camping. The Pinery (☎ 243-2220), a large park with 1000 sites, long had a reputation as a party spot but has been quietened down in recent years. The beach is 10 km long and trails wind through the wooded sections. Further north is Point Farms Park, about the size of Ipperwash.

Grand Bend is a Lake Huron resort town. It's a lively place in summer, with a few places for a drink along the shoreline.

Acting as the regional centre, **Goderich** is a small, green and attractive town with a distinctive circular main street. It bills itself as the prettiest town in Ontario.

At dusk, view the 'world's best' sunsets from near the Governor's House & Historic Gaol Museum. It's set on a cliff on the town bluffs over the water. And these sunsets really are spectacular. Also in town, on West St, is a Marine Museum (with displays on shipping and the lake), the Huron County Pioneer Museum and the expensive, resorty *Benmiller Inn* (☎ 524-2191).

The nearby village of **Blyth** is home to a major summer theatre festival which features primarily Canadian plays, both new and old. A unique B&B in town is the *Blyth Station House* (☎ 523-9826), in the converted train station. Rooms, all with private bathroom, start at $65. Several restaurants can be found along Queen St, the main street.

See after Owen Sound under the Georgian Bay & Lakelands section following for details of the northern Lake Huron region as far as Manitoulin Island.

Georgian Bay & Lakelands

North of Toronto, the lakes and woods, towns, resorts, beaches and cottages, all presided over by magnificent Georgian Bay and its varied shoreline, make up the playground of southern Ontario.

The mostly wooded hills, scores of lakes and rivers and numerous parks are scattered in and around prime farmland, making for fine summer fishing, swimming, camping and lazing – just what the doctor ordered. In winter the area is busy with winter recreation: skiing, snowmobiling and lots of ice fishing. In September and October, people tour the region to see nature's annual, brilliantly coloured tree show. Despite the emphasis on outdoor activities, this is generally a busy and developed area. For more space or wilderness, head further north, or to the larger parks such as Algonquin.

The district around Barrie and Lake Simcoe to Orillia and north-west to Penetanguishene, and then around Georgian Bay west to Collingwood, is known collectively as **Huronia**. The area north of Orillia (roughly between the towns of Gravenhurst and Huntsville along Hwy 11) and west to Georgian Bay is referred to as **Muskoka** or (incorrectly) as the Muskokas. The name is taken from one of the larger lakes of the region.

West from Collingwood along the south of Nottawasaga Bay, a smaller bay within Georgian Bay, is Owen Sound. Located at the southern entrance to the Bruce Peninsula, Owen Sound is the largest town in this area. The 'Bruce' is the narrow strip of land

running north which divides Georgian Bay from the main body of huge Lake Huron. From the tip of the peninsula at Tobermory, ferries may be taken to Manitoulin Island, with connections to the mainland of northern Ontario.

The following text leads first from Barrie west and north to Manitoulin Island, around western Georgian Bay, and then from Barrie north and east through the Muskoka-Huronia region, around eastern Georgian Bay.

The telephone area code for Huronia, Manatoulin Island and Muskoka is 705. East of Barrie and Hamilton everything is 519.

BARRIE
About 1½ hours north of Toronto is the town of Barrie, which is more or less the unofficial gateway to the big city's northward cottage country. On Friday afternoon, especially holiday summer weekends, expect a lot of traffic on Hwy 400, at least to Barrie and often beyond. Coming back into Toronto, the traffic is heavy on Sunday night.

There is nothing of particular note in Barrie itself, although the popular beach at Centennial Park (on Kempenfelt Bay of large Lake Simcoe) is convenient and generally busy.

The bus station (☎ 739-1500) is central, at 24 Maple Ave. From here buses go in all directions.

Information
There's a large Ontario Travel Information Centre (☎ 1-800-668-2746) just north of Barrie at 21 Molson Park Drive at Hwy 400, with details on regional points of interest. It's open all year.

A smaller, more locally oriented tourist office can be found at 17A Mulcaster St.

WASAGA BEACH
Wasaga is the beach resort closest to Toronto. Around Wasaga Beach and the strip of beaches (about 14 km long) running up along the bay are hundreds of cottages, a provincial park and several private campgrounds. The centre of activity is the decidedly unsubtle

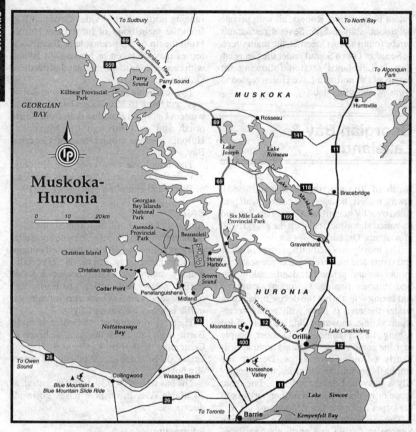

Muskoka-Huronia

0   10   20km

town of Wasaga Beach and the excellent beach (with fine swimming) at Wasaga Beach Provincial Park.

A popular weekend spot, Wasaga Beach is nearly empty during the week. Some areas of the beach are more for families; others (like those around the snack bars) attract the younger crowd. Wasaga Beach has two water slides, including one right on the shore in town.

Places to Stay

The local Chamber of Commerce (☎ 429-2247), with an office open all year at 35

Dunkerron St, should be able to help with finding accommodation. There are many motels around the district, including several along Main St or Mosley St. Rooms start at $40/55 for singles/doubles. They're slightly cheaper for a two-night stay, and cheaper still by the week. Also check on Rural Route 1. Others places to stay are on the beach. Lots of cottages with housekeeping facilities are available as well, but these are generally for stays of a week or longer.

Getting There & Away

Four buses run daily between Toronto and

Skiing in Ontario

Though the region north of Toronto tends to have milder winters and the topography is considerably less dramatic than that found in either Quebec or out in the far west around the Rockies, skiing is still a major winter activity. There are three main alpine centres, all offering daily equipment rental.

Closest to Toronto (about a two-hour drive) is Horseshoe Valley (☎ 835-2790; 283-2988 in Toronto). Take Hwy 400 up past Barrie to Horseshoe Valley Rd. Turn off and the ski hill is six km east. This is the smallest and lowest in elevation of the three and so is ideal for kids, families, the inexperienced or the merely out of shape. It's open every day and has night skiing until 10 pm. Plenty of lifts (including a quad chair) mean the lines move quickly even on busy days. A plus here is that there is also a good system of nearly 40 km of groomed cross-country trails. The trails close at 4.30 pm.

Mount St Louis Moonstone (☎ 835-2112; 368-6900 in Toronto) is one of the province's top ski resort/complexes, and the largest (in terms of number of ski slopes) in southern Ontario. It is at the village of Coldwater, about 10 or 15 minutes north of Horseshoe Valley continuing on Hwy 400. Take exit 131 to the right. Features include snowmaking, two fully licensed lodges (no accommodation) and equipment rentals. There are 42 runs, ranging through easy to difficult, with a 160-metre vertical drop.

Blue Mountain Resorts (☎ 445-0231; 869-3799 in Toronto), at Collingwood, is considered the most challenging of southern Ontario's ski centres and, being relatively far north, tends to have more natural snow and a longer season. The vertical drop here is 216 metres, with the maximum run length 1200 metres. Lifts include one quad, three triple and eight double chairs, as well as two pomas and a rope tow.

Collingwood is about a 2½-hour drive from Toronto. The slopes are 13 km west of town on Blue Mountain Rd. There is daily bus service from Toronto.

Cross-country (nordic) skiing is considerably less expensive; entrance fees to most places are in the range of $7 to $10 for the day.

For cross-country skiing north of the city, there is the aforementioned Horseshoe Valley, or for a relatively wild, undisturbed winter wonderland, Awenda Provincial Park (☎ 549-2231) in Penetanguishene is recommended. Both are open daily.

Close to Toronto are two good places to consider for cross-country skiing. Albion Hills Conservation Area (☎ 661-6600) is eight km north of the town of Bolton, which is north-west of Toronto. They rent equipment and have 26 km of trails winding through the woods. A good day can end with a snack in the coffee shop.

A second choice is to ski the grounds of Seneca College (☎ 833-3333, ext 5024) at their King Campus, at 13990 Dufferin St, in King City. They offer 'old, used and abused' skis and boots for rent. Call for trail conditions. When there is a lot of snow, the trails are open every day, and they are good, winding through the woods. There is no public transportation to the campus.

For the ski conditions report ☎ 314-0988 (alpine) and ☎ 314-0960 (cross-country) in Toronto. ■

Wasaga Beach. It's a 2½-hour trip, with a change of bus in Barrie. In Wasaga Beach, the bus travels right down the main road. The return fare is $43.

COLLINGWOOD

In the centre of the Blue Mountain ski area and right on the water, this little resort town has a reputation for being pretty, but really isn't. The surroundings are scenic enough, with the highest sections of the Niagara Escarpment nearby. The escarpment runs south, all the way to Niagara Falls. The caves along it near town are heavily and misleadingly promoted; they are not what you and I expect of that term, but are really more like overhangs. There is some good walking,

however; the hour-long trail by the caves loops over interesting terrain and offers excellent views. An admission fee is charged to the area around the caves, with an additional charge to actually see the caves.

A chairlift runs to the top of Blue Mountain, from where there is a choice of the chairlift or a slide-ride down in summer. The area is known for its 'blue' pottery, which is nice but not cheap. A bluegrass music festival is held here in summer.

There is a tourist office at 55 Hurontario St.

Places to Stay

Collingwood has an excellent Backpackers hostel, the *Blue Mountain Auberge* (☎ 445-1497), which is open all year but is often booked out. It's on Rural Route 3, near the ski hills north of Craigleith – about 2½ hours from Toronto. There are about 60 beds and a kitchen in a chalet-style building. The sauna is a bonus. Rates are $15 in summer, $17 in winter.

There are plenty of motels too. *Moore's Motel* (☎ 445-2478), on Rural Route 3, is a mid-size place with rooms from as low as $40 (but quite a bit more in season). Offering budget accommodation is the *Glen Lake Motel* (☎ 445-4676), on Rural Route 2, and the *Milestone Motel* (☎ 445-1041), at 327 First St. Both have rooms from $45. Of course, there are more expensive places in the area, including some resorts, lodges and inns with all the amenities.

SHELBURNE

A rather nondescript small southern Ontario country town between Toronto and Owen Sound, Shelburne comes alive once a year for the old-time fiddlers' contest. It's been held for two days in August since the 1950s. There's a parade and free music shows, and the contest semi-finals are only $5. Saturday night grand finals are $12.50 and these tickets must be reserved. For tickets call ☎ 925-3013. For rooms in people's homes for the weekend call ☎ 925-3135. For camping contact the Kinsmen Camp, Box 891, Shelburne, or Primrose Park (☎ 925-2848). **Durham**, slightly to the north and west of Shelburne, is a little town that since 1991 has staged an annual bluegrass festival in mid-August. It is sometimes held in one of the neighbouring villages such as Ayton.

OWEN SOUND

Owen Sound, with a population of just over 20,000, is the largest centre in the region, and if you're going up the Bruce Peninsula or north to Manitoulin Island, you'll pass it by. It sits at the end of a deep bay, surrounded on three sides by the Niagara Escarpment.

Although still a working port, it is not the shipping centre it was from the 1880s to the first years of this century. In those early days, before the railway, the town rocked with brothels and bars, and was battled over by the believers – one intersection had a bar on each corner and was known as Damnation Corner; another had four churches and was called Salvation Corner. The latter seems to have won out, because the churches are still there. In fact, for 66 long years from 1906 to 1972, you couldn't buy alcohol. There aren't too many merchant sailors on the waterfront now, but sections of it have been restored with marinas and restaurants.

Orientation & Information
The Sydenham River drifts through town, dividing it between east and west; the main street is Second Ave. There's a Visitor Information Centre (☎ 371-9833) at 1155 1st Ave West. A folder for a two-hour, self-guided historic walking tour of the city is available here or at City Hall. A Saturday market is held beside City Hall.

Harrison Park
This large, green park is right in town, along the Sydenham River. It has picnic areas, trails, fishing and even camping.

Tom Thomson Memorial Art Gallery
Thomson was a contemporary of Canada's Group of Seven and is one of the country's best known painters. He grew up here and many of his works were done in this part of the country. The gallery (☎ 376-1932), at 840 First Ave West, also displays the work of some other Canadian painters. From June to September it's open Tuesday to Saturday from 10 am to 5 pm (until 9 pm Wednesday) and on Sunday from noon to 5 pm. Admission is by donation.

County of Grey & Owen Sound Museum
Here you can see exhibits on the area's geology and human history. On display are a half-sized replica of an Ojibway Indian village and an eight-metre birch-bark canoe. The museum is at 975 Sixth St East.

Billy Bishop Heritage Museum
Home-town boy Billy Bishop, who became a flying ace in WWI, is honoured here. The museum is in the Bishop home, at 948 Third

Ave West. Billy is buried in town, at the Greenwood Cemetery.

Marine & Rail Heritage Centre
In the old train station at 1165 First Ave West, next to the information centre, this museum details the transportation and ship-building history of Owen Sound.

Mill Dam & Fish Ladder
In spring and autumn, it's interesting to see the struggle trout must go through to reach their preferred spawning areas – this dam and ladder were set up to help them on their swim upstream. It's a couple of blocks south of downtown.

Kelso Beach
North of downtown is Kelso Beach, on Georgian Bay. Free concerts are held regularly here in summer.

Inglis Falls
Six km south of town, off Hwy 6, the Sydenham River falls over the Niagara Escarpment. The falls, a 24-metre drop, are set in a conservation area which is linked to the Bruce Trail. The trail runs from Tobermory south to the Niagara River. See under Tobermory later for details. The segment by Owen Sound offers good views and springs, as well as the Inglis, Jones and Indian falls. It makes a nice half-day walk.

Festivals
The three-day Summerfolk music festival, held annually around the second or third weekend of August, is a major North American festival of its kind. The event is held in Kelso Park, right along the water, and attracts crowds of up to 10,000. Musicians come from around the continent. Tickets cost around $18 a day – and each day is a full one. There's camping nearby.

Places to Stay
Camping Very conveniently, there are campgrounds right in town. One is across the road from Kelso Beach, ideal for the music festival. Another is in *Harrison Park* (☎ 371-

9734), which charges $12 per site (without electricity), and you can use the heated pool – Georgian Bay is known for its cold water.

Motels Most accommodation is provided by motels. There are several on Ninth Ave, including the low-priced *Travellers Motel* (☎ 376-2680) with rooms from $38. The *Key Motel* (☎ 794-2350), 11 km south of town on Hwys 6 and 10, is costlier but still in the moderate range, with rooms from $41 to $55.

Places to Eat
There are a few places along the waterfront and most offer fish. The *Marketside Café*, at 813 2nd Ave East, serves unusual sandwiches, imaginative salads and very good desserts. It's open until 7 pm. *Belamy's*, at 865 Tenth St West, offers a bit of everything, from pasta to steak.

PORT ELGIN
Port Elgin is a little resort town on Lake Huron, west of Owen Sound. There are sandy beaches, the warm waters of Lake Huron, cottages and camping. **MacGregor Provincial Park**, with campgrounds and some walking trails, is five km south.

Further south is the **Bruce Nuclear Plant**, which is controversial, of course, as are all nuclear plants in Canada. They offer free tours and a film on nuclear power.

The **Saugeen River** has been divided up into canoeing sections ranging from 20 km to 40 km. Half-day and longer trips have been mapped out, with camping at several points along the river. A shorter trip is along the **Rankin River**.

SAUBLE BEACH
Sauble Beach is a summer resort with an excellent, sandy 11-km beach, warm shallow waters and entertainment diversions. The coast all along here is known for good sunsets.

There are plenty of hotels, motels and cottages for rent. Expect the many area campgrounds to be busy on summer weekends. Best is the *Sauble Falls Provincial Campground* (☎ 422-1952). Reservations are a good idea. Further north along the road are several commercial grounds – for example, *White Sands* (☎ 534-2781) in Oliphant. The sites at the back have trees and are quiet. Many of the private campgrounds tend to be noisy at night with young party goers – check out the neighbours if this is a concern! A walk around some of the side streets of the downtown area sometimes turns up a guesthouse sign or a seasonal B&B. Cottages tend to be cheaper than motels. *Chilwell's Cottages* (☎ 422-1692), at 31 Third Ave North, has six small cottages and is one of the cheapest, at $30 to $40 for doubles. Prices generally range from $40 to $75.

THE BRUCE PENINSULA

The Bruce, as it's known, is an 80-km-long limestone outcropping at the north end of the Niagara Escarpment. Jutting into Lake Huron, it forms the western edge of Georgian Bay, splitting it away from the main body of the lake. This relatively undeveloped area of the province offers some striking scenery, mixing rocky, rugged shorelines, sandy beaches, lakeside cliffs and green woodlands. The north end has two national parks. From Tobermory (at the tip of the peninsula), ferries depart for Manitoulin Island.

Dyer's Bay

If you have a car, a good scenic drive can be made via Dyer's Bay, which is about 20 km south of Tobermory. From Hwy 6, take Dyer's side road into the village and then the road north-east along the coast. It's not long, but with Georgian Bay on one side and the limestone cliffs of the escarpment on the other, it is impressive. The road ends at the Cabot Head Lighthouse. Before arriving there, you'll pass by the ruins of an old log flume where logs were sent over the edge. The road south of Dyer's Bay is also good, leading down to a 'flowerpot' known as the Devil's Monument. Flowerpots are top-heavy standing rock formations created by wave erosion. This secondary road continues to Lion's Head, where you can connect back with the main highway.

Dorcas Bay

On Lake Huron about 11 km south of Tobermory, there is a preserve owned by the Federation of Ontario Naturalists. This undeveloped area attracts many walkers and photographers for its wildflowers – up to 41 species of orchids can be spotted. To reach the site, turn west from Hwy 11 towards Lake Huron. You're there when you reach the parking lot with a few picnic tables and a toilet.

Bruce Peninsula National Park

The park (☎ 596-2233) protects and makes accessible some of the best features on the entire peninsula. For hikers, campers and lovers of nature, it's not to be missed. The park has several unconnected components, with segments on both sides of the peninsula, including Cypress Lake, some of the Georgian Bay coastline, the Niagara Escarpment between Tobermory and Dyer's Bay, and a great section of the Bruce Trail. See under Bruce Trail later for more details. Cypress Lake, with the campground, swimming and some shorter walking trails, is the centre of most activity.

Tobermory

This unpretentious fishing and tourist village (population 900) sits at the northern tip of the Bruce Peninsula, which protrudes into Lake Huron. On one side of the peninsula are the cold, clear waters of Georgian Bay, and on the other the much warmer waters of Lake Huron.

There is not much to see in town itself, but it is a busy place in summer. The Manitoulin Island ferry docks here. Aside from having its own charms, many people driving across Ontario and further west cut through Manitoulin because it's quicker than driving around Georgian Bay. Tobermory marks the end of the 780-km Bruce Trail and it is also a diving centre. The crystal-clear waters offshore contain more than 20 shipwrecks.

Activity is focused at the harbour area known as Little Tub. There's a Parks Canada centre here and a visitor information office (☎ 1-800-268-3838) just south of Little Tub on Hwy 6. Boats for tours of Flowerpot Island and all sorts of visiting yachts moor at Little Tub.

To reach Tobermory from the north, see under Manitoulin Island later.

Fathom Five National Marine Park This is Ontario's first partially underwater park, developed to protect and make more accessible this intriguing offshore area. More then 20 wrecks lie in the park's waters, scattered between the many little islands.

About five km offshore from Tobermory, **Flowerpot Island** is the best known, most visited portion of the park and is more easily enjoyed than the underwater attractions. The island, with its unusual, precarious-looking rock columns formed through years of erosion, can be visited by boat from mid-May to mid-October. There are various trails on the island, taking from a little over an hour for the shortest one to 2¼ hours for the more difficult. Look for the wild orchids. The island has cliffs, some picnic spots and six basic camp sites.

Reservations are needed for tenters, particularly on weekends, and you should bring all supplies with you, including water. Note that the mental image may not correspond with reality – there is little privacy, with boatloads of mainlanders arriving throughout the day. So much for the isolated island adventure.

Various companies and tugboats offer boat trips to the island allowing visitors to hop off and catch a later boat back. The cost is about $13; just ask around the harbour area. The glass-bottomed boat is the best known, but the waters are so clear that wrecks can be seen simply by peering over the side of any boat. The last boat tours depart at around 5 pm. Tours don't run in poor weather conditions.

Bruce Trail Tobermory marks the northern end of this 780-km footpath, which runs from Queenston (on the Niagara River) to this point (on the tip of the Bruce Peninsula, on Georgian Bay) over private and public lands. You can hike for an hour, a day or a week. The trail edges along the Niagara Escarpment, providing good scenery, and much of it is inaccessible from the road. UNESCO (the United Nations Educational, Scientific and Cultural Organisation) has designated the Niagara Escarpment a World Biosphere Reserve – an area that although developed preserves essential ecological features.

The most northerly bit, from Dyer's Bay to Tobermory, is the most rugged and spectacular. A good day's walk within the national park is possible. You may even get a glimpse of the rare Ontario rattlesnakes, though the chance of seeing one is slight and they tend to be timid, so don't let their existence deter you from a hike.

The Bruce Trail Association (☎ 529-6821 in Hamilton) puts out a detailed guide of the entire route for about $32, less for members. The head office is at Raspberry House, PO Box 857, Hamilton, L8N 3N9. There is also an office in Toronto. The Grey-Bruce Tourist Association has a $5 map of the top portion of the trail, and any local tourist office can tell you where there are access points.

Some parts of the trail are heavily used on summer weekends. Near Hamilton, at the southern end, there is a popular day walking area at Rattlesnake Point Conservation Area. Another southern one is at Terra Cotta, not far from Toronto. Yet another is at the forks of the Credit River.

There are designated areas for camping along the path, and in the gentler, busy southern sections there are some huts where you can even take a shower. In other sections there is accommodation in B&Bs or old inns. Either of the above trail offices can help with information about B&Bs along the trail. Prices start at $45/55 for singles/doubles. Remember the insect repellent, don't drink the water along the trail, and bring good boots – much of the trail is wet and muddy.

Diving The waters here are excellent for scuba diving, with many wrecks, geological formations and clear water. The water is also very, very cold. Even for snorkelling a wet or dry suit is required. G & S Watersports

(☎ 596-2200), at Little Tub in Tobermory, hires out equipment and offers a variety of diving courses. To rent snorkel equipment, including a basic wetsuit, costs around $22. The Ontario government puts out a pamphlet listing dive sites with descriptions, depths and recommendations. It's available free at the tourist office.

In 1993 a large section of well-preserved, 8000-year-old underwater forest was discovered at Colpoy's Bay. It is thought to have been submerged hundreds of years after the retreat of the last Ice Age, when the lake levels rose.

Other Activities Swimming in Georgian Bay in August can be good and warm, but not around here. Shallow Cypress Lake, in the park, is definitely a more sane choice. Further south on the bay, at **Wasaga Beach** and **Penetanguishene**, the water is quite pleasant. The waters along the Lake Huron shoreline are also warm, even on the west side of the Bruce Peninsula. Huron Kayak Adventures (☎ (519) 596-2950), based in Tobermory from mid-May to late-September, rents kayaks and offers tours and instruction.

Places to Stay *Tobermory Village Campground* (☎ 596-2689), three km south of the village, has four basic rooms with shared bathroom for $35. Camping costs $16.50.

At Cape Croker, an Ojibway reserve north of Colpoy's Bay, about halfway down the peninsula, there's a secluded recommended campground. Nature tours are available and Native Indian crafts are offered for sale.

There are a dozen or so motels in and around Tobermory but prices are a little high in peak season and reservations are recommended for weekends and holidays. The *Harbourside Motel* (☎ 596-2422) overlooks Little Tub and has rooms from around $50 during the week. The *Peacock Villa Motel* (☎ 596-2242), in a secluded spot a short walk from the harbour, has rooms at comparable prices.

Places to Eat There are plenty of restaurants in Tobermory, all specialising in variations of whitefish. All the motels have dining rooms too. The *Ferry Dock* restaurant is a cheap and pleasant place for breakfast with tables overlooking Little Tub Harbour.

MANITOULIN ISLAND

The world's largest freshwater island, Manitoulin Island is basically a rural region of small farms. About a third of the population is Native Indian. Tourism has become the island's main moneymaker and many southerners own summer cottages here.

The island is about 140 km long and 40 km wide, with a scenic coastline, some sandy beaches, 100 lakes (including some large ones), lots of small towns and villages and numerous hiking trails. It has so far remained fairly undeveloped. Visitors will soon find out that part of the reason for this is the difficulty of getting to the island and, once there, in getting around. Transportation is non-existent.

There are information offices in South Baymouth (where the ferry lands), Gore Bay, Mindemoya and Little Current (☎ (705) 368-3021). Little Current is the only one to remain open all year.

West of the ferry landing, at the village of **Providence Bay**, is the island's largest beach. Also here is the well known *Schoolhouse Restaurant*. Beyond **Meldrum Bay**, at **Mississagi Point** on the far western tip of the island, an old lighthouse (dating from 1873) provides views over the strait. There is a campground here, as well as a restaurant and a museum in the old lighthouse-keeper's cottage. Meldrum Bay has an inn with a restaurant. Along the north side of the island from Meldrum Bay to Little Current is some of the best scenery.

Gore Bay, on the rocky north shore, has one of the island's five small museums, displaying articles relating to the island's early settlers. See the prisoners' dining-room table from the jail. From the eastern headland at the edge of town, the lookout offers fine views. On the other side of town, the headland has a lighthouse and a campground. One of the main beauty spots, **Bridal Veil Falls**, is 16 km east.

The largest community is **Little Current**, at the beginning of the causeway north to the mainland towards the town of Espanola. The main tourist office for the island is here and can help you find a B&B. Rates are not bad on the island, relative to the southern mainland. There are two viewpoints of note near town and one good walk. The Cup & Saucer Trail, 19 km east of town, leads to the highest point on the island (351 metres), which has good views over the North Channel. Closer to town, four km west and 16 km south on Hwy 6, **McLeans Mountain** has a lookout with views towards the village of **Killarney**, on the mainland.

Activities
Two principal attractions of the island for many visitors are the fishing and boating. There are several fishing camps around the island. For cruising, the 225-km North Channel is superb. The scenery is great: one fjord, **Baie Finn**, is 15 km long, with pure white quartzite cliffs.

You can hire bicycles in Little Current, but that's 63 km away from the ferry landing. The one and only bus company running on the island recently ground to a halt. Ask at the tourist offices for any tours which may have started up.

Festivals
As mentioned, Manitoulin Island has a considerable Native Indian population. At the **Wikwemikong Reserve**, known as Wiky, the largest powwow (loosely translated as 'cultural festival') in the province is held on the first weekend in August, a three-day civic holiday. Native Indians from around the country participate. It's an all-inclusive event, with dancing and music, food and crafts. Wikwemikong is in the north-east part of Manitoulin Island.

Getting There & Away
Bus Getting to Tobermory or Manitoulin Island is a little difficult, particularly without a car. You must change buses in Owen Sound

for the Bruce Peninsula. From Toronto, and elsewhere, buses run frequently to Owen Sound but from there buses go to Tobermory on Friday, Saturday and Sunday only (and not at all in the winter). The complete trip takes almost the whole day. The schedule does vary each year, so call for the latest information. It's also worth asking if there are any special bus charters leaving on other days during the week. There is no train service up this way. Greyhound goes all the way around Georgian Bay from Toronto to Espanola, and from there down to Little Current (on Manitoulin).

Ferry From Tobermory, the *Chi-Cheemaun* runs over to South Baymouth, on the southern edge of Manitoulin. It's not uncommon to have to wait in line for a crossing. There are four crossings daily in midsummer, two in spring and autumn. From Tobermory, departure times are 7 and 11.20 am, and 3.40 and 8 pm. During the summer ferry season, mid-June to the beginning of September, the adult return fare is $18. Cars cost $60.75 return, $35 one way. There's a small charge for bicycles. The 50-km trip takes about 1¾ hours and there is a cafeteria on board. For reservations call ☎ 1-800-265-3163 or 1-800-461-2621 in French.

Car & Motorbike The island also makes a good short cut if you're heading to northern Ontario. Take the ferry from Tobermory, cross the island and then take the bridges to the north shore of Georgian Bay. The route can save you a few hours of driving around the bay and is pleasant, although more costly.

MIDLAND
North of Barrie, on the eastern side of Georgian Bay, is the small commercial centre of Midland (population 14,000), the most interesting of the Huronia region's towns. The Huron Indians first settled this area, and developed a confederacy to encourage cooperation among neighbouring Native peoples. The established Huron settlements attracted the French explorers and, more critically, the Jesuit missionaries.

Midland has a number of worthwhile things to see. Unfortunately, even though the town is quite small, getting to the cluster of sites out of the centre is difficult without your own vehicle.

Information

For information, see the Chamber of Commerce (☎ 526-7884), at 208 King St, opposite the bus station, just south of the town dock.

Little Lake Park

South of Yonge St, a short walk from downtown, Little Lake Park has 100-year-old trees, a small lake and a sandy beach.

Huron Indian Village

Within the park, the Huron Indian village (☎ 526-2844) is a replica of what the Native Indian settlements may have been like 500 years ago (before the French Jesuits arrived on their soul-saving mission). The **Huronia Museum**, adjacent to the village site, has a good collection of Native Indian and pioneer artefacts (check out The Slenderizer, circa 1958), as well as some paintings and sketches by members of the Group of Seven. A combined ticket to the museum and village is $5. It's open all year.

Sainte Marie among the Hurons

Away from the centre of town, this historic site (☎ 526-7838) reconstructs the 17th-century Jesuit mission and tells the story of a rather bloody chapter in the book of Native Indian/European clashes. Graphic depictions of missionaries' deaths by torture were forever etched in the brains of older Canadians by now-discarded school history texts. **Martyrs' Shrine**, opposite the Sainte Marie complex, is a monument to six martyred missionaries and the site of pilgrimages each year. Even the pope showed up in 1984. Sainte Marie is five km east of the town centre on Hwy 12. It's open daily from May to October and admission is $7.25. There's a cafe on the site.

Wye Marsh Wildlife Centre

Right next to the mission site, the centre (☎ 526-7809) provides boardwalks, trails and an observation deck over the marsh and its abundant birdlife. Most notable of the feathered features are the trumpeter swans, once virtually wiped out in the area and now being brought back. The first hatching in the wild as part of this programme took place in the spring of 1993. Displays provide information on the flora & fauna found in the area. Guided walks are offered free with admission ($6) and canoe trips through the marsh are also possible (for an extra $4). The site has a pleasant picnic area set amid indigenous gardens. It's open daily.

Organised Tours

From the town dock, 2½-hour boat tours depart aboard the *Miss Midland* (☎ 526-0161) for the inside passage to Georgian Bay and the islands around **Honey Harbour**. Cruises run from mid-May to the first week of October, with two trips daily during the summer months. A ticket is $14.

Places to Stay

The *Shamrock Motel* (☎ 526-7851), at 955 Yonge St, which runs west to east through the centre of town, and *King's Motel* (☎ 526-7744), at 751 King St, the main street running north to south, have rooms from $45. There are a couple of central B&Bs on King St, just across from the Huron village and museum. *B&B with the Artists* (☎ 526-8102) is at 431 King St and *Kylmore House B&B* (☎ 526-6063) is at No 427. Rates in both are a little high at $50 for a single. The Chamber of Commerce has a full list of local B&Bs.

Places to Eat

Riv Bistro serves moderately priced Greek food at 249 King St. Down at the town dock there's a popular pub offering hamburgers, fries and salads.

Getting There & Away

Penetang & Midland Coach Lines, or PMCL (☎ 777-9510 in Toronto, or ☎ 526-0161 in Midland), departs from the main bus station in Toronto and serves Midland and Penetanguishene.

PENETANGUISHENE

Slightly north of Midland, this town (pronounced 'pen-e-TANG-wish-een' but known as Penetang) is smaller but similarly historic. It has both a British and French population and past. Early French voyageurs, fur traders, set up around the British military posts, and both communities stayed. There is an information office (☎ 549-2232) at the town dock.

Discovery Harbour (☎ 549-8064) is a reconstructed naval base along Church St north of the centre. It was built by the British after the War of 1812 in case the US forces came back for more, but they didn't. The site features eight reconstructed ships, 19th-century naval buildings and costumed staff. In summer there are daily sailing programmes aboard the two schooners *BEE* and *Tecumseth*.

Overlooking the harbour is the **King's Wharf Theatre** (☎ 549-4221), which offers a varied season of plays and musicals throughout the summer. For somewhere to eat, try *Captain Roberts' Table* down by the water.

Between Penetanguishene and Parry Sound (to the north), the waters of Georgian Bay are dotted with 30,000 islands – the highest concentration in the world. This and the nearby beaches make it somewhat of a boating and vacation centre, and the dock area is always busy in summer with locals and out-of-towners. Three-hour cruises, which are popular not only in summer but also in autumn, when the leaves are all reds and yellows, depart from here and from Midland.

AWENDA PROVINCIAL PARK

Awenda (☎ 549-2231), right at the end of the peninsula jutting into Georgian Bay, is relatively small but good. It's busy with both day visitors and overnighters. The camp sites are large, treed and private. There are four fine beaches, all connected by walking paths. The first one can be reached by car; the second

and third are the sandiest. This is one of the few places around Georgian Bay where the water gets pleasantly warm.

There are also a couple of longer, less-used trails through the park, one offering a good view of the bay. Awenda is north of Penetanguishene, where food and other supplies should be bought. Firewood is sold at the park. Basic staples can be bought not too far from the park entrance but a vehicle is still needed.

Sometimes, particularly after heavy rain, water contamination from shoreline-dwelling beaver can result in bathers experiencing a nasty 'swimmer's itch'. It's worth asking about by phone before making the trip as the beaches are a main attraction of the park.

The camp sites cost $15, and reservations are advised for summer weekends (or arrive on Friday afternoon). The roadside signs on the approach indicating that the park campground is full are not always accurate, so persevering can be worthwhile. By evening on a Friday, however, it may well be choc-a-bloc until Monday morning. The park office has a list of commercial campgrounds in the district if it's booked out when you arrive. There are no electrical hook-ups.

CHRISTIAN ISLAND

Off the north-west edge of the peninsula and connected by toll ferry, this island, part of an Ojibway reservation, is the site of the well-preserved 350-year-old Fort Sainte Marie II. It was built by the Hurons in an attempt to protect themselves and some French soldiers and priests from the Iroquois. The Iroquois decided to starve them out. Inside, the Jesuits controlled the limited rations and exchanged food for the Hurons' attendance at mass. Within a year, 4000 Native Indians had starved to death, spelling the end of that band as a significant people in the area.

ORILLIA

Orillia, at the north end of Lake Simcoe, acts as the entrance to the Muskoka area and points beyond. Hwys 69 and 11 split just south of here and continue up to northern

ONTARIO

Ontario. It is also a major link in the Trent-Severn Canal System. From town, cruise boats ply the canal and Lake Couchiching.

Orillia was the home of Canada's well-known humorist, Stephen Leacock. He wrote here and in 1919 built a huge house, now operated as a museum and which can be visited all year. His *Sunshine Sketches of a Little Town*, based on Orillia, has been called the most Canadian book ever written.

The tourist office is at 150 Front St South. The new Casino Rama (☎ 1-888-817-7262), operated by the local Native Indian community just outside of Orillia, is Canada's largest gambling centre. It is open every day, all day and night.

In a different vein there are four and eight-day canoe trips of Algonquin Park offered from June to mid-September by the Orillia Home Hostel (☎ (705) 325-0970). All supplies are included, as is transportation to the lakes. The trips are always booked out, so call for details and reservations. The four-day excursion costs $150.

Places to Stay

There are about a dozen standard motels and inns. The area around the north end of Lake Simcoe also has three provincial parks with camping. All are busy, easy-going, family-oriented places. None of them offers much to do or dramatic scenery but they are the closest places to Toronto. Bass Lake (☎ (705) 326-7054) has a sandy beach, warm waters and a nature trail. There are also boat and canoe rentals, and fishing in the lake. The HI *Orillia Home Hostel* (☎ (705) 325-0970), at 198 Borland St East, is close to the bus station. There are 20 beds and some family rooms and the hostel is open all year. The basic room rate is $11.

Places to Eat

For drivers heading north and in need of a snack, stop at *Webber's*, a hamburger joint so popular that a pedestrian bridge had to be put up to enable patrons to cross the highway. It's on Hwy 11, south of the Severn River.

GRAVENHURST, BRACEBRIDGE & HUNTSVILLE

These three towns, discussed from south to north, are the principal centres of Muskoka. They supply this older, well-established and, in some sections, exclusive cottage country.

In Gravenhurst is the **Bethune Memorial House**, in honour of China's favourite Canadian, Dr Norman Bethune, who travelled throughout China in the 1930s as a surgeon and educator and who died there in a small village. The house details this and other aspects of his career and life. Through the summer, professional theatre is performed at the Muskoka Festival, in the restored Opera House. A restored 19th-century steamship, the *Segwun* (☎ (705) 687-6667) is based in Gravenhurst and provides touring cruises around some of the more well-known Muskoka Lakes (including Lake Rosseau, with its 'millionaires' row' of summer retreats). The ship is the oldest operating steamship in North America and was used around the area before the days of the automobile. There is an office at Sagamo Park in Gravenhurst, at 820 Bay St.

Other boats cruise around Lake Muskoka or Lake Joseph, including the *Lady Muskoka* departing from Bracebridge.

Huntsville is a commercial centre and the last major place for supplies for those going into Algonquin Park. It's also the shopping area for those with summer places around the large Lake of Bays. During the first three weeks of July, Huntsville hosts a Festival of the Arts which features classical music, jazz, theatre, dance and literary events. Call ☎ 1-800-561-2787 for programme information. All of these towns have numerous places to eat and many nearby motels and resorts.

ALGONQUIN PROVINCIAL PARK

Algonquin is Ontario's largest park and one of Canada's best known. It is also the oldest park in the province, having celebrated its 103rd birthday in 1996. About 300 km north of Toronto, it offers hundreds of lakes in approximately 7800 sq km of semi-wilderness. There are 1600 km of charted canoe routes to explore, many of them interconnected by portage paths. The one road through the park, Hwy 60, runs through the southern edge. Off it are lodges and eight campgrounds, as well as wilderness outfitters who rent canoes and just about everything else. Maps are available at the park.

If you want some peace and quiet and a bit of adventure, the park is highly recommended. Algonquin and the Temagami area represent the two wilderness regions closest to Toronto and southern Ontario and provide a good opportunity to experience what much of Canada is all about. There is a lot of wildlife in the park and not bad fishing either. Near the park gate is a logging museum. The park is open every day, all year.

Information

Located 43 km from the west gate of the park on Hwy 60, overlooking Sunday Creek, is the very good visitors centre (☎ (705) 637-2828). Various displays and dioramas illustrate the park's wildlife, history and geology. The centre also contains an excellent bookstore, which includes cheap trail-guide brochures, and a cafeteria. The centre is open every day from May to October, on weekends only the rest of the year.

On the reverse side of the canoe route maps there is camping advice and a lot of interesting information about the park. (It's handy reading material when you're inside the tent waiting for a storm to pass.)

Canoeing

Summer weekends are a busy time for canoeing, so a system of admitting only a certain number of people at each canoe route access point has been established. Arrive early, or book ahead. For reservations call ☎ (705) 633-5538 or write to the park at PO Box 219, Whitney, Ontario, K0J 2M0.

At two canoe-route access points off Hwy 60 within the park, Canoe Lake and Opeongo Lake, there are outfitters for renting canoes (about $20 a day) and gear. This is where most people begin a canoe trip into the park interior. To begin an interior trip from any other access point means transport-ing the canoe to it. (The interior refers to all areas of the park accessible only on foot or by canoe.) A good trip takes three to four days. The western access points – Nos 3, 4 and 5 on the Algonquin map – are good, with fewer people, smaller lakes and plenty of moose. The further in you get by portaging, the more solitude you'll find. A favourite spot is the camp site on the island in Timberwolf Lake, which is accessible either from the south or from the west.

Most rental places have ropes and mounting pads to enable renters to carry the canoe on the roof of their vehicle. To be safe, it is a good idea to bring enough of your own rope to secure the canoe. Different types of canoes are available. The heavy aluminium ones are the cheapest but their weight makes them unsuitable for portaging. They are also noisy and the seats get hot in the sun. For paddling around the main lakes, though, they are fine and virtually indestructible. If you want to get into the interior, where carrying weight becomes an issue, pay the extra to get a kevlar canoe (which weighs in at about 30 kg).

One of several outfitters outside the park boundaries is Rick Ward's (☎ (705) 636-5956) in Kearney, north of Huntsville; he rents canoes for just $18 a day, including paddles and life jackets.

Also recommended is Algonquin Outfitters (☎ (705) 635-2243), at Dwight by Oxtongue Lake, just outside the western edge of the park on Hwy 60. It also has a base at Lake Opeongo in the park. It can rent you everything you need, sell supplies and even offer guided trips. The park runs its own wilderness canoe trips, which include all equipment – canoe, food, supplies and even sleeping bags – for about $44 per day (less for longer trips). For details call ☎ (705) 633-5572.

Esprit Rafting (1-800-596-7238), based near Pembroke, east of Algonquin, offer a one-day canoe trip down the Barron Canyon in Algonquin Park for $75. It also runs a four-day whitewater canoe trip on the Petawawa River, which costs around $400, including all canoeing and camping equipment, meals and experienced whitewater

ONTARIO

guide. Both trips run between May and October. Also see under Orillia earlier for the good-value canoe trips organised by the HI Orillia Home Hostel.

Hiking

There are some interesting hiking trails within the park, ranging from short half-hour jaunts around a marsh to treks of several days' duration. Most of the short trails and lookouts are just off or near Hwy 60 and so can be enjoyed as part of a day trip. Hwy 60 can be taken through the park at no charge, but if you want to stop, a day fee of $6 is charged.

Algonquin Day Trippers (☎ (705) 767-3263), based south of the park in Baysville, offer a variety of guided day trips into Algonquin. They also do a night walk where you can listen for wolves and owls. Guided snowshoe and cross-country ski trips are offered to groups of six or more during the winter. See also under Organised Tours in Toronto for other Algonquin trips.

Places to Stay

Interior camping is $4.25 per person per night. At the campgrounds, where there are showers and real toilets, a site is $15 or more. Among the highway campgrounds, Mew Lake is suggested. It has its own warm lake for swimming, some fairly attractive camp sites by the far side of the lake away from the highway, some walking trails nearby, and a store within walking distance.

Getting There & Away

Bus For those without vehicles, the park is accessible by bus during the summer months. Take the Ontario Northland (☎ 393-7911) bus from the central Toronto bus station to the town of Huntsville. Transfer in the Huntsville station to a Hammond Transportation (☎ (705) 645-5431) bus into the park along Hwy 60.

Canadian Woodlands (☎ 469-4356) is a small outfit offering direct transport into Algonquin from downtown Toronto. Passengers can be dropped off at any access point

along the Hwy 60 corridor which runs through the park. A same-day return costs $50 and allows for around five hours in the park. A one-way trip costs $35. Guided walks along some of the shorter trails are also offered. Trips run from June to September, leaving Toronto at 7.30 am Monday, Wednesday and Friday. According to one reader, it's relatively easy to hitch into Algonquin from Huntsville, particularly during weekends.

SIX MILE LAKE PROVINCIAL PARK

Six Mile Lake (☎ (705) 756-2746), another of the many provincial parks in the region, is on Hwy 69 just north of Port Severn, about halfway between Orillia and Parry Sound. There is nothing particularly special about this over many of the other parks, but it is in a convenient location right by the highway and so may prove useful as a one-night stop-over point. There are 190 basic sites but no showers or electricity. There is swimming in the lake and boat rentals nearby. The park has access to a canoe route.

GEORGIAN BAY ISLANDS NATIONAL PARK

This park, consisting of some 50 islands in Georgian Bay, has two completely separate sections. The principal segment is not far from Six Mile Lake; take Hwy 400 from Toronto then Hwy 69 to Honey Harbour. Once there, water-taxis can be taken to the islands.

Beausoleil Island is the largest island and is the park centre, with campgrounds and an interpretive centre. Several of the other islands have primitive camping facilities, at just $7 a site. The islands are home to the eastern Massasauga rattlesnake, which is actually rather small and timid – and now endangered thanks to the proliferation of cottages and frightened men with axes.

Recreation includes swimming, diving, snorkelling and bass and pike fishing. Boating is also big in the area, what with all the islands and the Trent-Severn Canal system. Many boaters – and they range from those putting along in aluminium 14-footers (four-metre boats) to would-be kings in their floating palaces – tie up for a day or a night at the park islands, so they are fairly busy.

The park is really centred around the boating subculture and is otherwise not particularly interesting. For those seeking some sort of retreat, it is disappointingly busy and rather ostentatiously competitive. The water-taxis are not cheap (from $24 one way) and, while providing some flexibility in destinations and schedules, still offer only limited access.

For park information there is an office (☎ (705) 756-2415) in Honey Harbour, near the grocery store. In summer, a relatively inexpensive shuttle service runs over to Beausoleil.

Section two of the park, consisting of a number of smaller islands, is further north up the bay, about halfway to Parry Sound. This section, although quieter, is inaccessible to those without their own vessels.

PARRY SOUND
Parry Sound sits about midway up Georgian Bay and is the largest of the small district supply towns between southern Georgian Bay and Sudbury. There's a tourist office on the east side of Hwy 69 about 10 minutes' drive south of town. In town, there is a lookout tower with views over the bay. The town bills itself as the home of Bobby Orr who, for the uninitiated, was a superb ice-hockey player. He was a defenceman who changed the role of that position forever with his offensive prowess. Orr, who played for the Boston Bruins in the 1960s and 70s, showed that given the skills, a good defenceman can also be a substantial goal scorer.

Boat cruises around the 30,000 islands, on the *Island Queen*, push off from Government Wharf. The trips are about three hours long, departing in the early afternoon, and run from June to September.

Parry Sound is also known for its excellent and popular summer classical-music festival called the Festival of the Sound. Quality live theatre is presented in July and August.

There are dozens of motels and cottages

for rent in the area, some quite reasonably priced. The Parry Sound B&B Association (☎ (705) 746-5399) lists such places available in and around town.

Close to Parry Sound and accessible by a one-lane swing bridge is one of the largest of the Georgian Bay islands. **Parry Island**, 18 km long and 59 km around, is home to about 350 Ojibway Indians. At Oak Point, on the tip of the island, there's a small campground, a marina, a restaurant and a craft shop. There are good views out to the surrounding islands and plenty of secluded coves to explore. Canoes are available to rent for about $2 an hour. Call ☎ (705) 746-8041 for camping reservations.

KILLBEAR PROVINCIAL PARK
Lake Huron's Georgian Bay is huge, and grand enough to dwarf most of the world's waters. It's cool, deep, windy and majestic. The deeply indented, irregular shoreline along the eastern side, with its myriad islands, is trimmed by slabs of pink granite barely supporting wind-bent pine trees. This unique setting represents for many central Canadians the quintessential Canada. The works of the country's best known painters, the Group of Seven, have linked this landscape to the Canadian experience.

Killbear Provincial Park (☎ (705) 342-5492) is one of the best places to see what it's all about. There is shoreline to explore, three short but good walking trails, numerous little hidden sandy beaches and camping. Of course, it's popular; in July and August call ahead to determine camping vacancies. To help insure a quiet night consider asking for one of the radio-free campgrounds. Harold's Point is good. In September it may well be less than half-full. During autumn many visitors spend the day taking photographs and painting. May and June is also less busy. The park is highly recommended, even if an afternoon is all you have. From Parry Sound east to Burk's Falls is more lake and timberland with numerous cottages, both private and commercial. Out of season, things are pretty quiet up here.

ONTARIO

Northern Ontario

Northern Ontario is a vast, thinly populated region of lakes and forest. How large an area it is will quickly become evident if you're motoring around Lake Superior to or from Manitoba.

Commercial activity up here is almost all involved with natural resources – forestry and mining and their spin-offs. Sudbury is one of the world's major mining centres. Way up north beyond Sudbury, on James Bay, is the little town of Moosonee, one of the province's oldest European settlements, accessible by wilderness train. The big cities on the Great Lakes, Sault Ste Marie and Thunder Bay, are major ports and shipping centres. Outside the widely spaced towns, much of the land is wild, with clean waters and abundant wildlife. This is one of the best regions for really typically Canadian outdoor activities. Note, though, that summers are short.

The area telephone code for most of northern Ontario is 705, but for Thunder bay and west to Manitoba it is 807.

NORTH BAY

North Bay, with a population of 56,000, sits at the eastern end of big Lake Nipissing. At about 350 km north of Toronto, it is the southernmost of the north's major towns.

The Trans Canada Hwy, which connects Sudbury to the west and Ottawa to the east, passes through town. North Bay is also an access point to the many mining towns above it which straddle the Quebec-Ontario border. There is also some fine wilderness in the area, which attracts outdoor enthusiasts.

Orientation

Main St is the main street; south of town it becomes Lakeshore Drive. The centre of town is found between Cassells and Fisher Sts. Ferguson is the principal cross-street, and runs from the waterfront east to the North Bay bypass (which connects Hwys 11 and 17). Lakeshore Drive going south turns

into Hwy 11 for Toronto. Algonquin, leading north, becomes Hwy 11 for Timmins and also links to Hwy 17 east and west.

The bus station is at the corner of Second and Cassells Sts, and the train station (VIA Rail and Ontario Northland) is at the corner of Second and Fraser Sts.

All along the shore in town is a sandy beach, with scattered parks and picnic tables. Sunset Park is good at the end of the day. At Canadore College, north-west of downtown, one of several walking paths leads to Duchesnay Falls and good views.

Information

The tourist office (☎ 472-8480) is on Hwy 11 near the junction with Hwy 17 to Ottawa.

Dionne Homestead Museum

Beside the tourist office on the North Bay bypass, at Seymour St, the museum contains articles relating to the Dionne quintuplets. Born in 1934, they were to become the most famous Canadian multiple-birth story. The museum is actually the family log farmhouse, moved and restored. Also at this location is the Model Railroad Museum.

Boat Cruise

Cruises across Lake Nipissing aboard the *Chief Commanda II* follow the old voyageur paddle strokes to the Upper French River. A variety of trips are offered ranging from 1½ to five hours.

Places to Stay

The bulk of the city's accommodation is in motels. Many can be found along Lakeshore Drive in the south end of town. The *Star Motel* (☎ 472-3510), at 405 Lakeshore Drive, costs $40 to $50 for doubles but, like all of them, is cheaper in the off season. Across the street, the *Holiday Plaza* (☎ 474-1431) is a few dollars more but has newer rooms. Both are friendly. Others can be found further afield, on Hwy 11 both north and south of town.

Places to Eat

The *Windmill Café*, downtown at 168 Main

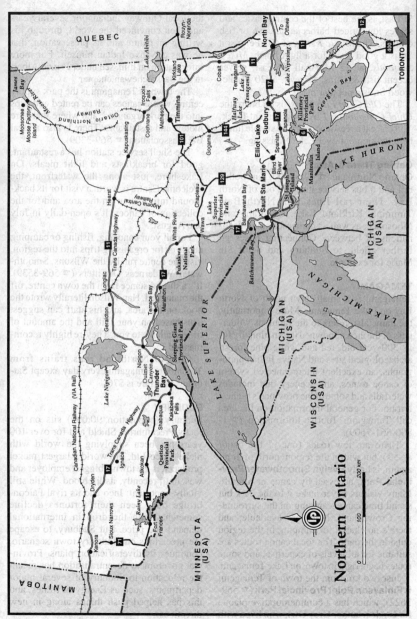

Northern Ontario

QUEBEC

James Bay

Moosonee
Moose Factory
Island

Moose River

Ontario Northland Railway

Lake Abitibi

Iroquois Falls

Cochrane

Kapuskasing

Matheson

Timmins

Kirkland Lake

Cobalt

Roux-Noranda

North Bay

To Ottawa

Temagami
Lake Temagami

Lake Nipissing

Killarney Provincial Park

Georgian Bay

TORONTO

400

11

12

17

69

Hearst

Gogama

Halfway Lake

Sudbury

Espanola

Spanish

6

144

Elliot Lake

Blind River

Manitoulin Island

LAKE HURON

101

Trans Canada Highway

Longlac

Geraldton

Nipigon

White River

Chapleau

Lake Superior Provincial Park

Wawa

Batchawana Bay

Sault Ste Marie

St Joseph Island

129

MICHIGAN (USA)

Algoma Central Railway

11

17

Pukaskwa National Park

Terrace Bay

Marathon

Batchawana Bay

LAKE SUPERIOR

MICHIGAN (USA)

LAKE MICHIGAN

Sleeping Giant Provincial Park

Ouimet Canyon

Thunder Bay

Lake Nipigon

Canadian National Railway (VIA Rail)

Shabaqua

Kakabeka Falls

Trans Canada Highway

Ignace

Quetico Provincial Park

Atikokan

Rainy Lake

Fort Frances

Sioux Narrows

Kenora

Dryden

17

11

71

MANITOBA

MINNESOTA (USA)

WISCONSIN (USA)

MICHIGAN (USA)

0   100   200 km

St East, is the best of the central basics and serves low-priced barbecue chicken or fish dinners. The *Magic Kettle*, at 407 Ferguson St, is a good place for a light lunch. *Mike's Seafoods*, at 22 Marshall St East, serves decent fish & chips. *Casey's*, at 20 Maplewood St, is a popular place.

The *Old Chief Fish House* is on board the *Chief Commander I* by Government Dock. You can eat a reasonably priced simple lunch here looking out over Lake Nipissing.

Getting There & Away

Ontario Northland (☎ 495-4200) runs both a rail and a bus service into and out of North Bay. Their rail lines link North Bay, Timmins, Kirkland Lake, Cochrane and Moosonee, as well as numerous small destinations in between. Connecting buses go further afield, to Sudbury and Sault Ste Marie for example.

TEMAGAMI

Temagami is a small town north of North Bay on Lake Temagami. More importantly, the name also refers to the fabulous wilderness of the area, renowned internationally for its 300-year-old, red and white pine forest, archaeological sites and Native Indian pictographs, an excellent interconnected system of canoe routes, and scenery that includes waterfalls and some of the province's highest terrain. For general information on the area call Temagami Tourist Information (☎ 1-800-661-7609).

There are few roads (one of the major assets), but within the region, north of Temagami, is **Lady Evelyn Smoothwater Provincial Park**, accessed by canoe or aircraft. Many visitors never make it to the park but spend time canoe camping on the surrounding Crown land. Maps are available, and there's no charge for camping in the region outside the park. The local canoe routes are suitable for all levels of expertise, and some routes begin right in town, on Lake Temagami.

Just two km from the town of Temagami is **Finlayson Point Provincial Park** (☎ 569-3622), which has a commemorative plaque for English author Grey Owl, who lived with the local Ojibway Indians for several years and then convinced the world, through his writing on nature and its preservation, that he was a Native Indian himself. For more information on him, see under Prince Albert in the Saskatchewan chapter.

The town of Temagami is the park supply centre, where canoes can be rented and trips into the park organised, and where there are motels and restaurants. There is also a local B&B association (☎ 569-3309).

The Shell service station has a restaurant, good for breakfasts and light meals. On Lakeshore, just along the waterfront, the Welcome Centre is worth a visit for its background information on the area and for the collection of canoes. It's open daily in July and August.

For all your canoeing, fishing or camping needs or for organising trips into the region, visit the centre run by the Wilsons, Smoothwater Wilderness Outfitters (☎ 569-3539). It's a short distance from the town centre, off the main road. Hap Wilson literally wrote the book on the area, and his staff can suggest trips based on your skill and the amount of time available to you. They're highly recommended.

Ontario Northland runs trains from Toronto to Temagami every day except Saturday. The fare is $76.

SUDBURY

Sudbury (population 90,000) sits on the rocky Precambrian Shield and for over 100 years has been supplying the world with nickel. Inco Ltd, the world's largest nickel producer, is the town's biggest employer and was, until recently, its lifeblood. While still vitally important, Inco and its rival Falconbridge have seen their fortunes decline somewhat with the drop in international demand and price. But Sudbury, to escape the precarious one-industry town scenario, continues its diversification plans. Provincial government decentralisation has meant the relocation to Sudbury of several major departments, such as Energy & Mines, and this has helped push things along in new directions.

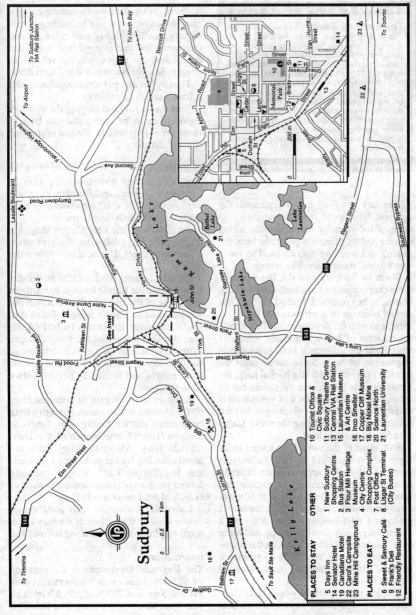

Sudbury

0   0.5   1km

To Timmins
144
To Sault Ste Marie
17

PLACES TO STAY
5   Days Inn
14 Senator Hotel
19 Canadiana Motel
22 Carol's Campsite
23 Mine Hill Campground

PLACES TO EAT
6   Sweet & Savoury Café
9   Frank's Deli
12 Friendly Restaurant

OTHER
1   New Sudbury Shopping Centre
2   Bus Station
3   Flour Mill Heritage Museum
4   City Centre
7   Post Office
8   Lispar St Terminal (City Buses)
10 Tourist Office & Civic Square
11 Sudbury Theatre Centre
13 Central VIA Rail Station
15 Laurentian Museum & Art Centre
16 Inco Smelter
17 Copper Cliff Museum
18 Big Nickel Mine
20 Science North
21 Laurentian University

0   200 m

🏵🏵🏵🏵🏵🏵🏵🏵🏵🏵🏵🏵🏵🏵🏵🏵

The Sudbury Basin

The town of Sudbury sits on the south rim of a ring of low hills outlining a unique and complex geological structure known as the Nickel Irruptive. The mines located around the outer rim of this boat-shaped crater produce most of the world's nickel, platinum, palladium and related metals, as well as large amounts of copper, gold, tellurium, selenium and sulphur. The inner basin area is roughly 60 km long and 30 km wide. Science North has a show offering possible explanations for its formation (which include a volcano or a giant meteor). ■

🏵🏵🏵🏵🏵🏵🏵🏵🏵🏵🏵🏵🏵🏵🏵🏵

The city has long had a reputation for ugliness. The rough, rocky landscape was debased for years by indiscriminate felling of trees and by merciless pollution from the mining and smelting operations. The result was a bleak, moonscape-like setting.

Much to Sudbury's credit, the worst of these characteristics have been (and are continuing to be) reversed. Indeed, the city has earned honours in environmental improvement, and with the development of parks and the creation of Inco's superstack to scatter emissions, the difference from years ago is impossible to miss. Some bleak areas do remain. From up at the Big Nickel park, the views indicate how barren the terrain can be around the mines. The lack of vegetation is mainly due to industrial discharges, but the naturally thin soil covering the rocky Canadian Shield never helped.

Still, most of the town is no longer strikingly desert-like, and in fact Sudbury is surrounded by a vast area of forests, hills and lakes, making it a centre for outdoor and sporting activities. On the east side of town, away from the mining operations, the land is green and wild-looking. There are over a dozen lakes just outside town, including large, attractive Ramsey Lake, at the southeast edge of the city. And Sudbury gets more hours of sunshine than any other industrial city in Ontario.

The downtown core, however, lacks character and there really isn't much to see.

Sudbury isn't a place worth making a major effort to get to, but if you're heading across country you'll probably pass through, and there are a few interesting things to see and do around the edges, mostly related to mining. Science North is a significant draw.

The city has a large French population and a Scandinavian community.

Note that in July and August, the Sudbury region tends to be sunny and can be hot. However, it is generally dry and nights can cool off sharply.

Orientation

The main streets downtown are Elm St (running east-west) and Durham St (going north-south). The core runs along Elm St from Notre Dame Ave to Lorne St.

On Elm St is the City Centre shopping complex and the Holiday Inn. The post office is across the street. The local bus routes start nearby.

Elgin St, running south off Elm St, divides Elm St East from Elm St West; at its southern end is one of the two VIA Rail stations. As you head east on Elm St, at Notre Dame Ave you'll encounter the brown-bulbed Ukrainian church. Further east the street changes names several times. It passes a commercial strip of service stations, fast-food restaurants, motels, and eventually becomes Hwy 17 to Ottawa.

South of town, Regent St becomes Hwy 69 for Toronto. It also passes through a long commercial district. Going west, Lorne St leads to Hwy 17, one branch of the Trans Canada Hwy. Along the way there are motels, the Big Nickel park, Inco Ltd, smelters and Copper Cliff. Hwy 11 running further north over Lake Superior is another branch of the Trans Canada Hwy.

Laurentian University with good views, lies on a hill on the far side of Ramsey Lake, south-east from downtown along Ramsey Rd.

Information

The Regional Development Corporation (☎ 673-4161) has a tourist information desk in Civic Square at 200 Brady St. It's open all year from Monday to Friday. The Rainbow

Country Travel Association (1-800-465-6655), at 1984 Regent St South, and the local Chamber of Commerce (☎ 673-7133), at 166 Douglas St West, also have information.

Science North

The large participatory science centre (☎ 522-3701) at the south-western end of Lake Ramsey has become a major regional attraction. This museum complex is conspicuously housed in two snowflake-shaped buildings built into a rocky outcrop at the lake's edge, beside Alex Baumann Park (named after an Olympic swimmer native to Sudbury). Bell Park runs adjacent to the north, back toward downtown.

Inside, after you enter by tunnel through the 2.5-billion-year-old Canadian Shield, is a collection of exhibits and displays on subjects ranging from the universe to insects, communications to fitness, animal life to rocks. Visitors are welcome to get involved with the displays through the many computers, the hi-tech equipment and the helpful, knowledgeable staff, many of whom are from the university.

Some highlights are the white-quartz crystal displayed under a spotlight (looking like a lingam in an Eastern temple), the excellent insect section (how about patting a tarantula?) and the bed of nails. The fitness test is fun but can be humbling. The 3-D film presented in the pitch black cave is also quite remarkable – just reach out and grab that image. There are major changing exhibits and a recent addition is a 200-seat IMAX theatre. Call ☎ 1-800-461-4898 to find out what's on and for ticket prices.

Also in the complex is an inexpensive cafeteria, a restaurant, and a science and book shop. At the swap shop, you can trade anything natural for anything else from nature's wonders.

Admission costs $8 at Science North, $8 at the Big Nickel or you can buy a cheaper combined ticket covering both sites. Another ticket also includes a bus tour around town (see Path of Discovery later). For information on all three attractions, call Science North. Opening hours are 9 am to 6 pm daily

in summer, till 5 pm in spring and autumn; from October to May, they're open from 10 am to 4 pm. Buses run from the centre of town to Science North every day; catch the No 500.

Big Nickel Mine

Just west of town on Hwy 17 West, up on the hill, the Big Nickel is the symbol of Sudbury. The huge nickel, however, is actually made of stainless steel. You can go down a 20-metre mine shaft, view equipment and see an exhibit of mining science, technology and history. Also in the mine is a vegetable garden and the country's only underground post office. The mine is open every day from mid-May to mid-October and keeps the same hours as Science North. Entry is $8, and city bus No 940 will get you there. From up at the Big Nickel, there's a good view of the surrounding area. The nickel can be viewed and photographed without buying a ticket.

Path of Discovery

Departing from the Big Nickel, this 2½-hour bus tour takes visitors on a geological tour around the city, on the rim of the Sudbury Basin, a 56-km-long, 27-km-wide depression or crater formed two billion years ago. The principal theories for the origin of the basin are volcanic activity or a crashing meteorite. The trip includes the only public access to Inco Ltd and part of their mining operations just west of town. Visitors get a look at the deepest open-pit mine in the country, as well as the grinding mill, smelter and refinery. Also included is a close-up look at the superstack, the world's tallest smokestack. A ticket costs $12; other ticket options that combine various attractions provide a small saving. Details can be obtained from Science North, which operates all three attractions. The Path of Discovery runs twice a day, at 10 am and 2 pm, through the summer months.

Copper Cliff Museum

On Balsam St in Copper Cliff, where Inco has its operation, this pioneering log cabin (☎ 674-3141) with period furnishings and tools is open in June, July and August, from 11 am to 4 pm Tuesday to Sunday.

Flour Mill Heritage Museum

This is a similar place – a pioneer house (☎ 674-2391) with period implements, artefacts and furnishings from the late 19th century. The museum is at 514 Notre Dame Ave and is named after the three flour silos on this street. It is open from 10 am to 4.30 pm Tuesday to Friday and on Saturday afternoon, from mid-June to September.

Laurentian University Museum & Art Centre

The centre (☎ 674-3271) exhibits changing art shows, often the work of local artists. There is also a permanent display of articles relating to the region's history. The centre is open all year from Tuesday to Sunday (afternoons only) and is closed on all holidays. Note that the centre is at the corner of John and Nelson Sts, not at the university campus.

Bell Park

After all the serious Sudbury sites, perhaps a bit of relaxation is in order, and Bell Park, walkable from downtown, fits the bill. This large green area with sandy beaches offers swimming practically in the centre of town. It runs off Paris St south of downtown. Walk or drive toward Lake Ramsey and turn east on Facer St, beside the hospital. Walking paths follow the shore of the lake south all the way to Science North, and others continue north from the hospital.

Organised Tours

The *Cortina* (☎ 522-3701, a 70-seat passenger boat docked next to Science North, offers daily hour-long cruises around Ramsey Lake. Adult tickets are $8. The dock is part of a boardwalk which rims a portion of the lake.

Laurentian University (☎ 675-1151), which has a planetarium, an arboretum, and sporting facilities which you can use (for a small fee), has tours.

Festivals

The Northern Lights Festival is a successful annual music event, featuring unknowns and rising stars from around the country. It takes place in early July in Bell Park. Other concerts and theatre are presented at Bell Park regularly through the summer at the bandshell. It's on the corner of Paris and York Sts and overlooks Ramsey Lake.

Sudbury, with its rocky, sunny landscape is prime blueberry territory. A walk off the road anywhere in the region will probably turn up a few berries. Celebrating them is the annual Blueberry Festival, held in mid-July. There are lots of outdoor events, and public feedings such as pancake breakfasts.

Places to Stay

Sudbury was never a city with an abundance of accommodation choices, and the selection has thinned further. Still, there are always the motels, and it's never so busy that finding one is a problem.

Camping Sudbury is surrounded by rugged, wooded, lake-filled land. There are quite a few government parks within about 50 km of town. The best bet is *Windy Lake Provincial Park* (☎ 966-2315), 26 km south of town. More commercial and designed for trailers and campers is *Carol's Campsite* (☎ 522-5570), just eight km south of town on Hwy 69. Also here is *Mine Mill Campground* (☎ 673-3661), again mainly for campers, but with some tent sites. *Halfway Lake Provincial Park* (☎ 965-2702), is about 90 km out on Hwy 144 north-west of town.

Hostels *Laurentian University* (☎ 673-6580), on Ramsey Lake Rd, rents rooms from mid-May to mid-August. Features include a cafeteria (which is closed on weekends) and use of the physical education facilities. The only problem is that the university is south-east of the downtown area, around the other side of Ramsey Lake. The views are good, though, and the area is pleasant and quiet. They charge $28/40 for singles/doubles. The No 500 bus from downtown runs to the university.

Hotels The bottom-end hotels are minimal with none which can be recommended. Down on Elgin St near the train station, on the strip belonging to the street people, there are a couple of basic cheapies. Surrounded by a lot of gritty urban life are the *Elgin*, at 196 Elgin St, and the *Ledo* (☎ 673-7123). The Ledo is reasonably clean and has 25 rooms, starting at $30/35 for singles/doubles. Ask in the bar about the rooms.

Moving up, a good choice is the central *Days Inn* (☎ 674-7517), at 117 Elm St West, with clean, comfortable rooms for $59/62. Also central is the similar *Senator* (☎ 675-1273). It's on the other side of downtown, at 390 Elgin St.

Motels The bulk of Sudbury's accommodation is in motels found around the edges of town.

Hwy 17 West is called Lorne St near town, and a few km from the centre there is a collection of motels along it. At 965 Lorne St is the *Canadiana* (☎ 674-7585), with a glassed porch and a black-and-white sign. Single and double rooms cost $45 and up. The *Imperial* (☎ 674-6459), at 1111 Lorne St, is a colourfully painted place that serves breakfast. Singles/doubles cost from $45/50.

The better motels are found south of town on Hwy 69. The *Comfort Inn by Journey's End* (☎ 522-1101) is here, at 2171 Regent St South, with rooms at $75. The *Brockdan Motor Hotel* (☎ 522-5270) is five km south on Hwy 69. Rooms cost from $47.

There are other motels on Kingsway leading to Hwy 17 East. One is the *Ambassador* (☎ 566-3601), with rooms in the $60 range.

Places to Eat
Frank's, a deli at 112 Durham St (near Larch St), is good and serves all three meals of the day. For the impecunious, the cheap *Friendly*, on ragged Elgin St, serves the basics without elegance or pretension. It's friendly, open long hours and good for breakfast.

The *Sweet & Savoury Café & Espresso Bar*, at 50 Durham St, serves well-cooked simple meals and is open for breakfast, lunch and dinner. They also have live jazz evenings and poetry readings. There's a health-food shop next door.

For good-value fresh seafood, *Seafoods North* is at 1543 Paris St, in a small shopping plaza. The front of the place is a seafood store; the restaurant, tucked at the back, offers good fish & chips or chowder at lunch and more complete meals at dinner. It's just south of Walford St – too far to walk from downtown.

Pat & Marios is away from the centre, on the corner of Lasalle Blvd and Barrydowne Rd, near two big shopping malls. This fairly dressy eating place is popular for Italian and finger foods.

For a bit of a splurge, consider the comfortable *Snowflake* restaurant at Science North. It overlooks Lake Ramsey. The menu is varied at lunch or dinner and a Sunday brunch is offered.

Regent St South (Hwy 69 to Toronto) is a commercial strip with several restaurants.

The Friday or Saturday *Sudbury Star* newspaper lists the weekend restaurant specials and Sunday brunches.

Entertainment
Backstreet, a pub at 28 Elgin St, has live blues. *The Edge*, north of downtown on Lasalle Blvd, is popular for live rock and alternative music. *Mingles*, at 762 Notre Dame Ave, is a dance club. The *Sudbury Star* on Friday has complete club listings.

Getting There & Away
Air Air Canada and Canadian Airlines fly into the airport in the north-east corner of the city.

Bus The Greyhound Bus Depot (☎ 524-9900) is about three km north of the downtown core, at 854 Notre Dame Ave. This as also the station for Northland Ontario buses (same phone number), which run north to Timmins and south to Toronto.

There are three eastbound buses a day for North Bay/Ottawa/Montreal, and three a day westbound for Sault Ste Marie/Winnipeg/Vancouver. There are several buses a day southbound for Toronto; ask for the express trip.

One-way fares are Ottawa $72, Sault Ste Marie $40, and Toronto $58.

Train There are two VIA Rail stations servicing Sudbury. The original (☎ 673-4771) is conveniently situated at the corner of Minto and Elgin Sts, about 10 minutes' walk from the centre of town. It's in the low, grey building that is mostly black roof.

Unfortunately, there is only one train which uses this station. The Budd car is the local nickname for the one-car train that makes the thrice-weekly trip from Sudbury through northern bush past Chapleau to White River, north of Lake Superior. The one-way fare is $63, but almost half price if you book seven days in advance. It's an interesting eight-hour trip through sparsely populated forest and lakeland. For many villages and settlements this is the only access. The train stops and starts as people along the way, often wilderness seekers with their canoes and gear, flag it down. A moose or bear on the track also means an unscheduled stop. There's lots of birdlife, including hill cranes and great blue herons. You might even do a bit of fishing or berry picking if you're stuck waiting for a freight train to pass. The train doesn't make money, so there's regular talk of cancelling it.

The other trains, such as those for Toronto or westbound, use a less central station known as Sudbury Junction (☎ 524-1591), which is about 10 km from the old downtown station. It is on Lasalle Blvd past Falconbridge Hwy, in the north-east section of town. Buses only go to within one km of the station.

There are three trips a week to Toronto: on Tuesday, Thursday and Sunday. The one-way fare is $71 with taxes.

Going north and west, the route heads straight up through basic wilderness to Longlac, on to Sioux Lookout and eventually across the border to Winnipeg in Manitoba.

No direct route runs to Ottawa, so you must go via Toronto.

Car Renting a car may be useful in Sudbury. Tilden (☎ 560-1000) has the best rates and will pick you up. The address is 1150 Kingsway. Hertz (☎ 566-8110) is at 450 Second Ave North.

Hitching Hwy 17, which becomes Kingsway in town, goes east to Ottawa. Regent St runs south from town into Hwy 69 south to Toronto. If westbound, head out along Lorne St, which eventually becomes Hwy 17 West.

Getting Around
Bus For transit information call ☎ 675-3333. The city buses collect on Lisgar St beside the post office, between Elm and Larch Sts, and this is a major transfer point. Outside the Eaton's store on Notre Dame Ave is the stop for regional buses to some of the surrounding small towns. Route 940 goes to the Copper Cliff Mine smelter site and the Big Nickel site, at quarter to and quarter past each hour.

AROUND SUDBURY
The area around and north of Sudbury is both one of the richest mining districts in the world and a destination for those seeking outdoor adventure and recreation. The fishing, camping and other activities attract visitors from the populated southern regions and the USA.

Some of the mines and smelters are open to the public, although the number of companies offering such tours seems to be decreasing. Ask at the tourist office for the *Mine Guide* of the area. For sportspeople, there are endless lodges, camps and guide services – usually fairly costly, especially the fly-in trips.

French River
South of Sudbury, the French River is famous for its fishing. There is also whitewater canoeing. One group which organises such trips here and elsewhere is Voyageur Canoeing (☎ (705) 932-2131) in Millbrook, Ontario. There is also whitewater rafting on the **Spanish River** near the town of Espanola.

Killarney Provincial Park

Killarney (☎ 287-2900) is one of the provinces's most impressive parks, and a visit is highly recommended, even if only for a day's paddle. Members of Canada's Group of Seven artists worked in the park, and a provincial artists' association was instrumental in its establishment.

Because the lakes are relatively small, the maximum number of overnight campers is low. The park's beauty is outstanding, so it's popular and often full. Try to go midweek, and make reservations, including booking a canoe, before arriving – call as far in advance as you can. Getting in on holiday weekends is nearly impossible.

The park is a uniquely mountainous forested area about 80 km south-west of Sudbury, on the shores of Georgian Bay. It's one of Ontario's three wilderness parks and has few conveniences. Access around the park is by canoeing, hiking or skiing. There is excellent scenery, with birch and pine forest edged by the **La Cloche Mountains**. Some lakes are lined on one side by white quartz mountains and on the other side by more typical reddish granite.

The lakes themselves offer astoundingly clear water with remarkable visibility, but unfortunately this is in part due to acid rain. Indeed, some of the lakes are essentially dead, devoid of life.

Portaging from lake to lake is relatively easy, as the trails tend to be short, at least for the first few, most-visited lakes. Two lakes could be explored from the dock at **Lake George**, making a fine day's outing for those without camping gear.

There is a campground at the park headquarters, on Lake George, and another at the village of **Killarney**, but to see more of the park, venture to the interior via portions of the 75 km worth of portages. There are places for pitching a tent at most of the interior lakes. Outfitters can be found at Killarney village and there is a small, rustic but comfortable lodge, the *Sportsman's Inn* (☎ 1-800-461-1117), with rooms from $65 double. Excellent fresh fish & chips can be had down at the dock area.

Halfway Lake Provincial Park

This is one of the many small, relatively developed parks with camping that surround Sudbury (☎ 965-2702). Within this park are various hiking trails of four, 10 and 34 km in length, as well as several scenic lookouts. The park is about 90 km north-west of Sudbury on Hwy 144.

Gogama

Continuing north up Hwy 144 about two-thirds of the way to Timmins, you reach the Arctic watershed, at Gogama, from where all rivers flow north to the Arctic Ocean. Did you notice it was getting a bit cool?

TIMMINS

Way up here in northern Ontario is Timmins, the largest city in Canada – in area that is. This notwithstanding, it's a small (population about 46,000) and particularly neat town. Originally the centre of the most productive gold-mining area in the western hemisphere, Timmins still acts in the same capacity, but the local mines now work copper, zinc, silver, iron ore and talc as well as gold. Kidd Creek Mines is the world's largest producer of silver and zinc and the main employer in town. One mine, now closed, was the country's deepest, going down nearly 2.5 km! There are still over 2000 km of underground workings in the area.

Forestry products are also important in this rough, rugged, cold region of primary industry. There are hundreds of lakes within the designated city limits, as well as 45 registered trap lines.

Sports are popular (winter sports, as there isn't really much of a summer), and the local arena has cranked out a number of top-rate figure skaters and hockey players. As in so many northern communities, drinking is also popular; as one resident said, there is really little else to do.

The first Europeans to settle this area were from Poland, Croatia and the Ukraine, and many of their progeny are still here. To them must be added numbers of Italians, Finns and Scots, all of whom came with the lure of gold in the 1920s. As in much of north-eastern Ontario, there is a large French population in and around town, and Native Indians, the original inhabitants, are a significant ethnic group. A multicultural festival is held in June.

Orientation

Timmins is actually made up of a number of small communities, the more important of which, strung together running from west to east over a distance of about 10 km, are Timmins proper, Schumacher, South Porcupine and Porcupine.

Hwy 101 passes through the centre of town (where it is known as Algonquin Blvd) on its way west to Lake Superior and east to Quebec. In town, the main streets are Third St (which runs parallel to the highway), Pine St and Cedar St. The central core is marked by the brick streets and old-style lampposts.

Information

The Chamber of Commerce (☎ 360-1900), east of town, on the main road in Schumacher, acts as the tourist office. In addition to the usual local information, it has details on numerous industrial tours of the Porcupine-Timmins area and sells the tickets for them. The address is 916 Algonquin Blvd East. Also ask whether the on-again off-again Ukrainian Museum is open. It had a good collection of artefacts relating to this important cultural group, many of whose members helped develop northern Ontario.

Timmins Museum

In South Porcupine, at 70 Legion Drive (near Algonquin Blvd East), this small but good museum (☎ 235-5066) doubles as an art gallery and exhibition centre, presenting changing exhibits ranging from paintings to masks to performances, and more. In the museum section, see the prospector's cabin, which gives an idea of the lives these people led. The history of the area is outlined. There is some old mining equipment outside, too. The museum is open every day (in the afternoon on the weekend). Admission is free.

Other Attractions

The disused, heritage-designated **Daily Press building** in Timmins, is worth a look and is considered one of the country's best examples of Moderne architecture, a variation on Art Deco.

Deadman's Point, on Porcupine Lake in South Porcupine, has the atmospheric cemetery where many of the town's people were buried after the great fire of 1911. There are good views over the lake.

The old storefronts of Schumacher, on First Ave between Pine St and Hollinger Lane, are being restored to the 1920s and 1930s period. This strip once had more bars per capita than anywhere else in the country.

Organised Tours

Gold Mine Tour The tour of the old Hollinger gold mine (☎ 267-6222) is the city's prime attraction. The mine was discovered in 1909 and was at one time the biggest producer in the western hemisphere – hundreds of millions of dollars worth of gold was dug out of here. The site has now been developed into a varied complex, with stores, a craft outlet, jewellery sales and a restaurant. The highlight remains the underground mine tour, which takes visitors down 50 metres in full mining gear and includes a rail ride and a simulated dynamite blast.

There are also some surface attractions worth seeing. Hollinger House is a relocated original worker's house; the company built these in number for the miners and their families. There are still a few in Timmins, a few blocks north of the highway. This one, though, holds artefacts and memorabilia of past eras. There is also an open-pit mine to see, and some trails past rocky outcrops from which minerals could be extracted. You can even try panning for gold.

All in all it's an interesting site, but tickets are not cheap. Tickets for the full tour cost $16, though there is a lower family rate. The full tour lasts about 1½ hours and includes both underground and surface portions. Tickets can be purchased for the aboveground attractions separately, at a rate of $6.

From May to October, tours run seven

days a week and there are five a day. Tickets must be bought ahead of time at the Chamber of Commerce. Pants and flat shoes are essential, and take a warm sweater; other equipment is supplied. The mine is between Timmins and Schumacher on James Reid Rd, which is off the 'back road' from Timmins to South Porcupine.

Kidd Creek Metallurgical Site & Buffalo Tour

Kidd Creek Mine runs tours of their concentrator and zinc smelter. It's a walking tour which shows how the valuable minerals – zinc, silver, lead and cadmium – are separated from the waste and then how the zinc is processed into shippable ingots. The same dress regulations apply as at the gold-mine tour. The tour, which lasts 2½ hours and costs $3, is only offered on Wednesday afternoon through July and August. Get information and tickets through the Chamber of Commerce (☎ 360-1900). The site is 26 km east of the centre of Timmins on Hwy 101.

Also at the Kidd Site, the employees keep a herd of bison which can often be seen from the road.

McChesney Lumber Tour

A third industrial-site tour is the trip through the now fully automated sawmill by the Mattagami River, where it has been since the turn of the century. Follow the processing of a log to the cut lumber that consumers get at the store. The sawmill is central, just off Algonquin Blvd. Tickets here are also $3 and the tour is about one hour long. Reservations and tickets are through the Chamber of Commerce, who coordinate all the company tours.

On all the tours described, very young children are not permitted.

Pulp Mill Tour

Tours are offered three times daily from Monday to Friday at the Abitibi-Price Pulp & Paper Mill in Iroquois Falls, north-east of Timmins. The mill is a major newsprint producer.

Places to Stay

East of town 35 km and then north three km is the recommended *Kettle Lakes Provincial Park* (☎ 363-3511), good for camping but also recommended for a day trip to see the 20 or so small, round, glacial kettle lakes. You need a car to get here.

Accommodation in Timmins is limited but includes several motels on each side of town. On the east side of town, in South Porcupine, the *Regal* (☎ 235-3393) is reasonable with rooms from $45.

In town are a couple of basic hotels and the good *Venture Inn* (☎ 268-7171), at 730 Algonquin Blvd East, where a double sets you back $70.

Places to Eat

There are plenty of places along the highway between towns and several around the central streets of Timmins.

Bentley's, at 36 Wilson Ave, is recommended for the soup-and-sandwich lunches. In Schumacher, the *McIntyre Community Centre* (☎ 360-1758) also known as the arena, serves a good breakfast. Later, sandwiches and various East European dishes are offered. The homemade pies and butter tarts are noteworthy. At the Italian *Porcupine Dante Club* (☎ 264-3185), 172 Cedar St South, you can get a satisfying, inexpensive Italian lunch or dinner – call to check the hours.

Casey's, east of town, is a popular chain restaurant and a place to have a beer. For a more expensive dinner out, try the *Airport Hotel*, an historic lodge out by Porcupine Lake in South Porcupine. Out the old lounge window you can see the runway – the lake. At one time this was a busy float-plane landing strip, hence the hotel name, and the bush pilots ate and slept at the lodge. A speciality is the fresh pickerel (walleye). There is still a flying school next to the lodge, so you may well see some landings and take-offs. Also, if you wander over, there are pilots who will, for a price, take visitors for a spin around in their planes. Try to get back in time for dessert.

Getting There & Away

Bus The train and bus stations (☎ 264-1377) are in the same building, at 1 Spruce Ave, not far from Algonquin Blvd. Ontario Northland has a daily bus service from Toronto ($96 via Sudbury). During the summer, a bus runs from Timmins to Cochrane for the Polar Bear Express.

Train There is no train service into Timmins itself, although Ontario Northland does get as close as the town of Matheson. From there a bus makes the one-hour trip into Timmins. A ticket from Toronto, including the bus transfer, costs $111.

THE POLAR BEAR EXPRESS

The *Polar Bear Express* is the best known line of the small Ontario Northland Railway service (☎ 1-800-268-9281). The *Polar Bear* heads north from Cochrane through northern wilderness to Moosonee, the oldest permanent settlement in the province, on the edge of James Bay (part of vast Hudson Bay). Three hundred years ago, this was the site of an important fur-trading centre.

Those taking the train have two choices. There is a one-day return trip or a slower two-day trip. The express runs primarily for tourists or those in a hurry. It leaves early in the morning and returns late the same day, taking 4½ hours each way and allowing for a look around Moosonee and Moose Factory. The slower local train, the *Little Bear*, caters to an odd mix of tourists, Native Indians, trappers and geologists.

The summer fare on both trains is $49.20 return (with tax), with reservations required. There are family, child and senior discounts. Trips can be booked from Ontario Northland Railway in Toronto, North Bay, Timmins or Cochrane. In Toronto, there is an information office in Union Station, the main train station, found on Front St.

Ontario Northland Railway also offers three and four-day tours (excluding most meals) out of North Bay and Toronto.

The *Polar Bear Express* runs daily (except Friday) from about 24 June to 4 September. The *Little Bear* operates all year but does not run every day. Outside of the summer season, the fare nearly doubles. Simple lunches and snacks can be bought on the train but you're better off taking your own food for the trip. If you've driven to Cochrane, there is free parking beside the train station.

Visitors should know that despite the train's name, there are no polar bears in the region.

Cochrane

Little Cochrane (population under 5000), roughly 100 km north of Timmins, is the departure point for the *Polar Bear Express*. The large polar bear statue at the entrance to Cochrane symbolises the importance of the train to the town.

Also in town is the **Railway & Pioneer Museum**, with some early railway, Native Indian and pioneer exhibits.

Places to Stay Cochrane has several motels and a provincial park campground to service the passengers. Drury Park, for camping, is close to the train station. Note that the half-dozen motels tend to fill up in midsummer, so arriving early in the day or calling ahead is not a bad idea. The *Northern Lites Motel* (☎ 272-4281), at $60 a double, has a handy restaurant on the premises. Another place to try is the slightly lower-priced *Country Haven B&B Inn* (☎ 272-6802), on a huge property about 23 km from the train station. The morning meal is included. Rooms are from $45.

Getting There & Away From Cochrane, Ontario Northland Railway connects south with Timmins (via Matheson and a bus ride), North Bay and other regional towns. There are also buses between these points. The Ontario Northland train runs between Toronto and Cochrane.

Moosonee

Moosonee, which sits near the tundra line, is as far north as most people ever get in eastern Canada. There are no roads. Once there, see the historic sites and the museums and, best of all, get out on the water on one of the boat tours.

Ontario Northland Railway can supply information on things to do and places to stay in Moosonee.

Moose Factory Island, out in Moose River, is the site of a Hudson's Bay Company trading post founded in 1672. It's two km and 15 minutes from town by boat. Moose Factory itself is a community of about 1500 people, mainly Cree, at the far end of the island. Things to see include some buildings at the historic site, a cemetery, an Anglican church dating from 1860 (with moosehide altar cloths and Cree prayer books) and one of the museums.

An inexpensive large 'freighter' canoe (☎ 336-2944) takes visitors to the island. More costly and extensive tours are available which include the trip to the island, a bus tour around it and other optional side trips (for example, to Ship Sands Island Bird Sanctuary, down the Moose River or out to James Bay).

On **Tidewater Island**, between the mainland and Moose Factory, is a provincial park. Trips here can be arranged and camping is possible.

Boat trips or the freighter canoes (for $15.50) also take people upstream to **Fossil Island** where fossils over 300 million years old can be found.

Back in Moosonee, the other museum, **Revillon Frères Museum**, documents the Hudson's Bay Company's rival, the North West Company, which was based in Montreal. The James Bay Educational Centre has some crafts by local Cree Indians.

Another attraction is the sometimes visible Aurora Borealis, also known as the northern lights.

Places to Stay If you're staying overnight in Moosonee, which is likely if you take the overnight train, there are a handful of places to stay, but they are not cheap.

Rooms at the *Polar Bear Lodge* (☎ (705) 336-2345) or *Moosonee Lodge* (☎ (705) 336-2351) go for around $60/78 a single/double.

Reservations are pretty well a necessity wherever you stay.

NORTHERN ROUTE

Hwy 11 runs west from Cochrane, eventually connecting with Thunder Bay. The province's most northerly major road, it cuts across rough, scrubby forest through several mining towns. There are campgrounds along the way.

The principal town along the route is **Kapuskasing**, with its circular downtown centre. In town, a river tour-boat runs upstream to **Beaver Falls** providing historical and geological commentary and allowing for glimpses of local wildlife like beaver and muskrat.

Hearst, as noted in the Sault Ste Marie section, is the northern terminal of the Algoma Central Railway.

WEST OF SUDBURY

From Sudbury, Hwy 17 (the Trans Canada Hwy) runs 300 km along the north shore of Lake Huron. Driving straight through, the trip takes slightly under four hours. There are a few things to see along the way if you wish to dawdle, and several smaller highways lead to more northern points. South of Espanola, Hwy 6 leads across Lake Huron's North Channel to Manitoulin Island.

Espanola

Espanola is the largest centre between Sudbury and Sault Ste Marie, and how it got its name is an interesting tale.

In about 1750, the Ojibway Indians of the district went on a raid down south, in what is now the USA but which at the time was under Spanish control. They brought back a captive woman, who later taught her children Spanish. When the French explorers arrived on the scene, I guess they were a little surprised to hear familiar Spanish being spoken. They called the settlement Espanole, which was subsequently anglicised to its present form.

Espanola is a pulp & paper town (EB Eddy, one of Canada's biggies, has a mill here) and acts as a gateway for the Manitoulin Island ferry. The island can be reached by road on this side but connects with southern Ontario by ferry (see Tobermory earlier).

During July and August, EB Eddy Forest

Products Ltd (☎ 1-800-663-6342) offers three different tours of their operations. Call for details and reservations or visit their information centre in Espanola. One trip lasts all day (nine hours) out in the bush, learning how the forest is managed. Good walking shoes are required.

Each of the other two tours is three hours in duration. One is through the pulp mill to see the paper-making process; the other is through a sawmill – the biggest this side of the Rocky Mountains. These last two tours are not open to kids under the age of 12 and safety gear (supplied) must be worn. Not every tour is offered every day, so be sure to check the schedule. All the tours are free.

Whitewater rafting is offered on the Spanish River. In town are a couple of standard motels and a few places to grab a bite.

Deer Trail

The Deer Trail refers to a driving route north from the highway at Serpent Lake through Elliot Lake, around a little-developed region along the Little White River and back south to Hwy 17 at Ironbridge.

Mississagi Provincial Park is about a third of the way around from Serpent Lake. At the park and at Flack Lake there are nature trails, the latter with good examples of fossils and a feature known as ripple rock. There are other areas of geological interest along the way, such as the tillite outcrops formed 1.5 million years ago and now found four km north of the Elliot Lake Uranium symbol.

Ask at the Blind River tourist office for information on other sites on the trail. There are over a dozen canoe routes in the district.

Elliot Lake

North of the Trans Canada Hwy, Elliot Lake is a mining town based mainly on uranium. It's a relatively new town, having been founded in 1954 when the ore was discovered. With the tough times the local mining industry has been suffering, Elliot Lake has been promoting itself as a fine retirement centre with a quiet, easy pace and especially low costs.

The **Mining & Nuclear Museum** (☎ 461-7240) features displays on the mining and applications of uranium but also has some area historical exhibits and a section on the wildlife of the region. The museum is open every day from June to September, on weekdays only the rest of the year.

Good views over the North Channel can be had from the Firetower Lookout, north of town five km up the Milliken Mine access road.

Blind River

Blind River, sitting almost exactly halfway between Sudbury and Sault Ste Marie, is a good place to stop for a break. Though small, it's a neat and clean little town with a few good places to find a meal. On the east side of town is a large, helpful tourist office (☎ 1-800-263-2546), with information on the entire region as well as on Blind River.

Beside the information building is the **Timber Village Museum**, outlining the history of logging in the area. There are also some interesting items from the Mississagi people, the original Native Indian inhabitants.

The veneer mill south of town offers tours, and Huron Beach, 13 km from Blind River, is a nice, sandy spot for a swim.

A roving event to watch for (the location changes each year) is the annual North Channel Fiddle Jamboree, held in July.

Places to Stay & Eat Camping is available near town; ask at the information office. Blind River also has five motels, and it's not likely they'd all be full up unless Madonna and Tom Cruise both came to visit. For food, *JR's* chip stand, beside the highway, has good burgers and fries, but there are several sit-down restaurants to choose from as well.

Tallest Tree

North up Hwy 129 toward Chapleau is Kirkwood Forest, where the tallest tree in Ontario is said to grow.

SAULT STE MARIE

'The Soo', as the city is called, sits strategically where Lake Huron and Lake Superior meet. Once a fur-trading outpost, the Soo is now an industrial town important as a shipping centre, for here, on St Mary's River, is a series of locks which enables ships to navigate the seaway system further west into vast Lake Superior.

Aside from the busy canal, the steel, pulp & paper, and lumber mills are major employers. The huge Algoma Steel mill, long one of the city's mainstays, has had to scale back considerably due to lost markets. Diversification has been assisted by the relocation of some provincial government offices from Toronto to the Soo.

The International Bridge connects the city with its twin in Michigan, USA. Going west to Winnipeg is slightly shorter via Michigan and Duluth than over the lake but is not as impressive.

With the bridge and the Trans Canada Hwy, the Soo is a convenient stopover and acts as a tourist supply centre. It is one of the more appealing of the northern cities, and there are some fine outdoor possibilities within range to complement it. With a population of around 79,000, it's the last big town until Thunder Bay to the west. Sudbury is 300 km to the east, a drive of between three and four hours.

Orientation

The approach to Sault Ste Marie from the east or west is a long row of eateries, service stations and motels. Hwy 17 North becomes the Great Northern Rd and then Pim St in town. Hwy 17 East becomes Wellington St, which is the northern edge of the downtown core. If you're passing through, use the bypass to avoid traffic hassles.

For visitors this is a dream town in terms of convenience. The downtown area is quite small and pleasant, with pretty much everything of interest either on or near the long, upgraded Queen St. South from Queen St is the waterfront area, which has also undergone a fair bit of renovation in the past few years. This process continues, and the slow,

thoughtful approach taken by the city is paying dividends in creating a central core popular with residents and visitors alike.

Many of the city's attractions, the bus station, the Station Mall (a large shopping centre) and several hotels are here, within walking distance of each other. Also in this general vicinity is the main tourist office.

A couple of buildings of particular note in town are the imposing courthouse in the middle of Queen St and the Precious Blood Cathedral, constructed of local red-grey limestone in 1875 and originally a Jesuit mission. Queenstown refers to the renovated downtown core.

Information

There is a huge, modern tourist information centre, Ontario Travel Information (☎ 945-6941) in town, on the corner of Huron St and Queen St West, just near the International Bridge leading to the USA. Here you can get maps, guides and advice and can change money. The office is open daily in summer.

The Chamber of Commerce (☎ 949-7152), at 360 Great Northern Rd (Hwy 17 North, near the large, white mushroom-like water tower), also has an information desk. It is, however, closed on the weekend. They also operate an information booth in Station Mall, by Spears department store.

The General Hospital is at 941 Queen St East.

Locks & Canals

If Sudbury is rock city, the Soo is lock city. At the south-west corner of downtown, at the bottom of Huron St (by the International Bridge), are the locks linking Lake Superior to Lake Huron. Joining the two great lakes is the narrow St Mary's River, with its rapids. It is here that in 1895 the locks were built, enabling lake freighters to make the journey hundreds of extra km inland.

Lake Superior is about seven metres higher than Lake Huron. The often continuous lake traffic (about 80 freighters a day pass through in summer) can be watched from a viewing stand or from anywhere along the locks for no charge. There are four

Sault Ste Marie

0   250   500 m

Map Key

1 Tourist Office
2 St Mary's Paper Mill
3 Municipal Fish Hatchery
4 ACR Station (Tour Trains)
5 Lock Viewing & Canals
6 Station Shopping Mall
7 Lunch Break
8 Post Office
9 Roberta Bondar Pavilion
10 Boat Tours
11 Norgama Museum
12 Mike's Restaurant
13 Bus Terminal
14 Sault Ste Marie Museum
15 Mary's Lunch
16 Art Gallery
17 Old Stone House
18 Algonquin Hotel
19 Bush Plane Museum

US locks, and one Canadian lock, found in the narrow channel between North St Mary's Island and South St Mary's Island. The Canadian lock, built in 1895, is the oldest in the lock system, but was put out of action in 1986 when part of the canal wall collapsed. Restoration work has been going on since 1994 and is scheduled for completion in May 1997.

Walk over the locks to South St Mary's Island, on which there is a circular walking trail. The paths, winding through the woods and under the International Bridge, make a nice retreat, with views of the shorelines, rapids and ships. It's a good picnicking spot. Further south, out in the river a stone's throw but inaccessible without a boat, **Whitefish Island** has been designated a National Historic Site. For 2000 years the Ojibway Indians fished these plentiful waters. Fishing is still popular, and anglers can be seen all along the canal and around the islands.

Boat tours (☎ 253-9850) of the locks depart from the dock beside the Civic Centre, off Foster Drive, which is parallel to and south of Bay St in the centre of town. Two boats operate several times daily from June to October. The two-hour cruise costs $15.50

for adults and for my money doesn't offer anything you can't see from shore. Still, being out on the water on a fine day can't be knocked. Longer dinner cruises are also offered.

Sea Lamprey Control Centre

Down at the locks is this small research centre where you can view some lamprey and the fish they victimise and learn more about these giant leeches. It's open from Monday to Friday, in summer only, and is worth a look. At night when it's closed, you can still peek into the lighted building and the tanks, though there really isn't much to see.

Municipal Fish Hatchery

Also down near the locks is the hatchery (☎ 759-5446); follow Huron St south towards the canal then turn left along Canal Drive to get to it. The hatchery raises chinook salmon, rainbow trout and brown trout and releases them into the river and surrounding waters to develop and maintain major sport fishing in the district. And it seems to be working. The region is getting a good reputation and sizeable fish are being taken right off the boardwalk in town. Despite this government cutbacks are threatening the operation. Free tours of the facility are offered from 9 am to 4 pm, daily from June to Labour Day and on weekdays only the rest of the year. The 20-minute tour around the various tanks and the fish at different stages of growth is quite interesting, but take a sweater with you – it's kept cold in there.

The Boardwalk

A boardwalk runs alongside the river off Bay St, behind the Station Shopping Mall, affording good views of the river and across to the USA. As well, there are places to fish and a number of city attractions to be found on or near the river. Near the foot of Elgin St, the large, white tent-like structure is the Roberta Bondar Pavilion, built to honour the Soo's very own astronaut. Doctor Roberta Lynn Bondar became Canada's first female astro-

naut aboard the Space Shuttle Discovery in 1992. The pavilion is the venue for regular concerts, exhibitions and, throughout the summer, a farmers' market on Wednesday and Saturday mornings. Along the boardwalk, see the plaque on Anna Jameson (1794-1860).

In 1836, this woman from Ireland left Toronto, where she lived with Robert Jameson, the attorney general. She took off unescorted to the Detroit area. From there she reached the Soo by boat, descended the rapids and attended a Native Indian assembly on Manitoulin Island. Through Georgian Bay and south to Lake Simcoe, she travelled back to Toronto and later home to Britain, where she published an account of the trip entitled *Winter Studies and Summer Rambles in Canada*. I'd say!

MS *Norgama*

This ship, now a museum (☎ 256-7447), was the last one built for overnight passenger use on the Great Lakes. It's open daily from mid-June until the beginning of September. It also has a restaurant on board. The ship is moored at the Norgama Marine Park dock, near the Roberta Bondar Pavilion.

St Mary's Paper Mill

The large paper mill (☎ 942-6070) on Huron St, at the south-western edge of downtown, offers free walking tours on Tuesday and Thursday afternoons. Register at the security gate.

Sault Ste Marie Museum

Housed in an Ontario heritage building at 690 Queen St East, on the corner of East St, this small, but well-put-together museum (☎ 759-7278) has various displays representing Native Indians, exploration, fur trading, lumbering, geology and other aspects of the area. Another section, on the Inuit, is good. In the turn-of-the-century exhibits, the cigarettes recommended for asthma relief are a lark. The museum is open from 9 am to 4.30 pm Monday to Saturday and on Sunday afternoons. Admission is $2.

Art Gallery of Algoma

This good local art gallery (☎ 949-9067), at

❀❀❀❀❀❀❀❀❀❀❀❀❀❀❀❀❀❀❀❀❀❀❀❀❀❀❀❀❀❀❀❀❀❀❀❀❀

Out of this World with Roberta Bondar

Five Canadians have been officially spaced out. Each has been part of the US NASA programme aboard the space shuttles. Marc Garneau was first in 1984 and repeated in 1996. Roberta Bondar made the voyage in the *Discovery* in 1992. Steve MacLean later that year and Chris Hadfield in late 1995, joined the select few. In mid-1996 Robert Thirsk was part of the longest shuttle trip to date – 17 days. His research will help lead to the space-station era and ensures Canada's on-going role in space exploration.

You want to know how you get to be the first and only woman on the Canadian astronaut team? Roberta Bondar was born in Sault Ste Marie in 1945. Besides getting top marks, she was athlete of the year in her last year at high school. At university she got a degree in zoology and agriculture while earning her pilot's licence and coaching the archery team. Continuing her education she bagged a Masters in experimental pathology, then a Doctorate in neurobiology. Just to stay well rounded she then finished off her Doctor of Medicine Degree.

For fun she parachuted and got her scuba diving certification. Soon she was an assistant professor and head of a clinic treating those with multiple sclerosis. But what she really wanted was to be an astronaut. So she applied when the National Research Council of Canada decided to begin a programme. So did 4300 other Canadians. She was one of the six picked. You don't want to know about the training or the 12 hour days.

As a 'payload' scientist she carried out studies on board the shuttle related to the effects of weightlessness on the human body. One finding she noted was that you needed velcro to hold your head to the pillow (she's funny, too!). Upon returning she wrote a book about her experiences, *Touching the Earth* which includes many of her own photographs. She calls herself an 'organised tornado'. ∎

❀❀❀❀❀❀❀❀❀❀❀❀❀❀❀❀❀❀❀❀❀❀❀❀❀❀❀❀❀❀❀❀❀❀❀❀❀

10 East St next to the public library, is worth a visit. There's an education room, a gallery workshop and two exhibition rooms of changing work. It's open all year from 10 am to 5 pm Monday to Saturday, and Sunday afternoon. Admission is by donation.

Bellevue Park

On the water two km east of town along Queen St, near the university, this is the city's largest park. There is a small zoo, picnic areas, sports fields and a marina.

Old Stone House

Also known as Ermatinger House (☎ 759-5443), this was built in 1814 by a British fur trader and his Ojibway wife. It's the oldest stone house west of Toronto and was where many explorers, including Simon Fraser and Alexander Mackenzie, put up for the night. Inside, the house has been restored and contains 19th-century furnishings. Someone there will answer questions. It's open every day in summer, from Monday to Friday during other seasons, and admission is free. The museum is at 831 Queen St East, near the corner of Pim St.

Bush Plane Heritage Centre

This two-in-one museum (☎ 945-6242) is in an old government hangar by the waterfront, at the corner of Bay and Pim Sts. The history of bush flying in Canada, a great story in itself, is tied closely to its role in forest-fire fighting. Many of the early small-plane pilots in the country were returning from the air force at the end of WWI. They also served in aerial mapping, surveying, medical assistance and rescuing. The museum has full-size planes on display, as well as some replicas, engines and parts. There are also maps, photographs and a tent set up as it would have been in the bush.

The centre is open daily from May to October, but on weekends only the rest of the year. Admission is $3 and tours are offered.

Ontario Forest Research Institute

The research centre (☎ 946-2981), at 1235 Queen St East, runs free tours of the laboratories, greenhouses and various displays at 2 pm Monday to Friday. The institute carries out wide-ranging studies on forest ecosystems in an attempt to determine the best ways of achieving sustainable forestry.

Forest Ecology Trail
Also operated by the government forestry service is this 2.5-km, self-guided nature trail out of the town centre off Hwy 565. There is an attendant to answer questions. Ask at the Ontario Forest Research Institute for details and directions.

Kinsmen-Crystal Creek Conservation Area
Known locally as Hiawatha Park, this is about a 10-minute drive from Great Northern Rd, north-west of downtown Sault Ste Marie. Stop at the big Hiawatha Lodge, where there is a swimming pond and waterfalls in Crystal Creek and from where there are lots of walking trails, ranging in length from two km to 10 km. Admission is free.

Gros Cap
About 20 km west on Hwy 550 is this ridge about 150 metres above Lake Superior and Blue Water Park. Hike up the cliffs for excellent views of Lake Superior, where there's usually a ship or two cruising by. Or take the Voyageur Trail (marked by white slashes), which winds up along the ridge edge providing views of St Mary's River and the lake. The trail will one day run all the way from Manitoulin Island to Thunder Bay, but so far stretches from Gros Cap 200 km east to Serpent River on Hwy 108 along the North Channel of Lake Huron.

Beside the park and parking lot is the *Blue Water Inn* (☎ 779-2530), a great place to eat, especially popular on the sporadic weekends when the Yugoslavian owner puts on big barbecues. The inn is open in summer only.

Agawa Canyon & the Algoma Central Railway
Together, these two make up the best-known and most-visited attraction in the area. The Agawa Canyon is a rugged wilderness area accessible only by the ACR trains. The 500-km rail line due north from town to Hearst goes through a scenic area of mountains, waterfalls, valleys and forests. The route, constructed at the turn of the century, was originally built to bring raw materials into

the plants of Sault Ste Marie. There are now several different options for passengers seeking access to the canyon and its surroundings. Note that the best views are from the seats on the left-hand side of the train.

The basic one-day visitor return trip to the canyon takes a full nine hours, with a two-hour stopover for a quick walk, fishing or lunch on the floor of the canyon. There is a dining car on board and snacks and drinks are also available. An adult ticket costs $46, with considerable reductions for children. The train departs at 8 am daily from June to October. This is the most popular trip, so booking a couple of days ahead is a good idea.

The trip is spectacular in the autumn, when the leaves have changed colour and the forests are brilliant reds and yellows. Normally the colours are at their peak in the last two weeks of September and in early October. Yet another possibility is the winter snow-and-ice run, which is added (on weekends only) from January to March.

There are also trips that run the full length of the line to the town of **Hearst** (population 5500), about a nine-hour trip. Hearst, perhaps surprisingly, is essentially a French town, with under 15% of the population listing English as their mother tongue. The town remains primarily engaged in lumbering, although it has its own small university.

Beyond the canyon, the track travels over less impressive flat, forested lakelands, various bridges and northern muskeg. This is a two-day trip with an overnight stay at the northern terminal. Alternatively, it's possible to stay in Hearst as long as you wish and return when ready, or not at all (mind you, there's not a lot happening in Hearst). There are motels and B&Bs in Hearst; ask about them at the tourist information centre in Sault Ste Marie. From Hearst, buses can be caught east or westbound.

Lastly, there is the passenger train used by anglers, trappers, hunters, lodge operators and various other local inhabitants. This train will stop anywhere you like or anywhere someone is standing and flagging it down, so obviously the going is slow, but some find the passengers a colourful lot and the train provides the only true access into the region.

The fare on this train is calculated by the mile – the current rate is 28 cents per mile.

Information on backpacking, canoeing, swimming, camping and fishing lodges in the canyon and beyond is available at the train station. All manner of supplies can be taken on board, including canoes, boats and a maximum of three cases of beer per person.

In Sault Ste Marie, the station (☎ 946-7300) is on the corner of Bay and Gore Sts, by the Station Shopping Mall in the centre of town. There is free parking at the station.

Hiking

The partially completed Voyageur Hiking Trail will one day run between Manitoulin Island and Thunder Bay. The longest completed segment goes east from the Soo (see under Gros Cap) to Serpent River, a small village south of Elliot Lake, a distance of about 200 km. This is not an easy strolling path; obtain complete information from the Voyageur Trail Association, which has an office in Sault Ste Marie (☎ 1-800-422-0552).

Organised Tours

City Tour Hiawathaland Sightseeing Tours (☎ 759-6200) has a ticket booth on the waterfront, next to the Holiday Inn, and runs four different bus tours in and around Sault Ste Marie. The double-decker bus city tour is a 1½-hour trip costing $8.75. Out-of-town trips stop at various beauty spots and sites. There is a night tour, and a trip out of town through some of the local forests.

Brewery Tour Northern Breweries (☎ 254-7373), downtown at 503 Bay St, offers free 45-minute tours of the facility and a chance to sample some of the various brews. This is one of the country's oldest beer companies and has been operating in northern Ontario since 1876.

Festivals

The annual Tugboat Race, held on the St Mary's River on the 1 July weekend, is a bit of good, silly fun. Competitors from both

sides of the river dress up their boats with flags and banners and putt for prizes and prestige.

Places to Stay

Camping There are several campgrounds close to town, though they are not rustic. *Ojibway Park* (☎ 248-2671) is a 10-minute drive east of Sault Ste Marie on Hwy 17 (called the Great Northern Rd in town). Tent sites cost $12 per night.

KOA (☎ 759-2344) tent & RV park is eight km north of town on Hwy 17. Turn west at the flashing amber light (Fifth Line). The park is on a river and is equipped with laundry, store and pool. Tent sites are $19 for two people.

A little further is *Pointe des Chênes* (☎ 779-2696), on St Mary's River; go 12 km west on Hwy 550 to Hwy 565, then 10 km south past the airport to the community park. There are 82 sites. Rates are comparable to KOA.

Hostels Hostelling International (HI) has an affiliate here in the *Algonquin Hotel* (☎ 253-2311), a fine budget hotel for those with or without hostel membership. The central location is superb, at 864 Queen St East (on the corner of Pim St), within walking distance of just about everything. The rooms are plain, with no extras, but they're clean and each has at least a sink. Singles/doubles are $19/21 with a hostel card, a dollar more without, plus tax. If four of you want to share a room, it's the same price as two. There is a popular bar downstairs – ask for a room on the upper floor if you don't want to hear it.

B&Bs The most central and least expensive place is run by *Lil & Oscar Herzog* (☎ 253-8641), at 99 Retta St, east of downtown off Wellington St. Singles/doubles are $22/28.

More upmarket, the *Top O' The Hill* (☎ 253-9041) at 40 Broos Rd, is in the north-eastern section of the city, about a 10-minute drive from downtown. Prices, including breakfast, are $45/55. Another possibility is the *Hillsview* (☎ 759-8819) where a double goes for $45.

Hotels See the Hostels section for details of the budget-priced Algonquin Hotel.

Also central and good is the *Days Inn* (☎ 759-8200), at 320 Bay St, right by the river. Singles/doubles here are $80/90. Facilities include a restaurant and a heated pool. Their Jolly Roger bar is the only brew pub in town.

Motels Sault Ste Marie's location means that a lot of people pass through, so it is one of those places with scores of motels. Most of them are on Hwy 17 either east or west of town, though some are downtown. Prices vary but average $40 to $45 for singles and $50 to $65 for doubles – generally, the closer to town, the more costly. Overall, these prices are quite good; they're lower than you'd find around Sudbury or southern Ontario, for example.

The *Shady Pines Motel* (☎ 759-0088), way out east at 1587 Hwy 17, is one of the cheapest around. Though ugly at the front, it's actually good. Big, modern rooms open onto a treed back yard with picnic tables and barbecues. Singles/doubles cost just $30/35.

The white place at 859 Trunk Rd (part of Hwy 17 East) is the *Travellers Motel* (☎ 946-4133). It has colour TV, and kitchenettes are available. Doubles cost from $40.

The *Holiday* (☎ 759-8608), at 435 Trunk Rd, is a pleasant looking place and costs $36/42. *Comfort Inn by Journey's End* (☎ 759-8000), at 333 Great Northern Rd, has doubles at $87. It's neat and busy and is part of a major chain. Other places can be found along Great Northern Rd, which leads north to the Trans Canada Hwy westbound.

Places to Eat

Most of the restaurants, many of which are the ubiquitous franchises, line the highway. However, those listed here are mainly local establishments found in the city centre. Queen St has a real assortment of good, atmospheric beaneries of the old lunch-counter type.

The *Coral Coffee Shop*, at 470 Queen St (near Spring St), is a basic classic. They have good prices for homemade soups, muffins,

chili and the like, and have cheap breakfasts and various specials. It's the only place we've ever seen with menus in braille. Tiny *Mike's*, with just half a dozen stools at 518 Queen St, has been serving its regular customers since 1932. Meals are under $7 at this friendly place caught in a time warp. At 663 Queen St East, near the corner of East St, the old-fashioned *Mary's Lunch* serves a lot of homemade stuff, including bread, and has the cheapest breakfast in town.

Germans missing a taste of home should try the *Lunch Break*, at 75 Elgin St, open on weekdays only.

Two town specialities are lake trout and whitefish, and both turn up on menus all over Sault Ste Marie. *Muio's*, on the corner at 685 Queen St East, is a cheap place to sample them. It also offers daily specials, such as a complete meal with cabbage rolls for $7.25. You can't beat that, and it's open on Sunday. Moving upmarket, Italian food is popular in town and *Suriano's* at 357 Trunk Rd is well patronised.

Barsanti Small Frye, 23 Trunk Rd (Hwy 17 East), is recommended for its basic good food, low prices, friendly waiting staff and style. They've been in the business for 75 years and have got it right. Conveniently, it's open long hours: 7 am to midnight daily. If you're just passing through, this may be the place to eat and run.

Getting There & Away

Air There are regular Air Canada and Canadian Airlines flights to Sault Ste Marie.

Bus The bus station (☎ 949-4711), serving Greyhound only, is downtown at 73 Brock St. There are four buses a day to Sudbury. From there, three buses daily depart for either Toronto or Ottawa. The through fare to Ottawa is $109, to Toronto $94. There are three buses daily to Winnipeg ($127). Ontario Northland goes to Wawa.

For buses to Detroit or Chicago, you must get to the city bus terminal. For details see Getting Around later.

Hitching The Soo is a major drop-off point

for those thumbing east and west. In summer there are plenty of backpackers hanging around town. If you're going west, remember that it's a long way from Sault Ste Marie to Winnipeg, with little to see in between. Nights are cold and rides can be scarce. Try to get a through ride to Thunder Bay (715 km) and then go on to Winnipeg from there.

Getting Around
The Airport The airport is 13 km west on Hwy 550, then seven km south on Hwy 565. There are airport buses between the airport and such major hotels as the Holiday Inn and the Empire Hotel.

Bus The city bus terminal (☎ 759-5438) is on the corner of Queen and Dennis Sts. The Riverside bus from downtown goes east to Algoma University, near Belvedere Park. A city bus leaves from the terminal and goes over the bridge into Michigan, USA. Long distance buses can be picked up here. Taxis will also take you across the bridge.

AROUND SAULT STE MARIE
Batchawana Bay
A relaxing afternoon or a full day can be spent north of town along the shore of Lake Superior around Batchawana Bay and beyond. The scenery is good and Batchawana offers beaches, swimming (the water is cool) and numerous motels, resorts and rental cottages.

It's 45 minutes' drive to **Chippewa Falls**, called the centrepoint of Canada, and it probably is close to being this. From the city up to Agawa Indian Crafts, a well-known landmark, it's about 75 km. With two sets of waterfalls, a couple of provincial parks and the shoreline, an enjoyable afternoon can be spent poking around. And you can visit the Montreal River garbage dump, about 25 km north-west of Batchawana Bay, where you can drive in and see the bears.

St Joseph Island
St Joseph lies in the channel between Michigan and Ontario, 50 km east of Sault Ste Marie. It's a rural island visited for swim-

ming and fishing and for **Fort St Joseph National Historic Site**. The British fort ruins date from the turn of the 18th century and are staffed by workers in period costume. The reception centre displays Native Indian, military and fur-trade artefacts. A large bird sanctuary surrounds the fort. The fort is open from the end of May to the middle of October. Check at the Soo tourist office for complete details.

Also on the island is the **Museum Village**, housing 4000 island articles exhibited in six historic buildings varying from an old general store to a log school. Another thing to keep an eye out for are the so-called pudding stones – red, black and brown speckled white rocks. The jasper conglomerates (to rockhounds) found around the shoreline were named by English settlers (obviously hungry) who felt they resembled suet and berry pudding.

St Joseph has several private campgrounds, a motel and a B&B. The island is reached by a toll-free bridge off Hwy 17.

NORTH AROUND LAKE SUPERIOR
From Sault Ste Marie to Thunder Bay, the Trans Canada Hwy is one of the few roads cutting through the thinly populated northern Ontario wilds. This huge area is rough, lake-filled timberland. So far, development has been slow to penetrate and the abundant minerals and wildlife remain undisturbed. There are areas where there's logging, but these are rarely seen. You may see signs of forest fires, which are common each year.

This quiet and beautiful part of the country is presided over by awesome Lake Superior – once known as Gitche Gumee (Big Sea Water) to the Ojibway Indians. The largest of the five Great Lakes (and one of the world's largest lakes), it's sometimes pretty, sometimes brutal. Even today, there are disastrous shipwrecks when the lake gets angry, and according to a Canadian folk song, Superior 'never gives up her dead'.

Several of the Canadian Group of Seven painters were inspired to work here, and descriptions reaching the poet Henry Wadsworth Longfellow had the same effect

Caribou, part of the reindeer family, differ from other deer in that both sexes have antlers

on him. Along the highway are many provincial parks, which make good places to stay and get a feel for the lake and surrounding forest.

Lake Superior Provincial Park

Hwy 17 runs for 80 km through this large natural park north of Sault Ste Marie, so (luckily) you can't miss it. It's a beautiful park, with a few things to see even if you don't stay. The rugged scenery is good, with rivers in the wooded interior and a shoreline featuring rocky headlands and sandy beaches. Several of the aforementioned Group of Seven painters worked in the park.

The provincial park (☎ 856-2284) has

three campgrounds, short and long hiking trails usually accessible from the highway, and seven canoe routes. Naturalists give talks and guided walks. The park also offers fishing. Various mammals live here, including the odd bear.

At **Agawa Bay**, see the Native Indian pictographs on the shoreline rocks, believed to commemorate a crossing of the lake. Note the crevices in the rocks along the path. Further along, stop at **Sand River** and walk down to the beach. Though the water is cold, the beautiful sandy beach, long and empty, looks as if it's been lifted from a Caribbean island.

For access to the less-visited eastern side of the park, where there is no road, inquire about the train which runs along the far eastern edge. It can be caught at Frater at the southern end of the park or at Hawk Junction. The latter is a small village outside of the northern boundary of the park east of the town of Wawa. The train line is part of the Algoma Central Railway. For more details see under Sault Ste Marie, Agawa Canyon.

Distance hikers and canoeists should hope for good weather – this is one of the wettest areas in Ontario. Trails are often enveloped in mist or fog, which lends a primeval, spooky air to the woods. As always, interior camping costs a few dollars less than using the campgrounds with facilities.

Wawa

Marked by the huge steel goose at the edge of town, Wawa is a small iron-mining centre. The name is an Ojibway word, meaning 'wild goose', bestowed on the town because of the thousands of geese which stop over on Lake Wawa during migrations.

There is nothing much to see here but the town does have several motels and places for a bite. In the restaurants, look for the locally caught fish (such as trout).

Wawa long had a big, bad reputation for hitchhiking. The story is told of one man who got stuck here so long waiting for a lift that he finally had to get a job. He ended up meeting a woman and getting married and still lives here! As traffic has picked up over the years and the locals have become less isolated, things aren't as bad they were, but if you are hitching, it's still better to get a ride through. There is nothing down at the highway and it can be a cold place at night, even in midsummer. Cyclists are a more common sight these days than hitchhikers.

Wawa is a supply centre for the surrounding parks. Motels are often full in the summer; a good one to try is the *Lakewood Motel* (☎ 856-2774), 15 km west of town at Catfish Lake. The *Pine Ridge Motel*, five km west of Wawa, serves a decent meal.

Chapleau

Chapleau is a small logging and outdoors centre inland from Wawa. There are numerous provincial parks in the area, three within 80 km. **Missinaibi Lake Park** (☎ 864-1710) is in the middle of **Chapleau Game Reserve**, the largest in the western hemisphere. The boreal forest is ideal for wilderness camping, canoeing or fishing.

The tourist offices around the area have a listing of canoe routes. There are 12 trips ranging from one to 14 days, with five to 47 portages. The longest one is a river and lake circle route going through part of the reserve; it's good for viewing moose.

Tourist offices can also help with information on the many lodges and fly-in camps which operate in the area.

White River

Back on the Trans Canada Hwy, this is called the coldest place in Canada, with temperatures recorded as low as -50°C. Get your picture taken near the thermometer.

Another bit of trivia has this as the original home of the bear which inspired AA Milne's *Winnie the Pooh* books. Apparently a Canadian soldier got a bear cub here and called it Winnipeg, after his home town. During WWI it ended up at England's London Zoo, where it became quite popular, and was subsequently immortalised in fiction.

White River has a couple of motels, moderately priced, for overnighters. VIA Rail connects the town to Sudbury. The station is on Winnipeg Rd, a short walk from the highway.

Pukaskwa National Park

Find out how tough you are. There is no road in this park (pronounced 'puk-a-saw') and access is by hiking or boat. From Heron Bay, off the Trans Canada Hwy near Marathon, is a small road, Hwy 627, which goes to the edge of the park at Hatties Cove. There is a small (67-site) campground and a visitor information centre (☎ (807) 229-0801). For day use, there is a picnic area, and swimming in a protected bay. In the lake itself, the water is cold and swells can be hazardous even for good swimmers.

The main attraction is the old 60-km coastal hiking trail, with primitive camping spots along the way. The terrain is rough but beautiful and the weather is changeable, switching quickly from sun to storm. The trail is often wet and slippery, black flies and mosquitos are guaranteed and bears are often a bother. Even the mice can be aggressive, digging into unattended supplies. Good luck.

The interior offers some challenging canoeing, including runs down the Pukaskwa and the less difficult, more accessible White River.

In the winter months it's possible to explore the headlands near Hatties Cove on snowshoe. There's also a six-km cross-country ski trail in the campground area. The park is open all year. Facilities are open from early June to late September.

Slate Islands Provincial Park

Situated offshore from the small town of **Terrace Bay** is this cluster of islands, home to the highest density of woodland caribou anywhere. The islands, without natural predators, support hundreds of caribou. At times there are too many for their food stocks and winters can take a heavy toll. The herd is studied by researchers looking into preserving the herds of mainland Ontario. Ask around Terrace Bay or the nearby provincial parks about trips over to the islands to see or photograph the caribou.

Nipigon

Nipigon sits at the mouth of the Nipigon River, where Hwy 11 meets Hwy 17, the Trans Canada. There really isn't anything here of note, but it is interesting that this was the first European settlement on Superior's north shore. European traders established a fur-trading post here, in the middle of the traditional Ojibway lands. East of town along Hwy 17, look for the Kama Lookout, with good views of the Lake Superior shore. This segment of the highway is also known as the Terry Fox Courage Hwy (for details, see the Thunder Bay section).

Ouimet Canyon Provincial Nature Preserve

About 45 km west of Nipigon and 40 km east of Thunder Bay, north-east of the highway, this park features a great canyon three km long and 150 metres both wide and deep. The walls on either side of the chasm are virtually perpendicular. Fences and viewing stations have been built right at the sheer edges for good, heart-pounding views. The canyon was scoured out during the last ice age and the bottom is home to some rare flora generally found only in Arctic regions. The canyon is definitely worth a quick stop; most times you'll find yourself alone. Walking trails meander around the top and there are some interpretive displays. Officially, there's no camping. There is no public transport out here, but that does help to keep it clean and serene.

THUNDER BAY

Situated on the northern shores of Lake Superior, and known as 'the Lakehead', Thunder Bay (population 113,000) is an amalgamation of the towns of Fort William and Port Arthur. Despite being so far inland, Thunder Bay is one of Canada's major ports and is as far westward as ships using the St Lawrence Seaway get. The main cargo switching hands here is prairie wheat going to market. The docks make the city the world's largest grain handler.

The city, halfway between Sault Ste Marie and Winnipeg – 720 km to either one – is a

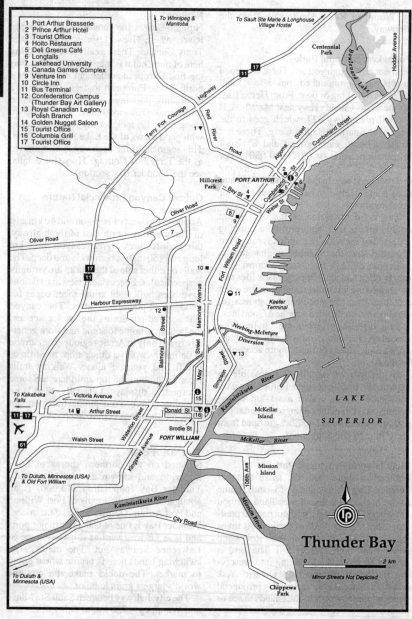

1 Port Arthur Brasserie
2 Prince Arthur Hotel
3 Tourist Office
4 Hoito Restaurant
5 Deli Greens Café
6 Longtails
7 Lakehead University
8 Canada Games Complex
9 Venture Inn
10 Circle Inn
11 Bus Terminal
12 Confederation Campus
   (Thunder Bay Art Gallery)
13 Royal Canadian Legion,
   Polish Branch
14 Golden Nugget Saloon
15 Tourist Office
16 Columbia Grill
17 Tourist Office

To Winnipeg &
Manitoba

To Sault Ste Marie & Longhouse
Village Hostel

Centennial
Park

Hodder Avenue

Boulevard Lake

Cumberland Street

Algoma Street

Highway

Red
River

Terry Fox Courage
Road

PORT ARTHUR

St

Cumberland St

Water St

Hillcrest
Park

Bay St

Oliver Road

Oliver Road

Fort William Road

Harbour Expressway

Memorial Avenue

Balmoral
Street

May
Street

Simpson Street

Keefer
Terminal

Neebing-McIntyre
Diversion

Kaministikwia River

McKellar
Island

LAKE
SUPERIOR

Victoria Avenue

Arthur Street

Donald St

Waterloo Street

Brodie St

FORT WILLIAM

McKellar River

Walsh Street

Kingsway Avenue

To Kakabeka
Falls

To Duluth, Minnesota (USA)
& Old Fort William

Mission
Island

Kaministikwia River

City Road

Mission River

To Duluth &
Minnesota (USA)

Chippewa
Park

Thunder Bay

0   1   2 km

Minor Streets Not Depicted

good stopping-off point. The place itself may not hold you long, but the setting is scenic and it makes a handy centre for experiencing some of the things to see and do in northern Ontario's rugged timberland.

The first Europeans here were a couple of Frenchmen who reached the area in 1662. For hundreds of years, this was a fur-trading settlement. In 1869 the Dawson, the pioneer's road westward, was begun. In 1882 the Canadian Pacific Railway arrived, and soon the prairie's first shipment of wheat was heading east.

Coming into town from the east on the Trans Canada Hwy, you'll pass mountains and see the city at the edge of the bay. Along the shoreline are pulp mills and grain elevators. Out in the harbour, ships are moored, and beyond is a long rock formation and an island or two. The unusually shaped mass of rock offshore is important in Native Indian legend and is said to be the Great Spirit, Nana-bijou, who turned to stone after a promise made to him was broken. Today the formation is known as the Sleeping Giant.

Orientation

Thunder Bay still has two distinct downtown areas, which are connected principally by Fort William Rd and Memorial Ave. The area between the two is pretty much a wasteland of fast-food outlets, the large Inter City Shopping Mall and little else.

Port Arthur (Thunder Bay North), closer to the lakeshore, appears more prosperous and is more modern and generally more attractive. The main streets are Red River Rd and Cumberland St. Port Arthur's Landing, off Water St, is a redeveloped waterfront area and includes parkland. The Pagoda tourist office is across the street. This half of Thunder Bay has a sizeable Finnish population, which supports several specialised restaurants on Bay St. Indeed, for a city its size, Thunder Bay has quite a large and varied ethnic population.

Though of equal age, Fort William (Thunder Bay South) looks older and is rather drab, without the activity of its cross-town counterpart. Main streets in this half of

the city are May St and Victoria Ave. The Victoriaville shopping mall is at this corner and is where most of the Fort William action occurs. The tourist office is nearby.

On each side of Thunder Bay is a commercial motel/restaurant strip.

Information

There's a visitor centre (☎ 983-2041) at the Terry Fox Lookout and Memorial about six km east of town on Hwy 11/17. It's open daily.

In Port Arthur, the main summer tourist office (☎ 684-3670) is central, in the 1910 Pagoda in the park on the corner of Red River Rd and Water St, and is open daily.

In Fort William, there's an office (☎ 625-3669) in central Paterson Park on the corner of May and Miles Sts. During the off season you can obtain information from the Visitors & Convention Bureau (☎ 1-800-667-8386), just next door to the tourist office at 520 Leith St. There is also an information booth at Old Fort William. The tourist offices have pamphlets outlining architectural walking tours for both sections of town. North of Superior Tourism (☎ 1-800-265-3951) is at 1119 Victoria Ave East, for any additional information required on the region.

Port Arthur General Hospital is at 460 Court St North.

Thunder Bay Museum

This small historical museum (☎ 623-0801), recently rehoused in the former police station at 425 Donald St East, contains Native Indian artefacts and a collection of odds & ends of local history. Topics covered include fur trading, mining and the early pioneers. There's also an Albertosaurus. The museum is not extensive but displays are well presented. It's open daily in the summer. Admission is free.

The Port

Thunder Bay Harbour is one of Canada's largest ports according to tonnes handled, with the greatest complex of grain elevators in the world. Terminals, elevators and other storage and docking facilities stretch along

45 km of central waterfront. At the Port Arthur shipyards, the huge freighters are repaired.

In the middle of the waterfront is the Keefer Complex, a cargo-handling facility where ships from around the world come and go. The terminal mainly handles resource materials and grains.

Very visible are the numerous grain elevators (some painted in pastels) operated by about half a dozen private companies. For those who have wanted to see a grain elevator all their lives, the Harbour Commission (☎ 345-6400) may be able to arrange tours.

Mission Island

Despite the industrial look of the port, there is life down there among the terminals. On Mission Island, south-east of Arthur St, the Lakehead Region Conservation Authority has created a sanctuary for water birds. During the spring and autumn migrations, thousands of birds can sometimes be seen on the 40 hectares of wetlands. To get there, cross the bridge off South Syndicate Ave and follow the signs.

Prince Arthur's Landing

Located in Port Arthur, by the lake opposite the Pagoda tourist office, the landing is a waterfront redevelopment zone. It contains the marina, the dock, a small art gallery and gift shop, and a restaurant in the old train station. Also in the train station, on the 2nd floor, is a large layout created by the model railroad club.

Still, the site is primarily parkland. There are some walking paths which meander around three piers. Best is the one out to Wilson St Headland, with views of the lake and dock areas.

Parks

Centennial Park Centennial is a large, natural woodland park at the eastern edge of Port Arthur, near Hwy 17. It's alongside Current River, which flows into Boulevard Lake before entering Lake Superior. The park is over the Boulevard Lake Bridge just off Arundel St. Entry is free. There are nature trails along the river and through the woods. On the grounds is a simulated logging camp of 1910 – not much to see, but the log cabins and buildings themselves are good. A small museum has a cross-cut section of a 250-year-old white pine tree on display. Various dates in history are marked at the corresponding growth rings. It's amazing to think what has gone on while this tree quietly kept growing. You'll find canoes and boats for rent here as well. Up the road from the park is the Bluffs Scenic Lookout, for a view of the lake and shore.

International Friendship Gardens This good-sized city park is off Victoria Ave near Waterloo St. Various local ethnic groups, such as the Finns and the Hungarians, have erected monuments and statues. There is a pond and some flowers but no extensive gardens. The park is west of downtown Fort William, on Victoria Ave.

Waverley Park Free summer concerts are held in the Rotary Thundershell on Wednesday evening and Sunday afternoon in summer at this city park. It's on the corner of Red River Rd and High St in Port Arthur.

Hillcrest Park Just to the west of Waverley Park, also on High St, Hillcrest has a lookout point for views of the harbour and to the Sleeping Giant.

Chippewa Park At the edge of Lake Superior and just beyond the southern end of Fort William, at the foot of City Rd, Chippewa Park has a beach, picnic and camp sites, a small amusement park, and a good indigenous-wildlife exhibit where many of northern Ontario's mammals can be seen from overhead walkways.

Sleeping Giant Provincial Park This is a larger, more natural and scenic park (☎ 977-2526) further out and on the east side of the city. Part of the Sibley Peninsula, the park arcs 35 km into Lake Superior. The setting and landscape are excellent, with woods, hills, shoreline and great views from several vantage points. On one trip in, just after dark, we saw three foxes at the road's edge. Moose also live in the park. Activities include swimming, fishing and camping, and there are some good walks, including one out along the top of the Sleeping Giant rock formation, from where there are fine views. One hike, taking a minimum of two days, cuts across most of the west coast of the peninsula.

An Ojibway legend tells the story of the formation of the Sleeping Giant. In one version, Nana-bijou, the spirit of the Deep Sea Water, showed the Ojibway a mine where silver could be found, as reward for their peaceful, spiritual way of life. But, he said, if ever they should tell the White people of the source of the silver, he would be forever turned to stone. Upon seeing the fine articles and jewellery made of silver, the Sioux, the Ojibway's historical enemy, sought to discover the metal's origins. When even torture failed to reveal the secret, the Sioux decided to send a man in disguise to live as an Ojibway. Eventually he was led to the mine. On his way back to his people with the great news, the Sioux stopped at a White man's encampment. They were enthralled upon seeing the silver sample he had with him. After plying him with alcohol, he agreed to take several of the men by canoe to the mine. A great storm came up, drowning everyone but the Sioux, whom the Ojibway later found floating around aimlessly. When the weather cleared, the open bay had been partially blocked by a huge rock formation, and the Ojibway knew that Nana-bijou's words had come to be.

The park makes a good stop if you don't want to go into town to sleep (see under Places to Stay). At the very end of the peninsula is the tiny community of Silver Islet where the old mining store has been transformed into the *Silver Islet Store & Tea Room*.

Thunder Bay Art Gallery
The gallery at Confederation College campus (☎ 577-6427), 1080 Keewatin St, off Balmoral St, collects, preserves and displays contemporary art by Native Indians. Works include paintings, prints, masks, sculptures and more. There are displays from the permanent collection, as well as travelling exhibits, which usually feature non-Native Indian artists. Norval Morrisseau, perhaps Canada's best known Native Indian painter, was born in Thunder Bay and some of his

work is on view. The gallery is open from noon to 8 pm Tuesday to Thursday, and from noon to 5 pm Friday to Sunday. Admission is free. The Northwood bus from Fort William goes to the campus door.

Canada Games Complex
The Canada Games recreational complex, at 420 Winnipeg Ave, includes an Olympic-sized swimming pool, a fully equipped weight room, a large water slide, saunas, whirlpools, a restaurant and a babysitting service. It's open daily.

Old Fort William
Some of Thunder Bay's best known attractions are some distance from downtown, as is Old Fort William (☎ 577-8461), perhaps the city's feature site.

The old fort settlement, with 42 historic buildings spread over 50 hectares west of town, not far past the airport and off Broadway Ave, is worth getting to.

From 1803 to 1821, Fort William was the headquarters of the North West Fur Trading Company. Here the voyageurs and Native Indians did their trading, and settlers and explorers arrived from the east. In 1821, after much haggling and hassling, the company was absorbed by its chief rival, the Hudson's Bay Company, and Fort William declined.

The fort re-creates some aspects of the early, thriving days of the fur trade through buildings, tools, artefacts and documents. Workers in period dress demonstrate skills and crafts, perform historical re-enactments and will answer questions. Interesting displays include the Native Indian camp and the woodwork of the canoe building. Animals can be seen at the separate farm section.

In mid-July the fort becomes the scene of the Great Rendezvous, a 10-day festival which re-creates the annual meeting of North West employees, voyageurs, Native Indians and traders. In August, keep an eye open for the Ojibway Keeshigun, a weekend festival of Native Indian culture.

A thorough but relaxed visit to the fort can take half a day or more. Entry is $7.25, with family rates available. In summer, free special-event days are held regularly. The fort is open daily from 10 am to 5 pm from the beginning of May to mid-October. Good, cheap homemade food (brick-oven bread and voyageur stew) is available in the fort's canteen.

Although the site is a long way out, city buses go close to the fort, departing from the terminal in either Fort William or Port Arthur every hour; the last bus from the fort leaves at around 4.30 pm, but check.

Kakabeka Falls

Set in a provincial park 25 km west of Thunder Bay off Hwy 17, the waterfalls, about 40 metres high, are worth a look. They're most impressive in spring, when the water in the river is at its highest, or after heavy rains. Sometimes the water flow is small, as it's dammed off for power. Walkways lead around and across the falls. Plaques tell the Ojibway legend of martyr Princess Green Mantle, who saved her village from the attacking Sioux by leading them over the falls.

Most people go to take pictures at the falls, but the park itself isn't bad, with camping, swimming at small beaches, and picnicking.

Mt Mackay

Mt Mackay is the tallest mountain in the area's north-western mountain chain, rising to 350-odd metres and offering good views of Thunder Bay and environs. The lookout is on an Ojibway reserve and an admission of $4 per car is charged to use the winding road to the top. The view of the city is good, but for seeing the Sleeping Giant you're better off at the Terry Fox Lookout, off the Trans Canada Hwy.

Mt Mackay is south-west of Fort William. Take Edward St to City Rd, towards Chippewa Park, and follow the signs. The road to Mt Mackay cuts through a portion of the residential area of the reserve. At the top there is a snack bar and gift shop. A walking trail leads further up to the peak. No city bus gets close enough to make public transportation to the mountain a viable option.

Legend has it that the local Ojibway had taken to some farming and were growing wheat. One harvest time, the crop was demolished by incessant flocks of blackbirds. The hunters were unable to replace the crop, due to early and heavy snows. The water froze, making fishing difficult, especially with the meagre bait available, and soon even this was gone. In desperation the daughter of the chief cut strips of flesh from her legs to give the fishers for bait. Enough fish were caught to stave off mass starvation but the girl died. In her honour, a visiting priest had the men build the small chapel which still sits atop Mt Mackay. Each year at Thanksgiving, the chapel is visited and prayers are offered for next year's crop.

Terry Fox Monument

Overlooking the Sleeping Giant on Hwy 11/17 just a few km east of town, this 2.7-metre high statue, and the segment of the Trans Canada Hwy north-west of town, honours the young Canadian who, in the early 1980s while dying of cancer, ran halfway across Canada to raise money for cancer research. After having one leg amputated, he made it from Newfoundland to Thunder Bay, raising millions and becoming a national hero before finally succumbing. Each year, cities across the country and around the world hold Terry Fox Memorial Runs to raise further funds for his cause.

There is a good visitor information centre here.

Activities

Canoeing Wildwaters Nature Tours (☎ 767-2022), out of town on Dog Lake Rd, offers canoe expeditions of various lengths and costs. They include wildlife, photography and fishing trips. There are trips into Wabakimi, the large wilderness park north west of Lake Nipigon, and expeditions that even go as far north as Hudson Bay. There's also a special trip for women only.

Fishing Fishing charters into Lake Superior (for salmon and trout) are available from the Thunder Bay Marina. Trout fishing is possible in nearby rivers and streams; the tourist office has a list of local fishing spots put out by the Ministry of Natural Resources.

From Thunder Bay to Kenora, near the Manitoba border, there are almost limitless fishing camps and lodges. Many people fly in to remote lakes. Tourist offices will have more information on these wonderful sounding but pricey trips.

Amethyst Hounding Amethyst (a variety of quartz) is a purple semiprecious stone that is found in several areas around Thunder Bay. There are many superstitions surrounding amethyst, including the early Greek one that it prevents drunkenness. The ever-practical Greeks therefore often fashioned wine cups from the stone. It is mined from veins which run on or near the earth's surface, so looking for the stone and digging it out are relatively easy.

Within about 50 km of the city are five sites where you can go looking for your own stones. Each site has some samples for sale if you should miss out on finding some. Shops in town sell jewellery and finished souvenir items made of the purple quartz. The tourist office has a list of all the mines and can direct you to stores around town which sell a range of stuff produced with the finished stone – mostly pretty tacky. The stone generally looks better raw.

Visits to all but one of the sites are free. You simply pay for the pieces you find and want to keep.

Thunder Bay Amethyst Mine Panorama is a huge property off East Loon Lake Rd, which is east of Hwy 587 South. The site is about seven km north of the Trans Canada Hwy, and the road is rough and steep in places. Entry is $1.

Three of the mine sites, all much smaller, are on Rd No 5 North, a little further east than East Loon. Located four km to six km north up from the Trans Canada Hwy, the three mine entrances can't be missed. You are given a pail and shovel and pointed in the right direction, then you're on your own – see what you come up with. All the sites are open daily from May to October and each has a shop on the premises.

Sauna You can get a sauna at Kanga's (☎ 344-6761), 379 Oliver Rd. Finnish saunas are popular in the region. At Kanga's

there are also some Finnish eats and good desserts. See also under Canada Games Complex earlier.

Organised Tours
In the Pagoda tourist booth, pick up a folder on a self-guided architectural walking tour of Port Arthur. The fire hall, some churches, various houses of note and other buildings are located and described. There is a similar brochure for downtown Fort William.

Thunder Bay City Tours (☎ 346-9881) offer 1½-hour tours of the town and some of its historic sites. In summer there are daily tours at 9 and 11 am, and 1 and 8 pm, leaving from Marina Park. Tickets are $15. Custom Boat Tours (☎ 626-6926) have a variety of boat tours including one and two-hour harbour cruises, which cost from around $15 per person.

Festivals
For 10 days in mid-July Old Fort William hosts a recreation of the Great Rendezvous, the annual get-together of North West Company employees, voyageurs, Native Indians and traders who congregated at the fort to trade pelts and generally carouse. Hundreds of appropriately dressed characters turn up to take part.

Harbourfest, also held in July, is an annual street festival centred around the marina. There's music, dancing, street theatre, markets and a firework display.

Mid-August sees the one-day Festa Italia, featuring food (of course), games and entertainment. It's held in the north-end Italian section of town.

Ask about the First Nation Powwow, featuring Native Indian dancers, held on Mt McKay around 1 July. The Indian Friendship Centre (☎ 345-5840) will have information.

Places to Stay
Camping Thunder Bay is one of those happy places where good camping can be found close to the city. On the west side of the city is *Trowbridge Falls* (☎ 683-6661) off Hwy 11/17 about half a km north up Copenhagen

Rd. It's run by the City of Thunder Bay, as is the adjacent Centennial Park.

Further west out of town off Hwy 17 (the Trans Canada), at the junction of Hwy 800, is a *KOA* campground (☎ 683-6221). A site costs $13.50. Look for the road to the Mt Baldy ski area: it's nearby on the opposite side of the road.

There's also camping south-west of the city, at *Chippewa Park* (☎ 623-3912), a short drive from Old Fort William. From the junction of Hwys 61 and 61B, go 3.2 km on Hwy 61B to City Rd and look for the signs. The park is right on the lake. There is a good wildlife collection here, with examples of most of the mammals found in the northern Ontario wilds. You can also camp further west at Kakabeka Falls Provincial Park. At Sleeping Giant Provincial Park there's a couple of possibilities. There is a large campground at Lake Marie Louise (☎ 977-2526), 32 km off Hwy 11/17 down Hwy 587, and a smaller campground just outside the park at Pass Lake (☎ 977-2646).

Hostels The Backpackers' *Longhouse Village Hostel* (☎ 983-2042) is excellent and open all year. It's a fair distance from town – 22 km east, at 1594 Lakeshore Drive (Rural Route 13) – but is well worth the effort. The location is green and quiet, the atmosphere friendly and relaxed. The couple who run it, Lloyd and Willa Jones, are the driving force behind Canada's link in the Backpackers chain of international hostels. Write to them (postal code P7B 5E4) for more information on this network.

The Jones' are knowledgeable about things to do around town. There is swimming and walking near the hostel and ask about Mackenzie Point and the waterfall in the woods.

Basic food is available and guests can use the kitchen. Rooms and beds are scattered all over the property in a variety of units, including a trailer, cabins, the main house and even a bus. The price is $14, or a tent can be set up on the lawn for $9. Couples and families can be accommodated.

From the highway, head down Mackenzie

Station Rd (easily walkable); the hostel is near the corner – perhaps the only one with an electric sign. Note that there are no city buses into town, but see the Getting Around section later for information on the Grey-hound bus.

There are beds available in the *Lakehead University Residence* (☎ 343-8612) from 1 May to 20 August. Singles/doubles cost $19/20. Breakfast is offered. The university is at 955 Oliver Rd, between the two downtown areas and slightly west. The cross-town city bus goes past the campus.

B&Bs The B&B situation in Thunder Bay has mushroomed over the past couple of years. There's now a local B&B association with around 16 members; contact the association through North of Superior Tourism (☎ 1-800-265-3951).

One well-established place, and a fine one for spending a night or two, is the *Unicorn Inn* (☎ 475-4200). It's out of town, about half-an-hour's drive, at Unicorn Road, Rural Route 1, South Gillies. See under Places to Eat later for directions. It has singles/doubles from $39/49. The rooms on the ground floor of an old farmhouse are comfortable and the breakfasts are worth waking up for. Call ahead to check availability. The *Cabbage Rose* (☎ 345-5242) is very close to the centre of Port Arthur, at 25 High St, north off Red River Rd. There are three rooms and singles/doubles are $45/55. A full breakfast is included. *Park Haven* (☎ 623-7175) is a stone's throw from the tourist office in Fort William, at 221 North Brodie St. Singles/doubles are $40/45.

Not far from Kakabeka Falls, north west of Thunder Bay at Pinebrook, is *Cedar Chalet* (☎ 683-6114). Rooms start at just $20 and go up to $55. There's also a camp site here, walking trails nearby and a sauna by the river.

Hotels Simpson St in Fort William has the central cheapies but none is recommended. That said, *Hotel Empire* (☎ 622-2912), at 140 Simpson St, with singles at $24 is the king of the skid-row specials.

Moving up and across town, the *Best Western Crossroads Motor Inn* (☎ 577-4241) is at 655 West Arthur St. Rooms at this good place are $67/74 for singles/doubles.

Top of the list of the corporate hotels is the *Prince Arthur Hotel* (☎ 345-5411), on the corner of Cumberland St and Red River Rd, right by the Pagoda tourist office. It's large, has several places to eat or drink and costs $75/79 a single/double. Some rooms look out over the lake.

Motels Most of the moderately priced accommodation is in the newer motel strips. There are two areas of heavy motel concentration, one on each side of the city, as well as a few rather good places in between the two downtown areas, along Memorial Ave. The *Circle Inn* (☎ 344-5744), at 686 Memorial Ave, and the *University Park Inn* (☎ 345-7316), at 439 Memorial Ave, have 50 rooms each and prices in the range of $47 a single. More upmarket is the nearby *Venture Inn* (☎ 345-2343), with rooms at $69/79.

The motel area in Port Arthur is on and around Cumberland St. It heads out to Hodder St, which then leads to the Expressway or Hwy 17 East. The motels are mainly found near the grain elevators along the lakefront. Cumberland St leads right into the downtown area of Port Arthur.

The *Strathcona* (☎ 683-8136), at 546 Hodder St, is a small, well-kept, blue-and-white place charging just $35/40. There are other, lower-priced places along Cumberland St.

The other motel district is along Arthur St, heading out of town from downtown Fort William past the airport. There are a few motels side by side on Kingsway Ave, off Arthur St, but these are priced higher than they're worth. The *Ritz Motel* (☎ 623-8189), at 2600 Arthur St East, is good and has some kitchenettes. Rooms cost $45 to $65 in this red-brick building close to town.

Places to Eat
Port Arthur At 11 South Cumberland St, *Deli Greens Café* is recommended for good

soups, salads and fresh sandwiches at tasty prices.

Nearby, at 230 Park Ave, which runs off Cumberland St south of Red River Rd, the well-established *Prospector* specialises in meat from a local cattle ranch. Steaks cost $12 to $20. Also on the menu is walleye, one of Canada's best eating freshwater fish. The restaurant opens daily at 5 pm, closing at 9 pm Monday to Thursday, 10 pm on Friday and Saturday and 8 pm on Sunday. They have a kids' menu, too.

Longtails is in the old CN train station in the dock area opposite the Pagoda tourist office. The menu features lake trout, salmon, steak and pasta dishes. Lunch costs around $10, dinner slightly more. There's an outdoor patio here too.

The *Hoito*, at 314 Bay St, is a Finnish place set up about 60 years ago. It is known for its homemade food served in plain surroundings. The large portions pack them in, even at lunch on the weekends. There are a couple of similar places in this Finnish neighbourhood, and around the corner on Secord St is a Finnish bakery. At 189 South Algoma St, near Bay St, the *Expresso* serves espresso and cappuccino.

The *Office*, in the Keskus Mall, Red River Rd, is a pub with inexpensive meals and live music at night. Away from the central core, at 901 Red River Rd (at the corner of Junot Ave), is the popular *Port Arthur Brasserie*, a brew pub where, in addition to the usual meals, they have a Sunday brunch. There are numerous restaurants on Memorial Ave which links the two parts of the city. Casual *Casey's* at No 450 or *East Side Mario's* at No 1170 are both geared to the young.

Fort William The *Columbia Grill & Tavern*, at 123 May St South, is a friendly, basic, all-purpose restaurant used by the locals. It gained some infamy in the early 1990s as the place where Laurie 'Bambi' Bembenek, the popular protagonist in one of North America's most captivating criminal cases, worked while on the run from US authorities. It's open daily from 8 am.

The *Royal Canadian Legion, Polish*

Branch, at 730 Simpson St, has a small coffee shop and bar where they serve up large, filling portions at low prices.

Victoria Mall, or the Victoria Centre, right in the centre of town, has a food fair. *Boston Pizza*, at 217 Arthur St West, serves pastas and ribs at moderate prices. The *Williams Restaurant*, at 610 Arthur St West, has a menu of standard Canadian and some Mexican-style dishes. The food is good and the portions large, but it's not low budget, with dinner costing around $20. From Sunday to Wednesday, there is an economical dinner package with an all-you-can-eat salad bar.

About half an hour south-west of the city, the *Unicorn Inn*, in a turn-of-the-century farmhouse, is the best restaurant in northern Ontario and has been ranked among the best in the country. Take Hwy 61 south of the city 20 km from the airport, then turn right onto Hwy 608 for South Gillies. The restaurant is on Unicorn Rd. Reservations (☎ 475-4200) are required for dinner, and calling even a week ahead is not too soon. It's dressy, and pricey – the fixed-price meals, from appetiser to coffee, cost over $30 per person. Main courses of seafood, fowl and beef are all offered. Bon appétit. A portion of the farmhouse also acts as a B&B.

Entertainment
Bars & Nightspots The *Innplace* is a popular hotel bar for pop and rock. It's in the Intowner, on the corner of Arthur and Brodie Sts.

The *Silver Saddle*, at 201 Syndicate Ave, is a popular country & western pub with live music nightly. The *Golden Nugget*, in the Victoria Inn at 555 Arthur St West, also has country music and line-dancing lessons on both Tuesday and Wednesday evenings. *Armani's*, a somewhat dressy restaurant and nightclub in the centre of Fort William, at 513 Victoria Ave East, has a casual rooftop bar in summer; it's not a bad place for a quiet beer.

Theatre A summer theatre programme, Moonlight Melodrama (☎ 623-7838), is

held in the theatre on the lower level in the Kekus Harbour Mall, 230 Park Ave, in Thunder Bay North. Check with the tourist office for exact dates.

Getting There & Away
Air Thunder Bay Airport is about 15 minutes' drive south-west of town, at the junction of Hwy 11/17 (the Trans Canada Hwy) and Hwy 61 to Duluth, Minnesota and the USA. Air Canada (☎ 623-3313) and Canadian Airlines (☎ 577-6461) offer flights to Winnipeg ($310) and to Toronto ($378). Bearskin Airlines (☎ 475-0066) services the region and other northern parts of the province.

Bus The Greyhound Bus Depot (☎ 345-2194) is closer to Fort William but lies in between the two downtown areas, at 815 Fort William Rd (near the Inter City Shopping Mall). It's a long walk north from central Fort William; grab the city bus. The Mainline bus goes past the door as it runs between Fort William and Port Arthur.

For Winnipeg ($82) and points further west, there are three buses a day, beginning early in the morning and running until the wee hours.

For Sault Ste Marie ($95) and points east, such as Toronto, there are also about three trips daily, and again the schedule is evenly spaced out over the 24 hours (with some departures at rather ungodly hours).

For Sudbury ($122), there is just one trip a day, departing in the early evening.

The Grey Goose bus line runs to Fort Francis and, via the USA, to Manitoba.

Car Avis (☎ 577-2847) is at 1480 Walsh St West. They charge $48 a day with 100 free km. Additional km are 20 cents each.

Budget Rent-a-Car (☎ 345-2425), at 899 Copper Crescent, has weekend specials which may be useful. There are several agencies with desks at the airport.

A circular tour of northern Ontario can be made by car from Thunder Bay by backtracking to Lake Nipigon and following Hwy 11 (the most northerly provincial route) through Geraldton and Kapuskasing, returning south via Timmins, Sudbury or North Bay. Provincial parks are found at regular intervals along Hwy 11. Towns are small.

Hitching Westbound travellers should head out to Arthur St; the airport bus will take you to a good spot. Alternatively, if you can get to Hwy 102 (Red River Rd-Dawson Rd) on the north edge of Port Arthur, you save a few km along Hwy 11/17 before the turn-off to Winnipeg. If you're eastbound, anywhere on Hwy 17 is OK. For $5 the eastbound Greyhound bus will take you to the edge of town, but tell the driver upon boarding where you want to get off because they don't like making surprise unscheduled stops.

Getting Around
The Airport An airport bus departs from the local city bus terminal, beside the Paterson Park tourist office (in Fort William, on the corner of May and Miles Sts) every 40 minutes until 12.20 am. The ride takes about 15 minutes.

A city bus, the 'Arthur' route, also goes from the Fort William side of town right to the door of the airport. It's much slower but costs less. Catch it anywhere on Arthur St.

Bus There is a good bus system which covers all areas of the city, and the drivers are some of the friendliest and most helpful in the country. Tell them we said so. For information call ☎ 344-9666.

In Fort William, the terminal for local buses is across the street from the tourist office, on the corner of May and Miles Sts. To get to the Port Arthur end of town, take the Memorial bus on May St or the Mainline bus along Fort William St (same thing going the opposite way).

In Port Arthur, the terminal is on the corner of Water and Camelot Sts (just down from Cumberland St), by the waterfront. The Pagoda tourist office is next door.

The cross-town bus from either end of Thunder Bay goes to the university. The Neebing bus goes to Old Fort William from the Fort William terminal.

For the hostel, there are no city buses, so

take the eastbound Greyhound bus from the terminal at 815 Fort William Rd. For $5 they'll take you along Lakeshore Drive to the hostel (or will at least let you off at Mackenzie Station Rd at the Trans Canada Hwy, from where it's a walk of one or two km straight to the hostel). Be sure to tell the driver beforehand that you want to get off at the hostel. There is a trip into town around noon and one back in the evening at around 7 pm, but ask about up-to-date scheduling.

City buses also go to and from the motel and fast-food strips on both sides of town.

WEST OF THUNDER BAY
Beyond Kakabeka, the traffic thins appreciably. At Shabaqua, the highway forks, the south branch leading to Atikokan and Fort Frances and the north branch heading for Kenora and the Manitoba border. Along the Trans Canada Hwy from this point, moose are often seen, especially at night, so drive with caution and with your eyes frequently scanning the shoulders of the road. In the Upsala region, a sign indicates the Arctic watershed. From here, water flows north. Another marks the beginning of a new time zone – you save an hour going west. Also note that you won't get much on the radio until you pick up Ignace stations.

Quetico Provincial Park
This huge wilderness park (☎ 597-2430), 100 km long by 60 km wide, is linked to another border park in Minnesota. Quetico is undeveloped for the most part but has one major organised campground. It offers excellent canoeing (1500 km of routes), primarily for those wanting peace and quiet. Portages tend to be short, averaging 400 metres. The use of motor boats is forbidden (except in a few areas by Native Indians) and you'll find no roads or logging within the park.

The park is a maze of lakes and rivers, with lots of wildlife and some Native Indian pictographs. Rocky shores and jack pines are typical of some parts, but there are large areas of bog in others and stands of red and white pine in yet others. The park can be accessed from several points, the principal one on the Canadian side being from the campground, Dawson Trail, off Hwy 11 where there is an information pavilion. There are outfitters (for canoes and equipment) and maps available in and around the park.

Atikokan

This is the supply town for the park. It has two small museums, a number of motels and lodges and plenty of casual places to find a meal. Rockhounds may want to explore the interesting old mine sites of Steep Rock and Caland. Fifteen different types of minerals can be found at the closed pit mines and waste dumps. Get a map at the tourist office, as the roads around the mines are rough and confusing.

There is a lot of wilderness camping in the district but you really need topographic maps. Between here and Ignace lies **White Otter Lake**, site of White Otter Castle, a locally well-known oddity built in 1904 by a Scottish immigrant named Jimmy McQuat. He did it all by himself and nobody knows why: he was a bachelor, yet this is a huge timber place with a four-storey tower, now being restored and preserved. It's on the north-western arm of the lake, accessible only by canoe.

Wilderness Adventures (☎ 807-597-2747) offers a variety of 'comfortable' adventure tours into the wilderness areas around Atikokan.

Fort Frances

Situated on Rainy Lake opposite International Falls, Minnesota, this is a busy border-crossing point into the USA. Both sides are popular outdoor destinations, with countless lakes, cottages, fishing, camping etc. In town you can visit a paper mill, the town's main business. A causeway across **Rainy Lake** towards Atikokan offers great views of the lake.

The **Fort Frances Museum** examines Native Indian history and the fur trade, as well as more recent developments. The museum (☎ 274-7891) also operates **Fort Saint Pierre**, a replica fur-trading post and

lookout tower at **Pither's Point Park**, on the eastern side of town. North Hwy 71 connects with Kenora and Winnipeg.

Ignace

Back on the Trans Canada Hwy is Ignace, with a number of motels and a couple of service station restaurants. It also has a large tourist office (on the west side of town, beside the old fire tower), good for regional information and for details on fishing and canoe routes, including the White Otter Lake district.

In the evening, head over to the garbage dump on the east side of town, north up Hwy 599 just past the golf & country club on the right-hand side. It's a great place to see bears. Although generally pretty blasé about the presence of people, they are unpredictable, so this is not recommended for cyclists. Drivers, you shouldn't get out of, or at least too far from, your vehicle. Bears may look clumsy but they can out dash any human – guaranteed.

Dryden

Like so many of the towns in the region, Dryden is fishing crazy – you may see a service station offering free minnows with every tank of gasoline purchased. If you don't hunt or fish, there isn't much here for a visitor. The paper mill, Dryden's major industry, offers interesting free tours on weekdays through the summer. On the radio, listen for the Sunday morning church sermon broadcast in Cree.

Kenora

Kenora, a pulp and paper town about 200 km from Winnipeg, is the closest town of any size to the Manitoba border. It is a centre for much of the local tourist activity, which consists mainly of summer vacation cottages, fishing and hunting. The setting is attractive, on the convoluted shores of Lake of the Woods.

There is a tourist office on the Trans Canada Hwy on the east side of town, about five minutes' drive from the central core, and another one about 20 km west of town. Main

St and Front St along the water are the main centres of activity. The harbourfront area of downtown has been re-done to good effect; the marina is here, as are the docks for two-hour boat cruises out on the lake. Less expensive is the little shuttle over to **Coney Island** for an afternoon's swim at the best sandy beach near town. There are other nearby beaches, such as popular **Norman Beach**, about three km from downtown, at the junction of Parsons St and the Trans Canada Hwy.

On Main St South, in Memorial Park, the small but good **Lake of the Woods Museum** features local history, notably the period around the turn of the century when Kenora changed rapidly. Tours can be taken of the paper mill, at 504 Ninth St North.

There's an international sailing regatta in late July, held in and around the 14,000 islands in the lake. A folk festival takes place in early July each year.

Many Native Indians, Ojibway, live in the area (referred to as Treaty 3 Territory), and it is they who hand-pick the Canadian wild rice (manomin) which grows locally; it's about $10 for half a kg in most places (natural-food stores) across the country and is delicious. Ask at the tourist office for a booklet on old Native Indian pictographs around the Kenora area. These paintings, done on rock using berry juices, tree gums and sap depict history and legends. Some of them are rea-

sonably accessible. Visitors are able to take part in a number of Ojibway events, including regional powwows. Call the Treaty 3 Territory cultural tourism hotline (☎ 1-800-461-3786). Some crafts can be purchased at the Ojibway Cultural Centre in Kenora.

There is camping just a few blocks from the centre of town, at Anicinabe Park on Sixth Ave South. It has showers, and there is a beach. Other provincial parks are nearby.

Motels can be found along the highway; there aren't any hotels in town to recommend. The *Whispering Pines* (☎ 548-4025), on the east side of town, has low-priced rooms, a beach and also camping.

Places to eat can be found along Main St, and look for the chip wagons around town and by the waterfront.

Sioux Narrows

About 80 km south of Kenora, on the eastern side of Lake of the Woods, Sioux Narrows is a local resort town. In addition to the residents from around the region, many US citizens and people from Winnipeg spend time here during the summer months. The town and its surroundings have a range of cottages, lodges, motels, campgrounds, and even houseboats for rent. Lake of the Woods fishing is renowned far and wide. Sioux Narrows Provincial Park (☎ 226-5223) has camping and contains some Native Indian pictographs.

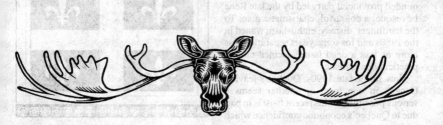

Quebec

'Kebec', an Algonkian Indian word meaning 'where the river narrows', is the heart of French Canada. This is the country's largest province and with the vast majority of the population being French, visitors will soon realise that Quebec is unlike the rest of Canada and North America and that the differences go far beyond language. The unique culture is reflected in various aspects of life including architecture, music, food and religion.

Even Montreal (Montréal, pronounced 'mor-eh-al'), where English is still widely used, has a decidedly different air to other Canadian cities, while historic Quebec City is noticeably European. But much of the beauty and appeal of the province lies in distinct regions outside these two intriguing population centres. Scenic, unspoilt Charlevoix is a protected area of natural beauty. The Laurentian Mountains are a year-round resort. Estrie or the Eastern Townships south of Montreal, settled by Loyalists, is a gentle, quiet region of farms, lakes and inns. The Gaspé region in the east with its rugged shoreline scenery is one of the overlooked areas of the country. The northern forests with their huge parks offer some excellent and accessible wilderness. Much of the far north is only now being developed.

Quebec is generally at odds with the rest of English-speaking Canada, particularly in its politics. Most people are familiar with the movement advocating Quebec separation from the rest of Canada. This desire was first formally channelled into the elected Parti Québecois (PQ) in 1976, a separation-minded provincial party led by the late René Lévesque, a colourful, charismatic man. To the hardliners' dismay, enthusiasm waned in the 1980s and for some years separation was more or less a dead issue, deemed neither practical nor realistic.

Now in the late 1990s, Quebec's leaving Canada in one form or another seems a serious possibility. This recent twist is in part due to Quebec's economic confidence which

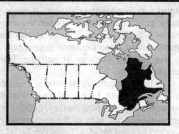

was in the doldrums for a number of years. But more so it is due to a sense that Quebec's differences and desires are neither understood nor appreciated by the rest of the country. Wrangling over constitutional matters and the failure of the Meech Lake Accord have brought these issues and sentiments to critical debate across Canada.

The federal election of October 1993 saw the Bloc Québecois party, which advocates separation, not only easily dominate Quebec but also become the official federal opposition party in Ottawa. It's cause-inspiring leader, Lucien Bouchard, left federal politics

and took over the PQ in 1996 determined to become leader of a new country. The PQ had previously won back the provincial leadership and so has a mandate to proceed as they see fit. Bouchard has vowed to work on the economy but wants also to proceed with the separation process. Montrealers, both English and French, the vast majority of whom are federalists, have thrown an unsettling, unexpected notion at the PQ: that of partitioning themselves into their own political entity.

Regardless of the intensity of the debate, all this has no bearing on visitors or their ability to enjoy the province's separateness.

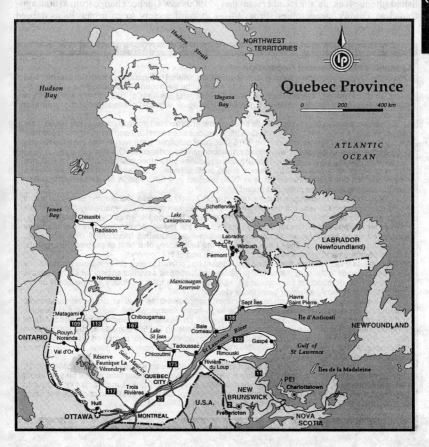

History

French explorer Jacques Cartier landed in Quebec City (then called Stadacona) and Montreal (then called Hochelaga) in 1534 (for information on the Native people see Population & People later in this chapter). Samuel de Champlain also of France first heard and recorded the word 'kebec' when he founded a settlement at Quebec City some 70 years later in 1608.

Through the rest of that century there were occasional disputes with the English, but by 1759 the English, with a final battle victory on the Plains of Abraham at Quebec, established themselves as the winners in the Canadian colony sweepstakes. From this point on French political influence in the new world waned.

The coming of thousands of British Loyalists fleeing the American Revolution and its effects resulted in the formation of Upper (Ontario) and Lower (Quebec) Canada with almost all the French settlers in the latter region.

The inevitable struggles of power and status between the two language groups continued through the 1800s with Lower Canada joining the Canadian confederation as Quebec in 1867.

The early and middle portions of the 1900s saw Quebec change from a rural, agricultural society to an urban, industrialised

Quebec's Move Toward Separation

One of the Quebecois leaders fighting for that province's political independence from Canada has said that until the issue is resolved to the separatists' satisfaction the notion of independence will never go away. And, he added, the relations between Quebec and the rest of the country will be like a never-ending trip to the dentist. Most Canadians now agree with that assessment of the separatist agenda.

In Quebec, the idea of leaving Canada first became an organised political cause in the 1960s. Late in that decade, a small group of French-Canadian radicals used terrorism and bombings to press their cause into national consciousness. The 1976 provincial elections were won by the Parti Quebecois (PQ) whose softly stated policy was based on securing independence for Quebec.

However, the PQ's win was based not so much on a desire by Quebec voters wanting independence as it was based on a real need for change at the political helm. This was shown to be true when a referendum on the independence issue in 1980 resulted in a 60% vote in favour of staying within Canada and the issue was publicly dropped.

In 1995 a second referendum under a revamped PQ party was held. Once again provincial voters opted to stay within Canada but the margin of victory was less than 1%. Immediately there was talk of following this up with a third referendum and the matter became known as the 'neverendum'.

In order to appease separatist leaning Quebeckers, the federal government has over the years transferred more and more of its powers to the provinces. Quebec has control over education, immigration and language. They have also been the beneficiary of a host of programmes, grants, transfer payments and more, to the ire of much of the rest of the country.

Since the last referendum, the federal government has offered to give the provinces a veto to any proposed changes to the constitution and to recognise Quebec as a distinct society, which has always been one of the demands of the separatists. However, what is meant officially and politically by the term a 'distinct society' has never been made clear.

The independence movement continues inexorably toward its goal of achieving separation. Warnings of economic hardships brought on by large-scale unemployment, migration out of Quebec, and loss of federal services and tax money largely fall on deaf ears among the committed. A fairly large segment of French-speaking Quebec (60%), if not seeing English Canada as the enemy, does see itself united in the desire for a fresh start, relieved of what are perceived as irreconcilable differences. At this point, it seems inevitable that some form of separation will come, but in what form cannot be guessed.

Although it is unlikely blood will be spilt, it will certainly not be an entirely smooth transformation if separation does become a reality. The Native peoples of Quebec, whose land claims take up about half of the province, have categorically voted against separation. Canada maintains that if Quebec separates it will be with the province's portion of the national debt, and at billions of dollars this could dampen the spirits of even the most enthusiastic new flag waver. ∎

one whose educational and cultural base, however, still relied upon the Catholic Church which wielded immense power and authority. About 90% of the population is Roman Catholic, though the Church's influence has declined sharply since the 1960s.

The 60s decade of questioning also brought the so-called Quiet Revolution during which all aspects of French society were scrutinised and overhauled. During this period Quebec began to assert more independence nationally and internationally. At the same time, the Canadian government embarked on their on-going quest to seek ways to ensure an harmonious, workable, long-term relationship between Quebec and the rest of the country. As part of this process, the national bilingualism policy was introduced. Just how difficult (impossible?) the task is has been painfully revealed over the past, sometimes bitter, three decades.

Climate
In Montreal and vicinity, July and August can be hot and sometimes muggy as well. East along the St Lawrence River, at Quebec City and beyond, hot days may be enjoyed but it's more likely weather will be sunny and warm. The further east or north you travel the cooler the weather becomes. Even in midsummer an evening sweater may be required. In most regions, particularly close to Montreal, anytime between May and October is suitable for travelling.

Everywhere across the province winters are cold and snow can be many metres deep. Other than in the south-east, summers are short and by September temperatures have dropped noticeably. Many people, however, do visit in the heart of winter for the top rate skiing.

Economy
Quebec's wealth has long been as much potential as actual. Despite abundant natural resources, manufacturing is the prime industry. There are vast amounts of hydroelectric power and the province is the main paper producer in North America. Roughly half the province is forest. Other important industries are aluminium, minerals, timber, tourism, dairy goods and apples and a local speciality, maple syrup.

The St Lawrence River (Fleuve Saint-Laurent) provides a link between the Great Lakes and the Atlantic Ocean, serving major Canadian and US ports.

Population & People
At the time of European exploration, the region along the St Lawrence River from Ontario to Quebec City was controlled by the Mohawks of the Iroquois Confederacy. North of and around Quebec City, the Montagnais were the principal aboriginal group. Further north was and is Cree homeland and beyond that the Labrador Eskimo, Naskapi and Inuit peoples are dominant. The Montagnais and Naskapi are also known as Innu. Around the southern portion of the Gaspé Peninsula, the Micmacs, found around much of the Atlantic Provinces, were the principal aboriginal group and they still live in the region although their numbers are small.

Today, the French dominate the province. Quebec is the only area of North America where people speaking French are in the majority. Outside of Montreal, English residents and immigrants are generally few, although parts of the Eastern Townships and the Gaspé and an area around the Ontario border near Hull still have English communities. Montreal has significant, Chinese, Greek, Haitian, Jamaican and Vietnamese communities. Most immigrants are assimilated into the Anglophone group.

Information
Provincial Symbols The provincial flower is the white lily, and the provincial bird is the snowy owl.

Tourist Offices General provincial tourist information can be obtained from Tourisme Quebec by calling toll free 1-800-363-7777 from anywhere in Canada and the USA. The mailing address is CP 979, Montreal, H3C 2W3.

QUEBEC

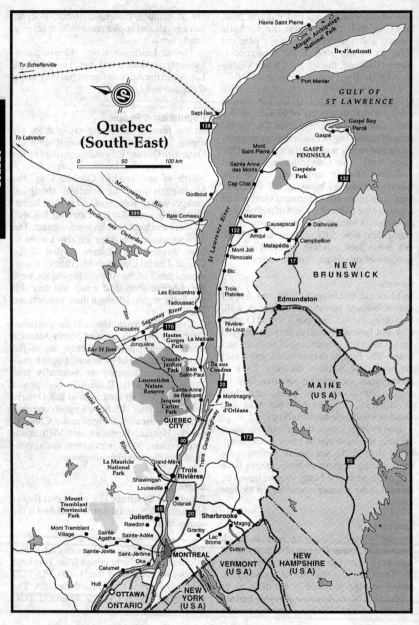

Quebec
(South-East)

To Schefferville

To Labrador

To Scheffersville

0   50   100 km

Manicouagan Riv

Rivière aux Outardes

389

Saint Maurice

Saguenay River

St Lawrence River

Trans Canada Highway

GULF OF
ST LAWRENCE

Havre Saint Pierre

Île d'Anticosti

Port Menier

Mingan Archipelago
National Park

Sept-Îles

138

Godbout

Baie Comeau

Les Escoumins

Tadoussac

Chicoutimi

Jonquière

Lac St Jean

Hautes
Gorges
Park

Grands
Jardins
Park

Laurentides
Nature
Reserve

Jacques
Cartier
Park

La Malbaie

Baie
Saint-Paul

Île aux
Coudres

Sainte-Anne
de Beaupré

QUEBEC
CITY

Mont Saint Pierre

Saints Anne
des Monts

Cap Chat

Gaspésie
Park

Gaspé Bay

Gaspé

Percé

GASPÉ
PENINSULA

132

Matane

Causapscal

Amqui

Mont Joli

Rimouski

Bic

Trois
Pistoles

Rivière-
du-Loup

Dalhousie

Campbellton

Matapédia

132

17

NEW
BRUNSWICK

Edmundston

2

MAINE
(USA)

95

La Mauricie
National
Park

Grand-Mère

Shawinigan

Louiseville

Trois
Rivières

Montmagny

Île
d'Orléans

20

173

Mount
Tremblant
Provincial
Park

Mont Tremblant
Village

Sainte-
Agathe

Sainte-
Jovite

Odanak

Joliette

Rawdon

Sainte-Adèle

Saint-Jérôme

Oka

Calumet

Hull

OTTAWA

ONTARIO

40

20

Sherbrooke

Magog

Granby

Lac
Brome

Sutton

MONTREAL

VERMONT
(USA)

NEW
YORK
(USA)

NEW
HAMPSHIRE
(USA)

There are few English signs or roadside markings in the province. Get hold of a good road map and watch for the conspicuous highway numbers and assorted symbols for attractions, ferries etc. The only hang-up is that the sometimes bizarrely obscure pictograms designed when bilingual signs were banned are often more use as passing-time riddles than travel aids.

Telephone The area code for Montreal and area is 514. In the eastern portion of the province including Quebec City, the area code is 418. This area extends north and east to Labrador. The western part of the province is 819. For emergency service in Montreal and Laval dial 911. Elsewhere call the operator on 0.

Time Quebec is on Eastern Time except for the far north-eastern corner south of Labrador which is on Atlantic Time.

Tax The provincial sales tax is 6.5%.

Activities
Tourisme Quebec offices usually have some general information booklets on the parks, historic sites, outdoor activities and adventure tour operators. Both national and provincial parks offer excellent camping, hiking, canoeing and wildlife observation. Northern and eastern portions of the province are popular fishing destinations with some renowned salmon rivers. Whale watching is centred around the Saguenay River. Sea-kayaking is increasingly popular from the north shore of the far eastern Saint Lawrence River area. Cycling is good around Estrie and the Gaspé and more and more parks are developing mountain-bike trails. The province is working on creating the world's longest bike trail. The Green Trail, which will total 2400 km, is partially complete. Whitewater rafting is popular along the Rivère Jacques Cartier near Quebec and the Rivère Rouge near Montreal. In winter, Quebec is one of North America's prime ski meccas.

Accommodation
Accommodation is pleasingly varied and relatively inexpensive in Quebec. While there is not a tradition of B&Bs, this form of lodging has increased considerably during recent years. Delightful small old hotels in the European mould abound in Montreal and Quebec City. In both centres as well as around the province, comfortable guest houses or tourist homes are plentiful. Modern hotels, motels and an array of government and private campgrounds round out the accommodation choices. Both HI and private hostels can be found across Quebec.

Montreal

Some cities take a bit of getting used to – you need time to know and appreciate them – but not Montreal. This city has an atmosphere all its own. It's a friendly, romantic place where couples kiss on the street and strangers talk to each other – an interesting and lively blend of things English and French, flavoured by the Canadian setting. There are about three million people in Greater Montreal – it's the second largest city in Canada after Toronto – and about 12% of all Canadians and 40% of Quebec's population lives here. Two-thirds of the population are French, making it the largest French-speaking city outside Paris, but the downtown core is surprisingly English.

Since its founding, Montreal has been a major port and a centre for finance, business and transportation. The four universities, two in each language, and numerous affiliates and colleges make it a major academic centre as well. It is also an arts centre particularly for French culture.

To the visitor, it is the mix of old with new and the *joie de vivre* that is most alluring. French culture prevails, giving the atmosphere a European tinge. The nightlife is great and there are 5000 restaurants in town.

The interaction of the English and the French gives Montreal some of its charm but is also responsible for some continuing conflict.

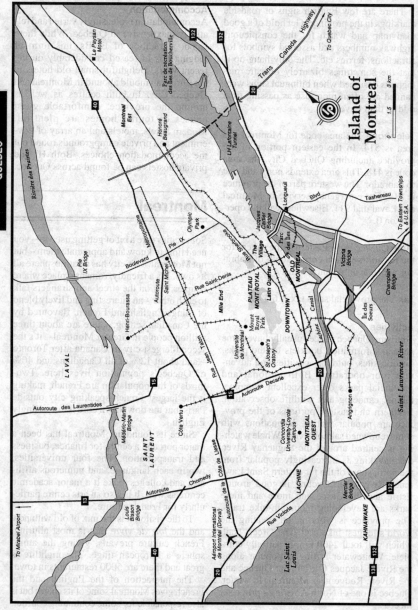

Island of Montreal

0   1.5   3 km

To Quebec City

Trans Canada Highway

132

132

20

To Eastern Townships
& U.S.A.

Tashereau

Longueuil

Blvd

Jacques
Cartier
Bridge

Parc
des Îles

Parc de récréation
des Îles de Boucherville

Le Paysan
Motel

Honoré
Beaugrand

Montreal
Est

LH Lafontaine
Tunnel

Victoria
Bridge

Champlain
Bridge

Île des
Soeurs

Rivière des Prairies

40

Pie
IX Bridge

Pie IX
Boulevard

Olympic
Park

Rue Sherbrooke

Saint Michel

Métropolitaine

Autoroute

Rue Saint-Denis

Mile End

PLATEAU
MONT ROYAL

Latin Quarter

The
Village

OLD
MONTREAL

DOWNTOWN

Canal

Lachine
Canal

LAVAL

Henri-Bourassa

Rue Jean Talon

Université
de Montréal

Mount
Royal
Park

St Joseph's
Oratory

15

Autoroute des Laurentides

15

Autoroute Decarie

Côte Vertu

Angrignon

Saint Laurence River

Médéric-Martin
Bridge

SAINT
LAURENT

Côte de Liesse

Concordia
University-Loyola
Campus

MONTREAL
OUEST

Chomedy

Autoroute

Côte de la

Autoroute de la

LACHINE

Mercier
Bridge

132

To Mirabel Airport

13

Louis
Bisson
Bridge

Aéroport International
de Montréal (Dorval)

40

20

Rue Victoria

Lac Saint
Louis

KAHNAWAKE

132

138

The French may have long dominated the social spheres but traditionally it was the English who ran businesses, made decisions, held positions of power and accumulated wealth. As Québecois awareness grew, this changed, and the French are now well represented in all realms of life. In fact, some recent laws are reactionary in their discrimination against languages other than French. The English are now voicing the need for balance and equality.

Regardless of these difficulties, Montreal exudes a warm, relaxed yet exciting ambience. It is as if the city itself has a pride and confidence in its own worth. Speak French if you can. If you can't, as long as you are not arrogantly defiant, you'll find most people helpful and likely to respond in English.

The city has a reputation for fashion savoir-faire, but this is not limited to the moneyed – a certain flair seems to come naturally to everyone.

Although the other seasons are temperate, a quick word about winter is in order. It can be cold, particularly in January, when the temperatures sometimes go as low as -40°C. There can be piles of snow too, although these don't disrupt things for long, and the Métro enables you to travel the city without taking one crisp breath of the outdoor air. The people are usually more gregarious when big storms hit, and afterwards, sunny skies make it all bearable.

History

Montreal's is a prominent and colourful chapter in the history of Canada. In many ways, the past is responsible for the politics here today. Before the French hit the scene, the Algonkian, Huron and Iroquois shared the area, not always peacefully. Jacques Cartier first visited in 1535 and found Hochelaga, an Iroquois village at the foot of the mountain. The first permanent European settlement didn't begin until 1642, when Sieur de Maisonneuve set up a religious mission named Ville Marie. The mountain had been named Mont Royal, which led to the city's present name. It soon became a fur-trading centre. The Native Indians weren't too thrilled with all this and attacks were a regular occurrence until just after 1700, when a treaty was signed. The fur trade boomed and Montreal became an exploration base. Today, Old Montreal preserves much of the city's 17th-century past.

The British had been battling the French for some time and took Quebec City in 1759. The French moved their capital upstream to Montreal but that didn't last long. The British captured it in 1760 and settlers followed.

Soon the rebelling American colonies were after the city. In 1775 General Montgomery took Montreal without firing a shot. It was in the hands of the revolutionary forces only until the British beat back another group trying to take Quebec City, at which time the revolutionaries fled Montreal. In the mid-1800s Montreal was the capital of the United Provinces of Canada. The late 1800s saw a big boom; the shipping and rail lines brought prosperity. By 1900 Montreal was the commercial and cultural centre of Canada. In the early part of the century there came a huge influx of Jewish Europeans – even today Montreal has the largest Jewish population in Canada. After both wars, immigrants of many nationalities arrived.

From the 1920s to the 1940s, Montreal gained a reputation as Sin City. This was due partially to Prohibition in the USA. Brothels, gambling houses and gangsters thrived and the nightlife was known far and wide; politicians and law-enforcers are said to have turned a blind eye. All this changed with the arrival of Jean Drapeau, who was elected mayor in 1954 and, except for a five-year period in the early 60s, was mayor right into the mid-80s. He cleaned up the city, encouraged redevelopment, and staged the World's Fair in 1967 and the Olympics in 1976. Still, he was touched by scandal and many dubbed him 'Emperor', claiming he was megalomaniacal. But Drapeau was popular and he certainly helped develop Montreal's international reputation.

For years, decades even, Montreal had been a stable city with little change in the downtown area. Returning after a long absence was always comforting, as though you hadn't really been away. Since the late 1980s, however, that equanimity has dissolved as redevelopment and modernisation strike markedly at points all over the downtown area. The changing and stylish look, a blend of European and North American forms, has sparked plenty of debate and continues to effect future projects and streetscapes.

Orientation

The city sits on an island roughly 40 km long and 15 km wide where the Ottawa River flows into the St Lawrence River. There are bridges connecting all sides with the mainland; this reinforces the impression of really not being on an island at all. Despite the size of the city and the size of the island, it's both easy to orient yourself and to get around Montreal.

In the middle of the island is Mont Royal, a 233-metre-high extinct volcano. The core of the city, which is actually quite small, is below this, in the south central section of the island.

The downtown area is bounded by Rue Sherbrooke to the north, Avenue Atwater to the west, Rue Saint Antoine to the south and Boulevard Saint Laurent to the east. This is the busy area of skyscrapers, shops, restaurants, offices and luxury hotels.

The small park, Square Dorchester (formerly Dominion Square, and often still called that), marks the centre of downtown. It's a peaceful spot surrounded by some new and many old buildings, some with green oxidised copper roofs.

The tourist office is on the north side of Square Dorchester along with the horse-drawn carriages, known as *calèches*, which can be taken around parts of town or up the mountain. On the south-west corner is the new Windsor Station/Molson Centre complex, the just completed hockey arena built around the venerable old Canadian Pacific railway terminal.

To the south is the top-end Marriot Château Champlain hotel. On the east side is the stone Sun Life Insurance building.

The Cathedral of Montreal (Marie-Reine-du-Monde Cathédrale, or Mary Queen of the World Cathedral) with its pastel, gilt-trimmed interior is on the corner of Boulevard René Lévesque (formerly Dorchester Boulevard) and Rue de la Cathédrale to the east of the square. Just to the east of the cathedral is the Queen Elizabeth Hotel below which is the CN-VIA Rail Central Station.

Parallel to Rue Sainte Catherine, wide Boulevard René Lévesque, is known for its tall towers. Place Ville Marie (sometimes referred to as the PVM) on the corner of Rue University across from the Queen Elizabeth Hotel, is one of the city's best known buildings. It's in the shape of a cross and is another landmark.

North, a block up Rue Peel from the square, is Rue Sainte Catherine, the principal east-west artery. North of Rue Sainte Catherine is Boulevard de Maisonneuve and then Rue Sherbrooke, the two other main east-west streets.

Sainte Catherine is one-way eastbound. It's the main shopping street with several department stores. At 705 Rue Sainte Catherine Ouest by the corner of Rue University, is one of the city's largest shopping complexes, the modern showpiece Eaton Centre – almost an attraction in its own right. The Promenade de la Cathédrale is an underground portion of the complex which runs beneath a church. The tough economy of recent years has brought some decline, however, and Sainte Catherine now has its share of vacancies, strip bars and pinball arcades.

Avenue McGill College, running north of Rue Sainte Catherine, was once a narrow student ghetto but has been (controversially) opened up presenting an imposing boulevard edged with some of the city's newest corporate and retail architecture. Structures aside, the channel of space leading from the city's main street to the campus of McGill University and beyond to the mountain is certainly impressive. A substantial number of statues and sculptures, including the eye-catching 'Illuminated Crowd', are found along the avenue.

Running north and south of Rue Sainte Catherine west of Rue Peel are Rue de la Montagne, Rue Crescent and Rue Bishop – the centre of one of the nightlife areas. There are many restaurants, cafes and discos here.

If you keep walking uphill on Rue Peel for a number of blocks you'll finally come to Avenue des Pins, across which is the edge of Parc du Mont Royal. You'll see some steps. At the top is an excellent view of the city, the river and the surroundings to the south – great views day or night. This is the city's largest park and is pleasant to stroll in on a warm day. The cross, on top and lit at night, is a city symbol.

Other good vantage points for views over the city are the Olympic Stadium Tower (charging an admission fee), the bar at the top of the Château Champlain hotel and the restaurant on top of the Radisson Hotel, 777 Rue University. There are also pretty good views from St Joseph's Oratory and from various points along the road around Mont Royal.

The area downtown and west to Loyola Campus on Rue Sherbrooke is pretty much English and residential. Westmount at the foot of the mountain is one of the city's wealthiest and most prestigious districts.

East of Rue Peel along Rue Sainte Catherine you'll see Square Phillips, a meeting place where guitarists busk and bask. Further east, just past de Bleury, is Place des Arts, a complex for the performing arts. A few more blocks east is Boulevard Saint Laurent (St Lawrence Blvd) known as The Main. This is one of the city's best known streets, with an interesting history and ethnic mix, and lots of restaurants. It is long and changes complexion in different areas but is always interesting and lively and gets relatively few tourists.

To the east of Boulevard Saint Laurent, Rue Sainte Catherine Ouest becomes Rue Sainte Catherine Est. East of Saint Laurent, streets are given the Est (East) designation, west of Saint Laurent they include the Ouest (West) designation in their name. All streets are divided in this way. East of Boulevard Saint Laurent the area has traditionally been predominantly French and it remains this way.

About seven blocks east (you can get a bus) is Saint Denis, the centre of a Paris-style cafe district sometimes called the Latin Quarter.

From Saint Denis east along Rue Sainte Catherine to Rue Papineau is Montreal's developing gay town known as The Village.

Two blocks east of Saint Denis is Rue Berri. Terminus Voyageur, the city's main bus station with US and Canadian destinations, is a block north on Rue Berri at Boulevard de Maisonneuve. A major transfer point of the Métro system, the Berri-UQAM station is also here and city buses roll in all directions from this subway stop.

Old Montreal is south-east of the downtown area; both Boulevard Saint Laurent and Rue Saint Denis lead into it.

There is a small but determined Chinatown clustered along Rue de la Gauchetière between Rue Saint Urbain and Boulevard Saint Laurent. Rue de la Gauchetière runs east-west past the train stations.

The streets of east-end Montreal and parts of the northern section are lined with distinctive two or three-storey apartment buildings with outside staircases. Such housing, peculiar to Montreal, was built in the 1920s and 30s. The stairs were put outside to save space inside.

Such an area is the Plateau Mont Royal. Known simply as the Plateau and bounded roughly by Avenue des Pins (Pine Avenue) to the south, Rue Saint Denis to the east, Boulevard Saint Joseph to the north and Avenue Parc to the west, this is the newer area for the young and/or hip.

Further north along Boulevard Saint Laurent, between Avenue Laurier and Rue Bernard, the Mile End district contrasts tradition with chic.

Anywhere from lower Rue Saint Denis, north through the Plateau and up this far is great for merely wandering and seeing Montrealers busy at life. Saturday is the most lively day.

QUEBEC

QUEBEC

Downtown Montreal

QUEBEC

PLACES TO STAY

4 Hôtel de Paris
5 Le Gite du Parc Lafontaine
7 Castel St Denis
8 Hôtel Manoir Sherbrooke
12 Manoir Ambrose
16 Ritz Carlton Kempinski
18 Hôtel Villard
21 Le Breton Hôtel
24 Hôtel St Denis
25 Hebergement l'Abri du Voyageur
33 YMCA
37 YCWA
45 Hôtel Travelodge
46 Hôtel Américain
47 Hôtel De La Couronne
48 Hôtel Viger Centre Ville
52 HI Auberge de Montreal

PLACES TO EAT

2 Café Méliés (Cinéma Parallele)
6 Le Commensal
9 La Casa Grèque
10 Bueno Notte
14 Maison de Cari (Curry House)
15 EggSpectation
19 Café Croissant de Lune
20 Le Bedouin
23 Da Giovanni
30 Dunn's
31 Joe's
32 Ben's
34 Bar B Barn
36 Chez La Mere Michel
38 McLean's Pub
44 Chinatown

OTHER

1 Lookout
3 St Louis Square
11 McGill University
13 Museé des Beaux Arts
17 McCord Museum
22 Terminus Bus Terminal
26 Contemporary Art Gallery/Place des Arts
27 Square Phillips
28 Main Post Office
29 Place Ville Marie
35 Canadian Centre for Architecture
39 Tourist Office/Infotouriste
40 Square Dorchester
41 Place du Canada
42 Cathedral of Montreal
43 Central Station (CN-VIA)
49 Place Bonaventure
50 Windsor Station
51 Molson Center
53 Dow Planetarium

Street Names Montreal is a bilingual rather than a French-speaking city. The bulk of visitors are English-speaking, English is widely used in the central area, and in addition, many of the streets were named by the British who dominated the city through its formative years. However, in this book, the Montreal street names are given in French. Many squares, parks and other sites are known by their French names. It may seem a little strange to read 'Rue Peel' instead of 'Peel St', but this has been done for the sake of consistency.

Boulevard René Lévesque was named in honour of the late Québecois leader and premier. This major street was formerly called Dorchester Boulevard and is still often referred to this way so you may hear either. Similarly Square Dorchester is still often referred to as Dominion Square.

Information

Tourist Offices Montreal has one central phone number for all its information offices (☎ 873-2015). From outside of Montreal information can be obtained on (☎ 1-800-363-7777) from 9 am to 5 pm Monday to Friday.

The main Montreal tourist office, Infotouriste, is central at 1001 Rue Square Dorchester on the north side of Square Dorchester. Square Dorchester is bounded by Boulevard René Lévesque, Rue Metcalfe and Rue Peel. Both the train station and the Métro are nearby and Rue Sainte Catherine is just a short walk away. Infotouriste is efficient and helpful and can supply information on all areas of Quebec. It's open daily through the year from 9 am to 5 pm but from June to September remains open until 7 pm. Aside from all the usual tourist office information, this centre also has a bookstore, moneychanger, souvenirs, post office and a fax machine, and can arrange sightseeing tours. For free accommodation reservations call ☎ 878-1000.

The other main information centre is also well located at 174 Rue Notre Dame Est in Old Montreal, not far from Place Jacques Cartier. It's busy but helpful, open from 9 am to 7 pm daily in season, 9 am to 5 pm with an hour and a quarter for lunch at 1 pm the rest of the year. This one deals mainly with Montreal. The tourist offices have a museum pass for sale which covers entry to 17 museums and galleries which may be economical if you intend on seeing a lot of the historical attractions. The airports also have information kiosks which are open all year round.

Note that Montreal's museums tend to be closed on Monday.

Money For exchanging money, Currencies International at 1230 Rue Peel on the corner of Rue Sainte Catherine is open every day and offers good rates. There's a Royal Bank at 360 Rue Sainte Catherine Est and a Bank of Montreal at 670 Sainte Catherine Ouest.

Post The main post office (☎ 846-5401) at 1250 Rue University receives poste restante.

Foreign Consulates There are a number of consulates in town of which only a few are listed here. Check the Yellow Pages for a detailed list.

France
  1 Place Ville Marie, (☎ 878-4835)
Germany
  1250 Boulevard Réné Lévesque Ouest,
  (☎ 931-2277)
Japan
  600 de la Gauchetière Ouest, (☎ 866-3429)
Netherlands
  1002 Rue Sherbrooke Ouest, (☎ 849-4247)
UK
  1000 de la Gauchetière Ouest, (☎ 866-5863)
USA
  1155 Rue Saint Alexandre, (☎ 398-9695)

Travel Agencies Travel CUTS, known in Quebec as Voyages Campus, has five locations including the main one at 1613 Rue Saint Denis (☎ 843-8511).

Bookshops & Maps Metropolitan News at 1109 Rue Cypress, west off Rue Peel near Square Dorchester in the centre of downtown sells newspapers from around the world and is open seven days a week.

Chapters Bookstore on the corner of Rues Stanley and Sainte Catherine has a vast selection of English books including a good travel section. Double Hook at 1235A Rue Greene is a good English bookshop featuring Canadian writers. For French books check out Librairie Champigny, 4380 Rue Saint Denis.

An excellent place for maps, English and French, as well as some travel books, is Aux Quartre Points Cardinaux, 551 Rue Ontario Est north of the bus station.

Medical Services Although there is no real discrimination, the best hospital for English patients is the Royal Victoria (Royal Vic) (☎ 842-1231) at 687 Rue des Pins Ouest (Pine West). For French patients, go to Hospital Notre Dame, 1560 Rue Sherbrooke Est (☎ 876-6421).

Warning Pedestrians, beware in Montreal! Might is right and drivers take full advantage of this. The careless may not get a second chance.

Old Montreal (Vieux Montréal)

This is the oldest section of the city, dating mainly from the 1700s. The square **Place Royale**, is where Ville Marie, Maisonneuve's first small fort-town, was built, when fighting with the Iroquois Confederacy was both lengthy and fierce.

The narrow, cobblestone streets divide old stone houses and buildings, many of which now house intimate little restaurants and clubs. Throughout the area are squares and churches and the waterfront is never far away. Old Montreal is a must for romantics, though it's unfortunately a bit crowded in peak season. With all the activity and history, it's a perfect area for just wandering where your feet take you. Do yourself a favour and don't bring your car down here – it's too busy and you won't find a parking spot.

The main streets are Rue Notre Dame and Rue Saint Paul. The area is bounded by Rue McGill on the west, Rue Berri on the east, Rue Saint Antoine on the north and the river on the south, with Boulevard Saint Laurent dividing the area east from west. The Métro stops in Old Montreal are Place d'Armes or Champs de Mars.

Near **Hôtel de Ville** (City Hall) and the Rue Notre Dame tourist office is the square **Place Jacques Cartier**, the centre of the area which in summer is filled with visitors, vendors, horse-drawn carriages and musicians. At the tourist office nearby, there's an *Old Montreal Walking Tour* booklet available, which is free and has all sorts of interesting historical tidbits, and points out the most noteworthy spots.

Many buildings are themselves marked with informative plaques. Some descriptions of the highlights follow. The old Bonsecours Market building at 350 Rue Saint Paul Est is once again a farmers' market.

Bird lovers may want to ask about the peregrine falcons which have been nesting on high building ledges around Old Montreal since the mid-1980s. Some years, observation posts manned by university students are set up with cameras focused on the nest. One year it was on the 32nd floor of the Stock Exchange.

Place d'Armes & Basilica Notre Dame The other major square in the area is Place d'Armes. A monument to Maisonneuve stands in the middle. On the square is Basilica Notre Dame, which you shouldn't miss. Built in 1829 and big enough to hold 5000 people, the church has a magnificently rich interior. The masses around Christmas, particularly Christmas Eve, are worth a special trip. There's a small museum at the back.

Église de Notre Dame de Bonsecours This church is on Rue Saint Paul. It's also known as the Sailors' Church and has several models of wooden ships hanging from the ceiling. From the tower in the church there's a good view. The vignettes in the small museum are also quite good. They tell the story of Marguerite Bougeoys, the first teacher in Montreal and founder of the Congregation of Notre Dame order of nuns.

Pierre du Calvet House Across from the

church at 405 Rue Bonsecours, Calvet House (☎ 282-1725), which dates from 1725, has been restored and is now a hotel and restaurant featuring the furnishings of that time.

Château de Ramezay On Rue Notre Dame, across from the Hôtel de Ville, is the Château de Ramezay (☎ 861-3708) which was the home of the city's French governors for about 40 years in the early 1700s. The building has housed a great variety of things since, but is now a museum with a collection of artefacts, tools and miscellanea from Quebec's early history. The house is open daily in summer, closed Monday the rest of the year. Admission is $5, students $3.

Montreal History Centre Also in Old Montreal is the Montreal History Centre (☎ 872-3207) in the old fire hall on Place d'Youville. Audiovisuals and displays depict some of the city's history, with tours running every 20 minutes. It's open daily 10 am to 6 pm from May to September, closed Monday the rest of the year and costs $2.25.

Musée Marc Aurèle Fortin Not far away is the Musée Marc Aurèle Fortin (☎ 845-6108), at 118 Rue Saint Pierre, which is less of a museum than a gallery dedicated to this Quebec landscape painter who lived from 1888 to 1970. He is especially known for his depictions of trees. Other painters are also represented in the changing exhibitions. This is closed on Monday throughout the year. Admission costs $4, students less.

Sir George-Étienne Cartier National Historic Park The Sir George-Étienne Cartier National Historic Park (☎ 283-2282) consists of two historic houses owned by the Cartier family. One details the life of the prominent 19th-century lawyer and politician and the changes in society in his lifetime, and the other offers a glimpse of a middle-class home during the Victorian era. It's at 458 Rue Notre Dame Est. Admission is $3 and the site is open every day in

QUEBEC

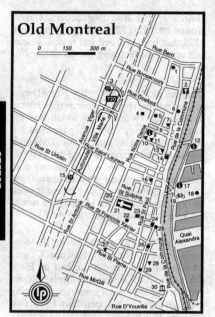

Old Montreal

0   150   300 m

Rue Berri

Rue Bonsecours

Rue Gosford

Rue Notre Dame

Rue de la Commune

Avenue Viger

Rue St Urbain

Rue Saint Laurent

Rue St Antoine

Rue St François Xavier

Rue St Sulpice

Rue St Paul

Rue St Pierre

Rue McGill

Rue D'Youville

Quai Alexandra

summer, and from Wednesday to Sunday for the rest of the year.

Pointe-à-Callière (Museum of Archaeology & History) Situated on the very spot where Sieur de Maisonneuve and Jeanne Mance founded the first European settlement, on the south side of Place Royale, this museum (☎ 872-9150) is an interesting archaeological and historical study of the beginnings of the city of Montreal.

For the most part, the museum is underground, in the actual ruins of buildings and an ancient sewage/river system. The first European cemetery is here, established just a few years after the settlement itself. Grave sites can be seen presented like a working dig.

Artefacts are cleverly laid out on levels of shelving according to their time period just as they would be unearthed, the oldest items from Montreal's prehistory on the bottom. There are also a few interactive exhibits, the best of which is a video monitor which allows visitors to have a 'conversation' with some of the original inhabitants via a ghost-like image.

The lookout at the top of the tower in the new building provides an excellent view of the Old Port. The tower can be visited without paying the museum entry fee.

The museum is at 350 Place Royale, use the Place d'Armes Métro stop. It is open from Tuesday to Sunday 10 am to 8 pm in summer, until 5 pm the rest of the year. Admission is $7 for adults, free for kids under 5.

Images du Future At 85 Rue Saint Paul Ouest is this centre of interactive arts and communications (☎ 849-1612). The multimedia presentations and facilities include holography, computer-generated films, satellite images and various other high-tech novelties, games and art forms. Admission is $10.75, less for children and it's open daily from the middle of May to the middle of October 10 am to 10 pm with shorter hours in winter.

Old Port (Vieux-Port) The Old Port waterfront is a district of riverside redevelopment south of Place Jacques Cartier which is still evolving and changing as construction and ideas continue. It covers 2.5 km of riverfront and is based around four quays *(quais)*. The Promenade du Vieux Port is a wide promenade along the river from Rue Berri Ouest to Rue McGill. An information booth (☎ 496-PORT) can be found at the entrance to Quai King Edward, pretty much in the centre of things. A number of the permanent features are listed here but each year, particularly through the summer, the port features a range of different temporary exhibits, shows and events. Check prices of the main attractions with the information number as they are not cheap and may be prohibitive to some. Cruise boats, jet boats and speed boats all depart for tours of the river from the various docks.

At the far eastern edge of the historic port on Victoria Pier is **Sailors' Memorial Clock Tower** now used as an observation tower open to the public and with a history exhibit. Quai Jacques Cartier includes restaurants, an open-air stage and a handicraft centre. Trolley tours of the port area depart from here. Also from Quai Jacques Cartier, a ferry goes over to **Parc des Îles** which is popular with cyclists (bikes can be taken on the ferry) and has a number of its own attractions (see that section later for details). If requested, a stop is made at **Parc de la Cité du Havre**, where there's a restaurant and some picnic tables.

On Quai King Edward at the foot of Boulevard Saint Laurent is a large flea market *(marché aux puces)*. It is also the site of the IMAX Theatre and **SOS Labyrinthe**, a two-km maze which is definitely not just for kids.

1 La Ronde
2 David M Stewart Museum
3 Clock Tower
4 Ferry Terminals
5 Velo-Aventure Bike Rental
6 Iberville Passenger Terminal
7 Biosphère
8 Metro Station
9 Casino

Ferry to Longueuil

Jacques Cartier Bridge

Saint Laurent River

Île Ste Hélène

See Old Montreal

Rue Berri

Ave Viger

Rue St Antoine

Rue Notre Dame

Rue de la Commune

Quai de l'Horloge

Parc des Îles

Quai Jacques Cartier

Pont de la Concorde

Île Notre Dame

Quai King Edward

Cité du Havre

Quai Alexandra

Rue McGill

Rue Pierre Dupuy

Beach

Parc des Îles & Old Port

0   0.5   1 km

At Quai Alexandra, a short distance east of Rue McGill, is the huge present-day port and container terminal. Also there is the Iberville Passenger Terminal, the dock for cruise ships which ply the St Lawrence River as far as the Magdalen Islands out in the Gulf of St Lawrence.

Lower Rue Saint Denis/Latin Quarter
Rue Saint Denis between Boulevard de Maisonneuve and Rue Sherbrooke, is the centre of a cafe, bistro and bar district with lots of open-air places and music bars. Originally an all-student area, more expensive establishments have now arrived but the young who still frequent it in numbers help to make the nights especially lively. Snoop around in the side streets, too, where little bars can be discovered. There are also some good small hotels in the area.

French is the tongue generally spoken here but don't let that deter you – it's a good chance to practise.

QUEBEC

Going south along Rue Saint Denis will lead you into Old Montreal.

North, up Rue Saint Denis just beyond Rue Sherbrooke, is Place Saint Louis, a small park dating from 1876 surrounded by fine Victorian homes built for the French elite of the time. West of the square is Rue Prince Arthur (see the following Plateau section). Saint Denis continues northward through the Plateau area.

Boulevard Saint Laurent & the Plateau

Away from the crowds and the well-known tourist haunts, the Plateau area is a multi-ethnic district of inexpensive housing, outdoor cafes, restaurants, discos and bars, and interesting, funky shops. This loosely defined area runs from Avenue des Pins north to about Boulevard Saint Joseph. Rue Saint Denis and Avenue du Parc mark the east and west edges. This portion of Montreal is in the midst of an energetic change, from being ignored to coming alive, and is well worth exploring on foot.

Still called St Lawrence by some and known by many as The Main, always interesting Boulevard Saint Laurent is the principal commercial strip of the district. Running north-south, it divides the city into east and west, historically French and English, and has long reflected various nationalities.

Stores are topped by apartments in the two to four-storey rows that line both sides of the street. Around Rue Sainte Catherine it's a little sleazy (but interesting), but from north of Sherbrooke it leads into the Plateau with a splash of upmarket shops and restaurants, and then past Avenue du Pins through a cornucopia of small businesses for countless blocks. Both Saint Denis and Saint Laurent pass through a mix of French, English and Portuguese communities with abundant bookshops, clothing stores, coffee shops and restaurants.

The area around and along Rue Prince Arthur is good for strolling and eating as is the section further north on and around Avenue Duluth.

Avenue du Mont Royal west of the Mont Royal Métro station for about 10 blocks to Saint Laurent contains numerous vintage and second-hand clothing stores for off-beat, street-fashion apparel. East of the Métro stop there are also some alternative shops, used-record stores and the like.

The Upper Main eventually leads to the Mile End area.

Mile End

Upper Saint Laurent leads into this unusual neighbourhood bounded by Rue Laurier to the south, Rue Bernard to the north, Avenue Parc to the east and Saint Laurent itself to the west. It's a blend of French, Greek and traditional Hassidic Jews.

Many upper-class French, a growing segment of Montreal's population, live in the Outremont neighbourhood just to the east of Parc du Mont Royal. There is a smattering of pricey boutiques and restaurants along a portion of Avenue Laurier. Further north, Rue Bernard has some noteworthy restaurants, bars and cafes. Avenue du Parc is the centre of the Greek community.

Further north around Rue Jean Talon at Rue Saint Denis, the busy Jean Talon Market is in the middle of an Italian area.

The Village

The city's homosexual community is revitalising Rue Sainte Catherine East between Rue Saint Hubert and Rue Papineau. New restaurants and stores continue to open in this long neglected part of town. Numerous bars and nightclubs catering to gays and lesbians can be found in the district as well as specialised hotels and shops. The area around Rue Amherst and Boulevard de Maisonneuve has an increasing array of antique and specialty shops worth a browse.

There have been some incidents of bashing in the neighbourhood. Take care and don't go wandering through parks alone in the middle of the night.

Mont Royal

Known as the mountain, this is the city's best and biggest park. It was designed by the designer of New York's Central Park. The **Chalet Lookout** has great views of the city: you can walk up to it from downtown (see the Orientation section earlier for details), or drive most of the way through the park and walk the rest. East of the lookout is the huge steel cross, lit up at night and visible from all over the city. Within the park is **Beaver Lake** (Lac des Castors), a depression-era 'make-work' project. The park has lots of trees and is used in summer for walking, picnicking, horse riding and Frisbee throwing. In winter there is skating, tobogganing and skiing. There are walking trails, some with views. Calèches can be hired for rides up to the lookout or around the park's trails.

If you're driving here, take Rue Guy from the downtown area to Chemin de la Côte des Neiges and then look for signs. To the left is another small park called **Parc Summit**. There is another good lookout here; this one has a good views of the western residential districts.

Underground City

To alleviate congestion and to escape the harsh winter, Montreal created a huge underground city in the city centre. Though much of it is actually underground, the term really covers anything connected by underground passageways. Thus you can go to the train stations, find a hotel, see a movie, eat out, go dancing or shopping, all without taking a step outside.

The notion is functional and innovative, but there's really not much to see. The shops are all modern and most of the system looks no different from a contemporary shopping mall, the differences being this is bigger and has the Métro going through it.

Major building complexes like Place Ville Marie, Place Bonaventure Place du Canada and the Molson Centre are all connected and within easy walking distance. Others, like Place des Arts and Complèxe Desjardins, are a Métro ride away. The Eaton Centre is also part of the network. The tourist office has a good map of the entire system; it may prove useful on rainy or snowy days.

Musée des Beaux Arts (Fine Arts Museum)

Beaux Arts (pronounced 'bose-ar') as it is known, is the city's main art gallery (☎ 285-1600), with both modern and pre-Columbian works. Europe, Africa, the Middle East and other areas are covered. There's also a display of Inuit art. The architectural style of the new gallery annex across the street is also worth a look.

It's at 1379 Rue Sherbrooke Ouest on the corner of Rue Crescent. It's open from 11 am to 6 pm but to 9 pm Wednesday. Like many of Montreal's museums, this one is closed on Monday. Admission to the general permanent exhibits is free but there is always some sort of special show on too. Admission to these is a steep $12 (or so), students and seniors $7.

Contemporary Art Gallery

Located in the centre of town by the Place des Arts Complex at 185 Rue Sainte Catherine, the gallery (☎ 847-6212) displays art from 1939 to the present with its substantial permanent collection and temporary shows.

It's the only public gallery in the country which specialises exclusively in contemporary art, and displays both Canadian and international work. On Tuesday and from Thursday to Sunday, the gallery is open from 11 am to 6 pm. It remains open on Wednesday until 9 pm and is free from 6 pm onwards. It is closed on Monday. Admission is $5; students and seniors pay less. There is a simple restaurant within the gallery.

Saidye Bronfman Centre

For a further look at contemporary art, this museum (☎ 739-2301), at 5170 Chemin de la Côte Sainte Catherine, on the west side of Mont Royal, has a collection to view. It's free and open from Sunday to Thursday.

Canadian Centre for Architecture

The centre (☎ 939-7026) is both a museum and working organisation promoting the understanding of architecture, its history and future. The numerous exhibition rooms feature permanent and changing shows of local and international architecture, urban planning and landscape design. It may sound dry but most people will find at least some of the displays (incorporating models, drawings or photographs) of interest.

A portion of the centre has been created in and around Shaughnessay House, built as home for a wealthy businessman in 1874 of the characteristic grey limestone seen so often around the city. A wander around its 1st floor is interesting for the details and architectural features. A highlight is the solarium garden and the wonderfully ornate tea room with intricate woodwork and fireplace (sorry, no refreshments served).

There is a busy bookstore here with books on famous architects and topics ranging from international styles to photography.

Don't miss the sculpture garden and lookout on the other side of Boulevard René Lévesque. About 15 sculptures of varying styles and sizes are scattered about a terrace overlooking parts of south Montreal. Directional markers set in the border wall point out various buildings of note below. The old banks, mills etc provide intriguing evidence of the centre's conviction that the study of architecture is the study of history and civilisation.

The centre is open from 11 am to 5 pm daily, until 8 pm on Thursday and closed on Monday and Tuesday. Admission is $5, $3 for students and seniors. On Thursday it's free all day for students and for everybody else from 6 to 8 pm. The address is central at 1920 Rue Baile near the corner of Boulevard René Lévesque and Fort. The Métro stop is Atwater and there is parking available.

McCord Museum of Canadian History
The McCord is the city's main history museum (☎ 398-7100) but it's not large; budget 60 to 90 minutes for a visit. Located at 690 Rue Sherbrooke Ouest, the two-level museum is well laid out, with exhibits dealing, for the most part, with Eastern Canada's early European settlement. One room exhibits the history of Quebec's Native people. The other displays highlight the

museum's collection which includes early Canadian costume and textiles and folk art. There are permanent and changing exhibits.

A highlight of the 700,000 photograph collection are those by William Notman, who, with his sons, photographed Canadian people, places and activities from 1850 to about 1930.

The 2nd-floor room entitled 'Turning Point: Quebec 1900' neatly encapsulates French Canadian history in Quebec. The gift shop has some quality items and interesting reading material.

Admission is $5, less for students. On Thursday from 6 pm to 9 pm admission is free. Other than Thursday, hours are 10 am to 5 pm but closed Monday. If you tire before seeing the entire photo collection (don't panic they are not all on display), there is a tea room, but don't plan to eat a full meal as food prices are high.

Marguerite d'Youville Museum
Mentioned more for the building itself, rather than the small museum (☎ 937-9501), this is a fine example of early Quebec stone architecture, particularly of the convents seen in number across the province. It's centrally located at 1185 Rue Saint Mathieu.

Founded by Mother d'Youville, this is home to the Grey Nuns, an active and hardy group from the colonial era. It was they who set out by canoe for what was to become Manitoba and founded a mission in St Boniface. That nunnery of 1850 is now a museum in the middle of the largest French community in western Canada.

The museum, open Wednesday to Sunday from 1.30 to 4.30 pm, contains Marguerite's tomb and some religious artefacts and other related articles.

Mt Stephen Club
Funded by the George Stephen House Foundation, this Renaissance-style mansion (☎ 849-7338) dating from 1880 was built for the man who gave it his name, the first president of the Canadian Pacific Railway. The 15 rooms inside are rich with quality materials and skilful artistry. The woodwork

is tremendous. Long the home of the private Mount Stephen Club, it is open to the public for a small fee from Thursday to Sunday, noon to 4 pm during July and the first week of August only. It's at 1440 Rue Drummond.

Château Dufresne Museum of Decorative Arts

Château Dufresne displays decorative art and handicrafts (☎ 259-2575). Each room in the substantial building dating from 1916-18 is furnished with objets d'art and finery. It's only open from 11 am to 5 pm Friday to Sunday. Admission is $3.50. The museum is in front of the Botanical Gardens on the corner of Boulevard Pie IX (pronounced 'pee neuf') and Rue Sherbrooke near the Olympic Park.

St Joseph's Oratory

The impressive modern-style basilica (☎ 733-8211), completed in 1960 and based on and around a 1916 church, honours St Joseph, patron of healers and patron saint of Canada, and Brother André, a monk said to have had the power to cure illness. Piles of crutches testify to the strength of this belief. Brother André's heart, which is on view here – a display ranking with the weirdest – was stolen some years ago but was finally returned intact. There is a small museum dedicated to Brother André and on Sunday there are free organ concerts at 3.30 pm. The site is open daily and is free.

The oratory dome, visible from anywhere in the south-west of Montreal, is at 3800 Chemin Queen Mary, off the western slope of Mont Royal. From downtown, take the Métro to Guy, then transfer to bus No 65.

For those seeking a quiet night, it is also possible to stay here (see Places to Stay for details).

Cathedral of Montreal

The Cathedral of Montreal or Marie-Reine-du-Monde (Mary, Queen of the World), is a smaller version of, and is modelled on, St Peter's Basilica in the Vatican. The cathedral was built between 1870 and 1894. It's situated on Boulevard René Lévesque just off

Dorchester Square near the Queen Elizabeth Hotel. Note the unusual canopy over the altar.

St James United Church

This church, at 463 Rue Sainte Catherine Ouest, is unusual in that the portals open onto the street but have stores and offices built in beside them. The church is actually behind the street.

Olympic Park

Ask any Montrealer and you'll find that the scandal, indignation and tales of corruption and government incompetence surrounding the buildings of the Olympic Sports Complex are as great as the structures themselves. Nevertheless, the complex (☎ 252-8687), created at enormous cost for the 1976 Olympic Games, is magnificent.

The showpiece is the multipurpose **Olympic Stadium** able to hold 80,000 spectators and often referred to as the 'Big O'. It certainly is a grand structure, even if it did take until 1990 to get it finished. The infamous retractable roof eventually arrived from Paris, France in late 1981 (five years after the Games) and then sat for several years before the money was found to hoist it into place. It then took yet more time to get it operating. In 1991, part of the roof support system collapsed sending chunks of concrete weighing 55 tonnes tumbling to the ground. I'm not making this up! Luckily no one was killed but they had to shut it down again and thoroughly safety check the place. The Kevlar it is made with has ripped many times resulting in expensive repairs and now it remains permanently shut. Talk continues about replacing it or again trying to make it retractable.

In summer, major league professional baseball and football is played in the stadium and it is also used for concerts and trade shows. All other visitors must take the tour.

A cable car runs up the arching **Montreal Tower** which overhangs the stadium to a glassed-in observation deck which provides outstanding views of the city and beyond for a distance of 80 km. A ticket to the top is

QUEBEC

$7.25. Combination tickets which include the tour and a laser show are available.

The **Sports Centre**, essentially a swimming complex, is also impressive with six pools including a 20-metre-deep scuba pool. Public swimming costs $3.50 at this huge, clean facility. The Métro stop for the pool is Viau. You are not going to believe this but, in 1993, part of the floor of one of the pools fell in, causing a few moments of panic during a therapy session with elderly non-swimmers, and forcing its temporary closure.

Also in the complex is **Olympic Village**, the housing sector with apartments and restaurants.

The **Tourist Hall** at the cable car boarding station is a three-storey information centre with ticket office, restaurant and souvenir shop. Guided tours of the site in French and English (☎ 252-TOUR) leave here every day. The fee of $5.25 chisels away at the local citizens' debt. It's worth it for those with a special interest in either architecture or sport.

On the grounds is the Biodome, another boldly designed stadium, originally built for cycling and later used for roller-skating.

The entire site is in Parc Maisonneuve on the extreme eastern side of the city, off Rue Sherbrooke on the corner of Boulevard Pie IX. The Métro stop is Viau (pronounced 'vee o'). A free shuttle bus runs from the Olympic site at the Biodome over to the Botanical Gardens.

Biodome

Housed in the former Velodrome cycling stadium at the Olympic Complex, the Biodome (☎ 868-3000), 4777 Avenue Pierre de Coubertin, is a captivating environmental museum which re-creates four distinct ecosystems and houses 4000 animals and 5000 plants. Under one roof visitors can enjoy, learn about and appreciate the necessity of the rainforest, the polar regions, the Laurentian Shield woodlands and the Gulf of St Lawrence ocean environment.

The rainforest section is particularly encompassing, with monkeys in huge live trees and alligators in rivers. Other highlights include the underwater views of riverscapes

where ducks may be seen competing with fish for food, the ocean microcosm and colourful tidal pools. The penguins are a natural favourite, too.

Admission is $9.50 for adults, $7 for seniors and $4.75 for children. Kids under age six are free. A good visit takes two hours. A two-day combination ticket is available for $13.50 which includes the Biodome, Botanical Gardens and Insectarium.

It is a popular attraction, far exceeding attendance expectations. Plan to go on a weekday, if possible, and avoid midday. You can bring your own lunch, there are picnic tables near the cafeteria. The gift/bookshop is quite tempting – beware.

A free bus shuttle runs between here, the Botanical Gardens and the Insectarium.

Botanical Gardens

The 81-hectare gardens (☎ 872-1400) are the third largest in the world after those in London and Berlin. Some 26,000 types of plants are grown in 30 garden settings and various climate-controlled greenhouses. The collection of 700 orchid species is particularly impressive, as are the Japanese Garden and bonsai and Chinese *penjing* with plants up to 100 years old. The Ming Dynasty style Chinese Garden is also a must. Other displays change with the seasons and there are often special temporary exhibits.

The gardens are open every day from 9 am to 6 pm with extended hours in summer to 8 pm. In summer a ticket is $7 and includes the gardens, the greenhouses and the Insectarium. In the low season prices drop a couple of dollars. Also see the combination tickets available listed under the Biodome. The gardens are next to the Olympic Buildings in Parc Maisonneuve. The Métro stop is Pie IX. A shuttle bus runs to the Olympic Park.

Insectarium

Whether you love or hate the creepy crawlies, this collection (☎ 872-8753) of bugs from around the world will fascinate you. The Insectarium is in the east end of the city at 4101 Rue Sherbrooke Est; take the Métro to Pie IX. It's open daily from 9 am to 8 pm in summer, winter opening hours are slightly shorter. Admission is $7 but check out the combination tickets available with the Botanical Gardens and the Biodome.

Just for Laughs Museum

The open, closed, re-opened international museum of humour (☎ 845-4000), with its changes and financial problems has become, in itself, a bit of a joke. Currently, it seems to be trying different routines to get a laugh, or at least an audience. Exhibits include videos of comics, animation clips and various changing interactive displays. There are also live performances including Friday night with comedians and other special shows. It's at 2111 Boulevard Saint Laurent in a reconverted factory space, admission is $10.

McGill University

On the corner of Rue University and Rue Sherbrooke, this is one of Canada's most prestigious universities. The campus is rather nice to stroll around, since it sits at the foot of the mountain. The **Redpath Museum** (☎ 398-4086) houses McGill's natural history collection, which includes animals, birds, fossils and rocks. It's free and open every day except Friday and Saturday. On Sunday, it's only open in the afternoon.

Dow Planetarium

The planetarium (☎ 872-4530) is at 1000 Rue Saint Jacques Ouest near Windsor Station. It offers laser shows as well as regular star and solar-system programmes; the shows are usually good and interesting. Admission costs $5.50, laser shows $7.

Habitat 67

At Cité du Havre, a jutting piece of land between Old Montreal and Île Sainte Hélène connected with the island by the Pont de la Concorde, is a residential complex known as Habitat 67. It was constructed for the World's Fair as an example of a futuristic, more livable apartment block. It has aged well, is still appealing with its block modular look, and remains a popular, if not cheap, place to live.

Parc des Îles (The Islands Park)

South of the city in the St Lawrence River largely in the area between the Jacques Cartier and the Victoria bridges are Sainte Hélène and Notre Dame islands (☎ 872-4537). They were the site of the immensely successful 1967 World's Fair, Man & His World. For the event Île Sainte Hélène was considerably enlarged and Île Notre Dame was completely created with landfill. They are now primarily parkland though a couple of vestiges remain of the fair and there are a number of other attractions of note.

There are a couple of different ways to get to the islands. If you're driving, two bridges lead to Île Sainte Hélène: the Pont Jacques Cartier and Pont de la Concorde. Definitely consider taking the Métro to the Île Sainte Hélène stop instead as they hit you pretty hard for parking. From the Métro stop, where there is an information desk, there are buses (use a transfer) to both island's attractions but you may find walking just as fast. Another possibility is to take the water shuttle (☎ 281-8000) across the river from the Old Port at Quai Jacques Cartier. The shuttle takes pedestrians and bikes for $2.75.

Île Sainte Hélène At the extreme northern end of Île Sainte Hélène is **La Ronde**, the largest amusement park in the province with restaurants and bars as well as an assortment of games and 30-some rides. 'The Monster', a roller coaster, is ranked as one of the world's best – hold on to your stomach. The gentle mini-rail offers good views of the river and city. A variety of concerts and shows are held through the summer often including circus performances and excellent firework displays. A schedule is available.

Full admission to La Ronde including all the rides is $20. There is also a ticket to the grounds and shows at half the price which offers limited rides (not the scary ones).

During the last two weeks of May, La Ronde is open only on weekends, from 11 am to 11 pm. Through the summer it's open daily from 11 am to midnight but stays open an hour later on the weekends.

There are also some portions of an old fort

near La Ronde. Inside the remaining stone ramparts is the **David M Stewart Museum** (☎ 861-6701) with artefacts and tools from Canada's past. Demonstrations are given by uniformed soldiers and others in period dress, and military parades are held daily in summer by the museum. Admission is $5.

Walkways wind around the island past gardens and among the old pavilions from the world's fair. One of them, the American Buckminster Fuller dome is now the **Biosphere** (☎ 283-5000). This is an interpretation centre on the Great Lakes-St Lawrence River ecosystem. It is designed to increase awareness about water and the need for its conservation. Using a range of exhibits and displays, topic's include the world's water and pollution. It's open 10 am to 5 pm except closed Monday and admission is $6.50.

Île Notre Dame This island which is largely parkland, has some attractions of its own. First among them is the **Casino de Montréal** (☎ 392-2746) which opened in 1993 and was so popular (and earning so much money) so quickly that expansion occurred almost instantly. It is open daily from 9 to 5 am and is busy pretty well continually. Weekend nights in particular can be hectic and long queues to get in are not uncommon. Further expansion completed in mid 1996 should alleviate these problems. There is now a European-style section and a glitzier US-style area. Entry is free and non-alcoholic drinks are available at no charge. Liquor is served at bar prices. There is also an upmarket restaurant and a couple of bars. Dress during the day is casual but no jeans, sweat pants, shorts etc. After dinner, it's more formal with most people looking pretty smart but you needn't rent a gown or tux. Driving is not a great idea as the free parking fills up quickly. Instead, take the Métro to Île Sainte Hélène and from there catch the bus, free with a transfer, or walk.

Also popular is the **artificial sandy beach** (☎ 872-6093) with room for 5000 people. The water is filtered and treated with chemicals. There are picnic facilities and snack bars at the site. It's open every day from 24

June to Labour Day from 10 am to 7 pm depending on the weather. Call to check if it's open – their idea of a bad day and hence not opening may not be the same as yours. A ticket is $6, less for children. To get there take the Métro to Île Sainte Hélène and from there a bus runs to the beach.

Also on Île Notre Dame is the **Outdoor & Nautical Centre** based around the former Olympic rowing basin. In summer you can rent windsurfers and paddle boats but perhaps it's more fun in winter when the area becomes a huge skating rink. There are lockers and a snack bar and you can rent skates – a lot of fun. There is also some cross-country (nordic) skiing; equipment can also be rented. The centre is open until 9 pm daily.

Much of the surrounding grounds are parkland which you can stroll around for free. At the **Gilles Villeneuve race track** (named after a Quebec racing-car driver) the occasional Formula 1 Grand Prix race is held.

Markets

There are four fairly central markets. At **Atwater Market**, south on Avenue Atwater, below Rue Sainte Catherine at the Lachine Canal, maple syrup is available, often from farmers who produce it. They can answer any questions about this traditional Quebec treat.

The **Marché de Maisonneuve** is on the corner of Rue Ontario and Avenue Létourneaux in the east end of the city.

More ethnically varied is the happening **Jean Talon Market** just south of Rue Jean Talon between Rue Henri Julien and Avenue Casgrain north of The Plateau in the middle of an Italian district. The original **Old Montreal farmer's market** is once-again operating in the restored Bonsecours Market Building at 350 Rue Saint Paul Est. All are open daily but Saturday is by far the best day to attend.

Montreal Stock Exchange

Tours are offered at this market of a different sort for $5 weekdays year round. The exchange is on the 4th floor at 800 Place Victoria. Ring ☎ 871-2424 for details, times and reservations.

Lachine

Out in Lachine, a suburb south-west of Montreal, is a national historic site called the **Fur Trade in Lachine** (☎ 637-7433). It's at 1255 Boulevard Saint Joseph on the corner of 12th Avenue along the pleasant waterfront. The museum tells the story of the fur trade in Canada, which was so critical to the development of the country. It's not a well known site and is about 10 km from the downtown area but makes a fine side trip and is accessible along a cycling route from Old Montreal. You can also take the Métro to Lionel Groulx and then bus No 191. Admission is free. Nearby, on Boulevard Saint Joseph but down near 7th Avenue, free walking tours are given along the Lachine Canal which was built for trade purposes. The tours run from Wednesday to Sunday only.

Kahnawake Indian Reserve

South of Lachine where the Mercier Bridge meets the south shore is the Kahnawake (pronounced 'con-a-wok-ee') Indian Reserve (☎ 632-7500) where some 5000 Mohawks live. This suburb-like reserve, about 18 km from central Montreal, was the location of a major confrontation which lasted for months between the Mohawks and the Quebec and federal governments through the summer of 1990 which made headlines internationally. The residents' support of the Mohawks in Oka over their land dispute exploded into a symbolic stand against the continuing mistreatment of Native Indians across the country.

There isn't much for visitors to see but in town is the **Saint Francis Xavier Church** with a small museum. It's free and is open daily from 10 am to noon and from 1 to 5 pm. Sunday mass at 11 am is sung in Mohawk. Some **Mission buildings** from the early 1700s can be seen and there is a gift shop or two with crafts.

Also on the site is a **Cultural Centre** with an extensive library relating to the Six Nations of the Iroquois Confederacy as well as exhibits dealing principally with this reserve and its history.

Cheap cigarettes and alcohol may also be purchased on the reserve. Canada's national game, lacrosse, is still popular here and you may see some boys playing on the sports fields around town.

Cosmodome (Space Sciences Centre)

This new interactive museum (☎ 978-3600) concentrates on space and new technologies. Multi-media exhibits focus on the solar system, satellite communications, teledetection, space travel and related subjects.

The centre is about a 20-minute drive and can be reached by public transportation using the metro and a connecting bus. It's at 2150 Autoroute des Laurentides in Laval, north of Montreal island.

Admission is $9.50, less for children and seniors. From 24 June to Labour Day, it is open daily 10 am to 6 pm but closed Monday the rest of the year. The centre also runs well-regarded two, three and five-day space camps, primarily aimed at youth who go through a sort of mini-NASA training.

St Lawrence Seaway

The seaway system of locks, canals and dams, opened in 1959, along the St Lawrence River enables ocean-going vessels to sail 3200 km inland via the Great Lakes. Across Victoria Bridge from the city is an observation tower over the first locks of the system, the Saint Lambert Locks, where ships are raised/lowered five metres.

There are explanatory displays. The observation area is open from April to December between 9 am and 9.30 pm, and it is free. In January, February and March the locks are closed – they're frozen like the river itself, until the spring thaw.

Canadian Railway Museum

This museum (☎ 632-2410) is at 122A Rue Saint Pierre in Saint Constant, a district on the south shore near Châteauguay. The museum, with Canada's largest collection, has examples of early locomotives, steam engines and passenger cars.

Admission is $4.50 and it's open daily from May to September and weekends to mid-October. To get there, take Champlain Bridge from town to Hwy 15, then Hwy 137 at the Châteauguay cut-off to Hwy 209.

Activities

Montreal is continuing to improve as a biking city. A map of routes and trails should be available at tourist offices. One route leads from the edge of Old Montreal, southwest all the way to Lachine along the old canal. Parks Canada (☎ 283-6054) runs guided historical trips along this bike path in summer from Thursday to Sunday.

At the Parc de Récréation des Îles-de-Boucherville there are 22 km of trails around the islands connected by bridges. The main entrance on Île Sainte Marguerite is connected by road to Montreal. A ferry (☎ 873-2843) connects Quai de Boucherville with Île Grosbois Thursday to Sunday, from 10 am to 4 pm for $3. Most of the trails offer good views of the city. Bikes can be rented at the park but the rental depot is not near the ferry terminal which means you pretty well have to take your own bike or have a car. Also note that the ferry does not run on Tuesday or Thursday.

The light-hearted, good-time Tour des Îles on the first weekend in June is a major biking event which now attracts about 50,000. Some riders wear wacky costumes in this long ride around the city. The organisers also set up Le Grand Tour, a longer ride around portions of the province. The tourist office will have details.

There is year-round indoor ice skating at l'Amphitheatre Bell (☎ 395-0555) at 1000 Rue de La Gauchetière (Bonaventure Metro stop). Admission is $5 and skates can be rented.

See under Olympic Park for swimming and Mont Royal for winter and summer activities.

Organised Tours

Sightseeing Tours Gray Line (☎ 934-1222), at the tourist office on Square Dorchester, operates 11 sightseeing tours. The basic city orientation tour takes 1½

hours, costs $17 and takes in some of the principal sights and the Mount Royal lookout. There are also tours aboard pseudo trolley buses. The deluxe bus trip is better value and costs $35 which includes admission into some of the attractions such as the Biodome. An eight-hour all-day trip is $43. Other bus trips are to the Laurentian Mountains north of Montreal and an evening tour.

Another company is Royal Tours (☎ 871-4733; formerly Murray Hill, sometimes still called that) also at 1001 Rue du Square Dorchester in the Infotouriste centre. They offer a lot of flexibility and you can choose from a number of options to customise the tour. On the summer Carousel tour, you can hop on and off the bus at different sights and take advantage of reduced admissions to some attractions. Like Gray Line, this is a reputable company.

The Amphi Tour (☎ 849-5181) offers a surprise. A bus tours the Old Port area for half an hour and then drives into the river! It then provides a port-area cruise for another half an hour. It operates daily from May to the end of October. The tour departs from Quai King Edward and reservations are essential.

Jet-Boat Tours A couple of companies offer bouncing, soaking boat trips through the nearby Lachine Rapids. Lachine Rapids Tours (☎ 284-9607), at 105 Esplanade de la Commune Ouest, have 90-minute trips leaving from Old Montreal, costing $48. Smaller and faster speed boat trips are also available.

Cruises Several companies offer straight boat trips. Montreal Harbour Cruises Ltd (☎ 842-3871) has river tours from Quai Victoria also called the Clock Tower Pier (Quai de l'Horloge), the pier at the foot of Rue Berri in Old Montreal. The basic trip around the port, Saint Helen's Island and the Boucherville Islands is $20. Longer sunset trips and later weekend night cruises with disco-dancing and drinks are other options. Another choice is their cruise aboard the *New Orleans*, a Mississippi-style paddlewheeler.

Tours aboard the comfortable *Le Bateau Mouche* (☎ 849-9952), a more deluxe, Parisian type vessel have been recommended. These tours depart Quai Jacques Cartier for the 90-minute narrated cruises. Call for details and reservations. Prices are comparable to the others.

Navimex (☎ 848-9136), cruise up to Quebec City.

Festivals

Some of the major festivals held in Montreal are:

January
  Fête des Neiges – This is a winter festival held at the end of January and based around the Old Port and Parc des Îles.
May-June
  International Benson & Hedges Fireworks – Held from between the end of May into July on weekends, this fireworks competition lights up the skies.
  Montreal Jazz Festival – This is held at the end of June and the beginning of July and is a major event with both internationally-known and local players. Indoors and out, concerts are held at various places around town, and many shows are free. There's usually quite a few performances around the Saint Denis area. Accommodation may be tight at this time as this event is a big draw.
  Fête Nationale – Formerly known as St Jean Baptiste Day (or Johnny Baptiste to the English), this event is held each year on 24 June and includes a major parade and holiday. Originally a religious holiday then transformed into a strident Québecois political demonstration, it has become more of a feel-good, beginning-of-spring celebration with some optimistic Quebec nationalism thrown in.
July-September
  Just for Laughs Comedy Festival – The bilingual comedy festival with both free and admission-charged performances is held in July. Over half a million attend with some 200 performers featured.
  Montreal World Film Festival – This is held in mid to late August and early September with screenings at cinemas around town.

Several big cycling races are held through the summer including one around the island and one through the streets.

Places to Stay

Montreal, like Quebec City, is popular with tourists in summer, so rooms can be hard to find and cost more than during the rest of the year. The period around Christmas and New Years is also very busy.

Camping There's not too much camping close to town. As you come from the west, before you actually get on the island of Montreal, on Hwy 338 in Coteau du Lac (exit 17 from Hwy 20) is *KEA* (☎ 763-5344). It's just off the highway around Dorion, about a 45-minute drive to downtown.

A 45-minute drive west of Montreal will also get you to *Camping D'Aoust* (☎ 458-7301) on Hwy 342 in Hudson-Vaudreuil. Take exit 26 coming from Montreal, exit 22 coming from Ottawa from Hwy 40 (the Trans Canada Hwy) then it's three km down the road on the right. A tent site is $16.

South of the city there is a *KOA* (Kampground of America) (☎ 659-8626), at 130 Boulevard Monette in St Phillippe. Take exit 38 off Hwy 15. Others can be found about 20 minutes from town south on Hwy 15.

Hostels The central HI *Auberge de Montreal* (☎ 843-3317) is well established but with a new location in the red and white former hotel at 1030 Rue Mackay south of Boulevard René Lévesque. The metro stop is Lucien L'Allelier. There are 250 beds and it's air-conditioned. Rooms vary with four to 10 beds and there are some for families. Cost is $17 and breakfast is offered in the summer. It's open all year with check in from 9.30 am to 2 am. Reservations are not a bad idea at any time but are strongly recommended from June through September when three weeks notice should be given. Walking tours of the city are offered and there is some parking.

The *Hotel de Paris and Auberge* (☎ 522-6861, 1-800-567-7217), listed with Backpackers, is conveniently situated at 901 Rue Sherbrooke Est. Primarily a fine, small hotel in a marvellous old turreted mansion, there is a newly renovated hostel section in the basement with beds at $14 (summer rate) including cooking and laundry facilities. There is also a cafe with *terrasse* on the premises. Forty other hostel beds and self-contained apartment rooms are available across the street in a second property.

At 1250 Rue Sherbrooke Est is *Le Gite du Parc Lafontaine* (☎ 522-3910), a hostel in a converted Victorian house facing the park where there are frequent free shows. The location is very convenient with the main bus station about a 10-minute walk away and Rue Saint Denis very close. Dorms are $19, singles/doubles $20.50 per person and there are family rooms. Weekly rates are offered. Sheets and blankets are included as is a continental breakfast. They have kitchen and laundry facilities and bicycles can be rented. It's open from 1 June to early September and is closed from 11 am to 3 pm.

Auberge Chez Jean (☎ 843-8279), affiliated with Backpackers, runs a place halfway between a B&B and a hostel out of a private apartment home. The cost is $14 a night including breakfast. Depending on demand, visitors may have a room to themselves or may be sharing. It is open from mid-June to mid-November. The address is 4136 Rue Henri Julien, north of Avenue Duluth, south of Rachel in the Plateau Mont Royal. Look for 'Jean' on the mailbox, it's the only sign. He is the owner and speaks quite good English.

See also the good, cheap *Hebergement l'Abri du Voyageur* listed in the following Small Hotels section.

The *YMCA* (☎ 849-8393) is at 1450 Rue Stanley. It's central too, and huge, with 350 beds. Singles/doubles are from $35/54 and they take both sexes. The cheap cafeteria is open from 7 am to 7 pm weekdays, 8 am to 2 pm weekends.

The *YWCA* (☎ 866-9941), for women only, is at 1355 Boulevard René Lévesque Ouest. Singles/doubles cost from $35/50 without bath or air-con and there is a kitchen on every floor. Good weekly rates are available. There is also a small restaurant and a pool which guests can use. On the Métro get off at the Peel stop.

Open all year and good value is the *Collège Francais* (☎ 495-2581 ext 196), also called Vacances Canada 4 Saisons, at 5155 Rue de Gaspé with a range of cheap beds. Dorms go for as little as $11.50. There are good-value rooms with four beds and a toilet, shower and sink at $12.50 per person or double rooms go for $16.50 per person. Inexpensive breakfasts are offered at a nearby restaurant or there is a cafeteria. Parking is available too. The college is near the corner of Avenue Laurier and Rue Saint Denis, north-east of downtown. The Métro stop is Laurier, 300 metres east of Rue de Gaspé. Although there are hundreds of beds it's busy in the summer months so call ahead to check availability.

The college also has another residence out of the centre in Longueuil (pronounced 'long guy') and perhaps of more interest, one in the Eastern Townships, where otherwise accommodation can be a little pricey.

McGill University, on the corner of Rue Sherbrooke and Rue University, opens its residences from 15 May to 15 August. The accommodation office (☎ 398-6367) is at 3935 Rue University. Singles (which is all there is) cost $37, for students $28. There are cafeterias and laundry rooms and some residences include breakfast but are more expensive. Rates go down with stays of more than one night and the weekly rates are good.

The residences of the *Loyola Campus* (☎ 848-4756) of Concordia University, at 7141 Rue Sherbrooke Ouest, is even cheaper. This campus is in Montreal Ouest. Buses run along Rue Sherbrooke from the downtown area. The student rate is $19 per person, single or double. Nonstudents pay $26/40 for singles/doubles.

The French *Université de Montréal* (☎ 343-6531), 2350 Rue Édouard-Monpetit north of the downtown area, offers singles/doubles at $31/39 for nonstudents or $21/30 for students with good weekly rates available.

Pretty inexpensive rooms are also available at *St Joseph's Oratory* (☎ 733-8211). Singles/doubles cost $25/40. Go to Pavilion Jean 23rd at 4300 Chemin Queen Mary.

Tourist Homes & Small Hotels Most standard hotels in the city are costly. The tourist homes and independent hotels are the alternative and there is a good, central assortment. Most of them are in the eastern portion of the downtown area. Nearly all are in older houses and buildings with 10 to 20 rooms. Quality ranges from the plain and functional to old-world-charm comfortable. Price is the best indicator of quality but sometimes just a few dollars can make quite a difference. Practically all the smaller ones have a variety of rooms with price differences depending on what facilities the room has – whether it has a sink or toilet or a full bathroom. Air-con adds a few dollars too. Prices are highest from June to October.

My first choice of location would be the convenient Saint Denis-bus station area where there are quite a few places offering good value.

Castel Saint Denis (☎ 842-9719) is at 2099 Rue Saint Denis, up the hill just south of Rue Sherbrooke. It's been renovated and redecorated a couple of times and is good value. It's not fancy but it's clean and convenient. Singles/doubles range from $40/45 without bath to $40/55 with bath before taxes.

At 1254 Rue Saint Denis in the cafe district, there's the larger more modern *Hôtel Saint Denis* (☎ 849-4526), with a range of 60 clean rooms starting at $49 double in the summer. Prices drop about $10 in the off-season. It's got air-conditioning and a restaurant.

Further south on Rue Saint Denis between Sherbrooke and Old Montreal, *Hôtel Américain* (☎ 849-0616), a small hotel at 1042 Rue Saint Denis, is good and European in style. It has 20 rooms at singles from $39 to $48 and doubles from $40 to $69. The rooms on the top floor are like those in tryst scenes in French movies but, as the manager has mentioned, there is nothing wrong with the other rooms. Montreal's gaytown is nearby and the hotel has become popular with out-of-towners who visit that part of the city, but straights also find the location convenient.

Cheaper rooms can be found at such places as the *Hôtel de la Couronne* (☎ 845-0901) across the street at No 1029.

East of Rue Saint Denis is *Le Breton* (☎ 524-7273), in an excellent location on a pleasant street. It's at 1609 Rue Saint Hubert, beside the bus station. Singles or doubles go from $42 to $60 depending on size and amenities. Some rooms come with TV, shower or bath. There are many other small hotels nearby including plenty of cheap tourist rooms.

Further south, at 1001 Rue Saint Hubert on the corner of Avenue Viger, is the inexpensive but good *Hôtel Viger Centre Ville* (☎ 845-6058). They have a wide variety of rooms from $45/48 singles/doubles. The least expensive of the 22 rooms come with sink, colour TV and fan. A continental breakfast is included and Old Montreal is within walking distance.

West of Rue Saint Denis there are places to stay on Rue Ontario. At No 307, *Hôtel Villard* (☎ 845-9730) has good rooms with good prices for singles at $35/40 and doubles $45/55.

On Rue Sherbrooke Est at Avenue Hôtel de Ville, between Boulevard Saint Laurent and Rue Saint Denis, are three tourist homes next door to each other, all in old houses. The *Hôtel Manoir Sherbrooke* at No 157 and the *Armor Tourist Lodge* (☎ 285-0140) are run by the same people. The latter is a large place, lined with natural wood inside. Both are busy places with prices changing with the season and varying with the features. In summer, singles/doubles without bath are $50/65 with continental breakfast included. *Hôtel Pierre* (☎ 288-8519) is at No 169. *Hotel de Paris* (☎ 522-6861) at 901 Sherbrooke Est has a wide range of rooms from budget at $50/55 in season to suites with kitchens at $95. Additional people cost $5 and rooms can accommodate six people. In another building across the street apartments are rented by the week.

At 258-264 Rue Sherbrooke Ouest, west of Rue Jeanne Mance, is the recently expanded wood and stone *Maison Casa Bella* (☎ 849-2777). The price range at this central hotel is quite wide with singles from $50 to $65, doubles from $50 to $80 but these prices include breakfast and parking.

There are also places scattered about the central downtown area. Several can be found along Rue Sainte Catherine near Boulevard Saint Laurent, where the men, painted ladies and some in-betweens appear at about 6 pm.

At 9 Rue Sainte Catherine Ouest is the *Hebergement l'Abri du Voyageur* (☎ 849-2922) a fine, low-budget place popular with international travellers. The rooms are simple but clean and there is a breakfast room with complimentary coffee and muffins. Rates are $21/32 for singles/doubles and $10 for additional people.

Villa de France (☎ 849-5043) at 57 Rue Sainte Catherine Est, is also a well-kept, friendly place which is quite OK if you're really on a budget. Without a bath, singles/doubles cost $35, with bath $45. Other places nearby tend to be a little dubious.

Going west, the *Manoir Ambrose* (☎ 288-6992), at 3422 Rue Stanley, is nicer and in a better location but it costs more, of course, with singles from $35 all the way up to $75, and doubles from $55 to $75. Compared to the sterile international hotels, it's still a bargain and has 22 rooms.

Next door on Rue Mackay south of Boulevard René Lévesque, the *Aux Berges* (☎ 938-9393) at 1070 Rue Mackay has an unusual approach, limiting itself to serving gay visitors. It's central but on a quiet street, has all amenities and has just been renovated. Rooms without bath are $65/80 with continental breakfast.

B&Bs Another alternative to the high-priced hotels are the B&Bs. This form of accommodation is more established in Montreal than anywhere else in the province. There are some individually operated places and some commercial establishments offering this style of lodging but the majority, by far, are listed by agencies. If you're staying a while, it's worth asking about a weekly rate. Also inquire if the breakfast is full or continental.

B&B Downtown Network (☎ 289-9749) is an agency run by Bob & Mariko Finkelstein which has been operating successfully for years. They have checked over 50 private homes for quality and hospitality beyond minimum requirements. Hosts range from students to lawyers, the places from mansions with fireplaces in the bedrooms, to Victorian homes, to apartments filled with antiques. Rates are quite reasonable at $30 to $40 for singles, $40 to $55 for doubles and triples are available too. For information and reservations, call or write to 3458 Laval Avenue, Montreal, H2X 3C8. There is now a toll-free number ☎ 1-800-267-5180 and Japanese is spoken.

B&B à Montreal (☎ 738-9410) run by Marion Kahn, is a similar organisation with some higher-priced homes as well, which offer something special. She also has some places in Quebec City which can be booked here.

A third organisation is *Montreal Oasis* (☎ 935-2312) run by Swedish Lena Blondel out of her own B&B place at 3000 Chemin de Breslay (off Avenue Atwater just north of Rue Sherbrooke). Almost all of her participant homes are in older houses in the central core and they pride themselves on the quality of their breakfasts. Ask about the places on quiet and particularly attractive Rue Souvenir, which is perfectly located near Rue Sainte Catherine, or about the historic home in Old Montreal. Prices range from $40 to $70 a single, $50 to $90 a double and, again, triples are available. Most of the places welcome children.

Bienvenue B&B (☎ 844-5897, 1-800-227-5897) is a smaller, agency which specialises in turn-of-the-century places around the interesting French area of Rue Saint Denis and Carré Saint Louis. Call or write to 3950 Avenue Laval, Montreal H2W 2J2. Avenue Laval is one block west of Rue Saint Denis and the office is a couple of blocks north of Rue Sherbrooke, a short walk from the Sherbrooke Métro stop. The owners, Carole Sirois and Allard Coté, operate a B&B themselves at the above address which is a great location very close to the Prince Arthur restaurant district. There are several other organisations – the tourist office will have a complete list. Prices are generally quite moderate.

Hotels & Efficiencies If you really like a more conventional, modern hotel but not the prices accompanying the usual downtown luxury choices there are a few possibilities. Also many hotels have lower weekend rates. Try the *Hotel Travelodge* (☎ 874-9090), central at 50 Boulevard René Lévesque near Boulevard Saint Laurent. Rooms are in the $70 range.

Comfort Suites (☎ 878-2711), at 1214 Rue Crescent, is $119 for two people weekdays or $75 on weekends. Other middle-priced hotels include the *Hôtel Montréal Crescent* (☎ 938-9797), at 1366 Boulevard René Lévesque, with prices from $75 to $90.

The central *Le Riche Bourg* (☎ 935-9224), at 2170 Avenue Lincoln, has good-value studio, one and two-bedroom suites with kitchen. A small studio single or double is $94 or $79 on weekends. The hotel is very well equipped with pool and roof-top balcony and a restaurant and grocery store. Weekly rates are available.

The following hotels are in the 'expensive' category. Despite the rather hefty prices, geared mainly to the business traveller, you will be charged outrageously for parking, telephone calls, drinks in the room fridge, and every other time you turn around. Some of the major hotels do have pretty good lower-priced weekend specials which may appeal to some for a splurge; prices are generally lower in summer when there is less commercial traffic.

Le Château Champlain (☎ 878-9000), Place du Canada, has rooms from $140 to $240. This hotel is right across the street from the Windsor train station. Ask for a room facing Square Dorchester and the view will be quite good. The top-floor bar also has windows overlooking the city. There's a restaurant and Vegas-style revues are often presented.

Nearby is the *Bonaventure Hilton* (☎ 878-2332), Place Bonaventure, with rooms from $135 to $375.

The *Ritz Carlton Kempinski* (☎ 842-4212), 1228 Rue Sherbrooke Ouest, with rooms from $180 to $340, has long been a hotel of distinction and reputation. The penthouse suite here is the most expensive place to stay in Canada (and it's probably not too shabby either). This seems to be the hotel of choice for business, entertainment and, if it's not an oxymoron, political superstars.

Motels There are two main motel districts in Montreal with others scattered here and there. All charge less in the low season (ie not in summer) but rates listed here are summer ones. The area closest to town is conveniently situated along Rue Saint Jacques. It's west of the downtown area, south and parallel to Rue Sherbrooke. Look around where Rue Cavendish runs into Rue Saint Jacques from Rue Sherbrooke. This area is about a 10-minute drive from the centre. Coming from the west (from places like Dorval Airport), Hwys 2 and 20 flow into Rue Saint Jacques.

The basic *Colibri* (☎ 486-1167), at 6960 Rue Saint Jacques Ouest, charges singles/doubles $39/45. It's the grey place behind Harvey's hamburger restaurant.

The *Motel Sunrise* (☎ 484-0048), at 6120 Rue Saint Jacques Ouest, just west of Boulevard Decarie, is good; singles/doubles cost $50/60.

The large, popular *Ideal Motel* (☎ 488-9561) at No 6951 charges $80 to $125 single or double.

Nearby at No 7455, the *Motel Raphaël* (☎ 485-3344), has been around forever and is beginning to show some wear with rooms at $45 for doubles and a swimming pool and restaurant.

The second district for motels is on Boulevard Tashereau on the south shore, across the river on the mainland. The street, also known as Hwy 134 and Hwy 132, stretches out of the city in both directions. Many of the motels are at the bridges – check at the Jacques Cartier (opposite Old Montreal) and Champlain in the west end. Victoria Bridge is between these two.

Located at 1277 Boulevard Tashereau is

La *Parisienne* (☎ 674-6291) with all the flags out front. Singles/doubles cost $55.

The *Falcon Motel* (☎ 676-0215) is at 6225 Boulevard Tashereau, with singles/doubles $35/45 in the deteriorated older section, more in the better, new section. There are several other places in the blocks around No 7000.

Back in town there are a few places in the East end. *Le Paysan* (☎ 640-1415), at 12400 Rue Sherbrooke Est, near Olympic Park charges single/double $35/56 weekdays and $45/64 weekends. *Le Marquis* (☎ 256-1621), at No 6720 Rue Sherbrooke Est is $60/80 and there are others in the area.

The *Motel Métro* (☎ 382-9780), at 9925 Rue Lajeunesse north of downtown, is a good bargain with standard singles/doubles for $45. More deluxe rooms with whirlpools are available. From the Metropolitan Hwy east take exit 73 (Rue Saint Hubert), go to Sauvé and then you'll see Rue Lajeunesse. Or get off at the Sauvé Métro station.

Places to Eat

The French have long been responsible for Montreal's excellent restaurant reputation, which various immigrant groups have only added to over the years. Many places have lunch specials – always the best bargains – and at dinner, a table d'hôte, a fixed-price complete dinner.

Many Montreal restaurants, generally in the lower and middle-price brackets, have a 'bring your own' wine policy. If you want to take advantage of this great idea and bring your own wine for a meal, you can get it in a *dépanneur* (convenience store) if there is no government outlet around or it's past closing time. In Quebec you can pick up a bottle of French wine, bottled in the province, for $7 to $9 at the liquor outlets, or from grocery stores where the price goes up a dollar or slightly more.

Many restaurants, particularly the better ones, don't start to get busy until around 8 pm and will stay that way for a couple of hours. If you're an early eater in this city, you may have the place to yourself.

A phenomenon to keep an eye, ear or nose out for are the so-called tam-tams. Translated directly, a tam-tam is a fuss, a bally hoo, or a ruckus. Beginning a few years ago, these unexpected, semi-spontaneous large outdoor parties feature some food stalls, craft stalls, live music, and illegal drinking and smoking. One regular location to check out is Parc Mont Royal (around the Georges Etienne Cartier monument) opposite Parc Jeanne Mance at Avenue Parc and Avenue Duluth, usually on a Sunday in the summer. The city authorities seem dead set against them (and all sidewalk food sellers) and make attempts to shut them down whenever found. However, many people find these bashes a lot of fun and vendors are determined to continue.

Central Area (Downtown) On the corner of Boulevard de Maisonneuve and Rue Metcalfe, *Ben's* is an institution. Montreal is known far and wide for its smoked meat and the Ben's name is familiar across the country. It's an informal deli, full of office workers at lunch time. Sandwiches are around $4, or $7 with French fries, pickle and coffee.

The *Bar B Barn*, at 1201 Rue Guy, is too small – it's usually packed, with a queue out the front – but they serve the best and biggest spareribs you've ever had. It's a comfortable, attractive place as well. The only other thing on the menu is chicken. This place is good value with meals costing from $11 to $16 and there's parking around the back.

Rue de la Montagne and Rue Crescent offer a range of places. At 2170 Rue de la Montagne *Katsura* is a popular Japanese place which is quite reasonably priced at lunch but more pricey for the evening meal.

Throughout Quebec, there was a long tradition of 'men only' drinking establishments known as taverns. These were generally small, grubby, congenial places offering cheap beer and good inexpensive meals. These have now passed into lore having become reincarnated as larger, brighter, cleaner establishments often known as brasseries and open to all. The central area contains several that are busy at noon weekdays with office and retail workers. One to try is the old, wood-panelled *McLean's Pub* at 1210 Rue Peel with meals ranging from $5.50 and up.

At 1459 Rue Metcalfe up from Rue Sainte Catherine is the well-known, long-established *Joe's* steak house. Good steak dinners range from $10 to $17; the meal includes a baked potato or French fries and an excellent all-you-can-eat salad bar. You can have just the salad bar to catch up on some greens for $7. All meals though are good value especially the filet mignon special offered Sunday to Tuesday.

Dunn's, at 892 Rue Sainte Catherine Ouest near Rue Peel, is a deli open (and usually pretty busy) 24 hours a day. It's good for a late night snack or the very cheap early morning breakfast, and the cheesecake is fabulous.

There are several East Indian restaurants in this central area. At 1241 Rue Guy is the good but expensive *Woodlands Azteca*. The South Indian vegetarian dishes are the best priced. The masala dosa, a crêpe filled with potatoes, onions and spices for $5, is good.

Nearby the *Phaya Tai*, at 1235 Rue Guy, is a fancier place offering tasty Thai food. Vegetarian main dishes are $6, seafood and meat dishes range from $8 to $12. The cosy, casual *Maison de Cari* (Curry House) over at 1433 Rue Bishop has dinner for three for a little over $40.

Very pricey, but mentioned because this is Montreal and people here like to eat, is *Chez La Mere Michel*, a city institution at 1209 Rue Guy for fine French food. It's been around so long an entire generation knows it as Mother Michael's. Dinner for two will set you back roughly $120 including wine, tax and tip. The three-course lunches are top value at $13. The service, the food and the style – everything is 1st class. Note that it is closed on Sunday and there is no lunch on Saturday.

For lingering over a coffee, there are numerous cafes in the Rue Crescent and Rue de la Montagne area. Recommended is *Egg Spectation* on the corner at 1313 Boulevard de Maisonneuve Ouest. This very attractive, comfortable, converted commercial space has excellent coffees and huge, delicious breakfasts and lunches of omelettes, crêpes or French toast for about $8. The French

toast special with fruit and English cream is hard to beat.

For a meal or making up your own, try shopping around *Le Faubourg* at 1616 Rue Sainte Catherine Ouest. This Parisian-style market/mall, which includes a bakery and liquor store, is devoted to food. Also see Markets earlier in this chapter.

Old Montreal Old Montreal is a fine place to splurge. Menus with prices are generally posted outside. The charm of many of these places is in some measure the location and restaurant decor rather than purely gastronomic excellence. Also, because this is a major tourist area, prices tend to be a little high. Nonetheless, it is such a great area that a meal out should not be resisted too strongly.

Good for lingering over a meal is the French *La Sauvagine* at 115 Rue Saint Paul near the corner of Rue Saint Vincent. Lunch prices range from $5 to $8, dinners from $13 to $18. The Dover sole is good with lobster soup and escargot from the 'prix fixe' menu. If you need help with the French menu, the waiters will explain. The only drawback is the price of the wine.

Also comfortable is *Le Père St Vincent* at 431 Rue Saint Vincent with French meals from soup to dessert priced at $18 to $25. The tables are arranged in a series of small, intimate rooms in an old stone house.

A third possibility for a special meal is the long running, *Gibby's* (☎ 282-1837), popular with Montrealers as well as visitors, at 298 Place d'Youville in a 200-year-old converted stable. The speciality is steak and atmosphere and, though a dinner is about $30 per person, reservations are suggested, at least for a weekend evening.

There are inexpensive places in this busy part of town too. At 273 Rue Saint Paul Est *L'Usine de Spaghetti Parisienne* has meals from $7 to $13, including all the bread and salad you can eat. On the corner of Rue Saint Paul and Boulevard Saint Laurent is the *Restaurant Le Coin du Vieux Montreal* with basics such as omelettes, hamburgers, and pizza. The club sandwich is recommended.

QUEBEC

At 160 Notre Dame Est, *Chez Better* has an array of sausages from mild to spicy and sauerkraut for $8, and imported beers.

The small *Café St Paul* at 143 Rue Saint Paul Ouest serves croissants and espresso and light lunches for $5. Highly recommended is the *Titanic* tucked in the basement at 445 Rue Saint Pierre well west of the busiest areas of Old Montreal. Catering to an established local clientele, the staff and atmosphere is friendly and casual but there is nothing nonchalant about the excellent food. Choose from an array of salads, creative sandwiches and pastas. A cream of vegetable soup, half baguette brie and tomato sandwich and a coffee is $7.50. It's open from 8 am to 3 pm Monday to Friday and credit cards are not taken.

Saint Denis/Latin Quarter Area The *Café Croissant de Lune* on the east side of Rue Saint Denis, downstairs at No 1765 just south of Rue Ontario, is a great place for breakfast. A café au lait and one or two of the fresh sweet buns or croissants will hold you for a few hours. At 2115 Rue Saint Denis, *Le Commensal*, open daily from 11 am to midnight, offering good self-serve vegetarian meals, salads and desserts priced by weight, is highly recommended. The food is good, the variety wide but keep an eye on how high you pile the plate or the cost will also mount up. Outlets of this restaurant can also be found at 680 Sainte Catherine Ouest and 1204 Rue McGill College.

Le Bedouin, at 1633 Rue Saint Hubert, is a small, unpretentious place with inexpensive Tunisian meals. Vegetables with couscous and mint tea or coffee is just $4 or there are complete dinners for two with North African wine.

A well-established, popular low-cost restaurant is *Da Giovanni* at 572 Rue Sainte Catherine Est. You can have a good, complete meal (from soup to dessert) featuring spaghetti for under $6. Other dishes such as fish or meat are available at not much higher prices. Arrive before 5.30 pm to avoid waiting in line. It closes at 8 pm and opens

for breakfast at 7 am. They have another outlet at 690 Sainte Catherine Ouest.

In the Village, *Nega Fulo* the bright yellow place at 1257 Rue Amherst serves up spicy Brazilian/Cajun dinners ranging from $12 to $20 and lunches at $8. Further east, at 1418 Rue Cartier just above Sainte Catherine *La Maison des Bières* is a small pub with well over 100 kinds of beer including many from Germany, Belgium and Britain as well as local brews on tap. Standard pub meals or mussels & frites are offered to a mainly business crowd. There are several pubs on Rue Ontario Est at Saint Denis.

The Main & The Plateau Just south of Rue Sainte Catherine on Boulevard Saint Laurent, known affectionately as The Main, are several of the city's best known French fries/hot dog places. Montrealers take these pedestrian items seriously and consequently they are produced with reasoned flair. The dogs are known as steamies because of the way they're cooked. If you ask for 'all dress', everyone will understand and you'll get the full Quebec treatment fully garnished with relish, mustard, onion and topped with chopped cabbage.

These give way north of Rue Sherbrooke to some of the city's newest, slickest dining establishments. Among the many is elegant *Bueno Notte* at No 3518 serving excellent Italian fare. The table d'hote is $25, the wines about $30.

Between the Latin Quarter and Plateau areas is Rue Prince Arthur a small, old residential street a portion of which has been converted into a pleasant eating enclave. The restaurant segment runs west from Place Saint Louis on Rue Saint Denis (just north of Rue Sherbrooke) to a block west of Boulevard Saint Laurent. Many small, inexpensive mostly ethnic restaurants line the 'pedestrians only' street. Greek and Vietnamese restaurants are most prominent but there are also French and Polish places among others. Most of the restaurants here have a 'bring your own' wine policy. The Greek places specialise in a Montreal favourite, brochettes, known to many as kebabs. Generally

MARK LIGHTBODY

MARK LIGHTBODY

RICHARD EVERIST

Left: The Big Nickel, Sudbury, Ontario
Right: Spanish aerocar, Niagara Falls, Ontario
Bottom: Niagara Falls from the top, Ontario

MARK LIGHTBODY

MARK LIGHTBODY

Top : Spring maple-syrup production, southern Ontario
Bottom: Brilliant autumn display, Ontario

the more traditional dishes such as moussaka are absent but vine leaves or spanokopita show up as appetisers and there is always Greek salad.

A fine Greek dinner can be had at *La Casa Grèque*, at 200 Rue Prince Arthur Est, for about $20 for two – good value.

For a bit of a splurge the *Akita*, a Japanese place at 166 Rue Prince Arthur Est, does everything well. Before 7.30 pm the set meal is good value.

Café Méliés at 3682 Boulevard Saint Laurent, in the Cinéma Parallèle, is a pleasant, comfortable spot to break the stroll with a coffee or low-priced quiche or sandwich on a grilled baguette.

Further north is a must: *Schwartz's* at 3895 Saint Laurent. It's a small, casual, friendly deli that's practically never closed. It is always packed and has absolutely the best smoked meat in town. They make it right on the premises and age it naturally without chemicals.

Avenue Duluth runs east-west off Boulevard Saint Laurent at about the No 4000 block. It's a narrow old street, once a red-light district, that has been redone as a restaurant centre. From just east of Boulevard Saint Laurent, running east to Rue Saint Denis and beyond, there are numerous good-value Greek, Italian and Asian eateries. A complete dinner at many of them is about $15.

Near Boulevard Saint Laurent at 65 Avenue Duluth Est, *L' Harmonie d'Asie* is a moderately priced Vietnamese place. At No 450 try *La Maison Grèque*, which is busy but large, with an outdoor area for good-value brochette dinners. There's a dépanneur nearby for grabbing a bottle of wine and at 430 Avenue Duluth Est, *Palais Gourmand*, a small chocolate factory for a hand-made dessert.

Rue Saint Denis above Avenue des Pins also has a plethora of eateries, generally new. All price ranges are represented. *Brulerie St Denis* at No 3967 makes superb coffees, roasting the beans on the premises, and try the strawberry cheesecake. Comfortably urbane *Ouzeri* at 4690 Rue Saint Denis is

recommended for its contemporary twist on traditional Greek food. Dinner for two before wine is about $35.

Mile End On Avenue Saint Viateur and Avenue Fairmont west of Boulevard Saint Laurent, superb still-hot bagels can be bought at one of three authentic open-fire bakeries.

Rue Bernard and Saint Laurent offer several good restaurants or comfortable places for coffee. *La Moulière* at 1249 Rue Bernard should be considered for its specialty of mussels served in about a dozen ways including one with cognac and green peppers. Main dishes including fish and meats are about $15 and there is a pleasant patio. *Le Bernardin* at 387 Rue Bernard is a good French bistro with meals at $50 for two before wine. There are a couple of good, cheap East Indian places on Saint Laurent just north of Avenue Fairmont and two or three Italian ones near Saint Viateur.

Avenue du Parc, running north up beyond the mountain, has numerous more traditional-style Greek restaurants (no kebabs or brochettes), many specialising in fish. Best of the lot is the casual but expensive *Milos* at 5357 Avenue du Parc. Very fresh fish makes up most of the menu. A dinner for two is in the $110 range with a range of Greek appetisers included. More economical meals can be had with four people because you select and order a whole fish which is priced by the pound.

Chinatown Montreal's Chinatown is small but well-entrenched. The district is centred on Rue de la Gauchetière Ouest between Rue Saint Urbain and Boulevard Saint Laurent, north of Old Montreal. A portion of the street is closed to traffic. The food is mainly Cantonese although spicier Sichuan dishes show up and several Vietnamese places can be found. Many offer lunch specials from as low as $6.

At 1068 Boulevard Saint Laurent, the *Cristal de Saigon* has cheap Vietnamese food but specialises in satisfying soups for about $4. Across the street at No 1071, the *Hoang Oanh* serves Vietnamese submarine sandwiches.

The *Jardin de Jade* at 57 Rue La Gauchetière Ouest has an immense buffet to match its enormous seating capacity spread over several rooms. The food may not be gourmet class but it certainly is plentiful ranging from dim sum to Sichuan to western pastries, and it's a bargain. In mid-afternoon the price is just $5.50 for all-you-can-eat. After 9 pm it is $7.50, at dinner, $11. Lunch is also offered. The food is the freshest on Saturday.

Entertainment

Montreal nightlife is good, varied, and comes in two languages. Clubs serve alcohol until 3 am – the longest opening hours in Canada, that's civilisation. Many bars don't start cooking until 10 or 11 pm and after that time there will be queues to get in.

The *Mirror* is a free weekly entertainment newspaper which can be picked up around town. *Voir* is the French equivalent. The Saturday *Montreal Gazette* also has club and entertainment listings as does *La Presse*.

For theatre and show details call ☎ 790-2787, an information line.

Live Music & Dance Clubs Rue Crescent, Rue de la Montagne and Rue Bishop are lively at night, with mostly disco-type places (no jeans allowed) but more casual places, too. This has long been the area for the English nightlife, whereas the French tend to party on Saint Denis. It's fun just to wander either area at night, maybe have a beer and people-watch. Recently a lot of the action has shifted to the Plateau with many clubs on upper Rue Saint Laurent and upper Saint Denis.

The *Sir Winston Churchill Pub* at 1459 Rue Crescent is popular and has dancing. *Thursdays* at 1449 Rue Crescent is a singles-style spot. Nearby, over on Rue Bishop, there are several pubs particularly south of Sainte Catherine.

Soundgarden at 1426 Stanley is a dance bar with different recorded music nightly. For the business and professional crowd, the *Pacha* at 1215 Boulevard de Maisonneuve Ouest on the corner of Rue Drummond is popular.

The *Salsathèque* at 1220 Rue Peel can be a fun place. It's a bright, busy, dressy place featuring large live Latin bands who pump out infectious Latin dance music. And if you like to see dancing, the patrons here will feast your eyes.

The *Yellow Door Coffee House* (☎ 398-6243), at 3625 Rue Aylmer, has survived from the 60s – US draft dodgers found refuge here. Folk music in a casual ambience is still presented but the schedule is erratic, call for upcoming concerts. It's closed through the summer.

The *Metropolis*, at 59 Rue Sainte Catherine Est, is the largest dance club in town, with bars spread over three floors and impressive sound and lighting systems but it's only open weekends. In Old Montreal at 104 Rue Saint Paul, *Les Deux Pierrots* is a huge, two-storey spot with local French singers and a casual atmosphere – and it's free.

Up in the Plateau Mont Royal there are a lot of clubs on Saint Laurent in the 4000 and 5000 blocks. The *Café Campus* at 57 Rue Prince Arthur Est is a popular student hang-out often with live bands, and *Rage* at 5116 Avenue Parc is popular with both live and recorded music.

Quai des Brumes at 4481 Rue Saint Denis is a fine place for live blues and rock.

There are numerous good spots for jazz in town. *L'Air du Temps* (☎ 842-2002) is in Old Montreal at 191 Rue Saint Paul Ouest on the corner of Rue Saint François Xavier. Solo music starts at 5 pm, groups after 9.30 pm; performers are mostly local musicians. There's no cover charge and the atmosphere and decor are pleasant. At *Biddles* (☎ 842-8656), 2060 Rue Aylmer, you might get a standard trio, a swing band or a vocalist. You can eat here too; there's no cover charge.

The *Grand Café*, at 1720 Rue Saint Denis, presents live jazz and blues at a modest price. Not far away at 311 Rue Ontario Est, local musicians play at *Café Thélème*.

Other Bars For a view of the city, try the top floor bar in the luxury *Château Champlain* on Square Dorchester. Drinks are costly but the view is fine and worth the price of at least one drink. The *Comedyworks* upstairs at 1238 Rue Bishop presents standup comics, usually several in a night. Admission is charged. *Finnegan's Irish Pub & Grill* at 82 Rue Prince Arthur East has a vast selection of Scotch and Irish draft beers. *Fûtenbulle* at 273 Rue Bernard Ouest is a casual, busy beer bar featuring dozens of fine brews from around the world which one reader has called one of the best of its kind on the continent. *Le Swimming* at 3643 Boulevard Saint Laurent is one of the nicest of the many pool (as in billiards) bars in the Plateau area.

Cinema There are several repertory film theatres around town, usually offering double bills and midnight movies on weekends. These theatres are generally cheaper than the chains showing first runs but a membership may be required.

The *Cinema de Paris* (☎ 875-7284), is central at 896 Rue Sainte Catherine Ouest. Most are of US origin but European films are regularly shown.

There is an IMAX (☎ 496-4629) large-format theatre in the Vieux Port (Old Port) area of Montreal. The *National Film Board* (NFB; ☎ 283-9000), at 1564 Rue Saint Denis, is worth a visit for serious cinefiles. There are regular screenings or individual monitors where you can watch the film of your choice. There is also a huge Canadian video collection available.

Theatre, Dance & More The *Centaur Theatre* (☎ 288-3161) at 453 Rue Saint François Xavier, generally has the best in English presentations. *Les Ballets Jazz de Montreal*, a Montreal modern dance troupe, has a good reputation and often performs in the city. *Place des Arts* (☎ 844-1211), Montreal's centre for the performing arts, presents an array of concerts, the symphony, L'Opera Montreal, and dance in three main theatres at the complex on Rue Sainte Catherine on the corner of Rue Jeanne Mance.

If Montreal's internationally famed *Cirque de Soleil* animal-free circus is in town a ticket is worth considering. The circus is based on acrobatics and a range of astounding acts of dexterity.

The Casino de Montreal, one of the 10 largest in the world, is open nearly all day and night. For more details see under Île Notre Dame earlier.

Spectator Sports Although there are alternatives, for all intents and purposes sports in this town means hockey or hockey.

The splendid new Molson Centre at the corner of Rue Mountain and Rue Antoine beside Windsor Station replaced the legendary but smaller Montreal Forum in March of 1996 as home to the Canadiens. The 'Habs', as the team is called, of the NHL are so popular it's been said that the crime rate goes down on game nights as people listen to the radio or watch it on TV in either French or English. A limited number of seats go on sale the first of the month for games during that month. Call the box office (☎ 989-2841) for more information. Otherwise seats are available through the legions of scalpers who begin lingering around the rink about noon on game days. Cost will depend on the opposition and importance of the game but all will be well above the list prices which range from $15 for a seat high in the rafters to $75 rink side. The season is from October to May.

The good, major league baseball team, the Montreal Expos of the National League, have a hard time drawing fans out to the Olympic Stadium (☎ 846-3976). If you want to catch a game, tickets are available through the season from April to September starting at just $6. The stadium is at 4549 Avenue Pierre de Coubertin in Olympic Park.

The once defunct football team of the teetering Canadian Football League (CFL) is back as the Alouettes with games also at the 'Big O' (same number as above). The season runs from the end of June to November.

Horse-racing can be seen at the Hippodrome Blue Bonnets (☎ 739-2741) at 7440 Boulevard Décarie most days but call for a schedule. Admission is $3.75.

QUEBEC

❀❀❀❀❀❀❀❀❀❀❀❀❀❀❀❀❀❀❀❀❀❀❀❀❀❀❀❀❀❀❀❀❀❀❀❀

The National Film Board of Canada

The National Film Board of Canada (NFB) has a formidable reputation as a cultural organisation responsible for pioneering filmmaking in all its aspects. The board was established by the Canadian government in 1939 to make and distribute films that convey the country's social and cultural realities to both Canadian and international audiences. Over the years it has been the recipient of more than 3000 awards, including nine Oscars.

The founder of the organisation, documentary filmmaker John Grierson, wanted the NFB to become the 'eyes of Canada'. Today it remains the only public producer in the world with the equipment and infrastructure to produce films from script to screen. Films produced by the board are available to the public through a network of offices and libraries across Canada and in major cities around the world.

The first genres the NFB excelled in were animation and documentary. In the 1940s, animator Norman McLaren joined the organisation and almost overnight the NFB achieved an international reputation for its innovative animation films. Researchers are now using the latest software programs to produce increasingly sophisticated computor-assisted animation techniques.

The NFB's research and development department has been responsible for an impressive number of important filmmaking breakthroughs. In 1964 the board's invention of the battery operated 16mm camera and lightweight synchronous sound recorder helped it to become the world leader in cinéma vérité –, a direct 'warts and all' approach to the documentary which allows crews to work with a minimum of intrusion.

Recent documentaries include Jacques Godbout's *Le Mouton Noir* (*The Black Sheep*), Alanis Obomsawin's *Kanehsatake: 270 Years of Resistance* and Aerlyn Weissman and Lynne Fernie's *Forbidden Love: The Unashamed Stories of Lesbian Lives*.

In the mid-1960s the NFB established the French Production Branch to produce films about the French community of Canada. Claude Jutra's 1971 film *Mon Oncle Antoine* has twice been chosen by critics as the best Canadian feature ever made. One of the board's priorities has been to make filmmaking accessible to under-represented groups.

In 1974 Studio D became the world's first production studio dedicated to making films by, for and about women. Some excellent films have been produced by Studio D, including Sherr Klein's *Not a Love Story: A Film About Pornography*, Terre Nash's *If You Love This Planet* (a documentary short which won an Oscar in 1983), Cynthia Scott's *The Company of Strangers* and Esther Valiquette's *Le Singe Bleu* (*A Measure of Your Passage*). In 1990 Studio D created a production unit for Native Indian women, and in 1991 Studio One was established to give voice to Native Indian filmmakers in general.

The head office of the NFB is in Ottawa and the operational headquarters are in Montreal. NFB films and videos can be ordered from anywhere in Canada on ☎ 1-800-267-7710. ■

❀❀❀❀❀❀❀❀❀❀❀❀❀❀❀❀❀❀❀❀❀❀❀❀❀❀❀❀❀❀❀❀❀❀❀❀

Things to Buy

The Canadian Guild of Crafts, at 2025 Rue Peel, has a small and rather expensive collection of the work of Quebec artisans and other Canadiana, as well as Inuit prints and carvings. It's free to look around.

Galerie Yves Laroche (☎ 393-1999), at 4 Rue Saint Paul Est on the corner of Boulevard Saint Laurent, has a fine varied collection of stone carvings. You can buy as well as look, but the pieces here are real collectibles and are not cheap.

Getting There & Away

Air There are two airports. Fortunately, very convenient Dorval, 20 km west of the centre of town, is now used for almost all passenger flights. White elephant Mirabel Airport, over 50 km north-west of the town's centre, handles charters and cargo. Dorval has a user fee of between $5 and $10 to finance upgrades. Expect to pay this upon departure.

Canadian Airlines' (☎ 931-2233) one-way fare to Halifax is $335 and to Winnipeg is $520 before taxes. Air Canada (☎ 393-3333) has virtually the same prices.

Cheap tickets to Florida, Mexico and parts of the Caribbean are often available out of Montreal.

Bus The bus station (☎ 842-2281) is central on the corner of Boulevard de Maisonneuve and Rue Berri, near Rue Saint Denis. It's right beside the Berri-UQAM Métro stop. The station serves Voyageur lines, Orléans Express and smaller Quebec regional bus companies. Greyhound from the USA, and Vermont Transit, which runs between Montreal and Boston (about seven hours away) with a transfer in Burlington, Vermont, also use the station. When dealing with Greyhound for US destinations, make sure you know which currency is being discussed.

Voyageur go to Ottawa every hour for $28 and Trentway Wager go to Toronto (about seven services daily) for $66. On both these routes there are sometimes cheaper return fares offered, so ask.

Orléans Express operates most buses in Quebec from Montreal eastwards. They have direct express runs to Quebec City and other slower trips which stop at smaller places along the way. Either way, a ticket is $36. Ask about possible return specials.

Limocar Bus serves the Laurentians north of Montreal and Autobus Viens goes south to the Eastern Townships.

In winter, two companies provide ski-shuttle day trips to the Laurentians for either downhill or cross-country. Royal Tours (☎ 871-8414) runs ski-bus expresses to Mont Tremblant. Buses can be picked up at various Metro stations or the central Infotouriste office. Tickets can include lift passes and are good value. Limocar runs a similar shuttle but to Mont Gabriel (with connections to nearby resorts) from the main bus station. Call for schedule information.

Train There are two train stations in the central area. You can walk underground from one to the other in 10 minutes. The main CN-VIA Rail station, also called Central Station, below the Queen Elizabeth Hotel on the corner of Boulevard René Lévesque and Rue Mansfield, gets all VIA Rail (☎ 871-1331) passengers. Use the Bonaventure Métro station.

There are four trains a day to Ottawa and six trains a day to Toronto, starting at 6.15 am. Fares are: Ottawa $36, Toronto $84, and Quebec City $44 plus GST.

For information about US destinations call Amtrak on ☎ 1-800-872-7245. Amtrak fares to New York vary depending on the month, day and how busy the route is. Cost

varies from $US45 to $75 one way, with cheap returns available. Booking well ahead increases the chance of a low price. Remember when inquiring about fares to US destinations to check whether prices are being given in US dollars. They probably are.

Windsor Station on the corner of Rue Peel and Rue de la Gauchetière, a few blocks from the CN-VIA station is used for local commuter trains. Use the same Métro stop.

Car The Trans Canada Hwy runs right through the city and Hwy 15 leads south to US 87 heading for New York. Hwy 401 joins Montreal to Toronto and beyond westward.

Car Rental Budget (☎ 866-7675) with offices around town and including in Central Station downtown, charges $40 per day with 100 free km, 14 cents per km over that for their economy cars. Tax is extra. Tilden (☎ 878-2771), at 1200 Rue Stanley, has similar rates.

For cheaper rates try Via Route (☎ 871-1166), at 1255 Rue Mackay or Mini-Prix (☎ 524-3009), at 2000 Rue Sainte Catherine Est. The latter has vans as well as cars. Getting a small group together could be quite economical.

There are many other companies and outlets all over town including at both airports. Prices tend not to vary a heck of a lot but differences can be found among the weekend specials and other multiple-day offers.

Car Sharing & Alternative Buses Allo Stop (☎ 985-3032), at 4317 Rue Saint Denis, is an agency that gets drivers and passengers together. Call a day ahead and tell them where you want to go or, if you're a driver, where you're going. Prices are good, considerably less than a bus ticket; it's $15 to Quebec City, for example. Allo Stop also goes to Toronto, New York and other cities. Passengers must pay a $6 membership fee, drivers a higher fee. Those with cars can have some of their expenses paid by taking along passengers. Allo Stop has offices in Toronto,

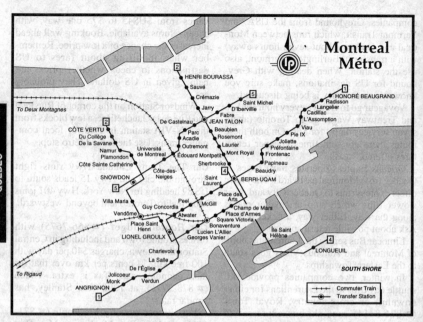

Montreal
Métro

HENRI BOURASSA
Sauvé
Crémazie
Jarry
De Castelnau
CÔTE VERTU
Du Collège
De la Savane
Namur
Plamondon
Côte Sainte Catherine
SNOWDON
Villa Maria
Vendôme
Place Saint
Henri
LIONEL GROULX
Charlevoix
La Salle
De l'Église
Jolicoeur
Monk
Verdun
ANGRIGNON

To Deux Montagnes

Saint Michel
D'Iberville
Fabre
JEAN TALON
Beaubien
Rosemont
Laurier
Mont Royal
Sherbrooke
Saint
Laurent
Place des
Arts
McGill
Peel
Guy Concordia
Atwater
Lucien L'Allier
Georges Vanier

Parc
Acadie
Outremont
Édouard Montpetit
Université
de Montreal
Côte-des-
Neiges

HONORÉ BEAUGRAND
Radisson
Langelier
Cadillac
L'Assomption
Viau
Pie IX
Joliette
Préfontaine
Frontenac
Papineau
Beaudry
BERRI-UQAM
Champ de Mars
Place d'Armes
Square Victoria
Bonaventure

Île Saint
Hélène

LONGUEUIL

To Rigaud

SOUTH SHORE

+++ Commuter Train
—●— Transfer Station

QUEBEC

Ottawa, Quebec City and many other points around Quebec such as the Saguenay and the Gaspé. This is an agency really worth checking out.

Another choice is the semi-underground Easy Ride (☎ 987-9615), at 92 Rue Sherbrooke Ouest with scheduled van and bus service to Ottawa ($12), Toronto ($30) and some US destinations.

Getting Around
The Airport The cheapest and quickest way to Dorval Airport is to take the Métro to Lionel-Groulx. Transfer to the No 211 bus outside. The first stop, about 15 to 25 minutes later, is the Dorval Bus Transfer Station. Switch here, with free transfer, to any No 204 bus which runs into the airport.

An alternative, at the same price, but slower unless you are near one of these bus lines is to take the Métro to Crémazie, then catch bus No 100 west towards the airport and ask the driver to let you off to catch bus

No 209, which will take you right in. The total cost for either of these routes is $1.75.

From the airport, catch the 204 East (Est) to the Dorval Bus Transfer Station and switch to the 211 Est. This will take you to the Métro. There is a maximum wait time of half an hour between buses, through most of the day waiting time will be much less. Bus Nos 204 and 211 run from 5 am to 1 am.

Autocar Connaisseur (☎ 934-1222) runs buses between Dorval and downtown luxury hotels for $9 one way and $16 return taking a little under half an hour. They also go between Mirabel Airport and downtown for $14.50 one way and $20.50 return. The latter trips take about 45 minutes. Buses also connect the two airports. A taxi from downtown to Dorval is roughly $25, from downtown to Mirabel, a hefty $60.

Bus & Métro The city has a fairly widespread, convenient bus-Métro system (☎ 288-6287). The Métro is the name for the city's underground train system. The Métro runs until 1 am and some buses run even later. One ticket can get you anywhere in the city as it entitles you to a transfer to any connecting bus or subway train. On the buses get a transfer from the driver, and on the Métro from the machines past the turnstiles. A strip of six tickets is $7.75 or single tickets cost $1.85 each. Buses take tickets, transfers, or correct cash only.

If you are in town for a calendar month and plan to use public transit frequently consider the monthly pass. It can be shared as no picture is required.

Métro routes are shown on the tourist map and stops are indicated above ground by large blue signs with a white arrow pointing down. The system runs basically east-west with a north-south line intersecting at Berri-UQAM. It runs on rubber tyres and is safe, clean, fast and quiet.

Car In town, most streets are one way and the drivers are aggressive. Watch the action at yellow lights. Driving the 'Metropolitan' (the Trans Canada Hwy, the No 40, through central Montreal) is an especially white-knuckle-inducing experience. Good luck. Don't drive to old Montreal – the streets are narrow and busy and there is little parking. Everywhere pedestrians are fair game; cross walks mean little to Montreal drivers.

Bicycle For rentals or repairs, Vélo Aventure (☎ 847-0666) on Quai King Edward at the Old Port is recommended. They're open every day from May to October and have good bikes in good condition. Roller blades (in-line skates) with all the padding necessary for novices are also offered. Rentals are by the hour or full-day and there are kids and family rates. Child trailers are available. Perhaps best of all, there is a major bike path going for miles from right at the door of the shop. Maps of the city's bicycle paths, one of which circles the entire island, are available from Vélo. Bicycles can also be rented at the Infotouriste office (☎ 393-1528) at Square Dorchester.

Bicycles can be taken on the Métro in the last two carriages of the train and on the water shuttles over to Park des Îles.

Calèche These horse-drawn carriages seen mainly around Square Dorchester, Old Montreal or up on the mountain, charge about $45 an hour. Four or five people can ride at a time. In winter, sleighs are used for trips up and around Mont Royal.

Around Montreal

OKA
This is a small town about 60 km west of Montreal, where the Ottawa River meets the St Lawrence River. It's on the north mainland shore, north of Dorion on the edge of Lac des Deux Montagnes, a bulge in the river. The place is well known for the Trappist monastery dating from the 1880s and the cheeses it produces. The cheese-producing has been largely taken over by business people and the monastery of 70 monks has been opened to visitors. There are religious artworks, a mountain with the Stages of the Cross and several old stone buildings. The chapel, gardens and boutique are all closed Sunday.

Oka became internationally known late in 1990 as the site of a major confrontation between Mohawk people and the federal and provincial governments. At first a local land squabble, this issue soon came to represent all the continuing problems such as land claims and self-government which Native Indians across the country would like to see properly resolved.

ROUGE RIVER
Not far north-west of Montreal near the Ontario border, the Rouge River is well known for white water rafting. Several companies offer day or weekend trips which most people reckon are a lot of fun. One to try is New World River Expeditions (☎ 242-7238, 1-800-361-5033) with an office in Montreal. They have an office in Calumet, Quebec

(near Hawkesbury, Ontario) on the river or you can call toll free. They have a lodge with pool and bar, so you're not roughing it in the bush the whole time. Esprit Rafting in Davidson, Quebec has hostel accommodation. Whichever of the several companies you choose, the basic trip is four or five hours.

SUCRERIE DE LA MONTAGNE

Situated in a maple forest, the sucrerie (☎ 451-5204) depicts a 1900-era Quebec sugar shack where sap is converted to maple syrup and sugar. A visit includes a tour and explanation of the process, a meal and folk music. The lunch package is $30, the dinner, $40. It's an interesting, popular place although the focus is on the restaurant.

To get to the site 70 km west from downtown without a car, take the train to Rigaud and then it's about a $10 taxi ride. If driving take Hwy 40 west to 300 Rang Saint-Georges, Rigaud.

THE LAURENTIANS (LAURENTIDES)

Between 80 km and 150 km north of Montreal, this section of the ancient Laurentian Shield is a mountainous, rolling lake-sprinkled playground. The land proved a dismal failure for lumber and mining, but when skiing caught on, so did this area as a resortland. The district today is used not only for the best in eastern skiing but for camping, fishing and swimming in summer. The many picturesque French towns dominated by their church spires and the good scenery

---

Skiing in the Laurentians

The Laurentians are without doubt one of the prime ski regions in the country. The region has the hills, the snow, the scenery, the experience and perhaps most of all, the relaxed, friendly sporting atmosphere that adds immeasurably to a day at the slopes.

With over 20 ski centres within 2½ hours of Montreal offering runs for the novice and the expert the alpine skiing is convenient and varied enough to offer something for everyone. Over a quarter of the 350 ski runs are now lit for nightskiing – a wonderful experience, and often less busy than the trails through the day.

Through a good winter, skiing can be enjoyed for four months with many lodges making artificial snow to complement what the sky provides. Although renowned for its downhill slopes, the region has plenty of good cross-country skiing as well and this can be tried and enjoyed for considerably less money. Equipment can be rented at a couple of sport shops around Montreal (try the yellow pages telephone book or the tourist office) and, more commonly, at the ski centres up north. Arrive early in the day for the best selection and help in getting fitted out. Renting the whole package – boots, skis and poles – runs to about $20 to $25 for a full day which isn't bad at all because the equipment tends to be good.

Tow prices vary from centre to centre but range from $25 to $44 a day with most about $30. Half-day tickets are sold at many resorts and there is a separate night-ski pass available which is less money. Children's tickets are also offered. Prices are lower during the week than on weekends and all prices rise for the period around Christmas and New Year.

Less than an hour from Montreal there are some fine places such as Habitant and, for beginners or the rusty, Olympia has a good selection of wide, easy runs. Go for it!

As a rough guide, the further from Montreal, the more challenging the hills can become although even resorts with deadly runs also offer some for novice or intermediate skiers so you don't have to get in over your head.

The grandaddy of them all is Mont Tremblant with the highest vertical drop in the Laurentians at 650 metres. The Mont Tremblant and Grey Rocks ski centres are huge offering multiple runs. Travel down one side of the mountain in the morning and then, when the sun shifts, ski down the other side. This resort, hoping to lure visitors from far and wide, is undergoing a major overhaul to bring all the facilities up to top rate international standards.

The Mont Tremblant area has some 150 km of mechanically set cross-country trails around the provincial park, Saint Jovite, and around the village of Mont Tremblant, itself. Many of the trails, even further south, say at Mont Rolland, are interconnected and some have warming huts at intervals along the way. ■

make it popular for just lazing and relaxing as well. Plentiful accommodation and restaurants provide a wide range of services, from elegant inns with fine dining rooms to modest motels.

The Autoroute Laurentienne, also known as Hwy 15, is the fastest route north from Montreal and is the way the buses go. The old Hwy 117 north is slower but more pleasant. A second major route goes north-east of Montreal to Joliette and then smaller roads continue further north.

The better known towns and resorts are all clustered near the highways. Cottage country spreads out a little further east and west. In general terms the busy area ends at Mont Tremblant Provincial Park. The smaller villages on the upper areas of Hwy 117 are quiet and typically 'Laurentian'.

To find less-developed areas or to camp, you pretty much have to head for the big parks, as most of the region is privately owned. Many of the towns have tourist offices so you can ask about things as you go. Outside the parks, campgrounds are generally privately owned too, and tend to be small and busy. Motels are next up the economic scale; the lodges are generally (but not always) quite pricey. There is a stable hostel in Val David and newer ones north of Mont Tremblant Village in Labelle and at Sainte Agathe.

The busiest times in the Laurentians are July, August, around Christmas, February and March. At other times, prices tend to be reduced, like the crowds. Autumn is a good season to visit, the hills are colourful and the cooler air is ideal for walking. The whole area (in all seasons) has a festive, relaxed atmosphere.

The area is served by Limocar Laurentides buses which leave from Montreal's main terminus. Stops are made in most main towns. In ski season, special buses operate to various hills, see under Montreal buses.

Year-round tourist information offices with accommodation assistance can be found in the villages of Saint Saveur des Monts, Saint Adèle, Sainte Agathe, Saint Jovite and at Mont Tremblant Village.

Saint Sauveur des Monts

Saint Sauveur des Monts, known simply as Saint Sauveur, the first stop-off on the way north, about 60 km from Montreal, is a small pleasant resort town with four nearby ski hills. Summer or winter, day or night, the main street, Rue Principale, with its restaurants, cafes, bars and shops is busy. Saint Sauveur has B&B, hotel and motel accommodation.

Mont Rolland

Mont Rolland is a recreation centre based at Mont Gabriel. There's excellent skiing in winter and in summer the mountain turns into a huge slide complex, a trend which many of the area's resorts have embraced. This one differs in that it is not a water slide, as such, but instead uses bobsleds sliding on ball bearings. Hang on tight!

The Rolland Paper Company, one of the oldest and most important paper makers in the country, is based here.

The *Auberge Mont Gabriel* on top of the mountain is one of the larger, more expensive lodges in the Laurentians.

Sainte Adèle

Sainte Adèle is one of the nicer-looking highway towns, with a popular recreation area, Lac Rond.

A museum recreates a story by one of the towns most illustrious sons, popular Quebec author Claude-Henri Grignon. Another museum, Musée Village de Séraphin, is a small recreated European pioneer village.

Places to Stay Accommodation, mainly good hotels, tends to be expensive here; cheapest is the *Auberge Familiale du Lac Lucerne* (☎ 228-4422) at 2469 Chemin Sainte Marguerite.

Sainte Agathe des Monts

With about 9000 people, Sainte Agathe is the largest town in the Laurentians and a busy resort centre. With numerous bars, cafes and restaurants, as well as shops for replenishing supplies, there is always plenty of activity.

QUEBEC

The local bakery, on Rue Sainte Agathe, is known far and wide.

At the edge of Lac des Sables, more or less in town, there is room for a picnic, and cruises of the lake depart from the wharf. Around the lake are beaches and places to camp. One km north of town, Village du Mont Castor is a modern townhouse development created in turn-of-the-century Québécois style using full-size logs. At the end of July, watch for the annual music and dance festival.

Places to Stay B&Bs, inns (auberges) and motels all tend to be quite busy, especially on weekends, so planning ahead is advisable. Very close to the centre on the lake at 242 Rue Saint Venant is the two-part *Auberge des Mats* (☎ 326-7692). One house is a B&B and the one next door, a hostel with its own kitchen. High season doubles are $70, hostel beds $22 with breakfast. Mountain bikes can be hired and the owners can organise various outdoor activities.

Another to try is the B&B *La Villa Verra* (☎ 326-0513) at 246 Saint Venant. South of town are some relatively modest motels such as the *Motel Clair Mont* (☎ 326-1444), at 1591 Rue Principale at $60 double.

Val David

Close to Sainte Agathe but to the east off Hwy 15, Val David is a considerably smaller town that's become an arts & crafts centre. Studios and workshops can be visited, and stores sell a variety of handicrafts.

Places to Stay There is an HI hostel, *Le Chalet Beaumont* (☎ 322-1972), at 1451 Rue Beaumont, in a rustic log chalet perched on a hill with great views. If you call from Montreal a shuttle bus will meet the bus from Montreal and take you to the hostel.

Saint Faustin

Saint Faustin with a population of about 1400 is the base for Mont Blanc. In summer, a large nature interpretive centre at Lac du Cordon with 15 km of walking and hiking trails can be visited. It's free and maps are available at the centre where there is information on the flora & fauna of the area. There is a maple-sugar shack here open in April and May where the production can be seen and the results sampled. Cabane à Sucre Millette (☎ 688-2101), is at 1357 Rue Saint Faustin.

A trout hatchery in a wooded setting can also be visited. The fish raised here are used to restock the rivers and lakes of the Laurentians. North of town, roads lead past Lac Supérieur into Mont Tremblant Park.

Saint Jovite

With 4000 people, Saint Jovite is the last major town in the region. Rue Ouimet is lined with cafes and restaurants. The busy area incorporating traditional architecture is known as the Petit Hameau district. The Musée de la Faune at 65 Rue Limoge has a collection of stuffed indigenous animals. In Weir, not far south of Saint Jovite, is the **Laurentides Satellite Earth Station**, an international telecommunications installation. There are free guided tours of the facilities and 10-storey-high antennae, as well as slide presentations. It's open daily from mid-June to Labour Day. Follow the signs from Weir.

Saint Jovite is a bit of a crossroads and acts as a supply centre for trips in to the Mont Tremblant area with its many lakes and skiing.

Mont Tremblant

North of Saint Jovite, Mont Tremblant lies just outside the provincial park of the same name. The mountain, with its 650-metre vertical drop, is the highest peak in the Laurentians. With over 60 runs, it's the region's major ski centre and marks the northernmost point of the easily accessible Laurentian destinations.

Intrawest who developed Whistler in British Columbia into a world-class facility has, since 1992, been totally overhauling Tremblant. It is now a major four-season resort with development and improvements continuing. Millions of dollars have resulted in state-of-the-art ski facilities as well as golf courses, water sports, and a range of possible activities from cycling to tennis. A chair lift runs to the mountain peak in summer and winter.

At the foot of the mountain, 146 km from Montreal, is Mont Tremblant Village, an accommodation centre with an abundance of restaurants, bars, typical 'terraces' (the glassed-in patios) and all amenities. Chemin Principal is the main street. The tourist office is one over on Rue du Couvent. For Tremblant information call ☎ 452-8681, or for reservations ☎ 1-800-567-6760.

Lac Mercier sits at the western edge of the village. Tour boats cruise larger Lac Tremblant north of town.

Lodging ranges from B&Bs through to luxury condos. It is generally expensive. With all the construction, it could take a couple of years before there is much accommodation at the budget end. For now, call the tourist office and ask about the B&Bs or consider staying at one of the nearby villages. In winter, the ski-package deals may be most economical but not at Christmas.

There are two main ski hills, Mont Tremblant itself, with the most runs and highest costs, and Gray Rocks to the southeast of the village.

Labelle
North of Tremblant, Labelle is a jumping off point for two undeveloped wildlife reserves as well as the western section of Tremblant Park. The second of the two Laurentian HI hostels is here, *Domain de Beau Sejour* (☎ 686-1323) at 1110 Chemin Saindon. For those not camping, this is the cheapest way to see some of the area. Dorms are $15.

Saint Donat
North-east of Sainte Agathe, this little lakeside town is a supply centre for the main entrance to Mont Tremblant Recreation Park which lies just to the north.

There are beaches on **Lac Archambault** and, in summer, 90-minute cruises around the lake.

Accommodation of all types can be found in and around town and is less expensive than in the towns along Hwy 117 to the west.

Bars and cafes along the main streets are lively at night.

Mont Tremblant Provincial Park
Opened as early as 1894, this is a huge area – over 1500 sq km – of lakes, rivers, hills and woods. There are many campsites in the park, some with amenities but most are basic. The most developed area is north of Saint Donat. Roads are paved, canoes can be rented, and the campgrounds have showers. Not too far from the entrance there are a couple of good walking paths with views and, a little further in, a fair-sized waterfall with nearby picnic tables.

Towards the interior, some campsites are accessible only by foot, canoe or unsurfaced roads some of which are rough old logging routes. The more off-the-track areas abound in wildlife.

In the far eastern section one September, we had whole lakes to ourselves, saw moose and heard nearby wolves howling as we sat around the fire. Nights were very cold so be prepared.

Mark Lightbody

LANAUDIÈRE
Lanaudière refers to the region north-east of Montreal and, though it is essentially still 'up north' or 'the Laurentians', it has cultivated its own identity. Without the quality ski hills and fewer large towns it is, though still popular, a less visited region. There are plenty of parks with walking trails over mountains and along rivers to enjoy. The southern area has its own cowboys. And food and lodging is noticeably cheaper than in the places further west along the Autoroute. For any specific area information call the Lanaudière tourist office on ☎ 1-800-363-2788.

Terrebonne
Believe it or not the Moulins region of south-west Lanaudière around the towns of Terrebonne and Mascouche and along the north shore of Rivière des Milles Îles is cowboy country. Here, about a 45-minute drive from downtown Montreal, there are

QUEBEC

about 30 ranches, thousands of horses and plenty of events for their fully Western-style riders to compete in. Throughout summer various horse shows, rodeos and gymkhanas are an almost weekly occurrence.

Pretty well every Saturday night at Tico-Smokey Ranch outside Terrebonne there is a competition of one sort or another. On Friday and Saturday nights, fans and riders meet for country music and dancing at the Chalet de la Vallée at 1231 Chemin Pincourt in Mascouche, but don't arrive too early – these cowboys don't have to get up before the sun.

Frequently throughout the summer there are major two-day rodeos with calf roping, steer wrestling and bronco busting. For a schedule of events and locations call the Lanaudière tourist office. Many stables in the area offer horses and trail rides, some not ending until midnight.

When your legs have had enough, the Wild West can be left far behind with a visit to the village of Vieux Terrebonne along the Rivière des Milles Îles, opposite Île des Moulins. Here along the waterfront are numerous restaurants and cafes.

Joliette
Joliette is a principal town and centre for the local tobacco-growing industry. You may notice that in some areas, the farmland is divided into long strips. These are known as *rangs* and were a traditional way of dividing up the land not seen outside the province.

There is also a lot of maple-syrup production in the area. In spring, many farmers allow visitors to the sugar shacks for a look-see and a taste. Sugar shacks can be found in Saint Esprit and Saint Jacques. Or you can see how it's done all year at Chez Madeleine in Mascouche, where they provide information and sell various maple goodies. I don't want to rush you, but it's said that, in time, acid rain could wipe out this traditional industry.

Joliette is the site of the annual Festival International de Lanaudière, a major international, classical-music festival, which draws crowds of thousands to the 50 or so concerts which take place throughout summer. Many

events are held at the new outdoor amphitheatre which has a capacity of 10,000. Free half-hour tours of the facility are offered.

Rawdon
Rawdon, the other main town, has **Moore Canadiana Village**, a re-created 1800s town, complete with workers in costume. Most of the buildings are authentic (the schoolhouse is from 1835). Other attractions include a museum and art gallery.

Lakeside Rawdon has long been a local beauty spot. Trails and observation points wind along the Ouareau River with the **Dorwin Falls**. Nearby there are other hilly, wooded areas good for walking. Ask at the tourist office in 1st Ave.

There are numerous lakes in the region, many with inns, resorts or campgrounds.

Berthierville
To the east of Joliette on the St Lawrence River is Berthierville, the birthplace of Gilles Villeneuve, the Formula 1 racing car driver. A museum details his exciting career on the Grand Prix circuit.

EASTERN TOWNSHIPS (ESTRIE)
The Eastern Townships area (Les Cantons de l'Est), the 'Garden of Quebec', generally known as L'Estrie by the French, extends from Granby to the New Hampshire border. The area is appreciated for its rolling hills, green farmland, woods and lakes – an extension of the US Appalachian region. The area has long been based on its fertile soil and resources but high-tech industries are increasingly important.

It's a popular resort area year round. In spring, 'sugaring off' – the tapping of trees for maple syrup, and then boiling and preparing it – takes place throughout the region. Summer brings fishing and swimming in the numerous lakes. During autumn, a good time to visit, colours are beautiful as the leaves change, and apple harvesting takes place with the attendant cider production. Skiing is a major winter activity with centres at Mont Orford and Sutton.

L'Estrie abounds in cottages and chalets

Maple Syrup

Liquid, golden maple syrup is a traditional, all-natural taste sensation. Quebec is the world's largest producer and Estrie, with its abundance of sugar-maple forests, has long been the centre of production.

It is believed the Native Indians, who had a spring date known as the sugar-making moon, passed their knowledge onto early pioneers. Production techniques vary but essentially in spring, when the sap begins to run, the trees are tapped and buckets hung from them to collect, drop by drop, the nearly clear sap. The liquid is then collected into large kettles and boiled at the 'sugar shack' for days, driving off most of the water. As it thickens, the colour becomes more intense and the sugar content rises to around 90%. It is then cooled, graded and bottled.

It is most often spread over vanilla ice cream or pancakes. A further refining results in maple sugar. The Montreal or regional Estrie tourist offices will be able to tell you where to see a demonstration of the process in early spring.

Acid rain has adversely affected the maple forests of Quebec and there is concern over the future of this small-farm industry. Maple syrup is also produced in eastern and central Ontario and New Brunswick. ■

both private and commercial, and inns. The region also has a reputation for its many fine but expensive dining rooms.

The Eastern Townships have a long history and, as evidenced by the place names, were until quite recently predominantly English. Though originally occupied by the Abenakis Indians much of the region was first developed by Loyalists fleeing the USA after the revolution of 1776. Later in the next century many Irish people arrived. Soon after, French settlers arrived to help with the expanding economy.

Many of the towns and villages are popular with antique-hunters; small craft-shops and galleries line many a main street. Another lure is the area's growing reputation for its spas and health centres where the stressed-out can be treated like Hollywood stars for a couple of days. Around the countryside on the smaller roads keep an eye out for the remaining wooden covered bridges and the round barns.

There is a B&B programme in the region (the tourist office will have the latest guide) and dozens of campgrounds. This region of the province is the only one where B&Bs make up the bulk of the accommodation but prices are not low. The more historic and deluxe choices offer supreme grace but prices rise accordingly.

The main L'Estrie tourist office (☎ 1-800-263-1068) is on the Autoroute (Hwy 10)

south from Montreal at exit 68. It's open daily all year. Other offices can be found in Magog, Granby and Sherbrooke.

L'Estrie is one of the good cycling regions in the province and rentals are available in Magog, Orford, North Hatley and other places. Both cycling and B&B maps are for sale at the regional tourist offices. One major cycling trail begins at Granby and runs to Waterloo and there are other established routes. There is also some good hiking including a 140-km long-distance trail network between Kingsbury and Mont Sutton. The district also produces some wines and most notably, mead, an ancient nectar made from fermented honey. A self-guided wine tour can be followed through the region.

Granby

This town is known far and wide for its **zoo**. I swear everybody in Quebec knows of it, if in fact they haven't seen it. It seems it has been there forever. Exhibits such as the insectarium containing 100,000 little creatures, the reptile displays and a cave with nocturnal animals have improved it considerably in recent years. It is now a major zoo with 1000 animals and admission to match. An adult ticket is $15. There is also good bird watching at Lac Boivin Interpretation Centre.

Granby is also well endowed with highly respected restaurants and hosts a gastronomical festival every autumn.

Lac Brome (Knowlton)

Nearby, south of Hwy 10 on Hwy 243, is the town of Lac Brome on the lake of the same name. Seven former English Loyalist villages, including Knowlton, make up the town of 5000. Many of the main street's Victorian buildings have been restored and it's become a bit of a tourist centre with craft and gift shops, etc. The good local history museum at 130 Lakeside St includes a tea room. A favourite meal in this area is Lac Brome duck and it shows up frequently on the better menus.

Sutton

Further south, Sutton is synonymous with its important ski hill, one of the area's highest. In summer, there are hiking trails in Sutton Park. The area around Sutton and south of Cowansville near the village of Dunham supports Quebec's wine industry and some of the wineries can be visited. This is also an important apple-growing region where casual work can be found in autumn. A 10-km cycling path runs south to the US border.

At the natural environment park there is the decidedly nonregional llama-breeding farm where rides on the haughty creatures can be attempted.

The Sutton area, again, is well known for its comfortable country inns and the fine restaurants, many of which specialise in using local produce.

The *Willow House* (☎ 538-0035), a B&B at 30 Rue Western, is priced about average at $60 double but is good for singles at $35.

Near the village of Sutton Junction Rural Route (RR) 4 sits what was once the farm of Madame Benoît, Canada's best known chef. She appeared on national TV for many years and wrote numerous cookbooks.

Lac Champlain

Although essentially a US lake, which divides Vermont from New York State, it does protrude into Quebec as well. Steeped in history, the area is popular with Canadian and US holidaymakers.

The lake is good for swimming and fishing and, in places, is scenic. At Platts-burgh, New York there is a good and busy beach, where on any summer weekend you'll find plenty of Quebeckers. The short ferry trip across part of the lake is quite pleasant and worth doing if you're travelling through the area.

Magog

Magog, sitting right at the northern tip of large Lac Memphrémagog, is an attractive town with 15,000 residents. The main street, Rue Principale, has a resort flavour with its many cafes, bars, bistros and restaurants.

On this same street, but just west of town, the tourist office can help provide information about the area. Daily boat cruises lasting a little over two hours are offered around the lake in summer.

There are numerous places to stay in and around town, but most are motels in the singles/doubles $50/65 range. The 10 B&Bs around town charge about the same. Hotels tend to be even more pricey.

Lac Memphrémagog

This is the largest and best known lake in the L'Estrie area. Most of the lakefront properties are privately owned. Halfway down the lake at Saint Benoît-du-Lac is a **Benedictine monastery** where monks continue the tradition of the ancient Gregorian chant. Visitors can attend services and there's a hostel for men and another nearby at a nunnery for women if you want to stay. One of Quebec's cheeses – L'Ermite, a blue – is made and sold here. Also try to taste the cider the monks make. Call ☎ 843-4080 for information.

Rock Island, the busy border crossing to the USA, is at the southern end of the lake and contains four of the Eastern Townships' best French restaurants.

Mont Orford Provincial Park

Just out of Magog, this is a good but relatively small park (though the largest in the Eastern Townships). Dominated by Mont Orford (792 metres), the park is a skiing centre in winter but fills up quickly with campers in summer as well. You can swim here, use the walking trails, and the chair lift operates throughout the summer.

Each summer, the Orford Art Centre presents the Jeunesses Musicales du Canada music and art festival. There is an *HI hostel* (☎ 843-3981) at the centre open through the summer.

North Hatley

Just east of Magog, North Hatley sits at the north end of Lac Massawippi, the shape of which can lead to the waters quickly turning very rough. The village was a popular second home for wealthy US citizens who enjoyed the scenery but even more the lack of Prohibition during the 1920s. Many of these huge old places are now inns and B&Bs. Try the Massawippi dark beer at the Le Pilsen pub. There's an English theatre in town and galleries, and antique and craft stores.

Sherbrooke

Sherbrooke is the principal commercial centre of the region and a fair-sized city in its own right. It's a bilingual town with several small museums, a wide selection of restaurants and a pleasant central core lying between the Magog and Saint François rivers.

The tourist office (☎ 564-8331) is at 48 Rue Depôt. The 18-km walking and cycling path along the Magog River known as Réseau Riverain, makes an agreeable stroll. It begins at the **Maison de l'Eau**, a museum on aquatic life, found at the edge of the Magog River at 755 Cabana St in Blanchard Park.

The **Musée des Beaux Arts** in the centre on Rue du Palais is a sizeable art gallery open every afternoon except Monday. The annual fall fair is a big local event held each August.

On the outskirts at Bromptonville, is the **Shrine of Beauvoir**, dating from 1920, a site of religious pilgrimages with good views over the city and the surrounding area. In **Lennoxville**, there's Bishop's, an English university. Also in Lennoxville are a couple of cottage breweries and some antique and craft shops to browse through. On Hwy 216 toward Stokes is the **Centre d'Interpretation**

de l'Abeille, the Honey Bee Interpretive Centre, a research facility open for visitors with displays about the little buzzers and the honey they produce. Other nearby attractions include the Magog River Gorge and the Frontenac Hydroelectric Plant.

Places to Stay & Eat Here, as elsewhere around the Eastern Townships, the motels, hotels and inns are not at all cheap. Alternative B&Bs can be found through the local tourist office although these, too, in Sherbrooke are not inexpensive. In summer, rooms are also available at low rates at the university. *Hotel-Motel La Réserve* (☎ 566-6464) at 4235 Rue King Ouest charges from $65 double.

Two well-established four-star eateries are *Au Petit Sabot* and *l'Élite*. For simpler fare there is the *Marie Antoinette* at 333 Rue King Ouest.

Getting There & Away The bus station (☎ 569-3656) is at 20 Rue King Ouest. Autobus Auger runs to Montreal, Magog and Granby. There are also buses to Trois Rivières.

South-west of town, several of the smaller area highways join Hwy 55 which leads south to Rock Island, a small town which is the major entry point into the USA, close to the states of New York, Vermont, and New Hampshire. During the summer, particularly on weekends, there can be major waits (as in hours) at this border. This is especially true going into Quebec as vehicles are checked for how much stuff was bought in the USA and duty collected. If possible find a smaller entry point, perhaps south of Coaticook.

East of Sherbrooke

East of Sherbrooke the rolling farmlands and historic cultured towns and villages give way to a much rougher, less-populated region of primary resource industry and untouched woodlands. Asbestos and Thetford Mines are mining centres. In the middle of the district is the large Frontenac Recreation Park for access into an unspoiled region. South of there, the Lac Mégantic area is a mix of mountains and scenic farmlands. Route 212 provides a scenic drive.

The south-eastern area is bounded by New Hampshire and Maine, USA.

MONTREAL TO QUEBEC CITY

Leaving Montreal behind, travelling east on Hwy 138, you begin to get a sense of what small-town Quebec is like. Stone houses with light blue trim and tin roofs, silver-spired churches, ubiquitous chip wagons called *cantines* and main streets with shops built right to the road, are some characteristics. The best section is from Trois Rivières onwards to the north-east.

A much quicker route is Hwy 40, a four-lane expressway that can get you from Montreal to Quebec City in 2½ to three hours. There are not many services along this route, so watch your fuel levels.

From Montreal there is also one fast and one slow route along the south shore to Quebec City and beyond. The old Hwy 132 edges along the river but isn't as nice as its north shore counterpart (Hwy 138), and the Trans Canada Hwy is fast but boring until Quebec City, where it runs a little closer to the water. At Trois Rivières, you can cross the river.

Saint Antoine de Padoue Church

This is on the north side of the St Lawrence River in Louiseville. It would be hard to miss, but take a peek inside too; it's one of Canada's grandest churches – very impressive. Next door, the seasonal tourist booth is helpful.

Odanak

Almost directly across the river from Louiseville is Odanak, a small Abénakis Indian village settled in the early 1600s. A museum right on Hwy 226 outlines their history and culture. Perhaps of even more interest is the annual powwow held in July.

Trois Rivières

Trois Rivières, over 350 years old and the largest town between Quebec's two main cities, is a major pulp & paper centre.

The attractive **old section** based around Rue Notre Dame and Rue Bonaventure with its reminders of a long history, is small but good for a stroll. Cafes and bars are abundant in this lively area. Rue des Ursulines and Rue Radisson are also main central streets. The St Lawrence River borders the southern edge of the area. There is a year round tourist office (☎ 375-1122) at 1563 Rue Notre Dame. Listen for the Blues Festival in July.

On Rue des Ursulines are several **old houses** now open to the public as small free museums and examples of various architectural styles. The **Ursuline Museum** at No 734 displays materials relating to the Ursuline Order of nuns who were prominent in the town's development. The Manoir Boucher-de-Niverville, an historic house at 168 Rue Bonaventure near the corner of Rue Hart has changing displays on the city's past.

The **cathedral** at 362 Rue Bonaventure, built in 1858, is the only Westminster-style church on the continent and is open daily.

The large, new, central **Folk Arts & Traditions Museum** (☎ 372-0406) at the corner of Rue Laviolette and Rue Hart has three major components. The pre-history collection has displays on fossils, early pottery discoveries and local Native Indians. Another has a vast collection of traditional Quebecois arts & crafts including textiles, furniture and toys. Lastly, the old prison on the site, used for 164 years, tells its grim story.

Two-hour **cruises** along the river aboard the MS *Jacques Cartier* depart from the dock in **Parc Portuaire** at the foot of Boulevard des Forges in the centre of the old town.

Also in the park is an exhibit with models and videos on the local pulp & paper industry but there are no tours of the plant itself. The exhibit is worth seeing.

Just north of town is the **Saint Maurice Ironworks National Park** which was the first major iron-ore operation in North America. Built in 1730, the forge ran sporadically, with a number of owners, until 1883. An information centre details the historic significance and also explains how the iron was produced and used.

There is an HI hostel in town, *Auberge la Flotille* (☎ 378-8010) at 497 Rue Radisson where dorms cost members/nonmembers $14.50/17.50 and there are double rooms. An inexpensive breakfast is available but there is also a communal kitchen and laundry facilities. Good, small tours are organised to local areas of interest. The hostel is about a 10-minute walk from the bus station. Several motels can be found on Boulevard Royal.

The station at 1075 Rue Champflour in the old train station is used solely for buses (☎ 374-2944), there is no train service. Voyageur Colonial and Orléans Express go to Montreal and Quebec City, Autobus Messier goes to Sherbrooke and other towns of the Eastern Townships.

Beyond the city, the road becomes hilly with gradients up to 17%. There are lots of camping places along the way as well as stands offering fruit, cider and wood sculpture – an old Quebec folk art. The old-style double wooden swings on many a front lawn are popular in Quebec but rarely seen in the rest of Canada.

Shawinigan & Grand Mère
These medium-sized towns further north up the Saint Maurice River are rather bleak, with little to hold the visitor. Both are industrial: pulp & paper has long been the backbone of the area. Both also have generating plants; at Shawinigan, you can visit the falls and the large hydroelectric power station.

Grand Mère has tourist information, and between 5th and 6th Aves, the rock in the shape of an old lady's head from which the town's name was derived. Boat tours out onto the river are available. If you're heading for any of the northerly parks, stock up here because the food and supply selection doesn't get any better further north.

Between here and La Mauricie National Park there isn't much in the way of accommodation, so you're pretty much stuck with one of the few ordinary motels in Grand Mère or Shawinigan. In both places a decent meal can be had before or after venturing out with the canoe.

Orléans Express bus line runs north from Montreal and Trois Rivières into both centres.

La Mauricie National Park
North from Trois Rivières, up past Shawinigan and Grand Mère, La Mauricie National Park (☎ 536-2638) is the only national park among the many large provincial wilderness parks north of the St Lawrence River. The park is 220 km north-east of Montreal.

The park covers 550 sq km, straddling northern evergreen forests and the more southerly hardwoods of the St Lawrence River Valley. The low, rounded Laurentian Mountains, probably the world's oldest, are part of the Canadian Shield that covers much of the province. Between these hills are many small lakes and valleys. Within the park, mammals include moose, fox, bear and beaver.

The park is excellent for canoeing. There are maps of five canoe routes, ranging in length from 14 km to 84 km, for beginners to experts. Canoes can be rented for about $15 a day at Lake Wapizagonke, itself scenic with sandy beaches, steep rocky cliffs and waterfalls. There's also fishing for trout and bass.

Hiking trails, guided nature walks and an interpretive centre are offered. The Route des Falaises hiking trail is a good one with fine scenery. Some of the trails go along or offer views of the Saint Maurice River, which is one of the last rivers in the province where logging companies still float down their timber to the mills. Along the edges of the river you can see the strays that get collected periodically.

There are three serviced campgrounds at $21 a night without power but firewood is included.

Interior camping (camp sites accessible only by foot or canoe found in the park interior) is $14 a night (without fire; additional cost with) and you need to pre-plan your route and register. On holiday weekends in summer, calling ahead to check on availability is a good idea. Reservations are not taken. Supplies are available in Grand Mère, but the selection is minimal; it's better to bring most stuff with you. There is good cross-country skiing in winter.

Two adjacent provincial parks also offer wilderness camping: one is to the north, one to the west, but road access is more difficult.

The English language is seldom spoken here, so be prepared to communicate in French.

La Domaine Joly de Lotbinière

This is a stately museum on the south shore of the St Lawrence River, between Lotbinière and Sainte Croix on the way to Quebec City from Trois Rivières. It was built for Henri Gustave Joly de Lotbinière (1849-1908), once the premier of Quebec. Not only is this one of the most impressive manors built during the seigneurial period of Quebec, it remains nearly as it was in the mid-1800s. It's now a government-operated museum containing period furniture and furnishings, and the grounds and outbuildings are a real treat in themselves. Lunch and afternoon teas are served.

Quebec City

Quebec City, rich in history, culture and beauty, is the heart of French Canada. If you're anywhere in the eastern part of the country, make the effort to visit.

The town is unique in several ways, most noticeably in its European appearance and atmosphere. It has the charm of an old-world city. Old Montreal has this feel to some degree, as does the French Quarter in New Orleans, but nowhere in North America is the picture as complete. The entire old section of town, essentially a living museum, has been designated a UN World Heritage Site. Quebec City is a year-round tourist centre but does get crowded in July and August.

As the seat of the provincial government and Laval Université, this is the centre of Québecois consciousness, in both its moderate and extreme manifestations. Quebec City

has been the Canadian centre of French nationalist thought for hundreds of years and many of today's 'intellectuals' and politicians speaking for independence are based here.

Although many people are bilingual, the overwhelming majority are French-speaking and 94% have French ancestors. But this is a tourist town, ranking with Banff and Victoria as one of the country's most visited destinations, so English is spoken around the attractions and in shops. However, if you can, speak French, as this will make you more friends and enable you to feel more comfortable away from the busiest areas. Exhibits at national sites are bilingual while, unfortunately, some provincial attractions are labelled only in French. Before buying any ticket, it is good to ask.

The city is also an important port, lying where the Saint Charles River (Rivière Saint Charles) meets the St Lawrence River. It sits on top of and around a cliff, an excellent setting with views over the St Lawrence River and the town of Lévis (pronounced not as in jeans but 'lev-ee') across the river.

Much of Quebec City's past is still visible. Its many churches, old stone houses and narrow streets make it an architectural gem. The old part of Quebec remains the only walled city in North America.

The climate in Quebec City must be mentioned as this is a city with both summer and winter attractions. Summers are much like those of Montreal or southern Ontario, though generally not as hot and always a bit shorter. The real difference is in winter: it gets cold. There may also be mountains of snow if you're visiting in winter, especially during January and February. You can't take enough sweaters. Life does go on, however – the locals don't hibernate.

History

One of the continent's earliest settlements, the site of Quebec City was an Iroquois Indian village called 'Stadacone' when the French explorer Jacques Cartier landed here in 1534. The name 'Quebec' is derived from an Algonkian Indian word meaning 'the river

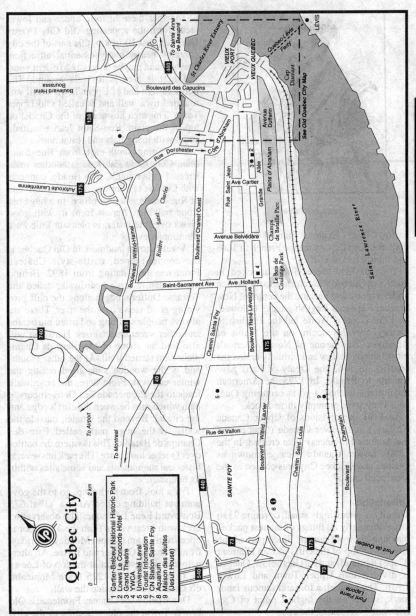

QUEBEC

Quebec City

0   1   2 km

1 Cartier-Brébeuf National Historic Park
2 Loews Le Concorde Hôtel
3 Grand Theatre
4 YWCA
5 Université Laval
6 Tourist Information
7 CN Station Sainte Foy
8 Aquarium
9 Maison des Jésuites (Jesuit House)

Jacques Cartier

narrows here'. Explorer Samuel de Champlain founded the city for the French in 1608 and built a fort in 1620.

The English successfully attacked in 1629, but Quebec was returned to the French under a treaty and became the centre of New France. Repeated English attacks followed. In 1759 General Wolfe led the English to victory over Montcalm on the Plains of Abraham. This is one of North America's most famous battles and virtually ended the conflict. In 1763 the Treaty of Paris gave Canada to Britain. In 1775 the American revolutionaries had a go at capturing Quebec. They were promptly turned back.

In 1791 the divisions of Upper Canada (Ontario) and Lower Canada (Quebec and the Atlantic Provinces) were created. In the 1800s Lower Canada became known as Quebec and Quebec City was chosen as the provincial capital.

Orientation

The city is surprisingly small, covering 93 sq km, with nearly all things of interest packed into one compact corner. Since part of the city sits on top of the cliffs of Cap Diamant (Cape Diamond) and part lies below, Quebec is divided into Upper Town and Lower Town. The Citadel, a fort and famous landmark, stands on the highest point of Cap Diamant overlooking the city.

Together these historic upper and lower areas form the appealing Old City (Vieux Québec). Just 10 sq km, this part of the city contains nearly every essential attraction. The best and maybe only way to orient yourself in this area is to walk around. The north-eastern end of Upper Town is still surrounded by a wall and is called Old Upper Town. This area lies north of the Citadel on top of the plain. Rue Saint Jean is a main street with many bars and restaurants.

Continuing south-east from Rue Saint Jean, Côte de la Fabrique is another main street. Further south, Rue Buade, connects with Côte de la Fabrique. At the eastern end of Rue Buade is a post office, in a huge old stone building. Across from it, with good views over the water, is pleasant little Parc Montmorency.

A well-known landmark in Old Quebec is the copper-topped, castle-style Château Frontenac hotel dating from 1892. Behind the château, a large boardwalk, called the Terrasse Dufferin edges along the cliff providing good views over the river. There are always people strolling and often musicians and other street entertainers. Here you will also find the statue of Monsieur de Champlain who started it all. At the other (south) end is the wooden slide used during the winter carnival. From here, the boardwalk leads to the Promenade des Gouverneurs, a path which runs between the cliff's edge and the citadel. Beyond the citadel, outside the walls, is the huge park called Parc des Champs de Bataille. This is where the battles over Quebec took place. The park has several historical monuments and some sites within its boundaries.

For a look from higher up, go to the government building called Anima 'G' at 675 Boulevard René Lévesque. The observation deck with great views from the 31st floor is open from 10 am to 4 pm Monday to Friday, from March to October and is free. An alternative is the restaurant at the top of Loews Le Concorde Hôtel, 1225 Place Montcalm off Grande Allée, outside the wall.

Down below the Chateau Frontenac is Old Lower Town, the oldest section of the city, sitting mainly between the St Lawrence and St Charles rivers and hugging the cliffs of Cap Diamant.

The focal point of this small area, at the north-eastern edge of Old Quebec, is Place Royale. From here, you can walk (it's not hard, or far) or take the funicular railway (elevator) for $1 one way to the top of the cliff of Upper Town. The funicular terminal in Lower Town is on Rue du Petit Champlain. Rue Sous le Cap and Rue du Petit Champlain, which are only 2.5 metres across, are two of the oldest streets in North America.

The ferry, which plies across the river to Lévis, docks in Lower Town not far from the Quebec Harbour.

Outside the wall in Upper Town are some places of note, including the National Assembly (Legislative Buildings) and some restaurants. The gates in the old wall are known in French as portes and are the only places where the Old Town can be exited. The two main streets heading west from Old Upper Town are Boulevard René Lévesque (formerly Saint Cyrille) and, to the south, Grande Allée, which eventually becomes Boulevard Wilfrid Laurier. Grand Allée, in particular, is busy at night with bars and numerous places to eat.

Lower Town, lying to the north, south and west of Upper Town contains residential, business and industrial areas.

Much further north in Lower Town are the highways leading east and west. In this section of the city you'll find some of the motels.

To the extreme south-west of the city you'll see signs for either Pont de Québec or Pont Pierre Laporte. Both these bridges lead to the south shore.

Information

There are several tourist offices where the staff are bilingual and well supplied with maps and other information.

The main office is at 60 Rue d'Auteuil (☎ 692-2471), just north of Rue Saint Louis. It's in the Parc de l'Esplanade, near the Porte

(Gate) Saint Louis. Usually they will help out with off-beat questions and will even make telephone calls for you and help with booking accommodation. Most of the workers are friendly, considering the crowds they get at peak times. In summer it is open from 8.30 am to 8 pm daily otherwise it closes at 5.30 pm.

A second tourist office (☎ 643-2280) is on Place d'Armes, on the north side of the Château Frontenac hotel. This one deals primarily with destinations elsewhere around the province.

Another is at 215 Rue du Marché-Finlay (☎ 643-6631) in Lower Town. It's on a large square, Place de Paris, near the water, east of Place Royale and deals mainly with the Place Royale area.

There is a post office outlet in the walled section of Upper Town, at the bottom of Rue Buade at No 3, opposite Parc Montmorency. The main post office is at 300 Rue Saint-Paul next to the train station.

Transchange, at 43 Rue Buade, is a central money changing office open daily.

Quebec has two French daily newspapers, *Le Soleil* and the *Journal du Quebec*. The English *Chronicle-Telegraph* is published each Wednesday. A good English/French bookstore is Librairie Garneau at 24 Côte de la Fabrique.

Historic Quebec City Nearly every second building in Old Quebec is of some interest; a list of all the sites in this area would fill a book. For a more complete guide, ask at the tourist office for the walking-tour booklet. Following are some of the most significant sites in the old section as well as some outside the walls.

Watch for a symbol in the shape of a key on buildings and businesses around town. It indicates something of historical note is on display. The tourist office has a guide to the 'key' locations as well.

Historic Old Upper Town not only has most of the city's interesting accommodation and restaurants but also many of the important sites and attractions.

QUEBEC

Old Upper Town

Citadel The French started to build here in 1750 when bastions were constructed for storing gunpowder. The fort (☎ 694-2815) was completed by the British in 1820 after 30 years work and served as the eastern flank of the city's defence system. The irregularly sided structure sits on the plain over 100 metres up from the river at an appropriate vantage point.

Today the citadel is the home base of Canada's Royal 22s (known in bastardised French as the Van Doos), a French regiment that developed quite a reputation through WWI, WWII and the Korean War. There is a museum outlining their history and a more general military museum containing documents, uniforms and models situated in a few different buildings including the old prison at the south-east end.

The entrance fee of $4.50 includes admission to these museums and a guided tour. The Changing of the Guard ceremony takes place at 10 am daily in summer. The Beating of the Retreat at 6 pm on Tuesday, Thursday, Saturday and Sunday during July and August is followed by the last tour. The citadel is still considered a working military site so wandering around on your own is not permitted.

Parc des Champs de Bataille (Battlefields Park) This is the huge park running southwest from the citadel. Its hills, gardens, monuments and trees make it pleasant now, however, the park was once a bloody battleground, the site of a conflict that may have determined the course of history in Canada. The part closest to the cliff is known as the Plains of Abraham and it was here in 1759 that the English finally defeated the French with both generals, Wolfe of the English and Montcalm of the French, dying in the process. In the park is the National Battlefields Park Interpretive Centre (☎ 648-4071/5641) focusing on the dramatic history of the park. It is housed in the Musée du Québec. The centre is open every day in summer but closed on Monday during the rest of the year. There is also a Martello

Tower (a small tower for coastal defence) in the park and a fountain with a lookout.

Musée du Québec (Quebec Museum) Towards the south-western end of the park at 1 Avenue Wolfe-Montcalm, is this museum/gallery (☎ 643-2150) with changing exhibits, mainly on Quebec's art. It shows both modern and more traditional art, ceramics and decorative works. It's small and not especially memorable, but it is free on Wednesday when it is open from 10 am to 10 pm. On other days it is $4.75 and open from 10 am to 6 pm although out of the summer season it is closed on Monday. The old prison nearby is now part of the gallery. Note that the museum also contains the Battlefields Park Interpretive Centre.

Fortifications of Quebec National Historic Site The largely restored now protected old wall site (☎ 648-7016) can be visited for free. In fact, you can walk a complete circuit on top of the walls, 4.6 km, all around the Old City. In the old Powder Building beside Porte Saint Louis, an interpretive centre has been set up, which provides a little information on the wall's history. Along the circuit are two other information booths, one on Terrasse Dufferin and one on the Promenade des Gouverneurs.

Parc d'Artillerie Beside the wall at Porte Saint Jean, Parc d'Artillerie (☎ 648-4205), a National Historic Site, has been used militarily for centuries. A munitions factory built cartridges for the Canadian Forces here until 1964. It's now an interpretive centre with a scale model of Quebec City the way it was in the early 1800s. In the Dauphine Redoubt, there are costumes and displays about the soldiers for whom it was built during the French regime. The Redoubt, built between 1712 and 1748, is a defence structure designed to protect a prominent point. In this case, the edge of the hill could be well guarded by the soldiers within. In the officers' quarters there's a history lesson for children. Admission is $2.60 with family rates offered.

Musée du Fort This is a small museum (☎ 692-2175), at 10 Rue Sainte Anne near Place d'Armes, dealing with more provincial military history. With the aid of a large model of 18th-century Quebec City, six sieges and battles are retold using sound & light (son et lumière). The half-hour show isn't bad, comes in English and French versions, and costs $5.50.

Musée Grévin Also facing Place d'Armes, the Musée Grévin, a wax museum (☎ 692-2289), depicts historical events like the landing of Columbus in America. Admission is $5.75, for students $4.75.

Ursuline Convent & Museum This convent (☎ 694-0694) on Rue des Jardins is the oldest girls' school on the continent. There are several buildings on the estate, some restored. The Ursuline Museum, which you enter at 12 Rue Donnacona, deals with the Ursulines and their lives in the 1600s and 1700s, and also displays paintings, crafts, furniture and other belongings of the early French settlers. A reader has written to say that the skull of General Montcalm is now on display. Admission is $3, students $1.50. The convent, chapel and museum are open daily from 9.30 am to noon and 1.30 to 4.45 pm but closed on Sunday morning and Monday.

Nearby, on the same street, is the Anglican **Cathedral of the Holy Trinity**, built in 1804, which is open in summer from 9 am to 8 pm Monday to Friday, 10 am to 8 pm Saturday and 11 am to 6 pm Sunday.

Latin Quarter The Latin Quarter refers to a section of Old Upper Town surrounding the large **Quebec seminary** complex. The seminary was originally the site of the Université Laval which outgrew the space here and was moved in the 1960s to Sainte Foy, south-west of the downtown area. Many students still live along the old, narrow streets which look particularly Parisian. To enter the seminary grounds, go to 9 Rue de l'Université. In the grounds are many stone and wooden buildings, several grassy, quiet quadrangles, a chapel and the **Musée de l'Amerique**

Francais (North American Francophone Museum). The latter, open daily in summer, $3, contains the university's museum collection and various artefacts relating to French settlement and culture in the New World. For tours and the museum, the entrance is at 2 Côte de la Fabrique.

Parc de l'Esplanade Just inside the Old City by Porte Saint Louis and Rue Saint Louis is this city park where many of the Quebec Winter Carnival's events are held. Calèches, the horse-drawn carts for sightseeing, line up for business along the edge of the park.

Other Things to See In the 1700s Upper Town began to grow after Lower Town was destroyed once too often in battle. **Place d'Armes** is the small square to the north of the Château Frontenac. It was once a military parade ground and is now a handy city orientation point.

Rue du Tresor is up, away from the water, off Place d'Armes. This narrow street, linking Rue Sainte Anne with Rue Buade, is jammed with painters and their wares – mostly kitsch stuff done for the tourists but some pretty good work too. At the end of Buade is the **Hôtel de Ville** (City Hall) dating from 1833. Next to the Hôtel de Ville, the park is used for shows and performances throughout the summer, especially during festival time.

On the corner of Rue Buade and Rue Sainte Famille is the **Basilica of Notre Dame**, dating from 1647. The interior is ornate and contains paintings and treasures from the early French regime. How times change; there is now a bilingual, multi-media historical presentation shown in the cathedral – for a price.

Old Lower Town
The oldest section of Quebec City, like the Upper Town, is well worth exploring. Get down to it by walking down Côte de la Montagne street by Parc Montmorency. About halfway down on the right there is a shortcut – the break-neck staircase – that

leads down to Rue du Petit Champlain. A second method is to follow the sidewalk beside the Musée du Fort toward the river and Lower Town and the staircase will lead you down. Alternatively, you can take the funicular from Terrasse Dufferin down; it also goes to Rue du Petit Champlain, to Louis Jolliet House. The house dates from 1683 and Jolliet lived in it when he wasn't off exploring the northern Mississippi. Rue du Petit Champlain, a busy, attractive street, is said to be the narrowest in North America and is also one of the oldest.

Place Royale This is the central and principal square of the Lower Town area with 400 years of history behind it. The name is now often used to refer to the district in general. When de Champlain founded Quebec, it was this bit of shoreline which was first settled. For the past few years the entire area has been under renovation and restoration, and the work is now nearly complete.

There are many houses and small museums to visit, some with period furniture and implements. The streets are full of visitors, people going to restaurants and cafes, and school children from around the province getting history lessons. It's not uncommon to see a bride coming down the church steps either. There are also galleries, craft shops and other stores.

Also on the square are many buildings from the 1600s and 1700s, tourist shops (don't buy film here, it's too expensive!) and in the middle a statue of Louis XIV.

At 25 Rue Saint Pierre, near the square, is an interpretive centre which gives a free outline of the history of Lower Town and Quebec City. See the Quebec City Information section earlier for details of the tourist office which specialises in this part of town. They can tell you of the many free events, concerts and shows which frequently take place in and around the Lower Town streets.

At 1 Place Royale, **The House of Wines** is a mouth-watering vintage wine store in a restored 1689 dwelling. It's free to visit and may include a sample drink. It's closed on Sunday and Monday.

Church of Notre Dame des Victoires
Dating from 1688, this house of worship on the square is the oldest stone church in the province. It's built on the spot where 80 years earlier de Champlain set up his 'Habitation', a small stockade. Hanging from the ceiling is a replica of a wooden ship, thought to be a good-luck charm for the ocean crossing and early battles with the Iroquois.

Royal Battery This is at the foot of Rue Sous le Fort, where a dozen cannons were set up in 1691 to protect the growing town. The Lower Town information office is just off the park here. The Canadian government has a coastguard base near the ferry terminal across the street.

Vieux Port (Old Port)
Built around the old harbour in Lower Town north and east of Place Royale, Vieux Port is a redeveloped multipurpose waterfront area still undergoing changes and growth. It's a large, spacious assortment of government buildings, shops, condominiums and recreational facilities with no real focal point but a few things of interest to the visitor.

Near Place Royale at the river's edge you'll see the MV *Louis Jolliet* and other vessels offering cruises downriver to the waterfalls Chute Montmorency and Île d'Orléans. You'll get good views of the city, but you can also get them from the cheap ferry plying the river between town and Lévis. Near the wharf is the Musée de la Civilisation.

Strolling along the waterfront leads to the Agora, a large outdoor concert bowl and site of many summer shows and presentations. A little further along is a warehouse-style building housing numerous boutiques. Nearby is a large naval training centre.

Musée de la Civilisation The large, striking waterfront museum (☎ 643-2158), 85 Rue Dalhousie, deals with both Quebec and broader historical and communication topics through permanent and changing exhibits.

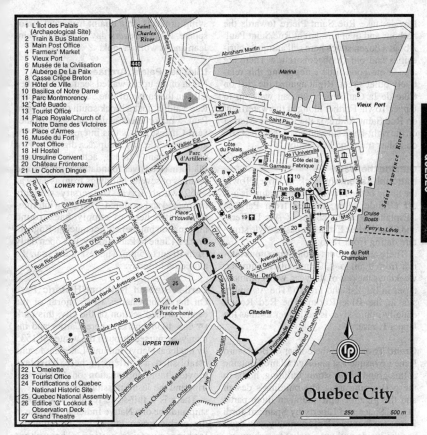

Map legend:

1 L'Îlot des Palais
   (Archaeological Site)
2 Train & Bus Station
3 Main Post Office
4 Farmers' Market
5 Vieux Port
6 Musée de la Civilisation
7 Auberge De La Paix
8 Casse Crêpe Breton
9 Hôtel de Ville
10 Basilica of Notre Dame
11 Parc Montmorency
12 Café Buade
13 Tourist Office
14 Place Royale/Church of
   Notre Dame des Victoires
15 Place d'Armes
16 Musée du Fort
17 Post Office
18 HI Hostel
19 Ursuline Convent
20 Château Frontenac
21 Le Cochon Dingue

22 L'Omelette
23 Tourist Office
24 Fortifications of Quebec
   National Historic Site
25 Quebec National Assembly
26 Edifice 'G' Lookout &
   Observation Deck
27 Grand Theatre

LOWER TOWN

UPPER TOWN

Old
Quebec City

0   250   500 m

QUEBEC

Human history and culture is explored through new and old artefacts and the creations of humankind.

It's spacious and well laid out. Aside from the static exhibits, it includes dance, music and other live performances.

It's definitely worth seeing and unlike many museums around the province there are English-speaking guides on hand. Admission costs $6 and it's open from 10 am to 7 pm daily from 24 June to Labour Day. The rest of the year it closes at 5 pm and it is not open at all on Monday. Note that on Tuesday out of the main season, it's free.

Old Port of Quebec Interpretation Centre
A short distance away, housed in a building at 100 Rue Saint André, is the Old Port of Quebec Interpretation Centre, a National Historic Site (☎ 648-3300). It's a large, four-storey exhibition depicting the local 19th century shipbuilding and timber industries, with good displays and often live demonstrations. Admission is $2.50.

Antique Shop District Rue Saint Paul, north-west of the Place Royale near the Old Port Interpretation Centre, is the location of a number of antique stores. From Place

QUEBEC

Royale, take Rue Saint Pierre towards the harbour and then turn left at Rue Saint Paul. About a dozen shops here sell antiques, curiosities and old Québecois relics. There are also some good little cafes along this relatively quiet street. Right against the cliff on Côte de la Canoterie, you can walk up to Upper Town. Further along at the waterfront on Rue Saint André, is the Farmers' Market on the right-hand side, and past that, the Gare du Palais train and bus station.

Outside the Walls

National Assembly Back in Upper Town, the home of the Provincial Legislature is just off Grande Allée, not far from Parc de l'Esplanade, on the corner of Ave Dufferin and Grand Allée Est. It is a castle-style structure dating from 1886.

There are free tours of the sumptuous interior from 9 am to 4.30 pm daily in summer, weekdays the rest of the year, with commentaries in English and French. The Assembly sits in the Blue Room. The Red Room, equally impressive, is no longer used as the Upper House.

Grand Theatre On the corner of Boulevard René Lévesque Est and Rue Claire Fontaine is this grand, three-storey building, home to the performing arts. The building's design and the gigantic epic mural in three parts: Death, Space and Liberty by Spaniard Jordi Bonet are features. Unfortunately, you can't see the inside without a ticket to a show.

Le Bois de Coulonge Park Not far west of the Plains of Abraham is this large area dedicated to the plant world. Long the private property of a succession of Quebec's religious and political elite, the area of woods and extensive horticultural displays is open to the public. It's wedged between Boulevard Champlain and Chemin Saint Louis with access from the latter only.

JA Moisan Épicier This is known as the oldest grocery store in North America. Dating from 1871, it still sells a good selection of groceries and more, including maple syrup products, in a quaint historical atmosphere. It's open every day at 699 Rue Saint Jean and is worth a look.

L'Îlot des Palais (Archaeological Site) North of the upper walled section of Quebec City on the corner of Rue Saint Nicholas and Rue Vaillier, just a block south of Rue Saint Paul, a major street which runs into Boulevard Charest Est, is this interesting idea for an historic site. It's set up as a dig of the first city intendant's house, actually a palace. Platforms lead over foundations, firepits and outlines of several buildings from as early as 1669 which Laval University students uncovered and explored. There's an interpretive centre here to supply background information but there is not much in English. From 24 June to Labour Day, it is open daily from 10 am to 5 pm. The rest of the year, it's closed on Monday.

Cartier-Brebeuf National Historic Park On the Saint Charles River, north of the central walled section of the city, this park (☎ 648-4038) marks where Cartier and his men were nursed through the winter of 1535 by the local Native Indians. Later the Jesuits established a settlement here. Displays provide more information on Cartier, his trips and the Jesuit missionaries.

There is a full-scale replica of Cartier's ship and one of a Native Indian longhouse in the park's green but rather unauthentic-looking riverside setting. Throughout summer it is open every day from 10 am to 5 pm and is $2.50. It's at 175 Rue de l'Espinay. From the downtown area take Rue de la Couronne north by car to the Laurentienne Expressway (Hwy 73 north) to the l'Espinay exit. By bus, go to Rue Julien from where you can walk to the park.

Maison des Jésuites (Jesuit House) South of the centre along the Saint Lawrence in Sillery this Jesuit and Native Indian site (☎ 688-8074) is at 2320 Chemin du Foulon. The first Jesuit mission was here in 1637 but it continued as a meeting place for the Native Indians and acted as a focal point for their relations with Europeans. Good displays illustrate the clash of cultures and there are outdoor replicas of Native Indian dwellings and a sweat lodge. This still-developing site is more satisfying than some of the others featuring Native Indian life. The re-creation of a typical pioneer garden is absorbing, too. A later resident, Francis Moore Brooke, wrote one of the country's early novels here. It's open 11 am to 5 pm from mid-May to September and admission is $2.

Together with the site below, the two make a not bad trip out of the centre especially if you wanted to cycle along Boulevard Champlain.

Villa Bagatelle Nearby at 1563 Chemin Saint Louis, this fine house and English garden present an example of 19th-century upper-class property and life. The house is largely given over to exhibiting art and afternoon tea is served. It's closed Monday and admission is $2.

Aquarium This is in the Sainte Foy district at 1675 Avenue des Hôtels (☎ 659-5264). They have about 250 species of fresh and saltwater fish. There's a cafeteria and, out on the grounds, picnic tables. It's open daily to 5 pm and costs $7.50 for adults and $3.50 for children.

Organised Tours

There is no shortage of tour possibilities here. Several companies offer bus tours of the city or full-day regional trips.

Gray Line (☎ 622-7420) runs numerous narrated tours from Place d'Armes. A 1¼-hour trip around town costs $13.25 and a four-hour trip to Sainte Anne de Beaupré, the falls Chute Montmorency and a short visit to Île d'Orléans, is $30. Several other companies offer similar tours which may offer more time around Île d'Orléans or some other variation. Gray Line seems to have the lowest prices. The tourist office has promotional pamphlets on the various tours available; there is also a ticket booth on Terrasse Dufferin representing many of the tour companies.

Maple Leaf-Dupont Tours (☎ 649-9226), with an office at 240 3rd Avenue, has six good, different multi-lingual tours in and around Quebec City by bus, foot or boat. There are city bus tours at $20 for two hours, and longer out-of-town trips including a whale-watching excursion. The city bus tour allows passengers to hop on and off at various locations. Free pick-up from your (or any) hotel is available so you needn't ever go to the out-of-the-way office.

Under a different number (☎ 622-3677), Maple Leaf offers two-hour walking tours twice daily for $11.50. Reservations are recommended. This company also runs the airport shuttle service.

In general, the less established operators tend to charge a few dollars less or provide longer tours for the same money.

Aventures Patriotes (☎ 835-9511), or contacted through the HI hostel, runs small hiking, canoeing, cycling trips and the like in the countryside of the Quebec City region. Groups are small and the prices good, making access to outdoor activities and historic and cultural sites fun and economical.

River Cruises Boat tours are also plentiful. A variety of boat tours is given on the big open-decked MV *Louis Jolliet*, which can carry 800 passengers. Tickets (☎ 692-1159) may be purchased at the kiosk, on the boardwalk behind the Château or at the booth along the waterfront near Place Royale.

The basic trip going downriver to Île d'Orléans and Chute Montmorency with a bilingual guide costs $20 and the boat is jammed with people. There are evening trips with music and dancing for $23 and dinner cruises, too. All these cruises are popular so getting a ticket early is a good idea.

Another company with a smaller vessel, the *Saint André* (☎ 648-9696), does similar 90-minute cruises around Quebec City and down the river at just slightly cheaper rates. For information call or see them at quay No 22 along the Old Port dock opposite the Agora.

There are many other companies all offering variations on the theme. Some go to Gross Île, others all the way to Tadoussac.

The ferry over to Lévis is, in a sense, a short cruise and provides a great view of the Château and costs next to nothing.

Festivals

Some of the major festivals and celebrations held in Quebec City are:

February
Winter Carnival – This is a famous annual event unique to Quebec City. The festival lasts for about 10 days in February, always including two weekends. If you want to go, organise the trip early as the city gets packed out (and bring lots of warm clothes). Featured are parades, ice sculptures, a snow slide, boat races, dances, music and lots of drinking. The carnival symbol and mascot is the frequently seen rolly polly snowman figure with a red hat called Bonhomme. The town goes berserk. If you take the train into Quebec City during Carnival, be prepared for a trip like no other. Activities take place all over Old Town and the famous slide is on the Terrasse Dufferin behind the Château.

In recent years, some celebrants have become overly unruly to the point of being problematic at times. Those with families may wish to inquire about participating in particular night-time festivities.

June
Les Nuits Black – This is a jazz & blues festival held at the end of the month with venues around town.

July
Summer Festival – This is held at the beginning and middle of July and consists basically of free shows and concerts throughout the town, including drama and dance. The tourist office should have a list of things going on. Most squares and parks in the Old City are the sites of some activity daily, especially the Parc de la Francophonie behind Hôtel de Ville at noon and in the evening.

August
Medieval Festival – Events with a medieval theme are featured during the popular five-day event held toward the beginning of the month on odd numbered years.

Quebec City Provincial Exhibition – Officially known as Expo Quebec, the Ex is held around the end of August each year and features commercial displays, agricultural competitions, handicrafts, a Black Jack parlour, horse racing and midway, the latter a large carnival with 55 rides and games of chance. The entrance fee is $7.50. Nearly three-quarters of a million people visit each year. Parc de l'Exposition (Exhibition Park) is north of the downtown area, off Route 175, Laurentienne.

Places to Stay

There are many, many places to stay in Quebec City and generally the competition keeps the prices down to a reasonable level. There are relatively few standard hotels – by far the bulk of the accommodation is in guesthouses, and small European-style hotels. As you'd expect in such a popular centre, the best cheap places are often full. Midsummer and Carnival time are the busiest times. If you can't find a place in the Old City, consider one of the motels slightly out of the centre or be prepared to stretch your budget.

Outside the peak periods, prices do drop. For accommodation assistance go to the tourist office on Rue d'Auteuil where they have lists of places and a phone you can use. Do not take their occupancy information as gospel, however. They may have a place down as 'full' when in fact a call will turn up a room, after everybody else has ignored it. The tourist accommodation guide also doesn't list all the places – a wander around will turn up others. Lastly, remember that morning is the best time to find a place and Friday and Saturday are often the worst.

Camping There are numerous campgrounds close to town. One is *Camping Municipal de Beauport* (☎ 666-2228) north of Quebec City. To get there, take Hwy 40 towards Montmorency to exit 321 and turn north. The park is not too far, on the left. It costs from $16 to $20 for tent and trailer sites. There are also a few places on Hwy 138 going east from Quebec City through the Sainte Anne de Beaupré area including *Parc du Mont Sainte Anne* (☎ 826-2323).

On the south shore, just one km west from the Quebec bridge, is *Camping du Pont de Quebec* (☎ 831-0777) with simple tent sites as well as electrical hook-ups.

There are many private campgrounds on this south shore road particularly west of Quebec City.

Hostels There are two well-established and busy hostels here.

The HI *Centre International de Séjour de*

Quebec (☎ 694-0775), is central at 19 Rue Sainte Ursule. Despite its great size with 300 beds, it's usually full in summer. Dorm bunks are $13 and there are some double and some family rooms. The pleasant, economical cafeteria offers all three meals. The hostel-run activities are worth looking into and the helpful staff is knowledgeable about things to do and how to get around.

Auberge de la Paix (☎ 694-0735) also well located at 31 Rue Couillard, is relatively small and quiet. It's open all year and has 60 beds. The European-style building is marked with a peace sign. The cost is $17 with breakfast, and $2 extra if you need a sleeping sheet and blanket. The doors close at 2 am. The location is perfect; there is a grocery store, a bar and restaurant all minutes away. It's best to arrive early in the morning to secure a bed. It's a short walk from the bus/train station but it's uphill all the way.

The *YWCA* (☎ 683-2155) at 855 Avenue Holland takes couples or single women. Singles/doubles cost $32/54 and they have a cafeteria and pool. The Y is often full, so reservations may be useful. Avenue Holland runs off Chemin Sainte Foy, which becomes Saint Jean in the old section. Bus No 7 along Chemin Sainte Foy goes past Avenue Holland. Walk south on Avenue Holland – it's not far.

The *Université Laval* (☎ 656-5632), between Chemin Sainte Foy and Boulevard Wilfrid Laurier to the east of Autoroute du Vallon, rents rooms in the summer from May to mid-August. Rates are $29 for singles and a few dollars less in a twin room. Student price is $18 or $25 for a twin. Bus No 800 from the Old City will get you there; it's about halfway between the bridges and the walled area.

Tourist Homes & Small Hotels Staying at one of the small, sometimes family-run hotels, often created out of old houses, adds to the charm of Quebec. There are literally dozens of them within the walls, which lets you stay in the centre of things while experiencing their individual characters. While certainly not a tradition in Quebec, more and more places are now providing the morning meal.

Most of the cheaper lodging is in one specific area. This area is roughly bounded by Rue d'Auteuil on the west, Rue Sainte Anne to the north, the Château Frontenac to the east and Avenue Saint Denis to the south. The two most fruitful streets as far as places to stay are concerned are Rue Sainte Ursule and Rue Saint Louis. Rue Sainte Anne and Rue Laporte are also good.

Many places are full by early evening in summer. Look for a room before 2 pm or phone ahead for a reservation. Prices at these places can be flexible, depending on the time of year and other factors such as on-going events. Consider bargaining if you're staying for more than a couple of days. Prices listed here are the summer high-season rates. Compared to the motels or larger downtown hotels here or in most cities, the places in this category still aren't bad value. Note too that most of the small places do have some parking available but it comes with an extra charge.

One of the best of the cheapies is *Auberge Saint Louis* (☎ 692-2424) at 48 Rue Saint Louis. The 27 rooms start at a reasonable $49 a single or double but go up to $89 with a full breakfast included. Parking is available but costs extra.

Further down at 72 Rue Saint Louis is the more basic *Maison du Général* (☎ 694-1905). There are 12 rooms which range in price from singles/doubles $33/38, without bath. As in many of these places, it's cheaper without TV, showers, the view or the biggest room. The cheaper rooms are sometimes noisier as they're often on the street but despite these drawbacks they always seem to be the ones to go first.

Also on Rue Saint Louis at No 71 is the super-renovated *Hôtel Le Clos Saint Louis* (☎ 694-1311, 1-800-461-1311) with 15 rooms at $55 to $95 for singles or doubles when things are busy, and dropping to $45 to $75 at other times. A continental breakfast is included.

Running off Rue Saint Louis is Rue Sainte Ursule, a pleasant, much quieter street. There are several places worth checking here. *Le Manoir La Salle* (☎ 692-9953) is at 18 Rue Sainte Ursule and has become one of the best buys because it has held its prices while those at so many other places have jumped. They have nine rooms at $30 to $40 for singles, $45 to $60 for doubles. Some may prefer the upstairs rooms to avoid having to go through the lobby to the bathroom, as is the case from the ground-floor rooms.

La Maison Sainte Ursule (☎ 694-9794) at No 40, looks and is more expensive, at $39 to $62 for singles and $48 to $89 for doubles. Kitchenettes are available – the only place offering this possibly big money-saving feature. The outdoor courtyard is pleasant.

Across the street at No 43 is *Maison Acadienne* (☎ 694-0280, 1-800-463-0280). Singles/doubles cost from $43/47 to $90/94 depending on the size of room and facilities. It's a good place and if you're lucky and have a small car you may get one of the parking spots around the back. A continental breakfast served out on the patio is available for $3.25.

La Maison Demers (☎ 692-2487) at No 68, charges from $35/50 for its eight rooms although the better doubles cost more and include a TV. Continental breakfast is included.

Further north-west off Rue Sainte Ursule is Rue Sainte Anne. *Maison Doyon* (☎ 694-1720) at No 9 has 16 rooms all of which have been spruced up with baths replacing simple washbasins. Singles are $50 and a room for four adults goes for $100, simple breakfast included.

There are numerous places by Parc des Governeurs to the south of the Château Frontenac. *Manoir Sur le Cap* (☎ 694-1987), at 9 Avenue Sainte Genéviève, has 14 rooms carved out of the old house, some of them have views of the park, others of the river and Lévis. Singles/doubles cost from $50 to $125 for four people.

The *Manoir de la Terrasse* (☎ 694-1592) is at 4 Rue Laporte close to the boardwalk. Singles or doubles are the same price and range from $40 to $70.

On the corner of Rue Saint Louis and Rue d'Auteuil is *Manoir de L'Esplanade* (☎ 694-0834), a large, old, refurbished place where prices are a little steep. The 36 rooms cost between $60 and $95 and the corner rooms can be noisy.

Hayden's Wexford House (☎ 524-0525), run by Michelle Pacquet, is a renovated historic house at 450 Rue Champlain, one km south of Old Lower Town. There's a public swimming pool nearby. Singles/doubles are $50/65 with full breakfast. Next door she has some fully equipped apartments suitable for four or five people at $80. Weekly rates are offered.

Motels Rare is the city with more motels than Quebec. Whether you have a car or not, they may be the answer if you find everything booked up downtown.

There are three major areas to look in for motels. All are out of the Old City, but not really far and not difficult to reach.

Beauport One area is Beauport, a section of Quebec City to the north of the downtown area. You pass by on the way to Sainte Anne de Beaupré or on a trip along the northern coast. The easiest way to reach it if driving from the downtown area is to head north up Rue Dorchester to Boulevard Hamel. Turn right (east); Boulevard Hamel becomes Rue 18 and then, further east, Boulevard Sainte Anne. This is Beauport. Look for when the numbers are in the 1000s. Most of these motels are off the road with the river running behind them.

At 1062 Boulevard Sainte Anne is *Motel Chevalier* (☎ 661-3876). Rooms cost from $49 to $60 for singles/doubles.

Motel de la Capitale (☎ 663-0587) charging $55/60 is at 1082 Boulevard Sainte Anne. Nearby, there's the *Motel Olympic* (☎ 667-8716), at 1078 Boulevard Sainte Anne, where prices range from $40 to an outrageous $90.

North-west of the centre at the intersection of Boulevard Henri IV and Hwy 138, up towards the airport, is *Comfort Inn* (☎ 872-5900) where rooms cost $90 for singles/

doubles. This Canada-wide budget chain is always reliable.

Boulevard Wilfrid Laurier The second major area for motels is along Boulevard Wilfrid Laurier, west of the city. The motel section runs just east of Boulevard Henri IV, which runs into the bridges from the south shore. Check around the 2800 numbers. Prices are generally quite a bit higher here, but it is closer to town.

The *Motel l'Abitation* (☎ 653-7267), at No 2828, has good prices with doubles from $50 off-season to $110 in season.

Further east after Boulevard Wilfrid Laurier turns into Grande Allée, there are a few smallish, reasonably priced places around the 600s addresses. The places closer to town are generally more deluxe and more expensive.

Boulevard Wilfrid Hamel The third area for motels is on Boulevard Wilfrid Hamel, marked only as 'Hamel' on street signs. To get to this area, head north up Boulevard Henri IV from the river or south from Hwy 40. It's about seven km from town. Start looking around the 5000 block, although the road is lined with motels. Some of these motels are in Sainte Foy.

Motel Pierre (☎ 681-6191) at 1640 Boulevard Hamel has rooms from $70 to $90. Low cost *Motel Plaza* (☎ 872-1552) is at 7175 Boulevard Hamel with singles/doubles from $35/45.

Places to Eat

There are dozens of restaurants in Quebec City and the food is quite good, but prices are generally high. Actually, it's not that they are overly costly it's just that they are mostly in the same category – suitable for a good night out. Still, there are some reasonably priced exceptions, and the costlier restaurants do generally provide good service in an attractive setting.

Most restaurants post their menus outside which is helpful when shopping around. If you're here for any length of time you're likely to find a favourite.

At dinner the set menus include soup, a roll, dessert and coffee. Many of these same dining rooms offer midday specials which aren't bad value at all. Some serve lunch until 3 pm and one place customarily offers it until 5.30 pm. Prices for the complete lunch can be as low as half the dinner cost although often portions are a might smaller. More modest places have the usual cheap lunches of pizza, sandwiches and the like.

The ethnic restaurants, which aren't numerous in Quebec City, provide an alternative. The Upper Town restaurants, within the walls as a rule, offer the least price range and tend to be costly. Outside the wall or down in the quieter sections of Lower Town less expensive and more casual places are easier to find.

Old Upper Town Getting a good, cheap, full morning meal has always been a bit of a problem here and paying a lot for breakfast seems to grate most travellers (this one included).

For the egg fix, a moderately priced (not cheap) restaurant which is always busy for any meal of the day is *l'Omelette*, at 66 Rue Saint Louis, specialising in – what else – omelettes. It has about a dozen varieties which are served with home-fried potatoes. Three breakfast specials are also offered which include juice, toast and coffee with a choice of cereal, eggs or croissants.

For a more French-style breakfast there is *Le Petit Coin Latin* at 8½ Rue Sainte Ursule near Rue Saint Jean. Open every day, this small cafe has croissants, muffins, eggs, café au lait and more, with low-priced lunch specials. It has an outdoor summer patio with a fixed-price dinner of $10 to $12. At 25 Rue Couillard, one block east of Rue Buade, *Chez Temporal* is a little cafe which serves coffee, croissants and great salads. It's perfect for snacks, breakfasts and light meals. The cafe feels very French – a good place to sit in the morning and plan the day. Note credit cards are not accepted.

One of the Old Town restaurants suitable for families is the *Café Buade* right in the middle of everything at 31 Rue Buade, just east of Rue des Jardins. In the downstairs section, simple, light breakfasts can be had for $3.10 to $4.75. The lunch and dinner fare is similarly straightforward and moderately priced.

Over on Rue Garneau opposite the Hôtel de Ville at No 48, *Croissant Plus* is busy day and night with snacks and light meals.

Along Rue du Tresor from Rue Buade you'll find the Place d'Armes. In the *Hôtel Auberge du Tresor* is a dining room – pleasant, done in wood with ceiling fans and white tablecloths. The evening meal will set you back around $20, which is about the norm.

One of the main streets for restaurants is Rue Saint Jean. There are many places to eat as well as night spots scattered along here, both inside the wall and further out. At 1136 Rue Saint Jean, near Côte du Palais, is *Casse Crêpe Breton*, a small restaurant specialising in crêpes of many kinds, starting as low as $3.05. It's a favourite because it has been here for years and hasn't been dressed up for the tourists at all. You sit right up at the counter and watch them put the tasty crêpes together. At 1087 Rue Saint Jean is the busy *Saint Alexandre Pub* with 200 kinds of beer and an array of pub-type grub.

For making a meal yourself try *Marché Richelieu*, a grocery store at 1097 Rue Saint Jean which offers breads from the in-house bakery, fruits, cheeses and even bottles of wine with screw top lids.

For excellent Asian fare, try *Apsara* at 71 Rue d'Auteuil. Dishes are about $10 or a complete dinner for two will cost around $36. Down at No 23, there's a cheap Lebanese spot, *Restaurant Liban*.

Not far from Rue Saint Jean, at 48A Rue Sainte Ursule, is *Le Saint Amour* with a $30 dinner table d'hôte, value lunch specials and a good reputation. The menu offers about six meat and six fish dishes daily. For a splurge you're probably better off in a place like this, on one of the quieter streets.

Café de la Paix, at 44 Rue des Jardins, is very French in decor and atmosphere and offers a varied menu of seafood, fowl and meats. It's very well established and is recommended and, while not cheap, is not

exorbitant either. The early bird dinners before 7 pm are good value. *Restaurant au Parmesan*, nearby at 38 Rue Saint Louis, is always busy and festive. They have a large menu of mainly Italian fare with most dishes from $14 to $20. They also have a huge collection of wine with about 2000 bottles to choose from, and live music.

At 34 Rue Saint Louis is *Aux Anciens Canadiens* in Jacquet House, Quebec's City's oldest house, dating from 1677. Aside from the historical aspect it is noteworthy for its reliance on traditional dishes and typically Quebécois specialities. It costs no more than many of the upper-middle places and is one of the few with a distinctly different menu. Here one can sample such provincial fare as apple wine, pea soup, duck or trout followed by dessert of maple-syrup pie. The special table d'hôte menu offered from noon to 5.30 pm is good value at $12.50.

Old Lower Town At 46 Boulevard Champlain, with a pig on the sign, is *Le Cochon Dingue*. They serve meals but it's a good place for a continental breakfast, with café au lait in a bowl (as it's served in parts of France) and croissants. At dinner French-style steak frîtes ($13) is a speciality.

Along Rue Saint Paul, an old quiet street away from the main tourist haunts, there are several inexpensive places although this area, too, has recently seen some redevelopment. The cafe at No 71 is good for light meals or a coffee. And at No 95 the *Buffet de l'Antiquaire* is a small simple place for things like sandwiches or hamburgers at nontourist prices. They even have a few tables out on the pavement.

At 77 Rue Sault au Matelot which runs perpendicular to Rue Saint Paul look for the *Le Lotus Royal* for Asian meals. This is one of the few places in town where there is a 'bring your own wine' policy. A little cheaper at $10 to $12, is the *Asia* at 91 Rue Sault au Matelot with Vietnamese and Thai meals. They also have a busier outlet on Grand Allée.

Moving upmarket, *Le Vendome*, at 36 Côte de la Montagne, is an expensive French

COLLEEN KENNEDY

MARK LIGHTBODY

MARK LIGHTBODY

MARK LIGHTBODY

Top Left: Old Montreal, Quebec
Top Right: Windswept shore of Ontario's Georgian Bay
Bottom Left: Mont Saint Pierre, Quebec, is renowned for sunsets.
Bottom Right: The incredible gannet colony on Bonaventure Island, Quebec

RICHARD EVERIST

MARK LIGHTBODY

JAMES LYON

Top: Québecois cowboy
Left: The Château Frontenac overlooking Quebec City's Lower Town, Quebec
Right: Former Expo '67 pavillion, now a casino, Montreal, Quebec

restaurant which has had a European-style menu since the 1950s.

Le Pape-Georges, a wine bar at 10 Rue Cul de Sac near the corner of Rue Notre Dame, sells wine by the glass.

Outside the Wall Outside the city centre, things are a little quieter and not so densely packed. Rue Saint Jean, west beyond the gate, has numerous bars, cafes, taverns and restaurants. There is Vietnamese, Lebanese and Mexican food available. This is a far less-touristed area, and prices are correspondingly lower. Walking and looking will turn up places all the way down to Ave Cartier.

On Rue Scott at No 821, south just around the corner from Rue Saint Jean, is *La Pailotte*, a good, casual (bring your own booze) Vietnamese place with complete dinners from $12. *Le Commensal*, 860 Rue Saint Jean, has a wide selection of good vegetarian food paid for by weight.

Further west, about six blocks, away from the tourists is Avenue Cartier which runs south down to Boulevard René Lévesque (formerly Boulevard Saint Cyrille Est). There are a few interesting cafes and restaurants here including a couple of Chinese if you feel like a change. On the corner on Boulevard René Lévesque is a small store called *Delices Cartier*. They have superb croissants which have even been described as being the best anywhere outside France. There is also a range of pastries and tortiéres (Quebec meat pies).

West, along Grande Allée from Old Quebec, past the Quebec National Assembly and other government buildings, and just past Rue d'Artigny, is a popular and lively strip of over a dozen alfresco restaurants. They make a good spot for a beer or lunch if you're out near the Plains of Abraham. All have complete lunch specials for $7 to $10 (from soup to coffee) and at most places, dinners range from $10 to $20. *Restaurant Patrimoine* at 695 Grand Allée and *La Vieille Maison du Spaghetti* at No 625 are long-term favourites.

The Farmers' Market The Farmers' Market is on Rue Saint André in Old Lower Town near Bassin Louise, not too far from Vieux Port (Old Port) or the train station. Under the covered open-air building you'll find fresh bread, cheeses, fruit and vegetables. The best time to visit is busy Saturday morning.

Entertainment

Though Quebec is quite a small city, it's active after dark and there are plenty of nightspots although they change faster than editions of this book. Many of the cafes and restaurants – some mentioned under the eating section – have live music at night. Others are clubs open only at night. Most of the nightlife is in the Old City or just outside the walls. Brasseries – taverns for men and women – close at midnight while bars stay open until around 3 or 4 am. *Voir* is a French entertainment paper appearing each Thursday with complete listings.

Rue Saint Jean is alive at night – this is where people strut. There are good places for just sitting and watching, and places with music.

Folk clubs known as *boîtes à chanson* come and go along and around Rue Saint Jean and are generally cheap with a casual, relaxed atmosphere. There are also lots of dance clubs around town but they change quickly, so ask.

At *Bar Le d'Auteuil*, at 35 Rue d'Auteuil, there is often live music. *Jules & Jim* at 1060 Rue Cartier decorated with stills from Truffault films is a nice place for a drink.

L'Inox at 38 Rue Saint Andre in the Old Port area is the city's only brew pub and has a pleasant outdoor patio but the *Thomas Dunn* pub at 309 Rue Saint Paul was preferred by one reader. Lastly, there are a couple of spots on Rue Saint Pierre in Place Royale.

The *Grand Théâtre de Québec* (☎ 643-8131), 269 Boulevard René Lévesque Est, is the city's main performing arts centre presenting classical concerts, dance and theatre among its shows.

Théâtre Capitole (☎ 694-4444) located at

972 Rue Saint Jean is another performing arts centre.

Cinema *Cinema Le Clap* (☎ 650-2527), at 2360 Chemin Sainte Foy in Sainte Foy, shows English, French and other international films, many with sub-titles. Théatre IMAX (☎ 627-4629), at 5401 Boulevard des Galeries, shows large format and 3-D films with digital wrap-around sound.

Just Sitting The restaurant/bar at the top of the Lowes Le Concorde Hôtel, 1225 Place Montcalm at the corner of Grande Allée, is good for views. Away from the clubs, if you just want to sit, Terrasse Dufferin behind the Château is perfect. It's cool, with views over the river.

Getting There & Away

Air The airport is west of town, off Hwy 40, near where Hwy 73 intersects it on its way north. Air Canada (☎ 692-0770) flies to Montreal and Ottawa as well as most major Canadian cities further afield. Canadian Airlines (☎ 692-0912) also serves Montreal and Ottawa and has nearly all the same routes covered.

Bus The station (☎ 525-3000), is at 320 Rue Abraham Martin at the main train station. Orléans Express has buses to Montreal nearly every hour during the day and evening; the fare is $36. There are also regular services to Rivière-du-Loup and then on to Edmundston, New Brunswick. The fare to Edmundston is $45. Rivière du Loup is the connecting point with SMT bus lines for destinations in Atlantic Canada. Intercar bus lines runs up the north coast to Tadoussac.

There are no direct buses to or from the USA. Most go via Montreal.

Train Odd as it may seem, small Quebec City has three train stations (☎ 692-3940). They all use the same phone number. The renovated and absolutely beautiful old Gare du Palais complete with bar and cafe on Rue Saint Paul in Lower Town is central and

convenient. It is used for trains going to and from Montreal and beyond Montreal westwards. Bus No 800 from Place d'Youville runs to the station. The station in Sainte Foy, south-west of the downtown area, by the bridges over to the south shore, is used by the same trains and is simply more convenient for residents on that side of the city.

Also of interest to travellers is the third station, the one across the river on the south shore in Lévis, right opposite Quebec City. The station is just up the hill from the ferry landing. VIA Rail ticket holders do not have to pay for the ferry. This station is used primarily for trains heading eastward to the Gaspé Peninsula or the Maritimes. Some Montreal trains also use the Lévis station.

To Moncton, New Brunswick there are three eastward trips a week, Wednesday, Friday and Sunday. It's an overnight trip, leaving at 10.30 pm and taking 12 hours. A ticket is $109.

For Montreal there are trips daily and the fare is $47.

Car For car rentals, Budget (☎ 692-3660) is at 29 Côte du Palais or there's an office at the airport. For sub-compact vehicles the rate is $45 a day with unlimited free km if you take it on a weekend. Rates are higher during the week. All rental agencies here suggest booking two days ahead.

Car Sharing Allo Stop (☎ 522-0056), at 467 Rue Saint Jean, is an agency that gets drivers and passengers together. Membership for passengers is $6, then you pay a portion of the ride cost to the agency three hours before the trip, and the rest goes to the driver. They offer good deals, such as to Montreal $15, Ottawa $29, Toronto $41, New York (from Montreal) $65, and Gaspé $35. There are even rides all the way to Vancouver – especially in May.

Allo Stop also has offices at the Saguenay River, Baie Comeau and Sept-Îles among others. If you'll be travelling around the province pick up a list of all their offices and phone numbers.

Ferry The ferry between Quebec City and Lévis runs constantly – all day and for most of the night. The one-way fare is $1.25, less for kids and seniors; it's $3 for a car. You'll get good views of the river, cliffs, the Quebec skyline and Château Frontenac even if the cruise only lasts a few minutes. The terminal in Quebec City is in Place Royale, Lower Town. In Lévis, the ferry terminal is right beside the VIA Rail station.

Getting Around
The Airport A summer-only bus service operated by Maple Leaf-Dupont (☎ 649-9226) saves you from paying the $32 taxi fare. The fare is $8.75. The bus makes four trips a day during the week with a reduced service on weekends. It leaves from major hotels, but will make pick-ups around town if you call at least one hour before flight time.

Another bus service, Autobus La Québecoise (☎ 872-5525) runs to the Mirabel International Airport in Montreal.

Bus There is a good city bus system (☎ 627-2511) which costs $1.80 with transfer privileges. The buses even go out as far as Sainte Anne de Beaupré on the north shore. The terminal, Gare Centrale d'Autobus, is at 225 Boulevard Charest Est in Lower Town and will supply you with route maps and information or you can call the above telephone number. Many buses serving the Old Town area stop in at Place d'Youville (known locally as Carré d'Youville) just outside the wall on Rue Saint Jean. Bus No 800 goes to the central bus and train station.

Bus No 800 also goes from downtown to Laval Université.

Car In Quebec City, driving isn't worth the trouble; you can walk just about everywhere, the streets are narrow and crowded, and parking is an exercise in frustration. The tourist office has a handy map of city operated parking lots scattered around the central area and which don't gouge too much.

Bicycle Vélo Passe-sport (☎ 648-0224), at 77 A Rue Sainte Anne in Old Upper Town,

has bicycles and rollerblades for rent. Bikes are $25 a day but hourly rates are available. Guided tours are also offered. Vélo Didacte (☎ 648-6022), is at 463 Rue Saint Jean. You may also see bikes for rent along Rue Saint Louis near the Château, too. The Auberge de la Paix at 31 Rue Couillard also has bikes for hire.

Calèche Horse-drawn carriages (calèches) cost $50 for about 40 minutes.

Around Quebec City

NORTH SHORE
About 15 km north-west of the city is the small town of **Wendake** which may be of interest as a half-day trip for those wishing to know more about the country's Native people. In the late 1600s, some Hurons, a group native to the lands of Ontario, came to this region of Quebec to escape European disease epidemics and tribal conflicts.

Things to see in this decidedly nontraditional, modern town include the Notre Dame de Lorette Chapel of 1731 which contains some articles from the first Jesuit mission set up for the Hurons. The Maison Aroünne at 10 Rue Alexandre Duchesneau has a small collection of Native Indian artefacts. It is open weekdays all year, and weekends too in July and August, and is free.

The main attraction is **Onhoüa Chetek8e** (this is not a spelling error!) (☎ 842-4308) billed as a reconstructed Huron village. This it isn't and the pseudo-teepee and totems are out of place. The longhouse and outdoor craft demonstrations, however, are good, particularly the traditionally Huron snowshoes and canoes. A visit is more worthwhile with a tour. Ask whether an English-speaking guide will be on hand.

A gift shop with books and tapes by Native Indian musicians and a restaurant serving traditional Native foods such as caribou, corn soup and bannock are part of the site at 575 Stanislas-Kosca St.

It's open from May to mid-October, daily from 9 am to 6 pm and a ticket is $4.

The Laurentians

As in Montreal, the Laurentians north of town are a summer/winter playground. **Lac Beauport** is one of the closest and most accessible resort lakes.

Laurentides Wildlife Reserve Provincial Park

Further north up Hwy 175, about 40 km from Quebec City, is this huge wilderness park with its wooded hills and mountains, and scores of lakes and streams. You can hike and fish and there are campgrounds along the road through the park. The road continues to Chicoutimi.

In the southern portion, **Jacques Cartier Park** (☎ 622-4444) is ideal for a quick escape from the city. In less than an hour's drive you can be camping, hiking trails or canoeing along the Jacques Cartier River. Near the entrance, an information centre provides details on the park's activities and services. Camping equipment, canoes and bikes can all be rented. In some backcountry sections simple overnight cabins have been set up. In winter there is cross-country skiing with shelter huts along some of the routes.

Île d'Orléans

East of Quebec, this 30-km-long, green island has long had a reputation for its picture of traditional rural Quebec life. It offers good scenery and views and some of the villages are over 300 years old with examples of wooden or stone houses and cottages in Normandy style. Then, as now, the prime activity was farming for the Quebec City market. A problem is it's proximity to downtown Quebec. Aside from all the visitors, city folks are building more and more homes here, especially at the western end. It's certainly no longer a sleepy, pastoral farming region. Still, there are some pleasing landscapes and there's lots of fruit, especially apples and strawberries. A view tower stands at the eastern tip. There's a *camp site* in the middle of the south-side at Saint Jean. The island is

linked to the mainland by a bridge at its north-west end and there is a tourist office here. For less changed rural-island escapes visit islands further down the river.

Chute Montmorency

About seven km east of Quebec City, along Hwy 138, just past the bridge for Île d'Orléans, are the Montmorency waterfalls, higher than those at Niagara but not nearly as impressive. They're set in the recently redeveloped Parc de la Chute Montmorency where there are good walking paths, stairs to the top of the falls, picnic grounds, an information centre with historical and geological displays but also, in a case of total overkill, cable cars and helicopter rides above the flowing water. There is some interesting history and it has been classed an historic site. A $5 admission is charged for the ride to the upper portions but you can walk the 487 stairs for nothing. There is a hefty parking fee as well. The falls are accessible by city bus. Catch the No 800 at Carré d'Youville (Square) and transfer at the Beauport terminal, No 50 to the top of the falls, No 53 for the bottom. Within the next 40 km or so there are three other impressive sets of waterfalls to consider. Also before Sainte Anne de Beaupré is the Bee Museum where mead is available, too.

Sainte Anne de Beaupré

This gaudy little tourist town is justly renowned for its immaculate and mammoth church. From the mid-1600s the village has been an important religious site. An annual pilgrimage takes place here in late July, attracting thousands of people when any nearby space becomes part of a huge camp. The beautiful basilica begun in the late 1920s replaced earlier chapels. Note the many crutches inside the door. There's good tile-work on the floor, and stained glass and ceiling mosaics.

Check the hotel across the street. It's designed like a chapel, stained glass included – yuk! Yet it does have an inexpensive cafeteria.

Also in town are a museum, a monastery with a seminary, a few other churches and a stations of the cross walk. There's a 360-degree painting of Jerusalem on the day Jesus died. Admission to see it costs $4. There are several low-cost restaurants near the church.

Intercar bus lines which runs up the north shore from Quebec City stops in town.

South a few minutes drive toward Quebec is *Motel Spring*(☎ 824-4953), a good, clean, low-priced bilingual motel and restaurant.

About three km north of town, towards Mont Sainte Anne, is *Auberge La Camarine*, a fine place for a splurge on a good French meal. It's run by a woman in an old Quebec-style house and offers complete dinners from $25.

Grand Canyon des Chutes Sainte Anne
Six km east of Beaupré, in a deep chasm, are the 74-metre-high Sainte Anne waterfalls (☎ 827-4057) in a natural setting. You can walk around and across them via a series of steps, ledges and bridges for $5. Though busy, this is quite a pleasant spot – less developed and more dramatic than the falls at Montmorency. The water roars loudest in spring but autumn is grand with the surrounding red and gold of the maple leaves. The site, with restaurant, is open from May to the end of October. In July and August it's open from 8 am to 6 pm, otherwise 9 am to 5 pm.

Mont Sainte Anne Park
A little further east, 50 km from Quebec, Mont Sainte Anne Park (☎ 827-4561) is best known as a ski area – it's the number one hill near Quebec City and one of the top slopes in the province. There are about a dozen lifts. In summer, there is a gondola to the mountain's summit. Or if you're up to it, bicycle and hiking trails wind to the top. There is a campground, and surprisingly, it's not overly busy even in midsummer. The Intercar bus line goes by the park enroute to Charlevoix but not into it and the camping is quite a distance from the highway.

Les Sept Chutes
A few km further east are these waterfalls at a defunct hydroelectric station and a dam. Trails wind along the river past the various falls and through the woods and there is information about the old power-production facilities. There's a restaurant and picnic tables as well. Admission is $6 for adults.

Cap Tourmente National Wildlife Area
Beyond Cap Tourmente village, south off Hwy 138, along the riverside is this bird sanctuary. Flocks of snow geese come here in spring and autumn but many other species as well as a range of animals and plants make these wetlands home. There is an interpretation centre (watch for the hummingbirds) and meandering walking paths. The area is open every day from 9 am to 5 pm. Admission costs are low.

SOUTH SHORE
Lévis
There's not much here for the visitor. It's a cross between a smallish town and a suburb of Quebec City. The ferry ride over makes a mini-cruise and the views of Quebec are good. Near the terminal is a train station (☎ 692-3940) for trips east and to Montreal. For more information about trains, see the Getting There & Away section of Quebec City.

Part of the way up the hill into town are the remains of a fort from where there are excellent views.

Between 1865 and 1872 the British built three forts on the south shore cliffs to protect Quebec. One, known as Pointe-Lévis Fort No 1 has been restored and operates as a national historic site with guided tours. It's on the east side of Lévis in Lauzon.

Eastward
Leaving Quebec City, the landscape is pretty flat but looking across the river you can see the mountains and hills; the large one with the ski runs is Mont Sainte Anne. Going along Hwy 132 through the little towns, Île d'Orléans lies just offshore. Without offering anything of particular note, **Saint Michel**

QUEBEC

Skiing Near Quebec City

The excellent skiing is the main draw of the Quebec City area through the winter.

Mont Sainte Anne (☎ 827-4561) at 800 metres with alpine runs down the north, south and west faces is the premier ski centre in the region, indeed in Eastern Canada. Despite the obvious downhill lure it also has a spectacular system of cross-country ski trails. Access to the cross-country area is eight km from the alpine centre on Route 360, in the village of Saint Ferreol les Neiges. For both types of skiing there are novice, intermediate and expert trails. The season runs from the end of November to the end of March. Numerous resorts, lodges and hotels can be found in and around the foot of the mountain. The tourist office has publications detailing winter vacation packages which include hotel and ski passes. Meals and the shuttle bus to the lifts may also be options.

The second major downhill centre is Stoneham (☎ 848-2411) in the village of the same name up Hwy 175 north of Quebec City. With 26 alpine slopes, it is half the size of Mont Sainte Anne. Ticket prices here are about 25% less.

Smaller, less expensive alpine centres are Centre de Ski Le Relais at Lac Beaufort and Mont Saint Castin also at Lac Beauport. These, too, have snow-making and a range of lifts and slopes of varying degrees of difficulty.

All four resorts offer rentals, lessons, child care, night skiing (a magical experience) and lodging right on the hill. The latter is a luxury that must be paid for but there is plenty of accommodation near the centres. The week between Christmas and New Year's and the March school break should be booked well in advance. Aside from Mont Sainte Anne, there are other cross-country ski centres but a very good day can be had right in town in the Parc des Batailles. Where else can you ski on a battlefield that determined the future of a country? ■

---

strikes me as attractive and a quintessential example of small-town Quebec.

Montmagny

About 60 km east of Lévis, along Hwy 132, Montmagny is the first main point of interest, primarily for two islands just offshore. The town is also of note for being on the migration route of the snow goose. Each spring and autumn thousands of these birds stopover on the shoreline around town. Bird watchers can feast their eyes and enjoy the festival initiated by the geese.

At 45 du Bassin Nord in town is the **Migration Education Centre** (☎ 248-4565) a dual-purpose interpretive centre (☎ 248-9196) with exhibits on migration, both bird and human. The first portion is a display on the Great White Goose. The second presents the history of European migration at Grosse Île and the surrounding south shore through a sound & light show. There is an English version. Admission is $5.

There is an extensive accordion collection at the free **Manoir de l'Accordeon** on the corner at 301 Boulevard Taché Est.

The Gare Fluviale or Marine Terminal in the centre of town on the waterfront has boats daily to Îsle Aux Grues and Grosse Île. Bikes and kayaks can be rented. A riverside bird sanctuary is adjacent.

In and around Montmagny there are numerous places to stay including lodges, motels and campgrounds. About a dozen places to eat can be found in town including the inexpensive bistro (or the costly dining room) in the *Manoir des Erables* at 220 Boulevard Taché Est.

Grosse Île and the **Irish Memorial National Historic Site** commemorates the significant role this small island has played in Canada's history. For 105 years, from 1832 until as late as 1937, Grosse Île was the major Canadian quarantine station for immigrants coming from Europe.

Through the last century and into the middle of this one, four million people passed through Quebec City en route to points across North America. Isolated Grosse Île was meant to screen out those amongst the thousands of people of varying nationalities with typhus, cholera and the like. In attempting to perform this service it became, in a sense, a city of woe. One of its most tragic periods was for the 15 years from 1832 when thousands of Irish died after taking the 'coffin ships' to escape the potato famine.

There are over 100 buildings or remains of buildings still on the historic site including churches, a school, the 'hotel' residences and hospital. And, of course, the cemeteries. Restoration is on-going. There are half or full-day excursions but, in either case, reservations are required. For information call ☎ 1-800-463-6769 or ☎ 248-4832 in Montmagny. Bilingual guides are available from the reception centre to lead visitors around the site which is open from May to October.

From Montmagny there are several different operators who run boats the short distance over to the park but these trips, some including a meal, can be pricey. For information on the various choices call the above numbers or try Croisières Lachance (☎ 248-7977) with a five-hour trip at $32. Taxi les Îles is a little cheaper. Asking around at the docks in Montmagny may turn up something else.

The only inhabited island in the archipelago, small **Île-aux-Grues** can also be visited. There are free ferry boats and pay water-taxi shuttles from the Montmagny dock. The island is mainly geared to those in need of a quick escape from the rat race and has a couple of costly inns and a restaurant. But a pleasant day can be spent cycling and walking on the 10-km-long island and there is also a campground, a couple of B&Bs and a cafe.

Saint Jean-Port-Joli

This small but spread-out town, with the big two-spired church right in the middle, is a centre for the Quebec art of woodcarving. Pretty well everything can be found along one street, Rue de Gaspé including the central seasonal tourist office. The impressive church dates from 1890 and the priest's house next door was built even earlier in 1872.

Good examples of the woodcarvers' art can be seen in the **Musée des Anciens Canadiens** at 332 Ave de Gaspé Ouest with an admission of $4. The museum has work done by some of the best known local sculptors, past and present. There is a gift shop and snack bar here too. It's open every day from May to November.

More recent carvings in the same style and in a variety of other styles can be seen in the many workshops and stores in and around town. Some carvers specialise in figures, others in religious themes, and still others in boats and ornate murals. Courses in carving can be taken as well. Other crafts produced and sold here are ceramics and textiles but they are distant seconds to the number of works in wood. **Faunart** at 377 Ave de Gaspé Ouest, shows works of art in many mediums by Denis D'Amours. Admission is charged at this gallery/store.

At 322 Rue de Gaspé Ouest is the **Maison Médard-Bourgault** the former home of a wood carver who left reminders of his work on the walls and in the furnishings of the old house.

On the east side of town, with the 1953 Constellation aircraft out the front, is the **Musée Les Rétrouvailles** with an assortment of farm and household articles from the past decades. There is a small admission fee.

In and around the centre you'll also find a

Wood carving by Pier Cloutier

restaurant or two, a few motels and a B&B. On the west side is *Auberge du Faubourg*, a massive accommodation complex with a restaurant. Further west is a good picnic area with views over the river. Campgrounds can be found in both directions out of town, closer heading east.

Orleans Express bus lines stop right in the centre of town at the Hotel St Jean. There's a daily bus to Quebec City.

East along the St Lawrence River

East along the St Lawrence River from Quebec City are some of the most scenic landscapes in the province as the shoreline becomes more typical of that found in Eastern Canada. With neat small farms and little villages dominated by the church – usually topped by a silver spire – this is rural Quebec. With few changes, life has been pretty much the same here for well over a century. You won't hear much English spoken in this part of the province.

From Quebec City you can take either the north or south shore up towards the Gaspé. Just don't take the super Hwy 20 from which you'll see nothing. The north side is discussed first followed by the attractions of the south shore.

There are ferries across the river at various points. The further east you go, the wider the river becomes and the more costly the ferry.

CHARLEVOIX (NORTH SHORE)

The north shore area is hillier, wilder and more dramatic than the south shore as the northern mountains come down close to the river. It also has the more physical points of interest.

Beyond Sainte Anne de Beaupré is the scenic coastal and mountain district known as Charlevoix. For 200 years this pastoral strip of hilly, flowery farmland counterbalanced with steep cliffs and woods wedged between northern wilderness and the river

has been a summer retreat of the wealthy and privileged. Though vestiges of this remain and prices are on the high side it is now a more democratic destination. UNESCO has classed it as a biosphere or heritage cultural and environmental region and this has meant worthwhile restrictions on the types of permitted developments.

It has long been a popular district with artists, and numerous galleries and craft shops may be found in the towns and villages. Inns and less-expensive B&Bs abound and there is no shortage of quality restaurants. Aside from the summer visitors, people from Quebec City enjoy Charlevoix as a place for a weekend break or a short holiday destination. Beginning around the middle of September the autumn foliage is remarkable.

Due to its popularity as well as upper-class tradition (and quality), prices for food and lodging are higher here than elsewhere up the St Lawrence but the terrain and parks make a short visit worthwhile even for those on tight budgets. There is plenty of camping, and alternatives to the more costly places do exist. Intercar and Orléans Express buses serve the area stopping at many of the small as well as the larger towns.

In 1995 a privately-owned tour train began operating between Quebec City and La Malbaie/Pointe au Pic. The *Le Touillard*, a 50s style train, departs Quebec in the morning and serves breakfast as it rolls to Charlevoix. There's a stop at Baie Saint Paul and at the end of the line, buses take passengers to sites and the casino before the return to Quebec by 9.30 pm. Tours run from spring until the end of October. The excursion on the well-appointed train (with bar) costs $89. Call ☎ 692-3999 for information.

Baie Saint Paul

Heading east along the St Lawrence River the first urban stop after Quebec City is Baie Saint Paul, with its old streets and big church. The tourist office (☎ 435-3681) in the Art Centre at 4 Rue Ambroise Fafard is open year round.

The main street of this attractive town, Rue Saint Jean Baptiste, is lined with historic houses some of which have been converted into galleries and restaurants. Artists' studios and craft shops are scattered around the side streets.

The Art Centre often has shows of Charlevoix painters. A major gallery is the Exposition Centre at 23 Rue Ambroise Fafard. Another to have a peek at is at 58 Rue Saint Jean Baptiste. This house/museum is where a local painter, René Richard, lived and worked and played host to some of the country's most prominent painters through the mid-1900s.

Down the street at 152 Rue Saint Jean Baptiste, the natural-history centre has displays on the flora & fauna and geography of the Charlevoix district. It's open from June to October. Remember that many of the exhibits are described in French but there is a slide show.

Bicycles can be rented in town at several locations and an afternoon's cycle around the area should be considered.

For spending the night, there is the excellent *La Balcon Vert* (☎ 435-5587) east out of the centre up the hill, off Route (Hwy) 362. Watch for the signs. With its restaurant, bar, woodsy setting, chalets, dorms and campground it is a retreat, hotel and hostel all in one. And, it has a fabulous view. It's open from about the end of May to the first week or so in October and makes a perfect base for exploring the region. A dorm bed is $14 and rates go down for stays of more than three nights. A private room or chalet for two is $40 and family rates are offered.

As the main town in the area, there are many hotels and B&Bs. *Gite du Voyageur* (☎ 435-3480), central at 44 Rue Amboise Fafard, is a bargain at $30/35 with breakfast. There are other similar modest places nearby along Rue Saint Joseph.

The immaculate white *Auberge La Grande Maison* (☎ 435-5575), covered in flowers at 160 Rue Saint Jean Baptiste, is more costly with rooms from $50 to $100. This attractive place is central and has its own restaurant.

About 20 minutes drive north of the centre, at 1493 Boulevard de Laval, is *Motels-Chalets Chez Laurent* (☎ 435-3895) where singles/doubles in the motel units start at $50 and there are fully equipped chalet cottages available.

The central area has numerous enticing cafes and restaurants.

Around Baie Saint Paul

Quiet, rural **Île aux Coudres** is what many people disappointed in better known Île d'Orleans are looking for. It's the gentle, easy paced kind of place where you go to spend an afternoon and stay for days. Once the base for whale hunting, the island is now mainly farmland with a number of small low-key historic sites and a windmill. At the terminal there is an information booth. Bicycles are ideal for exploring the island and can be rented. The difficulty is that the bike rental place is five km from the dock. Turn left at the blinking light after leaving the boat and keep walking. There are two campgrounds on the island and several motels and B&Bs.

Ferries run to the island from Saint Joseph de la Rive where there are a few places by the terminal to stay or to grab a bite. The pleasant trip takes 15 minutes and runs frequently, especially through the summer months.

Hwy 381, north from Baie Saint Paul, runs along the edge of huge Laurentide Park offering good scenery and steep hills.

Excellent hiking and rugged topography can be found in **Grands Jardins Provincial Park** which encompasses an area of mountains and taiga (northern evergreen forest) and includes a caribou herd amongst the wildlife. The park is 35 km from Baie Saint Paul and has the Thomas-Fortin information office at the entrance. There is camping or cottages in the park as well as bike and canoe rentals. There is little swimming but the hike up Mont de Lac des Cygnes (Swan Lake) is very fine and makes an excellent half-day outing. Sections of the park suffered a forest fire in the early 1990s and camping at Lac Athabaska amid the charred trunks certainly provides a unique perspective.

Going east along the Saint Lawrence, don't even consider taking Hwy 138 but take the coastal Hwy 362 which goes up and down hills beside the river. The scenery is superb around **Les Éboulements**, with farms running from the town's edge to the river. You may have to stop while a farmer leads cattle across the highway. Note the piles of wood used for the long winters and the many carving outlets.

Pointe-au-Pic

Seemingly a small, insignificant village, Pic was a holiday destination for the wealthy from as far as New York at the turn-of-the-century. The scenery, the isolation and the trendiness had many building fine summer residences along the shore. One such resident was William-Howard Taft, who was a US president. Some of these large, impressive 'cottages' along Chemin des Falaises have now been converted into comfortable inns.

Today, the main attraction is the posh **casino** at the *Manoir Richelieu*. The huge, once elegant, romantic hotel dating from 1928 is now busy with bus loads of gamblers but is still worth a look on its own. It offers one, two and three-day packages including some meals and entertainment but we're talking serious dollars. An exception to the prices is the Winston bar-restaurant on the ground floor with a low-cost breakfast – a good excuse for checking the place out. The adjacent casino with gaming tables and slots is open daily until 3 am and has no admission fee. It's not overly formal but shorts and jeans are not acceptable.

The **museum** at 1 Chemin du Havre, offers a good view and exhibits on the life and times of Charlevoix. A major part of the museum is the art gallery which has a permanent display as well as changing shows which promote the works of local artists. The museum is open daily in summer from 10 am to 6 pm, with shortened hours at other times, and admission is $4, less for students.

On Ave Richelieu is a small Protestant church.

Pointe-au-Pic has a considerable amount of accommodation, least expensive of which are the B&Bs. For a meal, or to savour some of the extremely impressive Belgian beer inventory, get comfortable at the *Au Petit Berger* at 1 Cote Bellevue. This very attractive Belgian restaurant has main dishes in the $10 range and exotic brews from a few dollars less.

La Malbaie

La Malbaie, the second largest town in the region, sits in the middle of Charlevoix about 140 km from Quebec City. There really isn't much to see and do here but there is a major tourist office at 630 Boulevard de Comport open daily which can help with information on the area and parks.

There are a couple of places for over-nighters but nowhere near the number as in Pointe-au-Pic.

In Cap-à-l'Aigle, east of town the good but expensive *Auberge des Peupliers* in a fine old house wrapped with a veranda has lunches at $12.50 and dinners costing $30 to $35. There is also a B&B down the street, the *Maison Victoria* (☎ 665-1022).

Just east of this village on Hwy 138 is Les Quatre Vent, considered by many to be Canada's biggest and best private garden. It's only open four Saturdays a summer and tickets sell out. For information contact Centre Ecologique, 337 Highway 138, Saint Fidèle, Quebec G0T 1T0, or ☎ 434-2209.

About 44 km north of La Malbaie is the impressive **Parc des Hautes-Gorges**, a geographically and scenically intriguing area of mountains cut through by the Malbaie River. The sheer cliffs along the river reach 700 metres high at places.

Most of the road is unsurfaced and rough making the drive over 1½ hours long. It leads to the gorge where there is an information centre with cafe and canoe rentals. The *campground* is often full but there are a number of undeveloped, cleared areas (sort of) where you can squeeze (barely) a tent in between the trees. The best sites, including some on stretches of beach, are reached by canoe.

Also departing from the information centre, 1½-hour cruises along the gorge cost $18. The same and more can be done by canoe. Many of those on cruises come as part of a one-day bus and boat package organised in Pointe-au-Pic. Organised hiking and bus excursions through the park with naturalist guides are offered out of Baie Saint Paul at the Natural History Centre, 152 Rue Saint Jean Baptiste. Most of these will be in French but some guides do speak English.

Fine hiking trails crisscross much of the park. Take supplies with you.

Saint Siméon

The ferry (☎ 638-2856) to Rivière-du-Loup on the south shore departs from Saint Siméon. At this point in the river, a crossing is 75 minutes. It's in this area that the river, on its way to the Atlantic, begins to get salty. The ferry is comfortable with lounges, an information desk and a capacity of 100 vehicles. Whales may be seen if you're lucky. There are five trips a day during summer, three or four in spring and autumn, but the schedule varies according to the tides. Visitors with vehicles should be at the dock an hour before departure but for walk-ons this is not necessary. For prices see under the south shore.

The ferry terminal is in the centre of town.

SAGUENAY RIVER & AREA

The Saguenay is the largest of Eastern Canada's few fjords – a spectacular saltwater inlet, edged in part by steep cliffs and running to a depth of 500 metres along a crack in the earth's crust. Ocean-going ships can ply the deep black waters as far as Chicoutimi.

A federal marine park protects the river and the waters around where the Saguenay empties into the St Lawrence. The land surrounding the fjord and part of the shore north of Tadoussac is contained within the provincial Saguenay Park.

At the confluence of the Saguenay River and the St Lawrence, shrimp and capelin abound, attracting beluga, minke, finback, and even some humpback and blue whales.

Now protected, the great beasts have sparked a revitalisation of the region and it has become one of the provinces most worthwhile visitor destinations. **Whale watching** and **fjord cruises** are the basis for the all the activity. A range of whale-watching trips run from the middle of May until mid-October but the surfacing giants can also be seen from shore at several locations. A community of the distinctive white beluga whales, normally found strictly in the far Arctic, live in and around the Saguenay River all year round. Once numbering 6000, only 500 beluga whales still remain and this area has become their refuge. In June, minkes and finbacks arrive from the Gulf of St Lawrence and, later in the summer, the huge blue whale shows up to feed on the krill which is produced in copious amounts where the two rivers meet. August to October is generally the best whale-watching period. Seals and sea birds are abundant and porpoises and dolphins also frequent the region.

A range of cruises up the fjord are also offered. These trips upstream past the cliffs are interesting, as you lose your ability to judge size and distance against the rock walls.

Regardless of where you're headed if you're going out on the water take a lot of clothes no matter how hot it is on shore. It is always breezy on the rivers and the water temperature here is low, even in July. Also, the waters can become stormy very quickly.

The parklands alongside the Saguenay and St Lawrence are also well worth exploring and there are some very fine trails and walks to enjoy as well as various viewpoints and geological features.

Baie Sainte Catherine

Baie Sainte Catherine at the mouth of the Saguenay River marks the eastern end of the Charlevoix district and together with Tadoussac acts as a centre for exploring the majestic Saguenay and surrounding waters.

The main point of interest on this side of the river is the **Pointe Noire Coastal Station** up the hill from the ferry landing. This whale-study post (☎ 237-4383) where the two rivers meet has an exhibit, a slide show and films, and an observation deck with a telescope for views over the mouth of the river. The centre is open daily from June to September and then weekends only into the middle of October and is free. This is one of the best places, cruises included, to see belugas. They are often seen in the Saguenay very close to shore especially during the tide shifts.

Of the many **boat cruises**, several of the larger operators with the bigger vessels, are based at the small port here. Some can also be boarded in Tadoussac and tickets can be bought in either town. Navimex Cruises (☎ 237-4274), with three boats each taking hundreds of passengers, has whale-watching trips and excursions up into the fjord. The three-hour trip runs from mid-May to mid-October and costs $30. In July and August it runs two cruises daily up the fjord to Cap Eternité. A ticket costs $40 and includes a meal. The return trip takes about 4½ hours. All its ships offer bars and all the extras.

Another major cruise company is Famille Dufour (☎ 235-4421) with similar trips. Information for all tours can be found at the dock.

There is some accommodation in Baie Sainte Catherine, mostly in fairly priced B&Bs. The *Auberge du Gite de l'Horizon* (☎ 237-4409), at 550 Hwy 132, the main street, charges $45 double. Nearby at No 526, is the *Gite aux Pignons Verts* (☎ 237-4331), a B&B at $35/45. Remember the area can be a busy place in midsummer so book a room early.

A couple of small, inexpensive eateries can be found along the highway here, too.

A ferry runs across the river to Tadoussac every 20 minutes from 8 am to 8 pm, then every 40 minutes through the summer months. The free 10-minute trip is not as frequent the rest of the year. It is not uncommon to see whales from the ferry.

Tadoussac

Across the Saguenay, Tadoussac, with a population of just 838, is about three times the size of Baie Sainte Catherine and though still a small town, acts as the regional centre. It's an attractive place and nearly all the numerous points of interest are within walking distance of each other. This is also headquarters for the whale-watching and river trips around the Saguenay waters. See under Saguenay and Baie Sainte Catherine above for more information.

The tourist information office (☎ 235-4977) is at 197 Rue des Pionniers in the middle of town. The hours are from 8 am to 8 pm daily in summer, closed weekends otherwise. All the sites and boat trips operate seasonally, and from the end of October to spring Tadoussac pretty much shuts up and visitors are few.

The quay and waterfront area along Rue du Bord de l'Eau facing out to Tadoussac Bay has offices for the various **boat trip** operators although tickets can be purchased at numerous places around town. It may be best to scout around at the water having a look at the various boats before you decide. Whatever you're preference, try to wait for a calm day. Of all the factors affecting the success of a trip this could be the most significant. Whales are best seen and even heard when the sea is not too wavy and it makes the captain's work locating them easier. Rain or shine, early or late doesn't make much difference, it's largely a matter of luck but it's rare that no whales are seen. Having tried different size boats, each has advantages and disadvantages but overall, the Zodiacs are recommended. They are fast, quiet, manoeuvrable, generally can get the closest and every seat is good. Take a lot of clothes, especially early and late in the season, nobody is ever too hot. The small and medium size boats are the second choice, the MV *Pierre Chauvin* is good and includes bilingual (if you ask) narration. If it's very cold and you're not prepared or the water is rough or you have children this is a good bet. Rates are pretty standard at $30 for most trips and a little lower out of peak season.

At 108 Rue de la Cale-Sèche is the **Marine Mammal Interpretive Centre** (CIMM). It's open daily from May to November and gives visitors some background information on the

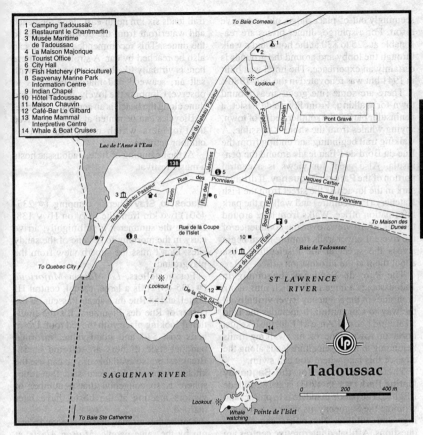

1 Camping Tadoussac
2 Restaurant le Chantmartin
3 Musée Maritime
  de Tadoussac
4 La Maison Majorique
5 Tourist Office
6 City Hall
7 Fish Hatchery (Pisciculture)
8 Sagvenay Marine Park
  Information Centre
9 Indian Chapel
10 Hôtel Tadoussac
11 Maison Chauvin
12 Café-Bar Le Gilbard
13 Marine Mammal
   Interpretive Centre
14 Whale & Boat Cruises

To Baie Comeau

Lookout

Rue des Forgerons

Champlain

Pont Gravé

Jaques Cartier

Lac de l'Anse à l'Eau

Rue du Bateau Passeur

Rue des Jésuites

Morin

Rue des Pionniers

138

Rue des Pionniers

Bord de l'Eau

To Maison des
Dunes

Rue de la Coupe
de l'Islet

Baie de Tadoussac

To Quebec City

Lookout

De la Cale Sèche

Rue du Bord de l'Eau

ST LAWRENCE
RIVER

SAGUENAY RIVER

Lookout

Whale
watching

Pointe de l'Islet

Tadoussac

0   200   400 m

To Baie Ste Catherine

QUEBEC

creatures found in local waters. Admission is
$4.75 for adults.

Maison Chauvin, at 157 Rue du Bord de
l'Eau, is a replica of Canada's first fur-
trading post and offers some history on the
first transactions between the Native Indians
and Europeans. It, too, is open every day but
through the warm months only.

Built in 1747 by the Jesuits, **La Vieille
Chapelle**, on Rue Bord de l'Eau, is one of
the oldest wooden churches in the country. It
is also known as the Indian Chapel.

The **Pisciculture** or fish hatchery located
at 115 Rue du Bateau Passeur is passed as

Tadoussac is entered from across the
Saguenay. Operated by the provincial government, the hatchery, which can be toured
at no charge, provides fish for the re-stocking
of Quebec's salmon streams and rivers.
Some of the Parc du Saguenay's walking
trails begin from behind the hatchery.

At 143 Rue du Bateau Passeur is the small
specialised **Musée Maritime de Tadoussac**
which through models, photographs and
other artefacts outlines the history of shipping on the St Lawrence and the development of the seaway.

Also in town is the **Tadoussac Hôtel**, a

seemingly out-of-place, huge, old, attractive resort. For a splurge, dinner prices are reasonable at $25 to $30 at the hotel and a walk through the lobby and around the grounds is certainly an experience. The hotel was built in 1941 but was renovated in the mid-1980s.

There are some fine green areas around town for **walking**. From Pointe de l'Islet, a peninsular park at the southern edge of town, spying whales from the shore is possible. A walking trail beginning and ending from the Rue du Bord de l'Eau leads around the peninsula. Also great for views is a central portion of the **Parc du Saguenay**. If driving, park in the lot across the street from the Fish Hatchery (Pisciculture) and walk to the park information office. Walks from here around the hill afford views over the confluence of the rivers. Longer trails running north begin across the street at the Pisciculture. Ask about them at the information office.

The Parc du Saguenay, beginning in Tadoussac, is a huge park which runs along both sides of the Saguenay River virtually all the way to Chicoutimi. It includes the land all around Lac de l'Anse à l'Eau, the lake just north of town. One of the walking trails beginning at the Pisciculture leads along the edge of this lake where you can swim.

The headquarters for the **Saguenay Marine Park** (☎ 235-4703) is at 182 Rue de l'Eglise. The park's mandate is to protect and promote the Saguenay, its waters, surroundings and wildlife. Naturalists can answer questions. Affiliated interpretive centres are found at Pointe Noire in Baie Sainte Catherine and at Cap de Bon Désir near Grandes Bergerons 22 km north-east of Tadoussac up the St Lawrence. At both centres whales can be seen from shore and there are displays on the mammals of the sea. At the latter you can wander along the rocky shore, picnic and keep an eye out to sea for a fin.

Between five and six km north-east of town, glaciers have sculpted massive sand dunes. The **Maison des Dunes Interpretive Centre** on Chemin du Moulin à Baude, part of the Parc du Saguenay, has information about their origins and is open daily from mid-June to the end of September. A walking trail leads six km north-east along the beach and waterfront from the downtown area to the dunes. This recommended side trip can also be reached by car. A stroll at the shore here is virtually like being at the ocean with salt air, seaweed and marine creatures to observe. Climbing the lovely, immense sand dune along the beach is an aerobic challenge.

Bicycles can be rented at Sepat, 188 Rue de Pionniers which organises various outdoor activities.

At the beginning of June, Tadoussac hosts a music festival.

Places to Stay There's camping (☎ 235-4501) two km from the ferry on Hwy 138. During the summer it is full nightly, arrive early in the morning to get one of the sandy sites. Don't miss the superb view from the playground.

For hostellers, *La Maison Majorique* (☎ 235-4372), is a large, casual, central HI hostel, at 158 Rue du Bateau-Passeur on the corner of Rue des Pionniers. It's the traditional-looking place with the red roof. Dorm beds cost $14 and good-value, informal banquet-style dinners are offered at $6. Breakfast is also available or you can use the kitchen yourself. It's been said the atmosphere is so congenial that a number of visitors meeting at the hostel have later married.

During the summer, there is a second place run by the same people, *Maison Alexis*, at 389 Rue des Pionniers about one km east of town.

Tadoussac also has a range of rooms for rent in people's houses ($30 to $40 average), B&Bs ($50) and hotel-motels ($50 to $80). Most are central. One B&B to try is *Maison Gauthier* (☎ 235-4525) at 159 Rue du Bateau Passeur. A couple of motels offer alternative low-end accommodation. At 188 Rue des Pionniers is the *Maison Clauphi & Motel* (☎ 235-4303). Another is the *Motel Chantmarin* (☎ 235-4242) at 414 Rue du Bateau Passeur which has an inexpensive restaurant. Rates at both start at $45 but may be more in peak season.

Places to Eat For a good, cheap breakfast check out the restaurant at *Motel de l'Anse à l'Eau* on Rue des Pionniers near the corner of Rue Bateau Passeur.

Café-Bar Le Gibard on Bord de l'Eau, the main waterfront street, is a small, casual place with excellent bagel-based lunches from $5 to $7.50. Whales can sometimes be seen from the window at high tide.

The restaurant in *Motel Chantmartin* beside the campground is a moderate, all-purpose place specialising in pizza (the vegetarian one is very good) but the menu is extensive.

Further up the road on the same side at 452 Rue du Bateau Passeur don't miss the chip wagon. It's run by connoisseur Claude Lapointe who knows life is a comic game but plays it seriously. He figures his fries can't be beat and he may be right. As you approach he'll say 'bonjour, Tremblay', betting that's your name so pretend along. The king of potatoes also knows a lot about the outdoors and enjoys a conversation.

Getting There & Away Intercar (☎ 235-4653) bus lines connects Tadoussac from Quebec City along the north shore and runs as far as Baie Comeau. The bus stops at the Esso service station on Hwy 138 near the campground. Autobus Tremblay & Tremblay runs up to Chicoutimi.

Up the Saguenay River
Just north-west of Tadoussac, Parc du Saguenay (Saguenay Park), which protects the river's edges almost all the way to Chicoutimi, begins. Visit the park information office (☎ 235-4238) off Rue du Bateau Passeur at the parking lot across from the entrance to Pisciculture at the western edge of Tadoussac. They can recommend walks and have information on some of the boat trips available. Good maps indicating walking trails and other details are available. Aside from the cruises of the fjord departing from the quay in Tadoussac there are others from various points along the river. There is camping in the park and guesthouses in the nearby villages.

On either side of the Saguenay, the roads northward are a long way from the river and are pretty uninspiring with little to see. The west side with access to more places of interest is the better choice.

From the village of Sacré Coeur, 10 km from Tadoussac on the east side of the river, a small road leads to L'Anse de Roche with a good view of the fjord and boat tours.

In the middle of the park on the west side of the Saguenay is L'Anse Saint John from where there are daily cruises through the summer for $18. *Auberge Chez Monika* (☎ 272-3115), at 12 Les Plateaux, is a place to stay with some hostel rooms and a kitchen. There are some good viewpoints and walking trails within a couple of km. Further west the area around Lac Ha! Ha! is where parts of the film *Black Robe* were filmed and there is camping on Petit Lac Ha! Ha!.

The main sites along the river are the cliff-side trails at Cap Éternité and Cap Trinité. Boat trips are also offered. At Cap Éternité, a rigorous hike, or rather a brutally long staircase, leads to a statue called Our Lady of Saguenay raised by a thankful, almost drowned soul in 1881.

Chicoutimi
Chicoutimi sits nestled between mountains on the west side of the Saguenay River about 1¼ hours from Tadoussac. Despite being one of the province's largest northern towns, working class Chicoutimi is quite small with a population of 60,000.

The tourist office (☎ 543-9778) is at 198 Rue Racine, the city's main street. There is not a lot to see around this ordinary town but the large number of students (there is a university and a community college known as a CÉGEP) liven things up.

See the **House of Arthur Villeneuve** (☎ 545-9400) at 669 Rue Taché Est. In the late 1950s when Monsieur Villeneuve retired as a local barber, he began painting. His depictions of the town and landscape along the river attracted a lot of attention and are now sold and collected around the world. The house, his former home, is a museum now known not so much for the paintings it contains but for the painting it is. The entire house has been painted inside and out like a series of canvases in Villeneuve's bright, naive folk style. It's open daily from mid-May to mid-October, admission is $3.

At 534 Rue Jacques Cartier Est is the **Musée du Saguenay-Lac Saint Jean** with displays on the history of the area including some Native Indian and Inuit artefacts. It's open every day in summer but closed on weekends for the rest of the year. Admission is charged.

You can visit the large (although no-longer operating) **pulp mill**, once the world's biggest, and adjoining museum. If you want a free tour in English, call ahead for reservations on ☎ 698-3158. The mill is at 300 Rue Dubuc.

From the redeveloped old harbour and market area, tour boats depart for trips down the Saguenay River.

Places to Stay For hostellers there is *Auberge de Jeunesse Saguenay* (☎ 543-1123) at 27 Bosse Ouest or low-budget accommodation in the community college (CÉGEP; ☎ 549-9520), at 534 Rue Jacques Cartier Est, from May to mid-August. Low weekly rates are offered.

Auberge Centre Ville (☎ 543-0253) at 104 Rue Jacques Cartier, has been recommended as a good, cheap central place, at least for males. There is a choice of basic rooms ($30) or more costly ones which have their own bathrooms. Either way a TV is included.

Also good value is *Motel au Parasol* (☎ 543-7771), at 1287 Boulevard Saguenay Est, with moderately priced rooms and a great view.

There are many other hotels, motels and some fine auberges (inns) around the region.

Places to Eat Rue Racine has numerous places to eat. *Au Café Croissant* is a good, inexpensive cafeteria-style place in the centre of town. *La Forchette* at 100 Morin, just off Racine is cheap and open 24 hours for standard fare. Many other restaurants including the main chains, can be found on Boulevard Talbot and Boulevard Saguenay leading into town.

At night the *Guiness Pub* at 455 Rue de l'Hotel Dieu is good and has a wide selection of beers. Along Rue Racine are several other places for raising a glass or kicking up the heels.

Getting There & Away Intercar bus line (☎ 543-1403), at 55 Rue Racine Est, connects to Quebec and Montreal and to Jonquière.

Jonquière

West from Chicoutimi along Hwy 170, Jonquière is about the same size as Chicoutimi and may be worth a look if you've come this far or are heading north. It has an enormous aluminium smelter and two paper mills.

The lookout at the **Shipshaw Dam** is a good stop. Turn right after crossing the Aluminium Bridge which is before downtown if you're arriving from Chicoutimi.

As well as a number of cheap hotels there is inexpensive summer accommodation at the community college at 2505 Rue Saint Hubert. There is also the central *Du Vieux St Pierre* hostel (☎ 547-0845), on Rue St Pierre at the corner of Rue St Hubert. The staff will help organise outdoor activities. Also ask about the resort-like *Île du Repos* hostel further north on the lake with its own restaurant and entertainment bar and nearby outdoor possibilities. Rue Saint Dominique, the main street, has a number of bars and cafes which are very busy at night.

Further north, Alma is on **Lac Saint Jean**, the source of the Saguenay. There's a wilderness park on the east side of the lake. On the west side at Mashteuiatsh, north of Roberval, is the **Piekuakami Ilnutsh Indian Reserve** (☎ 275-2473). There's a museum and outdoor adventures living with Native Indians in traditional ways can be organised.

The highway continues on through northern timberland and a huge nature reserve to the town of Chibougamou. From there the roads start to peter out.

NORTH-EASTERN SHORE & AREA
Les Escoumins
If you're going to the Gaspé and Trois Pistoles, the ferry here makes a logical choice. There is a motel, a couple of places for a munch and a bird-watching lookout.

Baie Comeau
Beyond Tadoussac on the north shore of the Saint Lawrence, the road continues northeast through hilly and less-populated areas to the newsprint town of Baie Comeau with a population of 26,000.

There isn't much to see here but in a small part of town known as the **Quartier Saint Amélie** there is another of the grand northshore hotels, Hôtel le Manoir. It's surrounded by a heritage district with much more modest houses dating from the 1930s.

For spending the night, there are several motels on Boulevard Lasalle west from the centre. *Motel Amigo* (☎ 296-3131), at 221 Boulevard Lasalle, is the most economical at $45.

Baie Comeau is one of the semi-remote industrial centres which seem to proliferate in this part of the country. As well as the pulp mill, there is a huge aluminium smelter, **Reynold's**, which runs free guided tours throughout the summer, twice on weekday afternoons.

But most associate the town with hydro-power because of the large projects along the Manicouagan River. Each of the three 'ginormous' **dams** operated by Hydro-Quebec – Manic Deux, Trois and Cinq – can be visited free. The first dam is 50 km north of town and the last one 200 km north. The scope and scale of these projects will really boggle the eyes and mind.

From Baie Comeau, Hwy 389 runs north past the Manicouagan projects and then beyond to Wabush and Labrador City on the border of Quebec and Labrador, Newfoundland. For details of these similarly awesome towns and Labrador, see the Labrador section in the Newfoundland chapter. There is also some more information on travelling the road to Labrador in that section. The **Grouix Mountains**, about 120 km north-

west of Manic Cinq reach as high as 1000 metres. This is a fascinating far-north landscape with lake-filled barrens and tundra.

Baie Comeau is connected by ferry to Matane across the river. For ferry details see under Matane.

Sept-Îles
Sept-Îles is the last town of any size along the north shore. It's a port city and international freighters make use of the docking facilities. In fact, despite the rather isolated location, this is Canada's second busiest port measured by tonnage.

Along the waterfront park a boardwalk fronts the shoreline and a tourist office. The tourist office (☎ 962-1238) is at 1081 Boulevard Laure Ouest and is open all year.

Vieux Poste on Boulevard des Montagnais is a reconstructed trading post where the French dealt with the Montagnais Indians whose land this traditionally was. There is also a small museum in town. The Native Cultural Centre has some traditional crafts for sale.

Offshore is the **Sept-Îles Archipelago Park** with its varied bird and sea life. Île Grand Basque can be visited for camping, hiking, beaches and a few other things to see. Nature trails cross the island. Camping costs $8. There are frequent ferries to Île Grand Basque, which cost $6, and water taxis to other places. Île du Corosol is a bird refuge.

Bicycles and kayaks can be rented in town at Location Rioux, 391 Ave Gamache. You can also take cod-fishing trips from Sept-Îles out among the many islands for about $15.

North-west of town is the huge, wild Reserve Faunique with camping.

The train from Sept-Îles permits access to part of Quebec's north and the western portions of Newfoundland's Labrador. See also the Labrador section of the Newfoundland chapter. The road continues eastward to Havre Saint Pierre.

Places to Stay & Eat For places to stay there is a HI hostel, the *Auberge Internationale Le Tangon* (☎ 962-8180), at 555 Rue Cartier and half a dozen motels in the expensive category. Further down the road in Havre Saint Pierre there is a campground. For something to eat there is both a Chinese and Vietnamese restaurant. The *Restaurant Saigon*, Rue Père Divet is about as far out of context as imaginable.

Getting There & Away Buses run between Baie Comeau and Havre Saint Pierre stopping at Sept-Îles en route. Call Autobus du Littoral on ☎ 962-2126 for the schedule. From Baie Comeau buses connect Quebec City.

The thrice-weekly train north from Sept-Îles to Schefferville via Labrador City, Labrador offers a fascinating trip through northern spruce forest and open tundra. The train crosses a 900-metre-long bridge, 50 metres over the Moisie River and past the 60-metre-high Tonkas Falls. The dome car is from the famous *Wabash Cannonball* train, a name often heard in US folk songs.

The route through the remote, rugged terrain was begun in 1950 and took 7000 workers four years to finish – a dirty job. These people had to be flown in, making the largest civilian airlift ever. For information in Sept-Îles call the Quebec and North Shore Railway (QNS&L) on ☎ 968-7505. The station is at 100 Rue Retty. For more information see under Labrador City.

Around Sept-Îles

A side trip from Sept-Îles (or Labrador City in Newfoundland) can be made to Fermont (Quebec), a mining town 27 km west of Labrador City, right on the provincial borders. Built in 1974, it has a unique design consisting of a 1.5-km-long, five-storey arched building which contains most of the town's commercial establishments. The housing is all built inside the windbreaking curve. Access is by the above-mentioned train which continues on to Schefferville, another mining town.

Havre Saint Pierre

This is the end of the road and the jumping-off point for visits to the island national park just offshore. This area, from Sept-Îles to Île

d'Anticosti, is one of the province's remote regions now attracting more visitors for the wild undeveloped land, animal life and outdoor adventure.

In town visit the national park's reception and information centre at 975 Rue de l'Escale (☎ 538-3285). In the former Hudson's Bay Company store at 957 Rue de la Berge, the Cultural & Interpretive Centre is a museum on local history and a place for visitors to pick up information on the area. The tourist office (☎ 538-2512) is here.

On the eastern outskirts of town is the *Camping Municipal* (☎ 538-2415). Out of town, 15 km, there is the *Auberge de la Minganie* hostel (☎ 538-2944), which can also help organise boat trips. Reservations are suggested. The bus from Sept-Îles will let you off at the hostel on its way to Havre Saint Pierre.

Chez Louis (☎ 538-2799) at 1045 Rue Boréal is a B&B. There are also a couple of inns and motels. In summer when the town is busy, some families in town rent out a room or two. Ask at the tourist office.

For the adventurous, there are ferries from town to Île d'Anticosti and along the coast to Labrador. Croisières Nordik, operated by Relais Nordik, (☎ 538-3230) also sail to Rivière au Renard on the Gaspé every day but Sunday with the *Nordik Passeur*.

Mingan Archipelago National Park

The park is made up of a string of 40 main islands no more than a couple of km from the mainland. A variety of sea birds can be seen and there are seals and whales. The major feature, though, is the appealing 'flowerpots' and other odd erosion-shaped limestone formations along the shores. Many visitors bring their own boats; kayaks are good, but a variety of commercial boat trips run from the mainland too. Some of the islands have hiking paths, picnic areas and/or wilderness camping sites. Fees are low but ask about drinking water. There is a visitor centre (☎ 949-2126) open through the summer months at 124 Rue du Bord de la Mer in Longue Pointe and park guides run interpretive programmes.

To Labrador & Newfoundland

From Havre Saint Pierre, a ferry skips along the barren north shore servicing about 10 of the 15 little fishing villages. The people eking out a living sometimes without even running water are a mix of French and Montagnais Indian. In Harrington Harbour, lodging is often available in people's homes but it's a matter of asking around. The ferry stops at Blanc Sablon, two km from the 54th parallel and the border of Labrador. These ferries run from April to mid-January depending on the ice situation.

From Blanc Sablon another ferry can be caught over to Saint Barbe, Newfoundland. See the Newfoundland chapter for details. For more information on the Quebec ferry call Relais Nordik Inc in Havre Saint Pierre on ☎ 538-3230 or in Sept-Îles on ☎ 968-4707. The ferry costs are quite low as they are partially subsidised by the government.

Île d'Anticosti

This large island at the mouth of the St Lawrence, halfway between the Gaspé Peninsula and the north shore, is a natural wildlife reserve. It's a remote, heavily wooded, cliff-edged island with waterfalls, canyons and good salmon rivers. For the first few editions of this book it remained practically totally unknown except to hunters attracted by the population of 120,000 white-tailed deer. Hunters who don't like to have to look too hard, it's presumed.

Recently, it has also been attracting more eco-sensitive visitors lured by its pristine ruggedness. About 150 species of bird have been recorded on the island and, as well as the canyons and waterfalls there is a major cave to be explored. Services are increasing and include basic campgrounds.

Anticosti was privately owned by different companies and individuals from 1680 to 1974. One of these was Henri Menier, a French chocolate whiz. Now there are about 300 residents, living mainly around Port Menier on the western tip, from where the island's lone road ventures to the interior.

Port Menier has a restaurant, lodging, tourist office, rental cars, gasoline and gro-

ceries. The Palaeontology Interpretation Centre has an assortment of fossils and the Eco-Museum has displays on the islands natural features.

There is a campground not far from Port Menier, towards West Point at the end of the island where there is a lighthouse. Potential campers should be well equipped and prepared for poor weather when planning trips anywhere in this region of the province.

L'Auberge Gite L'Antique-Costi (☎ 535-0111), is a fine place to stay with hostels beds at $15 and private rooms at $30/40 single/double breakfast included. There's a cafe bar and big stone oven where pizzas are cooked over a wood fire. It's at 26 Chemin de la Faune and is open from mid-June to mid-October.

The *Auberge Port Menier* (☎ 535-0352) charging $66 double for each of its 25 rooms is the only other game in town other than the full-package resorts.

The one basic road leads along the north coast past a four-km-long canyon, Chute Vaureal waterfall and a couple of simple camping areas. Ask in town about the cave at Rivière a la Patate which can be explored.

A daily (except Sunday) ferry runs between here and Havre Saint Pierre on the north coast of the Gulf of St Lawrence where the road eastward ends. It's operated by Relais Nordik (see the ferry for Blanc Sabon under To Labrador or Newfoundland section earlier). The cost is $40 per adult and $60 for a car one way. The same boat also sails to Rivière au Renard on the north shore of the Gaspé Peninsula. A longer, less frequent ferry runs to Port Menier from Sept-Îles. There are also flights into Anticosti. Safari Anticosti (1-800-526-5788) has one and two-day tour & flight packages from Gaspé which are not bad value at all given the high ferry prices.

SOUTH SHORE
Rivière-du-Loup

Rivière-du-Loup, on the south shore of the St Lawrence River, is a pleasant surprise for many people. Although a small, second-level city in the middle of nowhere, it's a lively

QUEBEC

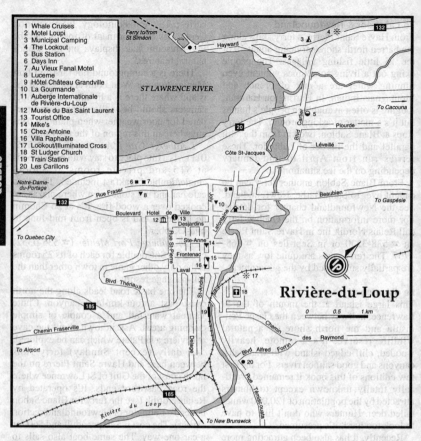

1 Whale Cruises
2 Motel Loupi
3 Municipal Camping
4 The Lookout
5 Bus Station
6 Days Inn
7 Au Vieux Fanal Motel
8 Lucerne
9 Hôtel Château Grandville
10 La Gourmande
11 Auberge Internationale
   de Rivière-du-Loup
12 Musée du Bas Saint Laurent
13 Tourist Office
14 Mike's
15 Chez Antoine
16 Villa Raphaële
17 Lookout/Illuminated Cross
18 St Ludger Church
19 Train Station
20 Les Carillons

ST LAWRENCE RIVER

Ferry to/from St Siméon

Hayward

To Cacouna

To Gaspésie

To Quebec City

Rivière-du-Loup

0   0.5   1 km

To Airport

To New Brunswick

and attractive town with an appealing and distinctively Québécois atmosphere. The massive stone church, Saint Ludger, in the upper portion of town dominates the skyline.

Much of the old town is built along winding, hilly streets offering views of the river to the mountains beyond. The location also makes it quite a busy stopping-off point for those going either through the Maritimes or further east into the Gaspé region of Quebec. There is free parking all around the central area, look for the signs with the letter 'P' on them.

The main street, Rue Lafontaine, leads up

the hill from Hwy 132 and Boulevard Hôtel de Ville. Many of the restaurants are found along it.

The tourist office (☎ 867-1272) is at 189 Rue Hôtel de Ville on the corner of Rue Hôtel de Ville and Rue Saint Pierre. It's open every day in summer and from Monday to Friday the rest of the year. You can't miss it coming into town. There is another office on Hwy 20 just west of the city.

Things to See Across the street from the central tourist office is the **Musée du Bas Saint Laurent** (Museum of the Lower St

Lawrence) at 300 Rue Saint Pierre on the corner of Boulevard Hôtel de Ville. The museum deals with local history and there's also a small art gallery. Admission is charged so note that all descriptions are in French.

Following Rue Frontenac, east off Rue Lafontaine, for a few blocks and you'll reach some waterfalls, a drop in the Rivière-du-Loup, and a picnic table or two.

The illuminated cross, another landmark and from which there are good views of the river, is easily seen but difficult to reach. From Chemin des Raymond turn left at Rue Alexandre, right at Rue Bernier and then left at Rue Sainte Claire. This is central and walkable from the centre of town.

Another **lookout**, less accessible without a vehicle, but with a great view of the St Lawrence and excellent at sunset is at the northern edge of town off Hwy 132 east past the large Auberge de la Pointe Hôtel. Follow the street signs to the small parking lot. A short walk through the woods leads to the viewing platform. Below, the waterfront park is a popular place for a picnic.

At 393 Rue Témiscouata are **Les Carillons**, a large collection of over 200 new and historic bells, some of which are enormous. All are oddly mounted and displayed on Hydro-Quebec pylons. The assortment can be visited daily in summer until 8 pm for a small fee which entitles you to ring the bells, from the smallest at 35 kg to the two-tonne monster.

Le Château de Rêve is a small amusement park with children's rides, a swimming pool and farm animals among other things. It's off Hwy 20, east of the centre.

Ask at the tourist office about boat tours and whale watching. Trips are made to several of the Lower St Lawrence islands which are protected nature sanctuaries. Lying just offshore, west from the city, the islands are good for walking and observing birds and seals. To the east, the river really begins to widen.

Places to Stay There is a convenient campground, *Camping Municipal* next to Ave Cartier beside the Auberge de la Pointe Hôtel

on the north side of town. It's geared to trailers as all sites have electricity but tents can be used.

The good HI hostel, *Auberge Internationale de Rivière-du-Loup*, (☎ 862-7566) is centrally located at 46 Hotel de Ville. Dorm beds are $12.50 for members and cheap breakfasts are available. It's closed from November to April.

Inexpensive lodging can also be found at the community college (CÉGEP; ☎ 862-6003) which rents out its simple rooms at $20/35 throughout the summer. It's at 325 Rue Saint Pierre.

Also inexpensive is the interesting looking *Hôtel Château Grandville* (☎ 862-3551) at 94 Rue Lafontaine on the corner of Rue Iberville, with rooms at $55/60 single/double in summer. This is north of the centre of town, nearer the motel district.

Most accommodation is in motels, the majority of which are just north of Boulevard Hôtel de Ville on Rue Fraser. They are scattered along here in both directions from the centre of town. Most are quite pricey but large and comfortable; some offer heated pools and good views of the river. They are all well kept and some are exceptional in appearance, the ultimate being the *Motel Loupi* (☎ 862-6898), at 50 Rue de l'Ancrage, which is the only motel I've ever seen that could be termed eccentrically spectacular. It's surrounded by immaculate terraced gardens complete with aviaries, a pool, swings, lawn chairs and a golf course. A double goes for $70 and up.

Also good is the *Days Inn* (☎ 862-6354) at 182 Rue Fraser. Across the street is *Camping Dubé* which has a pool. *Au Vieux Fanal Motel* (☎ 862-5255), at 170 Rue Fraser, has views of the river and a heated swimming pool which is good for the typically cool evenings. A double costs $65.

Another fine place at the same price is the *Motel Bellevue* (☎ 862-5229) right beside the ferry terminal and overlooking the river. Some rooms have kitchenettes. The perfectly good *Comfort Inn* (☎ 867-4162) at 85 Boulevard Cartier is about the same price but seems pedestrian in relation to the settings offered by the others. Others along Boulevard Cartier are cheaper.

Places to Eat There is good eating in this town. Many restaurants can be found along Rue Lafontaine along with a smattering of drinking places.

Mike's is a classy submarine-sandwich shop but with a dining room instead of a plastic take-away counter. The subs, pastas and pizzas actually make a pretty tasty and inexpensive meal for between $5 and $8. It's at 364 Rue Lafontaine at the corner of Rue Sainte Anne.

At No 433 *Chez Antoine* and, next door, the busier *Villa Raphaële* are both attractive, enticing places with more expensive complete dinners.

For breakfast head to *La Gourmande* at 120 Lafontaine. It's a cafe and bakery with bagels, croissants or toast, jam and coffee for $3. There are soups, salads and sandwiches at lunch.

A place for a casual dinner like steak-frites and a beer is *l'Estaminet* at 299 Rue Lafontaine.

The other major eating area is along Rue Fraser and serves the motel crowd. The *Lucerne* is a moderately priced place where you can comfortably take the kids.

Getting There & Away The bus station (☎ 862-4884) is at 83 Boulevard Cartier beside the Comfort Inn, a short walk from the centre. It's near the corner of Rue Fraser and Hwy 20, is open 24 hours a day and has coin lockers. Orléans Express runs west to Montreal, east to Gaspé and south to Edmunston. Some trips are express, others local, meaning they stop at towns along the way.

VIA Rail (☎ 1-800-361-5390) connects to Quebec City and to Campbellton, New Brunswick via the Matapédia Valley. The station is on Rue Lafontaine at the top of the hill near the corner of Fraserville.

The ferry (☎ 862-9545) to Saint Siméon on the north shore runs from early morning to early evening and the trip takes 1¼ hours. About seven services a day run in summer

costing $23 per car and $9 per person. In the middle of the summer, the first (7 am) and the last (8 pm) trips of the day are offered at good discounts. There is a restaurant and bar on board. Same-day return passenger-only fares, in other words a three-hour cruise, are reasonable. Keep an eye out for whales on the crossing. Boarding is on a first-come, first-served basis and hopeful passengers should be at the dock an hour before departure. This only applies to those with vehicles, walk-ons have no trouble arriving just before departure. The ferry, with a capacity of 100 vehicles, runs from April to January. Also offered is a five-hour cruise to the mouth of the Saguenay and back. For pedestrians, there is no bus to the ferry terminal about six km from the centre of town. If you want a cab try Taxi Capitol (☎ 862-6333).

I've heard of hitchhikers asking to have their ride requests broadcast over the ferry PA system before docking and being surprised by having their announcement meet with success.

Mark Lightbody

Towards New Brunswick
Hwy 185 with its pulp & paper mills and forests interspersed with farms provides a foretaste of New Brunswick. A highlight is the privilege of passing through and being able to say you've been to Saint Louis du Ha! Ha! (Haha is a French word traceable to the 15th century and meaning unexpected barrier or dead end – *Canadian Geographic*.) Also pleasant is the beautiful, green rolling landscape around **Lac Temiscouta**.

There is some camping and, most notably around Cabano, a number of motels where, as is so typical of Quebec, the amenities include a bar. In Cabano itself with a large cardboard mill, there are a couple of restaurants on the one main street near the edge of the lake. Fort Ingall historic site was built in 1839 as protection from possible US attack.

In the heart of the Temiscouta region a recommended place to stay and eat is the *L'Auberge Marie Blanc* (☎ 899-6747) in

Notre Dame du Lac. The address is 1112 Rue Commerciale. Built in 1905 by a lawyer for his mistress, Marie Blanc, the house has been operated as an inn since the early 1960s. It's open from the beginning of April until the end of October and the pricey dining room serves good food. Overnight rates are $60 double. There's a beach and access to a 60-km cycling trail along the lakeshore.

During the summer a ferry runs across the lake but this remains a largely undeveloped area.

Trois Pistoles

Just east of Rivière du Loup, Hwy 20 ends and you must take the smaller 132. At L'Isle Verte there is a lot of seafood for sale and smokehouses offering their produce, mainly salmon. There is also a ferry over to rural Île Verte where there is a small community.

The town of Trois Pistoles is dominated by a massive church and there's a good picnic site on the west side of town. If you want to linger, there are some eco-tour possibilities. Trips can be taken offshore to Île aux Basques which was used by Basques whalers in the 16th century and is now a reserve. Kayaks can be rented and guided paddling tours of the coast are offered. Also, cruises to the Saguenay for whale watching can be boarded here if you can't make it to Tadoussac.

For campers, there is a central *Municipal Campground* and two others nearby. There's a ferry (☎ 851-4676) here, going to Les Escoumins across the river on the north shore. The trip takes 1¼ hours and costs $23 per car, $9 per person. It runs from May to the middle of October, with three services a day in July and August when reservations are recommended.

The coast becomes more hilly and less populated as you head for the Gaspé Peninsula – it looks somewhat like the Scottish Highlands. To add to the similarity, people in the area, particularly between Saint Simon and Saint Fabien, cut and sell peat for garden fertiliser. The coast between Saint Fabien sur Mer and Bic is particularly scenic.

Bic

Bic was a little village in a beautiful setting a few km from Rimouski but has now become a sort of suburb. There are some good coastal views in the area and a visit to **Parc Bic** is recommended. The village has a good picnic spot and the park offers camping.

Parc Bic protects an unusual landscape of irregular, lumpy, conical mountains that edge the rough, rocky shoreline here. Numerous bays, coves and islands link land and sea. The park is a vegetation transition zone which makes for an interesting mix of southern deciduous and northern boreal forest. The park is also rich in wildlife. Of most interest are the sea birds and the colony of grey and harbour seals offshore. Bring binoculars if you have them.

Roads and walking trails (with a free map available in English) lead to mountain tops and beaches and cut through portions of forest. Guided walks are offered. The park is divided into three sections. The middle one, Secteur Rivière du Sud-Ouest, has the seasonal interpretation centre and campground. Picnic sites can be found in various places. The park is easily big enough to spend a couple of days exploring and day use is free. Note that it is officially closed from September to May but people do set up camp nearby and walk in during the day.

Boat tours around the river side of the park close to the seal and bird colonies are available.

Rimouski

Rimouski is a fairly large, growing industrial and oil-distributing town. The main street is Rue Saint Germain, which runs east and west from the principal cross street, Avenue Cathédrale. At this intersection is the Place des Veterans square where you will find the helpful tourist office (☎ 723-2322) at 50 Saint Germain Ouest.

Place des Veterans, marking the centre of town, is right by the highway near the **regional museum** in the neogothic **cathedral** from the 1850s. The museum, closed on Monday, presents varied and changing exhibits including the works of Canadian artists and a display on oceanography. The Maritime Institute is next door.

About five km east of the tourist office, along Hwy 132, is **Maison Lamontagne**, an 18th-century house now an historic site, set in parkland. It's open daily throughout the summer and displays period furniture and other items and represents a now almost extinct style of construction.

Ten km east of town in **Pointe au Père**, past the ferry terminal, is a maritime museum and lighthouse with displays on a shipwreck and other marine matters. Admission is $4.25. The nature reserve here is a good place to look for coastal flora & fauna.

South of town 30 km is the **Portes de l'Enfer** (Gates of Hell Canyon), a park with good walking alongside the canyon and its rushing waters.

Late summer is a good time to be passing through as the months of August, September and October each bring a different festival to the city.

Places to Stay *Auberge Internationale la Voile* (☎ 772-8002) is a HI hostel at 140 Saint Germain Est, a central and handy location above a strip of stores. It's closed through the afternoon and has kitchen facilities and family rates. A dorm bed is $13.

Gites du Centre Ville (☎ 723-5289) is an attractive central B&B at 84 Rue Saint Pierre with doubles at $48.

There are plenty of motels especially on Rue Saint Germain Ouest where there are also a couple of places with small, simple individual cabins for rent.

Places to Eat For eating, there is a pretty good selection. East of Avenue Cathédrale on Rue Saint Germain there are three or four popular restaurants and bars with outdoor tables and live music. Avenue Cathédrale also has a number of eateries and nightspots.

The well-established *Le Riverain*, at 38 Saint Germain Est, offers a bit of everything, is not expensive and works long hours daily. *Le Fromageon* at 61 Saint Germain Est is

a pleasant cafe good for snacks and light meals any time.

West of the centre on Saint Germain Ouest just past Rue Saint Louis, *Les Halles* is a complex with a deli, bakery, cheese shop, restaurant and more.

Restaurant Marie Antoinette on the highway and open 24 hours is always reasonable with a selection of Canadian standards. Just east of town you'll see quite a few fish shops *(poissoneries)* where bargains can be had on sole, cod, Atlantic salmon, shrimps and the biggest lobsters I've seen outside a museum. Some 2.5-kg brutes! Aside from fresh fish, many shops offer dried or smoked fish, and there are seafood restaurants too.

Getting There & Away The bus station (☎ 723-4923) is at 186 Rue des Gouverneurs in the north-eastern corner of downtown. Allo Stop, the car/drive sharing agency, has an office here at 106 Rue Saint Germain Est in the book store.

Rimouski is on the VIA Rail line (☎ 1-800-361-5390) but this is about as far as it goes. At Mont Joli, the line heads for Campbellton, New Brunswick. The station is on Rue de l'Evêché two blocks east of the cathedral. It's open from 11.15 pm to 2.15 am daily except Tuesday when it's closed. Nice hours aren't they?

A ferry (☎ 1-800-463-0680) departs from here for the 11-hour crossing to Sept-Îles on the north shore. This is not one of the regular daily crossing points such as those west at Trois Pistoles or east at Matane. It runs just once a week and goes way down river to Sept-Îles.

After leaving Rimouski the land becomes noticeably more wooded as you enter the Gaspé region.

Gaspé Peninsula

This is the rounded chunk of land that juts out north of New Brunswick into the Gulf of St Lawrence. To the people of Quebec it's 'La Gaspésie'. From west of Matane the

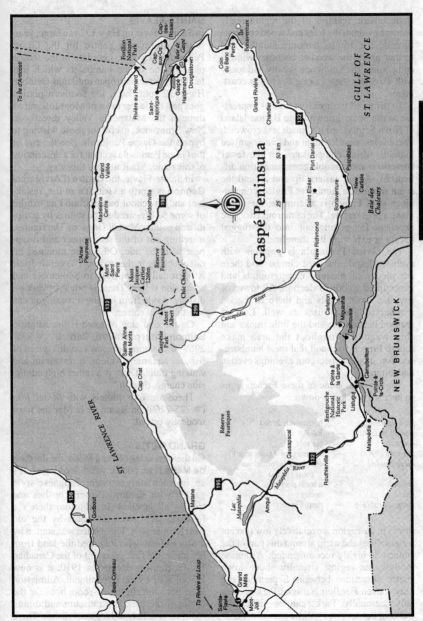

Gaspé Peninsula

characteristic features of the region really become evident: the trees and woods become forests, the towns become smaller and further apart, the weather becomes windier and cooler. The landscape is hilly and rocky with excellent views along the rough coastline.

To my mind the area is at least as impressive as the better known Cape Breton Island of Nova Scotia, and it's much less crowded. There is less development and less organised tourism, which compensates for the fewer attractions and possible communication difficulties. At the eastern tip and around the south shore are a number of English communities so if French is a struggle, these will make a petit respite! The numerous parks are excellent for getting out into the rugged terrain or exploring the shoreline.

The Gaspé Peninsula is popular with cyclists, despite the hard climbs, and there are plenty of hostels, campgrounds and unoccupied woods to sleep in. All towns of any size have motels and there is a good number of guesthouses as well. Lots of seafood is available and the little trucks and chip wagons throughout the area make superb French fries and real meat hamburgers. You should expect cool evenings even in midsummer.

You may see some of these French signs so here's a quick run-down:

pain de ménage	–	homemade bread
gîte du passant	–	B&B
à vendre	–	for sale
des vers	–	worms (not a tasty snack)
bière froide	–	cold beer (available at most stores)
crêtons	–	a local pork paté
miel	–	honey
sirop d'erable	–	maple syrup

Prices in the region are relatively low (except for gasoline) and a trip around this part of the country is highly recommended. A caution though, the region virtually shuts down visitor attractions between September and May – even Forillon National Park is open only seasonally. Parks can be visited for walking but services will be nonexistent.

SAINTE-FLAVIE

In Sainte-Flavie on Hwy 132 is a large, year-round information centre for the Gaspé Peninsula. If you're here late in the season pick up one of the pamphlets which lists facilities that remain open until mid-October. Hwy 132 splits here, the southern portion goes past the larger town of Mont Joli and on through the Matapédia Valley directly into New Brunswick, useful for those wishing to bypass the Gaspé Peninsula. See the end of the Gaspé Peninsula section for a description of this route. Via Rail goes this way.

In Sainte-Flavie, the **Centre d'Art Marcel Gagnon** is worth a visit. It's an inn, restaurant and art school based around an exhibit of some 80 life-sized stone statues by sculptor and painter Marcel Gagnon. The figures, marching out of the sea, appear and disappear with the tide. Others are mounted on rafts bobbing in the waves. The centre itself is open daily from May to September and admission is free. There is other artwork on display. Aside from having a meal, you can just sit with a coffee.

On the east side of town is the **Atlantic Salmon Interpretative Centre** (☎ 775-2969) with various displays on this queen of fish, an aquarium, videos, a restaurant and walking trails. There is a rather high admission charge, though.

There are four motels with *Motel Rita* (☎ 775-7269) on Route de la Mer the most modestly priced.

GRAND MÉTIS

On the west side of Grand Métis, the **Jardins de Métis** is an oddity worth looking at. It's an immaculately tended, Japanese-style garden with streams, flowers, bushes and trees – all labelled. In addition, there's a fantastic view over the coast by the old wooden mansion. The garden was started by a Mrs Reford, who inherited the land from her uncle, the first president of the Canadian Pacific Railway. Begun in 1910, it is now looked after by the government. Admission is $6 per adult. In the 37-room house at the centre of the park is a museum and dining room serving fish and regional dishes. There is also a more casual restaurant with views. The grounds close at 8 pm.

MATANE

A small, typical Quebecois town, Matane makes a good stopover. There's an information office at the lighthouse off the highway and it's open daily in summer and weekdays all year. The small museum is also here. Avenue Saint Jérôme and Boulevard Saint Pierre are the main streets. The promenade along the Rivière Matane where it flows under the Hwy and into the Saint Lawrence makes for a pleasant stroll.

Matane is a fishing town with salmon and shrimp among the catch. In mid-June is the shrimp (crevette) festival: a time when you can feast on them.

Salmon go up the river here to spawn, beginning in June. The government has set up a monitoring system where you can see the fish heading upstream and learn something of this curious phenomenon. An information office is in the little building by the dam, adjacent to the Parc des Îles and near the Hôtel de Ville at the top of Rue Saint Jerome. Nearby in the park is an open-air theatre used for summer shows.

The large shrimp-processing and fish-packing plant (☎ 562-1273) at 1600 Matane Sur Mer can be visited free through the summer. Reservations are needed on weekends and fish can be bought, fresh or smoked.

Matane Wildlife Preserve

The preserve (☎ 562-3700) can be reached south of Matane off Hwy 195. It's a huge, wild area with camping, canoeing, hiking, fishing, boat rentals and abundant moose. The park closes in early September. The road continues on to New Brunswick but don't follow it. Go around the rest of the Gaspé Peninsula.

Places to Stay

Motels are the primary accommodation with many strung out along or near the highway. Les Mouettes (☎ 562-3345), at 298 Rue McKinnon, is one of the cheapest at $50 for a double room. Priced similarly is the Motel Le Beach (☎ 562-1350) at 1441 Rue Matane sur Mer.

An alternative is the Hôtel L'Ancre at 292 Rue Saint Pierre, primarily a low-end drinking establishment but with basic accommodation for $18 single which is not recommended for women. A better choice for most people on a tight budget is the modern-looking Collège de Matane (☎ 562-1240), on the outskirts of town at 616 Ave Saint Redempteur. Rooms here are offered to visitors at the same price through the summer months.

Le Relais du Voyageur (☎ 562-3472) is a good-value central B&B at 75 Rue D'Amours with singles from $15.

West of town is Camping La Baleine with the whale model by the roadside. It's basic but clean and a tent site is $14.

Places to Eat

For the stomach, the all purpose Café Aux Delices at the corner of Rue Saint Jerome and Rue du Bon Pasteur in the centre of town is recommended. They've got Italian, Canadian and Chinese food, good breakfasts and they are open long hours every day.

Saint Jerome has a brasserie and a popular pizza place among others. For good seafood in the $10 to $15 range (main course) there is Les Délices de la Mer at 50 Avenue d'Amours open for dinner only.

Le Vieux Rafiot is the purple and grey nautical-looking place at 1415 Ave de Phare Ouest. It's a casual sort of pub with plenty of seafood and good prices on shrimp dinners all summer long.

Getting There & Away

Bus The terminus (☎ 562-1177) is at 750 Avenue du Phare Ouest in the Galeries du Vieux Port shopping centre along the highway in the centre of town. The office is in a corner of the Restaurant Bar Salons des Galeries. There are two buses a day for Gaspé and four a day for Quebec City.

Ferry The ferry (☎ 562-2500) link here to the north shore of the St Lawrence is the last

QUEBEC

in a series beginning at Quebec City and appearing periodically as the widening river travels north-eastwards to the sea. Call for information and reservations are recommended.

The ferry is a large vessel capable of handling 600 passengers and 125 cars. To Baie Comeau, there are four services a day through the summer. The trip takes two hours and 20 minutes and costs about $36 per car and driver. Bicycles are free and there is a cheaper same-day return fare.

Another boat goes to Godbout, a small town a little further west from Baie Comeau.

The ferry terminal is several km west of the town centre.

CAP CHAT

At Cap Chat with its big, sandy beach, the St Lawrence River meets the Gulf of St Lawrence. Rocher Cap Chat is a well-known landmark. This rock, said to resemble a crouching cat and which gave the village its name, sits by the shore on the west side of town, about a two-km walk along the beach from the centre.

Three km west of the central bridge is the odd looking hi-tech vertical axis windmill, the world's highest and most powerful. Bilingual tours are offered.

Basic roads lead south inland to two different wildlife regions with camping. Lac Joffre, Lac Simoneau and Lac Paul are good for trout fishing and there's salmon fishing in Rivière Cap Chat.

Places to Stay & Eat

A good place to spend the night is the *Cabines Goémons sur Mer* (☎ 786-5715), right on the beach. The cabins have kitchens and go for $37 double. Further east, the smaller, simpler *Cabines Sky Line* (☎ 786-2626) cost only $26/30 for singles/doubles. They are perfectly fine, though the location is not as good. The *Motel Fleur de Lys* (☎ 786-5518) is a more modern choice and has a restaurant which serves all day and is good for breakfast.

Le Cabillaud Restaurant on the east side of town and surrounded by flowers is a good

eating spot. It specialises in seafood with meals costing $15 to $20.

SAINTE ANNE DES MONTS

Sainte Anne is not one of the more pretty towns. But you can take advantage of its being a fishing centre by getting hold of some of the smoked or fresh fish for sale down by the dock opposite the church at the foot of Route du Parc. There is also a restaurant here. Beside the quay is Explorama (☎ 763-2500), a bilingual interpretation centre with exhibits on marine ecosystems and a large model of the Gaspé Peninsula. Admission is $5. There is a banking machine in the bank at the shopping centre at the corner of Boulevard Sainte Anne Ouest and Route du Parc.

Immediately south of town is the Saint Anne River Nature Reserve (Réserve Faunique) which runs along the river and into Gaspésie Park.

GASPÉSIE PARK

From Sainte Anne des Monts, Hwy 299 runs south to the excellent Gaspésie Park (☎ 763-3301). It is a huge, rugged and undeveloped area of lakes, woods and mountains. There's lots of wildlife like deer and moose and the fishing is good but the highlight is the great hiking.

The Interpretive Centre (☎ 763-7811) is open daily from early June to Labour Day and like the park itself, is free. Overnight camping does cost and is $13 in one of the four campgrounds. None of them is open past about 10 October but it is getting very cold here by then anyway. Backcountry camping is also permitted. Maps and information on the hiking trails are available at the centre which is somewhat inconveniently located in the middle of the park.

At **Gîte du Mont Albert** there is camping and a large, comfortable lodge (☎ 763-2288) with a highly praised restaurant. Singles/doubles in the hotel are $80 and start at that rate for chalets but go way up for the cabins suitable for eight people. Bicycles can be rented but this didn't strike me as ideal cycling country.

The roads leading through the park are rough and will take you to various hiking trails – some overnighters – and lookouts over the lumpy Chic Choc Mountains (Monts Chic Choc).

Mont Jacques Cartier, at 1270 metres, is the highest peak in this part of the country. It rises above the tree line and epitomises the conditions of the Gaspé Peninsula: cold, windy and often wet at the peak too.

Hiking it takes about $3\frac{1}{2}$ hours for the return trip, and is well worthwhile – the alpine scenery and views are fantastic and it is fairly common to see some of the herd of woodland caribou near the top. These are the last of the caribou found this far south; they seem to find the barren lands quite fine and happily munch on lichen all day. The trail is now tightly regulated in order to protect the herd from being disturbed.

Hikers can drive to a designated parking area along one of two routes each taking about 30 minutes from the Interpretation Centre where, alternatively, buses for $15 return can be boarded. They depart daily at 9 am. The Cartier parking area can also be reached from Mont Saint Pierre. From it, a $4 shuttle bus runs hikers six km to the beginning of the trail. The first bus is at 10 am, the last leaves the trail at 4 pm and no one is permitted on the summit between the end of the afternoon and the next morning. The buses operate from near the end of June to about the second week in September. The mountain is open until the end of the month but you must walk in. This late in the year the temperatures at the top can be well below zero. At the peak, naturalists are on hand to answer questions and talk about the caribou.

You can also climb **Mont Albert**, a steeper, more rigorous trail despite the mountain not reaching the same elevation as Cartier. Also excellent and not busy is the trail by Lac aux Americains up to Mont Xalibu, a fine half-day return walk with superb alpine scenery at the peak with mountain lakes and a waterfall in view on the way.

It is not uncommon to see moose in the early morning or evening feeding at Lac Paul.

You can enter the park at Sainte Anne des Monts and return to the coast highway at Mont Saint Pierre.

MONT SAINT PIERRE

Not far from Sainte Anne des Monts on Hwy 132 is this little white village nestled in a short bay. The setting is spectacular with rocky outcrops on one side and a nearby crescent-shaped beach on the other. The sunsets are also noteworthy.

This small community, far from any big city, is famous for hang gliding. Indeed, it is considered one of the best spots for the sport in North America. Each year around the end of June is the two-week hang gliding festival (La Fête du Vol Libre). A rough road goes to the summit of Mont Saint Pierre where there are three take-off stations and excellent views from the summit. A 4WD vehicle is recommended if you're not hoofing it up. Tours of the site are offered. Gliders and sea kayaks can be rented in town.

The cliffs east of town are etched with interesting rock patterns. The road runs along the bottom of the cliff and river's edge east (sometimes squeezed between the two) to about Gros Morne.

Auberge Les Vagues (☎ 797-2851), at 84 Rue Prudent Cloutier, is a hostel with room for 70 in summer but only 20 the rest of the year when heating is required. There's a kitchen and a grocery store down the street a few doors.

Alternatively, there are several motel-hotels in town. The motel restaurant *Au Delice* at 100 Rue P Cloutier is open early for breakfasts.

Gaspésie Park can be reached by unsurfaced road (with some logging trucks) from behind Mont Saint Pierre but having a good map is very helpful as the routes are not marked well.

EAST OF MONT SAINT PIERRE

East of Mont Saint Pierre there are lots of good picnic areas with coastal views. There are also plenty of campgrounds, motels or cabins with cuisinettes (kitchenettes). At the

QUEBEC

many small villages watch for the signs for *pain frais* or *pain chaud* (fresh or hot bread).

At L'Anse Pleureuse, turn off to Murdochville for tours of its **copper mine**. Rivière la Madeleine and Grand Vallée are particularly beautiful villages with grand settings perfect for picture-taking. At Cloridorme there is a good picnic site overlooking the Gulf of St Lawrence. Rivière au Renard is the largest fishing port in the Gaspé and the processing plant can be toured as part of a visit to the Fishing Interpretation Centre at 1 Renard Est. This is also a departure point for Nordik Passeur boats to Anticosti Island (see under Île d'Anticosti earlier). For those not visiting Forillon, Hwy 197 runs south cutting off the end of the peninsula. At L'Anse au Griffon watch for the house covered in bugs. And where else have you seen a grocery-lingerie store?

CAP DES ROSIERS

This is a small, old and interesting little village on the north shore. The **graveyard**, right on the cliff, tells the town's history: how the English came from Guernsey and Jersey; how the Irish settlers were Kavanaghs, O'Connors, etc; and how both groups mingled with the French. Generations later, the same names live on.

The **lighthouse**, built in 1858, is one of the highest in the country at 37 metres and is now classed as an historic site. It can be visited for a small admission fee.

Saltwater sport-fishing trips and whale-watching tours depart from the wharf (see under the following Forillon section for details).

There are a couple of places to stay. The *Chalets Cap Cabins*, (☎ 892-5641) costing about $28, are pleasantly rustic with views over the bay. There's another motel with great views and also a couple of restaurant in town.

FORILLON NATIONAL PARK

The park (☎ 368-5505) lies at the extreme north-eastern tip of the peninsula and is well worth a stop for its rugged seaside terrain and wildlife. In the woods there are moose, deer

and an increasing population of black bears. The shoreline cliffs attract numbers of sea birds, and offshore whales and seals are common.

There are good trails through the park, some with overnight camping. They range from rigorous 18-km one-way trails taking six hours to easy 30-minute walks. The Parks Service naturalists offer information programmes and free guided tours. Two boat trips are offered. The MV *Felix Leclerc* (☎ 892-5629) departs from the quay at Cap des Rosiers for $15 and takes in the rocky cliffs, sea birds, seal colonies and possibly whales. The MV *Norval* (☎ (892-5500) departs the harbour at Grand Grave for longer cruises costing $30 and concentrates on whales. For both, inquire if the guide is bilingual (some are).

The northern coast consists of steep limestone cliffs – some as high as 200 metres – and long pebble beaches. See **Cap Bon Ami** for the best of this topography. There is a telescope for whale watching – good from May to October – and sometimes you can hear them surface. Seals are common all year just offshore. Look to the left.

The south coast has more beaches, some are sandy, and small coves. **Penouille Beach** is said to have the warmest waters. Petit Gaspé is the most popular organised campground as it is protected from sea breezes and it has hot showers too.

The hike along the southern shore to **Cap Gaspé** is easy and pleasant, with seashore views. At the headlands, with a lighthouse, Percé Rock can be seen. Take the path one way and the road back, about two hours total.

At **Grand Grave**, the Haymen & Sons store is an interesting place for a snoop around.

The entrance fee to the park is $2.50 per adult. A tent site without electricity is $13.50 at one of the three campgrounds. Through July and August book ahead or arrive by late morning.

CAP AUX OS

On the south side of Forillon National Park, Cape of Bones got its name because at one time whale bones often washed ashore here. Hostellers can use the village as a base for exploring the park, otherwise there is no reason to stop here. The *HI hostel* (☎ 892-5153) at 2095 Boulevard Forillon is good and friendly – it's one of the most established places in the province and has a fine view overlooking the bay. It's a fairly large three-storey place which can accommodate 56 people and is open all year. During summer, it is generally full. You gotta love Quebec hostels, first they surprise people by often having coed dorms and then here they have condom machines in the washroom. Is this preventative or suggestive? (There are some rooms for families.) It's open 24 hours and breakfast and dinner are available. There is a grocery store a few minutes walk away. The bus stops at the hostel throughout the summer months. A drawback for those without vehicles is that it is a long way to any of the hiking trails although bicycles can be rented.

GASPÉ

After all the good scenery and attractive little villages, the town after which the entire peninsula takes its name seems pretty ordinary. It does, however, have all the amenities and services, gasoline stations and grocery stores. A fair bit of English is spoken too. Perhaps surprisingly, from here around the head of the peninsula and down along the Baie des Chaleurs, there are quite a few historic English towns which have stuck it out.

The **Jacques Cartier monument** at the north side of town right beside the hwy, is worth a look. It's different and well done. It was here that the explorer landed in 1534, met the Iroquois and claimed the area for the king of France. He took two sons of Chief Donnacona back to see Paris and later returned them. (They must have had a few stories to tell.) Beside the sculpture is a museum depicting the difficulties of those settling the Gaspé Peninsula, some maritime exhibits, crafts and a section on traditional foods. Admission costs $3.50. It's open daily but afternoons only on weekends.

The **Cathédrale de Gaspé** is interesting. It is the only wooden cathedral in North America. A fresco commemorates the fourth centennial of Cartier's landing. It's at the top of Rue Jacques Cartier about a 15-minute walk from the museum.

Continuing in a religious vein, the **Sanctuaire Notre Dame des Douleurs** is a church which has been a pilgrimage site since 1942. It's open daily from 7 am to 9 pm from early June to late October.

South of town there are beaches at Sandy Beach and Haldimand but the water is cool. There's camping by the Fort Ramsay Motel near the water.

For eating or sleeping most people will prefer to be in nearby Percé. But a place worth checking for a cheap bed through the summer is the central community college (☎ 368-2749) at 94 Rue Jacques Cartier. It is a regional college that rents its many residence rooms at reasonable rates. You can't miss it, it's the biggest building in town. Otherwise there are numerous motels. A cheap breakfast can be had at one of the motel dining rooms.

DOUGLASTOWN

Like some of the other small English towns of the region, Douglastown was established by Loyalists. Their ancestors continue to fish and farm.

PERCÉ

Named after the immense offshore rock with the hole through it (one of Canada's best known landmarks), this town is the main tourist attraction of the Gaspé Peninsula. It's a pleasant, very pretty place and the **Rocher Percé** (Pierced Rock) is truly an impressive sight. It can be seen on the approach into town from either direction. The Pic de l'Aurore (Peak of Dawn) hill dominates the north end of town. Although you can walk the length of the main street in 30 minutes it's not hard to spend a couple of days or longer here.

Even in July and August, Percé is the only place on the peninsula that gets busy. June or

September make good visiting times with the weather usually good, if not overly warm. By the middle of October, the town is shut up tight.

The tourist office (☎ 782-5448) is in the centre of town at 142 Route 132. It's open from the end of May to near the end of October. There's a laundrette at the wharf/shopping boutique complex nearly across the street from the tourist office.

You can also walk out to the rock at any time and it's even possible to walk around much of it at low tide.

The boat trips to green Île Bonaventure, an island bird sanctuary beyond Rocher Percé, are amazing value and highly recommended. For $13, one of a number of boats will take you out with a mini-tour of Percé, then around the cliffs of the island where seals may be seen and birds certainly will be, and then around to the dock. You can spend the day on the island walking the trails and catch a boat back later. A variety of sea birds nest on the island; over 200,000 birds can make some kind of noise (and smell)! The highlight is the gannet colony of 50,000 roosting on the cliffs just an arm's length from the trail. Among the boats, the small, slow, *Rocher Percé* is good and gets very close to the attractions. The more modern ones can't and they cost more. Going early in the morning to make the most of it is suggested. Boat tickets are sold all over town but can be purchased at the dock-side booths.

Wildlife Service rangers can answer questions and there is a small cafe but take a picnic. Some intriguing hardy plant life can also be seen and the views are marvellous.

The service also runs the free **Wildlife Interpretive Centre**, two km south of town on the Route d'Irlande and open from 9 am to 5 pm. There's a walking trail, film, aquariums and exhibits relating mainly to the sea birds. Naturalists are on hand to answer questions on the geology and flora & fauna of the area. Exhibits are bilingual.

Longer **whale-watching** boat tours are also available. Minke, fin, blue and humpback are species which frequent the area. The comfortable MV *Capitaine Duvall* charges

$35 for the 2½-hour trip but the Zodiac trips offered by Observation Littoral, 249 Route 132, are very good. Fishing trips can be arranged at the dock.

Behind the town are some interesting walks, for which the tourist office map is useful. Hike up to **Mont Sainte Anne** for a great view and to see the cave along the three-km path which begins behind the church.

Another area walking trail leads to the **Great Crevasse**, a deep crevice in the mountain behind the Auberge de Gargantua Restaurant. This three-km trail begins behind the restaurant which is two km north-west of town.

The museum, opposite the tourist office, is actually an art gallery featuring traditional and contemporary pieces. In town there are lots of souvenir shops selling glasswork, pottery and some good quilts.

At nearby beaches, rock hounds can look for agate, which is abundant. There is also diving in the area and an underwater park. Kayaks and bicycles can be rented at the booth by the swimming pool toward the south end of town.

Places to Stay

Accommodation here is pretty good value although prices can spike sharply upward during midsummer. Much of the budget category is in guesthouses in and around town. The tourist office will help in locating one, even calling places for you including some inexpensive farmhouses not far from the centre of town. There are also numerous campgrounds close at hand. Prices fluctuate with the season, the weather and the traffic.

Of the four convenient campgrounds, *Camping Côte Surprise*, two km south of town, has the most spectacular views. Two others are nearby and one is in town.

For hostellers, call in at *Chez Georges* (☎ 782-2980), centrally situated at 16 Rue Sainte Anne. Georges runs a guest house upstairs in his house and has a small hostel-like arrangement downstairs with bunks and a kitchen. A more agreeable, generous fellow you won't find. High season rates are $13 for the dorm beds and $35 double for the private rooms upstairs. Georges also drives a taxi and will give you a fair price on going just about anywhere.

There are other good value guesthouses which are centrally located. *Maison Avenue House* (☎ 782-2954) is on Rue de l'Église, which runs off the main street in the middle of town. Before the church, you'll see this fine house with five rooms of varnished wood at just $22 a single, and from $30 to $35 a double. The rooms are clean and have sinks. The guesthouse is in an excellent location and both English and French are spoken. Also good and cheap is *Maison le Havre* (☎ 782-2374), formerly known as the Haven before the Quebec language laws kicked in making English signs difficult to live with. It's on the main street, Hwy (Route) 132 at No 114 with rooms from $25 to $40.

Gite Maison Tommi (☎ 782-5104), a B&B at 31 Route 132, has singles/doubles for $30/40. Another serving breakfast is *Gite Rendez-vous* (☎ 782-5152) at 84 Hwy 132. A double is $45.

Right in the centre of town, the green and white *Fleur de Lys* (☎ 782-2772) is a reasonably priced motel charging from $35 to $55.

On the north edge of town at 104 Hwy 132, *Auberge Au Coin de Banc et Chalets* (☎ 645-2907) has rooms from $50 and a swimming pool.

There are many other places to stay, mostly motels but also some rustic cabins. The lower-priced ones are generally south out of the centre of town.

Places to Eat

Many of the hotels and motels have their own dining rooms and most offer cheap breakfasts. One to try is *Au Pigalle* at 158 Route 132 which opens at 7 am. It also has good-value fish for $10 to $12 and a table d'hôte for $14 to $20.

Les Fous de Basson is a casual cafe slightly south of the centre of town and beside the art gallery. For coffee, vegetarian meals or breakfasts of yoghurt, granola, croissants and the like, this is the place. At dinner, specials start at $11 or there is more

expensive seafood and the atmosphere is warm.

Forgettable but inexpensive meals are available all day at *Auberge La Table à Roland* at No 190 on the main street (Hwy 132) where there are Chinese dishes for $5.

The *Pantagruel*, five km east of town, has complete dinner buffets for $14. They feature fish, other seafoods and some regional dishes.

You can get a meal at *Resto-bar Le Matelot* at 7 Rue de l'Église but it's also a place to just have a beer and catch the night's entertainment.

There's a *bakery* beside the tourist office and another at 9 Rue Sainte Anne.

Entertainment

At night there is often folk music or jazz at *Les Fous de Basson Café*.

Getting There & Away

Bus Orléans Express (☎ 782-2140) buses link Percé to Matane, Rimouski and Quebec City. They also go to Edmundston and Campbellton, New Brunswick via Carleton and the south shore of the peninsula. There are two services a day in each direction. A ticket to Cap aux Os is $16, to Quebec City $71. The Petro Canada service station and depanneur (variety store) at the north end of the main street is used for the bus station.

Train From Montreal, VIA Rail (☎ 782-2747, 1-800-361-5390) serves the south side of the St Lawrence River with main stops at Lévis, Rivière-du-Loup, Rimouski and as far as Matane. The train then goes south through the Matapédia Valley and along the Baie des Chaleurs and up and around past Percé to the town of Gaspé. Many of the smaller places (along the entire route) are serviced. The one-way fare from Lévis to Percé for the 11-hour ride is $85 and it leaves Wednesday, Friday and Sunday. The station is 10 km south of town at Anse à Beaufils. A taxi is about $10.

THE BAY SIDE

The south shore of the Gaspé Peninsula

along the Baie des Chaleurs is quite different from the north coast. The land is flatter and less rocky and the weather is warmer. Farming and various small industries are important here. Also, unlike on the north side, there are quite a few English towns. Much of the French population is descended from the original Acadian settlers. The numerous small villages almost run together edged along the coast. The inland area is virtually uninhabited.

Chandler

Long a pulp & paper town, Chandler is still based on the huge Abitibi-Price newsprint mill which can be toured for free. Freighters carry the finished product to South America and Europe from the town's own port facilities. At least they try to, the wreck of the Peruvian ship visible from shore indicates they don't all make it. Chandler is a fairly large centre and has a couple of shopping malls.

Pabos Mills

There is an archaeological site, dig and uniquely designed interpretation centre at this French fishing village dating from the 1700s. Bilingual tours are offered from June to October.

Port Daniel

Residents of this pretty, former Micmac settlement are of Scottish, Irish and Acadian backgrounds. Secondary roads from town lead to the wildlife reserves of Port Daniel and Rivière Port Daniel. Sitting halfway between Chandler and New Carlisle, Port Daniel is also mentioned for the attractive blue-and-white *Maison Enright B&B* (☎ 396-2062). Off the main road just north of town is a beach.

Paspébiac

Descendants of Normans, Bretons and Basques live in this town. A waterfront historic site, open daily throughout summer, depicts the early life of the village as a fishing port. There are tours around the site which has a restaurant and trade shops.

New Carlisle

One of the area's English towns, New Carlisle was founded by Loyalists and has some grand colonial homes. Hamilton House from 1852, once home to the local member of Parliament, is open for tours. It's on the north side of the road at the east end of town. The house and grounds at 105 Rue Principal, once belonging to Judge Thompson, can also be visited.

Bonaventure

A small, pleasant Acadian town by the water and rocky beach, Bonaventure is the focal point for the area's farming community.

The Acadian museum, open all year, is worth a visit and has English bilingual booklets available to explain some of the Acadians' tragic yet fascinating history. For more on them see the New Brunswick chapter. A shop near the wharf sells various items made of fish-skin leather. It's soft, supple and attractive and no, it doesn't smell.

Near the museum on Avenue Grand Pré, the *Le Rendez-Vous* restaurant has good-value fresh-fish lunch specials Monday to Friday.

North of town, in **Saint Elzéar** (no public transportation) some of the oldest caves in the province were discovered in 1976. A visit to the site (☎ 534-4335) is recommended but you won't be able to afford eating for a few days. There is a free museum with displays and bones and a slide show but the guided tour of the cave (la grotte) is the only real attraction.

The four-hour trip, including safety equipment and a snack, is extensive and takes in the largest found variety of stalagmites and stalactites in Quebec. The cave is estimated to be 500,000 years old and it feels like it's never seen the sun. Warm clothing is essential or you'll freeze. Are you ready for the price now? It's $37 a ticket. Children aged 10 or more are admitted and their tickets are discounted. Reservations are required. The cave is open from the beginning of June until the end of October, and for some reason the museum opens a month later and closes a month earlier.

New Richmond

Nestled in the bay near the mouths of two rivers New Richmond with a population of 4000 is another Loyalist centre. On Boulevard Perron Ouest, west of the downtown area is the **British Heritage Centre**, a small re-created Loyalist village of the late 1700s. It consists of an interpretive centre, houses, a general store, a lighthouse and other buildings. The centre, which is open daily from mid-June to September, also covers the influence of later Irish and Scottish immigrants.

Carleton

About half the size of New Richmond, Carleton has a pretty location on the water backed by rounded hills. The setting, the sandy beach and the relatively warm air and water of Chaleur Bay have made Carleton a mini-resort. This is where the people of the Gaspé come for a day at the beach and to hang out.

From the docks there are boat excursions for fishing or sightseeing. At the central bird sanctuary, herons, terns, plovers and other shore birds can be observed along the sandbar. Walking paths and a road also lead behind the town to the top of Mont Saint Joseph which at 555 metres, provides fine views over the bay and across to New Brunswick. The oratory at the top can be visited and after the climb, the snack bar is a welcome sight.

The huge *Restaurant Le Heron* on the main street (you can't miss it) is a good, all-purpose eatery and the Orléans bus stops right out front.

Good food is available with a beautiful setting down near the water at the more expensive *Café l'Independant*, specialising in fish. There is also a good picnic site.

If you want to spend the night, a campground can be found out on the jutting spit of land near the centre of town and there are half-a-dozen motels which tend to be pricey. Furthest east out of town is the *Motel Shic Shoc* (☎ 364-3288) with basic rooms at $35 double and better ones at nearly double that. All have perfect views of the sea which can be walked to down a flight of stairs. Also economical is the *Auberge La Visite Surprise* (☎ 364-6553), a B&B at 527 Rue Peron, the main street.

Parc de Miguasha

The small peninsula here is renowned for its fossils. The park and Information Centre is set up around the 365-million-year-old fossil site and is free to visit. Guided walks take visitors through the museum and along a trail to the beach and the fossil filled cliffs. The site is open daily from June to October.

For those headed to Dalhousie, New Brunswick, a ferry just down the road from the park, makes a short cut by running across the Baie de Chaleurs. See Dalhousie in the New Brunswick chapter for details.

Pointe à la Garde

Although there is not really any village here, there is an excellent, year-round HI hostel, *Chateau Bahia*, (☎ 788-2048) at 155 Boulevard Perron (the highway). In addition to the building by the street (with dorms), the manager has built a stunning wooden castle in the woods. Here there are double, triple and family rooms and a dining room, where, during the summer months, Jean, the host, offers banquet-style dinners. Good breakfasts are offered daily and are included in the overnight price which ranges from $15. You can tent, too. The bus through town will stop 100 metres from the door if you ask the driver.

Pointe à la Croix/Listuguj

Formerly known as Restigouche, this has always been and remains a largely Micmac Indian community. Pointe à la Croix has a few motels and shops, a seasonal tourist office and the bridge over to Campbellton, New Brunswick. The town runs on New Brunswick time.

Listuguj is the Micmac part of town. At 2 Riverside West is the **Listuguj Arts & Cultural Centre** (☎ 788-5034) which outlines some aspects of their culture and history and the gift shop sells crafts. Outside there are re-creations of traditional buildings. The Micmacs are found all around the Atlantic

Provinces although their numbers are not large. These east coast Native Indians have traditionally produced fine basket work. The best pieces are now seen in museums but modern versions can be viewed or purchased on the reserve here. Ask about summer events such as the powwow. Across the street a fort is being built which will show the post-contact period of Micmac history.

Restigouche National Historic Park

A few km west of the bridge from Pointe à la Croix, the park (Parc Historique National La Bataille de la Restigouche) (☎ 788-5676) details the 1760 naval battle of Restigouche which pretty well put the kibosh on France's New World ambitions. An interpretive centre explains the battle's significance to the British and has salvaged articles and even parts of a sunken French frigate. The last few years of the war for control of the country are neatly chronicled. Don't miss the quote from Voltaire. The museum is open daily from early June until Thanksgiving in October. Admission is $3.

MATAPÉDIA VALLEY

From the village of Matapédia, Quebec, across the Restigouche River from the province of New Brunswick near Campbellton, the Matapédia Valley runs northward to Mont Joli or Matane on the St Lawrence

River. This peaceful, pretty valley is unlike any other portion of the Gaspé Peninsula. Alongside the Matapédia River and the railway line, traffic-free Hwy 132 passes through fertile farmland with a backdrop of green mountains for about 70 km. Aside from the good farming areas, the valley differs from much of the rocky, more sparsely vegetated peninsula by supporting broad-leafed maple and elm trees which add a lot of colour in the autumn. The river is renowned for its salmon fishing. There are several smallish towns along the way, a few sites to see and, around Lac Matapédia, a couple of picnic sites as well as a campground.

Routhierville

The first of many wooden bridges seen through the valley is in this small village. Some of them, known as settler's bridges, are covered, like the ones seen in greater abundance across New Brunswick. The picnic site here is about all there is. Fishing is the main attraction.

Sainte Florence

This larger town with a good-sized lumber mill is situated where the valley is broadening out and the landscape is more gentle. There's a place for gasoline and one *cantine* for burgers and fries.

The snow goose, found only in North America, has white plumage with black wing tips

Causapscal

Causapscal is the best place for a stop on the trip through the valley. It's a pretty town with a traditional look, a beautiful stone church and many older houses with typical Québecois silver roofs.

The Causapscal and Matapédia rivers meet here. There are a couple of covered bridges south of town and, in the centre, a pedestrian-only suspension bridge across the Matapédia. Again, sawmills are the main economic focus and the smell or smoke from the processing chimneys is ever present.

There is a tourist office near the interesting **Domaine Matamajaw** or Salmon Lodge Museum. The museum, in what was the lodge, the outbuildings and much of the riverfront property were all part of a private fishing estate built by Lord Mount Stephen of Canadian Pacific Railway fame in 1870. In the early part of the century a group of moneyed Canadian and US businesspeople bought the place and ran it as a private club for 60 years. Take a look in the lodge some of which remains much the way it was – some people know how to live. Other rooms are devoted to the Atlantic salmon, the impetus for all this. The site is open from 10 June to 10 September from 9 am to 9 pm daily and costs $4.

Across the street from the museum is a craft shop with some unique items – wallets, jewellery and more made of salmon and cod 'leather'. Other articles include tablecloths and rugs woven by local women and some homemade jams.

Fifteen km north are some waterfalls with riverside walking trails.

Places to Stay & Eat For spending the night or having dinner, there is the *Auberge La Coulée Douce* (☎ 756-5270) on the hill opposite the historic site. *Les Pignons Verts* (☎ 756-3754), at 100 Rue Morin, across the river and up the hill, is a B&B with less expensive rooms at singles/doubles $30/42. There are also a few cheaper rooms to let where the Orléans Express bus, linking New Brunswick to the St Lawrence shore, stops at 122 Rue Saint Jacques Sud. Also in town

are a couple of restaurants and the ubiquitous takeout cantines or chip wagons.

North of town is a campground and the *Motel Du Vallon* (☎ 756-3433) with doubles at $50, less out of season.

Amqui

The largest town in the valley doesn't have much to recommend it. All the basic needs can be met, and north of town beyond the bridge is a campground. Towards the end of summer you may see people standing by the side of the road waving jars. They're selling locally picked wild hazelnuts *(noisettes)* which are not expensive. Around **Lac Matapédia** there are some viewpoints over the lake and picnic spots.

Magdalen Islands

Out in the Gulf of St Lawrence, closer to the Atlantic Provinces than to Quebec, lies this lovely 100-km-long string of islands. The Magdalen Islands, or Îles de la Madeleine, comprise about a dozen islands, 120 km north-east of Prince Edward Island, and most of them are linked by long sand spits. In fact, the islands are little more than spits themselves, so excellent sand beaches line the shores.

Because of their remoteness, the quiet life, the superb seashore scenery of carved red and grey cliffs and the great beaches, the islands have appeal and have become quite popular with visitors, although Quebeckers make up at least 90% of the tourists. Most people stay two to four days and this enables them to look around most of the islands. More time can easily be spent walking the trails and beaches and exploring in depth.

The local people make their living mainly from fishing as they have always done but now the two months of busy tourism, July and August, are supplementing many an income. Sealing used to be important, but the commercial hunt has diminished under international pressure from those opposed to it. Some former hunters are now taking tourists

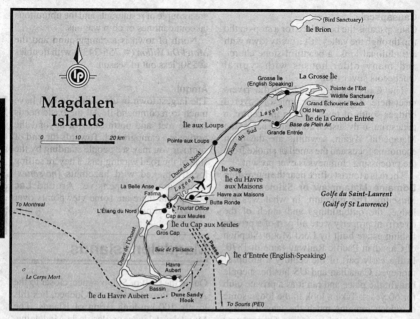

Magdalen Islands

out on the ice in early spring to see and photograph the baby seals. The Magdalens are considered the best place for this. Although expensive as a single purpose excursion, they are becoming the basis for popular brief trips to the islands.

Over 90% of the population of 14,000 speak various French dialects, but many Scottish and Irish descendants live on Île d'Entrée and La Grosse Île. The towns and the people too, are sophisticated despite the remote, isolated nature of the islands. Restaurants and living rooms could easily be transplanted from downtown Montreal. Unlike many fishing or farming regions, the islands seem quite prosperous and don't really have the old-time feel of, say, Prince Edward Island. Food and accommodation prices can, but need not, reflect these characteristics.

The main islands are Havre aux Maisons, which has an airport, and Cap aux Meules. At the town of Cap aux Meules, the ferry from Souris, Prince Edward Island, ties in and there is an information office (☎ (418) 986-2245).

Things to See & Do

Most of the islands' activities and sights revolve around the sea. Beach-strolling, and exploring lagoons, tidal pools and the cliff formations can take up days. More time can be spent searching out the best vistas, skirting around the secondary roads and poking around the fishing villages. The waters aren't tropical by any stretch of the imagination but are warmed (slightly) by the Gulf Stream. Swimming is possible in the open sea or, preferably, in some of the protected, shallow lagoons. Currents are strong and venturing far from shore is not advisable. With nearly constant breezes, windsurfing is good and several places offer boards and lessons.

Fishing expeditions can be arranged and diving on the reefs is possible.

There are also some historic points of interest such as the old churches and unusual traditional buildings such as the now-disappearing hay barns. Also around the countryside look for the old smoke houses (marked on the islands' map) now disused but once part of the important herring industry. Keep an eye out for the many fine and distinctive houses dotting the largely barren terrain.

In the evenings during the summer, you may be lucky to find a concert, a play, or an exhibition of some sort in one of the towns.

Festivals

At Grande Entrée, a lobster festival is held during the first week in July. Also in July watch for the annual sandcastle-building contests along a two-km stretch of beach on Havre Aubert.

Accommodation

From June to September the islands are busy and accommodation gets seriously scarce. If, upon arrival, you do not have a place booked (as most people appear to) go directly to the tourist office and have them find you something. After that first night and when settled a bit, you can always look around for something else. Before arrival, you could call the tourist office from Prince Edward Island and ask them to book a place in an area that appeals to you.

A good portion of the Magdalen Islands' accommodation is in people's homes or in cottages and trailers they rent out. These represent by far the most interesting and best value lodgings averaging $30 a single and $40 a double. The tourist office has a sheet listing many of these places but it is far from complete. The tourist office will call and book the ones they know (including ones not on the list) for you, still others can be found by following roadside signs or just asking people. The residents are friendly and enjoy even a broken French-English conversation.

More commercial accommodation is being established all the time but remains mostly in motel form at often more than double the guesthouse rate. Cottages go for

about $375 to $400 a week. The bulk of the places to stay are on either Cap aux Meules or Havre aux Maisons.

There are also about half a dozen campgrounds scattered around the islands. The campgrounds never seem full but remember this can be a wet and windy place. If you've got a cheap tent you're pushing your luck.

Food

Another of the islands' lures is the fresh seafood. One of the main catches is lobster; the lobster season runs from mid-May to mid-July. Snow crabs, scallops, mussels, perch and cod are other significant species. A local speciality available at many of the better restaurants is *pot-en-pot*, a dish of mixed fish and seafoods in a sauce baked in its own pie crust. The adventurous eater may want to try seal meat which is served a couple of ways.

All the major villages have some sort of a restaurant but out of Cap aux Meules choices are limited. Cantines with burgers, hot dogs and fries are seen here and there.

Cap aux Meules

Cap aux Meules, the largest town of the islands, and with the ferry terminal, is the commercial centre of the archipelago. It's quite busy and modern which can be a little disconcerting for those looking for something else. This first glimpse is, however, atypical of the rest of the towns, villages and landscapes around the islands. Supplies, banking and any necessary reservations should all be taken care of here.

The islands' tourist office is a short distance from the ferry landing on the corner of Hwy 199 and Chemin du Debarcadere. There really isn't anything of note to see in Cap aux Meules but the town has more hotels and restaurants than any other one place in the Magdalen Islands. The rest of this island is also fairly densely populated.

Places to Stay & Eat The half-dozen hotels and motels are all rather pricey and, as Cap aux Meules isn't particularly interesting, you'd be better off finding something away

QUEBEC

from town in the spacious, scenic country-side. Of course if you're arriving late this may not be feasible but the tourist office has a list of local tourist homes which make a stay more pleasant and easier on the wallet.

A number of inexpensive guesthouses can be found on the other side of the island in the Fatima or Étang du Nord areas. One place near the beach is *Lauretta Cyr* (☎ 986-2302). Of course nobody lives too far from the sea here.

Probably the least expensive place for dinner in town is the *Belle-Vue* with a choice of Chinese, Italian and some Canadian standards. More expensive and popular is the dressier *Pizza Patio* on the main street, Chemin Principal, a few blocks south from the ferry terminal. *Casse Croûte Raymond* is good for breakfasts, and fries and burgers. The *Auberge La Jetée*, at 153 Rue Principale, has something for everyone including some seafood.

La Belle Anse

The coastal area known as La Belle Anse on the north-west side of Cap aux Meules has some dramatic red cliffs and interesting coastal erosion features. There are some paths right along the cliffs offering excellent views. For a good and inexpensive meal go to the *Cooperative de Gros-Cap*, a lobster (*homard*) processing plant with a cafeteria-restaurant known as *La Factrie* upstairs with a large window overlooking the plant below. Just follow the road, Chemin de Gros Cap, north of the town of L'Étang du Nord. You needn't eat lobster, there is a selection of other seafoods with soups and salad all reasonably priced. It's open from noon to 9 pm daily, Sunday 3 to 9 pm. In Fatima, the small plain looking *Decker Boy Restaurant* on Chemins les Caps, is cheap and good. Try one of the chowders.

North of La Belle Anse at the good sandy beach at Anse de l'Hôpital is a small complex of tourist-oriented shops and a snack bar.

Île du Havre Aubert

South of Cap aux Meules, connected by long strings of sand at points barely wider than the road, is the archipelago's largest island.

The most lively area of the town of **Havre Aubert** is known as La Grave, an old section by the water at the south-eastern tip of the island. The main street is lined with small craft and gift shops, some restaurants and many old houses. There is a theatre here for summer productions in French only.

On any rainy day the interesting aquarium is packed with visitors disturbed from their seaside activities. A pool with various creatures which can be handled is a major attraction. The **Musée de la Mer** has displays on shipwrecks and various aspects of the islands' transportation and fishing history. Both are open daily in summer and have low admission fees.

Near town is the **Centre Nautique de l'Istorlet** with sail-boat and windsurfer courses and rentals. There is also a simple campground at the coastal property.

Places to Stay & Eat The *Auberge Chez Denis à François* (☎ 937-2371) has six rooms; singles/doubles cost from $44/50 and meals are available in its restaurant which is open to nonguests.

In La Grave, the *Café de la Grave* is a good place for simple, inexpensive meals or a coffee and cake. *La Saline* open at lunch and dinner time only is a pricier seafood restaurant where the local speciality, pot-en-pot can be sampled.

Île du Havre aux Maisons

All-told, probably the most scenic of the Magdalen Islands, Havre aux Maisons has a bit of everything. Definitely take the south shore road (Chemin des Montants) from Pointe Basse up around Butte Ronde and into a beautiful little valley. Excellent views, some traditional-style houses, smoke houses and a lighthouse are all seen along this route. There are several restaurants along the main road across the island.

Places to Stay & Eat For a place to stay on Havre aux Maisons, the *Auberge Les Sillons* (☎ 969-2134) is friendly, has a good location on Chemin Dune du Sud, and is reasonably priced at $50 a double and meals are available. *Nicolas Hubert* (☎ 969-4730) has a guest house at 235 Chemin de la Pointe Basse, about a km from the beach with rooms just $20/30.

The coastal area around Dune du Sud is also attractive and there are some fine places to stay in the area including some little cottages right on the water by a beach with huge sandstone arches.

Pointe aux Loups

On either side of this small community in the middle of the long sand spits connecting the north and south islands are stretches of sand beaches and dunes. For a quick dip, the water is warmer on the lagoon side.

La Grosse Île

This, the principal English section of the Magdalen Islands, was settled by Scottish pioneers. As soon as you arrive, you'll notice all the signs are in English. Despite generations of isolation, many of the local people barely speak a word of French! La Grosse Île, East Cape and Old Harry are the main communities.

Trinity Church, known for its stained glass depicting Jesus the fisherman, is worth a look. Out through the windows the eye captures the graves, the piles of lobster traps, some solitary houses and then the sea: the island's world in microcosm.

There is a commercial **saltmine** just off the main road en route to Old Harry. No tours are given but there is an information office open in the afternoon. Begun in 1983 the mine is 225 metres deep.

About 16 km off La Grosse Île is **Île Brion**, an ecological reserve, once but no longer inhabited by humans. It remains home to 140 species of birds and much interesting vegetation. On days that are not too windy it can be visited. Even camping is possible, but for details call the office of the Corporation for the Access to and Protection of Brion Island in Cap aux Meules on ☎ 986-4768.

Places to Stay Many of the people around La Grosse Île rent a room or two during the summer but are not listed in the guides.

Île de l'Est

Linking La Grosse Île and Grande Entrée is this wild region which boasts the islands' most impressive beach: from Pointe Old Harry, **La Grande Échouerie Beach** extends, a curving sweep of pale sand, about five km down Île de l'Est. A short road with parking areas and trails stretching down to the beach begins near the Old Harry harbour. From Hwy 199 (through Île de l'Est which, other than the beach is entirely a national wildlife refuge area) a few turn-offs lead to hiking paths.

Île de la Grande Entrée

On this island stop at Old Harry, a fishing wharf with about 10 boats and some spectacular shoreline cliffs, portions of which have caves in them. Walruses once inhabited the area but they were slaughtered indiscriminately. Sea Cow Lane is the site of the former walrus landing.

In the other direction from Old Harry don't miss **Saint Peter's by the Sea**, a beautiful, peaceful little church overlooking the sea and bounded by graves, belonging almost exclusively to members of the Clark and Clarke families. It's open to visitors and well worth a visit. On a breezy day the inside offers a quiet stillness broken only by the creaking rafters. It is all wood, including a richly carved door honouring drowned fishermen.

Across the street is a fine area for watching the sea explode into sparkling bits up onto the rugged, rocky shoreline.

Places to Stay & Eat *Club Vacances 'Les Iles'* (☎ 985-2833) is a resort built around the island's nature and the activities it affords: walking, windsurfing, boat tours, bird watching etc. Package deals include rooms, all meals and organised activities. The same package is offered to tenters at its campsites for $50 per person per day. Very little English seems to be spoken. If you just

QUEBEC

want to put up a tent, the fee is $12 a night and anybody can use the cafeteria-style restaurant.

At the far tip of the island are more colourful fishing boats to check out along the docks and a couple of places to eat. Best is the *Restaurant du C E P I M* where lobster is cheap and other seafood is offered.

Île d'Entrée

This is the one inhabited island not interconnected by land with the others. A ferry links it to the port at Cap aux Meules. The boat runs twice a day from Monday to Saturday: once early in the morning and once in mid-afternoon. Board in front of the coastguard building. The ferry crossing takes between 30 and 60 minutes. The virtually treeless island has an English-speaking population of around 175 and is primarily a fishing community. It's about four km long and less than one km wide with walking trails leading over much of it.

The gentler western section supports some farms before ending in high red cliffs. The eastern section is mountainous with the highest point, Big Hill, at 174 metres above sea level. A trail from Post Office Road leads up to the views from the top.

There is one *guesthouse* (☎ 986-4541) on the island, with cooking facilities, but call before arriving if you wish to stay. Also on the island are a couple of grocery stores and one basic snack bar.

Getting There & Away

Air Canadian Airlines flies in daily from Halifax; Air Alliance has two flights a day from Montreal, Quebec City, Sept-Îles, Gaspé and other points.

Ferry The cheapest and most common way to get to the Magdalen Islands is by ferry from Souris on Prince Edward Island. The boat leaves daily at 2 pm except Tuesday. On Tuesday the boat leaves at 2 am.

In midsummer, reservations are strongly recommended. Make them by calling ☎ (418) 986-3278. If not, arrive at least two hours ahead of time. I mean it, at least two

hours. The boat, the MV *Lucy Maud Montgomery*, with a capacity of 90 vehicles and 300 passengers is always completely full. If after waiting in line for hours you do not get aboard, they will give you a reservation for the very next ferry only. Sometimes at peak season there is another boat put into service but it leaves Prince Edward Island at 2 am. Nonetheless, it too will be packed.

For the return trip, reservations can also be made. It's advisable to do this on arrival or not long after. In peak season there will be at least several days worth of returning passengers choc-a-bloc as soon as you arrive. The return to Prince Edward Island departs at 8 am except on Tuesday when it leaves at 8 am. Again, the seasonal supplementary trip is at night.

This is not a cheap trip. The cost is $32 per person for the five-hour, 223-km cruise. It's the car fee that really kills you though. That's another $62. And these are both one-way fares only. Campers, trailers etc are still more costly. Bicycles can be taken for $7.50. Credit cards are accepted for payment.

The ship is well appointed, however, with a surprisingly inexpensive cafeteria. For those with a little extra money there is also a white-tablecloth dining room with meals in the $16 to $20 range and a full course (from soup to dessert) table d'hôte which is not bad value. The ship has some outdoor decks, various inner lounges and a bar with live entertainment.

Passenger boats operated by the same line cruise to the islands down the St Lawrence River from Montreal, but are expensive. There is also a passenger and cargo ship once a week from Montreal, which is less costly but still over $350 one way. The CTMA *Voyageur* taking cargo and 12 passengers departs Montreal once a week for Cap aux Meules and returns four days later. In Montreal call ☎ 937-7656. Meals are included in the price of the ticket. In the off-peak tourist season the price drops by about one third.

Getting Around

Five of the main islands are linked by road but distances are small and cycling is not uncommon. Bicycles can be rented at Le Pedallier in Cap aux Meules. The office is closed on Sunday.

There is a guided bus tour of the islands available out of Cap aux Meules and taxis will take you to specific parts of the island. Also, cars and motorcycles can be rented in Cap aux Meules or at the airport.

A ferry connects Île d'Entrée with the two principal islands.

One boat tour operator, Excursions en Mer, offers day-trips to Île d'Entrée, fishing excursions and trips around the coast to see the cliffs. Sea kayaks can be rented at Adventure Plein Air in Étang du Nord.

The Far North

Wherever you are in Canada, the north or far north are ambiguous terms. For the vast majority of people, two hours north of Montreal or a few hours drive north from almost any of the country's major cities, is considered the north. In Quebec, certainly, straying more than a couple of hundred miles beyond the main population centres puts you in the land of the boreal forest. And yet, if you travel as far north as possible on the most remote route in the middle of nowhere you might get half way up the province. The north is an immense, sparsely populated region, the most northerly sections of which are dotted with tiny Inuit and Native Indian settlements here and there accessible only by bush plane. The developed areas are based on massive industrial operations – mining, forestry and hydro-electricity.

Much of the accessible north has already been discussed in the text. These regions from west to east include the areas north of Baie Comeau, now connected by road to Labrador; Sept Îles with its train into Labrador and beyond; and the far eastern Gulf of St Lawrence with no roads but ferry access to Labrador. Many of the parks discussed between Quebec City and the Saguenay River are as far north as most people ever get. This section outlines some possibilities in

the north-west up to James Bay. Most tourism in the far north involves very expensive fly-in camps specialising in fishing and hunting. Some operators are now offering cultural and ecotours of various types but again they are prohibitively costly. For these trips inquire at tourist information offices in Montreal or Quebec. To experience wilderness and the northern coniferous forest, the various parks and reserves are the place to go. Most people visiting the James Bay area go to get a look at the colossal power stations. The roads are discussed below. Canadian Regional Airlines serves many of the north's major towns.

LA VÉRENDRYE RESERVE
North-west of Montreal, Highway 117 leads past Mont Tremblant Park into this massive, almost untouched wildlife reserve about six or so hours later. The wilderness canoeists who make up the majority of visitors tend to sigh and go into silent rapture when asked about it. Some supplies can be obtained in Mont Laurier or Maniwaki (south toward Ottawa) but most should be brought in. The interpretation centre at the park's south end has information on trails and canoe routes. The park has two campgrounds.

VAL D'OR
With a population of 24,000 this is a major town and centre for the local mining and forestry industries. The Mining Village of Bourlamaque is a re-created log village from the gold rush period. A mine shaft can also be toured. There are numerous motels and a nearby campground. The tourist office has a list of B&Bs.

ROUYN NORANDA
To the west, this copper mining and smelting town is about the same size as Val d'Or. Free tours of the Horne Smelter, one of the world's largest producers, can be taken in summer. There is also a reconstructed historic site here detailing the settlement era.

Nearby are several areas to enjoy nature such as Parc Aiguebelle. There are car rental agencies in town.

South of town, a main highway runs along the Ontario border to Temiscaming which is connected to North Bay and hence southern Ontario.

JAMES BAY

North of Val d'Or, past Amos and the many satellite villages, the surfaced road continues through wilderness to **Matagami**. This mining town is based on copper and zinc. Free tours are offered at the Noranda site. There are two motels in town.

From here the so-called Route de la Baie James, also paved, travels 620 km to Chisasibi on the waters of James Bay. Side roads on the way lead to Native Indian villages. Enroute are designated picnic spots, viewpoints and numerous lakes to stop at. The James Bay Municipality (MBJ in French) tourist office is at km 6 (six km out of town) along this road. Ask here about the gasoline stations and to reserve a site at one of the campgrounds. It is important to have accommodation prebooked. Campgrounds are located at km 38 and km 582 on the main road.

The MBJ covers a fifth of the province and is twice the size of England. At about the tip of James Bay, the forest gives way to the taiga vegetative zone. The true tundra is much further north, well beyond any road access.

The region began to open up in the mid 1970s with the commencement of work on the mega hydro-electric projects. The roads and all the recent settlements are related to these on-going controversial developments. Local Native peoples have long objected to the dams, mass flooding and resulting radical environmental changes. In the early 1990s, the Cree very successfully lobbied in New York, Quebec's main customer for power. Some projects have been scaled back, others shelved, at least for now.

Radisson, with 700 people, is the area's main town. From the vantage point in town much of the surrounding territory can be seen. To the east lies the string of reservoirs and massive power stations. A road, hundreds of km long stretching three-quarters of the way to Labrador, connects them. La Grand 2, just west of Radisson, produces half of Quebec's electricity. Free tours of the enormous site are given but reservations are required. They must be made through the MBJ tourist office in Matagami.

There are two hotels and a campground. South of town about 30 km is the other main road campground. The average temperature in July is 14°C.

Chisasibi, a Cree settlement on the coast at the mouth of La Grand Rivière also has a motel. La Grande 1, another power station, can be visited on the way. Again reservations must be made beforehand.

The other main road in the region is the unsurfaced Route du Nord (the North Route) which runs south-east off the Route de la Baie James, above Matagami, 437 km to Chibougamou. Before driving this lonely stretch ask about conditions and services. Gasoline is available at the Cree village of Nemiscau (Nemaska).

CHIBOUGAMOU

North-east of Val d'Or, Hwy 113 cuts through the forest toward central Quebec all the way to Chibougamou. It's a long, isolated trip, so take extra supplies. There is camping at Lebel sur Quevillon, a pulp & paper town. Canoes can be rented at the lake. Once in Chibougamou there are a few motels and hotels with attached restaurants.

From town, a secondary road continues 200 km through a reserve and past the Cree village of Mistissini before ending at Lac Albanel.

South of Chibougamou, Hwy 187 runs through Ashuapmushuan Wildlife Reserve, which has camping, to Lac Saint Jean and Chicoutimi. There are no towns until nearly Lac Saint John.

Newfoundland & Labrador

Unlike any other province, two distinct geographic areas make up this singular political entity. The residents, too, will remind you that Newfoundland (pronounced 'new-fen-LAND') is Newfoundland and Labrador is Labrador. The former is the island section of the province, the latter the larger northern mainland portion and each is always referred to separately. Though they have much in common, there are cultural, historical, geological and developmental differences. By far the majority of the population lives in more accessible Newfoundland and this is the region most visitors see.

Newfoundland has a unique character, and even a brief encounter with it is gratifying. It's a rugged, weather-beaten land at the edge of Canada, heavily influenced by the sea and the conditions of the not-too-distant far north.

From the often foggy shores, generations of fishers have headed out to sea and the waters legendary for cod and dozens of other kinds of fish. This more than anything has determined the life and culture of the province.

On the Grand Banks, lying south-east off the most populated region (the Avalon Peninsula), fishing boats gather from around the world as they have done since before Columbus even saw the 'New Land'.

Unfortunately, the huge, modern, hi-tech, floating factories now used by some nations, together with illegal practices, are a far cry from the traditional Newfoundland family trawler.

The early 1990s has seen the inevitable result of this with drastically reduced catches and the end of work for thousands of Newfoundland fishers. It is hoped the decimated cod schools will return and that in the meantime other species, particularly lobster, can help to tide people over. Fish farming is also being attempted but for many people the old way of life, relying on the sea, is gone for good.

Entered Confederation: 31 March 1949
Area: 404,520 sq km
Population: 568,474
Provincial Capital: St John's

- Walk the hilly streets of St John's, the oldest city in North America and the headquarters of the distinctive Newfoundland culture
- Enjoy traditional music and satirical theatre at local clubs found around the province
- View the icebergs around Twillingate and Notre Dame Bay
- Hike along the fjords in Gros Morne National Park
- Visit a 1000-year-old Viking settlement at L'Anse-aux-Meadows National Historic Park
- Discover the isolated fishing villages, called 'outports', along the shores of Labrador
- Explore northern Labrador's remote grandeur and be overwhelmed by the solitude

NEWFOUNDLAND

All of Labrador and the northern portions of the island are part of the Laurentian Shield, one of the earliest geological formations on earth – possibly the only area unchanged from times predating the appearance of animals on the planet.

Across the province, in both sections, the interior is mostly forested wilderness with many peat bogs and countless lakes and rivers. Almost all the people live along the coast, with its many isolated fjords, bays and coves.

History

In 1497, John Cabot sailed around the shores of Newfoundland in the employ of Henry VII of England. Not long after explorers under the flags of France and Portugal were also in the area. In the 15th and 16th centuries fishers from those countries, as well as Basques and Spaniards, regularly fished the offshore waters.

In 1583, Sir Humphrey Gilbert claimed Newfoundland for England and small settlements began developing over the next 200 years. Some autonomy was granted in about 1830.

The province has a rich aviation history hosting 40 pioneering transatlantic flights between 1919 and 1937 including those of Charles Lindbergh and Amelia Earhart.

During WWII, Canada, Britain and the USA all set-up military bases and airports.

The province was the last to join Canada, doing so as recently as 1949. By this time, fishing had become more modernised and pulp & paper, iron ore and hydro power had all added to the province's development.

Climate

Newfoundland's weather is cool throughout the year, Labrador's especially so, with the Arctic currents and north winds. There's heavy precipitation all year too, mainly around the coasts where fog and wind is common. Summer is short but July and August are generally quite warm. The sunniest and driest places are the central, inland areas.

Economy

The economies of Newfoundland and Labrador experienced an upheaval in the 1990s. Years of overfishing depleted the essential cod stocks to the point that, in 1992, federal fisheries officials imposed a ban on cod fishing off of eastern Newfoundland. A year later the moratorium was extended to southern Newfoundland in an effort to give the cod fishery a good chance to recover. The ban, however, devastated a province that was already enduring a 20% unemployment rate. More than 30,000 fisherman were put out of work and in many small coastal villages, as many as 80% of the families were on a government assistance programme called TAGS.

Tempering the bad news, were major oil and mineral discoveries. In Labrador's Voisey Bay near Nain, geologists turned up rich concentrations of nickel, copper and cobalt, and by the end of the decade Diamond Fields could easily become the second largest nickel producer in the world. Oil was discovered in Newfoundland's Terra Nova region and then there is Hibernia. Located in the Bull Arm west of St John's, the oil field was discovered in 1979 but 10 years of wrangling between the federal and provincial governments and the oil companies followed. A binding agreement was finally signed in 1990 and construction of a huge oil rig and loading system began to the tune of $5.8 billion. Oil production is slated to start in 1997 and the field is expected to average 125,000 barrels of oil a day.

Population & People

The people, of mainly English and Irish descent, have developed a distinct culture. Perhaps the most noticeable difference is the language with its strong lilting inflections, distinctive accent, unique slang and colourful idiom. A look at the map reveals descriptive and light-hearted names such as Nick's Nose Cove, Come-by-Chance, Main Tickle and Cow Head; names that reveal something of the history and the people that made it. To people in the rest of the country the residents of 'The Rock' are known

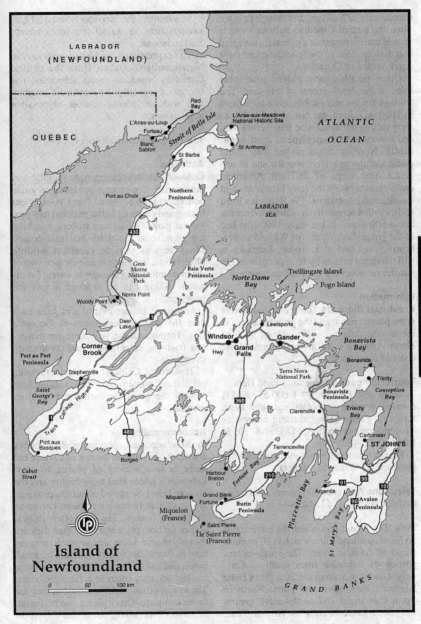

LABRADOR
(NEWFOUNDLAND)

QUEBEC

Red Bay

L'Anse-au-Loup
Forteau
Blanc Sablon

St Barbe

Strait of Belle Isle

L'Anse-aux-Meadows
National Historic Site

St Anthony

ATLANTIC
OCEAN

Port au Choix

Northern
Peninsula

LABRADOR
SEA

430

Gros
Morne
National
Park

Baie Verte
Peninsula

Norte Dame
Bay

Twillingate Island

Fogo Island

Woody Point
Norris Point

Deer
Lake

Lewisporte

Corner
Brook

Windsor

Grand
Falls

Gander

Bonavista
Bay

Port au Port
Peninsula

Stephenville

Saint'
George's
Bay

Trans Canada Highway

Hwy

Terra Nova
National Park

Bonavista

Trinity

Bonavista
Peninsula

Conception
Bay

360

Clarenville

Trinity
Bay

Port aux
Basques

480

Burgeo

Carbonear

ST JOHN'S

Cabot
Strait

Terrenceville

Harbour
Breton

Fortune Bay

210

Placentia Bay

Argentia

91

90

101

Miquelon
Grand Bank
Fortune

Miquelon
(France)

Saint Pierre

Île Saint Pierre
(France)

Burin
Peninsula

St Mary's Bay

80

Avalon
Peninsula

Island of
Newfoundland

0   50   100 km

GRAND   BANKS

NEWFOUNDLAND

humorously as Newfies, and though they are often the butt of Canadian humour there is no real malice meant: it's generally accepted that they are among the friendliest and most quick-witted of Canadians.

Other peoples have played prominent roles in the development of this land. The Vikings landed and established a settlement in 1000 AD. Inuit and Native Indian bands were calling the area home long before that, and historic sites mark some of these settlements. Newfoundland proper, the island portion of the province, was the site of one of the most tragic of all North American encounters between the early Europeans and the original inhabitants. The Beothuks lived and travelled across much of the province for about 500 years. In the early 1800s the last of the group died, victims of White diseases, hostility and bad luck. Today, Labrador is still inhabited mainly by Inuit peoples and in smaller numbers the Innu Indian people.

Information

Provincial Symbols The provincial flower is the pitcher plant, and the provincial bird is the marine Atlantic puffin. About 95% of North America's puffins breed around the coast of Newfoundland.

Tourist Offices The Newfoundland Dept of Tourism and Culture (☎ 1-800-563-6353) oversees tourism promotion and publishes a series of guides. Their mailing address is Visitor Services Section, PO Box 8730, St John's, A1B 4K2.

Tourist information booths across the province are known as 'chalets'.

Telephone Area code 709 covers all of Newfoundland and all of Labrador.

Time The island portion of the province is on Newfoundland Time which is 30 minutes ahead of Atlantic Time. The south-eastern portion of Labrador from south of Cartwright and down along the Straight of Belle Isle uses Newfoundland Time. Northern (from Cartwright and northwards), central and eastern Labrador are all on Atlantic Time.

In summer, the province uses daylight-savings time as do all provinces except Saskatchewan.

The expression '...and a half-hour later in Newfoundland', taken from the central Canadian broadcast media schedules, has become a regularly used comedic interjection with an infinite number of possible applications.

Tax The provincial sales tax is 12%.

Activities

Outdoor possibilities are wide-ranging and the tourism department publishes a guide outlining many of them. There is excellent hiking and camping in the national and provincial parks. Whale and iceberg watching are popular on the north and east coasts. Many regions provide excellent wildlife observation, with moose and caribou two of the most interesting animals to watch. Freshwater fishing can be enjoyed across the province.

Sometime between April and June each year the province celebrates St George's Day. Throughout the year there are numerous festivals, celebrations and community events.

Traditional Celtic-style music remains popular and numerous folk festivals are held around the province during the summer months.

Accommodation

In Newfoundland, accommodation prices are much like those in the rest of Canada but there is less variety of places to stay. Labrador's prices tend to be higher and the choices fewer. Scattered about the province are small, family-run guesthouses known as 'hospitality homes'. These are often the best choice for both price and fun. Often they are the only choice. Some are like small rooming houses, some are pretty much like small hotels and still others, probably the majority, are just an extra room in a family's home. The tourist office publishes lists but they are never complete. Other places can be found. In some of the small, out-of-the-way spots the pub manager might be able to suggest a couple of names.

The main alternatives to the types of places already mentioned are motel units. These are generally fairly new and reliable but more expensive and fairly uniform. The larger towns offer hotels as well.

Many visitors camp and the system of provincial parks is good, inexpensive and extensive with most parks within a day's trip of each other. Note that facilities at many of them are minimal, including a lack of serviced sites for recreational vehicles or showers. There are also some privately run campgrounds but nowhere near as many as you'll find in many other provinces. Potential tenters should have reasonably decent equipment as weather conditions don't allow for a casual hammock-in-the-tree style of camping.

Getting Around

Getting around the province presents some peculiar problems. The ever-growing road network connects major towns and most of the regions of interest to visitors but remains sketchy in many areas. Outside the two cities of St John's and Corner Brook and a few large towns, such as Gander and Port aux Basques, communities are small and the visitor traffic is light. Except for the one trans-island route, the public bus system consists of a series of small, regional services that usually connect with one or more major points. Although not extensive, this system works pretty well and will get most people to where they want to go.

There is no train service on the island but one line in western Labrador still operates.

The 905-km-long Trans Canada Hwy is the only road linking St John's, the capital, to Port aux Basques on the other side of the island. The road begins and ends at barren but strikingly attractive rocky coasts typical of the provincial shoreline. In between are vast areas of wooded lakeland, some of it quite scenic, and at the western end of the island there's a fertile valley edged by mountains.

It is a long haul from St John's to Port aux Basques, a 10 to 12-hour drive, but there are a few places worth stopping at on the way, and several towns break up the trip.

For many of the small, isolated coastal villages known as 'outports', the only means of transportation and connection with the rest of the province is by boat. Some of these villages are connected by a surprisingly inexpensive ferry service which runs regularly in a couple of areas and is for passengers and freight only. A trip along one of these routes provides a chance to see some of the most remote communities in North America. Visitors are few, but mainstream culture is seeping in at an ever-increasing rate.

For more information on outports and their connecting ferry services see the Outports section later in this chapter.

St John's

St John's, the province's capital and largest town with a population of 102,000 is not to be confused with Saint John which is a city in New Brunswick. It is a city that manages to feel like a town: invigorating yet warm, busy yet homey, modern centre and fishing village. Its splendid geographical location and its tumultuous, romantic history make St John's an inviting tourist destination.

As the oldest city in North America and England's first overseas colony, the establishment of St John's has been said to mark the birth of the British Empire.

St John's rises in a series of steps, sloping up from the waterfront. Everywhere there are stairs, narrow alleys and winding streets. Several of the downtown roads are lined with colourful, pastel clapboard town houses — the kind found all over the province. The more modern sections are mostly in the sprawling suburbs.

The land is inhospitable, the weather not much better and the economy still pretty much dependent on the whims of the sea. This will undoubtedly alter with the oil

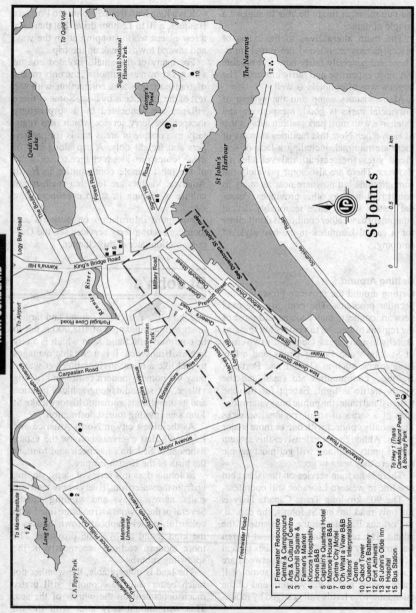

St John's

To Quidi Vidi

Signal Hill National Historic Park

George's Pond

Quidi Vidi Lake

The Narrows

St John's Harbour

To Airport

To Marine Institute

Forest Road

Logy Bay Road

The Boulevard

Kenna's Hill

King's Bridge Road

Signal Hill Road

Military Road

Gower Street

Duckworth Street

Prescott Street

See Downtown St John's map

Water Street

New Gower Street

Southside Road

Harbour Drive

Rennie's River

Portugal Cove Road

Bannerman Park

Queen's Road

Long's Hill

Harvey Road

Empire Avenue

Bonaventure Avenue

Elizabeth Avenue

Carpasian Road

Mayor Avenue

Memorial University

Prince Philip Drive

Freshwater Road

LeMarchant Road

Long Pond

C A Pippy Park

Confederation Parkway

To Hwy 1 (Trans Canada), Mount Pearl & Bowring Park

1 km

0.5

0

1 Freshwater Resource Centre & Campground
2 Arts & Cultural Centre
3 Churchill Square
4 Kincora Hospitality
   Home B&B
5 Captain's Quarters Hotel
6 Monroe House B&B
7 Centre City Motel
8 Oh What a View B&B
9 Visitors' Interpretation
   Centre
10 Cabot Tower
11 Queen's Battery
12 Fort Amherst
13 St John's Olde Inn
14 Hospital
15 Bus Station

field's exploitation, and the past few years have seen some quickening of controversial downtown development.

History

John Cabot in 1497 was the first to find the excellent and protective harbour that led to the city's development. As it's the closest point to Europe in the New World and because the famous Grand Banks teemed with fish offshore, a European settlement sprang up in 1528. Unfortunately, this brought to an end not only the lifestyle but the very existence of the Beothuk Indians.

From its inception, the settlement was the scene of battles, raids, fires, pirating, deprivations and celebrations.

The Dutch attacked in 1665. The French ruled on three occasions, but each time the English regained the settlement from them. In the 1880s it became a centre for shipbuilding and for drying and smoking fish. Its location has inspired more than trade, warfare and greed, however. The first transatlantic wireless cable was received here; 40 pioneering aeroplane crossings – including Earhart's and Lindbergh's – used the site, and even Pan Am's inaugural transatlantic flight touched here.

The wharves have been lined with ships for hundreds of years and still are, acting as service stations to fishing vessels from around the world. As befits a port of adventurers and turbulent events, the tradition of raising a glass is well established. Eighty taverns were well in use as long ago as 1775, and in the early 1800s rum was imported to the tune of over a million litres annually. Today the city might well lay claim to the most watering holes per capita.

In 1892 the Great Fire, lit by a dropped pipe, burned down more than half the town. In 1992 another major downtown fire burned a considerable section of Harvey Rd and its many old houses. The city has an infill housing policy which stipulates that new housing be designed to blend in with the existing historic character of the street. Examples of this may be seen on New Gower St east of the City Hall.

Orientation

On the approach to St John's, the highway passes the newer subdivisions, the large suburb of Mount Pearl, and then some of the older rectangular pastel houses which in sections look somewhat like stacked-up prefabs.

The road winds around slowly and then suddenly you end up in downtown, surprised at the beautiful setting and picturesque streets.

The main streets are Harbour Drive which runs right along the bay; Water St, lined with shops, restaurants and bars, one street up; and Duckworth St, further up still from the waterfront. The rest of the city continues to rise, rather steeply, up the hill away from the sea. It's said that everyone in town has strong legs.

In town, Gower St is noted for its many multicoloured Victorian terrace houses. These attractive old English and Irish style houses are now protected for their historic character. Although central, Gower St – not to be confused with New Gower St – is a little tricky to find but it runs parallel to, and in between Duckworth St and Queen's Rd immediately behind the Anglican Cathedral and then north-eastwards.

Beside City Hall, located on New Gower St near Adelaide St, is the 'Mile 0' sign marking the start of the Trans Canada Hwy.

At the north-eastern end of Water St is the small Harbourside Park, with a monument to Sir Humphrey Gilbert whose landing near here on 5 August 1583 marked the founding of Newfoundland and Britain's overseas empire. Lord Nelson and Captain Bligh also landed here. Across the street in a sharply rising park there's a War Memorial and benches with views.

Further east is the unmistakable Signal Hill, looming over both the harbour and the downtown area. At its base is a small group of houses known as the Battery, one of the oldest sections of the city.

Ships from many countries moor along the waterfront by Harbour Drive. Among the most commonly seen flags are the Russian, Spanish and Japanese. For a view over the

NEWFOUNDLAND

area, drive or walk to the top of the brown car-park building across the street.

The airport is about six km from town near Torbay.

Information

Tourist Offices The Tourist Commission's main office (☎ 576-8106) is in the City Hall Annex on New Gower St. It's open Monday to Friday from 9 am to 4.30 pm. Through the summer months there is an information office set up in the old railway car (☎ 576-8514) on Harbour Drive on the waterfront right in downtown. It's open daily from 8.30 am to 5.30 pm.

There is also an information desk at the airport.

For drivers, an information chalet can be found 70 km west of the city at the junction of the Trans Canada Hwy and Hwy 100 from Argentia. It's open daily during the summer from 8.30 am to 8.30 pm.

Money Several major banks can be found along central Water St.

Post There is a post office at 354 Water St.

Travel Agencies Travel Cuts (☎ 737-7926) has an office in the Thompson Student Centre at Memorial University.

Bookshops Breakwater Books at 100 Water St has a large and excellent selection of titles on the city and Newfoundland.

Medical Services St Clare's Mercy Hospital (☎ 778-3111) is central at 154 Lamarchant Rd.

Newfoundland Museum

Though small, the museum (☎ 729-2329) provides several good displays. There are a few relics and a skeleton – the only remains anywhere – from the extinct Beothuk Indian tribe who once lived here. Also on display are exhibits about the Vikings and the history of St John's. The museum, at 285 Duckworth St, is open 9 am to noon and 1 to 4.45 pm weekdays and 2 to 4.45 pm weekends. Admission is free.

Incidentally, a fine attraction nearby is the now nearly extinct Canadian traffic cop, gesticulating on the corner of Prescott and Duckworth Sts.

Murray Premises

The fully renovated Murray Premises on Water St and Beck's Cove is one of the oldest warehouses in the city. It was built in the 1840s, somehow escaped the fire of 1892 and today is a National Historic Site, where the original timber and brick can be seen among the many shops and restaurants. For a different view of the seal harvest and how the seals are utilised, stop in at the Canadian Sealers Association office here. The Newfoundland Museum no longer maintains exhibits in the building.

James O'Mara Pharmacy Museum

At 488 Water St in Apothecary Hall, the original Art Nouveau building, the pharmacy museum (☎ 753-5877) is a replica of an 1885 drug store (chemist's) complete with vintage fixtures, cabinets, equipment and medicines. It's open from mid-June to mid-September only and is free. Hours are 11 am to 5 pm daily.

Court House

By the Newfoundland Museum, the working court house on Duckworth St dates from 1904 and in the late 1980s had a major facelift. Now appearing pretty much as it did when first opened, it is one of the more imposing buildings in town.

City Hall

On New Gower St, five blocks west of the court house, (Duckworth St runs into New Gower St) is the new City Hall and 'Mile 0' sign, from where the Trans Canada Hwy starts westwards on its 7775-km journey across Canada to Victoria, British Columbia.

Masonic Temple

On Cathedral St, up the hill from the Newfoundland Museum on Duckworth St, is the striking, renovated temple from 1897, now a private men's club.

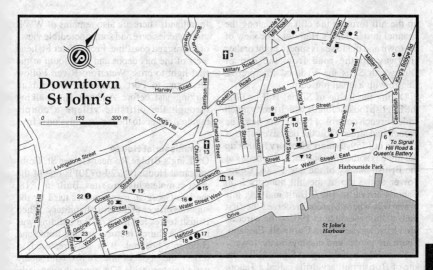

Downtown St John's

0   150   300 m

St John's Harbour

Harbourside Park

To Signal Hill Road & Queen's Battery

1   Colonial Building
2   Government House
3   Basilica of St John the Baptist
4   Prescott Inn B&B
5   Commissariat House
6   Zachary's Restaurant
7   Casa Grande Restaurant
8   Laundromat
9   Gower St House B&B
10 Fort William B&B
11 Duckworth Café
12 Stella's
13 Anglican Cathedral
14 Newfoundland Museum
15 Court House
16 Canary Cycles
17 Tourist Information Rail Car
18 Boat Tours
19 Classic Café
20 Mary Jane's Health Food
21 Murray Premises
22 City Hall, TCH 'Mile 0' &
    Tourist Information
23 Post Office

Anglican Cathedral

Across the street from the temple is the Anglican Cathedral of St John the Baptist (☎ 726-5677). Now a National Historic Site, the church was first completed in the mid-1800s. It was gutted in the Great Fire of 1892

and then rebuilt within the remaining exterior walls by 1905. Inside, note the stone walls, wooden ceilings and long, thin stained-glass windows. The address is 22 Church Hill. To enter, go to the side facing the harbour and into the doorway by the toilet. Ring the bell and someone will probably come to let you in. Tours are offered through the summer.

Basilica of St John the Baptist

Further north up Church St to Garrison Hill, and then right on Military Rd, you'll find this Roman Catholic church, also a National Historic Site. Built in 1855, it's considerably more impressive from the outside than the cathedral and, in fact, the Gothic facade dominates the cityscape. Inside, however, it's rather plain although the Italianate ceiling with gold-leaf highlights will catch the eye's attention and the pipe organ is a 'beaut'. There is a small museum on the premises which has articles relating to the history of the church.

Signal Hill National Historic Park

The view alone makes this site a must. East of town along Duckworth St, this park rises up the hill forming the cliff edge along the channel into St John's Harbour. The view of the town and out to sea is superb night or day. Halfway up the road from the end of Duckworth St is the Visitors' Interpretive Centre with a small museum.

During the Battle of Signal Hill in 1762 the English took St John's which pretty much ended French control of North America. The French had already lost the decisive battle of Quebec in 1759. **Queen's Battery** further up the hill has some cannons and the remains of the British battery of the late 1700s. **Cabot Tower** at the top of the hill honours John Cabot's arrival in 1497. Built in 1900, this tower was where Marconi received the first transatlantic message in 1901 – the wireless broadcast was sent from Cornwall, England. There are guides and displays in the tower.

From July to mid-August Signal Hill is the site of British military drills called a Tattoo. Every afternoon Wednesday through Sunday 60 to 80 soldiers dressed as a Royal Newfoundland Company go through their routines for the crowd on hand on a field next to the Visitor Centre. They end the demonstration by firing the historic cannons. The time changes from day to day so check at the Visitor Centre for a current schedule.

Admission into the museum is $2.25 or $5.50 per family but Cabot Tower and the rest of the park are free. Signal Hill is open daily in summer until 8 pm. Near the tower is Ladies Lookout which, at an elevation of 175 metres, is the highest point in the park.

Highly recommended in either direction is the 1.7-km walking trail connecting Cabot Tower with the Battery section of town down in the harbour. Going up, the trip takes about 90 minutes and climbs almost 200 meters. This walk should not be considered in winter or when any ice lingers or in heavy fog or at night. A slight stumble and it's a long way down.

Fort Amherst

Across the Narrows, at the base of the Southside Hills, is the remains of this fort which includes a lighthouse that was put into operation in 1810 as the first light in New-

foundland. There are also remains of WWII gun batteries here and some incredible views of the rugged coastline. From Water St, head west of the bus depot and turn south at the first light to cross Waterford River. Follow the signs to Fort Amherst. You end up parking just before Amherst and walking through the cliffside village a couple hundred meters to the fort. Admission is free.

Commissariat House

On King's Bridge Rd near Gower St, Commissariat House (☎ 729-6730) is one of the most complete historic sites. Built in 1818, the late-Georgian mansion was used by the supplies officer of the British military. When British forces left in 1870, the building was used as a church rectory, nursing home and children's hospital. It is now restored to reflect the style of the 1850s with many period pieces inside. The house is open daily in summer from 10 am to 5.30 pm. Admission is free.

Colonial Building

This building, on Military Rd, was the seat of the provincial legislature from 1850 to 1960. It's built of stone from Ireland which was formerly used as ships' ballast and contains many of the province's old records. The building (☎ 729-3065) is open in summer Monday to Friday from 9 am to 4.15 pm and admission is free.

Government House

Built in 1830, Government House, actually a residence, is beside Bannerman Park close to Commissariat House. The house was the official residence of the governor of Newfoundland until it became part of Canada and since then the lieutenant-governors have called it home.

CA Pippy Park

The north-western edge of the city along or near Confederation Parkway contains a number of attractions. The dominant feature is the huge 1343-hectare CA Pippy Park. Within the park, recreational facilities include walking trails, picnic areas and playgrounds.

At Long Pond marsh the bird-watching is good and mammals such as moose can sometimes be spotted in areas of the park. There is also a campground and snack bar.

The province's only university, **Memorial University** is here and provides some of its own points of interest. The university's Botanical Garden at Oxen Pond, at the western edge of the park off Mt Scio Rd, is both a cultivated garden and nature reserve. Together, these two areas provide visitors with a good introduction to the province's flora and varying natural habitats including boreal forest and bogs. The garden area is open from 1 May to 30 November, Wednesday to Sunday 10 am to 5.30 pm and admission is free.

Newfoundland Freshwater Resource Centre (NFRC) Also in CA Pippy Park the NFRC (☎ 754-3474) is the striking hexagonal balconied building across the street from the campground. The main feature is the 25-metre fluvarium, a glass-sided cross-section of a 'living' river, the only public fluvarium in North America. Viewers can peer through large windows to observe the natural, undisturbed goings-on beneath the surface of Nagle's Hill Brook. Numerous brown trout and the occasional eel can be seen. How much activity there is can vary considerably. Also, if the weather has been unsettled with high winds or if there has been any rain, the water becomes so cloudy that virtually nothing can be seen through the murkiness.

Within the centre are exhibits that closely examine plants, insects and fish of freshwater ecosystems and a demonstrative fish hatchery. Outside there are interpretive trails.

In summer the centre is open daily from 9 am to 5 pm with a feeding time scheduled at 4 pm. Tours are offered hourly. The rest of the year it is closed on Wednesday, Sunday morning and the daily hours are reduced. The rates are $2.75, less for seniors and children and a ticket includes a tour. The site is run by

a nonprofit environmental awareness group which has done some fine work along the Rennie River and Quidi Vidi Lake and are responsible for the development of some of the walking trails in the area.

Arts & Cultural Centre

The Arts & Cultural Centre (☎ 737-8210) complex about two km north-west from the downtown area on Prince Phillip Drive, beside the university, contains the Memorial University Art Gallery. The art gallery displays mainly contemporary Newfoundland and Canadian painting and sculpture. It's free and open from Tuesday to Sunday, noon to 5 pm and on Thursday and Friday nights until 10 pm. There is also a theatre at the complex.

Confederation Building

Just off Prince Phillip Drive, north-east of the arts centre, is the home of the provincial government. You can visit the building and the small military museum inside for free. It's closed on weekends.

Marine Institute

Although misleadingly named, the Marine Institute (☎ 778-0372) may be considered more worthwhile than the NFRC. Really it's more like a science and technology museum. The institute features primarily interactive exhibits. Although not on the scale of such facilities in the country's larger cities there is enough for a visit of over an hour with exhibits on such matters as fibre optics, magnets and the world's largest flume tank.

The institute is open daily with tours available in summer at 1:30 and 3 pm Monday through Friday. Also at the site is the province's only planetarium which presents its own shows featuring the heavens. The address is 155 Ridge Rd (at the top of the hill) in CA Pippy Park. You can visit only on a tour but there is no fee.

Bowring Park

South-west of the downtown area off Pitts Memorial Drive on Waterford Bridge Rd, this is another popular large city park. A couple of streams and walkways meander through the park. The Peter Pan statue is a replica of the famous one in Kensington Gardens in London, England and was made by the same sculptor.

Ocean Sciences Centre

Tours can be taken at this research unit (☎ 737-3708), which is part of Memorial University's science department. Ongoing research examines the life cycle of salmon, seal navigation, ocean currents and many other aspects of life in the colder ocean regions. There is a visitor interpretive centre and guided tours of the facility which take about an hour. Seals can be seen and there is a hands-on tank where various creatures can be touched.

It's open daily from 10 am to 6 pm in July and August and tours are offered every half an hour. Part of the tour is outside so bring appropriate clothes and footwear. Admission is $2.50. The centre is about eight km north of town just before Logy Bay at the end of Marine Lab Rd on the ocean. From town take Logy Bay Rd (Route 30) and then follow Marine Drive.

Museum of Transportation

This small museum in CA Pippy Park features a number of exhibits and artefacts collected by the Newfound Transport Historical Society and devoted to early transportation in the province. Stop by if you want to see pieces of railway rolling stock, engines or 'homemade marine transportation'. The museum is on Mt Scio Rd in the park. Hours tend to be irregular so it's best to call the tourist centre first.

Cape Spear

A 15-minute drive south-east of the city is Cape Spear, the most easterly point in North America. The area is preserved as the Cape Spear National Historical Site and located here is an 1835 lighthouse that has been refurbished inside, an interpretive center and the heavy gun batteries and magazines built in 1941 to protect the harbour during WWII. There is also a trail system that takes you along the edge of the headland cliffs, past 'the most easterly point' observation deck and up to the lighthouse. From there you can continue all the way to Maddox and Petty Harbour if you wish.

The coastal scenery at this spot is spectacular and through much of the summer there is an opportunity to spot whales. The interpretive centre is open from 10 am to 6 pm daily and there is a $2.25 fee to see the lighthouse. Everything else is free. You reach the cape from Water St by crossing the Waterford River west of the bus station and then following Blackhead Road for 11 km.

Quidi Vidi

Over Signal Hill, away from town, is the tiny, picturesque village of Quidi Vidi. This little fishing port has the oldest cottage in North America. **Mallard Cottage** (☎ 576-2266)

St John's on Ice

To many, a sight that almost equals seeing a 40-tonne humpback whale breaching, is a five-storey iceberg silently sailing past the St John's Harbour. Greenland glaciers produce up to 40,000 icebergs annually and the prime viewing area in Newfoundland is around Twillingate on the Notre Dame Bay. But an average of 370 icebergs drift as far south as St John's and in some years even more. In 1984, a total of 2,200 bergs reached the city.

The typical iceberg is 30 metres high and weighs 204,000 tonnes with only an eighth of it appearing above the water. Icebergs are often classified as 'slob ice', thick slush of small ice; 'bergy bits', small icebergs; and 'growlers', icebergs that are particularly dangerous because of their low profile and instability.

The iceberg season in St John's extends from May through June with an occasional berg appearing in early July. The best place to see them is at Signal Hill and Cape Spear. ■

dates back to the early 1700s and is now a National Heritage Site and a gift shop. Hours to tour it in the summer are 10 am to 10 pm daily. The rest of the year its closes at 5.30 pm. Admission is 50 cents.

You can walk to the village from Signal Hill in about 20 minutes or go around by road from St John's. Take Forest Rd, which runs along the lake and then turns into Quidi Vidi Village Rd.

Quidi Vidi Battery Built in 1762, this provincial historic site is up the hill from the village, guarding the bay. The French built it after taking St John's. It was later taken by the English and remained in military service into the 1800s. It's free and costumed guides are on hand daily in summer from 10 am to 5.30 pm.

Quidi Vidi Lake Inland from the village, this lake is the site of the St John's Regatta, which is held on the first Wednesday in August. Records show that the event started in 1818 and it's probably the oldest continuing sporting competition in North America. For those seeking more information there is the Regatta Museum (☎ 576-8058) on the 2nd floor of the boathouse at the lake.

The Rennies River flowing into the west end of the lake is an excellent trout stream. A conservation group, the Quidi Vidi Rennies River Development Foundation, is developing the area and a three-km walking trail from the lake along the river west to Long Pond has been set up. The foundation's Freshwater Resource Centre is at Long Pond. Trout leap from the river in the autumn as they get ready for spawning. There are other trails in the area and around Quidi Vidi Lake. The tourist office has a pamphlet with a map of the river system.

Organised Tours

For a relatively small city, the number and variety of tours available is noteworthy. The Newfoundland Historic Trust offers good walking-tours of the old city twice daily in summer at 10 am and 2 pm, leaving from the Murray Premises. The cost is $10 per person and there are group rates (☎ 738-3781).

McCarthy's Party (☎ 781-2244), a well established tour operator, offers three different excursions. The three-hour tour of the city costing $20 is good, but really doesn't provide too much that you can't do yourself for free. The other two, one to Cape Spear also for $20 and one in the opposite direction along Marine Drive, are more worthwhile. Plenty of humour, interesting historical tidbits and general information on the people and province is woven into the commentary.

Fleetline (☎ 722-2608) offers trips ranging from half-day around town to a full 10 days around the province which includes Saint Pierre and Miquelon islands. Another trip covers the Northern Peninsula. The company has an office in town but some trips leave from the major downtown hotels daily in summer.

City & Outport Adventures (☎ 747-8687) has a city tour, covering the usual sights for $20, and an outport tour that includes Cape Spear for the same price.

Other tours are done by boat. Dee Jay Charters (☎ 753-8687) is at the harbour near the railcar tourist chalet. It runs a good-value three-hour trip from the waterfront out to sea in search of icebergs in June and whales in July and August for $20, children half price. If the big highlights are not in the neighbourhood there is still bird-watching and sightseeing along the coast. Three trips are offered daily.

Also offering whale-sighting tours is O'Brien's (☎ 753-4850) out of Bay Bulls, 30 km south of St John's. Tours depart several times daily during the summer and charge $25. O'Brien's also run a shuttle bus from major hotels in St John's and charge an additional $10 for the ride.

Try to pick a calm day as it allows the boat to travel further. There are great views along the coastline, but it can get rough and cold, so take warm clothes – it may be balmy in the protected harbour but it's quite a different story once outside the Narrows. A sip of the Screech may help.

Bird Island Charters (☎ 753-4850) is similar but visits the Sea Bird Sanctuary Islands of the Witless Bay Sea Bird Ecological Reserve which includes the largest puffin colony on the east coast of North America. This sea bird reserve is one of the world's largest. Bird Island offers daily departures from Bay Bulls, south of town. There's a shuttle service from downtown hotels to get you to the dock.

Island Rendezvous (☎ 747-7253) based in suburban Mount Pearl, but operating out of the village of Garden Cove two hours from town, has a one-of-a-kind trip. Popular with local residents and taken mainly by couples, the two-day adventure visits one of the many now abandoned outport communities. Visitors are taken by boat to Woody Island, virtually a ghost town except for some people who use it as a base for seasonal fishing. Visitors are put up in a large old house run as a hospitality home. The days are spent poking around the old town and island and on a boat tour of Placentia Bay. The trip provides a glimpse into the traditional fishing village way of life as well as offering escape from what has replaced it. The cost is $123 and the office is at 42 McCrath St in Mount Pearl.

Finally, a delightful day can be spent sailing on a tall ship and there are several charters in St John offering such an outing from the waterfront. Both J&B Schooner Tours (☎ 682-6585) and Adventure Tours (☎ 726-5000) are on Pier 6 and offer several two-hours tours daily for $20 on different boats.

Festivals

Some of the major festivals are listed here. For other festivals – there are several during summer – ask at the tourist office.

June
  Discovery Days – The celebrations are held from around 18 June for two days to commemorate the city's birthday. Festivities include concerts (any Newfoundland event includes music), a parade, street dance and sporting events.
July-September
  Craft Fair – The Newfoundland & Labrador craft fair is held three times annually; the beginning of July, September and November, in the St John's Memorial Stadium.
  George Street Festival – Featuring music of all kinds this festival, performed on central George St, is held around the end of July.
  The Provincial Folk Festival – This three-day event, which takes place annually around the first week of August, should not to be missed for its great music. Dancers and story-tellers also perform in their respective traditions. The event is held in Bannerman Park with some portions held indoors if the weather is bad.
  Royal St John's Regatta – What probably began as a wager among a few fisherman to see who could row faster is now the oldest continuous sporting event in North America. The regatta officially begin in 1825 and is held on the first Wednesday of August. The entire town closes up that day and everybody heads to the shores of Quidi Vidi Lake to watch the competition among the rowers.

Places to Stay

Camping Conveniently located right in the city by the university there is camping in *CA Pippy Park* (☎ 737-3655). The charge is $5.50 for tenting, $11 for unserviced sites and $15 for serviced ones. The campground is off Higgins Line at the north-western side of the park near the Confederation Building.

The nearest provincial park with camping is Butter Pot, 30 km to the west along the Trans Canada Hwy. Unserviced sites in a very pleasant wooded setting cost $8. There is a beach, interpretive centre and trails including an easy climb up Butter Pot Hill.

Hostels The hostel situation in Newfoundland is very changeable and usually minimal, but check with the tourist office.

There are rooms for rent, though, at *Hatcher House* at Memorial University (☎ 737-7590, ext 20) through the summer months, mid-May to mid-August. Singles cost $13/18 for students/nonstudents with even cheaper doubles. Weekly rates are offered and all meals are available. There are buses to town but you can walk in less than half an hour, even if the roads are not direct. From the campus Newtown Rd leads downtown.

The owners of *Travellers B&B Hostel*

(☎ 437-5627), who have travelled on the cheap themselves, rent out a couple of rooms in their house on a large property about a 10-minute drive north out of the centre on Pine Line by Torbay. There's no public transportation but if you play you're cards nicely someone may pick you up. The price is $25 including breakfast. Call Donna or Jerry for availability of beds and exact location.

Tourist Homes & B&Bs Aside from the established places listed here, the tourist office should have an up-to-date list of places available in people's homes. There are usually places not mentioned in the printed provincial accommodation guides.

Gower St, not to be confused with New Gower St which runs into Gower at Bulley St, is an attractive, historic street and a fruitful place to look for a guesthouse.

Centrally located near the Anglican Cathedral, at 180 Gower St, is the *Gower St House* (☎ 754-0047). All the rooms are good and come with private bathroom, and one has a balcony. Check out the wood mosaic inlay of Cabot Tower in the floor beside the living room on the ground floor. Singles begin at $45 with a full breakfast which may include some traditional fare. Overnight costs drop in autumn, winter and spring. Other benefits here include the use of kitchen, laundry and parking facilities.

Nearby at 5 Gower St, the *Fort William B&B* (☎ 726-3161) is open all year with singles/doubles $50/62 and one housekeeping unit at slightly higher cost.

The *Oh! What a View* (☎ 576-7063) at 184 Signal Hill Rd is recommended as a neat, clean B&B with a spectacular view over the harbour and city. To take advantage of the location there are two decks from which guests can just sit and stare. There are four rooms at $45/55 including a continental breakfast of bread and muffins. Two of the rooms are in the basement but they are modern and comfortable. City buses run nearby but it is only a 10-minute walk into town. It's open summers only.

The *Prescott Inn* (☎ 753-7733) is a long-running B&B at 19 Military Rd, centrally

situated on the north-eastern side of the downtown area. It's a well-kept old house with balconies looking out over the harbour. There are rooms, suites and furnished apartments from $50 to $95 with full breakfast included.

At 36 Kings Bridge Rd is the year-round *Kincora Hospitality Home* (☎ 576-7415). It's a well-appointed Victorian house furnished with antiques. Singles/doubles cost $50/65 (more for a private bath) and include a continental breakfast.

More upmarket is *Monroe House* (☎ 754-0610) at 8A Forest St, behind the Newfoundland Hotel. It was built in 1900 and was once the home of the Newfoundland prime minister. The six rooms are spacious and tastefully decorated, the breakfasts substantial and in the evening there's complimentary wine. It's on a quiet street just a few minutes walk from the centre. If you seek some creature comforts and a little pampering this fits the bill at $59/69.

Away from the centre is the *Bird Island Guest Home* (☎ 734-4850 or 722-1675) at 150 Old Topsail Rd. From downtown take Cornwall Ave which turns into Old Topsail Rd. Rates are $45/55 with a continental breakfast included.

Also out of downtown there's the low-priced *Fireside Guesthouse* (☎ 726-0237) at 28 Wicklow St near the Avalon Mall Shopping Centre. Call for directions. Including a full breakfast, singles/doubles cost $35/40, making it one of the better buys, and it's just a short walk to an indoor swimming pool.

Hotels Hotels are not St John's strong point but with the good guesthouses this shouldn't pose problems. As a rule the hotels are fairly pricey and business-oriented but there are still some good, inexpensive places around town.

For a central and low-cost place, there's *Captain's Quarters* (☎ 576-7173 or 576-7468), at 2 King's Bridge Rd across the street from the Commissariat House. There are 20 rooms with singles/doubles at $35/40. On the first floor there is a cosy little pub with dart boards and fireplaces.

NEWFOUNDLAND

The *St John's Olde Inn* (☎ 722-1171), 157 LeMarchant Rd, has 15 rooms, six of them with fireplaces and chandeliers. At the recently renovated dining room you can get a $1.99 breakfast, and a pub has been added. Singles start at $30 for a room with a shared bath.

The historic *Hotel Newfoundland* (☎ 726-4980) with the imposing stone facade on Cavendish Square at the end of Duckworth St is the top-end classic in town. Run by Canadian Pacific Hotels, it's $138 for singles/doubles during the summer but there are special rates for the weekend.

About six km from downtown, at 102 Kenmount Rd, is *Hotel St John's* (☎ 722-9330). About a third of its 85 rooms come with kitchen facilities. Singles/doubles go for $65/71 and up. Also on Kenmount Rd but at No 199 is the *Best Western Travellers Inn* (☎ 722-5540), one of a chain seen across the country. They're fairly standard, reliable mid-range hotels. Here prices are $75/82 and children stay free.

Out by the airport on Airport Rd is the reasonable *Airport Inn* (☎ 753-3500 or 800-563-2489) at $45/50.

Motels The *1st City Motel* (☎ 722-5400) is at 479 Kenmount Rd, about six km from the city centre. Prices are $45 a single and $5 more for the double and additional people. The *Center City Motel* (☎ 726-0092) at 389 Elizabeth Ave near the university is a clean place with singles at $40. It has a restaurant and pub.

Greenwood Lodge & Motel (☎ 364-5300) towards Mount Pearl, off Route 60, is close to town. It has a games room and laundry facilities. Singles are $40.

Less costly is the *Crossroads Motel* (☎ 368-3191) at the junction of routes 1 and 60 at $38/43.

Places to Eat

The city has a good array of places 'to have a scoff' to use a local term for eating. Duckworth St in particular is an avenue of eateries. Every other storefront here seems to be a restaurant or cafe offering something slightly different than the one before.

At 190 Duckworth St is the comfortable *Duckworth Café* popular with the artsy and student crowds. They serve hearty soup-and-sandwich specials for $5.25, other light meals and there are lots of newspapers to read. Next door is *Vincent's* with a wide selection of teas, coffees and a giant café au lait for $2.65 as well as light dishes like hummus and pita bread for $2.75

Smaller, cosy *Stella's*, across the street at No 183, serves natural foods and vegetarian plates in the $6 to $12 range. The Caesar salad is good. Just up the street are two new places that are highly recommended by locals. *Le Petit Paris French Bistro* at 71 Duckworth St is a French restaurant with a pleasant outdoor patio overlooking the harbour while *Zachary's* next door is where you can order a traditional breakfast of fish cakes and toast for $4.

Head in the other direction to reach *Classic Café* open 24 hours at 364 Duckworth St. This is an excellent place, featuring a wide selection of seafood, fresh-baked goods and good prices. For $10 you can get a large basket of steamed mussels and two beers. Coffee and a giant muffin is $2.50 and there are always $5 lunch specials like grilled salmon.

Across the street is *Mary Jane's* with a back entrance off George St. This is a health-food store with a soup, sandwich and salad counter on the second floor. Salads are $4, most sandwiches are under $3. The counter is open from 11 am to 2.30 pm.

Keep in mind that many of the pubs serve very reasonable mid-day meals. *The Duke of Duckworth* at 325 Duckworth St is just one of many quiet English-style pubs that offer meat pies, sausages and sauerkraut or soup-and-sandwich combinations for under $6. You can wash it down with a refreshing pint of Harp.

St John's has (or used to have) some of the best fish & chips anywhere. People often bad mouth cod but it is *the* fish in this part of the world and fresh out of the sea it's excellent. These days with the lack of fish and the moratorium on fishing, getting fresh cod is not always possible. Sometimes the restaurants have it, at other times they must use frozen imported cod, which given the once boundless stocks is enough to make you wince.

For a quick sampling head to the junction of Harvey, LeMarchant and Freshwater roads, a short walk from the centre. The ever popular *Ches's* is at 5 Freshwater Rd, the *Big R* is at 69 Harvey, and *Scamper's* is at 1 LeMarchant.

House of Haynes at 207 Kenmount Rd is a casual dining room, offering other seafood like salmon, scallops and a local dish called 'brewis'. The latter is a blend of fish, onion and a bread-like mix that's soaked overnight. Another local speciality is cod tongues which are really closer to cheeks. They're often served deep-fried with very unimpressive results but, if you can, try them pan-fried.

Casa Grande is a nicely decorated Mexican restaurant at 108 Duckworth St. It holds about 10 small wooden tables encircled by wicker chairs and has dishes from around $8 and full dinners for $12.

For an East Indian meal try the *India Gate* at 286 Duckworth St which has an all-you-can-eat lunch buffet Monday to Friday from 11 am to 2 pm for $8.

For fine dining, the *Stone House Restaurant* (☎ 753-2380) at 8 Kenna's Hill has long been considered the number one choice. Specialities at this expensive restaurant are seafood, game and traditional Newfoundland dishes. It's in one of the city's oldest homes. For dinner with the best view in the city, head to the *Cabot Club* in the Hotel Newfoundland. Watching the lights emerge around the harbour at dusk is spectacular. Dinners range from $18 to $24.

Lastly, you may want to check out the farmers' markets which feature local produce for sale on Saturday throughout the summer. There's an all-day market at Churchill Square off Elizabeth Ave near the university and a second one from 9 am to 3 pm in the parking lot of Murray Premises in the city centre.

Entertainment

St John's is a lot of fun at night. You won't have to search too long in this town if you're thirsty because, per capita, there must be more watering holes here than anywhere. Political correctness in the sphere of alcohol is pleasantly absent in these parts and makes a refreshing change from the constant didacticism found in much of Canada. The elsewhere often forbidden 'happy hour' here becomes stretched to a laughable misnomer lasting from as early as 11 am to as late at 7.30 pm! Two for one specials abound across town and establishments are busy through the day especially on weekends.

George St is pretty crazy with crowds and queues at a variety of bars and is closed nightly at 10 to vehicle traffic, with the exception of the police and taxi drivers. The *Corner Stone* on the corner of Queen St has videos and live rock, *Sundance* with a western slant and country bands also has a large outdoor deck. *Jungle Jim's* has a 46-ounce frozen concoction called a Jumbo Hurricane and there is blues and jazz at *Fat Cat*.

The *Ship Inn* down the steps beside the Arts Council, 245 Duckworth St, is good with live music and *Schroeder's Piano Bar* on Bates Hill is an interesting little place.

There are also many Irish pubs offering live traditional music, including *Erin's Pub* at 184 Water St and *Blarney Stone* in the George St stretch.

For a complete run down of the music and bar scene in St John's, pick up a free copy of *Signal* found in bars and restaurants.

Live theatre or dance performances are staged regularly at the Arts & Cultural Centre (☎ 729-3900) on Confederation Parkway. The Resource Center for the Arts (LSPU Hall; ☎ 753-4531), at 3 Victoria St presents work by local playwrights.

In August, you can head out to Logy Bay where, across from the Ocean Sciences Centre, is the theatre for *Shakespeare By The Sea* (☎ 726-4585). Classic Shakespeare plays are performed at 6 pm on Friday through Sunday at the outdoor stage. Tickets are $10 and you should bring a blanket to sit on (and a coat if it rains).

NEWFOUNDLAND

Getting There & Away

Air Air Canada (☎ 726-7880) to Halifax costs $332 one way, to Montreal $447. Canadian Airlines (☎ 576-0274) flies to Charlottetown for $370. Obviously round-trip tickets save you considerably. The two biggies work with Air Nova and Air Atlantic respectively for local flights. For flights solely within the province also try Provincial Airlines (☎ 576-1666) and Air Labrador (☎ 753-5583).

Bus The bus system is a little confusing but if you can track things down it can work fairly well for you. The system, unlike that in other provinces, isn't monopolised by one or two operators but consists of a lot of small local and regional services. Finding out who they all are and where they go can take some digging.

The main bus station (☎ 737-5912, open 7.15 am to 5.30 pm; or for recorded information call 737-5911) is at the far south-west end of town at 495 Water St, underneath the overpass. It's about a 20-minute walk from town.

CN Roadcruiser operates just one route but it's the province's main one, running across Newfoundland along the Trans Canada Hwy to Port aux Basques and stopping at many places along the way. So many places, in fact, that the trip becomes somewhat of a marathon. To Port aux Basques there's one bus daily at 8 am which costs $84 one way. The trip takes about 14 hours. You can reach Grand Falls on that run for $48 or a 5.30 pm bus on Friday only. This distance takes about 6½ hours to cover. Note that across the province the CN Roadcruiser bus is often referred to as the CN bus.

For Argentia, Placentia and Freshwater there is Newhook's Transportation (☎ 726-4876), 13 Queen St, which runs buses daily down to the south-west Avalon Peninsula ($15 to Argentia.) Fleetline Bus Service (☎ 722-2608) goes to Carbonear and the lower Conception Bay area daily.

Bonavista North Transportation (☎ 579-3188), 1 Macklin Pl, runs up to the Bonavista Bay area and has a bus going to Newtown on Monday, Wednesday and Friday for $25 one way.

There are still others in St John's. Cheeseman's Bus Service (☎ 753-7022) and Foote's Taxi (☎ 364-1377) provide service from St John's to various points on the Burin Peninsula while North Shore Bus Lines (☎ 722-5218) runs up to Old Perlican. Contact the tourist bureau for information on new services.

The only train is in Labrador.

Taxi Share-taxis also run between St John's and the ferry terminal. In Argentia you can make dockside arrangements for getting to St John's.

Ferry The Marine Atlantic ferry for North Sydney, Nova Scotia, docks at Argentia on the south-west coast of the Avalon Peninsula. The MV *Joseph & Clara Smallwood* goes in each direction twice a week and runs from mid-June to October only. It departs Argentia on Wednesday and Saturday at 9 am, and North Sydney on Tuesday and Friday at 8 am for most of the summer but 4 pm in September. The crossing time is 14 hours, less if you have calm seas. An adult ticket is $51, a car $114. Rooms and beds are extra. You can take the less expensive ferry to Port aux Basques and then drive across the province twice but with gasoline at 66 to 70 cents a litre, calculate the savings first.

As on the sister ship to Port aux Basques, the MV *Caribou* (from Port aux Basques to North Sydney, Nova Scotia), passengers can enjoy the movie theatre, a bar with live band, a tourist booth, a children's play area, even miniature golf on the top deck – in short, the works. On the night trips most people flake out anywhere they can including all over the floor. Bring a blanket or sleeping bag and join the slumber party.

In July or August reservations are a good idea in either direction: call ☎ 902-794-5700 in North Sydney from anywhere in Canada or ☎ 709-772-7701 in and around eastern Newfoundland. In the US, call toll-free ☎ 800-341-7981. Usually one or two days' notice is all that is necessary.

If you're in a car, you'll get a free car wash as you board the ferry back to the Canadian mainland. This is to get rid of two bug varieties harmful to potatoes and found only in Newfoundland.

Car If you want a car when arriving at the airport (or in town) make sure you reserve. Reservations can be made at branches of the international chains in Nova Scotia or elsewhere, or you can phone the offices here in advance. Rates are about the same as anywhere else in Canada.

There are several car-rental agencies and most can be found along Topsail Rd. Budget (☎ 747-1234) is at 954 Topsail Rd; Dollar (☎ 722-7300) at 497 Kentmount Rd; and Rent-A-Wreck (☎ 753-2277) with cheaper, used cars is at 43 Pippy Place and 933 Topsail Rd and has small compacts for $32 a day plus 100 free km.

If you drive a car one way between St John's and Port aux Basques, you'll have to pay a return charge of at least $150.

Getting Around

The Airport There is no city bus to the airport which is about six km north of town on Route 40 going towards Torbay. Going by taxi, at about $12, is the only way. The official airport service is by Dave Gulliver Cabs (☎ 722-0003). Inquire about sharing and if you're lucky it may be cheaper.

Bus The St John's Transportation Commission runs the Metrobus (☎ 722-9400) city bus system. There are a few bus routes in and around town and together they cover most areas, No 3 does the central area. By transferring from this one to an adjoining loop, say the No 12 going west, you can get a pretty good city tour for just a couple of dollars. For hitching south on Avalon Peninsula, catch Nos 15 or 8 that will take you to Bay Bulls Rd. For the Trans Canada Hwy, take No 9 out to Avalon Mall.

The fare is $1.50 per ride. If you're in town for a while a 10-ride Metropass is $12.50.

Bicycle For two wheels, try Canary Cycles

(☎ 579-5972) at 294 Water St. Top-of-the-line mountain bikes are $13 for two hours, $20 for a day or $30 for two days.

AROUND ST JOHN'S

Marine Drive, north of St John's up towards Torbay, goes past nice coastal scenery. There are rocky beaches at both Middle Cove and Outer Cove – good for a walk or picnic.

Offshore around **Torbay** is a good whale-watching area. Puffins live and feed here also. Marine Drive ends at Pouch Cove but a gravel road continues to Cape St Francis for good views. West of town, head to Topsail for a great view of Conception Bay and some of its islands.

Ten km south of St John's is **Petty Harbour**. This is a very scenic harbour, filled with weathered boats, wharves and sheds on stilts and surrounded by high rocky hills. Several production companies have used it for movie settings. If you want to spend the night, *Orca Inn* (☎ 747-9676) has four rooms at $40/48.

In **Goulds**, at the junction of Hwy 10 and the road to Petty Harbour, don't miss Bidgood's, a supermarket with a twist. It's known for its Newfoundland specialities, especially with locals, who stock up on their favourite items before returning to jobs on the mainland. Where else can you buy caribou steak, moose in a jar or seal-meat pie? Depending on the time of year the selection may also include cod tongues, saltfish or lobster. There are jars of the province's distinctive jams – try partridgeberry or the elite of the island's berries, bakeapple. It's open daily, and until 9 pm on Thursday and Friday.

Bay Bulls and **Witless Bay** are excellent places from which to observe birds. Three islands off Witless Bay and southward are preserved as the Witless Bay Ecological Reserve and represent one of the top sea-bird breeding areas in eastern North America. Every summer more than a million pairs of sea birds gather to breed, including puffins, kittiwakes, murres, cormorants and storm petrels. Several operators run highly recommended trips out to the colonies.

No one is permitted on the islands but the boats do get close enough for you to consider taking ear plugs as well as a camera and binoculars. The din overhead is incredible. The best months for visiting are June and July which is also good for whale-watching – humpback and minke are fairly common here. Whales are seen in the vicinity until early August and the humpback is the most spectacular of all whales for its breaching performances. If you really hit the jackpot, an iceberg might be thrown in too.

Gatherall's (☎ 334-2887) runs a wildlife boat tour in Bay Bulls on the North Side Rd with several trips daily that include whale-watching and the bird colonies. The cost for the two-and-a-half-hour trip is $28. Also working out of Bay Bulls is Bird Island Charters (☎ 753-4850) and O'Brien's (☎ 753-4850). See Organised Tours earlier in this chapter for details on them. In Witless Bay, Murphy's Bird Island Tours (☎ 334-2002) charges $20 for the trip.

On Hwy 10 in Witless Bay there is a Tourist Chalet, open 9 am to 8 pm daily.

Cape Broyle further down the coast also has a bird-sanctuary trip run by Great Island Tours (☎ 432-2272). The trip includes a seaside view of an abandoned coastal village wedged into the cliffs. It also offers shuttle buses to and from St John's.

AROUND THE AVALON PENINSULA

The peninsula, more like an island hanging onto the rest of the province by a thin strip of land, is the most densely populated area of Newfoundland: nearly half its population lives here.

Conception Bay is lined with scores of small communities, but all around the coast you'll find fishing villages.

At Argentia in the south-west is the ferry depot connecting with Nova Scotia. The tourist office (☎ 227-5272) can suggest driving and camping tours of the peninsula.

Southern Avalon

Despite its proximity to St John's this section of the province is very good for viewing wildlife and has several good parks.

Down the coast there is excellent camping at **La Manche Provincial Park**, 53 km south of St John's. The park has 70 camp sites, many of them overlooking La Manche Pond along with a day use area and beach. A tent site is $8 a night. There are also two scenic trails that begin in the campground. The first is a 15-minute walk from the day use area to a small waterfall. The second follows the fire-exit track from site No 59 to the remains of La Manche, a fishing village that was destroyed in 1966 by a fierce winter storm. It's about a 30-minute hike one way.

Another 27 km south along Hwy 10 is **Ferryland**, a historical town where an interesting afternoon can be spent. Ferryland was one of the earliest English settlements in North America, dating to 1621 when Sir George Calvert, who later became Lord Baltimore, established a village here. The town lasted for a few years before the long cold winters sent Calvert to Maryland in search of warmer weather. Other English families followed, however, and maintained the colony until 1673 when a Dutch raid destroyed most of the town.

All this history can be seen at several places in Ferryland. As you approach, there is **Ferryland Museum**, open daily but afternoon only on Sunday, with local artefacts. Then head to the **Archaeological Dig Interpretation Centre**, opposite the playing field and open 9 am to 8 pm daily except Sunday when it opens at noon. Displayed inside are many of the artefacts that have been recovered and preserved. From the centre it's a short walk to the four main dig areas and the field laboratory where everything from axes to bowls are being recovered and restored. Guides in the lab will give you a free tour of the facility and the sites or you can just watch the archaeologists shift through the dirt. Workers are at the dig sites 8 am to 4.30 pm Monday through Friday and 8 am to 12.30 pm Saturday.

There is also an 1870 lighthouse that can be reached along a dirt road from the dig sites or you can climb the Gaze. The towering hill sits beyond the community museum and was named so by early settlers who use to climb it to watch for approaching warships or to escape the frequent pillages the area experienced. The view on a clear day is worth the climb.

The *Down Inn* (☎ 432-2808 or 432-2163) has 10 rooms at $35/45, including breakfast. Another 27 km to the south in Cappahayden, there is *Lawlor's Hospitality Home* (☎ 363-2164), open from June to August, with five rooms at $30/40.

In the interior of the peninsula is the huge **Avalon Wilderness Reserve** with an increasingly large herd of woodland caribou now numbering about 100,000. Permits, available at the La Manche Provincial Park office, are required to visit the area for hiking or canoeing. Caribou, however, can sometimes be seen right at the edge of Hwy 10. There are two posted areas for caribou crossings. The first is a 30 km-stretch between Chance Cove Provincial Park and Portugal Cove South and the second a 20-km stretch between Trepassey and St Stephens. Both areas feature wind-blown treeless terrain, where it's possible to see a good distance in any direction on a clear day. As migrating animals, caribou tend to move en masse and often you spot the animals grazing in groups of 10 to 30. Even spotting a lone individual is a real treat as they are quite impressive beasts and are rarely seen by those not living in the far north of Canada, Russia or Finland.

Camping is possible at **Chance Cove Provincial Park** south of Cappahayden. The campground is almost seven km towards the

⊕⊕⊕⊕⊕⊕⊕⊕⊕⊕⊕⊕⊕⊕⊕⊕

The World's First Flush Toilet
The digs at Ferryland have turned up some interesting artefacts, including, say archaeologists, what is probably the world's first flush toilet, dating back to the 1620s. Among the remains that have turned up from Lord Baltimore's colony is a privy that was strategically situated on the shoreline with a hole above the sea. Twice a day, the high tide came in and 'flushed' the contents away into the ocean, leaving nothing but a little salt water on the seat. ■

⊕⊕⊕⊕⊕⊕⊕⊕⊕⊕⊕⊕⊕⊕⊕⊕

coast from Hwy 10 and little more than a gravel parking area for those with recreational vehicles. But people with tents can walk up the bluff for an exceptional camp site overlooking the cove. These are some of the most scenic camp sites on the Avalon Peninsula and cost $8 a night. Also working out of the campground is Chance Cove Diving and Venture Tours (☎ 363-2257), which offers both whale-watching tours and diving tours. Within a short distance of the cove is a large concentration of wrecks only 36 metres deep. The rates are $30 per dive or $10 for a whale-watching trip.

Trepassey was the launching place of Amelia Earhart's first-woman-across-the-Atlantic flight in 1928. In town, you'll find a large food store, a commercial campground, the *Northway Lodge B&B* (☎ 438-2888) which has singles/doubles for $40 and the *Trepassey Motel* (☎ 438-2934) with 10 rooms for $55/59.

Continuing up the coast, the area from St Vincent's to St Mary's provides an excellent chance of seeing whales, particularly the humpback which feeds close to shore. Halfway between the two villages is **Point La Haye Natural Scenic Attraction**, a sweeping pebbled beach overlooking St Mary's Bay. In the 16th century Basque fishermen often visited the area to dry their cod. There are no official camp sites here but people occasionally camp on the beach.

On Hwy 90, **Salmonier Nature Park** is in the centre of the Avalon Peninsula, 12 km south of the junction with Hwy 1. Here you can see many animals found in the province, enclosed in the park's natural settings. A marked 2.5-km trail through the woods takes you past the animals – moose, caribou, beaver – as well as indigenous flora. There is also an interpretive centre with exhibits and touch displays for children. The park is open daily from June to September from noon to 7 pm.

Conception Bay
Like the rest of eastern Newfoundland, Conception Bay is rich in history and coastal scenery. The road winds along the densely

populated coastline and passes through dozens of towns and villages. Much of the early history of Canada was played out here. **Bay de Verde** in the north can be reached in half a day's drive from St John's. But, if time permits, there are places to stay. Fleetline Bus Service connects St John's with Carbonear with a bus daily except Sunday and makes stops along the way.

Despite its small size, **Brigus**, 80 km west from St John's, has quite a reputation for its pleasing old European atmosphere. A former resident, Captain Robert Bartlett, was renowned as one of the foremost Arctic explorers in the 20th century. He made more than 20 expeditions into the region, including one in 1909 during which he cleared a trail in the ice that enabled US Commander Robert Peary to make his celebrated dash to the North Pole. Bartlett's house, Hawthorne Cottage, is a National Historic Site and museum open daily during the summer from 10 am to 6 pm and there is a $2.25 admission fee.

Also in town is the Ye Olde Stone Barn Museum which has a set of displays on Brigus' 200-year history. It's open daily from 10.30 am to 5.30 pm and admission is $1. Nearby is the Brigus Tunnel that was cut through rock in 1860 so Bartlett could easily access his ship in the deep water cove on the other side.

With four places to stay and another one 20 km or so away there is more accommodation here than anywhere else on Conception Bay. The *Brittoner Guest Home* (☎ 528-3412), on Water St, is right in the middle of things with singles/doubles for $37/45 including full breakfast. *Seaport Cottage* (☎ 528-4943) has four rooms with singles at $30. For a bite to eat or afternoon tea there's *North St Cafe*.

Continuing north along Hwy 70, you'll quickly come to the turn-off to Hibbs Cove, nine km to the east at the end of Port de Grave Peninsula. Along the peninsula you'll see a very active fishing harbour. In the town of Port de Grave the fish market sells everything from cod tongues and crab to salt fish, salmon and scallops.

Hibbs Cove at the end is another picturesque harbour and home of the Fishermen's Museum. The small complex consists of a museum with pictures and artefacts depicting the trade at the turn of the century, a fishermen's home built in 1900 and a one-room schoolhouse. Hours are 10 am to noon and 1 to 5 pm daily except Sunday when it is open afternoons only. Admission price is $1.

Up past Cupid's, where the first official English settlement of Newfoundland was attempted in 1610, is **Harbour Grace** where the Spanish and French had been since the early 1500s. In the 1700s it was used by pirates. The old Customs House is now Conception Bay Museum with three floors of exhibits, including one on the aviation history of the area. Hours are 11.30 am to 4.30 pm daily and admission is free.

Many of the first attempts to fly across the Atlantic began in Harbour Grace beginning in 1919. In 1932, four years after her flight from Trepassey on the Avalon Peninsula to Europe, Amelia Earhart took off from here and became the first woman to cross the Atlantic solo. The airstrip is designated an historic site.

Carbonear Island has had a tumultuous history with international battles, pirate intrigues, shipwrecks and more recently, seal-hunt controversy. Carbonear Island is designated an historic site and there are many examples of old architecture in town. The annual Conception Bay Folk Festival here is not to be missed.

EJ Pratt (1883-1964), one of Canada's best-known poets, was born in Western Bay and a national historic plaque here commemorates him.

Further north up the coast, **Northern Sands Provincial Park** has beautiful beaches. On the inland side is a good spot for freshwater swimming, the ocean is too cold. The park has a 44-site campground with tent sites for $8 a night.

From Lower Island Cove there is some fine coastal scenery. At Bears Cove, near **Bay de Verde**, a short walk leads to dramatic views.

Trinity Bay

On the other side of the peninsula along Trinity Bay are several towns which exemplify the wonderful place names so often seen and enjoyed around the province. How about the absolutely lovely Heart's Delight or Heart's Content?

In **Heart's Content**, the Cable Station Provincial Historic Site tells the story of when the first transatlantic cable was laid here in 1866 and how the community played an important role in transatlantic communications for the next 100 years. The site is open daily during the summer and admission is free.

Both towns mentioned have a place to stay (nearby Heart's Desire doesn't). In **Heart's Delight** is *Farm House Hospitality Home* (☎ 588-2393). There are three rooms, one with a private bath, and rates begin at $40/45 with a light breakfast. Heart's Content has the small, more costly *Legge's Motel* (☎ 538-2929) which consists of seven self-contained housekeeping units and two cheaper simple motel-style rooms. Rates are $45/65 for singles/doubles.

At the bottom of Trinity Bay, **Dildo** (when you stop sniggering) is a good spot for whale watching. Pothead whales come in by the school and humpbacks, a larger species, can also be seen in summer. Both can be viewed even from the shore. In South Dildo, just a few km away, is the Whaling and Sealing Museum (☎ 582-2282), open 11 am to 5 pm Monday through Friday. Admission is $1.

Argentia

The south-west portion of the Avalon Peninsula is known primarily for Argentia with the large ferry terminal for boats to Nova Scotia. For ferry information see the St John's section earlier in this chapter. Newhook's Transportation connects both Argentia (☎ 227-2552) and Placentia with St John's by road.

There isn't much to see in Argentia and, surprisingly, given the presence of the ferry dock, very few places to stay. If you have a vehicle, it's 130 km to St John's or a good 90-minute drive. The problem is that by the time you depart the vessel it's often 10.30 pm or even later. You pass one motel along Hwy 100 in Argentia, but it is a less-than-desirable place to stay. One solution is to drive to **Fitzgerald's Pond Provincial Park**, 25 km north along Hwy 100. The park office stays open to midnight on nights the ferry arrives and turns its day-use area into additional camp sites when the campground becomes full. The rate is $8 for the unserviced sites.

Placentia

Nearby in Placentia, settled in 1662, are the remains of a French fort at **Castle Hill National Historic Site** (☎ 227-2401), with a visitors' centre and fine views. In the early 1800s Placentia was the French capital of Newfoundland and French attacks on the English at St John's were based from here. The site is open 8.30 am to 8 pm daily during the summer and until 4.30 pm the rest of the year. Admission is $2.25.

The old graveyard by the Anglican church offers more history as does the Placentia Area Museum (☎ 227-5568) found in O'Reilly House at 48 Riverside Drive. In a home built in 1902 and restored in 1989, the museum offers details of both the house and the area. It's open from June to September from 9 am to 8 pm Monday through Friday and noon to 8 pm on the weekends. Admission is $2 for adults and $3 for a family. The courthouse and the Roman Catholic church are other notable historic buildings. Plaques and cannons mark the sites of other former local fortifications. A boardwalk runs along the waterfront and there is a beach.

Near Placentia there is a section of the coast which is forested, a rather unusual sight here, as so much of the entire provincial coastline is barren and rocky. An excellent way to see the coastline is through Placentia Bay Tours (☎ 227-2136 or 463-8701), which offers trips on the tall sailing ship *Placentia Bay Queen*. The schooner actually departs Argentia and makes four to five three-hour trips a day that include whale watching. The cost is $25 per person.

Placentia has one hotel, the *Harold Hotel* (☎ 227-2107), on Main St, five km from the ferry terminal, at $48/54 and it has a restaurant. The *Rosedale Manor* (☎ 227-3613) on Riverside Drive has four rooms at $45/55 with a continental breakfast.

Cape St Mary's

At the southern tip of the peninsula is the **St Mary's Ecological Reserve**, an excellent place for seeing sea birds. An unpaved road leads the 16 km from Route 100 into the sanctuary where there is an interpretive centre and a lighthouse. A 30-minute walk from there takes you to views of Bird Rock, the second largest gannet-nesting site in North America. Its near-vertical cliffs rise more than 100 meters from the sea and provide ideal nesting conditions during the summer for some 53,000 sea birds, including kittiwakes, murres and razorbills. It's free and through the summer guides are present to answer questions.

Eastern Newfoundland

This is the smallest region of the province and consists of the area just west of the Avalon Peninsula on the edge of the main body of the island. Geographically it is also distinguished from the central portion of the province by the jutting peninsulas at each end: the Bonavista to the north and the Burin to the south. Like the Avalon Peninsula area, Eastern Newfoundland was settled early and the convoluted coastlines are lined with old fishing villages.

The ferry for the islands of Saint Pierre and Miquelon departs from Fortune in the south. To this day, the islands are French possessions and certainly not in name only. Spending a couple of days here is like a mini-trip to Europe.

BONAVISTA PENINSULA

The Bonavista Peninsula has some superb coastal scenery with many small, traditional fishing communities including some of the oldest in the province. Some people claim that historic Trinity is the oldest town in

North America. Several companies around the peninsula offer boat tours and Terra Nova National Park preserves a section of the peninsula in its natural state.

Clarenville

This is the access point to the peninsula and it's best to pass right through. The town does have a full range of services for travellers including large food stores, a laundromat (keep in mind there is none in Bonavista and in most communities on the peninsula) and a handful of hotels and B&Bs. The *Island View Hospitality Home* (☎ 466-2062) just north of Clarenville on Hwy 230 charges $39/45.

Up the Coast

Hwy 235, along the edge of **Southern Bay**, has some fine coastal scenery and a picnic spot with a view at Jiggin' Head Park. At the 300-year-old fishing village of **Keels** boat tours of the rugged and reddish coastline are available. Stop at the Foodstop General Store to book them. It's $40 per boatload for the two-hour tours and the boat holds up to five people.

Along the beaches here and around the Avalon Peninsula in late June and early July, millions of capelin – a small silver fish – get washed up on shore by the tides. This is partially due to the spawning cycle and partially to being chased by hungry cod. Anyway, the shore is alive with the fish, and people go down with buckets and bags to scoop up a free meal.

Bonavista

This largish town of 5000 residents is at the end of the peninsula where John Cabot landed on 24 June 1497 and first saw the 'new found land'. Later he drifted down to the St John's harbour and stopped there. For his troubles King Henry VII of England rewarded him with the royal sum of £10. It wasn't until the 1600s that Bonavista became a permanent village and from then on through the 1700s, the English and French battled over it like they did for other settlements along the coast.

Built over and around hills, Bonavista, with its narrow, winding streets is best explored by foot. Even the government tourist information says that street names are 'as rare as hen's teeth' and you'll likely get lost.

In the garden at the old courthouse, is a whipping post where instant justice could be meted out. Another historic site is the **Mockbeggar Property**, a restored home that once belonged to F Gordon Bradley, Newfoundland's first representative to the Canadian Senate. The site features a number of buildings and outlines aspects of traditional Newfoundland life. Hours are 10 am to 5.30 pm daily during the summer and admission is free. Signs on Hwy 230 will direct you to the house.

The **Cape Bonavista Lighthouse** dating from 1843 has been restored and is now a provincial historic site with guides in 19th-century period costume. Hours are 10 am to 5.30 pm daily during the summer and admission is free. Nearby is **Landfall Park** with its statue of John Cabot. The scenery at the end of the cape is dramatic and well worth the time to drive out to it. Or you can look into Landfall Boat Tours (☎ 468-2744) which operates on the cape and has three boat tours a day of the coastline. The two-hour tours are $30.

Dungeon Provincial Park is the site of an unusual rock formation on the shoreline. The park itself is little more than a parking area and an interpretive display but from the top of these headland cliffs you can view a handful of sea stacks along the coastline of Spillar's Cove. More impressive is the Dungeon, a hole along the shoreline that is 250 metres in circumference, 15 metres deep and has two channels where the sea roars in and out. In early summer whales may be seen off the coast.

Outside of town at the village of Maberly is **Maberly Provincial Park** on Hwy 238 with views of an offshore island where thousands of sea birds roost. Principal species are puffins, kittiwakes and murres.

Places to Stay The *Hotel Bonavista* (☎ 468-

1510) is on Hwy 230. Singles/doubles are $55/57 with children under 12 free. There are also a handful of B&Bs in the city, including *White's B&B* (☎ 468-7018) at $40/45 which has bike rentals. You can try camping at Dungeon Provincial Park but keep in mind the wind can be wicked out on the cape and from the number of cow pies I saw, its obvious that the beasts spill over from the surrounding dairy farms.

Getting There & Away Venture Bus Lines (☎ 722-9999 in St John's and 468-7459 in Bonavista) departs Bonavista at 7.30 am daily and then leaves St John's at 5.10 pm for the return trip. The bus stops at all points in between.

Port Union
The Fisherman's Protective Union was formed here in 1910 and a monument honours its founder. The province's largest fish-processing plant is here and one of Newfoundland's largest trawler fleets is still struggling to survive the cod moratorium in this ice-free port. For history of the town and fishing industry check out the Port Union Museum in the former train station. It's open 11 am to 6 pm Tuesday through Sunday.

Trinity
First visited by the Portuguese explorer Corte-Real in 1500 and established as a town in 1580, Trinity is one of the oldest settlements in the province and might be the oldest town on the entire continent. The village has a fascinating history which includes the first court in North America – convened in 1615. Many buildings along the town's narrow streets have been restored or renovated and indeed, much of the town has national heritage designation. It's easy to catch most of the sights with an afternoon walk.

The Interpretive Centre (☎ 729-2460), open 10 am to 5.30 pm daily in the summer, has information on the history, houses and buildings in town. From there swing past **Green Family Forge**, a blacksmith museum. They have been forging iron pieces here for shipbuilders since 1750 with the present building dating back to 1895. Hours are 11 am to 8.30 pm daily except Sunday when it is open 1 to 6 pm.

Trinity Museum is full of local artefacts as well as the oldest fire engine in North America, dating to 1811. It's open the same hours as the forge and admission is by donation. **Hiscock House Provincial Historic Site** is a restored merchant's home, furnished to the 1910 period. Hours are 10 am to 5.30 pm. **Ryan Building** is another provincial historic site that has been restored to portray the general store owned by the Rain family from 1902 to 1952. Hours are 10 am to 5.30 pm and there is no admission fee. Finally venture out to **Fort Point**, where you'll find four cannons embedded in the ground, the remains of the English fortification in 1745.

One of the more entertaining aspects of Trinity is the *Rising Tide Theater* (☎ 464-3232), which performs Wednesday, Saturday and Sunday at 2 pm near the Interpretation Centre. It's an outdoor drama on the history of the area with a Ryan slant. Tickets are $5 and worth it.

Organised Tours The increased tourism to Trinity has given rise to a number of different, and good, organised tours. Atlantic Adventures (☎ 464-3738) uses a sailboat for its whale-watching tours. Several are offered a day and the cost is $30 for the three-hour sail. Ocean Contact (☎ 464-3269), a whale-watching and research organisation, offers whale-watching expeditions in a nine-metre rigid hull inflatable and all-inclusive, expensive multi-day trips in its larger boat. Trinity Historical Harbor Tours (☎ 464-3355) has two-hour tours of the harbour for $16.

North East Treks (☎ 466-2036 or 466-3350) is a kayak outfitters based in Trinity during the summer. They provide a range of guided kayak trips in the area that run from one to five days and include equipment, meals and guides. The cost is $125 a day or $485 for five days. North East Treks also rent mountain bikes.

Places to Stay & Eat Ocean Contact operates from the *Village Inn* (☎ 464-3269), a very good place to stay with rooms from singles/doubles $40/50. Films and slides on whales and other sea life can be seen.

Alternatively, there is *Trinity Cabins* (☎ 464-3657), with housekeeping cabins in the $39 to $50 range for two people. There's a swimming pool or, for the brave, a beach nearby.

There are also two B&Bs in Trinity providing visitors with an unaccustomed and almost overwhelming accommodation decision. The more modest is the *Beach B&B* (☎ 464-3695), $42/47, while the *Campbell House* (☎ 464-3377) is a beautifully restored historic house with rooms at $50 to $70. In the village of Trinity East is the *Peace Cove Inn* (☎ 464-3738) in a restored turn-of-the-century house. A complimentary breakfast is included with a night's stay and lunch and dinner are available at extra charge. Singles or doubles start at $43.

Campers can head five km up Hwy 236 to pitch a tent at *Lockston Path Provincial Park* where the 22 unserviced sites are $8 a night. If you do, hike the 1.7-km Lockston Lookout Trail for the views of the area. For something even cheaper, as in free, head to *Trinity Loop Fun Park* (☎ 464-2171). This is a touristy haven of ferris wheels, pony rides and a miniature train. But they have large gravel areas where they allow anybody, especially RVers, to camp for free. Within the complex is a store, restaurant and a laundromat in a boxcar.

The best meal in town is at *Eriksen Premises* (☎ 464-3698) which is also a hospitality house. The delightful little restaurant on the first floor consists of two small rooms, offering afternoon tea or dinners ranging from $9 to $15.

Terra Nova National Park

This east coast park (☎ 533-2801), 240 km west of St John's and 80 km east of Gander, is split by the Trans Canada Hwy and typifies the regional geography. The rocky, jagged coastline on beautiful Bonavista Bay gives way to long bays, inland lakes, ponds, bogs and hilly woods. There's canoeing, fishing, hiking, camping, sandy beaches, even swimming in Sandy Pond.

You can rent bicycles in the park – a good way to get around. Lots of wildlife may be seen – moose, bear, beaver, otter and bald eagles – and, from May to August, icebergs are commonly viewed off the coast.

At both Newman Sound and Twin Rivers there are visitor centres open daily during the summer from 10 am to 8 pm with information about the park and small book stores. Vehicle entry fee into the park is $6 a day or $18 for four days. Terra Nova's main campground is *Newman Sound*, where sites are $11 a day. Also located here is *Newman Sound Convenience Store* (☎ 533-9133) with groceries, a laundromat and bicycle rentals. At the north end of the park is *Malady Head Campground* where sites are $10 a night.

Commercial lodging can be found outside the park, most notably at Eastport at the north end. *White Sails Cabins* (☎ 677-3400) has two-person units that begin at $40 while next door is *Squire's Cabins* (☎ 677-3224) not as nice and slightly higher priced.

Organised Tours At Newman Sound is Ocean Watch Tours (☎ 533-6024), recommended for their good-value boat tours. One trip explores the fjords and islands and sometimes stops in at old abandoned outports. It departs daily at 12.30 and 3.30 pm and the cost is $22. Another trip specialises more in wildlife and seeks out whales, seals, and birds. It leaves Newman Sound at 9 pm and is $26 per person.

Hiking & Canoeing Terra Nova has 14 trails totalling 56 km. There are some excellent days hikes in the park. The Malady Head Trail is a round-trip of four km to the edge of a headland cliff with stunning views of Southwest Arm and Broad Cove. Sandy Pond Trail is an easy three-km loop around the pond and through a bog. From Newman Sound Campground you can hike the Coastal Trail and see marine life along the shoreline.

There are also backpacking opportunities within the park. There are five backcountry camping areas at Dunphy's Pond and at the outports on Newman Sound. The camp sites are $7 per party and you must obtain a back-country permit from the visitor centres. To avoid backtracking, Ocean Watch will also drop backpackers at the Newman Sound outports during its regular trips. That would reduce the trek to South Board Cove to 17.5 kms and to Minchin Cove to 14 km.

There is also Sandy Pond-Dunphy's Canoe Route, a 10-km paddle that includes a short portage and access to three back-country camping areas. Canoes can be rented from Sandy Pond at Newman Sound.

BURIN PENINSULA

Jutting south into the Atlantic Ocean, the peninsula has been the base for European fishing boats since the 1500s. The Grand Banks off the peninsula (part of the continental shelf) teem with fish. Or at least they did until the early 1990s when stocks plummeted. The hilly, wooded northern area supplied timber for building and ships; the southern end is mostly barren, glacier-stripped rock interspersed with bogs and marshes.

Getting There & Away

Sadly the southern coast Marine Atlantic ferry, which used to skip along the province from Port aux Basques to Terrenceville on the Burin Peninsula, was suspended in July 1995. Terrenceville, already depressed from the moratorium on cod fishing, was hit hard by the lost of the ferry business and subsequently lost its bus service to St John's.

Without a vehicle, the only transportation to the peninsula is through van service. Cheeseman's Transportation with bus stations in St John's and Burin (☎ 891-1866), has a run that departs Burin at 8 am daily for $30. Slaney's (☎ 873-2511 in St Lawrence or 753-3287 in St John's) has a daily run that leaves St Lawrence at 8 am for $25. Foote's Taxi (☎ 832-0491) departs Fortune daily at 7.45 am for St John's, returning the same day. One-way is $30.

NEWFOUNDLAND

Marystown

Although the largest town on the peninsula, there is not much here for the visitor but Marystown does have a laundromat, restaurants, food stores, a handful of B&Bs and *Motel Mortier* (☎ 279-1600) with 138 rooms that go for $47 for a single or double. There is even a *McDonald's* here. There is also a tourist centre on Hwy 210 that is open daily from 8.30 am to 9 pm Monday through Friday and 10 am to 9 pm on the weekends. You can camp and swim at *Frenchman's Cove Provincial Park* 11 km away at Garnish. Sites are $8 a night.

Burin

Settled by fishers from Europe in the 1700s, Burin is one of the oldest towns on the south coast. It is a pretty town or rather a series of villages sparsely scattered around coves and the lumpy, treeless hills. The drive south to Burin is a scenic trip along a narrow winding road.

Burin is still struggling to maintain its important role in the Grand Banks and has a major trawler repair facility as well as a processing plant. Crab and lobster fishing have kept many of the trawlers afloat during the cod moratorium.

In the town of Burin itself, there is the **Heritage House**, on the corner of Main St and Union St, which consists of two historical homes and a small park dotted with marine engines and winches. Nearby is **Captain Cook's Lookout Trail**, picked up by turning off Main St at St Patrick's Elementary School and following the side street to its end. The trail begins by immediately skirting a small pond and then climbs to the high point where there are good views of the harbour. The English built fortifications here in 1812. It's a 20-minute walk to the top.

Freshwater Pond, which used to be a provincial park, is now a commercial campground. Little has changed except they now charge a vehicle entry fee of $2. The camp sites are still $8 a night.

St Lawrence

A little further down the coast, St Lawrence is a mining town with the only deposits of fluorospar in Canada. It was once the world's largest producer and although this is no longer the case, the mine still operates and the **St Lawrence Miner's Museum**, right on Hwy 220, outlines its history. It's open daily during the summer.

From St Lawrence to Lawn, Hwy 220 rises steadily over a series of hills and ridges to provide some grand views of the coast and numerous opportunities to hike to the top of rocky knobs for an even better view. There are small community parks with free camping at both Point au Gaul and Point May. *Point May Park* is an especially scenic spot to spend the night. Located right on Hwy 220 north of the town towards Grand Bank, the small park overlooks the French islands. The only facilities here are a pair of outhouses and a parking lot.

Grand Bank

Its role now diminished, this was one of the main centres of the early Grand Banks fishery and some of that history remains. The Burin Peninsula long-served as the base for the famous Banks fishing grounds. You can pick up the brochure *Grand Bank Heritage Walk* for a self-guided walk through town that will explain the varied 1880s architecture of the homes, churches and Water St storefronts.

The **Southern Newfoundland Seaman's Museum** (☎ 832-1484), on Marine Drive at the edge of town, depicts both the era of the banking schooner and the changes in the fishery over the years. It's collection of model sailing ships is impressive. Hours are 9 am to 4.30 pm Monday through Friday and 10 am to 6 pm Sunday. Admission is free. Also in town is **George C Harris House** at 16 Water St with rooms of local artefacts. It's open daily 10 am to 8 pm and is free.

If you're spending the night in Grand Bank, the big, old *Thorndyke* (☎ 832-0820), a designated historic home, makes a fine place to stay. It's at 33 Water St, just 6.5 km from the Fortune ferry. It's busy, so call for reservations. From the roof there are views over the town and bay and there is a restaurant on the premises. Rooms are $45 for singles or doubles. There is also *Granny's Motor Inn* (☎ 832-2180), a small motel on Hwy 220 charging $50/54.

There are a handful of take-outs and small restaurants in town and on Saturday in July and August the *Burin Peninsula Producers Market* is staged from 9 am to 2 pm on the old school grounds at 4 Main St. Along with the farmer's market there is often crafts, baked goods and sometimes entertainment.

Fortune

Fortune is the jumping-off point for trips to Saint Pierre and Miquelon and 20,000 people a year pass through on their way to the islands. Aside from looking after visitors, many of the town's people are employed at the large fish-processing plant. There is also a shipbuilding and repair depot.

The *Eldon House B&B* (☎ 832-0442), at 31 Eldon St, is open from mid-June to early September with four rooms at $35/40 including continental breakfast. You can also leave your car there while visiting St Pierre. The *Fair Isle Motel* (☎ 832-1010) with 10 rooms at $60 single or double is the alternative.

Saint Pierre & Miquelon

This is probably the oddest side-trip in Canada. Once called the 'Islands of 11,000 Virgins', these two dabs of land, lying 16 km west off Newfoundland's Burin Peninsula, belong to France. The tiny islands represent the only French holdings left in North America. The 6000 residents drink French wine, eat baguettes and pay for it in francs.

First claimed by France in the 1500s, the islands were turned over to the English along with Cape Breton after the Seven Years' War. They were then ceded to the French by the British in 1783 under the Treaty of Paris. Battles over fishing rights continued with Newfoundland and the islands changed hands a couple of times until 1815. Since then they have remained under French control. The disputes persist, however, and in 1989 there was a fairly serious flare-up with France getting involved in the bickering over territorial fishing limits.

An interesting aside is Saint Pierre's role during the Prohibition period in the USA. Canada would legally export what amounted

NEWFOUNDLAND

The Grand Banks

The fabulous portion of the Atlantic Ocean known as the Grand Banks, lying just south-east off Cape Race at the southern part of the Avalon Peninsula, is one of the prime reasons anybody ever bothered with the New World. After 500 years of serious plundering it remains one of the world's best fishing grounds. However, in the early 1990s the warning bells finally went off when it was realised that the dominant species, cod, had finally been reduced to alarming numbers. Biologists, fishers and government have now combined forces to work out a plan to allow the stocks to replenish.

The banks are a series of submarine plateaus stretching from north-west to south-east about 80 km out to sea from Cape Race. They cover an area about 500 km long by 300 km wide with a depth ranging from five to 350 metres. Though mostly in the Labrador Current, the waters are met by the Gulf Stream and this blending of the warm and cold gives rise to the legendary fogs. It also helps plankton (tiny marine plants and animals) to thrive and it is this food source that results in the millions of fish.

The main catch has always been cod but there is also halibut, flounder and herring among others. Boats come from around the world to fill their hulls, notably from Norway, Japan, Portugal, Spain and Russia. Canada has imposed restrictions and regulations but has an impossible task in trying to enforce its limits and authority.

It was in 1497 that John Cabot, an Italian working for England, first put down a net and couldn't believe his eyes when he saw it bulging with fish. It wasn't long before other Europeans began to arrive and set up fishing communities on the shores of Newfoundland. As well as the fog, nasty storms and marauding icebergs are hazards that fishers have had to contend with through the centuries.

In the past 20 years oil has been discovered on parts of the Banks and it is raising another potential threat to this unique biological resource. ■

to oceans of booze to the French island where US rum runners would pick it up to take home.

A few days make a good visit – exploring, relaxing, enjoying a different culture. Like much of the Newfoundland coast, the islands are barren and rocky (although there are some relatively wild areas as well as cliffs and sandy beaches).

As in so much of Atlantic Canada, the main source of livelihood has always been fishing and the supplying of fishing boats. The closing of much of the region's fishery, most notably the moratorium on cod fishing, has seriously undermined the economic viability of the islands. France has been paying some compensation to those put out of work and aims to boost the tourism industry. This money maker which has been increasing in importance for the past decade is where the island is placing its bets. France is building a new airport able to accommodate jumbo jets, and plans are being made to develop gambling casinos to lure even more visitors.

The archipelago consists of numerous islands. Saint Pierre, although not the largest, is the principal one; it's the most populated and its town of the same name is the largest on the island.

Miquelon is actually two islands separated by a narrow isthmus of sand. The northern section, Great Miquelon, has most of the people and a small town. The southern island called Langlade or Little Miquelon is quite wild. The remaining islands are all very small.

Canadian and USA visitors need neither passports nor visas for a visit, but good ID such as a birth certificate or driver's licence with photograph is recommended. For citizens of the European Union (EU), Switzerland and Japan, passports are required. All other nationals need both a passport and a visa.

Note that the time on the islands is half an hour ahead of Newfoundland time. Also keep in mind that making a phone call from Newfoundland to the islands is an international call as far as the long distance carriers are concerned and the area code for the

French islands is 508. They'll gladly take Canadian money on the islands but prices are usually quoted in francs. One dollar is worth roughly 3½ francs. On the plus side is the duty-free shop for alcohol, cigarettes, etc.

Information
The Saint Pierre Tourist office (☎ 412222 or 800-565-5118 off the islands) can provide a complete accommodation listing. Calling to the islands is like calling overseas. Other than any 800 numbers, you must dial 011 508, the country and area codes before the local number.

Things to See
In Saint Pierre you can see the **museum** which outlines the island's history and the cathedral. Also, visit the interesting **French cemetery**.

Outside town there is a lighthouse at **Gallantry Head** and good views from Cap aux Basques. Out in the harbour, a 10-minute boat ride away, is **Île aux Marins** with a small museum. You can take a bilingual guided tour around the island which had its own fishing village at the turn of the century.

Miquelon, 45 km away, is less visited and less developed. The people here are largely of Acadian background while Saint Pierre's inhabitants are French (mainly from Brittany and Normandy), and Basque.

The village of **Miquelon**, centred around the church, is at the northern tip of the island.

From nearby **l'Étang de Mirande**, a walking trail leads to a lookout and waterfall. From the bridge in town a scenic 25-km road leads across the isthmus to **Langlade**. The island of Langlade remains pretty much the same as it has always been. There are some summer cottages but no year-round inhabitants – human ones, that is. There are some wild horses and smaller animals such as rabbits, and around the rocky edges and lagoons you'll see seals and birds. Walks or horseback rides can be taken through the woods, along the beaches or through the sandy grasslands.

Festivals

Several annual holidays and festivals occur in July and August. On 14 July is Bastille Day. On 4 August, Jacques Cartier's arrival in the islands in 1536 is celebrated. The following week, a two-day festival on Miquelon recalls the Acadians' heritage and, later in the month, another two-day event on Saint Pierre celebrates the Basques' heritage. These, of course, are busy as well as interesting times to visit. From mid-July to the end of August folk dances are often held in Saint Pierre's square.

Places to Stay & Eat

Saint Pierre has a handful of hotels and the same number of guesthouses or pensions which are more reasonably priced and which generally provide breakfast. Accommodation can be tight in high season so you may want to check before you go.

Hotel Robert (☎ 412419), on the waterfront, is the largest place with 54 rooms that go for $104/122. Pensions include *Louis Vigneau B&B* (☎ 412042) at 12 rue Amiral Musekier with five rooms at $35 and *Bernard Arrossamena* (☎ 414086) at 16 rue Georges-Daguerre. At a couple of these places meals are available. Miquelon has its own tourist office (☎ 416187), one hotel *Motel Miquelon* (☎ 416310) near the ocean, as well as two pensions and a small campground at l'Étang de Mirande near town.

As might be expected on French islands, restaurants are numerous relative to the size of the population, and the food is good. In both Saint Pierre and Miquelon there are several places serving traditional French food. *Chez Dutin* on Saint Pierre has been recommended by a traveller. Saint Pierre has more choice and a number of less-expensive places for sandwiches, pizza and the like. *Le Maringoiun'fre* has good crêpes.

Getting There & Away

Air Saint Pierre flies from Montreal, Halifax and Sydney (Nova Scotia) during the summer. Information and reservations can be had through Canadian Airlines International.

Ferry Ferry transportation to the islands has been in a constant flux of change in recent years and it's best to double check times and companies before arriving in Fortune if you can. There used to be two boats serving the islands and a daytrip was possible throughout the week. Now there is only one ferry operating, MV *Anahitra*, and in 1995 many of its runs were dropped due to lack of passengers. From Sunday through Friday there is a single trip with the boat leaving St Pierre at 1.30 pm and returning from Fortune at 2.45 pm. On Saturday a daytrip is still possible with the ferry departing St Pierre at 8 am and 5 pm and leaving Fortune at 9 am and 6 pm.

Lloyd Lake's Travel Ltd (☎ 832-2006 or 800-563-2006) operates the ferry and has an office right at the dock in Fortune. Round-trip passage is $55 per adult and $27.50 for children.

St Pierre Tours, with offices in both St John's and Fortune, offers various package tours which includes ferry crossings, room and continental breakfast. It's $109 per person based on double occupancy of a room for a night at Hotel Robert or $85 per person for a night at one of the pensions. For round-trip transport from St John's, it's another $70 per person. The company also has a two-night package (one night at each island) for $169 per person based on double occupancy of a room. You can call St Pierre Tours at Fortune (☎ 832-0429) or stop at their office in St John's (☎ 722-3892) at 116 Duckworth St.

Getting Around

Between the Islands The MV *Anahitra* also travels to Miquelon twice a day, four times a week in July and August. The boat departs St Pierre Tuesday, Friday, Saturday and Sunday at 8.30 am and 5 pm. The return fare is $35 (roughly, depending on the value of the franc) less for children, and the trip takes about an hour.

Around the Islands In Saint Pierre rent a 'rosalie', a four-wheeled bicycle that comes in two sizes, two and four-person models are

NEWFOUNDLAND

available. There are regular bicycles as well, or small motorbikes. In both Saint Pierre and Miquelon, tours on horseback are offered.

Also on Saint Pierre there are tours by bus and mini-train, and on Miquelon a bus trip takes visitors around the island and across the isthmus to Langlade. In a couple of days much can be seen on foot.

Central Newfoundland

The vast, little-populated central area is the largest geographic region of the island portion of the province. For the visitor it is the area of least interest, although there are still some fine places to see, particularly the Notre Dame Bay coast and its intriguing, small islands. From Lewisporte, ferries depart for northern Newfoundland and Labrador. The southern area is mostly inaccessible, lake-filled woodland. One road leads down to the coast linking many small remote villages to the rest of the province.

GANDER

Gander, with a population of 13,000, is at the crossroads of the east-west Trans Canada Hwy and Hwy 330 which leads to Notre Dame Bay. Though there isn't a lot to do, it is a convenient stopping point whichever way you're going. Gander is best known for its airport and Canadian Forces base.

Gander served the first regular transatlantic flights and then, during WWII, was a major link for planes on their way to Europe. The first formation of bombers made in the USA for the UK left here in February 1940. The location was chosen because it is close to Europe but far enough inland to be free of the coastal fog that often plagues St John's.

Numerous USA and Canadian airlines also used it for transatlantic flights beginning in the 1930s. The airport, a major Aeroflot refuelling stop, is known for being the site of thousands of defections from Russia, Cuba and former Eastern Bloc countries: the plane touches down and passengers ask for political asylum. These days it is more likely the hopeful arrivals seek refugee status which permits them to stay in Canada until their case is heard.

There is a tourist chalet (☎ 256-7110) on the Trans Canada Hwy at the central exit into town and is open 9 am to 9 pm daily during the summer.

Aviation Attractions

There are three planes mounted and on display around town. On the west side of town is a Beech 18 from the Canadian navy. In the downtown area near the City Hall is a McDonnell CF100 Voodoo and out at the airport is the third, a Hudson Bomber.

Also at the airport is a small aviation display on Gander's history and, of more interest, there's a huge tapestry depicting the history of flight. It's in the passengers' waiting lounge but, if you don't have a ticket, ask the security officials and they'll let you in for a look.

The **Silent Witness Monument**, just east of town, south off the Trans Canada Hwy, tenderly marks the site of an horrendous early morning crash in December 1985 in which 248 US soldiers returning home from the Middle East for Christmas were killed along with eight crew members. The possible causes are still debated. The size of the swath of forest taken out by the crash is astounding.

Places to Stay

There is a campground 16 km north of town at *Jonathan's Pond Provincial Park* and another at *Square Pond Provincial Park* 34 km east of Gander. Tent sites are $8 a night. The *Cape Cod Inn* (☎ 651-2269) at 66 Bennet Drive is in a residential area close to downtown. A doubles ranges from $45 to $55, with breakfast. Other Newfoundland-style meals are available at extra cost.

There are numerous motels on the highway but they're decidedly pricey. The basic *Fox Moth* (☎ 256-3535) with some efficiency units is the cheapest with singles from $52. Also try *Skipper's Inn* (☎ 256-2534) where there is a dining room and rooms for $45/50.

Places to Eat

On Airport Drive in town are the usual fast-food outlets. The Chinese restaurant, *Highlight*, is better. It's in the little mall strip on the corner of Elizabeth St and Airport Blvd, the two main streets of Gander. It's very popular and, though the food is good, I suspect some people come just for the remarkably lavish decor.

Continuing east on Airport Blvd towards the airport at 136 Bennet St, beside the Gander mall, is the *Bread Shoppe*. This is a good bakery with a wide selection of breads and pastries and tables for its morning coffee drinkers.

Getting There & Away

Gander is a main stop for CN Roadcruiser (☎ 256-4874) which maintains a ticket office at the airport. A bus for St John's departs there at 5.02 pm daily while the bus for Port aux Basques departs at 12.46 pm daily.

NOTRE DAME BAY & AROUND

This coastal area north of Gander is the highlight of Central Newfoundland. Though relatively heavily populated it has especially scenic Newfoundland coastal topography. About 80 little villages are found around the bay nestled in small coves or clinging to the rocky shoreline. From Gander there are two road loops – one through Lewisporte, the other eastward to Wesleyville – which make good circular tours. A few of the towns have small museums dealing with various aspects of local history.

Offshore is a large cluster of islands, including Fogo, New World and Twillingate, which should not be missed and where whales and icebergs may be seen.

Gander Bay

If you go north along Hwy 330 (watch for moose), you'll reach the coast at Gander Bay which has a good place to stay. *Dorman's Cove Lodge* (☎ 676-2254), in a century-old house, is across the street from the sea in the village of Dorman's Cove. Singles/doubles cost $35/40 and there is a triple room as well.

Breakfast is included and the jams are terrific. Other meals are also available. The owners also run trips along the Gander River for nature watching, fishing or hunting. Canoes can be rented.

Change Islands

These two islands, reached by ferry from Farewell at the end of a what seems a long road from the main highway, don't change much, name notwithstanding. There are six (five on Sunday) 25-minute trips in each direction daily costing $5 per car and driver and $1.50 per person round trip. From Farewell the first ferry leaves at 8 am, the last at 9 pm with the others scattered evenly through the day. Check schedules as the times vary. There is no real town at Farewell but there is a restaurant at the ferry landing.

The two main Change Islands with a population of just 500 or so are connected by a short causeway at the northern end where the largest village is located. The islands are quiet with many traditional wooden houses and some old fishing-related buildings painted in a red-ochre colour common to the area. At the northern end is a small store and just one place to stay, the *Seven Oaks Island Inn & Cottages* (☎ 635-2247 during the summer). Singles/doubles cost $45/55 for the rooms, the two-bedroom cottages are $80. Meals are available and boat tours can be arranged. About 15 minutes from the ferry terminal is *TLP Restaurant & Bakery* for meals.

Fogo Island

Fogo, just to the east of Notre Dame Bay, is the largest of the area's islands. It is just 25 km long. Tread carefully because the Canadian Flat Earth Society has stated that Fogo is at the edge of the world! Indeed, say they, Brimstone Head is one of the four corners of the earth. Standing here looking out to sea it's not difficult to agree with them.

Like the Change Islands, Fogo is reached by ferry from Farewell. Again, there are five services daily (four on Sunday) leaving from 8.45 am to 9 pm. The fare is $9.50 for car and driver, $1.50 for adult passengers round trip. This trip takes about 55 minutes.

The island is pleasant for just exploring slowly and enjoying the coastal scenery. It has an interesting history being first settled by Europeans in the 1680s. There are about 10 villages on the island, together making up a population of about 4500. There are a couple of fine walking trails, a sandy beach at Sandy Cove and a small herd of caribou and some free roaming ponies on the island. At Burnt Point is a lighthouse. There are several fish plants on the island and visitors can have a look around them.

Icebergs can often be seen and in July there's a folk festival. A heritage house, once the residence of a merchant, has been converted into the small **Bleak House Museum** in Fogo and, of course, you can pick berries.

Places to Stay For those wishing to stay, *Alma's B&B* (☎ 627-3302), just minutes from the ferry terminal and 20 minutes from the town of Fogo, is the cheapest. The owners have two rooms for $43/48 breakfast included. Alternatively, there is the *Quiet Cannon Hotel* (☎ 627-3477) not far from the ferry terminal at Stag Harbour. They offer 10 rooms at $55/60 and have a restaurant. *Fogo Island Motel* (☎ 266-2556) rounds out the accommodation situation with rooms at $52/60. It's a good idea to book ahead before arriving in July and early August. In Fogo, there is *Beaches Bar & Grill* for seafood and traditional Newfoundland dishes.

New World Island

From the mainland, causeways almost imperceptibly connect Chapel Island, tiny Strong's Island, New World and Twillingate islands.

At **Newville** the tourist office is open 9 am to 9 pm daily during the summer and has maps of the area, advice on what to see and a sheet describing some of the trails and walks on Twillingate.

Dildo Run Provincial Park is good and central with camping and picnicking, set in a wooded area by a bay. Due to currents, swimming is not recommended. Sites are $8.

The western section of New World Island is far less visited and has some of the area's older houses in the small fishing villages clinging to the rough, rocky edges of the sea. At **Moreton's Harbour** is a small museum in an old-style house furnished in much the manner it would have been when the town was a prosperous fishing centre. It's open daily from 9 am to 8 pm except at lunch and dinner. There is one small, basic store in town but not much is stocked.

There are several very small parks around where picnicking and even camping are possible although facilities are minimal. One of them is **Wild Cove Park**, two kms north of Moreton's Harbour on the road to Tizzard's Harbour: look for the clearing surrounded by rocky hills right by the water on the left-hand side of the road. The facilities amount to a single picnic table and a pair of doorless outhouses but the cove is extremely scenic.

Twillingate Island

Actually consisting of two islands, north and south Twillingate, this is the area in all of Notre Dame Bay that gets the most attention and very deservedly so. It's stunningly beautiful, with every turn of the road revealing new ocean vistas, colourful fishing wharves or tidy groups of pastel houses perched on cliffs and outcrops.

The **Long Point Lighthouse** is a spectacular place with dramatic views of the coastal cliffs. This is an ideal place to watch for icebergs which are fairly common in May and June and not unusual in July. Seeing one in August is possible too, but fairly rare. They tend to drift southward from Labrador then eastward towards Bonavista Bay slowly melting in these warmer waters.

You can visit the 114-year-old lighthouse and a guide will lead you up the winding stairs of 44 steps to the top where you can enjoy the 360-degree view or watch the light flashing. Hours are 9 am to 4 pm Monday through Saturday and 4 to 7 pm on Sunday. Admission is free.

In Twillingate town, the **Twillingate Museum**, in what was formerly the Anglican rectory, provides an overview of the local history. Twillingate, one of the oldest towns in this part of the province, was settled by British merchants in the mid-1700s. One room displays articles brought back from around the world by local sea captains and includes a cabinet from India, a hurdy-gurdy from Germany and an Australian boomerang. Another room details the seal hunt and its controversy. There is also a craft shop at the museum. Hours are 10 am to 9 pm daily except Sunday when the museum opens at 2 pm. Admission is 50 cents. Next door is **St Peter's Church** which dates from 1844, and is one of the oldest wooden churches in Newfoundland.

Durrell Don't neglect to tour around unbelievably scenic Durrell. Many of the two-storey, box-like wooden houses are over 100 years old. The **Iceberg Shop** in a 130-year-old barn is an interpretation centre on the first floor and a craft shop on the top floor. Twillingate Island Tours (☎ 884-2242) also operates from the shop, offering four highly recommended boat trips a day to view icebergs and whales along the jagged local shores. The cost is $20 per adults, $10 for children.

Also here is the **Durrell Museum** perched way up on a hill. It has displays on what the fishing community of the early 1900s was like. It's open daily from 11 am to 9 pm and admission is 50 cents. Actually better than the museum are the views from this high point. Bring your lunch; there are a couple of picnic tables outside.

Fish, Fun & Folk Festival Held each year during the last week of July, the festival is a 'don't miss' event if you're anywhere near the region. The four-day event features traditional music and dance, some of which goes back to the 16th century. There are fishing exhibits, lots of great food and crafts as well. This is a busy time of year what with the possibility of whales and icebergs lurking offshore, so book early if it is at all possible.

Places to Stay *Sea Breeze Municipal Park* beside the Long Point Lighthouse is a glorious, very inexpensive place to bed down. The unserviced sites are $4 a night and the park includes a picnic shelter and hiking trails to highpoints overlooking the coast.

The *Hillside B&B* (☎ 884-5761), just up the hill from the Iceberg Shop at 5 Young's Lane, is a house built in 1874. It features fine views of the harbour and lighthouse. Singles/doubles are $30/40 with a light breakfast. Nearby at 56 Main St is *Toulinguent Inn* (☎ 884-2080) right on the water with three rooms at $35/45.

The *Anchor Inn* (☎ 884-2776), with views from on top of a hill, has some rooms in the lodge, some more motel-style rooms and some with cooking facilities at $55/60, but for $5 more housekeeping units are offered. There is also a dining room where fish is featured on the menu.

Harbour Lights Inn (☎ 884-2763) is the newest lodge, an historical house that was renovated in 1995. It's located right on the harbour and charges $55/60, light breakfast included. South of town at Little Harbour is *Beach Rock B&B* (☎ 884-2292) at $30/40.

Places to Eat The *R&J* has fish & chips and a great view of one of the many harbours. The *Anchor Inn* has a dining room and bar. There is also a Chinese restaurant, take-out cafes and foodstores in town.

AROUND TWILLINGATE

From Twillingate the road leads through Birchy Bay past timber and farming districts once roamed by the Beothuk Indians. The newest provincial interpretive centre, at Boyd's Cove, is devoted to the extinct tribe. **Beothuk Interpretation Centre** (☎ 656-7114) features displays, exhibits and a video theatre that explain the archaeological discoveries of a nearby Beothuk village. From the center you can then walk a short trail to the sites of the digs. The centre is open from 10 am to 5.30 pm daily during the summer and admission is free. From Hwy 340 head along the dirt road to South Boyd's Cove to reach it in two km.

LEWISPORTE

Lewisporte with a population of 4500 is the largest town along the coast and is known primarily for its Marine Atlantic ferry terminal. Other than the boats, there really isn't much reason to visit – though as a distribution centre it does have all the goods and services. West of Lewisporte, the bay becomes less populated and, as the road network declines, less accessible.

The **Bye The Bay Museum** (☎ 535-2657) in the large wooden Women's Institute Building on Main St displays articles from the area's history, including a long, colourful handmade rug depicting various facets in the life and times of Lewisporte. The ground floor of the building is a craft shop. Hours in the summer are 9 am to 9 pm daily except Sunday when it opens at 10 am.

Several people offer boat trips to the quiet, rocky **Exploits Islands** where local people have summer cottages, whereas Caribou Adventure Tours (☎ 535-8379) runs a safari-like trip to observe woodland caribou.

Places to Stay & Eat

You can camp in town at *Sunset Hideaway Campground*, which features showers and a swimming area or at *Notre Dame Provincial Park* 14 km from town on the Trans Canada Hwy. Both are $8 a night but keep in mind that Notre Dame will often fill up during the summer.

There are three guesthouses right on Main St. At No 92 *Northgate B&B* (☎ 535-2258), a short walk from the ferry terminal, is $40/50 including a breakfast of bread, muffins and homemade jams. On the way into town from Hwy 341 is *Brittany Inns* (☎ 535-2533) with 37 hotel, motel and housekeeping rooms from $57. There is a dining room.

For other places to eat try the mall near the junction of Hwys 340 and 341. There is a bakery here and a Sobey's grocery store which could be useful if you're getting on board one of the ferries. On Main St the *Oriental Restaurant* has dinners for under $7.

Beothuk Indians

Scattered around much of north central Newfoundland the Beothuks, a distinct cultural group, inhabited the area from about 500 years ago until 1829 when the last woman died. It was they, their faces painted red with ochre, who were first dubbed 'redmen' by the arriving Europeans, a name that was soon to be applied to all the Native peoples of North America.

Semi-nomadic, they travelled the rivers, notably the Exploits, in birch bark canoes between the inland lakes and the sea at Notre Dame Bay. They were not a violent people and there weren't large numbers of them. With White hostility, firepower, and diseases the ultimate tragedy unfolded. Before anybody had enough gumption or time it was realised there were just a handful of Beothuk Indians left. By the early 1800s there were only two women alive to leave what knowledge they could.

There is a museum dedicated to them in Grand Falls and also a re-created village. The museum in St John's also has a display, including a skeleton – the only known remains anywhere. The Beothuk Trail, Hwy 380, leads through some of their former lands. ■

Beothuk Bark Canoes

Getting There & Away

Bus The CN Roadcruiser bus running between Port aux Basques and St John's makes stops at Notre Dame Junction at the Irving service station south of town on Trans Canada Hwy. The bus for St. John's departs at 3.54 pm daily and the one for Port aux Basques at 1.25 pm. This is about 16 km from town and the ferry dock. Taxis meet the bus arrivals.

Ferry Two Marine Atlantic ferries (☎ 535-6876) depart for points north. One, a car ferry, goes to Cartwright on the Labrador coast and then on through Hamilton Inlet to large Lake Melville (which the Vikings may have visited) and on to Happy Valley-Goose Bay in the heart of Labrador where there is an important military base.

With a vehicle you can go from here across central Labrador to Churchill Falls and beyond to Labrador City at the Quebec border. The road continues south through Quebec to Baie Comeau.

The ferry to Goose Bay is a serious ride taking about 38 hours and only making the one stop en route. A variation is the direct trip with no stop in Cartwright. This knocks about three hours off the total travel time.

A one-way ticket is $88; add $145 for a car. Reduced rates are offered for children and seniors. Cabins are available at additional charge. There are two ferries a week in each direction (one direct, one with the stop) from mid-June to approximately mid-September that depart on Tuesday and Friday from Lewisporte.

The other boat, opening up a different part of Labrador, provides the coastal service which runs up the Northern Peninsula making a stop at St Anthony and then heading over to the coast of Labrador for a series of outport stops. This is strictly a passenger and freight service – no cars. Of course, except in a couple of places, there are no roads at any of these destinations anyway and that is their appeal.

This is approximately a 14 to 16-day return trip with Nain, the northernmost point, about 2100 km from Lewisporte. The ferries

run on this route from sometime in July to around mid-December when the coastal ice meets the Arctic pack ice and everything is sealed up until the summer thaw.

Towards the end of the season, throughout November and into December, the weather plays havoc with the schedule and the one-way trip can take weeks. With high winds and waves close to 15 metres high, the ship is often harbour-bound for days at a time.

Normally, it's a comfortable ship (actually there are two different ships which alternate trips) with four meals a day (you didn't forget 'night lunch' did you?) and a choice not unlike that found in any mainland restaurant but with prices slightly higher. Fares are low and determined by the number of nautical miles travelled. The rate is roughly 21 cents per nautical mile and an additional 10 cents per nautical mile for an economy two-berth cabin. To St Anthony it's 130 nautical miles thus a round-trip fare of $54, to Red Bay it's 194 miles or $80 and to Goose Bay it's 700 miles or round-trip $294. To head to Nain and back with a cabin would be $722.

There are 46 possible ports of call along the entire return route and the number of stops partially determines the length of the trip. You can get off at the village of your choice but keep in mind that most of them are not set up for tourists and that there's not a whole a lot to do while waiting for the ferry to return. At most ports, the ship usually needs one to two hours to unload and that is enough time for a good look around.

The low prices make the trip a real bargain. Because of that, and the chance to visit some of the country's most remote settlements and to see the fine scenery with granite cliffs and long fjords, the trip has become popular with visitors. Space is limited and, as most of it is required for local residents and their gear (everything from food to music cassettes to snowmobiles to toasters), reservations for the trip must be made from within Newfoundland.

Be prepared when making a reservation to pay a 25% deposit. Most likely a credit card will be necessary unless you are at a Marine Atlantic office. Most tickets are reserved through the Port aux Basques office (☎ 695-7081) and merely picked up at Lewisporte.

If you are driving, you can leave your car at the ferry terminal in Lewisporte. There is a security guard but a waiver must be signed discounting responsibility.

There are two trips in June, four trips a month in July, August and September, and three a month in October and November.

For either of the two ferry routes, arrive 90 minutes before departure in either Lewisporte or Happy Valley-Goose Bay and make reservations. For these and all information call the numbers (given earlier) or ☎ 709-695-7081 in St John's.

The federal government, which has developed air links to these northern communities, is talking about trying to phase out the boat runs – in a few years the voyage may not be possible.

GRAND FALLS & WINDSOR
These two small towns sit in pulp & paper country. Actually Windsor seems more like a suburb of Grand Falls and it is the latter which is of more interest to the visitor.

The tourist chalet information booth (☎ 489-6332) is on the highway a couple of km west of town and open from 8 am to 8 pm. The **Mary March Museum** (☎ 292-4522), on the corner of Cromer Ave and St Catherine St, is good and among other things outlines the life of the extinct Beothuk Indians. They lived in this portion of the province before the Europeans arrived but the clash of cultures spelled the end for this tribe. The museum is open daily from 9 am to 5 pm weekdays and 10 am to 6 pm on the weekends and is free.

Adjacent to the museum set in the woods is a re-creation of a Beothuk Indian village. It's open 9 am to 7 pm daily and admission is $2.

Overlooking the Grand Falls, a series of rapids and small cascades, is the **Salmonid Interpretation Centre**. The centre itself has exhibits and displays covering the biology and history of the Atlantic salmon. There is also an observation deck where you can watch the fish struggle upstream during its

spawning run. Hours are 8 am to 9 pm during the summer and admission is $3. You reach the centre from the downtown area by crossing the Exploits River from Scott St and then following the signs.

Not far west of town, **Beothuk Provincial Park** has an exhibit simulating a turn-of-the-century logging camp. The exhibit is free and is open from 10 am to 5.30 pm.

Places to Stay & Eat
There are a couple of expensive motels in town or the *Poplar Inn* (☎ 489-2546), a B&B at about half the rate with singles/ doubles at $35/40. It's at 22 Poplar Rd which runs off Lincoln Rd behind the Mt Peyton Hotel. The CN Roadcruiser stop is walkable, about three km away. At 78 Lincoln Rd on the way to the city centre is *Ye Olde Robin Hood Inn* (☎ 4849-5324) with rooms for $45/ 51.

Grand Falls' city centre is Church Rd and High St but most of the commercial district is now on the north side of the Trans Canada Hwy along Cromer Ave. Here you will find the fast-food chains, large foodstores and malls. Out by the tourist chalet is *Loung's Restaurant* with a $7 Chinese buffet served daily.

Getting There & Away
The CN Roadcruiser bus stops in town on Main St in Windsor.

SOUTH OF GRAND FALLS
Hwy 360 runs 130 km through the centre of the province to the south coast. It's a long way down to the first settlements at the end of **Bay d'Espoir**, a huge fjord. The cliffs at **Morrisville** offer the best views. **St Alban's** is the main town and is connected with Grand Falls by bus. **Conne River** is a Micmac Indian town. The region supports itself with a large hydroelectric plant, forestry and salmon farming. There are a few motels and a campground around the end of the bay.

Going further south you'll find a concentration of small, remote fishing villages. The scenery along Hwy 364 is particularly impressive, as is the scenery around **Harbour Breton**.

Places to Stay & Eat

Harbour Breton has a motel. A better choice is found in little English Harbour West at the *Olde Oven Inn* (☎ 888-3461) where singles/doubles are $40/50. The town is noted for its knitted sweaters. In Head Bay d'Espoir there are four motels, most charging $60 or more. The exception is *Pardy Cove Cottages* (☎ 882-2233) with units at $45 to $50 for one or two people. *Jipujikuek Kuespem Provincial Park* near the junction to Head Bay d'Espoir has camping.

Getting There & Away

The *Bay d'Espoir Bus Service* (☎ 538-2429 in St Alban's) links Grand Falls to St Alban's. A bus departs St Alban's on Monday, Wednesday and Friday at 8 am and arrives at Grand Falls at 11 am. The return trip departs Grands Fall at 4 pm. Hickey's Bus Service (☎ 885-2523 in Harbour Breton) does pretty much the same run on the same days from Grand Falls to Harbour Breton. At Pool's Cove you can board *Rencontre East Ferry* that makes two trips a day on Tuesday, Friday and Sunday and one the rest of the week to Bay L'Argent on the south side of Fortune Bay. This would save a considerable amount of backtracking for travellers without a car. The cost is $5.50 and includes a stop at Rencontre East. At Bay L'Argent, you can hike or hitch to Country Lodge on Hwy 210 to pick up bus transportation either to the Burin Peninsula or to St John's.

BAIE VERTE PENINSULA

Little-visited Baie Verte (Green Bay), north-west of Grand Falls, is a traditional region of small fishing and mining villages with a long history of human habitation. The Maritime Archaic Indians originally settled the edges of the peninsula and were followed by the Dorset Inuit who had a camp at or around **Fleur de Lys** from 1000 BC for several hundred years. There is a soapstone outcrop here from which the Inuit gouged the material for household goods such as lamps and for carvings. Evidence of their digging can be seen.

The Baie Verte area is pretty with green rounded hills edging the shore. Short ferry trips connect several of the islands. Springdale, the largest community in the area, has some accommodation and camping at *George Huxter Memorial Park* three km away. There is also *Flatwater Pond Provincial Park* with 25 sites in the middle of the peninsula 15 km south of Baie Verte on Hwy 410. Camping is $8 a night at both.

At **Baie Verte**, a relatively sizeable town at the north-west end of the peninsula, see the free Miners' Museum (☎ 532-8090) and tunnel. It doubles as the tourist office in town and is open 9 am to 8 pm daily during the summer. Just out of town, open-pit asbestos mining can be seen from an observation point off the main highway. The peninsula also has deposits of copper, gold, silver and zinc though much of it has been mined out. You can also visit some of the many abandoned mines nearby. In the past at little **Tilt Cove**, 5% of the world's nickel was mined.

La Scie is another good place to see an iceberg; boat trips are available.

Western Newfoundland

DEER LAKE & AROUND

There is very little here for the visitor but it's a convenient jumping-off point for trips up the northern peninsula. This is where you want to stock up on both gasoline and food before heading north.

There is a tourist chalet right on the Trans Canada Hwy which is open 8 am to 9 pm daily. In town the *Driftwood Inn* (☎ 635-5115), a large white, green-trimmed wooden building at 3 Nicholas Rd – an easy walk from Main St – is a good place to stay, although it's not cheap with rooms from $58 for a single. There is also *Deer Lake Municipality Park* which has 40 unserviced sites and showers. It's $9 a night. Most of the restaurants are fast-food chains on the Trans Canada Hwy but there is *Tai Lee Garden*, a simple, cheap Chinese place in the middle of Main St.

Between the town of Deer Lake and Corner Brook the road passes through scenic landscape alongside Deer Lake where many locals have summer cottages or trailers. Around **Pasadena Beach** there are some motels and cabins available for visitors.

NORTHERN PENINSULA

From Deer Lake the immense northern peninsula extends 430 km northward to Labrador along one of the most extraordinary, and beautiful roads in eastern North America. Called the Viking Trail, Hwy 430 extends between the coast and the Long Range Mountains to two UN World Heritage sites, another National Historic Site, two provincial parks, wonderfully barren far north topography and views over the history-filled Strait of Belle Isle to the coast of remote Labrador. There's lots of wildlife,

Moose

Though the moose is a fairly common animal across the country it is mainly found in the less populated, heavily forested northern regions. Nowhere in Canada are you as likely to see one as in Newfoundland. There are some 40,000 of them here and many of them live close to towns and roads including the Trans Canada Hwy. This, of course, increases the chances of getting a good look at one but also presents some hazards. There is more than one moose-vehicle collision a day across the province and smacking into a beast the height of a horse weighing 400 kg with antlers nearly two metres across is more wildlife than most people care for.

Moose tend to like the highways for a number of reasons. The open space makes walking easy, there is usually more breeze and fewer insects, and in spring the salt from winter de-icing makes a nice treat. For these reasons they also enjoy the train tracks, a habit which decreased their population at the rate of some 2000 per year until the train service was discontinued.

The areas of heaviest concentration are well marked and should be heeded particularly when travelling after dark, which is when most accidents occur. Ninety per cent of the run-ins take place between 11 pm and 4 am. If you do see a moose on or beside the road, slow down and if it doesn't want to move approach slowly with the lights off as they seem to get mesmerised by the beams.

I've seen them during the day on the Trans Canada Hwy on each of my trips. Get out and take pictures if you like, moose are generally not aggressive and are very impressive, if unusual-looking, animals. They can be unpredictable, however, and anything of this size should not be approached too closely or startled. During rutting (mating) season in October and November the males (bulls) can become very belligerent and downright ornery; it's a good time to stay in the car and well out of their way.

Calves are born in the spring, and throughout the summer it is not uncommon to see a cow moose with her young. Females and the young do not have antlers. Adult males grow a 'rack' of antlers each year in summer, only to have it fall off each autumn. ■

ranging from large mammals to specialised fauna, unbelievably various and abundant edible berries, spectacular fjords, excellent salmon fishing, small coastal fishing villages and very friendly people.

Even for those without a lot of time a trip from Port aux Basques to the northern peninsula if only as far as Gros Morne makes a memorable visit to Newfoundland. Many people make this region the focus of their trip to the Rock and never go further east than Deer Lake. L'Anse-aux-Meadows, a 1000-year-old Viking settlement (by far the oldest European landing site in North America, centuries ahead of Chris Columbus) has become somewhat of a pilgrimage site drawing a small but determined group from all over the USA and, to a lesser extent, Europe.

All of this has lead to a growing number of tourists in recent years which has meant an increase in services along the way. There are now motels, cabins and B&Bs from one end of the peninsula to the other to complement the campgrounds. It can be a wet, cool region with a lot of bugs as well, so if you're tenting be prepared for maybe the odd night in a motel.

It's roughly a five to six-hour drive from Deer Lake to St Anthony but even the price of gasoline is not as exorbitant as it once was.

Bus transportation is possible along the entire route.

Gros Morne National Park

Gros Morne National Park is a must for its spectacular, varied geography which has earned it status as a World Heritage Site. Special features include fjords that rival Scandinavia's, the majestic barren Tablelands, excellent mountain hiking trails, sandy beaches and historic little fishing communities. There is plenty of wildlife including caribou and moose, and offshore seals and, occasionally, whales. Part of the UN designation is due to the park's Precambrian, Cambrian and Ordovician rock and the evidence this rock supplies researchers with for the theory of plate tectonics.

Another factor was the site's 4500 years of human occupation.

Woody Point, Norris Point and Rocky Harbour are the principal commercial centres with Rocky Harbour being the main community, where there are all the amenities including a laundromat and grocery stores.

In the southern portion of the park, Hwy 431 leads to Woody Point and beyond to the Tablelands and Green Gardens. The village of Woody Point, site of a hostel, makes a good centre for seeing this portion of the park but keep in mind it's more than an hour's drive back to the main visitor's centre along winding roads around Bonne Bay.

Information The park has two information centres, a smaller one on Hwy 430 as you approach Wiltondale and the main one (☎ 458-2066) 25 km from the entrance on Hwy 430 at the exit to Norris Point. At either centre you need to purchase the vehicle permit ($4.25 a day) needed to enter the park. Maps, books and backcountry permits are available at both while the main centre also has an impressive interpretive area that includes a multi-image slide show. Both centres are open daily from 9 am to 10 pm during the summer.

Things to See & Do In the southwest corner of the park are the compelling **Tablelands**, by the road's edge, not far from Woody Point. This is a barren 80-km ledge of rock 700 metres high shoved up from beneath the ocean floor – a glimpse of them along Hwy 431 and a short trail to the base of the barren mountains.

Heading further west, **Green Gardens** is a volcanic coast that features sea caves and sea stacks. It's a hour-hike from the second trailhead of the Green Garden Trail to the coast. At the end of the highway is **Trout River**, a small, picturesque fishing community. Operating here is Tableland Boat Tours (☎ 451-2101) which runs trips up Trout River Pond past the Tablelands.

From the government wharf in Norris Point two-hour boat trips of **Bonne Bay** depart daily at 1 pm stopping over in Woody Point for more people to board before cruising the Arms. Book and purchase tickets for the tour at the Oceanview Motel (☎ 458-2730) in Rocky Harbour.

Near Rocky Harbour is a recreation complex with a 25-metre swimming pool and whirlpool. It has various swim times daily for $2.75 per adult.

Further up the coast past Sally's Cove, parts of the wreck of the SS *Ethie* which ran aground in 1919 can be seen on the beach. The storm and subsequent rescue sparked the writing of a song about the incident.

Western Brook Pond is the park's feature fjord with dwarfing cliffs nearly 700 metres high running vertically from the cool waters. Boat tours of the 15-km-long fjord are offered and definitely recommended. The 2½-hour trip takes you past sheer cliffs towering at the water's edge. The trips are very popular and you need to make reservations at the Ocean View Motel (☎ 458-2730) in Rocky Harbour at least a day in advance.

The tours run from June to the end of September with three trips daily at 10 am, 1 pm and 4 pm in the high season each taking up to 40 passengers. A ticket costs $23, less for kids. The dock is reached after an easy three-km walk from the road along the Western Brook Pond Trail.

The gentle, safe, sand-duned beach at **Shallow Bay** at the other end of the geographic spectrum seems almost out of place – as if transported from the Caribbean by some bizarre current. The water, though, provides a chilling dose of reality, rarely getting above 15°C.

At **Broom Point** there is a restored fishing camp depicting the inshore fishery of the 1960s. The three Nudge bothers and their families fished here from 1941 to 1975 when they sold the entire camp, including boats, lobster traps and nets, to the national park. Everything has been restored and now staffed with interpretive guides. Broom Point is open daily from 10 am to 6 pm from June to September.

Also keep in mind that the park staff hosts interpretive programmes, guided walks and evening programmes throughout the summer. The walks are a great way to help understand the fascinating geology of the park.

Hiking Gros Morne National Park maintains 22 trails that total 75 km and feature six backcountry camping areas for what arguably could be some of the best trekking in Newfoundland.

The gem of the park's trail system is **James Callahan Trail** to the peak of Gros Morne, the highest point in the area at 806 metres. The 16-km return trek is said to be a seven-to-eight hour hike but many people can cover it in less time. The trail is well maintained with steps and boardwalks but is still a tough hike, especially the steep rock gully that must be climbed to the ridgeline of the mountain. This is not a trail for tennis shoes. The views at the top and of 10-Mile Pond, a sheer-sided fjord, make the effort well worth it. There is backcountry camping in Fern Gulch along the trail and a popular backpacking trip is to set up there for a couple of nights and scale the mountain without the packs.

Green Gardens Trail is almost as scenic and challenging. The 18-km loop has two trailheads off Hwy 431 with each one descending a valley to the Green Gardens, a volcanic coastline. Plan on seven to 10 hours for the entire loop or book one of the three backcountry camping areas, all of them on the ocean, and turn the hike into an overnight adventure.

Shorter but just as scenic are: **Tablelands Trail**, that extends two km to Winterhouse Brook Canyon for a four-km return hike; **Lookout Trail** near Woody Point, a five-km loop to the site of an old fire tower above the treeline and **Western Brook Pond Trail**, the most popular trail in the park which is an easy six-km return hike to the western end of the fjord.

Other overnight treks include **Stanleyville Trail**, a round-trip of four km to the site of an old logging camp where there is backcountry camping. This easy trail begins in the Lomond Day-use Area off Hwy 431.

Western Brook Pond Trail and **Snug Harbour Trail** can be combined for a seven-km one-way hike to backcountry camp sites in the famous fjord. Or book passage on the tour boat and have them drop you off at the head of Western Brook Pond where there are several more backcountry camp sites.

Backcountry camp sites are $3 per person per night and must be booked in advance at the visitor centres. If you plan to do several trails, invest $10 in a copy of *Gros Morne National Park Trail Guide*, a waterproof map of the park with trail descriptions on the backside.

Places to Stay & Eat Within the national park are five campgrounds, located at Trout River, Lomond, Berry Hill, Green Point and Shallow Bay. The fees range from $11.25 a night to $7.25 for Trout River and Green Point, which do not have showers.

There is not one but three hostel possibilities, a dizzying unheard of array for Newfoundland. *Juniper Campground* (☎ 458-2917) in Rocky Harbour runs a nine-bunk hostel in a large cabin that includes a kitchen and showers. The cost is $10 a night. Alternatively, there is *Major's Hospitality Home & Hostel* (☎ 458-2537). In Woody Point there is the HI *Woody Point Hostel* (☎ 453-2470 or 453-7254). It's open from the end of May to October and features a kitchen and 10 beds for $10 a night for members, $12 for nonmembers. It is on School Rd, just up the hill from Irving Auto Service which doubles as the bus station, and is open all day.

Also in Woody Point is the *Victorian Manor* (☎ 453-2485), a hospitality home with rooms in the nice old house or newer two-bedroom efficiency cabins where you can cook your own meals. In the main house, the four rooms cost $40/45 with a light breakfast included. Laundry facilities and bike and canoe rentals are also offered.

Across the bay in Norris Point there are more choices. *Eileen's B&B* (☎ 458-2427) has two rooms available from June to September for singles/doubles $30/35 including

a light breakfast. A little more expensive is *Terry's B&B* (☎ 458-2373) at $40/45.

There are restaurants and grocery stores in both villages and a drug store (chemist) in Norris Point.

At Rocky Harbour, you could stay at *Gros Morne Cabins* (☎ 458-2020), 22 individual log cabins with kitchens and views over the ocean. Inquire at Endicott's variety store. The price is $55 for a one-bedroom place large enough for up to two adults and two kids. There is also *Ocean View Motel* (☎ 458-2730) at $55/60 a single or double and a number of B&Bs. *Ocean Acre Inn* (☎ 458-2272) is on the water and has four rooms at $35/45. *Evergreen B&B* (☎ 458-2692) is a pleasant place with laundry facilities and four rooms with shared bath that run $35/39.

For a munch, *Jackie's* has good home-made French fries and fruit pies and an outdoor deck. The *Narrows Head Restaurant*, not far from the campground in Trout River, is good for fresh and affordable seafood.

Getting There & Around Martin's Bus Service (☎ 453-2207) connects Woody Point with Corner Brook with daily runs Monday to Friday. It departs Trout River at 9 am, Woody Point at 9.30 am and Corner Brook for the return trip at 5 pm. One-way fare between Woody Point and Corner Brook is $9. In Woody Point, Martin's departs from Irving Auto Service.

The Viking Express bus (☎ 634-4710 in Corner Brook) departs Corner Brook at 4 pm for St Anthony via Deer Lake on Monday, Wednesday and Friday, overnights at St Anthony and then makes a return run the following day. It stops at Norris Point (across Bonne Bay from Woody Point) and at Ocean View Motel in Rocky Harbour on demand for those who want to continue north. Call the bus company in Corner Brook for a pick-up. The company also has a bus that begins in Rocky Harbour for Corner Brook, departing from the Oceanville Motel at 9 am Monday through Friday. In Corner Brook both buses depart from the Millbrook Mall

NEWFOUNDLAND

(see the Corner Brook section later in this chapter for more details.)

There is no longer ferry transportation across Bonne Bay from Woody Point to Norris Point. The only way to the other side of the bay is a 60-km drive.

The Arches

Out of the park back northward on Hwy 430, The Arches is worth stopping at for a stroll down to the beach which is littered with beautiful, smooth, coloured rocks about the size of footballs. The main attractions, though, are the three limestone arches and the remains of maybe three or four more formed some 400 million years ago. There are picnic tables overlooking the beach.

Table Point Ecological Reserve

North of Bellburns along the shore there are protected sections of limestone 470 million years old containing abundant fossils.

River of Ponds Provincial Park

On the Pond River which is good for salmon, there is a provincial park with a 40-site campground. The unserviced sites are $8 a night. If nothing else, pull in to see the display of whale bones estimated to be 5,000 to 7,000 years old. They're huge.

Hawke's Bay

At the turn of the century, there was a whaling station halfway to St Anthony from Deer Lake, Hawke's Bay. There are some excellent salmon waters here and at the salmon ladder, a device to aid the fish in getting upstream.

Just behind the tourist office, open from 10 am to 7 pm daily in summer, is *Torrent River Nature Park*. The park has a campground with 10 serviced sites for $7 to $15 a night as well as showers. Nearby the **Hogan Trail** begins along the Torrent River. Most of the three-km walking trail is on a boardwalk

Puffins can catch up to 10 small fish in succession and carry them crosswise in the bill to the nest

and leads over marsh and through the woods to the salmon ladder.

Maynard's Motel (☎ 248-5225 or 800-563-8811) has 20 units and another half-dozen with housekeeping facilities. Rooms cost $58/68. *Gloria's B&B* (☎ 248-5131) and *Baie View B&B* (☎ 248-270) both charge $35 for a single.

Port au Choix

Busy and interesting Port au Choix is one of the biggest towns between Gros Morne and St Anthony and a main stop for travellers on the Viking Trail.

The principal attraction is **Port au Choix National Historic Site** (☎ 861-3522 during the season), which preserves the history of two groups of peoples who lived thousands of years apart. Downtown beside the museum and visitor centre is a Maritime Archaic Indian cemetery dating from 3200 to 4300 years ago. The remains of about 100 individuals as well as tools, weapons and ornaments were discovered here accidentally in 1967. Some of these artefacts are on view in the visitor centre.

The other section of the park is a short distance away through town by road followed by a 20-minute walk along a trail. It deals with the Dorset Inuit people who settled on the Cape Riche Peninsula between 1500 and 2200 years ago. Excavation of this site, known as **Phillip's Garden**, was done in the 1960s and revealed the remains of several ancient houses. The trail continues for another 30 minutes beyond the site to the **Point Riche lighthouse**. You can also reach the lighthouse by car by turning onto the gravel road at the post office and following it for four km. This half of the trail to Phillip's Garden is much more scenic than the first half. The park's visitor centre is open daily during the summer from 9 am to 7 pm and admission into the exhibits is $1.

For a little more recent history, just out of town is a plaque outlining some of the tussles between the French and British for the fishing rights in the area which continued from the 1600s until the 1900s. In 1904 yet another treaty was signed in which the French relinquished their rights here in exchange for the privilege in Morocco.

Don't pass up Studio Gargamelle (☎ 861-3280), the workshop of artist Ben Ploughman. Outside he has an impressive whale skeleton exhibit, with the bones from an entire whale wired together.

Places to Stay & Eat In Port Au Choix the economical choice is the two-room *Jean-Marie Guest Home* (☎ 861-3023) located just off the Viking Trail and costing $40/50 with a light breakfast. An evening snack is included, too, and dinner is an extra option. To bolster the thin accommodation scene there is also a guesthouse in nearby Port Saunders, *Biggin's Hospitality Home* (☎ 861-3523), at $35/39.

In Port au Choix is the more expensive but well-kept *Sea Echo Motel* (☎ 861-3777) with 19 rooms. The dining room is quite good, friendly and has good-value lunch specials. Singles/doubles are $50/63.

The best meal in town is at *The Anchor Cafe*. Can't miss the place, the front half is the stern of a boat. A wide selection of seafood dinners are around $10 and a big bowl of seafood chowder with bread is $3.60. Across from the park visitor centre is *Wu's Takeout* for cheap Chinese.

About 50 km north of town right beside the provincial picnic park is a private campground, *Three Mile Lake Campground*. It's quiet, wooded and has a beach on the lake. There are 30 unserviced sites at $8 a night.

North from Port au Choix

Close to town the long, treeless mountain range to the east is quite close to the road although it's not as high as the peaks in Gros Morne National Park. After this close encounter, the mountains veer off to the east and don't have the same presence. The landscape becomes more and more barren until it appears pretty much like that found in the far Canadian north – an essentially flat, pond-filled primeval expanse. There is probably no other place in the country where this type of rugged terrain is as accessible.

At Plum Point a gravel road connects with

NEWFOUNDLAND

the eastern shore. At **Main Brook** there is *Tuckamore Lodge* (☎ 865-6361), an A-frame, B&B cottage with four rooms, a dining room, a fireplace and a sauna. Meals are available. Singles/doubles are priced at $60/70 with a light breakfast. Call ahead before driving across the peninsula because the lodge is mainly used as a base for multi-day package adventure tours which include trips to see birds, caribou, etc. It's also often used by hunters and anglers.

The main town over on this side is **Roddickton** and here, as in Main Brook, there are outfitters for hunting and fishing. There is also some hiking and a trip up Cloud Hill affords good views of the islands off-shore.

Back on Hwy 430, **St Barbe** is the site of a ferry to Labrador (see the Labrador section later in this chapter for details). From here on up the coast of Labrador is visible on clear days. *St Barbe Motel* (☎ 877-2444) is relatively new with 16 rooms that go for $50/55. Also in town is *Toope's Hospitality House* (☎ 877-2413) with three rooms at $30/35.

Pistolet Bay Provincial Park

With 30 sites in a wild but wooded area 20 km from the main road and 40 km from the Viking site, this is the place to stay if you're camping. The sites are not on the water but it's probably preferable to have the scrubby, stunted trees around to provide some wind-break. Be prepared for the mosquitoes and blackflies, they seem to have a real mean streak. There is a comfort station at the park with hot showers and laundry facilities and it's heated. What luxury! Sites are $12 a night.

Also on Pistolet Bay is the privately run *Viking Trailer Park* (☎ 454-3541) with serviced sites for camper vehicles. Sites are $10 a night.

Cape Onion

The closest town for milk and bread (and beer) is the fishing village of **Raleigh** while another eight km further north the road ends at Cape Onion. The cape reveals dramatic coastal scenery of islands, coves and also

'tickles', which in Newfoundland refer to narrow passages of water between two land formations. Also located here is the delightful *Tickle Inn* (☎ 452-4321 summer only). This seaside inn, built in 1890, features four rooms, a parlour warmed by a Franklin wood stove and excellent homecooked meals of local seafood and Newfoundland dishes. Singles/doubles are $40/45 and include a light breakfast. Other meals are by request and boat tours of the coastline or a nearby shipwreck can be arranged.

Saint Lunaire to Straitsview

There are five small, old fishing villages on the way to the historic site of L'Anse-aux-Meadows. You may see kids by the road's edge selling berries collected out on the barrens. In mid-August this will include the queen of all Newfoundland berries, the golden bakeapple sold here for $30 per gallon (4.5 litres – the people here still use imperial measurements, unlike those in much of the country) and fetching as much as $50 further south.

L'Anse-aux-Meadows
National Historic Park

This is a fascinating place (☎ 623-2608) made all the more special by the unobtrusive, low-key approach of the park developers. In an unspoiled, waterside setting – looking pretty much like it did in 1000 AD when the Vikings from Scandinavia and Greenland became the first Europeans to land in North America – are the remains of their settlement. Replicas of the sod buildings complete with the smoky smell almost transport you back in time.

These guys, led by Leif Eriksson, son of Eric the Red, built their own boats, sailed all over the North Atlantic, landed here, constructed houses which still remain, fed themselves and they were practically all just 20-something years old. Oops, let's not forget they smelted iron out of the bog and forged nails with it – 1000 years ago!

Allow two to three hours to browse through the interpretive centre with its artefacts, see the film and walk around the eight unearthed original wood and sod buildings and the three reconstructions.

Also captivating is the story of Norwegian explorer Helge Ingstad who discovered the site in 1960 ending years of searching. His tale and that of his archaeologist wife is told in the interpretive centre. A short walk behind the replica buildings leads to a small graveyard where lies the body of local inhabitant George Decker who made Ingstad's day by pointing out the mounds in the terrain.

Take time to walk the three-km trail that winds through the barren terrain and along the coast that surrounds the interpretive center. The park, 43 km from St Anthony's, is open 9 am to 8 pm daily from mid-June to the beginning of September (Labour Day) and until 4.30 pm to October. Admission is $2.50.

If you're totally captivated by the Viking experience, nearby is Viking Boat Tours (☎ 623-2464), which offers two-hour boat tours on a replica Viking ship. You don't have to row but they don't sail either, the Canadian Coast Guard won't allow it, so they motor around the bay looking at shipwrecks, icebergs and coastal scenery. The cost is $25 per person.

Places To Stay & Eat At the village of Gunner's Cove, five km from the historic site, is the recommended *Valhalla Lodge* (☎ 623-2018 summer only). The six Scandinavian-themed rooms are $40/50 with a light breakfast included. Even closer and also highly recommended is *Marilyn's Hospitality Home* (☎ 623-2811) at Hay Cove, practically across from the entrance to the park. Singles/doubles are $35/40 with a full breakfast. Other meals are by request.

There is no camping in the park but just past the entrance is a small roadside park where occasionally cyclists or hitchhikers will pitch a tent. In Straitsview, *Smith's Restaurant* serves meals of cod tongue, salt fish and brewis or scallops for under $3. Cod chowder, coffee and rolls is $6.

St Anthony

You made it! Unfortunately it's a little anticlimactic. With a population of 3500, and as the largest town in the north of the northern peninsula, it's functional and an important supply centre and fish-processing depot but it's not what you'd call pretty. There are, though, a couple of things to see.

At the Viking Mall downtown is a Sobey's grocery store for stocking up if you're taking the boat north or heading back down to Deer Lake. The Ultramar service station on the corner also doubles as a tourist centre with a few pamphlets on a rack.

The **Grenfell Museum** is the former home (☎ 454-8596) of Sir Wilfred Grenfell, a local legend and, by all accounts, quite a man. Born in England and educated as a doctor, he first came to Newfoundland in 1892 and for the next 40 years built hospitals, nursing stations and organised much needed fishing cooperatives along the coast of Labrador and around St Anthony. The fine old house with a large wrap-around porch outlines his life and work and displays mementoes and artefacts collected over the years. The museum is open daily from mid-June to the beginning of September from 9 am to 7 pm. Admission is $2.

Follow the main road through town and it ends at **Fishing Point Park**. The towering headland cliffs here are impressive and there are a handful of short trails, with names like Iceberg Alley and Whale Watchers Trail, that head to observation platforms on the edge of the cliffs.

In August, watch for the annual cod filleting contest held in town. Admission is free. These guys can clean fish!

Places to Stay & Eat There are two guesthouses and two motels in St Anthony. *Howell's Tourist Home* (☎ 454-3402), at 76B East St, has four rooms at a good rate of $31/39. Meals are available and it's open all year. A second choice is the *Trailsend Hospitality Home* (☎ 454-2024) at 1 Cormack St. Rates are $35/45 with a full breakfast.

Alternatively *St Anthony Haven Inn* (☎ 454-3200), at 14 Goose Cove Rd, has 22 rooms at $42 for a single but is a little run-down. The newer, larger *Vinland Motel* (☎ 454-8843) is $60/75.

The motels have restaurants or try *The Lightkeeper's Cafe*, the former lightkeeper's house at Fishing Point Park. Enjoy dinner while watching icebergs float by. During the summer it opens at 7 am. *Pizza Delight* also has an outlet here.

Things to Buy There are three craft outlets in town including Grenfell Handicrafts with parkas embroidered by hand, whale-bone and ivory carvings, and other articles. The Mukluk Factory has sealskin leather goods and some carvings and jewelry. A mukluk is a traditional Inuit soft winter boot made of sealskin or caribou hide and sometimes fur lined. Northern Crafts has a bit of everything.

Getting There & Away This is the final stop for the Viking Express bus (☎ 454-2630) and the ferry from Lewisporte en route to communities along the Labrador coast can be picked up here. For ferry information see the Lewisporte section earlier in this chapter. The bus departs St Anthony for Corner Brook at 10 am Sunday, Tuesday and Thursday. From Corner Brook connections can be made for the trans-island CN Roadcruiser bus to either Port aux Basques or St John's.

CORNER BROOK

With 22,500 people, this is Newfoundland's second largest town after St John's and there are a few things to see and do. Up high beside the waters of Humber Arm, it is fairly attractive despite the often all-pervading smell – a reminder that the focus of the town is the huge pulp & paper mill. The Corner Brook area is likely the sunniest region of the province and the warm, clear skies of summer can be a real treat.

Downtown is Main St by Remembrance Square and up along maple tree-lined Park St towards the Heritage District. There are a few restaurants here, the post office and, further along, City Hall.

Information

The large tourist office (☎ 634-5831) and craft shop can't be missed just off the Trans Canada Hwy near the turn-offs into town. Hours are 8 am to 8 pm during the summer.

Captain James Cook Monument

North-west of downtown up on some cliffs overlooking the Humber Arm is a National Historic Site commemorating Captain Cook and affording excellent views of the city and area. A map from the tourist office is necessary as the road access is pretty convoluted. Mr Cook certainly got around. He surveyed this entire region in the mid-1760s and his names for many of the islands, ports and waterways such as the Humber Arm and Hawke's Bay remain. His work here was so successful it led to the voyages to New Zealand and Australia. Replicas of some of Cook's charts are displayed.

Sticks & Stones House

On the opposite side of town, in a residential area, sits this folk art masterpiece – one man's life obsession that must be seen to be believed. It seems that for 30 years the owner, Clyde Farnell, spent every spare moment elaborately decorating the walls and ceilings of the house with found and discarded objects.

When he died and neighbours entered the house his secret floored them. The university

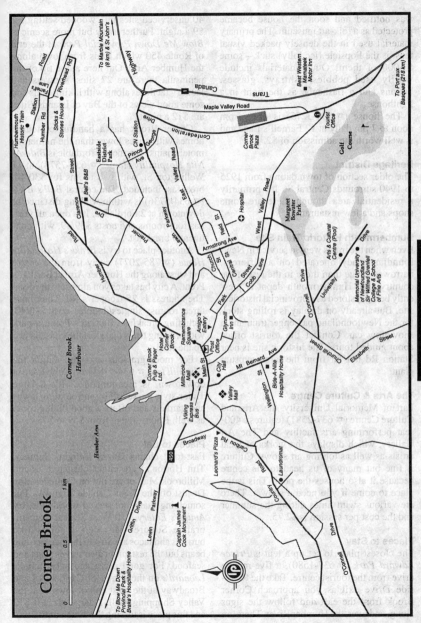

Corner Brook

NEWFOUNDLAND

was notified and soon the house became protected as a folk-art museum. The primary material used in the densely packed visual feast is the Popsicle (ice lolly) stick – some 53,000 of them! Other materials include wittily used pebbles, ashtrays, glasses, buttons and a flashcube as the light in a lighthouse.

The house (☎ 634-3275) is open from noon to 7 pm daily at 12 Farnell's Lane and is well worth the admission of $2.

Heritage District

The older section of town dating from 1925 to 1940 surrounds Central St. It's primarily a residential area though there are some shops and a few restaurants.

Humbermouth Historic Train Site

Even when the trains were in service in Newfoundland they operated on a different, narrower gauge than those in the rest of the country. The Humbermouth depot is presently being restored as a provincial historical site. But already on display is rolling stock for the Newfoundland passenger train and a snowplow car. Contact the tourist office about guided tours. The historic site is near Station Rd not far from the large gypsum plant.

The Arts & Culture Centre

Part of Memorial University, the Arts and Culture Centre (☎ 637-2581) features a 400-seat performing arts facility and The Art Gallery, which displays the works of local artists as well as touring art shows. Culture is fine but many of us head to the centre because it also houses the pool. This is the place to come if you need a shower. There are various swim times during the summer and the cost per session is $2.75.

Places to Stay

The closest place to set up a tent is *Prince Edward Park* (☎ 637-1580), a five-minute drive from the tourist centre. Take the Riverside Drive exit as you approach Corner Brook from the east and follow the signs along, and over, the Humber River. There are

40 unserviced sites in a wooded setting for $9 a night. Further away but more scenic is *Blow Me Down Provincial Park* at the end of Route 450 which leads from town along the Humber Arm. Out here at the tip of the peninsula there are 27 sites, showers and laundry facilities along with hiking trails and some good views of the Bay of Islands. Sites are $12 a night.

Corner Brook has a handful of tourist homes with prices lower than the numerous motel chains. The most affordable is *Bide-A-Nite Hospitality Home* (☎ 634-7578), at 11 Wellington St, with two rooms for $30/40, breakfast included. The central *Bell's B&B* (☎ 634-5736) is within walking distance of downtown at 2 Ford's Rd. It is open all year, has four rooms and costs $39/49, with continental breakfast.

Another place to try is *Brake's Hospitality Home* (☎ 785-2077) away from the centre and west along the Humber Arm at Bartlett's Point. A city bus takes you almost to the door. The address is 25 Cooper's Rd. They have three rooms; singles/doubles cost $30/40, including breakfast. Bartlett's Point, a park with walking trails that skirt the coast, is just up the road.

For more gracious accommodation the *Glynmill Inn* (☎ 634-5181), on Cobb Lane in downtown, is recommended. It's a large Tudor-style inn set off by surrounding lawns and gardens and offers a good dining room as well. Rooms range from $59 to $78.

Places to Eat

Fast-food chains (Pizza Delight, Subway, Tim Horton's) are either clustered around Millbrook Mall or are out on Confederation Dr just off the Trans Canada Highway. For something that's not served worldwide, try *Amigo's Eatery*, 710 West St near Remembrance Square. Mexican specials like burritos and tacos are $6 and include rice and beans but the restaurant also serves pasta and seafood. For good pizza and subs, there's *Leonard's* on the corner of Caribou Rd and Broadway at the west end of town near the Valley Shopping Mall. A large pizza is $12 and this place is tossing the dough until 2 am.

Also out this way is the *More or Less* store at 35 Broadway which is good for hiking and camping foods.

Getting There & Away

Corner Brook is a major hub for bus service throughout Newfoundland. The CN Roadcruiser station (☎ 634-8244), for points east and west along the Trans Canada Hwy, is in the north-east section of town on the corner of the Lewin Parkway and Prince George Ave. A bus heads west at 5.55 pm daily, a bus east at 11.25 am. Passage to Port aux Basques is $27, to St John's $67.

The Viking Express (☎ 634-4710) bus which goes up the northern peninsula arrives and departs from the Millbrook Mall shopping centre not far from Main St in the centre of Corner Brook. They have a ticket counter on the lower level next to Mary Brown's Chicken. A bus leaves Monday, Wednesday and Friday at 4 pm for St Anthony's. One way is $41. Another bus leaves at 5 pm Monday through Friday for Rocky Harbour in Gros Morne National Park. One way is $12.

Martin's Bus Service (☎ 634-4710) goes to Woody Point in Gros Morne National Park and also departs from the Millbrook Mall. The bus departs at 5 pm Monday to Friday and the ticket is $9. Eddy's Bus Service (☎ 643-2134) runs to Stephenville three to four times daily. It's office is at 9 Humber Rd and one-way fare is $10. Finally, if you need to reach Burgeo on the south coast, Devin's Bus Line (☎ 634-7777) provides service with an afternoon bus Monday through Friday.

AROUND CORNER BROOK

Marble Mountain, in the Humber Valley eight km east of town, has become an established major downhill ski centre; the area is also picturesque in the autumn with the colourful foliage. The half-km Steady Brook Falls Trail leads from the rear parking lot of Marble Mountain to the cascade that tumbles more than 30 metres. Marble Mountain Ski Area Trail is 3.5 km one way to the 500-metre summit of Skill Hill where there are good views.

For more serious walkers, including overnighters, there are numerous hikes in the **Blomidon Mountains** (also spelt 'Blow Me Down'), south of the Bay of Islands along Hwy 450 to Lark Harbour. These mountains were formed about 500 million years ago from brownish peridotite rock pushed up from the earth's mantle when the geographic plates of North America and Europe bumped together. What makes this special is that Newfoundland is one of the few places in the world where this type of rock is exposed and can be walked over.

Other features are the great views over the bay and islands and a small caribou population. Some of the trails especially ones up on the barrens are not well marked at all so bringing topographical maps and proper equipment is recommended. For a general description of the area purchase a copy of *Best Hiking Trails in Western Newfoundland* by Keith Nicol.

One of the easiest as well as most popular trails begins at a parking lot on the left side of Hwy 450 (500 metres from the bridge which crosses Blow Me Down Brook). The trail can be taken for an hour or so or, for more avid hikers, it continues well into the mountains where you're on your own. At Blow Me Down Park near the end of Hwy 450 there are also well-used marked trails which still provide fine views of the coastline.

South of town there is very good freshwater swimming at Stag Lake and also fairly warm waters at the **Blue Ponds Provincial Park** a little further out. Blue Ponds also has 61 camp sites at $8 a night.

STEPHENVILLE

Formerly a large military base town with the decaying evidence visible from the road, Stephenville with a population of 10,000, now relies mainly on the Abitibi-Price pulp mill. The town sits on St George's Bay between Corner Brook and Port aux Basques and acts as entrance to French Port au Port. There is not much here for the visitor but information can be had from the Chamber of Commerce (☎ 643-5854) on Hansen Memorial Hwy.

The Stephenville Festival is a three-week English theatre event, usually held in late July with local and internationally known participants. The festival offers theatre ranging from Shakespeare to modern Newfoundlanders' plays. Call the Arts & Culture Centre (☎ 643-4553) in regards to exact dates and tickets.

During lobster season (from April to July), the tasty devils are sold in the streets from trucks and trailers at good prices.

Places to Stay

For campers, there is the new *Indian Head Park* with swimming pool, nature trail and golf course. The wooded campground has 30 sites for $7 a night but no showers. To reach the park turn onto Massachusetts Ave from Hwy 460 and follow it around the airport to the coast.

Harmon House (☎ 643-4673), a B&B, at 144 New Mexico Drive not far from the hospital has singles/doubles at $40/50 with breakfast. Everything else is a motel, of which *Hotel Stephenville* (☎ 643-5176) is the cheapest at $45/55.

PORT AU PORT PENINSULA

The large peninsula west from Stephenville is the only French area of the province and has been since the early 1700s when it became known as the French Shore. It was used by the French for fishing in the **Strait of Belle Isle** right up until the early 1900s. **Red Island** was at one time France's most important fishing base in the New World.

Today, the further west you go the stronger the French culture is. At the south-west tip of the Port au Port Peninsula in **Cape St George** the children still go to French school preserving their dialect which is now distinct from the language spoken in either France or Quebec. Mainland, Lourdes and Black Duck Brook are also very French. In late July or early August each year there is a major French folk festival held in Cape St George with lots of music and other events.

In **Port au Port West**, a small community not far from Stephenville the Our Lady of Mercy Church is worth a look. Begun in 1914, it is the largest wooden building in Newfoundland. During July and August, a guide is on hand to show you around and provide some details and stories about the church. On the way there from Stephenville after going across the small bridge continue straight on the small road, don't follow the road around to the left or you'll miss the church like everybody else does. There is also the Lady of Mercy Museum with craft shop, a tea room and a collection of local artefacts. Hours are 10 am to 8 pm daily during the summer and admission is $1.

Along Hwy 463 on the way to Loudres, you will pass numerous small sheds selling lobsters during the season. At *Piccadilly Head Provincial Park* you'll find a rugged stretch of coast, hiking trails and 50 unserviced camp sites.

BARACHOIS POND PROVINCIAL PARK

Located right on the Trans Canada Hwy near the exits to Stephenville is this large provincial park, one of the few in Newfoundland that offers an opportunity for backpacking. From the campground a trail heads 4.5-km one-way to the top of Erin Mountain, a peak of almost 400 metres. On top there are excellent views of the surrounding area and backcountry camp sites.

Plan on two hours for the climb up. There are no fees for hiking or camping on the mountain but a night in the park's 150-site campground is $12. The park also has a swimming area, canoe rentals, showers, laundry facilities and a small store.

South-Western Newfoundland

Within the small south-western corner of the province the visitor is offered a remarkable variety of geography and history. It is well worthwhile spending some time exploring it rather than just doing the usual mad dash to or from the ferry. Hilly Port aux Basques built up and around a jutting, jagged peninsula and offering all the services including a major tourist office, is the centre of the region.

CODROY VALLEY

North of Port aux Basques beyond Cape Ray the broad green, fertile Codroy Valley runs from the coast north-east alongside the Long Range Mountains for about 50 km. This is one of the prime farming regions of the province and compared with the generally rugged, rocky landscape looks positively lush. A good spot for a view of the valley (accessible by car) is down near the sea by the town of **Searston.**

Further along, the road goes up a mountain at **Cape Anguille**; there are views as far as the mainland on a clear day. Back at the inlet, the estuary of the Grand Codroy River is an important wetland area for birds which is impressive at migration times when thousands of geese, black ducks and other species can be viewed. At **Grand Codroy Provincial Park** there is a beach, picnic areas, showers and the only full-service campground in the park system. Camp sites are $15 a night.

Despite its long period of settlement and the many quiet farms, the valley does have a nasty side to it. It can be the windiest place in Newfoundland and that's saying something. Along the highway winds can reach 200 km/h. They used to have to stop the trains at times to prevent them from blowing off the tracks.

PORT AUX BASQUES

For many visitors this is the first glimpse of Newfoundland. Approaching by ferry from Nova Scotia, the rocky, barren treeless landscape can look a little forbidding but also appealing in a rough, undeveloped way. For the many people heading to the province to enjoy its ruggedness, this uncommercialised port is a welcome sight.

The town itself, at least the older section built on and around the hills to the left of the ferry as it approaches, is very attractive with narrow, winding roads edged with the traditional wooden houses offering different views and angles at every turn.

Port aux Basques was named by Basque fishers and whalers in the early 16th century who came to work the waters of the Strait of Belle Isle which separates the province from Quebec. The French and Portuguese also used the port as a fishing station.

Today, Port aux Basques with a population of 6100, is the principal terminal for the Marine Atlantic ferry which links the island with the Canadian mainland. The ferry company is now the largest employer in town, though there are also freight-handling and fish-packing industries.

The town is also sometimes known as Channel-Port-aux-Basques.

Orientation

The ferry pulls into a small, well-protected bay. The town centre is to the south-east of the landing and back the way you came in. It consists of narrow, hilly streets overlooking the sea. To get to this old section of town, cross the bridge after leaving the ferry and turn left.

For the new part of town, turn right along the Trans Canada Hwy. Go past a number of gasoline stations and turn left at the Hotel Port aux Basques on the corner of Grand Bay Rd and High St. This will take you to the shopping mall, the centre of the new district.

Information

The tourist chalet (☎ 695-2262) with information on all parts of the province is on the Trans Canada Hwy a few km out of town on the way to St John's. Hours are 6 am to 11 pm daily during the summer.

Gulf Museum

In the city centre, at 118 Main St across from the Town Hall, is the two-storey museum (☎ 695-2460). The bulk of the collection is maritime artefacts – many from shipwrecks.

The showpiece of the museum is its astrolabe. This navigational instrument from the 17th century is a striking brass contraption

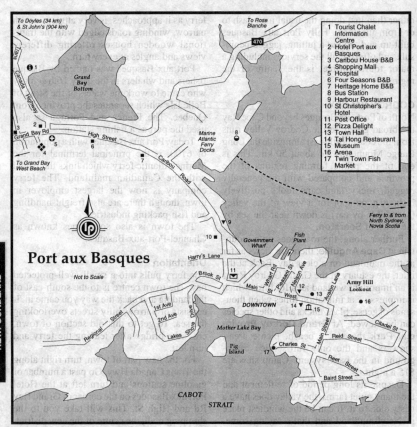

Port aux Basques

1 Tourist Chalet
   Information
   Centre
2 Hotel Port aux
   Basques
3 Caribou House B&B
4 Shopping Mall
5 Hospital
6 Four Seasons B&B
7 Heritage Home B&B
8 Bus Station
9 Harbour Restaurant
10 St Christopher's
   Hotel
11 Post Office
12 Pizza Delight
13 Town Hall
14 Tai Hong Restaurant
15 Museum
16 Arena
17 Twin Town Fish
   Market

about 17.5 cm in diameter made in Portugal in 1628. The design is based on a principal discovered by the ancient Greeks to allow for charting of the heavenly bodies. Variations on it have been used for nautical navigation since 1470.

The astrolabe is in remarkable condition and is one of only about three dozen in the world. It was found by a diver off Isle aux Morts, along the south coast from town in 1982 and is believed to have been on board either a Portuguese or Basque fishing boat.

Among some of the other items are some old photographs of the Codroy Valley taken

at the turn of the century and some soapstone relics taken from the Cape Ray Dorset Inuit site dating from around 100 to 500 AD. Hours are 2 to 9 pm daily from early July to late August and admission is $2.

Grand Bay West Beach

If you want to hit the beach in Port aux Basques, you head down Grand Bay West Rd and turn onto Klye Lane just before crossing the third bridge. At the end of Klye Lane you'll find a small park overlooking a wide, sandy beach. This is also the start of the Cormack Trail to JT Cheeseman Provincial

Park. Across from the park is *Steve's Horse Rides* (☎ 695-3920) where you can saddle up for $10 an hour.

Places to Stay

Campers have a good place close to town, close enough to be convenient when arriving late or leaving early. The *JT Cheeseman Provincial Park* 12 km along the Trans Canada Hwy north of town has 102 camp sites for $8 a night. There are no showers but the park features a wide sweeping beach and hiking trails. Whale bones found on the beach are now displayed in the park.

At the *Heritage Home* (☎ 695-3240) guesthouse (three rooms) you can stay in bed almost until the ferry blows the whistle. It's at 11 Caribou Rd beside the dock, and singles/doubles cost $37/42 with a continental breakfast. Also nearby is *Four Seasons B&B* (☎ 695-3826) at 82 High St with four rooms that are $40/45.

Further out is *Caribou House* (☎ 695-3408), a B&B, at 30 Grand Bay Rd about three km from the ferry and bus terminals. Prices start at $42/45.

St Christopher's Hotel (☎ 695-7034) with a fine view from its hilltop location on Caribou Rd is a larger, commercial hotel offering more amenities and a dining room. It features a family rate of $59 for one to four people in a room.

The *Gulfside Inn* (☎ 695-7091) and *Hotel Port aux Basques* (☎ 695-2171) are near the Trans Canada Highway and offer the same $59 family rate as the competitor.

For more reasonable prices you'll have to hit the highway. *Tompkins Motel & Tourist Home* (☎ 955-2901) in Doyles, 34 km away, is a start with rooms in the house from just $20 and motel rooms for $30. Further up the road is *Chignic Lodge* (☎ 955-2880) at $36/45.

Places to Eat

The *Harbour Restaurant*, on Main St is close to the ferry terminal and has good views of the waterfront if you're waiting for the midnight boat. The menu is mainly fried chicken

or fish & chips. It opens at 7 am with breakfast specials under $3.

At 116 Main St is the *Tai Hong* for Chinese with full dinners for under $6 and not far away is a *Pizza Delight*. If you're heading off for a camp site and want some seafood, there's *Twin Town Fish Market*, at the end of Charles St.

Getting There & Away

Bus The CN Roadcruiser bus service (☎ 695-4216) leaves once a day at 8 am from the ferry dock terminal for the 904-km trip to St John's. The trip takes about 14 hours and costs $84 one way. You can stop at any of the towns along the way (and there are plenty of stops). Connections can be made in other towns with other, more local, bus companies which service destinations other than those on the main route to St John's covered by CN Roadcruiser.

Corner Brook has a number of smaller lines, in particular buses to Gros Morne National Park and the Northern Peninsula. One-way fare to Corner Brook is $28.

If you're going to Gros Morne and Woody Point, you're better off getting a ticket past Corner Brook to Deer Lake because the connections in Corner Brook are poor. The bus from Corner Brook to Deer Lake doesn't leave from the station at which the CN bus from Port aux Basques arrives, but is inconveniently located across town with no city bus connections. But the Viking bus from Corner Brook stops at the same station in Deer Lake as does the CN bus. There is one possible problem though. The Viking bus from Corner Brook doesn't always stop at Deer Lake unless the driver knows there are passengers waiting. So, telephone back to Corner Brook to let Viking know that you are there!

Ferry Marine Atlantic (☎ 695-7081) operates both the ferry routes from Nova Scotia to Newfoundland: one going to Argentia and this one to Port aux Basques.

From the beginning of June to the middle of September there is a minimum of two trips daily and often three a day. In midsummer, reservations are a good idea and can be made by calling the above number in Port aux Basques or Marine Atlantic's North Sydney office (☎ 702-794-5700), Nova Scotia. Generally one or two-days' notice is sufficient. Early morning or late night trips are usually less busy and, if you're walking or cycling, there shouldn't be any trouble.

The fare is $19, less for children and seniors, $58 per car, more with a trailer or camper. The night ferry, which departs at 11.30 pm, saves you the cost of lodging because you can sleep anywhere and everywhere on board. Upon boarding there is a rush to the decks to secure a comfortable, quiet location away from hallways and most traffic. Bring a sleeping bag or blanket and a towel, there are free showers on board. In the cafeteria there is even a microwave oven if you're pinching pennies and want to use you're own tea bag. Otherwise the food is reasonably priced.

If it's a warm night, the outside decks can be pleasant and there are a few benches that you can stretch out on. For those with extra cash, berths and cabins are also available.

There are two ferries plying this route. The newer, large MV *Caribou* with a 350-car capacity is very deluxe; it's like a cruise ship complete with bar and live entertainment, movies, nursery and cafeteria – the works. Much smaller is the MV *John Hamilton Gray* which is used only during the summer peak season. It's considerably smaller taking just 165 cars and, while not quite as comfortable, is certainly alright. Both ships take from five to six hours for the summer crossing, longer in winter – up to 7½ hours.

There are no longer ferries from Port aux Basques travelling the south coast of Newfoundland (see the Outports section later in this chapter).

AROUND PORT AUX BASQUES
Cape Ray
Located 14 km north of the Marine Ferry Terminal and adjacent to JT Cheeseman Provincial Park is the small community of Cape Ray. The coastal scenery here, a mix of a surf-pounding beach and rocky headlands, is

excellent and leads up to the Cape Ray lighthouse. Outside the lighthouse is a plaque commemorating the first transatlantic cable which was laid in 1856. The lightkeeper's house is now a craft shop and nearby is the site of a Dorset Inuit camp dating to around 400 BC to 400 AD.

Hiking
The Port aux Basques-southern Codroy area offers some interesting hikes, due in part to the Long Range Mountains. The **Cormack Trail** is a long trail under development that someday will stretch from Port aux Basques north to Flat Bay near Stephenville. In Port aux Basque, you can pick up the trail at Grand Bay West Beach where there is a trail map. From there it's an 11-km trek along the coast to JT Cheeseman Provincial Park. Signs direct you through Cape Ray and the trail resumes at the lighthouse, reaching the Red Rocks area in 4 km.

Table Mountain Trail begins on the Trans Canada Hwy opposite the exit to Cape Ray, where a 'Table Mountain Digital Project' sign marks a rough dirt road. The six-km trail is actually this rugged road (don't even think about driving up it) that leads to the top of the 518-metre-high flat-top mountain. On top are the ruins of a radar site, air strip and buildings that the USA put up during WWII. The hike is not hard but plan on three to four hours for the 12-km round-trip walk.

Starlite Trail is another access route into the Long Range Mountains. It's 31 km north of Port aux Basques on the Trans Canada Hwy near the community of Tompkins and is a one-way hike of two km to a high point where there are views of the Codroy Valley.

SOUTH COAST
The often ignored Hwy 470, which heads east out of Port aux Basques for about 50 km, is a fine short excursion. If you've got an afternoon or a day waiting for a ferry this is an ideal little side trip for those with transportation. Edging along the shoreline the road rises and falls over the rounded, eroded windswept terrain looking as though it's fol-

lowing a glacier that ploughed through yesterday. There's not a tree in sight, just the cool pools and ponds (some the size of lakes) left in the many dents in the rock and muskeg (undrained boggy land). Visible along the other side of the road are half a dozen evenly spaced fishing towns.

Isle aux Morts (Island of the Dead) came by its name through the many shipwrecks just offshore which have occurred over some 400 years. The astrolabe, a navigational device and prize of the museum in Port aux Basques was found here.

Between Burnt Islands and Diamond Cove you pass a stunning waterfall plunging out of the hills north of Hwy 470. Look for a small 'Scenic Hike' sign for the start of a boardwalk that winds to almost the base of the falls. At the end are four picnic tables.

The highlight of the trip is the last village along the road, **Rose Blanche**, a very pretty, traditional-looking village nestled in a little cove with a fine natural harbour – a perfect example of the classic Newfoundland fishing community. To reach the Rose Blanche Lighthouse, turn left at the Town Hall and fire station and follow the sideroad to the H&P Lounge. A 'Lighthouse' sign will direct you to a trail that winds its way up the rocky slopes to the historic structure.

The original stone lighthouse dating from 1873 is unique and has been partially restored. Climbing the stairs inside is like being in a dungeon. Along the way is a small restaurant, the *Hook, Line & Sinker*, accessible only by foot and a friendly, casual place recommended for a light meal or just a tea.

For those who long to go that one step further, a trip can be taken by boat (ask around the docks) across the bay to the smaller village of **Petites** which has a population of about 30 families. Here, and visible from the Rose Blanche Lighthouse, is probably the oldest wooden United church in North America (although now the Anglicans have taken over) dating from about 1860. It's a plain and simple church kept in excellent condition and has registers of births, deaths and marriages to pore over for details of local history.

For those without a vehicle, Gateway Bus Lines (☎ 695-3456) in Port aux Basques offers a five-hour tour of the South Coast and Rose Blanche. The cost is $15 and includes a meal.

Outports

'Outport' is the name given to any of the tiny coastal fishing villages accessible only by boat. Some are on one of the two major intra-provincial coastal ferry lines, others are not. These little communities represent some of the most remote settlements left in North America. Change is coming at an ever quickening pace, but for the moment these outports harbour the rough Newfoundland life at its most traditional. These villages clinging to the rocky coastlines are perhaps the best place to see the unique culture of the Newfoundland people of European blood born in Canada.

Marine Atlantic has two runs from Lewisporte up the coast of Labrador. But one heads directly to Happy Valley-Goose Bay which is hardly an outport, with soldiers from a handful of countries stationed there. This ferry takes vehicles and passengers. The other run is for passengers only and leapfrogs from one outport to the next. This is the boat to be on. For details see the Labrador and Lewisporte sections in this chapter.

For places to stay on the north coastal trip, ask around beforehand or just take a chance on arrival. You can always stay on the ferry if you're continuing on without a stopover. This can be tiring if you're doing it on the cheap: sleeping on the floor or in a chair can be pretty uncomfortable after a few days, especially if the sea is rough. On a longer trip consider a cabin, the prices actually are quite fair. Ask about stopovers and how long the ticket is good for.

For details and schedules, call Marine Atlantic (☎ 695-7081) in Port aux Basques or Marine Atlantic (☎ 1-800-563-7381) from elsewhere in Newfoundland.

South Coast

In 1995, Marine Atlantic ferry dropped its South Coast run from Port aux Basques to Terrenceville on the Burin Peninsula and with it went one of Newfoundland's great travel adventures.

The province, however, stepped in and is salvaging portions of the run. The Intra Province Ferry Service (☎ 643-5105) connects Rose Blanche and the outports of La Poile and Grand Bruit with a passenger-only boat leaving Rose Blanche at 3 pm on Monday, Wednesday, Friday and Saturday and 2 pm on Sunday. Round-trip fare is $8.

On Thursday the boat departs La Poile at 8 am and heads west, stopping at Grand Bruit and reaching Burgeo at 2.45 pm where it returns to La Poile. You can overnight in Grand Bruit at *Blue Mountain Cabins* (☎ 492-2753) or *Dutch Inn* (☎ 492-2730), where a room or a cabin is $50 for a single. In Burgeo there's *Burgeo Haven* (☎ 886-2544) with four rooms at $40/50. To continue east, ferry transport is planned from Burgeo to Francois and another run from Francois to Hermitage, which is connected by road to Harbour Breton. In both Burgeo and Harbour Breton, there is bus service to Corner Brook or Grand Falls on the Trans Canada Hwy. Keep in mind this ferry service is new and thus very susceptible to changes in schedules and routes.

Labrador

Labrador is that part of Newfoundland – three times the size of the island – that is adjacent to the Quebec mainland. The Strait of Belle Isle separates Labrador from the Newfoundland Island. This vast, rugged land is one of the last incompletely explored areas in the country and one of the largest, cleanest, natural areas anywhere. For this reason it is beginning to attract more and more visitors to its varied regions.

The geological base of Labrador is the ancient Laurentian Shield – possibly the oldest unchanged region on earth. It's thought the land looks much the same as it did before life on the planet began. Four great caribou herds, including the world's largest with some 750,000 head, migrate across Labrador to their calving grounds each year.

Until recently, small numbers of Inuit, Native Indians and longtime European descendants known as 'liveyers' were the only human residents. They lived in little villages dotted along the rocky coasts as they had done for centuries, eking out an existence fishing and hunting. The interior was virgin wilderness.

Today a new people, with a completely different outlook and lifestyle, has arrived. White southerners have been lured by the overwhelming and nearly untouched natural resources.

And so, not far away from the more-or-less traditional way of life of the original inhabitants, lie some of the world's most modern, sophisticated industrial complexes. Most of the development has been far inland, near the border of Quebec. Labrador City and Wabush, with the latest technology, are two towns that produce half of Canada's iron ore. Churchill Falls is the site of an enormous hydroelectric plant that supplies power for north-eastern USA.

Happy Valley-Goose Bay is an older settlement first established as an air force base in WWII. It's now mainly a supply centre, you can get there from Lewisporte, Newfoundland by ferry. These four centres are home to more than half of Labrador's population of 30,000.

The east coast, accessible by boat from Newfoundland, is also interesting. Tiny villages dot the coast all the way to the far north. As in western Newfoundland, with some planning you can take a unique trip on the supply ferries.

Camping is an option all across Labrador but is mostly done in a van or camper. Tenting is possible but be prepared: although summers can be pleasantly warm, even hot, this is often a cold, wet and windy place. The amount of accommodation has been steadily

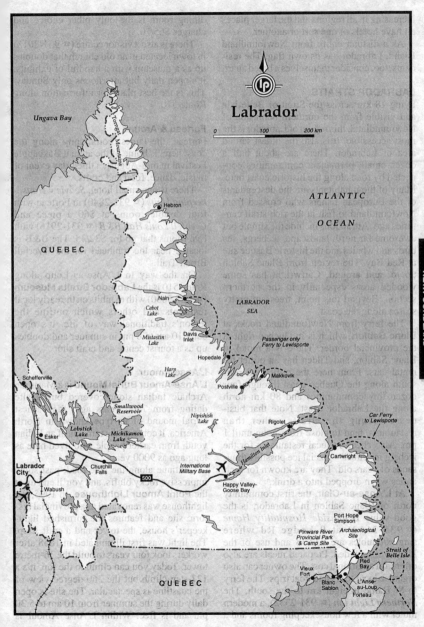

increasing in all regions and the larger places all have hotels of one sort or another.

As a distinct entity from Newfoundland Island, Labrador has its own flag. The residents, too, consider themselves a breed apart.

LABRADOR STRAITS

Lying 18 km across the Strait of Belle Isle and visible from the northern peninsula of Newfoundland, this region of Labrador is the most accessible. It is also the oldest settled area of Labrador. There are about half a dozen small, permanent communities connected by road along the historic coast here. Many of the inhabitants are the descendants of the European fishers who crossed from Newfoundland to fish in the rich strait centuries ago. Attractions include the simple but awesome far north landscape, icebergs, sea birds and whales and the historic Basque site at Red Bay. The region from Blanc Sablon up to, and around, Cartwright has some wooded areas especially in the northern section. Beyond this point, trees are pretty scarce along the coast.

The ferry from Newfoundland docks at **Blanc Sablon**, which is in Quebec right at the provincial border. There is a motel in Blanc Sablon, and Tilden has an outlet for rental cars. From here the only road runs south along the Quebec coast through four dozen tiny communities and 80 km north along the Labrador coast. Note that businesses along the straits, other than restaurants, tend to close from noon until 1 pm. Also check in local restaurants for the iceberg ice cubes – glacial ice possibly thousands of years old. They are known for their antics when dropped into a drink.

At **L'Anse-au-Clair**, the first community north of Blanc Sablon in Labrador, is the good-value *Beachside Hospitality Home* (☎ 931-2662) at 9 Lodge Rd where singles/doubles are $32/38 and use of the kitchen is included. Prepared meals are also offered at additional cost. The owner can also organise local tours and boat trips. The ferry to St Barbe is eight km to the south. The *Northern Light Inn* (☎ 931-2332), a modern motel with a few housekeeping rooms and a dining room is the only other choice and charges $65/70.

There is also a visitor centre (☎ 931-2013) in town located in an old church that doubles up as a museum with a handful of exhibits. It's open daily but afternoons only Sunday. This is the best place for information along Route 510.

Forteau & Around

Forteau, the largest community along the coast here, is home of the annual Bakeapple Festival in mid-August, a three-day event of music, dance, food and crafts.

There is one small hotel, *Seaview Housekeeping Units* (☎ 931-2840) in Forteau with four double rooms at $60 a piece and *Grenfell Louis Hall B&B* (☎ 931-2916) with five rooms that go for $32/35. The B&B is located near the trailhead for the Overfall Brook Trail.

On the way to L'Anse-au-Loup along Route 510 is the **Labrador Straits Museum** (☎ 927-5860) with exhibits on the early local residents and others which outline the region's traditional way of life. It's open daily 10 am to 8 pm in summer and doubles up as a tourist centre and craft shop.

L'Anse-Amour

L'Anse-Amour Burial Mound is a Maritime Archaic Indian stone-covered burial site dating from 7500 years ago, the earliest burial mound of its type known in North America. It contains the remains of an Indian youth from earlier people who lived here as long ago as 9000 years.

Continue along the side road, past some impressive rocky bluffs, and you'll end up at the **Point Amour Lighthouse**. In 1995, the lighthouse was renovated as a provincial historic site and features the furnished lightkeeper's house, the tower and a craft shop. The light was first illuminated in 1858 after workers took four years to build the 36-metre tower. Today you can climb to the top, it's a 127-step climb but the 360-degree view of the coastline is spectacular. The site is open daily during the summer from 10 am to 5.30 pm and is free. Within L'Anse Amour is

Davis B&B (☎ 927-5690) at $32/36, dinner upon request. The food is excellent and the couple are extremely knowledgeable about the area.

L'Anse-au-Loup

Between here and Red Bay is *Pinware River Provincial Park* with 15 camp sites for $8 a night and some picnic tables. Don't forget the insect repellent.

The best accommodation deal around is *Barney's Hospitality Home* (☎ 927-5634) with three rooms at $25/35 with a light breakfast included and other meals available at additional cost. Good meals can be obtained at *Beryl's Place*, open to 11.30 pm most nights.

From Pinware River Provincial Park to Red Bay, is some of the best scenery along Route 510. First you skirt the west side of the river, then cross over on a one-lane iron bridge and skirt the east from high above the rushing whitewater. This stretch of the Pinware is renowned for its salmon fishing and there are three lodges with guiding service in this area. Ten km from Red Bay, you enter a barren, rocky area that is full of blueberries and bakeapples in August.

Red Bay

Red Bay sits at the end of the road, Route 510, made distinctive by the rusting Quebec freighter in the harbour that ran aground in 1966. The National Historic Site here is the prime attraction of the region. The Red Bay Visitors Centre (☎ 920-2196) chronicles the discovery in the late 1970s of three Basque whaling galleons from the 1500s on the sea bed just off Red Bay. The ice-cold waters have kept them well preserved, making the area an underwater museum. Subsequent research has found that this was the largest whaling port in the world in the late 16th century, when more than 2,000 men resided here. Some of the excavated land sites can be visited by boat including a cemetery on nearby **Saddle Island** where there is a self-guided interpretive trail.

The visitors centre is open 9 am to 8 pm Monday through Saturday and noon to 8 pm on Sunday. Admission to the displays and video room is $2. The centre also runs the Saddle Boat tours at 10.30 am, 2 and 3.30 pm on Monday through Saturday and on demand on Sunday. Passage for the short ferry ride is $2.

Red Bay is also on the Marine Atlantic coastal ferry service route from Lewisporte and St Anthony. Accommodation amounts to a few cabins that are rented out at *Whaler's Restaurant* (☎ 920-2156), a very pleasant place to have a bowl of seafood chowder. The cabins are $65 single or double.

Hiking

There are a handful of pleasant dayhikes between Forteau and Cape Diable. The first is **Overfall Brook Trail** in the town of Forteau. The four-km trail is a one-way hike along the coast with views of the Point Armour Lighthouse in the distance. It ends at a 30-metre waterfall. East of the town is **Schooner Cove Trail**, a three-km trek from Route 510 to the cove that was once the site of Archaic Indians thousands of years ago and then a whaling factory.

On the west side of L'Anse-au Loup is **The Battery Trail**, a 2-km or 30-minute hike through a stunted tuckamore forest to the summit of the Battery, where a spectacular view of the Strait of Belle Isle can be enjoyed. Finally near Cape Diable is another marked hiking trail that climbs two km to a highpoint along a bluff.

Getting There & Away

Air Air Nova, an Air Canada partner, has flights from Deer Lake, Newfoundland, to Blanc Sablon. Also try Provincial Airlines from Corner Brook, Deer Lake or Happy Valley-Goose Bay. Blanc Sablon is also connected to Quebec destinations such as Sept Îles and Quebec City by Canadian Airlines and their partner Air Atlantic.

Ferry From 1 May to January, a vehicle and passenger ferry runs from St Barbe (Newfoundland) to Blanc Sablon (Quebec). It is operated by Northern Cruiser Limited (☎ 726-0015) out of St Barbe. From the

NEWFOUNDLAND

beginning of July to the end of August, when things are at their busiest, the boat runs two or three times a day, at other times service drops to once or twice daily. On Monday through Thursday and Saturday, the ferry leaves St Barber at 8.45 am. The two-hour trip is $8.50 per person, $17.25 for a car and more for trailers, vans etc.

A coastal freight service, the *Nordic Express*, operated by Relais Nordik Inc (☎ 968-4707 in Sept-Îles or 1-800-463-0680 from anywhere in north-western Quebec) runs up the Quebec coast from Sept-Îles on the Gulf of St Lawrence to Blanc Sablon with stops along the way.

The Marine Atlantic coastal service from Lewisporte on Notre Dame Bay, Newfoundland or St Anthony, Newfoundland up the Labrador coast makes a call at Red Bay as well but it's a passenger-only service. For details see the Lewisporte section earlier in this chapter.

Car The road running up and down the coast from Blanc Sablon is not connected to further destinations in either Quebec or Labrador. To the south, it continues for 74 km into an isolated area of Quebec known as the North Shore. Beyond Blanc Sablon, there are three villages; Middle Bay, St Paul and Vieux Fort, and they all have small stores that sell gasoline but not lodging. The scenery, however, is quite good. Within 19 km, you come to Brador River and cross it in front of an impressive waterfall thundering down into a narrow rocky gorge. From there the road climbs steeply into coastal headlands that feature a rocky, barren terrain. Several more waterfalls can be seen in the bluffs above before you reach an incredible viewing point high above the St Paul River. The town of St Paul is on the other side, 12 km from the end.

NORTHERN COAST

Beyond Red Bay all the way up to **Ungava Bay** are dozens of small semi-traditional communities and settlements accessible only by sea or air along the rugged, jagged and in some parts unspoiled mountainous coast.

This area of Labrador doesn't get a lot of visitors but offers the persistent a look at some of the most remote regions of North America.

Living off the land completely has pretty much disappeared especially now that the fishing industry has all but gone belly up. Between government moratoriums and lack of fish, making a wage from the sea is almost impossible. Some hunting and trapping is still carried on but these days unemployment is high and many people rely on government funds in one way or another. Still, the lifestyle remains unchanged in many ways due simply to the isolation and the small size of the villages. The people are a determined lot: they have to be.

The accommodation situation is a bit of an unknown as most travellers use the ferry as a floating hotel. For those wishing to get off and hang around somewhere until the next boat, it means winging it and asking around town for a spare bed.

Makkovik, an early fur-trading post, is a traditional fishing and hunting community. Both new and old-style crafts can be bought.

In **Hopedale** a National Historic Site preserves the old wooden Moravian mission from 1782. The site includes a store, residence, some huts and of course, the church. The *Hopedale Lodge* (☎ 933-3770 or 933-3833) has singles/doubles at $78/94 with meals at extra cost.

Nain

This is the last stop on the Marine Atlantic ferry and with a population of 1000 is the last town of any size as you go northward. Fishing is the main industry but the potentially massive Diamond Fields nickel mine nearby at Voisy Bay will obviously affect this community. As in the other smaller settlements, after the fishing season, hunting and trapping continue as they have for centuries. The **Piulimatsivik-Nain Museum** in one of the old mission houses, outlines both Inuit and Moravian history with artefacts relating to both traditions. Admission is free.

Again, there is a craft outlet and Nain has a hotel, the *Atsanik Lodge* (☎ 922-2910) at

⊕⊕⊕⊕⊕⊕⊕⊕⊕⊕⊕⊕⊕⊕⊕⊕⊕⊕⊕⊕⊕⊕⊕⊕⊕⊕⊕⊕⊕⊕⊕⊕⊕⊕⊕⊕⊕⊕

The Moravian Church
The Moravians developed in the mid-1400s as the Church of the Brotherhood. They broke from the Church of Rome and had to flee persecution in their place of origin, the then largely German-speaking provinces of Bohemia and Moravia, in what is now the Czech Republic. A strong evangelical movement, they set up missions in Asia, Africa, the West Indies, and North and South America.

Starting in the late 1700s they began ministering to the Inuit of the New World, doing some good but attempting to diminish the Native people's spirituality and culture at the same time. They were a prominent European group all along the Strait of Belle Isle on both the Newfoundland side and most notably on the coast of Labrador. They maintained an extensive mission community here until the 1950s. Many of their former buildings are still in use, some as historical sites. ■

⊕⊕⊕⊕⊕⊕⊕⊕⊕⊕⊕⊕⊕⊕⊕⊕⊕⊕⊕⊕⊕⊕⊕⊕⊕⊕⊕⊕⊕⊕⊕⊕⊕⊕⊕⊕⊕⊕

singles/doubles $73/84. There is often a guesthouse or two here as well.

North of Nain is another Moravian historic site in **Hebron**. Close to the northern tip of Labrador the wild **Torngat Mountains** are popular with climbers because of their altitude (some of the highest peaks east of the Rockies) and their isolation.

Getting There & Away
The Marine Atlantic passenger-only (no vehicles) ferry from Lewisporte, calls in at St Anthony on Newfoundland's northern tip and then 'bounces' along the Labrador coast from Red Bay, up into Goose Bay and then as far north as the town of Nain. Private vessels can be hired to reach still further north. This trip is really the only way to see something of isolated coastal Labrador and its changing older settlements. The trip length varies but is at least a week in each direction as the ferry drops in at somewhere between two dozen and over 40 communities unloading supplies and freight of every description. Space on this ferry is very limited and reservations must be made in Newfoundland. See the Lewisporte section earlier in this chapter.

CENTRAL LABRADOR
Making up the territorial bulk of Labrador, the central portion is an immense, very sparsely populated and ancient wilderness. Paradoxically, it also has the largest town in Labrador, Happy Valley-Goose Bay, in the south with a population of 7000.

Happy Valley-Goose Bay
Goose Bay was established during WWII as a staging point for planes on the way to Europe and has remained an aviation centre. Today there is a Canadian military base used by pilots from around Canada and Europe for testing high-tech planes, in particular controversial low-flying jets which the Innu say disturb their way of life.

The town has all the services including hotels but for the outsider there is not a lot to see or do and it is very isolated. The remote, forested landscape, however, attracts many anglers and hunters and there are numerous fly-in possibilities for camping.

For tourist information call the Mokami Regional Development Association (☎ 896-3100).

The **Labrador Heritage Museum** (☎ 896-2762) outlines some of the history of the area and includes a trapper's traditional shelter, samples of animal furs and some of the minerals found in Labrador. The museum is on the north side of town on the former Canadian Forces base.

At the **Northern Lights Military Museum** (☎ 896-5939), 170 Hamilton River Rd, some of the military history of the city is displayed. Also at the Northern Lights building visit the free Trappers Brook Animal Displays, lifelike displays of many of the animals and birds found in the region. Both exhibits are closed on Sunday.

Places to Stay & Eat The city has three fair-sized hotels, although none of them are cheap. The *Royal Inn* (☎ 896-2456) with singles/doubles from $57/67 is the most economical. It's at 5 Royal Ave and it also has some housekeeping units at a higher rate. There are also some hospitality homes but these seem to change quickly so try the tourist office lists. The *Davis' B&B* (☎ 896-5077) at 14 Cabot Crescent has two rooms for $35/45 with a light breakfast included.

The *Labrador Friendship Centre* (☎ 896-8302) is a native centre at 49 Grenfell St linked with Backpackers which offers rooms at $22. Meals are available, and if you are lucky you might be served caribou stew.

Getting There & Away To travel to Happy Valley-Goose Bay there is the choice of air, car or ferry.

Air Goose Bay is well served by air. Provincial Airlines serves Blanc Sablon and Goose Bay from Newfoundland's major towns. Labrador Airways connects to St Anthony and covers all the small communities along the Labrador coast.

Car From Happy Valley-Goose Bay, Hwy 500, which is a gravel road, runs westward through the heart of Labrador to Churchill Falls and then forks. Hwy 500 continues south to Wabush, Labrador City and Fermont, Quebec.

The road makes the entire inland area auto accessible for the first time. Drivers can take vehicles on the ferry from Happy Valley-Goose Bay to Newfoundland allowing for a complete circuit of the region. Potential users note that this road should only be travelled between June and October and that services are minimal. In fact between Happy Valley-Goose Bay and far western Labrador services are available only at towns. There are no road-side service stations. This makes for some pretty long stretches without a coffee or any other critical requirements.

The drive from Goose Bay to Labrador City takes about nine hours. The section between Goose Bay and Churchill Falls is rough and slow.

Cars can be rented in Happy Valley-Goose Bay at Avis and Tilden both with desks at the airport but not for travel on Hwy 500 due to its rough conditions.

Ferry The slow coastal service from Lewisporte ties in here but there is also a more direct car ferry from Lewisporte which makes the trip to Goose Bay direct or with just a stop at Cartwright on the way. See the Lewisporte section earlier in this chapter for details on this marathon 35 to 38-hour ferry ride.

WESTERN LABRADOR
Accessible from Quebec, everything in this area of Labrador is oversized in the extreme: mega-developments in a mega-landscape which the visitor can explore relatively easily.

Remember that there is a one-hour time difference between Quebec and Labrador City.

Labrador City/Wabush
These twin mining cities with a collective population of 12,000, just 15 km from Quebec, represent modern, industrial Labrador. The largest open-pit iron ore mine in the world is in Labrador City. Since 1958 a modern town has developed around this mine. Another open-pit mine operates in Wabush. You can tour both facilities. All the resource development in this part of the world is colossal in scale as the tours will reveal. Eighteen-metre-long dumptrucks with three-metre-high tyres are almost like absurd works of art.

There is a regional tourist chalet (☎ 944-7132) in Labrador City in the Arts & Cultural Centre which will help with information on Churchill Falls and other local spots as well as answering questions about the cities here.

The **Height of Land Heritage Centre** (☎ 944-2209) in a former bank is a museum. Also, paintings by Tom Thompson may be seen in the Labrador City Town Hall.

Most people want to see the land away from town and you don't have to go far to do that. The landscape, a vast expanse of low, rolling, forested mountains interspersed with areas of flat northern tundra, was scraped down by glaciers.

The **Wapusakatto Mountains** are just five km from town and parts have been developed for skiing. About 10 km from Labrador City is **Duley Lake Provincial Park** which even has a wide, long sandy beach and good swimming. There are 100 camping sites here too. Another park, 43 km from Wabush, on the Trans-Labrador Hwy is **Grand Hermine** also with a beach, tent sites for $10 a night and some fine scenery.

The 15-km-long Menihek hiking trail goes through wooded areas with waterfalls as well as open tundra. Outfitters can take anglers to excellent fishing waters.

Bus tours of the towns or surroundings are available. A real treat is the free lightshow – the aurora borealis, also called the northern lights – about two nights out of every three. Northern Canada is the best place in the world to see them because the magnetic north pole is here. Evidently these other-worldly coloured, waving beams are charged particles from the sun which are trapped in the earth's magnetic field.

Inuit belief is that the shimmering lights are the sky people playing a game of ball. Another is that the lights are unborn children playing. The Ojibway called the lights Waussnodae and believed them to be torches held by their dead grandfathers to light the way along the Path of Souls. The souls of the recently deceased walked this path, the Milky Way, to their final resting place.

Places to Stay & Eat There are several somewhat pricey hotels and motels, some with dining rooms. In Labrador City on Avalon Drive is the *Two Seasons Inn* (☎ 944-2661 or 800-670-7667) with singles/doubles for $77/82. The *Carol Inn* (☎ 944-7736) at 215 Drake Ave has 23 housekeeping units where you can do your own cooking at $75/85. The *Wabush Hotel* (☎ 282-3221) is the same price. Advance booking is recommended for all places. Ask around for guesthouses but don't bet on finding one.

Most of the eight or so restaurants are in Labrador City and include a couple of pizza places and *Ted's Pub*. Fish and sometimes caribou show up on menus.

Churchill Falls
Not quite halfway to Goose Bay is modern Churchill Falls. It is built around one of the largest hydroelectric generating stations in the world which was developed in the early 1970s. The diverted Churchill River falling over a 300-metre ledge powers the underground turbines and kicks out 550 megawatts, enough to supply almost the entire needs of the New England states. It's quite a piece of engineering. Tours (☎ 709-925-3211) are offered but must be booked at least one day in advance.

The town is connected by Hwy 500 to Goose Bay to the east and to Wabush to the west.

Banking, laundry, car repair and gasoline can all be taken care of in Churchill. This is the only place between Goose Bay and Labrador City with any services or supplies, so stock up.

For accommodation there is the central *Churchill Falls Inn* (☎ 925-3211) with a coffee shop and bar; booking ahead is recommended. Singles/doubles start at $72/82.

Getting There & Away Transportation here in central and western Labrador, while improving in giant strides, is still an adventure in itself.

Air Several airlines connect with Labrador City including Canadian Airlines with their regional partner Air Atlantic from Newfoundland and the rest of Canada. Air Alliance flies in from Quebec City.

Car Hwy 500 from Happy Valley-Goose Bay continues from just west of Churchill Falls south to Wabush and Labrador City and then to Fermont, Quebec. From there it becomes the mainly surfaced (with some fine gravel sections) Hwy 389 and then continues for 581 km south through the little-developed northern Manicougan District of Quebec, past Manic 5 with its huge dam to Labrador City. It can be driven in one day, but it's a long day. Some sections are slow due to roughness or the narrow winding road but it is generally smoother and in better

NEWFOUNDLAND

shape than the one from Goose Bay to Churchill Falls. Some small bridges are one-way traffic only.

There are motels and campgrounds along the way, for example at Manic 5, and a motel, restaurant and service station at Bassin Manic 5. For those going north from Baie Comeau, road conditions can be checked with the provincial police in that town. For those going south, if you are in any doubt or are wondering about updates or road improvements the police in Labrador can help.

Back at the Hwy 500 fork at Churchill Falls, a northern branch, the No 501, continues to Esker. Esker, halfway between Labrador City and Schefferville where the road ends, is really nothing more than a train station.

Tilden and Avis have offices in Wabush but cars may not be driven on Hwy 500.

Train Western Labrador is also accessible by rail. The route begins at Sept-Îles, Quebec (even further east than Baie Comeau). From there catch the Quebec North Shore & Labrador railway to Labrador City or beyond to Esker and Schefferville back in Quebec.

There are no other train routes in Labrador. With the opening of the road from Happy Valley-Goose Bay to Labrador City/Wabush the train is accessible to the eastern portion of Labrador.

In Labrador City the Quebec North Shore and Labrador railway station (☎ 944-8205) is at Airport Rd. The one-way adult fare to Sept-Îles is $49. Through the summer there are two departures weekly. The train has a snack car for light lunches.

See the Sept-Îles section in the Quebec chapter for more details of the train and trips around the Labrador City area.

Nova Scotia

In Nova Scotia, you're never more than 56 km from the sea, a feature which has greatly influenced the history and character of the province.

For generations the rugged coastline, with its countless bays and inlets, has provided shelter for small fishing villages, especially along the southern shores.

Inland, much of the province is covered with forest, while low hills roll across the north. The Annapolis Valley, famous for its apples, is gentle, scenic farm country – beautiful in springtime with lovely pink and white blossoms. The area also contains some of Canada's oldest and most captivating historical features.

The Bay of Fundy region is dominated by the world's highest tides. Along the impressive Northumberland Strait, wide sandy beaches washed by the warmest waters around the province offer a place to relax for a day or two.

The typical Maritime scenes and towns along the coast give way to Halifax-Dartmouth, one of the country's most attractive major metropolitan areas – a modern, cosmopolitan urban centre that retains an historic air.

Visiting rugged and mountainous Cape Breton Island, which shows another side of the varied topography, is the highlight of a trip to Nova Scotia.

Nova Scotia gets more visitors annually than any of the other Atlantic Provinces and its excellent travel-information network is well geared to tourists. In general, prices are a little higher here than in much of the Atlantic region and many of the lodgings and restaurants are a little more upmarket and sophisticated.

History
When Europeans first arrived in what was to become Nova Scotia, much of the land was inhabited by the Micmac Indians, the dominant people of the Atlantic region.

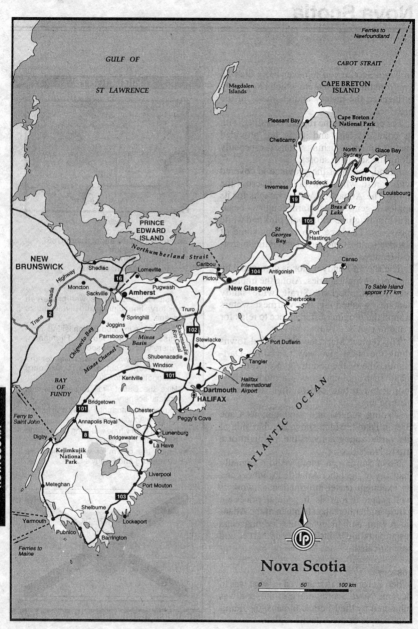

GULF OF

ST LAWRENCE

CABOT STRAIT

Ferries to
Newfoundland

Magdalen
Islands

CAPE BRETON
ISLAND

Pleasant Bay

Cape Breton
National Park

Cheticamp

North
Sydney

Glace Bay

Inverness

Baddeck

Sydney

19

Louisbourg

Bras d'Or
Lake

PRINCE
EDWARD
ISLAND

St Georges
Bay

105

Port
Hastings

Northumberland Strait

Canso

NEW
BRUNSWICK

Shediac

Caribou

To Sable Island
approx 177 km

Lomeville

16

Pictou

104

Antigonish

Highway

Moncton

Pugwash

Sackville

Amherst

New Glasgow

Trans

Canada

2

Springhill

Truro

Sherbrooke

Joggins

Chignecto Bay

Parrsboro

Minas Basin

102

Stewiacke

Port Dufferin

Minas Channel

Shubenacadie

Tangier

BAY
OF
FUNDY

Windsor

Kentville

101

Ferry to
Saint John

Bridgetown

Halifax
International
Airport

Dartmouth

101

Chester

HALIFAX

Digby

Annapolis Royal

Peggy's Cove

8

Bridgewater

Lunenburg

ATLANTIC OCEAN

Kejimkujik
National
Park

La Have

Meteghan

Liverpool

Port Mouton

103

Shelburne

Yarmouth

Lockeport

Pubnico

Barrington

Ferries to
Maine

Nova Scotia

0   50   100 km

The French created the first settlement at Port Royal in 1605 calling it Acadia.

Despite it changing hands with the English several times in the following 100 years, there were really no major British communities until the founding of Halifax in 1749. It was to here the first settlers and pirates came, followed by a contingent of Germans to the Lunenburg area. The Highland Scots landed in familiar-looking Cape Breton in 1773 and thousands more Scots followed to settle Nova Scotia, which means 'New Scotland'. In the late 1700s thousands of Loyalists and a significant number of US and Jamaican Blacks swelled the population.

The 1800s brought prosperity through lumbering and shipbuilding, especially for the export markets, and coal mining began.

Nova Scotia was one of the original provinces of Canada to join Confederation in 1867.

European immigration mushroomed after the two world wars and Nova Scotia entered the modern period.

Climate

The sea tends to keep the weather moderate. Summer and autumn are usually sunny, though the eastern areas and Cape Breton are often windy. Rain is heaviest on the east coast. The entire southern coast from Shelburne to Canso is often wrapped in a morning fog, which may take until noon or later to burn off. Winters can be very snowy.

Economy

A visitor may not notice it but manufacturing, mostly resource based, is the most important industry. Agriculture – with dairying, fruit and Christmas trees being the main products – is a significant part of the economy. Fishing remains important, with Lunenburg maintaining a major east coast fleet.

The catch includes cod, lobster and scallops. Nova Scotia, along with Newfoundland, has been hit hardest by the decline in fish stocks and the resulting moratorium on most cod fishing.

Mining, shipbuilding, tourism, and crafts are also major money makers.

Population & People

Many of the Micmac people remain on their original lands in Cape Breton. In other areas, French culture and language live on. But the majority (about 75%) of the province's people are of English, Scottish and Irish descent. In a few places you can still hear Gaelic spoken.

Information

Provincial Symbols The provincial flower is the mayflower, and the provincial bird is the osprey.

Tourist Offices Tourism Nova Scotia (☎ 1-800-565-0000 in Canada and 1-800-341-6096 from continental North America) operates the provincial information offices which are located in Halifax and five other strategic locations across the province. The mailing address is PO Box 519, Halifax B3J 2R7.

They have designated 10 different road routes through the province which best show the scenery and sights. These routes are generally on older, smaller roads, not the main highways, and each is marked with roadside symbols. A free booklet detailing all the routes is available and is worth having. Publications also detail accommodation and camping.

Telephone The area code for the province is 902.

Time Nova Scotia is on Atlantic Time.

Tax The provincial sales tax is 11%.

Activities

Aside from the varied seaside topography and intriguing history, Nova Scotia offers an assortment of good outdoor possibilities. The provincial tourist agency general guide provides some information on many activities with suggestions on where to look for further details.

Cycling is excellent in parts of the province, particularly around Cape Breton Island. Rentals are available around the province.

Due to the vast number of waterways, canoeing in the province is excellent. For paddling information visit the Nova Scotia Government Bookstore (☎ 424-7580) at 1700 Granville St, Halifax.

Sea-kayaking is becoming increasingly popular and outfitters are found at numerous coastal towns around the province.

For hiking, the national and provincial parks contain easy and strenuous trails. The Nova Scotia Government Bookstore also has good hiking reference books.

Also popular is whale watching along the Digby Neck area and along the north shore of Cape Breton. Diving is good all around the coast including Halifax Harbour.

Other outdoor pursuits include bird watching, rockhounding, fossil searching, and freshwater and deep-sea fishing.

Accommodation

Nova Scotia has a wide range of lodgings from backcountry camp sites to fine, historic inns and modern hotels. July and August are by far the busiest months during which time accommodation can be scarce in much of the province. The central and South Shore regions of the province are not as popular as the other areas, however, finding a room each night before dark is always recommended. From October to May many attractions, campgrounds and guesthouses are closed.

Halifax

Halifax sits by one of the world's largest natural harbours, midway along Nova Scotia's south Atlantic shore. With a population of 114,450 and nearly three times that in the surrounding metropolitan area, this, the capital of Nova Scotia, is the largest city east of Montreal. The historic central district, never more than a few blocks from the water is, however, pleasingly compact. Modern buildings nestle amongst heritage structures interspersed with numerous green areas and parks.

The port is the busiest on the east coast partially because it's a year-round harbour – ice forces most others to close in winter. Other major industries are manufacturing, oil refining and food processing. Canada's largest naval base is also here.

Residents are known as Haligonians.

History

Halifax's interesting history is longer than that of other Canadian cities. The area was first settled by Micmac Indians, and Halifax itself was founded in 1749 as a British stronghold with the arrival of 2500 people. The town was actually to be a military base counterbalancing the French fort at Louisbourg on Nova Scotia's south-east tip.

The harbour was used as a British naval base during the American Revolution (1775-83) and the War of 1812. During both world wars, Halifax was a distribution centre for supply ships heading for Europe, a function which brought many people to the city.

In 1917 a French munitions ship, the *Mont Blanc*, carrying a cargo of TNT collided with another ship in the harbour. The result, known as the Great Explosion, was the biggest explosion prior to the A-bombs being dropped on Japan in 1945.

The city was the home of Canada's first representative government, first Protestant church and first newspaper.

Orientation

The city lies on a peninsula between the harbour and an inlet called the North West Arm. The downtown area is hilly and there are parks everywhere. From Citadel Hill there are views of the town and waterfront – if the city is not lost in one of the frequent fogs.

The downtown area, dating from the earliest settlement, extends from Lower Water St on the waterfront and west up to the Citadel, a star-shaped fort on the hill. Cogswell St to the north and Spring Garden Rd to the south mark the other boundaries of

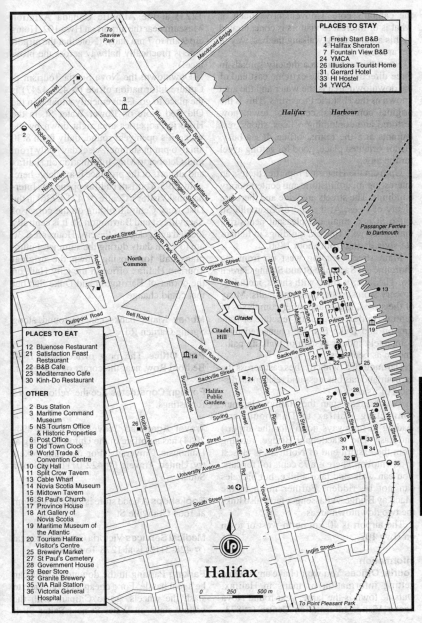

PLACES TO STAY

1 Fresh Start B&B
4 Halifax Sheraton
7 Fountain View B&B
24 YMCA
26 Illusions Tourist Home
31 Gerrard Hotel
33 HI Hostel
34 YWCA

PLACES TO EAT

12 Bluenose Restaurant
21 Satisfaction Feast Restaurant
22 B&B Cafe
23 Mediterraneo Cafe
30 Kinh-Do Restaurant

OTHER

2 Bus Station
3 Maritime Command Museum
5 NS Tourism Office & Historic Properties
6 Post Office
8 Old Town Clock
9 World Trade & Convention Centre
10 City Hall
11 Split Crow Tavern
13 Cable Wharf
14 Novia Scotia Museum
15 Midtown Tavern
16 St Paul's Church
17 Province House
18 Art Gallery of Novia Scotia
19 Maritime Museum of the Atlantic
20 Tourism Halifax Visitor's Centre
25 Brewery Market
27 St Paul's Cemetery
28 Government House
29 Beer Store
32 Granite Brewery
33 VIA Rail Station
36 Victoria General Hospital

Halifax Harbour

Passanger Ferries to Dartmouth

Citadel

Citadel Hill

Halifax Public Gardens

Halifax

0   250   500 m

To Point Pleasant Park

the capital's core. Conveniently, much of what is of interest to visitors is concentrated in this area, making walking the best way to get around.

From this central area the city spreads in three directions. At the extreme east end of the downtown area is the water and the area known as the Historic Properties. This is the original commercial centre of town, now restored and containing offices, shops, restaurants and the tourist office. It's a busy, visitor-oriented place, good for getting a feel for the city.

Up from the Historic Properties there's an interesting mix of historic and contemporary buildings. The streets are wide and there are plenty of trees. At the end of Granville St, Duke St is a small but pleasant pedestrian mall, lined with fine old buildings in Italianate-style dating from about 1860.

Main streets leading west up from the shoreline are Sackville St and Spring Garden Rd. The latter is lined with shops, including grocery stores, restaurants and malls. Many of the stores, hotels and other complexes of central Halifax, around the juncture of Barrington and Duke Sts, are connected by a completely indoor system of walking paths known as pedways.

Dartmouth, a twin city, lies east across the harbour and has business and residential districts of its own.

Two bridges span the Halifax Harbour, connecting Halifax to Dartmouth and leading to highways north (for the airport) and east. The Macdonald Bridge, running from the eastern end of North St, is closest to downtown. There is a 75 cents toll for cars. You can walk and take a bike, but bicycles can not be ridden. Further north is the MacKay Bridge. A passenger ferry also links the two downtown areas.

The airport is 40 km north-west of town on Hwy 102.

Information

Tourist Offices You won't have any trouble getting information or maps in Halifax. Outside town is the large, year-round Nova Scotia Visitor Information Centre (☎ 873-

1223) at the Atlantic Canada Aviation Museum near the airport on Hwy 102. Hours are 9 am to 7 pm daily. (Note that the airport here is practically halfway across the province!)

Downtown, the Nova Scotia Tourism & Culture information office (☎ 424-4247) is the place to go. Conveniently situated in the Old Red Store on Lower Water St, in the Historic Properties area right down by the water, it's open year round, daily from 8.30 am to 6 pm in summer, weekdays only from mid-October to May. Information on Halifax and all parts of the province is available here.

In 1995, Tourism Halifax opened its International Visitor's Centre (☎ 421-8736) in the Discovery Centre building on the corner of Sackville St and Barrington St. It is centrally located and geared to the city. Hours are 8.30 am to 8 pm daily during the summer. Future plans call for closing down the original Tourism Halifax office in the City Hall, on the corner of Barrington and Duke Sts, but that could change.

Money Major banks can be found along Spring Garden Rd.

Post Office The post office is at 1680 Bedford Row, near the corner of George St.

Foreign Consulates See the Yellow Pages for listings.

Travel Agencies Travel CUTS (☎ 494-2054) has an office in the Union Building at Dalhousie University. For discount tickets try United Travels (☎ 422-0111) in Scotia Square.

Bookshops A good store is The Book Room at 1664 Granville St.

Medical Services Victoria General Hospital (☎ 428-2110) is at 1278 Tower Rd.

Parking Parking in the downtown area can be a real hassle. For a cheap, central place to stash the wheels, go to Citipark with the yellow signs on Water St near Salter St. It will take campervans and has an all-day ticket for $5. From 4 pm through the night the flat rate is $3.

The Historic Properties

The Historic Properties is a group of restored buildings dating from 1800 to 1905. They were used in the original settlement of Halifax and now represent the town's seafaring past. Many of the buildings here are long two-storey places for easy storing of goods and cargo. Most now house shops and boutiques but there are also restaurants and bars.

Privateer's Warehouse, dating from 1800, is the oldest building in the area. Pirates brought their booty here for dealing and storage, hence the name. (The privateers were government-sanctioned and sponsored pirates who fed off the 'enemy'.) Among the other vintage buildings are the **Old Red Store** – once used for shipping operations – and a sail loft, now the tourist office.

Simon's Warehouse, built in 1850 of granite, was used as an office and warehouse building. It was also once used for storing liquor, and later by a junk and salvage dealer. Along the renovated dock area is the ferry to Dartmouth, which costs $1.10, and some of the 3500 commercial vessels that tie up here each year.

The blue **cable wharf** building along the pier by the ferry terminal is a centre for handicrafts and souvenirs. There are a couple of offices for boat tours, including the McNabs Island ferry.

Often moored at the wharf by Privateer's Warehouse is the *Bluenose II*, a replica of Canada's best-known boat.

The original *Bluenose* schooner was built in 1921 in Lunenburg and never lost a race in 20 years. In tribute, the 10-cent coin bears the schooner's image. The *Bluenose* has become nearly as familiar a Canadian symbol as the maple leaf.

The *Bluenose II* was launched in 1963 and now has a permanent berth at the Historic Properties when not on display at other Canadian ports. Two-hour harbour tours are given on the schooner, but when it's docked

you can walk on board to look at this beautiful piece of work for free.

Maritime Museum of the Atlantic

This large museum (☎ 424-7490) is a must for boat buffs but also has enough interesting displays to warrant a peek by anyone. It's spacious and contains full-scale examples of many regional vessels, with plenty of models, photographs and historical data as well. The lens from a Halifax lighthouse is impressive as are the painted figureheads taken from various ships, many of them wrecks. Also good is a portion of a boat you can enter which sways realistically as though out on the sea. There is a display on the *Titanic* and another on the Great Explosion.

The museum is open from 9.30 am to 5.30 pm Monday to Saturday (until 8 pm on Tuesday) and from 1 to 5.30 pm on Sunday. It's at 1675 Lower Water St, to the south of the Historic Properties, and admission is $3 or $6.50 per family.

Outside at the dock you can explore the CSS *Acadia*, a retired survey vessel from England. Also docked here is the HMCS *Sackville*, the last of 122 warships of its kind. It can be boarded daily, with donations going to its much-needed restoration work.

Ocean Touch Tank

Located near the HMCS *Sackville* at the dock area at the foot of Prince St, the small but popular touch tank affords landlubbers the opportunity of feeling a range of live sea mammals and plants. University students are on hand to answer questions and make handling suggestions. The tank is open daily from 10.30 am to 8.30 pm during good weather in July and August and until 3.30 pm in June.

Brewery Market

Also part of the restored waterfront, this complex is in the Keith's Brewery building (dating from 1820) at 1489 Hollis St. It now contains boutiques, restaurants and a couple of pubs. A farmers' market is held on the lower level on Friday and Saturday from 7

A Christmas Tree for Boston

Few cities have experienced such a sudden and unexpected turning point in their history as Halifax did with the Great Explosion. The day it occurred, 6 December 1917, was bright and clear and WWI was raging somewhere overseas in Europe, not in Canada.

Even after the two boats collided, the *Mont Blanc* – a French munitions ship filled with 300 rounds of ammunition, 10 tonnes of gun cotton and 180,000 kg of TNT – did not immediately explode. Rather it caught fire and its crew, only too aware of her cargo, took to lifeboats and rowed to Dartmouth. The ship then drifted unattended towards Halifax, drawing spectators to the waterfront to watch the spectacle.

At 9.05 am the ship exploded in a blinding white flash, the largest man-made explosion before the nuclear age. More than 1900 people were killed and 9000 injured. Almost all of the north-end of Halifax, roughly 130 hectares, was levelled. Most of the buildings and homes that were not destroyed by the explosion burned to the ground due to winter stock piles of coal in the cellars.

All 3000 tonnes of the *Mont Blanc* was shattered into little pieces. The barrel of one of the guns was found five km away, and the anchor shank, which weighed more than a tonne, flew three km in the other direction. The blast was felt as far away as Sydney, Cape Breton. The misery was compounded when Halifax was hit by a blizzard the following day that dumped 40 cm of snow on the city.

Relief efforts were immediate and money poured in from as far away as New Zealand and China. But most Haligonians remember the generosity of the USA state of Massachusetts, which donated $750,000 and instantly sent an army of volunteers and doctors to help in the recovery. Halifax was so grateful for the assistance in its hour of despair, that the city still sends a Christmas tree to the city of Boston every year as a token of appreciation. ∎

am to 1 pm in summer, and on Saturday only the rest of the year.

Historic Downtown Area

The tourist office has maps for a self-guided walking tour of the Historic Properties, the waterfront boardwalk and the old buildings west up the hill from the water. Most of the buildings which made up the early commercial area are marked with plaques giving a brief history. Using the map, it takes about an hour to do the circuit. Descriptions of some of the best sights follow.

Province House On Hollis St near Prince St, this fine example of Georgian architecture has been the home of Canada's oldest provincial legislature since 1819. There are free guided tours (☎ 424-4661) Monday to Friday from 9 am to 5 pm and on weekends from 10 am to 4 pm.

Government House This is between Hollis and Barrington Sts, near the corner of Bishop St. Government House has been the residence of the provincial lieutenant-governor

since 1807 (making it Canada's oldest). It was built by Governor John Wentworth.

St Paul's Cemetery Also known as the Old Burying Ground, the cemetery, first used in 1749, is across the street from Government House on Barrington St.

St Paul's Church St Paul's is on Barrington St near Prince St. It was the first Protestant church in Canada (dating from 1749) and the first church of British origin in the new land. It's open to visitors Monday to Friday from 9 am to 4.30 pm and on Saturday during the summer. A guide is on hand to answer questions. There are some intriguing curiosities here, such as the silhouette cast by a certain hole in the stained glass. Another is the piece of metal lodged above the door in the north wall, inside the porch. This is a piece of the *Mont Blanc* which exploded three km away in Halifax Harbour in 1917.

City Hall Built in 1890 at the opposite end of the sunken courtyard from St Paul's Church, City Hall is a gem of Victorian architecture. Visitors can join the mayor for tea Monday

NOVA SCOTIA

to Thursday from 3.30 to 4.30 pm in July and August.

Old Town Clock At the top of George St, at Citadel Hill, stands one of the city's most distinct symbols, the Old Town Clock. The inner workings arrived in Halifax in 1803 after being built in London, England. The tower was erected to a design by Prince Edward, the Duke of Kent, then Commander of the Citadel.

Citadel National Historic Site
The Citadel (☎ 426-5080), a huge, oddly angled fort on top of Halifax's big central hill, has always been the city's towering landmark. In 1749, with the founding of Halifax, construction of a citadel began.

In the mid-1750s, the British realised that the crunch was coming with France over possession of the new land. Halifax was a good location for British purposes: it could be used as a centre for ruling over Nova Scotia and, more importantly, as a military base from which to deal with the French, who had forts of their own in Louisbourg and Quebec City.

The fort that exists now was built between 1828 and 1861 and is actually the fourth one on the site. It is open daily from 9 am to 6 pm in summer, and from 9 am to 5 pm from early September to the middle of June. Admission is $3 in summer, free the rest of the year. The guided tours which include theatrical presentations are recommended. The guide will explain the fort's shape and how, despite appearances, it was not very well designed or constructed.

Also in the compound is the Army Museum, with exhibits relating to Atlantic Canada's military history.

Citadel Hill is a good park and a popular sunbathing spot. There are excellent views in all directions.

Nova Scotia Museum of Natural History
The Nova Scotia Museum is not actually a single museum but rather a series of them scattered around the province. This one (☎ 424-7353), at 1747 Summer St, west of the Citadel, is considered the headquarters of the provincial system. History, wildlife, geology, people and industry are all covered. The three-dimensional animal exhibits are excellent – you feel you can reach out and touch the displays. The fish-of-Nova Scotia exhibit is also well presented. There's a good history section, with an old stagecoach and a working model of a late-1800s sawmill.

From 1 June to 15 October it is open Monday to Saturday from 9.30 am to 5.30 pm (Wednesday to 8 pm) and on Sunday from 1 to 5.30 pm. Through the above months, admission is $3. The rest of the year it's free but closes at 5 pm each day and is closed Monday.

Maritime Command Museum
This museum (☎ 427-8250) is on the Canadian Forces Base (CFB Halifax), off Gottingen St between North and Russell Sts, near Macdonald Bridge. It's in the fine-looking stone building on large grounds protected by numerous cannons. You'll see mementos like uniforms, medals, etc from the military past of the Maritimes. It's open Monday to Friday from 9.30 am to 6 pm, Saturday and Sunday from 1 to 5 pm. Admission is free.

Art Gallery of Nova Scotia
The provincial Art Gallery (☎ 424-7542) is housed in the restored heritage Dominion Building of 1868 (once used as the post office), at 1741 Hollis St, across from Province House. Provincial and other Canadian works make up much of the large collection. There are both permanent and changing exhibits. Admission is $2.50 (free on Tuesday). During the summer the gallery is open Tuesday to Friday from 10 am to 5.30 pm, until 9 pm on Thursday and noon to 5 pm on Saturday and Sunday. There are tours daily at 2 pm in July and August.

Micmac Heritage Gallery
Owned and operated by the Micmac people, the gallery (☎ 422-9509) exhibits and sells a range of traditional and contemporary work by Native craftspeople, artisans and artists.

Two traditional skills, basketry and decorating with porcupine quills, are shown to good advantage in a number of different applications. The contemporary art gallery shows work from across the country.

The gallery is found in the Barrington Place Shops complex on the Granville Level, 1903 Barrington St.

Discovery Centre

The Discovery Centre (☎ 492-4422) is a hands-on science centre that in 1995 moved to a new location on the corner of Sackville St and Barrington St. On the first floor is the Tourism Halifax International Visitors Centre. The museum occupies the next two floors and is mainly geared to kids, featuring a range of hands-on exhibits in chemistry, physics and the like.

The centre is open Monday to Saturday from 10 am to 5 pm, Thursday until 9 pm, and Sunday from 1 to 5 pm. Outside the summer season it is closed on Monday (unless it is a school holiday). Admission is $4 per adult, $2.50 for children.

Nova Scotia Sport Heritage Centre

Essentially a sports hall of fame, the centre (☎ 421-1266) is at 1646 Granville St, Suite 101 in the Centennial Building. It deals with provincial heroes and teams through displays of trophies and photographs. Some of the old equipment is fun to look at. It's open Monday to Friday from 8.30 am to 4.30 pm and admission is free.

Halifax Public Gardens

The public gardens are a small but pleasant well-kept formal Victorian city park on the corner of South Park St and Spring Garden Rd. The park has a reputation as one of the finest Victorian-style gardens in North America. Bands give concerts in the gazebo on Sunday afternoon throughout the summer.

Point Pleasant Park

Point Pleasant Park is highly recommended. Walking trails, picnic spots, a restaurant, a beach and an old Martello tower – a round defence structure – are all found within this 75-hectare wooded sanctuary. There are lots of joggers and sunbathers in the popular park, and good views all the way around the perimeter. No cars are allowed.

The park is at the far southern end of town, at the tip of the peninsula. The No 9 bus links the park with the downtown Scotia Centre until 9 pm, or you can drive to the park's edge. Whichever way you come, check out the size of the houses along Young St.

At the city edge of the park is the Port of Halifax, a very busy terminal with containers piled high. Walk out to the lighthouse by the port for great views and a peek at the shipping activity; kids will be tossing in lines hoping for the big catch.

An interesting historical aside is that the park still belongs to the British government, which has rented it out on a 999-year lease at the rate of 10 cents per year.

York Redoubt

The remains of a 200-year-old fort make up this National Historic Site which overlooks the harbour from a bluff just south of the North West Arm (south of the centre). It was designed to protect the city from attack by sea and is built at the narrowest point of the outer harbour. The site was used in various capacities by the military as late as 1956.

Aside from the view, there are mounted guns, a Martello tower and historical information and displays. The grounds are open all year but the buildings are open only from 15 June to Labour Day, 10 am to dusk.

Seaview Park

At the north end of Barrington St, under the MacKay Bridge to Dartmouth, Seaview affords good views of the Bedford Basin. Footpaths wind through the largely open-style park. The park also has an interesting historic side to it. In the 1840s a Black community, known as Africville, was established here. Many of its members were former slaves from the USA. It remained until the 1960s, when the area was demolished and the residents moved south toward central Halifax. A visit after dark is not recommended.

McNabs Island

Out in the harbour and easily seen from York Redoubt, this small island makes a good break from the city. The island offers guided walks, beaches, picnic tables and hiking. There's also a teahouse for basic snacks or seafood. Ferries depart for the island through the day from the dock area, and tickets ($8.50) can be bought from Four Wind Charters (☎ 492-0022) at the Boat Tour Center by Cable Wharf Market.

Hemlock Ravine

A system of linked walking trails winds through this large wooded estate once called home by Edward, Duke of Kent, Queen Victoria's dad. It includes a view of Bedford Basin, and amidst the gardens are some very impressive 30-metre-tall trees. To reach it by car, drive along the Bedford Hwy (Hwy 2) past Birch Cove and then look for the signs. It's not far and, once there, feels a long way from a city.

Beaches

If you're looking for a beach, try Black Rock Beach, in Point Pleasant Park; Crystal Beach, 20 km west of town; or Queensland Beach, 35 km west of town.

Activities

Kayaking & Canoeing To rent a kayak in Halifax for exploring nearby waterways, call the Trail Shop (☎ 423-8736). Rates are $20 a day and $15 for each additional day. The Dartmouth Recreation Department (☎ 464-2228) offers canoe rentals during the summer at Graham's Grove waterfront.

Diving There are about 50 wrecks at the mouth of Halifax Harbour and good diving along the coast. For information and equipment rentals, try the Dive Masters Scuba Shop (☎ 465-2526), at 158 Wyse Rd in Dartmouth.

Organised Tours

A wide selection of tours by bus, boat or on foot is available. See the tourist office for a complete list, but some of the more established and interesting ones follow.

Acadian Lines (☎ 454-9321), a bus company, has tours in and around town and will pick you up from many area hotels or from the VIA Rail Station. The 2½-hour Historic Halifax Tour, which is offered at 8.45 am daily during the summer, takes in many of the essential sites. The cost is $12.

Double Decker (☎ 420-1155) offers 1½-hour city tours in London-style buses which leave from the Historic Properties three times a day during the summer. A ticket costs $13.

Cabana Tours (☎ 455-8111) has 70-minute city bus trips for $10 but also offers good, longer day trips to various points around the province (such as Peggy's Cove, Lunenburg and the Annapolis Valley). The Peggy's Cove trip takes four hours and costs $22. A full-day trip that includes Peggy's Cove and Lunenburg is $50.

Also offering a Peggy's Cove tour is Markland Tours (☎ 455-1082). The three-hour tour is slightly cheaper at $20 and they pick up at the HI Hostel. They also have a three-day tour of Cape Breton.

The beauteous *Bluenose II* (☎ 800-763-1963), perhaps the country's best known boat, takes visitors out on two-hour harbour sailing cruises for $20. Usually the sails are not unfurled until the boat is at the outer reaches of the harbour, and it only leaves on clear days. Ask about tickets at the dock or at the Red Store tourist office.

Murphy's on the Water (☎ 420-1015), from Cable Wharf at the Historic Properties, has various boat tours of the Halifax Harbour. The two-hour narrated trip aboard the *Harbour Queen* goes past both new and old city landmarks and at $15 is pretty good value. The boat carries 200 people and has both open and closed decks, a snack counter and a bar. From mid-June through August there are four runs daily. Out of peak season there are two trips daily, and in winter they close down completely. Dinner cruises are an option. Murphy's also operates the *Mar II*, a very handsome sailboat, for trips around the harbour. The one-hour sailing trips cost $16.

NOVA SCOTIA

A number of private entrepreneurs offer fishing trips, tours of the harbour or charters on yachts, the latter especially on weekends and holidays (in summer). Shop around the boats tied along the wharf area. There's likely to be one with moonlight sailings or some other unique angle which may appeal. Some offer whale-watching, but personally I'd be a bit sceptical, as this is not a prime area for that possibility.

Halifax Ghost Walk (☎ 469-6716) provides a two-hour walk beginning at 8.30 pm through July and August, from the Old Town Clock. The tour features tales of pirates, buried treasure and ghosts from the old city's lore and costs $8.50.

More matter-of-fact walking tours around the historic sections of the city are offered very cheaply by D Tours (☎ 429-6415). Their historic downtown walk is at 2 pm Monday to Friday during the summer and is $5.

Festivals

Some of the major events held in Halifax in July and August are:

Canada Day – Canada's birthday on 1 July is celebrated in high style in Halifax with parades, live entertainment, concerts and fireworks.

Nova Scotia Tattoo – This event is held in Halifax during the first week of July (or close to it) every year. It's called the province's 'greatest entertainment extravaganza'.

Halifax Natal Day – A major event held at the end of July or early August, featuring a parade, street parties, boat races, bridge walk, concerts and a fireworks display.

The DuMaurier Atlantic Jazz Festival – This festival takes place at the end of July.

Atlantic Fringe Festival – This festival in August draws more than 250 performers, from musicians and actors to comics and mimics, for a variety of events that are staged throughout the metro area.

Places to Stay

Camping You can camp right in the city of Dartmouth at the *Shubie Municipal Campground* (☎ 435-8328) in Shubie Park, on the shore of Lake Charles. It's on Jaybee Drive near the Shubenacadie Canal, and bus No 55 stops within two blocks of the entrance.

Facilities include showers and a laundromat. The fee is $14 a night for unserviced sites.

Laurie Provincial Park (☎ 861-1623) is on Route 2 six km north of Hwy 102, at the village of Grand Lake on Shubenacadie Grand Lake. It's strictly first come, first served – no reservations are taken. There are 71 sites for $9 a night.

Going west along Hwy 333 there are several campgrounds within 25 km of town. *Seaside Camping* (☎ 823-2732) on Route 333 at Glen Margaret, is open from June to October. Unserviced sites are $11 a night. Also at Glen Margaret is the large *Wayside Camping Park* (☎ 823-2547), with both tenting and RV areas. Unserviced sites here are $12 a night. *King Neptune Campground* (☎ 823-2582) is three km west of Peggy's Cove at Indian Harbour and has 35 unserviced sites for $11 a night.

Woodhaven Park (☎ 835-2271) is in Hammond Plains, a small town near Bedford just off Hwy 213, about 15 minutes' drive north of Halifax. Sites are $15 a night.

Hostels The HI *Halifax Heritage House Hostel* (☎ 422-3863) is perfectly located in a fine historic house at 1253 Barrington St. The hostel is an easy walk to the VIA Rail station or to downtown and the waterfront. There's room for 50 guests and features include cooking facilities, an outdoor patio and a small travel shop. Double and family rooms are available. Prices are $14 for members, $17 for nonmembers, and $29 for a double. Check-in is from 8 am to 4 pm, and 4 to 11 pm in the summer. From the airport, the Airbus goes to the nearby Hilton Hotel. From the bus depot, take the No 7 bus south from the corner of Robie and Almon Sts to the corner of Barrington and South Sts. The hostel can be seen from this corner.

The *YMCA* (☎ 423-9622) is in an excellent location at 1565 South Park St, across from the Public Gardens and very near Citadel Hill. Single rooms for men and women are $26 and a room for couples goes for $48. The weekly rate is cheaper. There's a small, cheap cafeteria and you can use facilities like the gym and swimming pool. It's open all year.

The *YWCA* (☎ 423-6162), for women only, is at 1239 Barrington St, right next door to the HI Hostel between the city centre and the VIA Rail station. There are 30 rooms; singles/doubles cost $26/47. Good weekly rates are available.

Halifax has the highest ratio of educational facilities per capita on the continent. This is good for the traveller, not just in the enjoyment of the erudite citizenry but in being able to take advantage of the abundance of economical rooms offered in dormitories during the summer months. All city universities are considering merging into one giant institution.

At *Dalhousie University*, rooms are available from mid-May to mid-August in the Howe and Sherref Hall residences. Contact Room 410 in the Dalhousie Student Union Building (☎ 494-8840 or 494-8876), 6136 University Ave. Both are on the campus: Howe residence is on the corner of Coburg Rd and LeMarchant St; Sherref Hall is on the corner of South and Oxford Sts. Reservations are required. Singles/doubles cost $35/51 including taxes and breakfast. All other meals are available.

Suites with kitchens are also available from mid-May to mid-August at *Fenwick Place*, an off-campus, high-rise residence at 5599 Fenwick St. The rate ranges from $42 to $63 and you also book them at the Dalhousie Student Union Building. It's central and close to the university.

The *Technical University of Nova Scotia*, or TUNS (☎ 420-245), also has rooms from mid-May to the end of August. Price is $23/36; students, $18/32. It's off Barrington St on Bishop St, a 10-minute walk east from the downtown core. Free laundry services are included and there is a cafeteria.

Mount St Vincent University rents rooms from May to late August; contact the Conference Officer (☎ 457-6286) at 166 Bedford Hwy (Hwy 2) on the campus. Rates are $22.50/32.50. They also offer excellent weekly and monthly rates, especially for students. Meals are available and there is a coin laundry. The university is a 15-minute drive west of town on the Bedford Hwy and overlooks the Bedford Basin.

Yet another university with accommodation is *St Mary's University* (☎ 420-5486), which is also cheap and not far from the centre, at 923 Robie St. Singles/doubles are $26/41 and there are two-room, self-contained units which are good for families at $79.

B&Bs, Tourist Homes & Hotels Halifax is blessed with plentiful, moderately priced, central accommodation. In fact, for quality and selection downtown, it's one of the country's best cities. There are many B&Bs and guesthouses in town and over in Dartmouth as well. Some especially fine ones, though more costly, are found in heritage houses and mansions.

Unlike many cities, there are no B&B agencies in Halifax, but everybody does quite well working independently. Through the summer months, this popular town does fill up, so don't leave finding a place until too late in the day.

The *Old 362* (☎ 422-4309), at 1830 Robie St, is top choice for a low-price B&B. It's small, with just three rooms, and isn't fancy but is pleasant and comfortable. Owner Carolyn Smedley has done some travelling of her own and understands what a budget traveller is looking for. Singles are $30 to $40 and doubles are $50, including a good breakfast. Guests may also use the upstairs facilities to make tea and coffee.

The plain, straightforward *Fountain View Guesthouse* (☎ 422-4169) is the bright blue place with white trim at 2138 Robie St, between Compton Ave and Williams St, across from the park and west of Citadel Hill. It's reliable, consistent and open all year. North Common is across the street and the Citadel is within walking distance. The seven rooms, all with TV, go for $24 to $28 a single and $30 a double. Each extra person costs an additional $5. It's popular, so try in the morning after guests have left.

The well-established *Waken 'n' Eggs B&B* (☎ 422-4737) is within walking distance of the downtown area, in a restored house at 2114 Windsor St. Cost is $35/45 with shared bath, $5 more for private facilities.

The spacious, comfortable *Fresh Start B&B* (☎ 453-6616) is in a big, old house at 2720 Gottingen St. It's tastefully decorated but not prissy. There are five rooms, priced from $40/45. Rooms with private bath are more costly. It's open all year and prices drop after the summer season.

The only drawback to this recommended place is the neighbourhood. The B&B's immediate surroundings are fine but much of Gottingen St and its side streets can be quite seedy. Some people will feel uncomfortable walking to and fro, and women alone, especially, should probably not consider doing so after dark. If you're driving, though, don't think twice about it, and there is on-site parking. Also, buses run on Gottingen St.

At 1520 Robie St, the *Illusions Tourist Home* (☎ 425-6733) is reasonably priced at $35/45 and centrally located. It's open only from April to October. This is one of the few guesthouses which permits smoking.

The *Running Lights Inn* (☎ 423-9873) is a three-storey house at 2060 Oxford St, just off Quinpool Rd. It's neat and clean, but a little overpriced for its style at $36/44 without bath, $55 for a double with. A simple continental breakfast is included. The more expensive top-floor unit comes with kitchenette. Smokers can indulge without being asked to step outside. This one is also open year round.

For hotels try the *Gerrard* (☎ 423-8614), at 1234 Barrington St, across the street from the HI Hostel. It's a small place in a good location, and the building is an historic residence built in 1860. There are nine rooms at $29/44, free coffee and on-site parking. The *Twin Elms Hotel* (☎ 423-8974), at 5492 Inglis St, near the park, has rooms at $25/40 with shared bath.

Top end The following places are in the next bracket up and tend to be larger, more expensive and often in heritage or historical houses or buildings.

The *Queen St Inn* (☎ 422-9828) at 1266 Queen St, near Morris St, is in a house dating from about 1860, with six tastefully decorated rooms at $45/50.

The *King Edward Inn* (☎ 422-3266, 1-800-565-5464) is an impressive-looking restored Victorian inn which looks almost out of place standing graciously at 2400 Agricola St. There are over 40 well-decorated singles/doubles from $55 to $77, with continental breakfast. The Citadel is an easy walk.

The *Lord Nelson Hotel* (☎ 423-6331), 1515 South Park St at Spring Garden Rd, has 174 rooms with rates beginning at $62 a night.

Immaculately kept and finished is the *Halliburton House Inn* (☎ 420-0658), 5184 Morris St. Built in 1820, it has antiques, a library and a pleasant garden. The 30 rooms start at $110/135 with suites at additional cost.

The central core also has a number of large corporate hotels. The *Prince George* (☎ 425-1986), for example, is ideally situated on the corner of George and Price Sts, close to the Citadel and the waterfront. A double here will set you back $160.

There are also places available out at the airport.

Motels Motels tend to be a little expensive and are clustered along the Bedford Hwy (Hwy 2), north-west of town along the bay called Bedford Basin. They offer good views of the bay and cool breezes; bus Nos 80 and 81 go into town, a 15-minute drive away.

The *Travellers Motel* (☎ 835-3394, 1-800-565-3394), open year round, is right at the city limits. The small, simple cottages (rather than the modern motel units) are $60/65 with shower, TV and pool.

The *Econo Lodge* (☎ 443-0303, 1-800-561-9961), the big brown place at 560 Bedford Hwy, has 33 fully equipped rooms at $58/68. Breakfast is available and there's a pool.

A third choice is the *Bluenose Days Inn* (☎ 443-3171 or 800-325-2525), 636 Bedford Hwy, which charges $50/58. Breakfast, at extra cost, is served from 7 to 11 am.

Further out is *Stardust Motel* (☎ 835-3316), 1067 Bedford Hwy, which has 51 rooms at $45/50, more for one with a kitchenette.

Places to Eat

Halifax has a good selection of restaurants offering a variety of foods in all price ranges, and generally the quality is high.

For breakfast, the *B&B Cafe*, on the corner of Barrington and Blowers Sts, offers the works for $2.99 but often has specials for even less. Or try the highly recommended *Mediterraneo Cafe* just down Barrington St which has a full breakfast for $2.25, and many pasta dishes such as cannelloni for $3.75.

Spring Garden Rd, between Grafton St and South Park St, has exploded in recent years with cafes, pubs and restaurants. *Second Cup*, in the Montreal Building at the corner of Queen St, is great for coffee and people watching. They have a couple of computers so you can go surfing on the Internet.

The *Midtown Tavern*, on the corner of Prince and Grafton Sts, is highly recommended – a good example of the Canadian workers' tavern. It's packed with friendly locals at lunch, most of them enjoying a sirloin steak, French fries and coleslaw and washing it down with draught by the glass. Steak and fries is $5, and a glass of beer after 4.40 pm is only 99 cents.

The *Bluenose*, on the corner of Duke and Hollis Sts, is another place packed with locals at lunch. Its menu ranges from Greek and Italian to full lobster dinners and there is beer on tap. Lunch specials are under $6, dinners start at $7.

Halifax is blessed with pubs, and many are good for a meal. The upmarket *Granite Brewery*, at 1222 Barrington St, brews its own beer, which is very good. The food, too, should not be ignored; try the jambalaya. Dinners start at $10.

Several pubs can be found in the mall area of Granville St on the corner of Duke St. Both the *Split Crow* and the *Peddlar's Pub* have outdoor sections and the latter has live music on Saturday afternoon. The Split Crow often has lunch specials like clams & chips for under $4.

Also for lunch or dinner, *Satisfaction Feast* is a well-established vegetarian restaurant. It's at 1581 Grafton St, in the pale blue building, open from 11 am to 9 pm. Dinners start at $8 and sandwiches $4. The spinach-and-cheese curry is definitely worth considering.

For East Indian food, the *Guru*, 5234 Blowers St, is good with main dishes starting at $8. The all-you-can-eat lunch buffets are very good value, particularly the vegetarian one, which is $7.95. Much cheaper is the *Samosa Plus*, at the corner of Barrington and Prince Sts. Lunch specials are $4, the all-you-can eat vegetarian buffet is $5.

For Vietnamese try the casual *Kinh-Do* at 1284 Barrington St. It offers tasty food, an extensive menu and low prices. There is a daily lunch special for under $5.

Another fine, inexpensive place to check out is *Kit's Deli and Restaurant*, at 1567 Grafton St near Spring Garden Rd. The Asian menu ranges from Sri Lankan and Korean to Singaporean-style dishes with a few other countries in between. Dinners range from $9 to $12. It's closed on Sunday.

Continuing with the ethnic places there is the small, cosy but much more expensive *Czech Inn*, a local favourite, at 5237 Blowers St, with schnitzels, borscht and the like. Entrees range in price from $8 to $13. Nearby, at 5215 Blowers St, downtown, the lower-priced *Hungary Hungarian* (run by the same man) specialises in goulashes.

And there is seafood here, of course. For a splurge try the *Silver Spoon*, on the 2nd floor of the stone building at 1813 Granville St. The menu is extensive and includes a range of seafoods. The good desserts can be enjoyed on their own in the downstairs cafe. The huge *McKelvie's*, at 1680 Lower Water St, and the *Five Fishermen*, 1740 Argyle St, are also established seafood places.

Cogswell St as well as its continuation, Quinpool Rd, are commercial streets with plenty of eating spots. If you crave fish & chips, the place is *Camille's*, at 6443 Quinpool Rd.

NOVA SCOTIA

The *Trident Booksellers & Café*, at 1570 Argyle St, with the large stained-glass piece in the window, is unbeatable for lingering with a coffee or pot of tea. The various coffees, from espresso to lattes, are good and cheap, and when you've finished with the newspaper, the other half of the cafe has a fine selection of books, new and used.

La Cave, tucked in the little doorway at 5244 Blowers St, is open until 4.30 am on weekends. In the basement, this small bistro offers good desserts and is particularly well known for its cheesecake.

For do-it-yourself ocean fare, go to *Fisherman's Market*, in the white building beside the ferry terminal. Boiled lobster is $8 a pound (500 grams) – a one-pounder being the usual meal and as small as they can legally catch them (they're also available live).

Mary Jane's Alternative Tastes is a health-food store at 1313 Hollis St, near Morris St.

Entertainment

Pubs & Live Music Halifax is lively at night and has an active pub and music scene. For a complete rundown of the music scene either stop in at the Tourism Halifax offices or grab a copy of *The Coast*, Halifax's offbeat magazine. This publication, offered free at restaurants and pubs, makes for interesting reading as well as providing a full schedule of music, film and stage performances in the city.

Privateer's Warehouse, in the Historic Properties (near the *Bluenose II's* docking area on the waterfront), with two restaurants, also has a busy, inexpensive bar on the lower level. The *Lower Deck* often presents Maritime folk music – good stuff.

At the corner of Grafton and Sackville is *Maxwell's Plum Tavern*, an English-style pub which boasts the largest selection of imported draught and single-malt Scotch in Atlantic Canada. Often on the weekends there is live blues or jazz.

More live music, especially bluegrass, can be enjoyed near the HI hostel at *Bearly's Beverage Room* on Barrington St.

On Spring Garden Rd there are several bars featuring live music. The *Thirsty Duck* is at 5470 Spring Garden Rd; go through the store and up the stairs. They've got burgers, fish & chips, etc, and draught beer at low prices. Just up the street is *My Father's Moustache*. Both feature roof-top patios and live music.

At 1740 Argyle is *My Apartment* for a dance floor with live rock bands nightly while *Birmingham Bar & Grill*, at Spring Rd and Park Lane near the Public Gardens, has jazz nightly along with an extensive list of imported beers.

The large, loud *New Palace Cabaret* (☎ 429-5959), 1721 Brunswick St, across from the Citadel, has rock and blues bands nightly.

The Harbour Folk Society (☎ 425-3655) presents informal concerts on the first Saturday of every month as well as an open mike Wednesday evenings at the *The Grad House*, 6154 University Ave.

The *Sheraton Hotel* at 1919 Upper Water St has a casino open daily.

Performing Arts The Symphony Nova Scotia plays the *Rebecca Cohn Auditorium* (☎ 421-7311), at 1646 Barrington St. The *Dalhousie Arts Centre* (☎ 494-3820) at the university is a major performance venue for theatre and dance. International artists and bands perform frequently at *Halifax Metro Centre* (☎ 451-1221) located on the corner of Duke and Brunswick Sts across from the Old Town Clock.

The *Neptune Theatre* (☎ 429-7070) is the city's leading theatre venue with a season that runs from September to mid-May. In 1997, the group will move to its new facility, an historic building on Barrington St that is being renovated. Halifax also has two dinners theatres; *Graton St Dinner Theatre* (☎ 452-1961) and *Historic Feast Company* (☎ 420-1840) located in the Historic Properties.

Cinema For repertory films there is the *Wormwood's Cinema* (☎ 422-3700) at 2015 Gottingen St.

Getting There & Away

Air Air Canada (☎ 429-7111) has services to Montreal ($325) and Toronto ($397). Canadian Airlines (☎ 427-5500) and Air Canada also both fly to St John's, Newfoundland.

Bus The principal Nova Scotian bus line is the Acadian line, which connects with the New Brunswick SMT lines. There are also a couple of smaller, regional lines which service specific regions only. They all use the Acadian bus station (☎ 454-9321) at 6040 Almon St, which runs south off Robie St, north-west of the Citadel.

One Acadian line runs through the Annapolis Valley and down to Yarmouth. Others cover the central region, the Northumberland Shore and parts of Cape Breton.

Following are the one-way fares to several destinations. To North Sydney (one express service daily and other milk runs) it's $45, to Yarmouth $41, Amherst $27, Saint John in New Brunswick $55 and Fredericton $61.

The MacKenzie Bus Line serves Nova Scotia's South Shore between Halifax, Lunenburg, Bridgewater and Yarmouth.

Zinck's bus company runs several services along the Eastern Shore from Halifax to Sherbrooke, stopping at all the small villages along the way. It runs once a day (except Sunday) eastbound and Tuesday to Saturday westbound.

Train The VIA Rail station (☎ 429-8421, 1-800-561-3952) is six blocks from the downtown area along Hollis St. It's on Terminal Rd by the big old Halifax Hilton Hotel and is a beautiful example of Canadian train-station architecture. The train is more useful for reaching out-of-province destinations than for getting around Nova Scotia. A train to Moncton, New Brunswick ($40) and eventually Montreal, departs at 2 pm daily (except Tuesday) along a route through northern New Brunswick that includes stops at Campbellton and Edmunston. The run to Montreal via Maine, USA has been dropped. By booking a week in advance the ticket to Montreal is $95.

Car Byways (☎ 429-0092), at 2156 Barrington St, charges $43 per day with 200 km a day and 14 cents a km beyond. Dollar Rent-Car (☎ 429-1892) with a desk at Citadel Inn Hotel, has compacts for $42 a day, 200 km a day and 12 cents a km beyond that. Keep in mind that by the time you add tax and insurance costs, the price is more than $50 a day.

Other rental places include Rent-A-Wreck (☎ 454-2121), 2823 Robie at Almon St, which offers HI members a discount, and Budget (☎ 492-7541), at the corner of Hollis and Sackville Sts in the Ultramar service station. The airport has several rental places.

Another option to consider is Alternative Passage (☎ 429-5169), at 5224 Blowers St. Basically they match up car owners with passengers. Typical fares from Halifax include Montreal ($50), Yarmouth ($18) and North Sydney on Cape Breton ($21).

Getting Around

The Airport From the centre of Halifax the airport is 35 km out on Hwy 102, north towards Truro.

There are no city buses to the airport but there is the Airbus (☎ 873-2091). It runs between the airport and the downtown centre, with stops at several of the major central hotels such as the Lord Nelson, the Prince George and the Sheraton. It also makes pick-ups at the Holiday Inn in Dartmouth. The fares are $11/18 one way/return. The bus makes 18 trips daily with the first run at 6.30 am and the last bus leaving the airport at 10.45 pm. Allow 90 minutes before flight time. When arriving at the Halifax airport, signs in the baggage area will direct you to the Airbus ticket window just outside.

An alternative is Share-A-Cab (☎ 429-5555 or 800-565-8669). Call at least four hours before flight time and they'll find other passengers and pick you up. The price works out about the same as the bus.

Bus Metro Transit (☎ 421-6600) runs the good, inexpensive city bus system. Fares are $1.30 or $24 for a 20-ticket booklet. Call for route and schedule information or pick up a *Metro Transit Route Guide* for free from the

Tourism Halifax centres. This large map of the area is easy to use with each bus route in a different colour.

The No 3 city bus on Robie St goes from the bus station into town.

Hitchhikers heading north towards Truro will want to pick up bus No 80 or 82 and get off near Hwy 102 north of Bedford. Those heading west, will want bus No 21 which ends at the village of Timberlea on Hwy 3.

Ferry Ferries runs continuously from near the Historic Properties dock. One boat heads across the bay to the city of Dartmouth, the other is a weekday service to Woodside. A ticket is $1.10 one way and the ride makes a nice, short mini-tour of the harbour. Ferries run every 15 minutes until 6 pm, then every 30 minutes. The last one is at 11.30 pm. On Sunday they run from noon to 5.30 pm.

Bicycle Bicycles can be rented at the Cycledelics (☎ 425-RIDE), 1678 Barrington St. Rates for the mountain bikes are $9/15 for a half day/full day. You can also rent mountain bikes at the HI Hostel (☎ 422-3863) at 1253 Barrington St for $13/22.

For any bike information or to join a bicycle tour of the city or Halifax region, call the Velo Bicycle Club (☎ 423-4345).

DARTMOUTH

Founded in 1750, one year after Halifax, when the ship *Alderney* put ashore 353 settlers, Dartmouth is Halifax's counterpart just across the harbour. However, the similarities end with the waterfront location of the central area. Dartmouth is a city of 70,000 people spread over a large area and, compared with Halifax, is more residential and the city centre less commercial. The downtown area lacks the history, charm and bustle of Halifax.

Having said that, Dartmouth does make for a cheap afternoon side trip and even a scenic one, thanks to the ferry. The Halifax-Dartmouth ferry, operated by Metro Transit (the bus people), is said to be the oldest saltwater ferry system in North America,

dating back to 1752 when it was just a rowboat. It is certainly the cheapest boat cruise on the harbour. For $1.10 you get a great view of both cities and then land at the centre of things in Dartmouth.

The fact that the city has 23 lakes within its boundaries will suit those seeking accessible water activities. Many of these lakes are good for swimming, seven have supervised beaches, some are stocked with fish and there's in-town boating and canoeing (see Kayaking & Canoeing in the Halifax section for details). Most popular of the beaches are Birch Cove and Graham's Grove, both on Lake Bannock.

Orientation

Aldernay Gate houses the ferry terminal, the Dartmouth Public Library, city offices, a food court and some shops.

Portland St, running up from the ferry terminal, is the main street. Several years ago it was completely overhauled, with trees planted and the sidewalks widened. Unfortunately there isn't much along it and the stores and businesses seem to be having a tough time. What there is includes several inexpensive restaurants, pizza joints, a couple of antique/junk shops and a bar or two of dubious character.

There are, though, a number of historic sites near the waterfront and the neighbouring downtown area. You can pick up a walking-tour guide at a tourist office in either city. Buildings in old Dartmouth are primarily made of wood, rather than of brick or stone as in Halifax.

Beside the large ferry terminal is Ferry Terminal Park, where a walking path leads along the water and puts you in view of Halifax-Dartmouth Industries, a shipyard, and Dartmouth Cove, the home of Canada's largest coastguard base. The distinctive red-and-white ships are used for search and rescue, icebreaking, maintaining coastal navigational aids and responding to any ocean emergency.

Micmac Mall is the largest shopping centre in the Maritimes.

Information

The main Dartmouth information office, Dartmouth Tourism (☎ 466-5352), is at 100 Wyse Rd, on the corner of Alderney Drive, to the west of the downtown area in Dartmouth. It is right beside the Dartmouth Heritage Museum and open daily from 9 am to 5 pm during the summer.

Practically across the street from the ferry terminal and Aldernay Gate is the Dartmouth Convention and Visitor's Centre (☎ 466-2875) at 101-12 Queen St which has information on the city and area. Hours are 9 am to 5 pm Monday through Friday.

World Peace Pavilion

Within Ferry Terminal Park is this unusual outdoor exhibit. The idea of the pavilion was conceived in 1989 by Metro Youth for Global Unity who invited each country in the world to send in a rock or brick to symbolize the earth we all share. More than 65 countries responded and the collection is well worth a look and at times even touching. The rocks range from a 280-pound piece of the fallen Berlin Wall that Germany sent and a stone from the Great Wall of China to a bit of rubble the USA contributed from a missile silo that was imploded in 1995 in accordance with the Strategic Arms Reduction Treaty.

Shubenacadie Canal

A little further around the corner from the shipyards is the Shubenacadie Canal Interpretive Centre, at 140 Alderney Drive. The canal connects Dartmouth (through a series of waterways, lakes and locks) with the Bay of Fundy, on the other side of the province. Built in the mid-1800s along an old Micmac portage route, much of the canal has now been restored. It's used by canoeists, but parks and various historic sites along it can be reached by road.

The interpretive centre has some information on the whole system but mainly deals with the historic marine 'railway' which moved vessels from the harbour inland a couple of hundred metres to where the interconnecting water system really began. From May to September it's open from 9 am to 5

pm Monday through Friday and 1 to 5 pm Saturday and Sunday. Admission is free.

For more details on the entire canal and its history and a look at two of the restored locks, visit the **Fairbanks Centre** (☎ 462-1826), 54 Locks Rd, at Lake Charles in north Dartmouth. It's open the same hours as the interpretive centre during the summer.

Dartmouth Heritage Museum

The museum (☎ 464-2300) is at the junction of Alderney Drive and Wyse Rd, about a 15-minute walk left off the Halifax ferry. It houses an eclectic collection pertaining to the city's natural and human history and includes some Native Indian artefacts and crafts, various tools and fashions and industrial bric-a-brac. The museum is free and during the summer is open from 10 am to 4 pm Monday through Friday, and 11 am to 4 pm on Saturday and Sunday.

Leighton Dillman Park

Beside the Dartmouth Heritage Museum is this park, basically a hillside. The park is part of the original common area of Dartmouth set up in 1788. You can climb to the top of Fairy Hill in the middle where there is a memorial cairn dedicated to the first settlers of the city and a great view of the harbour and Halifax on the other side.

Evergreen House

Built for a judge in 1862, Evergreen House, part of the Heritage Museum, is a fine example of a 19th-century house for the well-to-do. Many of the 20 rooms are open to the public and have been furnished in the style of the 1880s. Admission is free and the house is open from 10 am to 4 pm daily except Monday and Saturday in summer. The address is 26 Newcastle St, which is in the vicinity of the Shubenacadie Interpretive Centre.

Quaker Whaler House

At 59 Ochterloney St, near the museum and tourist office and within walking distance of the ferry, is the Quaker Whaler House, the oldest house in the Halifax area, having been built in 1786. The Quakers came to the region as whalers from New England. Guides in costume lead visitors around the house. Hours during the summer are 10 am to 4 pm daily except Monday and Sunday. Admission is free.

Cole Harbour Heritage Farm Museum

This museum (☎ 434-0222) is at 471 Poplar Drive, out of the centre. Built at the end of the 18th century, the farm includes five buildings, including the main house, blacksmith shop, barns and a carriage shop. The museum also includes walking trails and a tea room. Hours are 10 am to 4 pm daily during the summer except on Sunday when it opens at noon. Admission is free.

Bedford Institute of Oceanography

Just outside Dartmouth is this large government marine research centre (☎ 426-4093), which has set up a free self-guided tour for visitors. A walk around the exhibits concerning the fishery and various ocean studies takes a little less than an hour. There is also a video and some aquarium specimens to see. This is the country's leading oceanographic facility and as such has international standing and often carries out research with similar institutes from other countries. The centre is open Monday to Friday only, from 9 am to 4 pm. To get there from Dartmouth by car, take Windmill Rd to the Shannon Park exit, which is near the MacKay Bridge, or take bus No 51 from the Dartmouth ferry terminal.

Black Cultural Centre

Described as the first of its kind in Canada, the centre (☎ 434-6223) is a museum, cultural and educational facility all in one. Its principal aim is to preserve and present the history of Black people in Nova Scotia. Perhaps surprisingly, Nova Scotia was an early centre for Black communities in Canada and a significant depot of the Underground Railway (see the Windsor section in the Ontario chapter for details). There are various small exhibits, including some African musical instruments and a video. Of

more interest may be the scheduled events, lectures, concerts, etc, so call for information.

For those more interested in Black history in the province, pick up a copy of the *Black Heritage Trail* pamphlet here or at one of the major tourist offices. It lays out various routes around the province, detailing points of note, and provides some little-known historical information.

The centre is open year round from 9 am to 5 pm Monday to Friday and from 10 am to 4 pm on Saturday. It's in Westphal, just past the eastern border of the city of Dartmouth on Route 7, Cherrybrook Rd. This is about six or seven km south-east of central Dartmouth. Admission is $2.50.

Shearwater Aviation Museum

South of town on Pleasant St, at the Canadian Forces Base (CFB Shearwater), the aviation museum (☎ 460-1083) details the history of Canadian maritime military aviation. Some aircraft are on display, as well as pictures, uniforms and other salient objects. It's open during the summer from 9 am to 4 pm Monday through Friday and admission is free.

The Shearwater International Airshow is held here annually, usually in late August or early September.

Festivals

Festivals include a three-day multicultural festival held in June along the waterfront, featuring ethnic foods and arts; the Maritime Old-Time Fiddlers' Contest in early July; the Tattoo Festival, held along the waterfront in July; and the Dartmouth Natal Day Celebration in early August.

Places to Stay

There are places to stay on this side of the bay as well. They tend to be more scattered and less central than in Halifax. There is camping in the Shubie Beach Park.

Close to the harbour is *Martin House B&B* (☎ 463-7338), 62 Pleasant St, with rooms at $45/$54. Less expensive is *Caroline's* (☎ 469-4665), 134 Victoria Rd, not far from the Macdonald Bridge, with three rooms at $30/35 including a continental breakfast.

Places to Eat

Aside from the fast-food places with a view in the ferry terminal complex, there are a couple of places in the old section near the dock. *Tea and Temptations*, at 44 Ochterloney St, east of the ferry landing, is good for an afternoon break. *Incredible Edibles*, at the corner of King and Portland Sts, has good soup-and-sandwich lunches at about $5. Or else hit a pizza shop or take-away and head to Ferry Terminal Park for a picnic lunch.

Central Nova Scotia

The central part of Nova Scotia, in geographic terms, essentially takes in the corridor of land from the New Brunswick border down to Halifax. With a few exceptions it's an area to be passed through on the way to somewhere else. For many coming by road from elsewhere in Canada, this is the introduction to Nova Scotia. But don't turn against the province because of what you see from the Trans Canada Hwy, as it passes through flat, uninteresting terrain on the way to the province's main highway at Truro. Parrsboro is an interesting stop south-west of Amherst and there is some good scenery here along the shores of the Bay of Fundy.

AMHERST

Amherst is the geographic centre of the Maritimes and a travel junction. For anyone heading into Nova Scotia, passing by is a necessity, and Route 104 leads south towards Halifax and then cuts east for Cape Breton Island. Also from Amherst, it's not far to the Northumberland Shore and the north coastal route across the province. Route 16 to the ferry for Prince Edward Island is just across the border in New Brunswick.

There are two tourist offices in Amherst. Just off exit 1 of Route 104 is a huge provincial welcome centre (☎ 667-8429) that is open daily during the summer from 8 am to

9 pm. The centre features information and a booking service for all of Nova Scotia, an interpretive area and gardens out front. Within town is the Amherst tourist office (☎ 667-0696) in a railway car parked on LaPlanche St, from exit 2 off the highway. Hours are noon to 5 pm on Sunday and 9 am to 6 pm the rest of the week during the summer.

Amherst is a pleasant town with some fine buildings, and many from the 19th century have been restored. You'll find a number of these along Victoria St, the main street, whose intersection with Church St is the primary one in town. The local tourist centre has a walking tour map.

The **Cumberland County Museum** (☎ 667-2561) is at 150 Church St and has four exhibit rooms of local history. The most interesting displays are the articles made by prisoners of war at the Amherst Internment Camp during WWI, which included Leon Trotsky. Hours during the summer are 9 am to 5 pm daily except on Sunday when it opens at 2 pm. Admission is $1.

On the east coast there is a good beach at Lorneville on Northumberland Strait.

Places to Stay

Amherst is a great place to stay overnight with a range of moderately priced accommodations. *Brown's Guest Home* (☎ 667-9769) is at 158 East Victoria St and has three rooms with singles for $28 and doubles for $30 to $35. *Green Mansion* (☎ 667-2146), 113 Spring St, is a Victorian home built in 1907. There are three rooms at $25/42 including breakfast in the sunroom.

For a motel, try *Victorian Motel* (☎ 667-7211), at 150 East Victoria St. Rooms are $38/46.

Places to Eat

The classic *Hampton Diner* is recommended for good, cheap food and quick, courteous service. They've been open every day from 7 am to 9 pm since 1956! You can't miss it as you come into town from the highway off exit 1. Most sandwiches and hamburgers are $3, two eggs, potatoes and toast is $2.25.

At 7 Acadia St, *Bell's Delicatessen* features deli meats, big sandwiches and subs and homemade muffins and cheesecakes. It opens at 8 am and there is always a daily lunch special under $5.

Getting There & Away
Ticket agent and station for both the Acadian and SMT bus lines is the A&W Restaurant (☎ 667-2229) at 142 S Albion. There are two buses a day for Halifax at 2.55 pm and 7.10 pm; fare is $26.50. SMT will take you north to Moncton daily for $8.29.

CHIGNECTO
This region south and west of Amherst is named after the bay, the cape at the western tip and the large game sanctuary in the middle of it. This is one of the least visited, least populated areas of the province. The road network is minimal, although the Glooscap Trail tourist route goes through the eastern portion. It's an area with some very interesting geology and ancient history, which attracts dinosaur detectives, fossil followers and rockhounds. The Minas Basin shore has some good scenery and shoreline cliffs. The tides of the Minas Basin are high even by Fundy standards.

Joggins
A short distance from Amherst on Chignecto Bay is the village of Joggins, known for its seaside cliff full of fossils. It exposes one of the world's best Carboniferous-period fossil collections, consisting of trees, insects, reptiles and others that are 300 million years old. There is a footpath down to the beach and along the 50-metre sandstone cliffs but you're better off first visiting the **Joggins Fossil Centre** (☎ 251-2727) on Main St, which is open daily from 9 am to 6.30 pm from June through September. Here you'll see samples of what there is, including fossilised footprints, and learn more about the site. Admission is $3.50.

Guided tours of the fossil cliffs are not cheap, at $10, but they do last two hours and mean almost certain success in finding something of interest. One tour is offered daily but the times vary and are tied to the tides. The tourist office in Amherst has a schedule of the tours. This is a protected area, but small fossils which you find can be kept.

Cape d'Or
If you make it way down to the end of the peninsula, don't miss Cape d'Or Park at the lighthouse, and walk out to the point for a really spectacular view over the Minas Channel and Bay of Fundy. If you want to spend the night there are two nearby campgrounds and *Lightkeeper's Kitchen* near the lighthouse. The Kitchen serves breakfast and lunch and has four rooms available at $25/35.

Diligent River
At Diligent River there is Ward Falls Trail, a four-km hike up the river gorge. The trail is well maintained but steep in some places and towards the end passes the three-metre cascade.

Parrsboro
Parrsboro is the largest of the small towns along the Minas Basin shore and is a place to stay for a day or two. There are several museums, a fossil-laden shoreline to explore and a half dozen B&Bs and inns. In the centre of town, beside the Town Hall, is the tourist office, open 8.30 am to 7 pm during the summer. Among other things, the office has tide information for visiting rockhounds.

The area is interesting geologically and is known for its semiprecious stones, fossils and dinosaur prints. People scour the many local beaches and rock faces for agates and amethyst and attend the annual Rockhound Roundup, a get-together for rock, mineral and fossil collectors for the past 25 years, featuring displays, demonstrations, guided walks and boat tours.

Fundy Geological Museum At the museum (☎ 254-3814) you can find out why the Parrsboro beaches have been dubbed 'Nova Scotia's own Jurassic Park'. It features a glittering collection of minerals and fossils, of course, but also has models, hands-on exhibits and computer-aided displays that explain the fascinating geological history of the area. Naturalists on staff also lead special tours to the nearby beaches.

The museum is on Two Islands Road and is open year round. During the summer the hours are 9.30 am to 5.30 pm daily. Admission is $3 but often the tourist office has coupons that knock $1 off the ticket.

Two Islands Interpretive Site Continue on Two Islands Road away from town and you'll reach the site, dedicated to Wassons Bluff. In 1989, fossilized footprints of one of the oldest dinosaurs in the world were found in the eroding cliffs of the shoreline here. A trail leads to the beach and bluff and during low tide you can continue your dinosaur search out to the Two Islands.

Parrsboro Rock & Mineral Shop This is really the personal museum (☎ 254-2981) of Eldon George, who achieved international fame searching the nearby shorelines for gems and fossils. He loves to talk about his collection and has some interesting things on display, like the tooth of a duckbill dinosaur. The museum is on Whiteall Rd and hours during the summer are 9 am to 9 pm daily.

Partridge Island This is not only the most popular shoreline to search for gems (sort of a Mecca for rockhounds) but also a place steeped in history. Among others, Samuel de Champlain landed here in 1607 and took away (what else?) amethyst rocks from the beach. The island is south of town on Whiteall Rd and there is an interpretive display explaining how the powerful Fundy tides break up the layers of rock and expose new gem stones every year. More than likely there will be a dozen people searching the pebbled shoreline or the bluffs for agate, jasper, stilhite etc. Nearby is **Ottawa House Museum**, which preserves Sir Charles Tupper's summer home. Tupper was premier of Nova Scotia and later prime minister of

Canada. Hours are 10 am to 6 pm during the summer and admission is $1.

Ship's Company Theatre All the world's a stage or in this case, the entire boat is. The MV *Kipawo*, built in the Saint John Shipyard, was the last of the Minas Basin ferries. She ended her days on a beach of Newfoundland in 1977 before being salvaged and turned into a floating theatre. Throughout the summer a variety of plays are performed, most of them new works from Maritime writers. The box office (☎ 254-3000) is in town.

Places to Stay & Eat There are several B&Bs in town, the most affordable being the *White House* (☎ 254-2387), on Upper Main St, with rooms for $30/45.

Parrsboro has the usual take-outs and pizza place but also *Between Friends Cafe*, a pleasant eatery that serves soups, salads and sandwiches for under $4.

Five Islands Provincial Park

East of Parrsboro, the park offers camping, a beach and picnicking. Walking trails show the terrain's variety, some leading to the 90-metre-high cliffs at the edge of the Minas Basin, with views of the islands. Nearby tidal flats are good for clam-digging. The campground has 90 sites, most in a semi-open area with good views of the bay.

From here to the Trans Canada Hwy, you'll pass almost a dozen small takeaway stands, all of them offering fried clams. The clams are dug locally and were among the best I had in the Maritimes, no doubt because of their freshness.

Economy & Around

Closer to Five Islands than the town of Economy, Economy Mountain, at over 200 metres, affords good views. Six km north of Economy on River Phillip Rd, Economy Falls Trail leads four km into a gorge in the Cobequid Mountains, ending at this stunning 20-metre cascade. This is one of the best hikes in the area.

Just east of town along Hwy 2 is *The Dutchman's Cheese Farm* (☎ 647-2751), a combination cheese shop, restaurant and interpretive centre.

SPRINGHILL

Springhill is a small, modest, working-class town known to many Canadians for two things: horrendous coal-mining disasters and as the birthplace of one of the country's most popular singers, Anne Murray. The stories of both are told in museums.

Anne Murray Centre

More or less right in the middle of town, on Main St, is the centre honouring Springhill's best-known offspring. It's pretty well just for real buffs, though, with a rather high (relative to most provincial attractions) entrance fee of $5. For that you learn details of Anne Murray's successful career through pictures, videos, gold records and awards. There's also a gift shop, the only place that sells *From Springhill to the World*, a limited edition album she made just for the centre. The centre is open daily from May to October from 9 am to 5 pm.

Miners' Museum

Three km from the Anne Murray Centre (follow the signs), this site is a story of bravery, toil, guts and tragedy. A visit is worthwhile: interesting, educational and, to many people, emotional. Coal mining began here in 1834 and major accidents occurred in 1891 and again in 1956, claiming a total of 164 lives.

Two years later North America's deepest mine (4.3 km) had a 'bump', as cave-ins are called, and 75 miners were killed in what was one of the continent's worst mining accidents. The search for survivors lasted 6½ days and ended when 12 men buried underground were found alive. In 1970 all mining operations here ceased.

The Miners' Museum allows visitors a first-hand look down a mine, as well as displaying equipment, tools and photographs. The guides, all retired miners, lead the tour with a beautifully warm, human grace.

Admission is just $2.50 for seeing all the above-ground displays and $4 for the complete tour, which includes the guided talk and a trip down a shaft. Go for the latter – when you feel the cold, damp air at the opening, you'll be glad you're not going to work. The museum is open the same hours as the Ann Murray Centre.

TRURO

Truro (pop 13,000), with its central position in the province, is known as the hub of Nova Scotia. The Trans Canada Hwy passes through the north and east of town; Hwy 102 goes south to Halifax. The VIA Rail line goes by and Truro is also a bus transfer point.

The main part of town is around the corner of Prince and Inglis Sts, where some redevelopment has gentrified the streets.

The tourist office (☎ 893-2922) is in Victoria Square, a city park since 1860, at the corner of Prince and Commercial Sts. Hours are 8 am to 8 pm daily during the tourist season.

Victoria Park

Located in the heart of the city, this is the gem of Truro. At 400 acres, Victoria Park is more of a rugged nature reserve than a city park. Cars are banned, leaving most of park to walkers and cyclists. At minimum, hike the two km to view Joe Howe and Waddell Falls, two small cascades set in a rocky gorge. Boardwalks, staircases and observation platforms are everywhere in the gorge. If you feel energetic climb Jacob's Ladder, a stairway of 173 steps.

There is also a pool in the park open daily during the summer. The fee for swimming is $2.75. From the train station on Esplanade St, head south on Young St and then east on Brunswick St, where the entrance of the park is signposted.

Colchester Museum

At 29 Young St, in the centre of town, this large museum (☎ 895-6284) has exhibits on the region's human history, the founding of Truro and Elizabeth Bishop, a noted poet who grew up in the area. Hours in the summer are 10 am to 5 pm weekdays and 2 to 5 pm on the weekends. Admission is $1.

Tidal Bore

The Bay of Fundy is known for having the highest tides in the world, and an offshoot of these is a tidal wave or bore which flows up the feeding rivers when high tide comes in. The advancing tide is often pretty small but, with the right phase of the moon, can be a metre or so in height and runs upstream, giving the impression of the river flowing backwards. You can have a look for free at a few spots in and around town. The closest place is a lookout on the Salmon River, on Hwy 236, just west of exit 14 off Hwy 102. Better viewing of the bores is at Maitland on Hwy 215 if you are headed that way. Tide schedules are available at the tourist office or call their Dial-A-Tide hotline (☎ 426-5494).

Places to Stay

Right across from the bus station is *Willow Bend Motel* (☎ 895-5325), at 277 Willow St. Rooms in this pleasant motel are $40/48. *Berry's Motel* (☎ 895-2823) with similar rates is at 73 Robie St.

B&Bs are generally cheaper. The Victorian *Blue House Inn* (☎ 895-4150), at 43 Dominion St, is central, has three rooms and offers good value at $35/40 including a full breakfast and tea in the evening. The host will meet the train or bus if you call ahead.

Wentworth Hostel (☎ 548-2379), with lots of beds in a big rambling century-old farmhouse, is not quite halfway to Amherst, near Wentworth on Valley Rd. It features kitchen facilities, showers and 75 km of mountain-bike trails with a trailhead just outside the door. The hostel is signposted along the Trans Canada Hwy and its rates are $9.50 for members and $11.50 non-members.

Places to Eat

The cross streets of Esplanade St and Inglis Place have everything any budget traveller needs: a laundromat, beer store and two Chinese restaurants. This is the heart of Truro's commercial area and most of the restaurants and pubs are located here.

Within the Truro Centre, the train station mall along Esplanade St, there is the *Engine Room*, a lively pub and restaurant where sandwiches are $3 to $6 and most dinners are under $8. Across the street is *My Mother's Apron* which serves almost everything from Mexican and Italian to fish & chips with lunch specials for $5. There's also a farmer's market every Saturday from June to October. But for the cheapest eats anywhere, head to *Ryan's IGA* on Inglis Place. The large supermarket has a good lunch counter where sandwiches are under $2 and hot daily specials, like macaroni and cheese, are under $3. There are a few tables inside and a patio outside overlooking this busy commercial strip.

Just off the Trans Canada at exit 14 into Truro along Hwy 2 (which becomes Robie St in town) are the usual chain restaurants.

Getting There & Away

Bus The bus station (☎ 895-3833) is at 280 Willow St. It's near the hospital along the motel strip – you'll see the blue-and-white Acadian bus terminal sign. There are three buses a day to Halifax ($11) and four a day, with different stops, to Sydney ($38). To Saint John, New Brunswick ($44), there's an 8.40 am and a 2.15 pm bus daily, with a stop in Amherst.

Train The train station (☎ 1-800-561-3952) is in town on Esplanade St, near the corner of Inglis Place. All trains into and out of Nova Scotia pass through Truro, so connections can be made for Halifax, various points in New Brunswick and to Montreal. Trains to Halifax ($18) depart once daily except Wednesday and to Moncton daily except Tuesday. Purchasing tickets five days in advance usually saves a third or more.

MAITLAND & SHUBENACADIE CANAL

To the west of Truro on the Bay of Fundy is the little town of Maitland, at the mouth of the Shubenacadie River. Extending south along the river then through various locks and lakes, the continuous water system eventually leads to the city of Dartmouth and the ocean.

Opened in 1861, the canal is now a National Historic Site with a variety of sites and parks that can be visited along its course, including the Tidal Bore Park. It is also used by boaters and canoeists. Maps available at tourist offices list all the points of interest, walking trails, etc. The main interpretive centre is in Dartmouth, on the harbour.

Also in Maitland is **Lawrence House**, a provincial historical site. The grand house was built in 1870 for shipbuilder William Lawrence, who obviously did quite well for himself. From a small room on the second floor Lawrence could watch the progress of his vessels being built in the shipyard at the river's edge. Hours are 9.30 am to 5.30 pm daily, except Sunday when the home doesn't open until 1 pm. Admission is free.

STEWIACKE
At this little town south of Truro, you're halfway between the North Pole and the Equator.

SHUBENACADIE
Not far from Maitland or Truro, off Hwy 215 on the west side of the Shubenacadie River, is this park where the tidal bores can be watched daily. If that's not exciting enough for you then you can raft them. Zodiac rafts powered by outboard motors take six to eight passengers up the river and then ride the tidal bore as it sweeps through, literally a roller coaster in waves one to three metres high.

There is a $2 entry fee just to watch the action at Tidal Bore Park (☎ 758-4032 or 758-2177) while the two-hour-long raft trips are $45 per person.

Shubenacadie Wildlife Park (☎ 758-2040) is a provincial park housing examples of Nova Scotia's wildlife, including birds, waterfowl, foxes and deer, in large enclosures. It's off Hwy 102 at exit 10, 38 km south of Truro, just north of the town of Shubenacadie. It's open daily from 9 am to 7 pm from mid-May to mid-October and admission is $2 or $5 for the family.

South Shore

The South Shore refers to the area south and west of Halifax stretching along the coast to Yarmouth. It contains many fishing villages and several small historic towns. Some of the coastal scenery is good – typically rocky, jagged and foggy. The latter qualities have made the coast here and along the Eastern Shore as much a favourite with modern-day smugglers transporting illegal drugs as it once was to rum runners.

The first one-third of the area, closest to Halifax, is the city's cottage country and is quite busy. The tourist route through here, on the older and smaller roads, is called the Lighthouse Route and is probably the most visited region of Nova Scotia other than Cape Breton. Accommodations fill up fast, thanks to all that traffic in high season, so plan to find a place before dark each night.

MacKenzie buses service the region from Halifax to Yarmouth, with one departure in each direction daily. Yarmouth can also be reached via a northern route through the Annapolis Valley from Halifax on the Acadian bus line.

PROSPECT
South-west of Halifax is the quiet and little-visited Prospect, a small but attractive old coastal village. The view from the cemetery at the top of the hill on the approach to town is very impressive, especially if the fog bank is obscuring some of the islands and shoreline. There is a wharf, rocks to clamber over along the shore and a lighthouse.

PEGGY'S COVE
Canada's best known fishing village lies 43 km west of Halifax on Hwy 333. It's a pretty place, with fishing boats, nets, lobster traps, docks and old pastel houses that all seem perfectly placed to please the eye. Although not unlike many other such communities, Peggy's Cove does have a quintessential postcard quality about it.

The 415-million-year-old granite boulders (known to geologists as erratics) littering the surroundings add an odd touch.

The smooth shoreline rock all around the lighthouse just begs to be explored (but do not get too close – every year visitors are swept into the cold waters by unexpected swells). The ambience-creating fog completes the enticing effect. Count on the fog, too: it enshrouds the area at least once every three days and is present most mornings.

Peggy's Cove is a popular destination – probably one of the most visited in the Atlantic Provinces – and it's close to the capital too, so there are crowds which detract from its appeal. The best time for a visit is before 10 am. Many tour buses arrive in the middle of the day and create what has to be one of the worse traffic jams in the province. To ease that problem, there is a parking area with washrooms on the edge of town. Stop here and walk.

Surprisingly, the village, which dates from 1811, has just 60 residents and most of them are fishers.

See the pictorial in-the-rock monument by local artist DeGarthe outside his art gallery across from the provincial parking lot.

Located down near the lighthouse is *The Sou'wester Restaurant* with its huge gift shop of tacky souvenirs. Lobster dinners are $17 for a one-pounder and an order of fish and chips $7.45. The restaurant is huge but it can still be mobbed at times. The lighthouse is now a small post office which uses its own lighthouse-shaped stamp cancellation mark.

ST MARGARET'S BAY

A little beyond Peggy's Cove, large St Margaret's Bay is an area of small towns, craft shops and small sandy beaches, with a number of motels, campgrounds and cottages. Some visitors prefer to use it as a base for exploring the Halifax/Peggy's Cove region. It's a developed area where many people who work in the city live or have summer places.

Near the head of St Margaret's Bay is the start of the Bowaters Hiking Trail, which can

be used for a couple of hours or a full day's walk. At the top of the bay are the beaches. Queensland Beach, the one furthest west, is the largest and busiest and has a snack bar.

Places to Stay

One of the most attractive places to spend a night or two is the *Baybreeze Motel & Cottages* (☎ 826-2213 or 800-865-2615), nicely laid out by the water in Boutilier's Point. The cottages tend to be rented by the week but the motel units begin at $48 nightly for a double. The cottages are self-contained and some can sleep as many as seven.

MAHONE BAY

Mahone Bay, with its islands and history, has become a sort of city escape, with the town of the same name acting as the recreation/accommodation centre. It's a popular destination for a Sunday drive from Halifax, about 100 km away, or for an afternoon tea. The town has antique and craft shops and a decided tourist orientation. The approach from Halifax is noteworthy for the view of the three church spires by the roadside. You can see fine examples of Victorian gingerbread-house architecture around town, and the cemetery is interesting.

Along Hwy 3 on the east side of town is the tourist centre (☎ 624-6151), which is open 9 am to 7.30 pm daily during the summer. Among the many handouts here is a walking tour brochure of Mahone Bay. At 578 Main St is the **Settlers' Museum & Cultural Centre**, which deals mainly with the first German settlers to the area. Displays in two rooms cover the 1850s period. Hours are 10 am to 5 pm daily except Sunday when it opens at 1 pm. Admission is by donation.

Kayaking

Seakayaking is excellent in the island-studded Mahone Bay and located at 618 South Main St, just across from the harbour, is Mahone Bay Adventures (☎ 624-6632). The outfitters will rent singles for $40 a day and doubles for $60 a day. They also have canoes and offer a shuttle service up and down the coast.

For novices, there are half-day introductory lessons for $25, a day-long guided tour for $75 or a three-day B&B tour where you kayak from one inn to the next. All equipment, lodging and meals are provided and the cost is $350 per person.

Places to Stay & Eat

There are a dozen upmarket B&Bs, an indication of the trendiness and popularity of the Mahone Bay area. The *Fairmont B&B* (☎ 624-6173, or in Nova Scotia only 800-565-5971), 654 Main St, is central and reasonable for this area. The three rooms offered from May to October are $50/60 for singles/doubles.

Also in the centre of town is the *Heart's Desire B&B* (☎ 624-8766), at 686 Main St with doubles for $55 to $68 while just west of town, featuring a great view of the harbour from its porch, is *Edgewater B&B* (☎ 624-9382). The three rooms with shared bath are $45/55 and a full breakfast is included.

Among the shops are two pubs, a cafe and, at 621 South Main St, *Salt Spray Cafe* with a deck overlooking the harbour. Sandwiches here are about $5 but there is usually a daily special, like lasagne and salad, for under $7. For something a little more upmarket, try *Mimi Ocean Grill* just a little further on South Main St. Seafood dishes are around $10.

CHESTER

Chester, an old village with 1200 residents, overlooks Mahone Bay. Established in 1759, it has had a colourful history as the haunt of pirates and Prohibition bathtub-gin smugglers. It's now a small summer resort, and although there isn't a lot to do in town, a lot of visitors pass through each summer.

The centre of town is along Pleasant St between King and Queen Sts. The *Chester Playhouse*, which runs inexpensive comedies, musicals and dramas through July and August, is on Pleasant St. The tourist centre (☎ 275-4616) is on Hwy 3 north of town in the old train depot that is being renovated into a museum. Hours are 10 am to 7 pm daily during the summer.

Tancook Island

Offshore is Tancook Island, which can be reached by a 45-minute passenger-only ferry ride departing from the Chester wharf six times a day Monday through Friday and twice on Saturday and Sunday. The fare is $2 round trip. The islands – there is a Big & Little Tancook – are primarily residential but visitors are welcome to stroll around. Big Tancook has a tourist office, a simple food outlet and *Cove B&B* (☎ 228-2054), which has four rooms for $35/50. A walking-tour brochure available at the Chester tourist office outlines the paths which lead over much of the island.

The island is known for its plentiful cabbage and sauerkraut. Distinctive little cabbage-storage houses can be seen around the island.

Places to Stay

There is *Graves Island Provincial Park* (☎ 275-4425) for camping three km east of town near East River. The 64 wooded and open camp sites are on the ocean and are $12 a night.

At 78 Queen St, *Mecklenburgh Inn B&B* (☎ 275-4638) is a nice-looking place set in an old house built in 1890. Some rooms have private adjacent balconies. Prices are $50/60 with breakfast. For exploring, bicycles and a rowboat are available. It's open from mid-May to mid-October.

Another place to stay is the cheaper *Casa Blanca Guest House & Cabins* (☎ 275-3385), 463 Duke St, close to the centre. A single with shared bath is $44, including breakfast. A better deal is in nearby East Chester where the *East Chester Inn* (☎ 275-3017 or 275-4790) has seven rooms with shared bath. Singles range from $29 to $40, doubles $39 to $44 with a full breakfast.

Places to Eat

For a casual bite, there's the *Fo'c's'le Tavern*, and *Julien's Bakery & Cafe*, on the corner of Pleasant and Queen Sts. Julien's features fresh baked croissants daily.

Across the street from the Chester Playhouse is *Lost Parrot Cafe* for soups, salads and sandwiches in the $4 to $6 range while along the waterfront is the *Rope Loft* for seafood. A bowl of seafood chowder here is $5, pan-fried haddock $9.

NEW ROSS

At this small lumbering town in the interior of the province, 26 km north-west of Chester, is **Ross Farm Museum** (☎ 689-2210), a living agriculture museum of nine buildings set up like a working 19th-century farm. Hours during the summer are 9.30 am to 5.30 pm daily and admission is $3.

OAK ISLAND

What a story! This is treasure island with no treasure – so far. Said to be the burying place of the treasure of the infamous Captain Kidd or Blackbeard or Captain Morgan – maybe of Inca gold taken by the Spanish or ... the list goes on.

Despite nearly 200 years of digging, it's still up for grabs and has become one of the country's biggest and most captivating ongoing mysteries. Three farmboys stumbled upon a deep shaft in 1795, and since then, six lives and $4 million have been lost on 'the world's longest-running and most costly treasure hunt'. Before you grab your shovel and rush over, you need a permit which you can't get. The search – now using a lot of sophisticated equipment – is carried on by an international consortium determined to solve the mystery of the money pit once and for all.

But Oak Island Exploration Company (☎ 627-2376) does run tours of the site which explain some of the history and the incredible shafts, tunnels and chambers with their flooding systems. Some of the articles found thus far in the investigations are also shown. To get to the island, turn off Hwy 3 at Oak Island Rd. Hours are 10 am to 6 pm daily during the summer and admission is $5.

LUNENBURG

This attractive town of 2800 residents, best known for building the *Bluenose* sailing schooner in 1921 (which can be seen on the Canadian dime) is a UN World Heritage Site. Always a shipbuilding and fishing town, this well-preserved historic gem is now the centre of the provincial fishing industry and has one of the major fleets of the north Atlantic seaboard. The largest fish-processing plant in North America is here. From it come the Highliner supermarket seafood products.

Nova Scotia, like Newfoundland, has been hard hit by the dwindling fish stocks and severely curtailed limits imposed by the federal government. But Lunenburg has been able to turn more heavily to tourism to shore up its economy.

Lunenburg is an old town where Acadians lived until the mid-1700s. It was officially founded in 1753 when the British encouraged Protestants to emigrate from Europe. It soon became the first largely German settlement in the country. Much of its appeal today is in the fine, varied architecture.

Orientation & Information

The town's main street is Lincoln St. Montague St, running parallel to the harbour, is the street of most interest to the visitor. Along it are many of the town's commercial enterprises, including some interesting stores with gifts, crafts, antiques and prints for sale.

Many of the restaurants along Montague St have patios out the back facing Bluenose Drive, which runs right along the wharves. The Lunenburg Fisheries Museum is here, as are the boat tours. Further east along Montague St are the shipyards and commercial docks for the bigger trawlers. The principal intersection is with King St.

King St contains several banks, including the Royal with a 24-hour banking machine. Pelham St, one street back up the hill from Montague St, also has a number of shops. At No 134 is the oldest house in Lunenburg, **Bailly House**, constructed in 1760. This is where Earl Bailly lived and had his studio. He was one of the area's best known seascape painters, despite having had polio and having to wield his brush in his teeth. His brother now lives in the house, which can be visited to view some of the paintings.

Going up the hill along Lincoln St to

NOVA SCOTIA

Blockhouse Hill Rd is the **Lunenburg Tourist Bureau** (☎ 634-8100), open 9 am to 8 pm daily throughout the season, and a great view of the area.

Lunenburg is no Peggy's Cove, but in mid-season tourists flock down Montague St and tour buses rumble along Bluenose Drive at the waterfront. All of this is reflected in the prices for meals and rooms. It's almost impossible to find a double anywhere in town for under $50.

Lunenburg Fisheries Museum

The interesting provincial museum is down on the waterfront, on Bluenose Drive. It has one building, and two ships in the water for inspection: a dragger and a fishing schooner. In the building are exhibits on fishing and fish processing, and a 25-minute film on marine life. There's also an aquarium. It's open daily from 9.30 am to 5.30 pm from June to mid-October and admission is $4.50. Most people walk away thinking the museum is well worth the admission and if you purchase your ticket in late afternoon, it's good for the next day.

Churches

For a small town the churches are impressive, and there are five of them in the downtown area. St John's Anglican, on the corner of Duke and Cumberland Sts, is a real stunner. The beautiful black-and-white wooden place dates from 1753 and is one of the oldest churches in Canada. Tours are given through the summer. St Andrew's Presbyterian, on Townsend St, is the oldest Presbyterian church in the country.

The Zion Lutheran church has its own claim to fame. In it is one of the original bells from the fort at Louisbourg on Cape Breton Island. When at one time the federal government was considering ordering its return to the National Historic Site, it was removed from the church and hidden at the bottom of Lunenburg's back harbour.

Lunenburg Academy

The Academy, a school, is the huge black-and-white turreted structure on a hill seen rising above the town on your way in from Halifax. Built entirely of wood in 1895, as a prestigious high school, it is one of the rare survivors of the academy system of education. Now a National Historic Site, the Academy began offering tours for the first time in 1995 on Wednesday and a few Saturdays during August from 10 am to noon. Admission for the half hour tour is $3.

Activities

The public swimming pool is on Knickle Rd south-west of the centre.

The Dory Shop (☎ 634-9146), at Railway Wharf, rents boats by the hour or day – row, sail or motor, depending on your energy level.

Jo's Dive Shop (☎ 800-JO-DIVE-1), at 296 Lincoln St, has everything for the diver including rentals.

Bicycles can be rented and repaired at the Bicycle Barn (☎ 634-3426), located at Blue Rocks Road B&B almost two km from town. The hybrid and mountain bikes are $8 a half day and $15 a day.

Organised Tours

Several boat cruises are offered from down by the docks. Walter Flower Charters (☎ 527-7175) offers three-hour whale-watching trips departing from the Lunenburg harbour for $30 per person. Star Charters (☎ 634-3535 or 688-2351) has five trips daily on its two-mast, wooden ketch for $15.50 person.

Festivals

In July, a craft festival is held, and in mid-August the equally popular Folk Harbour Festival (☎ 634-3180) is a weekend of traditional music and dance. In late September the town tips a few pints during its Oktoberfest.

Places to Stay

Lunenburg is a popular destination, and during midsummer making reservations early in the day is strongly recommended. The tourist centre doubles as a booking agency for all the B&Bs and hotels, and late in the day will know who has vacancies.

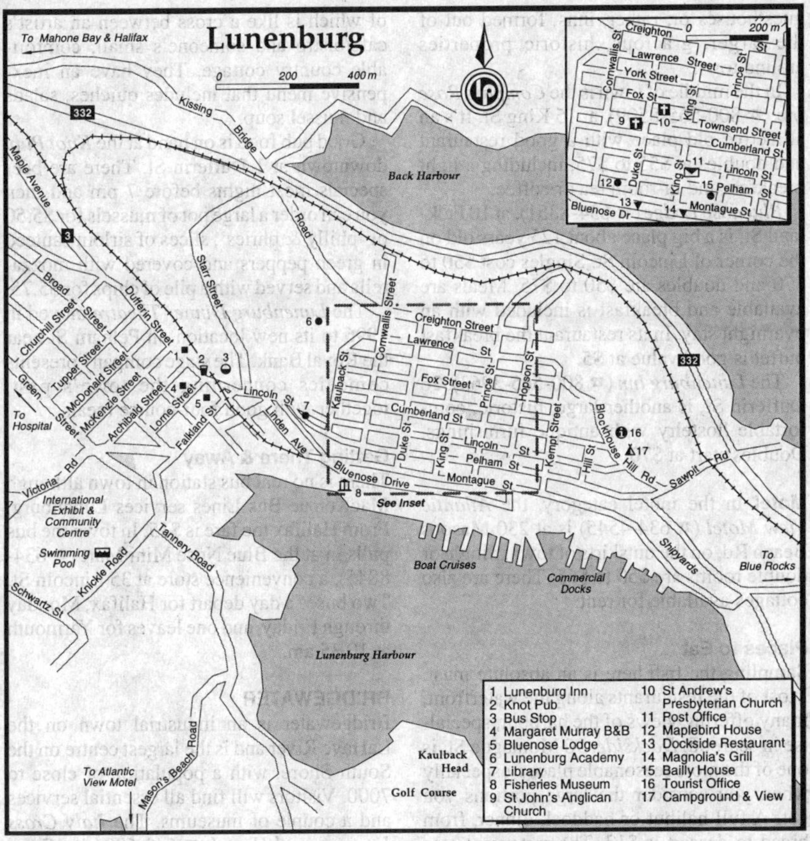
Lunenburg
0 200 400 m
To Mahone Bay & Halifax
332
Kissing Bridge
Maple Avenue
Back Harbour
3
Road
Starr Street
Broad Street
Dufferin Street
Churchill Street
Tupper Street
McDonald Street
McKenzie Street
Archibald Street
Lorne Street
Falkland St
Green Street
To Hospital
Lincoln St
Linden Ave
Kaulback Street
Cornwallis Street
Creighton Street
Lawrence St
Fox Street
Cumberland St
Duke St
King St
Lincoln St
Pelham St
Montague St
Prince St
Hopson St
Kempt Street
Hill St
Blockhouse Hill Rd
Sawpit Rd
332
Bluenose Drive
See Inset
Victoria Rd
International Exhibit & Community Centre
Swimming Pool
Tannery Road
Knickle Road
Schwartz St
Boat Cruises
Commercial Docks
Shipyards
To Blue Rocks
Lunenburg Harbour
Mason's Beach Road
To Atlantic View Motel
Kaulback Head
Golf Course
Creighton
0 200 m
Lawrence Street
York Street
Fox St
Townsend Street
Cumberland St
Lincoln St
Pelham St
Montague St
Bluenose Dr
Cornwallis St
King St
Duke St
Prince St
1 Lunenburg Inn
2 Knot Pub
3 Bus Stop
4 Margaret Murray B&B
5 Bluenose Lodge
6 Lunenburg Academy
7 Library
8 Fisheries Museum
9 St John's Anglican Church
10 St Andrew's Presbyterian Church
11 Post Office
12 Maplebird House
13 Dockside Restaurant
14 Magnolia's Grill
15 Bailly House
16 Tourist Office
17 Campground & View

Camping Right in town beside the tourist office, with great views, there is *Board of Trade Campground* (☎ 634-8100) for trailers or tenters. It's an ideal, incredibly convenient place which charges $12 for an unserviced site, $14 for a hook-up. It has 32 sites and does get full, so arrive early.

B&Bs Perhaps the most affordable accommodation in this high rent town is the *Margaret Murray B&B* (☎ 634-3974), a short distance west of the centre, off Dufferin St at 20 Lorne St. There are three rooms with shared bath at $30/40 for singles/doubles.

Also reasonably priced is the *Maplebird House* (☎ 634-3863), overlooking the harbour at 36 Pelham St in the centre of town. There are three rooms with shared bath that go for $45/50 light breakfast included.

Out on Blue Rocks Rd, 1.3 km from town, *Lamb & Lobster B&B* (☎ 634-4833) is appropriately named as the owner, William Flower, is a lobster fisherman and a shepherd. In the evening guests may be shown how the family collies round up the sheep. Singles/doubles are $40/50.

Inns There are also several more upmarket

guesthouses or, rather, inns, formed out of the larger, gracious, historic properties around town.

In the middle of town is the *Compass Rose Inn* (☎ 800-565-8509), at 15 King St. It's an attractive old place with a good restaurant and doubles at $55 to $75, including a light breakfast and in-room tea or coffee.

Bluenose Lodge (☎ 634-8851), at 10 Falkland St, is a big place about 125 years old on the corner of Lincoln St. Singles cost $50 to $70 and doubles are $50 to $75. Meals are available and breakfast is included with an overnight stay. In its restaurant the breakfast buffet is good value at $5.

The *Lunenburg Inn* (☎ 800-565-3963), 26 Dufferin St, is another large, historic, comfortable hostelry with antique furnishings. Doubles start at $70.

Motel In the motel category, the *Atlantic View Motel* (☎ 634-4545) is at 230 Masons Beach Rd, on the outskirts of town. Single or double rooms are $50 to $65. There are also cottages available for rent.

Places to Eat

Sampling the fish here is an absolute must. Most of the restaurants along the waterfront, many offering views of the harbour, specialise in seafood. *Dockside*, 90 Montague St, is one of the more reasonable places, especially when you consider the large portions you get. A full halibut or haddock dinner, from bread to dessert is $13. The restaurant also has an outdoor patio.

There are a number of places side by side here, many with menus posted, like *Peg Leg's*, a smaller restaurant with fresh pasta dinners for $8 to $10 and great desserts.

Fish or lobster is also available at the *Old Fish Factory*, overlooking the water from the Fisheries Museum building. It offers good, fresh seafood and a nice setting but dinners range from $12 to $20. At lunch, however, there is a seafood chowder and salad bar for $9 that is guaranteed to fill you up if you pile the salad high enough.

Away from the waterfront try *Magnolia's Grill*, at 128 Montague St, the eclectic inside

of which is like a cross between an artist's cafe/bistro and someone's small, comfortable country cottage. They have an inexpensive menu that includes quiches, salads and mussel soup.

Good pub food is on hand at the *Knot Pub*, downtown at 1 Dufferin St. There are beer specials most nights before 7 pm and then you can order a large pot of mussels for $5.50 or 'philly & phries', slices of sirloin sauteed in green peppers and covered with mozzarella and served with a pile of chips for $5.75.

The *Lunenburg Dinner Theatre* moved in 1996 to its new location on Pelham St near the Royal Bank. The stage company presents comedies concerning the town's past, together with good four-course meals.

Getting There & Away

There is no real bus station in town although MacKenzie Bus Lines services Lunenburg. From Halifax the fare is $15. In town the bus pulls in at the Blue Nose Mini Mart (☎ 634-8845), a convenience store at 35 Lincoln St. Two buses a day depart for Halifax, Monday through Friday, and one leaves for Yarmouth at 10.35 am.

BRIDGEWATER

Bridgewater is an industrial town on the LaHave River and is the largest centre on the South Shore, with a population of close to 7000. Visitors will find all essential services and a couple of museums. The *Italy Cross International Hostel* (☎ 543-6984 is 17 km south at 606 Somerset Rd. There are eight beds at this organic farm not far from the sea and area parks. The Mackenzie bus stops at Italy Cross.

The **Desbrisay Museum** (☎ 543-4033), on 10 hectares of parkland, has a small collection of goods relating to the early, mainly German, settlers of Lunenburg County. Hours are 9 am to 5 pm daily during the summer except on Sunday when it opens at 1 pm. Admission is free.

The **Wile Carding Mill** (☎ 543-8233) (carding is the straightening and untangling of wool fibres in preparation for spinning), on Victoria Rd, is an authentic water mill dating from 1860. Hours are the same as Desbrisay Museum.

The South Shore Exhibition, held each July, is a major five-day fair with traditional competitions between Canadian and US teams in such events as the ox pull.

Around **New Germany**, further up the river, are many Christmas tree farms. The trees are shipped from the Bridgewater docks to expectant households along the US seaboard.

THE OVENS

Route 332 south from Bridgewater edges along the LaHave River to the sea. It's a pleasant country road with the huge old trees and mammoth old riverside houses fondly associated with the history and good life of the Maritimes.

At the end of the road is The Ovens (☎ 766-4621), a sort of combination nature park and campground, which is highly recommended for its scenery and general easy-going atmosphere.

Gold was found here in 1861 and still can be found on Cunard Beach. Rent a dish at the office and try panning. In a different area, a trail leads along the shore past (and into) numerous caves. The camping is very good, with many camp sites right by the shore with fine views over the ocean and a rocky ledge to explore at low tide.

There is also a guided sea cave boat tour, done in inflatable Zodiac boats, a swimming pool, and a comfortable little restaurant which serves up inexpensive fish & chips. Admission into the park is $3 and an unserviced campsite is $16. The gold panning is $5 a day (pan included) and the sea cave tour is $12.50.

LAHAVE

From Riverport a 50-cent, five-minute ride by cable ferry takes you across the river to the town of LaHave, where a stop at *LaHave Bakery*, one of the best (physically and gastronomically) in the country, is a must. You can't miss it – it's just to the south of the ferry landing, on the main street.

Upstairs, the small *LaHave Marine Hostel* (☎ 688-2908), is a HI hostel for cyclists, backpackers or any like-minded soul looking for a cheap place to spend the night. It's open from May to October and the rate is $8/10 for members/nonmembers. Also based at the bakery is LaHave Outfitters, who run coastal boat excursions.

On the outskirts west of the village is the **Fort Point Museum**, a National Historic Site. It was here in 1632 that the first batch of French settlers soon to be known as Acadians landed from France. A fort, Sainte-Marie-de-Grâce, was built later the same year but very little of it remains today. The site was supplanted by Port Royal on the north coast and never became a major centre. A museum in the former lighthouse keeper's house at the site tells more of this early settlement and its leader, de Raizilly. It's open daily from 10 am to 6 pm June through August, and weekends in September. Admission is free.

LAHAVE ISLANDS

Just south-west of LaHave are the LaHave Islands, a handful of small islands connected to the mainland by a long causeway and to each other by one-lane iron bridges. The islands make a short scenic drive, and on Bell Island just past the Government Wharf is the **Marine Museum**. The museum is in the St John's Anglican Church and services are occasionally still held among the collection of marine artefacts. Hours are 10 am to 6 pm daily in July and August and admission is free.

Near the causeway to the islands along Hwy 331 is **Rissers Provincial Park** (☎ 688-2034), which features a very busy campground and an excellent long, sandy beach, although the water is none too warm. There is also a saltwater marsh with a board-walk trail. The 90 unserviced sites are each $12 a day.

Also nearby on Hwy 331 is Crescent Sea Kayak Tours (☎ 688-2806). Two-hour tours among the islands are $25 for a single boat and $40 for a double.

NOVA SCOTIA

LIVERPOOL

Situated where the Mersey River meets the ocean, as it does in Britain, Liverpool is another historic English-style town with an economy based on forests and fish. The tourist office (☎ 354-5421) on Henry Hensey Drive, just off Main St, in Centennial Park, has a walking-tour pamphlet which guides you past many of the notable houses and buildings in the downtown area and along the waterfront. The office also has a handful of bicycles that are free to use for touring the town. Hours of the centre are 9 am to 8 pm.

Perkins House (☎ 354-4058), built in 1766, is now a museum with articles and furniture from the colonial period. Hours during the summer are 9.30 am to 5.30 pm daily except on Sunday when it opens at 1 pm. Admission is free. Next door, the **Queen's County Museum** (☎ 354-4058) has some Native Indian artefacts and more materials relating to town history, as well as some writings by early citizens. Hours and admission are the same as Perkins House.

At **Fort Point**, marked with a cairn, is the site where Samuel de Champlain landed from France in 1604. There is also a memorial to the British privateers who were active in the local waters at the beginning of the 1800s, protecting the British trade routes from incursions by the USA.

There are four sandy **beaches** nearby: Beach Meadows, White Point, Hunt's Point and Summerville. All are within 11 km of town, and there are others further west.

An eight-km rail trail begins on West St behind the Municipal Offices in Liverpool and ends one km from Summerville Beach Provincial Park. The former railway line became a hike/bike trail after the CNR abandoned the route.

Places to Stay & Eat

For spending the night, there are B&Bs and nearby motels. *Lane's Privateer Inn* (☎ 354-3456), 33 Bristol Ave, is the white wooden building with balconies built in 1798 on Hwy 3 by the bridge over the Mersey River, just east of the centre. A double with continental breakfast is $52, and there is a good restaurant which specialises in seafood. They also have canoes and bicycles for rent. Next door the inn runs a B&B with rooms at $38/45. At 155 Main St is the *Liverpool Pizzeria*, which has medium pizza for $8, lasagne with garlic bread for $5. The *Liverpool Landing Pub* is on Legion St, across from the Canadian Tire store, with fish & chips for $6.

SEASIDE ADJUNCT
KEJIMKUJIK NATIONAL PARK

The main body of this large national park is in the interior north-west of Liverpool, south-east of Digby, but this undeveloped region of the south coast between Port Joli Bay and Port Mouton (ma-TOON) Bay is part of the same park. The 'Keji Adjunct' (☎ 354-2880) protects a beautiful, wild stretch of shoreline and the animals, most particularly the endangered piping plover bird, within it.

Services are nonexistent – no camping or fires are allowed, no toilets or drinking water are available. What you will find is pristine coastline, with two great beaches, coves, vistas, rock formations and an abundance of birdlife.

Two trails, one leading in from each end, provide the only access. Both tend to be a little wet. From **South-west Port Mouton**, an eight-km track leads to Black Point and the shore. From **St Catherine's River**, a little village, a three-km walk leads to the sea on the western side.

The **Port Joli Basin**, which is adjacent to the above park, also contains other sites of interest to nature lovers. The basin is composed of the harbour, Port Joli Bay, and the two coastal headlands which enclose it. At the end of the natural harbour, near the village of Point Joli, is the **Point Joli Migratory Bird Sanctuary**. Birders will find waterfowl, shorebirds and others in number, especially during migration periods. There are no facilities but visitors can explore on their own. In Port Joli ask for directions to the park.

LOCKEPORT

At the end of a jutting arm is the little town of Lockeport, with what is known as an historic streetscape. The town was founded by New Englanders in the 1700s but became prosperous in the mid-1800s through fishing and, more importantly, as a trading centre with the West Indies. It was during this time that the wealthy built the large, ostentatious homes seen at the waterfront. One street has five such homes, all impressive in their own way and all built by members of the Locke family between 1836 and 1876, using different architectural styles. The short street has been designated an historic site, although unfortunately none of the houses are open to visitors.

Before crossing the causeway into town you pass the **Crescent Beach Centre**, the striking building with the steeply pitched roofs. On the first floor is the tourist office (☎ 656-3123) open from 10 am to 9 pm daily during the summer. On the second floor is an observation gallery with a 360-degree view of the nearby saltwater marshes and the Lockeport Harbour along with interpretive displays and a viewing scope.

At the other end of Crescent Beach, a long sandy beach that was once featured on the Canadian $50 bill, is the **Little School Museum**. The former one-room school is now filled with local relics, including a replica of a 19th-century classroom. Hours are 10 am to 4 pm daily during the summer except Sunday when it opens at noon and admission is free.

If it's time to consider quitting for the day, there are a handful of options for spending a quiet night. The *Locke's Island Lodging* (☎ 656-3222), about 16 km down from Hwy 103, can't be missed. It's open all year and has three rooms, at $40/50 with a light breakfast included. In town is *Hillcrest B&B*, once run as a hotel in the late 1800s. It has three rooms with shared bath for $40/50.

The *White Gull Restaurant* offers seafood and an outdoor deck overlooking the Lockeport's inner harbour. Next door is the *Lobster Trap* if you want cooked takeaway lobsters.

SHELBURNE

This is one of the most attractive and interesting towns anywhere on the South Shore. The whole place is pretty much like a museum, with fine buildings and historic sites at every turn. It sits on a hill overlooking a good harbour, with a nice waterfront area and some good places to eat and stay.

This shipbuilding town with a population of 2245 is known as the birthplace of yachts. As well as the prize-winning yachts, though, it produces several other types of boats. Shelburne also boasts a towncrier, Perry Wamback, who has won national and international competitions.

Shelburne, like many towns in the Fundy region, was founded by Loyalists, and in 1783 had a population of 10,000, making it the largest community in British North America. Many of its inhabitants were former members of the New York aristocracy. Some of the Loyalist houses still stand. The so-called Loyalists were residents of the USA who maintained their allegiance to Britain during the period of the American Revolution. Life in the USA was not easy for those with loyalty to the British crown, and thousands left for Canada.

Water St, the main street, has many houses from 100 to 200 years old, and quite a few of the two-storey wooden homes are marked with dates.

Dock St along the harbour features several historic buildings and museums and the tourist office (☎ 875-4547), open from 9 am to 7 pm daily during the summer.

This is a major port, and boats from Quebec's Gaspé and the Magdalen Islands, from New Brunswick and Prince Edward Island, may be moored here. Recent cutbacks in fishing quotas have resulted in a marked decline in fishing activity. Individuals still cast for mackerel right off the dock, though. A little further out are the shipyards where repairs to the Marine Atlantic ferries and other vessels are carried out.

Ross-Thompson House

Built in 1784, this house (which has an adjacent store) belonged to well-to-do merchants who arrived from Britain via Cape Cod, and now acts as a small museum. Furniture, paintings, artefacts and original goods from the store can be viewed. The house is surrounded by gardens, as it would have been formerly. The Ross-Thompson House (☎ 875-3141) and all museums in town are open daily from 9.30 am to 5.30 pm from June to mid-October and are free.

Shelburne County Museum

Nearby is this Loyalist house dating from 1787, with a collection of Loyalist furnishings, displays on the history of the local fishery and other articles from the town's past. The oldest fire engine in Canada, a wooden cart from 1740, is quite something. There is also a small collection of Micmac artefacts, including typical porcupine-quill decorative work. The museum (☎ 875-3219) is on the corner of Dock St and Maiden Lane and open year round with shorter hours in the winter.

Dory Shop

Shelburne has long had a reputation for its dories, small boats first used for fishing from a mother schooner and in later years for inshore fishing and as lifeboats. Many were built here from the 1880s until the 1970s. At the museum you can learn about them and their history and see examples still being made in the workshop upstairs.

The large building across the street was once used as a warehouse and was also, at one time, one of the country's largest department stores.

Places to Stay

Just a few km west of town is a good provincial park, *The Islands* (☎ 875-4304). The 65 unserviced sites are in mature forest and there is swimming nearby. It's quiet during the week but has been known to get rowdy on weekends. A site is $9 a night.

The *Bear's Den* (☎ 875-3234) is a small, attractive and economical B&B on the corner of Water and Glasgow Sts, whose owner makes and sells teddy bears. You'll pass it on the way into the centre of town.

Singles/doubles cost $35/45, including a complete breakfast.

Another affordable B&B in town is *Harbour House* (☎ 875-2074) at 187 Water St. The owners are fluent in German and the three bedrooms are $35/45.

The *Toddle In* (☎ 875-3229) B&B is central, on the corner of Water and King Sts. Singles or doubles start at $60.

There are also a few motels at the edge of town, including the attractive *Cape Cod Colony Motel* (☎ 875-3411), 234 Water St, where rooms are $45/49.

Places to Eat

The *Toddle In* has a small, friendly dining room for inexpensive, fresh breakfasts and lunches.

Claudia's Diner, on Water St, open every day, is a low-priced restaurant with style and standard fare. The cinnamon rolls are good and a large bowl of lobster chowder is $5.50.

For a bit of a splurge the dining room in the *Coopers Inn* (dating from 1785) is very good. They offer just four dishes and four desserts nightly and do them well. Of course, seafood is on the menu but there's always an alternative. Dinners range from $15 to $17.50. *Charlotte Lane Cafe* offers pasta dishes for $9, or try the Swiss potato roesti which is grated potatoes sauteed and then smothered with cheese and egg for $6.

Getting There & Away

MacKenzie Bus Lines running between Halifax and Yarmouth stops at Scotia Lunch at 64 King St. A west-bound bus to Yarmouth stops at 12.45 pm daily and an east-bound bus for Halifax at 11.15 am daily except Sunday, when it passes through at 4.50 pm.

Elliot's Music & Repair (☎ 875-1188) in town rents out bicycles for $4 an hour or $20 a day.

BARRINGTON

The small village of Barrington, that dates back to 1760 when Cape Cod settlers erected their meetinghouse here, makes for an interesting afternoon or an ideal place to stay overnight. The town has four museums, all within walking distance of one another, all open daily and all free. There is also a campground, an HI hostel in the area and an historic B&B in town.

The tourist office (☎ 637-2625), in the middle of things, has an example of the Cape Island boat, the classic small fishing boat of the North Atlantic, originating on Cape Sable Island and now seen all around eastern Canada. The centre is open 9 am to 7 pm during the summer and usually there is free coffee and donuts on hand.

The most interesting museum is the **Woollen Mill**, restored to represent a small manufacturing mill of the late 1800s. It was the last woollen mill of its age to cease operating and, amazingly, not until 1962. Costumed guides lead you through the entire operation from cleaning the raw wool to spinning it into yarn and then show a video of the mill in operation in the 1950s.

The **Barrington Meetinghouse** reflects the town's early Quaker influence and was used as both church and city hall. There is an old cemetery next door and on the third Sunday of August a community service is still held in the meetinghouse.

The **Seal Island Light Museum** is a replica of the lighthouse found on Seal Island, 30 km out to sea, and is a record of the original and its keepers. Inside it houses the lens from the original lighthouse and other artefacts while from the top there's a vista of Barrington Bay.

Across the road from the Historical Society Centre, the **Western Counties Military Museum** has uniforms, medals and other artefacts.

Places to Stay & Eat

Also along Hwy 309 is *Bayberry Campground* (☎ 637-2181) with both secluded wooded camp sites and others overlooking the ocean. An unserviced site is $10 a night, $12 if you want to be on the water.

There is an excellent HI hostel, 6.5 km south of Barrington also on Hwy 309. The *Barrington Hostel* (☎ 637-2891) is in a two-storey structure with 10 beds on the top level and a kitchen area on the first floor. The whole place is warmed by a wood-burning stove and outside a trail takes you down to the ocean. The rate is $7.75 for members and $10.75 for non-members.

In town there is *MacMullen House* (☎ 637-3892), a B&B that was a hotel in the late 1800s. There are three rooms with shared bath for $35/45 and a cottage for $65.

In nearby Barrington Passage is the *Old School House* (☎ 637-3770), a hotel, restaurant, natural food store and bakery. Good sandwiches and salads are offered, with more substantial meals also available. The six inn rooms with shared bath are $35/45 otherwise there are cottages at $49 to $59.

BARRINGTON TO YARMOUTH

From Barrington there is not much of interest until Yarmouth. **Cape Sable** and **West Pubnico** were both once Acadian settlements and each has a small general museum. Pubnico remains French and is considered the oldest village in Canada still lived in by the descendants of its founders.

Yarmouth to Windsor

This region of Nova Scotia stretches from Yarmouth northward and along the south shore of the Bay of Fundy to Windsor and the Minas Basin. It consists, primarily, of two very distinct geographical and cultural regions.

The area between Yarmouth and Digby was one of the first European-settled areas in Canada. This municipality of Clare formed part of Acadia, the French region of the New World colonies. The 'French Shore' and its history are still very much in evidence today.

The best-known area, however, is the scenic valley of the Annapolis River, which runs more or less from Digby to Wolfville. It's famous for apples, and in springtime the blossoming valley is at its best.

The Evangeline Trail tourist route passes through the entire region, taking in both of these disparate districts.

YARMOUTH

With a population of nearly 8000, Yarmouth is the largest town in western Nova Scotia. It's also a transportation centre of sorts, where aside from the main highway and the district airport, ferries from Portland and Bar Harbour in Maine dock. It's an old city and recent town improvements have stressed its historical side. Whichever way you're going, chances are you'll be passing through, and this is a good place to stop.

There's a huge tourist office (☎ 742-5033) down at the ferry docks with both local and provincial information available along with a room reservation service and money exchange counter. They have a walking-tour guide of the city with a map and some historical information. The office is open 8 am to 7 pm from May through October.

Every Saturday through the summer, a farmers' market and flea market is held at the Centretown Square from 9 am to 3 pm, on the corner of Main and Central Sts.

Yarmouth County Museum

Open every day in summer (on Sunday from noon only), the museum (☎ 742-5539) at 22 Collins St, in a grey stone building that was formerly a church, is quite good and well worth the price of admission.

Most of the exhibits are to do with the sea – ship models, a large painting collection, etc. Many articles were brought back by sea captains from their travels in Asia, and include ebony elephant carvings from Ceylon and fine ivory work from Japan.

One of the highlights is a runic stone found near town in 1812 and believed to have been carved by Viking Leif Erikson some 1000 years ago. Other evidence has been discovered which suggests that the Vikings were indeed in this area.

In summer, the museum is open Monday to Saturday from 9 am to 5 pm and on Sunday from 1 to 5 pm; in the off season, hours are shorter and it's closed on Monday. Admission is $2 or $4 for a family.

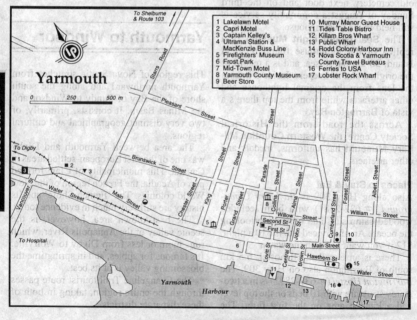

1 Lakelawn Motel	10 Murray Manor Guest House
2 Capri Motel	11 Tides Table Bistro
3 Captain Kelley's	12 Killam Bros Wharf
4 Ultrama Station &	13 Public Wharf
MacKenzie Buss Line	14 Rodd Colony Harbour Inn
5 Firefighters' Museum	15 Nova Scotia & Yarmouth
6 Frost Park	County Travel Bureaus
7 Mid-Town Motel	16 Ferries to USA
8 Beer Store	17 Lobster Rock Wharf
9 Yarmouth County Museum	

Firefighters' Museum

This museum (☎ 742-5525) at 431 Main St has a collection of beautiful fire engines dating from the 1930s. Admission costs $1; it's open from 9 am to 9 pm daily except on Sunday when the hours are 10 am to 5 pm.

The Wharves

As a major fishing port, Yarmouth's waterfront is lined with wharves. Beside the ferry terminal is the Public Wharf, where local fishing boats tie in. Many of the small boats of the herring fleet depart from here at around sundown. Also at the Public Wharf, vessels from around the world can sometimes be seen.

Next wharf over is the Killam Brothers Wharf, a waterfront park of sorts and the site of the **Killam Brothers Museum**. The Killam family began trading in 1788 and continued for more than a century on Yarmouth's waterfront. This shipping office was built in the 1830s and used until 1991. Now a museum, inside are the original desks, ledgers and scales that date back to the 19th century. Hours during the summer are 9 am to 5 pm Monday to Saturday and admission is free.

Around Yarmouth

The **Yarmouth Light** is 11 km from the ferry terminal at the end of Cape Forchu along Hwy 304. Signs from Main St will direct you all the way there. The original light was built in 1860 but torn down in 1964. The new one lacks any charm whatsoever, looking like a giant piece of penny candy. But the drive out is extremely scenic and interesting as you cross Yarmouth Bar where most of the lobster fishermen maintain their boat sheds and traps. At the end there is a small interpretive centre, open 10 am to 7 pm daily, and walking trails.

More walking trails can be enjoyed at the end of Wedgeport Peninsula, a 15-km drive from Yarmouth, via Hwy 3 north and then Hwy 334 south. The **Wedgeport Nature Trail** is a 5.4-km network of trails to Wedge Point and features observation platforms, boardwalks and 12 interpretive displays. The birding can be quite good here.

In the community of Wedgeport, Tusket Islands Cruise (☎ 663-4345) offers a four-hour boat tour for $30 which includes bird nesting colonies, seals, a stop at Harris Island and lots of shoreline scenery. The company also runs a lobster and clam bake to Harris Island.

Places to Stay

Camping The nearest campground is *Loomer's Campers Haven* (☎ 742-4848), four km east of the ferry terminal on Hwy 3 in Arcadia. This huge campground (250 sites) is geared primarily for RVers but you can pitch your tent here for $17 a night. There are showers, laundromat and a store on site.

Hostel The *Ice House Hostel* (☎ 649-2818) is 22 km north of Yarmouth next door to Churchill Mansion Inn just off Hwy 1 in Darling Lake. This HI hostel was indeed an ice house once when the mansion was the summer home of shipping magnate Aaron Churchill. There are only four beds but facilities do include a kitchen and shower. A bed is $8 a night while singles/doubles in the impressive mansion begin at $35/45.

B&Bs Just one block from the ferry is the seasonal *Murray Manor Guest House* (☎ 742-9625), at 225 Main St. There are three rooms and a kitchen guests may use. With breakfast, singles/doubles are $45/55.

In an historic house at 109 Brunswick St is the *Victorian Vogue B&B* (☎ 742-6398). Open year round, the Victorian charges $38/45 including a full breakfast.

If you have a vehicle, *Whittaker's B&B* (☎ 742-7649) is the best deal in the area. The farm house is three km from the ferry terminal on Peterson Rd on the west side of Yarmouth Harbour and has three rooms for $20/30. To reach it, follow the signs for Hwy 304 and the Yarmouth Lighthouse but continue towards Chegoggin when Hwy 304 swings south.

Motels The *Mid-Town Motel* (☎ 742-5333)

is central at 13 Parade St, and rooms begin at $40 for a single or double with a free coffee in the morning. Aside from the 21 standard rooms, there are a couple of efficiency units with kitchens.

The *Capri Motel* (☎ 742-7168), right off Main St at 8 Herbert St, was recently renovated and has singles that begin at $35. Also economical is the *Lakelawn* (☎ 742-3588), 641 Main St, where breakfast is available. Singles/doubles are $38/45.

Places to Eat

The cafeteria in the *Met*, a Woolworth's-style store at 386 Main St, near Lovitt St, is extremely inexpensive for Canadian basics, with everything under $6.

Not far away, in the big gabled place at 577 Main St, *Captain Kelley's* is a pub-style place which specialises in fish and beef. A haddock dinner is $9.50, Kelley's pub steak $5. Best of all is *Harris' Quick 'n' Tasty*, four km from town on Route 3 (Main St) towards Digby. It's a busy, good and reasonably priced seafood spot with fish cakes $6, haddock and chips $7 and affordable beer.

Overlooking the wharves at the foot of Jenkins St is *Tide's Table Bistro*. The service is a little slow here but the view is nice and the prices not bad; $4.50 for a bowl of seafood chowder or pasta dinners from $8.

Just up Jenkins St is *Yarmouth Natural Food Market*. The fast-food chains and large supermarkets are on Hwy 3 as you enter town.

Getting There & Away

Bus Acadian bus lines (☎ 742-9194), Nova Scotia's biggy, now departs from Rodd Colony Harbour Inn across from the tourist office. There is one run five times a week to Halifax, taking five hours via Digby and the Annapolis Valley. On Monday, Tuesday, Friday and Saturday it departs 6.45 am, on Sunday it leaves at 4 pm. To Digby, the fare is $13; to Halifax it's $41.

MacKenzie Bus Line (☎ 742-5011) also runs to Halifax, but uses the South Shore route and has a bus departing Monday through Saturday at 9.25 am and on Sunday

at 3 pm. These buses arrive at and depart from the Ultramar service station on the corner of Main and Beacon Sts. The fare to Halifax is $39.

Ferry There are two major ferry routes in and out of Yarmouth, both to the state of Maine in the USA; one connects with Bar Harbour and the other with Portland.

The Marine Atlantic (☎ 742-6800 in Yarmouth; 1-800-341-7981 elsewhere) ferry, the MV *Bluenose* to Bar Harbour, Maine, takes about six hours to travel the 160 km. It leaves Yarmouth at 4.30 pm daily during the summer months, less frequently the rest of the year and not at all during the winter. The basic one-way fare is $49 per adult, $64 per car and $11 per bicycle. There is also a one-day return trip, which is really a 12-hour cruise. Private cabins are available at additional cost. Ask Marine Atlantic for details.

The other ferry is operated by Maine's Prince of Fundy Cruises (☎ 742-6460 in Yarmouth; 1-800-341-7540 elsewhere in Canada) and it sails back and forth to Portland, Maine. The trip to Portland is 320 km – double the distance and therefore about twice the duration and more expensive – but you could win back the fare in the casino! This is a popular trip and for many is as much a holiday cruise as simple ferry transportation. Quite a few people just go and come back without even bothering to leave ship in port. Like the Bar Harbour boat, this is well appointed and comfortable, but the casino with floor show adds a touch of glamour. There are several other packages that include cabin and meals.

Sailing time is about 11 hours one way. Through the summer the ferry leaves Yarmouth daily (except Wednesday) at 10 am and Portland at 9 pm daily (except Tuesday). The basic fare is US$78, less in the off season. A vehicle is US$99. There is 10% discount for return trips, except on weekends. Please note these last fares are in US dollars.

Call ahead for either trip, as reservations will probably be required.

In Portland there is a Nova Scotia Tourist Office in the Portland Pier area, across from the old Thomas Block Building.

Getting Around

For car rentals there is a Budget (☎ 742-9500) at 150 Starrs Rd. For a sub-compact, you're looking at $50 a day plus 15 cents a km.

The Rodd Colony Harbour Inn near the ferry terminal rents bicycles for $11 a day while the tourist centre has a brochure outlining bike routes in the area.

FRENCH SHORE

From roughly Salmon River for 50 km up the coast along St Mary's Bay towards Digby is Old Acadia, also known as the Municipality of Clare. This is where the province's largest, mainly French-speaking Acadian population lives. It's an interesting region where traditional foods and crafts are available, a few historic sites can be seen and, in summer, festivals are held in some of the small villages. Because the towns are small, a visit through the area can be done quite quickly.

Among the crafts offered out of people's houses along the way, the best two are the quilts and the woodcarvings, both of which have earned good reputations.

For campers, there are several campgrounds between Yarmouth and Digby.

Cape St Mary's

A long wide arch of fine sand, the **Mavilette Beach** is marvellous. The marsh behind the beach is good for bird-watching. Across the street, the *Cape View Motel* (☎ 645-2258) has both regular motel rooms and some individual cabins. Prices are $40/50 in the units; the self-contained cottages are more costly.

From the *Cape View Restaurant* the beach looks great at sunset, and the food is good too. The menu is mainly seafood – clams are a local speciality – but also available is rapie pie, an old Acadian dish (for details see Church Point). Main dishes at dinner range from $9 to $13 and a rapie pie is $5.50.

Meteghan

This is a busy fishing port and there is a large commercial wharf where the boats moor. On the main street is **La Vieille Maison**, one of the oldest houses in the region and now set up as a museum depicting Acadian life here during the 18th century. It also doubles as a tourist centre (☎ 645-2389) and is open during the summer from 9 am to 7 pm daily.

The Wood Studio has carvings and quilts to see or buy.

For accommodation try the *Anchor Inn* (☎ 645-3390), a B&B in a big old house at just $22/33. For a light meal there is the *Meteghan Restaurant*.

Church Point (Pointe de l'Église)

Église Sainte Marie towers over the town and most other churches too. Built between 1903 and 1905, it is said to be the tallest and biggest wooden church in North America. It has an impressive multi-spired steeple and a very bright, airy interior.

In the corner by the altar is a small museum which contains articles from the church's history, including various vestments and chalices. A guide will show you around and answer any questions. The church museum is open 9.30 am to 5.30 pm daily from July to mid-October and admission is $1.

Nearby is the **Université de Sainte Anne**, the only French university in the province and a centre for Acadian culture.

The oldest of the annual Acadian cultural festivals, Festival Acadien de Clare, is held here during the second week of July.

Places to Stay & Eat For camping there is *Belle Baie Park* (769-3160), just out of town, where the best spots along the shore are saved for overnight tenters. An unserviced site is $15 a night.

There is an inexpensive B&B in town, *Chez Benoit Stuart* (☎ 769-2715) with singles/doubles for $20/30.

Just beyond the church, towards Yarmouth on the coast side of the road, with the Acadian flag outside, *Rapure Acadienne* is the place where all the local establishments get their rapie pie *(paté à la rapure)*. Inside, several women are busy preparing the three varieties: beef, chicken or clam. The result is difficult to describe but it's a type of meat pie topped with grated paste-like potato from which all the starch has been drawn. They are bland, filling and inexpensive and can be bought piping hot. In fact, they are all you can get here. A large rapie pie, enough to feed two people, is $5.

Nearby is *Tides Inn Restaurant*, featuring an extensive menu of seafood dishes such as haddock crepes and seafood casserole au gratin. Dinners range from $8 to $12. During the summer they stage a dinner theatre (☎ 769-2005) on Wednesday and Friday with one version in French and the other in English.

Belliveau Cove

There is a wharf on the attractive little harbour here, where the tides are particularly high. Stop at the pleasantly old-fashioned *Roadside Grill*, a comfortable local restaurant/diner with low prices for sandwiches and light foods but also lots of seafood – try the steamed clams, a local speciality, or the rapie pie, both under $6. The walls are adorned with stuffed animals and various memorabilia.

St Bernard

Here the grandest of the coast's churches stands – a mammoth granite Gothic-style monument which took 32 years to complete, beginning in 1910.

On Hwy 101, before you reach Digby, you pass some very affordable accommodations in old farm houses with a view of Digby Neck. Near Plymouth is *Stagecoach Inn* (☎ 837-7335) with six rooms for $29/36.

DIGBY

An old, attractive town with 2500 residents, Digby was built around a hill in the Annapolis Basin, an inlet of the Bay of Fundy. It's famous for its scallop fleet and busy with its terminal for the *Princess of Acadia* ferry, which plies the waters between Digby and Saint John, New Brunswick. The town is also well known for its 'Digby chicks', a type of smoked herring. In summer, historic Water St has a bit of a resort flavour, with many visitors spending a day or so having a look around and feeding on scallops.

The town was founded by United Empire Loyalists in 1783, and since then its life has been based on fishing. The central area is small enough for walking to be the best way of getting around. Up Mount St from Water St is Trinity Anglican Church and its graveyard. A couple of blocks away, at the south edge of the downtown section, is the old Loyalist cemetery on Warwick St.

From the top of the hill by the high school on King St between Church and Mount Sts, five blocks back from Water St, there is a good view of the area.

From the ferry landing, it is about five km to Water St in downtown Digby.

Information

There are two information centres in Digby. At Loyalist Park on Water St in the centre of town is the local tourist office (☎ 245-5714), open 10 am to 5 pm daily during the summer and until 8 pm on Thursday and Friday. Along Shore Road from the ferry terminal is the much larger provincial tourist centre (☎ 245-2201) with information about all of Nova Scotia as well as Digby. It is open 9 am to 8 pm during the ferry season.

Admiral Digby Museum

At 95 Montague Row, this small museum displays articles and photographs pertaining to the town's marine history and early settlement. It's open from 9 am to 5 pm daily in July and August but is closed on Sunday during other months. Admission is free.

Places to Stay

The *Admiral's Landing B&B* (☎ 245-2247 or 800-651-2247) is perfectly located at 115 Montague Row, opposite the Digby Bandstand, with views of the waterfront. Singles/doubles start at $35/40. Most rooms are equipped with at least a sink, and some have TV. It's open all year and the rates are lower after October.

Westway House (☎ 245-5071) is a B&B at 6 Carlton St, a quieter street but still within walking distance of things to see. Singles/doubles are $30/37, and outside there is a barbecue to use.

The *Thistle Down Inn* (☎ 245-4490 or 800-565-8081), another B&B, is the big old white house at 98 Montague Row. There are chairs out the back on the lawn from where you can watch the harbour. Doubles range from $60 to $65.

Lovett Lodge Inn (☎ 467-3917) includes breakfast in its rates of $35/40. It's eight km east on Hwy 101, in Bear River, a community known for its numerous art and craft shops.

There are also three motels in town and a few private campgrounds around Digby.

Places to Eat

There are a few seafood places where you can take advantage of the scallops and other local sea creatures. *Fundy Restaurant*, at 34 Water St, is pricey but does have two outdoor balconies providing views over the harbour area. Good seafood dinners range from $15 to $20.

The *Captain's Cabin*, on the corner of Water and Birch Sts, is more casual and much more affordable, offering similar seafood. Meals here range from $11 to $16.

Also on Water St is the lively *Red Raven Pub*. The tavern is also a restaurant, featuring an outdoor patio overlooking the wharf with dinner prices from $7 to $13. At night local bands often play. Lastly, consider buying some fresh seafood. There are several shops by the docks on Prince William St but the *Royal Fundy Seafood Market* has the best selection. If you're camping or have cooking facilities at the motel, even a bag of scallops can make a remarkably delicious dinner. They cost between $11 and $13 a pound. The Digby chicks, the heavily smoked herring for which the town is well known, will last up to two weeks and usually cost $1 each.

Getting There & Away

Bus The bus station is at the Irving service station on the corner of Montague Row (an extension of the main street, Water St) and Warwick St, a short walk from the centre of town. There is one bus Thursday through Monday to Yarmouth ($13) and two the other way to Halifax.

Ferry In summer, Marine Atlantic (☎ 245-2116) runs three ferry trips from Digby to Saint John, New Brunswick, daily, except Sunday when there are just two. One of the daily trips is at 8.15 pm. The crossing takes a little more than 2½ hours. Prices are a bit steep – $22 per adult passenger and $48 per car, with bicycles $10.50. Reservations are a very good idea for this trip, and arrive at the dock an hour before departure. Keep in mind this is not a year-round service with the last run generally in October. With two or more people it is probably cheaper to drive around.

DIGBY NECK

The long, thin strip of land which protrudes into the Bay of Fundy from just north of town is known as Digby Neck and is visible from much of the French Shore. At the far end are Long and Brier islands, the two sections that have become split from the main arm. Short ferry rides connect them, so a road links Westport (on Brier Island, at the far end) to Digby. The many small villages along the way are primarily fishing ports and there is some good scenery.

At Tiverton is **Island Museum**, a small museum and tourist information desk. It is open during the summer from 9 am to 8 pm if the volunteer staff hold out.

The most interesting sight on Long Island is **Balancing Rock**. The seven-metre high stone column is perched precariously on the edge of a ledge just above the pounding surf of St Marys Bay. It is such a striking sight that for years fishermen have used it as a landmark to return to port.

The rock became a tourist attraction in 1995 when a new trail was built from Hwy 217 to the bay. The round-trip walk is close to four km along a trail that includes rope railings, boardwalks and an extensive series of steps down a rock bluff to the bay. At the end there is a viewing platform that puts you within 15 metres of this balancing act. The trailhead is well posted along Hwy 217, two km south of the Island Museum.

Brier Island has three lighthouses, with picnic tables and shoreline views and numerous walking trails. Agates can be found along the beaches.

Whale Watching

What draws many people, though, is the sea life off Long and Brier islands. From June to October whale and bird-watching boat cruises run from Tiverton, East Ferry and Westport. Conditions make it a good location for seeing whales; the season is relatively long, beginning in May, building up in June and remaining steady, with a good population of three whale species – finback, minke and humpback – as well as dolphins, porpoises and seals, through August. The whale-watching trips here are the best and most successful of any in Nova Scotia.

There are now a half dozen operators who run whale-watching tours and surely more to come in the future. Still, reservations are a good idea and can be made by phone.

In Tiverton, Ocean Explorations (☎ 839-2417), doesn't use a boat but rather a Zodiac which, being small, allows for pulse-quickening close encounters and a manageable-sized tour group. Half-day trips are $40 if there four passengers, $35 if there are seven and $30 for nine or more. Pirate's Cove Whale Cruises (☎ 839-2242) uses an 11-metre vessel and offers at least two cruises daily. The cost of the three-hour trip is $33.

In East Ferry, Petite Passage Whale Watch (☎ 834-2226) has tours identical in length and rate as Pirate's Cove while in Westport, Brier Island Whales & Seabird Cruises (☎ 839-2995) works in conjunction with Brier Island Lodge to offer cruise-and-accommodation packages.

Hopeful passengers should take plenty of warm clothing (regardless of how hot a day it seems), sunblock and binoculars, if possible. An antimotion-sickness pill taken before leaving the dock may not be a bad idea, either.

Westport is about 90 minutes from Digby, so leave with plenty of time if you've a boat to catch and remember there are two ferries. They leave on the hour or half hour but are timed so that if you drive directly there is no wait for the second one. Return passage on the ferries is $1 each.

There is no public transportation along Digby Neck so you'll need a car or have to rely on hitching a lift.

Places to Stay & Eat

To make things a little less hectic, there are places all along Digby Neck. In scenic Sandy Cove is *Olde Village Inn* (☎ 834-2202 or 800-834-2206), three classic buildings built in 1830 to 1890 and restored as an inn and restaurant. There are a range of rates but the cheapest doubles start at $60. The inn is well posted along Hwy 217.

In Westport the most economical is the *Westport Inn* (☎ 839-2675), with three rooms ($35/45 for singles/doubles). All three meals are available, and for whale-watching, a box lunch is offered.

The *Brier House* (☎ 839-2879), also with three rooms, is on top of a 40-metre bluff; singles/doubles cost $35/45 with a full breakfast.

More upmarket is the *Brier Island Lodge* (☎ 839-2300). At this much larger place there are 23 rooms, most with an ocean view, and a restaurant open to non-guests. The menu offers a range of fresh seafood – try the fishcakes – but even hamburgers are available. They also have bicycles for rent. Doubles in the lodge range from $60.

ANNAPOLIS VALLEY

The Evangeline Trail through the valley is really not as scenic as might be expected, although it does pass through or by all the major towns and the historic sites. To really see the valley and get into the countryside, it is necessary to take the smaller roads parallel to Route 1. From here the farms and orchards, generally hidden from the main roads, come into view.

For those seeking a little work in late summer, there should be some jobs available picking apples. Check in any of the valley towns such as Bridgetown, Lawrencetown and Middleton. Line things up a couple of weeks before picking time, if possible. MacIntosh apples arrive first, at the end of August, but the real season begins around the first week of September.

ANNAPOLIS ROYAL

Known as Canada's oldest settlement, Annapolis Royal is one of the valley's prime attractions and is certainly worth a visit for the plentiful history. It's also a pretty little town to which many are attracted for the fine eating and lodging establishments.

The site of Canada's first permanent European settlement, founded by Samuel de Champlain in 1604, is actually out of town at nearby Granville Ferry. As the English and French battled over the years for the valley and land at the mouth of the Annapolis River, the settlement often changed hands. In 1710, the English had a decisive victory and

changed the town's name from Port Royal to Annapolis Royal (in honour of Queen Anne).

Despite the town's great age (in Canadian terms) the population is under 800, so it is quite a small community and easy to get around. It's a busy place in summer, with most things of interest located on or near the long, curving St George St. There is a waterfront boardwalk behind King's Theatre on St George St, with views over to the village of Granville Ferry.

A farmers' market is held every Saturday morning in summer.

A Nova Scotia Tourism Information Centre (☎ 532-5454) is at the Tidal Power Project site by the Annapolis River Causeway. Hours during the summer are 8 am to 8 pm. Pick up a copy of the historic walking-tour pamphlet.

Fort Anne National Historic Park

Right in the centre of town, this park preserves the memory of the early Acadian

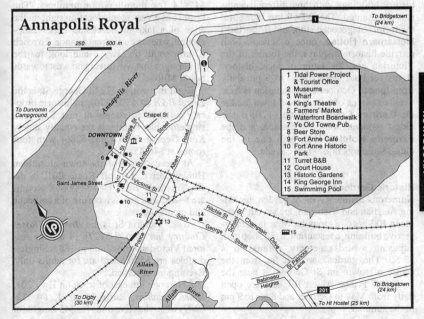

Annapolis Royal

To Bridgetown (24 km)

To Dunromin Campground

To Digby (30 km)

To HI Hostel (25 km)

To Bridgetown (24 km)

1 Tidal Power Project & Tourist Office
2 Museums
3 Wharf
4 King's Theatre
5 Farmers' Market
6 Waterfront Boardwalk
7 Ye Old Towne Pub
8 Beer Store
9 Fort Anne Café
10 Fort Anne Historic Park
11 Turret B&B
12 Court House
13 Historic Gardens
14 King George Inn
15 Swimming Pool

NOVA SCOTIA

settlement plus the remains of the 1635 French fort. Two gunpowder magazines can be entered and the ground fortifications of mounds and moats observed. A museum has replicas of various period rooms, artefacts, uniforms and weapons; the Acadian room was transferred from an old homestead. The museum is open 9 am to 6 pm daily from May to mid-October and admission is $2.25.

If you're around on a Sunday or Thursday night, join the fort's special Candlelight Tour of the Garrison Graveyard. Your park guide is dressed in black and sports an undertaker's top hat and cape, everybody on the tour is given a candle lantern. Then you all troop through the graveyard, viewing the head-stones in the eerie light and hearing tales of horror and death. The tour is $2 per person and very entertaining.

Lower St George St

One of the oldest streets in the country is St George, along the water. It contains many historic buildings, with three different centuries represented. The **O'Dell Inn Museum**, the former stagecoach stop, and **Robertson McNamara House**, once a school, both provide historic displays, the former of the Victorian era, the latter of local history. Hours for both are 9.30 am to 5 pm daily from June to October and admission is free.

Other places of note around town are the **de Gannes-Cosby House** (1708), the oldest wooden house in Canada, and the **Farmer's Hotel** (1710), also one of the oldest buildings in English Canada.

Historic Gardens

Numerous distinct types of garden, including Acadian and Victorian, are set out in the green 400-hectare grounds. There is an interpretive building, a restaurant, a gift shop and, adjacent, a bird sanctuary. Admission is $3.50. The gardens are not far from the centre of town, on St George St near the corner of Prince Albert Rd, and are open daily from May to October and 8 am to 9 pm in the summer.

Tidal Power Project

At the Annapolis River Causeway, this project offers visitors the chance to see a hydroelectric prototype harnessing power from the Bay of Fundy tides. There's also an interpretive centre on the second floor that uses models, exhibits and a short video to explain how it works. The site is free and open the same hours as the tourist centre on the first floor.

Places to Stay

The nearest campground is *Dunromin Campsite and Trailer Court* (☎ 532-2808) two km beyond the tourist centre on Annapolis River at Grandville Ferry. Unserviced sites go for $12.50 a night and there is a small store, laundromat, swimming pool and kayak rentals on site.

About 25 km from Annapolis Royal is the HI *Sandy Bottom Lake Hostel* (☎ 532-2497), in South Milford on Hwy 8. It's open from mid-May to mid-October and there is a kitchen, a shower and nine beds, which cost $12/14 for members/nonmembers. The hostel has a very scenic location right on the edge of a lake in Beachside Park Campground, where you can rent a canoe. To reach it, turn south on Hwy 8 and look for the hostel signs that will direct you west towards South Milford.

Right in town, at 372 St George St, is the *Turret B&B* (☎ 532-5770), an historic property with three rooms at just $30/40 a single/double. Nearby is the equally stately *King George Inn* (☎ 532-5286) with four rooms at $40/45.

At the east end of the town at Aulden Hubley Drive, just off Route 201, is the *English Oaks B&B* (☎ 532-2066). Rooms are $42/45 and guests have use of a barbecue and picnic tables.

At 82 Victoria St is the *Bread & Roses Country Inn* (☎ 532-5727), in a large restored Victorian house built in 1882. Singles/doubles are $55/65 and are for adults only. Evening tea is served.

About one km east of town on Hwy 201, *Helen's Cabins*, Rural Route 1, (☎ 532-5207) which has five units for $45 a night for singles or doubles with hot plates included for quick cooking. They are open from May to October.

The *Auberge Sieur de Monts* (☎ 532-5852), right beside the Habitation National Park in Port Royal, has two completely self-contained houses for rent at $55 a night, $50 if you rent for two or more days. Each sleeps four people and comes with kitchen, sitting room and bathroom.

At Victoria Beach, 26 km from Annapolis Royal, is the *Fundy View House & Cabins* (☎ 532-5015), with rooms in the house or in cabins with kitchens. Singles range from $25 to $30, doubles from $33 to $39.

Places to Eat

The *Ye Old Towne Pub*, on Church St just off St George St, by the wharf, is a busy place for lunch and a brew. Right next door is *Ye Olde Towne Restaurant*, a little more formal where dinners are $8 to $15 and a pot of steamed mussels $3.50.

The *Fort Anne Café*, on St George St opposite the historic site, is cheap and basic and good for breakfast. At lunch try the soups or a sandwich nearby at *Leo's Café*, 22 St George St. A salad and sandwich is $6.

Expensive and decorative *Newman's*, at 218 St George St, has a good reputation for its varied menu, which includes fresh fish, pasta and lamb. It features a dining terrace outside if the weather is good. Dinners range from $12 to $22 but its noted scallop linguini is only $8.

At 350 St George St, the *Garrison House*, in a house from 1854, is also good with dinners ranging from $9 to $15.

AROUND ANNAPOLIS ROYAL

Port Royal National Historic Site

Fifteen km from Annapolis Royal, this is the actual site of the first European settlement north of Florida. It has a replica, constructed in the original manner, of de Champlain's 1605 fur-trading habitation. It was destroyed by the English a few years after it was begun. Costumed workers help tell the story of this early settlement. The park (☎ 532-2898) is open from 9 am to 6 pm daily during the summer and admission is $2.50.

Delaps Cove

On the coast north of town is a series of typical small fishing villages, from Delaps Cove to the west all the way to the Minas Basin.

The Delaps Cove Wilderness Trail, about 24 km from Annapolis Royal, is a 15-km hiking trail that provides a good cross-section of the provincial coastal scenery. There are streams and waterfalls at various places and an assortment of birds and animals. Just west of Delaps Cove is an interpretive office (where you can get a map) but that's it for amenities.

KEJIMKUJIK NATIONAL PARK

This park, located well away from the tourist areas of the seacoast, contains some of the province's most pristine wilderness and best backcountry adventures. Less than 20% of Kejimkujik's 381 sq km is accessible by car, the rest is reached either on foot or by paddle. Canoeing, in particular, is an ideal way to explore this area of glacial lakes and rolling hills and the park is well set up for extended, overnight paddles. Portage routes are well marked, and the main lake, Kejimkujik, features red navigational buoys and many primitive camp sites are on islands.

Kejimkujik is 41 km south of Annapolis Royal via Hwy 8. At the main entrance, just south of Maitland Bridge, there is a visitor and interpretive centre (☎ 682-2772), where you can reserve primitive sites and purchase maps and books. Hours during the summer are 8.30 am to 9 pm and less the rest of the year.

Entry Fees

In 1995, Kejimkujik National Park tested a pilot program of individual entry fees. At other national parks entry is by motor vehicle permit, regardless how many people are in a car. Cyclists or visitors who walk in pay nothing. At Kejimkujik everybody pays. It's $2.25 for a daily pass, $6 a day per family or $6.75 for a four-day pass. Look for the same type of fee structure to be eventually adopted by all Canadian national parks.

Hiking & Canoeing

There are more than 40 primitive camp sites scattered along the trails and among the lakes of Kejimkujik. The main hiking loop is a 58-km trek that begins at the east end of Peskowesk Lake and ends at the Big Dam Lake trailhead. Most backpackers take three to four days to cover it, with September to early October being the prime time for such an adventure. A shorter loop, ideal for an overnight trek, is the 26-km Channel Lake Trail that begins and ends at Big Dam Lake.

The park also features more than a dozen lakes connected by a system of portages for flatwater paddling. Extended trips of up to seven days are possible in Kejimkujik with portages ranging from a few metres to 2.4 km in length.

You must stay in backcountry sites and book them in advance by calling or stopping at the visitor centre (☎ 682-2772). The sites are $7.25 per night plus a $3.25 reservation fee for each backcountry trip. They also require you to purchase a *Backcountry Guide*, a topographical map with route descriptions, for $5.

Canoes can be rented in the park at Jack's Landing from 8 am to 9 pm daily for $16 a day and $80 a week. You can also rent them at Loon Lake Outfitters (☎ 682-2220 or 682-2290) located just north of the park entrance on Hwy 8. Canoes are $15 a day or $75 a week and they also have tents, canoe packs and stoves for rent.

Places to Stay

Kejimkujik National Park has a huge camp-ground of 330 camp sites at Jeremys Bay, including a handful of walk-in camp sites near the shoreline for those who want to put a little distance between themselves and obnoxious RVers running their generators. The cost is $10.50 per night.

The *Whitman Inn* (☎ 682-2266) in Caledonia, five minutes from the park, is a comfortable place to stay for noncampers. It's a restored turn-of-the-century house that has an indoor swimming pool, saunas – the works – yet the simplest of the rooms are moderately priced at $45/50. All meals are available. Also keep in mind that the *Sandy Lake Hostel* is 19 km north of the park off Hwy 8 (see the earlier Annapolis Royal section for details).

BRIDGETOWN

Back along the Annapolis Valley, Bridgetown has many trees and some fine examples of large Maritime houses. A seasonal tourist office is in Jubilee Park, on Granville St. There's also the small **James House Museum**, an 1835 home among the shops along Queen St. In the museum is a tea room for an afternoon break. Try the rhubarb sparkle. Admission is free.

KENTVILLE

Kentville, with a sizeable population of 5500, marks the east end of the Annapolis Valley and acts as a focal point to a couple of nearby places of interest.

The town itself is functional and not of particular note but there are a few places to stay or eat. The tourist office (678-7170) is in the restored train station on Cornwallis Ave. Summer hours are 9 am to 5 pm daily.

At the eastern end of town is the **Agriculture Research Station** (☎ 679-5324), with a museum related to the area's farming history and particularly to its apples. There is a pleasant walking trail through the old growth woods, one of the few areas in the province with original forest. Hours are 8 am to 4.30 pm year round and guided tours are offered during the summer. Admission is free.

In town, local artefacts, history and an art gallery can be seen at **Old King's Courthouse Museum** (☎ 678-6237) at 37 Cornwallis Ave. The courthouse was the seat of justice from 1903 to 1980. Hours are 9.30 am to 4.30 pm year round and 11.30 am to 4.30 pm on Saturday and Sunday during the summer. Admission is free.

Kentville is about a two-hour drive from Digby and about one hour from Halifax.

Activities

Brent's Outdoor Adventure Shop (☎ 679-1700), at 15 River St, rents out kayaks for $35 a day and canoes for $30. They also offer weekend trips and evening kayaking clinics. Frame Break (☎ 679-0611), at 102 Webster St, rents mountain bikes for $25 a day or $45 for the weekend. They also lead tours into the valley.

Places to Stay & Eat

The *Grand Street Inn* (☎ 679-1991), at 160 Main St, just out of the downtown area towards New Minas, is the very attractive old grey and pink house. Doubles are $45, which includes a full breakfast as well as use of the swimming pool.

There are also two motels in town, the *Allen's Motel* (678-2683) being the most affordable with singles or doubles for $42. Not far away, on Main St in Port William, the *Country Squire* (☎ 542-9125) has four rooms in a Victorian home $35/45.

What many other Canadian towns desperately need, Kentville has; a few good pubs. The classic is *King's Arms Pub* on Main St where you can have a drink next to a fireplace or outside on the patio. Steak & kidney pie is only $4.25, a pot of mussels the same price. Happy hour begins at 4.30 pm when pints are $3.25 and half pints under $2.

Nearby *Paddy's* on Aberdeen St doubles as an Irish pub and a small brewery producing such gems as Annapolis Valley Ale and Paddy's Porter. Dinners range from $8 to $11 or just try the Paddy's Irish stew made with Guinness for $4.65.

NORTH OF KENTVILLE

The area up to Cape Blomidon, on the Bay of Fundy, makes for a fine trip for half a day or longer, with good scenery, a memorable view of much of the valley and a couple of beaches. At Cape Split there is an excellent, dramatic hiking trail high above the Minas Basin and Channel.

Canning

There is the *Farmhouse Inn* (☎ 582-7900) and a small, simple restaurant in tiny Canning, where there are so many large, overhanging trees Main St is dark even on a sunny day.

The Lookoff

From the road's edge at nearly 200 metres high, this could well be the best view of the soft, rural Annapolis Valley, its rows of fruit trees and farmhouses appearing like miniatures. Across the street is *Look-off Family Camping Park* (☎ 582-3373) where an unserviced site is $11.

Blomidon

At *Blomidon Provincial Park* (☎ 582-7319), there is camping and hiking trails that skirt dramatic 183-metre shoreline cliffs. A tent site is $12 a night. As at Kingsport's sandy beach further south, the water can get quite warm.

Scots Bay

The road continues north to Scots Bay, with a large pebbled beach. From the end of the road, a spectacular 13-km hiking trail leads to the cliffs at Cape Split. This is not a loop trail, so you must retrace your steps.

Halls Harbour

On the often foggy coast, Halls Harbour to the west is a classic, scenic little lobster village with a pier and a lobster pound. At the *Halls Harbour Lobster Pound* (☎ 679-5299) they cook live lobsters from noon to 8 pm daily from May to September and sell them at the best prices you'll ever find. All that's sold is the lobster, rolls and butter. There are picnic tables around the dock area.

WOLFVILLE

Wolfville is a quiet, green university town best known as the home of artist Alex Colville. With its art gallery, comfortable inns and impressive historic homes, there is a wisp of culture in the air.

The tourist office (☎ 542-7000) is in Willow Park, at the east end of Main St and open from 8 am to 8 pm daily during the summer. The bus stop for Acadian bus lines is in a place called Nowlan's Canteen, at the

NOVA SCOTIA

far west end of town on Main St on the corner of Hillcrest Ave. It's a bit of a walk into town.

Acadia University Art Gallery
The gallery (☎ 542-2202, ext 1373) in the Beveridge Arts Centre building, on the corner of Main St and Highland Ave, exhibits mainly the work of other Maritime artists. It also has a collection of the work (mostly serigraphs) of Alex Colville, some of which is always on display. Hours during the summer are noon to 5 pm weekdays and 1 to 4 pm on Saturday and Sunday. Admission is by donation.

Carriage House Gallery
In the middle of Main St, this commercial gallery has the works of local artists for sale, as well as some Colville prints.

Randall House Museum
Set in a house dating from the early 1800s, the museum (☎ 684-3876) deals with the early New England planters or colonists who replaced the expelled Acadians and the Loyalists who followed later. It is at 171 Main St and is open 10 am to 5 pm daily during the summer except on Saturday and Sunday when it opens at 2 pm. Admission is free.

Chimney Swifts
From May to late August, these birds collect to glide and swoop by the hundreds at dusk, before disappearing into a chimney to roost. There is a full explanation of the phenomenon at Robie Tufts Nature Centre on Front St, which features outdoor displays and a tall chimney where the birds display their acrobatic talents.

Places to Stay
Wolfville has a number of B&Bs in impressive Victorian homes but unfortunately most of that grandeur comes with a steep rate. Most modest is *Birchcliff B&B* (☎ 542-3391), 84 Main St, which has two rooms offered through the summer, at $30/40 a single/double.

Also within reason is *Seaview House* (☎ 542-1436), 8 Seaview Ave just off Main St. This Victorian home has three rooms for $42/60 and is within easy walking distance of the centre of town.

At the other end of the spectrum is *Victoria's Inn* (☎ 542-5744), 416 Main St, a very ornate place with rooms in the main lodge or the Carriage House. The best deals are rooms in the Carriage House ($69 for singles and $85 for doubles or triples). They also have a dining room.

Places to Eat
This being a college town you will find a few pizza and sub shops along Main St. There are also a couple of good coffee shops. Try *Front St Cafe* where a latte is $2. There is also soup, pastries, lots of reading material and occasionally live music at night.

Joe's Food Emporium on Main St is a lively place with an outdoor patio and a wide ranging menu. Pasta dinners are $5 to $9, a medium pizza $9 to $12 and a quiche-and-salad $6. They serve beer and wine as well.

For a real splurge *Chez La Vigne*, at 17 Front St, or *Action Cafe*, on Main St, are recommended. The owner/chef of the Chez La Vigne has been voted Canadian chef of the year. Dinners here set you back $12 to $24. Action Cafe is slightly more affordable and has an interesting salad bar during lunch.

GRAND PRÉ
Now a very small English-speaking town, Grand Pré was the site of one of the most dramatic stories in eastern Canada's history. The details of this sorry but fascinating tale can be learned at the National Historic Site north of the main highway and town, five km east of Wolfville.

Grand Pré National Historic Park
Grand Pré means 'great meadow' and refers to the farmland created when the Acadians built dykes along the shoreline, as they had done in north-west France for generations. There are 1200 hectares below sea level. It's a beautiful area and one you wouldn't want to leave involuntarily, especially after the

Left: Gros Morne National Park, Newfoundland
Right: Grounded fishing boat and lighthouse, Nova Scotia
Bottom: Coastline near Port aux Basques, Newfoundland

JIM DUFRESNE

JIM DUFRESNE

Top: Halifax waterfront, Nova Scotia
Bottom: Period-costumed guides, Louisbourg Historic National Park, Nova Scotia

The Acadians

The story of the Acadians is one of the most interesting, dramatic and tragic in Canada's history. It was played out in what are now five of the country's provinces, the USA, the West Indies and Europe. And although it began in the 1600s it is not over.

When the French first settled the area around the south Minas Basin shore of the Bay of Fundy in 1604 they named the land Acadia. By the next century these settlers thought of themselves as Acadians. To the English, however, they were always to be 'the French'. The rivalry and suspicion between these two powers of the New World began with the first landings and was only to increase in hostility and bitterness.

The population of Acadia continued to grow through the 17th and 18th centuries and, with various battles and treaties, changed ruling hands from French to English and back again. Finally, in 1713 with the Treaty of Utrecht, Acadia became English Nova Scotia. The Acadians refused to take an oath of allegiance, although for the most part they weren't much interested in France's point of view either and evidently wanted most of all to be left alone. Things sort of drifted along in this state for a while and the area around Grand Pré became the largest Acadian community. By this time the total regional population was not far off 10,000 with 3500 more people in Louisbourg and still others in Prince Edward Island.

Unfortunately for them, tensions once again heated up between England and France with squabbles and trade-offs taking place all over the east coast. When a new hardline lieutenant-governor Charles Lawrence was appointed in 1754 he quickly became fed up with the Acadians and their supposed neutrality. He didn't trust them and decided to do something about it. He demanded an oath of allegiance and, as the game had always been played, the Acadians said forget it. This time, though, the rules had changed.

In late August 1755, with the crowns of France and England still locked in battle and paranoia increasing, what was to become known as the Deportation or the Expulsion began. All told, about 14,000 Acadians were forced out of this area. Villages were burned, the people boarded onto boats.

The sad, bitter departure was the theme for Longfellow's well-known lengthy narrative poem, *Evangeline*, titled after its fictional heroine. Many Acadians headed for Louisiana and New Orleans, where their name became Anglicised to 'Cajun' (often heard in songs and seen on restaurant menus). The Cajuns, some of whom still speak French, have maintained aspects of their culture to this day. Others went to various Maritime points and north-eastern America, others to Martinique, Santo Dominigo, back to Europe, some even to the Falkland Islands. Nowhere were they greeted warmly with open arms. Some hid out and remained in Acadia. In later years many of those people deported returned.

Today, most of the French people in Canada's Atlantic Provinces are the descendants of the expelled Acadians and they're still holding tight to their heritage.

In Nova Scotia the Cheticamp area in Cape Breton and the French Shore north of Yarmouth are small strongholds. A pocket in western Prince Edward Island and the Port au Port peninsula in Newfoundland are others. New Brunswick has a large French population stretching up the east coast past the Acadian Peninsula at Caraquet and all around the border with Quebec.

There has recently been an upsurge in Acadian pride and awareness and in most of these areas you'll see the Acadian flag flying and museums dealing with the past and the continuing Acadian culture. There is another major National Historic Site dealing with the Acadians and their expulsion near St Joseph, New Brunswick, not far from the Nova Scotia border – a visit is recommended. Festivals held in some of these areas provide an opportunity to see traditional dress, sample foods and hear some of the wonderful fiddle-based music. ■

work that made it home. The park is a memorial to the Acadians, who had a settlement here from 1675 to 1755 and then were given the boot by the British.

It consists of an information centre, church, gardens, space and views, and free tours of the site are offered. The worthwhile gift shop has a selection of books on the Acadians, among other things.

A new stone church, built in the Acadian style, sits in the middle of the site as a monument to the original inhabitants. Inside, the history of those people is depicted in a series of colourful paintings done in 1987 by New Brunswick painter Claude Picard.

Walk down through the gardens to the old blacksmith's shed, where there are views of the surrounding gorgeous, fertile farmlands and pastures with green hills in the background, the air an aromatic mix of sea breeze and worked fields.

In the gardens are a bust of Henry Wadsworth Longfellow, honoured for his poem which chronicles the Acadian's saga, and a statue of Evangeline, now a romantic symbol of her people.

The park (☎ 542-3631) is open daily from 9 am to 6 pm from mid-May to October and admission is free. Acadian Days, an annual festival held sometime towards the end of July, consists of music, storytelling, arts & crafts. Many of the events are held at the historic park.

WINDSOR

Windsor is a small town on the Avon River, halfway between the North Pole and the Equator. At one time it was the only British stronghold in this district of French power and Acadian farmers.

Hwy 1 becomes Water St in town and the main intersection is with Gerrish St. Just off exit 6 of Hwy 101 is the tourist centre (☎ 798-2690), open from 9 am to 7 pm during the summer.

Nearby, off King St, there's an old blockhouse still intact amid portions of the British fort at **Fort Edward National Historic Site** (☎ 542-3631) dating from 1750. It was used as one of the assembly stations during the expulsions of the Acadians and is one of the oldest blockhouses in Canada. Around the structure are the earthen mounds of the fort and interpretive displays. The fort is open 9.30 am to 4.30 pm daily from June to October and admission is free.

Another site is **Haliburton House**, once the home of Judge Thomas Chandler Haliburton, one of the founders of written American humour. He created the Sam Slick character in Mark Twain-style stories. Although these aren't read much now, many Haliburton expressions, such as 'quick as a wink' and 'city slicker', are often still used. Haliburton's large estate is open from 9.30 am to 5.30 pm daily from mid-July to mid-September except on Sunday when it opens at 1 pm. Admission is free. It's on Clifton

Ave, which runs off Grey St, itself leading from Gerrish St just north of Lake Pesaquid, in the eastern section of town.

Shand House, part of the provincial museum system, is a small museum on Water St evoking the life of a well-to-do family at the turn of the century. It's on Ferry Hill and has the same hours and admission as Haliburton House.

Windsor calls itself the birthplace of ice hockey, though this has created a heated debate with Kingston, Ontario which makes the same claim. In Windsor, they say the boys of King's College School began playing the game on Long Pond around 1800. In 1836, Haliburton even referred to 'playing ball on ice' in his book *The Clockmaker*. These tidbits and more (the first pucks were slices of a thick pine branch and the Micmac Indians supplied hand-made hockey sticks to the North American market well into the 1930s) can be gathered at the **Windsor Hockey Heritage Society** (☎ 798-1800). The souvenir shop/museum is a storefront on Gerrish St and is only the first step towards a more permanent centre. Hours are 9 am to 5 pm daily and admission is free.

Tides

The tides in the bay and Avon River near Windsor are impressive – falling and rising up to 12 metres. At Poplar Grove, off Hwy 14 East, you can view a tidal bore. Ask at the tourist office for good times and locations for observing this phenomenon because it varies a lot. Port Williams, near Wolfville, is also a good place to see the difference between high and low tides.

Places to Stay

The *Meander Inn* (☎ 798-2325), 153 Albert St, is a good place for overnighters, with singles/doubles beginning at $25/40. The *Clockmaker's Inn* (☎ 798-5265), 1399 King St, is a Victorian home at $35/45 and bicycles for guests.

Getting There & Away

Acadian bus lines from Halifax to Windsor

continues on to Yarmouth, making numerous stops through the Annapolis Valley. In Windsor the bus stops at Donut Land, 18 Mission Dr. One-way fare to Yarmouth is $34, to Halifax $8.

Northumberland Shore

This is the north coastal district of the province, from the New Brunswick border to Cape Breton Island. The Northumberland Strait is between this shore and Prince Edward Island and has some of the warmest waters north of the US Carolinas. Hwy 6, also called the Sunrise Trail tourist route, runs along this strip of small towns, beaches and Scottish history.

On Hwy 104 right at the New Brunswick border is a large tourist office with maps and overviews of the driving trails around Nova Scotia.

Although there are no major attractions along this shore, it is busy, and as accommodation is not plentiful, places to stay fill quickly. It's strongly recommended that you find a place by lunch time in July and August.

PUGWASH

On the coast along the Sunrise Trail from Amherst is this small port, with good beaches nearby. On average, the water temperature along this coast is slightly over 20°C in summer. Pugwash's two claims to fame are the large salt mine, which produces boatloads of salt to be shipped from the town docks, and the colourful Gathering of the Clans festival, which takes place each year on 1 July. Street names in town are written in Gaelic as well as in English.

There are several craftspeople in town and their wares are sold along the main street or on Saturday when they set up tables at the **Pugwash Train Station**. Built in 1889, this is one of the two oldest stations in Nova Scotia and today serves as a tourist centre and library. Outside is the Caboose Cafe.

WALLACE

Wallace is not a major tourist attraction but there is an interesting town tidbit. The sandstone from the quarry just out of town has been used to build many fine buildings, including the Parliament Buildings in Ottawa and Province House in Nova Scotia.

Wallace does have a thriving lobster fishery and the delicacy can be purchased from several places in town. There is also a couple of B&Bs here and Grant's, a classic general store from another era.

MALAGASH

The Jost Winery (☎ 257-2636) off Route 6 is one of only two vineyards in Nova Scotia. Run by a German family, the winery began operation in 1970 and now, with 13 hectares, produces several varieties, with the Riesling style perhaps the best known. Free tours are offered at noon and 3 pm Monday through Saturday and 3 pm on Sunday during the summer. There is a store on the premises with a tasting bar and a deli and tables outside where you can enjoy lunch and a bottle of wine. The winery also rents bicycles at $5 an hour and $13 for three hours for touring the Malagash area.

Malagash was the site of the first rock salt mine in Canada, which operated from 1918 to 1949 and produced more than two million tons of salt. The **Malagash Museum** (☎ 257-2833) preserves that mining history with equipment and artefacts from the mine as well as a movie made during its peak production year in 1941. Hours are 10 am to 5 pm Tuesday through Sunday during the summer and admission is $2.

TATAMAGOUCHE

Despite having a population of just 726, Tatamagouche is somewhat of a visitor centre. Pretty well everything is along Main St, which is really the highway going east and west.

Not to be missed is the quirky **Fraser Culture Centre** (☎ 657-3285), a sort of museum-cum-art gallery. The showpiece is the room dedicated to Anna Swan who, at 2.4 metres tall and weighing 187 kg, was known as the giantess of Nova Scotia and went on to achieve some celebrity. Born in one of the surrounding villages in 1896, she parlayed her size into a lucrative career with Barnum & Bailey's circus and even ended up meeting Queen Elizabeth II in London, where Anna was married. Clothes, newspaper clippings and photographs tell the big story.

The centre also has some historical artefacts and several gallery rooms displaying the work of local artists. The tourist office is here, in another of the many rooms. Hours are 9 am to 7 pm daily during the summer and admission is by donation.

A few doors down is the less idiosyncratic **Sunrise Trail Museum** of local history, with emphasis on the shipbuilding industry, once of major importance here. The Acadian French settled this area in the 1700s and a display tells of them and their expulsion. Hours are 9.30 am to 5.30 pm during the summer and admission is $1.

In Tatamagouche, Oktoberfest is held at the end of September or beginning of October.

Places to Stay & Eat

For camping *Nelson Memorial Park* (☎ 657-2730) is just west of Tatamagouche and has 76 camp sites, showers and a beach. Tent sites are $10 a night.

Keep in mind that the *Wentworth Hostel* (☎ 548-2379) is only 27 kms south of town via Route 246 (see the Truro section).

For an unusual place to sleep in town, there's the *Train Station Inn* (☎ 657-3222), in the old train station on Main St. It features three rooms in the station that range from $50 to $68 for a single or double and two cabooses outside that have been converted into suites. They sleep two to four people and are $98 a night.

East of town on Barrachois Bay is *Barrachois Harbour B&B* (☎ 657-3009), with two rooms and a great location overlooking the fishermen's wharf. Rooms are $35/40 and you can purchase lobster from the boats when in season.

If you're looking for a bite, the *Villager Inn & Restaurant* has daily specials, some

seafood and quite good chowders. Most dinners are under $10. For breakfast there is the *Munch Inn and Sunshine Bakery* which opens at 7 am.

AROUND TATAMAGOUCHE

There are a couple of other small museums in the region. South down Route 311, **Balmoral Mills** (☎ 657-3016) has one of the province's oldest grist mills, which opened in 1874. Grinding demonstrations held at 10 am and 2 pm daily during the summer show the flour (oatmeal, barley, wheat) milling process from start to finish and the completed products are even offered for sale. It's open from 1 to 5.30 pm on Sunday and 9.30 am to 5.30 pm the rest of the week. Admission is free.

Another provincial historic site is outside the village of Denmark. The **Sutherland Steam Mill** (☎ 657-3365) was built in 1894 and was run continuously by family members until 1953. The sawmill is no longer a commercial entity but the machinery and steam engine are still operational and on the first Saturday of the month they cut lumber. Hours, season and admission is the same as Balmoral Mills.

This part of the province has a bit of a German colony, and at the *Bavarian Garden Restaurant* in Denmark, various made-on-the-premises German foods are offered. It's open every day in July and August but only on weekends in May, June and September. The Pork Shop next door sells a wide variety of German sausage, kassler, hams, etc.

PICTOU

Pictou (pronounced 'pik toe'), one of the most attractive and interesting towns along the North Shore, is where the Highland Scots first landed in 1773, to be followed by thousands in the settling of 'New Scotland'. In town, among the many older structures, are several buildings and historic sites relating to the early Scottish pioneers. Pick up a walking-tour brochure at the large tourist office at the rotary (roundabout) north-west of the town centre. Hours are 9 am to 8 pm daily.

Water St is the main street and reflects the architectural style of the early Scottish builders. Above it Church, High and Faulkland Sts are lined with some of the old, very large houses for which the town is noted.

Pictou, with it's stone buildings and scenic waterfront, is a haven for artists. Throughout town there are numerous art studios and craft shops, with most of them cluttered along Water St and Front St.

The ferry to Prince Edward Island leaves from just north of town at Caribou. For details see the Charlottetown Getting There & Away section in the Prince Edward Island chapter.

Hector Heritage Quay

Part of the waterfront has been redeveloped to preserve both history and access. At the boatyard, a full-size replica of the first ship to bring the Scottish settlers, the three-masted *Hector*, is being constructed. Begun in 1993, it will take about a decade to complete. Guides tell the story of the crossing and settlement.

Other features are the interpretive centre (☎ 485-8028), with varied displays and dioramas depicting the life of the Scottish immigrants, a blacksmith shop and a collection of shipbuilding artefacts. Hours are 9 am to 5 pm Monday through Wednesday, noon to 8 pm Saturday and Sunday. Admission into the interpretive centre and shipyard is $4 or $10 per family.

deCoste Entertainment Centre

This impressive preforming arts centre on Water St is the site of a range of live performances, from plays and comedies to the leading Scottish and Celtic musicians in Canada. For the current event or tickets call or stop at the box office (☎ 485-8848).

Grohmann Knives

The small family-run business (☎ 485-4224) at 116 Water St has a well-deserved reputation for the very fine outdoor and kitchen knives it produces. One of them, a classic belt knife available in many countries, is in the Museum of Modern Art in New York.

Many of the production stages are done by hand, as they were when the operation began in the mid-1950s, and can be seen on the free tours around the plant offered on demand (minimum four people) Monday to Friday from 9 am to 3 pm May to September.

Even if you don't take in the tour, stop at the factory outlet store, where there is a wide selection of knives for sale. On display is the folding knife Rudolph Grohmann hand-crafted in 1912 for his apprenticeship as a knifemaker. It would put any Swiss Army knife to shame as it features 108 tools and requires a half hour to fully open.

Northumberland Fisheries Museum

On Front St in the old train station, the museum tells the story of the area's fishing. The fisherman's bunkhouse is a good display. It's open daily from 9.30 am to 5.30 pm during the summer and admission is $1.

Hector National Exhibit Centre

Away from the town centre but within walking distance on Haliburton Rd, a continuation westward of High St, this centre (☎ 485-4563) presents a variety of ever-changing shows. Always on display are the quilts, pewter items and embroidery produced by the Pictou County Art & Crafts Association. The centre is open 1.30 to 5.30 pm Sunday and 9.30 am to 5.30 pm the rest of the week. Admission is $2.

McCulloch House

Built in 1806 for Thomas McCulloch, a minister and important educator, this home now displays articles pertaining to his career as well as items relating to other early Scottish settlers. The house is just up the hill from the Hector National Exhibit Centre. It is open the same hours as the centre and admission is free.

Beaches

There are a couple of very good beaches outside Pictou. The most popular is **Melmerby Beach** ('the Merb'), which is actually north of New Glasgow but draws visitors from far and wide. It's a long, wide

NOVA SCOTIA

sandy beach; there is a basic hamburger stand but no shade.

A better choice is **Caribou Beach**, which is equally sandy with gradually deepening water but is more scenic, with picnic tables along a small ridge above the beach and trees for when the sun gets too intense. It is much closer to town, north of Pictou near the Prince Edward Island ferry terminal. Both beaches are free and the water along this strip of ocean is as warm as any in Nova Scotia.

Festivals

The Lobster Carnival, a three-day event at the beginning of July, marks the end of the lobster season. The Hector Festival in mid-August is four days of celebration of the area's Scottish heritage, including concerts.

Places to Stay

Pictou has about a dozen possibilities for spending the night. Bear in mind that, while not crowded, the town has a steady stream of people passing through and most accommodation is full (or close to it) through the summer.

There are many B&Bs here, most of them located in large historical homes. Most economical and central is *The Sellers B&B* (☎ 485-5113), at 258 Faulkland St. The three rooms are $35/40 for singles/doubles and kitchen facilities are available if you want to cook your own lobster dinner.

The *Willow House Inn* (☎ 485-5740), 3 Willow St, is another B&B in a large historic house dating from 1840 and once belonging to the mayor. It features 10 rooms starting at $35/40.

Near the waterfront at 90 Front St is *Davies House B&B* (☎ 485-4864) in yet another grand old home. There are three rooms that begin at $35/40.

Away from the downtown area, near the tourist office by the traffic rotary, is *The Lionstone Inn* (☎ 485-4157). It has some newish motel units as well as a number of older individual cabins with their own kitchens. Singles are $45 but doubles and triples are just $5 extra.

Places to Eat

Right in the centre, at 11 Water St, is the *Stone House Café & Pizzeria*, where the food isn't great but the selection is wide. There is a nice outside patio and local entertainment is often on tap in the evenings. Dinners range from $10 to $13.

In the back of the Olde Theatre Place Mall, is the delightful *My Fair Deli*, which doubles up as a restaurant and a small lounge. The menu is interesting with such items as cajun burger for $3 and Jamaican pastry and rice for $4, the coffee is always fresh and there is beer on tap.

Relics is a friendly Scottish pub located in the Old Custom House Art and Craft Gallery. It features a menu of seafood, salads and sandwiches that start at $3. Also on the waterfront is *Settlers Pub & Eatery* on Caladh with a higher-priced menu. The restaurant has a deck overlooking the harbour and often live entertainment of traditional Maritime music.

Though out of the way and virtually impossible to reach without a car, one of the best known restaurants in the area is the *Lobster Bar*, across the bay from Pictou in Pictou Landing, where there is a Native Indian reserve and not a lot more. Driving involves a rather circuitous route over one of the bridges towards New Glasgow – get the map distributed at the Pictou tourist office.

It's a casual (take the kids), busy and not badly priced seafood house specialising in lobster. A full lobster meal costs about $20. They've been serving up fish, clams and all the rest since the late 1950s and have fed former US president Jimmy Carter as well as former Canadian prime minister Brian Mulroney and his wife Mila.

NEW GLASGOW

With a population of 10,000, New Glasgow is the largest town along the Northumberland Shore. It originally was, and remains, a small industrial centre. There is little to see in town, but it can be useful as a stopping point as it's close if you're coming or going to the ferry for Prince Edward Island.

Provost St, the main retail and shopping avenue, has a couple of restaurants. Temperance St, parallel to Provost St and up the hill from the river, is attractive, with lots of trees, some large older houses, a couple of churches and **Carmichael-Stewart House**. The latter, at 86 Provost St, is an historic building with a small free museum illustrating the town's history in shipbuilding and coal mining. Hours are 9 am to 4.30 pm Monday through Friday and 1 to 4.30 pm on Saturday.

Fraser's Mountain, not far from town, offers excellent views of the entire region. Drive east through town on Archimedes St and turn right on George St. Continue up the hill, veering left around the church, and keep going straight to the summit.

Nova Scotia Museum of Industry

The most interesting attraction is actually in neighbouring Stellarton. This impressive provincial museum (☎ 755-5425) features almost 14,000 artefacts in its collection which provide a cross-section of Nova Scotia's industrial heritage. There are several galleries that display everything from the Samson, the earliest standard gauge locomotive to operate in North America, and the first car to drive the streets of Halifax to Stellarton's glassworks industry that produced millions of soda bottles. The museum itself is located on the site of the Albion coal mine.

Hours are 10 am to 8 pm daily during the summer and admission is $5 for adults or $13 for a family. There is a tea shop in the museum with a pleasant outdoor patio.

Places to Stay

For spending the night, the *Wynwood Inn* (☎ 752-4527), 71 Stellarton Rd, a B&B since 1930, makes a fine choice. Actually an attractive old house, it's central and has a nice balcony. Rates start at $28/32 for singles/doubles, including a light breakfast.

Mackay's B&B (☎ 752-5889), at 44 High St, is also central but is more modest. Prices are $30/45.

There are motels on the highway outside town with most of them charging $55 a single.

ANTIGONISH

If you're coming from New Brunswick or Prince Edward Island, this is the place to spend the night. Antigonish (pronounced 'An-tee-guh-NISH') is also a good stop between Sydney and Halifax. A pleasant, small town with a few things to see, it has some good places to stay and the beach is nearby. It's a university and residential town with no industry.

Information

The tourist office (☎ 863-4921) is just off the highway at the west entrance to Antigonish, coming from New Glasgow at exit 32. It's open from 8 am to 8 pm.

Heritage Museum

Located in the classic Antigonish Depot that was built in 1908 by the Intercolonial Railway, the museum (☎ 863-6160) features displays pertaining to the early days of Antigonish. The most interesting exhibit is the 1864 hand-hauled fire engine the town once used to put out blazes. The depot is 20 East Main St and hours are 10 am to 5 pm weekdays and 1 to 5 pm on the weekends in July and August. Admission is free.

St Francis Xavier University

The attractive campus of this 125-year-old university is behind the cathedral near the centre of town. It's a pleasant place to walk.

County Courthouse

In 1984 this 129-year-old building was designated a National Historic Site. Restored in 1970, it still serves as the county's judicial centre. The design (by Alexander Macdonald) is typical of many of the province's courthouses from the mid-19th century.

Festivals

Antigonish is known for its annual Highland Games, held in mid-July. These Scottish games have been going on since 1861. You'll see pipe bands, drum regiments, dancers and athletes from far and wide. The events last a week.

NOVA SCOTIA

Festival Antigonish is a summer theatre festival, with all performances held at one of the university auditoriums.

Places to Stay

West of town, near Addington Forks and just off the Trans Canada Hwy, *Beaver Mountain* (☎ 863-3343) is a very quiet provincial park, good for camping. The 47 sites are up on a hill in a wooded area and are $9 a night.

Whidden's Campground & Trailer Court (☎ 836-3736), right in town on the corner of Main and Hawthorne Sts, is an unusual accommodation complex. It's a very large place and offers a real blend of choices. Tent camping is $16.50 for a night, full serviced sites $20 a night. There are also motel apartments with kitchens (from $60) and mobile homes with complete facilities ($68 a double plus $5 for each additional person). The grounds have a swimming pool and a laundromat for all guests to use.

For rooms at the central *University* from mid-May to mid-August, call the Residence Manager (☎ 867-3970). It has a dining room, laundromat and pool. Singles/doubles are $33/52 including a full breakfast and use of the university facilities.

There are also numerous inns, motels, cottages and a couple of B&Bs. *Green Haven* (☎ 863-2884) is a central B&B at 27 Greening St and close to the bus station. Singles/doubles are $30/35.

Another is the *Old Manse Inn* (☎ 863-5696), in a house dating from 1874 at 5 Tigo Park, a couple of blocks from the corner of Main and West Sts. It has five rooms at $30/36.

Most motels in town have singles that begin at $50. Head east for more affordable accommodations. *Chestnut Corner B&B* (☎ 386-2403), off Hwy 4 at Afton Station, is $30/35. *Hillside Housekeeping Cottages* (☎ 232-2888), 19 km east of Antigonish at Tracadie, has basic cottages that start at $40/46.

Places to Eat

A stroll down Main St and around the town will turn up several places for a bite. *The Pleasant Pheasant Bakery & Cafe* is a good choice for breakfast while the *Sunshine Café* at 332 Main St is good for soups, salads and vegetarian specialities as well as your double dose of café au lait in the morning. Light entrees are under $9, full dinners $14. Up the street is *Sunflower Health Food Store*.

Wong's is friendly and provides the local Chinese option, with full dinners in the $10 to $12 range. The *Venice*, just off Main St on College St is recommended for Greek dinners that range from $13 and pasta dishes.

West out of town along the Trans Canada Hwy, is the more costly *Lobster Treat* restaurant for the widest selection of seafood.

Getting There & Away

Bus The bus station (☎ 863-6900) is on the Trans Canada Hwy at the turn-off for James St into town, on the west side of the city, and is within walking distance of the downtown area. Buses include those to Halifax (four a day, $25), to Sydney (one morning and one afternoon trip, $23) and to Charlottetown (one daily, $38 including the ferry).

AROUND ANTIGONISH
Monastery

East of town in the small village of Monastery, the old monastery is now home to the Augustine Order of monks. It was originally a Trappist monastery established by French monks in 1825. Visitors are welcome to tour the chapel and the grounds.

Beaches

There are some good sandy beaches on the coast east or north from town. For the eastern ones, take Bay St out of town.

Driving Tours

There are several driving tours of the area, each no more than 80 km – a descriptive pamphlet is available from the tourist office. They try to take in some good scenery and points of historical note. One recommended 'off-the-track' route goes north along the coast to Cape George on Hwy 337, with some fine shoreline views. At Crystal Cliffs, along the way, there are huge cormorant roosts.

Eastern Shore

The 'Eastern Shore' designation refers to the area east from Dartmouth to Cape Canso, at the extreme eastern tip of the mainland. It's one of the least-visited regions of the province; there are no large towns and little industry, and the main road is slow, narrow and almost as convoluted as the rugged shoreline it follows. As in much of the province, the population is clustered in small coastal villages. Marine Drive, the designated tourist route, is pretty much the only route through the area, but despite published descriptions and alleged beauty spots, it is neither very scenic nor particularly interesting. There are some campgrounds and good beaches along the coast but the water on this edge of the province is prohibitively cold.

MUSQUODOBOIT VALLEY
A side trip away from the coast follows the course of the Musquodoboit River into the forested interior and along the valley's farming regions to the village of Upper Musquodoboit.

Along the road that heads south to Tangier on the coast there is **Moose River Gold Mines**. Prospecting in the area began in 1876 and Moose River Gold Mines reached their peak production between 1890 and 1909. In an attempt to reopen them in 1936, three men, including a Toronto barrister and a prominent Toronto doctor, became trapped 43 metres below after a cave-in. The rescue effort took 10 days and captivated the hearts of millions of people across Canada, the USA and Britain due to daily live reports of the Canadian Radio Broadcasting Company (later the CBC) that was carried by more than 700 stations. These broadcasts represented the first 'media event' in North America and for the most part changed the course of radio in Canada. Today the site is a provincial park with interpretive displays and mining equipment. Nearby is the **Moose River Gold Mines Museum** which has displays on the mines and the famous rescue. Hours are 10 am to 6 pm daily during the summer except Sunday when it opens at 1 pm. Admission is free.

MARTINIQUE BEACH PROVINCIAL PARK
Martinique, 4.8 km south of the village of Musquodoboit Harbour, is the longest beach in the province and a good place for a break.

Thanks in part to the beach, there are a number of interesting places to spend a night in and around Musquodoboit Harbour. Within town there is *Camelot Inn* (☎ 889-2198), a five-room inn overlooking a river that is fished for salmon. The inn features a restaurant on the 1st floor along with a fireplace lounge for guests. Singles are $34 to $45, and doubles are $52.

East of town is *Seaview Fishermen's Home* (☎ 889-2561), reached by departing Hwy 7 and heading south 13 km for Pleasant Point. The home, built in 1861, is surrounded by great coastal scenery that includes a lighthouse and a fisherman's wharf, where you can purchase lobster straight from the boat during the season. Rooms are $35/40.

JEDORE OYSTER POND
Quite the name for a town. See the small **Fisherman's Life Museum** – it's a model of a typical 1900s fishing family's house. It's open 9.30 am to 5.30 pm daily during the summer except Sunday when it opens at 1 pm. Admission is free. Also here on the water is the *Golden Coast Restaurant*, a place to buy fresh seafood to take away or to enjoy a seafood dinner. Dinners range from $8 to $15 and its seafood chowder, with chunks of lobster, scallops and haddock, is excellent.

SHIP HARBOUR
Off the shore here you'll see the buoys and nets of the local aquaculture industry. This is North America's largest mussel-farming centre. Fish-farming of every description is poised to become ever more significant as the natural stocks show the effects of centuries of indiscriminate hauling.

NOVA SCOTIA

TANGIER

A visit to **Willy Krauch's Smokehouse** (☎ 772-2188), a short distance from the main road in Tangier, is worthwhile. Begun by Willy, a Dane, and now run by his sons, it's a small operation with a big reputation. They smoke Atlantic salmon, mackerel and eel, but the ultimate is the Cape Breton smoked trout. You can keep it without refrigeration or it can be mailed, as it has been to Queen Elizabeth at Buckingham Palace. The shed is open every day until 6 pm.

Also in town is Coastal Adventures Sea Kayaking (☎ 772-2774), for lessons, rentals and guided trips. Their day clinic is an introduction to kayaking and includes a tour to offshore islands. The cost is $70. Half day rentals are $20, full day $35. They also have canoes and double kayaks.

TAYLOR HEAD PROVINCIAL PARK

Just east of the village of Spry Harbour, this day-use park has a very fine, sandy beach fronting a protected bay. The water, though, doesn't seem to warm up much. In recent years, the park has developed an extensive trail system along the shoreline of the point. The Headland Trail is the longest at eight km and follows the rugged coastline to scenic views at Taylor Head. The trail is a three to four-hour walk. Shorter is the Bob Bluff Trail, a three km return trip to views off the bluff at the end. Park entry is free.

LISCOMB PARK GAME SANCTUARY

North of Sheet Harbour lies this large preserve, 518 sq km in area. There's lots of wildlife and some good canoeing, swimming, fishing and hiking. At Sheet Harbour is *Sheet Harbour Motel* (☎ 885-2293) with singles/doubles for $38/42.

PORT DUFFERIN

Tiny Port Dufferin, population 157, is mentioned for the *Marquis of Dufferin Seaside Inn* (☎ 654-2696 or 800-561-2696), a highly regarded retreat featuring coastal views, breezes and tranquillity. Rooms are in a new motel-like strip alongside the original house. Singles/doubles are $60/65 and include a continental breakfast. The dining room in the restored house of 1859 serves good Maritime-style seafood meals such as fish casserole, haddock baked with eggs and shrimp. Dinners range from $11 to $16.

Port Dufferin is about two hours' drive from Halifax, Antigonish or the Halifax International Airport.

LISCOMB MILLS

In a green wooded area where the Liscomb River meets the sea is one of the provincial government's luxury resort lodges, *Liscomb Lodge* (☎ 779-2307). It has all the amenities, and prices to match; singles/doubles begin at $95/105. But you may want to have a look as the river here rushes through a maze of large boulders, making for a scenic setting.

SHERBROOKE

Inland towards Antigonish, the pleasant little town of Sherbrooke is overshadowed by its historic site, which is about the same size.

Sherbrooke Village (☎ 522-2400) recreates life 125 years ago through buildings, demonstrations and costumed workers. It's called a living museum and all of the houses, stores and various workshops are the original ones. The green, quiet setting helps to evoke a real sense of stepping back in time. The site is open daily from 9 am to 5.30 pm from 15 May to 15 October and admission is $4 per adult or $12 per family.

About half a km away is the **Sherbrooke Village Sawmill**, the former town mill, which is in working order and has a guide to answer questions. Across the street and a nice walk through the woods along a stream is a cabin in which the workers at the mill would have lived.

Sherbrooke itself, although not the major centre it was at the turn of the century, is one of the biggest towns in the area, so stop here for tourist information, groceries and gasoline. The **Sherbrooke Tourist Centre** (☎ 522-2192), right on Main St, also rents out bicycles for $5 an hour or $25 a day and canoes and kayaks for $6 an hour and $35 a day. The tide floods the St Mary's River up to Sherbrooke so you can literally carry the boats across the street and put in from a small park on the water. The tourist centre is open daily during the summer from 9 am to 9 pm.

Places to Stay & Eat

At *Try-Your-Tent-In-Place* (☎ 522-2581) you can rent a permanent tent with carpeting, table, chairs and a deck. The rate is $7/13 for singles/doubles. Regular tent sites are $8 at this campground just off Main St.

The central *St Mary's River Lodge* (☎ 522-2177) is $36/42 with shared bath facilities, and breakfast is available.

The *Bright House* restaurant, in a bright-yellow inn dating from 1850, specialises in roast beef and fresh seafood, and lunch costs around $10. It's open daily for lunch and dinner.

Regardless of whether you are going to partake in the dining room, do visit the adjacent bake shop for cinnamon buns, muffins, pies and various other sweets. It's open daily until 8 pm from May to October.

CANSO

With a population of just 1300, this town at the edge of the mainland is probably the largest on the whole eastern shoreline. Since the first attempted settlement in 1518, Canso has seen it all: Native Indian battles, British and French landings and captures, pirates, fishing fleets and the ever-present difficulties of life ruled by the sea.

A museum, **Whitman House** (☎ 366-2170), on the corner of Main and Union Sts, has reminders of parts of this history and offers a good view from the roof. The museum also doubles as the tourist office and is open from 9 am to 6 pm daily during the summer. Admission is free.

An interpretive centre on the waterfront tells the story of the **Grassy Island National Historic Site**, which lies just offshore and can be visited by boat. In 1720, the British built a small fort here to offer some protection from the French, who had their headquarters in Louisbourg. The island, however, was extremely vulnerable to military attacks and was totally destroyed in 1744. Among the ruins today is a self-guiding hiking trail with eight interpretive stops explaining the history of the area.

The visitor centre (☎ 295-2069) is open 10 am to 6 pm during the summer. The boat to Grassy Island departs from the centre twice a day at 10.30 am and 2 pm in July and August, and only once a day in June and September. Admission to the park is $2.25.

Cape Breton Island

Cape Breton, the large island adjunct at the north-east end of Nova Scotia, is justly renowned for its rugged splendour. It's the roughest, highest, coolest, most remote area of the province. The coast is rocky and rugged, the interior a blend of mountains, valleys, rivers and lakes. The nearly 300-km-long highway, the Cabot Trail, around the Cape Breton Highlands National Park is one of Canada's grandest and best-known roads. It winds and climbs to 500 metres between mountain and sea, providing access to a variety of physical, historical and cultural attractions.

The island offers more than natural beauty – it has a long and captivating human history encompassing the Native people, the British, the French and, especially, the Scottish, who were attracted to this part of the province because of its strong resemblance to the Scottish Highlands.

Except for the industrial centres of Sydney and Glace Bay, most towns are small enough to be considered villages. People in some areas still speak French; in others even Gaelic can be heard. Life is hard here and unemployment is very high. Fishing and mining have long been the main industries and both are in trouble.

For the visitor it is a very appealing, relatively undeveloped area, with the excellent national park in the highlands and a top historic site in Louisbourg.

North Sydney is the terminal for ferries to Newfoundland.

The Cabot Trail, understandably the most popular area, can be busy, even a little

NOVA SCOTIA

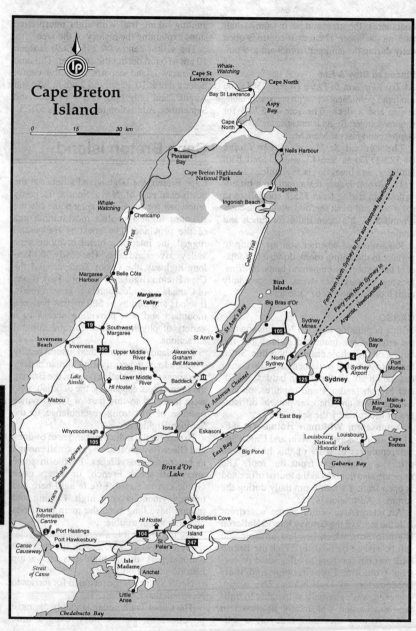

Cape Breton
Island

0   15   30 km

Whale-
Watching
Cape St
Lawrence
Cape North
Bay St Lawrence
Aspy
Bay
Cape
North
Neils Harbour
Pleasant
Bay
Cape Breton Highlands
National Park
Ingonish
Whale-
Watching
Ingonish Beach
Cheticamp
Cabot Trail
Ferry from North Sydney to Port aux Basques, Newfoundland
Ferry from North Sydney to
Argentia, Newfoundland
Belle Côte
Margaree
Harbour
Margaree
Valley
Cabot Trail
Bird
Islands
Big Bras d'Or
St Ann's Bay
Sydney
Mines
19
Southwest
Margaree
105
Inverness
Beach
Inverness
395
St Ann's
Glace
Bay
North
Sydney
4
Port
Morien
Upper Middle
River
Middle River
Alexander
Graham
Bell Museum
Sydney
Airport
Lower Middle
River
HI Hostel
Baddeck
125
Sydney
Mabou
Lake
Ainslie
St Andrews Channel
22
Mira
Bay
Main-a-
Dieu
East Bay
4
Whycocomagh
105
Iona
Eskasoni
Louisbourg
National
Historic Park
Louisbourg
Cape
Breton
Canada Highway
East Bay
Big Pond
Bras d'Or
Lake
Gabarus Bay
Trans
Tourist
Information
Centre
HI Hostel
Soldiers Cove
Port Hastings
104
Chapel
Island
Port Hawkesbury
St
Peter's
247
Canso
Causeway
Strait
of Canso
Isle
Madame
Arichat
Little
Anse
Chedabucto Bay

crowded in July and August, but it isn't difficult to get away if solitude is what you seek. The words most often used to describe the weather are windy, wet, foggy and cool. Summer days, however, can be warm and sunny. The sketchy public transportation system makes getting around Cape Breton difficult without a vehicle. From Port Hawkesbury and Canso, the Inverness (McKinnin) bus runs as far as Inverness on the north-west coast, going by Long Point and Mabou on the way. Acadian Bus Lines runs from Halifax or New Glasgow and Antigonish to Sydney, stopping at popular Baddeck along the way. Transoverland Ltd runs a bus route from Baddeck to Cheticamp through the Margaree Valley.

Information

A big and busy tourist office sits on the east side of the causeway in Port Hastings and is open 8.30 am to 8.30 pm daily. From here you can pick up information on all parts of Cape Breton or book rooms with a courtesy phone. If you need to make ferry reservations for a trip to Newfoundland, do it a few days before your planned departure.

NORTH COAST

From the Canso Causeway, Hwy 19, known as the Ceilidh (pronounced 'KAY-lee') Trail, goes up the northern side of the island to the highlands. The first part of the route is not very interesting but it still beats the Trans Canada Hwy (No 105), which goes straight up the middle.

At **Mabou**, things pick up. It's a green, hilly region with valleys following numerous rivers and sheltering traditional towns. This is one of the areas on Cape Breton where Gaelic is still spoken and actually taught in the schools. Right in the centre of little Mabou is the Gaelic & Historical Society Centre, in a storefront. Aside from information they have books, tapes and various items relating to their Scottish heritage. On 1 July a Scottish picnic is held, with music and dancing.

Right off Hwy 19 is *Clayton Farm B&B* (☎ 945-2719), a working farm in an idyllic setting outside Mabou. There are four rooms for rent with singles/doubles $40/50. Tents also pop up on a sweeping beach next to a small harbour just south of Port Hope off Shore Road. In Mabou, start the day at *Shining Waters Bakery & Eatery*. The homemade bread is a steal at $1.90 a loaf, while a full breakfast featuring thick slices of it is $3.75.

At the coast, off the main road, around Mabou Mines, the **Mabou Highlands** offers some good walking trails. To reach it, head for Mabou Harbour and then swing off on the gravel road marked with 'Mabou Mines'. You'll quickly return to the coast to pass a handful of houses and then follow a rough track as it climbs into the highlands. Within three km, you pass two posted trailheads, though the signs are easy to miss.

Between Mabou and Inverness on Hwy 19, the thirsty may wish to stop at **Glenora Falls**, where North America's only single-malt Scotch whisky is made, at the *Glenora Inn & Distillery* (☎ 258-2662). Free tours of the whisky operation take place daily during the summer on the hour from 10 am to 4 pm. You can have something to eat or even spend the night but the room rates are steep at $78 for a double.

INVERNESS

This is the first town of any size on the northern shore. There are miles of sandy beach with some nice secluded spots and few people and, surprisingly, the water temperature is not too bad, reaching temperatures of 19°C to 21°C, which is about as warm as it gets anywhere around the Atlantic Provinces – cool but definitely swimmable. Pilot whales can sometimes be seen off the coast.

Places to Stay & Eat

The *Inverness Lodge* (☎ 258-2193), in the centre, is a hotel and motel offering accommodation and a dining room. A double room costs $50. The *Gables Motel* (☎ 258-2314) is slightly less expensive with singles for $40, and at the north end of town try the comfortable *Cayly Café*, located next door to a laundromat.

NOVA SCOTIA

MARGAREE VALLEY

North-east of Lake Ainslie, in a series of river valleys, is a pretty and relatively gentle region known collectively as the Margaree Valley. With half a dozen different towns named Margaree this or Margaree that, it's an oasis of sorts in the midst of the more rugged, wild and unpopulated highlands.

In North East Margaree is the **Salmon Museum**, with information on the river, its fish and the human artifices they must avoid. An aquarium contains both salmon and trout. It is open daily from 9 am to 5 pm and admission is 50 cents. Also in town is the **Museum of Cape Breton Heritage**, whose displays about the Scottish and French settlers emphasise their textiles. It's open daily during summer from 9 am to 6 pm.

Places to Stay

As a small resort area, although thankfully a low-key one, there is a fair bit of accommodation and some places to eat scattered around the valley. Best known is the *Normaway Inn* (☎ 248-2987), a three-star luxury country inn operating since 1928. No doubt it is a fine place to stay and the food is said to be excellent. Rates range from $75 to $100 a double with the morning meal included. But check in after 4 pm and if there are any rooms available, they drop $25 from the room rate. This isn't usually the case in high season but is often possible in May and September.

Getting back to reality there's *Brown's Brunaich na H'Aibhne B&B* (☎ 248-2935), in Margaree Centre. Rates start at $32 a single and $40 a double or triple. In East Margaree is *Mill Valley Farm B&B* which features singles/doubles for $40/50 and a jacuzzi. Just south of Margaree Harbour on Hwy 219 is *Whale Cove Summer Village* (☎ 235-2202), with its own private beach on a small cove. The resort has 30 cabins with daily rates from $60.

Places to Eat

In Margaree Harbour, out of the valley on the coast, the *Schooner Village Tea House* serves light meals and inexpensive fish chowders.

BELLE CÔTE

From Belle Côte, where the Cabot Trail meets the coastline, northward to the Cape Breton Highlands National Park, another strong culture adds a different interest to the island. The people here are predominantly French, the descendants of the Acadians who settled the area in the 1750s after being expelled from the mainland by the British during the Seven Years' War. This region and one north around the coast from Yarmouth on the mainland are the two largest remaining French districts in the province.

The strength of this culture in Cape Breton is remarkable because of its small size and isolation from other French-speaking people. Almost everyone, it seems, speaks English, although an accent is sometimes detectable. Amongst themselves, they switch to French, keeping the language very much alive. Aside from the language, the French food, music and dance are worth sampling.

At Belle Côte look for the **Theatre of Scarecrow**, by the highway beside Ethel's Takeout restaurant. It's a humorous, quasi-macabre outdoor collection of life-sized stuffed figures. Watch out after midnight.

CHETICAMP

Just before the Cape Breton Highlands National Park, Cheticamp (population 3000) is the centre of the local Acadian community. It's a busy little town through which many visitors pass on their way to the park. From Cheticamp the Cabot Trail becomes more scenic, with great views and lots of hills and turns as you climb to the highest point just before Pleasant Bay.

The church, St Pierre, dominates the town, as is so often the case in French centres. It dates from 1883 and has the characteristic silver spire.

From the Government Wharf, across and down from the church, whale-watching cruises are run. The three-hour boat excursions by Whale Cruisers (☎ 224-3376) are pretty good value. They run three trips daily from May until the end of September at 9 am, 1 pm and 6 pm. The cost is $25. Others offering whale trips at the same price are

L'Escaouette (☎ 224-1959) and Seaside Whale & Nature Cruises (☎ 800-959-4253) while Acadian Whale Cruise is only $20. The most common species in the area is the pilot whale, also called the pothead, but fin whales and minkes are sometimes seen, as are bald eagles and a couple of species of sea birds. At the tourist office on Government Wharf they keep a chart of the whales spotted each day during the summer.

Over on Île de Cheticamp, Plage Saint Pierre is a good sandy beach with picnic tables and camping. The island is connected by road to the mainland at the south end of town.

The Acadians have a tradition of handicrafts, but in this area one product, hooked rugs, has long been seen as of particular beauty and value. Many of the local women continue this craft; their wares are displayed and sold in numerous outlets in and around town. A good rug costs $200 to $300 and up, so they aren't cheap but they are distinctive and attractive. Each is made of wool, and to complete the intricate work takes about 12 hours per 30 sq cm.

Les Trois Pignons

At the north end of town, this cultural centre and museum (☎ 224-2642) shows, among other things, the rugs and tapestries of many local people, including those of Elizabeth Lefort, who has achieved an international reputation. Her detailed representational rugs and portraits in wool hang in the White House, the Vatican and Buckingham Palace. Admission is $2.50.

Musée Acadienne

In the middle of town don't miss the Acadian museum, which has a small but interesting display of artefacts, furniture and some older rugs. It's interesting to see how the old motifs and designs are incorporated into the rugs made today.

Perhaps the highlight of the Acadian museum is its restaurant, with a large menu of mainly standard items, the low prices and freshness separating them from what's offered in run-of-the-mill places. The best dishes are the three or four traditional Acadian ones, all of which are excellent. The soup and meat pie make a great lunch. Fish cakes may be sampled (here, as in Newfoundland, fish means cod; other types are called by name). The desserts, which are all freshly made, include gingerbread and a variety of fruit pies. Everything is good and cheap (dinners under $9); the women who run the place and do the cooking and baking wear traditional dress.

The museum and restaurant (☎ 224-2170) are open daily 9 am to 9 pm from the middle of May to the end of October.

Places to Stay

Throughout July and August accommodation is tight, so calling ahead or arriving early in the afternoon is advisable.

As mentioned, there is camping on Île de Cheticamp at Plage Saint Pierre.

In the heart of town on Main St is *Albert's Motel* (☎ 224-2077) with $50 doubles. Just before the park, *Les Cabines du Portage* (☎ 224-2822) has six housekeeping cabins (includes kitchen), each with two double beds, at $50 a single or double plus $5 for each extra person. There are also three bigger, two-bedroom cabins for $60. Weekly rates are offered for all the cabins. The *Cheticamp Motel* (☎ 224-2711), on Main St on the south side of town, is well kept and friendly and has a dining room for breakfast. Singles/doubles are $40/45.

There is a growing number of bed and breakfasts in town, including *La Tete Ve Cheval* (☎ 224-3257) charging $30/40.

Places to Eat

Aside from the museum restaurant, there are quite a few other places for a small town. One of the main catches here is crab, which turns up on several menus, including *Harbour Restaurant*, which has a view and outdoor patio to complement the food. Lobster is also offered through the summer but be prepared for dinners that range from $13 to $16 though some pasta dishes are less. Very highly rated but more expensive again is the dining room at *Laurie's Motel*, which has been operating since 1938.

On the more affordable end is *Wabo's Pizza* next to the Government Wharf with large pizzas that start at $15 and subs for under $5. Right next door is *La Chaloupe*, a small cafe with a menu of fish, clams and scallops and a pub upstairs. Both places have outdoor seating overlooking the boat traffic.

Getting There & Away

Cheticamp is connected to Baddeck by bus with Transoverland Ltd. The buses also run from Baddeck to Sydney. The schedule can vary seasonally and buses may not run every day. There is, unfortunately, no bus service through or around the park.

CAPE BRETON HIGHLANDS NATIONAL PARK

In the middle of the highlands, this park not only has some of the most impressive terrain in the area but is also one of the most scenic places in Canada.

Summer conditions tend to be rather rainy, foggy and windy even while remaining fairly warm. The driest month is generally July, with June and September the runners-up. Maximum temperatures in midsummer usually don't exceed 25°C and minimums are around 15°C.

At either of the entrances, Cheticamp or Ingonish, there are information centres that are open daily during the season from 8 am to 8 pm and can provide maps (including topographical ones), hiking brochures and advice. Both have book stores and mountain bikes for rent for $5 an hour or $25 for eight hours. You can also purchase a motor-vehicle entry permit here; a one-day pass is $6, four days $18.

The Cabot Trail, one of the best-known roads in the country, gets its reputation from the 106-km park segment of its Cape Breton loop. The drive is at its best along the northern shore and then down to Pleasant Bay. The road winds right along the shoreline between mountains, across barren plains and valleys up to **French Mountain**, the highest point (459 metres). Along the way are lookout

points, the best of which is at the summit. If possible, save the trip for a sunny day when you can see down the coastline. From French Mountain the road zigzags through switchbacks and descends to Pleasant Bay, just outside the park. If you're driving, make sure your brakes are good and can afford to burn off a little lining. Despite the effort required, the park is a popular cycling destination. However, it is not suggested that it be used as your inaugural trip.

There are eight campgrounds in the park, some for tenters only. These tend to be small, with space for 10 to 20 people. Camping is $13 for a tent site, $15 for serviced sites. In the campgrounds, pick a site and set up. A warden will come around, probably in the evening, to collect the money.

Coming from Cheticamp there are a few park highlights to watch for. The top of **Mackenzie Mountain** affords great views of the interior. The **Grande Anse Valley** contains virgin forest.

In the small town of **Pleasant Bay**, the *Black Whale* restaurant is recommended for good, fresh seafood at reasonable prices in a casual, pleasant setting. The menu has everything from lobster to fish & chips; you can sit on the patio and watch for the regularly seen pilot whales just offshore. Seafood dinners, ranging from fresh haddock to poached sole, cost from $10 to $14. There are other places to eat, also specialising in seafood, and a couple of motels, both considerably more expensive than what's available in Cheticamp.

You can also book a whale sighting trip from the harbour of Pleasant Bay. Highland Coastal Tours (☎ 224-1825) has three cruises at 9.30 am, and 1.30 and 5.30 pm from mid-June to mid-September for $20 per adult.

Towards Ingonish, the short **Lone Sheiling Trail** leads through 300-year-old maple trees to a replica of a Scottish Highland crofter's hut, a reminder of the area's first settlers. The hut is actually visible from the road in case you're not in a walking mood.

From the village of **Cape North** out of the park, the extreme northern portion (also

•

called Cape North) of Cape Breton can be visited. In Cape North village there is a service station and food store and private campground in case the park is full. *Hide-Away Campground* (☎ 383-2116), on Shore Road off Cabot Trail, offers both wooded sites and open ones that put you on the edge of the bluff in full view of that rugged coastline you just drove along. Sites are $12 for tents and $14 for electricity, and there is even a small oyster bar in the campground.

Not far north from here, at Cabot's Landing Provincial Park on Aspey's Bay, is the spot where John Cabot is believed to have landed in 1497. A re-enactment is held annually on 24 June on the beach at Sugarloaf Mountain. At **Bay St Lawrence** whale-watching boat tours are run three times daily at 10.15 am, and 1.30 and 4.30 pm through the summer months with Whale Watch (☎ 383-2981). The cost for the 2½-hour tour is $25.

The road to Bay of St Lawrence ends at Meat Cove where there is *Meat Cove Campground* (☎ 383-2379). Sites are $12 a night and many say these are some of the most scenic sites in Cape Breton. From Meat Cove the trails head west to the Cape St Lawrence lighthouse and Lowland Cove.

A side trip is recommended to **Neils Harbour**, an attractive little fishing village. In fact, it's one of the nicest you're likely to see in Nova Scotia. Down at the wharf you can buy fish and lobster, or try something at the inexpensive *Chowder House*, by the water at the lighthouse.

At the eastern entrance to the park are **Ingonish** and **Ingonish Beach**, two small towns with accommodation and basic supplies. There are several campgrounds, both government and private ones, as well as motels and a park information office.

The beach at Ingonish Beach is a wonderful place, with a long, wide strip of sand tucked in a bay surrounded by green hills. The water can get pleasantly warm here after a few sunny days.

See the Getting There & Away section under Cheticamp earlier in this chapter for details of the limited bus service to the park.

Hiking

For as big and rugged as Cape Breton Highlands National Park is, the hiking is surprisingly limited with multi-day trails almost non-existent. The park has 27 trails and only two of them lead to backcountry camp sites. Fishing Cove Trail is an eight-km one-way walk that descends 330 metres to campsites on the mouth of rugged Fishing Cove River. Lake of Islands Trail is among the longer trails, 14 km one-way from Ingonish to primitive camp sites on the lake.

The backcountry camp sites are $11 a night and you must book them in advance at one of the two visitor centres.

Most of the other trails are shorter and close to the road. If the day is clear, many trails take you to ridge tops for impressive views of the coast. The best is probably Skyline Trail, a seven-km loop that puts you on the edge of a headland cliff right above the water. This trail is posted along Cabot Trail just beyond Corey Brook Campground. Other trails with ocean views from mountaintops includes Aspy, Glasgow Lake and Franey Mountain Trail.

For those who need to rent gear or are looking for guided overnight hikes, stop at Highland Hiking Expeditions (☎ 383-2933 in the summer only) right on Cabot Trail in South Harbour.

Cycling

The riding is tough but the views are spectacular when cycling through the park or other coastal roads in the area. Despite the heavy numbers of tourists and steep hills, considerable biking takes place here. If you need to rent, avoid the low-grade visitor-centre bikes and contact either Ingonish Mountain Bike Rental (☎ 285-2294) or Sea Spray Cycle Center (☎ 383-2732) in Dingwall. Sea Spray is an especially good outfitter that also has maps with suggested coastal routes for self-guided tours. Expect to pay about $25 a day.

Places to Stay & Eat

Eight km north of the park entrance, near Ingonish, is *Driftwood Lodge* (☎ 285-2558),

NOVA SCOTIA

run by Mrs Kulig. Rooms in the older building are cheapest and start at $20 for a single with shared bath. Doubles are $40 and $45 and she even has two-bedroom apartments with balconies overlooking the ocean for $65. Breakfast is served and a German-Polish lunch and dinner are available.

Also in Ingonish, the *Sea Breeze Cottages & Motel* (☎ 285-2879) has a dozen cottages of varying sizes and amenities, some completely self-contained. The six motel units are rented at $49 a double, the one-bedroom cottages begin at $58.

Ingonish Centre also has a few places, like *Deervale Cottages* (☎ 285-2212) where cottages start at $45, as does Ingonish Beach, where up on the hillside is the very expensive luxury government hotel, the *Keltic Lodge* (☎ 285-2880).

For a place to eat, *Coastal Waters Restaurant* in Ingonish is a sitdown place with sandwiches, hamburgers and seafood dinners. Even better, if the weather is nice, is *Muddy Rudder Seafood Shack*. The small eatery features steamed lobster, mussels, crabs and clams and has a handful of tables outside. It's located on Cabot Trail just before you cross Ingonish River and you can stop at the beer store in Ingonish on the way.

CAPE SMOKEY

From Ingonish south and up to Cape Smokey there is some fine scenery. At the peak on Cape Smokey, at a small roadside park with picnic tables, there are very good sea and coastal views. Also in the park is the trailhead for the Cape Smokey Trail, a round trip of 11 km where you descend 150 metres along the coast past several viewing points.

ST ANN'S

The interesting preserver and promoter of Scottish heritage, the **Gaelic College of Celtic Arts & Crafts**, is at the end of St Ann's Bay. Founded in 1938 and the only one of its kind in North America, the college offers programmes in the Gaelic language, bagpipe playing, Highland dancing, weaving and kilt-making and other things Scottish to students of all ages from across the land. Drop

in any time during summer and the chances are you'll hear a student sing a traditional ballad in Gaelic or another play a Highland violin piece; mini-concerts and recitals are performed throughout the day. You can stroll around the grounds, see the museum with its historical notes and tartans or browse the giftshop for books, music tapes or kilts. There is also a *cafeteria* serving light meals or tea.

A Scottish festival, the Gaelic Mod, is held at the end of August each year, with events daily.

BIG BRAS D'OR

After crossing the long bridge over an inlet to Bras d'Or Lake on the way towards Sydney, a secondary road branches off and leads to the coast and the village of Big Bras d'Or. Offshore are the cliff-edged **Bird Islands**, Hertford and Ciboux. The islands are home to large colonies of razorbills, puffins, kittiwakes, terns and several other species. Boat tours run from town from May to September. The islands are about 1.6 km from shore and take about 40 minutes to reach. The entire boat trip takes 2½ hours. Nesting time is June and July, so these are the prime months for a visit, but plenty of birds can be seen any time from May to September. Bald eagles can also be seen, as they nest in the vicinity as well. Binoculars are handy, but not necessary (they can be rented) as the tour boats go to within 20 metres or so of the islands.

The boat tours depart from *Mountain View By The Sea* (☎ 674-2384), where there are housekeeping cabins for rent, B&B rooms and a campground. The tour is $24 per adult and to camp is $10 a night.

NORTH SYDNEY

Small and nondescript, North Sydney is important as the Marine Atlantic terminal for ferries to either Port aux Basques or Argentia, Newfoundland. For details see under those destinations.

There isn't much in town but it makes a convenient place to put up if you're using the ferry. Tourist information is available at the ferry landing or you can also call the Cape Breton Tourist Association (☎ 539-9876) in Sydney.

The main street in town is Commercial St, where you'll find the stores and places to eat. For drivers, there is public parking behind the Town Hall, on Commercial St near the corner of Blowers St. On the waterfront off Commercial St, right in the centre of town at the foot of Caledonia St, is a boardwalk leading to the Ballast Grounds harbour area.

Places to Stay

North of town off the Trans Canada Hwy are a few privately owned campgrounds. The *Arm of Gold Campground* (☎ 736-6516), mainly for trailers, is closest to the ferry, at just 3.2 km away. A site is $9 a night.

With a view over the water, *Alexandra Shebib's B&B* (☎ 794-4876) is two km west of the ferry terminal. It's at 88 Queen St, which is called Commercial St in town. This is a nice place, open all year for $30/40.

Other than this there are several motels in the vicinity at about twice the above rate. One to try is the *Clansman Motel* (☎ 794-7226 or 800-565-2668), on Peppett St, off exit 2 on Hwy 125. Rooms are $48/58.

Places to Eat

There are a few basic restaurants in town, such as *Papa J's* or *Munchees* where you can get a plate of spaghetti for $6 or a slice of pizza for $3. If it's breakfast you're looking for, head to *Robena's Bakery and Restaurant* on Commercial St. Full breakfast is $3.50 and includes big slices of their homemade bread.

Getting There & Away

Bus There is no real bus depot in North Sydney; the depot proper is in Sydney. However, the Acadian line bus between Sydney and Halifax can be picked up at the North Star Inn, beside the ferry terminal, twice a day. There is also a local bus which runs back and forth between Sydney and North Sydney for $3. It, too, can be caught at the ferry dock, or at some points along Queen St. See Getting There & Away under

Sydney for information on the Transoverland buses to Baddeck.

Ferry For detailed information on ferry crossings, see the St John's and Port aux Basques sections in the Newfoundland chapter. Reservations may be required and are recommended in midsummer; call Marine Atlantic (☎ 794-5700) in North Sydney. The ferry terminal is central, at the end of Commercial St at Blowers St. The Trans Canada Hwy (Route 105) leads straight into or out of the ferry terminal.

SYDNEY MINES

Long known simply as the Mines, this small coastal town north-east of North Sydney was a depressed and dirty mining centre from as early as the 1700s. The mines were operating until recently and working in them was no picnic. Most of the shafts were out under the sea – one ran 6.4 km from shore below the ocean floor.

SYDNEY

Sydney is the third largest town in the province, the only real city on Cape Breton and the centre of the island's industrial sector. It's a very old town and, as the heart of a coal-mining district, has seen its share of grief and hardship. Until quite recently it was a drab, rather grim town with a hard-drinking, if warm and friendly, population. The people haven't changed but the appearance of the place has – there is more pride in the past and hope for the future. Though still somewhat at the whim of economic vagaries, it has the largest self-contained steel plant in North America, and numerous other industries, including machine works, foundries and pulp & paper manufacturing. Heritage buildings have been preserved and there is a variety of hotels and restaurants for visitors.

The main street downtown is Charlotte St, which has many stores and restaurants though a large mall has since popped up near the exit off Hwy 125. The Sydney River runs along the western edge of the downtown area. There isn't a lot to do, but with the ferry to the north and Louisbourg to the south,

NOVA SCOTIA

many people do pass by. On the way you could slip a few coins in the slots at the new casino in the Sydney Sheraton, 50 Dorchester St.

There is a tourist office (☎ 539-9876) south of town on King's Rd across from the mall which is open 9 am to 9 pm daily.

Northend

Just north of the city centre on Charlotte St, the Esplanade (which runs parallel to the river) and the adjoining streets is the old historic part of town, with half-a-dozen buildings from the 1700s and many built during the 19th century. On the Esplanade across from the Government Wharf, you can visit the oldest Roman Catholic Church in Cape Breton now a museum. Dating from 1828, **St Patrick's Church Museum** features the stone church with its three-foot thick walls and a variety of interesting artefacts inside, including the town's whipping post from the mid-19th century. Hours during the summer are 9.30 am to 5.30 pm and admission is by donation.

Cossit House, on Charlotte St, dates from 1787 and is the oldest house in Sydney. It's now a museum with period furnishings. It is open from 9.30 am to 5.30 pm and admission is by donation. Just down the road is the **Jost House**, also built in 1787 and now a museum housing a marine exhibit. Hours are 10 am to 4 pm Monday through Saturday during the summer.

At the Lyceum, the former cultural centre, 225 George St, is the **Centre for Heritage & Science**. The museum features the human and natural history of this region and houses an art gallery. The centre is open daily through the summer from 10 am to 4 pm and reduced hours the rest of the year. Admission is free.

Action Week is an annual event held in the first week of August. Festivities include music, sports and various other goings-on.

Places to Stay

Right in town is *Paul's Hotel* (☎ 562-5747), at 10 Pitt St. It has 24 rooms, some with shared facilities and the more expensive ones with private bath. Rates range from $28 to $40. Also quite central, at 169 Park St, is the *Park Place* (☎ 562-3518), a turn-of-the-century B&B with rooms at $32/40.

Heading south at 100 Kings Rd is *City Lodge* (☎ 567-3311 or 800-580-2489) with laundry facilities, pub and restaurant. Singles/doubles are $40/48. The larger, more modern choices are mostly along Kings Rd, which runs south of the centre along the Sydney River towards Hwy 125. Here you'll find numerous motels, most with restaurants attached. *Journey's End Motel* (☎ 562-0200 or 800-228-5150), at 386 Kings Rd, is $58/66.

Places to Eat

Charlotte St has an impressive selection of restaurants that offer cuisine from around the world. Along with the usual Chinese restaurants and a handful of pizza-and-pasta shops, there's *Sit & Gid's Lebanese Restaurant* where a falafal sandwich can be enjoyed for $4 or a serving of hummus and pita bread for $3. Across the street is *Ike's Delicatessen* and nearby is a pair of Greek restaurants, side-by-side. At *Island Greek Donair* a souvlakia is $3. *Joe's Warehouse*, also on Charlotte St, has a varied menu featuring steak and a large salad bar, and an outdoor patio with views of the water.

If it's Sunday, about the only thing open will be *Jasper's*, with several locations around town, including a central one on the corner of George and Dorchester Sts. This is an inexpensive 24-hour family restaurant where nothing on the large menu is more than $13 and most dinners are under $8.

Getting There & Away

Bus The Acadian bus line's depot (☎ 564-5533) is away from the centre a bit (walkable if necessary), across the street from the big Sydney Shopping Centre Mall on Terminal Drive. There are three buses a day to Halifax at 7.30 and 11 am, and 4.30 pm. A ticket is $48. The first and last buses go to the ferry terminal in North Sydney and make many other stops along the way.

For Charlottetown, Prince Edward Island, the fare is $61 and a change of buses is required.

Transoverland Ltd (☎ 248-2051 in Cheti-camp) runs buses to Baddeck, via St Anne's, and from there north through the Margaree Valley and up the coast to Cheticamp. Buses depart Monday, Wednesday and Friday at 3 pm and the fare is $9.

GLACE BAY

As part of the Sydney area's industrial region, the difficulties of Cape Bretoners have been and are reflected here. The district has a long, bitter history of hard work – when there is any – with low pay and poor conditions and, regularly, one of the highest unemployment rates in the country. The hardships, however, have resulted in a people who are able to smile at misfortune and are generally friendly and hospitable to strangers.

Glace Bay is one of the places where the coal-mining tradition survived until recently, but the mines are now shut and the population has decreased.

The **Miners' Museum** (☎ 849-4522), less than two km east from the town centre in Quarry Point, at 42 Birkley St off South St, provides a look at the history of local coal mining, with equipment displays and a rec-reated village depicting a miner's life at the beginning of the century. The highlight, though, is an hour-long underground tour led by a retired miner, that includes walking in the tunnel. It's $6 for the complete tour, less if you forgo (but don't) the mine visit. There is a restaurant at the site. The museum is open all year and daily during the summer from 10 am to 6 pm.

The **Marconi National Historic Site** marks the place where, in 1902, Italian Gugliemo Marconi sent the first wireless message across the Atlantic. It was received in Cornwall, England. There is a model of the original transmitting station, and other information on the developments in commu-nications that followed. The site is on Timmerman St at the area of Glace Bay referred to as Table Head and is open daily from 10 am to 8 pm during the summer. Admission is free.

MAIN-À-DIEU

Known as the Marconi Trail, the coastal road south of Glace Bay leads to the town of Louisbourg and its top-rate historic site, along the way passing a handful of small villages. One of them is Main-a-Dieu, which features a thriving lobster fleet and the most scenic harbour along this stretch.

At the north end of Main-a-Dieu is the **Fishermen's Museum**, two rooms packed with model ships and displays tracing the local history of this fishing village. It is open daily from noon to 5 pm in the summer and is located at the base of a scenic overlook of the village. Departing from the overlook is Moke Head Trail. It's a round trip of four kms to Moke Head and the views of Scatterie Island, where 30 families once lived. Along the way you past beautiful beaches and cross Mira River on a 20-metre bridge.

At the south end of town is the unique **Boardwalk Park**, where boardwalks connect a beach, observation decks, a pond and even a walk-through lobster trap. Based near Main-a-Dieu is Island Seafari (☎ 733-2309), which offers guided kayak trips, including a three-hour paddle of the harbour.

The main, more direct route running south of Sydney has half-a-dozen campgrounds along it.

LOUISBOURG

At the edge of the ocean with an excellent harbour sits Louisbourg (population 1400), the largest of the region's fishing towns and now famous for its adjacent historic fort. There are a couple of other things to see in the village as well.

The **Sydney & Louisbourg Railway Museum** (☎ 733-2720), which includes the tourist office, is at the entrance to the town. The museum has displays pertaining to the railway, which ran up to Sydney from 1895 until 1968, shuffling fish one way and coal the other. Hours are 9 am to 7 pm daily during the summer and admission is free.

On the waterfront, behind the fire station, is the **Louisbourg Playhouse** (☎ 733-2996). The theatre was originally built at the Fortress of Louisbourg in 1993 for the Walt

Disney movie *Indian Warrior*. After the film, it was totally dismantled, moved and given to the community. The playhouse is now a permanent performing arts centre for Louisbourg and hosts a variety of plays during the year.

Along the waterfront, examples of crafts can be seen and bought at a number of gift shops including the **House of Dolls**, which houses a collection of nearly 2000 miniature people. The gift shop/museum is open noon to 7 pm daily and admission is free. South of town are the ruins of Canada's oldest lighthouse with an interpretive display and walking trails.

Places to Stay & Eat

For those wishing to do more than a day trip, Louisbourg features a half dozen B&Bs and several motels. Being a major tourist designation, you'll find accommodations steeper in price and often filled during the height of the summer season. There is, however, a good campground in the heart of town. *Louisbourg Trailer & Campsite* (☎ 733-3631) is right on the waterfront and has 51 sites, most of them for RVers but there are a few tent sites for $5 a night.

On Main St (you can't miss it), *Ashley Manor* (☎ 733-3268) has three rooms at $32/40. *The Manse* (☎ 733-3155), 10 Strathcona St, and *Levy's B&B* (☎ 733-2793), 7 Marvin St, have identical prices and again include breakfast. The large *Coastal Inn Louisbourg Motel* (☎ 733-2844), 1225 Main St, charges $43/49.

There are a couple of places to eat with varied, reasonably priced menus which include numerous things from the sea. Most are along Main St including *The Picnic Basket* for homemade bread and soups and deli sandwiches. *Fortress View Restaurant* offers the usual fish & chips menu as well as $4 hamburgers while the *Grubstake* is the place for a good seafood dinner which ranges from $11 to $20.

Getting There & Away

There is now van service between Sydney and Louisbourg through two companies.

Louisbourg Shuttle Service (☎ 564-6200) departs from Cape Breton Tours, 24 King's Rd in Sydney, and charges $25 round trip. B&N Travel Services (☎ 562-9893 or 800-330-4223) picks up at the major hotels and the Sydney tourist office and charges $30 round trip.

LOUISBOURG HISTORIC NATIONAL PARK

This excellent, historic site (☎ 733-2280) is about 50 km south of Sydney on the southeast tip of Cape Breton Island and well worth the trek.

After the Treaty of Utrecht in 1713, the French lost their bases in Newfoundland. This left them Prince Edward Island, Saint Pierre and Miquelon islands, and Cape Breton Island, which became the centre for exporting cod to France. It was also chosen as the spot to build a new military base. Louisbourg, a massive walled fort and village complex, was worked on continually from 1719 to about 1745. It looked daunting but was poorly designed, and the British took it in 46 days during 1745 when it was barely finished. It was returned to the French three years later under the terms of another treaty, only to fall with the British siege of 1758. In 1760, after Wolfe (the British general who had led the Louisbourg onslaught) took Quebec City, the walls of Louisbourg were all destroyed and the city burnt to the ground.

In 1961, with the closing of many Cape Breton coal mines, the federal government began a make-work project: the largest historical reconstruction in Canada. Today the site depicts in remarkable detail what French life was like here in the 1700s. All the workers, in period dress, have taken on the lives of typical fort inhabitants. Ask them anything – what the winters were like, what they ate, what that tool is for, how this was made, who they had an affair with – and they'll tell you. There are many interesting buildings with appropriate contents. Three restaurants serve food typical of the time. Definitely go to the bakery and buy a one-kg loaf of soldiers' bread. It's delicious; one piece with cheese makes a full meal. (But take a plastic bag – they won't give you one because they didn't have plastic in 1750!)

You'll need a lot of time to see the park properly – plan on spending at least half a day at the site. The best times to visit are in the morning, when there's more going on and fewer tourists, and during June or September. Regardless of this, a visit is most interesting. Take in the movie in the interpretive centre first. Free guided tours around the site are offered through the day.

The weather here is very changeable and usually bad. Take a sweater and raincoat even if it's sunny when you start out, and be prepared for lots of walking. As well as the fort area itself, there are hiking trails around the grounds.

The park is open daily from 9.30 am to 5 pm in June and September and 9 am to 6 pm in July and August. Admission seems steep at $7.50 or $19.50 for the family but the fort is well worth it.

AROUND BRAS D'OR LAKE
Baddeck

An old resort town in a pastoral setting, Baddeck is on the north shore of the lake, halfway between Sydney and the Canso Causeway.

It's small but is a visitor centre of sorts as nearly everyone travelling Cape Breton spends some time here. Despite the large influx of tourists, the town remains attractive and the Alexander Graham Bell Museum is interesting.

Chebucto St, the main thoroughfare, has more or less everything on it and makes for a pleasant walk. On Water St, along the waterfront, the Government Wharf is lined with pleasure craft, sailing boats and tour boats offering cruises around Bras d'Or Lake. One of them, Amoeba Sailing Tours (☎ 295-1426), offers several tours daily on its tall-mast sailboat for $16 per person.

There is an excellent tourist office (☎ 295-1911) on the corner of Chebucto St and Shore Rd which is open daily during the summer from 9 am to 8.30 pm.

Alexander Graham Bell National Historic Site Alexander Graham Bell, the inventor of the telephone, had a summer place in Baddeck. This large museum (☎ 295-2069) is dedicated to him and his work. It's a national historic park that covers all aspects of this incredible man's inventions and innovations. Written explanations, models, photographs and objects detail his varied works. On display are medical and electrical devices, telegraphs, telephones, kites and seaplanes. You'll need at least two hours if you want to view all three exhibit halls. Hours are 9 am to 8 pm July and August, until 6 pm in September and 5 pm the rest of the year. Admission is $2.25.

The museum is set on a hillside amidst gardens and picnic tables, and there is a good view of the bay and part of the saltwater Bras d'Or Lake from the roof.

Kidston Island This small island lies just offshore and serves as a park for Baddeck. There is a fine swimming beach on Kidston, some nature trails and also a lighthouse. The

Alexander Graham Bell

NOVA SCOTIA

original lighthouse was built in 1875 and then moved across the ice to Shenacadie, which was experiencing more shipwrecks then Baddeck. The present lighthouse was built in 1915 but lost its lantern 60 years later when the Coast Guard was removing it for repair.

You reach Kidston Island thanks to the Baddeck Lions Club, who operate a pontoon boat at the Government Wharf. They make the short run to the island every 20 minutes during the summer from 10 am to 6 pm on weekdays and noon to 6 pm on weekends. The boat ride is free. Another way to reach the island is to rent a kayak at the wharf from the Outpost Store (☎ 295-2576). The rate is $9 an hour or $40 for the day.

Places to Stay There are a few B&Bs in and around town and half a dozen or so rather costly motels. All the central places are expensive.

The *Duffus House Inn* (☎ 295-2172), on Water St, has nine rooms furnished with antiques. The rooms start at $50/55 for singles/doubles with shared bath.

For a motel, the *Telegraph House* (☎ 295-1100), right in the centre of town, is very attractive in grey with white shutters, but a double with breakfast is $52 to $85 depending on the room.

Much more affordable is the *Restawyle Tourist Home* (☎ 295-3253) just south of town on Shore Rd. The B&B has four rooms, including a single for $25 and a double for $40.

The *Eagle's Perch B&B* (☎ 295-2640) is away from the centre, off Hwy 105 at exit No 9. Turn left at the stop sign and go for about five km. It's right on the Baddeck River and has canoes and bicycles for rent, so do-it-yourself transportation is not too much of a problem. Singles/doubles are $32/40.

Places to Eat Baddeck has a wide selection of good-quality eating places which tend to be a bit pricey. The best, and one that offers some cheaper possibilities while maintaining high standards, is the *Highwheeler Café/Deli/Bakery*, with a mouth-watering

selection of sandwiches, salads and bakery items. Deli sandwiches are $4.25.

The *Village Kitchen*, just off the main street, is a spot for an eggs-and-toast breakfast for $3 or in the evening the 'Steak & Stein' for $10. Moving up-market, the *Bell Buoy*, by the wharf, is good for seafood but is not cheap.

Lobster suppers, with a one-pounder and everything else you can eat from the buffet, are available in the centre of town in the old *Legion Hall*, on Ross St. At $25, they don't compare with the value of the real Prince Edward Island lobster suppers but the food is good and plentiful. They're open daily from June to October from 4 to 9 pm.

A surprise is the *Taj*, an East Indian restaurant in the grounds of the Bell Museum, with dishes from $7 to $10. Nearby on Main St is *Yellow Cello Cafe*, which offers vegetarian pizzas, sandwiches and subs as well as an outdoor deck to enjoy them at. A large pizza is $11 to $16.

For homegrown, there's the farmer's market every Saturday from 1 to 3 pm in the Baddeck Arena.

Getting There & Around Acadia buses serves Baddeck along its Halifax to Sydney run. A bus arrives daily at 8.50 am and then continues on to New Glasgow, Truro and Halifax. To New Glasgow, the fare is $26. Also from Baddeck, Transoverland Ltd buses run north through the Margaree Valley and then up the coast to Cheticamp. Buses out of town depart from the Ultramar service station at the east end of the central town area.

For seeing the immediate area, there's Island Eco-Adventures (☎ 295-3303) which rents mountain bikes by the hour or the day. They're located kitty-corner to the tourist office on Chebucto Rd.

Lake Ainslie
Just north of the Trans Canada Highway, via Hwy 395, and 40 km from Baddeck, is this large lake that attracts a healthy population of bald eagles, ospreys and loons. You can spend an afternoon following the 53-km

drive around Lake Ainslie, stopping at **Mac-Donald House Museum** (☎ 258-3317) on Hwy 395 along the east side. The 150-year-old farmhouse is maintained by the Lake Ainslie Historical Society and features furnished rooms and a barn full of farming machinery and tools. Hours are 9 am to 9 pm daily during the summer and admission is $2.

Nearby is *Glenmore International Hostel* (☎ 258-3622). The HI hostel is reached by turning onto Twin Rock Valley Rd from Hwy 395 and heading east for two km. If coming from the Trans Canada Highway, the road is reached immediately after you cross the second bridge. The small hostel is pretty basic; four beds on the first floor, seven more in a loft, kitchen facilities but no showers. Rates are $10 for members and $12 for non-members. The managers can help arrange sailing tours of Bras d'Or Lake or overnight tours of Cape Breton National Park.

Iona

This is a small village south of Baddeck, on the south side of the peninsula, by Barra Strait in Bras d'Or Lake (on Hwy 223). Iona (pop 130) is a bit out of the way but may appeal for that reason. The **Highland Village Museum** depicts the life of the Highland Scots at home, and here as pioneers. The 10 historic buildings include an example of the smokey peat-heated homes of the Scottish Highlanders in the early 1800s, the first pioneer houses in the new land, and the later houses in which new skills and materials were employed. Summer hours are 9 am to 5 pm Monday through Saturday and 10 am to 6 pm Sunday. Admission is $4 for adults or $8 for a family.

A Highland festival held on the first Saturday in August features the Celtic-based music of the island. Special events are scheduled through the summer, and something to watch for are he traditional suppers.

Next to the museum is the *Highland Heights Inn* (☎ 725-2360), a motel with rooms at the rather hefty rate of $60/68.

A short ferry ride connects with roads for the south side of Bras d'Or Lake.

SOUTH OF BRAS D'OR LAKE

This is a little-visited, sparsely inhabited area of small villages, lakes and hills. It's a farming and forestry region where many of the roads have not been paved.

Big Pond

On the south shore of East Bay, Big Pond has *Rita's Tea Room*, run by the hometown Cape Breton singer Rita MacNeil in a converted one-room schoolhouse. Adorning the walls are her music awards and records. Every July the Big Pond Concert, a sizeable annual Cape Breton music event, is held.

Bald eagles can frequently be seen along the Bras d'Or Lake shoreline, particularly in the Big Pond area. Big Pond Eagle Tours (☎ 828-3052), offers two-hour walking tours with local naturalists sighting and identifying a variety of birds but especially eagles. The daily tours are $15.

St Peter's

This town (pop 731) is on a narrow strip separating the Atlantic Ocean and Bras d'Or Lake along Hwy 4 and is the birthplace of noted photographer Wallace MacAskill. It was MacAskill's photo of the *Bluenose* that was used for the design of Canada's 10-cent piece. The home of his birth on Main St is now the **Wallace MacAskill Museum** and features 26 of his hand-tinted photographs. Hours are 10 am to 6 pm daily during the summer and admission is free.

Also in town is **St Peter's Canal**. Built in the 1850s, the canal includes a 91-metre, double-gate lock to assist vessels to move between the different water levels of the lake and the ocean. There is an outdoor exhibit explaining the lock and the history of the canal as well as a museum nearby. There is also a picnic area overlooking the canal where you can simply relax and watch the sailboats and cruisers pass by.

Joyce's Motel & Cottages (☎ 535-2404), 2.5 km east of St Peter's on Hwy 4, is a HI hostel. There are six beds along with a kitchen, laundry facilities and a swimming pool. The cost is $10 a night for members.

The French Corner

The extreme southern corner of Cape Breton, like the Cheticamp area, is largely French. The region all around Île Madame was settled by Acadians who had first tried to make Martinique in the West Indies home after the Expulsion but later returned to Nova Scotia. **Arichat**, on the ocean, is the largest town and has a restaurant and a traditional-style wooden Acadian inn called *L'Auberge Acadienne* (☎ 226-2200 or 226-2150), whose dining room offers some Acadian dishes. Rooms at the inn begin at $60 for singles or doubles. The **LeNoir Forge Museum** (☎ 226-2800), on Route 320, is a restored 18th-century French blacksmith shop, open from May to September. Admission is free.

Just down the road, **Petit-de-Grat** holds an Acadian festival every August, with music, food, etc. This small town is the oldest on Île Madame and was a busy trading port during Prohibition, but now it's a fishing centre.

East of Arichat on Hwy 320 is the *Acadian Campsite* (☎ 226-2447) with 48 sites, showers and laundry facilities. A site is $10 a night. From Little Anse, a trail leads to a lighthouse.

Port Hawkesbury

Though a fairly large town, there is little here for the visitor; it's essentially a modern shopping and industrial centre for the district.

SABLE ISLAND

Lying south of Cape Breton, about 177 km from the mainland, this is the 'graveyard of the Atlantic'. Countless ships from the 1500s to the present have gone down around the island, with its rough seas and hidden sandbars. The island, 32 km long by 1.5 km wide, is little more than a sandbar itself, with no trees or even shrubs. There are about a dozen inhabitants, a small herd of tough, wild ponies and lots of cranberries. The people maintain the two lighthouses, a meteorological station and a few other installations. The ponies are believed to be descendants from survivors of a 16th-century shipwreck.

NOVA SCOTIA

Prince Edward Island

Known as the Island, or PEI, Prince Edward Island is a pastoral, peaceful, wonderfully Irish-green expanse of quiet beauty. Mainlanders are seen on roadsides all over the island trying to capture the landscape on film: a few black and white cows here, some purple lupins there, perhaps a wave of sea in the distance. The pace of life here is slow. Laws against billboards further add to the old-country flavour of the island. Indeed, in some ways it has changed little from the descriptions in the internationally known novel *Anne of Green Gables*, written here by Lucy Maud Montgomery after the turn of the century.

This is not an exciting place; there is not a lot to do, particularly after dark, and if you get a week of rain, you'll be more than a little restless. But for a really lazy holiday, take the chance.

Prince Edward Island is the smallest and most densely populated province. You'd never guess this, however, as it's rural and the towns aren't big at all, though countless little-used roads crisscross every segment of land.

In March 1993, the province became the first in Canadian history to elect a woman premier. Catherine Callbeck led the Liberals to victory with a convincing 31 of 32 seats. In 1997, after much debate and protests among the Islanders themselves, PEI will be linked to New Brunswick and the mainland by the controversial Northumberland Strait Bridge, the world's longest at almost 13 km.

As in all of the Atlantic Provinces, the visiting season is short. This is perhaps noticed here more than anywhere, with many attractions, tour operations and guesthouses open only during the two midsummer months. Keep in mind, however, that on Labour Day weekend room prices are heavily discounted, sometimes as much as 50%, the crowds are gone and often you enjoy a touch of Indian Summer.

HIGHLIGHTS

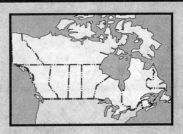

Entered Confederation: 1 July 1873
Area: 5657 sq km
Population: 131,600
Provincial Capital: Charlottetown

- Spend time in Charlottetown, the birth-place of Canadian confederation
- Visit the House of Green Gables near Cavendish, the setting for the story about Anne by Lucy Maud Montgomery
- Enjoy a summer's day on one of the north-coast beaches
- Dine out on casual, delicious lobster suppers, often held in church halls throughout the province
- Drive along the quiet, relaxed roads as they wind their way through bucolic land-scapes

✿✿✿✿✿✿✿✿✿✿✿✿✿✿✿✿✿✿

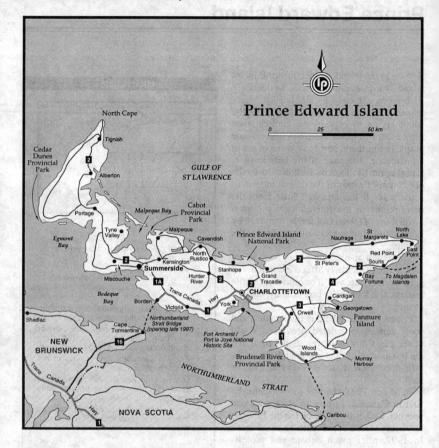

Prince Edward Island

0   25   50 km

GULF OF ST LAWRENCE

North Cape

Tignish

Cedar Dunes Provincial Park

Alberton

Portage

Malpeque Bay

Egmont Bay

Tyne Valley

Malpeque

Cavendish

Prince Edward Island National Park

Naufrage

St Margarets

North Lake

East Point

Red Point

North Rustico

Souris

Kensington

Stanhope

St Peter's

Bay Fortune

To Magdalen Islands

Summerside

Hunter River

Grand Tracadie

Miscouche

1A

CHARLOTTETOWN

Cardigan

Bedeque Bay

Borden

Trans Canada Hwy

York

Orwell

Georgetown

Panmure Island

Victoria

Shediac

Cape Tormentine

Northumberland Strait Bridge (opening late 1997)

Fort Amherst / Port la Joye National Historic Site

NEW BRUNSWICK

16

Wood Islands

Murray Harbour

Brudenell River Provincial Park

Trans Canada Hwy

NORTHUMBERLAND STRAIT

NOVA SCOTIA

1

Caribou

History

Aboriginal peoples have been here for about 11,000 years, before the land was separated from the mainland. The Micmacs, a branch of the Algonquin nations, arrived at about the time of Christ.

Jacques Cartier of France in 1534 was the first European to record seeing the island. Settlement didn't begin for another 200 years with a small French colony which grew somewhat with the British expulsion of the Acadians, mainly from Nova Scotia, in the late 1750s.

After the Treaty of Paris in 1763, the island became British and was renamed the Island of Saint John. In the early 1800s there was a marked rise in population with immigrants from the British Isles. The island became self-governing in 1769 and switched names in honour of one of the sons of King Edward III.

The island joined Confederation in 1873, deciding to forgo its independence for the economic benefits. The population has remained stable since the 1930s.

Climate

Conveniently, July and August are the driest

months of a fairly damp year. Because of warm ocean currents, the province has a milder climate than most of Canada and the sea gets warm enough for swimming.

Economy
PEI is primarily a farming community, with the main crop, potatoes, being sold all over the country. The rich, distinctively red soil is the secret, the locals say. Fishing, of course, is also important, particularly for lobsters, oysters and herring. The tasty, reasonably priced lobster suppers held throughout the province have become synonymous with the island.

The quiet, gently rolling hills edged with good beaches have made tourism a reliable moneymaker.

Population & People
Europeans of French, Scottish and Irish background make up nearly 90% of the population. The Native inhabitants at the time of colonisation, the Micmacs, now represent about 4% of the island's people.

Information
Provincial Symbols The provincial flower is the common lady's slipper, and the provincial bird is the blue jay.

Tourist Offices The head office of the Tourism Industry Association of PEI (☎ 1-800-565-0267 free from anywhere in North America, or 1-800-565-000 from Nova Scotia, or 1-800-561-0123 from New Brunswick) can be contacted at PO Box 940, Charlottetown, C1A 7M5. There are about a dozen offices around the island with the main one in the capital.

Telephone The area code for the province is 902. In the event of emergency dial 0, for which no money is required.

Time PEI is on Atlantic Time.

Tax The provincial sales tax is 10%.

Activities
If your idea of being active is flipping the pages of a book while lolling on a beach or maybe cracking the claws of a steaming lobster you've found your spot. You could drag yourself aboard a boat for a little deep sea fishing or if you're really feeling energetic cycle through the quiet, flat countryside. There are also a number of small museums and historic sites to look over.

Or you may just bask in having stepped out of the rat race.

Accommodation & Food
The island is covered with campgrounds – 13 provincial parks, one national park and numerous private campgrounds. Provincial parks charge $14 for an unserviced site, $17 for trailers. Privately owned places charge more but accept reservations. Government parks, which operate on a first-come, first-served basis, are usually better and are often full by the end of the day in July and August. The tourist office can give you vacancy reports.

Across the province there are few hotels, but fortunately the entire island has an abundance of good guesthouses. The quality is generally high and the prices excellent. PEI guesthouses and tourist homes offer some of the best accommodation deals in Canada. A double room averages about $35 or $40 and rarely goes above $45, and sometimes that includes breakfast. Many places are rented by the week. Much accommodation is in beautiful old wooden homes in the east-coast style. The tourist office has a complete list of these places and will make reservations for you.

There are nearly 40 outlets around the island for buying fresh seafood – good if you're camping and can cook your own food. Some guesthouses offer cooking facilities or use of barbecues.

Also look for the famous lobster suppers held in church basements or community halls or restaurants – these are usually buffet style and good value. Perhaps not as much fun, the restaurants offering lobster suppers at least do so on a regular basis and are

PRINCE EDWARD ISLAND

reliable, whereas the others are sometimes hit and miss. In the past couple of years more and more lobster supper venues have sprung up in response to the popularity and reputation of these casual seafood-based meals.

Getting Around

Bus Island Transit, the provincial bus service, shut down in 1993, leaving the province with virtually no public transportation. Ask about it though – with any government funds freed up, perhaps at least a limited service will resume.

Visitors can use the handy beach bus shuttle offered by Abegweit Tours and Beach Shuttle (☎ 566-3243). Both make runs between Charlottetown and the north coast beaches of the National Park and charge $12 round-trip. See Organised Tours or Getting There & Away in the Charlottetown section later in this chapter for details.

Bicycle With its winding country roads, gently rolling hills and short distances between towns, PEI is probably one of Canada's most popular destinations for cyclists. Hills here rarely exceed a 30 degree incline or a km in length and the highest point on the island at Springton is only 142 metres. Even if you didn't arrive with a set of wheels you can rent them in Charlottetown and put together a multi-day tour of the Island. For route suggestions ask at the bike shops or obtain a copy of *Prince Edward Island Cycling Guide* that is sold for $12 at Bookmark in the city centre or Coles Book Store in the Charlottetown Mall.

Smooth Cycle (☎ 566-5530), at the corner of Prince St and Kent St, rents hybrid bicycles for $22 a day or $75 a week. MacQueen's Bicycles (☎ 368-2453), 430 Queen St, has road bikes for $15 a day and $65 a week. Both shops rent panniers and helmets while MacQueen's also arranges bike tours.

You can rent bicycles in Cavendish village at Rent-A-Bike on the junction of routes 6 and 13 at the Petro Can service station. Bikes are $5 an hour and $17 a day and there's some good riding in this area, such as along the Gulf Shore Parkway.

Hitching Thumbing around the island is common, accepted and often done by residents. The island is relatively free of violence and you can generally hitch without expecting trouble. Your safety cannot be guaranteed, however, and hitching is not recommended without some reservations. Caution is advised.

Charlottetown

Charlottetown (population 45,000) is an old, quiet country town that also happens to be the historic provincial capital. It is Canada's smallest capital, with a downtown area so compact that everything is within walking distance. The slow-paced, tree-lined colonial and Victorian streets make Charlottetown the perfect urban centre for this gentle and bucolic island.

The city is the focal point of the large tourist trade as well as being the business and shopping centre for the province. In July and August the streets are busy with visitors but things are rather quiet out of season.

History

When the first Europeans arrived here in the early 1700s, they found the area settled by the Micmac Indians. Nevertheless, they established Charlottetown as a district capital of their own in 1763, named after Charlotte, Queen of Great Britain and Ireland (1744-1818).

In 1864, discussions to unite Canada were first held here. An agreement was finally reached in 1867, when the Dominion of Canada was born; Charlottetown became known as the birthplace of Canada. Though times are much less heady these days, many of the town's people are employed by various levels of government. Indeed, one out of four people across the island works directly for the government.

Orientation

Hwy 1 from Borden (never mind the approach into town – it's the only ugly

Charlottetown

1 Charlottetown Mall
2 International Hostel
3 Garden Gate Inn
4 University of PEI
5 Laundromat
6 Cairn's Tourist Office
7 SMT Bus Station
8 Seatrest Restaurant
9 Trius Bus Stop (to Wood Islands)
10 Doc's Corner Pub
11 Post Office
12 City Hall
13 Police
14 Government House
15 Confederation Court Mall
16 Confederation Centre of the Arts
17 Province House
18 St Paul's Church
19 Victoria Row Restaurants
20 St Dunstan's Basilica
21 Linda's Old Town Coffee Shop
22 Tourist Information Centre
23 Confederation Birthplace Park

To Souris
To Airport
St Peters Road
Brackley Point Road
Gordon Drive
Falconwood Drive
Woodward Drive
Garfield Street
Riverside Drive
Queen Elizabeth Hospital
Hillsborough River
Mount Edward Road
Confederation St
Gower St
Harley St
Beasley Ave
Spring Lane
St Pious 10. St
Landimouth Avenue
Kensington Road
Park St
Belmont St
Trans Canada Highway
Harbour
To Wood Islands, Montague & Georgetown
Trans Canada Highway
University Avenue
Belvedere Avenue
Nassau Street
Experimental Farm Road
Allen Street
Fitzroy Street
Kent Street
Grafton Street
Richmond Street
Sydney Street
Weymouth St
Upper Hillsborough St
Walthen Drive
Hillsborough St
Euston Street
Gerald St
Upper Prince Street
Prince Street
Eden Street
Summer St
Pond St.
Kirkwood Drive East
Queen Street
Pownal Street
Rochford Street
West St
Dochester Street
Water Street
King Street
Gt George St
North River Road
McGill Avenue
Highland Avenue
Churchill Avenue
Greenfield Avenue
Pond Road
Victoria Park
Goodwill Ave
York Lane
Park Driveway
Brighton Road
Queen Elizabeth Drive
Fort Edward
North River
North (York) River
To Borden

0   0.5   1 km

PRINCE EDWARD ISLAND

stretch of road on the island) becomes University Ave, the city's main street. University Ave ends at Grafton St and the large war memorial statue depicting three soldiers. Behind it, the entire block is taken up with the Provincial Archives, Province House National Historic Site and the large Confederation Centre of the Arts complex.

A block west along Grafton St is Queen St, parallel to University Ave. This is the other main street of Charlottetown and of more interest to visitors.

Off Queen St, south behind the Confederation Arts Building, is Richmond St. For one block east of Queen St, this is off limits to traffic during the summer and becomes a pedestrian mall called Victoria Row. Along it are street vendors, restaurants, crafts shops and galleries.

Four blocks south is the city harbour. From Richmond St south on and around Queen St to the waterfront is old Charlottetown. A number of buildings have been renovated and are now used as government offices, restaurants or shops. Many have plaques giving a bit of the history and the date of construction; some are over 100 years old. Great George St running downhill from Richmond St at Province House is particularly attractive.

At the foot of Great George St, south of Water St, is Peakes Quay and Confederation Birthplace Park. This redeveloped waterfront area now has restaurants, souvenir shops and is often the focal point of the city festivals. The main tourist centre is nearby.

West of town is the large Victoria Park, with Queen Elizabeth Drive running along its edge and the bay.

Information
Tourist Offices The tourist office (☎ 368-4444) for Charlottetown and the main office for the whole island was moved in 1996 to the Stone Cottage near Confederation Birthplace Commemorative Park at the foot of Hillsborough St just off Water St. It's open daily from 8 am to 10 pm during the summer season. Inside are courtesy phones to make local reservations.

There is a tourist information office (☎ 566-5548) at City Hall, on the corner of Queen and Kent Sts. This one is open from 8 am to 5 pm daily in summer and specialises in Charlottetown.

There is also the Cairn's Tourist Office & Visitor Centre on Pond St off University Ave north of the city centre.

Money Several of the big banks can be found in Confederation Plaza.

Post The central post office is at 135 Kent St.

Bookshops The Book Emporium at 169 Queen St has a selection of books on PEI and Anne of Green Gables.

Medical Services The Queen Elizabeth Hospital (☎ 566-6111) is on Riverside Drive just out of the centre.

Confederation Centre of the Arts
The architectural style of this large modern structure at the south-east corner of Queen and Grafton Sts is at odds with the rest of town, which has made it controversial since construction began in 1960. It houses a museum, an art gallery, a library and a theatre. The art gallery and museum charge $2 admission fees in July and August but are free for the rest of the year and are always free on Sunday. The gallery features shows from the collection of works by Canadian artists. Free tours of the centre (☎ 628-1864) are given all year. It is open daily through the summer from 9 am to 8 pm.

Province House
Next door to the previously mentioned arts centre, this neoclassical, three-storey, sandstone building is both a national historic site (☎ 566-7626) and the base of the current Provincial Legislature. The Confederation Room on the 2nd floor is known as the 'birthplace of Canada', for it was here in 1864 that the 23 representatives of the New World British colonies began working out the details for forming the Dominion of Canada.

Top: Loyalist graveyard, Saint John, New Brunswick
Left: Lobsters and beer, Prince Edward Island
Right: Sailboat at low tide, Fundy Bay, New Brunswick

Top: City hall, Fredericton, New Brunswick
Bottom: Tundra buggy, Churchill, Manitoba

This room and a couple of others have been restored to what they looked like in 1864. Inside or perhaps out at the entrance, you may also see costumed workers, each representing one of the original founders. Once daily in summer, there is a 'fathers of confederation' re-enactment. Check here or at the tourist office for current times of the presentation.

The current Legislative Chamber is also on this floor, and the summer breeze wafting in through open windows to this small, comfortable room lends an intimate informal atmosphere which is quite unlike that of the legislatures in Canada's larger provinces. Various rooms can also be seen on the 1st floor. Province House is open daily 9 am to 8 pm during the summer and admission is free.

St Dunstan's Basilica
This large basilica is south of Province House, on the corner of Great George and Richmond Sts. Built in 1898, the town's Catholic church is surprisingly ornate inside, painted in an unusual style, with a lot of green trim which blends well with the green and blue tints in the marble. Masses are said daily from June to the beginning of September.

St Paul's Church
On Church St east of Province House, this red, sandstone building dating from 1747 is the oldest Protestant church on the island.

Beaconsfield House
This beautiful yellow Victorian mansion (☎ 368-6600) at 2 Kent St was built in 1877. It is now the headquarters of the PEI Heritage Foundation. There are 11 historically furnished rooms along with a gift shop and a bookstore specialising in books about PEI. During the summer guided tours are given and afternoon tea is served on the large verandah. The house is open 10 am to 5 pm daily except Mondays from mid-June to Labour Day and shorter hours the rest of the year. Admission is $2.50.

Government House
Across Kent St is Victoria Park and Government House, another beautiful old mansion. This one has been used as the official residence of the province's lieutenant-governor since 1835. No visitors are allowed.

Organised Tours
Abegweit Sightseeing Tours (☎ 894-9966), 157 Nassau St, Charlottetown, offers double-decker bus trips around the island. They have three trips: the north shore, the south shore and Charlottetown itself.

The north shore trip takes about six hours and costs $30 all-inclusive. The city tour takes just an hour and costs $7. The south shore trip makes a stop at Fort Amherst National Historic Park and is also $30.

If you just want to go to the beach for the day, you can take the North Shore Tour bus. They'll pick you up on the way back. The cost is $10 return to Dalvay/Stanhope and $12 return to Cavendish Beach.

Peakes Wharf Boat Cruises (☎ 566-4458) departs from the marina at the wharf and has an hour-long harbour tour for $7.50 and a three-hour tour to see the seals off Government Island for $15. Schooner Adventures (☎ 629-7245) offers two-hour trips on the *Mercy Coles*, a traditionally built Maritime schooner. Tours are 10 am, 2 and 6 pm and begin at Peake's Wharf. The cost is $20.

Finally, walking tours of the historic Charlottetown area commence at City Hall (☎ 566-5548) at 10 am, 1 and 3 pm. Alternatively, the good self-guided tour brochure available at the tourist office covers the waterfront area and Peake's Wharf.

Festivals
All across the province, look for the local ceilidhs: mini-festivals at which there is always some music (usually of the traditional Celtic-based variety) and dancing. There is usually one a week. Ticketworks (☎ 566-1267), a ticket agency, has information and tickets for shows across the province. Some of the major events held in PEI from June to September are:

Charlottetown Festival – This festival is held each year from mid-June to mid-September. It's a theatrical event with drama and musicals. Each year *Anne of Green Gables*, which is called 'Canada's favourite musical', is performed. Tickets to any of the plays are available at the Arts Centre and are $20 to $32 for evening performances of 'Anne' and $16 to $30 for matinee shows. The festival also includes free outdoor performances, a children's theatre and dance programmes.

Blue Grass Music Festival – This is a new tradition which seems to be developing: this festival is held annually in July. It's a two-day camping event held at a park or campground. Tickets are not costly.

Provincial Exhibition – This event, held in the first week or two of August, features tractor pulls, a carnival with rides, harness racing, entertainment and games of chance along with the traditional horse and livestock shows.

National Milton Acorn Festival – This is a unique event worth considering. Sometimes known as Canada's People's Poet, Acorn was born and raised on PEI. The festival, held in the third week of August, includes poetry readings and music.

Festival of the Fathers – Held along the historic waterfront in late August, this festival celebrates the Charlottetown Conference for the confederation with street musicians, dances, traditional foods and a 10-tavern pub crawl.

Places to Stay

Camping Half a km outside Charlottetown there's the *Southport Trailer Park* (☎ 569-2287), at 20 Stratford Rd, overlooking the Hillsborough River. The nightly rate is $17.50, less if you're tenting or staying a week or longer. This is the only campground near town.

Hostels The good, friendly HI *Charlottetown Hostel* (☎ 894-9696), at 153 Mount Edward Rd, is about three km from the downtown area and close to the university. The barn-shaped building has room for 54 people and there's a kitchen with a microwave available for light cooking. Rates are $13 for members, $16 for nonmembers. The hostel is open from the beginning of June through Labour Day weekend and will have a list of all the hostels on the island.

The *University of PEI* (☎ 566-0442) has rooms from mid-May to the end of August. Reservations are a good idea. Rates begin at

Milton Acorn

Born in Charlottetown in 1923, Milton Acorn was to become somewhat the bad boy of Canadian literature. Despite living and working as a poet, he did not fit the usual academic mould and was always known for voicing his firmly held left-wing opinions. He supported a range of radical causes and his poems often reflected his political biases as well as his unwavering support of the working person. Spending much of his life in Montreal, Toronto and Vancouver, he became known as the People's Poet after being honoured as such by fellow poets. He died in his home town in 1986.

Dig up my Heart: Selected Poems 1952-1983 is the most complete and representative collection of Acorn's poetry, offering a good sampling of his subject matter and style. Personally, I prefer his numerous nature poems and reflective poems, some of which have a wonderful, easy lyricism. ■

$26 for a double, more if you want breakfast in the university cafeteria.

Tourist Homes Very central, at 234 Sydney St, the unassuming *Aloha Tourist Home* (☎ 892-9944) is in a large old house and has four rooms to rent. Singles/doubles are $32/36. There is a large kitchen that visitors can use. There isn't much privacy at the shared bathroom off the kitchen but the owner, Maynard MacMillan, is an affable, helpful host. Cyclists can stash their bikes in the garage.

Also central is the *Blanchard* (☎ 894-9756), at 163 Dorchester St with rooms at $20/30.

In behind the mall and provincial beer store, at 18 Pond St, is the spotless and friendly *Cairn's Tourist Home* (☎ 368-3552), in a modern house on a residential street. The home has three rooms available for $24/26.

Morais' Guest Home (☎ 892-2267), at 67 Newland Crescent, near the tourist office, will pick you up from the airport or bus depot. The owner speaks English and French. A double here goes for $38 but includes a light breakfast.

Some of the least expensive choices are on the eastern side of downtown, close to the racetrack. You might check along Edward St or York Lane. Houses here are smaller and less gracious than many but the area is still conveniently walkable to the city centre.

B&Bs In this category are many places much like the tourist homes but offering the morning meal. As a rule, they tend to be outside the city centre and in newer houses but there are also several more central, up-market places established in fine heritage homes and decorated with antiques and collectables.

The *Duchess of Kent* (☎ 566-5826 or 800-665-5826), in a heritage house from 1875 with period furnishings, is at 218 Kent St, in the centre of town. The seven rooms of varying features range in price from $48 to $60 a double, including the morning meal. Washrooms are shared, but there are so many that this is no hardship.

Some of the larger historic places have been converted to inns. One such is the *Dundee Arms Inn* (☎ 892-2496), at 200 Pownal St, in an impressive, restored turn-of-the-century mansion complete with antiques, dining room and pub. A double here ranges from $90 to $138 with a continental breakfast included.

Motels There are motels along Hwy 1 west of Charlottetown towards Borden. Also on this commercial strip are restaurants and service stations. Motels here usually cost at least $55 a double. The ones further from town tend to be more modest in appearance, amenities and price. Those in town provide more comforts and the price goes up accordingly.

Close to town on the south side is the *Garden Gate Inn* (☎ 892-3411). It's small and well off the highway but, like many of the motels, expensive at $58/65.

Three km from town on the Trans Canada Hwy is the *Queen's Arms Motel* (☎ 368-1110), with a heated pool. Rooms cost about $48 for a single, $98 for a housekeeping unit.

Further out, near the Hwy 2 junction, the

brown *Banbridge Inn* (☎ 368-2223 or 800-355-2223) offers doubles for $75 and rooms with kitchens for $95. There is a laundromat.

Places to Eat
For a small city there are a surprising number of quality restaurants but these mostly fall into the higher price bracket. Still, with the ocean minutes away, a fresh seafood dinner is not too outrageous and the low prices elsewhere around the island make up for costs here.

Cedar's Eatery, open every day and right in the middle of town on University Ave, is a fine little place. At the chunky wooden tables the speciality is Lebanese food, ranging from felafels to more expensive kebabs. But there is also standard Canadian fare: soups, salads, sandwiches, steaks and Old Abbey, a local beer. Dinners range from $6 to $14. Cedar's stays open late, one of the few places that does.

For breakfast, a simple meal or snack, the cheap and unpretentious *Town & Country*, at 219 Queen St, fills the bill with its basic Canadian menu. Also small and cheap but with a certain charm is *Linda's Old Town Coffee Shop*, at 32 Queen St. It opens at 7 am and a full breakfast is $2.50 to $3.50.

The most affordable seafood is at *Seatreat*, on the corner of University and Euston St. The restaurant features a basket of steamed mussels for $5, salmon or haddock dinners for $9, a bowl of fish chowder for $3.50 and, of course, lobster dinners.

There are probably a half dozen Chinese restaurants in town. My choice is *Dragon Garden* on University Ave near the tourist centre. Along with a full menu, they offer a lunch buffet for $6. For Mexican, there's *Pat & Willy's Bar & Grill* with an entrance near the corner of Kent St and Queen St. Dinners range from $8 to $11.

The *Old Dublin Pub*, upstairs at 131 Sydney St, has pub meals from $7, an agreeable outside deck and live entertainment at night.

Behind the Confederation Centre of the Arts is Victoria Row, a section of Richmond St that is closed off to vehicle traffic in the summer and lined with cafes with outdoor seating. *Island Rock Cafe* boasts Atlantic Canada's largest beer bottle collection (I believe them) as well as a menu that ranges from fettuccini prima vera to Thai chicken skewers. This can be a lively pub at night with dinners from $9 to $17. A couple of doors down is *Black Forest Cafe* if you want to finish your evening with a slice of double chocolate tort.

In Confederation Court Mall, on the corner of Kent and Queen Sts, the 2nd floor has a collection of cheap fast-food outlets offering pizza, chicken, burgers, etc. with a common eating area.

In the splurge category, the dining room of the *Dundee Arms Inn*, at 200 Pownal St, offers fine eating in a traditional setting with top-notch service. The *Claddagh Room* in the old historic area, downstairs at 131 Sydney St, is known for its seafoods with dinners ranging $16 to $20. Down at the edge of Confederation Commemorative Park on Charlottetown's waterfront is *Mackinnon's*, where you can buy fresh mussels, clams and oysters, as well as live or cooked lobster.

Cows, an island institution, has a location on Queen St near Grafton St. It is not a large place but it turns out good homemade ice cream. There are also outlets, open in summer only, in Cavendish and North River. People across Canada can be seen sporting the colourful, humorous Cows T-shirts. If you like them, there's a seconds shop for its shirts downstairs at the Queen St location.

A 10-minute drive west to Cornwall on the way to Borden is the *McCrady's Green Acres Motel & Restaurant* (☎ 566-4938). Run by an English couple, the restaurant serves English-style afternoon cream teas from 1 to 4 pm. Other menu items, like steak & kidney pie, are also good.

Entertainment

For a complete run down on the plays, dinner theatres, and what band is playing where in Charlottetown, get hold of a copy of *The Buzz*, the free entertainment guide for PEI.

Myron's, at 151 Kent St, off University Ave, is a popular spot, with different types of music featured each night. Further down Kent St is the *Tradewinds*, a much spiffier dancing spot which is open until 1 am. *Island Rock Cafe* often has live jazz and blues.

A Friday night spent at the Irish Hall (☎ 566-3273), 582 North River Rd, is a lot of of fun, with traditional Irish and Scottish music and dance. Things start around 8 pm on a regular basis through the year, but not every Friday – call to confirm. Admission is $5.

Live Irish and Maritime music can also be enjoyed at *The Olde Dublin Pub* with its outdoor deck at 131 Sydney St.

Getting There & Away

Air Charlottetown has a small airport, north of the city west off Hwy 2, about six km from the centre. Air Canada and Canadian Airlines connect PEI with the major Canadian cities and some New England US points like Boston. Air Canada flies one way to Toronto for $440 and Canadian Airlines flies to St John's, Newfoundland for $381 and to Montreal for $358. Round-trip fares are only $30 to $50 more. Prince Edward Air (☎ 436-9703) has a daily connection to Halifax.

Bus There are once-daily buses to and from PEI using each of the two ferries. Trius Bus Lines (☎ 566-5664), using the Wood Islands ferry, goes to New Glasgow, Nova Scotia, from where connections can be made to Acadian buses for points around Nova Scotia. The bus leaves at 7.45 am from an office at 205 Fitzroy St.

SMT Bus Lines (☎ 628-6432) uses the Borden ferry and connects with Moncton, New Brunswick. Tickets include the price of the ferry. For Moncton, a ticket is $30. The SMT depot is at 330 University Ave.

Beach Shuttle (☎ 566-3243) makes a run to the sand and surf of Cavendish. The bus departs daily at 9 am with pick-ups at the HI Hostel, the Cairn's Tourist Office & Visitor Centre, and the Dundee Arms Inn. It's $12 round trip and $8 one-way.

Train There is no passenger train service to, from or on the island.

Ferry Most people get to PEI by ferry, from either New Brunswick or Nova Scotia. There are two ferries linking the island with the mainland and they take cars, buses, bicycles and pedestrians. This will change in late 1997 when Northumberland Strait Bridge is scheduled to open, eliminating the ferry to New Brunswick.

The other route, run by Northumberland Ferries, joins Wood Islands (in the eastern section of PEI province) to Caribou, Nova Scotia. It is anticipated that this ferry will continue operating even after the bridge is completed. This 22-km trip takes 1½ hours and costs $9 per person return, $28.50 return per car and $5 per bicycle. In summer there are 20 runs in each direction daily. This route is busy – during peak season you may have a one or two-ferry wait. There's a cafeteria on board. The head office is in Charlottetown, at 54 Queen St, or call ☎ 1-800-565-0201 for reservations.

The ferry that links Cape Tormentine, New Brunswick with Borden in south-west PEI will operate until the controversial bridge opens. This 14-km trip takes 45 minutes and is run by Marine Atlantic, a government ferry system. The fare is $8 per person return, $19.50 per car and $3.75 per bicycle. There are nearly 20 crossings a day between June and September, slightly fewer the rest of the year.

This is one of Canada's busiest ferry routes and having to wait for two or even three ferries is not uncommon as reservations are not taken for this route. When the 13-km bridge does open, it will be easier to reach PEI but not any cheaper. Under the agreement signed between the government and the company building the toll bridge, the toll will remain the same as the fare for the ferry.

Charlottetown is about 60 km from Borden and the drive takes about 40 minutes.

Car A car, for better or worse, is the best and sometimes only means of seeing much of the island. There are several outlets in the capital. The supply of cars is limited and with the local bus system shut down, getting a car is not easy. They can all be booked up for a week, so try to reserve well ahead through an office of one of the major chains in whatever city you're in prior to your PEI visit.

Avis Rent-A-Car (☎ 892-3706) is on the corner of University Ave and Euston St.

Linking the Island

Almost nothing in the history of Prince Edward Island has Islanders so divided as the Northumberland Strait Bridge. Either they love it or hate it, there is nobody in between.

Expected to open in late 1997, the bridge will connect Cape Tormentine, New Brunswick with Borden. It's the narrowest point of the strait yet the bridge will still be almost 13-km long, allowing Canadians to claim they have the longest bridge in the world. There is a longer one in Denmark, but an island in the middle technically makes it two separate bridges.

At a cost of $900 million, the Northumberland project will include 44 spans. Each span is almost a city block long and is made from 8000 tonnes of steel-reinforced concrete that must be lifted into place. Once in place, each span will tower 20 storeys above the water.

When completed, PEI will be, for the most part, part of mainland Canada and that's the source of all the controversy. Those against the bridge say it will bring hoards of tourists who in turn will bring crime, litter and a growth of chain restaurants and tacky tourism attractions. Friends of the Island, an anti-bridge coalition, has gone to court to stop the construction, claiming the bridge will cause ice build-up in the strait that will harm lobster and scallop stocks.

But pro-bridge forces say the link is necessary because travel to and from the island is a nightmare for locals. During the summer you can wait for most of a morning to get a spot on the ferry. In the winter the boats often get stuck in the ice pack for hours. With the bridge, PEI companies will be able to compete more effectively with their competition on the mainland.

Meanwhile, the spans are being dropped into place one by one and there is no argument that once the toll gates open, PEI will enter a new era of uncertainty and change. ■

Their least expensive compacts cost $45 per day, with 100 free km.

There is also a Rent-A-Wreck (☎ 566-9955) at 114 St Peters with undoubtedly cheaper rates. But this office has moved several times in the past few years and never seems to have a person on duty when you call.

Getting Around

The Airport As there is no airport bus in town, the only transportation is a cab. A cab is about $5. See also Bus, Bicycle and Hitching in the following Around the Island section.

AROUND CHARLOTTETOWN
Micmac Indian Village

While not far at all by boat south from the city across the Charlottetown Harbour, the village site (☎ 675-3800) is a somewhat circuitous but scenic half-hour drive from Charlottetown on Hwy 19. Together with the historic site, it can make a worthwhile half-day trip from the city. The village re-creation is small and unsophisticated but this is part of its charm – it was run for ages by an old Micmac man and his homemade approach is in evidence.

A path winds through the woods past teepees, dugout canoes and sweat lodges, some of which have informative notes accompanying them. A series of traps displays traditional hunting techniques. The simple museum contains such things as arrowheads, baskets and clothing. A visit takes 30 minutes to an hour and costs $3.25. Hours are 9.30 am to 6 pm in July and August and 10 am to 5 pm in June and September.

Amherst National Historic Park

Very close to the Micmac Indian Village and Rocky Point is the site of the old French capital and more recently Fort Amherst (☎ 675-2220), built by the British in 1758 after they had taken over the island. There isn't really anything left to see other than foundations but the interpretive centre features exhibits and an audiovisual show. There are views of the city and three lighthouses and a beach within the park area. The interpretive centre is open from mid-June to

Labour Day from 10 am to 6 pm daily and admission is $2.25.

AROUND THE ISLAND

The island is small and, with a car, easy to get around. In one day it's possible to drive from Charlottetown up to the beaches for a swim, along the north coast all the way up to North Cape, then back along the western shoreline, over to Summerside and down to Borden to catch the evening ferry. And you're not even rushing!

There are about 12 tourist offices around the island, including one at each of the ferry terminals. Any one of them can arrange accommodation anywhere on the island within an hour.

Three equal-sized counties make up the island: Prince in the west, Queen's in the middle and King's to the east. Each county has a scenic road network mapped out by the tourist bureau. Though far from the only options, these routes do take in the better-known attractions and the historical and geographical points of note.

North of Charlottetown

The area north of the capital in Queen's County is where all the action is on Prince Edward Island (refer to the Cavendish Region map). The national park is here, with its camping and beaches, and most of the

> **Charlottetown Harbour**
> An old docker with gutted cheeks,
> time arrested in the used-up knuckled hands
> crossed on his lap, sits
> in a spell of the glinting water.
>
> He dreams of times in the cider sunlight
> when masts stood up like stubble;
> but now a gull cries, lights,
> flounces its wings ornately, folds them,
> and the waves slop among the weed-grown piles.
> **Milton Acorn**

island's main attractions are in this area. To feed and house the vacationers, many of the province's lodging and dining establishments are found not far from the north coast. After York, the description here covers areas from east to west *outside* the park, and then, again in the same direction, areas *within* the park boundaries.

YORK

Not far from Charlottetown, **Jewell's Country Gardens** in York has the *Potato Blossom Tea Room* which makes a pleasant afternoon stop for a sip and snack. They do some amazing things with potatoes in this restaurant, using the vegetable to make fruit scones, cinnamon rolls, even potato fudge. At breakfast there are always potato pancakes on the menu and for lunch you can order the special potato dish of the day. Lunches are around $7. There is also a small pioneer village and a glass museum.

GRAND TRACADIE

Little more than a crossroads at the southeastern edge of the national park and not far from its entrance on Route 6, this is a 'must stop' for *Beulah's Bake Shop*, a tiny shed beside the house and kitchen where all the cooking is done. The strawberry and raspberry pies are unbelievable and are cheap to boot. There are other things too, including bread and a variety of buns. Campers at Stanhope, stock up here.

STANHOPE

There is really nothing in this town, but near the park entrance are a couple of restaurants. There is one basic place, and another, more upmarket one in the old-time *Stanhope by the Sea* hotel, dating from 1817. You can also get a bite at the golf course, or at *Captain Dick's Pub*, next door to the hotel, which is open only on Friday night (but not every week).

Lobster

Unfortunately for this mottled green or bluish or blackish prehistoric wonder, somebody realised it tasted bloody good. This has meant that we've learned a lot about it. But the facts on this 100-million-year-old crustacean read like a joke book. It tastes with its feet, listens with its legs (of which there are 10), and has teeth in its stomach (which is found just behind the head). The kidney is in the head, the brain in the neck and the bones (shell) are on the outside.

Lobster is widely associated with the east coast of Canada but perhaps Prince Edward Island, with its famous lobster suppers, is most closely linked with this symbol of gourmet dining. It's now hard to believe but there wasn't much interest in the delicate meat until a good way into this century. In fact, they used to use lobster as fertiliser for the island's farms.

There are two fishing seasons, one in the spring ending in late June and one in the winter. Traps of wood, or now sometimes of metal mesh, baited with herring bits are dropped overboard to rest on the bottom and are checked soon after. The ingenious cage design allows the lobster's claws to narrow on the way in, but once inside they spread apart again and there is no way crawling back out is possible. The older wooden traps are available for purchase around the island at about $5 each and will one day be museum pieces. Huge holding tanks allow fresh, live lobster to be offered throughout the year.

The standard restaurant lobster in Canada weighs a pound or a little less than half a kg. Two and three pounders are often available but bigger ones are not often seen. Along the Quebec coast of the St Lawrence around Rivière-du-Loup I've seen five and six pounders (2.5 kg) for sale but tell me who's going to pick one of those suckers up and put it in a pot of hot water?

Most people are satisfied with the regular portion as it seems to be a rich food. The meat is lean, however, and is permitted on low-cholesterol diets, but hold the butter.

Lobster can be baked, broiled, even barbecued, but the best method is boiling. They should be cooked in boiling, salted fresh water for 12 to 15 minutes for the first pound, adding four minutes for every extra pound (half-kg). When done, the lobster has the characteristic orangey red shell, not unlike that of some of the bathers at Cavendish beach. Most meaty is the tail, followed by the larger claws. Though most people quickly discard it, the green mushy liver, known as tomalley, is considered a delicacy and one of the choicest parts to savour. ∎

Stanhope is one of the major accommodation centres, with dozens of places renting cottages, often by the week or longer. Weekly rates vary but most are between $350 and $450. The daily rate for most of the housekeeping units is around $50.

Campbell's Tourist Home (☎ 672-2421) in Stanhope is a B&B with a double for $40 and a weekly rate of $250.

From Stanhope to Cavendish there are about 10 privately operated campgrounds. (See also information on places to stay *within* Prince Edward Island National Park in that section later.)

NORTH RUSTICO

There is a post office and a government liquor store here as well as two supermarkets and a bank. Across the province, these liquor stores are the outlets for beer, wine and all alcoholic beverages.

PEI is the home of *Fisherman's Wharf Lobster Suppers*, probably the best known, busiest restaurant in the province. It's huge but in peak season it still gets crowded, with queues from 6 to 8 pm. It's a fun, casual, holiday-style restaurant offering good-value dinners. For $24 you are served a half-kg lobster and can help yourself to an impressive salad bar, unlimited amounts of chowder, good local mussels, rolls and a variety of desserts. If you get really lucky, along the back wall are tables with a view of the ocean.

At the wharf in North Rustico is *Aiden Doiron's* where you can get fresh seafood ranging from lobsters and mussels to scallops, salmon and mackerel. If there are two of you, consider feasting on a four or five-pounder lobster (2.5 kg), available live or cooked.

At Doiron's and in **Rusticoville** fishing charters can be arranged down at the quay. Boats often hold six to 10 people, who catch cod, mackerel and several other species during the three-hour trips. Most charters are $15 to $20 per person.

Outside South Rustico on the small Route 242 is the quirkiest of island attractions, **Jumpin' Jack's Old Country Store Museum**. It's in the middle of nowhere and doesn't charge admission. The museum is a junk collector's dream – an old two-storey house jammed with dust-covered articles of every description and function collected from far and wide for who knows how many years. It's open 10 am to 6 pm Tuesday through Saturday and 1 to 6 pm on Sunday in July and August.

North Rustico also has a lot of accommodation, including many tourist homes where it's possible to get something for less than a week fairly easily. A double room in someone's home can be had for $40 to $45.

North Rustico Harbour is a tiny fishing community with a lighthouse which you can drive to from North Rustico or walk to from the beach once you're in the national park. Located here is *Blue Mussel Cafe*. This pleasant dockside cafe has an outdoor deck overlooking the harbour, excellent chowder and a seafood menu that includes lobster dinners for $16 and two pounds (one kg) of mussels, steamed in wine and garlic, for $7.

The Rustico area is the base for one of the province's largest fishing fleets. Prince Edward Island's fishing industry is inshore (as opposed to offshore), meaning that the boats head out and return home the same day.

CAVENDISH

At the junction of routes 6 and 13, this little town is the area's commercial centre. You're in the centre of town when you see the service station, Cavendish Arms Pub, the church and the cemetery.

Also at the junction, as part of the police station and city offices, is the **Cavendish Visitor Centre** (☎ 963-2832). This new centre has a wealth of information on the area along with a courtesy phone to make reservations, exhibits on the national park and a small craft shop. During the summer, hours are 9 am to 10 pm.

This is also the home of Lucy Maud Montgomery, the author of *Anne of Green Gables*. For more information on this see the Prince Edward Island National Park section.

East of Cavendish is a large amusement park and close by are a wax museum, go-kart tracks, a Ripley's Believe It or Not Museum

Cavendish Region

Gulf of St Lawrence

Prince Edward Island National Park

St Peter's

St Peter's Bay

St Peter's Harbour

Savage Harbour

Tracadie

Tracadie Bay

Dalvay by the Sea Hotel

Dalvay

Stanhope

Brackley Beach

Winsloe North

Oyster Bed Bridge

York

Brackley

Charlottetown International Airport

Hillsborough River

CHARLOTTETOWN

Orby Head

Andy's Surfside

Inn

Bicycle Rentals

North Rustico Harbour

Rustico Island Beach

North Rustico

Cavendish

Bear Store

Rusticoville

South Rustico

St Ann

New Glasgow

Wheatley River

Hunter River

House of Green Gables

New London

Stanley Bridge

French River

New London Bay

0   5   10 km

PRINCE EDWARD ISLAND

and other tacky diversions, including a life-size model of the Space Shuttle. The growing number of these manufactured attractions in recent years is sad and definitely an eyesore in this scenic region of PEI.

At Stanley Bridge the **Marine Aquarium** has live samples of some of the native fish and a few seals. It isn't large, so to broaden the appeal there is a pinned butterfly display and a collection of 700 mounted bird specimens. Admission is $4 and hours during the summer are 9 am to dusk. Save it for one of the rainy days.

Just west of town on Route 6 is one of the more popular family attractions: **Rainbow Valley**, a recreational water complex which includes a variety of slides and boats. There are also animals, picnic areas and fast-food outlets.

Tourist homes, motels and cottages, some within the national park or close to the beach, can be found around Cavendish. Remember that this is the busiest and most expensive area for accommodation. See also the Places to Stay in the Prince Edward Island National Park section.

Just east of town is a restaurant complex all done in cedar shakes. It contains a few fast-food places, including one for breakfast. *Thirsty's*, across the street, is a bar. Nearby is Cavendish Rent-A-Bike (☎ 963-2075), where bicycles are $5 an hour or $17 a day.

The *Cavendish Tourist Mart* is a grocery store open from 8 am to 10 pm daily, good for all essential supplies. It also features a laundromat.

To the west of town, near the park entrance, **Cavendish Boardwalk** has some stores and a few places to eat, including pizza, chicken and 'sub' outlets.

Fiddles 'n' Vittles, three km west of town on Route 6, has been described as a fun place to eat; the food is good and they have half-price kids' dishes. The menu includes a variety of seafood but also steak, chicken and burgers, all at low or moderate prices.

Around Cavendish

Two lobster-supper houses are nearby in the village of New Glasgow, and in St Ann on Route 224. Both offer a lobster plus all-you-can-eat chowder, mussels, salads, breads and desserts. You may even get some live music to help the food go down. Neither is quite the operation of the one in North Rustico and the selection is not as large, but the price is lower.

The one in St Ann is an original and still operates in the St Anne's Church basement, as it has done for the past few decades. It's busy, casual and friendly and full of people from all over Canada, the USA and Europe. Lobster dinners are $21 and offered daily, except Sunday, from 4 to 9 pm.

NEW LONDON

Aside from the *New London Lobster Supper*, which runs from 11 am to 9 pm daily, New London is known for being the birthplace of Lucy Maud Montgomery, author of *Anne of Green Gables*. The house where she was born, in 1874, is now a museum and contains some personal belongings. Hours are 9 am to 7 pm during the summer and admission is $1.

Not far away in the village of Park Corner is a house which was once owned by Montgomery's uncle when she was a girl. This was one of her favourite places and she was married in the parlour in 1911. The home is now called the **Anne of Green Gables Museum** (☎ 886-2003) and contains such items as her writing desk and autographed first-edition books. There is also a tea room and craft shop here. The museum is at Silver Birch and open 9 am to 6 pm from June to October, later during the height of the tourist season. Admission is $2.50.

PRINCE EDWARD ISLAND NATIONAL PARK

Just 24 km north of Charlottetown, this is one of Canada's smallest national parks but has 40 km of varied coastline, including some of the country's best sand beaches.

Sand dunes and red sandstone cliffs give way to wide beaches (widest at Cavendish) and the warmest waters around the province. The Gulf Stream does a little loop around the island, causing water temperatures to be higher than those found even further south along the east coast. This is not quite tepid bath water but temperatures do get up to around a comfortable 20°C.

A day pass to the park costs $4 per person or $6 per family. The park maintains an information desk and the exhibits in the Cavendish Visitor Centre. There is also the Brackley Visitor Centre (☎ 672-2259) passed on the way to Brackley Beach on Hwy 15. It's open from 9 am to 6 pm daily during the summer and until 9 pm from July to mid-August.

Things to See & Do

House of Green Gables This is in the park near Cavendish and is, apart from the national park itself, the most popular attraction in the province.

The house is known as the place where Anne, the heroine of many of Montgomery's books, lived. The surrounding property was the setting of the 1908 novel *Anne of Green Gables* – a perennial favourite not only in Canada but around the world, having been translated into nearly 20 languages. The warm-hearted book tells the story of a young orphan, Anne, and her childhood tribulations in turn-of-the-century Prince Edward Island in a way that makes it a universal tale.

Everything relating to either the story or the author anywhere on the island has now pretty well become part of the Green Gables

industry, but despite that, the original charm of place and character do remain.

At House of Green Gables, actually a rather attractive and comfortable place, the over-popularisation reaches its zenith, with tremendous crowds arriving daily all through the summer. Bus loads of visitors arrive at the door continuously. Visiting first thing in the morning is highly recommended. Admission is $2.25 and the home is worth a visit for the period furniture and the feeling it gives of life here in the late 19th and early 20th centuries. The house is open from 9 am to 8 pm in high season, till 5 pm otherwise.

The quieter trails from the house through the green, gentle creek-crossed woods are worthwhile. 'Lover's Lane', particularly, has maintained its idealistic childhood ambience.

Not far away, near the United Church in Cavendish, you can visit the site of the house where Montgomery lived with her grandparents and where she wrote *Anne of Green Gables*. The farmhouse no longer stands, just the stone foundations and surrounding gardens.

Other Anne-related sites include the cemetery in Cavendish (where Montgomery is buried), the museum at Silver Bush in Park Corner on Route 20 (where Montgomery spent much time when it was owned by her uncle) and the museum in the Confederation Centre in Charlottetown (which contains some original manuscripts).

A Yen for Anne

Although Prince Edward Island is generally little known internationally, up to 10,000 of the island's annual visitors are now from Japan. This makes it easily one of the country's top destinations for the Japanese traveller. There is even a direct Tokyo-Charlottetown flight. Banff and the Rockies are also a major lure.

The attraction is partly because Charlottetown has become the twin city of Ashibetsu, a rural city in northern Japan. Student exchanges have taken place, as well as a number of tourist-related activities.

The main draw, however, is the Japanese fascination with *Anne of Green Gables*. The book has been found on Japanese school curriculums since the 1950s, and Anne's story has found a spot in the national psyche, especially among women, who identify strongly with Anne's character.

Also many Japanese now come to PEI to marry. Weddings and marriages in Japan can be prohibitively costly and are often difficult to prepare. Here couples enjoy the quiet countryside and, in some cases, the Christian church and ceremony to which many young people are attracted. Quite a few couples are married at Silver Birch in Park Corner, where Montgomery herself was married. Arrangements are handled by the local tourism ministry. ∎

Beaches There are several long stretches of beach in the park and they are all good. **Cavendish Beach**, edged with large sand dunes at the west end of the park, is the widest of them all. Although not really physically superior to the others it is easily the most popular and gets relatively busy in peak season. This does not mean crowded, however, for it is too big and the number of visitors too small for it ever to get over-congested.

Between Rustico and Cavendish is some of the park's most impressive terrain. At Cape Turner there is a good look-out area but don't miss **Orby Head** with its trails leading along the high red cliffs with great seaside views. There are other stopping-off points along this stretch of coastal road.

Brackley Beach, in the middle of the park, is also well attended, the others less so. Long, wide Brackley Beach backed by sand dunes is popular with locals, young people and visitors. There is a snack bar and change rooms by the boardwalk to the beach. Lifeguards are on hand but watch out for riptides.

Stanhope Beach, opposite the campground of the same name is similar to the more popular ones in appearance but seems to mainly attract the people of the nearby campground. There are no cliffs or dunes here, the landscape is flat and the beach is wide. At the entrance to the beach is a snack bar and change rooms with showers. A boardwalk leads to the beach which has lifeguards on duty through the day.

Dalvay Beach is the easternmost beach and a couple of short hiking trails begin in the area. Two called Farmlands and Bubbling Springs Trails are quite good, with a small graveyard, some remnants of old stone dykes and a spring for a cool drink found along the way. They can be combined for a four-km walk.

An appealing landmark is the **Dalvay by the Sea Hotel** (☎ 672-2048) built in 1895 and looking like something out of a novel by F Scott Fitzgerald. For a splurge this Victorian seaside lodge offers a varied menu – lobster bisqué to coq au vin. Reservations are required. If you're thinking of spending the night, the price of a double room (from $180 and up) includes dinner and breakfast.

All the north coast beaches tend to have red jellyfish. They are known locally as bloodsuckers but they aren't. Most are much smaller than a closed fist and, while unpleasant, are not really dangerous, although brushing against one can irritate the skin. There is virtually no shade to be had at any of the beaches, so for your own protection consider using an umbrella, a shirt, and lots of sunscreen lotion.

Kayaking Outside Expeditions (☎ 892-5425) is a Charlottetown-based outfitter that offers kayaking trips in the national park from June to October. Three-hour introductory trips, that begin with a lesson in kayaking techniques, are held three times daily at 9 am, 1 pm and near sunset. The cost, which includes all equipment, is $32. In Cavendish, phone them on ☎ 963-2391.

Places to Stay
Camping The national park has three campgrounds and, as you might expect, all of them are in heavy demand during the summer. There is no reservation system for sites so it's crucial you arrive early, preferably by early afternoon, if you're hoping to obtain one. To check availability call ☎ 672-6350.

Cavendish Campground is three km west of the town of Cavendish and has showers, a kitchen shelter and laundry facilities. Also beginning in the campground is the Homestead Trail, the park's longest at eight km. Being near the centre of things, this campground tends to the most popular and is often filled by noon. An unserviced site is $15, serviced $19.

Stanhope Campground across the road from the Stanhope beaches, has similar facilities and prices but features a more wooded setting and a well-stocked store. The relatively isolated *Rustico Island Campground* is near the end of the road to Brackley Beach. It has only unserviced sites and a kitchen shelter, no showers though there are some nearby at the Brackley Beach day-use building. A site is $10 a night.

Outside the park and occasionally adjacent to it are many private campgrounds. *Marco Polo Land* (☎ 963-2352), near Cavendish, has a range of amenities, including two swimming pools. An unserviced site is $17.50. At the other end of the national park, near Grand Tracadie on Route 6, the much smaller *Ann's Whispering Pines* (☎ 672-2632) has unserviced sites for $12. Both take reservations.

Other Accommodation Tourist homes, motels and B&Bs are found along the length of the national park. The prices are steep compared to what you pay elsewhere and the closer to the beach the accommodations are, the steeper it gets. Phoning for a reservation, even if only a few days in advance, helps considerably in obtaining a bed at night.

For these reasons, serious consideration should be given to visiting the national park after Labour Day if your schedule will allow it. The crowds are gone, the weather often provides those delightful Indian summer days and every B&B and motel is practically begging you to stay with them. By Sunday of that holiday weekend room prices are crashing. Two-bedroom cottages that were $100 in July can now be obtained for $60, B&B's that were asking $65 a few weeks earlier are teasing you with $30 doubles.

One of the best places to stay during the tourist season is *Andy's Surfside Inn* (☎ 963-2405 or 892-7994) inside the national park on the way to Orby Head from North Rustico. This large rambling house overlooking Doyle's Cove has been an inn since the 1930s and offers eight rooms at $30/35. A light breakfast is included and the kitchen is open to those who want to bring home a few live lobsters. The view from the porches is simply stunning.

On Route 6 west of North Rustico is *MacLure B&B* (☎ 963-2239) in a farm setting. There are three rooms for $35 to $40 a double with breakfast extra. *Parkview Farm Tourist Home & Cottage* (☎ 963-2027) is two km east of Cavendish and has rooms for $35/45 and cottages on the farm that sleep four people for $95.

Overlooking the bay near Rusticoville or 10 km east of Cavendish is *Beside the Sea B&B* (☎ 963-3148) on Hwy 6. There are three rooms for $45 for a double, full breakfast included.

The most affordable motel is *Tortuga Motel* (☎ 621-2020) at Oyster Bed Bridge, intersection of Hwys 6 and 7. The motel is pretty basic and a little far from the beaches if you don't have a car, but rooms begin at $35, about half what every other motel is charging.

West of Charlottetown

LADY SLIPPER DRIVE

The western third of the island is made up of Prince County. Lady Slipper Drive is 288 km long and is the marked tourist route around this portion of the island, pretty much circumnavigating the region.

The northern section of Prince County is, like so much of the province, pretty farm country, but the southern portion is rather flat, less scenic and possibly the least visited part of the island. The southernmost area, along Egmont and Bedeque bays, retains some evidence of its Acadian French history.

VICTORIA

Straddling Queens and Prince counties is this picturesque fishing village just off Hwy 1 and 35 km west of Charlottetown. Victoria is something of a haven for artists and features a number of studios and art galleries as well as Island Chocolates, a shop that produces excellent Belgian chocolates. The Victoria Lighthouse in town is now a one-room museum open noon to 5 pm daily except Monday while the community centre becomes the Victoria Playhouse (☎ 800-925-2025) during the summer.

You can purchase cooked lobster on the wharf and then enjoy them at a table overlooking the beach at Victoria Provincial Park. Or enjoy homemade soups, quiches or salads at *Landmark Cafe*. Those interested in spending a night or two can check into the

Victoria Village Inn (☎ 658-2483), a 19th-century home that has three rooms beginning at $43 for a double.

SUMMERSIDE

The second largest city in the province, Summerside has a population of 10,000. At one time residents of the capital would move to this side of the island in the hot months. Now Summerside is more a town in its own right, although the closure of the large military base here has caused a major economic setback.

The approach along Hwy 1A is much like that to Charlottetown, lined with motels, hamburger joints and a few campgrounds. But centrally, it's a quiet village with quaint old homes on streets trimmed with big trees. The one main street, Water St, has most of the commercial establishments.

The Lady Slipper Visitor Information Centre (☎ 888-8364) is on Hwy 1A two km east of Summerside and open 9 am to 8 pm daily during the summer. The walking-tour pamphlet of historic Summerside details some of the town's finer buildings from 1850 to the turn of the century.

For a week in mid-July each year there's the Lobster Carnival, with nightly feasts, contests, games and music. At the end of the month there is a hydroplane regatta. Sleman Park is the site of an airshow at the end of August.

South of Summerside, **Borden** is the terminal for ferries to Cape Tormentine, New Brunswick.

International Fox Museum & Hall of Fame

The controversial story of island fox farming is told at 260 Fitzroy St (☎ 436-2400), one block from Water St. In 1890, using two wild silver foxes captured on the island, a breeding and farming operation was begun. It was the first anywhere to successfully breed wild fur-bearing animals in captivity. The principles learned are now used around the world. Through the 1920s fortunes were made in Summerside in shipbuilding and in fur

farming. For a time, the latter was PEI's most important economic activity.

From May to September, the museum, created in Holman Homestead, a beautiful historic house with a lovely garden, is open from 9 am to 6 pm. Holman himself was a fox breeder, and there are still fox farms on the island today. One of them, Anglo Farms (☎ 882-2825) in the small village of Anglo Tignish, is also a B&B.

The College of Piping & Celtic Performing Arts

The school (☎ 436-5377), at 619 Water St, provides visitors with nearly continuous entertainment through the day – bagpipes, singing, dancing. Drop in any time Monday to Friday from 11 am to 5 pm and see what's happening. There are also exhibits and a lunch room for light meals. A ticket is $7 for the special Thursday night Scottish Ceilidh shows. The Thursday performance is usually held outdoors at the back of the building – bring a sweater! Watch for the International Highland Gathering at the end of June at the college.

EPTEK National Exhibition Centre & PEI Sports Hall of Fame

One of 22 national exhibition centres in the country, EPTEK (☎ 888-8373) features a small, changing art and history exhibit. A section on provincial sports figures is permanent. The centre, on the waterfront near Spinnaker's Landing, is open 10 am to 4 pm Tuesday through Friday and 1 to 4.30 pm Saturday and Sunday. Admission is $2.

Spinnaker's Landing

This is the boardwalk area along Summerside's waterfront, which includes the usual over-priced gift shops and the Whale's Tail Pub. But also here is The Boat Shed Interpretive Centre that has displays on the town's history and the traditional boat-building methods once employed here. Next door is the city's Lighthouse Lookout, which houses a visitor's centre on the first floor and observation platform at the top. Both the lighthouse and the Boat Shed are free and hours

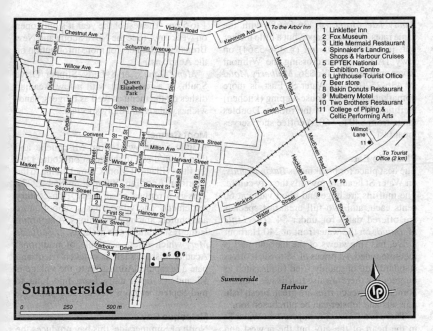

1	Linkletter Inn
2	Fox Museum
3	Little Mermaid Restaurant
4	Spinnaker's Landing, Shops & Harbour Cruises
5	EPTEK National Exhibition Centre
6	Lighthouse Tourist Office
7	Beer store
8	Bakin Donuts Restaurant
9	Mulberry Motel
10	Two Brothers Restaurant
11	College of Piping & Celtic Performing Arts

Summerside

0   250   500 m

are 9.30 am to 9.30 pm daily during the summer. The tourist centre offers an hour-long walking tour of the city at 2 and 6 pm daily during the summer. A ticket is $2 but includes entrance to the EPTEK Centre.

Spinnaker's Landing also contains a small outdoor stage area for free live music in summer. The Age of Sails performers also take to the stage with their historical comedy.

Harbour Cruises

Departing from Spinnaker's Landing are boat tours of the area for $12 per person. Harbour Cruises, which has a ticket office along the boardwalk, also has a sunset trip, featuring champagne and mussels, for $15.

Places to Stay

Summerside has a number of places to obtain a room, including a handful of moderately priced motels, a rarity in PEI.

For campers, there is *Linkletter Provincial Park* (☎ 888-8366), on Route 11, eight km

west of Summerside. There's a beach and a store for basic supplies.

In town, *The Arbor Inn* (☎ 436-6847) is a B&B at 380 MacEwen Rd. It's rooms vary from a simple single and two small, share-bathroom doubles to a deluxe suite with all the extras, including a whirlpool bath. The price ($35 to $60 a double) depends on the features of the room and includes breakfast.

Two farm B&Bs are located next door to each other just before Hwy 1A crosses the Wilmont River. *Blue Heron County B&B* (☎ 436-4843) offers four rooms in a grand farmhouse that are $40-50 for a double depending on the room. *The Island Way Farm* (☎ 436-7405 or 800-361-3435) is practically next door and also has four rooms in the same price range. Both include breakfast and maintain a riding stable for guests.

Motels offer some of the best rates in Summerside. The *Cairns* (☎ 436-5841), on the east side of town at 721 Water St, charges $38 and up for a double. Across the street is

PRINCE EDWARD ISLAND

Sunny Isle Motel (☎ 436-5665) with the same rates. A little cheaper, but a little further out, is *Glade Motor Inn* (☎ 436-5564) on Hwy 1A just before crossing the Wilmont River with doubles for $36. *Mulberry Motel* (☎ 436-2520), at 6 Water St East, is more upmarket and offers housekeeping (kitchen) facilities with some of the rooms. Doubles range from $40 to $60. A coffee shop serves breakfast.

Places to Eat
The best place for breakfast is *Bakin Donuts*, on Water St heading towards the city centre. The muffins are huge and good value at 60 cents each, and two full breakfast specials are offered daily for under $4. *The Little Mermaid*, on the waterfront at 240 Harbour Drive, has fine views of the harbour and is recommended. At prices of $6 to $9, it offers standard fare of mainly fried foods, such as burgers, but there are also fish dishes, and the homemade French fries are great. Fresh fish, mussels and lobster can be purchased too.

There is a *Chinese restaurant* on Water St in the heart of the city but the newest and most popular place in Summerside, especially at night, is the *Purple Parrot Pub and Restaurant* across the street. Dinners range from $7 to $12.

AROUND SUMMERSIDE
Miscouche
As you head west of Summerside along Route 2, the **Acadian Museum** (☎ 436-6237) in Miscouche has a small collection of early Acadian memorabilia. Dioramas and other displays relate the engrossing history of the Acadians before and after the mass expulsion from Nova Scotia by the British in 1720. An audio-visual exhibit provides more information. The museum is also a centre for genealogical research. A visit to learn something of this tragic story is worthwhile.

Most of the descendants of these early French settlers live in this section of the province. Six thousand still speak French as a first language. Admission to the museum is $2.75 and in the summer it's open Monday to Saturday 9.30 am to 5 pm and on Sunday

1 to 5 pm. The rest of the year it's only open on weekdays. (See the Nova Scotia and New Brunswick chapters for more information on the Acadians.)

Mémé Jane's, at 8 Lady Slipper Drive South, is a restaurant with a few Acadian dishes on the menu as well as burgers, sandwiches, salads and daily specials.

Mont Carmel
A little further west from Miscouche and then south down to the coast on Route 11 is the little village of Mont Carmel, home to the **Pioneer Acadian Village** (☎ 854-2227). This is a replica of an early 19th-century settlement. The village has a school, store and church, among other things. A highlight is the restaurant in the grounds, *L'Étoile de Mer*, which offers a couple of traditional Acadian dishes, such as chicken fricot and paté à la rapure. Admission to the village is $2 and it's open daily from mid-June to mid-September from 9.30 am to 7 pm.

Malpeque Bay
North of Summerside, this bay produces the world-famous oysters of the same name. About 10 million of them are harvested each year from the controlled 'farms' of the bay.

Cabot Beach Provincial Park (☎ 836-8901), north of Malpeque village, is one of the larger parks on the island and a popular place with the island residents. There is camping, a beach and lots of picnic areas.

AROUND PRINCE COUNTY
Tyne Valley is worth a visit. There are also a few craft places to visit, including a pottery. Also here, the *Doctor's Inn* (☎ 831-2164) is a fine country B&B whose good dining room is able to take full advantage of its surrounding organic garden. Rooms are $45 for a double and dinner is by reservation only. The inn also sells its organically grown vegetables and potatoes.

The *West Island Inn* (☎ 831-2495) is an attractive-looking historic place, with a big balcony and a gazebo with hot tub. A small double goes for $39, less in May, June, September and October.

Just north of Tyne Valley along Hwy 12 is **Green Park Provincial Park** (☎ 831-2370), which includes a beach, campground and the Green Park Shipbuilding Museum. The provincial museum preserves PEI's 19th-century shipbuilding industry, which at one time included almost 200 small shipyards where crews of 20 men were building boats in six months or less. On the grounds is an interpretive centre, a re-created shipyard with a partial constructed 200-ton brigantine in it and the Yeo House, the renovated home of a wealthy shipowner in the 1860s. Hours are 9 am to 5 pm daily during the summer and admission is $2.50.

A band of about 50 Micmac families live on **Lennox Island**, in Malpeque Bay. The scenery is good, and inside the Band Council Complex are paintings and artefacts dealing with the history of the people who were the first in Canada to be converted to Christianity. St Ann's Church, dating from 1875, can be visited, along with an Indian craft shop. The island is connected by road from the west side of the bay, near the village of East Bideford, north of Tyne Valley.

The inland town of **O'Leary**, right in the middle of Prince County, is a small commercial centre which sees few tourists. There is, however, the **PEI Potato Museum** (☎ 859-2039), on Parkview Drive in Centennial Park. Everything you ever wanted to know about the lowly tuber is carefully explained. You walk away with such gems of knowledge as man began cultivating the potato in Peru 4500 years ago and that French fries alone take up 85% of all potatoes grown in North America. There also several other historic buildings in the park and a kitchen that sells potato dogs; baked potatoes with hot dogs in them and covered with cheese. Hours are 9 am to 5 pm daily except the Sunday when the centre opens at 2 pm. Admission is $2.50 and, surprisingly, is worth it.

To the north in Bloomfield, is **MacAusland's Woollen Mill** (☎ 859-3005), the only woollen mill remaining on the Island and Atlantic Canada's only producer of virgin wool blankets. Tours of the mill are offered and pure woollen goods can be bought.

If you're near **Tignish** at meal time, drop in at the Royal Canadian Legion. It's cheap, and you're bound to find conversation. The Parish of St Simon and St Jude Church has an impressive pipe organ built in Montreal and installed here in 1882. It employs 1118 pipes.

Equally interesting is the convent behind the church that was built in 1868 and now is *Tignish Heritage Inn and Hostel* (☎ 882-2491). The huge brick building has 14 rooms, most with private baths, that are $40/55 for singles/doubles. There is also a dormitory with 20 beds for $15 a night. This is not an official HI Hostel but still has a kitchen, dining area and laundry facilities.

Near the village of Norway is **Elephant Rock**, a large erosion formation at the seashore. To find it, head north of the town on Hwy 14 and then follow signs that will lead you on a dirt road to the coast.

North Cape is a wind-blown promontory with a lighthouse. A wind turbine station has been set up to study the efficacy of wind-powered generators. The interpretive centre provides information and features an aquarium. Hours are 9 am to 8 pm daily and admission is $2. Upstairs there is a rather pricey restaurant. Even more interesting is the rock reef at North Cape which can be explored at low tide – look for sea life in the pools and watch for coastal birds.

About midway down the coast on the western shore along Route 14 is the village of Miminegash, in one of the more remote sections of the province. Right on Hwy 14 is the new **Irish Moss Interpretive Centre** (☎ 882-4313). It was begun by local women whose families have long been involved in the collecting or harvesting of the moss, a type of seaweed.

Almost half the world's supply of Irish moss comes from PEI. If you're dying to savour seaweed, there is the *Seaweed Pie Cafe* at the centre which has a standard lunch menu but also serves a special pie. The moss is in the middle layer of cream. Hours during the summer are 10 am to 6 pm daily except on Sunday when the centre is open from noon to 8 pm. Admission is $1.

Cedar Dunes Provincial Park (☎ 836-8901), at the south-east tip of Prince County, has a lighthouse, restaurant and beach and a campground. The lighthouse, dating from 1875, has been restored, and there is now a museum outlining its history. Overnight guests can stay at the inn, *West Point Lighthouse* (☎ 859-3605 or 800-764-6854), part of the former lightkeeper's premises, but rooms range from $70 to $110 a night. Alternatively there is a B&B called *Red Capes Inn* (☎ 859-3150), four km away on Route 14. A double at the inn is $38.

East of Charlottetown

THE KING'S BYWAY

The 374-km-long, circular sightseeing route around King's County (the eastern third of the province) is called the King's Byway. It's a lightly populated, rural region of farms and fishing communities. Much of this section of the province is peopled by ancestors of Scottish settlers rather than by the French of the western side or the Irish of the central district. The ferry to Nova Scotia is on the south coast, while the ferry to the Magdalen Islands is at Souris, on the east coast.

The shoreline is a mixture of parks, beaches, fishing ports and a few larger but quiet towns. The interior is crisscrossed with roads between farms.

ORWELL

Just out of town is the **Orwell Corner Historic Village** (☎ 651-2013), a restored and preserved 19th-century community. Originally settled by Scottish immigrants in 1766, the village includes a farm, blacksmith's, post office and store among other buildings still in their original settings. During the summer it's open from 9 am to 5 pm Tuesday through Sunday and costs $3. Concerts are held on Wednesday evening.

Nearby is **Sir Andrew MacPhail Homestead** (☎ 651-2789). The national historic site preserves the farm that MacPhail and his brother used to start the island's seed potato

industry and now features a restaurant in the wrap-around porch of the home. The site is open Tuesday through Sunday from 9 am to 5 pm. Admission is free.

WOOD ISLANDS

Down on the south coast, 'Woods' is where you'll find the PEI-Nova Scotia ferry terminal, and as such it's a busy visitor centre even though there isn't much in town itself. There are two tourist offices here with the one for PEI open from 7 am to 11.30 pm daily during the summer. The other is for Nova Scotia. The mainland is 22 km (75 minutes) across the Northumberland Strait.

The *Meadow Lodge Motel* (☎ 962-2022) is two km from the ferry landing, on the Trans Canada Hwy towards Charlottetown. A double room costs $51. In town there are about half a dozen places to eat.

MURRAY HARBOUR

Little visited and tucked out of the way, Murray Harbour is a fishing town with its own canning plant. Captain Garry's Seal Cruises (☎ 962-2494) departs from the town wharf to view PEI's largest seal colony, Bird Island and a mussel farm. The cost is $13.50. A similar tour is run out of Montague.

BRUDENELL RIVER PROVINCIAL PARK & AROUND

The campground in the park (☎ 652-2756) is just a bare field, but there's a lodge and a golf course for those not roughing it. At **Panmure Island Provincial Park** (☎ 838-4719), just south down the coast, there is a good beach, swimming and picnicking as well as a campground with laundry facilities. Unserviced sites at either park are $14.

Montague features one of the largest tourist offices on the island. The King's Byway Visitor Centre (☎ 838-2977) has racks of brochures and information as well as a vacancy board that will list openings in motels and B&Bs for the region. There is also an extensive set of displays and exhibits on PEI and a small video theatre where you can watch tapes on the topic of your choice. Hours are 9 am to 9 pm daily. From the

Montague marina *Cruise Manada* (☎ 838-3444) offers tours of PEI's largest seal colony for $13.50.

Cardigan, an old shipbuilding centre north of the park, has a lobster-supper house right down by the harbour; it's open 5 to 9 pm daily from June to October and includes chowder, salad bar and desserts as well as the lobster. The cost is $20.

BAY FORTUNE

The dining room at *The Inn at Bay Fortune* (☎ 687-3745) is considered to be one of the finest in the province. Main courses could be goat-cheese stuffed chicken in a walnut crust or mustard-crusted Atlantic swordfish. Dinners range from $19 to $26. There are also 11 comfortable guest rooms from $115 to $165 a night. This inn was once the home of Broadway playwright Elmer Harris.

The **Fortune River** flowing near Hwy 2 which cuts across the island is a good place for canoeing.

SOURIS

With a population of 1500, Souris feels like a real town after you've passed through so many small villages. It's actually one of the larger towns of the province and is the shopping and supply centre for the eastern region. First settled by the Acadian French in the early 1700s, it was named Souris, meaning 'mouse', due to several plagues. The name has been anglicised and the last 's' is pronounced. The town is an important fishing and processing port and is also important for the ferry (☎ 986-3278) which departs for the Magdalen Islands of Quebec, five hours and 134 km north in the Gulf of St Lawrence. See under Magdalen Islands in the Quebec chapter for more information on the ferry.

Main St, a strip with buildings from the 1920s and 1930s as well as some older distinctive architecture, is pleasantly slow, with cars stopping to let pedestrians cross. The shops, the newspaper office and a few simple restaurants are found here.

St Mary's Roman Catholic Church, built of island sandstone in 1901, is off Main St on Pacquet St and is the dominant structure in town. However, the Town Hall on Main St, the Georgian-style Beacon House and several other buildings are worth a look on the way by.

There is a tourist office at **Souris Beach Provincial Park**, a day-use facility with a wide sweeping beach at the south-west corner of town. Across the small bay, at the breakwater on the other side of town, is the large fish-processing plant and the dock for the red-and-white coastguard ship.

Places to Stay

For a small town, Souris gets quite busy due to the ferry traffic. There is a hostel, *The Hannan House* (☎ 686-4626), located right behind landmark St Mary's Church at 9 Longworth St. This excellent facility includes dorm rooms for $18 a night as well as 12 guest rooms at $45 for a double. It has full kitchen and laundry facilities, a lounge and TV room and mountain bikes for rent.

There are several B&Bs including the *Matthew House Inn* (☎ 687-3461) on Breakwater St, one block from the ferry. With period furnishings, en suite bath and more, this large restored Victorian home is a pleasant place to stay but is not in the low-budget category. Doubles range from $85 to $140, including continental breakfast. More affordable and nearly as nice is *Church Street Tourist Home* (☎ 687-3065) at 8 Church St right in the heart of town. Doubles are $35.

The good *Hilltop Motel* (☎ 687-3315, add 1-902 if calling from Quebec), gets full with ferry traffic even when the ferry arrives from Quebec at four or five in the morning. Checking in at that hour is OK, but call from the Magdalen Islands for a reservation before leaving or someone will probably beat you to the available bed. The motel has a restaurant that is good for breakfast. It's on the east side of town. Rates are $68 a double.

RED POINT PROVINCIAL PARK

Red Point is a small park with a sandy beach and some pleasant shaded tent sites. The beaches around here are known for the squeaking sound they make when you walk on them.

BASIN HEAD

Not even really a village, Basin Head is at the ocean's edge and is the site of **Basin Head Fisheries Museum** (☎ 357-2966). This provincial museum traces the history of the island's fishing industry with an interpretive centre, boat sheds with vessels on display and Smith Fish Cannery, which now houses a coastal ecology exhibit including salt water aquariums. Hours are 10 am to 5 pm daily during the summer and admission is $3.

EAST POINT

At East Point, the north-east tip of the island, cliffs are topped by a lighthouse, which can be climbed as part of a little tour for $2.50. Until the late 1980s it was run by a keeper, but is now automated like almost every other lighthouse in Canada. The assistant's old house nearby has a restored radio room and a gift shop. It's expected that in a few years the whole thing will have to be moved (as the lighthouse has been moved previously) because of the creeping erosion of the shoreline. The lighthouse is open from 10 am to 6 pm daily from 1 June to the end of September.

The north shore area of King's County all the way along towards Cavendish is more heavily wooded than much of the island but that doesn't mean the end of farms and potatoes altogether. There is a lot of fishing done along the coast here – you could try a charter in search of tuna. Inland there are a couple of trout streams worth investigating.

The people of the north-eastern area have a fairly strong, intriguing accent not unlike that heard in Newfoundland.

NORTH LAKE

This is one of the four fishing centres found along the north coast of King's County. Although small, the dock area and its lobster traps, storage sheds and boats is always good for a poke around. With autumn comes tuna season and quite a busy sport-fishing period, drawing anglers from abroad. Some of the world's largest bluefin tuna have been caught in these waters. Indeed the world-record catch, a 680 kg behemoth, was reeled in off North Lake in 1979.

CAMPBELL'S COVE PROVINCIAL PARK

Quiet and relaxing through the day, this small park, the best one in the county, fills up by evening in July and August. As always shade is at a premium, with about half the campsites offering some sun relief. Most campers are tenters as there are no electric hook-ups. Facilities are minimal so bring all necessary supplies.

The beach, with cliffs at each end, is excellent for beachcombing.

ST MARGARET'S

At the big church in St Margaret's, lobster suppers are held daily from 4 to 9 pm and are $21. Aside from the deep-sea fishing, there are some good trout streams along the road, and one of them, the **Naufrage River**, is just west of town. At the village of **Naufrage**, on the coast, there is another lighthouse and some colourful fishing boats around the wharf area.

ST PETER'S

The nets for commercial mussel farming can be seen stretched around St Peter's Bay. In town don't miss *Wilma's Bake Shop*, for bread, muffins and cinnamon buns.

MIDGELL

On Hwy 2 south of St Peter's Bay is the Midgell Centre (☎ 961-2963). Set up principally for the guests of the Christian centre, visitors are welcome to stay overnight at the hostel. There are 60 beds at $14 each. Light cooking is possible and there are showers and a lounge. It's open to visitors from 1 June to 1 September.

New Brunswick

New Brunswick, which celebrated its 212th birthday in 1996 is, along with Nova Scotia and Prince Edward Island, one of Canada's three Maritime Provinces. It was also one of the four original members of the Dominion of Canada established in 1867. Despite its long history, the province's essential characteristic is that it remains largely forested. Yet, for most visitors, it is the areas apart from the vast woodlands that have the most appeal.

From the Quebec border the gentle, pastoral farming region of the Saint John River Valley leads to the Bay of Fundy with its cliffs, coves and tidal flats caused by the world's highest tides. The eastern shore offers warm, sandy beaches and some of the finest salmon-fishing rivers anywhere flow out of the forested interior. The wooded highlands of the north contain one of the highest mountains in eastern Canada.

Saint John, the largest city, and Fredericton, the capital, both have intriguing Loyalist histories.

History

What is now New Brunswick was originally the land of the Micmacs, and, in the southern areas, the Maliseet (Malecite) and Passamaquoddy Native peoples.

The French first attempted settlement in the 1600s. The Acadians, as they came to be known, farmed the area around the Bay of Fundy using a system of dykes. In 1775 they were scattered by the English whose numbers rose by some 14,000 with the arrival of the Loyalists after the American Revolution. They settled the Saint John and St Croix river valleys and established Saint John.

Through the 1800s, lumbering and shipbuilding boomed and by the turn of the century other industries, including fishing, were developed. The Depression saw an end to prosperity and the power centre shifted to central Canada.

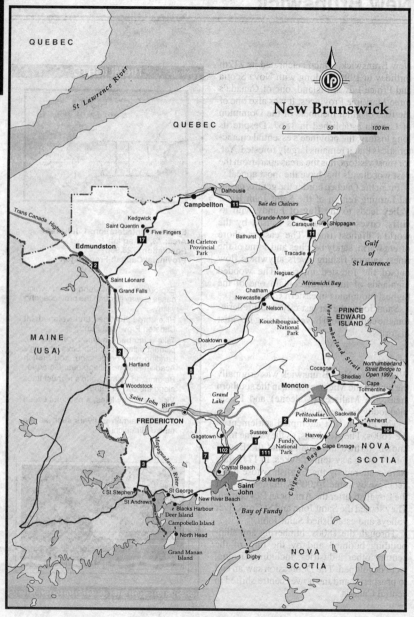

QUEBEC

St Lawrence River

QUEBEC

New Brunswick

0   50   100 km

Trans Canada Highway

Dalhousie

Campbellton   11   *Baie des Chaleurs*

Grande-Anse

Kedgwick   Caraquet   Shippagan   11
Saint Quentin   Five Fingers
17   Bathurst
Edmundston   Mt Carleton
Provincial   *Gulf of*
Park   *St Lawrence*
Tracadie

Saint Léonard   Neguac

Grand Falls   *Miramichi Bay*
Chatham
Newcastle
Nelson   **PRINCE EDWARD ISLAND**

MAINE (USA)   Kouchibouguac
National
Park

Doaktown

2   Cocagne   *Northumberland Strait Bridge to Open 1997*

Hartland   8   Shediac   Cape Tormentine

Woodstock   **Moncton**

Saint John River   2   *Petitcodiac River*   Sackville

FREDERICTON   Amherst
Grand Lake   104

Gagetown   Sussex   Harvey   **NOVA SCOTIA**
102   1
7   Fundy   Cape Enrage
111   National
Park
3   Crystal Beach
St Martins
St Stephen   New River Beach   **Saint John**

St Andrews   St George   *Chignecto Bay*

Blacks Harbour
Deer Island   *Bay of Fundy*   **NOVA SCOTIA**
Campobello Island
North Head

Grand Manan   Digby
Island

It has only been since the 1970s that New Brunswick has improved in infrastructure and further diversified its economy. The province's low costs and relatively inexpensive and bilingual labour have resulted in winning back some jobs from the rest of Canada. Moncton is doing particularly well.

Climate

Summers are usually not blisteringly hot and winters are very snowy and cold. The driest month of the year is August. Generally, there is more rain in the south.

Economy

Lumber and pulp & paper operations are two of the main industries. Manufacturing and minerals are also important, as are mixed farming and fishing.

Population & People

Today the numbers of Native peoples is small and the majority of the population has British roots. You may be surprised at how much French you hear spoken. Around 37% of the population have French ancestors and, even today, 16% speak French only. New Brunswick is Canada's only officially bilingual province. Roughly 60% of the province's residents live in urban areas.

Information

Provincial Symbols The provincial flower is the purple violet, and the bird is the chickadee.

Tourist Offices Tourism New Brunswick (☎ 800-561-0123) handles provincial tourist information. Their mailing address is Economic Development & Tourism, PO Box 6000, Fredericton, New Brunswick E3B 5H1. They have numerous offices around the province and can offer accommodation bookings.

Telephone The area code for the province is 506.

Time The province is on Atlantic Time.

Tax The provincial sales tax is 11%.

Activities

A copy of the province's *Outdoor Adventure Guide* or *Craft Directory* may be helpful and lists useful contacts. New Brunswick has good bird and whale watching, particularly in the southern regions. There is the Dorchester cycling loop in the south-east and the Saint John River Valley is also good for bike touring. Fundy National Park and Mount Carleton Provincial Park have numerous hiking trails and there is more walking in the eastern Bay of Fundy region. The tourist office can help locate canoeing waters and give advice on fishing, especially on the renowned salmon rivers.

Accommodation

The province has a complete range of accommodation, and Tourism New Brunswick can help with plans and reservations. Aside from national and provincial campgrounds and major hotels there is a selection of B&Bs, country inns, farm vacations and sports lodges and cabins.

Fredericton

Fredericton is the queen of New Brunswick's towns. Unlike most of them, it is non-industrial and a very pretty, genteel, quiet place. This the province's capital and about a fifth of the 45,000 residents work for the government. The small, tree-lined central area has some visible history to explore.

History

Three hundred years ago, the Maliseet and Micmac Indians lived and fished in the area. The French followed, setting up a pioneer village they called Ste Anne's Point in 1732 which eventually was burned to the ground by the British. In 1883, 2,000 Loyalists, fleeing the American Colonies, moved into the area at the end of the American Revolution. But Fredericton really came into its own the next year when the British Government decided to form a new province by splitting New Brunswick away from Nova Scotia.

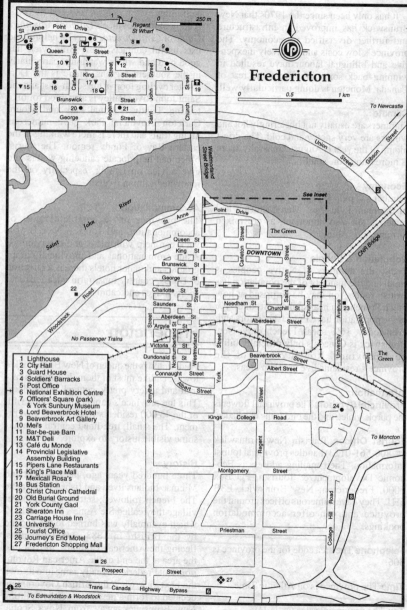

Fredericton

1 Lighthouse
2 City Hall
3 Guard House
4 Soldiers' Barracks
5 Post Office
6 National Exhibition Centre
7 Officers' Square (park)
   & York Sunbury Museum
8 Lord Beaverbrook Hotel
9 Beaverbrook Art Gallery
10 Mei's
11 Bar-be-que Barn
12 M&T Deli
13 Café du Monde
14 Provincial Legislative
   Assembly Building
15 Pipers Lane Restaurants
16 King's Place Mall
17 Mexicali Rosa's
18 Bus Station
19 Christ Church Cathedral
20 Old Burial Ground
21 York County Gaol
22 Sheraton Inn
23 Carriage House Inn
24 University
25 Tourist Office
26 Journey's End Motel
27 Fredericton Shopping Mall

Thomas Carleton, who was appointed lieutenant-governor, visited Ste Anne's Point and was impressed with how the village was strategically situated on the Saint John River, suitable to receive large ships and practically in the centre of the new province. In 1785, he not only made it the province capital and base for a British Garrison but renamed it 'Frederick'stown' in honour of Sir Frederick, Duke of York and the second son of King George III. Fear of an invasion from the USA kept the British regulars at Fredericton until 1869 but they never saw active service.

Long ago the town produced Canada's first English-speaking poet, Loyalist Jonathan Odell. Later, Lord Beaverbrook, who was to rise to international prominence as a publisher, was born here.

Orientation

The centre of the city is on a small, rounded peninsula which juts into the south side of the Saint John River. The city extends to the north side of the river, too, but this area is mainly residential and of little interest to visitors.

The Westmorland St Bridge connects the downtown area with the north shore. From the downtown side some fine big houses and a couple of church spires are visible across the river.

Further east along the river, the Princess Margaret Bridge, as part of the Trans Canada Hwy, links the two segments of the highway as it swings around the eastern edge of the city and over the river en route to and from Moncton. Not far beyond the bridge are the green woods and farmlands typical of the Saint John River Valley.

Coming into town from the west along the Trans Canada Hwy, take exit 292B (Regent St). Regent St will take you straight down to the centre of town.

In town, King St and the parallel Queen St are the main streets, just a block up from the river. Northumberland and Saint John Sts are the west and east edges of the small downtown area. The park on the corner of Queen and Regent Sts, called Officers' Square, is pretty much the centre of things.

As you head east from Queen St, out of the downtown area, there's a small strip of park known as The Green between the road and the river. This park extends eastwards for several blocks. Near the art gallery is a statue of Scottish poet Robert Burns. There are good views along the river here, and big shade trees to relax under. Several points of interest lie in The Green.

As you go further east, Queen St becomes Waterloo Row. Here it's the houses on the other side of the street that deserve your attention. Each is different from its neighbour and all are large and well maintained. Some have grand balconies, turrets and bizarre shapes. Nos 50, 82 and 146 are particularly impressive. The residence of the lieutenant-governor is around here; look for the coat of arms.

Back on The Green you'll pass the Loyalist Memorial beside Waterloo Row, commemorating the British founders. Not far away, on Brunswick St, is the old Loyalist Cemetery, similar to the one in Saint John.

Information

Tourist Offices The Visitors' Centre (☎ 452-9616) is in City Hall on Queen St. It's open Monday to Friday year-round from 8.30 am to 4.30 pm and until 8 pm during the summer.

There's a tourist bureau (☎ 458-8331) on the Trans Canada Hwy near Hanwell Rd, exit 289. It's open daily from early June to late September, from 8 am until 8 pm.

If you're driving in, the visitors' centres should be your first stop if for no other reason than they will give you a pass to park free at all municipal parking meters and carparks, including the lot right behind the City Hall.

Post Downtown, the post office, open Monday to Friday from 8 am to 5.15 pm, is at 527 Queen St, not far from Regent St.

Historic Walking Tour

A roughly six-square-block area of central Fredericton contains most of the city's attractions and is also the most attractive and architecturally appealing portion of the city. A walking tour around some of the following places plus other historical sites is outlined on the map of Fredericton, available at the tourist office. The walking tour includes 28 spots in the historic downtown area, starting from City Hall.

Officers' Square

This is the city's central park – on Queen St between Carleton and Regent Sts. The square was once the military parade ground and still sits amongst military buildings.

At 11 am and 7 pm Monday to Friday, from mid-July to the third week in August, you can see the full-uniform Changing of the Guard ceremony.

Also in the park during the summer is the Outdoor Summer Theatre, which performs daily at 12.15 pm on weekdays and 2 pm weekends. This free theatre-in-the-square is performed by a local group known as the Calthumpians, whose skits of history are laced with a good dose of humour.

On Tuesday and Thursday evenings in summer at 7.30 pm, free band concerts attract crowds. There might be a marching, military or pipe band, and sometimes classical music is played too. In the park is a statue of Lord Beaverbrook, the press baron and the province's most illustrious son.

On the west side of the square are the former Officers' Barracks, built between 1839 and 1851. The older section, closest to the water, has thicker walls of masonry and hand-hewn timbers. The other, newer end is made of sawn timber.

York-Sunbury Historical Museum

This museum (☎ 455-6041) is in the old officers' quarters, a building typical of those designed by the Royal Architects during the colonial period. The museum has a collection of items from the city's past spread out in 12 rooms: military pieces used by local regiments and by British and German armies from the Boer and both world wars; furniture from a Loyalist sitting room and Victorian bedroom; Native Indian and Acadian artefacts and archaeological finds. The highlight of the museum is a stuffed 19-kg frog. It was the pet of a local innkeeper.

Opening hours in summer are Monday to Saturday from 10 am to 6 pm but Tuesday and Thursday from 10 am to 9 pm; Sunday from noon to 6 pm. During the winter it's open only Monday, Wednesday and Friday from 11 am to 3 pm. Admission is $2.

Soldiers' Barracks

On the corner of Carleton and Queen Sts in the Military Compound you can see where the common soldier lived in the 1820s and also the Guard House (dating from 1828) where the naughty ones were sent. The Guard House now contains military memorabilia. A well-written, interesting history of it is available and admission is free.

School Days Museum

Also located in the Military Compound is the School Days Museum (☎ 459-3738) on the first floor of the Justice Building Annex.

Fredericton's Famous Frog

Move over Lord Beaverbrook. Without question, Fredericton's most beloved character is not the legendary publisher but a 19-kg frog. The famous frog made its first appearance in 1885, when it literally leaped into the small boat of local innkeeper Fred Coleman while he was rowing on Killarney Lake.

At the time the frog weighed a mere 3.6 kg but Coleman kept him at the inn by feeding it a steady (very steady) diet of buttermilk, cornmeal, whisky and june bugs. Little wonder it became the world's largest frog. With the leisurely life of a gourmand, this was one frog that definitely didn't want to return to being a prince.

Today the Coleman frog is forever enshrined in a glass case at the York-Sunbury Museum while in the gift shop Coleman frog T-shirts are the best selling item. ∎

What began as a collection by the New Brunswick Society of Retired Teachers is now this classroom museum featuring desks, textbooks and teaching aids from another era. Hours are 10 am to noon and 1 to 3 pm daily during the summer and admission is free.

Around the corner is Gallery Connexion (☎ 454-1433), a non-profit, artist-run centre showing contemporary and experimental art. During the summer the centre is open from noon to 4 pm Tuesday through Friday, and 2 to 4 pm on Sunday.

New Brunswick Legislative Assembly Building
Built in 1882, this government building (☎ 453-2527) stands on Queen St near Saint John St, east of Officers' Square.

When the Legislative Assembly is not in session, guides will show you around, pointing out things of particular merit, like the wooden Speaker's Chair and the spiral staircase. Hours are 9 am to 8 pm with the free tours leaving every half hour. When the assembly is in session, visitors are welcome to listen to the proceedings.

Regent St Wharf
Down at the river with an entrance off Queen St beside the Beaverbrook Hotel is the small wharf with a lighthouse and pier. The lighthouse contains a museum and the open top level affords views down the river. Admission is $2. At ground level (no admission charge) there is a snack bar and gift shop. The lighthouse is open daily in summer but it's only open on weekends from noon in the off-peak season.

Beaverbrook Art Gallery
Another of Lord Beaverbrook's gifts to the town is this gallery (☎ 458-8545), right opposite the Legislative Assembly Building on Queen St. There's a collection of British paintings including works by Gainsborough, Turner and Constable. They also have a Dali as well as Canadian and provincial works. The gallery is open Tuesday to Saturday from 10 am to 5 pm, Sunday and Monday from noon to 5 pm and daily during the summer. Admission is $3 per adult and $6 per family.

Christ Church Cathedral
Built in 1853, this is a fine early example of the 19th-century revival of decorated Gothic architecture. The cathedral is interesting because it's very compact – short for the height, yet with balance and proportion that make the interior seem both normal and spacious.

There is some good stained glass, especially around the altar, where the walls are painted above the choir. Free tours are offered. The church is just off Queen St at Church St, by the river, east of town.

Old Burial Ground
An easy walk from downtown is the Loyalist cemetery (dating from 1784) on Brunswick St on the corner of Carleton St. The Loyalists came from the 13 colonies after the American Revolution and were instrumental in settling this area. Many of the earliest Loyalists to arrive are buried here and it's interesting to browse around the grounds, open from 8 am to 9 pm daily.

National Exhibition Centre
On the corner of Carleton St at 503 Queen St in town, this building (☎ 453-3747) dates from 1881 and has been used as a post office, customs house and library. The exhibition centre on the 1st floor displays travelling exhibits which vary dramatically. Newoundland folk art, hooked mats, art photographs from the National Gallery and Japanese kites are some examples.

Upstairs is the New Brunswick Sports Hall of Fame with tidbits about achievements of local sportspeople, ranging from NHL hockey players to jockey great Ron Turcotte. Hours for both the Exhibition Centre and the Sports Hall of Fame during the summer are 10 am to 5 pm daily and until 9 pm on Friday. There is no admission fee.

Boyce Farmers' Market
The farmer's market is on George St between Regent and Saint John Sts. It's open Saturday

NEW BRUNSWICK

from 6 am to noon. A secondary opening with not as much activity is on Wednesday evening beginning at 4.30 pm. On Saturday there are nearly 150 stalls selling fresh fruit, vegetables, meat and cheese, and also handicrafts, homemade desserts and flowers. There is a restaurant here, too, open for breakfast and brunch.

Conserver House
Near the corner of Brunswick St, at 180 Saint John St, is this house (☎ 458-8747) dating from 1890, now used as a model and information centre for energy conservation. Tours and advice are free. The house is open Monday to Friday from 9 am to 5 pm.

NB Power Electricity Museum
If you got a charge from Conserver House, a visit to the museum (☎ 458-6805) at 514 Queen St will be worthwhile. Rather than the future and latest technologies, displays here feature primarily antique and obsolete equipment from the early days of electricity onwards. See what previous generations used to wash clothes and cook dinner. It's open July through August 9 am to 9 pm Monday through Friday, 10 am to 5 pm Saturday and noon to 4 pm Sunday.

Parks
In addition to the riverfront park and several smaller city parks, you can visit the following two. **Odell Park**, south-west of the downtown centre off Smythe St, covers 175 hectares and contains some primeval provincial forest. There are picnic tables, a kids' zoo and walking paths. **Killarney Lake Park** is about five km from town over the Westmorland St Bridge. A spring-fed lake is used for swimming and fishing.

Tula Farm
A 20-minute drive west of Fredericton on the Trans Canada Hwy leads to the impressive Tula sustainable agriculture education centre (☎ 459-1851). At the 29-acre project on Keswick Ridge overlooking the Saint John River Valley, visitors can witness ecologically sound farming practices along a self-guided interpretive trail. Wearing boots or other suitable footwear is suggested. From the Mactaquac/Keswick Ridge turn-off from the Trans Canada Hwy, cross the dam and take the first right onto Route 105. Take a second left onto McKeen Drive and look for the large 'Tula Farm' sign.

Activities
Rent a canoe for drifting along the river. In town, they're available is Fredericton Lighthouse (☎ 459-2515) at Regent St Wharf, which has boats for $5 an hour or $24 a day. You can also rent canoes at Hartt Island Campground (☎ 450-6057) west of the city on the Trans Canada Hwy. Canoes here go for $7.70 an hour or $30 a day.

The Small Craft Aquatic Centre (☎ 458-5513) has canoes, kayaks and rowing skulls for rent. The centre also offers guided canoe tours from one hour to three-day river ecology trips and instruction in either canoeing or kayaking. Two-hour paddles depart daily during the summer at 2 pm and are $25 for the first person, $20 for the second. Call for the full range of options on getting out on the river and maybe spotting some of the wildlife.

There are free swimming pools at Henry Park and Queen Square. There is a small admission fee to use the swimming pools at the YM-YWCA, 28 Saunders St.

Organised Tours
Throughout July and August, a member of an actors' group wearing a historic costume leads a good free one-hour walking tour around town, beginning at City Hall, four times a day. Ask at the tourist office for exact times.

From the City Hall you can also catch an hour-long city bus tour. The Fredericton Transit bus takes visitors through the downtown area, the campus of the University of New Brunswick and outlying areas of the city. The English tour departs daily at 1 pm, the French at 3 pm. The cost is $5 per adult or $12 for a family.

Finally, to see Fredericton from the water, call Checker Charters (☎ 452-0200) which has riverfront cruises on the Saint John River that range from two hours ($15) to all day. The tour boat is basically a houseboat and is docked at Regent St Wharf.

Festivals

Fredericton is a centre of the old craft of pewtersmithing. Examples can be seen any time of year at Aitkens Pewter, downtown at 81 Regent St, or you can arrange tours of the main plant there. Other craftspeople in the town do pottery and woodcarving. Some of the major events and festivals celebrated in the province between July and September are listed here.

NB Highland Games Festival – This two-day Scottish festival with music, dancing and contests is held each summer in late July.

Canadian National New Brunswick Day Canoe Race – This race is held annually in early August in the Mactaquac Headpond.

New Brunswick Summer Music Festival – Four days of classical music held at Memorial Hall at the University of New Brunswick campus in late August.

Handicraft Show – This free provincial handicraft show is held at Mactaquac Park on the weekend before Labour Day. All types of handicrafts are exhibited and sold.

The Fredericton Exhibition – This annual six-day affair starts on Labour Day. It's held at the exhibition grounds, on the corner of Smythe and Saunders Sts. The exhibition includes a farm show, a carnival, harness racing and stage shows.

Harvest Jazz & Blues Festival – This event transforms the downtown area into the 'New Orleans of the North' in early September when jazz, blues and Dixieland performers arrive from across North America.

Places to Stay

Camping The best place nearby is *Mactaquac Provincial Park* (☎ 363-3011), 20 km west off the Trans Canada Hwy on Hwy 105, on the north side of the river. There are 334 sites and a tent site costs $14. Also within the campground is a swimming beach, grocery store and a kitchen shelter. *Lake George Family Campground* (☎ 366-2933), 12 km south of the Trans Canada Hwy, via Route 635 and Route 636, on Lake George, has tent sites at $11, full-hook-ups

$13. The campground has a nice beach area as well as laundry facilities and a small store.

The closest campground to Fredericton is *Hartt Island Campground* (☎ 450-6057) 10 km west of the city on the Trans Canada. This is more like an amusement park as there are water slides, mini-golf course, batting cages, something called 'Bankshot Basketball', and, oh yea, camp sites. Tent sites are $17, full-service sites $22 a night.

South-east 30 km from town is the *Sunbury Oromocto Provincial Park* (☎ 357-3708) campground on Waterville Rd at French Lake, off Hwy 7.

Hostels Unfortunately, the HI hostel on York St closed down in 1995 due to budget problems. When or if it reopens is anybody's guess. The *University of New Brunswick* (☎ 453-4891) rents single and double rooms in the dorms, available from mid-May to mid-August. For tourists singles/doubles are $29/41, and for students the price drops to $13/24. Contact the Director of Housing at the above number. Facilities include a pool. The campus is within walking distance of the downtown area in a south-east direction.

Hotels & Tourist Homes There isn't a vast selection of budget places in town, but the ones that exist are good.

The *Manger Inn* (☎ 454-3410) is the nice yellow-and-black house at 269 Saunders St. This is a tree-lined residential street three blocks south of Brunswick St. Rates are $35 singles, one bed (two people) $40, two beds (two people) $45; kitchen facilities are available at an additional cost.

The *Carriage House Inn* (☎ 452-9924 or 800-267-6068) is over at 230 University Ave, also central but more expensive at $55/59 and breakfast is served in the solarium of this nice turn-of-the-century home. There's a shared TV room.

Moving upmarket, the venerable *Lord Beaverbrook* (☎ 455-3371), at 659 Queen St, is relatively moderate for a place of its class at $79/89. It has 165 rooms with all the amenities used mainly by business people and government officials. Fredericton's most impressive hotel is the *Sheraton Inn* (☎ 457-7000) at 225 Woodstock near Wilmont Park. Overlooking the Saint John River, this 223-room hotel often has room specials during the summer for $85 a night.

Motels The bulk of the city's accommodation is in motels around the edges of town.

On the west side of town on Rural Route 6, which is the Trans Canada Hwy West, there are several places. The *Roadside Motel* (☎ 450-2080) is along this strip with singles/doubles $40/45. Some rooms, however, are too close to the highway for a good night's sleep. On the east side of town across the river on Rural Route 8 (also known as Hwy 2 or the Trans Canada Hwy for Moncton) is the *Norfolk Motel* (☎ 472-3278) where rooms are only $31/34.

The *Comfort Inn by Journey's End Motel* (☎ 453-0800), part of a widespread chain, is at 255 Prospect St, one block north of the Trans Canada Hwy towards town off Regent St, and rooms start at $69. There are a few places to eat within walking distance.

The *Town & Country Motel* (☎ 454-4223) at 967 Woodstock Rd, about two km south from the Trans Canada Hwy, offers singles for $45 and doubles for $50 with views of the river.

Across the river in North Fredericton *Fort Nashwaak Motel* (☎ 472-4411) at 15 Riverside Drive has good views, singles for $38 and housekeeping units or individual cabins at $50 a double.

Places to Eat
There has been a small explosion of outdoor cafes and restaurants featuring outdoor decks in Fredericton. The best place to head for supper and fresh air is Pipers Lane, a courtyard of sorts between King St and Queen, west of York St. Surrounding this open area are almost a dozen restaurants, coffee shops, pubs and ice-cream parlours, half of them with outdoor seating.

Located in Pipers Lane is *Dimitri's*, good for an inexpensive Greek lunch or dinner of souvlakia, pita, brochettes, moussaka and the like. A plate of moussaka is $8.95 and

you can enjoy it on the restaurant's rooftop patio. Also featuring outdoor dining in this area is *Le Cafe* for Lebanese, Italian and Spanish dishes, and *Trumpers Vegetarian Foods*.

More outdoor dining can be enjoyed at *Mexicali Rosa's* at 546 King St and at *The Lunar Rogue*, a 'maritime pub' at 625 King which has British ales on tap and a nice selection of sandwiches and burgers from $4 to $6.

The *M&T Deli*, a small but comfortable and casual delicatessen with an interesting noticeboard, sits at the bottom of Regent St at No 62. It serves all the standards, including smoked meat from Ben's, the famous deli in Montreal. Various sandwiches, salads and quiches are served at the stools for about $4.25 and up. It's not open on Sunday.

On Queen St in the centre by the post office is the *Bar-be-que Barn*, which hops with locals at lunch time and in the evening. A plate of baby-back ribs here will set you back $9 but fill you up. They also have a children's menu.

Mei's, at 73 Carleton St, is the best Chinese restaurant in the city and is even open on Sunday until 10 pm. It offers some Sichuan-style dishes and have some combination plates (egg roll, fried rice and main course) for $6.50. Most full dinners run $11 to $14.

In the enclosed King's Place shopping mall on the corner of Brunswick and York Sts is *Crispins* which has cheap cafeteria-style lunches and shares a large eating area with the adjoining *McDonald's*.

For a tea try *Keay's*, at 72 York St, a sort of old-style counter eatery in a fruit market. For a café au lait head to *Cafe du Monde*, a quaint little restaurant on Queen St, kitty-corner to Officers Square. The restaurant adorns its walls with art and its menu with an interesting selection of salads, soups and vegetarian sandwiches and dishes. Dinners range from $9 to $14.

Away from the centre near the Trans Canada Hwy, the Fredericton Mall on Prospect St West off Regent St South has *Sobey's* grocery store and a liquor outlet.

Entertainment

Jocks and other sport freaks have their choice of sport bars in Fredericton, including two; *Upper Deck Sports Bar* and *Level II*, in Piper's Lane. Both have cheap beer, lots of billiards and live music on the weekends. At 625 King St is the *The Lunar Rogue*, a pub which presents live music on Thursday, Friday and Saturday.

The University of New Brunswick often has concerts and folk performers. Cheap films are also shown at the university in the Tilley Hall Auditorium.

Live stage performances can be enjoyed at the *Playhouse Theatre* (☎ 453-4697) on 686 Queen St. Most performances begin at 8 pm, Tuesday through Sunday in summer.

Getting There & Away

Air Fredericton is a small city, but as the provincial capital it does get a fair bit of air traffic. Many flights in and out are stopovers between various other points. Air Canada (☎ 458-8561) serves the city and has one nonstop flight daily from Toronto.

Bus The SMT bus station (☎ 458-6000) is on the corner of Regent and Brunswick Sts. Schedules and fares to some destinations include: Moncton at 11.05 am and 6 pm daily ($25); Quebec City via Campbellton at 3:05 and 8.15 pm ($60); Halifax, the same as Moncton ($60); and Amherst, which is also same as Moncton ($34).

Car For car rentals, Budget (☎ 452-1107) is at 407 Regent St. Their rate is $39 a day with 100 free km. Weekly rates with 1000 free km start at $227.

Delta (☎ 458-8899), at 304 King St, is slightly cheaper at $36 a day with 100 free km, then 14 cents per km. There is also a good weekend package available.

Getting Around

The Airport The airport is 16 km south-east of town. Arrange for a taxi from the Lord Beaverbrook Hotel and the rate is only $6.50. Plan on departing the hotel 60 minutes before flight time. Otherwise a taxi to the airport costs around $20.

Bus The city has a good system, Fredericton Transit (☎ 454-6287), and the $1 fares include free transfers.

The university is a 15-minute walk from the downtown area; if you want to take the bus, take No 16S south on Regent St. It runs about every 20 minutes.

For hitching on the Trans Canada Hwy you want the Fredericton Mall bus, which is also the Nos 16S or 11S.

For heading back into the city from these places catch the No 16N.

Bicycle Rentals are available at Key Cycle (☎ 458-8985) at 449 King St or Radical Edge (☎ 459-3478) on Queen St. You can also rent bikes at the Regent St Wharf from Checker Charter (☎ 451-0051) for $5 an hour or $25 a day and then load them on its cruise ship to be dropped along the Saint John River. There are bike paths on either side of the river that will return you to the downtown area. One-way fare is $2, bicycles are an extra $1.

AROUND FREDERICTON

Gagetown

A 45-minute drive from Fredericton is Gagetown, a charming little village located on the banks of Gagetown Creek just down from its confluence with the Saint John and Jemseg rivers. Founded shortly after the 1758 Moncton expedition drove the French settlers from the lower Saint John River Valley, Gagetown is one of the oldest English settlements in the area. Today the town is something of an artist's haven and supports almost a dozen galleries, pottery shops and **Loomcrofters**, the renowned weaving studio housed in a former British trunk house built in 1761. The studio (☎ 488-2400) is open daily during the summer from 10 am to 5 pm and inside you can watch looms weaving material that is sold as tartans, scarves, stoles and ties among other items.

Gagetown also serves as the gateway to what is commonly referred to as 'Ferry

Land'. Six small ferries, all of them free, operate in the lower Saint John River system and make for an interesting tour of this rural area. One of them operates at the south end of Gagetown, crossing the Saint John River from 6 am to midnight daily.

There are some good restaurants and places to stay that make spending a day here well worth it. *Loaves & Calico* (☎ 488-3018) is both an excellent cafe and an inn. Most dinners are about $9 and can only be topped by a slice of the restaurant's home-made pie. Rooms are $30/40. More up-market is *Steamer's Stop Inn* (☎ 488-2903), a large colonial-style home over-looking the river. The seven rooms are $55 to $65 for a double and include a full breakfast. Dinners range from $15 to $22. Just south of Gage-town on Hwy 102 in Queenstown is *Broadview B&B* (☎ 488-2266), offering rooms on a working farm for $35/ 45. There is also a restaurant here with the biggest portions in the valley. The roast beef dinner, which includes homemade soup, vegetables, juice, dessert and a endless supply of hot rolls, is $11.

A great way to see Ferry Land would be by bicycle. You can rent them at Steamers Stop Inn or from Ferry Land Adventures (☎ 488-3263). Make sure not to confuse this historic village with Gagetown, the largest military base in the country which is located nearby in Oromocto.

Sussex

Sussex is a small country town in the middle of some pastoral and productive dairy lands. Fortunately all the local cows aren't the size of the one seen on the outskirts of town.

On Hwy 2 at the exit into the centre is **Kings County Tourist Office** run by volunteer seniors and open from 9 am to 8 pm daily during the summer. In town one of the streets, Queen St, has been somewhat remodelled and is reminiscent of earlier decades. It's off Main St opposite the VIA Rail station. Here you'll find the licensed *Broadway Cafe*, a little sanctuary from the standard small-town greasy spoons, offering good, inexpensive lunch specials in a com-

fortable and casual atmosphere complete with an outdoor garden terrace. If nothing else, have a slice of the chocolate cheesecake with a café au lait. It's also open for breakfasts and until 9 pm Friday and Saturday. A breakfast bargain can be obtained at *Main Street Diner Cafe*, 600 Main St. It opens at 7 am and two eggs and toast is $2.20, a full breakfast with ham and homefries $3.

In town there is *Blue Bird Motel* (☎ 433-2557), across the street from the King County Tourism Office with singles/doubles for $46/52. Just to the east on Hwy 2 is *Pine Cone Motel* (☎ 433-3958), good at $45/49 and it has a campground.

The surrounding King's County has 17 of the appealing old wooden covered bridges often situated so prettily they look like pictures from a calendar. One, the 1908 Salmon River Bridge, is just five minutes north of the tourism office on Hwy 890. Five more are a short drive from Hwy 1 on the way to Saint John. If you have a spare afternoon, pick up the covered bridge map from the tourism office (you're going to need it) and then tour the country side looking for a dozen or so.

Mactaquac Provincial Park

Twenty-two km west of Fredericton is New Brunswick's biggest provincial park (☎ 363-3011). It runs along the 100-km-long pond formed by the Mactaquac Power Dam. The park offers swimming, fishing, picnic sites, camping and boat rentals. There's also a golf course where you can rent all equipment. The campground is huge at 334 sites but also busy and through much of the summer it will be full on the weekends. There is a $3 vehicle fee just to enter the park while camping is $14 a night for tents and $16 for sites with electricity.

Mactaquac Power Dam

The Mactaquac Dam across the park is responsible for creating the small lake and therefore the park's location. Its 400,000 kilowatt output is the largest in the Maritime Provinces. Free tours, lasting about 45 minutes, include a look at the turbines and an explanation of how they work. The gen-

Bald eagles can reach one metre in length and live along rivers, large lakes and tidewater

erating station (☎ 363-3071) is open seven days a week from 9 am to 4 pm.

Woolastock Wildlife Park

Just a few km west of the Mactaquac Park, Woolastock Wildlife Park (☎ 363-2352) is open daily from 9 am to 9 pm. The 1200-acre park has a collection of Canadian animals, many typical of this region. You'll see moose, bears, wolves, coyotes, foxes, caribou, hawks, owls and more. There are also some water slides, picnic areas and camping spots. If you camp, you get a discount on the ticket to the wildlife section. It's $13.50 for a tent site, $15 for electricity. Admission into the wildlife park is $5.75 for an adult and $18 for the family.

King's Landing Historical Settlement

The settlement (☎ 363-5090) is 37 km west of Fredericton, on the way to Woodstock. Take exit 259 off the Trans Canada Hwy. Here you can get a glimpse of (and taste) pioneer life in the Maritimes. A community of 100 costumed staff inhabits 11 houses, a school, church, store and sawmill typical of those used a century ago. The *King's Head Inn* serves traditional foods and beverages.

The settlement is open all year. From July through to Labour Day in September the opening hours are from 10 am to 6 pm daily. The rest of the year, it closes an hour earlier at 5 pm. Admission is $8 per adult and $20 for a family. A good tip to consider is that the ticket for King's Landing entitles you to free entrance to the Acadian Historic Village near the town of Caraquet.

Saint Croix Waterway Recreation Area

This area of 336 sq km is south-west of Fredericton near the Maine (USA) border. The town of McAdam is pretty much the commercial centre of this little-developed territory of woods and lakes. In McAdam itself, check out the Canadian Pacific train station dating from 1900. It's one of the finest in Canada and was made a National Historic Site in 1983.

Sixteen km from McAdam is **Spednic Provincial Park**, with rustic camping and access to some of the Chiputneticook chain of lakes. The Saint Croix River is good for whitewater canoeing. Other canoe routes connect lakes, and about 100 km of hiking trails wind through the area. There's another campground at Wauklehegan.

Fundy Shore

Almost the entire southern edge of the province is presided over by the ever-present, constantly rising and falling, always impressive waters of the Bay of Fundy.

The fascinating shoreline, the English-style resort town of St Andrews, the quiet Fundy Isles, the city of Saint John and the Fundy National Park make this easily one of the most appealing and varied regions of New Brunswick.

ST STEPHEN

Right at the US border across the river from Calais in Maine, St Stephen is a busy entry point for US visitors coming east. It's a small, old town that forms the northern link of what is known as the Quoddy Loop – a circular tour around south-eastern New Brunswick and north-western Maine around Passamaquoddy Bay. From St Stephen the loop route goes to St Andrews, St George and then goes on to Deer Island and lastly to Campobello Island which is connected by bridge to Maine. It's a popular trip taking anywhere from a day to a week, and includes some fine seaside scenery, interesting history and a number of pleasant, easy-going resort-style towns.

In St Stephen the Festival of International Cooperation is held in August with concerts, parades and street fairs. Note that there is a duty-free shop for alcohol and cigarette bargains opposite the Canadian Customs building.

St Stephen also has quite a reputation as a chocolate mecca due to being the home of **Ganong's** (a family chocolate business since 1873), whose products are known all around eastern Canada. Some say the chocolate bar was invented by the Ganong brothers and they are credited for developing the heart-shaped box of chocolates now seen everywhere on Valentine's Day. You can visit the old factory on the main street of town, Milltown Blvd. It's just a store now with not much to see but plenty to buy ranging from boxed chocolates to bars such as Pal O' Mine, a very sweet little number. The modern factory is away from the centre towards St Andrews on Chocolate Drive near the Charlotte Mall. It is not open to visitors and there are no tours except during the annual Chocolate Fest which occurs in August. The Ganong's Store is open daily during the summer and until 8 pm on weekdays.

Around the bay, a little north and west of St Stephen, on the border is **Salmon Falls Park**. This delightful little spot overlooks the rapids in the Saint Croix River and a fish ladder that assists spawning salmon to continue upstream. A gravel path connects the park to **Generating Station Park**, site of a former cotton mill. Both overlook Milltown Generating Station, one of the continent's oldest hydroelectric plants, operated by Power NB. Free tours are given from 1 June to 31 August, 9 am to 4.30 pm daily at which time you can view the plant's famed 'rope drive'.

Nearby at 443 Milltown Blvd, 2.8 km from the border-crossing, is the **Charlotte County Museum** with exhibits concerning the history of 200 years of settlement including the Loyalists and other ties with the USA. There are displays on shipbuilding and lumbering as well as other local industries. The museum (☎ 466-3295), an impressive mansion built in 1864, is open from 9.30 am to 4.30 pm Monday through Saturday during the summer.

Near the corner of Prince William St and King St, next to the Loyalist Burial Grounds, is a large tourist office for all of New Brunswick that is open daily until 8 pm and includes currency exchange.

Along Kings St towards the turn-off for Fredericton or St Andrews you pass a number of motels. The *Busy Bee Motel and Cabins* (☎ 466-2938) is the least expensive with some rooms for $30.

For a place to eat on Kings St try *Carman's Diner* or *McNay's White House* nearby where breakfasts of two eggs, homefries, toast and coffee are $3 and large subs are under $5.

ST ANDREWS-BY-THE-SEA

As its name suggests, this is a summer resort of some tradition and gentility. Together with a fine climate and picturesque beauty, St Andrews has a long, charming and often visible history – it's one of the oldest towns in the province and for a long period was on equal terms with Saint John.

History

The original group of Native Indians were the Passamaquoddies, very few of whom still live in the area.

White settlement began in 1783 after the American Revolution. Many British pioneers, wanting to remain loyal, deserted their new towns and set up home in the British territory around the fort in Castine, Maine – a very pretty area.

The new British-American border was changed and these people once again found themselves on American soil. The tip of the bay across the water was scouted and agreed

upon as being a place of equal beauty. So the pioneers loaded up ships and headed out, some even dragging their houses on rafts behind them, and St Andrews was founded in 1784.

Prosperity came first with shipbuilding and, when that was dying, continued with tourism. Oceanic research is now also a prominent industry. In the early part of the century, the Canadian Pacific Railway owned and ran the Algonquin Hotel, which more or less started St Andrews as a retreat. Soon moneyed Canadians and US citizens were building luxurious summer cottages alongside the 19th-century mansions of the lumber and shipbuilding barons. Nearly 100 of the beautiful houses first built or brought here from Maine are still used and maintained in excellent condition.

Orientation & Information

Water St, the main street, is lined with restaurants, souvenir and craft shops and some

A Native Indian family in traditional dress

places to stay. King St is the main cross-street; one block from Water St, Queen St is also important. There is an information office (☎ 466-4858) near the junction of Hwys 1 and 127 that is open 10 am to 6 pm daily in the summer. A second centre (☎ 529-3000) is in town at 89 Reed Ave, next to the arena and is open daily from 8 am to 8 pm.

Walking Tour

There are more than 200 houses over a century old in town, many marked with plaques. Pick up the walking guide from the tourist office – it includes a map and brief description of 34 particularly interesting places.

Algonquin Hotel

Also worth a look is the classic 1899 resort hotel with its veranda, gardens, tennis courts and pool. Inside, off the lobby, are a couple of places for a drink, be it tea or gin.

Opposite the hotel you may want to take a peek at the English-style thatched-roof cottage called Pansy Patch with its surrounding garden. Sometimes called 'the most photographed house in New Brunswick', Pansy Patch (☎ 529-3834) is now a rather high-priced bed and breakfast with rooms that begin at $85.

Blockhouse Historic Site

The restored wooden guardhouse (☎ 529-4270) is the only one left of several that were built here for protection in the War of 1812 and it almost didn't survive the 20th century. In 1993 arsonists set fire to the historical structure, resulting in the floors and ceiling being rebuilt out of white pine. The original hand-hewn walls survived and are the darker timber inside. Structures like this were easy to construct, practical to live in, and strong enough to withstand most attacks. The blockhouse is open daily during summer. Admission is free, and there are some good views through the gun holes on the 2nd floor. The park is at the north-west end of Water St. If the tide is out, there is a path that extends from the blockhouse out across the tidal flats that makes an interesting walk.

Huntsman Aquarium Museum

Out past the Blockhouse and then the Fisheries & Oceans Biological Station is the Huntsman Marine Science Centre (☎ 529-1202) with research facilities and labs. It's part of the Federal Fisheries Research Centre – St Andrews' most important business. Some of Canada's leading marine biologists work here.

The Huntsman lab also maintains its Aquarium Museum, that features displays of most specimens found in the local waters, including seals. There is a good seaweed display and one pool where the various creatures can be touched, even picked up. The high point of the day at the museum is feeding of the centre's harbour seals in a large tank, usually done at 11 am and 4 pm. It's quite interesting and great for kids. The centre, west of town on Brandy Cove Rd, is open daily from May to October and until 6 pm in July and August. Admission is $4 for adults, $2.75 for children.

Ross Memorial Museum

The Ross Memorial Museum (☎ 529-1824) is in a neoclassical house of some size on the corner of King and Montague Sts, downtown. It features the furniture, metal objects and decorative arts collections of its former owners, Mr & Mrs Ross, who lived in the house until 1945. It's open Tuesday through Saturday 10 am to 4.30 pm Tuesday through Saturday, and 1.30 to 4.30 pm Sunday. Admission is by donation.

Sheriff Andrew House

On the corner of King and Queen Sts is this restored middle-class home (☎ 529-5080) dating from 1820 and now redecorated in period style and attended by costumed guides. The back garden is also typical of this past era. It's open 9.30 am to 4.30 pm daily except on Sunday when hours are from 1 to 4.30 pm. Admission is free.

Sunbury Shores Arts & Nature Centre

This is a non-profit educational and cultural centre (☎ 529-3386) offering instruction in painting, weaving, pottery and other crafts in summer, as well as natural science courses. Various changing exhibits run through the summer. It is based in Centennial House, an old general store at 139 Water St. Hours are 8.30 am to 5 pm Monday through Friday and 1 to 4.30 pm Saturday and Sunday.

The centre also maintains a nearby conservation area with a walking trail, located off Water St past the Blockhouse.

Science-by-the-Sea Kiosk
Opened in 1994, this roadside exhibit showcases the scientific and historical wealth of the St Andrews area and directs you to local points of interest. It's located at Indian Point, not far from Passamaquoddy Park, and includes a telescope from which you can view much of the bay including Minister's Island.

Minister's Island Historic Site
Minister's Island was bought and used as a summer retreat by William Cornelius van Horne, builder of the Canadian Pacific Railway across the country and the company's first president and later chairman of the board. The island, his cottage of 50 rooms and the unusual bathhouse with it tidal swimming pool can now be visited.

Minister's Island is accessible at low tide, even by car, when you can drive on the hard-packed sea floor. A few hours later this route is under three metres of water. You can only visit the island on a guided tours through Friends of Minister's Island (☎ 529-5081). The two-hour tours are offered once or twice a day, depending on the tides, and the times are listed in the tourism office. Meet at the end of Bar Rd, off of Hwy 127 to Saint John, where a guide then leads the caravan across the tidal flats. The cost is $5 per person and you have to have your own vehicle.

Atlantic Salmon Centre
North of town about six km, in the village of Chamcook, the Salmon Centre (☎ 529-4581) tells the story of Atlantic salmon, prized by anglers and gourmets. Displays, including live fish, show the fish's history and life cycle. The centre's open from May to September daily, 10 am to 6 pm, and admission is $1.

Dochet's Island
In the Saint Croix River, eight km from town on Hwy 127, is Dochet's Island with a National Historic Site marking the place where in 1604 French explorer Samuel de Champlain spent his first winter in North America. The island itself is inaccessible without a boat, but looking at it from the shore makes an excuse for a good, quick sunset drive. There is also a plaque on the Maine shoreline across from the island.

Organised Tours
Whale-Watching Tours Two companies run whale-watching trips from the town wharf. Because the waters best for whale-watching are further out in the bay, it's better to take this tour from either Deer Island or Campobello if you happen to be visiting those places, where you'll spend more time actually watching the whales. In St Andrews, Fundy Tide Runners (☎ 529-4481) use a 24-foot Zodiac boat to zip you around on the bay. A pair of three-hour tours are offered daily and the cost is $40 per person. Quoddy Linke Marine (☎ 529-2600) has a more conventional and slower boat and charges $35 for its three-hour tour.

Kayaking Seascape Kayak Tours (☎ 529-4866) is a St Andrews-based outfitter that offers a variety of paddle trips, including half-day tours ($50) and extended overnight trips in the area.

Places to Stay
As a small but busy resort town St Andrews has plentiful accommodation with quite a range in type and price including many guesthouses and B&Bs. Motels can be found on Reed Ave and Mowat Drive.

Camping At the far east end of town on Indian Point is *Passamaquoddy Park* (☎ 529-3439) run by the Kiwanis Club, for tents and trailers. A tent site is $12 a night, electricity $17.

Near St Andrews are two provincial parks with beaches. *Oak Bay* (☎ 466-7552) is eight km east of St Stephen, north of St Andrews. There is a protected bay where the water warms up nicely for ocean swimming and there's interesting shoreline to explore at low tide. There is also *Island View Camping* (☎ 529-3787), on Hwy 127 from St Stephen, where tent sites have a nice overview of the St Croix River and are $15 a night.

B&Bs & Hotels The central *Heritage Guesthouse* (☎ 529-3875) is a modest but very appealing place at 100 Queen St that has been serving guests for many years. It is about average at $45/47. Breakfasts are offered. At 159 Water St is *McNabb House* (☎ 529-4368) with three rooms and charging about the same rates.

Away from the bustle of the downtown area is *The Mulberry* (☎ 529-4948) at 96 Water St. This colonial home has a pleasant porch and three rooms for rent. Rates begin at $45 and include a full breakfast. At the *Hanson House* (☎ 529-5947), a block off Water St at 62 Edward St, rooms begin at $40 a night and there are bicycles for the guests to use.

The *Shiretown Inn* (☎ 529-8877), 218 Water St, run by Best Western, has been a hotel since 1881 and now is a blend of the old with modern conveniences and a dining room. It's right in the middle of town and is a little pricier with doubles from $68.

The classic Canadian Pacific-run *Algonquin Resort Hotel* (☎ 529-8823) has rooms that start at $123 (you pay for the charm and the amenities). A walk through the lobby or maybe a drink on the porch will give non-guests a sense of the atmosphere.

The more affordable motels lie on the edge of town. Practically next door to each other are *Blue Moon Motel* (☎ 529-3245) and *Greenside Motel* (☎ 529-3039) on Hwy 127

Whales

Whales, the great mammals of the depths, first re-discovered by non-hunters in California then later up the coast in British Columbia, have now become major attractions around Atlantic Canada. Tours out to sea to photograph the awesome creatures depart from ports in places ranging from Quebec's Gulf of St Lawrence to Newfoundland's east coast. From most accounts, the trips are generally successful and well worth the uniformly reasonable cost, averaging $25 for a couple of hours.

Some of the best areas for such a trip are around the Bay of Fundy islands in New Brunswick or from the tip of Digby Neck in Nova Scotia. Also in Nova Scotia the north shore of Cape Breton up around the national park is good. Over in Newfoundland, Notre Dame Bay is 'fruitful', with some tours based out of Twillingate. Whales can even be seen up and down the coast out of St John's from where more tours originate.

In the St Lawrence River, Quebec, boat tours operate in the Saguenay River area. Although the huge blue, finback and minke whales are seen here, probably the principal species is the beluga, whose numbers are declining alarmingly due to horrendous pollution levels. Regulations now suggest that no boat approach belugas too closely as these whales have enough problems to deal with.

So you're much better off in the Bay of Fundy or on the open ocean in one of the Atlantic Provinces. Around the Grand Manan region the most commonly seen whales are the fin (or finback), one of the world's largest at 20 metres; the humpback (12 metres); the right (12 metres and less commonly seen); and the minke (eight metres). In addition porpoises and dolphins are plentiful. In this area the best whale-watching begins in early August and lasts until September.

From Westport at the tip of Digby Neck the season seems to begin a little earlier with good sightings reported in late June although by mid-July there are good numbers of all species.

The humpback, one of the larger whales of the east coast, is the one to put on the best show, breaching and diving with tail clearly visible above the surface.

Up around Cape Breton and in Newfoundland the smaller pilot or pothead whales, also sometimes known as blackwhales, are common and they're sometimes even seen from shore. Finbacks frequent these waters as well. Operators in these regions run trips in July and August.

Regardless of the weather or time of year take plenty of clothing, perhaps something for seasickness, and lots of film. ■

East (also known as Mowat Dr). Both have singles/doubles for $45/55.

Places to Eat

Right in the middle of town with a pleasant patio overlooking the boats in the harbour, the *Smuggler's Wharf* has a bit of everything but a lot of seafood. The stuffed sole ($9.95)

is worth trying. The best seafood chowder in town is at *Dalton's Fruit and Produce Co* on Water St. A huge bowl of the spicy chowder comes with bread and crackers and sets you back only $4.95. You can enjoy it on the outdoor patio.

For a burger and a dose of Elvis, there's *Chef Cafe* at 180 Water St with it's 1950s decor and classic juke box. The place is open

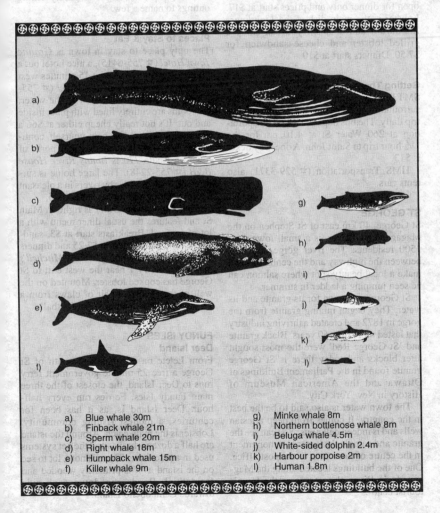

a)	Blue whale 30m	g)	Minke whale 8m
b)	Finback whale 21m	h)	Northern bottlenose whale 8m
c)	Sperm whale 20m	i)	Beluga whale 4.5m
d)	Right whale 18m	j)	White-sided dolphin 2.4m
e)	Humpback whale 15m	k)	Harbour porpoise 2m
f)	Killer whale 9m	l)	Human 1.8m

24 hours during the summer and the big selection of hamburgers start at $6.

More upmarket, the *Shiretown Inn*, dating from 1881, is a very well-kept place and has more expensive seafood meals. During lunch you can dine on the porch and watch the traffic on Water St. Perhaps the best meals are at the cosy *L'Europe*, a German-style white stucco place on King St which is open for dinner only and prices start at $17. Lobster is the main dish at the *Lighthouse Restaurant* and at lunch you can enjoy a grilled lobster and cheese sandwich for $7.50. Dinners start at $10.

Getting There & Around

SMT Bus Lines connects St Andrews and the surrounding area to Saint John with one bus trip daily. The bus departs HMS Transportation at 260 Water St at 4.10 pm for the 1½-hour trip to Saint John. A one-way ticket is $13.

HMS Transportation (☎ 529-3371) also rents cars.

ST GEORGE

St George, 40 km east of St Stephen on the Magaguadavic River, is a small town with 1500 residents. The river gorge and falls between the highway and the centre of town make a local beauty spot where salmon can be seen jumping a ladder in summer.

St George is known for its granite and its water. They began mining granite from the gorge in 1872 and created a thriving industry that lasted more than 60 years. Black granite and 'St George Red' were the most sought after blocks and today there is St George granite found in the Parliament Buildings of Ottawa and the American Museum of History in New York City.

The town water is also said to be the best in the country. It comes from deep artesian wells and is indeed delicious. You can see the granite and sample the water at a monument in the centre of town next to the post office. One of the buildings located along the Magaguadavic River also serves as the town's tourist centre.

Organised Tours

The Outdoor Adventure Company (☎ 755-2007 or 800-365-3855) is located on Route 770 right along the Magaguadavic River. The company not only organises trips but also serves as a booking agency for several smaller tour operators. It offers guided kayak trips, cycling outings on Deer Island, whale-watching trips, sunset cruises and fly fishing outings to name a few.

Places to Stay & Eat

The only place to stay in town is *Granite Town Hotel* (☎ 755-6415), a nice hotel but a bit pricey at $69/76. About 15 minutes west of town is the *Fundy Lodge Motel* (☎ 755-2963). It has a pretty location on the water; the rooms are entirely lined with pine, inside and out. It's not really cheap either at $66 a double but includes a help-yourself continental breakfast. Roughly 10 km north of town on Route 770 is *Bonny River House B&B* (☎ 755-2248). The large home is surrounded on three sides by rivers in a pleasant country setting and rooms are $40/45.

Fred's Downtown Diner is right on Main St and features the usual diner menu with a lot of seafood. Breakfasts start at $3, sandwiches and hamburgers at $2.25 and dinners at $11. If you're camping nearby, *Mitchell's Seafood* on Hwy 1 near the west exit to St George has cooked lobster. Mounted on the wall of the shed is a pair of claws from a 25-pound lobster that look like footballs.

FUNDY ISLES
Deer Island

From Letete on the mainland south of St George a free 25-minute government ferry runs to Deer Island, the closest of the three main Fundy Isles. Ferries run every half-hour. Deer Island is, as it has been for centuries, a modest fishing community. Lobster is the main catch. Around the island are half a dozen wharves and the net systems used in aquaculture. There is not a lot to see on the island as it is primarily wooded and residential. Roads run down each side towards Campobello Island.

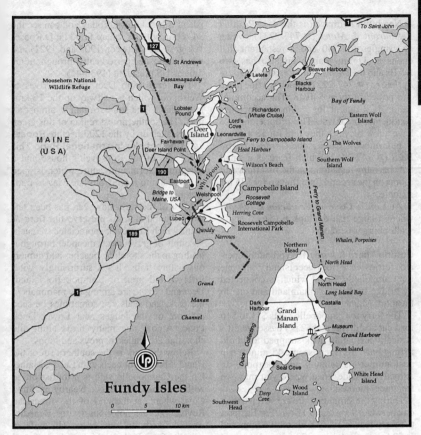

Fundy Isles

0   5   10 km

There is a tourist booth at the ferry landing. At **Northern Harbour** is a huge (it could well be the world's largest) lobster pound which at times contains 400 kg of live lobster.

At the other end of the island is 16-hectare **Deer Island Point Park** where whales and Old Sow, the world's second largest natural tidal whirlpool, can be seen offshore.

Whale-Watching Tours Whale watching is a popular activity from the islands. Cline Marine Charters (☎ 529-4188 or 747-2287), departing from Richardson on Deer Island, offers whale-watching tours at 8.30 am,

noon and 3.30 pm daily. The three-hour tours cost $40 per person. Cline Marine has offices in St Andrews and on Campobello Island as well. Three other operators, all on Grand Manan Island, also offer various whale cruises.

Places to Stay & Eat The best place to spend a night on the island is *Deer Island Point Park* (☎ 747-2423). You can set up your tent on the high bluff and spend an evening watching the Old Sow whirlpool. The campground includes showers, laundry facilities and even a small store. Tent sites are $12 a night.

Nearby in Fairhaven is the *45th Parallel Restaurant & Motel* (☎ 747-2231), which has singles for $40 and a restaurant that opens at 11 am. Fairhaven also has two B&Bs and the *Deer Island Log Guest House by the Sea* (☎ 747-2221) which is a fine place and priced fairly at $40/48. The accommodation is a quaint log cabin and includes continental breakfast. The proprietors also have a few bicycles they rent for $8 a day.

In Lambert's Cove is the *Gardner House B&B* (☎ 747-2462) which features a small but charming restaurant on the first floor and rooms on the second floor that go for $35 for a single.

At Lord's Cove is *Pendleton's Takeout* where a large fish & chips are $6.75 and a scallopburger is $2.95.

Getting There & Away Two privately operated ferries leave from Deer Island Point: one for Campobello Island which is connected by bridge to the USA mainland and one to Eastport, Maine.

The ferry to Campobello costs $11 to $16 for a car and driver and $2 per passenger. It's basically a floating dock strapped to an old fishing boat. It's a very scenic 45-minute trip past numerous islands and Eastport, an attractive seaside town where you may see freighters moored.

During the summer there are seven trips a day between 9 am and 6.15 pm. For Eastport the ferry leaves every hour on the hour and is $8 for car and driver, $2 for each passenger. Either ferry can be used as part of the circular Quoddy Loop tour around Passamaquoddy Bay through both Canada and the USA.

Campobello Island
Campobello is a gently scenic, tranquil island that has long been enjoyed by the wealthy as a summer retreat. Due to its accessibility and proximity to New England, the island has always felt as much a part of the USA as it does a part of Canada. Like many moneyed families, the Roosevelts bought property in this peaceful coastal area at the end of the 1800s and it is for this that the

island is best known. Today you can see the 34-room 'cottage' where Franklin D Roosevelt grew up (between 1905 and 1921) and which he visited periodically throughout his time as US president (1933-45).

The ferry from Deer Island arrives at Welshpool which is halfway up the 16-km-long island. The southern half is almost all park. The southernmost region of this green area is taken up by the 1200-hectare **Roosevelt Campobello International Park**. This is the site of the Roosevelt's house and a reception-information centre which is open daily 10 am to 6 pm from late May to mid-October.

Most of the park, however, has been left in its natural state to preserve the flora & fauna which Roosevelt appreciated so much. A couple of gravel roads meander through it leading to the shoreline, beaches and numerous nature trails. It's a surprisingly wild, little-visited area of Campobello Island. Deer and coyote are among the mammals in the park, and seals can sometimes be seen offshore on the ledges near Lower Duck Pond. Among the many birds along the shoreline are eagles, ospreys and loons.

Below the park at the southern tip of the island, a bridge connects with Lubec, Maine. On the Campobello side is a tourist office with currency exchange. Nearby is Snug Cove where, at the end of the American Revolution, the notorious traitor Benedict Arnold lived for four years. His wife, a socialite from Philadelphia, no doubt found life dull at Snug Cove, prompting the couple to move to Saint John in 1793.

Along the international park's northern boundary is New Brunswick's **Herring Cove Provincial Park**. Here too are several seaside walking trails and paths as well as a campground and a picnic area on an arching 1.6-km-long beach. It makes a fine, picturesque place for lunch.

Going up the island from Welshpool, **Wilson's Beach** has a large pier where fish can be bought, and a sardine-processing plant with an adjacent store. There are various services and shops here in the island's biggest community.

Head Harbour with its lighthouse at the northern tip of the island is the second busiest visitor spot. Whales can often be seen from here and many people put in some time sitting on the rocky shoreline with a pair of binoculars enjoying the sea breezes.

Cline Marine (☎ 529-4188), on Lighthouse Rd in Head Harbour, has a three hour whale-watching boat cruise daily at 9 am, 12.30 pm and 4 pm for $40 per person, as well as a one-hour sunset cruise at 7.30 pm.

Places to Stay There are a few places to stay in Welshpool as well as some cabins for rent at Wilson's Beach. Things tend to be pricier here than on the mainland. In Welshpool, the *Friar's Bay Motor Lodge* (☎ 752-2056) is reasonable at $30/36.

The *Quoddy View* (☎ 752-2981) has two cabins at Wilson's Beach from $50 and $55 each. The more expensive one has cooking facilities. *Herring Cove Provincial Park* (☎ 752-7010), on the north side of the island, has tent sites are $12 a night.

Grand Manan Island

South of Campobello Island, Grand Manan is the largest of the Fundy Isles – a quiet, peaceful, lovely, relaxed and interesting island. There is some spectacular coastal topography, excellent bird-watching, fine hiking trails, sandy beaches and a series of small fishing villages along this 30-km island. It's a marvellous place to spend a couple of days or a week away from the rest of the world observing nature.

On one side are ancient rock formations estimated to be billions of years old. On the other side, due to an underwater volcano, are volcanic deposits 16 million years old, a phenomenon which draws many geologists.

In 1831, James Audubon first documented the many birds which frequented the island. About 312 species, including puffins and Arctic terns, live or pass by each year, so bird watchers come in numbers as well. Offshore it's not uncommon to see whales feeding on the abundant herring and mackerel. Whale species include the humpback, finback (rorqual), minke and pothead.

Despite all this, the relative isolation and low-key development mean there are no crowds and little obvious commercialisation, making it a good place for cyclists.

One thing of possible interest to sample on the island is the dulce, an edible seaweed, for which Grand Manan Island is renowned. It's a very popular snack food around the Maritime provinces and most of it (and the best, say connoisseurs) comes from this island. Dulce is sold around the island mostly from people's homes. Watch for signs.

North Head The ferry terminal is at North Head. There are more business establishments in this village than elsewhere on the island but it is still small enough to walk through.

There are a few craft and tourist-oriented stores along the main drag but of most interest is the **Whale & Sea Bird Research Station** open daily from 10 am to 4 pm June through September, with a lot of good information on the marine life of the surrounding waters. Exhibits include skeletons and photographs and there are some books on whales and the island in general.

Ocean Search (☎ 662-8488) offers a different sort of whale-watching tour, using a sailing schooner, adding a marine biologist on board to answer questions and on some of the trips include an evening lecture. These upmarket, more in-depth tours are, naturally, more expensive than others but will be of interest to keen whale watchers. The seven-hour trips depart daily during the summer at 10 am, include lunch and are $70 for an adult, $35 for children.

Island Coast Boat Tour (☎ 662-8181) also runs trips from the North Head Fisherman's Wharf, offering four-hour whale-watching tours in a 12-metre vessel daily at 8 am and 12.30 pm July through September. The cost is $36.

North End Some of the most popular of the numerous short walking trails around the island are in this area, particularly the one to 'Hole in the Wall', an unusual rock formation. It begins north of North Head at the site of the old airport and leads through the woods to a natural arch at the cliff's edge. There are also great views of the coast from this vantage point.

Highly recommended is the somewhat pulse-quickening (especially in the fog) trail and suspension bridge out to the lighthouse at Swallow Tail on a narrow cliff-edged promontory. Further up-island, the rock formations (reaching 80 metres high at Seven Days' Work) and the lighthouse at Northern Head are also fine walks with seaside vistas. From either of the lighthouses whales may be seen, most easily on calm days when they break the surface most conspicuously.

Grand Harbour At Grand Harbour is the Grand Manan Museum (☎ 662-3524) open from mid-June to 30 September daily but only during the afternoon on Sunday. It has a marine section, displays on the island's geology, antiques and reminders of the Loyalist days, but the highlight is the stuffed-bird collection with examples of species seen on the island.

US writer Willa Cather worked here for many years and some of her personal belongings, including a typewriter, are still here. There is also a good book selection, including one on trails around the island. Bird checklists are available too. Admission is $2.25.

Dark Harbour This, the only village on the west side of the island, is the centre of the dulce industry. The seaweed is hand-picked at low tide along the shores of the island. It is then dried in the sun and is ready to eat.

Ross Island Uninhabited Ross Island can be visited at low tide. Or rather you can walk there at low tide, spend about four hours exploring the place, and then return before the tide gets too high. The island was the site of the first settlement on Grand Manan, established when Loyalists arrived from the USA in 1784.

Seal Cove In this small community is Sea Watch Tours (☎ 662-8552), one of the island's principal whale and bird-watching boat-tour companies. They've been around for 25 years and know the waters. Most of the trips are long (around six hours), so take lunch, an antimotion sickness pill and a warm sweater. Apart from whales there are seals and porpoises to see, a variety of sea birds and the coastal landscapes. Peak whale watching begins in early August and continues through September.

Down at the docks the tasty island-smoked herring can be bought at Helshiron Sundries, a small all-purpose store. Smoked fish is also available at a couple of other

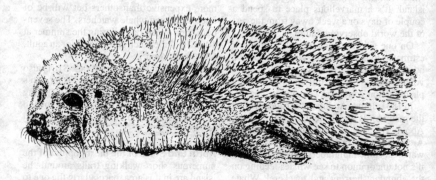

Seal pups are born with fluffy white coats which has made them victims to the fur trade

places around the island. You could try MG Fisheries in Grand Harbour.

Anchorage Park in Seal Cove is good for bird-watching – wild turkeys and pheasant are common.

Southwest Head The walk to the lighthouse and beyond along the edge of the 180-metre cliffs here should not be missed.

Hiking Thanks to the Friends of Grand Manan Trails, the island now features more than 18 marked and maintained foot paths that cover 70 km of some of the finest hiking in New Brunswick. The most extensive system of trails are found at the north end of the island and several can be linked for an overnight trek. Begin with the 10.4-km Seven Days Work Trail, reached from the Long Eddy Lighthouse off of Whistle Road north of the ferry terminal. This route ends at Whistle Beach where you pick up the Northwestern Coastal Trail that extends 11.6 km along the west side to Money Cove. At Money Cove you can either return to North Head along the Money Cove Trail or continue south to Dark Harbour on the Dark Harbour North Trail. Such a trip would be a walk of 29 to 33 km.

For more information obtain a copy of the brochure *Heritage Trails and Foot Paths on Grand Manan* that is published by Tourism Grand Manan.

Places to Stay There are over two dozen places to stay and the prices tend to be low. They're not glitzy but are comfortable; many of the cabins have a really unpretentious country feel to them. Many are in the Seal Cove area but others are scattered around the island.

The *Cross Tree Guesthouse* (☎ 662-8263) in Seal Cove has just three rooms and charges $30/40 or $45 for two people with two beds. Dinner is available at extra cost. Also in Seal Cove are the *Spray Kist Cottages* (☎ 662-3407) with units from $65 per day for a double or $350 per week. Nearby, and the same price, are the *Cliff by the Sea Cabins* (☎ 662-3133), five unique places

scattered amongst the trees in a superb setting. At both these places cooking facilities come with the cabins.

There are several places at North Head. The *Fundy Folly Guesthouse* (☎ 662-3731) is a good-value B&B at $40/48. The beach is within walking distance of the century-old house.

Lastly, at Grand Harbour the *Drop Anchor Cottages* (☎ 662-3394) has seven completely self-contained cottages with single bedroom units for $45 a night or $225 a week. There are many other places to stay on the island, and most are very reasonably priced. Weekly rates for the various cabins and cottages are around $275.

For camping the only place is the good *Anchorage Provincial Park* (☎ 662-3215), a large campground with 100 sites. Most people are tenters and, if you arrive early, there are some nice tent sites with trees edged into the woods. Otherwise you'll be out in the field where it can be very breezy. There is a kitchen shelter for rainy days, a playground and a long sandy beach. The park is near Seal Cove and it's $14 for a tents and $16 for sites with electricity.

Places to Eat Restaurants are not overly numerous on the island but there are enough casual, friendly and reasonably priced places.

North Head village has the widest selection with a couple of takeout places, two or three regular restaurants and a finer dining room in the *Marathon Inn*. The *Griff-Inn* is good for breakfasts and light lunches.

There are two more places in Grand Harbour halfway up the island, including *Fundy House Takeout* which serves pizza as well as clams & chips.

In Seal Cove is the small, plain *Water's Edge* which is not on the water but does have good food. There are burgers and pizza and other basic Italian dishes such as lasagne which are all homemade. Dinners start at $12.

Getting There & Away The ferry (☎ 662-3724) operated by Coastal Transport Ltd is from Blacks Harbour, south of St George on the mainland to North Head on Grand Manan Island. Actually, there are two ferries – one old and one new. The *Grand Manan V* is larger and quicker, knocking half an hour off the two-hour trip. Both ferries have snack bars, outdoor decks, inside chairs, and are operated by the government. The trip is an agreeable little cruise with good scenery, particularly near Blacks Harbour as the boat drifts by various islands and bays. Seeing a whale is not uncommon.

In summer, there are six trips Monday through Saturday and five on Sunday, but there are still usually queues if you have a car, and there is no reservation system. For walk-ons, bicycles, etc there is no problem. From September to the end of June the number of trips drops markedly. Actually the trip is free on the way over to Grand Manan. You just board the boat in Blacks Harbor and go. A ticket is needed to return to the mainland. There are advance-ticket sales at North Head but only for the first trip of the day.

For either boat the return fare is $8 per adult, less for children and $25 for a car. For campervans and trailers you pay according to their length.

Getting Around In Grand Harbour, Avis Green Taxi Service (☎ 662-8212) offers sightseeing tours of the island or you can arrange to be taken anywhere for hiking. Starboard Tours (☎ 662-8545), which operates out of Seal Cove also offers bus tours and hiking tours. The bus tour greets the 9.30 am ferry from Blacks Harbor daily except Sunday for a drive around the island. The cost is $22.

White Head Island

White Head Island, connected by a no-charge car ferry from Ingalls Head, is the only other inhabited island in the archipelago. A few families on the island make a living fishing. There are six 20-minute ferry services daily. The island has a good long sandy beach, another lighthouse to visit and some plant and animal life not found on Grand Manan. Note that the last ferry back

leaves at 4.30 pm. There is now accommodation on the island, *Cozee Cottage* (☎ 662-8226 or 662-3855), and a general store.

Machias Seal Island

Sixteen km south-west of Grand Manan is the small island bird sanctuary Machias Seal Island. Unlike at many other sanctuaries, visitors are permitted on shore here accompanied by a wildlife officer, but the number is limited to 25 people per day. The feathered residents include terns, puffins, razorbacks and several others in lesser numbers. Sea Watch also offers trips to this island, if the seas aren't rough.

BLACKS HARBOR

The jump-off spot for Grand Manan Island is Blacks Harbor. Sardine lovers will note that this seaport is also home of Connor Brothers, one of the world's largest producers of those delectable little fish-in-a-can. Their trademark brand is Brunswick Sardines and the company runs a factory outlet store in town. Load up!

NEW RIVER PROVINCIAL PARK

Between St Stephen and Saint John, about 35 km from the latter, is New River Provincial Park, a beautiful spot where you can easily set up camp for an extra day. The park is noted for having the best beaches along the Fundy Shore, a wide stretch of sand, bordered on one side by the rugged coastline of Barnaby Head. The park campground (☎ 755-4042) is across the road and features 87 sites, both rustic and serviced, in a wooded setting that allows everybody a little bit of privacy.

You can spend your day soaking up the sun or hiking Barnaby Head along a 5-km network of trails. The Chittick's Beach Trail leads you through coastal forest and past four coves, where you can check out the catch in a herring weir or examine tidal pools for marine life. Extending from this loop is the 2.5-km Barnaby Head Trail that hugs the shoreline most of the way and at one point puts you on the edge of a 15-metre cliff above the Bay of Fundy.

Camping at the park is $14 for tents and $16.50 for sites with electricity. It's $3.50 per vehicle to drive into the day-use area and beach or you can walk in for free.

SAINT JOHN

Historic Saint John (whose name is always spelt out in full, never abbreviated, to avoid confusion with St John's, Newfoundland) is the province's largest city and leading industrial centre. Sitting at the mouth of the Saint John River, on the bay, it is also a major year-round port.

As well as a refurbished downtown area, Saint John has a proud past. Known as 'the Loyalist City', it is the oldest incorporated city in the country. Evidence of this Loyalist background is plentiful and often very visible. The town museum, dating from 1842, is Canada's oldest.

History

The Maliseet Indians were here when the British and French began squabbling about furs. Samuel de Champlain had landed in 1604, and soon a fort was built and was changing hands between these two old-world enemies. However, the area remained pretty much a wilderness until 1755, when about 4000 British people loyal to the homeland and fleeing the revolutionary America arrived.

They built up and incorporated the city in 1785. It soon became a prosperous shipbuilding centre. Though now using iron and steel rather than wood, shipbuilding is still a major industry in town. The dry dock is one of the world's largest.

Fog very often blankets the city, particularly in the mornings. This helps to keep the area cool, even when the rest of the province is sweating it out in midsummer. In 1996 the city marked its 211th birthday as Canada's first incorporated city.

Orientation

Saint John sits on the waterfront at the mouth of the Saint John River. The downtown area, Saint John Centre, lies on a square peninsula jutting into the bay east of the river.

King Square, a small and pleasant park, marks the centre of town. Its pathways are placed to duplicate the pattern of the Union Jack. Streets on the east side of the park are designated that way, eg King St East.

Going west from the square are the principal downtown streets – which include Charlotte, Germain, Canterbury and Prince William – running south off King St. Modern Brunswick Square, a major city shopping mall, is on the corner of King and Germain Sts. One block further west at Water St is the Saint John Harbour. Here is the redeveloped waterfront area and Market Square with shops, restaurants and the Trade & Convention Centre. Across the street east from Market Square is City Hall.

South from King Square a few blocks is Queen Square, laid out in the same fashion. The district below the square is known as the South End. On Courtenay Bay, to the east, are the dry dock and the shipbuilding yards.

West over the Harbour Bridge (25-cent toll) is Saint John West, of equal size to the downtown area but (excepting a few sites) of less interest to the visitor. Many of the street names in this section of the city are identical to those of Saint John proper. To avoid confusion, streets here end in a west designation, such as Charlotte St West.

The famous Reversing Falls are here where the river flows into the harbour, under the bridge on Hwy 100. This side of town also has the landing for ferries to Digby, Nova Scotia and the city container terminals.

Further west going out of town is a mostly residential and industrial district built on rolling hills overlooking the river and the Bay of Fundy. A noteworthy exception to the character of this area is the Irving Nature Park.

North of town is large Rockwood Park, a sports and recreation area with a campground.

Information

Tourist Offices The Visitor & Convention Bureau (☎ 658-2990), on the 11th floor of City Hall at the foot of King St on the corner

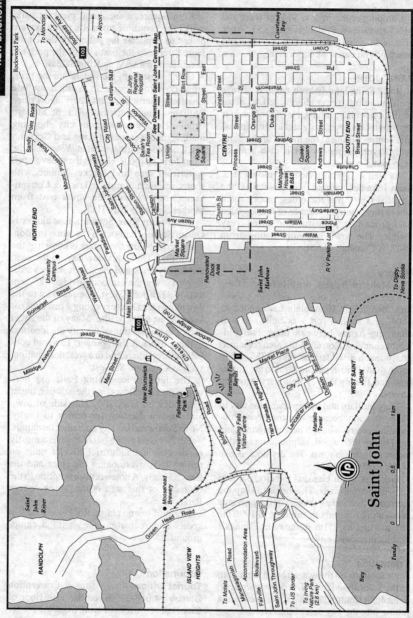

Saint John

of Water St, has an information desk and is open Monday to Friday year round.

Down at the waterfront at Market Square (just across Water St from City Hall) in summer there's the more convenient City Centre Tourist Information Centre (☎ 658-2855), in an old one-room schoolhouse which still has a couple of the original desks.

There is another information office, the Reversing Falls Visitor Centre (☎ 658-2937) at the falls. It's in Saint John West on Hwy 100, and is open from mid-May to mid-October.

A fourth alternative for information (☎ 658-2940) is on Hwy 1 (the Saint John Throughway) at Island View Heights in Saint John West. It's handy if you're coming from St Stephen or Fredericton and has the added advantage of a panoramic ocean view. It's open from mid-May to mid-October.

The tourist offices have coupons available upon request which are good for one-hour free parking at city lots. A list of places where the coupons can be used in the downtown area is provided.

Money Several banks including the Royal can be found on King St in central downtown.

Post The main post office with General Delivery is in Saint John West (☎ 672-6704) at 41 Church Ave West, Postal Station B, E2M 4P0.

Medical Services The Saint John Regional Hospital (☎ 648-6000) is at 400 Univeristy Ave.

Downtown Historic Walks
The central city and surrounding residential side streets have some very fine architecture and a stroll past the impressive facades is well worthwhile. The tourist office produces three separate self-guided walking tours:

Prince William's Walk This self-guided walk details the heritage commercial architecture of the downtown area and includes

many of those fine buildings you'll stroll by on the Loyalist Trail.

By the mid-19th century Saint John was a prosperous industrial town, the third largest in the world, important particularly for its wooden shipbuilding enterprises. In 1877, two-thirds of the city, including most of the mercantile district, was reduced to ashes by fire.

The replacements, primarily of brick and stone, are now considered some of the country's best examples of 19th-century commercial architecture. This walk takes in much of a preserved 20-block area.

Loyalist Trail The British Loyalists were really the founders of Saint John, turning a fort site into Canada's first legal city. Some of the early landmarks are still visible and interesting. The walking-tour pamphlet has a map and details of the best historical spots in the downtown area. Many of the places mentioned are no longer there; you just see the site of such and such – which is not exactly helpful unless you have a very active imagination.

Victorian Stroll Lasting about 1½ hours, this walk takes in the area south and west of King Square away from the commercial area and includes primarily Victorian houses, many of them very substantial dwellings.

Reversing Falls
The Bay of Fundy tides and their effects (see Tides in the Moncton section later in this chapter) are unquestionably an interesting and predominant regional characteristic. The falls here are part of that and are not only the biggest attraction in the city but one of the best known sites in the province. However, 'reversing falls' is a bit of a misnomer. When the high Bay of Fundy tides rise, the current in the river reverses, causing the water to flow upstream. When the tides go down, the water flows in the normal way.

To really see and appreciate this phenomenon you need to do two things; skip the touristy observation deck and free up about three or four hours. From one of the tourism centres pick up a *Reversing Falls Tide Table* brochure and then arrive about three hours after low or high tide. Pack along an easy chair, sandwiches and some of that bottled refreshment with the moosehead on it they brew just up the road. This is going to take awhile.

Head to Fallsview Park, reached on the east side of the bridge, at the end of Fallsview Rd off of Douglas Rd. This park puts you right above the river's narrowest gorge but, unfortunately, also right across from a pulp mill. Plug your nose. Given enough time (and enough beer), what you'll see is the river rush through in one direction, become calm during slack tide and then begin flowing in the other direction. Seen in its entirety, this is a remarkable display of nature's power. At high tide, this spot is a wild scene of rapids, whitewater and huge whirlpools with both waterfowl and harbour seals playing in the wicked current.

For a little more exciting look at the rapids check out Reversing Falls Jet Boat Rides (☎ 634-8987) at Market Square Wharf. They depart daily for a 30-minute ride to and through the whitewater. The cost of getting soaked is $18 per person but they do provide rain gear along with life jackets.

Loyalist House

On the corner of Union and Germain Sts, the Loyalist House (☎ 652-3590) dating from 1810 is the city's oldest unchanged building. The Georgian-style place is now a museum

depicting the Loyalist period and contains some fine carpentry. This attraction is open every day in midsummer, weekdays only in June and September, and by appointment through the winter. Hours are from 10 am to 5 pm and admission is $2.

Loyalist Burial Ground

This interesting site is just off King Square, in a park-style setting in the centre of town. Here you can see tombstones dating from as early as 1784.

Chubb Building

On the corner of Prince William and Princess Sts is the Chubb Building erected in the late 1800s. Chubb, the owner, had likenesses of all his children and half the town's politicians placed on the facade in little rosettes. Chubb himself is immortalised as a grinning gargoyle.

Old Courthouse

The County Court of 1829, which overlooks King Square at the corner of Sydney and King Sts, is noted for its spiralling stone staircase, rising three storeys without any support.

Old City Market

On Market St between Germain and Charlotte Sts is the colourful, interesting market which has been held here in the same building since 1876. Outside the door on Charlotte St, see the plaque outlining some of the

---

Tea with the Mayor

Most politicians are only seen for a few weeks before the election and then disappear until the ballot boxes are hauled out again. Not Shirley McAlary. She is the mayor of Saint John and every Wednesday during July and August she's serving tea at the Loyalist House on Union St from 2 to 3:30 pm. Literally.

'Milk or sugar,' McAlary dutifully asks a group of tourists who are stunned to learn that the mayor of this large city is actually there, handing them a tea cup and offering a plate of sweets. The tradition is carried on in other cities of Atlantic Canada but most observers agree that McAlary has taken political tea to new heights, arriving in a period costume that reflects the 185-year history of this Loyalist home and even (gasp!) serving the tea herself. 'Sometimes I serve as many as a 150 cups in an afternoon,' the mayor says.

Her present three-year term lasts to 1998. Whether she runs again is anybody's guess but whoever takes over the office, one thing is for sure, they'll be serving tea on Wednesday. 'It would be political suicide if they didn't,' says one city council member, sipping his tea. ∎

market's history. The heavy old roof beams show shipbuilding influences in their design.

Inside, the atmosphere is friendly but busy. Apart from the fresh produce stalls, most active on Friday and Saturday when local farmers come in, there are several good eating spots, a deli, and some antique stores. Good bread is sold, and dulce and cooked lobster are available.

An underground walkway leads to Brunswick Square. Market hours are 7.30 am to 6 pm Monday to Thursday, until 7 pm on Friday and to 5 pm on Saturday. The market is closed on Sunday.

Market Square

At the foot (western end) of King St is the redeveloped waterfront area known as Market Square. It offers views over the working dockyards and container terminals along the river.

In the adjacent complex is a major hotel, a convention centre, and shopping and restaurant hub. The indoor mall is actually pleasant to be in. There are about 15 restaurants in here with the better ones featuring patios along the outside wall in summer. There is also a library, art gallery, craft shop and some benches for just sitting. An enclosed walkway connects with City Hall across the street.

Barbour's General Store

This is a renovated old general store at Market Square. Inside it's packed with the kind of merchandise sold 100 years ago, including old stoves, drugs, hardware and candy. Most items are not for sale. Beside it, the Old School is a tourist information kiosk.

Partridge Island National/Provincial Historic Site

Out in the bay, Partridge Island (☎ 635-0782) was once a quarantine station for the Irish who were arriving after fleeing the homeland's potato famine. There are the remnants of some houses and a few old gun placements on the island.

In summer, 2½-hour tours are offered out to the island. They leave from the Market

Square wharf but service often seems sporadic – the boat doesn't go unless enough people show up and only if the tides are right. Call or stop at the Partridge Island ticket booth, a small lighthouse next door to Barbour's General Store. It's open Wednesday through Sunday from 9 am to 5 pm. The cost of the trip is $10 per person.

City Hall

On King St near Prince William St in the modern section of town is the new City Hall. On the top floor is an observation deck with a good view (on fog-free days!) of the city and harbour. Go to the 15th floor and then climb the steps to the 16th floor where you'll find the 'deck', an unused office, open from 8.30 am to 4.30 pm Monday to Friday.

New Brunswick Museum

West of town at 277 Douglas Ave, near the Reversing Falls, this is an eclectic place (☎ 643-2300) with an odd collection of things – some interesting, some not. There's a very good section on marine wildlife, with some aquariums and information on lobsters (you may as well know about what you'll probably be eating). There's a collection of stuffed animals and birds, mostly from New Brunswick. The displays on the marine history of Saint John are good, with many excellent models of old sailing ships.

In the other half of the museum is an art gallery which includes local contemporary work. Museum hours are from 10 am to 5 pm daily from May to September. It's closed on Monday for the rest of the year. Admission is $3.25, students $1.25 and families $8.

Carleton Martello Tower

In Saint John West, the national historic site Carleton Martello Tower (☎ 636-4011) is just off Lancaster Ave, which leads to the Digby ferry terminal. It's on Fundy Drive. Look for the signs at street intersections. A Martello tower is a circular two-storey stone coastal fortification. They were first built in England and Ireland at the beginning of the 19th century. In North America the British built 16 of them during the early 1800s.

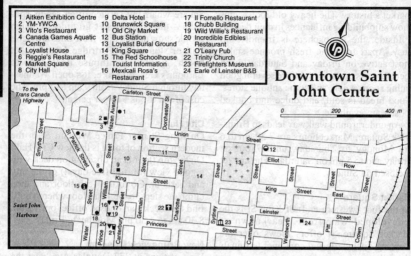

1 Aitken Exhibition Centre	9 Delta Hotel	17 Il Fornello Restaurant
2 YM-YWCA	10 Brunswick Square	18 Chubb Building
3 Vito's Restaurant	11 Old City Market	19 Wild Willie's Restaurant
4 Canada Games Aquatic	12 Bus Station	20 Incredible Edibles
Centre	13 Loyalist Burial Ground	Restaurant
5 Loyalist House	14 King Square	21 O'Leary Pub
6 Reggie's Restaurant	15 The Red Schoolhouse	22 Trinity Church
7 Market Square	Tourist Information	23 Firefighters Museum
8 City Hall	16 Mexicali Rosa's	24 Earle of Leinster B&B
	Restaurant	

Downtown Saint John Centre

Inside you can explore the restored powder magazine, barracks and the upper two levels that were added during WWII for the defence of the Saint John Harbour. Guides will show you around and provide background information. Go when there's no fog because the promontory sits on one of the highest points in the city and the view is outstanding. The tower is open 9 am to 5 pm daily from 1 June to 31 September. Admission is $2.25.

Moosehead Brewery

Moosehead Brewery used to claim it was the country's oldest independent beer maker, dating back to 1867, the year of Confederation. Now it also bills itself as the largest Canadian-owned brewery. This is due to the 1995 purchase of Labatt by a Belgium conglomerate and the fact that Carlton & United Breweries of Australia (producers of Foster's Lager) and Miller Brewing of the USA owns a hefty slice of Molson. This Oland family pride and their defiance of repeated takeover bids is felt throughout a tour of the Moosehead plant at 89 Main St West, just up the road from the Reversing Falls centre.

The tours are offered at 9:30 am and 2 pm daily and are free but so popular it's wise to

book them a day in advance at any tourist centre or by calling the Moosehead Country Store (☎ 635-7000). They begin with a movie and end with beer tasting. The country store, open Monday through Saturday, has great logo attire for all you mooseheads.

Telephone Pioneers' Museum

This museum (☎ 694-6388), in the lobby of 1 Brunswick Square, is small but good. It's open Monday to Friday from 10 am to 4 pm from mid-June to mid-September and is free. To find it, enter the mall off Germain St opposite Reggie's Restaurant.

Saint John Firefighters Museum

The city's newest museum is this partially restored 1840 firehouse, located at 24 Sydney St, overlooking King Square. Inside are old alarm systems, firefighting artefacts and, most interesting, historical photos that retell the story of the Great Saint John Fire of 1877. Hours are 10 am to 4 pm in July and August, other months visits are by appointment only. Admission is free.

Aitken Bicentennial Exhibition Centre

The centre (☎ 633-4870), which includes the

City of Saint John Gallery, is at 20 Hazen Ave across from the YM-YWCA in an attractive rounded sandstone building dating from 1904. It was built as a library and has six galleries which offer changing displays on art, science and technology. Many of the building's original features remain. Exhibits cover a range of topics from satellite images and wood sculptures to superconductivity and endangered species. There is also a very good children's interactive gallery called ScienceScape. In summer the centre is open daily from 10 am to 5 pm, otherwise it's closed on Monday. Admission is free.

Rockwood Park

On the north-east edge of the city centre, this is Canada's largest park contained wholly within a city at 870 hectares. Recreational facilities include picnic spots, wooded hiking trails, swimming areas, campground, nature centre, golf course, horse stable and a children's farm.

Cherry Brook Zoo The zoo (☎ 634-1440) has about 35 species of animals, including many endangered species. It's at the far northern edge of Rockwood Park in the north of the city and opens every day from 10 am to dusk. Admission costs $4, students $3 and families $10.

Lakewood Beach

On Route 111 south-east of town (15 minutes by car) there is swimming and a sandy beach at Lakewood Reservoir Park. Route 111 is called Loch Lomond Rd in town.

Irving Nature Park

For those with vehicles and an appreciation of nature, the park is a must (well worth the 20-minute drive south-west from the centre) for its rugged, unspoiled coastal topography. It is also a remarkable place for bird-watching, with hundreds of species regularly reported. Seals may be seen off-shore, too. Though the park is said to be on Taylors Island, this is not an island at all but rather a 225-hectare mountainous peninsula protruding into the Bay of Fundy. Four trails of varying lengths lead around beaches, cliffs, woods, mudflats, marsh and rocks. Good footwear is recommended. Also be careful along the ocean side on the rocks, as very large waves can occasionally catch the unsuspecting. The perimeter can be driven on a dirt road.

The park is free and open daily until dusk. To reach it take Route 1 west from town and turn south at Exit 107, Bleury St. Then turn right on Sand Cove Rd and continue for two km to the entrance. Other than toilets, there are no facilities at the park. Pick up a map at the tourist office before going.

Organised Tours

The Saint John Transit Commission (☎ 658-4700) offers three-hour bus tours around the city during the summer months. Departures and tickets are from Barbour's General Store at Market Square, Reversing Falls, and Rockwood Park Campground. There is one tour daily that departs Rockwood Park at 12:15 pm, the General Store at 12:30 pm and Reversing Falls at 1 pm. In September and October there are autumn foliage tours up the valley with lunch included. The Saint John Valley of New Brunswick is one of the best places in Canada for seeing the leaves changing colour. The cost of the bus tour is $15.

Also from Barbour's, in July and August, guided walking tours are offered around the historic portions of downtown. They are free and depart daily at 10 am and 2 pm.

For something different, there is Loyalist City Carriages (☎ 634-1097 or 696-6333) which offers 25-minute tours of downtown ($25 per couple) and 45-minute tours ($39 per couple). You pick up the horse-and-carriage service at Market Square near Barbour's General Store.

Festivals

Loyalist Days, an eight-day event held annually during the second week of July, celebrates the city's Loyalist background. Featured are a re-creation of the first arrival, period costumes, parades, arts & crafts, music recitals, lots of food and fireworks on the last night of the festival.

Each August the city hosts the very popular, highly regarded Festival by the Sea. For 10 days (the dates change) this performing arts event presents hundreds of singers, dancers and other performers from across Canada in concerts and shows put on throughout the city night and day. Many of the performances staged in parks and along the harbour front are free.

The Grand Ole Atlantic National Exhibition is held annually at the end of August in Exhibition Park and includes stage shows, livestock judging, harness racing and a large midway (fair ground).

Places to Stay

Camping Just north of Rothesay Ave, north of the downtown area, is huge *Rockwood Park* (☎ 652-4050) with its small lakes, picnic area, golf course and part of the University of New Brunswick's campus. It's an excellent place to camp, with pleasant camp sites and a view of the city. It could not be more convenient – close to the downtown area and the main roads out of the city. If only more cities had something similar!

The rate for tenters is $13 and $15 for those who need electricity, less for longer stays and the ticket office is also a mini-tourist centre.

Hostels The *YM-YWCA* at 19-25 Hazen Ave (☎ 634-7720), features single rooms that are clean but a little threadbare. Still you can't beat the price, $30 a night and $25 for students or those with a hostel card. Renters have full use of the facility which includes a swimming pool, a common room, an exercise room, and a snack bar with cheap food. There are 30 rooms; you get your own room key and the lobby is always open.

B&Bs Right in town at 96 Leinster St, a short walk from King Square in a turn-of-the-century three-storey building, the *Earle of Leinster B&B* (☎ 652-3275) has recently been renovated and now all seven rooms have a private bath. Rates begin at $36 and climb to $53 but include laundry facilities and a VCR with videos and popcorn. Calling

ahead is a good idea as the place tends to fill up in summer.

A little further away but still within easy walking distance of King's Square is *Garden House B&B* (☎ 646-9093) at 28 Garden St, near the Wall Street exit of Hwy 1. The 19th century Victorian home has three rooms, two with a shared bath, that are $35/$42. There are laundry facilities, and a baby-sitting service if you need it.

Near Queen Square is *Mahogany Manor* (☎ 636-8000) at 220 Germain St, a classic Victorian home with three rooms and private baths that begin at $55/60.

Over in Saint John West at 238 Charlotte St West is the *Five Chimneys B&B* (☎ 635-1888) for $50/55. This is about a 10-minute drive from the centre of town over the Harbour Bridge but a bit of a hassle by bus. It's four blocks from the ferry terminal for Digby, Nova Scotia and within easy walking distance to the Reversing Falls.

Manawagonish Rd has long been an important accommodation street in Saint John. Along this road are guesthouses, B&Bs, cabins and motels charging varying but mostly reasonable prices. The hassle is that it is a long way west of the downtown area beyond Saint John West, parallel to and north of Hwys 1 and 100. City buses do come and go into town from Manawagonish Rd but even in a car it's a 20-minute trip. One place to try is the *Manawagonish B&B* (☎ 672-5843), 941 Manawagonish Rd, from $40/45.

Hotels There are actually few hotels in Saint John and they tend to be in the middle or upper-price brackets. The *Courtenay Bay Hotel* (☎ 657-3610) with 125 rooms is central at 350 Haymarket Square and is not badly priced with rooms ranging from $57 to $85. *Keddy's Fort Howe* (☎ 657-7320) $71/79 is very good. It's on the corner of Main and Portland Sts.

Motels There are many motels along Manawagonish Rd and they tend to be less expensive than average. At times other than

June to September prices tend to fall even further.

Fundy Ayre Motel (☎ 672-1125), at No 1711, is small with only nine units, but they go for $55 a single or double with one bed. The rooms are tucked away off the road so they are quiet, and the very fine views of the Bay of Fundy and Taylors Island are a bonus.

Second choice is the *Island View* (☎ 672-1381) across the street at 1726 Manawagonish Rd. It also has kitchenettes as well as a heated swimming pool. Singles/doubles are $45/55.

Slightly closer to town at 1360 Manawagonish Rd is *Fairport Motel* (☎ 672-9700), which has rooms for $40/44 and a pleasant little restaurant.

Further out, still heading west, the road becomes Ocean West Way. At No 2121 you'll find the *Regent Motel* (☎ 672-8273). It has 10 rooms for $38 to $42.

On the east side of town is a strip of motels along Rothesay Ave on Hwy 100, which leads out to Moncton. It's north-east of the city centre but a little closer to it than Manawagonish Rd. Most of the places out this way are more expensive.

An exception is the small *Bonanza Motel* (☎ 633-1710), 594 Rothesay Ave, which is OK at $25/30.

Places to Eat

Saint John is not as limited as it once was when it comes time to tie on the bib.

For cheap eats there's *Reggie's Restaurant*, which has been around for more than a quarter of a century. At 69 Germain St near the Loyalist House, this is a classic downtown no-nonsense diner which specialises in smoked meat from Ben's, a famous Montreal deli. Also on the menu are chowders at $3.50 or less, dinners for under $6 and most sandwiches for under $3. It opens at 6 am for breakfast when you can have Reggie's Favorite – three sausages, an egg, home fries, toast, coffee and hot mustard, for $3.40.

Another pleasant little cafe is *Wild Willie's*, at the corner of Princess St and Prince William St. It opens at 7:30 am when you can order the Work-A-Day breakfast;

eggs, bacon and toast for $1.95. The cafe also has a nice selection of vegetarian sandwiches and dishes like vegetable chilli for $4.95.

Incredible Edibles, at 42 Princess St in the Brodie Building, is a nice spot for a bit of a splurge. It offers pastas, curries, omelettes and seafood. Specialities are the local desserts such as blueberry cobbler – a tasty fruit-based dessert with a crispy cake crust, usually topped with milk or cream. Most of the fresh pasta dinners start at $10 and often there are specials for under $10 but dinner for two, however, is unlikely to be under $50.

Not too far away is *Il Fornello* at 33 Canterbury. The Italian restaurant has a pleasant open setting where you would feel comfortable just sipping wine and watching the traffic go by. Speciality of the house is thin-crust pizza that starts at $7.50.

The Old City Market is a good place to be when hunger strikes. Aside from the produce there are numerous small restaurants or takeout counters and a delightful solarium eating area along King St. The *Lord's Fish Market* is good for fish, clams and scallops with chips or huge lobster rolls. *The Pasta Place* sells plates of pasta salad, *Jeremiah's* is a deli and sandwich bar, and *Slocum & Ferris* has a good salad bar and great sausage on the grill (try the Hungarian garlic).

On the corner of the market is *Billy's Seafood Company Fish Market and Oyster Bar*. The place is both a fish market and a quaint little restaurant with a three-stool bar inside. Billy's Fish Chowder is excellent at $5.25 a bowl, while the dinners start at $11.

A long time Italian restaurant is *Vito's*, on Hazen Ave on the corner of Union St. Spaghetti dinners start at $5, or try another pasta dish like Tortelline A la Vitos – tortelline stuffed with green peppers and mushrooms for $7.75. A large pizza starts at $13.

Market Square has a number of restaurants, four of them which have pleasant outdoor patios side-by-side overlooking the beach volleyball area of the wharf. *Grannan's*, not exactly budget, has a good selection of seafood with steaks too. Dinners range from $12 to $20, and if you're hungry for lobster there's the Lobster Feast – a cup of lobster stew, bucket of clams and two lobsters for $37. *Keystone Kelly's* is less expensive and more casual with various finger foods at $9 to $13 for a meal, while big glasses of beer and even bigger television screens can be had at *Don Cherry's Grapevine Restaurant*.

The *Bamboo East* at 136 Princess St offers Chinese food. The weekday lunch buffet is $6.95 and runs from noon to 2 pm; the weekend dinner buffet is $9.95 from 5 to 8 pm.

For afternoon tea or a light lunch there's *Sarah's Tea Room* just up Coburg St from Union St. Located in the Boyce Building in a charming section of the city, Sarah's features scones, homemade soups, salads, sandwiches and quiche. Hours are 11 am to 3 pm Monday through Saturday.

For a truly exceptional evening of dining, make reservations at *The Parkerhouse* (☎ 652-5054), on 71 Sydney St near King's Square, and ask for a table in the circular solarium. This stunning 1891 Victorian mansion is a fine restaurant on the 1st floor where patrons enjoy their candle-lit meals in small rooms of two or three tables. Dinners start at $16 and include such dishes as poached salmon and scallops Cinzano. Upstairs is a nine-room inn with rates that begin at $65 a night.

Entertainment

For an outdoor bar with a little bounce to it, try the *Sand & Slip*, on the wharf across from Market Square. This place overlooks the beach volleyball area where there are usually tournament games going on, however, if there isn't ask your waiter for a volleyball and kick off the shoes.

Practically across the street in Market Square and reached from a stairway at 59 St Patrick St is *Rocky's Pub*, a sports bar with a lively clientele, daily drinks specials, reasonably priced food and 19 TV screens.

Most of the action at night is around the corner of Princess St and Prince William St. *Gargoyles* is right on the corner and has them hopping to DJ music, especially on Travolta Tuesdays when the music is from the 1970s and so are the beer prices.

O'Leary's at 46 Princess is a good old fashion Irish pub with plenty of British and Irish brews as well as live music on Thursday, Friday and Saturday evening. On Wednesday it's open mike night, take a stab, you could be a star.

The *Imperial Theatre* is the new performing arts centre on King Square that opened in 1994 after having been restored to its turn-of-the-century splendour. Performances range from classical music to live theatre. Call the box office hotline (☎ 633-9494) for the schedule and ticket information.

Horse racing can be enjoyed every Wednesday evening and Saturday afternoon during the summer at Exhibition Park Raceway (☎ 633-2020) on McAllister Drive off Hwy 100 on the east side of the city.

⊕⊕⊕⊕⊕⊕⊕⊕⊕⊕⊕⊕⊕⊕⊕⊕⊕⊕⊕⊕⊕⊕⊕⊕⊕⊕⊕⊕⊕⊕⊕⊕⊕⊕

Tinsel in Saint John

No one will ever confuse Saint John for Hollywood, but it is uncanny how this east coast Canadian city is connected to that Tinsel Town on the west coast. Louis B. Mayer, founder of Metro-Goldwyn-Mayer (MGM) studios, immigrated to Saint John with his parents as a boy and eventually became one of Hollywood's most powerful men. His mother is buried in Saint John's Shaarie Zedek cemetery, whose chapel was donated by Mayer.

Actor Walter Pidgeon, one of Hollywood's leading men in the 1940s and known to most Baby Boomers as Grandpa in the television show *The Real McCoys*, was born here in 1898. So was Donald Sutherland, who had leading roles in such hits as *M.A.S.H.* and *JFK*.

Saint John was also the filming location of the movie *Children of a Lesser God* during the summer and fall of 1985 and many of the residents played extra roles in it. The film starred William Hurt and Marlee Matlin, who went on to win an Oscar for Best Actress for her performance. ■

⊕⊕⊕⊕⊕⊕⊕⊕⊕⊕⊕⊕⊕⊕⊕⊕⊕⊕⊕⊕⊕⊕⊕⊕⊕⊕⊕⊕⊕⊕⊕⊕⊕⊕

Getting There & Away

Air Air Canada (☎ 632-1500) to Montreal costs $275. Canadian (☎ 657-3860) flies to St John's, Newfoundland for $372.

Bus SMT Bus Lines (☎ 648-3500) is the provincial carrier. The station is at 300 Union St on the corner of Carmarthen St, a five-minute walk from the town centre. SMT Bus Lines connects with Orleans Express lines in Riviere du Loup, Quebec for Quebec destinations. For cities in Nova Scotia, SMT connects with Acadian Bus Lines.

To Fredericton there are two trips daily at 9.30 am and 6.25 pm, costing $15. That same bus is used for connections for passengers carrying on to Quebec City, for which the fare is $60. The bus to Moncton leaves at 11.15 am and 5.40 pm and the fare is $20. For Cape Tormentine (to Prince Edward Island), go to Moncton and transfer from there.

Buses also run to Moncton where VIA trains can be caught for Quebec or Nova Scotia. Combination road-and-rail tickets can be purchased at the SMT bus terminal. To Quebec City daily except Tuesday the bus/train fare is $114.

Ferry The Marine Atlantic ferry (☎ 636-4048), the *Princess of Acadia,* sails between Saint John and Digby, Nova Scotia, across the bay. Depending on where you're going, this can save a lot of driving around the Bay of Fundy through Moncton and then Amherst, Nova Scotia, but the ferry is not cheap. In comparison with the other Marine Atlantic routes around the region, and for the distance covered, the price is inexplicably high.

This route is heavily used by tourists which could be one explanation. For peak season of late June through mid-September fares are $30 per person one way and $47 per car and driver. Bicycles are $10.50. There is a very slightly reduced return passenger-only fare if you want to make a day cruise out of a trip there and back. Also, prices go down outside the summer season which is

from the middle of June to the first week of September.

Crossing time is about 2½ hours. In summer there are three services daily, 12.30 and 9 am, and 4.45 pm, except for Sunday when there is no 12.30 am crossing. Arrive early or call ahead for reservations, as the ferry is very busy in July and August. Even with a reservation, arrive an hour before the ferry sails or your space may be given away. Walk-ons and cyclists should be OK. There's a restaurant and a bar on board.

Car There are several choices for rentals. Delta (☎ 634-1125), at 378 Rothesay Ave, is open seven days a week, and charge $30 with 100 free km, then 12 cents per km. There is also a weekly price of $189 with 1000 free km.

Avis (☎ 634-7750) is located conveniently right behind the market building at 17 North Market St. For a middle-sized car, the rates are pretty much the same as the above. Ask about the weekend special which is quite good value. Drivers should note that west of the town centre, Hwy 1 crosses over the Saint John River. There's a toll bridge where you pay 25 cents. Further out westward, connections can be made with Hwy 7 (northward) for Fredericton.

Getting Around

The Airport The airport is east of town out along Hwy 111. There is an airport bus costing $7 that leaves, approximately 1½ hours before all flights, from top hotels like the Hilton on Market Square and the Delta Brunswick on Brunswick Square. For a share taxi call Vets (☎ 658-2020).

Bus Saint John Transit (☎ 658-4700) has 30 routes around the city. Major departure points for many buses are King Square in the city centre, Simms Corner at Bridge Rd, and Main in West Saint John. Bus fare is $1.25.

AROUND SAINT JOHN

North out of the city is a green rural area interspersed with deeply indented bays, rivers and islands, eventually leading to

Grand Lake and Fredericton. The Saint John River flows south through here to its mouth at the Bay of Fundy and the ferries connecting roads in the area are all free. The **Kingston Peninsula**, not far from Saint John, has scenery typical of the river valley landscapes and is particularly beautiful in autumn with the leaves changing colour. **Crystal Beach** is a popular spot for camping and swimming. If you're driving to Fredericton, don't take dull Hwy 7. Go along Hwy 102, which winds along by the river through small communities.

ST MARTINS

A rather uninteresting 2½-hour drive east of Saint John will take you to the worthy destination of St Martins, one of the province's historic towns, situated on the Bay of Fundy. It's a small, pretty, out-of-the-way place that was once the centre of the wooden shipbuilding trade. On entering the town you'll see a quintessentially Maritime, picturesque scene: **Old Pejepscot Wharf** edged with beached fishing boats waiting for the tide, two wooden covered bridges and a lighthouse. (If on the other hand, the tide is in, the boats will likely be out, working.) The **Quaco Museum** depicts the shipbuilding period. But keep going over one of the bridges and around the corner where a vast expanse of beach opens up. At the far end there are a couple of caves cut into the shoreline cliffs to explore. At the parking lot is a snack bar, right by the beach.

Hiking

The cliff-edged coastal region between St Martins and Fundy National Park and inland towards Sussex is a rugged undeveloped section of the province which has spectacular, wild beauty. Experienced hikers may wish to investigate the trail which runs mainly along the shoreline and extends some 40 km to the park. The hike takes three to five days.

From the park, Dobson Trail, another long-distance trek, leads north to the town of Riverview near Moncton.

Places to Stay & Eat

Back in town there is the *Fundy Breeze Lodge* (☎ 833-4723) for spending the night or having a meal in the restaurant. Doubles are $50. There is also a B&B, the *Bayview* (☎ 833-4723), for the same rate or camping just out of town at the *Seaside Tent & Trailer Park* (☎ 833-4413) where a tent site is $13.50. All three places are on Main St.

FUNDY NATIONAL PARK

Fundy National Park (☎ 887-6000) is one of the country's most popular parks. Aside from the world's highest tides, the park on the Bay of Fundy has an extensive network of hiking trails and some dirt roads for touring around in your car. Irregularly eroded sandstone cliffs and the wide beach at low tide make a walk along the shore interesting. There's lots of small marine life to observe and debris to pick over.

The park is home to much wildlife, including black bears, moose, beavers and peregrine falcons. The ocean is pretty cool here, so there is a saltwater swimming pool (not far from the eastern entrance to the park) where you can have a dip. If you are camping in the park the pool is free, otherwise admission is $2.75.

You can reach the park, 129 km east of Saint John and about halfway to Moncton, by following Hwy 114. Entering from the north you first reach Wolfe Lake Centre, open daily to 6 pm and on Friday 9 pm. At the south entrance is the park's Visitor Centre, and it is open from 8 am to 9 pm. Both have book stores and information counters where you can purchase your motor entry permit. It's $6 per vehicle for the day or $18 for four days.

Hiking

The park features 104 km of walking trails throughout its backcountry where it's possible to enjoy a short stroll down to the ocean or a three-day backpack. The most popular backpacking route is the Fundy Circuit, a three to four-day trek of 50 km through the heart of the park. Begin at the Visitor Centre

High Tides

The tides of the Bay of Fundy are the highest in the world. This constant ebb and flow is a prime factor in the life of the bay, the appearance of the shoreline and even how residents set shipping and fishing schedules.

The explanation for these record tides is in the length, depths and gradual funnel shape of the bay. As the high tide builds up, the water flowing into the narrowing bay has to rise on the edges. It is pushed still higher by the shallowing sea bed. A compounding factor is called resonance. This refers to the sloshing or rocking back and forth from one end to the other of all the water in the bay like in a giant bath tub. When this mass swell is on the way out of the bay and meets a more powerful incoming tide head on, the volume of water increases substantially.

The eastern end of the Bay of Fundy and around the Minas Basin is where the contrasts between the high and ebb tide are most pronounced with tides of 10 to 15 metres twice daily about 12½ hours apart. The highest tide ever recorded anywhere was 16.6 metres (54 ft), the height of a four-storey building, at Burncoat Head near the village of Noel, Nova Scotia. Other places around the world with noteworthy (that is, over 10 metres high) tides are the Bristol Channel in England, the Bay of St Malo in France, and Turnagain Arm in Alaska.

All tides, large and small, are caused by the rise and fall of the oceans due to the gravitational pull of the sun and the moon. Consequently, the distance of the moon and its position to earth relative to the sun determine tidal size. When the moon is full or new the gravitational forces of the sun and moon are working in concert, not at cross purposes, and the tides at these two times of the month are higher than average. When one of these periods coincides with the time (perigee, once every 27½ days) when the moon is at its closest to earth the tides are at their most dramatic.

Throughout the centuries various methods have been used around the bay to tap the tides as an energy source. Simple but successful grist mills spurned dreams of grandiose generating stations feeding the eastern seaboard. There is still no commercial electricity production but there is an experimental and working tidal power plant which can be visited at Annapolis Royal, Nova Scotia.

The times and heights of the tides change around the bay but local schedules are available at many tourist offices in the region.

Tidal Bore

A feature related to the tides is the tidal bore, a daily occurrence in some of the rivers flowing into the Bay of Fundy, most notably the Saint John River running through Saint John, the Petitcodiac River in Moncton and the Salmon River in Truro, Nova Scotia.

As the tide advances up a narrowing bay it starts to build up on itself forming a wave. The height of this oncoming rush can vary from just a few cm to about a metre. The power behind it forces the water up what is normally a river draining to the sea. This wave flowing upstream is called a tidal bore.

The size and height of the bore is determined by the tide, itself regulated by the moon. In the areas where the bore can be most interesting it is not difficult to get hold of a bore schedule. As with the tides, there are two bores a day, roughly 12 hours apart. While this is an interesting occurrence, especially in theory, the bores are not often overwhelming experiences to observe. Notice I resisted the term 'boring'. ■

---

to reserve a series of wilderness camp sites ($2 per person per night) along the route. From there the trail begins by heading north along the Upper Salmon River.

Another overnight trek is to hike Goose River Trail, an old cart track that extends from Point Wolfe 7.9 km to the mouth of the river, where there is backcountry camping. Enjoyable day hikes include Coppermine Trail, a 4.4-km loop to an old mine site, as well as Third Vault Falls Trail, a challenging one-way hike of 3.7 km to the park's tallest falls.

Places to Stay & Eat

The park has four campgrounds with individual sites and a fifth for groups. In the interior are Chignecto with serviced sites ($14 to $16) and tent sites ($9) and Wolfe Lake with tent sites ($7). Along the coast are the popular Point Wolfe with tent sites ($9) and Headquarters with serviced sites ($16) and tent sites ($11). Expect sea breezes and cooler temperatures at the coastal campgrounds.

In addition to the camping possibilities, there is the *Jeunesse Fundy HI Hostel*

(☎ 887-2216), a convenient facility just off Chemin Point Wolfe Rd near the golf course. The hostel has a kitchen, lounge area and beds that run $5 for members and $10 for non-members. There are also motel-style rooms and chalets at the *Caledonia Highlands Inn* (☎ 887-2930) within the park. The chalets have cooking facilities but tend to be a little pricey; $70 for singles or doubles. The *Fundy Park Chalets* (☎ 887-2808) are similar but are $65 for the unit that will hold up to four people.

At the small town of **Alma**, just east of the park on Hwy 114, there is the *Alpine Motor Inn* (☎ 887-2052) for $45/60 along with usual tourist services; food market, liquor store, bank and laundromat. At *Kelly's Bake Shop*, a sticky bun is a must. One is enough for breakfast and possibly lunch. *Collins Seafood* will sell you live or cooked lobsters to take back to your camp site.

CAPE ENRAGE

Heading east to Moncton take the smaller road, Hwy 915, as it detours closer to the coast and offers some fine views. At Cape Enrage, out on the cliffs at the end of the peninsula, the power of the elements is often strongly and stimulatingly in evidence.

For a different view of those cliffs, give Cape Enrage Adventures (☎ 887-2273 or 865-6081 in Moncton) a call. Instructors offer rappelling adventures at the cape. Gear and instruction is provided for you to descend, rather quickly, 45 metres down the cliffs to the beach. You can then scramble up the stairs to do it all over again and again. The cost is $30 for a three-hour outing.

SHEPODY NATIONAL WILDLIFE AREA

South of the town of Riverside-Albert and the village of Harvey at Marys Point on the Bay of Fundy is this gathering place for literally hundreds of thousands of shore birds. From mid-July to mid-August the beach is almost obliterated by huge numbers of birds, primarily sandpipers. Along the dykes and marsh there is a nature trail.

South-East New Brunswick

The corner of New Brunswick leading to Nova Scotia and Prince Edward Island is most interesting for its various geographic or topographic attributes. The regional centre is Moncton whose two principal attractions are places where nature appears to defy gravity. Outside the city are some fine, sandy beaches and, on the Petitcodiac River, The Rocks are the impressive result of seaside erosion.

MONCTON

Moncton, with a population of 57,000, is the third city of the province and a major transportation and distribution centre for the Atlantic Provinces. It's near the ferry for Prince Edward Island, and the train to Nova Scotia passes through it. Moncton is small and nondescript, but a much-needed face-lift has improved the downtown area while some aggressive marketing has resulted in the city's experiencing considerable economic growth and development. And due to a couple of odd attractions – Magnetic Hill and a tidal bore – it's worth a brief stop on your way by.

The first Europeans to settle in the area were Germans from Pennsylvania. Initially the town was called 'The Bend', after the turn in the Petitcodiac River, and specialised in shipbuilding. There's a fairly large French population and many people speak both of Canada's official languages. The Université de Moncton is the only French university outside Quebec.

Orientation

The small downtown area extends north and south off Main St. The river lies just to the south and the Trans Canada Hwy runs east-west north of town. Between Duke and Foundry Sts along Main St, the sidewalks have been gentrified and many of the old buildings contain restaurants and nightspots. Unfortunately for Moncton, as in several other towns around the province (or indeed,

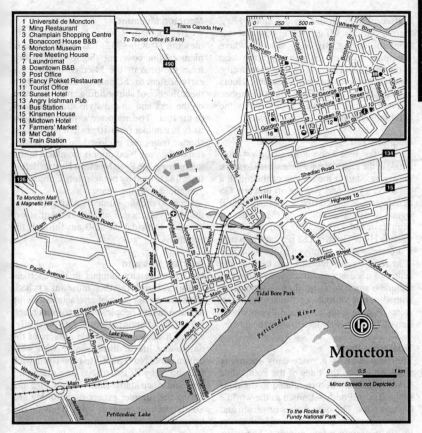

1 Université de Moncton
2 Ming Restaurant
3 Champlain Shopping Centre
4 Bonaccord House B&B
5 Moncton Museum
6 Free Meeting House
7 Laundromat
8 Downtown B&B
9 Post Office
10 Fancy Pokket Restaurant
11 Tourist Office
12 Sunset Hotel
13 Angry Irishman Pub
14 Bus Station
15 Kinsmen House
16 Midtown Hotel
17 Farmers' Market
18 Met Café
19 Train Station

Moncton

Minor Streets not Depicted

in many across the country), growth means new shopping malls and the national (or international) fast-food chains taking root. In Moncton, alone, there are 16 Tim Horton donut shops! Often, as is the case here, the downtown core suffers as consumers file to the malls and the development around the perimeter. Just to the east of the downtown centre across the bridge on Champlain St, an extension of Main St, is a mega-mall complex.

Lengthy Mountain Rd leading in and out to the west side of town from the Trans Canada Hwy is also a main street for service

stations, chain restaurants, fast-food joints and the same franchises seen in most Canadian cities. There are also some motels along here.

Information

There are two tourist offices in the Moncton area, one downtown and the other on the Trans Canada Highway. The main centre (☎ 853-3590) is in the new City Hall that opened in 1996 at 655 Main St across from the Blue Cross Centre. Hours for the office are 8 am to 6.30 Monday through Friday year round.

If coming in on the Trans Canada Hwy, there is a tourist office (☎ 853-3540) across from the Irving Big Stop station, where Mountain Rd meets the highway, north-west of the downtown area. This one has both city, regional and provincial information. Hours are 9 am to 5 pm daily from May to October.

There's another office south across the Gunningsville Bridge in Riverview.

Magnetic Hill

This is the best known attraction (☎ 384-0303) in the area. Gravity here seems to work in reverse: start at the bottom of the hill in a car or on a bike and you'll drift upward. Go as many times as you like, and maybe you'll figure it out. The hill is on the corner of Mountain Rd (Hwy 126) and the Trans Canada Hwy. There is a $2 per car fee, worth it if there are several of you in the vehicle.

In recent years the hill has become the centre of a variety of attractions which now include a small zoo next door, a water park with slides of various sorts, restaurants and stores. A mini-train links the different diversions. There are entry fees to everything here.

Tidal Bore Park

The tidal bore is a twice-daily incoming wave caused by the tides of the Petitcodiac River, which are in turn related to the tides in the Bay of Fundy – known as the world's highest tides. The bore rushes upstream and sometimes raises the water level in the river by six metres in a few minutes. The wave itself varies in height from a few cm to over 30 cm.

A good place to watch for it is in Tidal Bore Park at the east end of Main St where a large clock displays the time of the next bore. The pleasant park is filled with old men sitting on the benches until close to bore time when the water's edge gets really crowded with expectant visitors. Don't anticipate anything spectacular though – mostly the wave is not at all impressive, but the troop of street performers usually on hand help make this an entertaining event. The bore is best in spring and autumn, if it's raining or if the moon is right.

Moncton Museum

At 20 Mountain Rd near Belleview St, the museum (☎ 856-4383) has a collection of memorabilia covering the town's history, from the time of the Micmac Indians and early settlers to the present. Displays show the influence of shipbuilding and the railway on the area and an old-style street has been re-created. The museum's free and open daily in summer from 10 am to 8 pm, but has shorter hours and is closed on Monday the rest of the year. Next door is the oldest building in town, the **Free Meeting House** dating from 1821, used by numerous religious congregations over the years.

Free 90-minute guided walking tours of the city commence at the museum from Tuesday to Friday at 9.30 am through the summer.

Acadian Museum

On the university campus in the Clement Cormier Building, this museum (☎ 858-4088) has a collection of artefacts belonging to the Acadian people, the first French settlers of the Atlantic region. The displays offer a brief history and chronicle aspects of the day-to-day life of these people who were driven out of Nova Scotia to New Brunswick and abroad by British troops. The museum's free and open daily from 10 am to 5 pm during the summer except on Saturday and Sunday when it opens at 1 pm. It has shorter hours the rest of the year.

Thomas Williams' House

Built in 1883, this 12-room Victorian Gothic-style house remained in the family as a home until 1983 when it was bequeathed to the city as a heritage house. Much of the fine original work remains intact both inside and out, and the furnishings add to the overall effect. The tea room on the veranda is fun.

The house is open daily from 9 am to 5 pm in July and August except on Sunday when it opens at 1 pm. In May, June and September it's open only three or four days a week. It's at 103 Park St in the downtown area and admission is free.

Farmers' Market

On Saturday, from 7 am to 1 pm, a produce market is set up on Robinson St south of Main St year round and on Wednesday as well during the harvest season from mid-August to Thanksgiving.

Festivals

In early May there's the Acadian Art Festival, and in July a bluegrass and old-time fiddle-music festival is held.

Places to Stay

Camping The nearest campground to the city is *Green Acres Camping* (☎ 384-0191), just off the Mountain Rd exit (exit 488) of the Trans Canada Highway and within walking distance of Magnetic Hill. It's pretty much a grassy clearing but there is showers and a laundromat. A tent site is $14.

Hostels The *Kinsmen House* (☎ 382-7520), a non-profit community group takes in travellers at 138 Cameron St between St George and Main Sts. Rooms here are $25/30 and include a light breakfast.

The *Université de Moncton* (contact Housing Services on ☎ 858-4008) rents rooms during summer in two of the residences. They have shared washrooms and there is a cafeteria. Cost is $25/35 for students and $18/30 for seniors.

Tourist Homes The lack of hotels is partially offset by quite a few guesthouses and B&Bs. During the summer, these are often full by the end of the day.

McCarthy's B&B (☎ 383-9152), at 82 Peter St, with three rooms is good and inexpensive at $28/38. Note that it is open only from May to October. Peter St is just under two km north of the downtown centre.

Within walking distance (but a fair jaunt of seven or so blocks) is the *Bonaccord House B&B* (☎ 388-1535) at 250 Bonaccord St. It's the appealing yellow-and-white house on the corner of John St with a porch, and the four rooms are $35/45.

Very central at 101 Alma St is the *Downtown B&B* (☎ 855-7108), open all year with three rooms at $39/49.

Mountain View Tourist Home (☎ 384-0290) is at 2166 Mountain Rd. It has three rooms at the reasonable price of $30/40. It's a simple, no-frills place and a fair distance from the city centre.

Hotels At 46 Archibald St in a central location near Main St, is the yellow, wooden *Canadiana Inn* (☎ 382-1054). It's a beautiful place – as if you've stepped back in time – with wood everywhere and hanging lamps and, indeed, it's more than 100 years old. There are 17 rooms beginning at $55/60.

The *Hotel Beauséjour* (☎ 854-4344) on Main St is the largest and most expensive place in town and is primarily for business clientele. Rooms here begin at $89.

Motels There's no shortage of motels, and a fair range of prices. Not far from town is the good *Beacon Light Motel* (☎ 384-1734), at 1062 Mountain Rd, reached by taking Hwy 126. Doubles cost $52 and there are some kitchenette rooms available. Mountain Rd has a couple of other places as well.

On Hwy 2 near Magnetic Hill are numerous motels. The *Atlantic* (☎ 858-1988) has rooms that start at $25/30. The *Restwell* (☎ 858-0080) in the other direction (east) is from $45 to $55. Features here include a pool and some kitchenette rooms.

Also decent is the *Moncton Motor Inn* (☎ 382-2587), 1905 Main St, an older place but clean and well kept, with a view of the river. It has a swimming pool and is just a five-minute drive into town. Singles/doubles here are $52/57.

Right in the centre of town within walking distance to either the bus or train station, is the *Midtown* (☎ 388-5000) which is in a quiet location at 61 Weldon St. It's pricier at $54/59 and also has some kitchenette rooms.

There are several other motels strung out along Rural Route 1, towards and in River Glade.

Places to Eat

At 700 Main St, *Crackers* is a nice place for sandwiches, salads, ribs or Italian food. The large Caesar salad at $5 makes a good lunch and there is a wide selection of tempting desserts. At night it becomes a sort of club and is open very late on weekends.

Rye's Delicatessen at Main and Westmoreland Sts has great bagels and nightly specials that might be fettuccine on Tuesday and steamed mussels on Friday. They also have a happy hour that begins at 4 pm and features pints for under $3.

Robinson St just north of Main is a small pedestrian area that features a couple of espresso shops. *Cafe Robinson* is a cosy spot to have coffee or a croissant sandwich. A large café au lait is $2.25 and there are tables outside.

At *Fancy Pokket*, a Lebanese restaurant on the corner of Main St and Lester, you can feast on an all-you-can-consume buffet at lunch for $5 and at dinner for a few dollars more.

The food counter at the *Metropolitan* store at the Highfield Mall on Main St has the lowest prices in town with meals at about $5. Nearby the *Traveller's Café* in the bus station has cheap breakfasts with two eggs, toast and coffee for $3 and the good-value dinners are under $7.

Probably the best known restaurant is *Cy's*, a very well established seafood place at 170 Main St. It is not cheap and may be a little over-rated, but the seafood is good. On the corner of Main and Westmoreland Sts is *Boomerang's Steakhouse*, a restaurant with an Aussie theme, happy hour crowd and large frozen drinks. Steak dinners start at $12.

Mountain Rd has numerous eating spots, including almost a dozen Chinese restaurants, three alone near the corner of Mc-Sweeney Ave. One is *Ming Garden* which claims to have a 101-item buffet (no, I didn't count them). The all-you-can-eat affair is $8 for dinner Monday through Thursday, $7 during lunch. Also along this stretch of Mountain Rd is every chain restaurant imaginable.

Entertainment

Central Main street has several bars catering to the young with live bands and dancing. *Spanky's* has live rock.

More live music can be enjoyed at the *Angry Irishman* on the corner of Main and Foundry Sts. The pub features Beamish stout and John Courage ale on tap, a friendly crowd and live Irish music on the weekends.

The *Coliseum* is home to major shows, concerts and sporting events.

The impressive Capitol Theatre at 811 Main St, a 1920s vaudeville house, has been restored and is now the city's *Performing Arts Centre*. Call the theatre box office (☎ 856-4379) for a schedule of performances, which includes both Theatre New Brunswick and Symphony New Brunswick on a regular basis throughout the year.

Getting There & Away

Bus The station for SMT Bus Lines (☎ 859-5060) is at 961 Main St between town and the train station on the corner of Bonaccord St. Some schedules with one-way ticket prices are: Fredericton, 11.55 am and 5.50 pm daily ($25); Saint John, 12.20 and 5.55 pm daily ($20); Halifax, 2 and 8.15 pm daily ($35); and Prince Edward Island, 2.05 and 8.05 pm daily ($30).

Train The VIA train station (☎ 857-9830) is south-west of the downtown area near Cameron St a couple of hundred metres off Main St. Look for it behind the building at 1234 Main St or behind Sobey's grocery store at the Highfield Mall. It's only open from 9.30 am to 7 pm on weekdays and 10 am to 7 pm on weekends. Regular one-way fares are $43 to Halifax and $130 to Montreal. If you purchase your ticket a week in advance you save considerably. There is no train service to Saint John and only one train to Montreal now as the run through Maine, USA, has been dropped. The *Ocean*, goes through northern New Brunswick, including Campbellton and Quebec, on its way to Montreal daily at 6.42 pm except on Tuesday. The train to Halifax departs daily at 11.10 am except Wednesday.

Getting Around

Codiac Transit (☎ 857-2008) is the local bus system running daily except Sunday.

AROUND MONCTON
Covered Bridges

Within 100 km of Moncton, 27 of the province's historic covered bridges can be seen. Two driving trips south of Moncton, called the Scenic Trail and the Covered Bridge Trail, take in many of these bridges (see Covered Bridges in the Sussex section earlier in this chapter).

Dobson Trail

Just south of Moncton in Riverview, this 60-km hiking trail leads you through the Albert County hills and maple forests down to Fundy National Park. The entire trail is a three-day, one-way hike to where it connects with the Laverty Falls Trails in the national park.

To reach the northern trailhead, take the causeway across the Petitcodiac River to Riverview and then turn east on Hwy 114. Turn south on Pine Glen Rd and in three km you reach the trailhead marked by a white sign on one side of the road and a small parking area on the other. The first section of the trail is the 9.4-km trek to Beaver Pond where you'll find areas to make camp and a new hut.

For information contact the Trailmaster, Edwin Melanson (☎ 855-5089) in Riverview.

Hillsborough

Hillsborough, about 20 km south-east of Moncton, is a small town overlooking the Petitcodiac River. From here the Salem-Hillsborough Railroad (☎ 734-3195), a restored steam engine, pulls antique coaches beside the river to Salem eight km away. It takes an hour for the return trip. The fare is $6.50, less for kids. The train runs at 1.30 and 3 pm every Sunday in July and August and on a few weekends in September.

The Rocks Provincial Park

Continuing south-east from Hillsborough, you'll encounter the park at Hopewell Cape, the point at which the river meets the Fundy waters in Shepody Bay. The 'rocks' are unusual erosion formations known as 'flowerpots'. The shore is lined with these irregular geological forms, as well as caves and tunnels, all of which have been created by erosion from the great tides.

An exploratory walk along the beach at low tide is well worthwhile – check the tide tables at any tourist office. You can't hit the beach at high tide but the rock towers are visible from the trails above. Camping is not allowed.

Saint Joseph

Here, 24 km south of Moncton, is the Acadian Odyssey National Historic Site (☎ 758-9783), which tells the enthralling but difficult history of the Acadians, the early French settlers of the Bay of Fundy region, most of whom were expelled by the British in 1755. The exhibits, including paintings, crafts and life-size models, are well done and, unlike those at many such history-based sites, also devote some attention to the subjects' lives through the years to the present.

Saint Joseph is in the Memramcook Valley, the only area near the Bay of Fundy where some Acadians live on what was the land of their forebears before the mass banishments.

The site is open from June to mid-October, from 9 am to 5 pm daily and entry is free. It's between Moncton and Dorchester off Route 106 and, if you're interested in the Acadians it's worth the slight detour.

SACKVILLE

Sackville is a small university town that's in the right place for many travellers passing by to swing through as a pit stop. There is a tourist office (☎ 364-0431) on York St just up from Main St. Hours are 8 am to 8 pm daily during the summer and usually there is free coffee and donuts.

In the centre of town is **Mount Allison University** and the park on campus is good for stretching the legs. Among the facilities open to the public is the Owens Art Gallery and the pool and athletic centre. The gallery is open daily 10 am to 5 pm except on Saturday and Sunday when it opens at 1 pm. On the edge of town, off East Main St, is the **Sackville Waterfowl Park** on a major bird migration route. Boardwalks have been built over portions of it and there is another trail and some interpretive signs.

Also in the Sackville area is the **Tintamarre National Wildlife Reserve**. The Wildlife Service office (☎ 364-5044), at 63 E Main St, has a few displays on the reserve and information for those wishing to see more.

If you stay the night, consider a show at *Live Bait Theatre*, Sackville's professional stage company which often performs comedies. Call the box office (☎ 536-2248) for tickets and schedule.

Places to Stay & Eat

Mt Allison University (☎ 364-2247), right in the centre of town, opens rooms to overnight guests from May to August, and cost $23/43, a few dollars less for students. It also serves inexpensive meals.

There's a good B&B at 146 West Main St called the *Different Drummer* (☎ 536-1291). It's a fine old Victorian house; each of the four rooms is furnished with antiques and has a bath. Breakfasts include homemade muffins and bread. Singles/doubles cost $45/49. *Borden's Motel* (☎ 536-1066) is the same price while *Cosmic Tree* (☎ 536-3504) has singles for $38.

At the *Marshland's Inn* (☎ 536-0170) at 59 Bridge St, you can get a very good dinner whether you're spending the night there or not. Rooms begin at $50/55. On York St, across from the university, the little *Vienna Coffee House* is the place for a coffee or a light meal. The favourite among locals is *Mel's Tea Room* on Bridge St which has the charm of an 1950s diner with the jukebox and prices to match.

FORT BEAUSÉJOUR NATIONAL HISTORIC PARK

Right by the Nova Scotia border at the shoreline, the park (☎ 536-0720) preserves the remains of a French fort built in 1751 to hold the British back. It didn't work. Led by Colonel Monckton, the fort was taken over before it was even finished. Later it was used as a stronghold during the American Revolution and the War of 1812. There are some pretty good displays within the fort and some evocative pictures set in the surroundings. The views over the marshy end of the Bay of Fundy alone make a trip out here worthwhile. Hours for the interpretive centre are 9 am to 5 pm daily June through mid-October and admission is $2.25.

SHEDIAC

Just 22 km north-east of Moncton on the coast, Shediac is a popular summer resort town with a population descended mainly from the Acadian French. The beaches here are blessed with warm waters due to sand bars and shallow water. Most popular are Parlee Beach (east of Shediac) and Pointe du Chêne, with water temperatures of around 20°C all summer. The waters of the Northumberland Strait are possibly the warmest north of the Carolinas in the USA.

There are other beaches on the small coastal roads and north and south of Shediac, and lots of camping places.

The area also is a lobster centre of some repute and Shediac is home to the annual lobster festival in July. You can enjoy it even on pizza!

The tourist office is at the west end of Main St, just before you cross the causeway across the Scoudouc River into town. You can't miss it, there's a giant lobster outside. It's open daily during the summer.

There is little to see in town itself, but at night the many lights and the decorative seagulls add a festive touch. **Pascal Poirer House**, built in 1835 is the oldest house in town and is now open as a small museum. The home was the birthplace of Poirer, a noted writer and the first Acadian senator, and was moved to Shediac from Grande

Digue. Hours are 1 to 9 pm Tuesday through Sunday from June through August. Admission is free.

Places to Stay & Eat

For camping there is a lot of choice in the area but best is probably *Parlee Beach Park* (☎ 532-1500), a grassy campground beside the provincial beach where a tent site is $12 per person. Reservations should be made for holiday weekends, but for any weekend, arrive as early as possible on Friday.

Aside from camping, the big white *Hotel Shediac* (☎ 532-4405) is a central, middle-range place dating from 1853. Singles/doubles begin at $45/48. A less expensive option is the *Neptune Motel* (☎ 532-4299) at $35/45. There are also a couple of places with cabins rented by the week.

East of town is a strip of eateries and takeaways. You'll find clams and lobsters, cooked or fresh, dead or alive. *Fisherman's Paradise* packs them in with fair (but that doesn't mean cheap) prices. The *House of Lobster* is more upmarket with the boiled lobster dinner at $25 and other seafood dinners starting at $16.

Lobsters can be bought at various outlets and at the wharves. The largest is *Shediac Lobster Shop* passed after just crossing the Scoudouc River on Main St. This being a tourist town, expect to pay anywhere from $6 to $8 a pound.

CAP-PELÉ

East of Shediac there are a series of less used beaches such as the one at Cap-Pelé where there is also a water slide. Further south at Murray Corner is a provincial park with more sandy beaches.

CAPE TORMENTINE

Further east of Shediac and also on the coast is Cape Tormentine with the terminal for the ferry to Borden, Prince Edward Island. In 1997, the ferry is expected to be replaced by the Northumberland Strait Bridge.

Just north of Bayfield is a very long, almost empty beach with the remains of an old wreck at one end.

North & East New Brunswick

North of Fredericton and Moncton lie the province's vast forests. Nearly all the towns are along the east coast or in the west by the Saint John River along the US border. The interior of northern New Brunswick is nearly inaccessible rocky, river-filled timberland.

Inland, highways in this area can be quite monotonous with thick forest lining both sides of the very straight roads. Fortunately these routes need not often be used. In the eastern section of the province the coastal roads are where pretty well everything of interest lies. Kouchibouguac National Park protects a variety of littoral environments and their natural flora & fauna. Most of the larger towns of the east coast are pulp & paper centres with not a lot to hold the visitor's attention. Newcastle sticks out as a place to break up the trip.

The Acadian Peninsula with its little-touristed islands and French population based around Caraquet is one of the most geographically appealing regions with the Baie des Chaleurs shoreline. The peninsula also has a major historic attraction. Campbellton and Dalhousie at the edge of the northern uplands are access points to the province of Quebec.

KOUCHIBOUGUAC NATIONAL PARK

The highlights of this park (pronounced 'koo she boo gwak') are the beaches, lagoons and offshore sand dunes stretching for 25 km. The sands are good for beach combing, bird watching and clam digging. Seals are often seen offshore. For swimming, the water is warm but much of it is too shallow for adults. There are, though, a number of designated swimming areas with deeper waters.

The park also has populations of moose, deer, black bears as well as some smaller mammals. Other features are the bird life around the salt marsh and a bog where there is an observation platform.

The park is 100 km north of Moncton with an entrance just off Hwy 11. The visitor centre (☎ 876-2443) is open daily from mid-May to mid-October from 8 am to 8 pm and features interpretive displays and a small theatre as well as an information counter and gift shop. Entry fee into the park is a $6 daily motor-vehicle permit or a four-day pass for $18.

Check with the centre for the variety of programmes offered at the park, including a three-hour tour in a large Voyageur canoe where you paddle to offshore sand bars to view birds and possibly seals. The tours are offered four times a week and are $25 per adult, less for children.

Cycling Kouchibouguac features hiking trails and canoe routes but what really sets it apart from other national parks is the 32-km network of bikeways – crushed gravel paths that wind through the heart of the park's backcountry. From Ryans day-use area, where bikes can be rented, it's possible to cycle a 23-km loop and never be on the park road for any of it. Bicycles are $4 an hour and $20 a day. *Ryan Rental Center* (☎ 876-3733) also rents out canoes and kayaks for $5.50 an hour and $23 a day.

Camping Kouchibouguac has two drive-in campgrounds and three primitive camping areas. The camping season is from May to October and the park is very busy throughout July and August, particularly on weekends. Get there early in the day to obtain a camp site as they are handed out on a first-come-first-serve basis. There is talk of installing a reservation system so a call in advance might be a good investment in the middle of July.

South Kouchibouguac is the largest campground, located 12 km inside the park near the beaches and featuring 219 sites along with showers and a kitchen shelter. The rate is $14 a night during the summer. *Cote-a-Fabien* is on the north side of Kouchibouguac River, away from the bike trails and beaches, and does not have showers. A site here is $12 a night.

If the park is full, a good alternative is the *Daigles Park* (☎ 876-4540) a private campground two km outside the park in Saint Louis-de-Kent. An unserviced site is $10 a night.

The three primitive campgrounds in the park have only vault toilets and a pump for water and are $10 a night for two people. *Sipu* is located midway along the park's longest trail, the 14-km Kouchibouguac River Trail. *Petit Large* is on a bike path and *Pointe-a-Maxime* is along the shore and can be reached only by canoe.

MIRAMICHI BAY

North of the national park, in and around Miramichi Bay, are more beaches. Folks here, like those further south and in north Prince Edward Island and Nova Scotia where the same claim is made, say the waters are the warmest north of either Virginia or the Carolinas in the USA. In any case, the water at all these places is quite suitable for swimming in, having been warmed by spin-off currents of the Gulf Stream.

MIRAMICHI CITY

In late 1995, six communities including Chatham and Newcastle were amalgamated to form Miramichi City.

Chatham

This portion of the new city was a prosperous town when it was the centre of the wooden shipbuilding industry, but the development of steel ships put an end to that and the Canadian Forces base recently closed. There is little to recommend for visitors, but the revamped downtown area along Water St by the Miramichi River is pleasant enough in a quiet way.

Approaching town on Hwy 11, you pass a tourist centre (☎ 778-8444) that is open May to September from 9 am to 7 pm daily. Two blocks away from the waterfront the WS Logge Cultural Centre (☎ 773-7645), in a restored Victorian house at 222 Wellington St, is primarily a locally oriented art gallery.

At 149 Wellington St on the corner of University Ave, the Natural History Museum

(☎ 773-7305) has a small idiosyncratic collection and free admission. It's open from mid-June to mid-August.

In **Douglastown**, halfway between the Chatham bridge and the Newcastle area is the Rankin House Museum (☎ 773-3448), three floors of artefacts relating to early life in New Brunswick. The Rankin House also doubles up as a tourist centre and anchors the Lower Town Walk, a posted route past other historical buildings along Douglastown's waterfront.

North of Douglastown in Bartibog on Hwy 11 is **MacDonald Farm Historic Site** (☎ 778-6085). Overlooking the Miramichi River, the farm dates back to 1820 when Alexander MacDonald, a Scottish settler, built the stone house so typical of Scotland. Also on site is a barn, net shed and spring house while costumed guides continue the traditional activities of cooking over an open hearth, soap making and so on. Hours are 9.30 am to 4.30 and admission is $2.25.

Newcastle

Though the site of another huge paper mill, Newcastle is pleasant – a good place to break up the trip north or south. Around the attractive town square are some fine old wooden buildings and shops. Here in the central square park bounded by Castle and Henry Sts is a statue to Lord Beaverbrook, one of the most powerful press barons in British history and a statesman and philanthropist of no small reputation. Beaverbrook was born Max Aitken in 1879 and spent most of his growing years in Newcastle. Beaverbrook House (☎ 622-2511), his boyhood home at 225 Mary St, is now a museum. Among the many gifts he lavished on the province are the 17th-century English benches and the Italian gazebo in the square here. His ashes lie under the statue presented as a memorial to him by the town.

Across the river in **Nelson**, at the recently developed waterfront park called Ritchie Wharf there is a boardwalk and Murray House Museum (☎ 622-9100) which also doubles up as a tourist centre. Hours are 9 am to 7 pm daily during the summer.

Each summer the Miramichi Folk Song Festival, begun in the 1960s and the oldest one in North America, is held. Through traditional song, the local history and culture are preserved. It's good fun, and worth catching.

Places to Stay South of town off Hwy 8 is another of Lord Beaverbrook's gifts – a provincial park called The Enclosure. The campground in the park is now privately run as *Enclosure Campground* (☎ 627-4071) and is a pleasant place to pitch a tent. There is no fee for using the park's day use area.

Across the river in Nelson is the large *Governor's Mansion* (☎ 622-3036), without a doubt the most intriguing hostel and inn in New Brunswick. The huge house, with three floors of antiques, model ships and history, was built in 1865 and was the home of J Leonard O'Brien, the first Irish lieutenant governor of the province. On the grounds is an Ogham stone that dates back to the 4th century and exhibits early writing of the Celts. Numerous bedrooms on the second and third floor are $12 to $15 a night. A full breakfast is a few dollars more.

MIRAMICHI RIVER

South-west of Miramichi City, the Southwest Miramichi River extends beyond Doaktown, about halfway to Fredericton. The river runs 800 km and the waters are crystal clear. The area, in particular the main river, is renowned for Atlantic salmon fishing. Together with the Restigouche and Saint John rivers, it has gained the province an international reputation amongst serious anglers. Even Prince Charles has fished the Miramichi! Both residents and visitors need licences and there are special regulations for nonresidents.

Doaktown has become more or less the unofficial fishing centre for the region. In town is the Atlantic Salmon Museum (☎ 365-7787), which is actually pretty interesting and includes pools of live salmon ('king of the freshwater game fish') on the 1.5-hectare grounds. Hours are 9 am to 5 pm daily June through September.

One of Canada's best fly-fishing shops is here, WW Doak & Sons. It sells about 60,000 flies a year, many tied on the premises. Other points of interest include the Glendella Mansion (a rather unexpected sight) and Doak Historic Park, concerning local history and with a preserved house from the 19th century and costumed interpreters for the farm section. Hours for the historic park (☎ 365-4363) are 9 am to 5 pm daily during the summer and admission is free. Near town is an 1870s covered bridge, one of the province's oldest.

South of town at McNamee is Clearwater Hollow Expeditions (☎ 365-7636) which offers a series of good one and multi-day outdoor adventures in and along the river. This family business has economical hiking, cycling and wilderness canoe trips with all equipment available, or will act as outfitter and supply shuttle transportation. Cabin accommodation is offered at $50 for up to 4 people and some hostel-type rooms are in the planning stages.

ACADIAN PENINSULA

The large peninsula, which extends from Chatham and Bathurst out to two islands at the edge of the Baie des Chaleurs, is a predominantly French area which was first settled by the Acadians who were the unhappy victims of the colonial battles between Britain and France in the 1700s. The descendants of Canada's earliest French settlers proudly fly the Acadian flag around the region and many of the traditions live on in music, food and the language which is different to that spoken in Quebec.

For visitors, by far the most interesting section and best scenery is around Caraquet.

Getting There & Away

Transportation around this part of the province is very limited although there is some service. SMT Line buses, which cover pretty well the entire province, are not seen in this region at all. Instead, a couple of individuals run vans around the Acadian Peninsula from Monday to Friday.

The Gloucester Coach Lines (☎ 395-5812) runs between Tracadie and Bathurst via Shippagan and Caraquet once each way every weekday. In Caraquet, the bus stops at the Irving service station on Boulevard Saint Pierre Ouest. In Bathurst, a Gloucester bus departs the SMT station at 1.15 pm Monday through Friday for the return trip around the peninsula. A ticket from Bathurst to Caraquet is $10.

The Tracadie Coach Lines (☎ 395-5639) has a bus that leaves the Irving service station in Tracadie at noon Monday through Friday and reaching Newcastle/Chatham at 2.30 pm. The fare is $15.

The drivers for both of these coach lines can be reached at these numbers only in the evenings and on weekends – the rest of the time they are out driving the routes.

Tracadie

From Neguac, north-east of Chatham, the road passes by a mixture of old houses and modern bungalows. It's not a wealthy area and there isn't much to see as the road is too far inland for coastal views. In the little town of **Tabusintac** is Le Musee Historique de Tracadie (☎ 395-1500) on the second floor of the huge Academie Ste-Famille building on Main St. This unusual museum, the only one of its kind in Canada, offers a glimpse of leprosy in the 19th century through photos and artefacts. Hours during the summer are 9 am to 6 pm daily except on the weekends when it opens at noon. Admission is $2.

In Tracadie notice the Quebec-style double silver-spired Saint Jean Baptiste church. Just across the river at the north side of town is a tourist office.

Shippagan

At the tip of the mainland, Shippagan has the Aquarium and Marine Centre (☎ 336-3013), the highlight of which is the aquarium. Examples of many of the species, including seals, found in the Gulf of St Lawrence region are displayed. There is also a freshwater exhibit and displays showing all the electronic equipment used by today's fishing industry.

The centre is open from 10 am to 6 pm daily during the summer. Admission is $5 for adults and $11 for a family.

Adjacent to the centre is a marina with a restaurant and the tourist office in a small lighthouse. The tourist office is open the same hours as the Marine Centre.

A causeway connects Île Lamèque, a boggy island where the collection and shipping of peat competes in importance with fishing. Île Miscou, reached by a short free ferry ride, is less populated with quiet stretches of sandy beach. At the far tip is a lighthouse.

Caraquet

The oldest of the Acadian villages, Caraquet was founded in 1757 and is now the main centre of the peninsula's French community. Stretched out more or less along one street, it has one of the oldest churches in the province, Sainte Anne du Bocage. Down at the dock area on Boulevard Saint Pierre Est is a big fish market with fresh, salted, and frozen seafood for sale.

Acadian Museum In the middle of town, with views over the bay from the balcony, is this museum (☎ 727-1713) with a neatly laid out collection of artefacts donated by local residents. Articles include household objects, tools, photographs and a fine wood stove in the corner. Most impressive is the desk/bed which you can work at all day and then fold down into a bed when exhaustion strikes. It belonged to a superior at the Caraquet Convent in 1880.

The museum is open daily in summer from 10 am to 8 pm except on Sunday when it opens at 1 pm. Admission is $3.

Other Attractions Behind the museum is the *Théâtre Populaire d'Acadie* which puts on shows in midsummer. The tourist office (☎ 727-1705) is attached to the theatre. In August there is an Acadian Festival with a variety of events. A few km east out of town near Caraquet Park is the Sainte Anne du Bocage religious shrine.

Places to Stay Back a bit from the street at 143 Boulevard Saint Pierre Ouest is the *Hotel Paulin* (☎ 727-9981), an old red house with a green roof, by the water. It's open all year with singles/doubles at $40/45, and there is a restaurant for lunches and dinners.

Out close to the shrine is *Maison Touristique Dugas* (☎ 727-3195) with rooms beginning at $22/29 and camp sites for $10 a night. It's at 683 Boulevard Saint Pierre Ouest, also called RR2. Also for camping there is a provincial park close to the shrine.

Acadian Historic Village

The Acadian Historic Village (Village Historique Acadien), 14 km west of Caraquet, is a major historic museum (☎ 727-3467) set up like a village of old, with 26 buildings and workers in period costumes reflecting life from 1780 to 1880. The museum depicts daily life in a typically post-expulsion Acadian village and makes for an intriguing comparison to the obviously prosperous English King's Landing historic village outside Fredericton.

A good two hours is required to see the site, and you'll want to eat. For that there are two choices: a cafeteria or restaurant at the Dugas House, the latter serving Acadian dishes.

The museum is open from 10 am to 6 pm daily in summer. It's on Hwy 11 towards Grande-Anse. Tickets are $8 or $20 for the family. After Labour Day, when most of the custom guides have departed, tickets are $3.25 and $6.50 for the family.

The previously mentioned Gloucester Coach Lines van from Bathurst goes right by the door.

Grande-Anse

This small town boasts the popular Pope's Museum (☎ 732-3003), which houses images of 264 popes from St Peter to the present one, as well as various religious articles. There is also a detailed model of the Basilica and St Peter's Square in Rome.

The *Auberge de l'Anse* (☎ 732-5204) is a B&B on the main route, eight km from the Acadian Historic Village site. Doubles are

$30 to $40. There are also a couple of inexpensive motels and a restaurant in town.

GRANDE-ANSE TO BATHURST

All along the route from Grande-Anse to Bathurst the rugged, shoreline cliffs are scenic and include views across the bay to the mountains of the Gaspé Peninsula. There are some beaches (the one at Maisonnette is good), picnic sites and, at **Pokeshaw Provincial Park**, coastal erosion including a sea stack to see. If you're making a return trip to Bathurst, follow this same route both ways, as going around the rest of the peninsula is not worthwhile.

Near **Janeville** there is a restored grindstone mill which can be visited. For camping *Chapman's Tent & Trailer Park* (☎ 546-2883), 14 km east of Bathurst on Hwy 11, is highly recommended for its open sites overlooking the beach and ocean. An unserviced site is $9 a night.

BATHURST

Bathurst, yet another industrial town, but based on extremely rich zinc mines as well as lumber and pulp & paper, has little to recommend it to the casual visitor. Really quite small with about 15,000 people, the town is split into three sections: South, East and West Bathurst by the Nepisiguit River and the Bathurst Basin. The principal street is Main St in South Bathurst and this is where a couple of restaurants can be found.

St Peter Ave has the range of food-chain places and service stations as well as the War Museum (546-3135), displaying weapons, uniforms and photos and a reproduction of a WWI trench. Hours are 11 am to 9 pm daily during the summer and admission is free.

On the coast north-east of the harbour at the edge of the city is the **Daly Point Reserve**, a mix of woods and salt marshes with several trails that can be followed for observing birds. An observation tower provides views to the Gaspé Peninsula and along the Acadian Peninsula shoreline.

Some 20 km north of town towards Dalhousie in **Petit-Rocher** is the New Brunswick Mining & Mineral Interpretation

Centre (☎ 783-8714). This mining museum has various exhibits, including a deep shaft to descend, and features the local zinc-mining industry. The site is open daily from 10 am to 6 pm June through August and a tour takes about 45 minutes. It's on Route 134 and there is an admission fee.

Places to Stay & Eat

At Salmon Beach, just east of Bathurst is *Carey's By The Sea* (☎ 546-6801), a small resort with a great restaurant run by Johnny and Tomi Carey. Tomi is the author of six cookbooks and the pair host a cooking show, *Carey's Magic Kitchen*, that is taped in the restaurant. The cottages are extremely comfortable and begin at $30 for a double while another, which can sleep four people, is $40. Dinner at the restaurant ranges from $10 to $19 but is well worth it. Their frozen drinks (try the Moonlight Margarita) is the only civilised way to begin a meal.

Getting There & Away

You can walk to the old downtown section at the end of Nepisiguit Bay from the VIA Rail station (☎ 546-2659) which is at 690 Thornton Ave on the corner of Queen St. The station is open only when there is a train – 7 to 11.30 am daily except Wednesday and 4 to 9 pm daily except Tuesday. SMT Bus Lines (☎ 546-4380) is at 15 St Peter Ave on the corner of Main St. A bus departs north at 4.15 pm daily for Campbellton and south at 1.30 pm daily for Moncton.

DALHOUSIE

Dalhousie is a small, agreeable town on the north-east coast of New Brunswick on the Baie des Chaleurs opposite Quebec. The town's main industry is newsprint, and there are a few things to do.

William St and the parallel Adelaide St near the dock are the two main streets with most of the commercial enterprises. On the corner of Adelaide St at 437 George St is the **Restigouche Regional Museum** (☎ 684-1313) with local artefacts and history. Hours are 9 am to 5 pm weekdays and admission is free.

The cruise boat *Chaleur Phantom* departs from the town wharf at the foot of Renfrew St on a nature cruise at 9 am in the bay and a scenic cruise at 2 and 7 pm along the Restigouche River. The three-hour nature cruise to view birds, seals and possibly whales is $15 per person or $20 per couple.

Places to Stay

Two km east from the ferry dock at the end of Victoria St is *Inch Arran Park* (☎ 684-1333) right on the water with camp sites, a swimming pool, the tourist office, the beach and fine views across the bay. An unserviced site is $10 a night and there is a laundromat across the street.

Getting There & Away

You can take a car ferry from across the bay to Miguasha, Quebec. The ferry (☎ 444-1792), which leaves every hour on the hour from 9 am to 9 pm cuts about 70 km off the driving trip around the bay. The trip takes about 20 minutes and costs $12 for a car and driver and $1 for each passenger. It runs from the end of June to sometime in September.

CAMPBELLTON

Campbellton, on the Quebec border, is in the midst of a scenic area at the edge of the Restigouche Highlands. The Baie des Chaleurs is on one side and green, rolling irregularly shaped hills seem to encase the town on the remaining sides. Across the border is Matapédia and Hwy 132 leading to Mont Joli, 148 km into Quebec.

The last naval battle of the Seven Years' War was fought in the waters just off the coast here in 1760.

Main streets in this town of about 10,000 residents are Water St and Roseberry St, around which the commercial centre is clustered. Campbellton is truly a bilingual town with store cashiers saying everything in both French and English.

Nearby, **Sugarloaf Mountain**, rising nearly 400 metres above sea level and dominating the skyline, is the principal attraction and provides excellent views of the town and part of the Restigouche River. It looks remarkably like its namesake in Rio. From the base, it's a half-hour walk to the top; another trail leads around the bottom.

There's camping in Sugarloaf Provincial Park and skiing in winter. A large provincial tourist centre (☎ 789-2367) is located on Water St near the town square in which a focal point is a huge statue of a salmon surrounded by man-made waterfalls.

About 10 km west of town towards Matapédia is **Morrisey Rock**, another place for a good view of the scenic river area.

Places to Stay

There are 65 semi-serviced sites in a pleasant wooded setting at *Sugarloaf Provincial Park* (☎ 789-2366) on Route 270, off Hwy 11. A site is $15 a night.

There is the HI *Campbellton Lighthouse Hostel* (☎ 753-7044) at 1 Ritchie St in the central waterfront district along the Restigouche River. It's open from early June to September. There are only 20 beds in this converted lighthouse, so calling ahead to check availability is advisable. The rate is $10 for members, $15 for nonmembers and $5 if you just want to pitch your tent outside.

The *Auberge Maritime Inn* (☎ 753-7606 or 800-561-1881), at 26 Duke St, is a good choice if you'd like to be right in the centre of town. Singles begin at $48.

Between here and Dalhousie on Hwy 134 are numerous motels and campgrounds, many with attractive seaside locations. Others are found on Hwy 134 West.

Sanfar Cottages (☎ 753-4287) is west of town at Tide Head on Route 134. There are 12 cabins here, at $40 for two people, and a light breakfast is included.

Places to Eat

In the centre of town along Roseberry St is the usual assortment of chain restaurants and for a cheap breakfast, *Art's Dog Cart*. This funky little place has only stools and counters but Art will cook you a full breakfast, including coffee, for $2.50.

Getting There & Away

The SMT bus stop is at the Pik-Quik variety

store on Water St near Prince William St. The VIA Rail station is conveniently central on Roseberry St. There is one train daily except on Wednesday going south to Moncton and Halifax and one daily except Tuesday heading the other way to Montreal.

MT CARLETON PROVINCIAL PARK

This 17,427-hectare park is the largest and wildest in the province, offering visitors mountains, valleys and rivers in a wilderness setting. The main feature of the park is a series of peaks and ridges, including Mt Carleton, which at 820 metres is one of the highest peaks in Maritime Canada. This range is actually an extension of the Appalachian Mountains from the USA and plans are currently underway to extend the 3200-km Appalachian Trail, which begins in the state of Georgia, from Maine into New Brunswick.

Access to Mt Carleton Provincial Park is via Hwy 180 from **Saint Quentin**, a town that's south-west of Campbellton along the Restigouche River. The park is roughly 130 km south of Campbellton and 43 km from Saint Quentin, the last place to purchase gasoline, food and beer.

At the entrance is a visitor centre (☎ 235-2025) for maps, information and park-entry permits. The centre is open 7 am to 10 pm daily during the summer and the motor-vehicle permits are $3.50 a day.

Hiking

Day hiking is the best way to explore Mt Carleton. The park has a 60-km network of trails with the vast majority of them loops winding to a handful of rocky knobs that are the peaks.

The easiest peak to climb is **Mount Bailey Trail**, a 7.5-km loop to the 563-metre knob that begins near the day-use area. Most hikers can walk the route in two to three-hours and there is a picnic table at the top so pack a lunch.

The highest peak is reached from the **Mount Carleton Trail**, a 10-km route that skirts over the 820-metre knob, where there is a firetower. Along the way is a back-

country camp site located near three beaver ponds and in full view of the mountain. Plan on three to four hours for the trek and pack along your parka. The wind above the treeline can be brutal at times.

The most scenic hike is **Sagamook Trail**, a 6-km loop to the 777-metre peak. There are eight view points along the loop and the vast majority of them allow you to gaze down on Nictau Lake and the highlands area to the north of it. Plan on three hours for this trek. The trailhead is conveniently located near Mt Carleton Lodge so you can enjoy a cold beer or a hot toddy afterwards.

Places to Stay & Eat

Armstrong Brook Campground is a large facility on the north side of Nictau Lake with toilets, showers, kitchen shelter but no serviced sites. It's $9.25 a night to camp here.

Along the south side of the lake, near the Sagamook Trailhead, is *Mount Carleton Lodge* (☎ 235-1915), which has cabins for rent, a restaurant and bar, and canoe rental. A cabin is $60 for a single or double.

Saint John River Valley

The Saint John River, which has been likened to the Rhine, begins in Maine, USA, on the north-western corner of New Brunswick and flows south for over 700 km before entering the Bay of Fundy at Saint John.

It winds along the western border of the province past forests and beautiful lush farmland, through Fredericton between tree-lined banks, and then around rolling hills to the bay. The valley that protects it is one of the most scenic places in the province. It's particularly picturesque and gentle from just north of Saint John to near Woodstock.

There are bridges and ferries across the river at various points. The Trans Canada, Hwy 2, follows the river up to Edmundston and then crosses into Quebec.

Because of its soft, eye-pleasing landscape and because the main highway connecting the Atlantic Provinces with central Canada runs along the river, not surprisingly, it is a busy route in summer. So much so that accommodation can be difficult to find in July and August. It is advisable to stop early or use the tourist office's toll-free reservation service to book ahead. In the off-peak season there is no problem at all.

Aside from the bigger centres, some small towns along the route have a B&B or two. There are also campgrounds along the way. There is a choice of two routes, the quicker Trans Canada Hwy mostly on the west side of the river, or Hwy 105 on the east. The slower route is not any more scenic but does go right through many of the smaller villages.

WOODSTOCK

A small town set in a rich farming area, Woodstock acts as a tourist crossroad. The Trans Canada Hwy goes through town, as does the road to Maine, USA. Hwy 95 to Bangor, Maine, and then Hwy 2 is an alternative and shorter route to Montreal than going north through Edmundston and then along the St Lawrence River. Main St through Woodstock has some fine, old large Maritime houses.

There is a bluegrass music festival held in town in summer.

Places to Stay & Eat

For spending the night, there is a bit of choice here and prices aren't bad. At 698 Main St is the *Down Home B&B* (☎ 328-1819) in a 19th-century Victorian home with three rooms, one with a private bath. Rates are $50/60.

Away from the centre but with a quiet, country location is the *Froelich's Swiss Chalet B&B* (☎ 328-6751). The house looks as though it might have been lifted from the Alps. A double is $45 and includes breakfast. It's about 15 km from town on Route 105, nine km south of the Grafton Bridge. Among the motels there's the *Motel Haven* (☎ 272-2100) on Route 2 with rooms at $30/32.

On the north side of town is the *Hometown* (you can't miss it), a good spot for a meal.

HARTLAND

Hartland is an attractive little town with a nice setting and, though there is not much else to see, it does have the grand-daddy of New Brunswick's many wooden covered bridges, now considered historic sites. This bridge at 400 metres long is the longest in the world. There are 74 of these bridges dotted around the province; the tourist office has a complete listing if you're interested. The bridges were covered to protect the timber beams used in the construction. With such protection from rain and sun, a bridge lasts about 80 years. They are generally high and wide because cartloads of hay pulled by horses had to pass through. Nearly all of the bridges that remain are on secondary or smaller roads.

Halfway between here and Grand Falls is a provincial park at Kilburn.

Places to Stay & Eat

The *Ja-Se-Le Motel* (☎ 375-4419 or 800-656-1144) (named with letters from the names of the original owner's daughters), north of town, is the only local motel. It has a pretty good restaurant serving mainly German food, but you can get the standard Canadian breakfast of eggs, bacon and toast. Rooms are $36/42. There is also a couple of B&Bs in town. Try *Campbell's B&B* (☎ 375-4775), overlooking the Saint John River and just three km from the famous covered bridge on Hwy 105. Rooms range from $30/45.

GRAND FALLS

A town with 7000 residents, Grand Falls consists essentially of one main street and the falls that make it an interesting short stop.

In a park in the middle of town, the falls drop about 25 metres and have carved out a gorge 1.5 km long with walls as high as 70 metres. At the site is the Malabeam Reception Centre that doubles as a tourist office (☎ 473-4538). Hours during the summer are 9 am to 9 pm. Among the displays inside is a scale model of the gorge showing the extensive trail system that follows the edge of it. Entrance to the park and centre are free but there is a $2 admission for a 253-step stairway that leads down into the gorge.

The falls are best in spring or after a heavy rain. In summer, much of the water is diverted for generating hydroelectricity. The dam for this also takes away from the rugged beauty the site once would have had. The area at the bottom of the gorge reached by the staircase is more scenic than the falls themselves and permits a glimpse of how the pre-development days would have looked.

The town celebrates its primary resource, the potato, in a festival each year around 1 July.

Places to Stay & Eat

At 142 Main St is the *Maple Tourist Home* (☎ 473-1763), a B&B with doubles for $45. Along the highway to the north of town are several motels and camping.

For something to eat there are a couple of quick places down the main street, Broadway. *Bob's Deli* has salads and baked goods. At *Grits Bar & Grill* at Broadway and Main St, most dinners are under $8 and there always seems to be a beer special going on. *LaBouffe Restaurant*, also on Broadway, serves café latte and croissant sandwiches.

AROUND GRAND FALLS

East of Grand Falls around the farming community of New Denmark is the largest Danish population in North America. In the middle of July there's a festival celebrating all things Danish. In town, there is a small museum while the *Valhalla Restaurant* serves Danish foods all year.

Hwy 108, the Plaster Rock Hwy, cuts across the province to the east coast. The highway sluices through forest for nearly its entirety. Animals such as deer and moose are commonly seen on or beside the road – take care at night. There are some camping spots along the way.

SAINT LÉONARD

As the name suggests, Saint Léonard is primarily a French town, like many in this region. Some are old Acadian settlements although the Acadian descendants are more concentrated in the north-east of the province.

In Saint Léonard is the Madawaska Weavers group, formed in 1939 and still using hand looms to make fabric for items such as ponchos and scarves. Visit the centre at Main and Saint-Jean Sts.

From here, Hwy 17 runs north-east through the dense forests of northern New Brunswick.

EDMUNDSTON

If you're coming from Quebec there's a good chance this will be the first town in the Maritimes you get a look at, as the border is only about 20 km away. From here it is three hours' drive to Fredericton. Maine is just across the river and there is an international bridge on Dupont St at the south end of town not far from City Hall.

Edmundston is an industrial pulp & paper centre with numerous mills in and around town. It's split pretty well in half by the Madawaska River and the old central district on the west side of the river is built around some low hills which give it some character.

The population of about 13,000 is 85% French-speaking. Nearly all of them, like most of New Brunswick's French, speak English.

The main intersection downtown is that of Church St and Canada Rd. Within a few blocks of this corner are many of the shops, a couple of restaurants, City Hall plus an indoor shopping mall. Victoria St, between the highway and this central section, is also a busy commercial street.

Clustered around exit 18 from the highway is the tourist office, a shopping mall, some fast-food restaurants, a Canadian Tire store (hardware, sports and automotive parts) and nearby a motel.

There is no inner-city bus service so you'll have to do some walking here, but the distances are not great.

The local citizens have a somewhat whimsical notion of Edmundston as the capital of a fictitious country known as Madawaska whose inhabitants are known as Brayons. Evidently this traditional community uniting

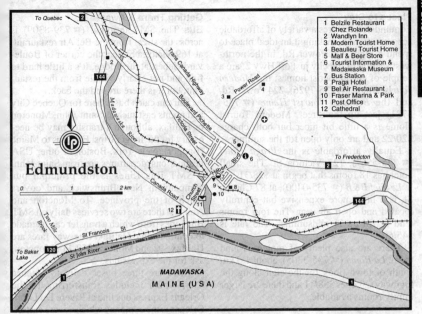

Edmundston

To Quebec

Trans Canada Highway

Madawaska River

Boulevard Pichette

Victoria Street

Power Road

Hébert Blvd

Canada Road

Church Street

Too Mile Brook

St Francois St

St John River

Queen Street

To Fredericton

To Baker Lake

MADAWASKA
MAINE (USA)

1 Belzile Restaurant
  Chez Rolande
2 Wandlyn Inn
3 Modern Tourist Home
4 Beaulieu Tourist Home
5 Mall & Beer Store
6 Tourist Information &
  Madawaska Museum
7 Bus Station
8 Praga Hotel
9 Bel Air Restaurant
10 Fraser Marina & Park
11 Post Office
12 Cathedral

0   1   2 km

concept has historical origins in a period during the late 1700s when the region existed in a sort of political vacuum between the border-bickering of the US and British governments.

Information
The local tourist office (☎ 735-2747) is in the museum building on the corner of Boulevard Pichette and Boulevard Hébert.

Madawaska Museum
At 195 Boulevard Hébert on the corner of Boulevard Pichette is the Madawaska Museum (☎ 737-5064) which outlines the human history of the area from the time of the original Maliseet (Malecite) Indians through colonial times to the present. The museum also has displays on local industries such as the timber trade. It's open daily from 8 am to 8 pm in summer, but has reduced hours the rest of the year. There's an admission fee.

Petit Témis Interprovincial Linear Park
This unique park stretches from Edmundston to Cabano in Quebec and features a 62-km bicycle trail that winds along the Madawaska River and Temiscouata Lake. A pleasant afternoon can be enjoyed cycling just a portion of it; the best place to start is at Fraser Marina just off Victoria St on the east side of the river in Edmundston. At the marina there is a picnic area, a foot bridge to the west side of the river, a boat launch as well as two bike rental shops. Outdoor Adventures (☎ 739-6800) rents canoes and kayaks, as well as bicycles.

Festivals
Each year on the nine days preceding the first Monday in August is the 'Foires' Festival, which celebrates the physically nonexistent republic of Madawaska. There are cultural, social and sporting activities as well as some good traditional Brayon cooking to sample.

Places to Stay

Edmundston features a variety of affordable accommodation, making it an ideal place to spend a night. On Power Rd, in the northwest section of the city just off Hwy 2, are a couple of cheap tourist homes; the *Modern Tourist Home* (☎ 735-7926), 224 Power Rd, and the *Beaulieu Tourist Home* (☎ 735-5781) just up the street. Modern Tourist Home is a little bit nicer but both charge $20/22 and are only open for the summer.

Equally affordable is the *Praga Hotel* (☎ 735-5567), 127 Victoria St. The small hotel has 18 rooms that begin at $28/31.

Le Fief B&B (☎ 735-0400), at 87 Church St, is a little more expensive but centrally located and open all year. The four rooms tend to fill up in midsummer. The rate is $45/60.

There are also plenty of motels around town. *La Roma* (☎ 735-3305), about 1.5 km south of town (look for the sign along the highway) charges $38/41 and there are larger family rooms available.

Places to Eat

The central downtown area has very few restaurants. The *Bel Air*, with the sign that can't be missed, is on the corner of Victoria St and Boulevard Hébert. It's been here almost 40 years, is open 24 hours, and has become a city landmark. The extensive menu offers Italian, Chinese, seafood or basic Canadian fare. Chinese dinners are under $7, most other dinners are under $10 and the portions are pretty filling. Adjoining the Bel Air is *Steak & Seafood Paradise*, more upmarket with dinners starting at $10.

There are also a couple of Chinese places along Victoria St. *Pizza Delight* has a large outlet at 180 Boulevard Hébert at exit 18 just off the Trans Canada Hwy.

The locals flock to *Belzile Restaurant Chez Rolande*, a 10-minute drive from the centre at 815 Victoria St, for sandwiches, burgers etc and a couple of French Canadian specialties such as poutine (fries topped with melted cheese curds and gravy) and their 'famous' sugar pies. Hamburger plates or fish & chips are under $5.

Getting There & Away

Bus The SMT terminal (☎ 739-8309) is across the street from the Bel Air restaurant, at 169 Victoria St near the corner of Boulevard Hébert at the bridge. It's a little hard to find and not clearly visible from the restaurant, but it is there around the back.

You can catch buses here for Quebec City and points east such as Saint John, Moncton or Halifax, although a transfer may be necessary for the longer trips. For trips to Maine (Bangor), New York, Boston or other USA destinations, departures are from Saint John.

SMT Bus Lines is the principal bus company in New Brunswick and covers much of the province. To Moncton and Amherst there are two services daily on SMT Bus Lines from which a transfer can be made to continue onto Halifax. One-way fares are Halifax $92 and Moncton $57. For Moncton, ask for the express bus.

There are three buses daily to Quebec City, which includes transferring to the Orleans Express bus line at Rivere Du Loop. Orleans is the company which covers eastern Quebec. The one-way fare is $44.

SAINT JACQUES

Seven km north of Edmundston, about halfway to the Quebec border, is the small community of Saint Jacques which has a couple of places of interest. Les Jardins de la Republique Provincial Park (☎ 735-4871) offers good camping and has picnic sites along the river.

Also here is the New Brunswick Botanical Gardens (☎ 739-6335), put together by a group from the well known Montreal Botanical Gardens in Quebec. With both natural and cultivated sections running along the edge of the Madawaska River, it makes a refreshing, tranquil respite from the highway if you've had a long drive. The garden is open from early June to the middle of October every day until dusk, and there is a snack bar.

There are a couple of motels here, a few km from the commercial strip around Edmundston. One, *Motel Guy* (☎ 735-4253), is on the Trans Canada and charges $42/44.

Manitoba

Manitoba, Canada's fifth province, probably gets its name from the Algonkian Indian languages – in Lake Manitoba there is a strait where the water hits the limestone edges, making an odd echoing sound; the Native Indians associated this sound with the 'great spirit' ('manito') and named the spot 'Manito Waba', which means Manito Strait. Manito Waba became Manitoba.

The province is the first of the three prairie provinces as you head westward. The southern half is low and flat; the western edge is best for farming. The Canadian Shield, which covers about half the country, cuts across northern Manitoba, making this rocky, hilly forested lake land.

Winnipeg, the capital, has had a long and interesting history which greatly influenced the development of the west in general. The city has a variety of things to see and do, and many are within walking distance of each other along architecturally diverse streets.

Winnipeg is a major cultural centre and offers plenty of choice in accommodation and eating out. Neighbouring St Boniface is the largest western French community in Canada. Scattered across the province are large parks, ideal for exploring the terrain. Way up on Hudson Bay, Churchill with its intriguing wildlife is one of the destinations most alluring to visitors.

Fishing and hunting attract many visitors to this province, especially from the USA.

History

The Assiniboine and Cree First Nations were the principal groups inhabiting the region upon the arrival of Europeans. The Chipewayen of the northern sections and around Hudson Bay soon became involved with the fur traders. The Ojibway, found mainly across Ontario, also moved as far west as the great lakes of Manitoba.

Unlike in much of the country, early European exploration and settlement occurred not

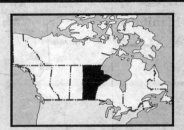

HIGHLIGHTS

Entered Confederation: 15 July 1870
Area: 650,090 sq km
Population: 1,091,942
Provincial Capital: Winnipeg

- Enjoy Winnipeg's museums and take in the Folk Festival in early July
- Take part in the cultural life of western Canada's largest French community
- Visit the far-north natural attractions of Churchill, which include polar bears, caribou and beluga whales
- Drive past fields of nodding sunflowers in the south-eastern part of the province
- Explore some of the 3000 sq km of Riding Mountain National Park with its multitude of forests, lakes, rivers and meadows

in the more hospitable south but along the cold, remote coasts of Hudson Bay. By the early 17th century fur-trading posts had been set-up. Much of Manitoba, first called

MANITOBA

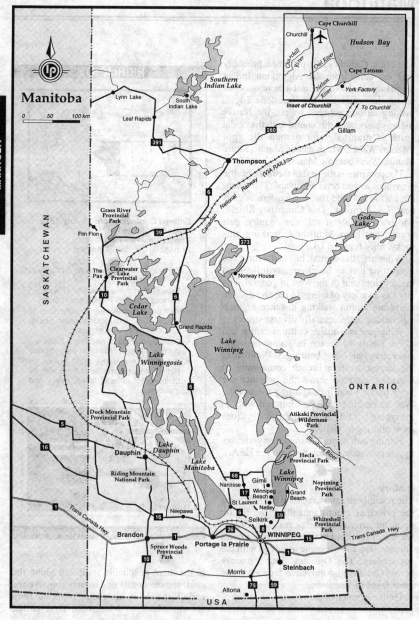

Manitoba

0   50   100 km

Southern Indian Lake

Lynn Lake

South Indian Lake

Leaf Rapids

391

Thompson

6

Grass River Provincial Park

Flin Flon

39

The Pas

Clearwater Lake Provincial Park

10

Cedar Lake

Grand Rapids

Lake Winnipegosis

Norway House

373

Lake Winnipeg

Canadian National Railway (VIA RAIL)

280

Gillam

To Churchill

Gods Lake

ONTARIO

Duck Mountain Provincial Park

5

16

Dauphin

Lake Dauphin

Lake Manitoba

Atikaki Provincial Wilderness Park

Bloodvein River

Riding Mountain National Park

1

Trans Canada Hwy

68

Narcisse

17

Neepawa

16

Brandon

Portage la Prairie

Spruce Woods Provincial Park

10

Morris

Altona

75

59

Gimli

Winnipeg Beach

St Laurent

Netley

6

Selkirk

Lake Winnipeg

Grand Beach

59

WINNIPEG

15

Steinbach

1

Trans Canada Hwy

Hecla Provincial Park

Nopiming Provincial Park

Whiteshell Provincial Park

USA

Inset of Churchill

Cape Churchill

Churchill

Hudson Bay

Churchill River

Owl River

Nelson River

Cape Tatnam

York Factory

Rupert's Land, was granted by Charles II of England to the Hudson's Bay Company.

Led by Lord Selkirk, agricultural settlement began in 1812 in the area which is now Winnipeg. Conflict between farm expansion and land rights of the Métis resulted in two major rebellions against the federal authorities. Louis Riel, who is still a controversial figure, was leader of the Métis and led the uprisings.

In the late 19th century, British settlers arrived to grow wheat and Winnipeg began its growth to become a major centre. Immigration increased until the Depression. Since the 1950s, the north has been opened up and mining and hydro-electricity have become important ingredients in the province's development.

Climate

The winters are long and cold, but the summers can be hot and are usually very sunny. Generally there is a decrease in temperature as you go from south-west to north-east. There's about 130 cm of snow a year.

Economy

Manufacturing is the main source of income. Food processing and clothing factories are also important contributors to the provincial economy. Wheat is the major agricultural product, with various other grains and cattle following closely behind. In the northern Shield area there are rich deposits of gold, copper, nickel and zinc.

Population & People

Several Indian groups shared the region before Europeans arrived. Most prominent among them were the Cree, mostly of the north, and the Assiniboine in the south. Today, Native peoples make up about 7% of the population. The major ethnic backgrounds are British, German, Ukrainian and French. The southern portion of Manitoba contains 95% of the population, with more than half living in or around Winnipeg.

Information

Provincial Symbols
The provincial flower is the prairie crocus, and the provincial bird is the grey owl.

Tourist Offices
Travel Manitoba is the provincial tourist agency. Their main office is at 155 Carleton St, 7th Floor, Winnipeg, Manitoba R3C 3H8. The toll free number for information on the province and free material is ☎ 1-800-665-0040. Travel Manitoba offices can also be found at major border crossings. Winnipeg and other towns have their own tourist offices which are good for obtaining local information.

Telephone
The area code for the province is 204.

Time
Manitoba is on Central Time.

Tax
The provincial sales tax is 7%.

Activities

Fishing is a major outdoor activity. Travel Manitoba produces several publications dealing with details of where and how to fish. The province also offers abundant canoeing possibilities. To this end the tourist office has an excellent guide detailing canoe routes including some wilderness trips.

Riding Mountain National Park offers good hiking and riding and is home to a herd of bison. A variety of wildlife viewing is possible at Churchill, famed for its polar bears.

Accommodation

Travel Manitoba produces a booklet on accommodation and campgrounds in Manitoba. A useful map indicating all the campgrounds is also available from tourist offices. In addition there is a farm vacation programme, a range of lodges and resorts, fly-in camps and B&Bs. Addresses for many of these can be found in the Travel Manitoba publications.

Winnipeg

Winnipeg sits in the geographical centre of the country but it feels very much like a western town. Due primarily to its layout and architecture, Winnipeg also has a somewhat US ambience. Indeed, Winnipeg is often compared to Chicago – its mid-western, grain-handling, transportation counterpart.

Winnipeg also feels much bigger than it is, although with 650,000 residents, it is the fourth largest Canadian city. About half of Manitoba's population lives here.

The city has some fascinating history which visitors can explore in museums and at various sites. If you're crossing Canada you'll have to pass through the city, and Winnipeg makes a pleasant stopover.

Summers are very hot and winters are very cold. The corner of Portage Ave and Main St is said to be the windiest corner on the continent.

History

The Cree Indian people called the area 'Winnipee', meaning 'muddy water'. They shared the land now occupied by Winnipeg with the Assiniboines, before de la Vérendrye, the first European trader, arrived in 1738. In the early 19th century the area was the centre of fur-trading rivalry between the Hudson's Bay Company and the North West Company.

In 1812 Lord Selkirk led Scottish and Irish immigrants to the area to create the first permanent colonial settlement. Later, Fort Garry was built. Louis Riel, a native son and one of Canada's most controversial figures, led the Métis in voicing concerns over their way of life. He is considered the father of Manitoba. The railway arrived in Winnipeg in 1881.

The 1970s saw urban redevelopment upgrade the provincial capital. In the 1980s, the main street, Portage Ave, underwent a massive change, with the building of a mega-mall complex taking over several blocks. The wide downtown streets, edged with a balance of new and old buildings, give a sense of permanence as well as of development and change.

Orientation

As you approach Winnipeg from the east, the trees start to disappear. With about 50 km to go, the flat prairie land that stretches to the Rockies appears. Near town is a sign marking the longitudinal centre of Canada.

Once in Winnipeg, Main St is the main north-south street. Portage (pronounced 'Port-idge') Ave, the major east-west artery, is also the main shopping street, leading westward towards the airport and eventually to the westbound Trans Canada Hwy. The downtown core spreads out evenly from their junction. Most of the hotels and restaurants and many of the historic sites are within a 10-block square around this point. The railway station is central, on the corner of Main St and Broadway Ave. The Legislative Building and other government buildings are on Broadway Ave, too.

The corner of Portage Ave and Main St has many office buildings and examples of newer architecture. Portage Place, a redevelopment project of stores and offices, runs from Carlton St all the way to Vaughan St and has transformed much of the north side of Portage Ave. Enclosed walkways (known as skywalks) over Portage Ave connect Portage Place to major department stores on the south side. Many of the downtown side streets are one-way streets, which alternate in direction as a rule.

To the north-east of the city core is the old warehouse area which is known as the Exchange District. Nearby, north up Main St, the Centennial Centre is an arts and cultural complex.

The small Chinatown is also in this area. The Chinese Cultural Building/Dynasty Building, at 180 King St, has a small oriental garden retreat. The Mandarin Building, on the corner of King St and James Ave, contains a replica of the Chinese Nine Imperial Dragon Mural and a statue of Buddha. The two buildings are linked by the China Gate, which runs above King St.

MANITOBA

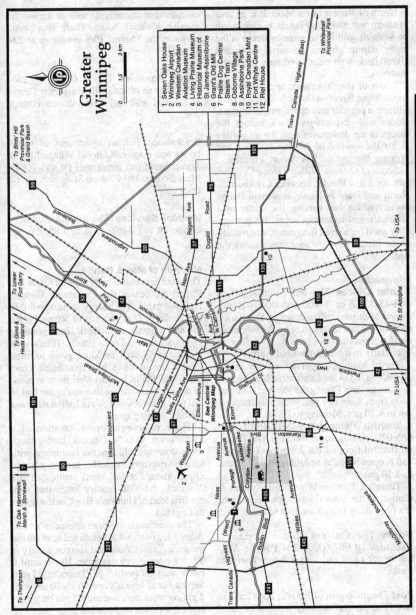

Greater Winnipeg

0   1.5   3 km

1   Seven Oaks House
2   Winnipeg Airport
3   Western Canadian
    Aviation Museum
4   Living Prairie Museum of
5   Historical Museum of
    St James-Assiniboine
6   Grant's Old Mill
7   Prairie Dog Central
    Steam Train
8   Osborne Village
9   Assiniboine Park
10 Royal Canadian Mint
11 Fort Whyte Centre
12 Riel House

To Birds' Hill
Provincial Park
& Grand Beach

To Lower
Fort Garry

To Gimli &
Hecla Island

To Oak Hammock
Marsh & Stonewall

To Thompson

To Whiteshell
Provincial Park

Trans Canada Highway (East)

To St Adolphe

To USA

To USA

See Central
Winnipeg Map

North of Rupert St on Main St is an area of cheap bars and dingy hotels. Further north on Main St, you'll find some evidence of the many ethnic groups, primarily Jews and Ukrainians, who once lived here in greater numbers.

South of the downtown area, across the Assiniboine River on Osborne St, is Osborne Village, a popular area containing boutiques, stores and restaurants. Back across the bridge in the downtown area, the art gallery is on the corner of Memorial Blvd and Portage Ave and the bus station is nearby.

South of Osborne Village, along Corydon Ave for a few blocks, between Cockburn St North and Daly St North, is a small Italian district which has become the centre of a little cafe and restaurant scene. It's particularly good for a stroll in summer, when many of the places have outdoor patios along the street.

Information

Tourist Offices The main tourist office (☎ 945-3777 or 1-800-665-0040) is the Travel Manitoba office down at The Forks, the historic site and market by the riverside, not far from the train station. The office is open daily in the summer until 9 pm.

Travel Manitoba operates another office (☎ 945-5813) in the Legislative Building on Broadway Ave. During the summer it's open daily from 8 am to 7 pm. Winter hours are 8 am to 4.30 pm, Monday to Friday.

Tourism Winnipeg (☎ 943-1970 or 1-800-665-0204) can also be found at The Forks, on the 3rd floor of the Johnston Terminal, and is open Monday to Friday from 8.30 am to 4.30 pm.

There's a Tourism Winnipeg Information Centre on the main floor of the airport too. It's open daily from 8 am to 9.45 pm.

Money The Custom House Currency Exchange (☎ 987-6000), 231 Portage Ave, has better rates and longer hours than the banks.

Post The main post office is at 266 Graham Ave. The general delivery window is open on Saturday morning as well as during the regular weekday hours. There is a postal outlet in the Pharma Plus drugstore at 234 Donald St.

Travel Agencies Travel CUTS (☎ 269-9350), has an office in the University Centre at the University of Manitoba on Portage Ave.

Bookshops For an assortment of travel books and maps call Global Village Map & Travel Store (no storefront) (☎ 453-7081). Mary Scorer, 389 Graham St, is also a good bookstore.

Medical Services The Health Sciences Centre (☎ 787-3167) is at 820 Sherbrooke St.

Museum of Man & Nature

This excellent museum (☎ 956-2830), at 190 Rupert St, beside the Centennial Concert Hall, has exhibits of history, culture, wildlife and geology. The dioramas of Native Indian life and animals are realistic, incorporating sights, sounds and even smells. Take a look at the grizzly claw necklace given to artist Paul Kane in 1848 by Assiniboine chief Mah-Min. Plains Indians wore them as proof of their bravery: to get one you either had to kill four grizzlies or a Sioux Indian who was already wearing one!

There is an excellent re-creation of a 1920s town, with 'sod' house, barber shop, drug store and old cinema (complete with Chaplin movies). In another section, you can climb aboard a full-sized replica of the *Nonsuch*, the 17th-century ketch that took the first load of Hudson's Bay Company furs to England.

The museum is worth an afternoon's visit. Admission costs $4. A combined ticket to the museum, planetarium and science gallery is $9. It's open every day from 10 am until 6 pm in summer (until 9 pm Thursday). From September to June it's open from 10 am until 4 pm on weekdays and until 5 pm on weekends. It's closed on Monday.

MANITOBA

Planetarium

The planetarium (☎ 943-3142), housed within the museum, has good programmes on space, the solar system and different aspects of the universe. There are also laser rock shows, fashion shows and other performances which utilise the unique equipment. The usual programmes are $3.50; the laser rock shows are more expensive. Ring for information and programme times.

Touch the Universe

In the museum basement is a 'hands-on' science gallery with participatory displays designed to help reveal how our senses perceive the world. The staff put on demonstrations on a range of scientific topics. Admission is $3.50, less for children.

Ukrainian Centre

The Ukrainian Centre (☎ 942-0218), at 184 Alexander Ave, near the Museum of Man & Nature, contains a gallery and museum. Set up to preserve and present the culture of the Ukraine, the museum has costumes, textiles, ceramics as well as painted Easter eggs (*pysankas*). The gallery displays both old and contemporary works. A specialised library holds 60,000 volumes relating to this important Canadian immigrant group.

The centre is open Tuesday to Saturday from 10 am to 4 pm, and on Sunday from 2 to 5 pm. Admission is free.

Holy Trinity Ukrainian Orthodox Cathedral

Within this church with the bulbous Byzantine domes is the provincial branch of the Ukrainian Museum of Canada (☎ 334-6531). Examples of traditional arts & crafts are displayed. The cathedral is at 1175 Main St. Call for opening times, as they vary seasonally and by day of the week.

The Forks

This very successful redevelopment project has made The Forks the busiest people place in Winnipeg. The fetching location at the forks of the Red and Assiniboine rivers, behind the VIA Rail station off Main St near Broadway Ave, has in one way or another been the site of pretty much all of Manitoba's history. The staff, who are on duty every day by the round office structure of the national-historic site (☎ 983-2007), can provide information on what's gone on through the years at this river junction. Native Indians first used the area some 6000 years ago. The early explorers and fur traders stopped here, forts were built and destroyed, and Métis and Scottish pioneers later settled The Forks.

The site is essentially a riverside park. The Riverwalk is a path with historic notes written on plaques in English, French and Cree. Parts of the trail also provide views of the city along the way. The Forks is also a recreation area, with shops, restaurants, bars and events all centred around overhauled turn-of-the-century stables, warehouses and factory buildings.

The Market Building is buzzing with produce stalls, craft shops, galleries and cafes. It's a fine place for a coffee and cinnamon bun breakfast with a newspaper. The Johnston Terminal is similar but also houses the **Manitoba Sports Hall of Fame** (☎ 985-1921) for sports buffs.

Walking tours are offered from The Forks Pavilion. Bicycles and canoes can be rented at the site; a paddle along the historic river, perhaps past the Basilica over in St Boniface, is not a bad way to spend a couple of hours. A water bus runs back and forth across the river, too, or to Osborne Village with a stop at the dock behind the Legislature. Full-scale boat tours of the river depart from nearby. In winter there is skating on the river or you can walk over the ice to the impressive-looking St Boniface Basilica. Cross-country ski trails are groomed along the river. Take a break and warm up beside the fire in the Pavilion.

City buses connect the downtown area to the site near the Market Building, but it is quite walkable. On weekdays the No 99 bus runs from here up to Broadway Ave and around by the Art Gallery. The No 96 bus, which runs on weekends, links Portage Ave to The Forks.

MANITOBA

MANITOBA

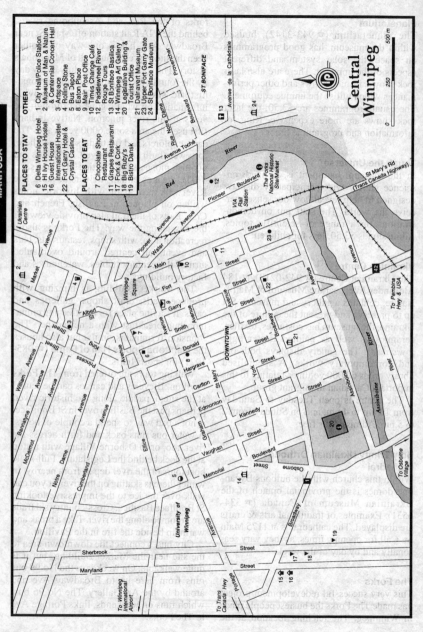

Central Winnipeg

PLACES TO STAY

6 Delta Winnipeg Hotel
15 Hi Ivy House Hostel
16 Guest House
   International Hostel
22 Fort Garry Hotel &
   Crystal Casino

PLACES TO EAT

7 Chocolate Shop
   Restaurant
17 Grapes Restaurant
18 Fork & Cork
18 Big Ruby's
19 Bistro Dansk

OTHER

1 City Hall/Police Station
2 Museum of Man & Nature
   & Centennial Concert Hall
3 Artspace
4 Rolling Stone
5 Bus Depot
8 Eaton Place
9 Mair Post Office
10 Times Change Café
12 Paddlewheel River
   Rouge Tours
13 St Boniface Basilica
14 Winnipeg Art Gallery
20 Legislative Building &
   Tourist Office
21 Dalravet Museum
23 Upper Fort Garry Gate
24 St Boniface Museum

Manitoba Children's Museum

Here's a museum (☎ 956-5437) set up just for kids, especially those between the ages of three and 11 years. Located at The Forks, the museum has a whole range of hands-on exhibits that encourage play and learning at the same time. Included are a fully functional television studio, an exhibit on exploring computer technology, a tree that preschoolers can climb to spot life-sized animals and birds, and a refurbished 1950s diesel engine. The museum is open daily from 10 am to 6 pm (until 9 pm Thursday and Friday) and admission is $4.75.

Legislative Building

The Legislative Building (☎ 945-5813), on Broadway Ave on the corner of Osborne St, is one of the world's great examples of the neoclassical architectural style. It was built using rare limestone and is now one of the most valuable buildings in North America. 'Golden Boy', a bronze statue perched jauntily at the top of the building, is covered in 23½-carat gold and has become a city symbol. His torch lights up at night. Inside are two massive bronze bison either side of the staircase. There are good, free tours throughout the day and the building has a cheap and pleasant cafeteria.

Behind the Legislative Building, a park with a monument to Louis Riel, the Métis leader, runs beside the river. At night this is an area for commercial sex as it has been for many, many years.

Macdonald House (Dalnavert)

Near the Legislature, this beautiful Victorian house at 61 Carlton St is also called Dalnavert (☎ 943-2835). It was built in 1895 for the son of John A Macdonald, Canada's first prime minister, and is decorated with period pieces. It's closed on Monday and Friday. Admission is $3.50 and there's free parking around the back. From June to September the house is open all day; the rest of the year it's open only in the afternoons.

Winnipeg Art Gallery

Shaped like the prow of a ship, this gleaming building (☎ 786-6641), at 300 Memorial Blvd, near Portage Ave, contains a good collection of Inuit art and shows mainly Canadian works, including those by young, little-known artists. The gallery is well designed and laid out. During the summer it's open daily from 10 am to 5 pm; the rest of the year it's open Tuesday to Sunday from 11 am to 5 pm (until 9 pm Wednesday). Admission costs $3 but is free all day Wednesday. There's a restaurant on the roof which you may want to investigate.

Exchange District

This is one of the city's most interesting areas. It's a 20-block area of fine turn-of-the-century commercial buildings and warehouses, many now restored for housing and business. There's some very substantial architecture here, as well as distinctive old advertising signs painted directly onto the brick walls of numerous buildings. Though rarely seen in most of Canada today, such billboards seem to be undergoing a mini-revival in this part of Winnipeg.

The various Edwardian and Victorian buildings here arose to fill the needs of the many stock and commodity exchanges which boomed in the city from 1880 to the 1920s. Market Square, on the corner of King St and Bannantyne Ave, is a focal point of the area and there's often something going on here on weekends, for example you may find a flea market or some live music.

Artspace (☎ 947-0984), just across from Market Square at 100 Arthur St, is a massive building housing more than 20 local arts groups. There are film and theatre groups, craft shops, gallery space and Winnipeg's Cinémathéque (☎ 942-2776), which shows a good range of Canadian and European films.

The tourist office has maps of an informative walk in the district (see the Organised Tours section later in this chapter for more details). The area also contains many of the city's theatres and some clubs, so it doesn't close up after dark. Unfortunately, the recession of the early 1990s has taken its toll and much of the redevelopment of the area has stalled or even slipped back, with many buildings now sitting partially vacant.

Portage Place

The city's downtown redevelopment indoor shopping mall runs along the north side of Portage Ave for three blocks. It's a three-storey affair, connected to large department stores on the south side of the street by enclosed overhead walkways. Aside from being a place to shop and hang out, the mall has three first-run movie theatres, and an IMAX cinema (☎ 956-IMAX) on the 3rd floor for large-format film presentations. There are also some places to eat in the complex.

This development is part of a major plan to keep the inner city viable and prevent the population from becoming too suburbia oriented.

Winnipeg Square & Eaton Place

Each of these is another large shopping complex. The first is underground beneath the corner of Portage Ave and Main St. It connects by skywalk or tunnel with many of the area's buildings, including Eaton Place, which lies between Portage Place and Winnipeg Square along Hargrave St.

If you had spent a winter in Winnipeg, you would know why these indoor, protected retail centres are so commonplace. There are food fairs in both, as well as several restaurants covering a variety of price ranges.

Winnipeg Commodity Exchange

Canada's largest and oldest commodity futures market (☎ 949-0495) is here, with a visitors' gallery which overlooks the trading area. It's on the 5th floor of the Commodity Exchange Tower, 360 Main St. You can see grains and other crops being traded and prices fluctuating with the Chicago markets. Don't forget to find out how pork bellies are doing! Guides can explain some of this very different world to you at no charge. The exchange is open Monday to Friday from 9.30 am to 1.15 pm.

Gambling Centres

Situated on the 7th floor of Hotel Fort Garry, 222 Broadway Ave, is the somewhat swish, upmarket Crystal Casino (☎ 957-2600), featuring many of the classic games such as roulette, blackjack, baccarat and, of course, the slot machines.

The casino is open from noon to 2 am Monday to Saturday and from 2 pm on Sundays. There is a rather restrictive, semi-formal dress code in effect. Men should sport a jacket and tie, women the equivalent. Because the casino has proven so lucrative for the provincial government, they have built two more casinos, or rather electronic bingo and slot-machine palaces, around town. The McPhillips Station, with an old-west train station motif, is in the city's north end. Aside from the many, varied slot machines, this casual, no-dress-code, no-alcohol monument to the one-armed bandit features a McDonald's. Club Regent, with a sort of Caribbean Island-paradise theme, is located in suburban Transcona.

Both are open daily from noon to 2 am, and they are busy. The government allocated at least $2 million in 1996 to gambling-addiction programmes.

Upper Fort Garry Gate

In the small park on Main St, near Broadway Ave and across from the train station, is the old stone gate and some remaining wall (restored in 1982) of Fort Garry. Since 1738, four different forts have stood on this spot, or nearby. The gate dates from 1835 and was part of the Hudson's Bay Company's fort system. There are also some photographs and written descriptions.

St Boniface

Primarily a residential district, St Boniface, across the Red River on Boulevard Provencher, is one of the oldest French communities in Canada. There's not much to see, but the imposing façade of the **St Boniface Basilica**, dating from 1908, is worth a look. The rest of the church was destroyed by fire in 1968. Churches were built and rebuilt on this site from as early as 1818. In front, facing the river, is a cemetery used by the local French from the early 19th century to the present. Louis Riel, the Métis leader, was born in St Boniface and is buried here.

Next door, at 494 Rue Taché, is the **St Boniface Museum** (☎ 237-4500), in what was the nunnery around 1850. This is the oldest building in Winnipeg and evidently is the largest oak-log construction on the continent. It contains artefacts and relics pertaining to Riel and to other French, Métis and Native Indian settlers as well as to the Grey Nuns, who lived and worked here after arriving by birch-bark canoe from Montreal, a trip of nearly 3000 km.

There is also some information on Jean Baptiste Lagimodière, one of the best-known of the voyageurs (early French fur traders/explorers) who canoed between here and Montreal. There is a diorama of a Métis hunter's camp, with an example of the famous Red River Cart, which could be floated across rivers by repositioning the

wheels. Also in the museum are some articles that were saved from the destroyed basilica.

Admission is $2. In summer, it's open from 9 am to 9 pm Monday to Friday, from 9 am to 5 pm on Saturday, and from 10 am to 9 pm on Sunday and holidays. In winter it closes at 5 pm every day.

The tourist office has a booklet on the area of St Boniface which includes a map and self-guided walking tour. To get there from downtown, take the bus east along Portage Ave across the bridge and then walk along the river to the church and museum. From The Forks it's a short, pleasant walk to St Boniface.

Taché Promenade follows the Red River along Rue Taché, past much of St Boniface's history. A few plaques indicate the major points of interest and provide some details about the Grey Nuns.

Gabrielle Roy House, 375 Rue Deschambault, was built in 1905 by Léon Roy, the father of Gabrielle, a well-known

---

The Métis & Louis Riel

The Métis are people of mixed Native Indian and French blood, almost always the result of unions between White men and Native Indian women. Many Métis can trace their ancestors to the time of western exploration and fur-trading, when the French voyageurs travelled the country, living like (and often with) the Native Indians.

The term is also used more loosely to include English-Indian mixed bloods, in order to avoid the term half-breed.

As time passed and their numbers grew, many Métis began to use the St Boniface/Winnipeg area as a settlement base, living a life which was part European, part traditionally Native Indian. This unique juxtaposition soon became an identity, and those born into it began to think of themselves as a distinct people with their own needs. The ensuing rebellions against the political authorities were the almost inevitable product of this consciousness.

Born in St Boniface in 1844, Louis Riel led the Métis in an antigovernment uprising in 1869, partly to protest the decision to open up what they saw as their lands to new settlers and partly to prevent possible assimilation. When complaints went unheeded, he and his men took Upper Fort Garry. Government troops soon reversed that, and to the Canadian government, Riel became a bad guy. Land was allotted to the Métis, however, and the province of Manitoba was created. As part of the turning twists of Riel's fate, he was then elected to the House of Commons, but was forbidden to serve.

There is some question about what transpired in the next few years. Riel may have spent time in asylums. In any case, he took refuge in Montana for several years from the stress of personal persecution and political machinations. Later he returned to lead the again-protesting Métis in their 1885 struggle in Saskatchewan, where they had fled seeking greater autonomy. They again lost the battle. Riel surrendered and, after a dramatic trial, was called a traitor and hanged. The act triggered French anger and resentment towards the English that has not yet been forgotten. Riel's body was returned to his mother's house in Winnipeg and then buried in St Boniface. Riel is now considered the father of the province.

Important sites relating to the Métis and Riel can be seen in Winnipeg, St Boniface and Saskatoon and vicinity. ∎

Canadian fiction writer who used the house as the setting for some of her works. Outside the house there is a small plaque but nothing much to see unless you're a literary fan.

At 340 Boulevard Provencher is the **French-Manitoban Cultural Centre** (☎ 233-8972). The centre is open daily and is responsible for organising, creating and promoting a variety of French cultural events around the city. There's a bar, and a restaurant serves French Canadian food at lunch time.

Royal Canadian Mint

The real money is made south-east of town, at 520 Lagimodière Boulevard, on the corner of the Trans Canada Hwy (☎ 257-3359). This ultramodern, glass, pyramid-shaped building contains some of the most modern minting machinery in the world. Free tours every half-hour show the procedures used in cranking out two billion coins a year. The mint produces Canada's coinage as well as coins for many other countries, especially in Asia. It's open May to September, Monday to Friday from 8.30 am to 5 pm, and Saturday from noon to 5 pm. (No free samples!)

Western Canadian Aviation Museum

One of the country's largest aviation museums, the WCAM (☎ 786-5503) is at 958 Ferry Rd, opposite the Winnipeg International Airport. They have a good collection of 25 planes from over the years but only some of them are on display at any given time. The museum is open Monday to Saturday from 10 am to 4 pm, and on Sunday afternoons. Admission is $3, and a tour is offered for a small additional fee. From the 'Flight Deck', traffic at the Winnipeg Airport can be observed.

Police Museum

At the Winnipeg Police Academy (☎ 986-3976), 130 Allard Ave, a small museum features uniforms, 'wanted' posters, a Harley Davidson and a jail cell from 1911. It's free, but call about opening hours.

Riel House National Historic Park

At 330 River Rd, in a residential area known as St Vital, quite a distance south of downtown, Riel House (☎ 257-1783) details Louis Riel's life here in the 1880s.

The restored and furnished traditional French Canadian-style log farmhouse, built in 1881, belonged to Riel's parents. He was brought here to lie in state after his execution in Saskatchewan in 1885. A staff interpreter offers information on the Riels and on the Métis in general.

To get there, take the No 16 bus from Portage Ave going west; after passing through Osborne Village, it will take you nearly to the door. The site looks out of place beside the modern bungalows which surround it. Opening hours are 10 am to 6 pm, daily in summer, on weekends only in September (it's closed for the rest of the year). Admission is free, but phone to be sure it is open before making the trip out there.

Seven Oaks House

The oldest habitable house in the province, Seven Oaks House (☎ 339-7429) was built (without nails) in 1851. It's about four km north of Portage Ave and Main St, at 115 Rupertsland Ave. Seven Oaks House is open daily from the last weekend in May to Labour Day.

Historical Museum of St James-Assiniboine

This small museum (☎ 888-8706), 3180 Portage Ave, has a collection of Native Indian, Métis and pioneer artefacts from the area at the turn of the century. It's open from 10 am to 5 pm daily, but is closed on weekends after Labour Day until the following spring. Admission is by donation. On site is a 100-year-old log house with authentic furnishings.

Ross House

Ross House (☎ 943-3958), the first post office in the west, is an example of Red River log construction. It's open from mid-May to Labour Day, Wednesday to Sunday from 11 am to 6 pm, and is free. It can be found in Joe Zuken Heritage Park, on the west side of Mead St between Sutherland and Euclid Sts.

North Point Douglas & Selkirk Ave

This section of the city, the North End, is the only area west of Montreal to be classified an historic area. Many of the houses are over 100 years old, and plaques and monuments commemorate various historical events.

It's north up Main St, just north and east of the junction of Hwy 42, which leads over the river and north out of town. Selkirk Ave has long been the commercial centre of the city's north end and the first home of a range of immigrant groups. See Organised Tours later in this chapter for details of free walking tours of the area.

Assiniboine Park

Assiniboine is the largest city park and is open from 7 am until dark. The grounds hold an English garden, and a 40-hectare zoo with animals from around the world. See the statue of Winnie the Bear, a bear purchased in White River, Ontario by a soldier from Winnipeg on his way to England to serve in WW I. The bear ended up at the London Zoo and is said to have been the inspiration for AA Milne's *Winnie the Pooh*.

Other features are the conservatory (with some tropical vegetation) and, nearby, the Leo Mol Sculpture Garden and a small art gallery. The sculpture garden displays a very good range of work by the internationally regarded Mol. There are also numerous playing fields. At the beginning of July, watch for the free evening outdoor Shakespearean performances.

The park is south of the Assiniboine River and just south-west off Portage Ave, about seven km west of the downtown area. Entrances are off Corydon Ave West (at Shaftsbury) or at the west end of Wellington Crescent.

Assiniboine Forest

South of the Assiniboine Park, between Shaftsbury and Chalfont Aves, this largely undeveloped forest area is even larger than the park itself. In the middle is a pond with an observation area for bird-watching, and deer may be seen along the winding trails.

Grant's Old Mill

Grant's is a reconstruction of an 1829 water mill (☎ 837-5761), which is thought to be the first use of hydropower in the province. There's not really very much to see, although grist (grain) is ground every day and offered for sale. The mill is open daily from May to Labour Day. It's on the corner of Booth Drive and Portage Ave West, near Sturgeon Creek.

Living Prairie Museum

At 2795 Ness Ave, north of Grant's Mill, the Living Prairie Museum (☎ 832-0167) is really a park, or rather a preserve, where a 12-hectare area of now very scarce, original, unploughed tall prairie grass is protected and studied.

Within this small area, 200 native plants can be found, as well as a variety of animal and birdlife. The interpretive centre at the site is open daily through the summer, and naturalists are on hand. Walking trails and guided walks are offered. Admission is free.

Fort Whyte Centre

The centre (☎ 989-8355), at 1961 McCreary Rd in a conservation area with a marsh, lake and woods, is an environmental education facility. Walking trails, exhibits, demonstrations and slide shows on local wildlife are part of the programme. A freshwater aquarium depicts the province's different aquatic life. It's not a bad place to get a glimpse of some of the features of rural, undeveloped Manitoba as well as some of the province's fauna. Trails lead through replicas of various provincial wetland areas, where birds, waterfowl and even the odd mammal such as deer may be viewed. Admission is $3.50 for adults, $2.50 for students and seniors. It's open daily and is about a 20-minute drive from downtown.

Other Parks

There are numerous parks in and around the city, some quite large. Aside from the ones mentioned, there is Little Mountain Park, which has hiking trails and examples of local forest and prairie vegetation. It's two km east of Sturgeon Rd off Oak Point Hwy.

Activities

Swimming A couple of swimming pools in the city are open to the public. There's Central Outdoor Pool, administered by the City of Winnipeg Parks & Recreation Department, at 200 Isabel St, and the Pan-Am Pool (☎ 986-5890) at 25 Poseidon Bay. Built for the Pan-American games in 1967, the latter pool is one of the country's largest.

Other In summer the larger city parks are good for walking and cycling. In winter there is skating on the rivers, and for that perhaps the best spot is on the Red River near The Forks, in front of the St Boniface Basilica.

Organised Tours

One hour walking tours of the Exchange District leave from the Museum of Man & Nature on Tuesday to Sunday during July and August. Tours cost $4 per adult. Call (☎ 986-4718) to check times.

Free walking tours (☎ 586-3445) of Selkirk Ave are offered in the summer at 10 am and 2 pm Tuesday to Saturday. Tours leave from the Amphitheatre on Selkirk Ave, four blocks west of Main St. (See North Point Douglas earlier in this chapter).

Gray Line together with Paddlewheel River Rouge (☎ 942-4500) have six boat and bus tours ranging in length and price. The basic downtown double-decker bus tour lasting 3½ hours is $17.

The lower-priced boat tours depart from a wharf down by The Forks Historic Site, at the foot of the Provencher Bridge on the corner of Water Ave and Gilroy St. The ticket office is also here.

There are straight along-the-river cruises ($10.75 for a two-hour cruise), or more costly evening dinner-dance cruises ($11.75 plus cost of meals, which start at $12.50, and the cruise lasts for three hours), on a replica paddlewheeler. Another travels down to Lower Fort Garry. The MS *River Rouge* also has dinner cruises, dance cruises and Sunday afternoon cruises.

Festivals

The following are some of the major festivals:

Le Festival du Voyageur – If you happen to be out here in the dead of winter, Le Festival du Voyageur, in mid-February, is a 10-day event commemorating the early French voyageurs or fur traders with concerts, a huge winter street party, a Governor's Ball with period costumes, arts & crafts displays and lots of outdoor activities.

The Red River Exhibition – Held in late June at the Winnipeg Arena, this festival is a week-long carnival, with an amusement park and lots of games, rides and exhibits.

Winnipeg Folk Festival – This annual festival (☎ 231-0096) is probably the country's biggest and best known. It takes place for three days in summer, usually early July, with more than 200 concerts plus a craft and international food village. The festival is held at Birds Hill Park, 20 km north of downtown.

Black-O-Rama – Held in mid-July, this is an annual summer festival of music, dance and poetry of West Indian origin.

Winnipeg Fringe Festival – This is a nine-day event held in the Exchange District in late July, featuring international fringe theatre, comedy, mime, music and cabaret.

Folklorama – This is the city's big, popular festival of nations. The tourist office will have up-to-date details on this August event which celebrates the city's surprising number of ethnic groups through two weeks of music, dance, and food in pavilions throughout downtown Winnipeg.

Places to Stay

Camping There are a few places to camp around town but most are a long way out, off the main highways or up at the beach areas around Lake Winnipeg.

Jones Campground (☎ 864-2721) is 13 km west on Hwy 1. Unserviced sites are $10. *Conestoga Campsites* (☎ 257-7363) is a little closer to town, south-east of Winnipeg, at Lot 143 St Anne's Rd. Sites are $10.50. Both campgrounds are open from May to mid-October.

Hostels The HI *Ivy House Hostel* (☎ 772-3022) is good and central. It's in an old turreted house at 210 Maryland St, near the corner of Broadway Ave and Sherbrook St, not far from the bus station. The hostel sleeps 40 and has kitchen and laundry facilities.

During the summer it's open from 8 am to midnight and in the winter from 8 am to 10 am, and 4 pm to midnight. The rates are $12 for members, $16 for nonmembers. Nearby, over on Sherbrook St, is the hostelling regional office (for memberships, etc).

From the airport, catch the No 15 bus to the corner of Sargent and Maryland Sts. From there, take bus No 29 to the corner of Broadway Ave and Maryland St. From the train station, walk west along Broadway Ave, or take the No 29 bus to the corner of Broadway Ave and Sherbrook St and walk a block west.

Just a few doors away, at 168 Maryland St, in a large, comfortable three-storey house dating from 1912, is the Backpackers *Guest House International* (☎ 772-1272 or 1-800-743-4423), run by Bill Macdonald. It, too, can accommodate about 40 people in a variety of rooms, including four for couples. There's a good kitchen, laundry facilities and a TV and video library. The price here is $11 (no membership required), and it is open all day through the summer months. Both hostels can be full (or close to it) in July and August, so calling ahead is not a bad idea. Notification prior to arrival is necessary at Backpackers from November to March because the winter months are slow and Bill is not always at home.

The *University of Manitoba* rents rooms from mid-May to mid-August. Rooms are around $19 per person per night. For information, contact the conference coordinator (☎ 474-9942) at 26 MacLean Crescent, Pembina Hall.

B&Bs The provincial B&B Association (☎ 661-0300) is based in Winnipeg, and many of its members are also here. In addition there are independent operators in the city and around the province – the tourist office has a fairly extensive list. Prices aren't bad at all, with most in the range of $35/45 for singles/doubles. Breakfast may vary from a light breakfast to a complete hot meal.

Casa Antigua (☎ 775-9708), at 209 Chestnut St, is in a pleasant old tree-lined residential area near Portage and Broadway Aves. A single here is $35. Dinners are offered and Spanish is spoken.

More upmarket is *West Gate Manor* (☎ 772-9788), at 71 West Gate, in the historic well-to-do area of Armstrong Point. It's about a 20-minute walk south-east of the Art Gallery or bus station to this quiet neighbourhood. The tasteful, well-decorated rooms go for $38 to $45 a single, $50 to $55 a double.

The *Riverside* (☎ 233-3218), at 476 St Mary's Rd, has singles/doubles for $30/40. Hosts Mary and Walter Pederson will pick up from the train station or airport for a small fee. English, Danish and Japanese are spoken.

Over in St Boniface, the French area of town, is *Voyageur House* (☎ 231-1783), at 268 Notre Dame St. There are three rooms, with shared bathroom, at $35/45. Pick up from the airport or bus station can be arranged and bicycles are available. English, French and German are spoken.

Hotels – bottom end Winnipeg has an abundance of small, older hotels in the downtown area. Unfortunately most of these are very basic, catering to locals on the skids and some which are more likely to be rented by the hour than the night. None of them are recommended for women travelling alone. The low end of the middle price bracket offers better-calibre alternatives.

A few blocks up Main St towards Portage Ave from the railway station is the *Winnipeg Hotel* (☎ 942-7762). Rooms cost around $30.

Many of the cheapies are clustered around the Exchange District near the intersection of Notre Dame Ave and Albert St. Two are the *Royal Albert Hotel* (☎ 943-8750) and the *Oxford Hotel* (☎ 942-6712), but neither is particularly savoury. The downstairs bars are the primary feature. Rooms start at about $30; rooms with a bath cost more.

A cut above the budget accommodation is found down in Osborne Village, the *Osborne Village Motor Inn* (☎ 452-9824). The 32 rooms are quite reasonably priced, at $36/39. This is a better neighbourhood – in fact, it is quite a lively area with good restaurants and

MANITOBA

stores. The hotel features live music, however, so be prepared for some bass thumping in at least some of the rooms until last call.

Hotels – middle Winnipeg is also well served by moderately priced hotels with clean, safe rooms in a conveniently central location.

The *Balmoral* (☎ 943-1544), on the street of the same name, is on the corner of Notre Dame Ave and has rooms at $33/40.

The *Gordon Downtowner Motor Hotel* (☎ 943-5581) is very central, at 330 Kennedy St, a few blocks from Portage Ave. It has a restaurant, a couple of bars and free parking. Rates are $46/52.

Similar is the *St Regis* (☎ 942-0171), at 285 Smith St, just south of Portage Ave, with rooms at $45/49.

The always reliable *Carlton Inn-Best Western* (☎ 942-0881), at 220 Carlton St, has rooms from $61/66.

Hotels – top end The *Delta Winnipeg* (☎ 956-0410), at 288 Portage Ave, has rooms for $129/144. The *Westin* (☎ 957-1350), at 175 Portage Ave East, has doubles from $145.

The attractive *Hotel Fort Garry* (☎ 942-8251), built in 1913, is the city's classic old hostelry. It's at 222 Broadway Ave, close to the train station whose passengers it was meant to serve. The casino is here. A double also costs around $145. Look out for weekend packages, when doubles go for as little as $69, at both the Fort Garry and the Westin.

Motels The *Assiniboine Garden Inn* (☎ 888-4806), at 1975 Portage Ave, on the park, has singles or doubles for $46 and a dining room offering food at good prices. *Down's Motor Inn* (☎ 837-5831), at 3740 Portage Ave, charges $40/48. There are others along Portage Ave going away from the downtown area.

Pembina Hwy (Hwy 42) going south out of town has many motels. The *Capri* (☎ 269-6990), at 1819 Pembina Hwy, charges $39/48. The cheaper rooms are in one of the small, quiet cabins at the back and there is a swimming pool. Some of the units have cooking facilities. *Comfort Inn by Journey's End* (☎ 269-7390), at 3109 Pembina Hwy, is immaculate, for $71/76.

There are many other, more expensive places that are large, well appointed and well maintained. Generally, the larger the place, the more it costs.

Places to Eat

The cheapest place to eat in town is the *cafeteria* in the Administration Building, in the cluster of government offices between Main and King Sts on William Ave. Different lunches are served each day. The cafeteria is on the 2nd floor and opens from 8.30 am to 4.30 pm Monday to Friday. Non-employees shouldn't have any problems getting in unless you look like you've slept in the woods for a week. The *Golden Boy Cafeteria* in the Legislative Building is similar and is definitely open to the public.

Downtown on a Sunday you'll find most things closed, but there are several *Salisbury House* restaurants around town which tend to open early and close late every day. There's one at 212 Notre Dame Ave, another at 354 Portage Ave, and one in the bus station. This local chain began in 1931 and has remained successful serving cheap, plain food in a cafeteria-style setting. They're good places for breakfast but their reputation has been built on their hamburgers, which are known as 'nips'.

West along Portage Ave away from the centre at No 1405 is *Rae and Jerry's*, a Winnipeg institution. This diner-style place has been serving up Canadian and US standards with panache for many years.

The *Chocolate Shop Restaurant*, at 268 Portage Ave, is a likeable place for lunch, dinner, coffee and sweets or for the popular teacup and tarot card readings. It's moderately priced.

The *Old Swiss Inn*, at 207 Edmonton St, offers steaks, veal and seafood. The food is good, priced from $16. *Hy's*, at 216 Kennedy St, is a well-known steak house.

The popular *Grapes*, at 180 Main St, near the railway station, is a big bar/restaurant with lots of wood and plants. The menu offers a bit of everything at moderate prices. While certainly OK, the food's not great; it's more the place, the people and the drinks that make it work.

Down in the Exchange District there are a few eating spots to be found. The *King's Head Tavern*, at 120 King St, is a busy British-style pub. One section of it is now the *Moti Mahal*, serving East Indian food. There's an *Old Spaghetti Factory*, at 219 Bannantyne Ave, which is always reliable and good value, though it doesn't have stupendous food.

At 180 King St is the Chinese Dynasty Building, with the Heritage Gardens out the front. Slightly beyond is the city's tiny Chinatown, on Rupert, Pacific and Alexander Aves. The restaurants are mainly on King St. *Marigold*, at 145 King St, is the biggest and poshest. The moderately priced *Foon Hai*, at 329 William Ave (at Adelaide), has both Cantonese and Sichuan dishes and is open late every day.

The Forks Historic Site is a pleasant place for a bite, and along with the food stalls and the small cafes of the Market Building, there is *Branigan's*, for a more substantial meal. Weekend brunches are offered. They also have a lounge which is open late. In the nearby Johnston Terminal, *Right On Billiards Café* is a place for coffee, desserts and perhaps a quick game of pool.

There are several worthwhile places in the area around Sherbrook St and Broadway Ave. *Big Ruby's*, at 102 Sherbrook St, is a comfortable restaurant offering moderately priced pasta dishes, salads, specialty burgers and a good selection of wines.

Bistro Dansk, at 63 Sherbrook St, is a perennial Danish favourite, with well-prepared food, good lunches under $10 and pricier dinner specials. It's open from 11 am to 3 pm and 5 to 9.30 pm daily (closed Sunday).

Down near the corner of Broadway Ave, at 218 Sherbrook St, the *Fork & Cork* is a more expensive but congenial spot for a dinner out. The speciality is fondue (try the bouillon fondue for $15), but there are other items on the menu as well.

There are plenty of good restaurants with a range of prices in Osborne Village and along Corydon Ave, in the Italian area; both are south of the downtown area. *Messob*, at 106 Osborne St, serves very cheap Ethiopian fare from 11.30 am to 11.30 pm every day. *Carlos & Murphy's*, at 129 Osborne St, is a well-established Mexican place with an outdoor patio, a big menu and moderate prices. *Baked Expectations*, at 161 Osborne St, is primarily for sweets. The *Toad in the Hole*, at 112 Osborne St, is a popular pub.

Sofia's Caffé, at 635 Corydon Ave, has a wonderful little summer courtyard outback and very reasonable prices for basic Italian fare. *Bar Italia*, on the corner of Cockburn St, is good for sipping a cappuccino.

Zine's Infocafé, at 875 Corydon, offers a variety of coffees, sandwiches and desserts and the chance to use the internet for $4 per hour. There's also a good selection of Canadian and international magazines and newspapers for sale.

Many of the better downtown hotels have Sunday brunches at noon, which are good value.

Out of the downtown area, St Boniface has several French restaurants. *Le Café Jardin*, at 340 Boulevard Provencher, is a small place which offers low-priced French Canadian lunches.

Pembina Hwy leading south out of town has numerous restaurants, including many of the familiar franchises.

Entertainment

To find out what's going on in the city, the *Winnipeg Free Press* has complete bar and entertainment listings on Friday, or look for the free entertainment monthly the *Interchange*.

Casinos Winnipeg, which pioneered permanent legal gambling houses in Canada, has three places at which to wager. The *Crystal Casino* is on the 7th floor of the Hotel Fort Garry, at 222 Broadway Ave. It's open from noon to 2 am Monday to Saturday and from noon on Sunday. There are two other casinos where you can call upon Lady Luck (for more information see Gambling Centres earlier in this chapter).

Music The *Pyramid*, at 176 Fort St, presents new and/or young alternative bands, as does the *Albert* at 48 Albert St. Cover charge varies but is generally low. At 65 Rorie St is *Wise Guys*, a casual place for a simple meal and local bands.

On the corner of Main St and St Mary Ave, close to the railway station, the inexpensive *Times Change Café* is good for jazz and blues. Live shows are on Friday, Saturday and Sunday nights.

There are several nightspots on Mc-Dermot Ave near Rorie St, such as the *Rolling Stone* for rock or blues bands. The *Bank*, at 195 Bannatyne Ave, near the corner of Main St, is a dance club in the old Imperial Bank building.

The *Palladium* is out of the centre, at 2935 Pembina Hwy. This huge disco has lots of flashing lights, and a band on weekends.

The boat *River Rouge* has night cruises, with pop bands from Wednesday to Saturday and jazz music on Sunday and Monday nights.

The *West End Cultural Centre* (☎ 783-6918), at 586 Ellice Ave, often has cheap folk or classical concerts in a relaxed, casual atmosphere.

The *Centre Culturel Franco-Manitobain* (☎ 233-8972) presents all kinds of interesting shows, concerts and productions. It's in St Boniface; call for information. Some performances require a knowledge of French, some transcend language and still others use French and English.

Performing Arts The *Royal Winnipeg Ballet* (☎ 956-0183 or 1-800-667-4792) has an excellent international reputation. Their new home is on the corner of Graham Ave and Edmonton St, and they offer student rates on tickets.

The *Winnipeg Symphony Orchestra* plays at the Centennial Concert Hall (☎ 956-

1360), 555 Main St, from November to May. The *Manitoba Opera* (☎ 942-7479) presents three or four operas every year in Winnipeg.

Plays, dance, mime and more are presented at the *Gas Station Theatre* (☎ 284-2757), at 445 River Ave, in the centre of Osborne Village.

Cinema The *Cinema 3* (☎ 783-1097), on the corner of Ellice Ave and Sherbrook St, is a good, low-priced repertory cinema. The *Cinémathéque* at Artspace, 100 Arthur St, has an ever-changing selection of good Canadian and international films.

Spectator Sports In summer and autumn, the Winnipeg Blue Bombers play professional football in the Canadian Football League (CFL). Games are played at the Winnipeg Stadium, on the corner of Portage Ave and King Edward St, west of the downtown core. The Winnipeg Goldeneyes play Northern League baseball at the stadium during July and August. For information on stadium events call ☎ 780-8080.

Things to Buy
Factory Outlets Shoppers should know that Winnipeg has a surprising array of factory retail outlets. Canada's only Ralph Lauren factory store is here. Other such outlets include Arrow, Izod Lacoste and Woolrich.

For cheap camping equipment, and a stupendous range of army surplus in the basement, have a rummage in United Army Surplus Sales on the corner of Portage Ave and Memorial Blvd.

Native People's Art Winnipeg is a focal point for Native people's art, as is Churchill in the far north of the province. To see or perhaps purchase some contemporary work, check out the following stores/galleries: Northern Images, in Portage Place, for Inuit art & crafts; Upstairs Gallery, 266 Edmonton St, with one of the country's largest collections of serious Inuit art; Four Winds Trading, at The Forks Market, for more popular, less expensive Native Indian crafts.

Getting There & Away

Air The international airport is about 20 minutes north-west of the city centre. Several airlines serve Winnipeg, both for local trips and for destinations in the USA.

Canadian Airlines (☎ 632-1250) flies to Sault Sainte Marie at least three times daily. Air Canada (☎ 943-9361) also serves Winnipeg.

Canadian Airlines flies to Churchill three times a week but it's not cheap. If you want to go, book at least two weeks in advance for the best deal. For more information about Churchill, see the relevant section later in this chapter.

Bus The station for both Greyhound and Grey Goose lines is the Mall Centre Bus Depot, at 487 Portage Ave. It's open from 6.30 am to midnight and there are left-luggage lockers and a restaurant in the station.

Greyhound (☎ 783-8840) covers all Ontario destinations (or at least to the required connecting point) and many western cities. There are three buses daily eastbound for Thunder Bay ($81) and beyond, four buses a day for Regina ($58) and two for Saskatoon. Be sure to ask which buses are express and which are the mail runs, because on a trip to Saskatoon, for example, the difference can be three hours.

The Greyhound desk also handles the small Beaver Bus Line, which serves Fort Garry, Selkirk and other points north of town. There's at least one bus an hour.

Grey Goose buses (☎ 784-4500) go to Regina, Thunder Bay and many of the small Manitoba towns in the area and further north.

Train The VIA Rail station (☎ 1-800-561-8630) is centrally located, where Broadway Ave meets Main St. In summer there's a tourist information booth in the station. The western route goes to Edmonton and Jasper and then down to Vancouver. The eastern route goes north, way over Lake Superior en route to Sudbury and the major cities of Ontario. There is no train at all to Regina.

For Edmonton the fare is $178 and the train departs on Sunday, Wednesday and Friday. There are three trains a week to Sudbury ($207). For Churchill trains see that section later in this chapter.

Car Executive car rentals (☎ 478-7283), at 104 Pembina Hwy, have the cheapest rates going; from $28 per day with 150 km free, or $175 for the week with 150 km free.

Budget (☎ 989-8505) is on the corner of Sherbrook St and Ellice Ave. Dollar (☎ 949-3770), at 1380 Sargent St, offers weekend and holiday rates and has a student discount policy.

Hitching For hitching west out of town, take the express St Charles bus along Portage Ave. After 6 pm, take the Portage Ave-St Charles bus.

For hitching east on Hwy 1, catch the Osborne Hwy 1 bus or the Southdale bus on Osborne St South, on the corner of Broadway Ave.

Getting Around

The Airport Very conveniently and economically, a city bus departs for the airport every 20 minutes from Vaughan St on the corner of Portage Ave. It's called the Sargent No 15 airport bus and costs $1.35, exact change.

A taxi from the airport to the centre of town is about $12. There is an airport limo, which runs from 9 am to nearly 1 am to and from the better hotels, but it costs more than a cab.

Bus All city buses cost $1.35, exact change. For transit information, call ☎ 986-5700 (24 hours a day). Routes are extensive but you need a transfer, which is obtained from the driver, if you're changing buses.

Bicycle There are bicycle routes through town and some out of town. Ask at the tourist office for details. The hostels rent bicycles.

AROUND WINNIPEG

The Prairie Dog Central

The Prairie Dog is a 1900s-style steam train which takes passengers on a three-hour, 50-km trip north to Grosse Isle and back. From

June to September the train makes two trips a week, on Sunday at 11 am and 3 pm. It costs $13, less for kids. The station (☎ 832-5259), which is a bit hard to find, is on Portage Ave West near Kenaston Blvd, just behind Manitoba Hydro and across from the Viscount Gort Motor Hotel. There is free parking at 1661 Portage Ave.

Lower Fort Garry

Lower Fort Garry (☎ 785-6050), 32 km north of Winnipeg on the banks of the Red River, is a restored Hudson's Bay Company fort dating from 1830. It's the only stone fort from the fur-trading days that is still intact.

Although the fort was a failure as a fur-trading post, it remained in use as a police training centre, a penitentiary, a lunatic asylum, a Hudson's Bay Company residence and, later, a country club.

The buildings are historically furnished and the grounds are busy with costumed workers who'll answer questions. Go early in the day to avoid the crowds, and see the film at the entrance for the historical background – you should allow one or two hours for a visit. Admission to the fort costs $4. It's open from 10 am to 6 pm daily from mid-May to Labour Day. During the rest of September it's open on weekends only. There's a restaurant and a picnic area.

To get there, take the Beaver line bus from the main station and tell the driver you're going to the fort – the fare is about $7 return.

Selkirk

Beyond the fort, halfway to the lake from Winnipeg, is Selkirk, 'Catfish Capital of the World'. The lunkers that are taken out of the Red River here would certainly turn heads in the southern USA, where the fish is considered prime eating. The Marine Museum of Manitoba (☎ 482-7761) is also here, with six high-and-dry ships, including a restored steamer and an icebreaker.

Oak Hammock Marsh

Southern Manitoba has several important, very large marshes. These critical wetlands are home to thousands of waterfowl and other birds and act as way stations along major migration routes for thousands more.

Oak Hammock Marsh is a swamp area north of the city, about halfway to Lake Winnipeg and eight km east of Stonewall, 15 km west of Selkirk. It's noted as one of the best bird sanctuaries on the continent; over 280 species can be seen. You can amble about on viewing boardwalks or take out a canoe, and there is an information centre with interpretive displays.

East of Winnipeg

Dugald, not far east of Winnipeg along Route 15, is the home of the **Dugald Costume Museum**, a collection of 15,000 items of dress and accessories dating from 1765 to the present. The various garments are displayed on soft mannequins in realistic settings. One section offers a view of hundreds of accessories and workroom restoration activities. The costume museum is open daily from 10 am to 5 pm during summer; it's closed on Monday and Tuesday at other times of year. Admission is $3 and there's a tea room and gift shop.

Also here is a restored pioneer home dating from 1886, furnished as it would originally have been.

South of Winnipeg

South and slightly west of Winnipeg and bordered by North Dakota is an area known as the **Pembina Valley**. The Red River flows northward through this prime farming region.

Morris is the site of a major annual rodeo, second in size only to Calgary's. It takes place for five days at the beginning of August.

This is also sunflower country, and a festival to mark this is held in **Altona** on the last weekend in July. The Mennonites of the area supply some very fine homemade foods for the occasion.

Three km east of the village of Tolstoi, near the Minnesota border on Hwy 209, one of the best remaining examples of **tall grass prairie** in the region can be seen. The 130-hectare area was purchased by the Manitoba

Naturalists' Society, making it the largest single protected acreage of this increasingly rare prairie plant life. Trails for walking and hiking are accessible year round. Call ☎ 945-7775 for details.

Eastern Manitoba

The border region of Manitoba continues with the same rugged woodland terrain as is found in neighbouring Ontario. Toward Winnipeg this begins to give way to the flatter expanse more typical of the southern prairies. In the north-east, the sparsely populated timberlands continue through a series of gigantic government parks. The southern area of this side of the province is primarily farmland.

MENNONITE HERITAGE VILLAGE
South-east of Winnipeg, about an hour's drive down through sunflower country, is the town of Steinbach. Two km north of the town on Hwy 12 is a museum featuring the Mennonites, a religious utopian group originating in Europe which reached Manitoba via Pennsylvania and Ontario. An information centre gives some of the history of the movement.

But the bulk of the site is a re-created late 19th-century Mennonite village with some century-old buildings. Various special events are held through the summer.

There's a restaurant on the grounds, which serves good, fresh traditional Mennonite food. The village is open from 1 May to 30 September. For more information on the Mennonites, see Kitchener in the Ontario chapter.

LA BROQUERIE
Just out of Steinbach, this little village with a population descended from French and Belgian pioneers celebrates its Gaelic roots on 24 June (Fête Nationale, formerly known as St Jean Baptiste Day) and during the provincial Fête Franco-Manitobaine.

WHITESHELL PROVINCIAL PARK
Due east of Winnipeg and lying along the Ontario border is this 2590-sq-km park. Though some parts are heavily commercialised (particularly around Falcon Lake), other areas, especially northward, are less developed. The park contains 200 lakes, and all kinds of outdoor activities are available, summer and winter. There are some good hiking trails – some short and others as long as 60 km. The park headquarters (☎ 369-5246), in the village of Rennie, on Hwy 44 in the south-west corner of the park, offers information including recommendations for hiking, etc.

The park has 17 campgrounds, and there are moderately priced lodges which are rented by the day or week – a quarter of the province's fishing lodges are found within the park. More expensive, well-equipped resorts can be found at several locations.

Near the park headquarters in Rennie, the Alf Hole Goose Sanctuary is worth a visit, particularly during the spring and autumn migrations. There is a visitor centre, and an observation deck overlooking the small lake where a couple of hundred geese spend the summer.

At Bannock Point, not far north of Betula Lake, are centuries-old Native Indian petroforms: rock formations in the shapes of fish, snakes and birds.

ATIKAKI PROVINCIAL WILDERNESS PARK
Heading up north, the province quickly becomes rather wild. This wilderness park (☎ 345-2231) is best visited by canoe. In it, along the Bloodvein River, there are remnants of Native Indian cliff paintings thought to date back 6000 years. Access to canoe routes is through Wallace Lake, which can be reached by car along a rough road.

NOPOMING PROVINCIAL PARK
More accessible but still offering a taste of the true northern wilderness is Nopoming Provincial Park (☎ 534-7204), north of Whiteshell. This park has a few campgrounds and at least a sketchy road system.

The park also contains some woodland caribou, though you are unlikely to see them in the summer months.

Lake Winnipeg

Canada's fifth largest lake, with its southern tip lying about 50 km north of Winnipeg, is far and away the dominant geographic feature of the province. It begins just beyond suburban Winnipeg and ends in virtually untouched northern wilderness.

The easily accessible southern region is where Manitobans play in summer. The two prime recreational features are the fine, sandy beaches, and the numerous parks and wetlands ideal for wildlife observation, most notably bird-watching. Oak Hammock Marsh is listed under the Around Winnipeg section earlier in this chapter, as it is very close to the city.

The eastern shoreline is lined with beaches, including the unofficial centre of summer fun, **Grand Beach**, which is very popular and a good place to relax. The excellent beach has light-coloured sand, and dunes as high as eight metres. The lagoon formed behind the dunes is home to hundreds of species of birds.

The other side of the lake is less accessible to visitors, as much of the land is privately owned; many people have cottages in the area. However, there are some good, popular public beaches, such as **Winnipeg Beach**. This is the resort centre for the west side of the lake. A provincial park protects the best strip of sandy beach for public use and there is good windsurfing out in the bay. In and around Winnipeg Beach is an abundance of camping areas, motels, restaurants and all other services. The government park is best for campers in tents.

At the southern end of the lake, Netley Marsh is home to a huge number of waterfowl.

Places to Stay & Eat
There is camping at Grand Beach Provincial Park (☎ 754-2212) and further south at Patricia Beach (☎ 754-2212). *Lakeshore Heights* (☎ 754-2791) is a B&B off Hwy 59 near Grand Beach, 90 km from the city. For detailed directions, call the above or call ☎ 475-8173 in Winnipeg. Most of the commercial services and motel accommodation are available just south of the park, in Grand Marais. The *Grand Marais Inn* (☎ 754-2141) has rooms from $48.

Organised Tours
North and east of the beach districts, a mini industrial tour circuit can be made. At Pine Falls, the Generating Station (☎ 474-3233) is open for tours through the summer. Call for the schedule. Also here, the Pine Falls Paper Company (☎ 367-2432) offers guided trips around the mill. South down Hwy 11 is the village of Lac du Bonnet and an underground research lab belonging to Whiteshell Laboratories (☎ 1-800-665-0436). Whiteshell also has an above-ground plant, at Pinawa, and is involved with nuclear research, among other things. At Pinawa, pregnant women and young children are not permitted on the tours, which might tell you all you want to know. Anyone, though, can visit the underground site for the 1½-hour tours of the laboratory, which is built down below the water table in the rock of the Canadian Shield.

NETLEY MARSH
In the other direction, in more ways than one, is Netley Marsh, formed where the Red River drains into the southern end of Lake Winnipeg. This is one of the major waterfowl nesting areas on the continent, and hunters and watchers bring their conflicting points of view to enjoy the 18 species of duck and the flocks of geese. Autumn is a particularly good time, as the birds collect in number, but this is also hunting season. The Breezy Point Observation Tower, within the Netley Creek Provincial Recreation Park, allows for views over a section of the marsh. Netley is 16 km north of Selkirk.

The Canadian Shield

The 'Shield' is one of Canada's most dominant physical characteristics. It surrounds Hudson Bay on the east, south and west in a vast U pattern, with a shield-like shape around the perimeter. In the north, it runs from the Atlantic Ocean on the coast of Labrador 3000 km west past Lake Winnipeg north-west to Lake Athabaska, to Great Slave Lake, Great Bear Lake and on to the Arctic Ocean. From the Hudson Bay areas, it stretches south from Lake Superior to the St Lawrence River around Kingston.

And just what is it? A mass of ancient, stable rock, the first region of the continent raised permanently above the sea. The predominantly igneous, fossil-free, stratified rock from the archaeozoic period is among the world's oldest. The entire region was scraped and gouged by glaciers, resulting in an almost uniformly flat to undulating rocky surface very sparsely and intermittently covered with soil. Rarely across its expanse does it rise more than 500 metres above sea level. Many of the dips, dents, cracks and pits in the surface are filled with water – lakes, rivers and ponds of every shape and size. In several sections, as much as 40% of the surface is fresh water.

The southern sections tend to be forested, and in Manitoba, these boreal woodlands extend as far north as Churchill. Further north the trees begin to diminish, and eventually disappear altogether, leaving lichen and mosses as the principal vegetation.

The southern areas, bordering as they do much of the heavily populated regions of the country, have become part of the Canadian mental landscape. Synonymous with outdoor living, camping, cottages, hiking, fishing and wildlife, this generally inhospitable but wildly beautiful land is part of the quintessential Canada. ∎

Interlake

The region north of Winnipeg, wedged between massive Lake Winnipeg to the east and Lake Manitoba to the west, is known as the Interlake. The southern region of this area has been detailed in the Around Winnipeg section earlier in this chapter. In the northern Interlake region, to the east of Lake Winnipegosis, the population thins markedly, the cottage communities disappear and the real north begins.

GIMLI

Ninety km north of Winnipeg, on the western shores of Lake Winnipeg and marked by the Viking statue, this fishing and farming community is made up largely of the descendants of Icelandic pioneers. Once known as the Republic of New Iceland, the area was settled by Icelanders around 1880. The **Gimli Historical Museum** outlines the history and possesses some artefacts of the local settlement, as well as items suggesting the influence of the Ukrainians, a major early immigrant group in the western provinces. Every summer, around the beginning of

August, **Islendingadagurinn** (the Icelandic Festival) is held, with three days of games, contests, parades and folk music.

The wide, sandy beaches of the southwestern shore continue into the Gimli area.

Gimli has a couple of standard motels.

HECLA PROVINCIAL PARK

Further north (Gimli is halfway from Winnipeg) is Hecla Provincial Park (☎ 378-2261), situated on an island jutting out and almost across Lake Winnipeg. A causeway leads to Hecla Island, the principal island, with its campgrounds and villages. Hecla Village was the site of an Icelandic settlement in 1876. A museum and short walking trail detail some of the historical highlights.

The island is well populated with moose, although deer and smaller mammals are also commonly seen. The Grassy Narrows Marsh teems with waterfowl. Numerous hiking trails wind through the woods and along shorelines.

Another park adjacent, **Grindstone**, is still under development.

Places to Stay & Eat

Solmundson Gesta Hus (☎ 279-2088) is a B&B in Hecla Village. A double goes for

$55. At the northern tip of the island is Gull Harbour, where the campground is situated and where all supplies can be purchased.

SNAKE PITS

Snake lovers, you're in luck. Here in Manitoba is the world's largest population of red-sided garter snakes, concentrated in wiggling mega-dens of up to 10,000 of the little funsters. Researchers, pet dealers and those with a taste for the macabre come from distant continents to view the snake pits, which are about six km north of Narcisse, off Hwy 17 due west of Gimli.

In fact, the pressure of attention on them has resulted in a drastic decline in the numbers of snake dens, and harvesting regulation is occurring. The mating ritual, when tens of thousands emerge from their limestone sinkhole lairs to form masses of entwined tangles, takes place around the last week of April and the first two weeks of May, or when the weather has warmed enough to perk up the slitherers. The greatest intensity of activity occurs when the snow has melted and the first hot, sunny days of spring have arrived. Autumn is the other time of the year when viewing is good. Early in September, after a fancy-free summer, the snakes return to their dens, but remain at the doors until the cold autumn weather forces them to crawl inside for the winter. The snakes are not dangerous and can be picked up – no screaming please – but may not be removed from the site.

The **Narcisse Wildlife Management Area** protects one area of the snake pits and provides a walking trail and parking lot six km north of Narcisse – just follow Hwy 17. It is just under a two hour drive from Winnipeg. Bring the camera and the kids, and make a day of it by visiting nearby **Komarno**, where there's a statue of the world's largest mosquito. Packing a lunch (or at least a snack) and something to drink is not a bad idea, as there isn't much around, although well water is available.

Other locations for snake pits are around Chatfield and Inwood.

PEGUIS & FISHER RIVER

North of Narcisse, Hwy 17 leads to two fairly isolated Native Indian Reserves: Peguis and Fisher River. This is an undeveloped area, with few services and little in the way of tourist development. The **Peguis Powwow** is a five-day event featuring games, song, crafts and various activities, to which the Cree and Ojibway of the reserves invite the public. Call the Manitoba Association of Friendship Centres (☎ 943-8082) for exact dates and more information. There is some camping in the area, and Hecla Provincial Park is just over 40 km to the east.

LAKE MANITOBA SHORELINE

Much less developed than Lake Winnipeg but with a series of small towns and some cottage communities, Lake Manitoba also has some fine, sandy beaches, particularly at Twin Lakes (in the south), around the town of Lundar and at Silver Bay (west of Ashern). St Laurent, a predominantly French and Métis community, is a regional supply town.

The area between the lakes is important for beef cattle, and some of the farms take in overnight guests.

NORTHERN WOODS & WATER ROUTE

This is a series of roads now linked as one which connects Winnipeg with British Columbia, running across northern portions of Saskatchewan and Alberta. Most of the roads are surfaced, though there are stretches of gravel. There are no cities, but many small communities, nine provincial parks and numerous campgrounds along the way. You'll find lots of lakes and woods up here, as well as fishing areas and wildlife. Nights are cool.

From Winnipeg, the route heads to The Pas (in the north-west of the province), continues to Prince Albert (in Saskatchewan, near the Prince Albert National Park) and on into Alberta, and ends up at Dawson Creek, British Columbia. The road is marked on signs as 'NWWR'.

Northern Manitoba

Two-thirds of the province still lies north-wards of The Pas, above the two big lakes at the 53rd parallel. Northern Manitoba is rugged, resource-based, lake-filled timber-land which slowly evolves into the treeless tundra of the far north. Flin Flon, The Pas and Thompson are important towns. Way up on Hudson Bay is Churchill, remote but one of the province's top draws.

THE PAS
Once an important meeting site for Native Indians and British and French fur traders, The Pas is now a district centre and acts as a 'gateway to the north'. Although lumber is important, this is a rich agricultural area as well. During summer, days are long and sunny.

The small **Sam Waller Museum**, at 306 Fischer Ave, provides some historic back-ground on the area. It's open Wednesday to Sunday from 1 pm to 5 pm.

Christ Church (☎ 623-2119), on Edwards Ave, was founded by Henry Budd, the first Native Indian ordained by the Angli-can Church. On one wall, the Lord's Prayer and the 10 commandments can be seen written in Cree. Call and someone will arrange to let you visit.

Also of interest is Opasquiak Indian Days, an annual festival put on by The Pas Native Indian Band in mid-August. Included in the events are traditional contests and games and a 30-km canoe race. Call The Pas Friendship Centre (☎ 623-6459) for exact dates.

Within the Clearwater Lake Provincial Park, deep crevices and huge chunks of rock fallen from cliffs can be seen along the Caves Trail. It's called Clearwater for a reason: the bottom can be seen from over 10 metres.

Places to Stay
Camping is possible not far from town, in Clearwater Lake Provincial Park. There are about half-a-dozen motels or hotels in town, and finding a vacancy shouldn't be a problem. The *Wescana Inn* (☎ 623-5446), across the road from the bus station, is clean and comfortable and has singles/doubles for $61/67.

Getting There & Away
The Pas is connected to Winnipeg by air, Grey Goose buses and VIA Rail. Driving takes about eight hours if you take Route 327 and Hwy 6. The bus takes a longer route. VIA Rail continues on to Thompson and Chur-chill.

FLIN FLON
Further north, right on the Saskatchewan border, Flin Flon is a copper and zinc-mining centre. The unusual name is taken, it's said, from the protagonist of a novel some pros-pectors found up here in 1915. A goofy statue of the character, Josiah Flintabbatey Flon-atin, greets visitors at the edge of town.

Also here, on Hwy 10 as the town is entered, is a tourist office and campground run by the Chamber of Commerce (☎ 687-4518). At the tourist office, have a look at the examples of birch-bark biting. This is an old Cree women's craft which has almost disap-peared. Using their teeth, they etch patterns, often of animals, into the bark. You can sometimes see examples of this art in some of the better Native Indian craft outlets around Saskatchewan.

The town of about 10,000 residents is built on the rocky Canadian Shield, meaning you'll be going up and down hills as you make your way around town.

The Hudson Bay Mining & Smelting Company surface mine in town can be toured from June to August. Copper, zinc, gold and silver are produced.

The city is surrounded by typical northern rocky, wooded lakeland. There are canoe and camping outfitters in town and the huge Grass River Provincial Park (☎ 472-3331) is not far east. The fishing is excellent. The Grass River system is ideal for canoeing with about 150 lakes strung along the river. Woodland caribou, moose and deer are among the animals resident within the park. The river has been used for centuries by

Native Indians and, later, European explorers and traders.

About halfway between Flin Flon and Grass River, south of town, is **Bakers Narrows Provincial Recreation Park**. It offers camping and canoeing and, with its beach and quiet, is also good for a relaxing day.

Flin Flon has a couple of older hotels in the centre, on Main St, and a couple of motels around the edges. The *Royal Hotel* (☎ 687-3900), at 93 Main St, has rooms for $35/45. The *Victoria Inn* (☎ 687-7555) is more expensive and has a full range of facilities.

Buses run to The Pas and Winnipeg.

THOMPSON

The last town northwards connected by road, Thompson (population 15,000) is a nickel-mining centre. There is virtually nothing but wilderness on the long road up here, whether you've come from The Pas or along Lake Winnipeg. And just out of town in any direction, civilisation disappears quickly. If driving, make sure you have the necessary supplies, water and fuel, as services are few to nil, especially on Hwy 6 north of Lake Winnipeg.

You can visit the Inco nickel mine but the tour does not descend into the earth; it shows instead all the surface operations. The Heritage North Museum, in an impressive log building, has exhibits and artefacts relating to natural history, the fur trade and early White settlement. The Thompson Folk Festival is held annually on the weekend closest to the summer solstice, usually around 22 June.

Anna's B&B (☎ 677-5075), at 204 Wolf St, is a good place to stay, and they will pick up guests from the airport or station. English and Dutch are spoken and a single goes for $35. There is a city-operated campground close to town.

VIA Rail, en route to Churchill, serves the city, as does Grey Goose Bus Lines.

Calm Air (☎ 1-800-839-2256) flies to Churchill from here four times a week, Tuesday to Friday mornings. A return flight is $250 if you book 14 days in advance.

GILLAM

Situated about halfway to Churchill on the train line, Gillam exists because of its hydro-power development.

CHURCHILL

If you've come this far, you've come for Churchill. Other than Winnipeg, this is the province's most interesting draw, especially for international travellers. It is one of Canada's few northern outposts that is relatively accessible, made so by the train line running all the way up from Winnipeg.

Despite its forbidding, remote location and extremes of weather – July and August are the only months without snow – Churchill has always been of importance. The area is one of the oldest, in terms of European exploration, in the country. The first Hudson's Bay Company outpost was set up here in 1717 (and was named after Lord Churchill, Governor of the HBC and later the first Duke of Marlborough). Much of the exploration and settlement of the west came via this route. Explorers, traders and the military have all been here and it was once one of the largest grain-handling ports in the world. The railway was completed in 1929, giving the prairies an ocean port that is closer to Europe than Montreal. The town has had some tough years due to the decline in grain-handling. The population is now just over 1000 and is relying more on its natural resources to draw business.

Tourism has become very important, and the town bills itself as the Polar Bear Capital of the World. It sits right in the middle of a polar bear migration route, which means the great white bears often wander into the township. During September and October, visitors are taken out on the frozen tundra in large motorised buggies to see the huge and very dangerous bears.

Possibly of more economic significance is the recently opened communications satellite launching and monitoring station, SpacePort Canada, operated by Akjuit Aerospace. It's hoped that the facility, built at a cost of $250 million, will be able to tap into the burgeoning small-satellite telecommuni-

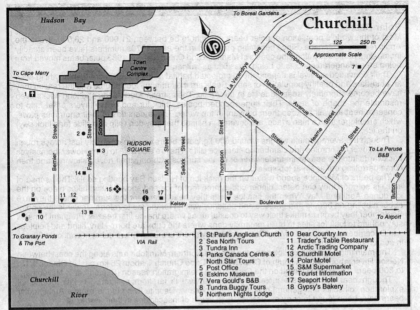

MANITOBA

Map legend:
1 St Paul's Anglican Church
2 Sea North Tours
3 Tundra Inn
4 Parks Canada Centre &
   North Star Tours
5 Post Office
6 Eskimo Museum
7 Vera Gould's B&B
8 Tundra Buggy Tours
9 Northern Nights Lodge
10 Bear Country Inn
11 Trader's Table Restaurant
12 Arctic Trading Company
13 Churchill Motel
14 Polar Motel
15 S&M Supermarket
16 Tourist Information
17 Seaport Hotel
18 Gypsy's Bakery

cations business. The port's far-north location means less fuel is needed to get satellites into polar orbit. Situated about 20 km east of town, the launch facility is on the site of the former Churchill Research Range which operated from 1957 to 1985.

The raggedy township itself, with its port and grain elevator to the west of the train station, sits at the juncture of the Churchill River and Hudson Bay. It feels small and naked in comparison to the vastness all around and the immense Arctic sky above. Facilities are minimal; there are no luxury hotels here, no pavements, no traffic lights, and no trees.

All the motels and information offices are within walking distance of the train station. Overlooking Hudson Bay at the north end of town, the large Town Centre Complex houses everything from a high school and library to recreational facilities, which include a swimming pool and a movie theatre.

Information

There is a tourist information office on Kelsey Blvd, opposite the train station. Up towards the Town Centre Complex, in the same building as the Royal Bank, Parks Canada (☎ 675-8863) operates a visitor centre and a small, general museum. Films on Churchill and the polar bears are shown. Park staff also perform live shows (appalling but quite funny) about the history of the region. There are also some displays of furs and articles relating to the Hudson's Bay Company. The company was so widespread in area and influence that it's been said the initials HBC stand for 'Here Before Christ'.

Natural Attractions

The area around Churchill is wild and starkly beautiful: the coastline is heaped with huge quartzite boulders worn smooth by the retreating glaciers, and in summer the tundra is covered in red, orange and violet wildflowers. There is an incredible variety of

Polar Bears

Most of the world's population of polar bears, thought to be between 21,000 and 28,000, live in the Arctic regions of Canada. Since becoming protected in the early 1970s numbers have been steadily increasing, particularly along the coasts of Manitoba and Ontario, and in 1983 polar bears moved from being an endangered species to being classified as 'vulnerable'.

Their continued survival is dependant on protected habitat and, perhaps more than anything else, an abundant and healthy population of seals. Seals are their primary food source and the reason they have become supremely adapted to life in the Arctic. Their streamlined heads and long necks even resemble the shape of seals. Their huge rounded bodies, thick fur and heavy layers of fat help to conserve heat as well as keep them buoyant in the water. The undersides of their enormous paws, which are bigger than a man's face, are covered in hair so that they don't slip and slide (and look silly) on the ice.

Though the average male weighs around 600 kg, polar bears can run incredibly fast across rough ice, leap over tall hurdles and clamber up steep ice cliffs. They're also able to gently lower themselves backwards into the sea, swim underwater or on the surface with only their noses showing, and then come barrelling out again at top speed.

The bears of Manitoba spend winter on the pack-ice of Hudson Bay hunting seals. Their sense of smell is so good they can detect dinner under three feet of ice and snow. Mating takes place on the ice during April and May. When the sea ice melts they head inland for the summer where they laze about nibbling on berries and grasses and patiently waiting for the ice to reform. Towards the end of September they begin to make their way to coastal areas where the ice first freezes. Pregnant females stay behind to look for sites to build maternity dens where the cubs are born – tiny, blind and helpless – in December or January. In March the small family (there are usually two cubs) moves onto the ice in search of seal pups.

The main migration route followed by the bears of Northern Manitoba runs along the coast between Nelson River, about 200 km south of Churchill, and Cape Churchill, about 25 km east of Churchill. Up to 300 bears have been sighted on the Cape during the migration season (September to November).

Though bear numbers are increasing, their survival is far from assured. Threats include oil exploration, oil spills and general pollution of the oceans. Despite living in the remote Arctic, polar bears have been found to carry excessively high levels of insecticides in their tissue. ■

---

wildlife to see, from polar bears to beluga whales, and during winter it's one of the best places in the world for watching the aurora borealis (northern lights). Other wildlife in the Churchill area includes seals, beaver, caribou, grey wolves, lemmings and Arctic foxes. Apart from all that, the air itself is so unbelievably clean it'll make the hairs in your nostrils stand up and sing. At deadline, the brand new 11,000 sq km Wapuska National Park was opened south-east of town.

Polar Bears Towards the end of September and into October the polar bears of the region start to make their way from their inland summer retreats to coastal areas where the ice first freezes. After a summer diet of berries and grasses they're keen to get onto the ice to hunt for seals again. As many as 150 polar bears pass close to Churchill.

The township is an attraction for the animals (food and fun), but it's also thought that the older bears force the younger ones to move inland and that this could be why they sometimes lumber into town. Local police and government authorities maintain a 24-hour vigil from September to November to protect bears and humans from each other. An alert system has been set up (if you see one, ☎ BEAR) and if bears do come into town they're trapped and carted off to the out-of-town polar bear 'jail' and later released onto the ice.

To be certain of seeing polar bears at close range, safely, a tundra buggy tour (booked well in advance) in October or early November is the only sure option. See under Organised Tours.

Beluga Whales During the summer, from around mid-June until the end of August, up

MANITOBA

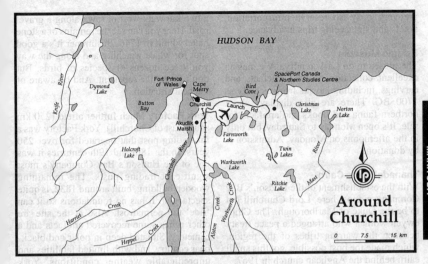

HUDSON BAY

Around Churchill

to 3000 beluga whales move into the Churchill River. It's thought that the whales are drawn by the warmer water temperatures. They spend the summer feeding on large schools of capelin, calving, mating and checking out *Homo sapiens.*

Adult belugas are glossy white and about three to five metres long. Though they're easily spotted from the shore of Hudson Bay, a boat trip is the best way to see them. The whales come right up to the boat and a special microphone dropped over the side allows passengers to hear their extraordinary song. Early whalers who heard them through the hulls of their ships called them sea canaries. Belugas were heavily hunted right up until 1968; now only Inuit hunters are allowed to take a small number.

Birds From the end of May to mid-June, it's possible to see up to 200 species of birds in and around Churchill. Even a casual observer is likely to see about 100 species in the space of a week. The rare Ross's gull (its breast turns pale pink in the mating season) nests in Churchill. More common visitors include Pacific and red-throated loons, Smiths' longspurs, Arctic terns, yellow war-

blers and snow geese. From late June to mid-August it's also possible to see up to 40 species of rare tundra butterflies.

Cape Merry, the Granary Ponds by the port, Bird Cove and Akudlik Marsh, four km south of Churchill, are all excellent bird-watching spots.

Visitor Tips As wildlife is the principal attraction bring a camera, lots of film and binoculars, if possible. Mosquitoes and black flies are ferocious in July and August, so be prepared to do battle. Repellent-saturated jackets and head-nets can be bought at local stores. Repellents with 30% to 50% DEET are recommended.

Average temperatures are -2.3°C in May, 6.1°C in June, 12°C in July, 11.5°C in August, 5.7°C in September and -1°C in October. You don't want to know about the rest of the year – lets just say that -50°C is normal. Even though temperatures can get to the high 20s in July, it is advisable to bring warm clothing – sweaters, gloves and reasonable footwear – for any visit. By early September, the snow is flying.

Summer (June, July and August) and the prime bear season (October and November) are very busy, so reserve transportation, hotels and sightseeing trips in advance.

Eskimo Museum

The museum, on La Verendrye Ave, has an excellent collection of Inuit artefacts and carvings, including kayaks from as early as 1700 BC. There are also displays about northern fauna and books and artefacts for sale. It's open Monday to Saturday, but only in the afternoons on Monday. Admission is by donation.

Thanadelthur's Cairn

With the establishment of the Hudson's Bay Company outpost here, Lord Churchill got to be the Duke of Marlborough. The Chipewyan woman who arranged a peace treaty between the warring tribes of the region, which made the post possible, got this small cairn behind the Anglican church in 1967.

National Historic Sites

Fort Prince of Wales This is one of four National Historic Sites in the Churchill area administered by Parks Canada. The partially restored stone fort, built on the peninsula head opposite Cape Merry, was originally built to protect the fur-trading business of the Hudson's Bay Company from possible rivals. It took 40 years to build but was surrendered to the French without a shot being fired because it was never seriously manned. From July to September, guides are on hand to tell the fort's story. The fort is included on many of the trips run by tour companies.

Sloop's Cove Private operators run trips to Sloop's Cove, four km upriver from the fort. The cove was used by European boats out on whaling excursions and on trading trips with the local Inuit. Names of some of the early Hudson's Bay Company people, including that of Samuel Hearn, the local 18th-century governor, can be seen carved into the seaside rocks.

Cape Merry The third site, Cape Merry, is on the headland northwest of Churchill. It's

a two km walk west of town along a gravel road. Here you can see the remains of a stone battery built in 1746. In summer it's a good spot for whale watching and along the way you'll see dozens of species of birds. But don't forget the repellent. And be aware of the bear situation.

York Factory Much further afield (250 km south-east of Churchill), York Factory was a fur-trading post that operated for over 250 years. In the 18th and 19th centuries it was one of the Hudson's Bay Company's most significant trading posts. The remaining wooden building, built around 1832, is quite spectacular. It has no foundations so it can 'ride' the permafrost. Also at the site are other ruins, some recovered artefacts and a cemetery. Situated deep in polar and black-bear country, and with limited facilities and unpredictable weather conditions, York Factory is accessible only by air or (for the very determined and experienced) by canoe.

Bird Cove

Bird Cove, about 15 km east of town and accessible by vehicle (tours are available), is one of the best spots for viewing birdlife. Along the way (and with a short hike), you can see the wreck of the *Ithaca*, a freighter which went down in a storm in 1961 at the western edge of the cove. Visitors are advised to take care when walking on the beach because the tides rise and fall very quickly. The decks of the freighter are rusted through and are not safe to walk on.

Boreal Gardens

About 1.5 km east of town on Shore Rd, the gardens and greenhouses here produce some food for local consumption. Free tours are offered on Sunday afternoons from 2 to 4 pm during July and August.

Northern Studies Centre

Housed on the site of the old rocket range 25 km east of town, the centre (☎ 675-2307) offers a variety of Arctic studies courses and is a base for researchers from around the world.

Organised Tours

The list of companies offering tours in and around Churchill is astounding for a place of its size. Many are based in town, but several others work out of Winnipeg. It's worth calling to see if things are busy and whether reservations are required. Options include tours for viewing whales, birds, icebergs, historical sites or bears. In the winter you can even go on dog-sled trips. If you're planning ahead, arrangements can also be made at travel agencies in Winnipeg.

Sea North Tours (☎ 675-2195), in Churchill, specialises in boat and sea-life tours. A 2½-hour boat tour, which includes Fort Prince of Wales and the whales, costs around $40. Churchill Wilderness Encounter (☎ 675-2248) is a smaller operation run by Bonnie Chartier who is an authority on the wildlife (birds in particular) of the area. She offers birding trips, whale-watching and polar-bear tours.

North Star Tours (☎ 675-2629), also in town, has bus tours and tundra-buggy trips. In general, the boat and bus tours are not exorbitantly priced, though the most popular tundra-buggy trips to see the polar bears are not cheap (around $70 for an afternoon).

Tundra Buggy Tours (675-2121 or 1-800-544-5049) is another company to try. The buggies are shortened buses of varying sizes, generally carrying 20 or so passengers. They have lots of big windows and ride on huge, deeply treaded tyres which protect the delicate tundra. Some trips include an overnight stay in a Tundra Buggy Lodge. Remember that the only time you will see polar bears on the tundra is from mid-September to early November.

A variety of year-round walking tours are offered by Adventure Walking Tours (☎ 675-2826) in Churchill. Run by a biologist, the tours range from just an hour to a full day and can take in four distinct eco-zones – marine, sub-Arctic forest, tundra and boreal forest.

From June to November Steve Miller of MidWest Helicopters (☎ 675-2576) guarantees that you'll see polar bears from the air, or he'll give you your money back. There's a minimum half-hour bear flight for $110 per person or a longer 1¼-hour flight over tundra and boreal forest with a photography stop included. A 15-minute mini-tour ($40) takes you over the township, Prince of Wales Fort and hundreds of beluga whales swimming in the river.

B&B Scuba (☎ 257-3696), in Winnipeg, organise diving tours with the whales.

For booking Churchill tours in Winnipeg, try Frontiers North (☎ 663-1411) and the Great Canadian Travel Company (☎ 949-0199). The Winnipeg tourist office can also help with a listing of hotels and tour operators in Churchill.

Festivals

The hardy may like to participate in the July Dip in the Bay event, part of which requires relay team members to jump into the not-so-balmy Arctic waters.

Places to Stay

Churchill is not a cheap place to visit. However, there are about half-a-dozen places to stay and a few more places to eat. Accommodation costs are mostly around $70/80 for singles/doubles. Reservations are recommended.

Best bargain and within walking distance of the town centre is *Vera Gould's B&B* (☎ 675-2544), at 87 Hearne St. A single in this modern bungalow is $30, with a very full breakfast (which often includes pancakes with Quebec maple syrup or toast with home-made jams). She has room for six people in three rooms and is very busy. Book ahead.

La Peruse (☎ 675-2254), at 100 Button St, run by Vera's daughter Anne, has two rooms with shared bathroom. From June to September rooms are $36/60. During prime polar bear season (October to the first week of November) both singles and doubles are $60. During summer, guests can pay less by choosing to do a little work around the house. Again, call ahead from Winnipeg.

The *Northern Nights Lodge* (☎ 675-2403), at 101 Kelsey Blvd, charges $58/68. It's open from June to November only. The renovated *Bear Country Inn* (☎ 675-8299), at 126 Kelsey Blvd, has rooms at $68/78. All rooms have cable TV. Slightly more expensive for pretty much the same thing is the *Polar Motel* (☎ 675-8878), at 16 Franklin St. Rooms are $77/84.

The *Seaport Hotel* (☎ 675-8807), at 299 Kelsey Blvd, costs $75/85. There's a coffee shop, dining room and a bar on the premises. The *Tundra Inn* (☎ 675-8831), like the Polar Motel, is on Franklin St. Rates are the same as the Seaport and it, too, has a place for light meals. On the corner of Kelsey Blvd and Franklin St, is the *Churchill Motel* (☎ 675-8853) with rooms at $70/80.

Many of the hotel rooms are monopolised by temporary professional workers doing government or research work; others are taken by bush pilots, photographers and the like. The scarcity is likely to intensify as the satellite programme gets busier.

Places to Eat
There isn't a lot of choice in town at feeding time. *Gypsy's Bakery*, east along Kelsey Blvd, is the best place in town for breakfast or lunch. The bakery serves very good soups, sandwiches and homemade pastries. It's open daily until 8 pm. The *Trader's Table*, at the other end of Kelsey Blvd, is the most pleasant restaurant for dinner, but isn't cheap. You'll find steak, Arctic char (the local fish) and desserts featuring locally grown berries on the menu. An evening meal costs around $20.

Most of the hotels have dining rooms and there's a cafeteria in the Town Centre Complex. The *S&M Supermarket* sells a pretty good range of fresh fruit and vegetables.

Things to Buy
Various outlets sell contemporary Inuit arts & crafts. The Arctic Trading Company has interesting souvenirs such as carvings and Inuit-style boots called *mukluks*. Also have a look around the Northern Store, formerly Hudson's Bay. The Eskimo Museum has some articles for sale, including jewellery.

For something a little bit different have a look at Myrtle's caribou hair sculptures in the Town Centre Complex.

Getting There & Away
There is no road to Churchill; you must either fly in or catch a train. Canadian Airlines (☎ 632-1250 in Winnipeg) has three flights a week from Winnipeg. The regular return airfare is $778, but savings of hundreds of dollars are offered on flights booked at least two weeks in advance. Calm Air (☎ 1-800-839-2256) flies between Winnipeg and Churchill about four times a week. In summer there are extra flights.

There are three trains a week from Winnipeg, departing at 9.55 pm on Sunday, Tuesday and Thursday. They arrive in Churchill two days later at 8.30 am. The straight return fare for the cheap coach seat is $385 for the 1½-day, 1600-km trip. If booked seven days or more prior to departure, the fare drops to $231. Booking just seven days ahead shouldn't be a problem, as this train is rarely full, but be careful in midsummer.

Getting Around
There are a few places in town where you can rent vehicles. Polar U Drive (☎ 675-2727), on Franklin St, hires cars for $60 per day. Tamarack Rentals (675-2192), on the corner of Button St and Kelsey Blvd, has mini-vans for $55 per day. Neither place charges mileage. The Polar Motel rents bicycles at $20 per day.

Western Manitoba

From Winnipeg westwards towards the Saskatchewan border, the flat prairie landscape dominates. Get used to it – it lasts until halfway through Alberta! The terrain is neither totally barren nor treeless, though, and there are a couple of government parks in this section of the province to consider visiting on the way.

WHITE HORSE LEGEND
Not far out of Winnipeg along the Trans Canada Hwy, where Hwy 26 runs north off the highway, is a statue of a white horse. Native Indian legend has it that a Cree rode

this way on his white horse with his new bride, hotly pursued by his failed rival in love, a Sioux. Eventually overtaking the couple, the scorned man killed both bride and groom. The young woman's spirit entered the horse, which continued to roam the prairie for years, a living reminder of the tragic couple.

PORTAGE LA PRAIRIE

Portage is a farm centre; on the way there, look for the crop identification markers indicating wheat, flax, mustard, etc. Other common crops include barley, sunflowers and rapeseed (often known as canola these days, for political reasons). The latter two are grown for their oils, used in cooking and prepared-food production.

The main street in Portage is Saskatchewan Ave, East and West. There is a museum on the site of **Fort La Reine**, originally built by explorer de la Vérendrye in 1738. Also at the fort is Pioneer Village Museum, which depicts life in a simple 19th-century village. Exhibits include a replica of the famous Red River Cart, essentially the truck the pioneers used to travel across from Quebec to Manitoba's Red River Valley. It was an ox-drawn cart made entirely of wood. Because of the dust of the trails, the axles were not oiled, and it is said that the creaking and squeaking of a caravan of carts could be heard for miles. The site is open daily from May to September.

Portage La Prairie Kampgrounds (☎ 267-2228) is west of Winnipeg on Hwy 1 (the Trans Canada Hwy), 16 km east of Portage La Prairie; at $12 for a tent, it's good value. The site is grassy and quiet, with lots of trees. On the west side of town along the main road, there are a couple of places to eat, some motels and the Greyhound Bus Depot, but disembarking really can't be recommended.

North of town, along the southern shores of Lake Manitoba, is another of the province's essential wetlands. Eight km long, Delta Marsh is internationally known and is one of the most significant waterfowl staging marshes in North America. Public access to much of it is limited by research and wildlife management controls, but there is camping at the eastern edge, just north of the town of St Amboise.

Delta Marsh Canoe Trips (☎ 243-2009), based in St Amboise, offer one to three-day guided trips from May to September.

The Trans Canada Hwy splits into two segments 11 km west of Portage. The Yellowhead Route runs north along the southern edge of Riding Mountain National Park and on to Edmonton, Alberta. The southern portion, the original, heads due west to Brandon and on to Calgary, Alberta.

SPRUCE WOODS PROVINCIAL HERITAGE PARK

Within the park just south of the highway is a 25-sq-km area of desert-like sand dunes as high as 30 metres, which supports the northern prairie skink (Manitoba's only lizard), the western hognose snake and two species of cacti not found elsewhere in the province. There are more hospitable areas in the park, too, with woods, lakes and camping areas. Walking trails lead to some of the more interesting sections of the park, including the dunes and underground-fed pools. Alternatively, horse-drawn carts can be taken from the information centre to these attractions.

BRANDON

The second largest city in the province, with a population of 40,000, Brandon has little to attract the visitor, although it is considered a good place to live. Primarily a commercial centre, it's situated four km south of the highway.

Agriculture Canada, a federal government department, has a research centre here which investigates everything from cattle breeding to barley pasture weed control. In one form or another, this experimental farm has been operating since 1886. The town also has a university and a large railyard.

The main street is Rossen Ave, and the Assiniboine River flowing through town keeps it a fairly green-looking place. There is a tourist information booth on the Trans Canada Hwy.

MANITOBA

The Greyhound Bus Depot is on the corner of Rossen Ave and Sixth St.

The Brandon Folk Music & Art Festival takes place around the beginning of August.

COMMONWEALTH AIRCRAFT MUSEUM

At the airport is the Commonwealth Aircraft Museum, which tells the story of the thousands of recruits from around the British Commonwealth who were trained as pilots and navigators in Canada from 1939 to 1945 before heading over to Europe. There are 13 original training planes housed in the old Brandon hangar. Small training centres such as this one dotted the prairies.

Other displays include photographs, aircraft engines and other artefacts and memorabilia. It's open daily and there is a small admission charge.

Places to Stay & Eat

Numerous places to eat and sleep can be found along the highway if you don't want to haul into Winnipeg. In town, there is a *YWCA* at 148 11th St, and along 18th St there are a variety of restaurants.

AROUND BRANDON

Royal Canadian Artillery Museum

South-east of Brandon on Route 340, there is a Canadian military base, in Shilo. On the base, for those with a special interest, is the Royal Canadian Artillery Museum, with a vast collection of uniforms, guns, ammunition, vehicles and more, dating from 1796.

There are both indoor and outdoor exhibits. The museum is open daily through the summer, but only in the afternoons on weekends and holidays. The rest of the year it is closed on weekends.

Grand Valley Provincial Recreation Park

Just 10 km west of Brandon is this privately operated park, campground, picnic area and waterslide. Perhaps of more interest is the Stott Site, within the park. A provincial heritage site, it was a Native Indian bison kill area dating back some 1200 years. Displays offer information on how it was used, and a Native Indian encampment has been re-created. There are also some live bison to send one's imagination to a time when the prairies saw herds of thousands. When they moved, the earth literally shook.

West to the Border

From Brandon west, there are a few small towns, such as Virden, of no real interest to the visitor. In some areas, derricks can be seen pumping oil. Remember that during the summer, clocks move back one hour at the Saskatchewan border because Saskatchewan, unlike the rest of the country, does not use daylight-savings time.

Neepawa

North of Brandon, Neepawa was the childhood home of well-known writer Margaret Laurence. Her home, at 312 First Ave, has been set up as a type of Laurence museum and minicultural centre, with a gallery and space for artists.

RIDING MOUNTAIN NATIONAL PARK

Also north of Brandon, 300 km north-west of Winnipeg, Riding Mountain is the major attraction of western Manitoba. Covering nearly 3000 sq km, it is a huge island of a park rising from the surrounding plains. Much of it is highland, set on a forested escarpment that runs from North Dakota to Saskatchewan. Within the park are deciduous forests, lakes, rivers and meadows. Around **Clear Lake** is the developed area, but most of the park is wilderness. There are over 300 km of walking, cycling and horseback riding trails in the park, providing access to various sections of interest. At **Lake Audy** is an enclosed small herd of bison. Elk and moose are plentiful.

Canoeing is good and rentals are available. The park is patrolled by rangers on horseback, and a couple of companies run horseback tours. Trips range from an afternoon's outing to three-day camping treks. Try Breezy Hill Horse Camp in **Kelwood** for short evening rides. For longer trips there is High Mountain Outfitters (☎ 967-2077), also in Kelwood. Note that the eastern section of the park is the highest,

The Bison

In the days before the European's arrival in the west, huge herds of bison roamed from what is now Manitoba to the Rocky Mountains, from Texas to the shores of Great Slave Lake. On the wide-open grassy plains of the prairies, herds could number in the hundreds of thousands.

The name buffalo is very commonly, if not nearly always, used in relation to the North American bison, but this is incorrect. A buffalo is a type of heavy oxen found across Africa and Asia.

The bison is a large, shaggy form of wild cattle. An old bull can weigh as much as 900 kg and full-grown females average over 500 kg. To the western Indians, the bison were stores with legs, but were also beings with spirits, to be respected. Bison were the principle source of food. The hides and hair made clothes, tents and bedding. Horns were used in crafts and rituals, the bones as knives. Nothing went to waste – even the 'chips' (dried excrement) were burned as fuel.

Aside from eating the fresh meat, much was prepared and preserved during the summer for the long winters. It could be cut into strips, pounded with herbs and dried in the sun to create a type of jerky. I tried this once myself using beef, with great success, but had to endure the sideways glances of neighbours as I strung the strips out on my city clothesline. Native groups from more northern areas added currants and berries and boiled fat to the dried meat to form pemmican, a nutritious mix which kept many a fur-trader and explorer alive.

Bison would be hunted in a number of ways. Sneaking up on them, often disguised as an animal, and then firing arrows, was one simple method. Later, they were chased on horseback. (The horse, icon of the west, was unknown in North America before the arrival of the Spanish. Until then, Native Indians roamed the prairies on foot, aided only by domesticated dogs, who pulled materials and supplies.)

When possible, hunters made use of the lay of the land, such as at Head Smashed In, Alberta or the Stott Site (mentioned in Grand Valley Provincial Recreation Park). Animals would be herded and rushed over cliffs. While effective for the Indians' needs, none of these methods appreciably diminished the bison's numbers.

Through the late 19th century, Europeans with rifles and horses slaughtered the immense herds to near extinction, often for nothing more than amusement. For the Plains Indians, the demise of the bison led to starvation and meant the end of their way of life. In Canada, the largest remaining wild herd is found at Buffalo Woods National Park. Smaller groups and individual specimens can be seen at various parks and zoos around the country. ■

so the views are best. **Wasagaming**, on the south shore of Clear Lake, is a casual resort town with all the amenities. The park information centre is here (☎ 1-800-707-8480). Also of note is the First Nation Celebration, held in early June, which provides an opportunity to see traditional Native Indian dance, costume, games and crafts.

For camping, there are serviced campgrounds as well as some backcountry opportunities. Motels and cabins can be found in and around Wasagaming. The

modest *Manigaming Motel* (☎ 848-2459) has doubles from $50.

DAUPHIN

North of the park up Hwy 10, Dauphin is one of many Ukrainian centres found all across the prairie provinces. South-west of town is Selo Ukraina (Ukrainian Village), the location of the country's **National Ukrainian Festival**, held at the beginning of August each year. Dancing, traditional costumes and lots of food are part of the festivities.

Saskatchewan

Saskatchewan is a Cree Indian word which refers to the Saskatchewan River and means 'river that turns around when it runs'.

Prior to the arrival of Europeans, first the fur traders and explorers, then the farmsteading settlers, the region was primarily Cree territory. They were a semi-nomadic people whose life was inextricably linked with the herds of bison which roamed the vast plains.

Tourism is not a major industry in Saskatchewan but many people do pass through. Each of the two major cities has some interesting things to consider on a stopover, and there are several good historical parks around the province which give a glimpse into the Native Indian way of life. Prince Albert National Park is accessible Canadian timberland. The southern region has some intriguing landscapes and desert-like topography.

Many people find the scenery monotonous; the south of the province is mercilessly flat, often without a tree in sight. But such wide-open space is a scene much of the world cannot even imagine. And the sight of golden, ripening wheat rippling to the horizon in all directions can be beautiful. The sunsets, sunrises, cloud formations and night skies are all fantastic. There's a lot of space. You might hear people out this way say 'the Rocky Mountains are nice but they get in the way of the view'.

In the north of the province, 55 canoe routes have been mapped out, and there are canoe outfitters at Lac la Longe and in Flin Flon, just over the border in Manitoba. The northern half of Saskatchewan has over 100,000 lakes and few roads.

Between this area and the bald, open prairie of the south is a transition zone stretching across the province, covering the lower middle section of Saskatchewan in rolling hills and cultivated farmland. This range, called the parklands, contains some large government parks and both the North and South Saskatchewan rivers.

HIGHLIGHTS

Entered Confederation: 1 Sept 1905
Area: 651,903 sq km
Population: 988,928
Provincial Capital: Regina

- Experience the seemingly endless skies and uncluttered space of the vast Canadian prairies
- Visit Wanuskewin Heritage Park to gain an appreciation of Native Indian culture and history
- Canoe and hike in Prince Albert National Park, once the home of the naturalist Grey Owl
- Enjoy outdoor theatre along the river in Saskatoon
- Explore Cypress Hills, a camping retreat and the location of Fort Walsh, an historic RCMP base

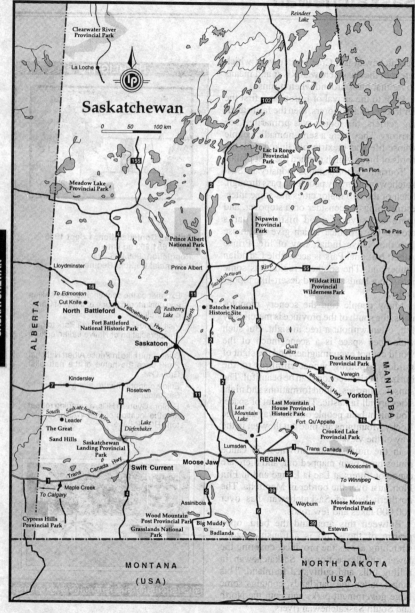

Reindeer Lake

Clearwater River Provincial Park

La Loche

Saskatchewan

0   50   100 km

Meadow Lake Provincial Park

Lac la Ronge Provincial Park

Flin Flon

Nipawin Provincial Park

The Pas

Prince Albert National Park

Prince Albert

Saskatchewan River

Wildcat Hill Provincial Wilderness Park

Lloydminster

To Edmonton

Cut Knife

North Battleford

Redberry Lake

North Saskatchewan Hwy

Batoche National Historic Site

Fort Battleford National Historic Park

Yellowhead Hwy

Saskatoon

Quill Lakes

Duck Mountain Provincial Park

Veregin

Kindersley

Rosetown

Yellowhead Hwy

Yorkton

Last Mountain Lake

Last Mountain House Provincial Historic Park

Crooked Lake Provincial Park

South Saskatchewan River

Leader

The Great

Sand Hills

Saskatchewan Landing Provincial Park

Lake Diefenbaker

Fort Qu'Appelle

Lumsden

Trans Canada Hwy

Trans Canada Hwy

REGINA

Moosomin

Moose Jaw

To Winnipeg

Swift Current

Weyburn

Moose Mountain Provincial Park

Maple Creek

To Calgary

Assiniboia

Cypress Hills Provincial Park

Wood Mountain Post Provincial Park

Grasslands National Park

Big Muddy

Badlands

Estevan

ALBERTA

MANITOBA

MONTANA

(USA)

NORTH DAKOTA

(USA)

Drivers should watch for the Mohawk service stations, which sell an ethanol-blended gas made partly from wheat and said to cut undesirable emissions by as much as 40%.

History

When Europeans first arrived in the late 17th century, the region was divided by Native Indians of three distinct language groupings. Most prominent among them were the Chippewa, Cree and Assiniboine. They aided the first explorers and traded furs. White settlers homesteaded in numbers from about 1880 and the plains were converted from bison range to farmlands. After 1890, most of the Native people had been designated to reserves and the traditional way of life was pretty much over. By 1930 the developing agricultural area together with the railway had meant the migration of nearly a million Europeans.

After WWII the significance of wheat production increased. Farms had to be huge to make it viable and urbanisation began. With mineral and energy reserves, the economy diversified.

The province is home to the Socialist movement in Canada and has maintained its allegiance to those ideals more or less since the 1930s.

In recent years, the population has remained constant or even decreased as farming continues to decline and the towns and cities can not fill the employment gap.

Climate

The weather in Saskatchewan is changeable and extreme. June can be particularly severe with tremendous thunderstorms, hailstorms and even tornadoes. Summers are generally warm and short, with maximum temperatures reaching 40°C. August and September tend to be warm, dry months, but even then the nights are cool. Winters are long and cold: the temperature can get down to -50°C.

Economy

Saskatchewan and wheat are pretty much synonymous. The province is the greatest grower of wheat in North America and, with over a third of Canada's farmland, produces two-thirds of Canada's crop. Besides wheat, grains such as barley and rye are important, as are sunflowers and beef cattle.

In the past few years, oil has become increasingly important; you'll see the slowly cranking rigs in the fields. The province also has the richest potash deposits in the world. Along the Trans Canada Hwy, some of the soil is jet black – this is natural because the area was once totally submerged under water. Occasionally you'll see large patches of white stuff which looks like snow. This is sodium sulphate and occurs only in certain climatic conditions. It's used in various industries, such as detergent preparation.

Population & People

Despite having no major cities, Saskatchewan is now mainly urban with less than 25% living on farms. Regina and Saskatoon, about equal in size, are by far the largest centres. The ethnic background of most of today's residents is British, German, Austrian, Ukrainian and Scandinavian. This is readily noticeable in the numbers of fair-skinned blondes.

Evidence of aboriginal inhabitation dates from at least 10,000 BC.

The Cree remain the largest of the Saskatchewan Native people but there are also Dakota, Saulteaux, Nakota and Dene. The far north of the province – part of the Canadian Shield – is rocky timberland and a wilderness of lakes and forests inhabited by few people. Of those who do live here, many are Métis.

Information

Provincial Symbols The provincial flower is the lily, and the bird is the sharp-tailed grouse.

Tourist Offices Tourism Saskatchewan is the provincial body which supplies the public with visitor information. Its main office (☎ 787-2300) is at 500-1900 Albert St, Regina, Saskatchewan S4P 4L9. They operate a North America-wide, toll-free number (☎ 1-800-667-7191).

They offer a series of booklets on attractions, fishing, outdoor activities, events and accommodation and more. Major towns all have city and region tourist information offices.

Telephone The area code for the province is 306.

Time Saskatchewan is on Central Time and, unlike the rest of the country, does not go on summer daylight-savings time.

Tax The provincial sales tax is 9%.

Activities
The principal outdoor activities in the province are canoeing and fishing, both of which are done primarily north of Saskatoon in the woodlands. *Outdoor Adventure*, a booklet available from Tourism Saskatchewan, lists outfitters and activities throughout the province.

Accommodation
The *Saskatchewan Accommodation Guide* lists campgrounds through to major hotels. There are a few B&Bs scattered around the province, mostly in small towns, and they are not expensive.

The national and provincial parks offer good camping and are supplemented by privately operated campgrounds. It's also possible for visitors to stay on a farm, which can be a reasonably priced arrangement; the relevant tourist offices have more information.

Regina

Regina (population 184,000) is Saskatchewan's capital. It is the largest city and acts as the commercial, financial and industrial centre of the province, but it's still a relatively small, quiet town that pretty much closes down after dark.

Wascana Creek and its parkland run through town, providing a change from the golden grain fields stretching in all directions.

Two interesting facts about the city: Regina is the sunniest capital in Canada and, oddly, every single tree you see here was planted by hand. It's for good reason that this part of the world is known as the bald prairie.

History
The Cree Indians originally lived in this area, butchering bison and leaving the remains along the creek. It became known as Wascana, a Cree word meaning 'pile of bones'. Later, European settlers were prompted to dub the settlement Pile O'Bones. In 1882 the city was made capital of the Northwest Territories and its name was changed to Regina in honour of Queen Victoria. The Northwest Mounted Police used the city as a base from the 1880s, and in 1905 it became the capital of the newly formed Saskatchewan.

In 1933, the Cooperative Commonwealth Federation (CCF), a socialist party, held its first national meeting in Regina and called for the end of capitalism. In 1944 it became the first socialist party to form a Canadian provincial government. The CCF merged with the New Democratic Party (NDP) in 1961 to form Canada's left-wing party.

Orientation
The city's two main streets are Victoria Ave, running east-west, and Albert St, going north-south. Both streets are lined with fast-food restaurants and service stations. East of the downtown area, Victoria St becomes Hwy 1 East (the Trans Canada Hwy) for Winnipeg. South of the downtown area, Albert St leads to both Hwy 6 (southbound) and Hwy 1 West. Albert St north leads into Hwy 11 for Saskatoon.

The downtown core is bounded by Albert St to the west, 13th Ave to the south, Osler St to the east and the railway tracks to the north. Victoria Park sits in the middle of the downtown area. Scarth St and 12th Ave, which edge the park, are important shopping streets.

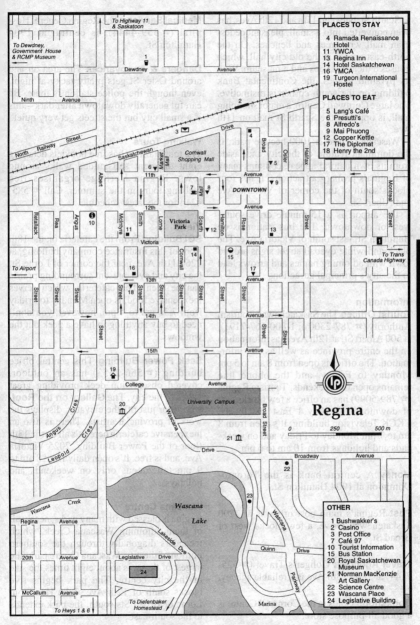

SASKATCHEWAN

Regina

LP

0   250   500 m

PLACES TO STAY
4 Ramada Renaissance
   Hotel
11 YWCA
13 Regina Inn
14 Hotel Saskatchewan
16 YMCA
19 Turgeon International
   Hostel

PLACES TO EAT
5 Lang's Café
6 Presutti's
8 Alfredo's
9 Mai Phuong
12 Copper Kettle
17 The Diplomat
18 Henry the 2nd

OTHER
1 Bushwakker's
2 Casino
3 Post Office
7 Café 97
10 Tourist Information
15 Bus Station
20 Royal Saskatchewan
   Museum
21 Norman MacKenzie
   Art Gallery
22 Science Centre
23 Wascana Place
24 Legislative Building

Scarth St, between 11th and 12th Aves, has been converted into a small, pleasant pedestrian mall with trees and benches. On the north-east corner is the old city hall, which houses a theatre, shops and a museum. With its pyramid shapes, the Continental Bank building on the south corner is distinctive. The large Cornwall Centre, a major shopping mall, is opposite the Scarth St mall on 11th Ave.

Wascana Centre, a 1000-hectare park, is the dominant feature of the city and, aside from its own natural appeal, contains many of Regina's primary attractions. It lies four blocks south of the corner of Victoria Ave and Albert St.

The airport is a 15-minute drive southwest of downtown. The bus station is on Hamilton St, just south of Victoria Ave. The black-and-white eyeball street signs around town with adjoining names and arrows lead to the city's principal attractions.

Information

Tourist Offices The Saskatchewan Tourism Authority (☎ 787-2300 or 1-800-667-7191), at 500 Albert St, at 12th Ave, has information on the entire province as well as city information. The office is open from 8 am to 5 pm Monday to Friday, and the phone line remains open on weekends. Tourism Regina (☎ 789-5099) has an office a few blocks east of downtown on Hwy 1 East just by the CKCK Television building. It's open from 8 am to 7 pm Monday to Friday and on weekends and holidays from 10 am to 6 pm.

Money A central bank is the Toronto-Dominion at 1904 Hamilton St.

Post Regina's main post office is at 2200 Saskatchewan Drive, a few blocks west of Broad St.

Travel Agencies Goliger's Travel (☎ 525-7144) at 1802 13th Ave is a reliable agency.

Bookshops Coles in the Cornwall Centre is a good all-purpose store.

Medical Services The Regina General Hospital (☎ 359-4444), is central at 1904 Hamilton St.

Dangers & Annoyances The area on and around Osler St gets pretty tacky at night, even though the police station is there. Be careful generally downtown after dark – this is a small city but the streets get very quiet.

Walking Tours

The tourist office has free booklets detailing eight different self-guided walks around town. Regina Heritage organises free walking tours in the summer. Call ☎ 585-4214 for the latest schedule.

Views

SGI Building From the cafeteria on the 18th floor of this insurance company building, at 2260 11th Ave, near the corner of Lorne St, the city and ever-present surrounding prairie can be seen. The cafeteria, which serves inexpensive food, is open Monday to Friday from 7.30 am to 4 pm, however, you don't need to buy anything to have a peek out the windows.

Sask Power Building This central office building (☎ 566-2553) has an outdoor, covered observation deck providing great views of the city. The **Gallery on the Roof**, a corridor just off the elevator, displays the work of provincial artists. There is also an inexpensive cafeteria here. It's all on the 13th floor of the Power Building, 2025 Victoria Ave, and is free. It's open daily from 8 am to 9 pm (afternoons only on weekends and holidays).

Wascana Centre

Regina is blessed with many parks, nearly all of them adjoining Wascana Creek, which meanders diagonally through the southern portion of the city. Wascana Centre park, the largest of these, is about eight times the size of the city centre. The park begins five blocks south of 12th Ave. Take Hamilton, Lorne or Broad Sts south; the park extends to the south-east.

The predominant feature is the artificial Wascana Lake. But as well as the lake, the picnic areas and sports fields, the green park contains many of the city's points of interest.

It's hard to imagine now, but originally there was nothing here but a small creek called Pile O'Bones, surrounded by treeless prairie.

The headquarters of the park, Wascana Place (☎ 522-3661), is on Wascana Drive, west of Broad St, east of Wascana Lake and north of the marina. There's not really much of interest here, but there is an information office and a good view from the 4th level of the building.

A little ferry, which is cheap, runs to Willow Island on the lake, a good site for picnics. Catch it off Wascana Drive by the north end of the lake. Boats can be rented beside the Wascana Pool building off College Ave. There is no swimming in the lake but the pool is open to all. There are flower gardens in the section north of the Legislative Building.

A waterfowl park off Lakeshore Drive, east of the Centre of the Arts, has 60 species of birds and helpful identification displays. A boardwalk leads into the marsh, and naturalists are on duty through the week. The waterfowl park is open from 9 am to 9 pm from 1 May to 1 November.

The tourist office has a map of the Wascana Centre and a booklet detailing six walks through the park. There is also a good, low-cost restaurant with an outdoor patio, the *Park Place* restaurant, at the Wascana Marina. Free Sunday afternoon concerts are given at the Bandshell.

The University of Regina is on the northeast side of the park.

Saskatchewan Science Centre

In the park is the Saskatchewan Science Centre (☎ 791-7914), with its series of exhibits, hands-on participatory displays and demonstrations on the planet, its place in the solar system, physical laws and life.

The Science Centre is in the interesting, overhauled old Regina Power Plant (see the bank of old dials and meters in the lobby),

on the north shore of the lake, east of Broad St near the corner of Wascana Drive and Winnipeg St. A bus up Broad St from downtown will get you to within a two-block walk of the door. The centre also houses a snack bar, a restaurant and a nifty little store.

A large-format **IMAX movie theatre** (☎ 522-4629) and the **Kalium Observatory** are other features of the centre, and have their own programmes. Stargazing nights, held two or three times a month at the observatory, are worthwhile and cost just a couple of dollars.

Entry to the Science Centre is $7.50 per adult, with lower senior and family rates. IMAX shows are $6.75 each, or you can buy a money-saving combination ticket. In summer the centre is open daily from 10 am to 9 pm. During the winter it's open from 9 am to 4 pm Monday to Friday and from noon to 6 pm on weekends.

Provincial Legislature

Just off Albert St, on the park's west side, this beautiful building was built in 1919 in loose English Renaissance style at a cost of $3 million. Inside, 34 kinds of marble were used. The building is open all day, every day, and there are free tours given on the hour (except at lunch time) from June to Labour Day. While at the Legislature, take a look at the **Native Heritage Foundation Gallery**, in the east wing on the main floor. The gallery exhibits and promotes Native Indian art and is open daily.

Royal Saskatchewan Museum

Also in the park, the museum is just south of the corner of College Ave and Albert St (☎ 787-2815). Upstairs there are realistic displays of North American wildlife, particularly animals native to Saskatchewan, with good explanations accompanying the exhibits. Downstairs the displays outline the biology of insects, birds, fish and animals and attempt to explain their behaviour. Space is also given to palaeontology (fossils) and archaeology.

The First Nations Gallery presents thousands of years of Saskatchewan's Native

Indian history. There are often films on a variety of topics.

The museum is open daily from the beginning of May to the beginning of September; call for the off-season schedule. Admission is free and a visit will take about one hour.

Norman MacKenzie Art Gallery

Next door to the museum is the Norman MacKenzie Art Gallery (☎ 522-4242), which specialises in Canadian painting, much of it by local artists. Exhibits change and may be historical or contemporary. The collection also contains works from US and European artists and good touring exhibitions are staged. The gallery is free and is open daily from 11 am to 6 pm (until 10 pm Wednesday and Thursday).

The art gallery is the venue for dramatic performances of *The Trial of Louis Riel*, which are held during August (see the Entertainment section later for details).

Diefenbaker Homestead

Although not in its original location, but on Lakeshore Drive west of Broad St in the park, this house is the boyhood home of former prime minister John Diefenbaker and is furnished with pioneer articles, some from the politician's family. It's open daily and admission is free.

Regina Plains Museum

Yes, Virginia, there is life away from the park. The Regina Plains Museum (☎ 780-9435) is on the 4th floor of the old City Hall, on the corner of Scarth St and 11th Ave. There are several employees who will guide you around, lovingly telling stories about items from Saskatchewan's past. The museum deals with the various people in the city and province's life: the Native Indians, Métis and European settlers.

Through the summer, the small museum is open daily from 10 am to 4 pm. The rest of the year it's closed weekends. Admission is $2, less for seniors.

Government House

Government House (☎ 787-5726) is the restored home of the lieutenant-governor of the Northwest Territories and Saskatchewan from 1891 to 1945. Indeed, Saskatchewan's current lieutenant-governor works (but doesn't live) in this house.

The Northwest territorial government was set up in 1870 to oversee the huge tract of land which was passing from the control of the fur-trading companies. You can imagine what a sight this building must have been in the dusty village of Regina in the 1890s.

Government House contains furnishings from the turn of the century, and interpreters are on hand to show visitors around.

The site is north-west of the centre, at 4607 Dewdney Ave, slightly west of Lewvan Drive. It's open Tuesday to Sunday from 1 to 4 pm. Admission is free.

RCMP Centennial Museum & Depot

This museum (☎ 780-5838) details the history of the Royal Canadian Mounted Police from 1874, when they first headed west to keep the peace. It was in this part of the country that their slogan 'we always get our man' became legend. On display are uniforms, articles, replicas and stories of some of the famous and/or notorious exploits of the force.

The training facilities and barracks, known as the depot, can also be seen. Mounties still police many of Canada's western and more remote towns and communities, as well as having various federal responsibilities, such as being part of the national security forces. Tours run almost hourly until 3.30 pm, Monday to Friday. In addition, a daily drill takes place each weekday at 1 pm.

Open daily, the museum is on Dewdney Ave West, beyond Government House, not far from the corner of McCarthy Rd. From downtown, city bus No 8 goes to the museum.

Also at the depot you can see the popular Sunset Ceremony, a formal drill spectacle of drumming and marching surrounding the flag-lowering. It's a bit slow – call it a long hour – but the uniforms are colourfully impressive, and hey, the Mounties are one of Canada's best known symbols! The ceremony, like everything here, is free, but is held only once a week, at 6.45 pm, in July and August. Ask at the tourist office for details, or call the museum. Additional ceremonies take place at the Pile O' Bones Sunday event (see Festivals later for details) and on 1 August at the Legislature.

City Hall
Regina's seat of local government (☎ 777-7305), at 2476 Victoria St, is open on weekdays from 8 am to 4.30 pm, with free guided walks available. Call ahead to make arrangements.

Sports Museum & Hall of Fame
In the former Land Titles building, a heritage site, this small provincial museum (☎ 780-

9232) is at 2205 Victoria Ave, across from Victoria Park. It honours local athletes and teams, with a tribute to Gordie Howe, a local boy made good and one of the greatest players in hockey history, as one of the features. The museum is open daily (in the afternoons on weekends) and admission is free.

Historical Telephones
SaskTel, the provincial telephone company, has an historical display area on the main floor of their building at 2121 Saskatchewan Drive. It's free and is open all day, Monday to Friday.

Fire Hall
Displays of old firefighting equipment can

The Royal Canadian Mounted Police
The 'Mounties', for better or worse, are one of Canada's two most enduring and clichéd symbols (the other is the beaver). No doubt the traditional scarlet uniforms are striking, particularly when worn by a handsome young man atop a fine chestnut steed. Alas, the opportunities for appreciating this sight are somewhat rare now, as the garb of lore is pretty much exclusively ceremonial and the horses have been largely replaced by gasoline-driven horsepower.

Still, this emblem of the west, much like the US cowboy, does have its origins in reality. Originally formed as the North West Mounted Police in 1873, the force was charged with bringing peace and order to the developing west, then known as the North West Territories. Their headquarters was set up in 1882 at a tiny settlement beside Pile O'Bones Creek, later to become Regina. Perhaps the best-known police force in the world, they developed a reputation for always 'getting their man'. What with the Native Indians caught in the middle of the rapidly changing west, the ever-increasing numbers of arriving pioneers and the coming of the railway, they had their hands full, and generally earned the respect of most. Canada did largely manage to avoid the full-scale Indian wars that plagued the westward expansion in the USA.

Now involved in counterintelligence and thwarting international smuggling, terrorism and narcotics, the Mounties' actions are more controversial if less visible.

Traditionally attired Mounties can be seen in Regina at the RCMP Museum and, often, around the Parliament Buildings in Ottawa. Contrary to some international perceptions (and suggested by many a postcard), they are not seen on horseback in front of Niagara Falls, thief in hand, with beavers industriously gnawing away in the background. ■

be seen in this modern, working fire station (☎ 777-7830) at 1205 Ross Ave. It's open to the public on weekdays and is free.

Antique Mall

For a mooch around on a rainy day or a Sunday when things are pretty quiet, try the Antique Mall, a grouping of 25 or so antique booths and dealers. It's open all year at 1175 Rose St, near Sixth St. Note that on Sunday, even this isn't up and running until after noon.

Farmers' Market

A smallish farmers' market is set up two days a week through the summer along Scarth St on the east side of Victoria Park. Produce and baked goods (including jams and pies) as well as some crafts are offered for sale. Hours are 11 am to 4 pm on Wednesday and 8 am to 1 pm on Saturday.

Other Attractions

A pass can be bought at the YMCA for use of their courts, gym or pool. The tourist office can give you information about swimming at public pools. There's one in Wascana Centre, just south of College Ave.

The Devonian Pathway is 11 km of paved bike routes through four city parks. It begins and ends at Rotary Park, off the Albert St bridge. Bicycle rentals are available from Joe's Cycle (☎ 347-7711), at 2255 Albert St, for $20 per day.

The Regina Astronomical Society has a telescope set up on Broad St opposite the CBC building, by Wascana Centre, and is open on Wednesday night in summer for public viewing. Also ask about the Kalium Observatory at the Science Centre.

The Saskatchewan Wheat Pool (☎ 569-4411) can help you plan a visit to a grain elevator or a livestock saleyard.

Festivals

Some of the festivals held here from April through to November are:

Saskatchewan Indian Federated College Powwow – Should you be in town in April, consider attending this event which is held in the Agridome of the Exhibition Grounds. It features dancers from around North America, as well as traditional Native Indian crafts and foods.

Mosaic – This three-day multicultural event with ethnic foods, music and entertainment is held in early June.

Regina Folk Festival – This three-day festival, based in Victoria Park but with concerts elsewhere around town, is also usually held in early June. Call ☎ 757-7684 for ticket information.

Buffalo Days – This six-day celebration is a big annual event held towards the end of July or beginning of August. Stores put up special decor and some workers wear pioneer garb. A talent stage is set up to offer free entertainment and the days are filled with competitions, pancake breakfasts, a beard-growing contest and parades, peaking with a big concert/barbecue in Wascana Park on what is known as Pile O'Bones Sunday. The amusement park features rides, music shows, a casino and various displays and exhibits. A fireworks display wraps up the festival.

Agribition – This is a five-day agricultural and livestock show held at the end of November.

Places to Stay

Camping As you approach Regina from the east on Hwy 1, there are a few camp sites, which are geared mainly to trailers and recreational vehicles, not tenters. They might prove useful for a short stay but are definitely not rustic.

There's much better camping to be had in the Qu'Appelle Valley, about an hour's drive north-east of Regina. You'll find camp sites at *Echo Valley Provincial Park* (☎ 332-3215), eight km west of Fort Qu'Appelle, and at the *Katepwa Campground* (☎ 332-4264), 26 km north of Indian Head on Hwy 56 at Katepwa Beach.

Hostels The HI *Turgeon Hostel* (☎ 791-8165), is in a fine old house once belonging to William Turgeon, an Acadian Frenchman who was Attorney General in 1907. It's at 2310 McIntyre St, not right downtown but quite central. McIntyre St is a residential street near Wascana Centre. The rates are $12 for members, $17 for nonmembers. It has 50 beds, as well as cooking and laundry facilities, and stays open until midnight.

The men-only *YMCA* (☎ 757-9622), at 2400 13th Ave, rents small, quiet rooms for $17. There is a cheap cafeteria and a pool you can use (see Activities earlier). Note that in summer it is not unusual for all the rooms to be booked out.

The *YWCA* (☎ 525-2141), at 1940 McIntyre St, for women only, is quite a bit more expensive, at $34. There is a kitchen and a steam room.

B&Bs *B & J's* (☎ 522-4575), at 2066 Ottawa St, only about three blocks from the downtown area and near the General Hospital is good value. In this two-storey house on a resiential street, there are four rooms at $25/35.

Daybreak Bed & Breakfast (☎ 586-0211) is a short drive south-west of town at 316 Habkirk Drive. There are two rooms and prices are also around $25/35. Free transport to and from the airport is offered.

Hotels The last of the basics that can be considered even half decent is the *Empire* (☎ 522-2544), 1718 McIntyre St, on the corner of Saskatchewan Drive. It's an easy walk north-west of the central downtown area. The clean, simple rooms have no toilet or bath but do have a sink. Rooms are $30, but they can't be recommended for women alone. Any other cheap hotels around town are pretty grim.

A good budget hotel suitable for anyone is the central *Plains Motor Hotel* (☎ 757-8661), 1965 Albert St, at the corner of Victoria Ave. Rooms cost $34 to $48 and each room has its own bath and colour TV. There is a restaurant and free parking. The neon tower atop the hotel sign indicates the weather forecast – blue means clear, green means precipitation and orange means unsettled weather. If the lights are running up, the temperature will rise, and vice versa.

Moving upmarket, the *Travelodge* (☎ 565-0455), 1110 Victoria Ave East, is good and has nearly 200 modern rooms. Rates are $46/58. Other hotels in the downtown area are costlier. The *Regina Inn* (☎ 525-6767), at 1975 Broad St, is right in the centre of town and is moderately priced, with rooms from $60. The *Sands Hotel & Resort* (☎ 569-1666) – though no one can quite figure out where the resort is or what it could possibly be – is at 1818 Victoria Ave and has singles and doubles from $67.

The totally upgraded *Hotel Saskatchewan* (☎ 522-7691), on the corner of Scarth St and Victoria Ave, costs from $95, with weekend specials for $67. The *Ramada Renaissance* (☎ 525-5255) features a three-storey-high indoor water slide, a swimming pool and whirlpools. Prices start at $65 for singles and go way up, but there are weekend specials. It's central, at 1919 Saskatchewan Drive.

Motels Most of the motels are on Hwy 1 east of town. The *Siesta* (☎ 525-8142), on the corner of Park St and Victoria Ave, by the Pump Bar, has rooms from $32.

The *North Star* (☎ 352-0723), a few km from town, is the last motel on the north side of the highway. It is pale blue and set back from the road. Rooms cost $25/30 with air-conditioning.

The *Coachman Inn Motel* (☎ 522-8525) is closer to town. It's the orange place at 835 Victoria Ave. Rooms vary from $40 to $45.

The *Sunrise* (☎ 757-5447) is near the overpass on Hwy 1 East, just out of town. Rooms with TV and air-conditioning cost from $40.

Places to Eat

There's a pretty decent range of places to eat in town, and a number of places offering international cuisine have recently added to the variety. Most choices listed here are in the central area, many of which are closed on Sunday. However, the Saturday newspaper is full of ads for Sunday brunch buffets around town, and most of the eateries around the outskirts remain open on Sunday.

A basic friendly place for breakfast is the *Town & Country*, at 1825 Rose St, open from 6.30 am daily. *Henry the 2nd* at 2425 13th Ave, opposite the YMCA, is a new place serving specialty sandwiches, salads and soups. There's an outdoor patio and a bar with billiard tables.

SASKATCHEWAN

The *Sandwich Tree*, at 1829 Hamilton St (and three other locations around town), is an office workers' kind of lunch place offering excellent sandwiches with such tasty ingredients as avocado, shrimps and bean sprouts. *Olga's Deli & Desserts*, at 1856 Hamilton St, has bagels, blintzes and coffees. It's open every day for breakfast and lunch and is inexpensive.

Upstairs at the 1928 Market Mall, a restored building on Lorne St near the corner of 11th Ave, is the huge Italian restaurant *Presutti's*, an inexpensive, casual place with an outdoor patio and wood-burning oven. Pizzas, pastas and the like are specialities.

For Chinese food, there's *Lang's Café*, at 1745 Broad St. It's open for lunch and closes late. The decor is plastic but the food is cheap and not bad. A Vietnamese place, the *Mai Phuong*, at 1837 Broad St, has an inexpensive lunch buffet.

The *Copper Kettle*, at 1953 Scarth St, opposite Victoria Park, is open daily from 7 am to 1 am and offers pizzas, Greek dishes, cheap breakfasts and a $5.95 lunch buffet. *Grabbajabba* at 1881 Scarth St, is a good place for coffee and dessert.

In the pedestrian section of Scarth St, *Alfredo's* has outdoor tables and serves vegetarian and pasta dishes. The *Elephant & Castle* is a British-style pub in the Cornwall Centre, which you enter on the corner of 11th Ave and Scarth St. Part of the restaurant façade is from the bank building built on the site in 1911. Also in this shopping mall is a cheap food fair, found on the 2nd level.

The *Park Place* restaurant at the Wascana Marina, in the park near Broad St, has some pleasant outdoor tables and offers sandwiches and buffalo burgers. It's open every day.

For a steak, there is the well-established *Diplomat* at 2032 Broad St. It's open from 11 am to 2 pm and again from 4 pm to midnight (except Sunday).

Entertainment

Music & Pubs *The Plains*, in the Plains Hotel, 1965 Albert St, has live bands (often blues on weekends) and there is a late Saturday afternoon jam. There's also live blues at the *Crow's Nest*, downstairs from the Italian restaurant Presutti's, at 1750 Lorne St. *Café 97*, at 1834 Scarth St, features jazz.

The *Long Branch Saloon*, at 1400 McIntyre St, and the *Seven Oaks Inn*, at 777 Albert St, both feature country music. *Lauderdale's*, in the Regina Inn, 1975 Broad St, has dance music. Also check the local papers and lampposts for rock and alternative music options.

On the eastern edge of town, at 1832 Victoria Ave East, *Brewsters* brews its own beer. Closer to downtown, and not far from the RCMP Museum, is the *Bushwakker Brewing Co*, at 2206 Dewdney Ave which runs between Albert and Broad Sts. On offer are several of their own brews, including an oatmeal stout.

The fine, old train station at 1880 Saskatchewan Drive is now the *Casino Regina* (☎ 1-800-555-3189), open daily until 3 am.

Performing Arts *The Trial of Louis Riel*, held in the MacKenzie Art Gallery (☎ 522-4242), 3475 Albert St, is a theatrical dramatisation of the 1885 court battle fought over this leader of the Métis. One of Canada's most famous historical figures, Riel led two uprisings against the government. The re-creation of the trial highlights issues that are still important, as well as demonstrating the animosity between the country's French and British settlers.

It's worth catching, if your timing is right, and has become one of the longest-running shows in the country. There are shows three nights a week in July and August. Tickets ($10) are available at the tourist office or at the door.

Applause Dinner Theatre is a popular dinner theatre which doesn't cost an arm and a leg. Two-act musical comedies are presented with dinner. It's in the Regina Inn, 1975 Broad St.

The *Saskatchewan Centre of the Arts*, in the Wascana Centre at 200 Lakeshore Drive, is a venue for concerts and performances ranging through folk, musicals and rock to opera and the symphony orchestra.

SASKATCHEWAN

Cinema There's a repertory cinema (☎ 777-6016) on the lower level of the Central Library at 2311 12th Ave.

Spectator Sports In summer and autumn, the Saskatchewan Roughriders (☎ 525-2181) play professional football at Taylor Field as part of the Canadian Football League (CFL).

Curling is a major winter sport on the prairies, and the Curlodrome at Exhibition Park holds major competitions (known as bonspiels) through the snowy months.

Getting There & Away
Air Air Canada (☎ 525-4711) has flights east and west. There's no longer an Air Canada office in town, but any travel agency can organise tickets. Standard one-way fares include $404 to Vancouver and $397 to Thunder Bay. Canadian Airlines also serves Regina. Athabaska Airways flies to Saskatoon, Prince Albert and some of the smaller northern towns.

Bus The bus station is downtown on Hamilton St, just south of Victoria Ave. There are left-luggage lockers and a quick-lunch counter. Three bus companies operate out of the station. Greyhound (☎ 787-3340), for daily interprovincial trips, runs west to Calgary and Vancouver and east to Winnipeg and Toronto.

The Saskatchewan Transportation Company (☎ 787-3340) covers the small towns in the province and runs to Saskatoon and Prince Albert. There are three trips a day to Saskatoon ($25). The 240-km trip takes three hours.

Moose Mountain Lines has one route into rural Saskatchewan.

The hostel has cheap bus tickets available to members for trips around the province.

Train There is no train service in or out of the city.

Car Dollar Rent-A-Car (☎ 525-1000) is central, at 1975 Broad St, on the corner of 12th Ave. They also have an office at the airport. Other companies are Thrifty, Hertz and Avis.

Hitching For hitching east, take the No 4 bus from downtown.

Getting Around
The Airport The airport is about a 15-minute drive from downtown, and the only way to get there is by taxi, which costs about $8. There are half-a-dozen car-rental agencies at the airport.

Bus Regina Transit (☎ 777-7433) operates the bus routes around the city. Buses run from 6 am to midnight Monday to Saturday and from 1.30 to 8.30 pm on Sunday. Call for route information.

Bicycle Rentals are available from Joe's Cycle (☎ 347-7711), at 2255 Albert St, for $20 per day. The Devonian Pathway is a system of 11 km of paved bike routes through four city parks.

AROUND REGINA
Lumsden
North-west of Regina, Lumsden sits nestled and protected in a convoluted, lumpy, hilly little valley on the main road (Route 11) to Saskatoon. The Franciscan Monks here run the St Michael's retreat. The Heritage Museum outlines the history of the Qu'Appelle Valley.

Qu'Appelle Valley
The Qu'Appelle Valley runs east-west from the town of Fort Qu'Appelle, north-east of Regina, and makes a good contrast to the prairies. Following the Qu'Appelle River and interspersed with lakes, this valley is one of the green and pretty playgrounds of Saskatchewan.

There are several provincial parks and historic sites along the glacially formed valley. North of Lumsden, in Craven, the **Last Mountain House Provincial Historic Park**, is a fur-trading post dating from 1869 to 1871. Staff, displays and reconstructed buildings tell the story of the site.

SASKATCHEWAN

It's open from the beginning of July to the beginning of September each afternoon from Thursday to Monday. The **Big Valley Jamboree**, held here annually in the middle of July, is one of the province's big country-music festivals, drawing acts from around the country and the USA. Beer gardens, free camping and booths selling all manner of western garb are part of the three-day event.

Later in the summer, in August, another event worth catching is the **Craven Valley Stampede**. Chuck-wagon races, roping contests and country & western music are some of the features. There isn't much in Craven, but as it is only 37 km north-west of Regina, you can find accommodation in the city.

Fort Qu'Appelle

Fort Qu'Appelle, a town of nearly 2000 people, lies north-east of Regina, by the Qu'Appelle River. The museum, at the corner of Bay Ave and Third St, has a collection of Native Indian artefacts, pioneer articles and some things from the old Hudson's Bay Company post (from 1864), which is adjacent to the museum. It's open every day through the summer. At Qu'-Appelle Crafts, 310 Broadway, Native Indian crafts produced for the commercial market can be seen or purchased. Each year in early or mid-August a large **Native Indian powwow**, takes place at the Standing Buffalo Reserve, nine km west of town. Dance competitors come from far and wide. Call ☎ 332-4685 for exact dates.

Also west of town is the **Echo Valley Provincial Park** (☎ 332-3215) with a campground, swimming and trails around the valley.

East Saskatchewan

MOOSE MOUNTAIN PROVINCIAL PARK

West from Manitoba along the Trans Canada Hwy and south down Hwy 9, Moose Mountain (☎ 577-2144) is a place to consider camping the night or stopping for a break from the unchanging pancake landscape. The park provides an oasis of woods on the highest plateau in this area of the province. It is a fairly developed area, however, with golf courses, water slides and the like available around the park's main gate. The central and western portions of the park are quieter, and walking trails can be found in these parts.

South of the park is **Cannington Manor Historic Park**. The park records an English settlement here between the years 1882 and 1900. The park is open daily from 10 am to 6 pm.

There are a couple of motels in nearby Kenosee.

CROOKED LAKE PROVINCIAL PARK

An alternative is Crooked Lake (☎ 728-7480), which is further west but not so far from the Trans Canada Hwy. The park is 30 km north of the highway, along the eastern stretches of the Qu'Appelle Valley and Qu'Appelle River. Again, there is camping.

YORKTON

The onion-domed churches of Yorkton, due north of the Crooked Lake Provincial Park, reflect the area's Ukrainian heritage. The town is a major retail and distribution centre in eastern Saskatchewan. There's a branch of the provincial museum system here, depicting the struggles of the various immigrant groups of the province.

St Mary's Church is worth seeing, particularly the painted dome.

Every May the town hosts the Yorkton Short Film and Video Festival – the oldest continuously running short-film festival in North America.

Nearby are two provincial parks: **Good Spirit Provincial Park**, with good swimming, and the larger **Duck Mountain Provincial Park**, on the border of Manitoba.

The *Corona Motor Inn* (☎ 783-6571), at 345 West Broadway Ave, has been recommended. Rooms cost around $46 for doubles. The inn has a restaurant and bar.

Veregin and the Doukhobours

Veregin is a small, essentially unknown town, more or less in the middle of nowhere, but it has a rather unexpected international and intriguing history. The town and its surrounding area were settled between 1898 and 1899 by the Doukhobours, a determined and somewhat extraordinary religious sect from Russia.

At the turn of the century, with help from writer Leo Tolstoy, a good many of these people left their homeland and the persecution there to come to Saskatchewan in search of religious freedom and seclusion. Here, under the leadership of Peter Veregin, they created a small but successful community.

Bliss was not to last, however, and soon the Doukhobours were in trouble with their neighbours and government again. They resisted all mainstream authority, be it church or state. Partially based on fact, but somewhat exaggerated, are the well-known tales of nude demonstrations and arson which have, rightly or wrongly, come to be closely associated with the group.

After about 20 years here, many of the Doukhobours moved to British Columbia, where there's still a community. In the 1950s some of them returned to Russia, or headed to new lands once again, this time settling in Paraguay. ■

VEREGIN

Veregin lies near the provincial border with Manitoba. It is north of Yorkton, and 265 km north-east of Regina.

In town is the **Doukhobour Heritage Village**, a series of mainly reconstructed buildings and homes which reveal aspects of the settlers' lives at the beginning of the 1900s.

Houses and the Prayer Home are decorated in typical traditional fashion and include some attractive textiles. The museum contains many other artefacts, as well as photographs. Bread baked in the old-style brick ovens can sometimes be purchased.

The village is open daily from mid-May to mid-September, on weekdays only through the winter. There is a small admission charge for visitors.

There is also a statue of author Leo Tolstoy, commemorated for his assistance in the Doukhobours' emigration.

Southern Saskatchewan

Running across the southern section of the province is the Red Coat Trail, a highway route from Winnipeg, Manitoba to Lethbridge, Alberta. The trail is named after the Mounties and roughly parallels the route they took in coming to tame the west.

Tourist offices have a pamphlet which highlights the historical and geographical points of interest along the way. Here, as in much of the province, the towns themselves don't have much to interest visitors but the government parks do have areas of geographic, historic or cultural significance.

MOOSE JAW

Moose Jaw is a small, fairly typical farm-supply town but with some industry as well. Theories on the origins of the once-heard, never-forgotten name are numerous and nebulous; 'moosegaw' is a Cree word meaning 'warm breezes', so this possibility has some credence.

Information

The tourist office (☎ 693-8097) is at 88 Saskatchewan St East. During the summer they also operate a booth out on the Trans Canada Hwy, beside the statue of the moose. Moose Jaw has long had a bad reputation as a place to get stuck hitchhiking. It ranks right up there with Ontario's Wawa and Nipigon.

Things to See & Do

The downtown area has a number of heritage buildings from the town's boom days in the 1920s; the tourist office produces a pamphlet for a self-guided historical walking tour along Main St and nearby. Painted murals with an historical theme can be seen on 23

SASKATCHEWAN

buildings in the core area. The Mural Centre, with more information on the project, is at 445 Main St. Situated halfway between the railway towns of Winnipeg and Calgary, Moose Jaw was selected as a major Canadian Pacific Railway terminal in the late 19th century.

There are four **Western Development Museums** around the province, each specialising in an aspect of provincial history. The one in Moose Jaw concentrates on the development of transportation in the west, with old carts, cars and trains. Admission costs $4.

Also here is **Wild Animal Park**, a zoo really, with mainly indigenous animals including bison. This was the site of Chief Sitting Bull's victory celebration after the famous 1876 Battle of Little Bighorn (in what is now Montana, USA).

Curiosity-seekers might enjoy the **Sukanen Ship & Pioneer Village Museum**, 13 km out of town, with plenty of pioneer relics and remains and the ship built way out here for sailing on the sea. The odd collection also contains old cars and tractors. It's open in summer only.

The town also hosts a major **international band** (pipe, brass, marching, etc) and **choral festival** in May. There is an armed forces base in Moose Jaw, which is home to the famous Snowbirds, an aerial acrobatic squadron which performs at air shows across the continent. The **Saskatchewan Air Show**, largest on the prairies, is held here each July.

Places to Stay

For camping, the *Besant Trans-Canada Campground* (☎ 756-2700) is a 20-minute drive west on the Trans Canada Hwy. There are both tent and trailer sections within the park, and a small pond for a swim.

There are about 10 motels and hotels in town and a B&B. The *Prairie Oasis Campground* (☎ 692-4894) is a family-oriented recreation centre (water slides, etc) with mobile homes which can be rented from around $40 a night. It's at the corner of Ninth Ave North-East and Hwy 1.

ESTEVAN

Near the US border, Estevan (population 10,700) is one of the largest towns in southern Saskatchewan. It's a town with energy – it has the world's largest deposits of lignite coal, three electrical generating stations and some natural gas pockets and is surrounded by oilfields.

Local attractions include the sandstone rock formations at **La Roche Percée**, once a site of Native Indian religious observance, and the **Estevan Brick Wildlife Display**, which has samples (stuffed) of most local species, including bison and antelope.

Ask at the tourist office about rockhounding or visiting the dam and coal mines. There are about half a dozen standard motels.

South of town, in North Portal, Chicago gangster Al Capone used to hang out in the Cadillac Hotel – this was a big booze-smuggling area during the Prohibition days (1920-33) in the USA.

WEYBURN

From Weyburn, a farming supply centre with nearly 10,000 residents, the so-called CANAM International Hwy leads northward to Regina and beyond, and southward through North and South Dakota and Wyoming. A promotional pamphlet lists the attractions of a trip along the designated route.

There isn't a lot in Weyburn, but there is a park with camping facilities and tourist information, and a small museum, the Soo Line Historical Museum, which has some Native Indian artefacts and articles from the pioneer days.

Weyburn is the birthplace of Canadian author WO Mitchell and the setting for his best-known book, about a boy growing up, *Who Has Seen The Wind*.

BIG MUDDY BADLANDS

Off Hwy 34 south of Regina and Moose Jaw, near the US border, this vast, hot area of sandstone formations, hills and valleys was once used by stagecoach robbers, cattle-rustlers and all the other bad-guy types you see in western movies. In fact, the outlaw Butch Cassidy used to ride here.

Food, accommodation and camping is available in the small town of **Bengough**. There is another campground in Big Beaver, and guided tours of the badlands are available.

ASSINIBOIA

South of this small centre at the junction of Hwys 13 and 2 are two historic parks which may be of interest. At **St Victor's** are prehistoric Native Indian petroglyphs (carvings in rock). **Wood Mountain Post Provincial Historic Park** has more recent history, with displays on the North West Mounted Police and the Sioux people. Wood Mountain was where Sitting Bull brought his Sioux warriors after the Battle of Little Bighorn. There are some reconstructed buildings and tours are given. Note that the park is closed on Tuesday and Wednesday, and closes for the season at the beginning of September.

GRASSLANDS NATIONAL PARK

Not yet completed, this park preserves noteworthy flora & fauna as well as remarkable geological and historical features. It's a two-section park lying between Val Marie and Killdear, south of Swift Current and west of Assiniboia. The eastern block is west of Wood Mountain Post Provincial Park. Information on this section of the park can be found at the Rodeo Ranch Museum, in Wood Mountain. The western section of the park runs south-east from the town of Val Marie, at the junction of Hwys 4 and 18. Information and the latest details on the park are available at the Park Service Office and visitors' centre (☎ 298-2257) in Val Marie. Basic wilderness camping is permitted. As yet, there are no facilities in the park.

Surrounded by ranchland, the park protects a section of original, natural, short-grass prairie land. But this is not the only characteristic. Also protected in the park are the Killdear Badlands, 70-Mile Butte, which is the second highest point in the province, cliffs and coulees (gulches, usually dry), a prairie-dog town and some historic Native Indian sites.

SWIFT CURRENT

Though a fairly large town, Swift Current has little for the visitor. Still, a bed or a meal can be found without difficulty. Country music fans may want to check out the **Canadian Country Music Hall of Fame** (☎ 773-7854), off the Trans Canada Hwy, or the fiddle championships which are held in September.

GREAT SAND HILLS

Just west of Swift Current (or north of Gull Lake and Maple Creek) is a semidesert area with dunes and near-arid vegetation. The best viewing area is near the little village of **Sceptre**, in the north-western section of the hills near the town of Leader. Antelope and mule deer may be seen. There are farm B&Bs in the area; ask in Swift Current.

SASKATCHEWAN LANDING PROVINCIAL PARK

Straight north up Hwy 4 from Swift Current, the section of the Saskatchewan River here was used as a crossing point by the early European explorers and, later, the White settlers. The Interpretive Centre, a stone house

Whitetail deer

SASKATCHEWAN

built by the North West Mounted Police, provides some details on this and on the Native Indian sites within the park. There is also camping.

EASTEND

Not far from the town of Eastend, south-west of Swift Current on Hwy 13, is the partially excavated site of the first *Tyrannosaurus rex* skeleton found in Saskatchewan. Access to the site is by guided tour only. Frenchman

Valley Tours (☎ 295-3606) offers several tours a day from July to September. Tours include a visit to the field research station which contains palaeontological displays and a working lab. Tickets costs $25 per person and reservations are required.

CYPRESS HILLS PROVINCIAL PARK

This is a small region on the border of southern Saskatchewan and Alberta which offers geographical respite from the prairies. It's a

---

Wheat

Since it's all you're looking at, I suppose a word about the golden grain is in order.

Wheat, brought to the New World by European settlers, was largely responsible for the development of the Canadian prairies. It is the primary crop across Manitoba, Saskatchewan and Alberta but by far the bulk of it is grown in Saskatchewan.

So productive are the fields here that Canada is the world's sixth largest producer after Russia, China, the USA, India and France. The majority of wheat is produced for the export market. Russia, despite its own massive wheat production, is one of Canada's most important clients. Canadian wheat is sought after for its quality and high protein content.

Because of the cold climate the principal variety grown is hard red spring wheat, a bread wheat which is planted in spring and then harvested in August and September. The other main type is durum wheat whose characteristics make it especially suitable for the production of pasta.

In late summer, when the ripened wheat is golden brown it is not uncommon to see the huge self-powered combines cutting and threshing through the fields at any hour of the night or day, often in teams. At night in particular, with the bright light beams skimming across the fields from the droning machines, it's quite a memorable sight.

The Canadian Wheat Board markets the crop. This organisation represents the farmers, the consumers and the government in buying, selling, setting quotas and regulating export. Needless to say, the Board's actions are hotly debated.

Farmers are paid when they deliver their bushels to the grain elevators, where the entire crop is pooled and then sold by the Board. Once that is accomplished the wheat is carried to ports by train and loaded onto freighters for destinations far and wide.

Grain Elevators

The unique, striking, columnar red, green or grey grain elevators seen along rail lines across the province are the classic symbol of mid-western Canada. These vertical wheat warehouses have been called the 'castles of the New World' and to this day are the artificial structure most visible across the plains.

Very simple in design and material and built solely for function they have been described as Canada's most distinctive architectural form. Western painters, photographers and writers have taken them as objects of art, meditation and iconography.

Across much of the province they have represented the economic life of the town and district and indeed have topped in size, if not in importance, that other traditional landmark, the church.

The first grain elevators were built in the 1880s. While Canada was becoming the 'breadbasket of the world' at the turn of this century, the number of elevators mushroomed, reaching a peak of nearly 5800 in 1938. Through consolidation and changing conditions that number is now down to just under 2000. This decline has concerned many individuals and groups who hope to prevent (not just lament) any further major loss of elevators.

Formerly made all of wood, they are now built from materials such as steel and cement. The classic shape, about 10 metres square and 20 metres high, is being experimented with as well, in an attempt to improve efficiency.

The stark beauty of elevators catching the light or looming out of the horizon is certainly an unmistakable part of the prairie landscape. ■

pretty area of small lakes, streams and green hills up to 1400 metres high. Much of the land is a park which stretches across the provincial border. There's some organised camping on the Alberta side, around the lakes; tenting costs around $10, but it gets crowded in summer.

A dirt road links this area to **Fort Walsh**, where there's a national historic park. The fort, built in the late 1870s as a North West Mounted Police base, is a remnant of the district's rich but sad history.

The hills, always a sanctuary for animals, were at one time also a welcoming retreat for the Plains Indians. Information at the old fort tells the story of the time when 'a man's life was worth a horse and a horse was worth a pint of whisky'.

MAPLE CREEK

At the northern edge of Cypress Hills, Maple Creek is worth a look for its old western main street. Many of the storefronts in this ranching district town are heritage vintage. The **Old Timer's Museum**, 218 Jasper St, is the oldest in the province. It has artefacts on the RCMP and some on the Native Indian and pioneer communities.

If you're around here in late summer, ask about the weekend-long **Cowboy Poetry Gathering**. Begun in 1989, the poetry event has become a surprise success attracting storytellers and singers who carry on the tradition of cowboy (and cowgirl) narrative. You can also see the work of artisans such as saddlemakers and silversmiths. On Saturday night there's a big western dance.

There are a couple of motels in and around town, and there is the *Willow Bend Trailer Court*, a campground geared to those with campervans or recreational vehicles.

Saskatoon

Saskatoon (population 195,000) is a small, quiet city sitting smack in the middle of the Canadian prairies. The clean, wide streets, low skyline and flat surroundings give the city a western flavour. The South Saskatchewan River meandering through green parkland helps create the atmosphere of a very peaceful, easy-paced community. The largest employer in town is the university, and Saskatoon has pretty much become the provincial cultural centre, with an active arts community.

As the second city of the province, however, Saskatoon is also a farm-trading centre, acting as a transportation, communication and commercial hub. In addition, the city has a major agricultural research centre, called Innovation Place.

There isn't a lot here for the visitor, and after a short look-see you'll have a feel for the place. It's an attractive little city with a few things to see, and the Wanuskewin Heritage Park makes it an even better and more convenient crossroads for the traveller. Accommodation is reasonable and you can get a reasonable meal.

Just off the main thoroughfares, residential streets are lined with small, neat, square houses – some old, some new. Seven bridges link the city across the river.

History

In 1883, 35 members of the Temperance Colonisation Colony from Ontario founded a settlement on these Cree lands. The town stayed (though the ban on alcohol didn't), taking its name from the Cree word 'misaskwatomin', for one of the indigenous berries still enjoyed today in pies and jams. In 1890 the railway hit town and growth continued until the Depression. The city has had its ups and downs since then, but is now well established and diversified beyond its agricultural roots. Uranium mines and some of the world's largest potash deposits are found nearby.

Orientation

The South Saskatchewan River cuts through the city diagonally from north-east to southwest. The small main downtown area lies on the west bank; the university is on the opposite side.

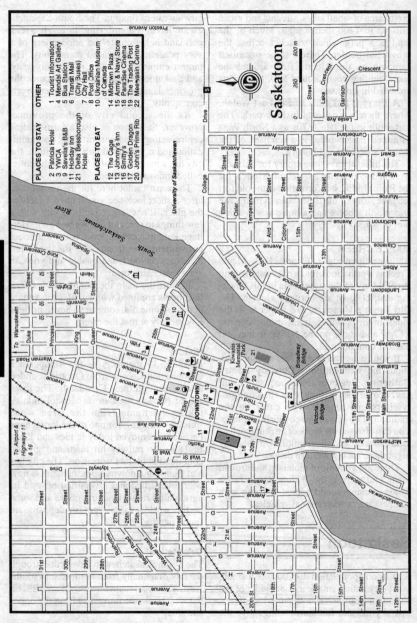

Saskatoon

PLACES TO STAY
2   Patricia Hotel
3   YWCA
9   Savella's B&B
11 Holiday Inn
21 Delta Bessborough Hotel

PLACES TO EAT
12 The Cage
13 Johnny's Inn
16 Smitty's
17 Golden Dragon
20 John's Prime Rib

OTHER
1   Tourist Information
4   Mendel Art Gallery
5   Bus Station
6   Transit Mall
    (City Buses)
7   City Hall
8   Post Office
10 Ukrainian Museum
    of Canada
14 Midtown Plaza
15 Army & Navy Store
18 Paradise Cinema
19 The Trading Post
22 Meewasin Centre

Idylwyld Drive divides the city's streets into their east and west designations. Out of town in each direction, Idylwyld Drive becomes Hwy 16, the Yellowhead Hwy. The city is split into north-south sections by 22nd St, and the streets on either side are marked accordingly.

The downtown core extends to the river to the south, First Ave to the west, 25th St to the north, and Spadina Crescent and the river again (it changes direction) to the east.

Streets run east-west, avenues north-south. The main street is Second Ave. Another important street is 21st St East with its blend of new and old architecture and lots of stores, framed by the Bessborough Hotel at one end and the Midtown Plaza, the old CN train station, at the other.

At 23rd St East, between Third Ave North and Second Ave North, is the Greyhound Bus Depot, in a block open only to bus traffic. Most bus routes can be picked up here. Note though that the transit mall, a few blocks further west, is the city bus terminal.

Behind the Bessborough Hotel is one of the city's large parks, Kiwanis Memorial Park, running beside the river. At each end of the attractive park, which is used by cyclists and joggers during the summer months, Spadina Crescent continues on along the river.

Just west of Idylwyld Drive on 20th St West is an old commercial area, now in some decay. It was formerly a largely Ukrainian area, and there are some remnants of this past, along with the newer immigrant establishments (mostly Chinese, found in the side streets running off 20th St). Also in the area are a couple of cheap hotels, many pawn-shops and a second-hand bookshop.

Faring better is Broadway Ave, another old shopping district and actually the town's oldest. For several years it has enjoyed some re-gentrification. A range of stores and restaurants can be found along this small historic section of Broadway St, which is south of the river from downtown, over the Broadway Bridge. The area of interest runs from the bridge south about half a dozen blocks to Main St East.

Information

Tourist Offices The Tourism Saskatoon office (☎ 242-1206) is in the old CP train station at No 6 305 Idylwyld Drive North. During the summer it's open from 9 am to 7 pm Monday to Friday and from 10 am to 7 pm weekends. There is a seasonal information booth open daily from May to August at the corner of Ave C and 47th St.

Post Office The main post office is at 202 4th Ave N.

Medical Services The Royal University Hospital (☎ 665-1000) is on the grounds of the university, just north of downtown.

Wanuskewin Heritage Park

Five km north of the city alongside the South Saskatchewan River, this is the premiere attraction in the Saskatoon area and, indeed, the entire province. The 100-hectare site (☎ 931-6767 or 1-800-665-4600) around the remarkably attractive and scenically diverse Opamihaw Valley presents and interprets the area's rich archaeology, prehistory and the Northern Plains Indian culture. Wanuskewin (pronounced wah-nus-KAY-win, which is Cree for 'seeking peace of mind') is a fascinating cultural, historical and geographical centre all in one. Two dozen prehistoric archaeological sites have been unearthed, attracting attention from researchers around the world. It's now known that hunters and gatherers lived in the area at least 6000 years ago. Active digs can be visited and there is an archaeological lab on site.

The visitor centre, developed in conjunction with provincial Native Indian groups, tells the story of the regional Native peoples and their way of life on the once buffalo-filled prairies. Displays also outline more recent history and Native Indian life as it is now. Most of the site workers are Native Indian. During the summer there are daily dance performances at 1.30 and 3.30 pm.

Best of all is the land itself, left untouched to reveal why so many people over so many years found it a sacred place. Virtually invisible from the surrounding prairie, four trails lead the visitor down and around the valley amid wildflowers, songbirds and such park highlights as the old buffalo trail, a buffalo jump, the mysterious medicine wheel and tipi rings. The site harbours a rich concentration of flora & fauna, including a small herd of deer.

From June to September visitors can camp out in the park in a traditional tipi. An overnight stay, including breakfast and admission to the park, costs just $23 for hostel members. Full price is $39 for adults and $20 for children. There are one, two and three-night packages available which might include learning how to build and raise a tipi, listening to traditional stories, guided walks along Wanuskewin's ancient trails, cooking Native Indian foods and making crafts such as dream catchers.

If visiting for the day, a suggestion is to arrive early in the morning – the earlier, the better. There will be few people, if any, and a walk around the trail system at this time is sure to be quiet and peaceful – the way the Native people would have found it. Also, if

it is midsummer, the air will be fresh and cool and the odds of seeing some of the wildlife markedly increased. When it gets busy after lunch, the visitor centre can be viewed.

For the trails, wear flat comfortable shoes, and in high summer take a juice or water bottle because it can get extremely hot. To thoroughly see the site – walk the trails, watch a performance, and take a break for lunch – allow around six hours.

The restaurant provides an opportunity to try Native Indian foods such as buffalo, wild rice and Saskatoon berry desserts. The buff stew with bannock, an unleavened bread, is inexpensive and good.

Getting to the site presents some difficulties for those without a car. The city has considered a weekend bus run to the park. Call the park or city bus information (☎ 975-3100) for the latest news on transport options. If you're staying at the Patricia Hotel, mention to the managers that you'd like to go to Wanuskewin and they may be able to arrange transportation, especially if there's a bunch of you.

South-western Saskatchewan is known for its cattle ranches and wheat fields

Taxis by the meter cost about $20 one way, although you may be able to negotiate a cheaper rate. Cycling is another option, but this is not really cheap either – $20 for the full day. Bikes can be rented at several outlets, including Joe's Cycle, Bike & Blade, the Ramada Renaissance Hotel and the Bessborough Hotel.

Taking one (with lock) from the Ramada Renaissance is not a bad idea, as it can be picked up at 9 am and doesn't need to be returned until 9 pm. Riding steadily at a good clip, the trip takes almost exactly an hour one way. The ride makes a good introduction to the park – an oasis surrounded by vast, open prairie.

Follow Warman Rd out of the centre (just keep going and going) and then look for signs with the park symbol (a buffalo in a circle). These signs are also seen if you're driving north out of the city along Idylwyld Drive, which becomes Hwy 11. For those with more time and a map, the pleasant Meewasin cycling trail can be used for part of the trip.

The site is open daily from 9 am to 9 pm from the end of May to Labour Day, and from 9 am to 5 pm daily for the rest of the year. Admission is $6 for adults, less for seniors and children, and there is a family rate.

Western Development Museum

You open the door of this museum (☎ 931-1910) and suddenly you're looking down Main St, circa 1910. It looks like a movie set, with stores, workshops, a hotel, a printing shop and other establishments. The general store is good. Don't miss the model of men playing chess. There are all manner of goods, tins, relics and supplies on display, as well as old wagons, cars and farm machinery.

The museum is at 2610 Lorne Ave, quite a way south of town. To get there, take a No 1 Exhibition bus from Second Ave downtown. When leaving the museum, get on the bus going the same way as when you arrived. It loops around, then goes back a different way. The museum is open daily. Admission costs $4, less for seniors and kids; it may be

worth showing a HI hostel card too. There is a cafe at the site. Call to check opening hours.

Ukrainian Museum of Canada

This museum (☎ 244-3800), at 910 Spadina Crescent East, preserves and presents a Ukrainian heritage through articles donated by Ukrainian immigrants. The highlight is the collection of fantastic textiles used in formal and everyday dress and for other household purposes. In style, colour and design, they rival South American textiles.

Also interesting is the exhibit on symbolic, festival or special-occasion breads (such as wedding breads). Other items are the painted eggs (pysanka) and a brief history of the pioneers' arrival.

The museum is open Tuesday to Saturday from 10 am to 5 pm and on Sunday and holidays from 1 to 5 pm. Admission is $2.

There are branches of this museum in other Canadian cities, such as Winnipeg and Edmonton, but this is the main one.

Ukraine Museum

A small museum (☎ 244-4212) at 202 Avenue M South, this one has examples of Ukrainian crafts and dress, and through the exhibits portrays aspects of Ukrainian culture from prehistoric times to the mid-20th century. It's open daily in summer, on the weekend in winter. Admission is $2.

The adjacent Byzantine-style Ukrainian cathedral can be visited; ask at the museum.

Marr Residence

Just a block from the river, at 326 11th St East, sits the oldest building (☎ 665-8688) in Saskatoon still in its original location. Built in 1884, it was used as a hospital the following year, during the North West Rebellion. Admission is free; call for opening times.

Meewasin Valley & Centre

The pretty, green Meewasin Valley follows the South Saskatchewan River down the middle of the city. (Meewasin is a Cree word meaning 'beautiful valley'.) From behind the Bessborough Hotel, the valley park runs in both directions and on both sides of the river for a total of 17 km.

There are pleasant views of the river. The **Meewasin Valley Trail** is good for walking and cycling, and picnic tables are scattered among the trees, where black-and-white magpies flit. Bridges span the river at several places and the trail follows the banks on both sides. Many of the city's attractions and events are along the river. The university lies along the east shore.

The **Meewasin Centre** (☎ 665-6888), 402 Third Ave South, is at the bottom of Third Ave South, on the corner of 19th St East. It's really a museum about the river and the city's history, with some good displays.

Although it's hard to imagine, the river is melted glacier ice from the Rockies far to the west near Lethbridge, Alberta. It flows north from Saskatoon, joining the Assiniboine River on its way to Winnipeg. The Meewasin Centre is open daily, and has good maps of the trail with its various parks. Admission is free.

Mendel Art Gallery & Conservatory

These are at 950 Spadina Crescent East, a short walk along the river from the downtown area. The gallery (☎ 975-7610) has three rooms of changing exhibits, usually featuring Canadian works. One of the three galleries shows historical works, while the other two display contemporary art. The small conservatory has a few palms, amongst other plants. Admission is free and the centre is open daily from noon to 9 pm. There is a coffee shop and gift store on the premises.

University of Saskatchewan

There are a few things to look at on the campus (☎ 966-4343), which is on a huge tract of land along the river. There's a small biology museum, an observatory for stargazing (open Saturday evenings after dusk), two art galleries and other small faculty museums. The Natural Sciences Museum has some life-size replicas of dinosaurs. For opening hours and information on free tours of the campus and many of the points of interest, call during office hours.

Also on campus is the **Diefenbaker Centre**, detailing aspects of former prime minister's Diefenbaker's life. It has changing exhibits on Diefenbaker, as well as other historical and craft exhibits. The centre is open daily, but afternoons only on weekends and holidays. His grave site is next to the centre.

The **Little Stone School**, dating from 1887, is the oldest public building in the city. It can be visited Saturday and Sunday afternoons. A costumed interpreter provides information. It's free, as are all the university sights. If you're going to stroll around the campus, pick up a copy of the architectural pamphlet *Building the University*, which offers details of the various structures and their dates of construction.

Forestry Farm Park & Zoo

This park (☎ 975-3382) is eight km northeast of the downtown area, across the river and along Attridge Drive and then Forest Drive. The zoo inside the park is home to around 300 animals, mostly those found in Saskatchewan and other parts of Canada: wolves, lynx, caribou and bison. There are also gardens, picnic sites, a restaurant and a new fishing lake. In winter the park has a ski trail. The park is over University Bridge; for specific details of how to get there, ask at the tourist office or call the park, but there are signs to follow along Attridge Drive. There is a vehicle charge of $2 and tickets for the zoo are $3. It's open 365 days a year, until 9 pm through the summer months.

Beaver Creek Conservation Area

About 13 km south of the Meewasin Valley (from the Freeway Bridge) is the Beaver Creek Conservation Area, a large park protecting some of the river valley and its wildlife. Walking trails run through the area and the information centre provides geographical and historical background. The park contains some of the little remaining uncultivated prairie in the province. Beaver Creek is open daily from May to August and admission is free.

Saskatchewan Railway Museum

The province's railway history is here (☎ 382-9855), spread over 2.5 hectares. There are engines, cabooses, even transplanted railway buildings. Smaller artefacts have also been collected from around Saskatchewan. It's open on weekends only from 1 pm to 6 pm. Admission is $2. The site is four km south-west of town via Hwys 7 and 60. Call for detailed instructions.

The Berry Barn

Located on a working farm 11 km south-west of town, the Berry Barn (☎ 382-7036) sells a range of foods made with the Saskatoon berry. Light meals are offered at tables overlooking the Saskatchewan River. There's also a substantial gift shop upstairs. In season, you can go into the fields and pick your own berries. Call for hours (they vary), information on the harvesting time and directions.

Activities

There are numerous city-operated swimming pools around town; the tourist office will help locate a convenient one. In winter there is a skating rink on the parkland beside the Bessborough Hotel.

Organised Tours

Northcote River Cruises (☎ 382-1166) offer one-hour boat tours with historical narration, leaving from the lookout behind the Mendel Art Gallery. They run on the hour through the afternoon and early evening daily in June, July and August. There are weekend trips only in May and September. The cruise costs $6.50, less for kids. Guided walks of the university and some of its attractions are offered on Monday and Friday from June to August; call ☎ 966-8384 for information.

Borealis Outdoor Adventures (☎ 343-6399) runs weekend and longer bicycle trips around the province.

Festivals

Some of the major events held from June through to September are:

Shakespeare on the Saskatchewan – This is a successful and popular summer-long theatre programme, held in a tent near the river by the Mendal Art Gallery. Each year, one play by the Bard is presented for the season. Performances are in the evening and advance tickets are advised; call ☎ 653-2300 for bookings.

Saskatchewan Jazz Festival – This festival (☎ 652-1421) is held at the end of June or beginning of July and takes place at various locations around town. Most of the concerts and performances are free. Emphasis is on conventional jazz, but bands range from Dixieland to free form.

Louis Riel Day – This is a one-day event held in the first week of July, with various outdoor activities and contests taking place by the Bessborough Hotel.

The Exhibition – This is an eight-day event in mid-July, with livestock competitions, exhibits, concerts, rides and parades.

International Fringe Theatre Festival – At the end of July, look for this week-long festival, showcasing varied, experimental and inexpensive theatre, including drama, mime, comedy and dance.

Folkfest – This three-day festival (☎ 931-0100) takes place in late August or early September. The fee of $9 gets you into 25 multicultural pavilions set up around the city presenting food, crafts, music and dances. A free shuttle bus does the circuit around the various pavilions.

Places to Stay

Camping Quite close to the centre is the *Gordon Howe Campsite* (☎ 975-3328), on Ave P south of 11th St, operated by the City Parks Department. It's quite green and although geared to those with trailers and campervans, there are tent sites for $8 per night. It's open from April to September. There is a small store for basic supplies. A five minute drive north-west of town on Hwy 16 is *Saskatoon 16 West RV Park* (☎ 931-8905). It's open from April to October and sites are $13 for tents.

Hostels Some rooms at the neat and central *Patricia Hotel* (☎ 242-8861), on Second Ave between 24th and 25th Sts, have been converted to hostel dormitories with bunk beds. A bed costs $12 with a membership card or $17 without. The hostel rooms are above the bar and on weekends there's live music; don't figure on sleeping before 2 am, or consider an ordinary hotel room (from $21) higher up. The bar is quite inexpensive, as is the restaurant in the basement, where there is lots to look at while you eat the good, cheap food. The hotel lobby has a TV lounge area.

The *YWCA* (☎ 244-0944), on the corner of 25th St East and Fifth Ave North, rents rooms all year round to women ($38 a single). Look for the blue sign near Third Ave. They have a pool and a small kitchen.

There is accommodation available at the University of Saskatchewan (☎ 966-8600), 25-minutes walk north-east of town along the river, from the beginning of May to the end of August. A shared room is $19.50; a single room is $24.

B&Bs The Country Vacation Association (☎ 672-3970) has a full list of B&Bs in the area. *Savelia's* (☎ 653-4646) is quite central at 330 6th Ave North, just south of 25th St. There are three rooms with shared bathroom at $30/40 a single/double. A full breakfast is included. *Brighton House* (☎ 664-3278) is north of downtown, near the river, at 1308 Fifth Ave North. Rates are $35/45. Bicycles are available and transport can be arranged for a small fee.

For a real taste of prairie hospitality you can stay on a 40-hectare farm complete with cows, pigs, sheep and goats. *Chaplin's Farm* (☎ 931-3353) is about 11 km south-east of Saskatoon and has rooms for $35/45. Overnight camping costs $7. Call ahead for reservations and directions.

Hotels – middle The *Patricia Hotel* (☎ 242-8861), 345 Second Ave North, between 24th and 25th Sts, is the best and cleanest of the cheap places. In fact, this is one of the best budget hotels in the country – central, friendly and well run. It's good value, with rooms from $21 to $30, depending on the facilities (see also under hostels). The sports bar and restaurant on the premises are both good and inexpensive. Note that some rooms can be a little noisy on weekends if they are above the bar and a live band is on hand.

The *Senator* (☎ 244-6141) is right in the centre of town, on the corner of Third Ave

South and 21st St East. It's old but has been renovated. The rooms are good and cost $40/44. It has a beautiful pub-style bar and a rooftop eating area.

There are a couple of cheapies on Second Ave at 20th St, but neither is recommended; ditto for those on 20th St West.

Moving up the scale, there are several moderately priced places. The *Westgate Inn* (☎ 382-3722) is at 2501 22nd St West, with rooms from $38 to $45.

The *King George* (☎ 244-6133), at 157 Second Ave North, is large, one block from the bus station, and costs $40 to $44. There's a laundromat in the basement.

Hotels – top end There are quite a few expensive hotels out around the airport, as well as these two, more central ones.

The *Holiday Inn* (☎ 244-2311), at 90 22nd St East, has doubles for $89. The classic *Delta Bessborough* (☎ 244-5521), a city landmark at 601 Spadina Crescent East, is a better choice at $100 for a double. It's a large, chateau-like place at the bottom of 21st St, by the river.

Motels The *Travelodge* (☎ 242-8881), near the airport at 106 Circle Drive West, on the corner of Idylwyld Drive, is like the others in the chain. The motel section has rooms from $64.

The following motels are all quite close to town. The *Colonial Square Motel* (☎ 343-1676) is at 1301 Eighth St East, near the university. Rooms cost $48 to $52.

Comfort Inn by Journey's End (☎ 934-1122), at 2155 Northridge Drive, is near the airport. It offers good value, with rooms from $47 to $55.

The *Circle Drive Suites* (☎ 665-8121), 102 Cardinal Crescent, at the corner of Airport Drive, has rooms from $40. It's clean and some of the rooms offer simple kitchens. For those who want to sleep during the day and travel at night, they also offer a day rate: $25 for a room from 8 am to 5 pm.

Places to Eat
The *Cage*, at 120 Second Ave North, is a

basic, all-purpose restaurant but it has a varied menu and the decor and furniture are a cut above the usual. Breakfasts are good value and will hold you long past lunch. The Cage stays open 24 hours (except Sunday, when it's closed all day).

Next door is the *Gotta Hava Java*, a good place for a caffeine fix and a piece of cake.

Smitty's, a pancake house, is an admirable place for breakfasts. It's at the corner of Idylwyld Drive and 20th St West.

The best meal in town, and suitable for any budget, can be had at the downtown *Saskatoon Asian*, a small, nondescript-looking place at 145 Third Ave South. The menu offers mainly Vietnamese dishes, but there are also some Thai-influenced items and Chinese plates to round out the options. It's open every day from lunch to 10 pm.

The *Keg*, 301 Ontario Ave North, at the corner of 24th St, is a medium-priced place serving very good steaks. There's an outdoor patio and a popular bar adjoining the restaurant.

John's Prime Rib, at 401 21st St East, is also good for steak, but isn't cheap.

The *Artful Dodger*, at 119 Fourth Ave South, is an English-style pub with typically British meals for around $7.

D'reen's (☎ 931-8880), at 718 Broadway Ave, is a bit more expensive but serves a good mix of continental and nouvelle cuisine. Some vegetarian dishes are included on the menu. Blackboard specials change daily. It's open every day, but only for lunch on Sunday. Reservations are suggested for dinner.

There are a number of restaurants along 20th St West, an area once mainly Ukrainian but now sporting a small Chinatown. The better Chinese places can be found on or near Ave C, a few blocks from Idylwyld Drive. The large *Golden Dragon*, at 334 Ave C South, has been around for years.

Around the outskirts, and for those with wheels, Eighth St East and 22nd St West both offer abundant choices. The Saskatoon Brewing Company sells beer made on the premises in the casual *Cheers Brew Pub*, at 2105 Eighth St East.

For a choice of prime rib of beef, steak or seafood, and a good atmosphere, the *Granary*, at 2806 Eighth St East, is a good choice, with meals around $15. For Greek food, *Cousin Nik's* at 1100 Grosvenor Ave, about half a block from Eighth St East, is recommended. It's open every day for dinner and is priced in the mid-range.

The *Taj Mahal* (☎ 978-2227), at 1013 Broadway Ave, is the best Indian restaurant in town. Reservations are recommended and it's closed Sunday. *Seafood Sam's* is a wacky sports bar, at 819 2nd Ave North, featuring seafood, Chinese dishes and Sam -- restauranteur and hockey fan.

Out of town, *Taunte Maria's Mennonite Restaurant* (☎ 931-3212), on the corner of Faithful Ave and 51st St, offers basic, healthy farm food for any meal of the day.

Entertainment

Live Music *Bud's*, at 817 Broadway Ave, has live rhythm and blues nightly and a Saturday afternoon jam. *Amigo's*, at 632 10th St East, features alternative local and regional bands.

For country music, *Texas T*, at 3331 Eighth St East, is a popular place; they have live music every night -- and a volleyball court. The *Sutherland Bar*, 810 Central Ave, plays classic recorded rock on Thursday, Friday and Saturday nights and has two volleyball courts!

For jazz, check out the *Bassment*, at 245 Third Ave South. They bring in some good acts and it's not expensive.

Performing Arts The Saskatoon Symphony plays at the *Centennial Auditorium* (☎ 938-7800), 35 22nd St East, and other venues regularly from September to May. Large-scale theatrical productions and dance performances are also held here.

Saskatoon is also home to a French theatre company and a dance troupe. *La Troupe du Jour* performs an international repertoire throughout the province and *La Ribambelle* specialises in French Canadian folk dancing.

Spectator Sports The Saskatoon Blades play Western League (which includes four

Canadian provinces and two US states) junior hockey from September to March at Saskatchewan Place. The Saskatoon Riot play Prairie League professional baseball from mid-June to September at Gordie Howe Park.

Things to Buy

A store that might be worth checking out is the large old Army & Navy, on the corner of 21st St East and Third Ave South. This is one of Canada's oldest discount department stores and is a real classic with three floors of cheap goods.

Another place to have a peek at is the Trading Post, 226 Second Ave South. It specialises in crafts and souvenirs, with an emphasis on Native Indian goods. There is some junk, but also some good stuff, including fine, wool Cowichan-style sweaters, Inuit prints and sculpture, some jewellery, woodcarvings and British Columbian jade.

Dreamcatchers, at 217 20th St West, is a smaller place offering a variety of local Native Indian crafts, clothes and a good selection of Native Indian music.

Getting There & Away

Air The airport is eight km from the centre, in the north-east of the city, off Idylwyld Drive. Air Canada (☎ 652-4181) and Canadian Airlines (☎ 665-7688) both fly in and out of Saskatoon. It's about a two-hour flight to either Winnipeg, Calgary or Edmonton. Athabaska Airways (☎ 665-2700) serves Prince Albert and various small northern towns from Saskatoon and Regina.

Bus The big Greyhound Bus Depot (☎ 933-8000), for various destinations all over Saskatchewan, is on the corner of 23rd St East and Ontario Ave. The station has a cafeteria and small store. The washrooms even have showers, which people with tickets can use.

Services include: Regina, daily at 8 am, 1.30 and 5.30 pm ($25); Winnipeg, two a day, one in the morning and one in the evening ($80); and Edmonton, four a day,

including one late at night ($60). There are also three buses a day to Prince Albert.

Train You won't be too happy with this station's location – it's way out, a long way west from downtown on Chappell Drive. The taxi fare is about $10, but a city bus runs to town at a quarter to and quarter past each hour, from Elevator Rd (behind the curling rink, which is across from the station). It doesn't run very late at night, however. For train information call ☎ 1-800-561-8630.

You'll be even less happy with the Saskatoon timetable. Trains run to Edmonton ($83) and on to Jasper and Vancouver three times a week, on Monday, Thursday and Saturday at 2.15 am. To Winnipeg ($117) and on to Toronto, trains also run three times a week, but on Monday, Wednesday and Saturday at 3 am.

There is no longer a train service to Regina.

Car For car rentals, Budget (☎ 1-800-268-8900) is at 234 First Ave South. There are other local and well-known companies around town and at the airport. Two are Dollar and Thrifty.

Getting Around

The Airport A taxi to the airport is about $8.50. Alternatively, catch the No 1 bus from the Transit Terminal, a section of 23rd St East between Third Ave North and Second Ave North blocked off to all traffic but the buses. Tell the driver you're going to the airport because you'll need to transfer to a No 21 en route. There is a bus every half-hour through the day.

Bus All routes and schedules can be accessed through city bus information (☎ 975-3100), although most things of interest to the visitor are within walking distance of the centre of town. Many of the bus routes begin at the Transit Terminal. There are signs for all the bus routes, benches to sit on and lots of people milling about waiting. One of the drivers will be able to help you with any destination questions. City fares are $1.10.

For the train station, which bus you catch will depend on the time of day, so ask. None goes right into the station, but they do go within two blocks or so (see Train under Getting There & Away for details).

Bicycle Bicycles can be rented at Joe's Cycle (☎ 244-7332), 220 20th St West, and at Bike & Blade (☎ 665-2453), 205 Idlywyld Drive. The Bessborough Hotel and the Ramada Renaissance also rent bikes. The rate is the same but a day's rental is longer, because the staff don't have to close up and go home.

AROUND SASKATOON
Redberry Lake
Redberry Lake, about an hour's drive north-west of Saskatoon, is a prime bird-watching location. The lake and its islands are all protected as a federal bird sanctuary. Of most interest are the large, white pelicans and the small, scarcer piping plover, but there are many others. Bird-watching tours can be taken and boats and canoes or windsurfers can be rented. The town of **Hafford** has all the conveniences.

Thirteen km east of town on Hwy 40 is the sanctuary interpretive centre. From here, displays on the white pelicans and closed-circuit TV of their nesting sites can be seen, and then guided boat tours can be taken out on the lake. The centre is open daily.

Little Manitou Lake
Near the town of Watrous, about 120 km south-east of Saskatoon, Little Manitou Lake contains mineral water denser than that of the Dead Sea. It was called Lake of Healing Waters by the Plains Indians and in the 1930s and 40s became a popular Canadian resort. Manitou Springs Mineral Spa (☎ 946-2233) has three pools of heated mineral water and offers massage therapy. It's open year round and is connected to a resort hotel. The spa costs $10 per day.

There are a couple of modest motels in Watrous.

Batoche National Historic Site
North-east of Saskatoon, 80 km up Hwy 11 and then along Route 225 off Hwy 312 from the town of Rosthern, is the site of the 1885 Battle of Batoche, fought between the government and the Métis (led by Louis Riel).

The visitor centre tells the story of the battle, and includes an audiovisual display on the Métis from the 1860s to the present. Also here are the few remains of the village of Batoche, including the church and some of the trenches dug for military purposes. The site is open from 9 am to 5 pm every day from mid-May to mid-October. Admission is free.

Batoche was the centre of a Métis settlement and its provisional government in the late 19th century; many of these people had left Manitoba after running into difficulties over land there.

Batoche is about halfway between Saskatoon and Prince Albert. Driving through this area you'll see the remains of 19th-century wooden farm houses.

North of Batoche
Just north of Batoche on Hwy 11, **Duck Lake** is worth a stop. Throughout the town, which has been revamped with antique street lamps and brick sidewalks, painted murals tell some of the area's cultural and historical stories. One outlines the tale of a Cree, Almighty Voice, and how he and a White policeman ended up dying over the killing of a cow. The Duck Lake Regional Interpretive Centre, at the north end of town off Hwy 11, has an artefact collection relating to the pioneers, Native Indians and Métis of the region.

Further west, **Fort Carlton Historic Park** provides more information on the fur trade, the treaties signed with the Plains Indians and the Riel rebellion.

Northern Saskatchewan

The area north of Saskatoon seems like the northern portion of the province and we refer to it that way, but really this is central Saskatchewan. Geographically, Prince Albert National Park isn't even halfway to the northern border, so technically north begins somewhere beyond that point.

From Saskatoon, the Yellowhead Hwy, a branch of the Trans Canada, which comes from Winnipeg, runs north-west through North Battleford on its way to Edmonton and British Columbia. Pick up a copy of the Yellowhead map and pamphlet, which has some historical background, from the tourist office.

Between Saskatoon and Prince Albert is a farm belt which runs the width of the province. Prince Albert seems a long way north, and indeed, the growing season is short. At Prince Albert the land begins to change, and Prince Albert National Park just north of town marks the start of the vast boreal (northern) forest which takes up the northern half of Saskatchewan.

Saskatchewan has over 100,000 lakes, and a good percentage of these are in the wilderness regions north of Prince Albert. This rugged region of the province is much like the north of the country everywhere from Newfoundland westward. It forms part of the rough, rocky Canadian Shield.

The national park and several others in the region are about as far north as most visitors (or residents) get.

Ask at a provincial tourist office for the booklet titled *Heart of Canada's Old Northwest*, which provides a more detailed look at the region north and west of Saskatoon, including historical information and sites and other things to see and do.

PRINCE ALBERT

Prince Albert (population 35,000) is the most northerly town of any size in the province. Forests lie to the north, the flat grain fields to the south. It also sits right in the middle between Alberta and Manitoba. Known as PA, it acts as the jumping-off point for trips into the huge Prince Albert National Park. In 1776 a fur-trading post was built here among the Cree. The town was founded in 1866 by a churchman who came to set up a mission,

and was named after Queen Victoria's husband.

There's a visitor information centre (☎ 764-6222) south of town at 3700 Second Ave West. The Tourism and Convention Bureau (☎ 953-4385) is also here.

In Prince Albert itself, there are a couple of quite minor attractions. The **Historical Museum** (☎ 764-2992), in the old fire station at the end of Central Ave, has displays on the city's past. The museum tea room overlooks the North Saskatchewan River, which flows through town to be joined, not far east, by the South Saskatchewan River.

The **Lund Wildlife Exhibit**, at 98 River St West, has been here forever and contains an astonishing collection of stuffed animals. It's open daily from June to September. Admission is $3.

Prince Albert is the location of a major maximum-security prison. (The locals could have opted for a university but they chose a penitentiary instead.) The **Rotary Museum of Police & Corrections**, beside the tourist office at 3700 Second Ave West, outlines related history.

In mid-August, Prince Albert hosts a large powwow at the Exhibition Grounds and in mid-September there's a Métis Fall Festival. Check with the tourist office for exact dates.

Places to Stay

There's camping at *Whispering Pines Campground* (☎ 763-3863), five km north-east of town, just off Hwy 2.

The *Marlboro Inn* (☎ 763-2643 or 1-800-661-7666) is right downtown at 67 13th St East. Singles/doubles are $50/55. *Comfort Inn by Journey's End* (☎ 763-4466), on the corner of 2nd Ave West and Marquis Rd, just across from the tourist office, has rooms for about the same price.

Lindsay House (☎ 764-4337), at 1904 1st Ave East, is a large Victorian B&B with three rooms at $40/45. *Aurora's B&B* (☎ 764-8997), at 619 Fourth Ave East, has one room for $25 per person.

Places to Eat

Amy's on Second, at 2990 2nd Ave West, is

known far and wide for excellent food. Specialties might include grilled pickerel or steaming hot wild-rice soup. There's a cosy open fire and local art on the walls. Lunch, including cheesecake and coffee, costs around $15.

Freckles Deli, at 30 13th St West, is a good place for breakfast. *Venice House*, at 1498 Central Ave, serves cheap lunches and dinners (pasta, steak, ribs). For a reasonable Chinese meal try *Koko House*, at 3433 2nd Ave West.

AROUND PRINCE ALBERT

East of town, 18 km out on Hwy 55, the **Weyerhaeuser Pulp & Paper Mill** (☎ 953-5194) can be visited. The free two-hour tour showing the pulping, bleaching, drying and more is definitely an industrial tour, not a stroll in the park. Wear suitable clothes and footwear and be prepared for some noise.

In 1988, De Beers, the diamond company from South Africa, staked a claim on some land 40 km or so from Prince Albert. Since then, with obvious respect for De Beers' expertise, millions of hectares nearby have been staked for diamond searching and processing of ore has begun at some of the sites.

The area north of town is known as the lake district, a relatively undeveloped area of woods, bush, lakes and cottages. Aside from those found within the national park, other mega-lakes of the region are **Candle Lake** and **Montreal Lake**.

Further north are three immense parks: **Nipawin** to the north-east, **Meadow Lake** to the north-west and **Lac la Ronge** directly north. The latter provincial park completely surrounds enormous, island-filled Lac la Ronge, which has the reputation of being one of the most attractive lakes in the province. Beyond these areas is untouched wilderness.

PRINCE ALBERT NATIONAL PARK

The national park (☎ 663-5322) is a huge, primarily wilderness tract of softly rolling terrain where the prairie of the south turns to the woodland of the north. Among the geographic features are huge cool lakes, spruce bogs and forested uplands. There are trails of greatly varying lengths, and good canoeing routes provide access to much of the park – the system of interconnected rivers and lakes is well suited to paddlers. There's fishing, a range of camping possibilities and, in winter, cross-country ski trails.

Grey Owl

Naturalist Grey Owl was somewhat of a legend through the 1930s for his writings and lectures on conservation and for his love of the wilderness. He toured widely across North America and the United Kingdom, encouraging preservation and appreciation of the environment.

His first book, *The Men of the Last Frontier*, was published in 1931. *Tales of an Empty Cabin*, published in 1936, is possibly the best-known work, but in between there were several others.

Upon his death, in 1938 in Prince Albert, it was discovered that his identity and lifestyle as a Native Indian had been assumed and that in fact he was Archibald Stansfield Belaney of Hastings, England – this only enhanced the legend surrounding him. He had emigrated to Canada, become a trapper and guide, married an Iroquois woman and been adopted as a brother by the Ojibway tribe.

His wife, Anahereo, who died in 1986, was awarded the Order of Canada for her work in conservation. Her ashes are buried by the graves of Grey Owl and their only daughter, beside the cabin where they lived and worked in Prince Albert National Park. Much of his research was done in the park.

The small, simple, one-room cabin on Ajawaan Lake has become a pilgrimage site of sorts. From the cabin (known as Beaver Lodge), the couple worked to restore the nearly obliterated beaver population. It sits right on a beaver lodge by the lake's edge.

It is still a fairly inaccessible spot, which can be reached one of two ways. First is the Grey Owl Trail, a 20-km hike along Kingsmere Lake. Alternatively, you can canoe from the end of the road, on Kingsmere River upstream to Kingsmere Lake. From there, paddle across the lake to the north end, where there is a choice of either a three-km walking trail or a one-km portage to Ajawaan Lake, from where the cabin can be reached by paddling. ■

Other highlights are **Lavallee Lake** (with the second largest white-pelican colony in the country), the herd of wild bison in the south-western grassland portion of the park and the cabin occupied for seven years by the controversial conservationist **Grey Owl**.

The park's southern border is about 50 km north of Prince Albert.

Information

The park's service centre, where you'll find lodgings, groceries, gasoline, canoe rentals and swimming, is the village of **Wakesiu**, on the huge lake of the same name. The park information office is also here.

Places to Stay

There are many campgrounds in the park, but it is a popular place and fills up on any midsummer weekend, especially holiday weekends. It's best to arrive as early as possible on a Friday.

One campground is geared to RVs, the rest to tenters. The smaller campgrounds are simple and quiet, or there is backcountry camping for canoeists and hikers.

The HI *Waskesiu Hostel* (☎ 663-5450) is on the accessible eastern side of the park, directly north of Prince Albert. Members pay $12, nonmembers $17, and there is a family rate available. Meals can be provided (with advance notice), and there are cooking and laundry facilities. The hostel accommodates up to 60 people and is within walking distance of the park facilities. It's open from the beginning of May to the beginning of September.

LAC LA RONGE PROVINCIAL PARK

La Ronge (☎ 1-800-772-4064) is Saskatchewan's largest provincial park. Aside from the main lake, it contains about 100 more, and a portion of the Churchill River known for its falls and rapids. Boat tours take visitors along the river and to some of the more impressive sights, or you can rent a canoe – some of the 55 provincial canoe routes are here. Campgrounds can be found along the western side of the lake and at the northern edge, at Otter Lake.

On the west side of the park is the village of **La Ronge**, now a small resort centre for the park. Free tours are given of the La Ronge Wild Rice Corporation, which processes the rice gathered by local producers. It's open from mid-August to mid-October. If you are not familiar with Canadian wild rice, don't miss giving it a taste. Long used by Native peoples, it is black-hulled and has a mild, nutty flavour. Also here, the Mistasinihk Place Interpretive Centre, on La Ronge Ave, has displays on the life, crafts and history of the people of the north. It's not open on weekends. Among the four or five motels is the *Drifters Motel* (☎ 425-2224), on Hwy 2 on the way into town.

FLIN FLON

Just over the border in Manitoba, Flin Flon has several canoe outfitters for canoeing the northern lakes. For more information on Flin Flon, see that section in the Manitoba chapter.

MEADOW LAKE PROVINCIAL PARK

Similar to Prince Albert National Park, this one (☎ 236-7690) runs along a chain of lakes by the Alberta border. Nature trails and a series of longer hiking trails allow for wildlife viewing. There is a lot of fauna in the park, and good beaches on many of the lakes. Aside from campgrounds, visitors can stay in simple, privately operated rental cabins.

The park is north of Meadow Lake off Hwy 55, and is part of the Northern Woods & Water Route, a road system that begins in Manitoba and ends in British Columbia.

FORT BATTLEFORD NATIONAL HISTORIC PARK

This historic site is five km from the town of North Battleford, about 140 km north-west of Saskatoon off the Yellowhead Hwy. The North West Mounted Police built the fort in 1876 to help settle the area and police the Native Indians, traders and White settlers. Inside the walls are five buildings you can visit to see police and Native Indian artefacts, tools and memorabilia. The barracks contain an information display and there are guides in costume around the park. The Fort

Battleford National Historic Park is open daily from 20 May to 9 October. Admission is $3.

AROUND NORTH BATTLEFORD

In North Battleford, across the North Saskatchewan River, the interesting **Western Development Museum** deals with agricultural history.

There is some interesting landscape around the Battlefords, with a little more topographic variety than you'll find in much of this region of Saskatchewan.

Good camping can be found at *Battlefords Provincial Park*, north of North Battleford.

From the Battleford area, Hwy 16, the Yellowhead, runs north-west to Lloydminster (on the border) and then on to Edmonton, Alberta.

A short stop can be made at **Cut Knife**, 50 km west of the Battlefords on Hwy 40, which was the site of a battle between the government authorities and the Native people in early summer 1885. About 15 km north of town through the Poundmaker Reserve, plaques mark the site of Chief Poundmaker's grave and outline the story of the skirmish. In Cut Knife itself, you can't miss the huge eight-ton tomahawk. A small campground is adjacent.

Alberta

Not so long ago Alberta was a vast, sparsely inhabited wilderness. Today it has two of the largest cities in Canada – Edmonton and Calgary. Its huge wheat farms, cattle ranches and rich deposits of minerals and fossil fuels are the basis of its wealth. For the visitor, Alberta's main attractions are its wildlife, historic sites, diverse scenery and the wide range of recreational pursuits it offers.

Alberta, the most westerly of the prairie provinces, is bordered in the north by the Northwest Territories, in the east by Saskatchewan, in the south by Montana, and in the west by British Columbia. The east is a continuation of the Canadian prairies. The northern area is filled with rivers, lakes and forests; it's a rugged and largely inaccessible region especially in the north-east. The south-western edge of the province rises from foothills into the Rocky Mountains; while much of the rest of the south is dry and flat with badlands (barren, convoluted arid land) in some areas.

Although Edmonton is the most northerly of Alberta's major cities it is still geographically in the centre of the province.

History

From 9500 to 5500 BC, Alberta – particularly the southern portion – was occupied by the Plains Indians. For millennia they lived a nomadic life walking great distances hunting the vast herds of bison which they used for food, clothing and shelter.

From our cinema and TV screens many of us have an image of these people pursuing the herds on horseback. This period in fact only lasted from about 1750, when the horse was introduced, to the end of the 19th century when most of the bison had been destroyed.

The Plains Indians included the Blackfoot, Blood, Peigan, Atsina (also called Gros Ventre), Cree, Sarcee and Assiniboine. The Sioux came from the south in the late 1800s.

HIGHLIGHTS

Entered Confederation: 1 Sept 1905
Area: 661,185 sq km
Population: 2,545,550
Provincial Capital: Edmonton

- Take in the unbeatable outdoor activities and scenery of the Rocky Mountains
- Visit the famous resort towns of Banff and Jasper
- Have your breath taken away by the beauty of lakes such as Moraine and Peyto
- Explore the badlands with its unusual rock formations, or check out the former dinosaur stomping grounds around Drumheller and Dinosaur Provincial Park
- Spend an afternoon at Calgary's Glenbow Museum, one of the country's best
- Learn about the history of the Plains Indians at Head-Smashed-In Buffalo Jump, a UN World Heritage Site
- Enjoy some of Edmonton's major events and festivals

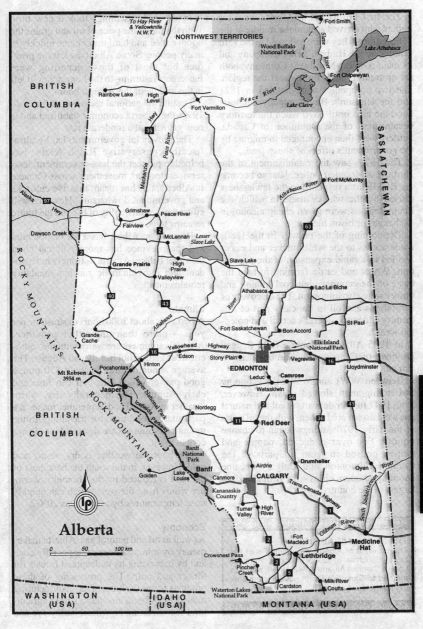

ALBERTA

Alberta

0   50   100 km

The first Europeans in Alberta were fur traders who arrived around the middle of the 17th century. They were followed in the 18th century by the Hudson's Bay Company and its main rival the Northwest Company; both set up trading posts throughout the region. The two companies amalgamated in 1821 and the Hudson's Bay Company administered the area until 1870 when the territory became part of the Dominion of Canada. Settlers were then encouraged to migrate by the government's offers of cheap land.

The 1870s saw the establishment of the Northwest Mounted Police, later to become the RCMP, as a response to the lawlessness caused by the whisky trade in which the Plains Indians were given cheap alcohol in exchange for bison hides.

The coming of the railway in the 1880s made access to the west quicker and easier and led to a rapid expansion of the population. Wheat and cattle farming formed the basis of the economy but coal mining and timber were also important. The discovery of natural gas and oil in the early part of this century added to Alberta's actual and potential wealth.

In 1905 Alberta became a fully fledged province of Canada with Edmonton as its capital.

Between WWI and WWII the economy and immigration slowed down. However, from 1947 further deposits of oil and natural gas were discovered. Then, with the oil crisis of the early 1970s, things began to change rapidly. For over a decade, people and money poured in from all parts of the country. Edmonton and Calgary became booming, modern cities – the fifth and sixth largest in the country.

⊛⊛⊛⊛⊛⊛⊛⊛⊛⊛⊛⊛⊛⊛⊛⊛
The Naming of Alberta
The province of Alberta was named after the fourth daughter of Queen Victoria, Princess Louise Caroline Alberta (1848-1939), who was married to Canada's fourth governor general, the Marquis of Lorne. ∎
⊛⊛⊛⊛⊛⊛⊛⊛⊛⊛⊛⊛⊛⊛⊛⊛

In the mid-80s things took a new turn. With the fall in the price of oil and grains the boom ended and hard times came quickly to many people. Some Albertans left the province but most of those departing were Easterners returning to the homes they'd left in the middle of the Alberta boom.

Despite the national recession of the early 1990s the Alberta economy stabilised and is now growing at a moderate rate.

The provincial government, led by ultra-fiscally conservative Ralph Klein, has helped to pioneer the less-government, less-services, less-tax movement across Canada. In Alberta, this has meant massive cutbacks and government downsizing. How this will effect the overall quality of life and the future remains to be seen.

Regardless, Albert has a lot of potential and the province has more political clout than ever before. Alberta's strongly independent and individualistic rancher mentality remains intact.

Climate
Alberta has about 2000 hours of sunshine per year – more than any other province. Alberta's summers are warm with the southern areas getting hot in July and August. The average annual rainfall is about 450 mm, a good part of which falls between June and early August. The generally dry, warm weather in August and September makes it a particularly good time for travelling. In the mountains summers are short and it's always cool at night.

In winter the weather is dry, sunny and cold. However, in the south the harshness of the cold is reduced by the chinooks: warm, dry winds from the west which can quickly raise temperatures by as much as 20°C.

Economy
As well as oil and natural gas, Alberta makes money by mining minerals, especially coal, and by harvesting its widespread forests for timber and pulp. The processing of these products forms the basis of its manufacturing industries. Alberta also has a strong agricultural sector resting on wheat, barley, rye and

Chinook

The chinook is a warm, dry, south-westerly, winter wind which blows off the eastern slopes of the Rocky Mountains. These winds can change the snowy streets of Calgary, for example, to slush and puddles within hours. The name is derived from the Chinook Indians who lived along the north-west Pacific coast, mainly in what is now Washington state. In the days of the fur trade a language developed which mixed Chinook and other Native Indian words with French and English and was known as Chinook jargon.

In British Columbia (as well as Oregon and Washington states) chinook is also the name given to a Pacific salmon (elsewhere called spring, quinnat, king or tyee salmon). ∎

beef. Tourism is the third highest source of revenue. Visitors can take advantage of the lowest gasoline prices in Canada.

Population & People

European became the dominant ancestry after the agricultural settlement from 1890 to 1914. The largest ethnic segment remains British but surprisingly, about half the population has neither an English nor French background. Prominent nationality groups are German, Ukrainian, Scandinavian and Dutch. Today, Native Indians represents about 3% of the population. Edmonton and Calgary are home to well over half of all Albertans, a largely urban lot despite the cowboy and rancher image.

Information

Provincial Symbols Alberta's provincial flower is the wild rose, while the lodgepole pine is the province's official tree. The great horned owl is Alberta's provincial bird, and the big horned sheep is its official mammal.

Tourist Offices Unlike anywhere else in Canada, tourism and tourist offices in Alberta are no longer overseen solely by the government. Tourism offices are now run by the Alberta Tourism Partnership (ATP), a blend of private associations and independent operators with some government input. The numbers of tourist Visitor Information Centres and government campgrounds is expected to decrease with the new system. The main Alberta Tourism Partnership office is in Edmonton. They can supply general information as well as addresses for the pro-

vincial regional tourism offices if specific, specialised details are required.

The ATP also has information on national parks and the extensive provincial parks system. Also ask about the Alberta Forest Service which has set aside recreation areas and campgrounds within the government forest land (covering nearly 390,000 sq km) that it administers.

Alberta Tourism Partnership
Visitor Sales & Services, 3rd Floor, Commerce Place building, 10155 102nd St (☎ 427-4321). The mailing address is Box 2500, Edmonton, Alberta T5J 4G8. There is also a North America-wide, toll-free number; call ☎ 1-800-661-8888 for information.

Telephone The area code for Alberta is 403.

Time Alberta is on Mountain Standard Time, one hour behind Saskatchewan and Manitoba.

Tax There is no provincial consumer sales tax. There is, however, a 5% tax on accommodation.

Activities

With its mountains, rivers, lakes and forested wilderness areas Alberta provides plenty of opportunities for independent or guided outdoor recreational activities. Tourism Alberta's free brochure, *Accommodation & Visitors' Guide*, lists companies offering fishing, horse riding, cycling, canoeing, whitewater rafting, hiking, rock climbing and mountaineering. It's available from any Visitor Information Centre. In addition, there are a range of good, detailed books available on specific activities and locations at better bookshops.

National & Provincial Parks Alberta has five national parks three of which are in the Rocky Mountains: Banff, Jasper and Waterton Lakes. Wood Buffalo National Park, the largest and least accessible, is in the far north-east while Elk Island National Park, the smallest, is just east of Edmonton. Camping in the parks operates on a first-come, first-served basis and sites cost between $5 and $17 depending on the facilities available. For more information on the national parks see the Facts about the Country chapter. Material is also available at tourist offices or at information centres in each park.

Hiking & Cycling There are lots of hiking and cycling trails in the national and provincial parks and in other recreation areas such as Kananaskis Country. Two of the more spectacular cycling routes are the Icefields Parkway between Banff and Jasper, and the Bow Valley Parkway between Banff and Lake Louise. *Backcountry Biking in the Canadian Rockies* (Rocky Mountain Books, Calgary, 1987) by Gerhardt Lapp is a useful book. Edmonton and Calgary have also set aside trails within their city boundaries for hiking and cycling.

Canoeing & Kayaking Some of the more popular places for canoeing are the lakes and rivers in Banff, Jasper, Waterton Lakes and Wood Buffalo national parks and Writing-on-Stone Provincial Park. In Jasper National Park there is whitewater kayaking and rafting on the Athabasca, Maligne and Sunwapta rivers. The two major universities offer canoeing information in their respective areas as well as rentals:

Campus Outdoor Centre
    P153 Van Vliet Centre, University of Alberta, Edmonton T6G 2H9 (☎ 492-2767)

Outdoor Recreation Centre
    University of Calgary, 2500 University Drive NW, Calgary T2N 1N4 (☎ 220-5038)

To find out more about whitewater rivers contact Alberta White-Water Association Division (☎ 453-8585/6; fax 453-8553), Percy Page Centre, 11759 Groat Rd, Edmonton T5M 3K6.

Hydrological and topographical maps are available from Maps Alberta (☎ 427-3520), 2nd Floor, 108th St, Edmonton.

Skiing The best downhill skiing areas are Nakiska in Kananaskis Country; Mt Norquay, Sunshine Village and Lake Louise in Banff National Park; and Marmot Basin in Jasper National Park. Many of the hiking trails in the national and provincial parks become cross-country ski trails in winter.

Rock Climbing & Mountaineering The Rocky Mountains provide plenty of challenges for the climber, from beginners to advanced. Mt Rundle near Lake Louise is a popular destination. Organisations based in Banff, Calgary, Canmore and Jasper offer instruction and guided climbing. Contact:

Canadian School of Mountaineering
    629 9th St, Canmore T0L 0M0 (☎ 678-4134)
Jasper Climbing Schools
    PO Box 452, Jasper T0E 1E0 (☎ 852-3964)

Accommodation
Campers should get a copy of *Campgrounds in Alberta*, a free booklet available at Visitor Information Centres. It gives an alphabetical listing of places and their campgrounds, both government and private. In national parks sites range from $5 to $17, in provincial parks from $7.50 to $18, and in private campgrounds from $10 to $25 depending on facilities.

Also available is the *Alberta Accommodation & Visitors' Guide* which lists hotels and motels in the province. Both are published annually.

Hostelling International (HI) has 18 hostels in Alberta. For information about HI hostels in southern Alberta contact Hostelling International Southern Alberta (☎ 283-5551), 203 1414 Kensington Rd NW, Calgary T2N 3P9. For northern Alberta contact Hostelling Association Northern Alberta (☎ 439-3139), 10926 88th Ave, Edmonton T6G 0Z1.

A number of B&B agencies operate booking services in the province; a sample follows:

Alberta's Gem B&B
    Mrs Betty Mitchell, 11216 48th Ave, Edmonton T6H 0C7; has B&Bs throughout the province and other areas of Western Canada (☎ 434-6098)
Edmonton B&B
    Pat & Dave Yearwood, 13824 110A Ave, Edmonton T5M 2M9; offers accommodation in Banff, Calgary, Canmore, Drumheller, Edmonton, Hinton, Jasper and other locations (☎ 445-2297)
High Country B&B Association
    PO Box 61, Millarville T5M 2M9; offers accommodation in Calgary and the south-west of the province (☎ 931-3514)

Edmonton

Edmonton, Canada's fifth largest city, sits astride the banks of the North Saskatchewan River at just about the geographic centre of Alberta. The city was founded on the abundant resources of the surrounding area and these remain the basis of the economy. As an early aviation centre Edmonton was once known as 'The Gateway to the North' but that title changed to 'Oil Capital of Canada' in the 1970s when the entire province boomed and shrugged off its cowboy image. They were heady days. The city experienced explosive growth; the downtown area was totally transformed and modernised. Calgary has the head offices and oil and gas management but Edmonton has the technicians, the scientists and the wells – some 7000 of them within a 160-km radius.

Since then the vagaries and fluctuating fortunes of the oil and gas industries have meant a series of minor up and downs for the city. The 1990s have brought more diversity, stability and a manageable, ongoing prosperity. The city continues to develop albeit at a modest pace, in all aspects, slowly forging its own identity. New sports and cultural facilities are being added as other cities, particularly in the east, remain in budget crisis.

It's proximity to Jasper and other national parks and its transportation links to the far north attract visitors in addition to those lured by its range of attractions and shopping. The city averages over six hours of sun per day. Summers are short, generally dry and warm with daytime temperatures averaging 22°C. In January, the coldest month, the average daytime high is -11°C.

History
Until the arrival of European explorers and fur traders in the late 18th century the area was populated by the Cree and Blackfoot nations for over 5000 years.

In 1795 the Hudson's Bay Company built Fort Edmonton, which grew as a fur-trading centre until about 1870, when the Canadian government bought the land from the company and opened up the area for pioneers. By 1891 the railway had arrived from Calgary and in 1892 Edmonton was officially incorporated as a town, then in 1904 as a city. In 1905, with the creation of Alberta, Edmonton – then with 8000 residents – became the capital.

With the discovery of gold in the Yukon in 1897, Edmonton was the last outpost of civilisation for many gold seekers coming overland on their way north to the Klondike. In 1938 North America's first mosque was built here by 34 Muslims. WWII brought a large influx of people, many to work on the Alaska Hwy. Though mainly of British descent, many residents have German backgrounds. Ukrainians, too, have had a large hand in the development of the region and for this reason the city is sometimes humorously referred to as Edmonchuk.

It was in the late 1940s and 50s that real development in Edmonton began, when wells started hitting oil with great regularity. The rise in oil prices in the early 70s gave a further boost to development and brought a dramatic change in the city skyline.

ALBERTA

The rapid changes to the city caused some problems which continue. Many of the city's 25,000 Native Indians have little education or job training and the changes made life harder for them in particular. However, the establishment of educational programmes has meant more of these people are completing high school and going on to trade school or college. Despite the lack of much physical evidence around town, the city does have a fairly long history and the indigenous people played a major part in it.

Greater Edmonton now has a population of nearly 800,000 and ethnic diversity continues. The steep prices of the '70s and early '80s have levelled off and the cultural life of the city has grown dramatically. Rivalry with Calgary remains unabated.

In 1995 the city celebrated its 200th year of development from trading post to modern city.

Orientation

From Edmonton the Rocky Mountains are about 300 km to the west, the lake country and Alaska Hwy are to the north, Lloydminster in Saskatchewan is to the east and Calgary to the south. The North Saskatchewan River, which starts in the Columbia Icefield in the Rocky Mountains, drifts through the centre of town.

All avenues go east-west; streets run north-south.

North of the River Edmonton's main thoroughfare, Jasper Ave (101st Ave), is very long and has mainly stores and restaurants. Both Jasper Ave and 102nd Ave go west from downtown through the West End, a wealthy district of fine homes. The major commercial street here is 124th St. They then lead on through largely middle-class residential areas to Stony Plain Rd, a commercial strip which becomes the Yellowhead Hwy to Jasper. The strip includes motels and lots of fast-food restaurants.

North-west of the downtown area, off Kingsway Ave, is the municipal airport. The northern boundary of the airport is the Yellowhead Trail, which then joins the

Yellowhead Hwy east to Saskatoon and west to Jasper.

Though the city is spread out, the downtown centre with the Greyhound Bus Depot, VIA Rail station, restaurants and hotels is quite small. The central area of town is bounded by 104th Ave to the north and 100th Ave to the south. The western edge is marked by 109th St, the eastern side by 95th St. The area is easily walkable. The central core tends to be pretty quiet evenings and weekends.

The main intersection is Jasper Ave and 101st St. On 99th St, two blocks north of Jasper Ave, is the civic centre with several municipal buildings. Opposite the civic centre is Sir Winston Churchill Square, one block north of which is City Hall with its glass pyramid. To the east are the art gallery and law courts.

Another block north to 104th Ave will bring you to the main post office and the VIA Rail station below the CN Tower. To the west, covering four blocks between 105th St and 109th Sts, is the huge new City Centre Campus of the Grant MacEwan Community College. With its concrete towers, this is one of the city's more striking and unusual architectural complexes. It will accommodate around 27,000 part and full-time students by the year 2000 and should help liven downtown Edmonton's nightlife.

The downtown area consists of many mirrored, 1970s-design, high-rise buildings. The southern end of 100th St is the office section. Many of Canada's banks have buildings in the area. This is also the theatre and shopping district, with the Eaton Centre and the large Edmonton Centre housing all types of stores.

Beneath the downtown area are underground pedestrian walkways called 'pedways' which connect shopping malls, hotels, restaurants and the VIA Rail station.

The eastward redevelopment of the city centre during the 70s and 80s stopped at 97th St (though this is now beginning to change) and for a few blocks east some of the streets are sleazy, especially 96th St. The bars and hotels here aren't recommended. Along the

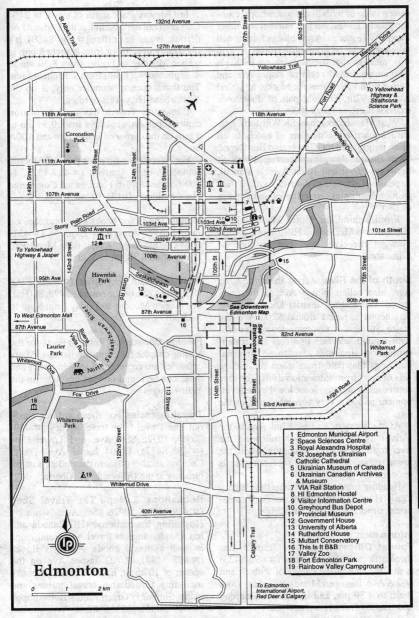

132nd Avenue

127th Avenue

St Albert Trail

Yellowhead Trail

97th Street

82nd Street

Manning Drive

To Yellowhead
Highway &
Strathcona
Science Park

Fort Road

118th Avenue

118th Avenue

1

Kingsway

124th Street

116th Street

109th Street

Capilano Drive

111th Avenue

Coronation
Park

2

135 Street

107th Avenue

148th Street

3

4

5   6

7

8

Stony Plain Road

102nd Avenue

11

103rd Ave

103rd Ave

10

102nd Avenue

9

101st Street

95th Ave

142nd Street

12

Jasper Avenue

100th   Avenue

105th St

15

75th Street

Hawrelak
Park

Groat Rd

Saskatchewan Drive

90th Avenue

13   14

North   Saskatchewan   River

87th Avenue

16

See Downtown
Edmonton Map

87th Avenue

Buena Vista Rd

104th Street

82nd Avenue

To
Whitemud
Park

Laurier
Park

Whitemud   Dve

17

Fox Drive

113 Street

99th Street

See Strathcona Map

63rd Avenue

Argyll Road

ALBERTA

18

Whitemud
Park

122nd Street

2

19

Whitemud Drive

40th Avenue

Calgary Trail

1	Edmonton Municipal Airport
2	Space Sciences Centre
3	Royal Alexandra Hospital
4	St Joseph's Ukrainian Catholic Cathedral
5	Ukrainian Museum of Canada
6	Ukrainian Canadian Archives & Museum
7	VIA Rail Station
8	HI Edmonton Hostel
9	Visitor Information Centre
10	Greyhound Bus Depot
11	Provincial Museum
12	Government House
13	University of Alberta
14	Rutherford House
15	Muttart Conservatory
16	This Is It B&B
17	Valley Zoo
18	Fort Edmonton Park
19	Rainbow Valley Campground

LP

Edmonton

0   1   2 km

To Edmonton
International Airport,
Red Deer & Calgary

eastern side of 97th St are pawnshops, cash-for-goods stores, and a number of other inexpensive places. A few blocks further will take you to the HI Edmonton Hostel. Also in this area is the small down-on-its-heels Chinatown, based north of Jasper Ave and 97th St, and the Farmer's Market at 102nd Ave and 97th. The old part of downtown extends north as far as 103A Ave.

West a few blocks from Sir Winston Churchill Square are a number of hotels in all price ranges, and the Greyhound Bus Depot. West of the downtown centre, 124th St between 102nd and 109th Aves is a small, expensive shopping district, with a few fashion boutiques, art galleries and a bistro or two.

From behind the Hotel Macdonald at 100th St and McDougall Hill, there is a good view of the river and southern side of Edmonton.

South of the River Across the river, 82nd Ave, also called Whyte Ave, is the main street. The historic district known as Old Strathcona is based around 82nd Ave and 104th St. This lively mini-downtown area with a good selection of stores and restaurants contains many restored original buildings that date from when the village was distinct from Edmonton itself. The area continues to undergo some low-key redevelopment and is a very agreeable part of the city.

At the western end of 82nd Ave is the University of Alberta, and following the river south-west, Fort Edmonton, where the town began. Most of the southern side is residential.

Heading south, 104th St joins the Calgary Trail (Hwy 2) which leads to the international airport, Red Deer and Calgary.

Information

Tourist Offices Edmonton Tourism has three offices. The central one (☎ 496-8423) is at City Hall at the corner of 99th St and 102 A Ave. It is open Monday to Friday from 9 am to 4.30 pm, and in summer Saturday and Sunday from 11 am to 5 pm.

In Gateway Park south of town, at 2404 Calgary Trail northbound, at the Leduc #1 oil derrick, is another office (☎ 496-8400). It's open daily in summer from 8 am to 9 pm; in winter Monday to Friday from 8.30 am to 4.30 pm and weekends from 9.30 am to 5 pm The third, open in summer only, is on the Yellowhead Hwy west of town.

Edmonton Transit has an information centre (open on weekdays from 9.30 am to 5 pm) on the corner of Jasper Ave and 100A St.

For information on other parts of Alberta, contact Alberta Tourism (☎ 427-4321, 1-800-661-8888), 3rd Floor, in the Commerce Place building, 10155 102nd St.

Money The major banks have branches on Jasper Ave. American Express (☎ 421-0608), 10305 Jasper Ave, is open Monday to Friday from 8.30 am to 5.30 pm.

Post The main post office (☎ 944-3271), 9808 103A Ave on the corner of 99th St (Hull St), is open Monday to Friday from 8 am to 5.45 pm.

Foreign Consulates Refer to Facts for the Visitor chapter for complete listings. Many countries are represented in Edmonton and these can be found under Consulates in the Yellow Pages.

Travel Agencies For cheap airfares check out The Travel Shop travel agency (☎ 439-3096), 10926 88th Ave, and Travel Cuts (☎ 488-8477), 12304 Jasper Ave. Travel Cuts has another office in the student's union building at the University of Alberta.

Bookshops & Maps The Travel Shop (☎ 439-3809), 10926 88th Ave, is run by Hostelling International (HI)-Canada and has a wide range of travel books and maps as well as travel goods. Audrey's Books (☎ 423-3487), 10702 Jasper Ave on the corner of 107th St, has two floors of books including Canadiana, travel guides and maps. Similar is Greenwood's Bookshoppe (☎ 439-2005), 10355 82nd Ave, in Old

Strathcona. Map Town (☎ 429-2600) at 10815 100th Ave is an excellent source of maps and atlases of all kinds for Canada and beyond.

Medical Services Royal Alexandra Hospital (☎ 477-4111) is at 10240 Kingway Ave.

Useful Organisations If you're interested in conservation issues in Alberta contact the Western Canada Wilderness Committee (☎ 497-7617), 9526 Jasper Ave.

Parking Parking is a problem in downtown Edmonton but you can get free parking permits and a map of parking lots from the Visitor Information Centres.

Work If you're looking for temporary work there are lots of personnel agencies listed in the Yellow Pages. There's also a paper, *Careers & Jobs*, available free around town.

Walking Tours
To explore the city on foot get a copy of the free booklet the *Greater Edmonton Visitor Guide* from the Visitor Information Centre. It has four walking tours of the city including one of Old Strathcona. For a more detailed look at Old Strathcona get a copy of the booklet *A Walk Through Old Strathcona*.

Parks
On each side of the North Saskatchewan River is parkland. This appears to be one long park, though it's actually a series of small parks joined together. You can walk, jog or cycle all day along the system using the many trails and bridges. In some, like **Whitemud Park**, south-west of downtown, and **Strathcona Science Provincial Park** north-east of town, the paths become cross-country ski trails in winter. Whitemud Park also has a hang-gliding area. One of the easiest ways to get there from the south side of town is to head south on 99th street and then turn right (west) along Whitemud Drive.

The 61-hectare **Hawrelak Park**, Edmonton's largest, is south-west of downtown

on the southern banks of the North Saskatchewan River off Groat Rd. It has a lake used for boating and fishing in summer, and for ice-skating in winter. The annual Edmonton Heritage Festival is held in the park at the end of July. Throughout the parkland are dozens of picnic spots. Many of the city's other sights are in this green belt area.

Provincial Museum
This excellent museum (☎ 453-9100), at 12845 102nd Ave west of downtown, is set in attractive, spacious grounds, and is very well laid out. The natural-history section describes the natural forces that have shaped Alberta and its life forms, present and past. It has a large display of fossils and minerals.

The anthropology section covers the Native Indians of Alberta, their way of life and relationship with nature. There are drawings, photos and displays. Displays include examples of how various plants and animals were used for medicine, food, clothing and dwellings. There are amulets incorporating the wearer's umbilical cord and many artefacts and crafts.

The museum also has frequent cultural shows and dancing, and free film programmes. To get there, take bus Nos 1 or 2 west along Jasper Ave. In summer, it's open Sunday to Wednesday from 9 am to 9 pm, Thursday to Saturday, 9 am to 5 pm. The rest of the year it is closed on Monday. Admission is $5.50.

Government House
The large and impressive former residence of provincial lieutenant-governors beside the museum is now used for government conferences. It can be visited on Sunday between 1 and 4.30 pm if there are no government functions taking place. The grounds and gardens overlook the river. For information call ☎ 427-2281.

Rutherford House
This provincial historic site (☎ 427-3995), on 11153 Saskatchewan Drive by the university, was built by Alexander Rutherford, the first premier of Alberta. Completed in 1911,

the mansion is said to symbolise the end of the pioneer architectural style. The building has been restored and contains many antiques. Costumed interpreters provide background. Admission is $1 and it's open daily in summer from 10 am to 6 pm, in winter from noon to 5 pm. Several buses service the campus including Nos 32 and 35.

Alberta Legislature

The Alberta Legislature (☎ 427-7362), on the corner of 97th Ave and 108th St, is built on the site of the original Fort Edmonton. A beautiful Edwardian building from 1912, it is surrounded by fountains and manicured lawns overlooking the river. Its dome has remained one of the permanent landmarks of Edmonton. Free tours, lasting about half an hour, are given daily, offering interesting details about the building and the government. In summer they are available weekdays between 8.30 am and 5 pm, on weekends between 9 am and 4.30 pm. Call for the schedule at other times of year. To get there catch bus No 43 west along 100th Ave.

Fort Edmonton Park

On the southern side of the river in Fort Edmonton Park (☎ 496-8787), is a reconstruction of the old Hudson's Bay Company fort and the surrounding town, circa 1885. The fort contains the entire post of 1846 which was built to promote the fur trade (not as a military fort), and was presided over by Chief Factor John Rowland, head of Saskatchewan District from 1828 to 1854. It lacks some authentic feel but the carpentry, meant to re-create the times through furniture, tools and constructions, is excellent.

Outside the fort is a street re-creating downtown Edmonton between 1871 and 1891, when the railway arrived. It's quite interesting, with good explanations of the buildings, though hard to visualise as the early Jasper Ave. Along the wooden sidewalks are examples of the various merchants and their goods. A newspaper office and a schoolhouse are represented. Check all the cabinets, bottles and vials in the chemist's. Rides on the train and horse-trailer are included in tickets which cost $6.50 (children $3.25).

From the middle of May to the end of June, Fort Edmonton is open Monday to Friday from 9 am to 4 pm, weekends from 11 am to 6 pm; July to early September it's open Monday to Friday from 9 am to 6 pm, weekends 11 am to 6 pm; September to May it's open Monday to Friday 9 am to 4 pm, weekends 1 to 4 pm.

To get there take bus Nos 32 or 132 west along 102A Ave or south on 101st St.

On the grounds beside the fort is the **John Janzen Nature Centre** (☎ 496-2939) where you'll find a few examples of both living and dead local animals, insects and reptiles. Among the educational exhibits in simulated natural environments best is the live bee display. In summer the centre's open daily from 10 am to 6 pm. Admission is free.

Valley Zoo

North-east of Fort Edmonton Park, this zoo (☎ 496-6911) in Laurier Park, at the southern end of Buena Vista Rd, has about 500 animals and birds, but it's mainly a children's zoo with models of storybook characters. It's open daily in summer from 10 am to 6 pm, and admission is $5 (children $2.50). Winter opening hours are shortened.

Muttart Conservatory

South of the river off James Macdonald Bridge, the Muttart Conservatory (☎ 496-8755), 9626 96A St, is comprised of four glass pyramids, three large and one small. Each contains a different climate and the plants that go with it; one is desert, one temperate, one tropical while the fourth has regularly changing exhibitions to mark the changing seasons. If you walk up the hills you can look without going in, but you miss the best part – the feel and smell. The conservatory is open from 11 am to 9 pm Sunday to Wednesday, 11 am to 6 pm Thursday to Saturday and costs $4.25, children $2. It's on bus routes Nos 45 and 51.

There are some interesting photos to be taken of the conservatory and it offers good views of the city.

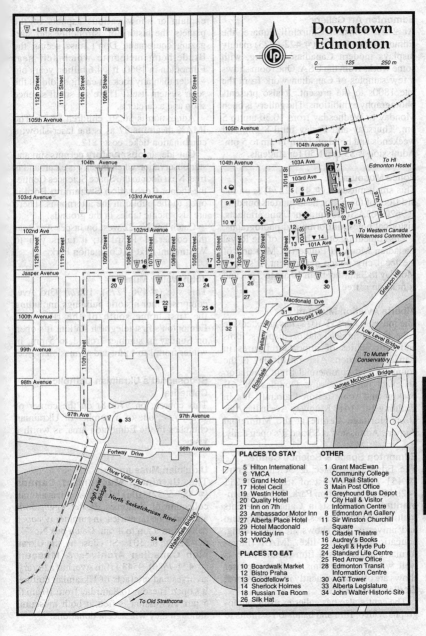

Downtown Edmonton

0   125   250 m

= LRT Entrances Edmonton Transit

To HI Edmonton Hostel

To Western Canada Wilderness Committee

To Muttart Conservatory

North Saskatchewan River

High Level Bridge

Waterdale Bridge

James McDonald Bridge

Low Level Bridge

To Old Strathcona

ALBERTA

PLACES TO STAY
5   Hilton International
6   YMCA
9   Grand Hotel
17 Hotel Cecil
19 Westin Hotel
20 Quality Hotel
21 Inn on 7th
23 Ambassador Motor Inn
27 Alberta Place Hotel
29 Hotel Macdonald
31 Holiday Inn
32 YWCA

PLACES TO EAT
10 Boardwalk Market
12 Bistro Praha
13 Goodfellow's
14 Sherlock Holmes
18 Russian Tea Room
26 Silk Hat

OTHER
1   Grant MacEwan
    Community College
2   VIA Rail Station
3   Main Post Office
4   Greyhound Bus Depot
7   City Hall & Visitor
    Information Centre
8   Edmonton Art Gallery
11 Sir Winston Churchill
    Square
15 Citadel Theatre
16 Audrey's Books
22 Jekyll & Hyde Pub
24 Standard Life Centre
25 Red Arrow Office
28 Edmonton Transit
    Information Centre
30 AGT Tower
33 Alberta Legislature
34 John Walter Historic Site

Edmonton Art Gallery

At 2 Sir Winston Churchill Square, the Edmonton Art Gallery (☎ 422-6223) mainly displays modern Canadian painting, with some works from the USA. One room shows a few samples of Canadian work from the late 1800s to the present. It also presents photography exhibitions. The gallery is open Monday to Wednesday from 10.30 am to 5 pm, Thursday and Friday until 8 pm, and weekends and holidays from 11 am to 5 pm. Admission is $3 or $1.50 for students.

Police Museum

This small museum (☎ 421-2274) is on the 3rd floor of the police headquarters building at 9620 103A St, downtown. Using artefacts, historical notes, uniforms and photographs, it tells something of the history of the Royal Canadian Mounted Police (RCMP) and of the local city police department. It's open Monday to Saturday from 10 am to 3 pm and admission is free.

Alberta Aviation Museum

The museum (☎ 453-1078) has an extensive collection of models, photos, displays, films and biographies of important figures in Canadian aviation. Also on display is the country's first commercial flight simulator, an exact duplicate of a Douglas DC-6B cockpit and some restored aircraft. It's in Building 14, 11410 Kingway Ave in the Aviation Heritage Centre at the Municipal Airport. Admission is $3 and it's open daily.

Edmonton Space & Science Centre

The Edmonton Space & Science Centre (☎ 451-7722) is west of town at 11211 142nd St in Coronation Park. The city **planetarium**, the largest in Canada, presents multimedia programmes on the solar system and universe. The shows are entertaining, educational and life-like. IMAX (large-format cinema) has a film theatre here as well, with changing films. Rock-music laser shows are offered frequently in the **Margaret Ziedler Star Theatre**.

The centre also has galleries using photographs, video, film and hands-on exhibits to explain or show various aspects of the planets, the history of astronomy and star-gazing equipment. Don't miss seeing the Bruderheim meteorite which fell near Edmonton in 1960. It's 4.6 billion years old – older than any rock on earth; as old as the solar system itself. There's a small science shop and a cafeteria.

Admission is $6.50, children $4.25. The IMAX theatre is $7 as is the laser show; a combination ticket costs $12.

Outside, an **observatory** permits sun and star observation when the sky is clear, and is free. Next door to the Space Sciences Centre, the indoor **Coronation Swimming Pool** is open to the public in the afternoons. There are also picnic tables in the grounds.

Catch bus No 22 west on Jasper Ave near the corner of 103rd St; it takes you to Westmount next to Coronation Park.

John Walter Museum

This site (☎ 496-7275), 10627 93rd Ave, comprises four historic buildings, including the first home south of the river and Edmonton's first telegraph station. It's open on Sunday in summer from 1 to 5 pm, in winter from 1 to 4 pm, and admission is free.

St Josephat's Ukrainian Catholic Cathedral

This church, on 97th St on the corner of 108th Ave, one of a number of Ukrainian churches in the Edmonton area, is worth a visit.

Ukrainian Museums

The **Ukrainian Museum of Canada** (☎ 483-5932), 10611 110th Ave, has a small collection of costumes, Easter eggs, dolls and very fine tapestries. In summer it's open daily from 9 am to 4 pm. Catch bus Nos 41 or 42 north on 101st St. Close by, the **Ukrainian Canadian Archives & Museum** (☎ 424-7580), 9543 110th Ave, has a library, archives and artefacts of Ukrainian culture. It's open Tuesday to Saturday from 10 am to 5 pm. Admission is free at both museums although they will accept donations.

West Edmonton Mall

If you thought a shopping centre as an attraction had no place in this guidebook, think again. 'West Ed' (☎ 444-5300), 8770 170th St on the corner of 87th Ave, is really something else; it's so overwhelming it's worth taking a look. More than just the world's largest shopping mall and largest indoor water park, it's a self-contained city complete with roof. You could live, OK, exist, inside for years.

There are over 800 stores, a hotel, an amusement park, a water park with beach and waves, an ice rink with skate rentals, a mini-golf course, cinemas, submarines in simulated oceans, restaurants galore and lots more, plus thousands of people. Two features to see are the Drop of Doom, a ride in Fantasyland guaranteed to put your stomach in your mouth (and that's just watching!), and the ersatz New Orleans Bourbon St, complete with statues of prostitutes.

If you get too tired to make it around everything you can rent yourself a little powered scooter.

To get there take bus No 10 west on Jasper Ave downtown; the journey time is about 25 minutes.

Wild Waters Aquatic Park

This waterslide complex (☎ 447-4476) is at 21515 103rd Ave (Yellowhead Hwy west). It's open daily (weather permitting) in summer from 10 am to 7 pm. Admission is $13, children $10.

City Farmers' Market

This city food market is in downtown Edmonton on the corner of 102nd Ave and 97th St at the edge of Chinatown. It's open daily but is best on Saturday until 3 pm.

Old Strathcona

The area south of the river, by 82nd Ave (also called Whyte Ave) and 104th St, was once the town of Strathcona. It amalgamated with Edmonton in 1912. Though now absorbed into the city, this area is rich in historical buildings dating from 1891. There are about 75 houses built prior to 1926 in the residential district and about 40 buildings of note in what was the commercial core. This is now one of the most vibrant and interesting areas of town with numerous cafes, restaurants, bookshops and buskers.

You can pick up a walking-tour map of the district at the Visitor Information Centre downtown or at the Tourist Information Office (in the Old Strathcona Caboose) on the corner of Saskatchewan Drive and 103rd St in End of Steel Park. The Old Strathcona Foundation Office (☎ 433-5866) at 8331 104th St also has local information. The Foundation also leads cemetery tours.

From 105th St east, 2nd Ave has been spruced up with brick sidewalks and old-style lamp posts making a pleasant change from the high-rise buildings of the downtown area. Within walking distance are several small attractions. Strathcona Square in the renovated Post Office building with the clock tower at 82nd Ave and 105th St has restaurants, shops and a pub.

Model & Toy Museum The intricate, miniature world displayed makes this museum (☎ 433-4512), at 8603 104th St in a residential area, a fun half-hour.

Primarily made of cut and folded paper, 400 detailed models include the Kofuku Ji Pagoda of Japan, the Sydney Opera House and planes and ships. A $2 donation is asked and it's open afternoons.

C&E Railway Museum The Strathcona station (☎ 433-9739) from 1891 contains artefacts and memorabilia from the early rail era. In summer it's open daily from 10 am to 4 pm and admission is by donation. The station is located at 10447 86th Ave.

Telephone Historical Centre The history of the phone in Edmonton is told using real equipment and interactive displays. The wall exhibit on switching technologies is a behind-the-scenes eyeful. The museum (☎ 441-2077) is located at 10437 83rd Ave and is closed Saturday morning and all day Sunday. Admission is $2.

ALBERTA

1	Knox Church
2	Old Strathcona Foundation Office
3	Old Strathcona Farmer's Market
4	Telephone Historical Information Centre
5	New York Bagel Café
6	Uncle Albert's
7	Strathcona Hotel
8	Strathcona Square
9	Veggies
10	Princess Theatre
11	Commercial Hotel
12	CPR Station (Old)

Activities

For information on park and recreation facilities like outdoor swimming pools, skating and skiing areas or bicycle paths, call Edmonton Parks & Recreation (☎ 496-4999). (See also Parks earlier.)

The Kinsmen Sports Centre (☎ 496-7300), 9100 Walterdale Hill, has public swimming and other programmes. Admission is $4. It's open Monday to Friday from 5.30 am to 10 pm, weekends 7 am to 10 pm. Mill Woods Recreation Centre (☎ 496-2900), 7207 28th Ave, has a wave pool, saunas, ball courts and other facilities. It's open weekdays from 5.30 am to 9 pm, Saturday 6 am to 9 pm, Sunday from 8 am to 9 pm. A swim in the wave pool costs $4.90. The Commonwealth Stadium Sports & Fitness Centre (☎ 496-2929), 11000 Stadium Rd, has a gym and ball courts.

Edmonton has an extensive network of bicycle routes and the best area to cycle is on the paths by the river. A map showing these routes is available from the Visitor Information Centre.

You can go horse riding in Whitemud Park; contact the Whitemud Equine Centre (☎ 435-3597) for details. You can also go hot-air ballooning up to 300 metres – every day if the weather is fine – with Windship Aviation (☎ 438-0111), 5615 103A St.

Organised Tours

Royal Tours (☎ 488-9040), 203 10441 124th St, offers three tours of Edmonton. The 3½-hour, historical tour of the city visits the Alberta Legislature, the university and Old Strathcona and costs $27. The 2½-hour ecological tour which looks at the city's parkland and goes out to the Provincial Museum costs $24. The day tour combines the two and costs $45.

On Sunday and holidays in summer, Edmonton Transit operates the Fort Edmonton-Valley Zoo shuttle between the zoo and the University of Alberta, for the basic fare. This route takes a circular tour of Edmonton, passing many of the city's sights. It leaves the university every hour on the hour from 11 am to 5 pm, and leaves the zoo hourly on the half hour from 11.30 am to 5.30 pm.

The North Saskatchewan Riverboat Company (☎ 424-2628) has a 400 passenger paddlewheeler for tours along the river. The docking site is Rafter's Landing across the river from the Macdonald Hotel.

Nite Tours (☎ 453-2134) does night trips around the city featuring pubs and clubs or comedy shows. Tickets cost around $20.

The HI Edmonton Hostel (☎ 429-0140) organises group outings on an ad hoc basis.

Festivals

Edmonton has many festivals throughout the year; the following are some of the bigger ones. The Visitor Information Centre has details on exact times and locations as these change annually.

June

Jazz City International Jazz Festival – There are concerts all over town, many outside and free during this week-long event.

The Works –This is a major visual arts celebration and exhibition featuring events around town including in city parks.

July

International Street Performers Festival – Amazing buskers bring the streets alive during this multi-day event.

The Klondike Days – This, Edmonton's biggest festival held towards the end of July, celebrates a less than honourable period in Edmonton's history. In the gold-rush days of 1898, unscrupulous entrepreneurs lured gold seekers to the city with tales of a trail, the Klondike Trail, from Edmonton to Dawson City in the Yukon, which didn't really exist. Many people didn't make it through and some returned to settle in Edmonton. During the festival, locals dress up the streets, the stores and themselves in period style; stages dot the road and are alive with singers and dancers; parades run through the streets; the Northlands Coliseum presents nightly entertainment of rock, pop or country & western music; a Klondike village, with old-time stores and a gambling saloon, is set up in Northlands Park; and the Citadel Theatre puts on 'heroes & villains' melodramas. The street festivities last five days; the Northlands Park exhibition goes on for another five days. Contact the Edmonton Klondike Days Association (☎ 426-4055), 1660 10020 101A Ave, for information.

Edmonton Heritage Festival – This three-day festival, held late July, early August in Hawrelak Park, celebrates the city's ethnic diversity. Call ☎ 488-3378.

August

Folk Music Festival – In early August the city holds this festival in Gallagher Park with blues, jazz, country & western and bluegrass as well as traditional folk music. Ask at the Visitor Information Centre or call ☎ 429-1899.

Fringe Theatre Event – Well worth catching, this event has a 10-day programme that brings all kinds of live alternative theatre to the public with over 800 performances of 150 productions in 14 theatres, in the parks and on the streets. Many of the performances are free and no ticket costs over $10; there's no booking, you choose a theatre and stand in line. The festival takes place in Old Strathcona around the middle of August. Contact Chinook Theatre (☎ 448-9000), 10329 83rd Ave, or ask at the Visitor Information Centre.

Cowboy Poetry & Western Art Festival – Now an established annual event at Exhibition Park in Stony Plain, it features all things Western, new and old, from story telling to leather carving.

Dreamspeakers – Held at Sir Winston Churchill Square in late August, this is a Native Indian and artistic festival which includes poetry, storytelling, dancing, live musical performances plus traditional food and craftwork. Films made by Native Indian filmmakers are also shown. For information call ☎ 439-3456.

Places to Stay

Camping Several camping areas, some run by the Alberta government, are close to town. *Ardrossan Campground* (☎ 922-3293), 18 km east of Edmonton on the Yellowhead Hwy, has 24 camp sites for $7. There are firepits but nothing else, and no water. Similar is *Bretona Campground* (☎ 922-3293), 18 km south-east of Edmonton near Sherwood Park on Hwy 14 at the junction of Hwy 21, with 28 camp sites.

The privately owned *Half Moon Lake Resort* (☎ 922-3045) 21524 TWP, Rd 520, Sherwood Park, charges $13.50 for a tent site and has every convenience including showers and laundromat. The resort is very large and there is swimming in the lake. It's 29 km south-east of Edmonton; follow 82nd Ave east to Wye Rd, then head south. Closer to town is *Rainbow Valley Campground* (☎ 434-5531), 14340 56th Ave off Whitemud Drive in Whitemud Park. It has a laundromat and showers and tent sites for $13.

Hostels HI *Edmonton Hostel* (☎ 429-0140), 10422 91st St, is within walking distance of the centre of town. It has a well-equipped kitchen, a view across the river to the southern side of Edmonton and a pub nearby. It sells a few basic staples and issues daily transit passes for Edmonton's public transport system. The phone is open 24 hours but only ring after midnight if you're stranded. A dorm bed costs $12.50 for members, $17.50 for nonmembers.

The hostel has discounts to many of the sights, restaurants, sports and recreation centres, retail outlets and pubs; also on car rental. It also sells half-price tickets to the

ALBERTA

Edmonton Trappers home baseball games and rents out bikes for $12 a day including helmet. They might even be able to tell you where to find work.

To get there from downtown, walk east on Jasper Ave or 103rd Ave (which eventually turns into Jasper Ave anyway) to 91st St, just before the bridge. The hostel is down a few doors on the left. Between the downtown area and the hostel are a couple of run-down blocks which are not great at night, especially for women alone.

The central YMCA (☎ 421-9622), 10030 102A Ave opposite the Edmonton Centre and next to the Hilton Hotel, is close to the Greyhound Bus Depot and VIA Rail station and takes in men and women although you won't see many women. Singles/doubles cost from $27/38 and there are cheaper weekly rates. Dormitory accommodation is $20 with a maximum of three nights. It also has a TV room, gym facilities including pool, and a very cheap cafeteria which is open from 6 am. The recently opened new Y's are for fitness facilities only.

The YWCA (☎ 423-9922), 10305 100th Ave on the corner of 103rd St, is also central. It takes women only and charges $13.50 in a dorm, $29.50 for a single or, with a private bath, $36. Doubles with private bath are $46. Sheets are supplied in all the rooms. There's a good, cheap cafeteria that anyone can use.

The University of Alberta, in south-west Edmonton, rents out rooms in the summer in Lister Hall opposite the Jubilee Auditorium. It has good facilities and cheap cafeterias. The rates are $25/32 (including tax) for a single/twin, and weekly or monthly rates are available. Contact Guest Services (☎ 492-4281), 44 Lister Hall on the corner of 87th Ave and 116th St. Also part of the university, St Joseph's College (☎ 492-7681), on the corner of 89th Ave and 114th St, has singles/twins for $20.75/31.50 (including tax).

B&Bs The Visitor Information Centre has details of B&Bs in Edmonton. See also the agencies, through which you can make bookings, listed under Accommodation at the start of this chapter.

Norma's Place (☎ 434-6832), 5220 104A St in south Edmonton is reasonably central and has singles/doubles for $35/45 with full breakfast. Also recommended is Chez Suzanne (☎ 483-1845), at 18603 68th Ave not far from West Edmonton Mall. Rates are $35/45 and you can make tea or coffee anytime. The rooms have telephones which can be handy. The hosts can offer advice and suggestions on Edmonton. Both the above can host families.

More upmarket is This Is It (☎ 439-8481) central in Strathcona at 11013 87th Ave. The large, well-restored home charges $80/88 with full breakfast.

Hotels – bottom end Edmonton is not blessed with a great selection of cheap central hotels. But there are a few basic places that survived the downtown's redevelopment which may fit your bill. None is recommended for single women.

The Grand Hotel (☎ 422-6365), 10266 103rd St on the corner of 103rd Ave right beside the bus terminal, is probably the best of the downtown cheapies. There are three grades of room; for singles/doubles with bath you'll pay $30/35. Simpler rooms are less. The hotel is very clean and all rooms have colour TV. There's a bar and a restaurant with cheap breakfasts on the premises. Hotel Cecil (☎ 428-7001), 10406 Jasper Ave, is a little rougher, especially in the bar. It's old and worn but clean, and the rooms are fine. Some have a bath; all have sinks and are basic but comfortable. Rates are from $25/35 (including tax). Downstairs there's a friendly, cheap restaurant. There are a few more in the old part of downtown east of 97th St, but they're not recommended.

In south Edmonton a cheapie to try is the Strathcona Hotel (☎ 439-1992), 10302 82nd Ave on the corner of 103rd St, which has bathless rooms for $17/23. Rooms have no TV or telephone. It's a great old timbered building dating from 1891 and is registered as an Alberta Historic Resource. The Commercial Hotel (☎ 439-3981), 10329 82nd Ave, has live music in the bar downstairs and rooms cost $25/28.

ALBERTA

Hotels – middle The good value *Quality Hotel* (☎ 423-1650), 10815 Jasper Ave, has apartments as well as rooms available. A continental breakfast is included in the price of $45/50. The *Quality Inn Downtown* (☎ 428-6442), 10209 100th Ave, also offers a free breakfast and parking from $54/65. The *Ambassador Motor Inn* (☎ 423-1925) is very central at 10041 106th St. The well-equipped rooms cost $50/60.

At the *Alberta Place Suite Hotel* (☎ 423-1565), 10049 103rd St, all rooms come equipped with a kitchen. Single bachelor rooms are $75, the single bedrooms for two are $85 and include a continental breakfast. It has a sundeck, exercise room, laundry, and indoor parking.

Hotels – top end Good value is the *Inn on 7th* (☎ 429-2861), 10001 107th St which has a licensed restaurant and rooms for $99. Next to the Citadel Theatre downtown is the *Westin Hotel* (☎ 426-3636), 10135 100th St on the corner of 101A Ave, with singles and doubles from $99.

One of Edmonton's older and more elegant hotels is the *Hotel Macdonald* (☎ 424-5181) at 10065 100th St. Still run by a railway, now Canadian Pacific, it has rooms from $129. *Hilton International* (☎ 428-7111), 10235 101st St near the corner of 102A Ave, has singles and doubles from $99 to $135. Pedways connect the hotel with the Edmonton Centre and Eaton Centre.

Motels The bulk of the city's mid-price range accommodation is in motels. Most motels have plug-ins (electric sockets for engine heaters) for your car – a good thing for Edmonton winter mornings. There are two areas near town where most motels are located.

One area is along Stony Plain Rd and the Yellowhead Hwy, west of downtown. To get to this area head out along Jasper Ave or 104th Ave which turns into Stony Plain Rd; further west, Stony Plain Rd becomes the Yellowhead Hwy. The other area is along the Calgary Trail south of the city and most of the motels there are reasonably priced.

Royal Scot Motel (☎ 447-3088) is at 20904 Stony Plain Rd, about 1.5 km from Edmonton. It has singles/doubles from $36/40 or $5 extra for a kitchen. *Rest E-Z Inn* (☎ 447-4455), 21640 Stony Plain Rd, is a little over three km from town. It has 40 units with colour TV, priced at $35/38.

South of town try the *Derrick Motel* (☎ 434-1402), 3925 Calgary Trail North, which has rooms for $35/40. Kitchenette and waterbeds are available. *Chateau Motel* (☎ 988-6661), 1414 Calgary Trail South-West, has 40 units with colour TV and telephone; a kitchenette is extra. Rates are $34/40.

Out at the international airport the *Nisku Place Motel* (☎ 955-3078) is good and will pick-up free of charge from the airport. Rooms are $43/49.

Places to Eat

Budget The *cafeteria* in the Alberta Legislature serves plain, decent food at the best prices in town. It's open Monday to Friday from 7 am to 4 pm, with lunches from 11.30 am to 1.30 pm.

Sarah's Café in the YWCA is open daily to both men and women, resident or not. There's not a lot of choice but prices are good: breakfast specials are $2.50, omelettes $4. The YMCA has a similar place open Monday to Friday from 7 am to 4 pm.

The *Silk Hat*, 10251 Jasper Ave, opened in 1940 and was one of Edmonton's first restaurants. It still has the old, small wall jukeboxes at the booths (although they don't always play the right song) and movie posters on the walls and is a hang-out for a lot of local characters. Three pancakes go for $4 and lunch specials are $4.95. It's open Monday to Friday from 7 am to 9 pm, Saturday from 8 am to 10 pm, and Sunday from 10 am to 9 pm.

At 10089 Jasper Ave on the corner of 10th St on the 8th floor of the Bank of Montreal Building, the *Nest* is recommended for inexpensive, light meals accompanied by a very fine view. It's open Monday to Friday only until 5 pm.

ALBERTA

The *Boardwalk Market*, on the corner of 103rd St and 102nd Ave, a renovated old building also containing offices and stores, has a food court with stalls selling all kinds of food including Chinese and East Indian.

In Old Strathcona there are quite a few good eating places on and around 82nd Ave. On the corner of 104th St and 82nd Ave, *Uncle Albert's* is popular. It has pancakes for $5 and fish & chips from $6.25. The *New York Bagel Café*, 8209 104th St next to Uncle Albert's, is recommended. This is a small, comfortable little spot with tables on the sidewalk, serving excellent cappuccinos and light foods. *Veggies*, 10331 82nd Ave, is a vegetarian restaurant (in fact most of the dishes are vegan), which is good for lunch and dinner. Felafels are $4.25, curry $8.95. Other ethnic places, cafes and bakeries can be found along 82nd St as far east as 99th St.

Middle Where 101A Ave and 100A St meet, right in the centre of town, a small restaurant district and people-place sanctuary sits amidst all the office towers. Trees have been planted and there are benches for lingering. Most of the restaurants have outdoor sections. The *Bistro Praha*, 10168 100A St, is a European-style spot with salads $4 and main meals like schnitzel about $14. During nonmeal hours it's pleasant for a good coffee with a cake or pastry and a flip through a newspaper. It also serves wine by the glass. *Goodfellows* down a few doors on the corner makes its own corned beef on the premises and offers a variety of sandwiches at lunch. At dinner the menu is more formal and prices rise.

Nearby at 10012 101A Ave and dwarfed by the tower blocks around it, is the *Sherlock Holmes*, a British-model pub good for both food and British and locally brewed beers. A ploughman's lunch is $5.95 and fish & chips $7.95. It's open daily.

A collection of mid-range eateries can be found in the Boardwalk Market. The *Old Spaghetti Factory* is a combined bar and restaurant with decent food at moderate prices in an interesting environment: lots of plants, Tiffany lamps and an old streetcar (tram). Spaghettis cost from $8 to $10 which includes bread, salad and coffee or tea. It's open Sunday to Thursday from 4 pm, Saturday from noon. Next door is *Bones* for ribs (from $10 to $15), open Monday to Friday from 11.30 am to 4 pm; and a few doors down, *La Crêperie* which offers a range of crepes for $8 to $13. There are other places here both more and less expensive. Walk through the building and have a look.

For German food try the alpine-like *Strathcona Gasthaus* on 101 St just south of 82nd St. A meal costs between $10 and $16.

One of the best eating buys in Edmonton is at one of the places with a lunch buffet or Sunday brunch. Some of the larger hotels put on big spreads at reasonable prices. Check the weekend newspapers for places and times. The *Inn on 7th* (☎ 429-2861), 10001 107th St has lunch buffets every weekday. A good feed at one of these could last you till the next day's breakfast. For about $9 you can eat from a choice of hot and cold buffets. Lunch is from 11 am to 2 pm.

One traveller has recommended the *Steak & Ale Restaurant*, 14203 Stony Plain Rd, for its good food and choice of 90 Canadian and imported beers.

The *Russian Tea Room*, 10312 Jasper Ave, is ideal for a late afternoon pick-me-up, especially for teas, coffees, sandwiches ($4 to $6) and cakes ($4). It's open daily.

Top End The *Chateau Beirut* at 11223 Jasper Ave has very good Lebanese food at night sometimes accompanied by entertainment. A dinner for two before wine is about $40. In Old Strathcona at 9602 82nd Ave, *Unheardof*, which serves steak, chicken and seafood is similarly priced. *La Bohème*, 6427 112 Ave, offers good French food and wine. Main dishes are between $10 and $16. If you find the atmosphere inspiringly romantic you don't have to leave; the owners have a B&B in the historic building.

The posh *Harvest Room* in the Hotel Macdonald has main dishes ranging in cost between $19 and $25.

Entertainment

See, and *Culture Shock* are local art and entertainment papers free around town. *Nightlife*, also free, is a broadsheet listing the latest in drama, comedy and concerts. For daily listings see the entertainment section of the *Edmonton Journal* newspaper.

Theatre & Nightlife Edmonton offers a wide selection of live theatre. The *Citadel Theatre* (☎ 425-1820), 9828 101A Ave, Edmonton's foremost playhouse, is actually a complex of theatres featuring mainstream drama, comedy, experimental productions, concerts, lectures and films. Its season is from September to May. Depending on the production, theatre tickets cost from around $20 to $50. The *Chinook Theatre* (☎ 448-9000/9011), 10329 83rd Ave, puts on experimental plays and organises the annual Fringe Theatre Event.

The *Jubilee Auditorium* (☎ 427-2760, 433-7741), 11455 87th Ave, is the venue for the Edmonton Opera and the Edmonton Symphony Orchestra (one of Canada's best). Tickets cost from around $35. The *Francis Winspear Centre for Music* on Sir Winston Churchill Square scheduled to open in 1997 will be a major concert-hall addition to the city.

Mayfield Inn Dinner Theatre (☎ 483-4051), 16615 109 Ave, puts on musical productions. *Yuk Yuk's* (☎ 481-9857), on Bourbon St in the West Edmonton Mall has off-beat, standup comedy from Tuesday to Saturday. Laser-light concerts are held at the *Space & Science Centre* (see earlier for details).

There are lots of venues around town catering to different musical tastes. In Old Strathcona *Blues on Whyte* in the Commercial Hotel (☎ 439-3981), 10329 82nd Ave, features live blues music as does the *Sidetrack Café* (☎ 421-1326), 10333 112 St, which also has local rock groups.

The *Yardbird Suite* (☎ 432-0428), 10203 86th Ave, is the jazz bar in town. Admission varies but is only $2 for the Tuesday jams.

Visitors often enjoy a night at the *Cook County Saloon* where you get a real taste of the west with country music and line dancing. Free lessons are given Tuesday and Thursday nights – more fun than cow chip bingo! It's on 103th St at 80th Ave.

A few British-style pub/restaurants, like the *Jekyll & Hyde* (☎ 426-5381), 10610 100th Ave, offer singalong sessions.

The *Metro Billiard Café* at 10250 106th St attracts a young university crowd with pool tables, rock music and video games.

Cinema The *Princess Repertory Theatre* (☎ 433-5785), 10337 82nd Ave near 104th St, is Edmonton's main outlet for good, varying films. It charges nonmembers $5 or $7 depending on the film. On Saturday it shows matinees, mostly for kids. The cinema itself is an historic site – it was the first marble-fronted building west of Winnipeg and at one time showed first-runs of Mary Pickford films.

The *Edmonton Film Society* regularly shows classic films in the Provincial Museum auditorium (☎ 453-9100). Tickets are $4. The *Edmonton Art Gallery* shows commercial and classic films, borrowed from the National Film Theatre, for the price of admission to the gallery.

Spectator Sports If you're here during the ice-hockey season from October to April, try to see a home game of the Edmonton Oilers at Northlands Coliseum (☎ 471-2791), 7428 118th Ave on the corner of 73rd St. Tickets are $15 to $60. Alternatively, you could see the Edmonton Eskimos play football, from July to October, at the Commonwealth Stadium (☎ 448-3757), 11000 Stadium Rd. Tickets are $18 to $28. The Edmonton Trappers of the Pacific Coast Baseball League play their home games at Telus Park (☎ 429-2934), 10233 96th Ave, from April to August. Admission is $6.50 to $9.50.

Getting There & Away

Air Edmonton International Airport is around 30 km south of the city along the Calgary Trail, about a 45-minute drive from the centre of town. This larger airport handles most flights. Edmonton Municipal

ALBERTA

Airport, three km north of downtown off 97th St near 118th Ave, is generally used for smaller planes and therefore shorter flights, particularly within Alberta. City buses run between there and town. Talks of amalgamating the two and closing the 'muni' to public air traffic are ongoing.

Edmonton is well served by airlines. Canadian Airlines (☎ 421-1414), Main Floor, 10060 Jasper Ave, and Air Canada (☎ 423-1222) fly to the NWT, Vancouver and major cities in eastern Canada. Time Air (☎ 421-1414), in partnership with Canadian Airlines, is Alberta's commuter airline. It has daily services to Grand Prairie, Calgary, Lethbridge, Medicine Hat, Red Deer and other destinations in Western Canada. Delta Air Lines (☎ 426-5990), 10135 100th St, connects Edmonton with Alaska and many points in mainland USA. Northwest Airlines (☎ 1-800-225-2525), 10024 Jasper Ave, flies to Winnipeg and destinations in mainland USA.

Air Canada operates a 40-minute commuter service to Calgary with flights all day long. If you're not on business you'll probably find the regular one-way fare a bit pricey at $161 (including tax) but there are cheaper flights available in off-peak times. Standard, one-way fares (including tax) to other cities are Toronto $802, Vancouver $375, and Yellowknife $484.

Bus The large Greyhound Bus Depot (☎ 421-4211), 10324 103rd St on the corner of 103rd Ave close to the VIA Rail station, is very central. It's open from 5:30 am to midnight and has left-luggage lockers ($2) and a fast-food restaurant. As always, bus fares are usually cheaper than train tickets. Greyhound goes east to Winnipeg twice a day; the one-way fare is $132. Greyhound also goes to Jasper $45, Calgary $33, Vancouver $113, Prince George $87, Yellowknife $177, and Whitehorse $227. From Whitehorse you can catch buses to Fairbanks, Alaska.

Another bus line serving Calgary is Red Arrow (☎ 424-3339, 425-0820), with its office in the Howard Johnson Hotel, 10010 104th St. The office is open Monday to Saturday from 7 am to 9.30 pm, and Sunday from 10 am to 9.45 pm. It has four buses a day leaving from outside the hotel; the one-way fare is $33 (including tax). The deluxe buses with kitchenettes can also be caught at the Riviera Hotel at 5359 Calgary Trail.

Train Entry to the VIA Rail station (☎ 422-6032 for arrival/departure information; ☎ 1-800-665-8630 for fares and reservations), at 10004 104th Ave on the corner of 100th St is through the CN Tower entrance and down the stairs. The station is open Monday, Thursday and Saturday from 7 am to 3.30 pm; Tuesday and Friday from 8.30 am to 9 pm; Wednesday from 8.30 am to 4 pm; and Sunday from 10.30 am to 9 pm. There's a small shop and left-luggage lockers ($1).

Trains depart three times a week eastward to Saskatoon, Winnipeg, Toronto, Ottawa and Montreal and westward to Jasper, Prince George and Prince Rupert. At Prince George' you can connect with BC Rail to Vancouver. The one-way fare, no advance (including tax) to Jasper is $87, to Prince George $126, and to Vancouver $206.

Car The downtown addresses of some of the car-rental companies operating in Edmonton are:

Budget
    10016 106th St (☎ 448-2000)
Rent-A-Wreck
    11225 107 Ave (☎ 448-1234)
Thrifty
    10036 102nd St (☎ 428-8555)
Tilden
    10131 100A St (☎ 422-6097)

Rent-A-Wreck is the cheapest charging $30 a day plus 10 cents a km after the first 200 km. Budget charges $34 a day plus 14 cents a km after the first 200 km. Thrifty charges $38 a day with unlimited km. These prices don't include tax or insurance which can raise the cost quite a bit. The companies often have special deals so ring around.

Getting Around

The Airports City buses don't go as far south as the international airport, but you can take the Grey Goose Airporter Bus (☎ 463-7520). It leaves from the Hotel Macdonald every half hour from 5.15 am to 12.15 am for a one-way fare of $11 or $18 return. It also picks up and drops off at other top hotels and the Greyhound Bus Depot. A taxi from downtown to the international airport costs about $37.

City buses run to and from the municipal airport. Take bus Nos 41 or 42 north along 101st St to Kingsway then change to bus No 23. A taxi from downtown costs about $9.

A shuttle bus connects the two airports.

Bus & LRT Edmonton Transit (☎ 496-1611 for information about fares, routes and schedules) operates city buses and Canada's smallest subway system, the Light Rail Transit (LRT). The LRT has 10 stops running north-east from the university, east along Jasper Ave, north along 99th St then north-east all the way to 139th Ave in Clareview. Between Clareview Station and Stadium Station the LRT travels overground; from Churchill Station to Grandin Station it runs beneath the surface.

A single one-way fare is $1.60 on the LRT or buses. You can transfer from one to the other but you must get a transfer receipt when you pay your fare and use it within 90 minutes. You can also buy a day pass for $4.75. From 9 am to 3 pm Monday to Friday, and from 9 am to 6 pm Saturday, the five subway LRT stations, Churchill to Grandin, form a free zone.

There is an information centre (open weekdays from 9.30 am to 5 pm) at Central Station on the corner of Jasper Ave and 100A St. There's another (open weekdays from 8.30 am to 4.30 pm) at Churchill Station, on the corner of 102nd Ave and 99th St. You can buy passes and ticket books at them.

Buses cover all parts of the city but not all routes operate on Sunday or holidays. Bus No 46 goes from downtown to the university and back. Bus No 12 goes from downtown south-west to the Valley Zoo in Laurier Park.

Taxi Two taxi companies are Yellow Cab (☎ 462-3456), and Alberta Co-Op Taxi (☎ 425-8310). The fare from downtown to the West Edmonton Mall is about $14. The flagfall (drop) is $2, then it's 10 cents for every 105 metres.

Bicycle River Valley Cycle & Sports (☎ 465-3863), 9124 82nd Ave, rents out bikes for $7 an hour or $21 per day. It also does guided history tours by bike. HI Edmonton Hostel also rents out bikes (see Places to Stay earlier for details).

AROUND EDMONTON

Alberta Railway Museum

This museum (☎ 472-6229) has a collection of steam and diesel locomotives and rolling stock depicting the railways from 1877 to 1950. There is also an artefact exhibit. Admission is $3, children $1 and it's open daily in summer from 10 am to 6 pm. A ride on the train which operates holiday weekends is an extra $1. To get there, drive north on 97th St (Hwy 28) to Namao then turn east onto Hwy 37 for seven km, then south onto 34th St for about two km.

Elk Island National Park

In the northern Beaver Hills, 45 km east of Edmonton on the Yellowhead Hwy is this 194-sq-km tract of original forest preserved in 1906 as a wildlife sanctuary. For those interested in Canadian fauna, the park is a must for its high concentration of animals. There are free-roaming herds of elk and plains bison and a small herd of endangered wood bison. Bison can often be seen from the road and almost certainly along one of the walking trails. About 35 other mammals also inhabit the park and many of these can also be seen on an early morning or evening hike. Autumn is a particularly good time for wildlife viewing as much of the vegetation has thinned out. The park is a popular weekend spot with camping, hiking, cycling, canoeing and swimming in summer and cross-country skiing in winter. The park can be reached in under an hour from town so

ALBERTA

renting a car for one day, perhaps late afternoon to late afternoon with a night in the park would be a good, relatively cheap way of seeing it. Read the guide to bison viewing as they can be very aggressive. Parts of the park close for the season by October and re-open in spring. For information contact the Superintendent (☎ 992-6392), Elk Island National Park, RR 1, Site 4, Fort Saskatchewan T8L 2N7.

Ukrainian Cultural Heritage Village

This village (☎ 662-3640), 50 km east of Edmonton on the Yellowhead Hwy, pays homage to Ukrainian immigrants. There is a replica pioneer home and other exhibitions of the first settlers in the area. From mid-May to the beginning of September it's open daily from 10 am to 6 pm with reduced hours at other times. Admission is $5.50.

Vegreville

The Ukrainian community in this town (120 km east of Edmonton on the Yellowhead Hwy) has constructed the world's biggest *pysanka* or painted Easter egg. Built of aluminium, over seven metres tall and 5.5 metres wide, the egg sits just off the highway on the eastern side of town. The Ukrainian Pysanka Festival takes place in early July.

Polar Park

Polar Park (☎ 922-3401), 22 km south-east of town on Hwy 14, is a park with a collection of mainly regional and northern animals: snow leopards, polar bears and caribou are some of the 100 species. There are good walking and cross-country ski trails. It's open daily all year from 9 am to 9 pm and admission is $5, less for seniors and kids. Nearby there is excellent walking in the hilly and marshy Blackfoot Recreation Area and Grazing Reserve which is not far from Elk Island.

Red Deer

Halfway to Calgary, this large town is in the centre of grain and cattle country. An international folk festival is held here every July and an international air show every August.

Travellers to either Calgary or Edmonton may find Red Deer a useful stopping-off point. During either Calgary's stampede or Edmonton's Klondike Days it might be worth considering Red Deer as a base. Accommodation will not be as tight and is not likely to be as expensive either. Either city is about an hour and a half away on the two-lane highway.

Edmonton to Jasper

Jasper is 370 km from Edmonton along the Yellowhead Hwy. On the way there are commercial and government campgrounds as well as numerous motels, lodges and guest ranches.

About 30 km west of Edmonton is **Stony Plain** where the Multicultural Heritage Centre (☎ 963-2777), 5411 51st St, has displays on different pioneer groups and their crafts; you can even try some traditional food. It also has an art gallery.

For about 100 years, since prayers at **Lac Sainte Anne** by the Roman Catholic Mission to end a drought were answered, it has been believed that the waters of this lake have God-given curative powers. Here, 50 km west of Edmonton (about 25 km north off the Yellowhead Hwy), an annual pilgrimage takes place in July drawing about 10,000 people from around the province and across North America. It's a five-day event.

Edson, a small gas, oil, farming and forestry community, sits about mid-way along the highway. Another 85 km west brings you to **Hinton**, home of the Athabasca Nordic Lookout Centre, reputedly one of the best cross-country ski centres in North America. It has night-time skiing and a luge run. For more information, contact the Alberta Forest Service (☎ 865-2400), Hinton Ranger Station, 227 Kelly Rd, Hinton T7V 1H2.

Northern Alberta

The land north of Edmonton is a vast, sparsely populated region of farms, forests, wilderness areas, lakes, open prairies and oilfields. The Cree, Slavey and Dene were the first peoples to inhabit the region and many of them still depend on fishing, hunting and trapping. The north-east has virtually no roads and is dominated by Wood Buffalo National Park, the Athabasca River and Lake Athabasca. From its headwaters in British Columbia, the mighty Peace River makes its way to Lake Athabasca in the north-east of the province. The north-west is more accessible with a network of highways that connect Alberta with northern British Columbia and the Northwest Territories.

PEACE RIVER & AROUND

From Edmonton, Hwy 43 heads north-west to connect with Hwy 34 then Hwy 2 to Dawson Creek (a distance of 590 km), the official starting point of the Alaska Hwy. Numerous campgrounds and several provincial parks line the route. The scenery is generally flat or gently undulating with dairy and cereal farms, and with grain silos in nearly every town. **Grande Prairie**, a large sprawling community, is an administrative, commercial and agricultural centre. Most of the accommodation is centred on 100th St and 100th Ave.

Hwy 2 heading north directly out of Edmonton is a more interesting route as it follows the southern shore of **Lesser Slave Lake** part of the way. Just north of McLennan, **Lake Kimiwan** and its surrounding marshland is a special place for bird watchers. It's in the middle of three migratory routes and nearly 300,000 birds pass through each year. The interpretive centre, next to Hwy 2, is open May to September, and a boardwalk takes you through the bird habitats. For information call ☎ 324-2004.

The Peace River is so called because the warring Cree and Beaver Indians made peace along its banks. The town of **Peace River** sits at the confluence of the Heart, Peace and Smoky rivers. The Visitor Information Centre, on Hwy 2, is open July to September daily from 9 am to 9 pm. The town has several motels and two campgrounds. Greyhound buses leave daily for the Yukon and Northwest Territories. West out of town Hwy 2 leads to the Mackenzie Hwy.

MACKENZIE HIGHWAY

The small town of **Grimshaw** is the official starting point (though you might bypass it if you come via Peace River) of the Mackenzie Hwy (Hwy 35) north to the Northwest Territories. The relatively flat and straight road is paved for the most part though there are stretches of loose gravel or earth where the road is being reconstructed.

The mainly agricultured landscape between Grimshaw and Manning gives way to endless stretches of spruce and pine forest. Come prepared, as this is frontier territory and services become fewer (and more expensive) as the road cuts north through the wilderness. **High Level**, the last settlement of any size before the border, is a centre for the timber industry and workers often stay in the motels in town during the week. Between High Level and Enterprise in the Northwest Territories the only service station is at Indian Cabins.

LAKE DISTRICT

From St Paul, over 200 km north-east of Edmonton, to the Northwest Territories border lies Alberta's immense lake district. Fishing is popular (even in winter when there is ice-fishing) but many of the lakes, especially further north, have no road access and you have to fly in. St Paul, gateway to the lake district, is a trading centre. Its claim to fame is the only **flying-saucer landing pad** in the world. It's still waiting for its first customer. The region around St Paul has lots of provincial parks and campgrounds.

Hwy 63 is the main route into Alberta's north-eastern wilderness interior. The highway, with a few small settlements and campgrounds along the way, leads to **Fort McMurray**. Originally a fur-trading outpost, it is now home to one of the world's largest oil fields. The Visitor Information Centre (☎ 791-4336), 400 Sakitawaw Trail, organises guided tours of the oil-processing plants.

WOOD BUFFALO NATIONAL PARK

Established in 1922 and nearly 28,000 sq km in size, Wood Buffalo (☎ 872-2349) is

ALBERTA

Canada's largest national park and one of the world's largest parks. Bigger than Switzerland, the world heritage site lies two-thirds in Alberta and one-third in the Northwest Territories. Vegetation in this vast wilderness park ranges from boreal forest to plains, bogs and marshes. If you want to get a glimpse of what the early fur traders overcame, this is a good place to look.

The park is home to the world's largest free-roaming bison herd – about 3000 – and is the only nesting ground of the rare whooping crane. Though few in number and endangered, conservation efforts have resulted in their population stabilising. Moose, caribou, bears and wolves abound as well as many smaller animals, and over a million ducks, geese and swans pass by in autumn and spring on their migratory routes. At nearby Fort Smith rare white pelicans nest by the Slave River rapids. Other major features include the Peace-Athabasca Delta, Salt Plains and underground caves and sinkholes.

Most of the scenic areas in the park are not visible from the roads and the roads themselves are not always open. On the shores of Lake Athabaska, **Fort Chipewyan** is the oldest continuing European settlement in Alberta.

Fort Smith and Fort Chipewyan each have visitor centres or contact the Park Superintendent (☎ 872-2349), Box 750, Fort Smith, Northwest Territories X0E 0P0. The road to Fort Chipewyan is only passable in winter. In summer there is no road access. Also note that bugs can be a serious problem so come prepared for battle.

Activities

You can go swimming at **Pine Lake**, hike on the marked trails, or explore the deltas of the **Athabasca** and **Peace rivers** by canoe. The park staff run field trips and overnight camping trips or buffalo-watching hikes. In winter there are cross-country ski trails.

Outfitters and guides provide supplies, equipment or tours into the park. One to contact is Northern Visions (☎ 872-3430), PO Box 1086, Fort Smith, NWT X0E 0P0.

Places to Stay

There are few comforts in Wood Buffalo National Park. The small *Pine Lake Campground* (☎ 872-2349 in Fort Smith), 56 km south of Fort Smith, in the most developed area of the park, has 36 sites at $10 and pump water. In addition there are a couple of campgrounds just outside the park's border: one 17 km north-east of Fort Chipewyan at Dore Lake operated by the Alberta Forestry Service, and the other near Fort Smith (see also Fort Smith & Wood Buffalo National Park in the Northwest Territories chapter). Within the park there are numerous designated basic camp sites for individual campers which offer some primitive facilities such as an outhouse and sometimes a firepit. The more adventurous may set off on their own and camp anywhere they find agreeable.

Getting There & Away

Air Northwestern Air (☎ 872-2216 in Fort Smith) has a scheduled air service between Fort Smith, Fort Chipewyan and Edmonton.

Road The park is accessible by road but not from Alberta. By road, travel up the Mackenzie Hwy north-west of Edmonton to the Northwest Territories where Hwy 1 then Hwy 2 lead to Hay River on the southern shore of Great Slave Lake. South of Hay River, Hwy 5 heads east to Fort Smith along which two roads head south into the park. North of 60 Bus Lines (☎ 874-6411) plys between Hay River and Fort Smith.

Calgary

Calgary protrudes conspicuously from the flat plains of south central Alberta. Farms are minutes away, the rising foothills of the Rockies just visible to the west. But the streets of the city centre by the Bow River, headquarters of the oil industry, are lined with office towers. Calgary is young and modern having recreated itself from regional town to major Canadian city in the last 25 years. With a population reaching 740,000 this is Alberta's second city and it continues to grow rapidly. It is an economic centre with a university, professional sport franchises and an increasingly diverse cultural life. Still, the frequently seen cowboy boots and hats reveal the strong ties to the recent past.

The people generally are educated, well paid and work in high-tech, energy and resource based industries. It's also said there are more single people here than anywhere else in Canada. Perhaps this is why tanning salons and fitness centres are so prevalent – and busy.

The city's climate is dry and sunny. It gets hot in summer but remains amazingly cool in the shade. In winter the warm chinook winds periodically blow off the mountains, drastically raising temperatures – at least temporarily.

One of Alberta's greatest assets, Banff National Park, is just 120 km to the west. Edmonton is 294 km to the north.

History

The name Calgary, meaning 'clear, running water' in Gaelic, comes from Calgary Bay on the Isle of Mull in Scotland. The area was initially home to the Blackfoot but they were joined in the 18th century by the Sarcee and the Stoney. In the 1800s there was war between them and trouble with European trappers and traders, so the Northwest Mounted Police were sent to cool things down.

They established Fort Calgary in 1875. The Canadian Pacific railway came this far in 1883. Settlers were offered free land and the population jumped to 4000 by 1891. Soon, cattle herders from the USA were pushing north looking for better grazing. Calgary became a major meat-packing centre and cowboy metropolis. Slowly, with moderate growth, it became a major western transportation and distribution point and is still the leading cattle centre. But since the late 1960s the city has had to deal with some dramatic ups and downs, exploding from a fair-sized cow town to a brand-new city of steel and glass. Through this period Calgary was labelled everything from a rootless boom town to a major new urban centre to a depressed area.

The reason for Calgary's changeable fortunes is simple: oil. Oil had originally been discovered as far back as 1914, but it wasn't until the late 1960s that the black gold was found in vast quantities across the province. Coupled with the energy crisis of the 1970s which bumped prices up sharply, the industry boomed. The city took off, becoming one of the fastest growing cities in the country. It became the headquarters of 450 oil companies and home to more US citizens than any place outside of the USA.

After a brief breath-catching period, the cultural side of the city began to develop as well. However, during the 1980s things turned tough. With the bottom falling out of the oil market and 70% of the workforce relying on it, things turned sour quickly. Just when the city was struggling, attempting to maintain what it had become, Calgary's fortunes and reputation were boosted when it hosted the Winter Olympics in 1988. And by 1993 there was an upturn in the fortunes of the oil and gas industries. In 1995 it surpassed Montreal in the number of head offices it houses. Only Toronto has more. The city has a broader economic base now and is ready to move into the next century as one of the country's major cities.

Orientation

Calgary lies on flat ground. It began at the confluence of the Bow and Elbow rivers and has spread equally in all directions; indeed the city is now the country's second largest in area. The downtown core is still bounded by the Bow River to the north. The Elbow River cuts through the southern portions of the city.

Whoever dreamt up the street-numbering system must have thought it great, but it's a jumble and will take you a few days to get a grip of. The city is divided into four geographical segments: north-west (NW), north-east (NE), south-west (SW) and south-east (SE). These abbreviations are important

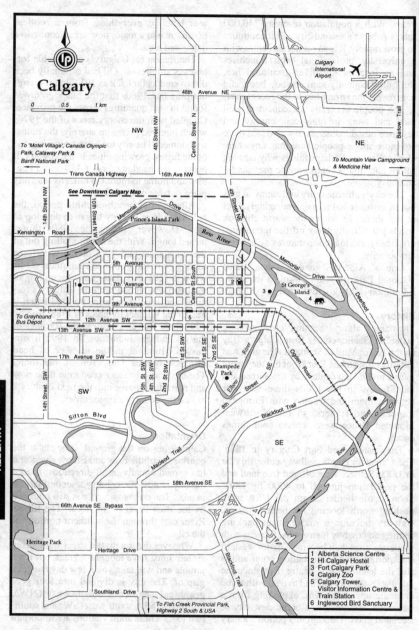

Calgary

0   0.5   1 km

NW

NE

Calgary
International
Airport

To 'Motel Village', Canada Olympic
Park, Calaway Park &
Banff National Park

Trans Canada Highway   16th Ave NW

To Mountain View Campground
& Medicine Hat

See Downtown Calgary Map

Prince's Island Park

Memorial   Drive

Bow River

Kensington   Road

Memorial

Drive

5th Avenue

7th Avenue

St George's
Island

9th Avenue

To Greyhound
Bus Depot

12th Avenue SW

13th Avenue SW

17th Avenue SW

Stampede
Park

Ogden Road

Blackfoot Trail

Sifton Blvd

8th Street

Macleod Trail

Bow River

SE

58th Avenue SE

66th Avenue SE Bypass

Heritage Park

Heritage Drive

Southland Drive

Blackfoot Trail

To Fish Creek Provincial Park,
Highway 2 South & USA

1 Alberta Science Centre
2 HI Calgary Hostel
3 Fort Calgary Park
4 Calgary Zoo
5 Calgary Tower,
  Visitor Information Centre &
  Train Station
6 Inglewood Bird Sanctuary

ALBERTA

as they're marked on street signs and included in addresses.

The Bow River and Memorial Drive divide the city between north and south, approximately. Centre St divides the northern part of the city and downtown between east and west; Macleod Trail divides the southern part of the city between east and west.

All city streets run north and south, all avenues run east and west. The downtown streets are all one way except for 7th Ave. Here all cars go west to east but there's one bus and taxi lane which goes the opposite way. The Light Rail Transit (LRT – known as the C-Train) also runs along 7th Ave.

Downtown Around the downtown centre the 'Plus 15 Walking System' refers to pedestrian bridges and over-the-street walkways (enclosed sidewalks) which are at least five metres above the ground. Various buildings and shops are connected in this way.

The Calgary Tower, right in the centre of town on 9th Ave at Centre St, is a good orientation point. If you look across the street up Centre St, you're looking north towards the downtown area. Ninth Ave is lined with modern offices, expensive hotels, banks and parking lots as well as hosting the train station, Calgary Convention Centre and Glenbow Museum & Art Gallery complex.

Eighth Ave between 3rd St SW and 1st St SE is a very long pedestrian mall – Stephens Ave Mall, also called 8th Ave Mall. It's lined with trees, benches, shops including the large department stores, restaurants and fast-food places. There are also a lot of vendors selling crafts, odds & ends and souvenirs. At its western end Stephens Ave Mall connects with Barclay Mall (3rd St SW) which heads north towards the YMCA, Eau Claire Market and Prince's Island Park. Eau Claire is a redeveloped part of downtown containing a mix of shops, restaurants, clubs and open spaces.

Around Centre St, before it heads north over the river, between 1st St SW and 1st St SE, is the small, vibrant Chinatown with grocery stores and video shops as well as restaurants.

The western downtown area is mainly offices and businesses. The eastern section was the last to undergo redevelopment. It used to be the saviour of the impecunious with its cheap bars and tatty hotels of which a few vestiges remain but generally it's pretty cleaned up. The Single Men's Hostel and a couple of old hotels remain; the HI Calgary Hostel is down this way as well. Among the older buildings, a couple of fine ones are the City Council building dating from 1907 on 7th Ave SE and the Anglican church dating from 1904 on 7th Ave SE at 1st St SE. The latter replaced a temporary cathedral built in 1884. One of the newer complexes is the large Centre for the Performing Arts on the corner of 9th Ave and 1st St SE with the park nearby.

Stone lions on each side mark the Centre St Bridge over the Bow River, which has the greyish-green colour of Rocky Mountain waters. The river marks the northern edge of the downtown area. To the west of the bridge is Prince's Island, a park. Over the bridge, on the northern side, are stairs on both sides leading up to the cliff. There's a footpath along the cliff and good views of the city, especially if you take the stairs on the western side. If you're driving, turn left on 8th Ave NW, then head back towards the river.

Note that most places in the downtown area are within walking distance of each other. Those who find the modern glass and steel central core too business oriented and a little sterile should investigate some of the following areas.

North The city north of the river is primarily residential. The Trans Canada Hwy cuts east-west across here along 16th Ave NE and 16th Ave NW. In the north-west the University of Calgary is off Crowchild Trail (Hwy 1A). To the north-east, off Barlow Trail is the international airport. Just north-west over the river, off Memorial Drive, is the older district of Kensington which has restaurants, cafes and some nightclubs.

South South of Calgary Tower, over the railway tracks, is another section of the city – a sort of mini-downtown. It's between 10th Ave SW and 17th Ave SW and on 4th St SW running north-south. There are quite a few restaurants in this area. Five blocks to the east is Stampede Park.

Heading west from Stampede Park is 17th Ave SW. It's lined with a wide range of restaurants as well as a variety of other businesses including many antique shops. Fourth St SW, south of 17th Ave SW, has boutiques, a few galleries and yet more eating places and night spots.

Further south is Macleod Trail (Hwy 2) which eventually heads to the USA. The most exclusive section of Calgary is east of Macleod Trail around the Bow River.

Information

Tourist Offices The Visitor Service Centre (VSC; ☎ 263-8510, 1-800-661-1678), is on the ground floor of Calgary Tower at the junction of 9th Ave SW and Centre St. It's run by the Calgary Convention & Visitors Bureau, has maps of the city and pamphlets on things to do and will help you find a place to stay. It's open daily in summer from 8 am to 8 pm. There are also offices at both the arrivals and departures areas of the airport.

Money There are several banks on Stephens Ave, but the Hong Kong Bank of Canada in the Good Fortune Plaza on 3rd Ave SE in Chinatown is open on Saturday. American Express (☎ 269-3757) is at 421 7th Ave SW.

Post The main post office (☎ 292-5512), 220 4th Ave SE, is open Monday to Friday from 8 am to 5.45 pm.

Foreign Consulates Many countries are represented diplomatically in Calgary. Check in the Yellow Pages for the various consulates and embassies. A list of Ottawa addresses can also be found in the Facts for the Visitor chapter at the beginning of this book.

Bookshops & Maps The Hostel Shop (☎ 283-8311), 1414 Kensington Rd NW, open daily, has travel and outdoor-activity guides and maps, as well as travel goods. Map Town (☎ 266-2241), 640 6th Ave SW, has travel guides and a wide range of maps. Topographical maps are available from Maps Alberta (☎ 297-7389), 703 6th Ave SW, plus some good publications on the province's flora & fauna. A good second-hand bookshop is the Best Little Wordhouse in the West at 223 10 St NW, Kensington.

Medical Services Calgary General Hospital (☎ 268-9111) is north-east of the downtown area, over the river in the Bow Valley Centre at 841 Centre Ave NE; take bus No 3.

Calgary Tower

This building (☎ 266-7171), 101 9th Ave SW, at the foot of Centre St downtown, acts as a landmark and symbol of the city. It may not dominate the skyline but can be seen from far away. The 191-metre tower houses a revolving restaurant, an observation gallery and, at the very top, a cocktail lounge. While the elevator ($5) takes just 58 seconds, walking the 762 emergency steps takes a bit longer.

The observation gallery is open from 8 am to 10 pm daily in summer, from 8.30 am the rest of the year.

Glenbow Museum & Art Gallery

The Glenbow Museum & Art Gallery (☎ 268-4100), 130 9th Ave SE, is excellent and well worth a visit. The collections are varied and interesting, the displays effectively laid out. The complex shows part of human history through artefacts and art.

The 2nd floor contains frequently changing exhibitions of international, national and local art; there is always some Inuit art and a painter's work on show.

The 3rd floor has historical displays, mainly to do with the Canadian west. There is a superb collection of Native Indian dress and jewellery. Woodcarving from coast to coast is also represented. There's a section with Inuit tools and a kayak, the traditional

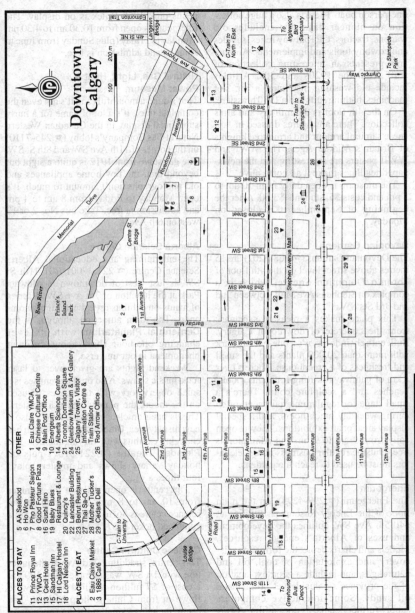

Downtown Calgary

0   100   200 m

PLACES TO STAY
11 Prince Royal Inn
12 YWCA
13 Cecil Hotel
15 Sandman Inn
17 HI Calgary Hostel
18 Lord Nelson Inn

PLACES TO EAT
2   Eau Claire Market
3   1886 Café
5   AA Seafood
6   Ho Won
7   Pho Pasteur Saigon
8   Good Fortune Plaza
16 Sushi Hiro
19 Baby Blues
    Restaurant & Lounge
20 Quincy's
22 Lancaster Building
23 Beirut Restaurant
27 Thai Sa-On
28 Mother Tucker's
29 Cedars Deli

OTHER
1   Eau Claire YMCA
4   Chinese Cultural Centre
9   Main Post Office
10 Energeum
14 Alberta Science Centre
21 Toronto Dominion Square
24 Glenbow Museum & Art Gallery
25 Calgary Tower, Visitor
    Information Centre &
    Train Station
26 Red Arrow Office

one-person boat. There is also a huge collection on pioneer days that includes old wagons, tractors, CP Railway relics, saddles and cowboy tools and implements. Another area presents an interesting collection of stuff from the 1920s and 30s. Articles include old washing machines, a car, slot machines, bathing suits and a 1930 brassiere.

On the 4th floor is the military and arms collection. There are figures dressed in Japanese samurai armour and armoured knights of Britain's Middle Ages. The WWI and WWII posters are interesting and the newspaper headlines make it all come alive.

The museum is open daily from 10 am to 5 pm and costs $5, students $3.50. After the beginning of September it is closed on Monday.

Devonian Gardens

The Devonian Gardens (☎ 268-5207) are 15 metres above street level on the 4th floor of Toronto Dominion Square, which is a complex on Stephens Ave Mall, between 2nd and 3rd Sts SW.

This place makes a pleasant sanctuary from the concrete of downtown Calgary. Built entirely indoors, it's a one-hectare park with more than 20,000 plants and the smell and freshness of a greenhouse. There's over a km of pathways skirting fountains, pools, benches and a sculpture court. There's a small stage for regular entertainment, often during weekday lunch hours, and a special display area for art exhibitions. They're open daily from 9 am to 9 pm and admission is free. Outside regular business hours, elevators must be used to reach the gardens.

Energeum

The Energeum (☎ 297-4293), on the main floor of the Energy Resources Building at 640 5th Ave SW, outlines the development and uses of Alberta's energy resources. Models and charts depict the formation, discovery and exploitation of coal, oil and natural gas, and include a good explanation of the province's valuable yet problematic oil sands. Some interactive computers supply further details, as does a film. A gorgeous pink 1958 Buick is on display. The Energeum is open from 10.30 am to 4.30 pm Monday to Friday (plus Sunday from June to August) and admission is free.

Natural Gas, Light, Heat & Power Museum

That's quite a mouthful (and it's not even the complete title). It's a lot of name for a fairly superficial display in the Canadian Western Natural Gas Company's lobby (☎ 245-7110) on the corner of 11th Ave SW and 8th St SW. The gas stove from 1912 is quite a sight but beyond that, the few home appliances and old photographs don't amount to much. It's open Monday to Friday from 8 am to 4 pm and admission is free. Take bus Nos 2 or 13 west on 6th Ave.

Alberta Science Centre

The entertaining and educational Alberta Science Centre (☎ 221-3700), 701 11th St SW, is just west of downtown in Mewata Park at the junction of 7th Ave SW. A series of hands-on exhibits reveal natural phenomenon. The main attraction, though, is the **Centennial Planetarium** with its ever changing one-hour show about different phenomena in our universe.

Weekend nights are given over to laser rock-music shows. Also on the premises is a small observatory with telescopes focused on the moon, the planets and star clusters. This is open on clear nights. There's also a new display area, **Discovery Hall**, which has changing exhibits with varying themes. The **Pleiades Theatre** (☎ 221-3707) puts on holiday variety shows and mystery plays four times a year.

The centre is open daily in the summer from 10 am to 8 pm. Admission to the science centre is $6, to the planetarium $6; a combined ticket is $7.

Chinese Cultural Centre

This centre, straddling 2nd Ave at the junction with 1st SW, was completed in 1993 at a cost of $7 million. Skilled artisans were flown in from China to help build it. The centre includes a small museum (open daily from 11 am to 5 pm, admission $2) and you can watch people playing chess in the main hall.

Prince's Island Park

This is a pretty park on an island in the Bow River north of the downtown area, connected to both sides of the river by pedestrian bridges. It's a cool, quiet spot with lots of trees and flowers, picnic tables and jogging and cycling paths. This is a good antidote to a hot summer's day in Calgary. As the signs say, the water in the Bow River is dangerous for swimming: it moves fast and is cold. The tranquil but pricey River Café serves sit-down meals. The bridge to the island from downtown is at the top (northern end) of 3rd St SW.

Heritage Park Historical Village

This is an area of 26 hectares portraying life in a town of the Canadian west prior to 1914 and on a good day offers views of the Rockies, too. The park (☎ 259-1900), 1900 Heritage Drive at the junction of 14th St SW, south-west of downtown, sits on a peninsula jutting into the Glenmore Reservoir formed by the Elbow River.

The reconstructed frontier village includes a Hudson's Bay Company fort, a working grain mill, an 1896 church and many stores full of artefacts and antiques. The well-laid-out grounds have a ranch house, a teepee, a trapper's cabin and other housing. The old schoolhouse with its desks and slates is interesting. There is an excellent collection of horse-drawn buggies in section E, which includes stagecoaches, traps and surreys, and the chemist's and general store are particularly good. Also, be sure to see the two-storey outhouse.

The park actually covers more than just pioneer days, encompassing development into the early 1920s. There are old cars, a railway exhibit of old coaches and a working steam engine.

Around the site are several eating places and you can buy fresh bread from the bakery. From May to June the park is open weekdays from 10 am to 4 pm, weekends to 6 pm; from the end of June to early September it is open daily from 10 am to 6 pm; then on weekdays till 5 pm until early October. Admission is $6, children $3 and $1.50 extra with the train ride. To get there take the C-Train to Heritage Station and transfer to the No 20 bus.

Fort Calgary

This is not really a fort but a 16-hectare park (☎ 290-1850), at 750 9th Ave SE, east of downtown, where Calgary's original settlement began. In the park is an interpretive centre (☎ 232-1875), the remains of the fort and two of Calgary's earliest houses. The interpretive centre tells the story of Calgary's development; there are displays and a video show on the Northwest Mounted Police every 30 minutes in the theatre and a re-created store and carpentry shop. The centre is open daily from 9 am to 5 pm and admission is $2.

Here in 1875, where the Bow River meets the Elbow River, the first detachment of the Northwest Mounted Police arrived. They built a fort and called the developing settlement the 'Elbow'. Later it became Fort Calgary and remained a police post until 1914, when it was sold to the Grand Trunk Railway. All that remains of the fort are a few foundations. Plaques give some of the history.

The fort site is pleasant and has good views. You can follow paths down to the river and walk across the footbridge to St Patrick's Island and on to Calgary Zoo. The park is open every day and is free.

To the east, across the Elbow River, is **Hunt House**, probably the oldest building on its original site in the Calgary area. It was built by the Hudson's Bay Company in 1876 for one of its employees. Next door the larger **Deane House**, was built in 1906 for the commanding officer of Fort Calgary and is now a restaurant.

Calgary Zoo

The zoo (☎ 232-9372), one of Canada's largest and best, is east of downtown on St George's Island and the northern bank of the Bow River. It brings together 1200 species

ALBERTA

of mammals, birds, amphibians and reptiles, many in enclosures simulating the animals' natural habitats. Underwater viewing areas allow you to see polar bears, seals and other creatures as they behave beneath the water. Special blacked-out rooms enable you to see nocturnal animals. There is a section on Australian animals and pens for large, exotic mammals like tigers, giraffes and Himalayan cats. Call ahead to check on feeding times. Hundreds of tropical birds are kept in greenhouses full of plants and flowers of warmer climes. Picnic areas dot the zoo and island and there is a cafe at the site.

The **Botanical Garden** in the zoo has changing garden displays, a tropical rainforest and a good butterfly enclosure. The three-hectare **Prehistoric Dinosaur Park**, an extension of the zoo, contains fossil displays and life-size replicas of dinosaurs in natural settings.

The zoo is open year-round and charges $7.50, $3.75 for children under 16. In summer it's open from 9 am to 7 pm, in winter 9 am to 5 pm. Catch the C-Train east along 7th Ave to Zoo Station.

Inglewood Bird Sanctuary

This 32-hectare sanctuary (☎ 269-6688, 237-8811) is south-east of downtown at the end of 9th Ave, on a forested section of the Bow River flats. The area is home to at least 266 species, and is a resting spot for those on the migratory trail. Trails lead through the sanctuary which is open daily from 7 am to 9 pm and admission is free. Bus No 411 goes within a few blocks of the sanctuary (Monday to Friday only) or the No 1 from downtown gets close, too.

Calgary Stockyards

The stockyards (☎ 934-3344), 100 2635 Portland St SE, are one of the centres for western livestock dealing. If you want to see what goes on, there are cattle auctions on weekdays. Take bus No 24 from downtown.

Grain Academy

Operated by the Alberta Wheat Pool, the Academy (☎ 263-4594) tells the story of the province's grain through film, models, tools and guides. The entire grain handling system is outlined. The Academy is open Monday to Friday 10 am to 4 pm and Saturday noon to 4 pm from April to September and is free. It's located at the Round Up Centre, Stampede Park.

Museum of the Regiments

Museum of the Regiments (☎ 240-7674) is

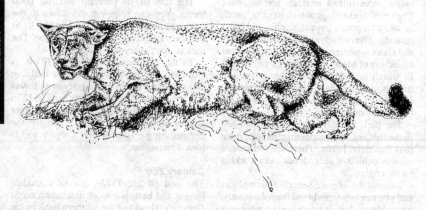

Among cats of the Americas the puma, often called a cougar, is second in size only to the jaguar

at the Canadian Forces base, Currie Barracks, 4520 Crowchild Trail SW between 33rd Ave SW and 50th Ave SW. It pays homage to Calgary's home regiments: Lord Strathcona's Horse, Princess Patricia's Light Infantry, the Calgary Highlanders and the King's Own Calgary regiment. There are collections of uniforms, weapons, badges, toys and memorabilia from both the 19th and 20th centuries.

Entry is free and it's open daily, except Wednesday, from 10 am to 4 pm. As it's on the base, you may be asked for identification – calling ahead is a good idea. To get there take bus Nos 18, 108, 111 or 112 from downtown.

Fish Creek Provincial Park
On the south-western edge of Calgary, quite a way from downtown, is this huge tract of land more than eight-sq-km in size, running along Fish Creek, which flows into the Bow River. It acts as a shelter for many animals and birds as well as people on weekends. Park interpreters present slide shows and walking tours to explain some of the local ecology.

For details drop into the administration office or call Calgary Parks & Recreation (☎ 268-3888). To get there from downtown head south on the Macleod Trail.

Calaway Park
This large amusement park (☎ 240-3822/24), about 10 km west of town on the Trans Canada Hwy, features over 20 rides, a cinema with a 180° screen, restaurants and entertainment events. It costs $9.95 to get in to see the shows, or $17.50 including rides.

Winter Olympics Site
Calgary hosted the 15th Winter Olympics in 1988, a first for Canada. Some of the locations and facilities were already in place, others were specially built for the Olympics, but they all remain in use.

A 15-minute drive west of town on the Trans Canada Hwy, **Canada Olympic Park** (☎ 247-5403) is interesting to visit. There you can see the 70 and 90-metre ski jumps –

from the top you realise how crazy those guys are – and the bobsled and luge runs built of concrete. If you don't want to try the real thing yourself there are simulators that recreate the sensation of bobsledding or skiing. Some of the facilities are now used as an Olympic training centre. You can look around for free or take a guided tour of the park for $6. The **Olympic Hall of Fame** (☎ 247-5452), is open daily from 10 am to 5 pm and admission is $3.75. A combined ticket costs $8.

The adjacent downhill ski area is open to the public in winter. But the real alpine skiing took place 55 km west of town in Kananaskis Country (see that section later).

Bow River
The Bow River begins as clean, clear barely melted ice in Bow Lake in the Rockies not far from Banff, and flows swiftly through Calgary. From Calgary it slows and warms and eventually reaches Medicine Hat near the Saskatchewan border. There it melds with other meandering rivers, changes name and eventually slips into Hudson Bay.

The Bow River in its middle section – the 60 km from Calgary east to Carseland – is considered one of the best trout-fishing rivers in North America and the best dry fly-fishing river in the world. The fish, mainly brown and rainbow trout, are numerous and big, too. And the river will just float you along with no effort required. It sounds good even for those who don't fish. Swimming is out, though – the water here is still far too cool.

A good access point is just at the southern edge of Calgary's city limits under the Hwy 22X bridge. There are numerous fishing-guide services in town as well as sporting-goods stores for fishing tackle and information. One place to try that combines the two is Country Pleasures (☎ 271-1016), 570 10816 Macleod Trail South.

Tsuu T'ina Museum & Reserve
The Tsuu T'ina Indian Nation have a community about 30 minutes south-west of town at the end of Anderson Rd. There is a small

museum (☎ 281-4455) which can be visited for free or more in-depth tours are offered around their huge tract of land. Guides will talk about the peoples past, culture and current status. There are some historical sites to see, and bison grazing. These tours are prohibitively expensive for individuals so call first to see what can be arranged and try to have a few people together to help defray costs.

IMAX Theatre

Calgary's new IMAX Theatre (☎ 263-4629), 132 200 Barclay Parade SW, is in the Eau Claire Market just south of the Bow River. These specially designed theatres show films up to 10 times the size of a normal 35 mm movie with very impressive results.

Aero Space Museum

Visitors with a keen interest in planes and aviation history may enjoy this collection (☎ 250-3752) of civil and combat aircraft and engines. Members carry on a lot of restorations and are currently working on several major projects. The museum is open weekdays from 10 am, noon on weekends and is located at 64 McTavish Place NE.

Activities

Calgary has 180 km of bicycle and hiking trails, many in the parks and nature areas. Maps and information are available from Parks & Recreation (☎ 268-3888, 268-23009). Budget Rent-a-Car (☎ 263-0505), 140 6th Ave SE, rents bikes for $6/18 per hour/day. The R'n'R shop in the Eau Clair market rents quality bikes and rollerblades but the prices are a little high.

Two leisure centres run by Parks & Recreation have giant wave pools, year-round skating, racquet courts, hot tubs, climbing walls and more. They are: Village Square Leisure Centre (☎ 280-9714), 2623 56 St NE, and Southland Leisure Centre (☎ 251-3505), 2000 Southland Drive SW near the corner of 19th St SW. Downtown, the Eau Claire YMCA (☎ 269-6701), 101 3rd St SW, has the latest in keep-fit facilities. Admission is $6.50 outside of peak hours. Call Bungee

Canada (☎ 286-4334) at Canada Olympic Park if you want to dive 37.5 metres into a specially designed 3.6-metre-deep pool for $50.

Horse riding, including lessons, is available in Fish Creek Provincial Park with Happy Trails (☎ 251-3344) riding stable. A one-hour trail ride costs $15.

Organised Tours

The cheapest bus tour of town is to take the No 10 bus from along 6th Ave. For $1.25 this city bus goes on its 2½-hour circular route past old and new areas, the highest point of the city with views to the foothills, the university and some wealthy districts in the north-west.

Brewster's Gray Line (☎ 221-8242), 808 Centre St SE, runs tours of Calgary and various Rocky Mountain locations from Calgary. The tour of Calgary takes about four hours, covers about 50 km and costs $33. It includes Fort Calgary, Canada Olympic Park and the downtown area, with admissions included in the ticket. A history of the city is given. Their tour to Banff takes nine hours and costs $57 including a ride on the gondola up Sulphur Mountain. White Stetson Tours (☎ 274-2281), 6312 Travois Crescent NW, does similar city and mountain tours.

Two new small tour companies are recommended. Hammerhead Tours (☎ 547-1566) operates two trips, one west to the Drumheller Badlands and Tyrrell Museum for $45 and one south to Head-Smashed-In Buffalo Jump for $49. Both are full day trips with a small group in a van, and take in various attractions along the way. They pick-up at several locations around town including the International Hostel and the Calgary Tower. The office is at 4714 14th St NW and trips are run June to October.

Working in conjunction with the HI Calgary International Hostel is True North Tours (☎ 275-4979). They operate the Rocky Express which is a six-day trip through some of the highlights of the mountains with accommodation in various hostels along the way. The price is $149 plus the hostel rates. Vans are used and the optional group meals can really keep costs down. Call the Calgary Hostel (☎ 269-8239) for details and reservations. Bookings and connections can also be made at the Banff hostel. Reservations should be made about two or three weeks in advance. Trips run from the beginning of June to the middle of October.

Other trips may be arranged through the hostel including hikes and mountain-bike tours. The Visitor Information Office runs walking tours of the central area. For those with a specialised interest, the Old Town Calgary Society (☎ 265-4171), 1 917 9th Ave SE, can help with further historic information.

Whitewater rafting on either the Kananaskis or Red Deer rivers is available through Rainbow Riders Adventure Tours (☎ 850-3680), 3312 3rd Ave NW. The cost is $45 for about 2½ hours. Calgary Helicopters (☎ 291-0017), 575 Palmer Rd NE, offer tours of the city for $85 per person and of the Rocky Mountains for $325.

Festivals
The following are some of Calgary's major festivals.

July
  Calgary Stampede – Dating from 1912, this is a wild 10-day festival that starts with a huge parade in the second week of July each year. Most organised events take place in Stampede Park south-east of the downtown area, but many of the streets are full of activity too. Stampede Park comes alive with concerts, shows, exhibitions, dancing and eating. There is also an amusement area with rides, a gambling hall and lots of contests. Highlights are the chuck-wagon race and the rodeo, which is said to be the biggest and roughest in North America. Events include rides on bucking broncos and bulls, and calf-roping and branding. At night the Stampede Stage Show takes over, with singers, bands, clowns and dancers. Tickets for the main events go early and range in price from about $16 to $45. Prices all over town go up, so beware. And the town and nearby countryside are packed for the duration of the celebrations, so if you plan to be here at this time, it's a good idea to book ahead for somewhere to stay or arrive early. For more information or tickets call or write to Calgary Exhibition & Stampede (☎ 269-9822, 1-800-661-1260), Box 1060, Station M, Calgary T2P 2K8.

Calgary Folk Festival – During this festival in late July there are free weekday lunch-time performances in Stephens Ave Mall, Century Park Garden and Olympic Plaza. In the evenings there are performances in venues around town including Kensington Delicafé and King Edward Hotel. The main events take place on Prince's Island. Both three-day and one-day passes are available. The festival includes local, national and international artists. For details call ☎ 261-4060.

August
  Dragon Boat Festival – Watch for this at the beginning of the month in Glenmore Park. It's a very colourful race on the water based on a traditional Chinese event.
  International Native Arts Festival – This takes place in the middle of August and includes traditional dancing, music and arts & crafts by the indigenous peoples of North America and around the world.

Places to Stay
The prices quoted here are the regular ones but in some places they rise when special events are on, such as the Calgary Stampede.

Camping There are several campgrounds near the city for both RVs and tents. *Whispering Spruce Campground* (☎ 226-0097) is in Balzac along Hwy 2 about 15 minutes north of the city. It's convenient and large enough to always have space, but maintenance and cleaning are virtually non-existent. It's open from mid-May to the end of October and has tent sites for $14. *Mountain View Campground* (☎ 249-7372), on a farm three km east of Calgary on the Trans Canada Hwy, is open all year. It has showers, laundrette, barbecue, even a small zoo, and tent sites for $14. *Calaway Park* (☎ 249-7372), 10 km west of Calgary on the Trans Canada Hwy, has full facilities including showers and laundromat, and unserviced sites for $14.

The quietest place is south of Calgary, five km east of Okotoks on Railway St. *Okotoks Wilderness Campground* (☎ 938-6036) has sites for $12 and there are showers and hiking trails. To get there go 33 km south on Hwy 2 and take the Okotoks turn off, then turn left at the lights and travel for about a km; the campground is just past the car wash.

ALBERTA

Hostels The popular HI *Calgary Hostel* (☎ 269-8239), 520 7th Ave SE just east of downtown not far from Fort Calgary, is open 24 hours. It is a large hostel complete with laundrette, kitchen and snack bar but still often gets full in summer, especially for men. Reservations are suggested. The hostel organises a lot of events and activities and offers a variety of cost-saving ideas. There is also a shuttle bus to hostels out of town. See under tours earlier for other trips. Rates are $14 for members, $19 for nonmembers.

The central *YWCA* (☎ 263-1550), 320 5th Ave SE, is for women only. The single rooms are $27/32 without/with bath, doubles are $30/40 without/with bath. A dormitory bed is $18. The rooms are clean, you can use the pool or gym and there's a cafeteria which is open every day.

The *University of Calgary* rents rooms in the residences from early May to the end of August. For details and information contact the University Housing Office (☎ 220-3203), Room 18, Dining Centre, University of Calgary, 2500 University Drive NW, Calgary T2N 1N4. Dormitory accommodation, meaning a small simple room starts at $27. There are also two sizes of apartments with kitchens. In the smaller ones it's $40/25 unshared/shared, and in the larger apartments it's $52/34. There are good facilities on campus, including a gym and a cheap cafeteria. The university which is north-west of the centre off Crowchild Trail is serviced by the C-Train.

B&Bs The Visitor Information Centre keeps a list of B&B places and will make a booking for you. An association which checks and lists houses offering B&B in the city is the B&B Association of Calgary (☎ 2531-0065), 6016 Thornburn Drive NW, Calgary. See also the agencies listed under Accommodation at the start of this chapter. The *Accommodation & Visitors' Guide* lists about 30 B&Bs in Calgary. The rates start from singles/doubles $30/50. A central and inexpensive one is the *Tumble Inn* (☎ 228-6167) at 1507 6th St SW. A room is $35/45 with full breakfast.

Hotels Central Calgary doesn't have an abundance of lodgings in any price range. Many of the hotels are around the edges of the city but the downtown ones are concentrated on here. The south-east section, once a rough and tumble area, was the centre for cheap hotels but as the area was cleaned up most of the small, older places disappeared. There are still a few and, though they tend to be for long-term residents, may have a few available rooms.

The *Cecil Hotel* (☎ 266-2982), on the corner of 4th Ave SE and 3rd St SE, is a low-budget place that's been around for a long time, but it can be noisy and a bit rough and some of the patrons are prone to a couple of drinks too many. Rooms are $22/32 with no TV, no phone and no bath, but a sink in each room. At the bar downstairs you can get simple food. The *St Louis Hotel* (☎ 262-6341), 430 8th Ave SE, is another basic place, but the budget conscious will find it cheap at $25/30 with bath and TV. There's a busy bar and simple restaurant downstairs. Neither of these places is recommended for women.

South-east, in walking distance of downtown and Stampede Park in the district of Inglewood, is the *Shamrock Hotel* (☎ 290-0084), 2101 11th St SE, which has very clean rooms with TV and telephone and costs $39/49. Don't be put off by the industrial landscape close by.

The *Lord Nelson Inn* (☎ 269-8262), 1020 8th Ave SW, is very central and has full facilities, including a fridge in each room. Rooms are $65/70. *Prince Royal Inn* (☎ 263-0520), 618 5th Ave SW, is a modern all-suite hotel. There's a laundry service and rooms have a kitchenette, fridge, telephones and cable TV. Rates are $90/$100 to $120 for a double with breakfast, and at weekends you can get singles/doubles for $50. You can also rent by the week or month.

The *Sandman Inn* (☎ 237-8626), 888 7th Ave SW, a good, standard mid-range hotel is $68/72. It has full facilities including gym, swimming pool, licensed restaurant and bar.

Westward Inn (☎ 266-4611), 119 12 Ave SW, is within walking distance of Stampede Park and has rooms for $70.

ALBERTA

Motels Much of the good moderate accommodation is found outside the centre of town in motels. Calgary has dozens of them in all parts of the city, but there are some areas of very heavy concentration, making it easy to shop around. One of these is along Macleod Trail south of the city. Macleod Trail is a commercial strip with service stations, fast-food restaurants, motels and furniture shops.

Cedar Ridge Motel (☎ 258-1064), 9030 Macleod Trail South, is reasonably priced. Singles/doubles cost $50/60. *Flamingo Motor Hotel* (☎ 252-4401), 7505 Macleod Trail South near the corner of 75th Ave SW, is marked by – you guessed it – a large pink flamingo. Rooms cost from $55/65 with a TV in each room, a laundry, pool and a sauna. The treed grounds are pleasant and there are restaurants nearby.

Travelodge Calgary Macleod Trail (☎ 253-7070), 9206 Macleod Trail South near 90th Ave SE, is a two-storey building containing a pool, whirlpool and sauna. Rooms have air-con, cable TV and telephones and cost $70/80.

Another motel area is in the north-western section of the city on and just off 16th Ave (the Trans Canada Hwy). South-east of the University of Calgary, 16th Ave meets Crowchild Trail; linking the two on a diagonal, forming a triangle, is Banff Trail (also called Hwy 1A). Because of the many motels in and around this triangle, the area is called 'Motel Village'. It's a fair way from downtown but it is linked by the C-Train and city buses.

One of the cheapest motels is *Savory Lodge* (☎ 289-0295), 2373 Banff Trail NW. It has 30 rooms, most of them at $40/45; those with kitchenettes cost $5 extra. There's a restaurant and a pub. The *Avondale Motel* (☎ 289-1921), 2231 Banff Trail NW, has a licensed restaurant, swimming pool and laundrette. Rooms are $64/70. *Budget Host Motor Inn* (☎ 288-7115), 4420 16th Ave NW, is simple but fine and has free coffee. Rooms are $59/65. *Econolodge* (☎ 289-2561), 2440 16th Ave NW, has a Latin American look about it. Some of its 55 rooms have kitchenettes but there's no extra charge. Rooms cost from $65/75.

Places to Eat
The Saturday edition of the *Calgary Herald* newspaper has ads for breakfast and lunch buffets. The growing number of Calgary's different ethnic groups is reflected in the variety of food available.

Downtown Stephens Ave Mall has numerous places, some that set up tables in the mall in fair weather. One, the long running *Prospector*, 205 Stephens Ave West, is good for breakfast.

For lunch or dinner, check out the 2nd floor of the nearby Lancaster Building at 304 Stephens Ave Mall on the corner of 2nd St SW. There are 17 food kiosks serving cheap Chinese, Mexican, Indian, deli and other foods. Curry dishes or tacos are around $4.50. You get street views, too. Similar is the food court at Eaton's, 510 8th Ave SW (next to the Devonian Gardens).

Also in the Lancaster Building but downstairs, is the agreeable *Unicorn Pub* with an Anglo-Irish flavour. It's a busy, friendly place which serves moderately priced food like fish & chips for $6.50 and steak & kidney pie for $7.50, and the locally brewed Warthog Ale. It's open Monday to Saturday from 11 am to 1 am. The restaurants in the Bay department store nearby on the corner of 1st St SW and Stephens Ave Mall are cheap.

Beirut Restaurant, 112 Stephens Ave Mall, offers the usual sandwiches plus Lebanese dishes, with starters for $3 to $5 and felafel for $8.

Swartzie's Bagel Noshery, 509 8th Ave SW is good for coffees and a wide range of bagels and toppings all under $5. There are good pizzas for $8 to $18 at *Baby Blues Restaurant & Lounge*, 937 7th Ave SW. Try the pizza with spinach. Live music is also featured at night.

1886 Café, on the corner of 3rd St SW and 1st Ave SW, is an interesting little place in the old Calgary Water Power Company building, established in 1886. It's a worn, white wooden building by the river near the walking bridge for Prince's Island. The YMCA recreation centre and the Eau Claire

ALBERTA

Market have helped revive the area and attract a lot of people. The cafe is extremely popular and is recommended – if you can get in. It's open for breakfast and lunch daily from 7 am to 3 pm and serves mainly omelettes for around $5.50; or try the breakfast sundae ($6.25), consisting of muesli, yoghurt and three types of fruit. There are many places for a munch in the Eau Clair Market itself, including the *Good Earth Café* offering vegetarian and health food dishes. The *YMCA* here on Eau Claire Ave has its own cheap cafeteria too.

Alberta in general, and Calgary in particular, has long had a reputation for steak – this is the heart of cattle country after all. For a downtown dinner featuring beef – prime rib or steak – try *Quincy's*, 609 7th Ave SW. It offers an attractive wood-lined dining room and moderate prices. Main courses are $15 to $20 and seafood is offered. A less expensive way to sample the local cattle is with a city lunch specialty known as beef dip. This consists of thinly sliced roast beef served plain in a long bun usually with fries and a bowl of 'sauce' to dip the meat into. In the better places this dip is nothing but juice from the roast, it should *not* be like gravy. Prices are about $5 to $7. Try either *Dusty's Saloon* at 1088 Olympic Way SE or the *Unicorn Pub*.

Sushi Hiro, near the corner of 7th St SW at 727 5th Ave SW, is a well regarded Japanese restaurant. Appetisers go for $5 to $7 and main dishes from $8 to $17. It's open Monday to Saturday from 5 to 11 pm, but is also open for lunch from 11.30 am to 2 pm.

There is a small Chinatown on 2nd and 3rd Aves at Centre St. Now largely based in a number of new shopping complexes the area is particularly lively on a Sunday around noon when the whole area is packed and lots of fresh pastries are on offer. *Diamond Bakery*, downstairs in the Good Fortune Plaza on 3rd Ave SE, is a tiny place offering tasty Chinese and Western treats and sweets from around 75 cents. The small and old *Ho Won* and *AA Seafood* on Centre St offer dim sum lunches for around $6. These places are giving way to newer, larger eateries such as the cavernous, but pleasant, *Regency Palace* in the Dragon City building, 328 Centre St. Dim sum begins at $2.50 per item here but there is an extensive menu of complete dishes. The Vietnamese *Pho Pasteur Saigon* at 207 1st St SE is recommended for its 18 kinds of beef noodle soups. Toss on the plate of vegetation that comes with it, add some sauce and you've a tasty, filling meal for under $4.

South of Downtown South across the train tracks below 9th Ave, *Cedars Deli* on the right side, just after the underpass on 1st Ave SW, is worth the short walk for good, cheap Lebanese food in a green and white setting. It has good starters for around $3.50 to $4.25 and a felafel plate for $5.25. It's closed on Sunday.

Thai Sa-On, 351 10th Ave SW, is a good Thai restaurant with lunch-time specials for $5 and main dishes at dinner from $8. It's open Monday to Saturday. Nearby at *Mother Tucker's*, 347 10th Ave SW, you can get huge sandwiches and salads for $6.50 to $8 and seafood dishes for $13 to $18. It's a very popular place and has music at night.

Further south are a couple of good areas for food searching. There's a variety of places along 17th Ave SW from 4th St SW westward for about 10 blocks. *Nellie's Kitchen*, 738 17th Ave SW near 7th St SW, is a small, pleasant cafe with good sandwiches for about $2.50 to $6 and has a patio out the back. Similarly priced, *Bagels & Buns* across the street at 807 17th Ave SW, is also good for informal breakfasts and lunches and is very popular. There are several Italian places nearby. Fourth St SW itself, between 17th and 25th Aves SW, has lots of restaurants – Greek, French, Indian, delis, etc. Just take a wander.

Other Areas North of the river off Memorial Drive within walking distance of downtown, Kensington, a district based on Kensington Rd and 10th St NW, is an old city neighbourhood with plenty of restaurants and is well worth checking out. *Sam's Deli & Pub* at 1167 Kensington Cres is a busy inexpensive place near the Plaza cinema. There are several coffee bars and patios in the area to linger at with a drink or meal.

Outside the central area, the commercial strips along Macleod Trail south and the Trans Canada Hwy east-west across the north of the city have many familiar food chains.

Well known *Peter's Drive-In* at the corner of 16th Ave NE (Highway 1) and 2nd St NE makes milkshakes worth stopping for even if you're just going right through town.

Entertainment

For complete entertainment guides pick up a copy of *Vox* or *Cityscope* available free around town and read the local newspapers. The Friday edition of the *Calgary Herald* has a lift-out called *What's Up* which tells you what's happening on the weekend and beyond.

Theatre & Nightlife The city has several live theatre venues. The *Lunchbox Theatre* (☎ 265-4292), in the Bow Valley Square on the corner of 6th Ave and 1st St SW, is a professional performing arts stage catering to downtown shoppers, workers and passers-by at lunch hours during the week. The season is from October to May. Shows vary from comedy to drama to musicals, and change regularly. They start around noon, usually with an additional afternoon pro-gramme each week. Admission is $8.

The *Calgary Centre for the Performing Arts* (☎ 294-7455), known as The Centre, is on Stephens Ave Mall on the corner of 1st St SE. It has performances by Alberta Theatre Projects (☎ 294-7475); it also has ballet, the Calgary Philharmonic Orchestra and more. The *Garry Theatre* (☎ 233-9100), 1229 9th Ave SE in Inglewood just east of the down-town area, puts on comedy and drama – old and new. *Pumphouse Theatre* (☎ 263-0079), 2140 9th Ave SW, puts on experimental plays. The *Alberta Science Centre* has laser shows and the Pleiades Theatre there puts on variety shows and mystery plays (see Alberta Science Centre section earlier). *Stage West* (☎ 243-7077), 727 42 Ave SE, is a theatre restaurant that showcases well-known stars from south of the border.

In summer the Calgary Philharmonic Orchestra has a series of free community concerts at various locations around the city. There are also free concerts by various musi-cians in McDougall Centre Park, 455 6th Ave SE. Big-name concerts are held in the Cana-dian Airlines Saddledome in Stampede Park and in the Jubilee Auditorium, 1415 14 Ave SW; tickets cost from around $35.

Many of Calgary's popular nightspots are along 17th Ave West. *Morgan's Pub*, 1324 17th Ave SW near 4th St SW, is a good spot for rock as is the *Ship & Anchor Pub* at 535. For alternative music, there's the *Republik* at 219 17th Ave West. There are other places along the street, some with dancing. On 11th Ave SW, between 4th and 6th Sts SW, (known as Electric Avenue) there is a con-centration of pubs and clubs catering to the young. Downtown, the *King Edward Hotel*, on the corner of 9th Ave SE and 4th St SE, is the city's prime blues bar. The *Unicorn Pub* has Irish music. *Dusty's Saloon*, 1088 Olympic Way SE offers live country music.

North over the river *Kensington's Deli-café*, 1414 Kensington Rd NW in Recreation Square next to the Hostel Shop, is a good restaurant and nightspot. It has cheap food, a relaxed atmosphere, live music and an outdoor patio. It's open daily. Nearby is *Pancho's* for rock 'n' roll and blues.

Bottlescrew Bill's at the corner of 1st St SW and 10th Ave SW has a vast selection of brews from around the world. There is an extensive wine by the glass selection as well. But the real wranglers will catch the annual July 'prairie oyster' cook-up at adjacent *Buzzard's*. For the uninitiated, the traditional cowboy oyster is a bull's testicle, sliced, sauteed and ready to eat. By most accounts the event is a real ball. On the corner of 10th Ave SW and 4th St SW is *Claudio's* for a beer and a game of pool and the pizza is good.

South of town the *Lake Bonavista Inn*, 747 Bonavista Drive SE, with views of the lake and mountains, is a more upmarket place for a drink. There are three casinos in town including the *Stampede Casino*, the largest, at the Big Four Building in Stampede Park. It's open until 3 am.

ALBERTA

Cinema The repertory *Plaza Theatre* (☎ 283-3636), 1113 Kensington Rd NW, has two different shows a night plus midnight performances on Friday and Saturday. It presents off-beat US and foreign films. Tickets are $6.50. The film and video department (☎ 260-2781) of *Calgary Public Library*, 616 Macleod Trail SE, sometimes screens free films. The *University of Calgary* often has films, mainly foreign, in either the 148 Science Theatre or the Boris Roubakine Recital Hall.

Spectator Sports The Calgary Flames (☎ 261-0475), arch rivals of the Edmonton Oilers, play ice hockey from October to April in the Canadian Airlines Saddledome. Tickets cost from $12 to $50. The Calgary 88s who play in the World Basketball League also use the Olympic Saddledome as a home base. The Calgary Stampeders (☎ 289-0205) of the CFL play Canadian-style professional football from July through to September in McMahon Stadium in north-west Calgary off Crowchild Trail. Tickets range from $20 to $41. The Calgary Cannons (☎ 284-1111), play their baseball home games at the Foothills Baseball Stadium from April to September.

Things to Buy
Many visitors are taken by the Western apparel seen in and around town, especially that worn around Stampede time or in country music bars. The Alberta Boot Co is the only Western boot manufacturer in the province. Visit the factory and store at 614 10th Ave SW. For cowboy hats, shirts, skirts, vests etc check out Riley and McCormick, 209 8th Ave SW. Howdy pardner.

Getting There & Away
Air Calgary International Airport is about 15 km north-east of the centre of town off Barlow Trail, a 25-minute drive.

Air Canada (☎ 265-9555), 333 5th Ave SW, and Canadian Airlines (☎ 235-1161), 407 2nd St SW, fly to many Canadian and US cities. The flights with Alaska Airlines (☎ 1-800-426-0333), American Airlines (☎ 1-800-433-7300) and Delta Airlines (☎ 263-0177), 905 530 8th Ave SW, connect Calgary with points in Alaska and mainland USA. Northwest Airlines (☎ 1-800-225-2525) flies to Winnipeg and destinations in mainland USA. United Airlines (☎ 1800-241-6522) has an office at the airport.

Air Canada operates a 40-minute commuter service to Edmonton with flights all day long. The regular one-way fare is a bit pricey at $161 (including tax) but there are cheaper flights available in off-peak times. Advance booking return fares (including tax) to some other cities are: Toronto $464, Winnipeg $370, Montreal $670, and Halifax $812. Discount fares are advertised in the travel section of Saturday's *Calgary Herald*.

Bus The Greyhound Bus Depot (☎ 265-9111), 850 16th St SW at the junction with 9th Ave SW, is a bit away from the centre. It's walkable but most people opt for the free city shuttle bus which goes to the door. It has a small shop, cafeteria and left-luggage lockers ($2) and is open daily from 5 am to 1 am. There are frequent Greyhound buses to Edmonton for $33; Vancouver via the Okanagan or Fraser Canyon for $99; Banff, $17; Drumheller, $19; and Winnipeg, $132. Fares include tax.

Red Arrow Express (☎ 531-0350) offers four luxury buses a day to Edmonton from its Calgary terminal at 205 9th Ave SE. The fare is $33 one way.

Train Despite the closure of VIA Rail's southern route it is still possible to travel by train from Calgary to Vancouver via Banff on the privately owned 'Rocky Mountaineer'. But it isn't cheap: to Vancouver the one-way fare costs from $625, double occupancy, including some food and an overnight stop in a hotel in Kamloops. The service runs between the beginning of May and mid-October. For information contact a travel agent or Rocky Mountaineer Rail Tours (☎ 604-606-7200, 1-800-665-7245), Suite 130, 1150 Station St, Vancouver.

The train station is conveniently located in the Calgary Tower.

Getting Around
The Airport The best way to and from the airport is the Airporter Bus (☎ 531-3909), which runs from 5.30 am to 11.30 pm between all major downtown hotels and the airport and costs $8.50, $15 return. One departs every 20 minutes from the Westin Hotel at 320 4th Ave SW. Alternatively you could take the C-Train north-east to White-horn then catch bus No 57 to the airport. A taxi to the airport costs about $23.

Bus & LRT Calgary Transit (☎ 262-1000), 240 7th Ave SW, operates the bus and Light Rapid Transit (LRT) rail system. The office has route maps, information and tickets and is open Monday to Friday from 8.30 am to 5 pm. Maps are also available at the tourist office. The Calgary LRT train is known as the C-Train. One fare entitles you to transfer to other buses or the C-Train. The C-Train is free in the downtown area along 7th Ave between 10th St SW and 3rd St SE. If you're going further or need a transfer, buy your ticket from a machine on the C-Train platform. A single one-way ticket costs $1.50 but you can get a day pass for $4.50.

The C-Train goes north-west to the university, north-east to the airport and south to Macleod Trail. Bus Nos 3, 17 and 53 go north-south along Centre St between the northern areas of the city and downtown. Bus No 19 runs east-west along 16th Ave (the Trans Canada Hwy). Bus No 10 goes south along the Macleod Trail.

Taxi For a cab call Alberta South Co-Op Taxi Lines (☎ 531-8294) or Yellow Cab (☎ 974-1111). It costs $2.10 for the first 220 metres and 20 cents for every 220 metres thereafter.

Car Various rental outlets can be found around town. Rent-A-Wreck (☎ 237-6880) with the lowest overall rates, charges $29.95 per day plus 12 cents for every km over 200 km. Thrifty Car Rental (☎ 262-4400), at 117 5th Ave SE, requires $50 a day with unlimited km. Budget (☎ 226-1550), 140 6th Ave SE, charges a flat $49.99 per day. These are weekday rates, weekends are less.

Hitching Thumbing within the Calgary city limits is illegal and subject to very heavy fines. The law's enforced, so forget hitching here. If you're heading west to Banff take bus No 105 from downtown and ask the driver if there's a connecting bus going further. If not, walk to the city boundary before attempting to hitch.

AROUND CALGARY
Drumheller
Little known Drumheller is slowly getting the attention it warrants. A small city in a strange setting 122 metres below prairie level, Drumheller is about 150 km north-east of Calgary in the Red Deer River Valley dinosaur country. Thousands of years of wind, glacier and water erosion have created the captivating surrounding badlands which reveal millions of years of the earth's animal and geological history.

The area is renowned for its fossils of dinosaurs, petrified wood and weird land formations. More complete dinosaur skeletons of the Cretaceous Age (from 64 to 140 million years ago) have been found in the region than anywhere else on the planet. These characteristics combined make the area one of the most intriguing in the province and a visit is well worthwhile. Even a quick one-day side trip is manageable from Calgary under two hours away but two days or more is better.

The Chamber of Commerce Information Office (☎ 823-2171) is at 60 1st Ave W and is open daily. There is also a Visitor Information Office south of the centre in the same building as the Greyhound Bus Depot and both are open Monday to Saturday from 6 am to 9 pm, Sunday from 9 am to 9 pm. Buses run to Calgary three times weekly and return the same days. See under Calgary Organised Tours for inexpensive trips to Drumheller.

Just out of town on the west side is Newcastle Beach for picnicking and swimming. Ask if Prehistoric Park with its life size models set amidst the coulees has re-opened. Vandals had caused its closure.

ALBERTA

Drumheller Dinosaur & Fossil Museum
This small museum (☎ 823-2593), 335 1st
St East, gives a good introduction to the
prehistoric life and geology of the badlands
and has remains and fossils on display. The
main display is an Edmontosaurus, a four to
five-tonne, nine-metre-long, duck-billed
dinosaur pieced together from fossils found
in 1923.

The museum is open daily in May and
June from 10 am to 5 pm, in July and August
from 10 am to 6 pm. Admission is $2.

Dinosaur Trail & Hoodoo Drive Drumheller is at the beginning of Dinosaur Trail
(Hwy 838), a 48-km loop around the area. It
takes in all the attractions but you'll need a
car or bike to cover it. The scenery along the
trail is really interesting, as are the views
from the top of **Horsethief Canyon** and
Horseshoe Canyon. There are trails
leading down into the canyons where you
can poke around in the petrified oyster beds.
In **Midland Provincial Park,** north-west of
Drumheller, you can go on self-guided
walking tours. There's no camping in the
park. Twenty-seven km north-west of
Drumheller, at the turn of the trail, you can
take the free cable-operated ferry *Bleriot*
across the river. It's been running since 1913.

The Hoodoo Drive, about 25-km long (it
only goes one way so you must return by the
same route) takes in the **hoodoos**, about 18
km south-east of Drumheller on Hwy 10.
Here can be seen the best examples of these
weird, eroded, mushroom-like columns of
sandstone rock. This area was also the site of
a once prosperous coal-mining community.
The Atlas Mine is now a provincial historic
site and is being preserved. Take the side trip
(which includes 11 bridges in six km) to
Wayne for a beer at the fabled Last Chance
Saloon.

Both roadways have numerous other stops
of interest.

Royal Tyrell Museum of Palaeontology
This excellent museum (☎ 823-7707), along
Dinosaur Trail (Hwy 838) north-west of
town, uses displays, videos, films, comput-

ers, fibre optics etc to outline the study of
early life on earth. Fossils of ancient creatures including flying reptiles, prehistoric
mammals and amphibious animals help trace
the story of evolution; best of all is the extensive display of over 30 complete dinosaur
skeletons. In 1995 the museum received the
remains of a giant prehistoric sea monster.
The 100 million-year-old whale-like creature was found in the oilsands of northern
Alberta. The museum is open daily from 9
am to 9 pm in summer while the rest of the
year it's open Tuesday to Sunday from 10 am
to 5 pm. Admission is $5.50.

Passion Play Each year in early July the
classic story of Jesus Christ is told in the Old
World-like setting of Drumheller's outskirts.
There are only about half a dozen of the
outdoor performances and they're always
sold out so ask for details in advance by
calling the tourist office.

Places to Stay & Eat A few km south of
Drumheller the small communities of
Rosedale and Wayne each have small municipal campgrounds with minimal facilities but
they're only $5. Six km north of town the
campground at Nacmine is good. Further
out, 23 km, the *Bleriot Ferry Campground*
(☎ 823-1749) has pump water and sites for
$5. In town the *Shady Grove Campground*
(☎ 823-2576), 25 Poplar St on the northern
side of the river, is open year round, has most
facilities including showers, and charges $10
for a site but is a bit shabby. A little further
north the *Dinosaur Trailer Park* (☎ 823-
3291), near the corner of Dinosaur Trail and
Hwy 9, has tent sites for $15 and showers.

Situated in an old hotel the central HI
Alexandra Hostel (☎ 823-6337), 30 Railway
Ave, holds 55 people and has showers, laundromat and kitchen. It costs $13.50 for
members, $18 for nonmembers. Family
rooms are available. Bikes can be rented.

Drumheller has several hotels on and
around Railway Ave, but one of the better
value places is the *Badlands Motel* (☎ 823-
5155) just north of town on the Dinosaur
Trail. It has log cabins from $42/46. There

are many B&Bs in and around town at $50 double.

For breakfast it's the *Diana Restaurant* at 388 Centre St. Down a few doors from Centre on 3rd Ave is the *Morning Star* for an evening cappuccino. The *Bridge Restaurant*, near the bridge serves good Greek food; try the chicken with feta cheese. Also under $10, the *Sizzling House* at 160 Centre St has surprisingly good Chinese food. Lastly, there is a cafeteria at the Tyrrell museum.

Things to Buy The Fossil Shop, 61 Bridge St immediately north of the bridge, is worth visiting for a look around and perhaps a purchase of a 75 million-year-old souvenir. There are all kinds of bones and dinosaur fragments to examine and the staff are very knowledgeable. Perhaps unexpectedly, some of the findings offered for sale are not at all expensive.

Southern Alberta

Southern Alberta is cattle-ranching country, although wheat is very important, too. Here you can visit the badlands with their unusual rock formations and vestiges of prehistoric beasts around Drumheller and Dinosaur Provincial Park, or see Head-Smashed-In Buffalo Jump where the Blackfoot used to hunt the herds of buffalo. In the south-east corner rising out of the prairies is Cypress Hills Provincial Park. In Writing-on-Stone Provincial Park you can see hoodoos and ancient petroglyphs. To the west are the spectacular Alberta Rockies.

BAR U RANCH
Located near the village of Longview west of High River the Bar U (☎ 395-2212) is a National Historic Site marking the significance of ranching to the development of the west. There is a visitors centre, and guided tours around the range are offered daily. Inquire about special events and demonstrations. Admission is $4.

LETHBRIDGE
Lethbridge, on the Crowsnest Hwy, is the largest town in southern Alberta, the third largest in the province, and a centre for the local agricultural communities. The main streets are 5th and 6th Sts South and 3rd Ave South. One of the city's landmarks, High Level Bridge, is the world's longest and highest trestle bridge. It spans the Oldman River Valley which eventually runs into Hudson Bay. The parkland along the Oldman contains 62 km of walking and cycling trails. When you walk around town you'll see some people dressed in early 19th-century clothing. These are Hutterites, members of a Protestant sect who live on collective farms and eschew many aspects of modern society.

Information
The Visitor Information Centre (☎ 320-1223) is on Brewery Hill at the western end of 1st Ave South. For information about the south-western region of Alberta visit the Chinook Country Tourist Association (☎ 320-1222), 2805 Scenic Drive South at the junction with Mayor Magrath Drive South. The main post office (☎ 320-7133) is at 704 4th Ave South on the corner of 7th St South. The Toronto Dominion Bank on the corner of 4th Ave South and 5th Ave South is open on Saturday from 9 am to 4 pm.

If you're interested in learning about Native Indian culture contact the Sik-Ooh-Kotok Friendship Society (☎ 328-2414, 327-0087), 10 535 13th St North.

Things to See
The **Nikka Yuko Japanese Gardens** (☎ 328-3511), on the corner of 7th Ave South and Mayor Magrath Drive South, were built to symbolise Japanese-Canadian friendship. These authentic gardens consist of ponds, rocks and shrubs but no flowers. The buildings and bridges were built in Japan and reassembled here. Young women in traditional Japanese costume greet you at the entrance and recite their oft-repeated descriptions. The gardens are open from mid-May to early October and admission is $3, students $2.

ALBERTA

Southern Alberta

   Top: Little barn on the prairie, Saskatchewan
 Middle: Grain silo in Denholm, Saskatchewan
Bottom: Practising steps for the Prince Albert Powwow, Saskatchewan

MARK LIGHTBODY

MARK LIGHTBODY

TOM SMALLMAN

Top: Hoodoos, a feature of the badlands of southern Alberta
Left: Moraine Lake near Lake Louise, Alberta
Right: Statue of businessmen, Stephens Ave Mall, Calgary, Alberta

On the western side of the city beside Oldman River is **Indian Battle Park**, named after a battle between the Blackfoot and the Cree, the last battle in North America between Native Indians. Within the park is **Fort Whoop-Up** (☎ 329-0444), a replica of Alberta's first and most notorious illegal whisky trading post. In 1995 after tremendous July floods the fort along with many other parts of town suffered major water damage.

Around 25 of these outposts were set up in the province between 1869 and 1874 for the purpose of trading whisky, guns, ammunition and blankets for buffalo hides, furs etc from the Native Indians. The existence of these trading posts led directly to the formation of the North-West Mounted Police who arrived in 1874 at Fort Macleod to bring law and order to the Canadian West.

Fort Whoop-Up is open Monday to Saturday from 10 am to 6 pm, Sunday from noon to 8 pm and admission is $2. Also in the park, the small **Sir Alexander Galt Museum** (☎ 320-3898), at the western end of 5th Ave South, displays artefacts from Lethbridge history. It's open daily from 10 am to 4 pm and is free.

In town under the High Level Bridge is the **Helen Schuler Coulee Centre and Nature Reserve**, with a small exhibition centre and trails amongst the woods and coulees along the river. It's free, is quiet and cool and offers a range of flora & fauna.

The **Birds of Prey Centre** (☎ 345-4262), about 10 km east of Lethbridge off the Crowsnest Hwy in Coaldale, is a rehabilitation centre for injured predatory birds such as owls, hawks and bald eagles. The admission fee of $4 goes to help wildlife conservation.

Places to Stay & Eat
The two closest campgrounds to downtown are *Bridgeview Campground* (☎ 381-2357), 910 4th Ave South off the Crowsnest Hwy north-west of town, and *Henderson Lake Campground* (☎ 328-5452), in Henderson Park off Parkside Drive (7th Ave South).

Both have showers and laundrettes and charge $14 for a tent site.

Ruth at the *Chelsea House B&B* (☎ 381-1325), 9 Dalhousie Rd West, near the university, has some hostel-style rooms for $20.

The *YWCA* (☎ 329-0088), 604 8th St South, is for women only, has a laundrette and gym and charges $22/40 for a single/double.

The *University of Lethbridge*, south-west of downtown over Oldman River, offers accommodation between May and August, with fully appointed apartments in Aperture Park costing $33/54 for singles/twins or rooms with shared facilities in University Hall for $27/48. For details contact Housing Services (☎ 329-2244), University of Lethbridge, C420, 4401 University Drive, Lethbridge T1K 3M4.

The *Alec Arms* (☎ 327-3142) is a basic, cheap, central hotel at the corner of 5th St and 4th Ave. Motels line Mayor Magrath Drive.

For good fish & chips, try *Bill's Fish Market*, 543 13th St, on the corner of 6th Ave. The more central *Bagel Café* at 313 6th St South is good and inexpensive for breakfasts and light lunches. Many restaurants can be found along the commercial strip, 3rd Ave.

Getting There & Around
The Greyhound Bus Depot (☎ 327-1551), 411 5th St South, is open daily from 9 am to 7 pm. Some sample one-way fares (including tax) are Calgary $28 and Regina $71. For information about local buses call the Transit Infoline (☎ 320-3885).

FORT MACLEOD
On Oldman River about 50 km west of Lethbridge, two hours south of Calgary, is the town of Fort Macleod. **Fort Macleod Museum** (☎ 553-4703), 219 25th St, is a replica of the North-West Mounted Police fort of 1874, the first in the region. The fort is patrolled by Mounties wearing traditional red uniforms, four times daily in July and August. Inside there is a small local history collection. Admission is $4.

For trivia enthusiasts Fort Macleod is the home town of Joni Mitchell, the popular singer/songwriter whose most famous songs include Big Yellow Taxi, Both Sides Now and Woodstock.

HEAD-SMASHED-IN BUFFALO JUMP

About 18 km north-west of Fort Macleod, Head-Smashed-In Buffalo Jump (☎ 553-2731), on Spring Point Rd off Hwy 2, is a UN World Heritage Site and the most significant attraction of southern Alberta. It's the oldest, biggest and best preserved bison-jump site in North America. For thousands of years Blackfoot used it to run bison, their 'living department stores', through drive lanes over the edge of the cliff. They then used the meat, hide, bone, horns and nearly everything else for their supplies and materials. Head-Smashed-In was one of a series of communal-kill sites and was last used for this purpose in the early 19th century. According to legend a young brave wanted to view a killing from beneath the cliff but became trapped and was crushed by the falling bison, hence the name Head-Smashed-In.

The interpretive centre, which is built into the hillside, provides explanations of the site and how the Blackfoot's work was achieved. There are nearly two km of outdoor trails. A 10-minute film, a dramatised re-enactment of the buffalo hunt, is shown regularly during the day and sometimes Native Indians perform traditional music. The centre is open daily from 9 am to 8 pm and admission is $5.50 for adults. Allow an hour for the trails and 1½ hours for the indoor displays. A small restaurant serves bison, prairie chicken and sandwiches. The site gets quite busy by late morning so arriving early is advisable and you may see deer and more birds on the trails before the sun gets too hot. See under Calgary for inexpensive tours.

TIPI VILLAGE

West of Fort Macleod near Brockett, off Highway 3, the Peigan Native Indians operate an arts & crafts centre and provide guided walks to a tipi village and along a trail offering insights into their culture, history and the surrounding land.

CROWSNEST PASS

Further west of Fort Macleod the Crowsnest Hwy heads through the prairies and into the Rocky Mountains to the Crowsnest Pass and the British Columbia border. At the turn of the century this was a rich coal-producing region which gave rise to a series of small mining towns. In 1903 one of these, Frank, was virtually destroyed when part of nearby Turtle Mountain collapsed and buried most of the town killing around 70 people. This and a number of other mining disasters, plus the fall in demand for coal, eventually led to the demise of the coal industry although one mine, at Bellevue, continued to operate until 1961.

The **Frank Slide Interpretive Centre** (☎ 562-7388), overlooks the Crowsnest Valley 1.5 km off the Crowsnest Hwy and 27 km east of the border. As well as displays on the cause and effects of the slide, it has exhibits on the coming of the railway and turn-of-the-century life and mining technology. It's open daily from 9 am to 8 pm (from 10 am to 4 pm in winter) and admission is $3.25. If you want to learn more about life in coal-mining communities **Leitch Collieries** near Coleman and the **Bellevue Mine** are also worth visiting.

CARDSTON

Cardston, south-west of Lethbridge at the junction of Hwys 5 and 2 and adjacent to the Blood Indian Reservation, is a centre for the Mormons. The town gets its name from Charles Ora Card who founded it in 1887. The huge, renovated, box-shaped **Alberta Temple** (☎ 653-4142), 348 3rd St, was built in 1923 and, although only Mormons can enter the temple itself, there's a visitor centre open daily in summer. The **Remington Alberta Carriage Centre** (☎ 653-5139), south of Lee Creek off Main St, was opened in 1993 and records the history of 19th and early 20th-century horse-drawn transportation. The collection has 200 carriages, wagons and sleighs. The centre includes a museum, carriage factory, blacksmith and stable. It's open daily from 9 am to 8 pm (to 5 pm in winter) and admission is $5.50.

WRITING-ON-STONE PROVINCIAL PARK

This park is south-east of Lethbridge close to the US border; the Sweetgrass Hills of northern Montana are visible to the south. To get to the park take Hwy 501 east off Hwy 4 from the town of Milk River, a distance of 42 km. The park gets its name from the carvings and paintings made by the Plains Indians over 3000 years ago on the sandstone cliffs along the banks of Milk River. This is North America's largest collection of rock art.

You can see some of these **petroglyphs and pictographs** for yourself if you follow the two-km hoodoo trail along the north of the valley, but the best are to be found in a restricted area (to protect them from vandalism) which you can only visit on a guided tour (free) with the park ranger. In the valley is a police outpost dating from 1887 which has been restored to its original condition.

The river is used for canoeing and swimming (there's even a small beach beside the river) and in winter there's cross-country skiing. The park also provides a wide variety of habitats for wildlife, which includes more than 160 species of birds, 30 kinds of mammals, four kinds of amphibians and three kinds of reptiles, not to mention the fish in the river. You can obtain details on all of these from the information office in the park or by contacting Writing-On-Stone Provincial Park (☎ 647-2364), PO Box 297, Milk River T0K 1M0.

The campground by the river has sites for $12 with running water and gets busy at weekends.

On the way to the park from Lethbridge, dinosaur enthusiasts may want to stop at **Devil's Coulee** near Warner where dinosaur nests and eggs were uncovered in 1987. There is an interpretive display and an active dig.

DINOSAUR PROVINCIAL PARK

No, this isn't Jurassic Park but as a World Heritage Site, it's the next best thing. The six-sq-km Dinosaur Provincial Park (☎ 378-4342) is a 76.5-million-year-old dinosaur graveyard and is a must if you're passing by. It's 48 km north-east of Brooks, roughly halfway between Calgary and Medicine Hat, off Hwy 544.

The badlands of the park are a dry, convoluted lunar landscape, but they weren't always like this: at one time the area was a tropical rainforest on the shores of an inland sea where dinosaurs thrived.

More than 300 complete skeletons have been found, and many have been sent to museums around the world. In 1995 fossil hunters made a spectacular find of a wonderfully preserved 75 million-year-old ostrich-like dinosaur. The Ornithomimid is one of only four in its condition in the world.

Entrance to the park is free and there are hiking trails and a driving loop to follow. Access to a third of the park is restricted but there are guided walks through these strange, eroded landscapes and an interpretive two-hour bus tour for $4.50 each. These popular excursions operated from late May to October should be booked at the Field Station early on the day of departure.

The **Tyrell Museum Field Station** has four display areas where nearly complete skeletons have been uncovered, dusted off and encased in glass. Archaeologists are on hand to answer questions.

A full day can easily be spent exploring. Wildlife can be seen, wildflowers are abundant and good photographs are easy; the hoodoos especially make a good subject. Take plenty of water along in summer (walking in the valley can be as hot as hell), a hat, sunscreen and insect repellent.

There are three pretty good *campgrounds* in the park by a creek which makes a small, green oasis in this stark place. A tent site costs $13. A laundrette and hot showers are available. These sites fill up regularly. There are two other provincial campgrounds in the region otherwise accommodation is available in Brooks.

ALBERTA

KINBROOK ISLAND PROVINCIAL PARK

This is a good camping spot on the way to or from Calgary. It's off the Trans Canada Hwy, 13 km south of Brooks then two km east off the secondary road 873 beside Lake Newell. The artificial lake is home to many species of waterfowl including Canada geese, blue herons, cormorants and pelicans. You can swim and fish, or simply escape the very flat, totally treeless stretch of highway between here and Medicine Hat. The campground (☎ 362-2962/4525) has 167 sites and running water.

MEDICINE HAT

This city, on the banks of the South Saskatchewan River at the junction of the Trans Canada and Crowsnest highways, was formed in 1883 when the Canadian Pacific Railway, drilling for water, hit natural gas.

Dall ram

Enough of it was subsequently found to prompt Rudyard Kipling to label it 'the city with all hell for a basement'. Even today the downtown street lamps are lit by gas.

The Visitor Information Centre (☎ 527-6422), 8 Gehring Rd SW south of downtown off the westbound side of the Trans Canada Hwy, is open daily throughout the year: summer hours are 8 am to 9 pm, winter 9 am to 5 pm. The Greyhound Bus Depot (☎ 527-4418), downtown at 557 2nd St SE, is open daily. It has left-luggage lockers and a cafeteria. Most of the accommodation is along the Trans Canada Hwy.

From the Visitor Information Centre or from the highway you can see the **'world's tallest teepee'**, a tribute to Native Indians. It's actually made of metal and was used ceremonially at the 1988 Olympic games in Calgary. There is a small cultural display and a trail around a Native Indian archaeological site by the teepee. Medicine Hat is also notable for its parks and walking trails, some of which line the South Saskatchewan River, and the fine, old red-brick buildings of downtown. If you miss Calgary's Stampede, there's one here during the last week of July or first week of August at the Exhibition & Stampede Grounds (☎ 527-1234), five km south-east of downtown off 21st Ave SE.

CYPRESS HILLS PROVINCIAL PARK

This park, an oasis of forest surrounded by seemingly endless prairie, straddles the Saskatchewan border. It is described in the Saskatchewan chapter.

The Alberta Rockies

Much of the Rocky Mountain area of Alberta, running along the British Columbia border, is contained and protected within two huge, adjacent national parks, Banff to the south and Jasper to the north. The Icefields Parkway links the two, though there is no real boundary. Adjoining the southern boundary of Banff National Park is Kananaskis Country, an outdoor recreational area.

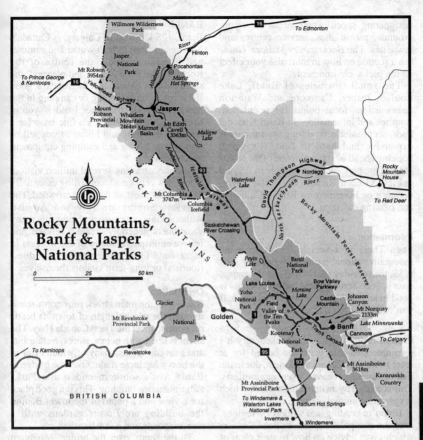

Rocky Mountains, Banff & Jasper National Parks

To the south on the US border is the less-visited Waterton Lakes National Park.

The entire area is one of spectacular beauty with some of the best scenery, climbing, hiking and skiing in the world. The national parks offer jagged, snow-capped mountains, peaceful valleys, rushing rivers, natural hot springs and alpine forests. The opaque emerald-green or milky-turquoise colour of many Rocky Mountain lakes will have you doubting your eyes. The parks also have modern conveniences or backcountry trails to choose from and wildlife abounds, particularly in Jasper National Park.

Banff National Park was Canada's first national park and is the best known and most popular. It covers an area of 6641 sq km and contains 25 mountains of 3000 metres or more in height. The skiing and climbing are world famous. Jasper National Park is larger, wilder and less explored but, like Banff National Park, offers excellent hiking trails. Waterton Lakes National Park, the smallest of the national parks, contains wildlife, scenery and activities to match its northern neighbours.

In order to preserve the region, the Canada Parks Service controls visitors' impact by designating specific park areas for camp-grounds, picnic sites, service centres and townsites. The *Backcountry Visitors' Guide* has a section on how to minimise your effect on the parks' environment.

The small townsites of Banff, Lake Louise, Jasper, Canmore and Waterton Lakes act as focal points for orientation, supplies and information. In Banff National Park, accommodation during the summer is expensive and hard to find. It's worth booking ahead or staying in one of the towns outside the park such as Canmore in Alberta or Field, Golden, Radium Hot Springs, Windermere or Invermere in British Columbia and making day trips.

Information

Fees There is a vehicle fee to enter the mountain national parks. The one-day pass is $8, the four-day pass is $16 and the annual pass is $60. Seniors rates are less. A pass is good in any of the regional national parks. If you're cycling or on a bus there is no charge.

Precautions When in the backcountry it's recommended that water be boiled for at least 10 minutes before drinking it, due to the risk of catching 'beaver fever' or giardiasis. This is caused by an intestinal parasite which is spread by animal waste.

If you're heading into wilderness regions, read the pamphlet *You are in Bear Country* which gives advice on how to steer clear of dangerous encounters with bears and what to do if this becomes unavoidable. You can get a copy from Visitor Information Centres.

The trails heavily used by horse trips are a real mess; long-distance hikers will want to avoid them. Ask at the park-warden offices or the Visitor Information Centres which trails are used most by the horses.

Tenters should note that pretty well all the campgrounds in and around the Rockies are covered in pebbles or stones which are rather lumpy for sleeping on the ground. A sleeping pad or foam mattress of some description is more-or-less essential. Also, you can expect to bend or snap a few tent pegs.

BANFF

Banff, 138 km west of Calgary, is Canada's No 1 resort town in both winter and summer and as such is really the centre of the Rockies. The town is neat and pleasant, the surroundings unbeatable. It makes a good R&R spot after travelling or camping in the backcountry. On the other hand if you're keen to get exploring, it's a fine base for a range of day trips and hikes. Stores sell or rent skiing, hiking and camping equipment and supplies.

Despite attracting several million visitors a year, it's very small, consisting essentially of one main street, so it can get crowded. The heaviest months are July and August. Although this can cause problems, the many vacationers generally create a relaxed and festive atmosphere. Many of the workers in and around town are newcomers, 'gorbies' (tourists) or long-term visitors themselves.

Orientation

Banff Ave, the main street, runs north-south through the whole length of town. It heads off north to meet the Trans Canada Hwy. The street is lined with hotels, stores, restaurants and souvenir shops, many of which cater to the heavy Japanese trade. Over the bridge at Banff Ave's southern end is the Parks Administration building. This is a good place for a view and a photo of the town. Behind the building are flower gardens with a stream, ponds and a few benches.

To the south, over the bridge, Mountain Ave leads to Sulphur Mountain and the hot springs, while Spray Ave leads to the Banff Springs Hotel, the town's most famous landmark. To the west, Cave Ave goes to the Cave & Basin Hot Springs; these were the first springs found in the area and led to the creation of the national park.

The side streets in town are mainly residential but the central ones also have eating spots and a few shops. Safeway, the best grocery store in town, is on Elk St.

Information

Tourist Offices The Park Information Office and the Chamber of Commerce both have counters in the Visitor Information Centre (☎ 762-1550), 224 Banff Ave near the corner of Wolf St in the centre of town. Before doing any hiking, check in here: there are detailed maps and the staff will tell you about specific trail conditions and hazards. Anybody hiking overnight must sign in. The office also has the leaflet, *You are in Bear Country*. Free naturalist programmes and guided hikes happen regularly. The centre is open daily from 8 am to 8 pm in summer.

Money If you need to change money the Foreign Currency Exchange (☎ 762-4698) in the Clock Tower Village Mall is open daily from 9 am to 9 pm.

Post The main post office (☎ 762-2586), 204 Buffalo St on the corner of Bear St, at the southern end of downtown, is open Monday to Friday from 9 am to 5.30 pm.

Bookshops & Library The Book & Art Den (☎ 762-3919), 110 Banff Ave, is an excellent bookshop with all manner of guides and books on the mountains, hiking, canoeing and the history of the area.

The public library (☎ 762-2661) is at 101 Bear St opposite the post office.

Medical Services Mineral Springs Hospital (☎ 762-2222) is on Bow Ave near the corner of Wolf St.

Emergency The Banff Warden Office (☎ 762-1470; in emergencies ☎ 762-4506), is open 24 hours daily year round.

Work Employment is usually easy to come by in and around Banff in the hotels, bars, restaurants and ski areas. However, working without a permit has become more difficult for non-Canadians and many establishments are now having to ask for proper documentation. If you want to be absolutely sure of being able to earn some money, inquiring at home for the correct visa is advisable.

Some employers offer accommodation, but don't expect great pay. At some of the hotels accommodation may be included or offered at modest rates. Look for classified advertisements in the local newspaper *Crag & Canyon* and signs in the windows.

Laundry Johnny O's Emporium, open daily at 223 Bear St, makes doing the chore a little more agreeable as they have a TV lounge, restaurant and pinball games to pass the time.

Warning Police are very strict in Banff and after 1 am, cars are often checked for drunk drivers and drugs. The fines are heavy. Drinking on the street or even carrying an open beer can or bottle is illegal. Hitchhikers should be aware they may often be thoroughly checked out. Cars are frequently broken into so don't leave valuables in them, especially at night.

Lastly, a warning from a reader about the elk in Banff:

The elk in Banff seem tame and, yes, they do stand in people's gardens munching away at the flowers, but they are still wild animals and will charge if they feel threatened. People have been attacked and it's advisable to stay 100 metres away particularly during the rutting and calving seasons.

Linda Broschofsky

Museums
Banff Park Museum The park museum (☎ 762-1558), 93 Banff Ave by the Bow River Bridge at the southern end of town, is housed in an old wooden building dating from 1903. The museum has been declared a National Historic Site and contains a collection of animals, birds and plants found in Banff National Park. Included are two small stuffed grizzlies and a black bear so you can study the difference. There's also an 1841 graffiti-carved tree. The museum is open daily from 10 am to 6 pm in summer (from 1 to 5 pm the rest of the year) and admission is $2.25 for adults. At 11 am and 3 pm daily there is a free half-hour tour.

Natural History Museum This museum (☎ 762-4747), on the 2nd floor of the Clock Tower Village Mall at 112 Banff Ave, has displays on early life forms, including Canadian dinosaurs. It has video and slide

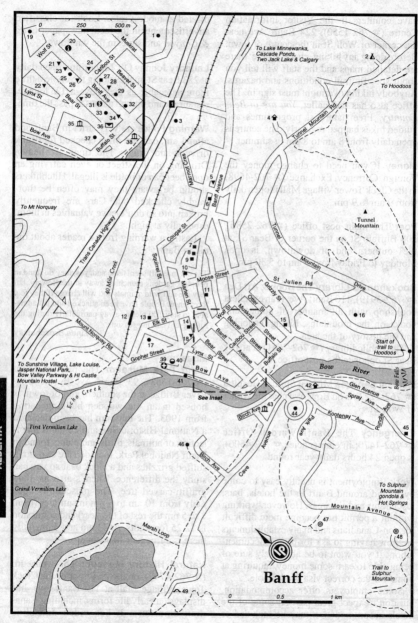

Banff

presentations, fossils and features a model of the notorious Sasquatch, the abominable snowman of the Rockies. The Sasquatch of Western Canada is said to be about three metres tall and to have been spotted over 500 times. You can also read descriptions of Castleguard Cave, one of Canada's biggest at 12 km long, which is in the north of Banff National Park. The museum is open daily in summer from 10 am to 10 pm and is free.

Luxton Museum Luxton Museum (☎ 762-2388), 1 Birch Ave in the fort-like wooden building to the right as you head south over the bridge, is worth a visit. It deals mainly with the Native Indians of the Northern Plains and the Rockies but also covers indigenous groups from all over Alberta. The museum has life-sized displays, models and re-creations depicting aspects of their traditional cultures. Note the woven porcupine quills, the old photographs and the human scalp as well as the stuffed animals. There is also an interesting shop. Admission is $4.50 adult and the museum is open from 9 am to 9 pm daily in summer, from 10 am to 5 pm the rest of the year.

Whyte Museum The Whyte Museum complex (☎ 762-2291), 111 Bear St between Buffalo and Caribou Sts, contains an art gallery and a vast collection of photographs telling the history of the area. The archives also contain manuscripts, oral history tapes and maps. On the property are four log cabins and two Banff heritage homes, one dating from 1907 and one from 1931. There are guided tours, including one of the heritage homes, Tuesday to Sunday. The foundation presents films, lectures and concerts regularly. It's open daily in summer from 10 am to 6 pm with reduced hours through winter. Cost is $3, seniors and students, $2.

Banff Centre

The Banff Centre (☎ 762-6300), on St Julien Rd east of the downtown area, contains one of Canada's best known art schools with facilities for dance, theatre, music and the visual arts. Exhibits, concerts and various other events are presented regularly. Throughout the summer during the Festival of the Arts, students, together with internationally recognised artists, present their works in workshops and performances. There is something almost every day with some events free. The Visitor Information Centre has a complete schedule.

PLACES TO STAY					
2	Tunnel Mountain Village Campground	18	Banff Coffee Co	25	Sundance Mall
4	HI Banff Hostel	21	Smitty's Family Restaurant	29	Silver City
6	Spruce Grove Motel	22	Melissa's Restaurant	31	Bank of Montreal
7	Irwin's Motor Inn	23	Joe Btfsplk's Diner	32	Clock Tower Village Mall
8	Red Carpet Inn	24	Rose & Crown	33	Barbary Coast
9	High Country Inn	26	Grizzly House	35	Whyte Museum
10	Mrs McHardy B&B	28	The Balkan Restaurant	36	Main Post Office
11	Mr & Mrs Harnack B&B	30	Magpie & Stump	37	Public Library
13	Mrs C Riva B&B	34	Le Beaujolais	38	Banff Park Museum
14	Holiday Lodge			39	Mineral Springs Hospital
15	Tan-Y-Bryn	**OTHER**		40	Bus Terminus
27	Mt Royal Hotel			41	Canoe Dock
42	YWCA	1	Buffalo Paddock	43	Luxton Museum
45	Banff Springs Hotel	3	Banff Warden Office	44	Parks Administration Building
		12	Train Station	46	Martin Stables
PLACES TO EAT		16	Banff Centre	47	Middle Springs
		17	RCMP	48	Upper Hot Springs
5	Bumper's Beef House	19	Safeway Groceries	49	Cave & Basin National Historic Site
		20	Visitor Information Centre		

ALBERTA

Harmony Drug

In this drugstore at 111 Banff Ave take a look at the old photos, dating from about 1915, all around the ceiling. Some were taken by Byron Harmon, who once owned the drugstore and ran a photography business. Many of that business's early photos are for sale around town, and reproduced in books or as postcards.

Buffalo Paddock

Just north-west of Banff on the Trans Canada Hwy (entrance from the westbound lane only), this 40-hectare enclosure of poplar forest contains a small breeding herd of wood bison. Admission is free and you can drive through, but *don't* get out of your vehicle. Evening or early morning is the best time to visit; during the middle of the day the beasts tend to keep a low and docile profile, out of view. Nearby, at the airport alongside the Trans Canada watch for the elk often seen lazily grazing on the grass runway.

Sulphur Mountain & Gondola

Sulphur Mountain gondola (☎ 762-5438) runs to the summit and provides spectacular views of the surrounding mountains, Bow River and Banff townsite from an altitude of 2285 metres. You can walk up in about 1¼ hours if you don't fool around, and are rewarded with a free lift down; tickets are only needed going up.

The lower terminal is just over three km south of Banff on Mountain Ave, near the Upper Hot Springs. To get there, you can hitch fairly easily or take the Brewster Gray Line bus from town. The walking path starts under the gondola cables. The gondola runs from 9 am to 8 pm in the summer, with shorter hours in the winter. Tickets are $9 for adults.

Upper Hot Springs

There is a soothing hot pool and steam room at the Upper Hot Springs spa (☎ 762-1515), three km south of town near Sulphur Mountain. You can also get a massage. Admission to the pool is $5 and you can rent bathing suits ($1.50) and towels ($1). In summer the very busy hot springs are open daily from 8 am to 11 pm. Shorter hours are kept the rest of the year. Ahhhhhh.

Cave & Basin National Historic Site

It was the discovery of the hot sulphur springs in a cave here that led to the creation of Banff National Park. The swimming pool and complex (☎ 762-1557), south-west of town at the end of Cave Ave has been rebuilt to the original style of 1914 but there is no bathing at the site. Visitors can see (and smell) the cave and sulphurous waters as well as view exhibits and a film. Admission is $2.25 for adults. It's open daily from 9 am to 7 pm between the end of May and early September (from 9.30 am to 5 pm the rest of the year).

The attractive grounds can be walked around for no charge and both natural and man-made pools can be seen. It's a good place for picnics as there are tables, a fine view and a snack bar. Several pleasant short walks begin here: the 400-metre **Discovery Trail**; the 2.7-km **Marsh Loop**; and the 3.7-km **Sundance Trail**.

Lake Minnewanka

Lake Minnewanka, the largest lake in the park, 11 km east of Banff townsite, is a scenic recreational area surrounded by forests and mountains with hiking, swimming, sailing, boating and fishing available. Lake Minnewanka Boat Tours (☎ 762-3473; 762-6767 for bus pick up) has a 1½-hour cruise on the lake to Devil's Gap for $20.

Activities

Hiking There are many good short hikes and day walks around the Banff area. From the Visitor Information Centre get a copy of *Drives & Walks* which describes trails in and around Banff. For longer, more remote hiking, the leaflet *Backcountry Visitors' Guide* has a map showing trails in the whole park. Some good walks begin more or less right in town, like the ones to Tunnel Mountain and the hoodoos; others begin a little further out.

You can take a pleasant, quiet stroll by **Bow**

River just three blocks west of Banff Ave beside Bow Ave. The trail runs from the corner of Wolf St, along the river under the Bow River Bridge and ends shortly thereafter on Buffalo St. If you cross the bridge, you can continue left through the woods along a trail to **Bow Falls** – it's not far.

For a good short climb to break in the legs and to view the town and area, walk up stubby **Tunnel Mountain** east of the downtown area. There's a trail leading up from St Julien Rd; you can drive here, but it's not a long walk from downtown to the start of the path. From the southern end of Buffalo St a trail between Bow River and Tunnel Mountain heads north to the **hoodoos**.

Just west of downtown off Mt Norquay Rd is the two-km **Fenland Trail** loop which goes through marsh and forest and connects the town with First Vermilion Lake. If you follow Banff Ave north from town towards Lake Minnewanka for about five km you come to **Cascade Ponds**, just past the Trans Canada Hwy. There you can follow the trail north to join the **Bankhead Interpretive Trail** or climb up beside the waterfall for good views.

One good hike that's not difficult is the **Johnston Canyon Trail**, 25 km north-west of Banff on the **Bow Valley Parkway** (Hwy 1A), that branches off, then later rejoins, the Trans Canada Hwy en route to Lake Louise. The 12-km trail goes by many waterfalls, including two large ones, to some underground-fed crystal-clear, blue-green pools known as the Ink Pots. Here in the meadow is an ideal picnic spot. The first 2.7 km of the trail, mainly stairs, is busy as it winds through the woods by the falls and is well worthwhile as a short walk on its own. Along the Bow Valley Parkway watch for impressive **Castle Mountain**, a huge piece of rock that catches the late afternoon light. From Castle Mountain you can follow the **Rockbound Lake Trail** which is 18 km return, takes about six to seven hours and has some strenuous patches. The trailhead is opposite HI Castle Mountain Hostel.

At **Sunshine Village** you'll find long and short trails. On one of the trails you can walk across the boundary into British Columbia. A popular trail is the overnight trip to nearby **Egypt Lake**. From Sunshine Village it's a long, steady climb with great scenery over **Healy Pass**, including views to Mt Assiniboine (3618 metres) in British Columbia. You'll see lots of butterflies and flowers in the alpine meadows. You can take hikes to the higher lakes and fish for cutthroat trout. At the lakes is a basic hut that sleeps about 10 people, but you should register in Banff before you go because it may be booked out. There's tenting around the hut so a place inside is not essential. **Mt Norquay** offers good hiking trails.

Swimming, Fishing, Lazing Johnson Lake, north-east of town off Lake Minnewanka Rd, is ideal for whiling away an afternoon. The shallow water gets warm enough for a dip, there are picnic tables by the shore and you can even cast a line in here and there by following one of the lakeside paths. On the far side there's a rope hanging from a tree you can use to swing out over the water just like Huckleberry Finn. Also see Lake Minnewanka listed above. People wishing to fish should get a permit at the visitor centre.

Canoeing & Rafting You can go canoeing on **Two Jack Lake** north-east of Banff, the **Vermilion Lakes** (which have lots of wildlife) west of town, **Echo Creek, 40 Mile Creek** and **Bow River**. Rocky Mountain Raft Tours (☎ 762-3632), rents canoes for $12/36 per hour/day from Canoe Dock by the river on the corner of Bow Ave and Wolf St. It also offers a one-hour rafting tour on the Bow River from Bow Falls to the hoodoos for $22.

Numerous companies offer whitewater rafting on area rivers. Wet 'n' Wild (☎ 1-800-668-9119) has exciting trips down the Kicking Horse River from Golden. Half-day trips are $45, full day $69 with lunch and transport from Banff. Kootenay River Runners (☎ 762-5385), on the corner of Bear St and Caribou St, also has half-day and full-day trips.

ALBERTA

Cycling You can cycle on the highways and on some of the trails in the park. Contact the Visitor Information Centre for trail conditions and permits. Excursions for a few hours, a day or several days with overnight stops at campgrounds, hostels or lodges are all possible. No cycling is allowed off the trails. Two good, short cycling routes close to Banff are along **Vermilion Lakes Drive** and **Tunnel Mountain Drive**. For a longer trip the scenic, 24-km **Bow Valley Parkway** connecting Banff and Lake Louise is very popular.

Rocky Mountain Worldwide Cycle Tours (☎ 678-6770) has trips along the Icefield and Bow Valley parkways for $80, and others. For bicycle rentals see the Getting Around section later.

Horse Riding In Banff the most popular routes are south of Bow River on the trail beside **Spray River**, the **Marsh Loop**, the **Sundance Trail**, the trail alongside **Cave Ave** and the one to **Middle Springs**. Holidays on Horseback operated by Warner Guiding & Outfitting (☎ 762-4551), 132 Banff Ave, offers horse-riding trips from one hour to one week in length. Rates start at $20 per hour. They have three other offices including one at the old-west-like Martin Stables (☎ 762-2832), on Birch Ave off Cave Ave toward the Cave & Basin site where the horses can be seen.

Climbing Quite a few companies offer climbing courses and organised tours into the mountains. Beginners can start by using the climbing wall Monday, Tuesday or Thursday from 7 am to 9 pm at Mountain Magic Equipment (☎ 762-2591), 224 Bear St. It has classes here for $15 from Monday to Friday and outdoor classes from $40. Experienced climbers can use the wall free of charge.

The Canadian School of Mountaineering (☎ 678-4134) is just outside the park in Canmore at 629 9th St. A weekend of rock climbing costs $140 for beginners or $200 for those at the intermediate level; it also has snow and ice climbing. Most fees include

dormitory accommodation, breakfast, equipment and instruction. Banff Alpine Guides (☎ 678-6091) offer climbing instruction and guided climbs from $250 a day but you really need your own group. The Alpine Club of Canada (☎ 678-3200) in Canmore can provide information and/or a guide.

Skiing Two of the finest ski centres in Canada are here. They have runs for skiers of all abilities and run shuttle buses from Banff. The least expensive, most convenient ski holiday is a package which includes accommodation and lift passes and sometimes a few extras.

Mt Norquay, nine km north of Banff along Mt Norquay Rd, has difficult runs and moguls and offers night skiing. The season is from early December to April. A day pass is $32. For information and snow report contact Mt Norquay (☎ 762-4421), PO Box 1258, Banff T0L 0C0.

Sunshine Village, 22 km north-west of Banff, has all natural snow; tons of it, which means the longest ski season lasting about seven months from mid-November to late-May. It has 62 runs, 60% intermediate and one which is eight km long. A day pass is $41. For information call or write to Sunshine Village (☎ 762-6500) PO Box 1510, Banff T0L 0C0. For the snow report call ☎ 762-6543.

CMH (☎ 762-7100), 217 Bear St, specialises in four to 10-day heli-skiing trips to some of the best and most remote areas in the western mountain ranges. These superb trips are in the $5000 range. Both companies use ski areas in BC.

Organised Tours
Brewster Gray Line (☎ 762-6767) does a three-hour tour of Banff for $33. The bus goes to the hoodoos, Bow Falls, Tunnel Mountain Drive, Buffalo Paddock and Sulphur Mountain.

Brewster Gray Line also runs tours to Lake Louise, the Columbia Icefield and Jasper. The tour to Lake Louise goes via the Vermilion Lakes and Bow Valley Parkway stopping at Johnston Canyon and Castle

Mountain. The round trip takes four hours and costs $36 but you can do it cheaper one way. The tour to the Columbia Icefield in Jasper National Park takes approximately 9½ hours one way and costs $65. The longer return trip to Jasper takes two days and requires an overnight stay there; you travel to Lake Louise, then along the Icefields Parkway stopping at the Columbia Icefield with time allowed for a ride on the Athabasca Glacier, though that's not included in the price. The return fare is $90 and accommodation is extra. All rates are cheaper outside the peak season.

For budgeters, ask about Bigfoot's Backpacker Adventure Tours booked through the Banff HI hostel. They have economical tour/transportation trips to Kamloops and Vancouver with stops along the way.

Rocky Express Tours runs good, six-day low-cost adventure bus trips between Calgary, Banff and Jasper. For details see under tours in Calgary. Booking can also be arranged through the HI hostel in Banff. In midsummer two to three weeks advance registration is advised.

Helicopter tours offering spectacular views of the park are also available. Some popular sights are Mt Assiniboine, the Goat and Sundance mountain ranges, Hidden Glacier and the Three Sisters. Operators include Mountain Wings (☎ 678-6465) with a mountain-top afternoon tea trip, and Canadian Helicopters (☎ 678-2207) with heli-hiking among their many options. There are several other companies and all are based in Canmore. Rates start at $80 for a 20-minute flight.

If you're driving, you can buy self-guiding auto cassette tapes that describe the journey between Banff and Jasper via Lake Louise and the Columbia Icefield Parkway. They're available at Miles High Image Centre (☎ 752-5221), 119 Banff Ave for $22.

Places to Stay

Generally, accommodation here is fairly costly and in summer hard to find. Booking ahead is strongly recommended. The numerous motels are usually expensive, the hotels more so. If you're not camping or hostelling, B&Bs and private tourist homes can be a reasonable alternative. They are often more interesting as well as good sources of local information.

To avoid accommodation in Banff some people stay in the towns of Canmore or Golden just outside the park, where the rates are lower, and then enter the park on a day basis.

Camping There are many campgrounds in the area around Banff. Most are only open between May or June and September. Note that they are all busy in July and August, and availability is on a first-come, first-served basis so book in by noon or you may well be turned away. Campgrounds with showers are always full first.

Tunnel Mountain Village is not bad. Tunnel Mountain is close to town and has three sites all with showers, two for RVs only and one for tents at $15 per site. At night you may hear coyotes yelping and howling. At Two Jack Lake there are a couple of campgrounds. *Two Jack Lakeside*, 12 km north-east of Banff on Lake Minnewanka Rd, is open from July to early September and costs $15 per site. One km north, *Two Jack Lake Main* has 381 sites at $12 each. Both campgrounds have running water but no showers. Along the Bow Valley Parkway there is a campground at Johnston Canyon, about 26 km west of Banff, for $15 with showers. It's wooded and secluded though trains whistle by at night. Castle Mountain two km north of Castle Junction costs $12.

Alternatively, there are those who unfold sleeping bags anywhere in the woods surrounding Banff, including just up the road towards Sulphur Mountain. If you do this *don't* ever light a fire or use the food bag for a pillow. Who knows what animal is on the prowl?

Hostels HI *Banff Hostel* (☎ 762-4122), on Tunnel Mountain Rd three km from the downtown area, has 154 beds in small rooms, a cafeteria, laundromat and a common room with a fireplace. Members pay $17, nonmembers $22. The *YWCA* (☎ 762-3560), 102 Spray Ave, is more central but the facilities aren't as good. It takes men and women, can hold up to 60 people and has a cafeteria but no cooking facilities. Dorm beds are $19, and rooms are $49/52 without/with bath.

HI *Castle Mountain Hostel* on the Bow Valley Parkway, holds up to 36 people, has pit toilets, hot showers and volleyball courts. For members a dorm bed is $11, for nonmembers $16.

B&Bs & Tourist Homes The Chamber of Commerce desk in the Visitor Information Centre has a list of people offering B&B and tourist-home accommodation. They can be contacted at 224 Banff Ave, PO Box 1298, Banff, Alberta T0L 0C0. Some places rent out rooms in their houses, others in small separate cabins.

The prices for B&Bs and tourist homes vary, depending on their size and facilities, your duration of stay and the season, but are generally in the $25 to $80 range for a single or double. Banff has quite a few but you should telephone around first. Some prefer at least a week's stay, some prefer not to take young people or may ask if you're married.

A real bargain is *Mr & Mrs Harnack* (☎ 762-3619), 338 Banff Ave, with six rooms from $25 single or double. They also have two larger self-contained cabins out the back. *Mrs C Riva* (☎ 762-3431), 328 Elk St, has one room ($40) and one cabin ($50) with accommodation for up to eight people. Also try *Tan-Y-Bryn* (☎ 762-3696), 118 Otter St, with room for 20 people in eight rooms. Cost is $25 to $45 all year.

Marten St has several tourist homes. *Holiday Lodge* (☎ 762-3648), 311 Marten St, run by George Baptist, is one of the nicest in town. George is a good source of information about Banff and cooks a great breakfast. Out the back are two cabins with cooking facilities which hold four people. Rooms cost between $40 and $80. *Mrs McHardy* (☎ 762-2176), 412 Marten St, offers cabins with hot plates for $45 a double.

Hotels Banff has no cheap hotels. Downtown, *Rundle Manor Apartment Hotel* (☎ 762-5544), 348 Marten St, has rooms for $115 a single or double and more costly ones with kitchens. Children under 16 years of age can stay in their parents' room for free. The *Mt Royal Hotel* (☎ 762-3331), 138 Banff Ave, with a sauna and hot tub is $150 single or double. The historic *Banff Springs Hotel* (☎ 762-2211), on Spray Ave south of downtown, has everything including a golf course, tennis courts, riding stables, bars, restaurants and fresh sushi. Singles or doubles cost from $165 to $337.

Motels Most accommodation is in motels, many of which are on Banff Ave north of Elk St; they are not cheap either but are not as costly as the hotels. There are many places geared for skiers, which offer kitchens and can be good value if there are four of you or more. Of course, there are many deluxe places too if you're looking to really splurge.

The cheapest motel in town is the *Spruce Grove Motel* (☎ 762-2112), 545 Banff Ave, with standard rooms with colour TV from $39 to $65 depending on season. *Red Carpet Inn* (☎ 762-4184), 425 Banff Ave, is close to town and charges $80/90. It has a licensed restaurant and spa and is usually full in summer. Close by, *Irwin's Motor Inn*, 429 Banff Ave, has covered parking and charges $120.

High Country Inn (☎ 762-2236), 419 Banff Ave, has air-con and heated parking and rooms for $90/95. If you don't want to stay in town, *Johnston Canyon Resort* (☎ 762-2971) is one of the cheaper motels but it's 26 km west on the Bow Valley Parkway. Singles or doubles cost from $55 to $75, more with a kitchen. Groceries are available. The resort is open mid-May to the end of September.

Places to Eat
Like any resort town, Banff has plenty of restaurants. It's a good place to catch up on a meal or two if you've been in the backcountry. There are plenty of places to choose from but prices tend to be a bit high.

Places to Eat – bottom end For reasonably priced meals try *Café Alpenglow* in the HI Banff Hostel and the *cafeteria* in the YWCA. Their breakfast specials cost around $4. If you make an early start you can have the breakfast special in the *Summit Restaurant* atop Sulphur Mountain for $3.95 between 8.30 and 9.30 am.

There are several places opposite the Visitor Information Centre. *Joe Btfsplk's Diner* (pronounced 'bi-tif-splik'), 221 Banff Ave, is a US-style diner with juke boxes on the walls, open daily and busy from 8 am to 10 pm. It has breakfast of two eggs, bacon and toast for $6, burgers from $6.25 and is good.

At *Smitty's Family Restaurant*, 227 Banff Ave, the five pancakes with syrup at $5.29 and the special at $4.25 are good breakfast value. It's open daily from 6.30 am to 10 pm but find lunch and dinner elsewhere.

On the upper level of the Sundance Mall is *Fossil Face Café* serving healthful and organic soups, salads, sandwiches, hot dishes and desserts daily. A lunch is $6 and it's a nice place to sit and write a postcard.

For those of you who would rather be eating chocolate, go to *Welch's Chocolate Shop* at 126 Banff Ave. It's great for on the trails, and besides, you're burning off calories, right?

The *Banff Coffee Co* at the corner of Wolf and Bear Sts has snacks and good coffee.

Places to Eat – middle For something spicier try the popular *Magpie & Stump*, 203 Caribou St on the corner of Bear St. Built like an old-style saloon with cosy brown colours inside, it serves mainly Mexican (including vegetarian) food like tacos, enchiladas and burritos from $10. It also serves steaks and is open from noon till midnight. Meals are cheaper at lunch time.

Also up the ladder a rung is *Melissa's Restaurant*, 217 Lynx St near the corner of Caribou St, looking sort of like a wood cabin inside and sort of like an English cottage outside. The menu includes pizza, burgers, steaks and seafood with main dishes between

$8 to $20. It has a bar and is open daily from 7 am to 10 pm.

The *Balkan Restaurant*, 120 Banff Ave, is a moderately priced Greek-style restaurant with a very good reputation, open daily from 11 am to 11 pm. It offers Greek dishes like moussaka and souvlaki plus pastas and seafood. Dinner including side dishes and salad costs between $9 and $18.

Places to Eat – top end For a splurge, try *Grizzly House*, 207 Banff Ave, open daily from 11.30 am to midnight. It's basically a fondue place with prices for main courses starting from $17. It serves a variety of food including beef, seafood and escargots. Appetisers like onion soup are $4.95 while rattlesnake fondue, at the top of the price list, is $56!

Bumper's Beef House, 603 Banff Ave north of downtown behind a service station, serves good prime rib or barbecued ribs for around $18, and has a salad bar and casual atmosphere. *Le Beaujolais*, 212 Buffalo St on the corner of Banff Ave, is expensive but highly rated. A French dinner for two is $80 *before* wine, tip and tax. The restaurant is open daily from 6 to 11 pm.

Entertainment
Banff is the social and cultural focus of the Rockies. You can find current listings in the free *Bow Valley This Week* newspaper or the monthly *Wild Life*.

The *Banff Centre* (☎ 762-6300), St Julien Rd, presents movies, theatre and concerts throughout the year, but especially from June to late August during the Festival of the Arts, when it puts on over 80 performances.

The theatre (☎ 762-4214) in the *Rundle United Church*, 104 Banff Ave on the corner of Buffalo St, shows the one-hour movie *Challenge*, at 4, 7 and 9 pm daily in summer. (For a description see Entertainment under Jasper later.)

The *Rose & Crown*, 202 Banff Ave on the corner of Caribou St, is a British-style pub and restaurant which has live rock music and one room where you can play darts. *Silver City*, 110 Banff Ave, is a bar with live music at weekends; it's open from 4 pm to 2 am. *Barbary Coast*, upstairs at 119 Banff Ave, has rock music nightly.

Many of the larger hotels and motels provide their own live entertainment.

Getting There & Away

Bus Greyhound (☎ 762-6767) buses run from the Brewster Transportation Depot, 100 Gopher St, near the police station. There are six buses daily to Vancouver. Some Vancouver buses stop at Lake Louise village, some also stop in Kelowna or Kamloops. One bus makes the journey via Radium Hot Springs. You can stop off at Lake Louise for free with a ticket on to Vancouver provided you let the company know beforehand. Note that some buses go to Lake Louise village, and others go all the way down to the lake which can be helpful. The one-way fare including tax to Lake Louise village is $9. For Calgary, there are five daily at $17. Brewster Transportation (☎ 762-6767) has one bus a day to Jasper; it takes about 4½ hours and the one-way fare is $40. It also operates a bus daily between Calgary's international airport and Banff for $30. Laidlaw Transportation (☎ 762-9102) also goes once to Calgary's airport but picks up at hotels.

Train VIA Rail no longer goes through Banff. However, the privately owned 'Rocky Mountaineer' travels via Banff between Calgary and Vancouver. The basic one-way fare from Banff to Vancouver is $565 double occupancy which includes some meals and an overnight stop in a hotel in Kamloops. The service runs between the middle of May and early October. There are seven trips a month in June, July and August. For information contact a travel agent or Rocky Mountain Rail Tours (☎ 604-606-7200; or 1-800-665-7245), Suite 130 1150 Station St, Vancouver V6A 2X7.

The train station is the ochre building at the northern end of Lynx St past the police station, close to the downtown area.

Car The major car-rental companies have offices in Banff. Their addresses are:

Avis
 Cascade Plaza, Wolf St
 (☎ 762-3222, 1-800-879-2847)
Budget
 204 Wolf St (☎ 762-4565)
Hertz
 Banff Springs Hotel, Spray Ave
 (☎ 762-2027, 1-800-263-0600)
Tilden
 Corner of Lynx St & Caribou Ave
 (☎ 762-2688, 1-800-387-4747)

Budget charges $42 a day with 100 free km and then 15 cents per km. Insurance is $12.95 a day. Weekly rates are $235 with 1000 free km. Tilden's prices are about the same with slightly higher km fees. Rates vary all the time so ring around. During the busy summer months the weekends especially can be booked out, so reserving in advance is a good idea.

Getting Around

Bus Banff Explorer Transit Service operates two bus routes through town. One goes along Spray and Banff Aves between Banff Springs Hotel and the RV parking lot north of town for $1; the other goes from the Luxton Museum along Banff Ave, Wolf St, Otter St and Tunnel Mountain Rd to Tunnel Mountain Village One Campground for $2. Buses go every half hour.

Brewster Transportation has a bus departing the Banff Springs Hotel for Sulphur Mountain hourly between 9.40 am and 4.40 pm. It only goes as far as the Upper Hot Springs; if you're going to the gondola it's a short walk from there to the lower terminal. The one-way fare is $4. There is also a shuttle between the hotel and downtown.

Bicycle Park n' Pedal (☎ 762-3191), 229 Wolf St, rents bicycles and is open from 9 am to 9 pm. Most bikes cost $6/24 per hour/day. Peak Experience (☎ 762-0581), 209 Bear St, rents mountain bikes for $7/24 while Performance Ski & Sports (☎ 762-8222), 208 Bear St, charges $6/24. Bactrax Bike Rental (☎ 762-8177) at the Ptarmigan Inn, 339 Banff Ave, charges $5/20; it's open from 8 am to 8 pm.

Hitching Hitchhiking is common in and around town.

LAKE LOUISE

About 57 km north-west of Banff is Lake Louise, known as the jewel of the Rockies. Before you get to the lake is the uninspiring village of Lake Louise which is really nothing more than the Samson Mall shopping centre and a service station. Though small, the convenient strip of shops has everything from groceries, restaurants and liquor to a place to buy film. Get what you need and carry on to the lake itself, five km away by road. There's no transport; if you're walking, it takes about 45 minutes on the footpath.

Lake Louise itself is a much-visited but stunning lake sitting in a small glacial valley, surrounded by treed snow-capped mountains. A visit is best early in the morning when it's less crowded, and chances of the classic reflection in the water are better. One of the Rockies' best known and original hotels, the Chateau Lake Louise, is situated grandly at one end of the lake. There are also some very fine nearby walks and hikes.

Information

The Visitor Information Centre (☎ 522-3833) in the village is open daily during the summer from 8 am to 8 pm (from 9 am to 5 pm in winter). It has an exhibition on the geological and natural history of the Rocky Mountains. Next door at Samson Mall are camping equipment rentals and a laundrette which offers showers. Woodruff & Blum bookshop (☎ 522-3842) has general guides to the Canadian Rockies, as well as hiking, cycling and climbing guides and maps.

Things to See & Do

Mt Whitehorn East of the village along Lake Louise Drive is Mt Whitehorn. A gondola (☎ 522-3555) takes you to the top from which there are hiking trails and views of Lake Louise and Victoria Glacier. The gondola ride costs $9 for the round trip and there's a buffet restaurant and snackbar. Mt Whitehorn is an important ski centre in winter.

Moraine Lake Lesser known Moraine Lake, about 15 km (mostly uphill) from Lake Louise, is for many, the more impressive of the two. Surrounded by peaks and a deep teal in colour, it is defyingly gorgeous. There is an attractive lodge, gift shop and numerous trails at the lake. Again, there is no bus but with all the traffic, hitching isn't too bad.

Hiking The main Lake Louise trail follows the northern banks of the lake westward to the end of the lake and then beyond to the **Plain of Six Glaciers**. On the way, between the lake and the lookout at the end of the trail, is a teahouse.

For a more rigorous venture take the switchbacks up to **Mirror Lake**. There's another teahouse here and good views from **Little Beehive** or **Big Beehive** (not real beehives, but mountains shaped like them). From there you can climb still higher to **Lake Agnes**, then around the long way to join the Plain of Six Glaciers trail and back along Lake Louise to the hotel. These trails can be followed for a couple of hours or turned into a good day's walk.

For a shorter stroll, there's a less-used path on the southern banks of Lake Louise beginning by the boathouse which goes up through spruce forest and offers excellent views of the lake and the hotel.

The roughly 20-km hike through the **Valley of the 10 Peaks** between **Moraine Lake** and Lake Louise is highly recommended.

Take a quick detour to **Larch Valley** where there's a stream and superb scenery. Before Larch Valley a trail heads west past **Eiffel Lake** into Yoho National Park. Better still, hike to Moraine Lake from Lake Louise via **Paradise Creek** and **Sentinel Pass**. This is a full day's hike with some steep parts but is an excellent route, with great scenery. You can do it the other way round but that's doing it the easy way. Getting up through Sentinel Pass is a long, scree-filled trek but well worth it. At the top, 2600 metres high, it's cool and breezy. Once at Moraine Lake you can hitch-hike back to Lake Louise along Moraine Lake Rd.

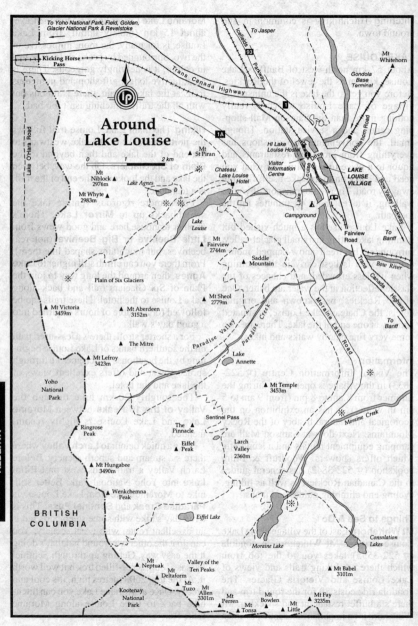

To Yoho National Park, Field, Golden,
Glacier National Park & Revelstoke

To Jasper

Mt Whitehorn

Kicking Horse
Pass

Gondola
Base Terminal

Trans Canada Highway

**Around
Lake Louise**

White Horn Road

HI Lake
Louise Hostel

Mt St Piran

Visitor Information
Centre

Lake
Louise
Drive

**LAKE
LOUISE
VILLAGE**

0   1   2 km

Mt
Niblock ▲
2976m

Lake Agnes

Chateau
Lake Louise
Hotel

Bow Valley Parkway

Mt Whyte ▲
2983m

Lake
Louise

Campground

Fairview
Road

To
Banff

Mt
Fairview
2744m

Saddle
Mountain

Bow River

Plain of Six Glaciers

Lake Agnes

Mt Sheol
2779m

Paradise Creek

Moraine Lake Road

To
Banff

▲ Mt Victoria
3459m

▲ Mt Aberdeen
3152m

The Mitre

Paradise Valley

Paradise Creek

Lake
Annette

▲ Mt Lefroy
3423m

Yoho
National
Park

Mt Temple
3453m

Sentinel Pass

Moraine Creek

Ringrose
Peak

The
Pinnacle

Eiffel
Peak

Larch
Valley
2360m

▲ Mt Hungabee
3490m

Wenkchemna
Peak

Eiffel Lake

**BRITISH
COLUMBIA**

Moraine Lake

Consolation
Lakes

▲ Mt Neptuak

Valley of the
Ten Peaks

▲ Mt Babel
3101m

Mt
Deltaform

Mt
Tuzo

Kootenay
National
Park

Mt
Allen
3301m

Mt
Perren

Mt
Tonsa

Mt
Bowlen

Mt
Little

Mt Fay
3235m

ALBERTA

There are other trails in the area as well: the brochure *Drives & Walks* lists and describes them.

It is common to see pikas (plump, furry animals also called conies) and the larger, more timid marmot along these trails. You often hear ice rumbling on the slopes, too.

Skiing Lake Louise has a large ski area with skiing on four mountain faces and has many chairs to feed the 50 plus runs. It could well be the most scenic ski area in Canada, too. A day pass is $42. For information call or write to Lake Louise Ski Area (☎ 522-3555), Box 5, Lake Louise T0L 1E0. For the snow report call ☎ 762-4766. Many of the hiking trails become cross-country ski trails in winter.

Several companies offer heli-skiing, where a helicopter flies you to a mountain and you ski out. Selkirk Tangiers (☎ 837-5378) based in Lake Louise has day trips.

Climbing Rock climbing on the **Back of the Lake**, a backwater crag, is popular. Access is easy and there are lots of different routes with interesting names like Wicked Gravity and Chocolate Bunnies from Hell. Other places to climb, of varying degrees of difficulty, include **Mt Fairview**, **Mt Bell** and **Eiffel Peak**.

Places to Stay
Camping The two campgrounds in Lake Louise are run by the Canadian Parks Service and are both on the Trans Canada Hwy. The tenting campground, off Moraine Lake Rd, is open year round with sites for $12.50; the RV campground is open mid-May to October with sites for $16. Both have flush toilets but no showers although there is a pay shower in the laundrette at Samson Mall. People should not crawl in the dryers however!

Hostel The HI *Lake Louise Hostel* (☎ 522-2200), on Village Rd north of Samson Mall, has eased a little pressure on accommodation. There's room for 105 people and it has a kitchen, showers and laundromat. Dorm beds cost $17.50 for members, $22.50 for nonmembers. It also has private rooms.

Hotels Hotels are serious dollars. *Paradise Lodge & Bungalows* (☎ 522-3595) is a good choice. It's a short walk to the lake on Lake Louise Drive, it's very pretty and as as economical as any at single/double from $130. *Lake Louise Inn* (☎ 522-3791, 1-800-661-9237), 210 Village Rd, has more facilities including a gym. Rooms start from the same price.

Much less, and a good place if you're caught needing a room, is the *West Louise Lodge* (☎ 343-6311) 11 km west of Lake Louise on the highway in BC. Rooms here start at $70 in high season.

Places to Eat
Aside from the Samson Mall, there are places for a bite in the Chateau Lake Louise. The tiny coffee shop has moderately priced snacks and good coffee. *Lake Louise Station* is a restaurant in the historic train station of 1884. It's open daily for lunch and dinner and is one km from the mall on Sentinel Rd.

Getting There & Around
The bus terminal (☎ 522-3876) is at the Samson Mall. Greyhound runs west to Golden and Vancouver and east to Banff and Calgary four times a day. The fare to Banff is $9. Brewster Bus Lines goes to Banff three times a day for $11.50 and then on to the Calgary airport. They also have an express to Jasper daily for $34. A taxi to the lake is about $8 one way.

ICEFIELDS PARKWAY
This 230-km road (Hwy 93) opened in 1940 which links Lake Louise with Jasper is one of the most spectacular stretches of asphalt in Canada. The highway follows a lake-lined valley between two chains of the Eastern Main Ranges which make up the Continental Divide. The watershed rivers from the Continental Divide flow eastward towards the Atlantic Ocean and westward towards the Pacific Ocean. The mountains here are the highest, most rugged and maybe the most scenic in all the Rockies. The highway is good but slow, as animals such as goats, bighorn sheep and elk are often beside or even on it.

You can drive the route in a couple of hours but stopping at the many viewpoints, picnic spots and sights or hiking on one of the many trails can make it a full day or longer. Visitor Information Centres have trail details. Cycling the Icefields Parkway is very popular. Because of the terrain it's easier to go from Banff to Jasper than vice versa.

On the way see **Peyto Lake**, one of the world's most beautiful glacial lakes; again, early in the morning is the best viewing time. Further north, around **Waterfowl Lake**, moose are plentiful.

About halfway between Lake Louise and Jasper is the **Athabasca Glacier**, a tongue of the vast **Columbia Icefield**. The icefield itself covers an area of 325 sq km and parts of it are over 900 metres thick. Its meltwaters flow into the Mackenzie, Saskatchewan and Columbia rivers.

The Columbia Icefield Visitor Information Centre across the highway from the glacier has a display and film on glaciers for free. In summer the centre is open May to September daily from 10 am to 5 pm (7 pm between mid-June and late August).

You can walk to the toe of the glacier from the Information Centre. For a further look, Athabasca Glacier Icewalks, with an office in the Information Centre, is recommended. It has a three-hour trip for $25 and a five-hour trip to various destinations in the snowfields for $30. It also has an office (☎ 762-5385) at 208 Bear St, Banff. Call either place for the schedule as they don't do both everyday. Brewster has 1½-hour rides out on the ice in big-tired snocoaches for $20.50. They too have an office here and one in Banff (☎ 762-6735).

Other points of interest are **Sunwapta Falls** and **Athabasca Falls**, closer to Jasper.

Places to Stay

The route is lined with a good batch of rustic HI hostels charging $10 for members, $15 for nonmembers. Most are quite close to the highway in scenic locations; they're small and without showers but there's usually a 'refreshing' stream nearby. Choices include the excellent HI *Mosquito Creek Hostel*, on the Icefields Parkway about 27 km north of Lake Louise, with cooking facilities and a sauna. HI *Hilda Creek Hostel* (☎ 762-4122), seven km south of the Visitor Information Centre, has 21 beds and a kitchen. HI *Athabasca Falls Hostel* (☎ 439-3089) is about 30 km south of Jasper and has 40 beds.

You can also find campgrounds and moderately priced motels along the way.

JASPER

Jasper, 369 km west of Edmonton, is Banff's northern counterpart. It's smaller with fewer things to see and do and its setting is less grand, but some people prefer its quieter streets and less full-scale pandering to tourists. It's a good connecting point, with the Yellowhead Hwy and VIA Rail running east to Edmonton; west to Prince George; and the Icefields Parkway going south to Lake Louise. The town is a good supply centre for trips around Jasper National Park, which is teeming with wildlife and has excellent backcountry trails of various lengths.

Glaciers are Cool but Icefields are Awesome

The Columbia Icefield contains about 30 glaciers and is up to 350 metres thick. This remnant of the last Ice Age covers 325 sq km on the plateau between Mt Columbia (3747 metres) and Mt Athabaska (3491 metres) off the parkway connecting Banff to Jasper. This mother of rivers straddling the Great Divide is the largest icefield in the Rockies and feeds the North Saskatchewan, Columbia, Athabasca, Mackenzie and Fraser river systems with its meltwaters. They flow to three oceans.

The mountainous sides of this vast bowl of ice are some of the highest in the Rocky Mountains with nine peaks over 3000 metres. One of its largest glaciers, the Athabasca, runs almost down to the road and can be visited on foot or by specially designed bus-like vehicles. The water you see at the toe of the glacier fell as snow on the icefield about 175 years ago. ∎

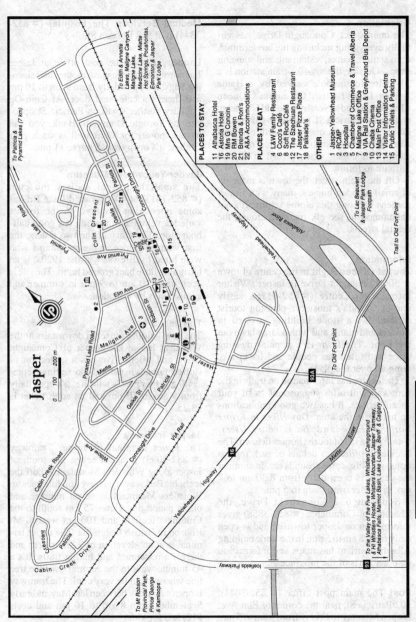

Jasper

0   100   200 m

PLACES TO STAY
11 Athabasca Hotel
16 Astoria Hotel
19 Mrs G Concini
20 BM Bowen
21 Brenda & Ron's
22 A&A Accommodations

PLACES TO EAT
4   L&W Family Restaurant
6   Coco's Café
8   Soft Rock Café
12 The Szechuan Restaurant
17 Jasper Pizza Place
18 Palisade's

OTHER
1   Jasper-Yellowhead Museum
2   RCMP
3   Hospital
5   Chamber of Commerce & Travel Alberta
7   Maligne Lake Office
9   VIA Rail Station & Greyhound Bus Depot
10 Chaba Cinema
13 Main Post Office
14 Visitor Information Centre
15 Public Toilets & Parking

To Edith & Annette
Lakes, Maligne Canyon,
Maligne Lake,
Medicine Lake, Miette
Hot Springs, Pocahontas,
Edmonton & Jasper
Park Lodge

To Patricia &
Pyramid Lakes (7 km)

Pyramid Lake Road

Pyramid Ave

Connaught Drive

Patricia St

Geikie St

Colin Crescent

Cedar St

Elm Ave

Robson St

Maligne Ave

Miette Ave

Patricia St

Geikie St

Maligne Lake Road

Willow Ave

Cabin Creek Road

Patricia Crescent

Cabin Creek Drive

Connaught Drive

VIA Rail

Hazel Ave

Yellowhead Highway

Yellowhead Highway

Athabasca River

Miette River

Icefields Parkway

To Lac Beauvert
& Jasper Park Lodge
Footpath

Trail to Old Fort Point

To Old Fort Point

93A

To Old Fort Point

To the Valley of the Five Lakes, Whistlers Campground
HI Whistlers Hostel, Whistlers Mountain, Jasper Tramway,
Athabasca Falls, Marmot Basin, Lake Louise, Banff & Calgary

To Mt Robson
Provincial Park,
Prince George
& Kamloops

93

ALBERTA

Orientation

The main street, Connaught Drive, has virtually everything including the bus terminal, train station, banks, restaurants and souvenir shops. Outside the toy-like train station is a 21-metre totem pole carved by a Haida artisan from British Columbia's Queen Charlotte Islands. Nearby is an old CN steam engine. On Patricia St, parallel to Connaught Drive, traffic runs one way north of Hazel Ave. No, it's not just you – the street numbers along Connaught, when posted at all, are difficult to follow.

Off the main street, the town is made up of small wooden houses, many with flower gardens befitting this alpine setting. It's not uncommon to see elk roaming around the central streets.

Information

Tourist Offices Right in the centre of town at 500 Connaught Drive is Jasper's Visitor Information Centre (☎ 852-6176), easily one of Canada's most eye-pleasing tourist offices. It's a stone building covered in flowers and plants and with a large lawn out the front. The lawn is a popular meeting place and often has people and backpacks lying all over the place.

The centre has information on trails in the park and will offer suggestions to fit your specifications. It has two good publications on hiking in the area: *Day Hikes in Jasper National Park* and *Backcountry Users' Guide* and a list of tourist homes in town. The booklet *Profiles* has details of park regulations, wildlife, campgrounds etc. In summer the centre is open daily from 8.30 am to 7 pm, in winter from 9 am to 5 pm.

South at 632 Connaught Drive, the Chamber of Commerce (☎ 852-3858) gives information on Jasper townsite and is open daily from 8 am to 5 pm. In the same building Alberta Tourism has maps and information on other parts of the province.

Post The main post office (☎ 852-3041), 502 Patricia St, near the corner of Elm Ave, is open Monday to Friday from 9 am to 5 pm.

Medical Services The hospital (☎ 852-3344) is at 518 Robson St.

Laundry Beside the post office at Jasper Laundromat you can wash clothes and sleeping bags; it's open daily from 9 am to 10 pm and there's a cafe next door. At Coin-Op Laundry, further south on Patricia St opposite the Toronto Dominion Bank, you can have a shower for $2 as well as wash your clothes; it's open from 8 am to 11 pm.

Jasper-Yellowhead Museum

The small historical society museum (☎ 852-3013) at 400 Pyramid Lake Rd has some interesting displays on the town's varied development, making it a good half-hour stop. The story of the two sisters, the first women guides in the mountains who were hired by Brewster in the 1920s, is an intriguing little background tidbit. The site is open daily 10 am to 9 pm in summer and admission is by donation.

The Den

The new wildlife museum downstairs at the Whistlers Inn at the corner of Connaught Drive and Miette Ave has a collection of stuffed animals in natural-like settings representing Jasper park's wildlife. It's open daily from 9 am to 10 pm and an adult ticket is $3.25.

Jasper Tramway

The lower terminal of Jasper Tramway (☎ 852-3093) is about seven km south of Jasper along Whistlers Mountain Rd off the Icefields Parkway. The busy gondola goes up Whistlers Mountain in seven minutes and offers panoramic views 75 km south to the Columbia Icefield and 100 km west to Mt Robson in British Columbia. The upper terminal is at an elevation of 2285 metres and there's a restaurant and hiking trails. It's a 45-minute walk to the summit over the tree line where it can be very cool. The tramway is open every day between late May and early September from 8 am to 10 pm and costs $12, less for kids.

Patricia & Pyramid Lakes

These lakes, about seven km north-west of town along Pyramid Lake Rd, are small and relatively quiet. They have hiking and horse-riding trails, picnic sites, fishing and beaches; you can rent canoes, kayaks, sailing boats and windsurfers. In winter there's cross-country skiing and ice skating. It's not uncommon to see deer, coyotes or bears in the vicinity.

Lakes Annette & Edith

Off the Yellowhead Hwy, three km north-east of town along Lodge Rd, Lake Annette and Lake Edith, at about 1000 metres, can be warm enough for a quick swim. There are beaches, hiking and bike trails, picnic areas and boat rentals in the wooded parks around the lakes.

Jasper to Maligne Lake

About 11 km east of Jasper on the way to Maligne (pronounced 'ma-LEEN') Lake you pass **Maligne Canyon**, a limestone gorge about 50 metres deep, with waterfalls and interesting rock formations. You can walk from the cafe down to the floor of the canyon. A further 21 km brings you to **Medicine Lake** whose level rises and falls due to the underground drainage system; sometimes the lake disappears completely.

Maligne Lake, 48 km south-east of Jasper at the end of Maligne Lake Rd, is the largest of the glacier-fed lakes in the Rockies and the second largest in the world. It's promoted as one of the most scenic of mountain lakes but this is perhaps unwarranted. It's a very commercial, busy destination and the classic view with the island is some km out in the lake, accessible only by boat. You can, however, go horse riding near it for a good view, or hire a canoe for $10 an hour from Maligne Tours (☎ 852-3370). Alternatively, take the 40-km, 1½-hour boat tour to Spirit Island with Maligne Tours for $29 ($47 with transfers to/from Jasper). Make a reservation in Jasper at the Maligne Lake Office, 626 Connaught Drive, open daily from 8.30 am to 9 pm. There are also some fine hiking trails in the lake's vicinity and excellent cross-country skiing in the highlands around the lake between November and May.

Miette Hot Springs

A good spot for a bathe is Miette Hot Springs (☎ 866-3939), 61 km east of Jasper off the Yellowhead Hwy near the park boundary. Miette has the warmest mineral waters in the Canadian Rockies. The modern spa has two pools, one deep and one suitable for children. It's open in summer daily from 8.30 am to 10.30 pm and costs $4; you can hire bathing suits for $1.50 and towels for $1. In the summer of 1995 it was closed temporarily due to a mudslide.

Activities

Hiking Hikers are generally fewer in Jasper than in Banff and wildlife is more plentiful. If the weather has been wet you may want to avoid the lower trails where horse trips are run; they make the path a mud bath. Topographic maps are available for all routes. As well as the hikes around the lakes mentioned earlier there are many others. The leaflet *Day Hikers' Guide to Jasper National Park* has descriptions of most of the walks. If you're hiking overnight you must obtain a park-use permit (free) from the Visitor Information Centre.

Off the Icefields Parkway, about 10 km south-east of Jasper, is the small **Valley of the Five Lakes**. The eight-km loop around the lakes is mostly flat and makes a pleasant two to three-hour stroll. Alternatively, you can take the trail that heads off north from the loop to **Old Fort Point** about two km from Jasper. The **Mt Edith Cavell** and **Miette Hot Springs** areas also have good day hikes. There are quite a few two and three-day hikes in the park. One is the 45-km **Skyline Trail** which starts at the north-western end of Maligne Lake and finishes on Maligne Lake Rd about 13 km from Jasper. Approximately 26 km of the trail is at or above the tree line and has great scenery. The trail has plenty of wildlife too; watch out for grizzlies.

There are also a few four, seven and 10-day hikes.

Cycling As in Banff National Park you can cycle on the highways and on some of the trails in the park. No cycling is allowed off the trails. Journeys of a few hours, a day or several days with overnight stops at campgrounds, hostels or lodges are all possible. For more information get a copy of *Trail Bicycling Guide, Jasper National Park* from the Visitor Information Centre.

A good cycling route close to town is along **Maligne Lake Rd** to Maligne Canyon or further to Medicine Lake. A popular, scenic but fairly tough trail ride is through the Valley of the Five Lakes to Old Fort Point, a distance of about 23.5 km. For bicycle rentals see the Getting Around section later.

Climbing Jasper Climbing School & Mountaineering Service (☎ 852-3964) PO Box 452, Jasper T0E 1E0, is run by Helen & Hans Schwartz and has three-hour to five-day, beginner-to-advanced climbing schools. These run from May to September; in winter you can go waterfall ice climbing or ski mountaineering. The three-hour rappelling adventure for beginners is $25.

One-day guided climbing tours go to Mt Morro, Messner Ridge, Mt Athabasca, Mt Andro-meda and Mt Edith Cavell. Cost depends on the size of the group but is $100 and up per person.

Whitewater Rafting Calm to turbulent rafting can be found on the **Maligne River**, **Sunwapta River** and the **Athabasca River** near Athabasca Falls. Numerous companies offer trips of varying lengths. Maligne River Adventures (☎ 852-3370) does a 13-km trip on the fast, rough Maligne River for $50 per person; you can book a ticket from Maligne Lake Office, 626 Connaught Drive. Letter writers have described it as exciting. Whitewater Rafting Ltd (☎ 852-4386/ 7238), with an office at the Esso station, 702 Connaught, has 3½-hour trips to Athabasca Falls and four-hour rides on the Maligne or Sunwapta rivers. Prices start from $40.

Skiing Jasper National Park's main skiing area is **Marmot Basin** which lies 19 km south-west of town off Hwy 93A. It has good downhill runs for both beginners and experts, and plenty of scenic cross-country trails. Call ☎ 852-3816 for information or ☎ 488-5909 for a snow report. A day pass costs $40.

Near Maligne Lake the **Moose Lake Loop** (eight km) and the trail in the **Bald Hills** (11 km) are an easy introduction to cross-country skiing in the park as well as offering great scenery. The skiing season goes from December to May.

Organised Tours
There are three main companies in town which book tickets for the various tours and activities. Jasper Travel Agency (☎ 852-4400), in the Via Rail station, coordinates and sells tickets for tours, river trips, sightseeing and adventures. Maligne Lake Tours (☎ 852-3370), 626 Connaught Drive does the same. The third is Jasper Adventure Centre (☎ 852-5595) at 604 Connaught Drive in the Chaba Theatre.

Brewster's Gray Line (☎ 852-3332) has a three-hour drive to some of the local sights including Jasper Tramway, Whistlers Mountain, Pyramid and Patricia lakes and Maligne Canyon. The trip costs $30. Its Maligne Lake cruise takes five hours and costs $50. It also has tours along the Icefields Parkway to Lake Louise for $59 one way, taking 7½ hours.

Another company with tours of the park's sights is Jasper Heritage Tours (☎ 852-5254). Jasper Raft Tours (☎ 852-3613), offers one and two-hour tours on the Athabasca River from $31, with descriptions of the natural and human history of the region. The cost includes the bus trip.

If you're driving, there are two self-guiding auto-cassette tapes available. One covers Jasper to the Columbia Icefield, and one from the icefield to Banff. Produced by Rocky Mountain Auto Tours, these can be purchased for $12.95 each from Exposures, 612 Connaught Drive.

ALBERTA

Places to Stay

In general, prices here are better than those in Banff, but hotel and motel prices are still fairly steep. The B&Bs and tourist homes are the best bet after the campgrounds or hostels.

Camping Jasper National Park has 10 campgrounds all operated by the Canadian Parks Service and all at ☎ 292-4444. Closest to town is *Whistlers Campground* about three km south off the Icefields Parkway on Whistlers Rd. It's quite good, with electricity, showers and flush toilets but, though large (it has 781 sites), it does get crowded. In summer, films and talks are presented nightly. Sites cost from $13 to $19.

A herd of wapiti (American elk) lives in the campground at certain times of the year. In the autumn a male looks after a large number of females – the harem – and his bawling instructions are heard far and wide.

Two km further south on the Icefields Parkway, *Wapiti Campground*, beside the Athabasca River, is the only campground in the park open during the winter. It has sites for $14 to $15.50. Two other campgrounds reasonably close to town are *Wabasso Campground* 17 km south on Hwy 93A, with sites for $12, and *Snaring River Campground*, 17 km north on the Yellowhead Hwy, with sites for $10.

Hostels HI *Whistlers Hostel* (☎ 852-3215) is 6.3 km south of Jasper on Skytram Rd towards the Jasper Tramway; the last two km are uphill. The hostel is one of the few big modern ones in the Rockies and has showers, a laundromat and a large kitchen. There's a midnight curfew but the hostel is much more relaxed than it once was and is generally full all summer. Ask about the shuttle bus into town. Members pay $14, nonmembers $19. In winter there may be some long-term guests who are working in and around town.

HI *Mt Edith Cavell Hostel* (☎ 439-3089) is also south of Jasper on Mt Edith Cavell Rd, 11 km from the junction with Hwy 93A. It's open from mid-June to October and charges $9 for members, $14 for nonmembers.

HI *Maligne Canyon Hostel* (☎ 852-3584), 11.5 km north-east of town on Maligne Canyon Rd, is small but good with members paying $9, nonmembers $14.

Tourist Homes The Visitor Information Centre has a list of over 50 tourist homes, all clean, most in or close to town, most charging similar prices, most open year round. National Park regulations disallow breakfast being served but some places may offer a muffin with the often offered tea or coffee. In July and August many of these places fill up early, so it's a good idea to book ahead. Most places charge from $35/40 for a single/double and may offer lower rates in the off season.

The cheapest of the lot is *R M Bowen* (☎ 852-4532), 228 Colin Crescent, with a couple of double rooms with TV for $25 each. *Mrs G Concini* (☎ 852-3744), 312 Patricia St, has two rooms available for $40 each with shared bathroom. *Brenda & Ron's* (☎ 852-3882), 200 Patricia St, has one double room available for $45, also with shared bathroom. *A&A Accommodations* (☎ 852-5260), 110 Connaught Drive, offers two rooms at $50 with TV, private bathroom and complimentary coffee. German is spoken. *Joe & Sheila Couture* (☎ 852-4949), central at 734 Connaught Drive have rooms at $30/50.

Hotels, Motels & Bungalows In town the *Athabasca Hotel* (☎ 852-3386), 510 Patricia St, has basic singles/doubles for $65/70 and more deluxe rooms for $91/95. The *Astoria Hotel* (☎ 852-4955), 404 Connaught Drive, has doubles at $110. Both hotels have a pub and restaurant and provide entertainment. Deluxe *Jasper Park Lodge* (☎ 852-3301), with small cabins beside Lac Beauvert north-east of town, is Jasper's answer to the Banff Springs Hotel. It has everything including a world-class golf course. Singles/doubles start from $275, suites from $632.

In Jasper many of the motels are north along Connaught Drive. Out of town some places offer motel-type rooms and bungalows (usually wooden cabins).

ALBERTA

Patricia Lake Bungalows (☎ 852-3560), on Patricia Lake Rd about five km north of town, at $80 in summer, is more reasonable out of peak season. A little further north along the road *Pyramid Lake Resort Bungalows* (☎ 852-3536) has rooms from $100. It's beside the lake and has a licensed dining room. *Tekkara Lodge* (☎ 852-3058) is one km south of Jasper off Hwy 93A at the confluence of the Miette and Athabasca rivers. You can either stay in the lodge or in one of the cabins. Rooms cost from $75. It has a licensed restaurant and is open May to the end of September.

Other Accommodation Hostelers and those seeking a place with easy access to outdoor activities might consider *Blue Lake Adventure Lodge* (☎ 1-800-582-3305) about an hour's drive east of Jasper, 25 km north of Hinton. The lodge is situated in Switzer Provincial Park. Accommodation is in cabins, chalet rooms or by camping. Summer and winter sports equipment can be rented including bikes and canoes, and various adventure courses are offered. Meals are available. Cost for two adults in a cabin is $57, or $77 for four plus taxes, less out of summer.

Places to Eat

Coco's Café at 608 Patricia St is a comfortable place good for breakfasts of muesli at $3 or muffins and cappuccino. At lunch there are sandwiches and burritos. *Papa George's* in the Astoria Hotel, 404 Connaught Drive, has standard breakfasts for $6.

The *Soft Rock Café* in the tiny mall at 622 Connaught Drive is a fine little place for casual light lunches and inexpensive snacks. A soup-and-sandwich lunch goes for about $4.

Jasper Pizza Place, 402 Connaught, with the rooftop patio, has excellent pizza for $9 to $13 and salads are available, too. The *Szechuan Restaurant* at 504 Patricia St has been recommended for its tasty large portions costing $6 to $11. For a good, more expensive dinner try *Palisade's* on the corner of Patricia and Cedar Sts. The menu lists plenty of seafood and Greek specialties but

also has pastas. All the main dishes are in the $10 to $14 range.

Many of the hotels and lodges have their own dining rooms.

For a wide selection of bulk and natural foods check out *Nutter's* at 622 Patricia St.

Entertainment

Chaba Cinema (☎ 852-4749), 604 Connaught Drive opposite the VIA Rail station, shows the one-hour movie *Challenge* at 4 pm daily in summer. Shot largely on the Columbia Icefield and narrated by Peter Ustinov, the film chronicles whitewater kayaking, heli-skiing, ice-climbing and other activities in the Rockies. Admission costs $6.50.

The *nightclub* in the Athabasca Hotel regularly has live rock bands and dancing. For disco music head to *Champs* in the Sawridge Hotel; it's open nightly. The *Astoria Bar* in the Astoria Hotel is famous for its imported draught beers.

Getting There & Away

Bus The Greyhound Bus Depot (☎ 852-3926) is situated in the VIA Rail station on Connaught Drive. Three buses go to Kamloops, Vancouver and Edmonton daily. The one-way fares (including tax) are: Kamloops $47; Vancouver $86; and Edmonton $45. Greyhound doesn't run buses between Jasper and Banff.

Brewster Transportation (☎ 852-3332), at the same station, has one bus a day to Banff; it takes about 4½ hours and costs $40 one way. It also goes to Lake Louise. The Calgary fare is $49.50. These prices include tax.

Train The ticket office (☎ 852-4102) in the VIA Rail station is open Monday and Saturday from 8.30 am to 4 pm; Tuesday and Thursday from noon to 4 pm; Wednesday from 8.30 am to noon, and from 4.30 to 8.15 pm; and Friday and Sunday from noon to 8.15 pm. From here trains go west to Prince George and Prince Rupert, south-west through Kamloops to Vancouver and east through Edmonton to Saskatoon, Winnipeg and beyond. The train to Vancouver leaves

Monday, Thursday and Saturday at 3.30 pm; to Winnipeg on Tuesday, Friday and Sunday at 2.55 pm; and to Prince Rupert on Wednesday, Friday and Sunday at 8.10 pm. Some sample one-way fares (including tax) are: Kamloops $86; Edmonton $80; Winnipeg $217; and Vancouver $137.

The private 'Rocky Mountaineer' tour train runs between Jasper and Vancouver via Kamloops. It only operates between the beginning of May and the middle of October and the number of trips varies with the month. The one-way fare to Vancouver is $565 double occupancy with some meals and an overnight stay in Kamloops included. See under the Vancouver and Banff Getting There & Away sections for further details.

Car Car rental in Jasper is available through the following:

Avis
  Petro Canada, 300 Connaught Drive
  (☎ 852-3970)
Budget
  Shell, 638 Connaught Drive (☎ 852-3222)
Hertz
  Avalanche Esso, 702 Connaught Drive
  (☎ 852-3888)
Tilden
  Via Rail Station, 607 Connaught Drive
  (☎ 852-4972)

Tilden rents small cars for $50 a day with 100 km free, plus 22 cents for each extra km. Budget's rates are $49 a day with 100 km free, plus 23 cents for each extra km.

Getting Around
Bus Although Jasper doesn't have a public transport system, small 24-seater buses, run by Maligne Tours (☎ 852-3370), do go from outside the Maligne Lake Office, 626 Connaught Drive, to various places around Jasper National Park. Some destinations and one-way fares are: Maligne Canyon and hostel $6; Maligne Lake $10; and Skyline Trail (southern trailhead) $10.

The Rocky Ride shuttle bus (☎ 852-3215) connects Jasper with the Whistler Campground and Hostel twice a day for $2.25.

Bicycle Jasper has lots of places with bicycles for hire. Beyond Bikes (☎ 852-5922), 4 Cedar Ave, has mountain bikes for $5 an hour, $12 per day and $18 for 24 hours. Freewheel Cycle (☎ 852-3898), 600 Patricia St, rents mountain bikes for $5 an hour, $15 for a half-day or $20 a day. Other places include Sports Shop (☎ 852-3654), 416 Connaught Drive beside the CIBC Bank, Saito Sports & Hardware (☎ 852-5555), 625 Patricia St and the Jasper Park Lodge.

KANANASKIS COUNTRY
Adjacent to the south-western corner of Banff National Park and 90 km west of Calgary, Kananaskis Country has been set aside as an outdoor recreational area. The 4000-sq-km region offers facilities for skiing, climbing, cycling, hiking, horse riding, boating, camping and picnicking. Kananaskis Country is most notable for the downhill skiing at **Nakiska** on Mt Allan (☎ 591-7777), off Hwy 40, where the 1988 Olympic Winter Games were held. Skiers today can use the slopes there when no competitions are being held. Cross-country skiing is also good with trails throughout Kananaskis Country.

The fast-growing town of **Canmore**, off the Trans Canada Hwy and squeezed between Banff National Park and Kananaskis Country, is the main focus for the area. As well as campgrounds, hotels and motels it has tour companies offering outdoor activities throughout the Rockies. The *Rocky Mountain R&R* (☎ 678-3535) backpackers hostel is here, too. It's at 278 St Barbara Terrace in the old hospital, a 15-minute walk from downtown. Dorms are $20. It's run by a group promoting community health.

The main access road to Kananaskis Country is Hwy 40 which does a loop through the area. It runs south of the Trans Canada Hwy through Peter Lougheed Provincial Park to link with Hwy 541, then Hwy 22. At the junction of Hwys 541 and 22 you can either head north to Calgary or south to the Crowsnest Hwy. The other main route into Kananaskis is Hwy 66 from south-eastern Calgary.

ALBERTA

WATERTON LAKES NATIONAL PARK

This 525-sq-km national park and UNESCO World Heritage Site in the far south-western corner of Alberta, 130 km from Lethbridge, was opened in 1895. The land rises from the prairie into rugged, beautiful alpine scenery with many lakes, waterfalls and valleys. Spotting wildlife is common and there are more than 800 species of wildflowers. Ask about the cougar situation and make sure little Fido doesn't wander off. Waterton Lake, a central feature, is the deepest in the Rockies. The park gets considerably fewer visitors than its two more northerly sisters, Banff and Jasper and the town of Waterton is smaller and much more low-key than Banff.

Waterton is joined with the Glacier National Park of Montana to form the Waterton Glacier International Peace Park. Each park is operated separately, however, and entry to one does not entitle you to entry to the other. The park entry fee to Waterton Lakes is not valid for Glacier; and to get to the latter you have to leave Waterton Lakes, head south on Hwy 6 (Chief Mountain Hwy) and go through US customs and immigration at the border.

The park information office (☎ 859-2224), on the highway just before you get to Waterton, is open daily May to September from 8 am to 8.30 pm. There are 255 km of hiking trails, some of which are also good for cycling and horse riding, while in winter many become cross-country skiing trails. Ask about the six-hour return Crypt Lake hike, one of the Rockies' best.

Waterton Inter-Nation Shoreline Cruises (☎ 859-2362 in summer, 285-2180 in winter), operates cruises on Upper Waterton Lake with boats holding up to 200 passengers. A limited operation begins in May with no stops in the USA; the full schedule operates between 1 July and 30 August with most cruises stopping at Goat Haunt in Montana. The fare is $16. There are also cruise/hike trips offered.

In the north-east of the park you can visit **Bison Paddock** containing a small herd of plains bison. The **Akamina Parkway** provides a scenic 16-km route west from Waterton along the Cameron Valley to Cameron Lake, while the 15-km **Red Rock Parkway** follows the Blakiston Valley to Red Rock Canyon.

Places to Stay

The park has three government campgrounds. The *Waterton Townsite Campground*, on Hwy 5 at the southern end of town, is the largest with full facilities and sites for $17. There are also a few privately owned campgrounds just outside the park. Waterton has a number of lodges and hotels.

Northland Lodge (☎ 859-2353), on Evergreen Ave and open mid-May to the end of September, is the cheapest. Single/double rooms without/with bathroom are $46/65. *El Cortez Motel* (☎ 859-2366), on Mountview Rd, is clean and reasonably priced with rooms for $60. The town's showpiece accommodation is the venerable railway *Prince of Wales Hotel* (☎ 859-2231), overlooking the lake. Even if you can't afford the $120 rooms it's worth a wander round. In 1995 it was designated a National Historic Site. When it first opened you could get a room for $8!

British Columbia

British Columbia, known simply as BC, contains some of the most varied and spectacular scenery in the world. The Rocky Mountains are in the east, the northern interior is full of mountain ranges, forests, lakes and wilderness. The southern interior has a small desert, while the lush Pacific coastal area has rainforests and countless inlets and islands. In short, the range of landscapes provides habitats for wildlife and opportunities for outdoor activities to suit every taste.

The general atmosphere in BC, particularly on the south-west coast, is slightly different than that of the rest of Canada. The culture, more lifestyle-conscious than in the east, partially reflects the influence of California.

These factors combine to make tourism – in a province with many lucrative industries – the second largest money-maker.

As in California, much of the early settlement was due to gold fever around the 1850s. The bulk of the population is of British ancestry, although Vancouver has a large Asian community.

BC is Canada's most westerly province. It's bordered in the north by the Yukon and the Northwest Territories; in the east by Alberta; in the south by the three US states of Montana, Idaho and Washington; in the north-west by Alaska; and in the west by the Pacific Ocean.

Victoria, the province's capital, is at the southern tip of Vancouver Island, which lies south-west of the mainland. The city of Vancouver, the province's business centre and by far BC's largest city, sits alongside the ocean near the mouth of the Fraser River.

The Trans Canada Hwy (Hwy 1) is the major route connecting Vancouver and southern BC with the rest of southern Canada. The busiest section is between Hope and Vancouver, where the road follows the Fraser River. The Yellowhead Hwy (mainly Hwy 16, also including part of Hwys 37 and 5) links Prince Rupert in BC's north-west

HIGHLIGHTS

Entered Confederation: 20 July 1871
Area: 948,596 sq km
Population: 3,282,065
Provincial Capital: Victoria

- Spend time in scenically beautiful Vancouver, where the mountains meet the ocean
- Explore Vancouver Island with its rugged west-coast beaches, lush rainforests, ample hiking and camping opportunities, and the refined 'old-world' charm of Victoria
- Take in the unsurpassed hiking, camping or skiing which is found across the province
- Enjoy the many lakes, vineyards and orchards of the sunny Okanagan Valley
- Visit the Native Indian sites of the Pacific north-west, especially the Queen Charlotte Islands, which is the home of the world's largest original group of totem poles
- Meander through the Kootenays, where lakes and rivers are abundant, skiing is fabulous and the scenery is spectacular

BRITISH COLUMBIA

with Prince George in the east, Jasper and Edmonton in Alberta, then Saskatoon and Winnipeg.

The Cassiar Hwy (Hwy 37; also called the Stewart-Cassiar Hwy) links the north-west of the province with the Yukon, meeting the Alaska Hwy near Upper Liard, just north of the BC/Yukon border.

Hwy 97 from Washington state in the USA connects south-central BC with the north via Kamloops, Prince George and Dawson Creek. From Dawson Creek, Hwy 97 is also known as the Alaska (or Alcan) Hwy; it connects northern BC with Fairbanks in Alaska via Whitehorse in the Yukon.

The bulk of the province is mountainous lying inside the Western Cordillera, which runs roughly north-west to south-east. Within the cordillera there are three major mountain ranges – the Rocky Mountains to the east, the Cassiar (north) and Columbia (south) mountains in the centre and the Coast Mountains to the west.

The province contains scores of freshwater lakes and fast-flowing rivers plus several plateaus, the largest of which is the Fraser Plateau in the south-west. Estimates vary, but about 60% of BC is covered by forest, consisting mainly of varieties of coniferous trees – western red cedar and Douglas fir which occur in the moist coastal regions while pine, hemlock and spruce are more often found in the drier, higher interior.

History

The earliest known inhabitants of BC are believed to have arrived from Asia between 12,000 and 10,000 years ago, after the end of the last Ice Age. Some settled along the Pacific coast while others settled in the interior east of the Coast Mountains.

The Pacific coast Native Indians included the Bella Coola, Cowichan, Gitskan, Haida, Kwakiutl, Niska, Nootka, Salish and Tsimshian groups. With plenty of animal, marine and plant life available, they were able to evolve a highly sophisticated culture and an intricate network of trade. They also developed a rigid class system.

Inland, with its greater extremes of climate, the people led a nomadic, subsistence way of life. To the north they followed the migratory herds of animals such as the caribou and the moose; to the south they followed the bison. In the south, around the Fraser, Columbia and Thompson rivers, salmon was also an important resource. Most of these people were Athapaskans (now called Dene, pronounced 'de-nay'), which included such groups as Beaver, Chilcotin, Carrier, Sekani and Tahltan. Other important groups were the interior Salish (divided into the Lillooet, Okanagan, Shuswap and Thompson) and the Kootenay (or Kootenai).

Towards the end of the 18th century, European explorers appeared off the west coast in search of new sources of wealth. The Russians and Spanish came first and were soon followed by the British explorer Captain Cook, who was looking for a water route across North America from the Pacific to the Atlantic – the legendary Northwest Passage.

He was unable to find it, but his account of the riches to be had from furs brought traders eager to cash in on the lucrative market. The most famous of these were Alexander Mackenzie, Simon Fraser and David Thompson, who explored routes overland from the east. A series of trading posts was established which, by the 1820s, came under the control of the Hudson's Bay Company.

In the meantime, initially to counter the Spanish presence, Captain George Vancouver had explored and claimed Vancouver Island for Britain. Then in 1849, following years of dispute with the USA, it became a crown colony.

The discovery of gold along the Fraser River in 1858 brought in a flood of people seeking their fortune and led to mainland BC also being declared a crown colony. A second wave of fortune hunters came when gold was discovered further north in the Cariboo region. Although the gold rush only lasted a few years, many of those who came in the wake of the miners remained behind to form more permanent settlements. In 1866 the two colonies were united and, after much discussion, joined the Canadian Confederation in 1871 as the province of British Columbia.

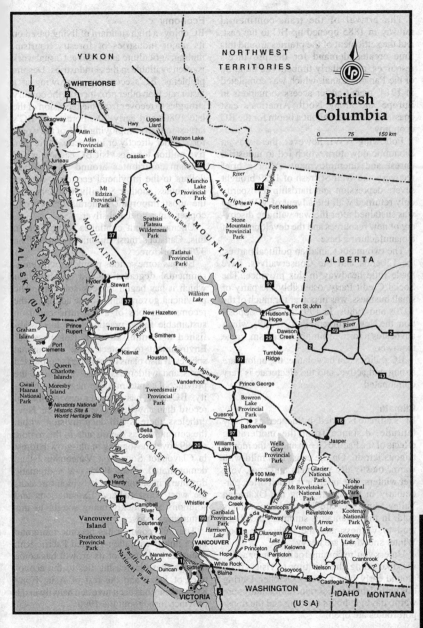

British Columbia

0   75   150 km

YUKON

NORTHWEST
TERRITORIES

WHITEHORSE

Skagway

Atlin
Atlin
Provincial
Park

Juneau

Cassiar

Upper
Liard

Watson Lake

Mt
Edziza
Provincial
Park

Muncho
Lake
Provincial
Park

Alaska Highway

Liard Highway

Fort Nelson

Spatsizi
Plateau
Wilderness
Park

Stone
Mountain
Provincial
Park

Tatlatui
Provincial
Park

Hyder   Stewart

Williston
Lake

Fort St John

Hudson's
Hope

Peace River

Dawson
Creek

New Hazelton

Prince
Rupert   Terrace

Graham
Island

Port
Clements

Queen
Charlotte
Islands

Gwaii
Haanas
National
Park

Moresby
Island

Ninstints National
Historic Site
& World Heritage Site

Kitimat

Smithers

Houston

Yellowhead Highway

Vanderhoof

Tweedsmuir
Provincial
Park

Bella
Coola

Prince George

Bowron
Lake
Provincial
Park

Quesnel

Barkerville

Tumbler
Ridge

Jasper

Williams
Lake

Wells
Gray
Provincial
Park

Glacier
National
Park

Mt Revelstoke
National
Park

Yoho
National
Park

Golden

Kootenay
National
Park

Port
Hardy

Campbell
River

Courtenay

Port Alberni

Whistler

Cache
Creek

100 Mile
House

Kamloops

Revelstoke

Vernon

Arrow
Lakes

Kootenay
Lake

Garibaldi
Provincial
Park

Harrison
Lake

Okanagan
Lake

Kelowna

Nelson

Cranbrook

Vancouver
Island

Nanaimo

Strathcona
Provincial
Park

Port Alberni

Pacific Rim
National
Park

Duncan

Sidney

VANCOUVER

Hope

Princeton

Penticton

Osoyoos

Castlegar

VICTORIA

White Rock

Blaine

WASHINGTON
(USA)

IDAHO   MONTANA

The arrival of the trans-continental railway in 1885 opened up BC to the east; and the settlement of the prairies around this time created demand for the province's resources, particularly timber. The building of the Panama Canal, which was completed in 1914, meant easier access to markets in Europe and along North America's east coast. This brought about a boom for the BC economy.

Following WWI, however, there was an economic downturn which led to industrial unrest and unemployment. After a brief recovery, the Wall St crash of 1929 brought severe depression and hardship. Prosperity only returned with the advent of WWII and was sustained after the war with the discovery of new resources and the development of a manufacturing base.

The two major Canadian political parties, the Liberals and the Conservatives, have made little headway in this province. The Social Credit Party, ostensibly the party of small business, was in power for much of the 1970s and 1980s. In 1991 its main opposition, the New Democrat Party (NDP), which advocates a form of limited socialism, came to power.

BC politics can be volatile; the unions are strong and active, and the electorate is very opinionated.

Climate

BC's climate is varied, influenced as it is by latitude, distance from the moderating effects of the Pacific Ocean and by the mountainous terrain. On the coast it is mild with warm, mostly dry summers and cool, very wet winters. The interior is much drier, particularly in the south along the Okanagan Valley; summers are hot and the winters cold. In the mountains, summers are short, tend to wetness and the nights are cool. Winter snowfalls are heavy.

Unless you're coming for the winter activities like skiing, the best time to visit is from around early June to early October. During this period there is less rain, temperatures are warm, daylight hours are long and the transport routes are open.

Economy

BC enjoys a high standard of living based on its major industries of forestry, tourism, mining, agriculture and fishing. Casual work is often available in these industries. Despite problems, BC's economy is growing at a faster rate than other provinces as the country struggles to recover from the recession of the late 1980s and early 90s. Forestry is BC's largest industry employing 18% of the workforce either directly or indirectly. More than five million tourists visit BC each year and tourism contributes around $4.5 billion dollars to the provincial economy. Mining contributes another $4 billion dollars with the most important minerals being coal, copper, zinc, gold and silver.

Unemployment continues to be high in this, Canada's most unionised (more than 37%) workforce.

BC has some serious problems with environmental degradation and pollution for which it has begun to seek solutions. The provincial government is now acting on the recommendations of a scientific panel on sustainable forest practices and has established a Commission on Resources & Environment to protect plant and animal species. It also plans to increase the protected parks and wilderness areas to 12% of the province. Despite massive negative publicity, BC now has a better environmental record than anywhere else in Canada. Nevertheless, there is still deep division within the community as the dispute in the middle of 1993 over the logging of old-growth forest in Clayoquot Sound on Vancouver Island demonstrated. Also, 1995 saw a dramatic downturn in salmon stocks which threatens the west coast fishery. Explanations and solutions are quickly being sought to this disturbing discovery.

The BC economy has become more and more linked with the so-called Pacific Rim countries and much of its growth has come through these increasing ties to the economies of Japan and the rest of Asia. Hong Kong money has been invested heavily in the province throughout the 1990s.

Top: The brilliant colour of ripening canola, southern Alberta
Middle: Horseshoe Canyon, part of the badlands near Drumheller, southern Alberta
Bottom: Downtown Calgary from Prince's Island Park, Alberta

DEANNA SWANEY

MARK LIGHTBODY

NICK ROBINSON

A	
	C
B	D

A: Boya Lake, northern British Columbia
B: Native woodcarving at the village of K'san, British Columbia
C: Thunderbird Park behind the museum in Victoria, British Columbia
D: Red squirrel, Yoho National Park, British Columbia

Population & People

With nearly 3.3 million people, BC is Canada's third most populous province, and the fastest growing. Vancouver is Canada's third largest city with a population of more than 1.6 million. The overwhelming majority of people live in the south of the province mainly in the small area in and around Vancouver in the south-west corner of the mainland and Victoria on the southern tip of Vancouver Island. The north is virtually empty in comparison.

Britain and Ireland are the ancestral homelands of most British Columbians. However, successive waves of migrants, especially since WWII, have produced a multiracial society with people coming from dozens of ethnic backgrounds. There are large groups whose origins are Ukrainian, German, Scandinavian, Dutch, Italian, Chinese, Japanese, East Indian or Indochinese, and many other smaller groups. In more recent years most migrants have come from other parts of Canada rather than from abroad, while Vancouver has also had a large influx of Hong Kong Chinese.

Twenty-eight Native Indian groups (often referred to as First Nations) live within the province and they have become more assertive over historical land claims and the right to govern themselves. The decline in their numbers has been reversed by the introduction of better health provisions, but problems of poverty, unemployment and alcoholism remain.

Information

Provincial Symbols The provincial flower is the Pacific dogwood, and the provincial bird is the blue-black Stellar's jay.

Tourist Offices Tourism BC is the name of the body which operates the province's comprehensive tourism infrastructure and also produces a mountain of literature covering just about everything the visitor needs to know. It oversees a broad network of well-signposted tourist offices – called Travel Infocentres – throughout BC, many of which operate as an arm of, or in conjunction with, the local Chamber of Commerce. Some are open year-round (mainly those in towns) but the majority are seasonal, only opening their doors between April or May and the first weekend in September. For information on travel and accommodation reservations in BC contact Tourism BC (☎ 685-0032 or 1-800-663-6000 in North America; fax 387-1590), Parliament Buildings, Victoria V8V 1X4.

The province is divided into nine tourism regions, each with its own central tourist association. For those seeking detailed information on a specific area, Tourism BC can supply addresses for any or all of these nine associations. Most tourist offices have information booklets on all regions.

Telephone The area code for metro Vancouver, east to Hope, north to Whistler, and north-east along the Sunshine Coast is 604. The rest of the province is 250. If, in your travels, you notice a forest fire, telephone the operator (☎ 0) and ask for Zenith 5555.

Time Most of BC is on Pacific Standard Time, three hours behind Eastern Standard Time. Two areas bordering Alberta, however, are on Mountain Standard Time: one is in the north-east around the Peace River; the other, in the south-east, covers the Rocky Mountains north from the Montana border to Vermount.

Tax There is a general provincial sales tax of 6%. Beer, wine and spirits have a tax of 10% while accommodation tax varies between 8% and 10%. There is no provincial tax on food bought in restaurants, or on books.

Activities

For general information about activities contact tourist offices.

Canoeing With the Pacific Ocean to the west and so many inlets, lakes and rivers there are plenty of opportunities to go canoeing on BC's waters. Some of the more popular spots are Bowron Lakes and Wells Gray provincial parks, and Slocan and

Okanagan lakes; and for ocean canoeing around Vancouver, the Gulf Islands and the Queen Charlotte Islands. There are dozens of destinations for whitewater canoeing (some are listed in the following section). Write to the Recreational Canoeing Association of BC (☎ 275-6651), 1200 Hornby St, Vancouver, V6Z 2E2, for details.

Caving Exploring caves may not be everybody's idea of fun, but there are two main places where the inexperienced can do it. They are the Cody Caves in the Kootenays north of Nelson, and the Horne Lake Caves on Vancouver Island. Gold River, also on Vancouver Island, offers further excellent caving opportunities.

Cycling You can either go cycling on your own or in organised group tours. Many places in BC have bicycles for rent. The leaflet *Trail Bicycling in National Parks in Alberta & British Columbia* lists trails where cycling is allowed.

In Vancouver one of the most popular spots for cycling is along the 10-km road in Stanley Park. Around BC other favourite areas are the Rocky and Kootenay mountains for mountain-biking; the Fraser River Valley; the Gulf Islands; and along Vancouver Island's east coast. For information and maps contact the Cycling BC (☎ 737-3034), 1367 West Broadway, Vancouver V6H 4H9.

Fishing Fishing, both the saltwater and freshwater variety, is one of BC's major tourist attractions. Particularly popular are the waters around Vancouver Island (where several places claim the title 'salmon capital of the world') and the Queen Charlotte Islands; the Fraser, Thompson, Nass, Skeena, Kettle, Peace and Liard rivers; and the lakes of the High Country, Cariboo, Chilcotin and Okanagan Similkameen regions. Commercial operators offer boat rentals or charters or there are all-inclusive packages which include transport and accommodation. For further information contact BC Tourism.

Fishing is controlled by law and you will have to obtain a licence. This is a simple procedure; they are widely available from sporting good stores and outfitters inexpensively and on the spot. There are short-period licences and annual permits.

Hang Gliding British Columbia's rugged mountains, offer some of the best terrain for hang gliding to be found anywhere. Back-country roads take you to launch sites throughout the province. Mt Seven, south-east of Golden, has been the site of several world and Canadian hang-gliding records. Some of the best sites for hang gliding are the south-east of Vancouver Island, Salt Spring Island, the Fraser Valley, the Kamloops area, the Okanagan Valley, the Kootenay Mountains, and in the north around Dawson Creek.

For more information contact the Hang Gliding Association of BC (☎ 980-9566), 933 Adderley, North Vancouver. The *Western Canada Hang Gliding Site Guide* describes launch sites and landing zones in detail.

Hiking Almost any kind of hiking experience is possible in BC: from short walks of a few hours along well-marked, easily accessible trails to treks of one or two weeks in remote terrain where you have to take your own food and equipment and be flown in by helicopter. There are well over 2000 km of maintained trails in the national and provincial parks giving you access to many of the province's most outstanding scenic features.

Close to Vancouver there are many good walks: in the Coast Mountains, Garibaldi Provincial Park and around Whistler to the north; and in the Cascade Mountains to the east. From Manning Provincial Park the Pacific Crest Trail goes all the way to Mexico! On Vancouver Island the trails in the Pacific Rim National Park as well as Strathcona Provincial Park offer opportunities to see both marine and land wildlife, as do those in South Moresby Gwaii Haanas National Park Reserve in the Queen Charlotte Islands.

In the south-east of the province there is a host of walks (varying in degree of difficulty) in the provincial and national parks in and around the Rocky, Columbia and Cariboo mountains. Finally, to the north, for the adventurous, there is Tweedsmuir Provincial Park and in the far north Spatsizi Plateau and Kwadachi wilderness parks.

Many of these areas are also very good for rock-climbing or mountaineering.

Sailing Sailing is another popular form of recreation and, though the best time is from mid-April to mid-October, in the sheltered waters of BC's Pacific coast it's possible almost year-round. Coastal marine parks provide safe all-weather anchorage and offer boat hire. Inland, some of the more favoured places include Harrison, Okanagan, Arrow and Kootenay lakes in the south, and Williston Lake in the north.

Scuba Diving The rich and varied marine life in the waters along BC's 7000-km Pacific coast make scuba diving a very rewarding activity. The best time to go is winter when the plankton has decreased and visibility often exceeds 20 metres. The water temperature drops to about 7°C to 10°C in winter while in summer it reaches 15°C. At depths of more than 15 metres, though, visibility is good throughout the year and temperatures rarely rise above 10°C.

The best places to dive are in the waters off the Pacific Rim National Park on Vancouver Island's west coast; in Georgia Strait between Vancouver Island's east coast and the mainland's Sunshine Coast north of Vancouver; and in Queen Charlotte Strait off Vancouver Island's north-east coast.

Skiing BC's climate and mountainous terrain provide great conditions for downhill and cross-country (nordic) skiing in the many skiing resorts and provincial and national parks. Most of the downhill ski resorts are equipped with chair lifts which serve vertical rises that range between 400 and 700 metres plus a few around the 1100-metre mark. The cross-country resorts offer about 1500 km of prepared trails with thousands more km of unmarked trails. Many of the ski resorts have hotel accommodation either on the mountain or nearby. It's also possible to go heli-skiing or skitouring to the remoter parts of the province. Pick up a copy of Tourism BC's brochure *British Columbia Skiing* (free from any Travel Infocentre), which lists all the major downhill and cross-country skiing centres in the province. Most of these centres are in the south, from Vancouver Island eastward through to the Rocky Mountains.

Near Vancouver to the north are Blackcomb, Whistler and Grouse mountains and the Cypress Bowl and Seymour Ski Country resorts; Hemlock Valley and Manning Provincial Park resorts are to the east. On Vancouver Island you can ski on Cain, Washington and Arrowsmith mountains and Forbidden Plateau. In the Okanagan Valley region the ski resorts include Apex Alpine, Silver Star, Big White Mountain and Baldy Mountain.

In the Rocky Mountains area in the south-east of the province the main ski resorts are at Rossland-Trail, Fernie Snow Valley, Kimberley, Panorama, Fairmont Hot Springs and Whitetooth.

In the centre of BC along the Yellowhead Hwy between Prince Rupert and the Alberta border there is access to a number of secondary ski areas, including Hudson Bay Mountain near Smithers, and Tabor and Purden mountains near Prince George. These are less crowded and accommodation is cheaper than the resorts to the south.

Surfing In Pacific Rim National Park on Vancouver Island, Long Beach reputedly has the best surfing in BC.

Whale Watching Killer (orca) whales inhabit the waters off the west coast around Vancouver Island. Tours run south from Victoria and also north in Johnstone Strait particularly around Robson Bight, an ecological reserve. Pacific grey whales migrate between Baja California and Alaska, travelling north in spring and south in the autumn.

They may be seen anywhere around the island but best are trips from Ucluelet or Tofino.

Whitewater Rafting BC's topography means that there are many rivers throughout the province suitable for this increasingly popular sport. Check with the local Travel Infocentre for details of where to go and which companies to use. You don't need to be experienced. Commercial rafting is regulated by the provincial government and operators are allowed only on rivers that have been checked over by experts, guides must meet certain qualifications and companies must provide equipment that meets government requirements. Trips can last from three hours up to a couple of weeks. Wilderness rafting averages about $200 per day for everything, while half-day trips start from about $45.

The more favoured rivers are the Fraser, Thompson and Chilliwack close to Vancouver; to the east in the High Country near Kamloops the Adams and Clearwater rivers; in the Rockies the Kootenay, Kicking Horse and Illecillewaet rivers; the Chilko and Chilcotin rivers in the Cariboo region west of Williams Lake; and in the north the Skeena, Spatsizi, Stikine, Alsek and Tatshenshini rivers.

National & Provincial Parks BC has six national parks and more than 340 provincial parks covering 9% of the province, an area nearly twice the size of Switzerland. A new national park to be situated on several Gulf Islands is in the planning stages. *Road Map & Parks Guide*, produced by Tourism BC and available free at Travel Infocentres, lists them all with their location and facilities. There are also publications and maps on individual parks which you can get by visiting or writing to the following:

BC Parks
    Parliament Buildings, Victoria, BC V8V 1X4
Ministry of Environment, Lands & Parks
    Visitor Services, 4000 Seymour Place, Victoria V8V 1X5 (☎ 387-5002; fax 387-5757)
Outdoor Recreation Council of BC
    Suite 334, 1367 West Broadway, Vancouver, BC V6H 4A9 (☎ 737-3000/58; fax 738-7175)
Parks Canada Information Services
    Western Regional Office, Room 520, 220 4th Ave SE, PO Box 2989, Station M, Calgary, Alberta T2P 3H8 (☎ (403) 292-4401; fax (403) 292-4746)

Four of the national parks are close to each other in the south-east – Yoho, Kootenay, Glacier and Mt Revelstoke. Yoho and Kootenay adjoin Alberta's Banff National Park in the Rocky Mountains while Glacier and Mt Revelstoke are to the east in the

Despite their size (up to 2.5 metres long and 410 kg) grizzlies can run as fast as 48 km per hour

Columbia Mountains. The Trans Canada Hwy passes through all four.

Pacific Rim National Park stretches along Vancouver Island's west coast and is divided in two by Barkley Sound and includes the Broken Group Islands. South Moresby Gwaii Haanas National Park, inaccessible by road, is in the Queen Charlotte Islands.

Provincial parks occur throughout BC. They vary enormously in size from, for example, the 6568 sq km of Spatsizi Plateau Wilderness Park in the north-west to the one hectare of Ballingall Islets between southern Vancouver Island and the mainland. Most of them can be reached on sealed or gravel roads in conventional vehicles, while for some you will need a 4WD vehicle. Some parks have no road access at all and you'll have to hike in. You can take a ferry to a few of them.

Some of the national and provincial parks are open all year, but the majority are closed during winter and only open from April or May to September or October. Many have vehicle (RV) and tent camp sites, picnic areas and toilets and offer activities such as hiking, swimming, boating and fishing. At most of them a camping fee, between $6 and $17, is charged during the peak visiting season. Near the more popular parks there are motels and privately run campgrounds.

Some places considered historically significant have also been set aside as parks. Examples of these are Barkerville east of Quesnel, Fort Rodd Hill near Victoria and Fort Steele in the south-east near Cranbrook.

Much of the forests of the province can be used for recreation and camping at no cost. Because these areas are not well publicised they are generally not busy and camping spots may be found when others in the area are fully booked. Most tourist information centres around the province will have copies of the good maps available for the local forest district. The Ministry of Forests (☎ 387-6656; in Vancouver ☎ 660-7500), Integrated Resource Branch – Recreation Section, 1450 Government St, Victoria, V8W 3E7, may also have information available.

Accommodation

Super Camping is a free guide available at Travel Infocentres. It gives region by region lists (not comprehensive) of private and government-owned campgrounds and their facilities, opening periods and prices. There is a fee for camping in nearly all provincial and national parks during the summer season.

Hostelling International has five hostels in BC – Kamloops, Penticton, Vancouver, Victoria and Whistler – as well as a number of associate ones. For information contact Hostelling International, BC Region (☎ 604-684-7111; fax 604-684-7181), Suite 402, 134 Abbott St, Vancouver, V6B 2K4.

Also, available from Travel Infocentres is the free brochure *Accommodations*, published annually, which lists places to stay approved by Tourism BC. Most of the hotels and motels listed begin in the moderate price range. It also includes YM-YWCAs, some campgrounds and some B&Bs. Near the back of the brochure is a listing of regional B&B agencies to contact.

For more information on B&Bs throughout the province get in touch with British Columbia B&B Association (☎ 276-8616), PO Box 593, 810 West Broadway, Vancouver, V5Z 4E2. It's also worthwhile obtaining a copy of the *British Columbia B&B Directory*, which is a free booklet listing B&Bs across the province. It's available at Travel Infocentres, but is very popular, so not all offices may have a spare copy. If it's not on display, ask.

Vancouver

Vancouver lies nestled between sea and mountains in the extreme south-western corner of British Columbia. Its physical setting and features make it easily one of the most scenically attractive cities in Canada, if not the world. The hilly terrain it's built on and the many bridges offer beautiful views of the ocean, sheltered bays and of the city itself.

The parks are numerous and large. One, Stanley Park, is the size of the downtown business area. Sandy beaches dot the shoreline and, like the towering mountains just out of the city, can be used for sports and recreation. Few cities can match Vancouver for its number and variety of interesting sights.

The port, the busiest on North America's west coast, operates all year round in the beautiful and practical natural harbour. It handles nearly all of Canada's trade with Japan and Asia. This connection has been strengthened by the numbers of mainly Chinese immigrants of the early 1990s. The city is now the most Asian in North America.

The US border is just 40 km to the south. Along with the city's physical resemblance to San Francisco, the attitudes and lifestyles of Vancouverites are more Californian than elsewhere in the country. The mild climate, at least in Canadian terms, further extends the comparison with California, and attracts many eastern Canadians. The average January temperature is 2°C, the July average 17°C. It rarely snows and is not often oppressively hot. The only drawback is the rain, particularly in winter when it rarely stops and the cloud cover obliterates the view of the surrounding mountains. Even in summer a rainy spell can last for weeks. But when the sun shines and the mountains reappear, most people here seem to forget all the soakings they've had.

History

The Vancouver area was first inhabited by Salish Indians. The first European to see the region was the Spanish explorer Don Jos Maria Narvaez in 1791. There wasn't a real settlement until 1865, when the Hastings Timber Mill was built. In 1867 a town sprang up around 'Gassy' Jack Deighton's bar. Gastown, as it became known, was the centre around which Vancouver grew.

In 1884 the Canadian Pacific Railway (CPR) chose Vancouver for the western terminal of the newly built national railway. Soon after the town became incorporated, taking its name from Captain George Vancouver, a British explorer, who had sailed

right into Burrard Inlet in 1792. On 13 June 1886 a fire almost completely destroyed the city in less than an hour, killing 21 people. Reconstruction began immediately and by 1889, with the CPR's work done, the population jumped to 8000. The city became the port for trade to Asia, and the population rose to 42,000 by 1901.

In the next 10 years, the city boomed with the development of the fishing and wood-processing industries. Immigrants poured in. The completion of the Panama Canal increased Vancouver's significance as a port.

WWII catapulted the city into the modern era, and from then on it changed rapidly. The western end became the high-rise apartment centre it now is. In 1974 Granville St became a mall. Redevelopment included housing as well as office buildings and this set the basis for the modern, liveable city Vancouver is today.

In 1986 the city hosted Expo 86, a very successful world's fair. A few prominent structures remain, while the rest of the area where it took place is now being redeveloped. In April 1993 the city's international reputation was enhanced when it hosted the summit meeting between Boris Yeltsin and Bill Clinton. Through 1995 the city continued to grow in size and international stature with increasing numbers of countries locating consulates here.

Orientation

Vancouver proper is built on a strip of land bounded on the north by Burrard Inlet and on the south by the Fraser River. The city, however, spreads south and east to include suburbs such as Richmond, Burnaby, New Westminster, Surrey, Coquitlam and Langley. To the north of Burrard Inlet lie West Vancouver and North Vancouver. The many bays, inlets and river branches, as well as the Pacific coastline, are a major feature of the city.

Generally, the avenues in Greater Vancouver run east-west; the streets go north and south. Some of the streets in the downtown area as well as many of the avenues in the Greater Vancouver area are given east or

Vancouver

1 Capilano RV Park
2 Canyon Court Hotel
3 BC Rail Station &
   Royal Hudson Steam Train
4 North Vancouver Museum & Archives
5 Globetrotter's Inn
6 Exhibition Park
7 Pacific Central Station & Bus Depot
8 HI Vancouver Jericho Hostel
9 Shaughnessy Village
10 Vancouver General Hospital
11 Vandusen Botanical Gardens
12 Nat Bailey Stadium
13 Vancouver International Centre
14 Burnaby Heritage Village

west designations. So Hastings St, for example, is divided into West Hastings St and East Hastings St. As a rule the dividing cross street is Main but this varies a block or three either side in some cases.

Downtown The real downtown area, in the north-western section of the city, is actually a peninsula, cut off from the southern portion of the city by False Creek. Robson Square, a three-block complex of offices, restaurants, shops and theatres, is pretty well the centre of downtown. It lies on the corner of Robson and Howe Sts. Robson St and, two blocks north, Georgia St, are the two principal north-west/south-east streets. Both streets run into Stanley Park, however Georgia St continues through the park to Lions Gate Bridge which spans Burrard Inlet, joining it to the separate municipalities of North and West Vancouver.

The main north-east/south-west streets are, from west to east: Burrard, Howe, Granville and Seymour. North of Georgia St, bordered by Howe and Burrard Sts, is the main office, banking and financial district. Robson St is an interesting area with a blend of many ethnic shops, designer clothing stores and restaurants.

The area south of Robson St and west of Howe St all the way to Sunset Beach on English Bay is primarily residential in the form of high-rise apartments.

This high-density area to the west of the downtown shopping area is known as the West End – *not* to be confused with West Vancouver on the North Shore, or the West Side, which is that part of Vancouver south of False Creek and west of Main St. Davie St, between Robson St and the beach, is a secondary commercial and shopping street which also runs into Stanley Park.

On and around Granville and Seymour Sts, which run north-east from False Creek all the way to West Hastings St, are some of the cheaper hotels.

Much of Granville St, from Nelson St north to West Hastings St, is closed to cars. It's not a true mall as trucks and buses are

still permitted and it has never worked very well as a central showcase. It's fairly drab and quiet during the day, but at night it's a lively focal point for some of the city's street scene. Musicians and various buskers line the street, teenagers by the dozen parade, various eccentrics and misfits appear and street kids beg for money. The southern end towards the bridge is something of a red-light area, with a mix of sex shops and bars advertising 'exotic' dancers. A couple of large legitimate cinemas also draw crowds to the area, so it's quite a mix.

Also on Granville St are the two main department stores, Eaton's and the Bay. Below these, towards Burrard Inlet, is the modern underground shopping mall called the Pacific Centre.

Yaletown on Hamilton and Mainland Sts at Davie St is currently the 'hot' part of town with old warehouses being converted to hip bars, restaurants and apartments.

Georgia St near Granville St is the area with some of the city's top hotels. At the northern end of Granville and Seymour Sts is West Hastings St.

Further north, at the bottom of Granville St near Burrard Inlet, is Granville Place and Harbour Centre. Here you'll find modern shopping complexes with views of the harbour. At the water's edge at the foot of Howe St is the impressive Canada Place with its jagged white 'sails'.

Hastings St is lined with bottom-end hotels, bars, restaurants, pawnshops and army surplus-type shops. For a couple of blocks either side of Main St it's the total dregs with many down-and-outs (see the Dangers & Annoyances section later). Gastown is north of West Hastings St between Columbia and Richards Sts. This is the interesting, tourist-oriented, restored area of old Vancouver.

Chinatown is very close by to the south, in the area around Pender, Gore and Carrall Sts.

The Pacific National Exhibition (PNE) stadium and exhibition grounds are further east on East Hastings St, near the Second Narrows Bridge.

Greater Vancouver To the south of the West End and downtown, over False Creek, lies most of Vancouver – this vast area is primarily residential.

West Heading west after crossing Burrard Bridge or Granville Bridge is the area of Kitsilano, very popular with young people and students as well as professionals. When a young person from BC's interior moves to the city, this is where he or she wants to be. The main artery through the area is West 4th Ave. It's lined with shops, restaurants and cafes, few of which are pricey. The other important thoroughfare is West Broadway, south of West 4th Ave.

There are beaches all along English Bay, from Kitsilano past Jericho Beach and Spanish Banks to the University of British Columbia (UBC) campus. Just before the campus is one of the expensive areas of town, with good views of the city. UBC is at the far western end of the 'hump' sticking out into the Strait of Georgia. You can walk around the coast all the way to Wreck Beach, south of the university (but wait until the tide is out).

South Between Kitsilano and Sea Island – where Vancouver International Airport is located – are some of the city's most exclusive areas, such as Shaughnessy Heights. Estates line South-West Marine Drive, facing out to Sea Island.

Further south is the rapidly growing largely Asian municipality of Richmond, built on a portion of the Fraser River Delta. On the southern side of Fraser River is Burns Bog; this is used for peat extraction so very little building goes on.

Still further south is the port of Tsawwassen, where you can catch a ferry to Vancouver Island, the Gulf Islands or Seattle.

East East of downtown running south from Powell St, Commercial Drive is Vancouver's main Italian street. It's the focal point for a developing arty, student and professional neighbourhood.

Burnaby, east of Vancouver proper, is another residential area and contains Simon Fraser University. The Trans Canada Hwy runs through the centre of Burnaby on its way from Vancouver east to Chilliwack and north-west to Horseshoe Bay.

South-east of Burnaby is the city of New Westminster, an area along the Fraser River with many old wooden houses and lots of industry. On the southern side of the river from New Westminster is Surrey.

North Over Lions Gate Bridge and Second Narrows Bridge lie West Vancouver and North Vancouver, both essentially middle-class residential areas, although parts of the western area are very exclusive. The shore of Burrard Inlet in North Vancouver is lined with commercial docks. In North Vancouver the principal north-south street is Lonsdale Ave. To the east is Lynn Canyon Park, and beyond is Mt Seymour Provincial Park. To the north along Capilano Rd are Capilano Canyon, the Lions Peaks (from which Lions Gate Bridge takes its name), Grouse Mountain and the edges of the Coast Mountains. Further west and north lie Cypress Provincial Park, Horseshoe Bay (from where you can take a ferry to Vancouver Island) and the Sunshine Coast (which is also reached by ferry from Horseshoe Bay).

Information

Tourist Offices The Travel Infocentre, Plaza Level, Waterfront Centre, 200 Burrard St, is open in the summer daily from 8 am to 6 pm, and the rest of the year Monday to Friday from 8.30 am to 5 pm, Saturday from 9 am to 5 pm. Though usually busy, the staff are friendly and helpful but don't forget to take a number! They will help you with bookings for accommodation, tours, transport and activities. Call ☎ 683-2000 for information or ☎ 683-2772 for bookings. At the infocentre get a copy of *The Vancouver Book*, the official visitors' guide, which has information on shopping, accommodation, entertainment, local transport, etc and is free. Also useful is the monthly booklet *Where Vancouver*, available around town, often at hotels.

On the corner of Georgia and Granville Sts is an information booth open in summer Tuesday to Friday from 10 am to 6 pm. Travel information is available in Tsawwassen at the ferry dock. There are information booths at either end of the George Massey Tunnel under the Fraser River on the way to Tsawwassen. If you're coming from the east along the Trans Canada Hwy you'll see the signs as you get closer to town. Another infocentre is south on Hwy 99 just inside the US border.

The HI Vancouver Hostel has a notice board that lists rides, plane tickets, goods for sale and sometimes job offers.

Money Changing foreign currency or travellers' cheques is no problem. If you need to do any banking outside normal business hours quite a few banks around town open Saturday including: Canada Trust, on the corner of East Pender and Main Sts, open from 9 am to 5 pm; Royal Bank, 269 East Pender St, open from 9 am to 3 pm; Toronto Dominion, on the corner of East Pender and Columbia Sts, open 9 am to 4 pm; and Royal Bank, 2907 West Broadway, open from 9.30 am to 3.30 pm.

Thomas Cook has a number of offices in Vancouver including one (☎ 687-6111) at 1016 West Georgia St and another at Suite 130, 999 Canada Place. American Express (☎ 669-2813) is close by at 1040 West Georgia St. They're open on Saturday too.

You can also find currency-exchange offices, usually in the heavily touristed areas and often open every day. Downtown, International Securities Exchange (☎ 683-9666), 1169 Robson St, is open Monday to Thursday from 9 am to 7 pm, Friday and Saturday from 9 am to 9 pm, and Sunday from 10 am to 7 pm.

Vancouver Airport provides banking and money-changing facilities too (see the Getting There & Away section later).

Post The main post office (☎ 662-5725), 349 West Georgia St between Homer and Hamilton Sts, is open Monday to Friday from 8 am to 5.30 pm. It has no separate poste-restante counter: you just join the queue, show some identification and the person behind the counter will look for your mail. The post office also has a good philatelic desk and a photocopier.

The American Express office, 1040 West Georgia St, will keep a card-holder's mail for a month.

Foreign Consulates The following is a partial list of the extensive number of countries with diplomatic representation in Vancouver. For a complete listing see under Consulates in the Yellow Pages. The Facts for the Visitor chapter at the beginning of this book also has a section on consulates and embassies based in Ottawa.

Australia
    Suite 602, Canada Place, 999 Canada Place, V6C 3E1 (☎ 684-1177)
France
    Suite 1201, 736 Granville St, V6Z 1H9 (☎ 681-2301)
Germany
    Suite 704, 999 Canada Place, V6C 3E1 (☎ 684-4258)
Japan
    900 Board of Trade Tower, 1177 West Hastings St, V6E 2K9 (☎ 684-5868)
New Zealand
    Suite 1200, 888 Dunsmuir St (☎ 684-7388)
Switzerland
    Suite 790, World Trade Centre, 999 Canada Place V6C 3E1 (☎ 684-2231)
UK
    Suite 800, 1111 Melville St, V6E 3V6 (☎ 683-4421; fax 581-0693)
USA
    1095 West Pender St, V6E 2M6 (☎ 685-4311)

Travel Agencies Travel CUTS, the student travel organisation, has four offices in Vancouver: one at Suite 501, 602 West Hastings St (☎ 681-9136), another at 1516 Duranleau St, Granville Island (☎ 687-6033) and one on the campus of each university, UBC and Simon Fraser.

Bookshops Vancouver has a number of very good bookshops. Duthie Books (☎ 684-4496), 919 Robson St, on the corner of Hornby St, has a range of books including a travel and Canadiana section. It has several other branches including one at UBC. Book Warehouse (☎ 685-5711), 1150 Robson St, has good quality books, many at bargain prices. It's open seven days a week from 10 am to 10 pm. World Wide Books & Maps (☎ 687-3320), 736A Granville St, down a flight of stairs, has a variety of travel guides, atlases and maps for Canada and abroad. Another good bookshop is Blackberry Books (☎ 685-6188/4113), 1663 Duranleau St on Granville Island. It's open daily from 9 am to 9 pm and has two more outlets in Kitsilano. Also in Kitsilano at 2667 West Broadway, the Travel Bug (☎ 737-1122) has travel guides and maps plus language tapes and accessories.

Smith Books and Cole's are general chainstore bookshops, both with branches downtown in the Pacific Centre Mall.

Library The huge, new, architecturally controversial Vancouver Public Library (☎ 331-4000), is at the corner of West Georgia St and Hamilton St. Looking somewhat like the Roman Coliseum, the airy, striking building is open Monday to Wednesday from 10 am to 9 pm, and Thursday to Saturday 10 am to 6 pm. In winter (October to March) it's open on Sunday from 1 to 5 pm.

Medical Services Vancouver General Hospital is at 855 West 12th Ave. The emergency number is ☎ 875-4995; call ☎ 875-4000 for patient information.

Dangers & Annoyances Hastings St, for a couple of blocks either side of Main St, is not a good area. After dark it's advisable to stay out of the side streets. By day it's safe albeit grubby and has a few places you may want to visit. Granville St south of Robson St also gets a bit tacky with boarded up storefronts and unsettling with homeless streetkids in some numbers.

If you're driving, traffic congestion and finding a place to park can be a problem (see the Car section under Getting Around later).

Useful Organisations The Western Canada

Gassy Jack

In the mid-19th century the men working in the sawmills along the shores of Burrard Inlet weren't allowed to drink alcohol on mill property. They had to travel a long way into town, New Westminster, to find somewhere to imbibe. An enterprising former riverboat captain, John Deighton, saw his opportunity and landed in his canoe close to the mill area with his wife, a few animals and a small barrel of whisky. He began selling the whisky almost immediately and soon became a huge success. He was called 'Gassy Jack' because he talked so much; the community that developed around his saloon, became known as Gassy's Town then Gastown. ■

Wilderness Committee (☎ 683-8220), 20 Water St in Gastown, has information and maps on hiking trails in wilderness areas and books on environmental awareness issues relating mainly to Western Canada. It helped to open up walking trails in old-growth forest areas such as the Carmanah and Clayoquot valleys and Meares Island. It also has a nature walking guide to Stanley Park.

The British Columbia Automobile Association (BCAA) (☎ 268-5600), 999 West Broadway, has a 24-hour breakdown service for its own members and those of other automobile associations.

Disabled persons can call the Handicapped Resource Line (☎ 875-6381). The Gay and Lesbian Centre (☎ 684-6869) is at 1170 Bute St.

Downtown

Gastown The name is taken from 'Gassy' Jack Deighton, an English sailor who forsook the sea to open a bar servicing the developing timber mills. When a village sprang up around his establishment it was called Gassy's Town. The name stuck and Vancouver was on its way. The Gastown area today is bounded by Columbia and Richards Sts, with Water St the main thoroughfare. Burrard Inlet is just to the north. A statue of Gassy Jack has been erected in Maple St Square, where Cordova and Water Sts meet.

Downtown Vancouver

0   250   500 m

SeaBus to
North Vancouver

Burrard
Inlet

Centennial
Pier

CHINATOWN

GASTOWN

WEST END

Burrard Bridge

Sunset Beach Park

Vanier
Park

False Creek

Granville
Island

Cambie Bridge

Granville
Bridge

To Stanley
Park & North
Shore

To Paul's Guest
House & Queen
Elizabeth Park

2nd Avenue

BRITISH COLUMBIA

PLACES TO STAY		4	Bud's Halibut & Chips	14	Vancouver Aquatic
		5	Ciao!		Centre
8	Riviera Motor Inn	6	Pepita's	15	Granville Island Public
9	Barclay Hotel	7	Saigon		Market
12	HI Vancouver	10	Fogg 'n' Suds	23	Duthie Books
	Downtown Hostel	11	Fresgo's	26	Burrard Station
16	Travelodge	20	Bread Garden	28	Travel Infocentre
17	Cecil Hotel	21	Heidelberg House	29	Canada Place
18	Hotel California	22	White Spot	30	Granville Square
19	YMCA	32	Jolly Taxpayer Hotel &	31	Waterfront Station
24	Hotel Vancouver		Pub	33	Pendulum
25	Hyatt Regency	38	Elephant & Castle	35	Vancouver Art Gallery
27	Day's Inn	49	Kilimanjaro	36	Robson Square
34	Hotel Georgia	51	Water St Café	37	Pacific Centre
39	St Regis Hotel	52	Old Spaghetti Factory	40	Granville Station
41	Dufferin Hotel	53	Brother's Restaurant	43	Vancouver Public
42	Kingston Hotel	61	Only Seafoods Café		Library
44	YWCA	62	Bodai Vegetarian	45	Queen Elizabeth
47	Niagara Hotel		Restaurant		Theatre & Vancouver
54	Dominion Hotel	63	Miu Jay Garden		Playhouse
55	New Backpackers		Vegetarian	46	Main Post Office
	Hostel		Restaurant	48	Harbour Centre
64	Patricia Hotel	66	Pho Lu Zuan	50	Steam Clock
65	Harbourfront Inn	67	Max King Bakery &	56	Stadium Station
70	Vincent's Backpackers		Restaurant	57	BC Place Stadium
	Hostel	68	Hon's Wun Tun House	58	GM Place
		69	Punjab Restaurant	59	World's Thinnest Office
PLACES TO EAT					Building
		OTHER		60	Dr Sun Yat-Sen
1	Great Wall Mongolian				Chinese Classical
	BBQ	13	HR MacMillan		Garden
2	Café Slavia		Planetarium &	71	Science World
3	Musashi Japanese		Vancouver Museum	72	Main Street Station
	Restaurant			73	Pacific Central Station
					& Bus Depot

The whole Gastown area gradually became a skid row, but in the 1970s it was restored and renovated, simply pushing Vancouver's seedier characters a little further south to Hastings St. The old Victorian buildings now house restaurants, bars, boutiques and galleries. The brick streets have been lined with old lamps. Street vendors and buskers add to the holiday feel of the area which is lively day and night. The historic flavour is only a little marred by the parking lot several storeys high in Water St.

At the western end of Water St is the world's first clock run by steam. You can see it work through the side glass panels and will hear it toot every 15 minutes.

Chinatown About 35,000 people of Chinese descent live in the area around West Pender St, roughly bordered by Abbott and Gore Sts.

For the most part it's genuine, serving the locals. Even some of the young people don't speak English. Through the day the streets are full of people going in and out of stores of hanging ducks and chickens or oriental remedies and groceries. There are restaurants and bakeries as well. The colours, signs and occasional old Chinese-style balcony can make you believe for a second that you're in Hong Kong, especially when you see the Chinese characters on signs for banks and Hertz Rent-a-Car. There are tourist and souvenir shops interspersed with the community businesses. For years the area has contended with the run-down Hastings and Main St blights and this is finally taking a toll. Trade is slowing down in Chinatown and much of the new population and investment has headed to Richmond. Now at night it's a pretty quiet area.

BRITISH COLUMBIA

World's Thinnest Office Building Called the Sam Kee, this building at 8 West Pender St, near the corner of Carrall St, has made it into Ripley's *Believe It Or Not* and the *Guinness Book of Records*. It's easy to miss not only due to narrowness but because it looks like the front of the larger building behind, to which it is attached.

Dr Sun Yat-Sen Classical Chinese Garden This is the only full-scale classical Chinese garden (☎ 689-7133) found outside China. Its design is subtle but exquisite in execution and effect. Modelled after the Ming Dynasty gardens, best represented in the city of Suzhou, it makes a real sanctuary in the centre of the city. The Taoist principles of Yin and Yang are incorporated in numerous ways throughout the garden.

The guided tours are included in the admission and are well worthwhile. If possible, go during the week when it won't be too busy. It's at 578 Carrall St behind the Chinese Cultural Centre in Chinatown. It opens daily from 10 am to 6 pm and admission is $4.50. The last of the hourly tours begins at 4:30 pm. The adjacent park, built by local artisans using Chinese materials, is similar in design and has free entry.

Robsonstrasse Robsonstrasse is the local name given to the section of Robson St between Howe and Broughton Sts. At one time mainly German, the area is now known for its many ethnic restaurants and shops. There are some Italian, French, Japanese, Vietnamese and Danish places among them. For more detailed information on restaurants, see the Places to Eat section. The area around Granville St has some exclusive fashion shops.

Stanley Park The city's main green area, a 400-hectare park, is one of the best in the country. With its wooded hills, parkland, trails, sports fields, swimming pools and

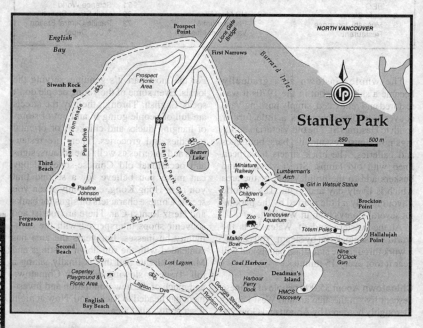

Stanley Park

beaches, there's something for everyone. The 10-km sea wall that encircles the park makes a good walk, run or bicycle ride even if you don't go all the way round. From various points there are good views of downtown Vancouver, the North Shore and out to sea towards the islands.

Along the western side are several sandy beaches; Lions Gate Bridge extends from the northern tip, and the road through the park to the bridge is usually busy. Just to the west of Lions Gate Bridge is **Prospect Point**, a popular point for views of the Narrows and passing ships. There's a restaurant here as well, which is a nice spot for a coffee on the terrace. Near **Brockton Point** there is a good collection of totem poles. Off the southern side, near the yacht club, is **Deadman's Island**, once used, it's said, by a northern Native Indian tribe as a camp for women captured in raids. Later it became a burial ground for Chinese people and Native Indians.

Vancouver Aquarium Within the park is the very busy Vancouver Aquarium (☎ 268-9900), Canada's largest, with 8000 sea creatures. Most popular are the dolphins and killer whales that put on shows several times a day. There is also a special (controversial) tank for beluga whales. Other exhibits include octopuses, crocodiles, eels, piranhas and a wide variety of local sea life and freshwater fish. The aquarium is also used for research. It's open every day from 9.30 am to 8 pm July to early September, from 10 am to 5.30 pm the rest of the year and admission is $11 for adults.

Vancouver Art Gallery The city's art gallery (☎ 682-5621), 750 Hornby St, is right at the centre of things. It has a large collection of work by Emily Carr, a one-time resident of the area and one of Canada's best-known painters.

There's also a survey collection of other Canadians, and some US and British paintings. The gallery is open 10 am to 6 pm Monday to Wednesday, 10 am to 9 pm on Thursday and Friday, 10 am to 5 pm on Saturday, and from noon to 5 pm on Sunday. Admission costs $6, but Thursday between 5 pm and closing it's pay what you want.

Pendulum Worth a look (duck your head) is the swaying 26-metre sculptural piece called Pendulum in the Hong Kong Bank of Canada. It's on West Georgia St opposite the Vancouver Art Gallery.

Canada Place Canada Place, built to coincide with Expo 86, juts into the harbour at the foot of Howe St. It resembles an ocean liner with tent-like sails and has become a major city landmark. At the northern end are the promenade shops and restaurants, and outside, good views across Burrard Inlet. The complex contains the World Trade Centre, the Vancouver Trade and Convention Centre, the Hotel Vancouver, the Pan Pacific Hotel, and is also a terminal for cruise ships. Also here is the CN IMAX Theatre (☎ 682-4629) with a five-storey-high screen showing films made exclusively for such theatres. Canada Place is very close to Waterfront Station.

BC Place BC Place Stadium (☎ 669-2300 for general information, ☎ 661-7373 for events), 777 Pacific Blvd South, is the unmistakeable large sports arena covered by a translucent dome-shaped roof. The roof is 'air-supported', which means it is inflated by huge fans (no, not sports fans) and kept in place by criss-crossed steel wires, hence its quilted appearance.

Concerts, trade shows, sports events and other large-scale gatherings are held during the year in this 60,000-capacity stadium which is also the home ground of the BC Lions football team.

To get to the stadium catch either bus No 15 or No 17, or take the SkyTrain to Stadium Station.

GM Place Situated right beside the stadium across Georgia St this sports arena, built in 1995 with a major financial commitment from General Motors, makes the area the major focus for the city's professional sports.

It is home to the Vancouver Canucks of the National Hockey League (NHL) as well as the Grizzlies of the National Basketball Association (NBA).

Royal Diamond Casino Tucked in behind the stadium by False Creek in the Plaza of Nations complex with restaurants, a theatre, offices and a marina is the casino (☎ 685-2340). The alcohol-free, casual-dress gambling hall is open nightly from 6 pm to 2 am with blackjack, roulette and other games of chance.

Concord Pacific Place This refers to the massive redevelopment project on the large tract of land along the waterfront at False Creek between the Cambie and Granville bridges. Formerly an area of disused railway lines and warehouses, it will contain apartments, parks, a theatre and museums as part of a 25-year plan. An arts and recreation centre is being created from the old rail Roundhouse. The site is to be Canada's first fibre optic community with direct links to the so-called information highway.

Science World A structure that remains from Expo 86 is the geodesic dome just off Quebec St near Main St Station. It now houses Science World (☎ 268-6363), a museum where you can get involved through touching and testing the displays. Aimed primarily at children, hands-on exhibits and experiments help explain scientific and physical phenomena. One of the main features is the OMNIMAX film theatre. Science World is open every day from 10 am to 6 pm except Saturday when it's open till 9 pm. The admission fee is $9 and the OMNIMAX theatre costs $9; a combined ticket is $12.

Views One of the best views of the city and surroundings is from the top of the **Sheraton Landmark Hotel**, 1400 Robson St, in the revolving restaurant and lounge. If you're eating, the elevator up is free. The hotel is one of the city's highest buildings. A second spot is the more-advertised observation deck (☎ 689-0421) and restaurant atop the **Harbour**

Centre Tower at 555 West Hastings St. The deck is open from 8.30 am to 10.30 pm (summer) and is reached by an external glass-walled elevator, which takes 50 seconds. The cost is $7, students $4; the ticket is valid all day so you can come and go. If you're going to eat in the restaurant, the ride up is free. Take a SkyTrain to Waterfront St or bus Nos 10, 14, 16, 20 heading towards the harbour on Granville Mall.

The commercial harbour area stretches along Burrard Inlet from Stanley Park to the Second Narrows Bridge. The plaza at Granville Square beside the SeaBus terminal, or Canada Place's observation deck, offer a view where you watch the many types of vessels moving in and out of the harbour.

West Side
Granville Island On the southern side of False Creek, under the Granville Bridge, this formerly industrial little island has been redeveloped into a busy blend of businesses, restaurants, galleries, and theatres. The Granville Island Information Centre (☎ 666-5784), 1592 Johnston St, is open daily from 9 am to 6 pm.

Major attractions include two important performing-arts centres, numerous theatre companies and, on the north-western tip, the popular Public Market, open daily 9 am to 6 pm, with fresh fruit, vegetables and fish. A few prepared-food counters sell small meals and snacks.

There are shops where local painters, jewellery makers and weavers make and display their crafts. Prices are fairly reasonable. You can also view the art galleries in the Emily Carr College of Art & Design (☎ 844-3800), 1299 Johnston St.

The Granville Island Brewing Co (☎ 688-9927), 1441 Cartwright St, is a small company producing naturally brewed beer (ie without chemicals), and gives free tours at 1 and 3 pm with a sample at the end.

On the north-eastern edge of the island it's interesting to have a look at the attractive, pricey, floating houses. To get to the island from either Water St in Gastown or Granville St downtown, catch the No 50 False Creek bus. The bus stops near the information centre. Alternatively, you can take the False Creek miniferry (see the Getting Around section for details). Much of the island's activity is shut down on Monday.

Vanier Park Vanier Park, on English Bay south of False Creek and below Burrard Bridge, is home to the Vancouver Museum, HR MacMillan Planetarium and the Vancouver Maritime Museum. Also in the park are the Vancouver Archives, Academy of Music, Canadian Coast Guard and Burrard Civic Marina. The park is a popular area and when the weather's fine you'll see people strolling, jogging, cycling, walking their dogs or simply sitting and watching the ships moving between English Bay and False Creek.

Vancouver Museum This museum (☎ 736-4431), 1100 Chestnut St, just west of Burrard Bridge and also called the Vancouver Centennial Museum, specialises in local history. On display are old photos of BC and sections on the archaeology of the area, concentrating on the Salish Indians and ethnology. There are a few examples of most Native Indian crafts. The basketry is impressive, especially those made of cedar and pine roots. The part of the museum showing the European exploration and settlement of Vancouver is interesting. The last of the Hudson's Bay Company forts – Fort Victoria – was here.

The museum is open daily May to September from 10 am to 7 pm; from October to April it's open Tuesday to Sunday from 10 am to 5 pm. Admission costs $5, or $2.50 concession. To get there (and to the Vancouver Maritime Museum close by) take bus No 22 from Burrard St downtown.

HR MacMillan Planetarium The planetarium (☎ 738-7827), part of the Vancouver Museum complex, has regularly changing, entertaining and educational shows which are projected onto a 20-metre dome. Make reservations for these popular shows.

Adult admission is $5. There are also music-laser shows for $7.50 at 8.30 pm Sunday to Thursday and at 9.30 pm Friday and Saturday. The planetarium is closed on Monday during the winter, but open daily in the summer months. On Friday, Saturday and Sunday afternoons when the sky is clear the Gordon Southam Observatory (☎ 738-2855) is also open to the public and is free.

Vancouver Maritime Museum This museum (☎ 257-8300), 1905 Ogden Ave at the foot of Cypress St, is a five-minute walk from the Vancouver Museum. It is divided into two sections. The museum itself is strictly for boat buffs – with lots of wooden models and some old rowboats on display.

The other section, a designated historic site, displays the *St Roch*, a 1928 RCMP Arctic patrol sailing ship which was the first to navigate the legendary Northwest Passage in both directions. There are interesting guided tours on the ship every half-hour or so. From the museum wharf you can take a miniferry to Granville Island. The site is open daily May to September from 10 am to 5 pm and admission is $5, $2.50 concession.

Old Hastings Mill Store Built in 1865, this was the first store (%y228-1213) on Burrard Inlet. It survived the Great Fire of 1886 and was moved in 1930 to where it stands today at 1575 Alma St on the corner of Point Grey Rd at the eastern end of Jericho Beach. It's the large, off-white, barn-like building with brown trim. It houses a small collection of Native Indian artefacts and some local memorabilia and is open daily in summer from 11 am to 4 pm, weekends only the rest of the year from 1 to 4 pm. Admission is by donation.

University of British Columbia The University of British Columbia (☎ 822-2211), often just called UBC, is at the most westerly point of Vancouver, on the spit jutting out into Georgia Strait. The huge campus serving 30,000 students is spread over 400 hectares much of which is still forest. Bus Nos 4, 10 and 14 heading south on Granville St run up to the university every 10 minutes or so; the journey takes about 30 minutes.

As well as the attractive grounds, there are several points of interest.

UBC Museum of Anthropology This museum (☎ 822-5087) is excellent. The exhibits include art and artefacts from cultures around the world. Asia, Africa and the Pacific are all well represented but the emphasis is on the work of BC's Coastal Indians, which includes a terrific totem pole collection – both indoors and out. The collection has some fine sculptures and carvings. Many of the items are stored in glass filing cabinets. Everything is numbered and catalogued, so you can look up details and cross-references yourself. The museum is open daily in summer from 11 am to 5 pm, till 9 pm Tuesday. It's closed Monday, between early September and the end of June. Admission is $6 and free on Tuesday between 5 pm and 9 pm.

Nitobe Memorial Gardens These beautiful Japanese-style gardens (☎ 822-4208) are near the museum. Designed by a leading Japanese landscape architect, they're a perfect display of this symbolic art form. Get a guide at the gate when you buy a ticket. The gardens are open daily from 10 am to 6 pm in summer, and Monday to Friday from 11 am to 3 pm the rest of the year. Admission is $4 for adults.

Near the gardens, **Totem Park** has carvings and buildings representing part of a Haida Indian village. Admission is free.

Wreck Beach Along South-West Marine Drive, heading south past the Rose Garden and the Museum of Anthropology, are markers for trails into the woods. Follow one of the trails marked No 4, 5 or 6 down the steep steps to Wreck Beach, a pleasant and quiet – if notorious – nude beach. This is probably the best known stretch of sand in the country even though most people have never seen it. Since the 1960s it's been a bit of a hang-out and some of that original ambience remains. You can buy pizza, beer and other attitude adjusters and its undeveloped natural appearance seems a long way from the big city.

Aquatic Centre If you don't fancy that, try the UBC Aquatic Centre (☎ 822-4521) back on the campus, off University Blvd, which has pools, saunas and exercise areas, and is open to the public.

Queen Elizabeth Park This 52-hectare park, between Cambie and Ontario Sts and near 33rd Ave, is the city's second largest park. Up the hill to the Bloedel Conservatory there are great views of the city in nearly every direction. There's a well-designed sunken garden surrounded by small cliffs which has some fantastic plants, one with leaves a metre across.

Next to the parking lot is an unusual, Oriental-looking garden consisting of many pools and fountains. The garden is mostly cement, but is dotted with wooden frames holding plants and flowers. There is a restaurant and a cheaper coffee shop. Catch bus No 15 heading south-east on Robson St to get there.

Bloedel Conservatory The conservatory (☎ 872-5513) has three climate zones including desert and tropical beneath its plastic dome. For the admission prices of $3 or $1.50 for students, however, you may consider it's not really worth it with all the flowers and gardens around for free. It's open weekdays from 9 am to 8 pm, weekends from 10 am to 9 pm.

Vandusen Botanical Gardens These 22-hectare gardens (☎ 878-9274), 5251 Oak St between 33rd and 37th Aves, are not far from Queen Elizabeth Park. The gardens contain a small lake and a large collection of ornamental plants from around the world. They're open daily from 10 am to 9 pm in summer. The admission price is $5, students $2.50. Take bus No 17 south on Burrard St from downtown.

Museum of Exotic World In the category of wonderfully eccentric is this 3561 Main St storefront assemblage (☎ 876-0073) of the planet's oddities. Souvenirs, photographs and clippings culled from the personal collection of owner/operator Harold Morgan after a lifetime of travels fill every inch of the two-room space. It's stunningly colourful and a browsers delight. Harold provides guided talking tours to anyone who walks in the door. It's free and open every day.

North Vancouver

North and West Vancouver together make up the North Shore. There are three principal ways to experience this side of the inlet. You can take the SeaBus for city views, stroll Lonsdale Quay and spend a few hours eating and sightseeing around lower North Vancouver. Or, with a vehicle, tour along Marine Drive through West Vancouver, possibly all the way to Horseshoe Bay stopping at parks and enjoying the harbour alongside some of Vancouver's wealthy neighbourhoods. Lastly, you can visit one of the provincial parks for some fine vistas and real hiking.

For information on any of this see the North Van Travel Infocentre (☎ 987-4488) in a former house at 131 East 2nd St.

Lonsdale Quay Market The Lonsdale Quay Market (☎ 985-6261) is the centre of the North Shore SeaBus terminal complex which includes a water's edge park, offices and apartments. The 1st floor is devoted to fresh and cooked food; the 2nd floor is mainly speciality shops but has a restaurant with good views. As you leave the ferry, there's an information booth to offer guidance on the North Shore's attractions. The local bus terminal is here as well.

The market is open daily 9.30 am to 6.30 pm except Friday when it stays open to 9 pm. To get there catch the SeaBus from the downtown terminal at Waterfront Station.

North Vancouver Museum & Archives

The small museum (☎ 987-5618), 333 Chesterfield Ave, offers rather good changing exhibits on a wide range of subjects such as transport, antiques and Native Indian crafts. Admission is by donation and it's open Wednesday and Friday to Sunday from noon to 5 pm; Thursday it stays open till 9 pm.

Capilano Suspension Bridge This bridge (☎ 985-7474), 3735 Capilano Rd on the left-hand side going north, spans the Capilano River for almost 140 metres at a height of 70 metres. Open daily in summer from 8 am till 9 pm, it's very tourist oriented and, with little else in the small park, is really not worth the $7.50 (students $4) admission.

To get there from downtown take bus No 246, marked 'Highlands', going west on West Georgia St or bus No 236 from Lonsdale Quay to Edgemont Village; you then change to bus No 232. (This bus also goes to Capilano Salmon Hatchery and Cleveland Dam; in summer No 236 also goes all the way to Grouse Mountain.) If you're driving, head north over Lions Gate Bridge to Marine Drive in North Vancouver, then turn left (north) at Capilano Rd.

Capilano Salmon Hatchery The hatchery is a fish farm (☎ 666-1790) run by the government to help stop the depletion of valuable salmon stocks. Although you can't see the holding pools, there are exhibits with good explanations of the whole process. Salmon in various stages of growth are on display in tanks, and you can see how they are channelled from the river into the hatchery when they head upstream to spawn. Admission is free. It's in Capilano River Regional Park, off Capilano Rd not far north of the suspension bridge.

Cleveland Dam The dam (☎ 224-5739) blocks Capilano Lake, which supplies much of Vancouver's drinking water. You'll get good views of the Lions, two peaks of the Coast Mountains. There are picnic areas and trails and it's free. The dam is slightly further north of the salmon hatchery, up Capilano Rd which becomes Nancy Greene Way.

Grouse Mountain Grouse Mountain (☎ 984-0661), 6400 Nancy Greene Way (the northern extension of Capilano Rd), is famous for its Swiss-built Superskyride cable car which operates daily in summer from 9 am to 10 pm, the rest of the year it's 11 am to 5 pm weekdays, till 7 pm weekends.

BRITISH COLUMBIA

From the top – 1110 metres – you can see all of Vancouver, the coast, part of Vancouver Island and northward over the mountains. It's an expensive ride at $14.50. There are restaurants at the top and bottom of the mountain. There are a lot of trails on the mountain some of which should be taken seriously. A woman died here in August, 1995 after getting lost.

If you take the Superskyride, make sure it's a clear day. If it's raining, foggy or at all hazy with low clouds, forget it: by the time you reach the top you won't see a thing. Go in late afternoon; then you can see the city by day and night. (See Capilano Suspension Bridge earlier for details on how to get there.)

In winter there is day and night skiing (see the Activities section later).

Royal Hudson Steam Train This 1930s steam engine pulls restored coaches on a 5½-hour return excursion to Squamish. The route follows the coast northward along the shore of Howe Sound through some beautiful scenery. The cost is $35 return. A variation is to take the train one way and cruise back on the MV *Britannia*; the fare is $60 return. The train leaves from BC Rail's station (☎ 1-800-663-8238), 1311 West 1st St at the southern end of Pemberton Ave, North Vancouver. A shuttle service to the station is available. Call for schedule details. (See Organised Tours in the Activities section later for details.)

Park & Tilford Gardens These 1.2 hectares of flower gardens, at 1200 Cotton Drive south-west of Lynn Canyon Park, were developed by the distillery of the same name. There are some unusual tree specimens, tropical birds and lots of flowers. Although free, these gardens are not highly recommended; they're used mainly by wedding photographers. They're open daily from 9.30 am till dusk.

To get there take bus No 239 from Lonsdale Quay to Phibbs Exchange, then change to No 232 heading east to Brooksbank, where the gardens are located.

Lynn Canyon Park Set in thick woods, this park popular with residents, gives a good glimpse of the rainforest vegetation so different from that found in eastern Canada. There are many hiking trails, and you can find your own picnic and swimming spots. Over Lynn Canyon is a **suspension bridge**; although not as big as Capilano, it's much the same and is free. The **Lynn Canyon Park Ecology Centre** (☎ 987-5922), 3663 Park Rd, has displays, films and slide shows about the biology of the area. It's open daily from 10 am to 5 pm.

To get to the park take bus Nos 228 or 229 from Lonsdale Quay. If you're driving go over Second Narrows Bridge, take Lynn Valley Rd then go right (east) on Peters Rd, where you'll see signs that lead you into the park.

Mt Seymour Provincial Park This park, 13 km north-east from downtown, is a quick, close escape from the city. There is a road up most of the way and a chair lift goes to the peak. The park has several hiking trails and the views of Vancouver's surroundings are beautiful. Some areas are very rugged, so visitors going on overnight trips should register. There's also skiing here in winter.

There are parking lots for RVs but no real tent campground; you can pitch a tent along the many alpine trails. From Lonsdale Quay take bus Nos 229 or 239 to Phibbs Exchange then No 215. If you're driving head over the Second Narrows Bridge and turn right (east) onto Mt Seymour Parkway.

West Vancouver

West of the Capilano River and up the hillsides are the communities of West Van. Marine Drive passes by the Park Royal shopping centre into **Ambleside** with its waterside park on Burrard Inlet. Further west is **Dundarave**, a commercial strip with a number of restaurants and cafes amid the shops, some with balconies overlooking the water. Northward up the hill and on the other side of the Upper Levels Hwy are the expensive houses of the **British Properties** with good views over the harbour. Marine Drive follows the coast to Horseshoe Bay (see the Around Vancouver section for details).

Lighthouse Park Here in a stand of original coastal forest are some of the largest trees in the Vancouver area. Also see the knoll of arbutus trees. Trails lead to the lighthouse and bluffs. The park is at Point Atkinson, eight km to the left (west) on Marine Drive after going over Lions Gate Bridge. Catch bus No 250 going west on West Georgia St.

East Vancouver

Simon Fraser University The university sits atop Burnaby Mountain in Burnaby, about 20 km east of downtown. Its intriguing modern architecture and excellent vistas make it a worthwhile place to visit. The design, incorporating unusual use of space and perspective, was – and remains – controversial. There are huge courtyard-like quadrants and many fountains, including one on a roof. Some areas of the complex are reminiscent of Mayan ruin sites in Mexico. For information on tours around the university, call ☎ 291-3111. To get there, catch bus No 10 or 14 on East Hastings St then change near Boundary Rd to bus No 135, which will take you to the university.

Museum of Archaeology & Ethnology On the campus, this museum (☎ 291-3325) features a collection of Pacific Coast Indian artefacts and has a cheap cafeteria. The museum is open Monday to Friday from 10 am to 4 pm, and admission is by donation.

Burnaby Heritage Village Located at 6501 Deer Lake Ave, beside Deer Lake, this museum (☎ 293-6501) is in Burnaby's Century Park, close to the Trans Canada Hwy. It's a replica of a village community which attempts to preserve both the artefacts and atmosphere of a south-western BC town in the years 1890 to 1925. There's an old schoolhouse, printing shop, drugstore and other establishments; a large, working steam-train model is next to the village. The restored carousel with 36 wooden horses is a highlight. Friendly, informed workers are

---

The Arbutus Tree

Gnarled and peeling, the distinctive arbutus is Canada's only broad-leafed evergreen. It's found only along the shores of the Straight of Georgia rarely more than eight km from the sea. It's a small, generally twisted and bent tree which sheds its bark rather than its leaves. Coastal residents often grow this quirky attractive specimen ornamentally. ■

---

in period dress. It's open daily from 10 am to 4.30 pm during summer, shorter hours the rest of the year. Admission is $6, $3.50 for students and seniors. Catch bus No 120 on East Hastings St.

Teleglobe Canada The displays and exhibits here focus on videos, satellite and undersea international communications, telecommunications artefacts and related electronic equipment. The gallery, open Monday to Friday from 8 am to 4 pm, is in the Vancouver International Centre, 3033 Beta Ave, Burnaby, off Canada Way, 13 km from downtown. Call ☎ 293-4200 for details. To get there, go south of the Trans Canada Hwy on Willingdon Ave and turn left onto Canada Way; Beta Ave is the second turning on the left. Alternatively, take the SkyTrain to Nanaimo Station then catch bus No 25.

New Westminster

South-east of the centre on the Fraser River, 'New West' founded in 1859 was BC's first capital. The waterfront esplanade has been overhauled and together with the Westminster Quay Public Market has become a casual people place with restaurants and bars as well as shops. The small downtown area is here, too, just north of the SkyTrain stop.

Activities

Swimming & Water Sports You can swim at a number of city beaches, for example Second and Third beaches in Stanley Park, English Bay and Sunset beaches downtown, or at Kitsilano and Jericho beaches on the southern side of English Bay. Kitsilano Beach is the largest and most popular and where the beach culture scene is at its peak. On a hot summer day as many as 10,000 hit the sands. The prime spot to see and be seen is apparently around the lifeguard section; other areas attract those who prefer a little more material used in the construction of their bathing suits. For swimming, the saltwater Kitsilano Pool is generally busier than the waters of English Bay. (At one portion of the beach you might catch one of the semi-pro or professional volleyball tournaments which occur regularly through the summer months.) For details on infamous Wreck Beach see the UBC section under West Side earlier.

The Vancouver Aquatic Centre (☎ 665-3424), 1050 Beach Ave near Sunset Beach, has an indoor heated swimming pool, whirlpool, diving tank, gym and sauna. It's open from 6.30 am and admission is $3 but it's always closed in August. There's another aquatic centre at UBC (see that section earlier) and one (☎ 926-8585) in West Vancouver at 776 22nd St. Kitsilano Beach has an outdoor heated saltwater pool (☎ 731-0011). It's open in summer Monday to Friday from 8.45 am to 8.45 pm, and on Saturday and Sunday from 10 am to 8.45 pm. Admission is $3.50.

If you've got the energy for canoeing or kayaking, the Fraser and Chilliwack rivers offer plenty of opportunities for the beginner to the experienced. At Granville Island you can hire canoes. Ecomarine Ocean Kayak Centre (☎ 689-7575), 1668 Duranleau St, hires out solo kayaks for $19 for two hours or $39 a day. It has another outlet at the Jericho Sailing Centre at Jericho Beach in Kitsilano near the HI Hostel and also does educational tours of the islands (see the Organised Tours section later).

In North Vancouver, on Indian Arm, Deep Cove Canoe & Kayak (☎ 929-2268), 2156 Banbury Rd, has rentals and will teach you how to use a canoe. At Deer Lake, east of town in Burnaby, you can rent solo canoes for $12 an hour from Deer Lake Boat Rentals (☎ 255-0081).

Windsure Windsurfing School (☎ 224-0615), 1300 Discovery St at the Jericho Sailing Centre, gives lessons and also rents boards. English Bay is a popular area for salmon fishing, for which the west coast is famous. Boats and equipment are for hire and there are guided charters. A good place to investigate is on Granville Island where there are a number of operators. Try Corcovado Yacht Charters (☎ 669-7907) at Suite 104, 1676 Duranleau St or Granville Island Boat Rentals (☎ 682-6287).

Scuba diving is popular north-west of the city off Lighthouse Park and at Porteau Cove 24 km north of Horseshoe Bay, both in Howe Sound; and at Indian Arm at the eastern end of Burrard Inlet. A number of outfits offer equipment, training and trips including AB Divers World (☎ 732-1344), 1817 West 4th Ave, and Diving Locker (☎ 736-2681), 2745 West 4th Ave, both in Kitsilano.

Skiing Vancouver has some great downhill and cross-country skiing a short distance away.

Grouse Mountain (☎ 984-0661) is the nearest to the city and is notable for its nighttime skiing, when most of the downhill runs

Snowboarding on Mt Seymour

are illuminated and open till 10.30 pm. The day pass for an adult is $30.

For information on Whistler and Blackcomb mountains see the North of Vancouver section later.

Other nearby ski resorts include Cypress Bowl (also with night-time skiing) and Hollyburn (☎ 926-5612 for either resort) both in **Cypress Provincial Park** on Vancouver's North Shore. Cypress Bowl has downhill but is best known for its cross-country trails. **Mt Seymour** (☎ 986-2261), in North Vancouver, is a semi-wilderness provincial park only 16 km from downtown. The park's 3.5 sq km contain downhill runs, groomed cross-country trails and a tobogganing slope. It also has night-time skiing. Garibaldi Provincial Park (☎ 929-1291) has cross-country skiing only (for details see the North of Vancouver section later).

Further out, Hemlock Valley (☎ 797-4411) is a two-hour drive east along the Fraser Valley on Hwy 7; and Manning Park (☎ 840-8822) in Manning Provincial Park, is a 2½-hour drive east on the Trans Canada Hwy to Hope, then the Crowsnest Hwy into the park (for details see that section later).

Hiking Hiking is available in many of the provincial parks around Vancouver. Cypress Provincial Park is the closest, just eight km north of West Vancouver off Hwy 99. It has eight hiking trails including the Baden-Powell, Yew Lake and Howe Sound Crest trails. Mt Seymour Provincial Park, 15 km north-east of downtown, has 10 trails varying in difficulty and length. On clear days both parks offer magnificent views. At both parks you should be prepared for continually changing mountain weather conditions.

There's hiking in Garibaldi Provincial Park (for details see the North of Vancouver section later).

Golden Ears Provincial Park is 48 km east of Vancouver. Take Hwy 7 as far as Haney, then turn left (north) and follow the 13-km road to Alouette Lake. The park has 11 hiking trails, plus camp sites and picnic areas.

Cycling A good way to get around town and Vancouver's numerous parks and beach areas is by bicycle. Some areas with designated bicycle paths are the 10-km sea-wall promenade in Stanley Park; the route from Granville Island, through Vanier Park to Kitsilano Beach; and if you want to keep going west you could take Point Grey Rd to Jericho Beach Park then follow the shoreline to Spanish Banks. (See also the Getting Around section later for details on bicycle rental.)

Rockclimbing One of Canada's fast-growing sports can be practiced at Cliffhanger Indoor Rock Climbing Centre (☎ 874-2400), 106 West 1st St.

Strolling In the heart of the city, Sunset Beach at sunset is beautiful and busy and there are cafes near the corner of Denman St. A stroll is highly recommended. The sea-wall promenades in Stanley Park, Vanier Park and Jericho Beach Park are also worth a leisurely walk.

Organised Tours

The Gray Line Bus Company (☎ 879-3363) offers a wide selection ranging from city tours to 10-day tours of the Rockies. Most begin at the Hotel Vancouver, and all major hotels sell tickets. A two-hour trip on a British double-decker bus costs $19. The most complete tour of Vancouver is the Double Decker/Canyon & Peaks Tour: it costs $29, lasts 3½ hours, will acquaint you with varying districts and stops at a few attractions. The same tour is offered in a choice of five languages – Cantonese, French, German, Japanese and Spanish – for $31. For $87.50 you can go on a day trip to Victoria.

Another company with local area tours is Town Tours (☎ 278-5251). A tour of Vancouver including Stanley Park and Gastown costs $29 and lasts for 3½ hours. They also do a full-day tour to Victoria, including the Butchart Gardens, for $83.

The best-value bus tour is operated by the Vancouver Trolley Co (☎ 451-5581). The full trip costs $17 and lasts two hours but you can get on and get off at 17 stops along the way.

Pacific Coach Lines (☎ 662-7575), at Pacific Central Station, operates a number of one-day excursions for about the same price as a normal bus ticket. Destinations include Vancouver Island and the Sunshine Coast.

Dominion Tours (☎ 298-1133) has a four-hour night tour that takes you to Grouse Mountain for $42 and a salmon barbecue option is offered.

First Tours (☎ 688-7246; 1-800-663-1500), near the foot of Denman St, offers a sight-seeing tour by boat and train. The seven-hour trip past good scenery goes up Howe Sound to Squamish. You can travel to Squamish on the MV *Britannia* and return by the *Royal Hudson* steam train, or vice versa. The cost is $60, $50 for students. You can go both ways by train for $35 return. These tours are available between the start of June and the middle of September.

Harbour Ferries (☎ 688-7246) has 1½-hour cruises for $16, and longer more costly evening dinner sailings around False Creek, English Bay and Burrard Inlet. Boats leave from their office at the north foot of Denman St by Stanley Park.

Ecomarine Ocean Kayak Centre (☎ 689-7575), 1668 Duranleau St, Granville Island, has educational tours of the islands in Georgia Strait and in Clayoquot Sound on the west coast of Vancouver Island. The one to the central Gulf Islands lasts three days and costs $395.

Keep an eye out for small adventure companies operating through the hostels.

Festivals

Following is a list of some of the major events in Vancouver during the year. *The Vancouver Book*, available from the Travel Infocentre, has an up-to-date list of current events.

January
Polar Bear Swim – This popular, chilly affair has been taking place on English Bay Beach annually on 1 January since 1819. If you can't handle the water, watching is allowed.

February
Chinese New Year – In mid-February Chinatown provides the setting for one of Vancouver's most colourful events, with dancers, music, fireworks and food.

June
International Dragon Boat Festival – This annual event takes place in False Creek over three days in late June. It attracts nearly 2000 competitors from around the world and about 150,000 spectators. As well as the boat races there's music, theatre and international cuisine.

July
Vancouver Folk Festival – Held on 1 July, this is the province's largest multicultural festival. The main events take place in Gastown, Robson Square and the Orpheum Theatre – all free. There is music, dance, performances and, of course, traditional costumes and foods.

Vancouver Sea Festival – During this festival in mid-July there are concerts, parades, fireworks and salmon barbecues, which take place on the shores of English Bay. For details and times call ☎ 684-3378.

Vancouver Folk Music Festival – Also in mid-July, the Folk Music Festival is three days of music, including concerts and workshops, from some of the best North American folk musicians. It attracts about 30,000 visitors and most of the action takes place at Jericho Beach Park. For information about tickets call ☎ 879-2931.

August
Abbotsford International Air Show – Known as Canada's National Air Show, it has been voted the world's best. The three-day event, held in early August, has everything that flies, from fighters to the Concorde. It's held 56 km south-east of Vancouver in Abbotsford near the US border.

Gay Pride Day – Also in early August watch for the outrageous feature parade drawing 15,000 along Denman St.

Festival of the Written Arts – Held in early to mid-August in Sechelt, north up the Sunshine Coast beyond Horseshoe Bay, this event features writers from across Canada speaking to and meeting those attending.

Pacific National Exhibition – Known as the PNE (☎ 253-2311), this big fair, the second largest in Canada (Toronto's CNE is the biggest) features a little bit of everything – sports, competitions, international exhibits, concerts and shows, as well as amusement park rides. It starts off each year with a two-hour parade. The exhibition lasts about two weeks, from late August to Labour Day. The PNE takes place in Exhibition Park on East Hastings St near the Second Narrows Bridge. Catch bus No 14 or 16 from downtown.

September

Vancouver Fringe Festival – This popular theatre event presents drama, musical theatre, comedy and dance from around the world. It takes place over two weeks from early to mid-September in various theatres around Main St, between East 6th and East 17th Aves in the Mount Pleasant area. Call ☎ 873-3646 for information.

October

Oktoberfest – The German-based Oktoberfest takes place in the Commodore Ballroom, 870 Granville St, over three weekends from early to mid-October. There's the usual oompah and Tyrolean music, Bavarian dancers, beer and more beer.

Places to Stay

It must be stressed that accommodation in Vancouver throughout the summer is very tight – in all price categories. Weekends are especially bad. Booking ahead is well advised and usually just a couple of days is sufficient. Also note that the booking agency at the airport is not a comprehensive source on vacancies and often tends to concentrate on the pricier lodgings. In winter you may get places a little cheaper, and if you're staying a week it's worth asking for a reduction, any time of the year.

Camping There are no government-run campgrounds in the Vancouver area and except for one, the trailer (RV) parks right in Vancouver do not allow tenting. The closest camping areas that do are south of the city, on or near Hwy 99, which runs to the US border. There are also a couple near the Tsawwassen ferry terminal.

The *Capilano RV Park* (☎ 987-4722) with everything including jacuzzi and tent sites from $18 is at 295 Tomahawk Drive, North Vancouver. Exit onto Capilano Road South off Highway 1 from downtown. *Timberland Motel & Campground* (☎ 531-1033) at 3418 King George Hwy (Hwy 99A), Surrey, has sites for tents and trailers. A site costs $12 and there's a laundry and showers. The campground is a half-hour drive from Vancouver, six km from the US border.

South of the middle arm of Fraser River, *Richmond RV Park* (☎ 270-7878), 6200 River Rd, Richmond, near Hollybridge Way is one of the closest to town. It's open from April to October and has sites from $15 for two people; it's $2.50 extra per person. *ParkCanada RV Inns* (☎ 943-5811), 4799 Hwy 17, Delta, is north-east of the Tsawwassen ferry terminal. It has free showers and sites from $14.

On the eastern side of town is the *Four Acres Trailer Court* (☎ 936-3273), 675 Lougheed Hwy, Coquitlam, which has some places for tents at $6. It has showers and a laundry and is about 25 km from the city centre. (The Lougheed Hwy is also called Hwy 7.)

Hostels Travellers have an ever-increasing array of hostel choices including some real dogs trying to cash in on the increase in traffic. Those are not listed here. Most of the good hostels are pretty much full through the summer and quite busy the rest of the year.

Greenpeace

Originally called the Don't Make a Wave Committee, Greenpeace was founded in Vancouver in the early 1970s. Stressing the need for a balance between economic development and environmental conservation, it first drew attention when members hired a fishing boat to go to Amchitka Island in Alaska to protest against a hydrogen bomb test. In the mid-1980s, it was the focus of world attention when its ship the *Rainbow Warrior* was blown up in New Zealand by French agents attempting to end Greenpeace's activities against nuclear testing in the South Pacific.

Greenpeace is now a global organisation with 59 offices in 31 countries. It continues to campaign on such diverse environmental issues as commercial whaling, the proliferation of nuclear power, the logging of temperate and tropical rainforests and the dumping of radioactive and other waste. In British Columbia, there are offices in Vancouver and Victoria. Toronto also has an office. ■

Although the HI *Vancouver Jericho Beach* (☎ 224-3208; fax 224-4852), 1515 Discovery St, Kitsilano, is away from the centre of town, its location is great. It's close to the beach in Jericho Beach Park on English Bay, about 20 minutes from downtown by bus. The hostel is open 24 hours, although there is a 'quiet time' between 11 pm and 7 am. With 288 beds, it's the largest in Canada and has complete facilities. The rates are $15 for members, $19 for nonmembers. Ask about the places in town where the hostel card will get you reductions. From downtown take bus No 4 south on Granville St, it continues south over False Creek, runs west along West 4th Ave then turns onto Marine Drive. Turn right (north) onto Discovery St and you'll come to it – it's the big white building on the left.

The new *HI Vancouver Downtown* hostel (☎ 684-4565) in a former nunnery and health-care centre has opened at 1100-1114 Burnaby St at the corner of Thurlow. There are 212 beds with no more than four in any one room. Family rooms are available. Prices are $17.50 members, $21 nonmembers. Facilities include a patio out back, library and games room. This very convenient hostel is walkable from anywhere in the downtown area and is also open 24 hours.

Popular *Vincent's Backpackers Hostel* (☎ 682-2441), 927 Main St, is next to the Cobalt Motor Hotel and above The Source, a store. This is not in the best of areas but is within walking distance of downtown and not too far from the Main St SkyTrain station, Science World and Pacific Central Station. Take bus No 3, 8 or 19 from downtown along Main St. The office is open 9 am to 11 pm, there's no curfew and the rates are low at $10/20/25 a dormitory/single/double. It takes 75 people and offers weekly rates.

Vincent has a new place – the *New Backpackers Hostel* (☎ 688-0112) centrally located in the big, former hotel at 347 West Pender St. This is generally a more spacious place and the little outdoor courtyard, good for reading, is pleasant but the $10 beds still fill up and you may have to wait for a shower. Singles/doubles are $25/35.

The smaller, very clean *Harbourfront Inn* (☎ 254-0733), 209 Heatley Ave, has dorm beds for $15 and double rooms for $35. Heatley is a few blocks east of Chinatown, turn north off East Hastings to the hostel. It can only take 25 people, so call ahead. If it's full you can sleep on the patio at the back for $5. There are two shared bathrooms and a kitchen.

Over in North Van, the golden *Globetrotter's Inn* (☎ 988-2082), at 170 West Esplanade, has re-opened after a few years' absence. It's a five-minute walk to the SeaBus at Lonsdale Quay and close to all amenities. They have a kitchen and laundry and a range of rooms. Dorms are $15, singles are $30 and doubles are $40 to $45.

The *YMCA* (☎ 681-0221) is right downtown at 955 Burrard St. Depending on whether you'd like a TV, singles are $33 or $35, doubles are $53 or $55. Single rooms can also be rented by the week for $167/174 without/with TV. These rates include tax. Women and couples are allowed and quite a few travellers stay here. The only drawback is the constant unlocking of doors. There are gym and pool facilities and a small inexpensive restaurant serving good-value breakfasts and sandwiches.

The new *YWCA* (☎ 895-5830), at 733 Beatty St between Georgia and Robson Sts near the BC Place Stadium is really like a hotel and accommodates men, women, couples or families. There are 155 rooms in various configurations ranging from singles with bathroom down the hall to family rooms and others with five single beds. A basic single is $49. A single sharing a bathroom with the room next door is $61. Doubles start at $59 and go to $93 with a private bath. There are 'double doubles' with two double beds for $86 with shared bathroom and ones with private baths are available. Tax is extra. Each room has a fridge but there are also communal kitchens as well as TV lounges and a laundry. Fitness facilities are offered but are off the premises. The stadium SkyTrain stop is a five-minute walk.

The *University of British Columbia* rents rooms from about the first week in May to the end of August. Singles/doubles with shared bath are $20/40 or you can get self-contained apartments for $85. Contact the Conference Centre (☎ 822-1010), Gage Towers, 5961 Student Union Blvd, UBC Campus, Vancouver. The pleasant campus has a cafeteria, some cafes, laundromat, pub and sports facilities. *Simon Fraser University* also rents out rooms from May to August. They're all fully furnished and bathrooms are shared; singles with sleeping bag cost $19, with bedding $30, doubles with bedding $49. Contact Housing & Conference Services (☎ 291-4503), Room 212, McTaggart-Cowan Hall, Burnaby, V5A 1S6.

B&Bs B&B accommodation has really mushroomed across the country, perhaps more so in BC than anywhere. The Travel Infocentre has information on agencies who select, inspect and book individual houses. The *Accommodations* guide also has a list of over a dozen agencies operating in Vancouver. B&Bs here are not cheap averaging $75 to $95 double with shared bath. There are some as low as $65 and rates do drop a bit out of season.

A good registry to try is *Old English B&B Registry* (☎ 986-5069), 1226 Silverwood Crescent, North Vancouver V7L 1L3, with rooms from $65. Two other established ones are *AAA B&B* (☎ 875-8888), 658 East 29th Ave, Vancouver V5V 2R9, and *Town & Country B&B*, (☎ 731-5942), 2803 West 4th Ave, Vancouver V6K 1K2.

Other operators run independently and many have advertisements at the Travel Infocentre. Some are very central but nearly all have only two or three rooms, so you may have to call several to get a room.

One place which is recommended is *Paul's Guest House* (☎ 872-4753), south of the downtown area at 345 West 14th Ave, two blocks from Cambie between Alberta and Yukon Sts in a quiet residential area. Paul speaks 11 languages and that should cover most guests! Breakfast includes all the eggs you can eat. It's very clean and friendly and there's a laundry service, TV room and free coffee or tea during the day. Singles are $50

and doubles $50 to $60 from May to September dropping to $30/40 the rest of the year. If this place is full, he has another nearby or can find you something similar in the area.

Hotels – bottom end For whatever reason, many people prefer one of the older, cheap central hotels to the hostels or universities. Vancouver, despite its rapid growth, has a great number of them, right in the downtown core. Many are well kept and offer good value, many serve the downtrodden and those on very low incomes or government assistance, whose numbers are greater here than in any other Canadian city.

There are more very basic cheapies than you can shake a stick at in the Gastown, Chinatown and Hastings St areas. A few of these are all right for serious budget travellers or those seeking some big city grittiness. Rooms are rented by the day, week or month.

The main downtown area has a better selection of hotels, ranging from basic ones through moderate to expensive.

The best low-cost hotel in town is the recommended, excellent value *Kingston Hotel* (☎ 684-9024) at 757 Richards St. It was the city's first B&B hotel and still offers the morning meal (although it's just enough to get the eyes open). Prices depend on your room and facilities: singles cost from $35 to $50, doubles from $45 to $65. Extras offered are the sauna and guests' laundry and the overnight parking subsidy.

Nearby at 435 West Pender St on the corner of Richards St is the *Niagara Hotel* (☎ 688-7574) with a sign depicting Niagara Falls tumbling four floors. It's old but good, with singles/doubles at $45/$48 without bath, $50/57 with.

Down the street, the central, worn *Piccadilly Hotel* (☎ 669-1556), 620 West Pender St, with a good pub has 45 small simple but clean rooms. Singles/doubles cost $30/40. It's not geared to visitors and is often full with permanents.

In Gastown, the old *Dominion Hotel* (☎ 681-6666), 210 Abbot St on the corner of Water St, dates from 1899. The rooms go for $47 with shared bath or $59 with private bath. There are many others in the area but most are bottom of the line.

Hastings St on either side of Main St is a less-than-wholesome part of town (especially at night), but the *Budget Inn – Patricia Hotel* (☎ 255-4301), 403 East Hastings St, breaks ranks. It's large, clean, well kept and very good value with rooms from $36/45. Some rooms have fine views of the harbour.

The southern end of Granville St, past Nelson St towards the bridge has a number of hotels. It's generally a seedy area with a lot of sex shops, but backpackers will find some places OK. One of them is the *Hotel California* (☎ 688-8701), 1176 Granville St. The refurbished rooms at $39/45 are fine. The busy bar downstairs has loud rock music nightly. The *Cecil Hotel* (☎ 683-8505), 1336 Granville St near the bridge, has simple rooms which aren't bad at $39/45 for singles/doubles but not for female travellers. The popular bar downstairs features 'exotic' dancers.

Hotels – middle The *Dufferin Hotel* (☎ 683-4251), 900 Seymour St, with prices beginning at $50/60 is a good choice and gets the Kingston's overflow. There's a dining room and free parking, which is a plus. The *St Regis Hotel* (☎ 681-1135), 602 Dunsmuir St on the corner of Seymour St, is similar and all rooms come with bath and there is a bar and restaurant. Rooms are from $50/60.

Recommended *Shaughnessy Village* (☎ 736-5511) at 1125 W 12th Ave is indescribable with limited space and must be seen. In more or less equal measure this high-rise complex is a B&B, hotel, resort, apartment building and fun centre all rolled into one. And it attracts an equally broad range of guests in sufficient numbers to fill the hundreds of rooms nightly. Even the room-price list is three pages long. The tiny ship-like studio cabins are about single/double $60/75 with breakfast and come packed with every amenity. Weekly rates are offered. Ask for one of the limited parking spots when you book the room.

Back to normality, there's a *Travelodge* (☎ 682-2767) at 1304 Howe St near Gran-

ville Bridge and not far from Sunset Beach. It has a dining room and heated outdoor pool. Rooms are $89/99.

Down Robson St towards Stanley Park are several good, moderately priced hotels. The *Barclay Hotel* (☎ 688-8850), 1348 Robson St, has air-con, TVs and a licensed lounge. Singles/doubles cost $65/85.

Riviera Motor Inn (☎ 685-1301), 1431 Robson St, has apartments with fully equipped kitchens. From some of the apartments you get a good view of the North Shore. Rooms cost from $78/88.

The *Shato Inn Hotel* (☎ 681-8920), a couple of blocks from Stanley Park and English Bay Beach, at 1825 Comox St off Denman St also has some rooms with cooking facilities. Rooms are $70/80; $20 extra for the kitchen.

Hotels – top end The *Day's Inn* (☎ 681-4335), 921 West Pender St, is central and has a bar, restaurant and free parking. Rooms start at $110/125.

One of the older, more elegant hotels with its wooden panelling and chandeliers is the *Hotel Georgia* (☎ 682-5566), 801 West Georgia St. It has air-con rooms with TV, movies and a minibar. Singles cost from $130 to $160 and doubles from $140 to $170.

The *Four Seasons Hotel* (☎ 689-9333), 791 West Georgia St, is in the Pacific Centre building. To get to reception you take the escalator left of the statue of the Buddha. Prices depend on the size of the bed as well as the number of people! Rooms start from $200/225.

The largest hotel in Vancouver with 644 rooms is the *Hyatt Regency* (☎ 683-1234), 655 Burrard St, where rooms cost $195/220. Despite the rising skyline the *Hotel Vancouver* (☎ 684-3131), 900 West Georgia St, remains a city landmark recognisable by its green copper roof. This Canadian Pacific hotel is one of the largest in Vancouver and has just about everything including a pool, saunas and three restaurants. Its rates are $180/195.

Motels There are three distinct areas where you'll find motels around Vancouver. They're all outside the downtown area but not a great distance away, and with a car they're very accessible.

The closest strip to downtown is along East Hastings St around Exhibition Park and east into Burnaby. This is a convenient area, close to Second Narrows Bridge leading over Burrard Inlet to North Vancouver. The *Best Western Exhibition Park* (☎ 294-4751), 3475 East Hastings St on the corner of Cassiar St, has rooms from $100 single or double.

The second motel area is along Kingsway, a major road which branches off Main St south of 7th Ave. It is the former highway and runs south-east out of downtown through Burnaby, New Westminster and across the Fraser River. It's also called Hwy 1A and is south of the Trans Canada Hwy. One of the closest motels to town is the *Biltmore Motor Hotel* (☎ 872-5252) at 395 Kingsway. It has air-con, TV, licensed restaurant and coffee shop. Rooms are from $70 single or double.

The other motel area is on the North Shore, over Lions Gate Bridge. Look along Marine Drive and north up Capilano Rd. There are also a couple of spots on the Esplanade, which runs east-west along the North Shore, past the SeaBus terminal.

Avalon Motor Hotel (☎ 985-4181) is at 1025 Marine Drive, North Vancouver, about five minutes' drive east of the bridge. Rooms are $70/75.

The good-value *Canyon Court Motel* (☎ 988-3181) is at 1748 Capilano Rd, North Vancouver close to Lions Gate and Grouse Mountain. Singles range from $75 to $85, doubles from $85 to $95. All rooms are cheaper after 1 October. There's a laundry, free coffee, swimming pool and at extra cost, kitchens.

One of the more central motels is *City Centre Motel*, 2111 Main St, a 10-minute walk south of Main St Station. It has singles/doubles for $55/60 and offers free coffee. If you're staying a week or more you might be able to negotiate a reduction.

Places to Eat
With its continuing increase in population and sophistication Vancouver's reputation as a good town for eating is true now more than ever. As in many places known for good restaurants, the quality and variety filters down through all budget levels. Coffee shops, selling a variety of gourmet coffees and snacks are found all over this caffeine-mad town.

Robson St This is one of the main eating areas of Vancouver and has a cosmopolitan collection of restaurants including Indian, French, Greek, German, Chinese and Thai.

The *Bread Garden* at 812 Bute by the corner of Robson St has an excellent selection of fresh sandwiches, salads and casseroles all under $6. There's another outlet on Denman at Comox St.

Heidelberg House, 1256 Robson St, has been serving various German specialities for years. The moderately priced menu includes goulashes, schnitzels and a variety of sandwiches. The lunch buffet is $8, $2 more at dinner.

Fogg 'n' Suds is a busy bar and grill at 1323 Robson with beers from around the world. There are two outlets in Kitsilano, too.

For good, inexpensive meals, the *Saigon*, open every day at 1500 Robson St on the corner of Nicola St, is a very popular Vietnamese place. Its menu includes curries and seafood, and it has lunch specials for $6.

Robson Public Market, 1610 Robson St, open 9 am to 9 pm daily has a bakery, cheese shop, fruit stalls, and delicatessens.

Robson St also has lots of coffee shops. Ubiquitous *Starbuck's* with an outlet at No 1100, is popular. *Grabbajabba* is similar.

Denman & Davie Sts Denman St, near Stanley Park, is a lively, pleasant street to visit around evening meal time. There's a good selection of eateries, particularly towards the Georgia St end, and lots of people strolling and menu-reading. The choice includes Mexican, French, Greek and many others.

The *Great Wall Mongolian BBQ* at 717 Denman St creates giant stir-fries while you watch using ingredients that you have selected. The lunch ($6) and dinner ($10) all-you-can-get deals are hard to beat for the fresh and spicy blends. *Musashi Japanese Restaurant*, 780 Denman St between Robson and Alberni Sts, is cosy, casual and cheap. It's closed Monday.

Café Slavia, 815 Denman St, is a small, friendly, inexpensive place with a Slavic slant; it serves food like goulash and perogies (dumplings) for around $7. *Bud's Halibut & Chips*, 1007 Denman St, is a good place for fish & chips ($7 to $10). It's open daily from 11.30 am to 9 pm and is often packed.

Ciao! at 1074 Denman St is a small Italian-style cafe with sandwiches and sweets for $3 to $4. Close by at No 1110 is *Falafel King*, for Middle-Eastern fare and fresh fruit juices.

Open daily till midnight, *Pepita's* at the corner of Denman and Davie streets is one of the city's most established Mexican restaurants. Quesadillas are from $5 and main dishes like enchiladas are $11. You also get complimentary corn chips and salsa.

Davie St, particularly around Bute St, has developed its own little restaurant and coffee-shop scene. *Fresgo's* at 1126 Davie St is a local favourite for its large portions and low prices on Canadian standards.

Gastown Area For soup-and-sandwich lunches, try the *Cottage Deli*, 131 Water St, which has views of Burrard Inlet; or the corner of Carrall St near the statue of Gassy Jack, where there are several good-value cafes.

At *Brother's Restaurant*, 1 Water St, the decor has a monastic theme and the waiting staff are dressed in monks' habits. It serves seafood, pasta and poultry and includes items like 'Monastery burger'; starters are $5 to $9 and main meals $8 to $18. It's open daily from 11.30 am to 11 pm.

The *Old Spaghetti Factory*, 53 Water St, is good value. This is a branch of the popular Canada-wide chain. The eye-catching decor includes some old machinery, stained-glass

Tiffany lamps and even a 1910 Vancouver streetcar (tram). Starters cost between $2.50 and $4.50 and main meals go for $8 to $13. It's open Monday to Saturday from 11.30 am to 10 pm, Sunday until 9 pm.

More upmarket *Water St Café*, 300 Water St opposite the steam clock, is very busy and has a large sidewalk seating area. This was once the Regina Hotel, built in 1875 and the only major building to escape the Great Fire of 1886. The food's good with lunch-time main dishes of pasta and fish for $11.

If you like East Indian food, Water St offers several choices. *Kilimanjaro*, at 332 Water St in the Le Magasin shopping complex, serves African dishes based on Indian cuisine. There's a restaurant upstairs and a bistro downstairs. It's a very attractive place with quality food; main meals cost $8 to $15.

The seemingly out of place *Bodai Vegetarian Restaurant*, 337 East Hastings St, and the *Miu Jay Garden Vegetarian Restaurant* close by at No 367, serve lots of appetising, filling soups and dishes, some of which include simulated meat. Lunch-time dim sum specials at the latter go for $5.50.

The *Only Seafoods Café*, on Hastings St near the corner of Carrall St, is a Vancouver institution – it's been going since 1912 and has hardly changed. There's no toilet, no liquor licence and seating for only 25, mostly on stools. Once almost always busy it has suffered with the continuing disintegration of the neighbourhood but still draws all types of people. They'll boil, steam or fry whatever fish you choose. Fish & chips costs $7 to $9. It's closed on Sunday.

Chinatown The city's central Chinatown, sadly, has seen better days. While there's still a fair bit of bustle through the day, things really die off at night and some restaurants don't even bother opening for dinner. The new Chinese activity centre is now based out of the city in Richmond in the malls along Cambie Road and No 3 Road. Still you can get a reasonable meal here and it's not a ghost town.

Ming's, 147 East Pender St, has excellent dim sum between 11 am and 2 pm daily. A wide variety of dishes, each priced at about $4, are served from a cart whirled around by the waiting staff. Arrive early for the best selection. *Hon's Wun Tun House* on East Keefer St is a Chinese fast-food place selling bowls of noodles from $3.75; it's also famous for its 'pot-stickers' – quick-fried dumplings. It's very popular and is open Monday to Saturday from 8.30 am to 1 am, Sunday from 8.30 am to 8 pm.

Max King Bakery & Restaurant, 277 East Pender St, has tasty pastries and cakes starting from 80 cents. Try the lotus-seed cream cake.

Vietnamese restaurants have begun to appear in the Chinatown area. The reasonably priced *Pho Lu Zuan*, 207A East Pender St, is one but try the *Saigon Brochette* at 217 Carral St tucked in the very pleasant courtyard called Gaoler's Mews at the corner of Water St. It's open daily, lunch specials are $6.95, dinners from $10.

Elsewhere Downtown Two British-style restaurants-cum-pubs serving dishes like bangers & mash or fish & chips for $7 are the *Jolly Taxpayer Hotel & Pub*, 828 West Hastings St near Howe St, and the *Elephant & Castle*, 700 Dunsmuir St, on the corner of Granville St.

The *Vieux Montreal Café* at 317 East Broadway specialises in Quebecois food such as tortiere (meat pie) and the low brow favourite, hot chicken sandwich. It's a casual place for a $12 meal with live music, open daily but in the evening only.

A splurge can be had at the *Ferguson Point Tea House* in Stanley Park. With its wicker furniture, hanging plants, large windows and a view over English Bay, the atmosphere is right out of *The Great Gatsby*. The best prices are at lunch time, from 11.30 am to 2.30 pm Monday to Friday. Dinner is served from 5.30 to 10 pm seven days a week. The mostly seafood main meals cost between $10 and $17. Also in Stanley Park, near Lions Gate Bridge, *Prospect Point Café* has a varied menu, again mostly seafood. Main meals cost between $10 and $16; fish & chips are around $9. The food's a little overpriced, but the cafe is in a great spot with an outdoor patio and views across Burrard Inlet, and there is also a cheap snackbar.

On Granville Island a good restaurant to try for snacks, reasonably priced lunches or full meals is *Isadora's Co-operative Restaurant*, 1540 Old Bridge St. It has a small play area for children and some of the money you spend on food goes to help community organisations. The food is Pacific Northwest featuring salmon, and local herbs and vegetables. Various sandwiches from $6.75 and main dishes are $10 to $15. It is open daily.

For lunch or a snack you could try one of the eateries in the food court on the ground floor of the Royal Centre Mall on the corner of Burrard and Dunsmuir Sts, downstairs at the Pacific Centre Mall, or the Harbour Centre on West Hastings St, also downstairs. They have basic Chinese, Italian, Mexican, Japanese etc places, at reasonable rates.

White Spot, a Vancouver institution famous for its hamburgers, is a chain of family restaurants begun in 1928. With numerous locations in Vancouver, it serves standard food at reasonable prices every day. In the central area there's one at 1616 West Georgia St on the corner of Cardero St, one at 580 West Georgia St on the corner of Seymour St, and another on the corner of Burrard and Robson Sts. A sandwich with fries or salad is a meal in itself and costs from around $6, omelettes are $5.50.

Kitsilano Once the sole domain of students and alternative lifestylers with their cafes and second-hand stores, Kits now has its share of professionals and expensive properties. The blend makes for fine eating. Between Burrard and Alma Sts, West 4th Ave has a large, varying selection of eateries with many nationalities represented. West Broadway also has numerous spots for stomach satisfaction.

At 1754 West 4th Ave near the corner of Burrard St is the *Heaven & Earth Curry House*. It serves meat or vegetarian dishes, priced at about $9 to $10. It looks a little run down on the outside but the place is established and good and is open only in the evenings for dinner. At No 1938, *Sophie's Cosmic Café*, 2095 West 4th Ave on the corner of Arbutus St, is a happening place with queues sometimes out on the street. The walls are covered in all sorts of memorabilia including an old billiard-table top. It sells an impressive range of burgers, including vegetarian felafel burgers, from $6.50 or steak sandwiches for $8. It also does salads and enchiladas.

Ristorante Simpatico, 2222 West 4th Ave, is a very attractive, Greek-style taverna, also offering – as its name suggests – Italian food. There's spinach pie or hummus with bread for $3.75; or moussaka for $9.

Naam Restaurant, 2724 West 4th Ave near the corner of MacDonald St, is the city's oldest vegetarian health-food 'new age' restaurant. It's very casual, has live folk music every night and is open 24 hours. Main meals are around $7 to $9, or you could have a tofu hot dog for $4. It also has good cakes and pies for $3.50.

Nyala Café, 2930 West 4th Ave, provides Ethiopian food to be eaten without the use of cutlery: you use bread instead. Main dishes of lamb, poultry, beef and seafood are $9 or $11, vegetarian main meals are $7 to $9 and there's a buffet on Sunday evening. Saturday night between 10 pm and 2 am there's African or Caribbean music and dancing.

Over on West Broadway the 3000 block area is sometimes known as Little Greece. Among several popular places, is the very good Greek *Ouzeri*, at No 3189 on the corner of Trutch St. It's open till the early hours serving in casual tapas style. A meal is in the $12 range. The ethnic mix also includes *Andale's*, 3211 West Broadway, serving a variety of tasty Mexican and Spanish dishes. Enchiladas start from $9 and paella $14. The restaurant is brightly decorated and even the lamps are wearing sombreros.

Good for lunch and snacks, *Greens & Gourmet*, 2681 West Broadway, is a vegetarian and health-food restaurant charging by weight.

Little India The Vancouver area has the largest East Indian community in the country and the majority are Sikhs from the Punjab. The focal point of the population is the Punjabi Market south on Main St between 48th and 51st Aves. Here you'll find East Indian groceries, and shops selling saris, spices and East Indian music, but the area is small and surprisingly low-key. *The Himalaya Restaurant* in the Pabla's Trade Centre market, 6587 Main St, has inexpensive buffets but the masala dosa for $5 from the menu is a better choice. Most dishes are around $7.

Zeenaz Restaurant, 6460 Main St, offers East African-style East Indian food – the spices used are more delicate. Lunch and dinner buffets are $8.95/11.95 and there is an à la carte menu. It's closed Tuesday.

North on Main at No 2313 the comfortable *Nirvana* in the same price range has been recommended and has a range of vegetarian dishes. The *Punjab Restaurant*, 796 Main St on the corner of Union St, a few blocks south of Chinatown, has stood the test of time. It serves good Indian food at reasonable rates: starters are around $3.50, vegetarian main meals around $10, non-vegetarian around $12. It's small, quiet and popular.

Commercial Drive There are several interesting neighbourhood restaurants and cafes along a portion of Commercial Drive, between East 6th Ave and Parker St, popular with the mix of artists, professionals and various alternative types who live in the area. *Joe's Café*, 1120 Commercial Drive, long popular for snacks and conversation with an array of characters from punks to media personalities, is one with a measure of notoriety. The newer *Hot Pepper Café* at No 1206 is popular, and has good breakfasts. *La Quena* coffee house at No 1111, presents an array of political, social and musical evenings.

This traditionally Italian district has some fine upmarket Italian food on offer. *Spumante's* at 1736 Commercial Drive serves excellent hearty fare in a tasteful setting. Meals range up from $20. There are also Mexican and Vietnamese restaurants to choose from.

North Vancouver Lonsdale Quay Market has lots of places to munch at or to buy food to take away. The British-style *Cheshire Cheese Inn* on level 2, sells traditional British food like steak & kidney pudding and shepherd's pie, for $7.95. *Sailor Hagar's* nearby at 235 West 1st St is a brew pub.

Several restaurants are concentrated near the corner of Lonsdale Ave and Esplanade. *Corsi Trattoria*, 1 Lonsdale Ave, is an Italian place where everything is made on the premises, including the pasta and bread. Appetisers are from $4.50 and spinach fettucini $10. It's open Monday to Friday for lunch from noon to 2 pm, and daily for dinner from 5 pm to midnight. Nearby *Anotoli's* sells Greek dinners for $11.

Frankie's Inn, 59 Lonsdale Ave, is a basic eatery with the usual Western food, but there's a Vancouver twist: Japanese dishes like sukiyaki, tempura and teriyaki are available, served with chopsticks. Breakfast specials are $3.25. This spot is popular with workers from the nearby docks. It's open Monday to Friday from 9 am to 6 pm, Saturday from 9 am to 4 pm.

At 69 Lonsdale Ave, the *Jägerhof* specialises in schnitzels and also serves deer and moose meat. On the walls it has old framed photographs and prints, and mounted animals' heads. Meat platters with soup or salad cost $16.

North up the hill at 2039 is *Tandoori Garden* for Indian food using the tandoori oven. Most dishes are about $10. There are numerous cafes and plenty of Greek places notably around 13th Street.

Entertainment

The best source of information on entertainment in Vancouver is the *Georgia Straight*, which comes out every Thursday. The weekly *WestEnder* and the monthly *Playboard* give reviews and dates of events in the visual and performing arts. These are all free around town. The daily newspapers (the *Vancouver Sun* and the *Province*) also have complete entertainment listings, including theatre, dance and concerts. The Travel Infocentre will also be able to help you.

Theatre Theatre, from mainstream to fringe, is flourishing in Vancouver. Next to the main post office, in Hamilton St, the *Queen Elizabeth Theatre* (☎ 280-4444) puts on major international productions; the *Vancouver Playhouse* is part of the same complex. The *Metro Theatre* (☎ 266-7191), 1370 South-West Marine Drive, and *Firehall Arts Centre* (☎ 689-0926), 280 East Cordova St, put on plays by Canadian and foreign playwrights. The *Arts Club* (☎ 687-1644) has more experimental productions with three locations in town – two in Johnston St on Granville Island, and the other at 1181 Seymour St on the corner of Smithe St. Also on Granville Island, the *Waterfront Theatre* (☎ 685-6217), 1410 Cartwright St, is the venue for a number of local theatre companies.

Punchlines Comedy Theatre (☎ 684-3015), 15 Water St, has stand-up comedy shows at 9 pm Tuesday to Sunday, with an extra show on Friday and Saturday at 11 pm. Another place offering offbeat comedy is *Yuk Yuk's Comedy Club* (☎ 687-5233) at 750 Pacific Blvd near Cambie Bridge. It has one show on Wednesday (amateur night) and Thursday at 9 pm; two on Friday and Saturday at 9 pm and 11.30 pm. The entry price varies depending on the performer.

Several fringe theatres worth checking out are the *Vancouver East Cultural Centre* (☎ 254-9578), 1895 Venables St (east along Prior Street), *Vancouver Little Theatre* (☎ 876-4165), 3102 Main St, and *Station St Arts Centre* (☎ 688-3312), 930 Station St.

The two universities have theatrical events during the year which give drama students the chance to practise their craft. The universities also put on professional productions. Call Simon Fraser University (☎ 291-3514) and UBC (☎ 822-2678) for details.

For theatre tickets check the little booth on ground level in Robson Galleria, 1025 Robson St. It sells tickets for local shows at half price, usually close to showtime. It's open from noon to 1 pm and from 4.30 to 6 pm Monday to Saturday. Otherwise you can call the Vancouver Ticket Centre (☎ 280-4444) for normal-priced tickets.

Cinema At 919 Granville St, the *Paradise* cinema (☎ 681-1732) shows commercial films at half price every day and the *Denman Place Discount Cinema* (☎ 663-2201), 1737 Comox St, shows three films for $3 on Tuesday.

Vancouver also has a selection of low-cost repertory theatres which show a mix of North American and overseas films. You may need to buy a cheap membership. *Hollywood Theatre* (☎ 738-3211) is at 3123 West Broadway; tickets are $3.50 from Tuesday to Sunday, $2.50 on Monday. *Ridge Theatre* (☎ 738-6311), 3131 Arbutus St on the corner of 16th Ave, charges $4. A third is the *Pacific Cinémathèque* (☎ 688-3456), 1131 Howe St.

Music In summer, every Friday at noon, there are concerts at the *Orpheum Theatre* (☎ 665-3050) at 884 Granville St. The programme varies each day but you might hear folk, blues, jazz or classical music. The Vancouver Symphony Orchestra often performs here.

Downtown around Richards and Seymour Sts, and in Yaletown around Davie and Hamilton Sts, it's bustling at night. The *Railway Club* (☎ 681-1625), 579 Dunsmuir St on the corner of Seymour St, is a pub-like place with live music seven nights a week and good-quality, often original jazz sessions on Saturday afternoon between 4 and 7 pm. *Richard's on Richards* (☎ 687-6794), 1036 Richards St, is a popular, dressy singles bar with a hefty but varying entry charge. The *Yaletown Brewing Co* on Hamilton St at the corner of Helmcken St is a popular place with its own beer.

Nearby, Granville St is interesting after dark with lots of street activity. The *Commodore Ballroom* (☎ 681-7838), 870 Granville St, can accommodate over 1000 people and plays everything from punk to Lambada. At 1300 Granville St, on the corner of Drake St, the *Yale* (☎ 681-9253) is one of the best blues bars in the country. It's open with live music seven nights a week from about 9.30 pm to 1.30 am.

There is a fair bit of nightlife in the Gastown area. The *Town Pump* (☎ 683-6695), 66 Water St, has local rock bands. The inexpensive *Gastown Music Hall* (☎ 685-1333), 6 Powell St, is a long-standing casual bar with live rock and reggae. The *Twilight Zone* (☎ 682-8550), 7 Alexander St, often rewards those in outlandish dress with free admission and features industrial, alternative, or tribal music depending on the night. Don't go punk on ska night!

The *Picadilly Pub*, 620 West Pender, has live R&B on Friday night. There's live, mostly traditional jazz at the *Hot Jazz Club* (☎ 873-4131), 2120 Main St. Admission is $10, less for students. The *Glass Slipper* (☎ 877-0066) at 2714 Prince Edward St behind the Biltmore Hotel has more contemporary jazz and world music nightly.

A gay bar that's been around for a long time and has music mostly nights is the *Royal Hotel* (☎ 685-5335), 1025 Granville St. One with various events and parties is *Denman Station* (☎ 669-3448) at 860 Denman St.

Most clubs close at around 2 am, and pubs around midnight or 1 am.

Spectator Sports The BC Lions (☎ 589-7627) play Canadian-style professional football from July to September in BC Place Stadium. Tickets are from $15 to $43. The Vancouver Canadians (☎ 872-5232), the local baseball team, play their home games at Nat Bailey Stadium, 4601 Ontario St next to Queen Elizabeth Park. Admission is $6.

The Grizzlies (☎ 589-7627) of the National Basketball Association (NBA) had their inaugural season in 1995/96. They play at GM Place. If you're here during the ice-hockey season, October to April, try to see a home game of the Vancouver Canucks (☎ 254-5141) at GM Place. Tickets to their games cost between $23 and $58.

Things to Buy

Several shops in Vancouver sell Native Indian wares, but most have fairly poor-quality stuff. Hill's Indian Crafts at 165 Water St is different. It's open seven days a week from 9 am to 9 pm and has a good selection of carvings, prints, masks, and the excellent Cowichan sweaters for about $190. These sweaters are hand-knitted and 100% wool. Originally from the Lake Cowichan area on Vancouver Island, they are now made in many places.

The Inuit Gallery, 345 Water St, sells Inuit sculptures, drawings and tapestries and Northwest Coast Native Indian masks, carvings and jewellery. It's open Monday to Saturday from 10 am to 6 pm, Sunday from noon to 5 pm. The art is free to look at, big bucks to buy. Images for a Canadian Heritage, 164 Water St, and the Marion Scott Gallery, 671 Howe St, are similar.

There are a number of good places selling camping and outdoor equipment, guidebooks and maps, mainly in the Kitsilano area. There's Gulliver's at 137-4255 Arbutus St and Wanderlust at 1929 West 4th Ave. Mountain Equipment Co-operative (☎ 872-7859), 130 W Broadway, sells all kinds of outdoor equipment at reasonable rates. It doesn't hurt to ask about HI member discounts.

Getting There & Away

Air Vancouver International Airport is about 10 km south of the city on Sea Island – between Vancouver and the municipality of Richmond.

On arrival, when you leave the baggage claim area, to the right there is a Royal Bank foreign-exchange office and an information desk through which you can book accommodation and organise transport. Ahead of you are the car-rental counters. The departure area has a bookshop, newsagent and small post office (open Monday to Friday from 9 am to noon, and 1 to 5 pm). There's also a Royal Bank 24-hour automatic-teller machine (ATM) which will change the notes of all major currencies, and an ATM for American Express card holders.

When leaving Vancouver you have to pay an airport improvement fee (AIF): $5 if you're flying within Canada, $10 to the USA and $15 to the rest of the world.

Major Canadian airlines fly to Vancouver, as do many US and Asian airlines. Some

Canadian and foreign airlines with offices in Vancouver are:

Air Canada (and Air BC)
  1040 West Georgia St (☎ 688-5515)
Air China
  1040 West Georgia St (☎ 685-0921)
Air India
  Suite 6, 601 West Broadway (☎ 879-0271)
Canadian Airlines International
  1030 West Georgia St (☎ 279-6611)
Cathay Pacific
  605 West Georgia St (☎ 682-9747, 661-2907)
Garuda
  Suite 930, 1040 West Georgia St (☎ 681-7034)
Hawaiian Airlines
  157-10551 Shellbridge Way, Richmond
  (☎ 231-8100)
Korean Air
  Suite 1010, 1030 West Georgia St (☎ 689-2000)
Lufthansa
  Suite 1401, 1030 West Georgia St
  (☎ 1-800-563-5954)
Singapore Airlines
  Suite 1111, 1030 West Georgia St (☎ 689-1233)

Fares can be cheaper if notice is given and may vary with the day of the week. Those given in this section are all full economy fares. Some one-way fares (including tax) with Canadian Airlines are Edmonton $375, Toronto $950, Whitehorse $550, Yellowknife $768, and Seattle $168.

A US$5 inspection tax is added to the Seattle flight; you go through US customs and immigration in Vancouver, not on arrival in Seattle.

Air Canada prices are virtually the same as those for Canadian Airlines. Air BC is a local airline run by Air Canada, serving Vancouver Island, points in the interior and Seattle. The pre-tax fare from Vancouver to Victoria is $112 return.

You can also fly to Seattle on United Airlines (☎ 1-800-241-6522). The flight time is about 45 minutes and some flights carry on to San Francisco or various US connections from either point.

Many people going across the continent find it cheaper to go, say, Seattle to Buffalo rather than Vancouver to Toronto. You may want to do this to get a flight to New York – it's likely to be cheaper from Seattle than from a Canadian point. Bus connections can be made between the Canadian and US airports at either end. Flights to Asia also may be cheaper from US west coast cities than from Vancouver.

Northwest Airlines (☎ 1-800-225-2525) and Alaska Airlines (☎ 1-800-426-0333) fly to Alaska. American Airlines (☎ 1-800-433-7300) and Horizon Air (☎ 1-800-547-9308) fly to many destinations in the western states of the USA.

See the introductory Getting There & Away chapter for information about flights from Australia, New Zealand and Asia into Vancouver.

Bus The bus station is part of Pacific Central Station (see the Train section following). Greyhound (☎ 662-3222), Pacific Coach Lines (☎ 662-8074) and Maverick Coach Lines (☎ 662-8051, 255-1171) stop here. Some examples of one-way fares with Greyhound (including tax) are: Kelowna (four daily), $47; Banff (four daily), $97; and Calgary (five daily), $99.

Pacific Coach Lines has eight buses daily to Victoria, leaving the bus station every hour at 10 minutes to the hour from 5.50 am to 8.45 pm. The one-way fare is $23 including ferry and the journey takes about three hours.

Maverick Coach Lines operates eight buses daily to Nanaimo for $18 one way (including ferry); the trip takes 3½ hours. It also has buses to Powell River, Squamish, Whistler and Pemberton. If you're heading for the USA, Quick Coach Lines (☎ 244-3744) operates a daily bus shuttle to downtown Seattle for $28, Seattle's SeaTac Airport for $35 and Bellingham Airport for $17. Buses leave downtown Vancouver from most major hotels.

You can also catch a city bus to White Rock close to the US border. Take bus No 351, 352 or 354 south on Granville St.

An alternative bus service is Bigfoot's Backpacker Adventure Tours (☎ 488-0484, or book through the HI hostel) which does a three-day trip to Banff via Kamloops with interesting stops along the way. Price is $45

to Kamloops or $84 for the whole trip. Hostel accommodation enroute is included. They also have a two-day camping trip to Whistler.

Train There are a number of train services operating out of Vancouver which travel across the country, to the Rockies or through the province.

VIA Rail Vancouver is the western terminal for VIA Rail. Pacific Central Station is off Main St at 1150 Station St between National and Terminal Aves. The closest main intersection is the corner of Main and Prior Sts. The station is marked 'Canadian National' and has a small park in front of it. It's a magnificent building inside but was underused until the main bus station re-located here in 1993. There's a McDonald's, a small shop and a car-rental outlet. For 24-hour information on fares and reservations call the toll-free number ☎ 1-800- 561-8630. The ticket office is open restricted hours: Monday and Thursday from 8 am to 8 pm; Tuesday, Wednesday and Friday from 8 am to 3.30 pm; Saturday from 12.30 to 8 pm; and Sunday from 8 am to 1.30 pm. Left luggage is open from 8 am to 10 pm (closed between 3.30 and 4 pm).

The route east goes through Kamloops ($71), Jasper ($148) and Edmonton ($206). Fares include tax. Trains leave Monday, Thursday and Saturday at 8 pm. Stopovers are permitted but you must re-reserve.

VIA Rail also provides a bus service between the towns of Kamloops and Penticton, Edmonton and Calgary and Saskatoon and Regina. This provides a connection to major towns no longer part of the rail system.

There is no rail connection with Seattle.

Rocky Mountaineer The privately owned *Rocky Mountaineer* train travels through some of the country's most scenic landscapes from BC to Alberta on no-longer used classic VIA lines. Leaving VIA Rail's Pacific Central Station it rolls northward to Kamloops where it splits in two. After an overnight stop, one portion goes to Jasper, the other down through Banff and on to Calgary. Both sections then return the same way. A whole series of tours are possible ranging from the basic two-day trip to extensive 12-day excursions. Anyway you do it won't be cheap but it is comfortable and some meals and accommodation are included. The basic one-way trip to either Banff or Jasper is $565, to Calgary $625 per person, double occupancy. The southern route to Banff is considered the more scenically dramatic.

The service runs between the middle of May and early October. There are seven trips a month in summer. For information contact a travel agent or Rocky Mountaineer Railtours (☎ 606-7200; reservations 1-800-665-7245), Suite 130, 1150 Station St, Vancouver in the main train station.

BC Rail British Columbia has its own railway system (☎ 984-5246) which heads north from North Vancouver to Squamish, Whistler, Lillooet, 100 Mile House, Williams Lake, Quesnel and Prince George, where it connects with VIA Rail (from Prince George you can go west to Prince Rupert or east to Jasper). The train to Prince George runs Sunday, Wednesday and Friday. It leaves North Vancouver at 7 am and arrives in Prince George at 8.30 pm. The one-way/return fare is $171/342 which includes all meals and tax.

A daily train to Whistler leaves at 7 am arriving at 9.34 am and the fare is $27/54 with tax and a meal. Both are busy and reservations are advised.

Trains leave from BC Rail's station, 1311 West 1st St at the southern end of Pemberton Ave, North Vancouver. To get to the station take bus No 239 west from the SeaBus terminal at Lonsdale Quay.

Car If you're coming from the USA (Washington state), you'll be on Hwy 5 until the border town of Blaine. At the border is the Peace Arch Provincial and State Park. The first town in British Columbia is White Rock. Hwy 99 veers west, then north to Vancouver. Close to the city, it passes over two arms of the Fraser River and eventually turns into Granville St, one of the main thoroughfares of downtown Vancouver. In the centre of town Granville St becomes a pedestrian mall, and ordinary traffic is forbidden. Remember there is a network of one-way streets around here too.

If you're coming from the east, you'll almost certainly be on the Trans Canada Hwy, which takes the Port Mann Bridge over the Fraser River and snakes through the eastern end of the city, eventually meeting with Hastings St before going over the Second Narrows Bridge to North Vancouver. If you want to go downtown, turn left when you reach Hastings St.

If you're coming from Horseshoe Bay in the north, the Trans Canada Hwy heads through West Vancouver and North Vancouver before going over the Second Narrows Bridge into Burnaby. If you're heading downtown leave the highway at the Taylor Way exit before you get to Second Narrows Bridge; from there Hwy 99 takes you over Lions Gate Bridge into Stanley Park.

Car Rentals There are many car-rental companies in Vancouver; the larger ones have several offices around town and some also have offices at the international airport. Some have discount coupons which are available at various outlets including the Travel Infocentre. Check the yellow pages for a thorough listing of car-rental companies. Following is a list of a few companies and their central address:

Budget
    450 West Georgia St (☎ 668-7000)
Lo-Cost
    1105 Granville St (☎ 689-9664)
Rent-A-Wreck
    180 West Georgia St (Sandman Hotel)
    (☎ 688-0001)
Thrifty
    1400 Robson St (☎ 688-2207)
Tilden
    1140 Alberni St (☎ 685-6111)

Lo-Cost charges from $55 a day with 200 free km then $0.12 per km plus insurance and

BRITISH COLUMBIA

tax, while Rent-A-Wreck charges $59 a day with unlimited mileage on the midsize cars. Rates vary depending on the size and type of car, when you rent (rates are usually lower at weekends) and how long you intend to rent for. Note that all agencies are very busy through the summer so plan ahead where possible or go first thing in the morning.

Car Sharing Check the newspaper classifieds or the Yellow Pages for car driveaways. Also check the notice boards at the hostels for opportunities to share car rides.

Ferry BC Ferries operates the ferry routes between the mainland and Vancouver Island and the main route is from Tsawwassen to Swartz Bay, which is just north of Sidney. There are about 15 ferries in each direction daily in summer leaving every hour on the hour between 7 am and 10 pm. The trip takes about 90 minutes. Sunday afternoon, Friday evening and holiday Monday are the busiest times and if you have a car there is often a one or two-ferry wait. To avoid long delays it's worth planning your crossing for other periods if you can.

Ferries also operate to Nanaimo from Tsawwassen and Horseshoe Bay. The one-way fare on all routes is $6.50 per adult, $2.50 for a bicycle and $27 per car. Call ☎ 227-0277 for information.

To get to Tsawwassen by city bus catch the southbound bus No 601 from the corner of Granville St and West 4th Ave to the Ladner Exchange. From the exchange take bus No 640 to the ferry terminal. Another quicker way is to catch the SkyTrain to Scotts Road Station and there catch the No 640. The fare either way is $1.50, or $3 if you travel in peak traffic time. From Swartz Bay you can take bus No 70 into Victoria. For Horseshoe Bay from Vancouver take bus No 250 or 257 northbound on Georgia St.

Hitching Hitching on the Trans Canada Hwy is illegal until 40 km past the city limits. One possibility is to take bus No 9 along East Broadway to Boundary Rd, then walk south to Grandview Hwy (which connects with the

Trans Canada Hwy) and stick your thumb out. Alternatively, take the SkyTrain to Scott Rd Station then bus No 502 to Langley along the Fraser Hwy before getting onto the main route.

Getting Around
For BC Transit information call ☎ 521-0400 or obtain one of the two publications they produce on getting around the city. One is the *Transit Guide*, a map of Greater Vancouver showing the bus, train and ferry routes. It costs $1.25 and can be bought at newsagents and bookshops. *Discover Vancouver on Transit* lists many of the city's attractions and how to get there (and includes Victoria). It's free and is available at the Travel Infocentre.

The Airport There are two ways of getting between the airport and downtown by bus, but the quickest is to take one of the Vancouver Airporter (☎ 244-9888) buses. They run from the Pacific Central Station and all major central hotels for $9 ($15 return with no time limit). Tickets can be purchased from the driver. Buses leave every 30 minutes starting at 6.15 am and take about 30 minutes. Buses for the downtown hotels leave the airport from level 2, the last one departing about 12.15 am; for the bus station, buses leave from bay 9 on level 1.

To get to the airport by city bus, take No 20 south on Granville St to 70th Ave. From there transfer to bus No 100 which will take you to the airport. From the airport, do the reverse. The total travel time is one hour and the fare is $1.50 ($3 during peak traffic time).

A taxi between downtown Vancouver and the airport takes about 25 minutes and costs around $26.

Bus, SkyTrain & SeaBus Vancouver doesn't have a subway, but does have an integrated bus network, light-rapid-transit (LRT) system using the SkyTrain, and ferry links using the SeaBus. Try to avoid buses at rush hour as the traffic jams are unbelievable.

The transport system is divided into three zones: the inner zone covers central Vancouver; the next zone includes the suburbs of Richmond, Burnaby, New Westminster, North Vancouver, West Vancouver and Sea Island; the outer zone covers Ladner, Tsawwassen, Delta, Surrey, White Rock, Langley, Port Moody and Coquitlam.

During off-peak times (between 9.30 am and 3 pm and after 6.30 pm Monday to Friday, and weekends and public holidays) you pay a flat $1.50 for a single journey good for bus, SkyTrain or SeaBus. In peak times it depends on how many zones you travel across: $1.50 for one zone, $2.25 for two, $3 for three. All-day transit passes are $4.50 (good for unlimited rides on the bus/Sky-Train/SeaBus after 9.30 am weekdays and all day weekends). Buy passes at the SeaBus or SkyTrain stations or from shops displaying the 'FareDealer' sign.

SkyTrain The SkyTrain connects downtown Vancouver with Burnaby, New Westminster and Whalley in Surrey. The trains are fully computerised (ie there's no driver!) and travel mostly above ground along a specially designed track. From downtown they operate between 5.50 am and 1.17 am during the week, between 6.40 am and 1.17 am on Saturday, and 8.47 and 12.17 am on Sunday. The trains are scheduled to connect with buses. They leave from Waterfront Station.

SeaBus These super-modern catamarans zip back and forth across Burrard Inlet between Waterfront Station downtown and Lonsdale Quay in North Vancouver. They leave every 15 minutes on weekdays, every half hour at other times. The trip lasts only 12 minutes but gives good views of the harbour and city skyline. Try to avoid rush hours when many commuters crowd aboard. Beautiful Waterfront Station was originally the western terminal for the Canadian Pacific Railway.

False Creek Miniferries Two companies operate miniferry shuttles across False Creek. From 10 am to 8 pm daily False Creek Ferries (☎ 684-7781) runs between the Vancouver Aquatic Centre on Sunset Beach at English Bay, Granville Island, the Vancouver Maritime Museum on Kitsilano Point and Stamps Landing near the Cambie St bridge. From the aquatic centre to the maritime museum costs $1.50 one way. Aquabus (☎ 689-5858) travels between the Arts Club Theatre on Granville Island and Hornby St via Stamp's Landing and the Concord/Yaletown dock near BC Place.

Car If you're driving, you'll notice the city doesn't have any expressways: everyone must travel through the city. Congestion is a big problem, especially along Lions Gate Bridge (probably best avoided altogether), Second Narrows Bridge and right downtown. On a wet or snowy day it's worse: try to avoid rush hours. It's also costly to park and/or very difficult to find a parking spot in the inner city. You're better off parking the car out a bit and catching a bus or SkyTrain into the centre; it'll probably be quicker too.

Taxi Unless you're staying at a big hotel the best bet is to phone for a cab; trying to hail one in the streets is likely to prove unsuccessful. Three of the companies are Black Top (☎ 683-4567), MacLure's (☎ 731-9211, 683-6666) and Yellow Cab (☎ 681-3311/1111). The flag fall is $2.10 and $1.18 for every km thereafter.

Bicycle Cycling is a good way to get around town, though riding on the sidewalk is illegal and bikes are not allowed on the SeaBus. Get a copy of the Bicycling Association of BC's cycling map of the city (see the Activities section at the start of the chapter). One of the most popular routes is along the 10-km road in Stanley Park, which has a number of rental places close by, including:

Action Rentals
    1793 Robson St (☎ 683-5648)
Bayshore Bicycles
    745 Denman St (☎ 688-2453)
Kitzco Beachwear & Rentals
    1168 Denman St (☎ 684-6269)

BRITISH COLUMBIA

Spokes Bicycle Rental & Espresso Bar
1798 West Georgia St (☎ 688-5141)

There are others so check the Yellow Pages.
Rates start at $5 an hour, $15 for four hours
or $20 a day.

AROUND VANCOUVER
Reifel Bird Sanctuary
The 340-hectare bird sanctuary (☎ 946-6980) is on Westham Island, 10 km west of
Ladner, south of Richmond. Each year, over
240 bird species pass through, including
herons, eagles, falcons and swans. There are
about three km of pathways and an observation tower. The sanctuary is open daily from
9 am to 6 pm in summer, to 4 pm in winter.
Admission is $3.25. There's no public trans-
port to the sanctuary. If you're driving, head
south on Hwy 99 then, after passing through
the George Massey Tunnel, head right
(south-west) on River Rd and follow it till
you come to Westham Island Rd.

Buddhist Temple
More than simply a temple, this Chinese
Buddhist centre (☎ 274-2822), in Richmond
at 9160 Steveston Hwy, consists of a temple,
garden, small museum and library. You may
also catch an art show or tea ceremony. The
temple is ornate and has some fine work, but
compared to the temples of Asia it may seem
modern and sterile. The centre is free and
open daily from 10 am to 5 pm. It's accessible
by bus from the city: No 403 on Howe St.

Steveston
This little town, in Richmond on the coast
near the Buddhist Temple, is heavily promoted as a quaint fishing village. There's
certainly nothing overly wrong with the
place and you can get some reasonable fish
& chips, but a quaint fishing village it's not.
There's a wharf where some of the fishing
fleet moors and a place to buy fresh seafood.
It has lots of historical buildings and the
Steveston Museum (☎ 271-6868) is open
Monday to Saturday from 9.30 am to 5 pm and
is free. To get to Steveston catch bus Nos 401,
402, 406 or 407.

White Rock
Still further south, on Semiahmoo Bay south
of Surrey and about two km from the US
border, is the suburb of White Rock so-
named because of the large white rock on its
beach. All summer long the beach, with
expanses of sand and warm waters, is quite
a scene; strut your stuff if you've done your
sit-ups. Take the SkyTrain to 22nd St Station
then catch bus No 353 to the beach, or catch
bus No 354 heading south on Granville St.

Fort Langley Historic Park
The 19th-century fort (☎ 888-4424) is at
23433 Mavis St, Fort Langley, 48 km east of
Vancouver along the Trans Canada Hwy. It
was erected in 1827 and served as a Hudson's
Bay Company post until 1858, long before
Victoria or Vancouver were established. It
was here in 1858 that BC was proclaimed a
crown colony. Most of the buildings were
restored in 1956 and you can see the old
palisades, furnishings and utensils. The park
is open in summer from 10 am to 4.30 pm
and admission is $4.

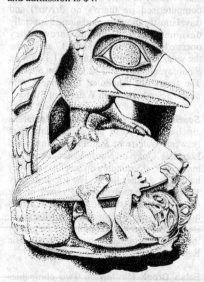

'The Raven and the First Men'
carved by Haida artist, Bill Reid

Take the SkyTrain to Scott Rd Station, catch bus No 501 to the Exhibition Centre in Fort Langley, then bus No 507 to the park.

Vancouver Zoological Centre

The 48-hectare site (☎ 856-6825) known before political correctness as the game farm, off 264 St in Aldergrove about 12 km south-east of the fort, has 60 different kinds of animals in large, open pens, including tigers, lions, elephants and buffalo. It's open daily from 8 am to 8 pm and admission is $9.

Horseshoe Bay

North of Vancouver the small coastal community of Horseshoe Bay marks the end of Marine Drive and West Vancouver. It's a pretty spot and with the Nanaimo ferry terminal's traffic and city daytrippers, is quite busy and commercial.

On Bay St by the water is *Ya Ya's Oyster Bar* for various seafoods including fish & chips and beer brewed on the premises. Next door is a popular pub.

The road from Vancouver splits at Horseshoe Bay. You can head further north up the Sunshine Coast by catching the ferry to Langdale, or take Hwy 99 north-east to Squamish, Garibaldi Provincial Park and Whistler (see the North of Vancouver section for details).

North of Vancouver

SUNSHINE COAST

The name refers to the coastal area north of Horseshoe Bay to Lund, 23 km north of Powell River. It's a narrow strip of land separated from the mainland by the Coastal Mountains. The scenery is excellent: hills, mountains, forests, inlets, harbours and beaches. Slow and winding Hwy 101 edging along the coast is broken at two separate points where you'll need to take a ferry – from Horseshoe Bay to Langdale and from Earl's Cove to Saltery Bay. The highway ends completely at Lund. At Powell River there is a ferry over to Comox on Vancouver

Island. For information about the ferries, call BC Ferries (☎ 277-0277) or pick up a copy of their schedules from one of the Travel Infocentres.

The region remains quiet but is increasingly busy with both commuters and visitors. For the latter, it can be part of an interesting circuit from Vancouver around Vancouver Island and back. BC Ferries offers a circular ferry ticket known as the Sunshine Coast Cirlepac which includes all four ferries around the loop at a good reduction from full fare. Economical bus service is available between Vancouver and Powell River with the two ferries included. See under Getting There & Away in the Vancouver section for more detail.

Sechelt and Powell River are the commercial and activity centres of the coast. Aside from the good hiking, camping and fishing in the area, these towns are bases for some of the world's best diving although it is not for novices and local guides should be used. Around Egmont near **Earl's Cove**, diving spots include wrecks and a beautiful bronze mermaid.

In **Powell River** the Travel Infocentre (☎ 485-4701) is at 4690 Marine Ave. The Beach Gardens Resort Hotel (☎ 485-6267), 7074 Westminster Ave, rents boats and diving equipment and runs charters out to diving spots such as the submarine cave formations in Okeover Inlet near Lund. From Powell River there is a 65-km canoeing circuit which takes five to seven days. North of Lund, **Desolation Sound Marine Park** has abundant wildlife, diving, canoeing and wilderness camping.

Accommodation around Powell River includes hotels, motels and campgrounds. Two work-for-stay alternatives may be of interest. *Fiddlehead Farm Hostel* (☎ 334-8044) accessible by boat makes a fine retreat for a few days of canoeing and hiking. All meals are included in the daily dorm ($20) or tent ($15) rate with some work around the farm required. Pick-up can be arranged for the Powell River bus station or Comox ferry terminal. For information and reservations call or write to Linda Schreiber, Fiddlehead

Farm, PO Box 421, Powell River V8A 5C2. A similar arrangement can be found at *Theodosia Mariculture*, the oyster and clam farm of Hendrik & Marijke Beune, situated in the south-east corner of Desolation Marine Park. In return for fours hours work a day they offer room and board. Minimum stay is a week. To contact them by phone, call the marine operator by dialling 0, ask for channel 64 then Zenobia N111373.

HORSESHOE BAY TO WHISTLER

You can't drive quickly to Whistler – the road is narrow, hilly and winding; besides you'll be enjoying the views.

Squamish

This is the main town in this resort area. The Travel Infocentre (☎ 892-9244), 37950 Cleveland Ave, is open year round. Nearby there is great windsurfing in Squamish Spit and rock-climbing on Stawamus Chief and Smoke Bluffs. Squamish is the destination for the *Royal Hudson* steam train (see the Organised Tours section under Vancouver earlier for details).

The new Squamish Hostel (☎ 892-9240), at 3840 Buckley Ave, which is walkable to the centre, makes a good base for enjoying the area's outdoor attractions. It's open all year, charges $15 and rents mountain bikes. The owner can help organise various activities.

Shannon Falls Provincial Park

South of Squamish, the Shannon Falls tumble over a 335-metre cliff just off the road. There's hiking, rock climbing and camping in summer, skiing in winter. Nearby at Brittania Beach is the BC Museum of Mining which includes a tour of the mine.

Garibaldi Provincial Park

This park is a 195-sq-km mountain wilderness, 64 km north of Vancouver. Most of the park is undeveloped and it's a full-day's hike from the parking lot off Hwy 99 to the campground. For more information and a map stop at one of the Travel Infocentres in Squamish or Whistler.

Garibaldi Provincial Park has five hiking areas – Diamond Head, Garibaldi Lake, Cheakamus Lake, Singing Pass and Wedgemount Lake – covered by more than 60 km of developed trails. Garibaldi is a wilderness park so you should take your own supplies and equipment, especially if you intend to go far from developed areas.

Brandywine Falls Provincial Park

About 10 km south of Whistler (look for the sign) is a waterfall with some interesting pioneer lore. Evidently, they threw bottles of brandywine into the falls – mesmerised by the fine view? It's quite a scenic little place with hiking trails and a campground.

WHISTLER

Just outside the northern end of Garibaldi Provincial Park is this major resort area geared mainly for skiing, which is available all year round. In summer you can go hiking, cycling, canoeing, take the cable car up the mountain or visit an aquatic park. Ask about the 'singing tunnels', an old mine site, which you can visit. Whistler Village has a sort of contrived feel about it – it is very new – but people being active and having fun generally create a light, relaxing atmosphere. The village is really made up of hotels, lodges, restaurants and bars and the bills can certainly add up.

The Whistler ski district has three centres, Whistler Village, Blackcomb and Whistler's South Side. The latter is the least expensive while the village has the most action and socialising – with the larger hotels it is also more costly. Together the three areas make up Canada's largest ski resort. Blackcomb Mountain (☎ 932-3141; in Vancouver ☎ 687-1032) has the largest downhill ski area in North America, offering 1600 metres of continuous skiing. Whistler Mountain is a close second with 1530 metres. The usually reliable snow, the vertical drop and mild Pacific air combine to provide some of the most pleasant skiing to be found anywhere, from novice slopes to glacier skiing. The latter is available pretty well all year, providing the country's only summer skiing.

Heli-skiing companies based in Whistler Village offer services to more than a 100 other runs on glaciers near the resort. There are cross-country trails as well.

On Blackcomb Mountain the day pass for an adult is $40. For a snow report call ☎ 932-4211. On Whistler Mountain (☎ 932-3434; in Vancouver ☎ 685-1007) the skiing and facilities (including the base station at Whistler Village and the 10-passenger, high-speed, enclosed cable car) make it one of the best resorts in the world and the price is the same. For a snow report call ☎ 932-4191; in Vancouver call ☎ 687-6761.

Places to Stay

There are about two dozen inns and lodges in and around Whistler Village. They're all new and for the most part in the mid or upper price ranges. HI *Whistler Hostel* (☎ 932-5492) is in a beautiful setting on Alta Lake (West) Rd about four km by foot from Whistler Village. It costs $14.50 in summer, $17.50 in winter for members and a few dollars more for nonmembers. The office is open from 7 to 11 am and from 5 to 11 pm. With just room for 35 people it's a good idea to book ahead especially during ski season. The BC Rail train will stop at the hostel upon request.

Whistler Backpackers Guest House (☎ 932-1177), 2124 Lake Placid Rd in Whistler, is close to the centre of things. Private and shared rooms start from $16 a day in winter, $13 in summer.

The *Shoestring Lodge* (☎ 932-3338) 7124 Nancy Greene Drive has shares from $17 and doubles from $55 depending on the time of year. Nesters Road about one km north of the village has several moderately priced pension-style B&Bs. A reader has suggested that in summer, renting a condo can be very good value; inquire at tourist information.

Getting There & Away

Maverick Coach Lines (☎ 255-1171) has six buses daily to Whistler from Pacific Central Station in Vancouver. It's about a two-hour drive from Vancouver, along the edge of scenic Howe Sound and into the Coast Mountains from Squamish. The fare is $14/26 one way/return. Also see under Getting There & Away in the Vancouver section for information on Bigfoot's alternative bus service. Once in Whistler you don't need transport to get about.

On BC Rail the return fare to Whistler is $54 (see the Vancouver Getting There & Away section for more details).

Vancouver Island

The attractions of Vancouver Island, the largest island off the west coast of the Americas, range from its rugged wilderness to the grand rooms of its provincial legislature.

The island is 450 km long and has a population of over 500,000 people, most of whom live along the south-eastern coast.

The geography is scenically varied. A mountain range runs down the centre of the island, its snow-capped peaks setting off the woods and many lakes and streams. The coast can be either rocky and tempestuous or sandy and calm.

South of the island, across the Strait of Juan de Fuca, the sea is backed by the substantial Mt Olympus (2428 metres) in Washington state's Olympic National Park.

Across Georgia Strait, which runs along the island's eastern shore, the mainland's Coast Mountains form the skyline. The open west coast is fully exposed to the Pacific. The waters around the island are filled with marine life, much of which is commonly seen and some, like the salmon, eaten. Crab is a BC culinary delicacy and the world's largest octopuses are found here.

Vancouver Island also has a diverse birdlife, with over 440 different species. The bald eagle is widespread and can be seen near rivers and lakes; the golden eagle is an endangered species but can still be seen along the coast.

The central north-south mountain chain divides the island into distinct halves. The sparsely populated west coast is rugged, hilly, forested and cut by deep inlets. The

Ferry to
Prince Rupert

COAST MOUNTAINS

▲ Mt Waddington
4016m

Port
Hardy

Cape Scott
Provincial
Park

Port
McNeill

Telegraph
Cove

Quatsino
Sound

Port
Alice

Cape
Cook

19

19

Sayward

Kyuquot
Sound

Zeballos

Whistler

Garibaldi
Provincial
Park

Campbell
River

Lund

101

Powell
River

Saltery Bay

Squamish

Gold
River

28

Courtenay

Mt
Washington
(1606m)

Comox

Egmont

Sechelt

99

PACIFIC OCEAN

Strathcona
Provincial
Park

Nootka
Sound

Qualicum Beach

19

Gibsons

Horseshoe
Bay

Clayoquot
Sound

Meares
Island

Tofino

Pacific
Rim National
Park

Ucluelet

Broken
Group
Islands

Barkley Sound

4

Parksville

Port Alberni

1

Nanaimo

Ladysmith
Chemainus
Crofton

Bamfield

West Coast Trail

Lake Cowichan

Pacific
Rim National
Park

Port
Renfrew

14

Duncan

VANCOUVER

Tsawwassen

Gulf
Islands

Sidney

VICTORIA

Sooke

San
Juan
Islands

Juan de Fuca Strait

Olympic Peninsula

WASHINGTON
(USA)

Vancouver Island

0   50   100 km

more gentle eastern side is suitable for farming. The island's industries – forestry, mining and fishing – and nearly all of the principal towns are found along this side of the ridge. Up the east coast the resort towns and villages have plenty of campgrounds, motels, hotels and guesthouses. However, don't imagine the entire east coast to be urban sprawl: it's still quite undeveloped in places, especially north of Campbell River.

The island has the mildest climate in the country. It's particularly moderate at the southern end, where the northerly arm of Washington state protects it from the ocean.

There is substantially less rain in Victoria than in Vancouver. August and September, when the sky is usually blue, are excellent months during which to visit.

Vancouver Island is a popular tourist destination and Victoria especially can get crowded in mid-summer. For those seeking quieter spots, a little effort will be rewarded.

VICTORIA

Victoria, the second largest city in the province and the provincial capital, lies at the south-eastern end of Vancouver Island, 90 km south-west of Vancouver. Although bounded on three sides by water, it is sheltered from the Pacific Ocean by the Olympic Peninsula across the Juan de Fuca Strait in Washington state. It is a gentle and genteel town-like city.

Both visitors and residents alike seem to indulge the British and resort flavour that has arisen. With the mildest climate in the country, its clean streets, the interesting history, and its flowers to attract people, it's not surprising that two million tourists visit Victoria annually. This quiet, traditional seat of civilisation was once described by Rudyard Kipling as 'Brighton Pavilion with the Himalayas for a backdrop'.

Although it is the provincial capital and home to an important university and naval base, Victoria is not an industrial city. About 30% of its 300,000 or so residents work in tourist and service-oriented businesses, while another 20% work in the public sector. The island is also a major retirement centre, with retirees making up around 20% of the population. Along with Vancouver, it is one of the faster-growing cities in the country.

History

The first residents were the Salish Indians. Although Captain Cook landed on Nootka Island on the west coast in 1778, it was not until 1843 that James Douglas, acting for the Hudson's Bay Company, founded Victoria in the name of the queen as a fur-trading post. The town boomed as a drop-off point when gold was discovered in the Cariboo area in the late 1850s. Soon Victoria was full of merchants and brothels, and home to one 'Gassy Jack' Deighton, who later played an important role in Vancouver's development.

The gold rush ended, however, and the Canadian Pacific Railway never fulfilled its promise of a railway link. But it did build the fabulous Empress Hotel, and when the hotel opened in 1908, the tourist trade began in earnest. Without the railway connection, industry was forgotten. As the seat of emerging political power and with an increasing reputation as a graceful social centre, Victoria blossomed in its own way.

Today there are still more British-born residents in Victoria than anywhere else in Canada, and they have entrenched their style rather than forgotten it. Rising numbers of immigrants and visitors from around the world are imparting an increasingly cosmopolitan air.

Orientation

The city lies at the south-eastern tip of Vancouver Island, actually closer to the USA than to the Canadian mainland. The downtown area is simply laid out and really not very large. Bounded on two sides by water, the central area of the city with very few high-rise buildings, is easy and pleasant to explore on foot and you'll have little trouble getting your bearings.

The focal point is the Inner Harbour, a section of Victoria Harbour surrounded by several of the city's most important structures. The Empress Hotel faces out over its lawns to the waterfront. Across the way are the enormous provincial Parliament Buildings. In between the two, on the corner beside the Netherlands Centennial Carillon, is the Royal BC Museum. To the east of the museum is Thunderbird Park, with its totem poles, and south of this is Beacon Hill Park, the city's largest. Surrounding the park and extending down to the ocean are well-kept residential houses, many with attractive lawns and gardens.

Along Wharf St, north of the Empress Hotel, is the central Travel Infocentre, on the corner of the Inner Harbour. Following Wharf St along the water will take you through the Old Town, the restored original area of Victoria.

Meeting Wharf St at right angles are Fort, Yates and Johnson Sts. Just up a few steps from Wharf St is Bastion Square, the Old Town's square, lined with historic buildings.

Parallel to Wharf St and a couple of blocks east is Government St, one of the major downtown thoroughfares and containing numerous government buildings. Near Yates St is Trounce Alley, once the tiny byway where miners sold their gold. It has been renovated and has many boutiques – some selling gold.

To Duncan,
Victoria
General Hospital &
Campgrounds

To Airport, Sidney, Swartz Bay
Ferry Terminal & Butchart Gradens

Gorge Road

Trans Canada Highway

To Motels & Fort
Victoria RV Park

Fernwood Road

Pleasant Street

Hillside Avenue

2

Skinner Street

Catherine Street

Bay Street

Bay Street

Queens Avenue

**Upper
Harbour**

Caledonia Avenue

Discovery Street

4

Chatham Street

3

Store Street

Tyee Road

Harbour Road

Esquimalt Road

5

Herald Street

6

Fisgard Street

7

Cormorant

9

Street

Quadra Street

Cook Street

Chambers Street

1

10

11

12

Pandora Avenue

Johnson Street

Yates Street

**Victoria
Harbour**

**Laurel
Point**

**Songhees
Point**

**Inner
Harbour**

Walking Path

Wharf Street

Government

Broad St

Douglas Street

Blanshard Street

View Street

Fort Street

58

60

62

63

64

Belleville

Quebec

Avenue

Kingston Street

Superior Street

Menzies Street

Broughton Street

57

56

Courtney Street

Burdett Avenue

59

Rockland
Avenue

61

To Government
House &
Craigdarroch
Castle

St Lawrence Street

Montreal Street

Michigan Street

Oswego Street

Simcoe Street

Niagara Street

Dallas Road

Toronto Street

68

69

65

67

66

Fairfield Road

Humboldt Street

Southgate Street

Richardson Street

Moss Street

See Inset

**Beacon Hill
Park**

Government

Battery Street

70

Dallas Road

Walking
Path

13

14

Pandora Avenue

15

16

Johnson Street

17

18

19

21

22

23

Yates Street

20

24

26

27

28

25

Wharf Street

29

30

31

32

Langley St

Government

Broad Street

View Street

33

34

Fort Street

35

Broughton Street

36

Courtney Street

37

38

Douglas

41

39

40

42

43

Blanshard St

Humboldt Street

46

47

48

49

44

45

50

Belleville Street

51

52

53

54

55

0   50   100 m

**Inner
Harbour**

![Lonely Planet logo] (lp)

Victoria

0   100   200 m

BRITISH COLUMBIA

PLACES TO STAY		20	Harvest Moon Café	33	Victoria Eaton Centre
		23	Day & Night	36	Post Office
3	Paul's Motor Inn	24	Periklis	39	Victoria Clipper Ferry
4	Imperial Inn	27	Eugene's Restaurant		Terminal
9	Fairfield Hotel		& Snack Bar	40	Travel Infocentre
15	Hotel Douglas	29	Le Petit Saigon	44	Royal London Wax
18	Salvation Army Centre	30	Koto Japanese		Museum
19	Victoria Regent Hotel		Restaurant	45	Pacific Undersea
21	HI Victoria Hostel	32	Murchie's		Gardens
28	Dominion Hotel	35	Pagliacci's	47	Miniature World
34	Ritz Hotel	38	Sticky Wicket Pub	48	Victoria Conference
37	Strathcona Hotel	41	Sam's Deli		Centre
43	Green Gables Hotel	42	Smitty's Family	49	Crystal Garden
46	Empress Hotel		Restaurant	50	Bus Station
55	Crystal Court Motel	58	Da Tandoor	51	Parliament Buildings
57	YM-YWCA	62	Barb's Place	52	Royal BC Museum
60	Backpackers Victoria			53	Helmcken House & St
	Hostel	**OTHER**			Anne's Pioneer
65	Helm's Inn				Schoolhouse
66	Beaconsfield Inn	1	Spinnaker's	54	Thunderbird Park
67	Shamrock Motel	2	Point Ellice House	56	Royal Theatre
68	James Bay Inn	7	The Bay	59	BC Ferries
		10	Swans Hotel	61	Art Gallery of Greater
PLACES TO EAT		11	McPherson Playhouse		Victoria
		12	Market Square	63	Fisherman's Wharf
5	Herald St Caffé	13	E&N Railiner Station	64	Black Ball Ferry
6	Foo Hong	22	Crown Publications		Terminal
8	The Ocean Phoenix	25	Victoria Express &	69	Carr House
14	Café Mexico		Victoria Star Ferry	70	'Mile 0' Trans Canada
16	John's Place		Terminal		Highway
17	Chandler's Seafood	26	Bastion Square		
	Restaurant	31	Munro's Books		

One block east is Douglas St, the main commercial street of Victoria. The area around Douglas St, Government St and Bastion Square is the centre of the business area, with banks, offices and department stores.

City Hall, built in 1890, is on the corner of Douglas St and Pandora Ave. The brownish-purple building with its mansard roof, clock tower and flowers is worth noting.

East again is Blanshard St, running near the edge of the downtown area. Going further leads you into residential areas. Marine Drive, along the waterfront east of town, is a wealthy district with parks and beaches.

The northern boundary of the downtown area is marked by Fisgard St, between Government and Wharf Sts, which has a small Chinatown with Oriental-style street lamps and buildings, Chinese characters on the street signs and, of course, restaurants. The

area is remarkably neat and clean but very colourful due mainly to the brightly painted facades of the buildings. Fan Tan Alley, halfway along, has a few small shops and connects Fisgard St with Pandora Ave. In the 1860s when this, Canada's first Chinatown, was in its heyday and much bigger, the alley was lined with opium dens and gambling houses – it's a lot quieter now with no evidence of these early vice-filled days. To keep it that way it's locked at night.

Following Fort St east up the hill and then along Oak Bay Ave will lead you through the 'tweed curtain' to the wealthier, very British area of Oak Bay. The Infocentre has information on walks to take in this attractive and traditional district.

Both Douglas and Blanshard Sts lead north out of the city: the former to the Trans Canada Hwy and Nanaimo, the latter to Hwy 17 (Patricia Bay Hwy), Sidney and the Swartz Bay ferry terminal. To the north-west is Gorge Rd, an area of heavy motel concentration. It forms part of Island Hwy 1A, which cuts across both Douglas and Blanshard Sts, runs along the northern side of the gorge and meets up further west with Craigflower Rd and the Trans Canada Hwy.

Victoria International Airport is in Sidney, about 20 km north of Victoria on Hwy 17. The bus station is at 700 Douglas St, on the corner of Belleville St and opposite Crystal Garden.

The city has many attractions. The more popular of the commercial variety are listed below. They're all about the same price and not cheap, choose carefully. People with special interests may find others worth visiting.

Information
Tourist Offices The Travel Infocentre (☎ 382-2127), 812 Wharf St, is by the water at the Inner Harbour, across the road from the Empress Hotel. It has dozens of pamphlets, maps and information on shopping, sightseeing, transport, where to stay and where to eat. It's open daily from 9 am to 9 pm but Sunday to 7 pm. There is also an office two km south of the Swartz Bay ferry terminal on Patricia Bay Hwy, and another in Sidney.

If you'd like to find out more about Victoria before you arrive contact Tourism Victoria (☎ 382-2127), 710 1175 Douglas St, Victoria V8W 2E1.

Money The major banks have branches along Douglas St. The Toronto Dominion Bank, 1070-1080 Douglas St, is open on Saturday from 9.30 am to 4.30 pm. You can change money at Money Mart, 1720 Douglas St, opposite the Bay department store, and at Currency Exchange (open seven days a week from 7 am to 9.30 pm), 724 Douglas St opposite the Budget car-rental office. You can also change money at American Express, 1203 Douglas St. US currency is accepted in many establishments but usually at a poorer exchange rate.

Post The main post outlet is at 905 Broughton St at the Broughton Square complex. It's closed Sunday.

Bookshops & Maps Crown Publications (☎ 386-4636), 546 Yates St, sells maps, federal and provincial publications on Canadiana, as well as books on Native Indian culture and on nature, and travel guides. It's open Monday to Friday from 8.30 am to 5 pm and Saturday from 9.30 to 5 pm. Maps BC (☎ 387-1441), 3rd Floor, 1802 Douglas St, is a government office with maps and atlases of the province.

Munro's Books (☎ 382-2464), 1108 Government St, is in a beautiful old building originally built for the Royal Bank and restored in 1984. It is now classified as a heritage building; the atmosphere inside is almost ecclesiastical and is worth a look even if you aren't in the market for a book. It sells a whole range of books and has a good Canadiana section. In summer it's open Monday to Friday from 9 am to 9 pm, Saturday from 9 am to 6 pm and Sunday from 11 am to 6 pm.

There are also a number of second-hand bookshops along Fort St, including Renaissance Books next to Da Tandoor restaurant.

Medical Services The Royal Jubilee Hospital (☎ 595-9200; 595-9212 in an emergency) is at 1900 Fort St. Victoria General Hospital (☎ 727-4212; 727-4181 in an emergency) is at 35 Helmcken Rd, north-west of the downtown area, off the Trans Canada Hwy.

Useful Organisations Greenpeace (☎ 388-4325), 202-620 View St, has details of environmental issues and helps organise information nights. Friendly by Nature (☎ 388-9292) in Bastion Square, has information on environmental issues in BC and sells T-shirts etc.

Left Luggage Left-luggage lockers beside the bus station, 700 Douglas St, cost $2.50; tokens are obtained from inside the station.

Dangers & Annoyances At night, Broad St between Yates and Johnston Sts, is often occupied by prostitutes and drunks. Some drunks also hang out on the corner of Yates and Douglas Sts.

Walking Tours Ask about the free walking tours at the Travel Infocentre or buy a copy of the booklet Victoria on Foot (Terrapin, Victoria, 1989), by Barrie Lee, which gives details of walking tours around the Old Town.

Inner Harbour

Royal BC Museum This excellent museum (☎ 387-3701), 675 Belleville St, is a must see, even for people who normally avoid such places. The wide variety of displays is artistically arranged, beautifully lit and accompanied by informative, succinct explanations. There are good sections on geology, vegetation, wildlife and ethnology. Many of the models and exhibits are incredibly realistic.

In the areas devoted to the BC Native Indians, see the detailed models of villages, the documentary 1914 film *In the Land of the War Canoes* on the Kwakiutl people, and the rock on which a man 'fell from the sky'. Also look at the Haida craftwork in argillate, a dense black carbon shale. The pipes represent some of the best Native Indian art anywhere.

There's a town made up of 19th and early 20th-century buildings and goods, including a Model T Ford. Chaplin movies are shown in the old movie theatre. The museum also has an interesting collection of artefacts from the 1920s through to the 1970s. Outside there is a garden of BC's native wildflowers.

Admission is $5, or $3 for students. The museum provides free tours and is open daily from 9.30 am to 7 pm in summer and from 10 am to 5.30 pm in winter.

Helmcken House This house (☎ 387-4697), in Eliot Square beside the Royal BC Museum, is the oldest in BC to have remained unchanged. The rooms are shown much the way they would have appeared in the early 1850s. John Helmcken, a doctor and politician, was very active in the local community. The house contains much period furniture and examples of decorations and implements. Staff members are friendly and helpful. It's open daily in summer from 11 am to 5 pm and admission is $4.

St Anne's Pioneer Schoolhouse Also in Eliot Square, this schoolhouse, operated as part of the Royal BC Museum, is one of the oldest buildings in Victoria still in use. Built sometime between 1840 and 1860, it was moved to its present site in 1974 from the grounds of St Anne's Academy.

Thunderbird Park This small but interesting strip of grass beside the Royal BC Museum has a collection of both plain and painted wooden totem poles, some of which are labelled. In the Thunderbird Park Carving Studio you can watch Native Indian artists at work and talk to them too. The studio is run on a volunteer basis with help from the Royal BC Museum.

Parliament Buildings The multi-turreted Parliament Buildings (☎ 387-6121), 501 Belleville St facing the Inner Harbour, were designed by Francis Rattenbury and finished in 1898. On top of the main dome is a figure of Captain George Vancouver, the first British navigator to circle Vancouver Island. Rattenbury also designed the Empress Hotel and the Parthenon-like Royal London Wax Museum, which was once a Canadian Pacific railway ticket office. The buildings are open daily from 8.30 am to 5 pm and free 30-minute guided tours are offered every day in summer.

The paintings in the lower rotunda depict scenes from Canadian history. Around the upper rotunda are paintings of four of BC's main industries. The Legislative Chamber is where all the laws of BC are made (there is no Senate in the provincial parliament). You can view the debates from the public gallery when the session is in. In the Legislative Library is the dagger used to kill Captain Cook in Hawaii, while on the lawn are a statue of Queen Victoria and a sequoia tree from California planted in the 1860s. The buildings are lit spectacularly at night, by more than 3000 lightbulbs.

Pacific Undersea Gardens A sort of natural aquarium, the gardens (☎ 382-5717), are found on the harbour at 490 Belleville St.

Visitors descend beneath the water's surface to view a range of corralled sea creatures such as octopuses, eels, crabs etc. Children especially find it intriguing. Admission is $6.75.

Royal London Wax Museum This museum (☎ 388-4461), 470 Belleville St, in front of the Parliament Buildings, contains more than 200 wax models of historical and contemporary figures. It's open daily from 9 am to 9 pm and admission is $7.

Miniature World At Miniature World (☎ 385-9731), 649 Humboldt St, beside the Empress Hotel, you'll find numerous layouts depicting in exact detail various themes, such as the world of Dickens. The highlight is a large model train representing the development of the Canadian Pacific railway from 1885 to 1915. Miniature World is open daily from 9 am to 8 pm and admission is $7.

Douglas St
Beacon Hill Park Just south-east of the downtown area, along Douglas St, this 62-hectare park is Victoria's largest. Bus No 5 will take you there. The park is an oasis of trees, flowers, ponds and pathways. Trees of this size you don't see anywhere but on the west coast. Also in the park is the 'world's tallest totem'; and a cricket pitch. The southern edge overlooks the ocean and offers good views of the coastline. At the lookout above Dallas Rd is a marker indicating the direction of places such as Seattle, and noting the elevations of mountains. At the south-western corner of the park, the path along the water meets the **'Mile 0' marker**, the Pacific terminal of the Trans Canada Hwy.

Crystal Garden This site (☎ 381-1277), 713 Douglas St, is one of the more popular commercial attractions. The principal draw is the colourful tropical-like garden complete with 65 varieties of international endangered animals and birds as well as free-flying butterflies. Designed by Francis Rattenbury, it was fashioned after London's Crystal Palace and built in 1925. Once a focal point for the

social elite, it was restored in 1977 as a visitor attraction, but remains a venue for splashy events. It's open daily from 10 am to 9 pm in July and August; the rest of the year it closes at 5.30 pm. Admission is $6.50 and there is a restaurant.

Carr House South of the inner Harbour a short walk leads to the birthplace of Emily Carr, one of Canada's best-known painters. Carr House (☎ 383-5843), at 207 Government St, shows something of her upbringing and background and also displays some of her work, both in painting and literature. Many of her paintings incorporated subject matter drawn from the culture of the west coast Native Indians, particularly the totem poles. There is also a video about her life and career. It's open daily from 10 am to 5 pm and admission is $3. Note that the Victoria Art Gallery usually has an Emily Carr exhibit.

Old Town
The original Victoria was centred along Wharf St and Bastion Square. This was where the first fur-trading ships moored. Wharf St was once busy with miners, merchants and all those fortune seekers heading for the Klondike.

Bastion Square was where Fort Victoria was situated and held the courthouse, jail, gallows and brothel. The whole area has been restored and redeveloped. The square is pleasant for strolling around or sitting in and people-watching. Many of the old buildings are now restaurants, boutiques, galleries or offices. The same is true of those in Wharf St.

Further north along Wharf St you'll come to **Market Square**, a former warehouse on the corner of Johnson St, dating from the 1890s. Renovated in 1975, this compact, attractive area now has two floors of over 40 shops and restaurants, built around a courtyard shaded by trees. Take a look at the **holograms** in the store which bills itself as an art gallery. They're pretty amazing, easily superior to those generally seen.

Emily Carr

Emily Carr was born in Victoria in 1871 to prosperous parents. Her parents died when she was young and by 16 she was 'waging war' with the family to permit her to attend art school in San Francisco. As her dedication to painting was deemed unladylike, she was forced to make a living from teaching.

Her career as an artist took a pivotal turn when, in 1898, she accompanied a churchman to his mission at Ucluelet on Vancouver Island. The life and arts of the Native Indian village had a profound effect on Carr. Inspired by what she saw she began using both the landscape and the Native Indians as her subject matter. She soon realised, however, that she needed to learn technique so headed to London to study landscape painting.

Carr returned to Canada but found that the power of nature and that of the Native culture were still missing from her painting. Working virtually alone she left, at age 39, for Paris to absorb some of the more modern painting techniques and styles. She found what she was looking for and her work took on her unique use of colour, brush stroke and subject matter.

Back home her new paintings were not taken seriously and were even found to be offensive. Students were removed from her art classes and her income steadily declined. At the age of 42, after a disastrous exhibition of paintings depicting the forests of Vancouver Island, she became a social outcast. To make ends meet she became a landlady in central Victoria.

It wasn't until the late 1920s that her scorned 1912 paintings were shown in eastern Canada and, in a sense, discovered. She then met the members of the increasingly well-known and influential school of painters called the Group of Seven, and with renewed energy and confidence continued her development as an artist. Until the latter 1930s she revisited many of her cherished Indian locales and painted some of her best-known works.

As her health failed and she became bed-ridden she took to writing. Her book *Klee Wyck* is a collection of stories recalling her life among the Native Indians. The title means 'laughing one', the name given to her by the Kwakiutl people. *The Book of Small* chronicles her childhood in Victoria, and *The House of All Sorts* describes her years as a landlady.

Her house in Victoria is open to the public, and some of her paintings can be viewed at the Art Gallery of Greater Vancouver as well as at all of the major galleries across the country. Carr produced a rich body of work unlike that of any other Canadian artist and is regarded as Canada's first major woman artist. ■

Maritime Museum This collection of artefacts, models, photographs and naval memorabilia is for nautical buffs only although everybody will find the elevator inside the front door worth a look. The museum (☎ 385-4222), 28 Bastion Square near Government St, is open daily from 9.30 am to 4.30 pm and admission is $5, $3 for students.

Victoria Eaton Centre Although this is a shopping centre, it's worth a wander round. The complex incorporates the facades of original buildings. As well as shops and eateries, it has fountains, pools and a rooftop garden. It occupies two blocks between Government and Douglas Sts.

Rockland Area
Art Gallery of Greater Victoria The gallery (☎ 384-4101), in a Victorian mansion at 1040 Moss St, 1.5 km east of the downtown area, just off Fort St, is best known for its excellent Asian art, including the Japanese and Chinese collections. It also has artworks from other parts of the world and from widely varying periods of history including pre-Columbian Latin American objects through to contemporary Canadian paintings. Emily Carr's work is usually displayed and there are some good Inuit pieces. Take bus No 10, 11 or 14 from the downtown area. It's open Monday to Saturday from 10 am to 5 pm, Thursday from 10 am to 9 pm and Sunday from 1 to 5 pm. Admission is $5, $3 for students and seniors. It has a restaurant too.

Government House This house is the official residence (☎ 387-2080) of the province's lieutenant-governor. The impressive grounds are open to the public except when British royalty is in residence. The building is not far from the Art Gallery of Greater

Victoria, away from the downtown area, at 1401 Rockland Ave. Take bus No 1 from downtown.

Craigdarroch Castle Near Government House, but off Fort St, 1050 Joan Crescent, this rather impressive home (☎ 592-5323) was built in the mid-1880s by Robert Dunsmuir, a coal millionaire, for himself and his wife. The interior remains decorated in the manner of that time. It's now a museum and has been restored. Admission is $6 (students $5) and it's open daily in summer from 9 am to 7 pm, the rest of the year from 10 am to 4.30 pm. To get there take bus No 11 or 14.

Butchart Gardens
If you're coming from the east, you'll probably notice the signs for this attraction beginning in Banff. They are without question the most publicised of all Victoria's sights. No doubt the gardens are beautiful and extensive, but admission is costly at $13 (students $6.50). Whether it's worth it depends on you and your budget. Flower fans should consider the little-known Horticultural Centre of the Pacific (☎ 479-6162), 505 Quayle Road as an alternative.

Parts of the gardens are sectioned into specialities like the English Rose Garden and the Japanese Garden. There are hundreds of species of trees, bushes and flowers. You can walk through in about 1½ hours, but linger as long as you wish. In the evenings from June to September the gardens are illuminated. There are also concerts and puppet shows around dusk. On Saturday night in July and August there is a spectacular fireworks display set to music and there's no extra charge to watch it.

Open daily year round from 9 am till dusk, the gardens (☎ 652-4422), 800 Benvenuto Ave, are about 21 km north-west of downtown in Brentwood Bay. City bus Nos 74 and 75 go within one km during the week and three km on Sunday.

Dominion Astrophysical Observatory
On the way to the Butchart Gardens you

could visit this observatory (☎ 363-0012), where you can peer out to space through a 183-cm telescope. There is a museum and equipment used to record earthquakes. The observatory is open Monday to Friday from 9.15 am to 4.30 pm, and from 7 to 11 pm Saturday night and admission is free. It's north-west of the centre, at 5071 West Saanich Rd, on Little Saanich Mountain.

English Village
This gimmicky but effective re-creation of some English Tudor-style buildings is in Lampson St, across Victoria Harbour from the Empress Hotel. The highlights are the replicas of Shakespeare's birthplace and the thatched cottage of his wife, Anne Hathaway. The cottage (☎ 388-4353), at 429 Lampson St, and the rest of the 'village' are furnished with authentic 16th-century antiques. It is open daily from 9 am to 10 pm in summer, and from 9 am to 5 pm in winter. Admission is $6.50. Take bus No 24 from the downtown area.

Point Ellice House
This beautifully kept house (☎ 387-4697), built in 1861, was sold in 1868 to Peter O'Reilly, a member of government and a very successful businessman. Many of the house's immaculate furnishings now on display belonged to him and his wife. Admission is $4 and it's open mid-June to the end of September, Thursday to Monday from 11 am to 5 pm. It's north of the downtown area, at 2616 Pleasant St, off Bay St, at Point Ellice Bridge. Take bus No 14 from downtown. To reserve for the pricey afternoon tea call ☎ 380-6506.

Craigflower Farmhouse & Schoolhouse
The farmhouse (☎ 387-4697) was built by Kenneth McKenzie in 1856. It was the central home in the first farming community on Vancouver Island and its construction heralded Victoria's change from a fur-trading settlement to a permanent one. Built to remind McKenzie of Scotland, the house was decorated with the many furnishings he had brought from his homeland. Because the

family entertained frequently, the house became a social centre for Fort Victoria and the Esquimalt Naval Base. Admission also includes a visit to the historic schoolhouse.

The farmhouse is open daily from noon to 4 pm and admission is $4.50. It's a little north-west of town, on the corner of Craigflower and Admiral's roads, near Gorge Water. To get there catch bus No 14 from town.

Fort Rodd Hill National Historic Park

This scenic 18-hectare park (☎ 363-4662) overlooking Esquimalt Harbour contains some historical points of interest. There are the remnants of three turn-of-the-century gun batteries. These artillery installations were built to protect the naval base in the bay and, until 1956, when such a defence system was deemed obsolete, were regularly upgraded. There are information signs around the park, as well as guides. The park is open daily from 10 am to 5.30 pm, Wednesday to 8.30 pm. Admission is $3, ask about the candlelight tours.

Also in the park is **Fisgard Lighthouse**, which still works and has been in continuous use since 1860. It was the first lighthouse to shine its beam across the water in Western Canada.

The park is at 603 Fort Rodd Hill Rd, off Ocean Blvd, about 12 km north-west of downtown , on the western side of Esquimalt Harbour. To get there catch bus No 50 which takes you to within one km of the park.

Fisherman's Wharf

The wharf area is on Victoria Harbour, west around the bay from the Inner Harbour, along Belleville St past Laurel Point, and is worth a look. It's a busy spot, with fishing boats and pleasure craft coming and going. You can sometimes buy fresh seafood from the boats or the little shed, and near to it is Barb's Place selling fish & chips (see Places to Eat later). Take a look at the mix of houseboats moored at one end of the dock.

Scenic Marine Drive

Starting either from Fisherman's Wharf or Beacon Hill Park, the Scenic Marine Drive, with great views out over the sea, skirts the coast along Dallas Rd and Beach Drive. The road heads north past some of Victoria's wealthiest neighbourhoods and the retirement community of Oak Bay where you could stop for afternoon tea at the Blethering Place (see Places to Eat later).

You'll see several parks and beaches along the way, though access to the shore for much of the way is restricted because of private housing right on the coastline. The Gray Line double-decker buses include Marine Drive in their tours.

Views

At the northern end of Shelbourne St, **Mt Douglas Park Lookout** provides views of the Saanich Peninsula, the Georgia Strait and the islands in it and Washington state. There are good views at **Mt Tolmie Park Lookout**, off Cedar Hill Cross Rd; it is near the University of Victoria.

Activities

Swimming One of the best swimming places is the **Sooke Potholes**, about an hour's drive west of Victoria on Hwy 14, by the town of Sooke, on the southern shore. Watch for signs at Milne's Landing. You can find your own swimming hole but the water ain't balmy. There's good picnicking and some walking trails too. Don't get caught drinking alcohol because the fines are heavy for drinking in a public area.

Also popular is **Thetis Lake Municipal Park**, not too far north-west of town (about 20 minutes driving), off the Trans Canada Hwy. It's very busy at the main beach but if you hike around the lake you'll find a quiet spot.

Whale Watching A number of operators run killer (orca) whale-watching trips from the Victoria area. Ocean Explorations (☎ 383-6722), has trips in speedy Zodiacs to the three pods of the resident southern community. The three-hour tour departing from their mooring on Inner Harbour costs $70. Seacoast Expeditions (☎ 383-2254) departing from the Ocean Pointe Resort across the Johnson St bridge on the Inner Harbour has a similar trip and for $10 extra offers a money-back guarantee of seeing killer whales. They also have a cheaper two-hour trip but chances of seeing orcas is not as good. The Zodiac trips are recommended but for more warmth and comfort and even an on-board meal try the *Pride of Victoria* (☎ 592-3474) cruise at $79. They depart from the Oak Bay Beach Hotel.

Sea lions, seals, porpoises and a variety of birds are also often seen. Note that there is excellent killer-whale watching from the Alert Bay/Telegraph Cove area and gray-whale watching from the Tofino area at less cost than the Victoria trips.

Fishing The waters around Victoria are renowned for deep-sea fishing with salmon being the top prize. The Travel Infocentre can supply information and you should also check the Yellow Pages. There are freshwater lakes and streams within an hour or two of Victoria as well as up-island that are good for trout and/or salmon fishing. Saanich Inlet has one of the highest concentrations of salmon in the world.

Scores of charter companies offer deep-sea fishing trips of varying lengths. Most supply all equipment, bait and even coffee. Duffy's Salmon Charters (☎ 727-2375), run by Duff Johnson has minimum four-hour trips for $200 but four adults can go.

Scuba Diving The Georgia Strait provides opportunities for world-class diving. The undersea life is tremendously varied and has been featured in *National Geographic*. Several excellent shore dive sites are found near Victoria, including Saanitch Inlet, Saxe Point Park, the Ogden Point Breakwater, 10-Mile Point and Willis Point for deep diving. Race Rocks, 18 km south-west of Victoria Harbour, offers superb scenery both above and below the water. Diving charters and dive shops in Victoria provide equipment sales, service, rentals and instruction. Poseidon Diving Systems (☎ 655-3213) is at 10001 5th St in Sidney.

Other Activities Windsurfing is popular, especially in Cadboro Bay near the university, and at Willow's Beach in Oak Bay. Rentals are available at both for around $13; some places offer lessons too. Oak Bay is also a popular canoeing spot. Ocean River Sports (☎ 381-4233), 1437 Store St, rents canoes and kayaks, sells equipment and runs courses. Sports Rent (☎ 385-7368), 611 Discovery St, hires canoes and kayaks from $30 per day.

A few people offer horseback trips in the nearby highlands and lake areas. Some include overnight camping. Ask at the Travel Infocentre. Lakeshore Trailrides (☎ 479-6853), 482 Sparton Rd, has one-hour rides for $20.

The Crystal Pool & Fitness Centre (☎ 380-4636), 2275 Quadra St, on the corner of Wark St – an easy walk from the downtown area – has a pool, a sauna, a whirlpool and locker rooms. Entry to the pool is $3.50. Call for the schedule.

Scenic Marine Drive makes a good bike trip (see Bicycle under the Getting Around section later for bike-hire details).

Organised Tours

Some companies offer a variety, from bus tours of downtown Victoria to quick trips around the island. Other companies only do one kind of tour, such as day and evening harbour boat trips or rides by horse-drawn carriage. There are also tours up-island to view wildlife, hiking trips and self-drive tours using recorded tapes. The Travel Infocentre has details on many of the options.

Gray Line (☎ 388-5248), 700 Douglas St, offers a variety of tours here, as they do in so many North American cities. Its city bus tour costs $14 for 1½ hours and takes in some of the major historical and scenic sights. Many of its bus tours include admission to attractions like the Butchart Gardens. You can buy tickets, and buses depart, from in front of the Empress Hotel. Heritage Tours (☎ 474-4332), 713 Bexhill St, offers more personalised city tours in limousines seating six people for $69 for 1¼ hours, or $87 for two hours. The rate is per car, not per person.

Tallyho Sightseeing (☎ 479-1113) gives 45-minute city tours in a horse-drawn carriage for $11 per person leaving from the corner of Belleville and Menzies Sts.

In the past few years a number of good, small, specialised tour companies have developed trips focusing on nature or wildlife aimed at the more adventurous traveller. They tend not to be expensive, make a unique experience more accessible and represent good value.

Freedom Adventure Tours (☎ 480-9409), Box 8606, Victoria V8W 3S2, has four camping and hiking trips ranging from one to three days which may include Long Beach at Pacific Rim National Park or the rainforest of the Carmanah Valley. The one-day rainforest hike is $40 with a discount for hostellers.

Seagull Expeditions (☎ 360-0893), 213-951 Topaz Ave, is a transportation service offering two-day or five-day camping tours of the island for budget travellers. The itinerary includes the Pacific Rim National Park and Strathcona Provincial Park, with opportunities for hiking and sight-seeing. The bus carries 24 people and leaves from 1905 Store St near the HI Victoria Hostel. The five-day trip costs $99 and covers the travel expenses only. Food is not included or the very low camping costs. Arrangements can be made for pick-up at the Nanaimo ferry and various drop points. Coastal Connections (☎ 480-9560), focuses on half and full-day hikes. Guides Graham and Glen know their stuff and provide informative commentary on either the rainforest, rocky uplands or coastal environments depending on which of the seven trips you choose. One nine-hour trip flies into the Carmanah Valley for a hike for $199, other half-day excursions are as low as $35, food and transportation included. HI-Hostellers should ask for the discount prices.

The Blackfish Wilderness Expeditions (☎ 383-3113), 511 Mary St, offers three different day trips on the water in and around island wildlife sanctuaries in their 15-metre-long replica of a traditional native whaling canoe. A three-hour trip costing $45 includes a visit to a sea-lion reserve where whales may also be seen.

Intertidal Explorations (☎ 595-4774), at Renouf House, 2010 Stanley Ave, offer kayak trips ranging from a half-day ($40) paddle to Discovery Island to extensive four-day trips around some relatively secluded Gulf Islands. Groups of three or more qualify for a good discount.

Festivals

May

Victoria Day Festival – Held during the fourth week of May to celebrate Queen Victoria's birthday, it features a parade, performances by the town's ethnic groups, stage shows and many sporting events. Many people dress in 19th-century-style clothes, and some shopkeepers dress their windows in period manner. Call ☎ 382-3111 for information. The Swiftsure Lightship Classic, a sailing race, ends the event. Call ☎ 592-2441 for information. The last weekend can get pretty wild – a real street party.

June

Jazz Festival – In late June the Victoria Jazz Society (☎ 388-4423) puts on its annual jazz festival at various locations around town.

June/July

Folkfest – Held at the end of June and beginning of July this celebrates Canada's cultural diversity. Dance and musical performances take place at Centennial Square.

June/August

Victoria International Festival – This festival, offering classical music performed by Canadian and foreign musicians, lasts through the summer till mid-August. For information contact the McPherson Playhouse (☎ 386-6121).

August

First Peoples' Festival – This takes place in August beside the Royal BC Museum and along Inner Harbour. It lasts three days and includes traditional craftwork, dancing, a potlatch and war-canoe rides. For information call ☎ 383-2663.

August/September

Fringe Theatre Festival – Featuring more than 50 performances in various locations around town, the festival includes drama, comedy, acrobatics, jugglers and street performers. It takes place in late August and early September. For details call ☎ 383-2663.

September

Classic Boat Festival – During this festival, held on the first weekend in September each year, vintage wooden boats powered by sail or engine compete in various categories. The competition is held on the Inner Harbour. Free entertainment is provided on the quayside for the spectators. For information call ☎ 385-7766.

October

Salmon Run – Observe the fish and take part in events and educational displays marking the annual salmon migration at Goldstream Provincial Park (☎ 391-2300), north of town.

Places to Stay

Camping Closest to town is *Fort Victoria RV Park* (☎ 479-8112), 340 Island Hwy, off Island Hwy 1A, 6.5 km from the city centre. Take bus No 14 or 15 from the downtown area; there's a bus stop at the gate. The park caters mainly to RVs. It does have a few tent sites but there are no trees, and open fires are not allowed. It has full facilities including free showers and charges $19 for a tent site.

A little further out, *Thetis Lake Campground* (☎ 478-3845), 1938 Trans Canada Hwy, on Rural Route 6, is about a 15-minute drive north-west of the city centre. All facilities are available, including a laundry and shower. There's a store, and you can swim in the nearby lake. A site for two people is $15 including tax; electricity is $2 extra. The campground is open all year.

The best one is *Goldstream Provincial Park* (☎ 391-2300), on the Trans Canada Hwy, about 20 km north-west of Victoria. A tent site costs $15.50 for one to four people and you can go swimming, fishing or hiking. Take bus No 50 from Douglas St. South of Goldstream Provincial Park, about 3.5 km off the Trans Canada Hwy, at 2960 Irwin Rd, on Rural Route 6, is *Paradise Campground* (☎ 478-6960). It's part of a nature sanctuary and is open from early June to the end of September. It has full facilities, canoe and kayak rentals, and charges $18 for two people.

The Travel Infocentre can tell you of other campgrounds not too far from town.

Hostels Hostels have boomed here in recent years and there is now more choice than anywhere other than Vancouver. Despite this, most of them are full through the summer. While in town ask about the small hostels around the island, some of which are

in relatively remote places while others are more accessible.

The HI *Victoria Hostel* (☎ 385-4511), 516 Yates St, is in the old part of town just up from Wharf St. It has room for over 100 people, family rooms, a larger common area, kitchen, laundry and a good notice board. Memberships are available. A bed costs $15 for members and $19 for nonmembers. The hostel is open Sunday to Thursday from 7.30 am to 2.30 am but the office closes at midnight. In peak season it's advisable to book in before 4 pm.

Selkirk Guest House International (☎ 389-1213), 934 Selkirk Ave in Esquimalt over the Johnson St Bridge, is affiliated with Hostelling International. A dorm bed costs $14 for members, $18 for nonmembers and the private rooms start at $35. Travellers with kids can be accommodated economically and should feel right at home in this family operated hostelry. Features include a garden complete with hot tub on the shore of The Gorge. The No 14 bus from Douglas St gets you within two blocks.

The *Backpackers Victoria Hostel* (☎ 386-4471), 1418 Fernwood Rd, has dormitory beds for $12, doubles for $30 and the 'honeymoon suite' for $35. It has weekly and monthly rates too. There's a $10 deposit for the key. The former manager has put together an excellent guide of things to do around town. The hostel has no curfew and is close to the shops and restaurants of Fernwood Village. Buses east along Fort St will take you there; the No 10 Haultain bus goes right past the door.

Nearby on a residential street is small *The Cat's Meow* (☎ 595-8878) at 1316 Grant St. Here a dorm is $17 and a private room for two is $42, both with breakfast. The manager, Daphne, will help in discovering things of interest around town. This hostel may move in the next year or so but intends to keep operating.

Also in the neighbourhood is *Renouf House* (☎ 598-1515) at 2010 Stanley Ave. This is an excellent choice for either the hostel-style dorm rooms at $18.50 (bunk & breakfast) or the private rooms (B&B) at single/double $35/45 with shared bath. Other rooms offer private bath. It's a friendly, casual and comfortable place which also offers kayaking (one of the owners makes them) or sailing tours through Intertidal Explorations.

If they are full, *Christine's Place* run by the sister of one of the owners is a more upmarket B&B in an immaculately renovated house around the corner. The cost is a little higher and without being told you'll likely find yourself removing your shoes at the door. Call the Renouf for bookings.

The *YM-YWCA* (☎ 386-7511) are both in the same building at 880 Courtney St, but the residence is only for women. There are 31 beds in single and double rooms with shared bathrooms. Singles/doubles are $33/49. It has a cafeteria that anyone can use and a heated swimming pool.

The *University of Victoria* rents rooms from the start of May to the end of August. Singles/doubles are $37/52, including breakfast and free parking. You can make use of the university's facilities and there are several licensed cafeterias on campus. Contact Housing & Conference Services (☎ 721-8396) at the University of Victoria, PO Box 1700, Victoria V8W 2Y2. Catch bus No 14 on Douglas St to the campus: it takes about 20 minutes.

The *Salvation Army Centre* (☎ 384-3396) is in a modern building at 525 Johnston St, on the corner of Wharf St, and is for men only. A bed in a dormitory costs $15, while a private room is $19, breakfast included.

B&Bs This form of accommodation is very big in town and makes a good alternative to standard hotels and motels. There are several B&B associations that approve members, list them and make reservations at one central office. Check the listings of B&B agencies in the *Accommodations* brochure available from Travel Infocentres. Prices are between $45 and $75 for singles and between $55 and $120 for most doubles, though some go up to as much as $190.

A couple of associations to try are *All Seasons B&B Agency* (☎ 655-7173), PO Box 5511, Station B, Victoria V8R 6S4; and *Victoria Vacationer B&B* (☎ 382-9469), 1143 Leonard St. Many B&Bs advertise independently and have pamphlets at the Travel Infocentre. A few of them are listed here.

North-east of the centre, *Renouf House* (☎ 595-4774) is a 1912 heritage home at 2010 Stanley Ave. It can cater to people with special diets and has homebaked bread. Rooms cost from $35/45. The *Marion Simms B&B* (☎ 592-3070), 1730 Taylor St, about a 10-minute bus ride from downtown is recommended. Rooms are $35/55, the good breakfasts are enormous and the owners are friendly and helpful. *Breland B&B* (☎ 383-0927), also south of the centre at 544 Toronto St, is close to the shops and sights. Rooms cost from $39/54 and parking is available. *Battery St Guest House* (☎ 385-4632) is south of the centre, near Beacon Hill Park, at 670 Battery St. It's an old house dating from 1898 which now is run by Pamela, a Dutch woman. Rooms are $45/75. *Craigmyle Guest House* (☎ 595-5411), 1037 Craigdarroch Rd, about 1.5 km east of the downtown area, is next to Craigdarroch Castle. Rooms are $65/80.

Hotels – bottom end There are a few reasonable places right in the downtown area. The city really fills up in summer and room prices rise; after 1 October many prices drop.

Some of the older hotels like the *Fairfield Hotel* (☎ 386-1621), 710 Cormorant St on the corner of Douglas St, and the *Ritz Hotel* (☎ 383-1021), 710 Fort St, are cheap but not really geared for short-term visitors though if there's a vacancy they will let the rooms out for about $40.

Hotel Douglas (☎ 383-4157), centrally located at 1450 Douglas St, on the corner of Pandora Ave, has rooms from $65/70. It shares its lobby with an art gallery and has a restaurant and bar downstairs.

Opened in 1897, *Cherry Bank Hotel* (☎ 385-5380), 825 Burdett Ave, is east of the downtown area, up the hill a few blocks, opposite the law courts. It's simple but reasonable value at $45/65 with a shared bathroom, or $51/71 with a private bathroom. Prices include breakfast but rooms have no TV or telephone. There's a popular restaurant and a bar on the premises.

More airy is the *James Bay Inn* (☎ 384-7151). It's the big old place with bay windows at 270 Government St, a few blocks south of the downtown area, in a residential area of small, attractive houses. Rooms with a shared bathroom are $72, while those with a private bathroom cost from $89. It has a TV room, bar, restaurant and food machines downstairs.

Hotels – middle At the *Strathcona Hotel* (☎ 383-7137), 919 Douglas St, a couple of blocks east of the Inner Harbour, rooms start at $60/70. All the rooms have private bathroom, telephone and TV. It has free parking, several bars and a restaurant. At the *Dominion Hotel* (☎ 384-4136), 759 Yates St, singles/doubles start from $80. It has free parking and a restaurant. Attractive *Green Gables Hotel* (☎ 385-6787), 850 Blanshard St, is close to the Inner Harbour and has an indoor pool, as well as a sauna and restaurant. Singles/doubles cost from $99 to $150.

Hotels – top end *Beaconsfield Inn* (☎ 384-4044), 998 Humboldt St, is a few blocks east of the downtown area and a couple north of Beacon Hill Park. It's in an Edwardian mansion and the rates include breakfast. Rates start from $130 for a single or double and rise dramatically.

The *Empress Hotel* (☎ 348-8111), 721 Government St, looks out over the Inner Harbour and is the focal point of Victoria. As you face the building, the reception area is to the left of the main entrance. Even if you're not staying here, the Empress Hotel is worth a visit. Singles/doubles are priced from $195/230 to $275/320.

Victoria Regent Hotel (☎ 386-2211), 1234 Wharf St, near the corner of Yates St, specialises in suites. Rates start from $155 for single or doubles. There's underground parking and the staff is friendly and helpful.

Oak Bay Beach Hotel (☎ 598-4556), 1175 Beach Drive, is a seaside hotel east of the downtown area, overlooking Oak Bay. It provides a shuttle service into the centre and lunch-time cruises. Rooms range from $125 to $236. *Laurel Point Inn* (☎ 386-8721), 680 Montreal St, west of the downtown area, near Laurel Point, is generally considered the best of all and is one of the most expensive. Singles/doubles start from $155 and go up to $495.

Motels Douglas St, being one of the main roads into Victoria, has a lot of motels, many of them just to the north of town.

The *Doric Motel* (☎ 386-2481), 3025 Douglas St, is a five-minute drive north of the downtown area. It has TV, laundry and free coffee. Rooms are $60/70; a kitchen is $6.50 extra. *Paul's Motor Inn* (☎ 382-9231), 1900 Douglas St, has a 24-hour restaurant. Singles/doubles are priced from $80/85. The *Imperial Inn* (☎ 382-2111), 1961 Douglas St, costs $70/80 and has a restaurant and bar.

Crystal Court Motel (☎ 384-0551) is at 701 Belleville St, on the corner of Douglas St, across the road from the Greyhound Bus Depot and Crystal Garden. Rooms are $68/70, and a kitchen costs just $2 more. It's clean and the rooms have a TV, radio and telephone. The staff are friendly and helpful but note that you have to pay with cash or travellers' cheques. The motel is white, blue and gold.

Helm's Inn (☎ 385-5767), 600 Douglas St, has one-bedroom and studio suites with kitchen from $90/100. Opposite is the *Shamrock Motel* (☎ 385-8768), 675 Superior St, where rooms are $89/99.

A good area for motels not far north-west of the downtown area is along Gorge Rd, which forms a section of Island Hwy 1A. From Gorge Rd it's about a five-minute drive to town.

At the *Capri Motel* (☎ 384-0521), 21 Gorge Rd East, rooms are $60. *Travellers Inn on Gorge* (☎ 388-9901), 120 Gorge Rd East, has a sauna, heated pool and laundromat. Rooms are $49, those with a kitchen are $10 extra.

Places to Eat

Though a small city, Victoria has a varied array of restaurants, due in part to its many visitors, and prices are generally good. As befits a tourist town, especially one with British roots, there are numerous cafes and tea shops. Some dining rooms offer good lunch specials but are fairly pricey in the evenings. The pubs in town are also good for reasonably priced meals.

Places to Eat – bottom end The *Public Cafeteria* in City Hall, on the corner of Douglas St and Pandora Ave, has daily specials for $5 or you could try the *cafeteria* with a wider selection in The Bay department store. The modest and casual *Day & Night*, 622 Yates St, is good for any meal, with good-value plain food, including one of the cheapest breakfasts in town. Sandwiches and pasta dishes start from $4. *Smitty's Family Restaurant*, 850 Douglas St, is an old standby and best for cheap pancake breakfasts for around $7 including coffee. It's open from 6 am to midnight.

Sam's Deli, under the maroon awnings at 805 Government St, on the corner of Wharf St and diagonally opposite the main Travel Infocentre, is a perfect spot to have an espresso and write a postcard. There are a dozen tables outside on the sidewalk and more inside, where the walls are covered in 1920s and 1930s posters. This is a popular place with a European flavour. It serves good-value soups (from $3.25), salads ($4) and sandwiches ($3).

It's worth joining the crowds at colourful *John's Place*, 723 Pandora St, for the large portions at breakfast or lunch. A quality meal costs about $7.

In Bastion Square, opposite Harpo's nightclub, is *C'est Bon*, a small French-style cafe which has lunch-time specials of soup, croissant and coffee for $4.85. Mel Gibson once ate here when shooting a film close by. It's closed Sunday and Monday.

The fish & chips are excellent in Victoria and there are several outlets for them. *Barb's Place*, 310 St Lawrence St, at Fisherman's Wharf, is a wooden shack on the dock serving fish & chips in newspaper for $6 to $10. Fresh crabs can be bought from the boats nearby. At *Cook St Fish & Chips*, 252 Cook St near Beacon Hill Park, fish & chips with coleslaw costs $8.95. *Brady's* at 20 West Burnside by the corner of Harriet is one of the top fish & chip shops in town and is open daily.

The *Sticky Wicket Pub*, on the corner of Douglas and Courtney Sts, has nachos ($5.75) and pizza (from $6) and a variety of Canadian, US and UK beers. It's open from 11.30 am to 11 pm.

Another cheap but good place is the busy *Eugene's Restaurant & Snack Bar*, 1280 Broad St. Simple, basic Greek foods at about $4 to $8 are served cafeteria-style. It's open Monday to Friday from 8 am to 10 pm and Saturday from 10 am to 9 pm, but closed on Sunday.

Market Square, 560 Johnson St, has several places to munch at. Among them is the *Café Mexico* for quick Mexican items such as tacos from $7. It's a pleasant little place, is licensed and has a patio overlooking the courtyard. *Bavarian Bakery* has good bread (around $2).

The *Mount Royal Bagel Factory*, 1115 North Park St but with the door on Grant St in the Fernwood Village area has fresh Montreal-style bagels.

Places to Eat – middle Perhaps the most happening place in town is the *Rebar* at 50 Bastion Square with an eclectic contemporary international menu and funky decor to match. It's busy all day for breakfasts, coffees, desserts, salads and the main dishes ($8 to $10) which are all well prepared.

For dinners the *Spare Rib House*, in the Cherry Bank Hotel, 825 Burdett Ave, is good. It serves rib dinners (from $12), steaks and seafood. There's a children's menu ($3.95) and live honky tonk piano entertainment.

Pagliacci's, 1011 Broad St, between Fort and Broughton Sts, is mainly Italian. A complete dinner is about $20 and the food is good. It has live music most nights and is another of the 'in' spots in town, so it's best to book for the evenings, as there are often queues.

Herald St Caffé, 546 Herald St, is a small Italian restaurant serving delicious pastas for around $12 to $15. It also has vegetarian dishes, great desserts and a wine bar and gets busy after 10 pm.

For East Indian food, *Da Tandoor*, 1010 Fort St is recommended. It's open for lunch Thursday and Friday from 11.30 am to 2 pm and for dinner daily from 5 to 10.30 pm. Most of the meat dishes and breads are baked in tandoori clay ovens. Vegetarian dishes are also available. Main dishes are in the $8 to $16 range.

Periklis, 531 Yates St, is a Greek place with starters $3 to $6 and main courses between $10 and $24. It's open for lunch Monday to Friday from 11.30 am to 3 pm, and daily in the evenings from 5.30 pm till late, and with belly dancers on weekends.

Chinatown, marked by the Gate of Harmonious Interest over Fisgard St, has its share of eating spots. *Foo Hong*, 564 Fisgard St, is small and basic yet has good, simple Cantonese food from $4.50 to $7.50. The *Ocean Phoenix* at 509 Fisgard St, closed Monday, offers a small, neat dining room, an extensive menu and good food. Cantonese lunch specials are $6 and dinner items range from $7 to $11. There are several other places on Fisgard to have a look at.

Le Petit Saigon at 1010 Langely St is recommended for Vietnamese meals. It's open daily for lunch and dinner but no lunches on Sunday. A complete dinner for two is about $35, a single lunch would run $7 to $10. The menu includes meat, fish and vegetarian dishes.

For afternoon tea a popular place with the locals is the *Blethering Place*, 2250 Oak Bay Ave, away from the centre of town in Oak Bay Village. It has Devonshire teas for around $10 and is open every day from 8 am to 10 pm. *Murchie's*, at 1110 Government St, between View and Fort Sts, is a quality west coast, tea & coffee merchant which also serves a decadent assortment of pastries and chocolates. Scones with strawberry jam and Devonshire cream cost $2.75. *Milestone's*,

812 Wharf St, right on the harbour, below the Travel Infocentre, has a few tables outside and is a good spot for an afternoon beer and view.

Places to Eat – top end The Empress Hotel has an array of eating options. The formal dining room, the *Empress Room* is predictable, top quality and very pricey. Soups start at $7 and meat and seafood main courses range from $25 to $32. The more interesting *Bengal Lounge* is a real treat. It serves seafood and poultry and every day a different curry for $14 (other daily specials are cheaper). The service and the style make it worth the price. There is a tiger skin on the wall and it's right out of the days of the British Empire. Downstairs, the *Garden Café* lunch is cheaper. Finally, the tradition of afternoon tea is upheld in the lobby of the hotel, but you have to be suitably attired – a 'dress code is in effect'. There are regular sittings between 11 am and 5 pm for the $20 affair.

Chandler's Seafood Restaurant near the Victorian Regent Hotel and the corner of Yates and Wharf Sts is an established dining room specialising in ocean fare. Starters run from $6 to $10 and main dishes $14 to $27. It also has a bar.

The *Harvest Moon Café*, 1218 Wharf St, may be of special interest to visitors as it features BC foods and wines. Menu items may include caribou and salmon but change with the seasons. It is not inexpensive with main dishes in the $20 bracket. It's open every day.

At 607 Oswego St overlooking the Inner Harbour, the *Harbour House Restaurant* is a formal, elegant seafood and steak house in the same price range.

Koto Japanese Restaurant, 510 Fort St, just up from Wharf St, serves mainly seafood and has a sushi and salad bar; main courses cost from $16 to $26. There's a detailed, colourful display in the window of the kinds of dishes available in the restaurant. It's open for lunch Monday to Saturday from 11.30 am to 2 pm and for dinner daily from 5 pm.

Entertainment

Monday Magazine, the weekly entertainment paper available free around town, has extensive coverage of what's on.

Theatre Victoria has a number of live theatres that provide venues for plays, concerts, comedies, ballets and operas. The *McPherson Playhouse* (☎ 386-6121), 3 Centennial Square, on the corner of Pandora Ave and Government St, regularly puts on plays and comedies. The box office is open Monday to Saturday from 9.30 am to 5.30 pm. The elegant *Royal Theatre* (☎ 386-6121), 805 Broughton St, between Blanshard and Quadra Sts, hosts a range of performances, including the ballet, symphony, dance and concerts. Other theatres worth checking out are the *Belfry* (☎ 385-6815), 1291 Gladstone Ave, north-east of the downtown area, and the *Phoenix Theatre* (☎ 721-8000), on the University of Victoria campus.

Open Space Gallery, 510 Fort St, presents young poets, dancers and musicians.

Music One of the most popular nightclubs is *Harpo's* (☎ 385-5333), 15 Bastion Square on the corner of Wharf St, above Rebecca's. It has live bands playing a variety of music, including rock, celtic rock, ska, reggae and blues. The cover charge is generally about $5, but may be higher depending on who's performing. It's open Monday to Saturday from 9 pm to 2 am.

In the same building as the Strathcona Hotel, 919 Douglas St, there are several clubs that feature live music including the *Forge* a long-standing rock and blues nightclub and *Big Bad John's* more for country & western fans. Both charge about $5 and stay open until 2 am. *Steamers Pub* on Yates St just below Government St is a good blues bar and has Sunday afternoon sessions.

Merlin's Nightclub (☎ 381-2331), 1208 Wharf St, is on the Inner Harbour, down the stone staircase, opposite Bastion Square provides a different form of entertainment each night, including a Ladies' Night every Wednesday.

Pagliacci's is popular not only for its food but also for the entertainment it provides. It's the centre for jazz in Victoria but varies this with comedy sessions. For information about jazz around town call ☎ 658-5255.

Pubs If you like a beer then Victoria's pub scene should please you. The city has a number of 'brew pubs' – pubs that brew their own beer – and although they're admittedly a bit trendy, the beer is good.

Spinnaker's, which opened in 1984, was Canada's first brew pub. It's at 308 Catherine St, right on the water of Victoria Harbour, off Esquimalt Rd, west of the downtown area. It has a variety of excellent beers made in-house and starting from $3.25 To get there on foot, cross Johnson Bridge into Esquimalt Rd, then turn left into a pathway that follows the shoreline round to the pub. There are good views back towards town. Bright yellow *Swans Hotel*, opposite Johnson Bridge, on the corner of Pandora Ave and Store St, has a variety of homemade beers; a half-pint glass of stout is $2.90. Two other brew pubs are the *Garrick's Head*, 69 Bastion Square, and the *Sticky Wicket Pub* in the Strathcona Hotel, 919 Douglas St.

Cinema Commercial cinemas such as the *Cineplex Odeon*, 780 Yates St, are reduced to $4.25, nearly half price, on Tuesday.

Things to Buy

There are a number of craft shops along Douglas and Government Sts selling Native Indian art and craftwork such as sweaters, moccasins, carvings and prints. Be careful: the good stuff is expensive. There are lots of imitations and lots of junk.

Canadian Impressions (☎ 383-2641), 811 Government St, has some quality items and Native Indian crafts. The small Indian print greeting cards make good, cheap little presents and some are even signed by the artist. Also see the prints upstairs costing between $25 and $180. Canadian Impressions has another shop at the airport.

Sasquatch Trading Company (☎ 386-9033), 1233 Government St, has a good selection of Cowichan sweaters. These hand-spun, hand-knitted sweaters average between $140 and $200 but are warm and should last a decade or more. No dyes are used. Other stores selling quality sweaters are Hills Indian Crafts (☎ 385-3911), 1008 Government St, Cowichan Trading (☎ 383-0321), 1328 Government St and Indian Craft Shoppe (☎ 382-3643), 905 Government St.

In Fort St, between Cook and Quadra Sts, there are a number of antique and bric-a-brac shops.

For chocolate lovers, Roger's Chocolates, 913 Government St, dating from 1885, offers a treat to both nose and tongue. Try one (or more) of the Victoria creams – chocolate-covered discs in over 20 flavours at $1.75. Everything on sale here is made on the premises. It's open Monday to Friday from 9.30 am to 8 pm, Saturday from 9.30 am to 5.30 pm and Sunday from 11 am to 5 pm.

Getting There & Away
Air Two airlines with offices in Victoria are: Air Canada (☎ 360-9074), 20 Centennial Square; and Canadian Airlines (☎ 382-6111) 901 Gordon St. Air Canada and Canadian Airlines connect the airports of Vancouver and Victoria. The normal, one-way, pre-tax economy fare is $232 for harbour to harbour return, but weekend return specials can lower this to $112 return. The one-way fare to Seattle on Canadian Airlines is $198 plus tax.

If you're flying to Vancouver and beyond, the cost of a ticket from Victoria is just a few dollars more than one from Vancouver itself, so it's not worth paying the ferry price to catch a flight directly from Vancouver.

Horizon Air (☎ 206-762-3646 in Seattle; 1-800-547-9308), flies to Victoria daily. North Vancouver Air (☎ 1-800-228-6608) links Vancouver, Victoria and Tofino.

Bus Although Greyhound has no service on the island or to the mainland it does have an office (☎ 385-5248), in the bus station at 700 Douglas St where you can get information and purchase tickets. The one-way fare (including tax) on Greyhound to Calgary is

$121 and to Edmonton $136. There are reductions on some fares if you book in advance.

Pacific Coach Lines (PCL) (☎ 385-4411) and Island Coach Lines (☎ 385-4411) also operate out of the same station. PCL runs to Vancouver, some of the southern BC mainland and to Seattle. There's a bus to Vancouver every hour between 6 am and 9 pm; the one-way fare, which includes the cost of the ferry, is $22.50/42 one way/return. It's the same price to Vancouver Airport; it connects with the airport shuttle bus at Delta Pacific Resort. The bus to Seattle, via Sidney and Anacortes, leaves at 10 am and gets there at 5 pm. The one-way fare, including the cost of the ferry, is $39.

Island Coach Lines, sometimes referred to as Laidlaw Lines, covers Vancouver Island. There are eight buses a day to Nanaimo and northern Vancouver Island. The one-way fares are: Duncan $9.25; Nanaimo $16.25; Port Alberni $28; and Port Hardy $78.

Train The Esquimalt & Nanaimo Railiner (or E&N Railiner), operated by VIA Rail (☎ 383-4324; 1-800-561-8630), connects Victoria with Nanaimo, Parksville as well as Courtenay. There is one train in each direction per day – northbound from Victoria at 8.15 am, southbound from Courtenay at 1.15 pm. The journey, through some beautiful scenery, takes about 3½ hours. The *Malahat*, as the train is known, is very popular so book ahead. Some one-way fares are to Nanaimo $19, Parksville $24 and Courtenay $36. Seven-day advance purchases are much cheaper.

For the full schedule, get a copy of the E&N Railiner pamphlet from the station, a travel agency or the Travel Infocentre. The station, 405 Pandora Ave, is close to town, right at Johnson Bridge, near the corner of Johnson and Wharf Sts. It's open from 7.30 am to noon and from 1 to 3 pm.

Ferry BC Ferries (☎ 656-0757, 24 hours), 1112 Fort St, on the corner of Cook St, runs frequent trips from Swartz Bay to Tsawwassen, on the mainland. The 38-km crossing takes about 1¾ hours. There are between 10 and 15 sailings per day: the schedule varies according to the season. The passenger fare is $6.50, while a car costs $25 or $27 weekends and holidays. Bus No 70 from the downtown area to the ferry terminal costs $1.50.

BC Ferries also operates between Swartz Bay and five of the southern Gulf Islands: Galiano, Mayne, Saturna, Salt Spring and Pender. There are about three or four services a day. The return fare to the southern Gulf Islands is $4.50 per person, $2 for a bicycle and $17.25 for a car.

BC Ferries also links other more northerly islands in the Georgia Strait to towns along the coast up-island. For ferries north to Prince Rupert see Port Hardy at the end of the Vancouver Island section.

The *Victoria Clipper* and *Victoria Clipper II*, run by Clipper Navigation (☎ 382-8100), 1000 Wharf St, sail between Seattle and Victoria. The clippers are water-jet-propelled catamarans and don't take cars. The journey lasts about 2¾ hours and the fare one way in summer is $70; it's a little cheaper the rest of the year. For those with cars, the Victoria Line (☎ 480-5555), 185 Dallas Rd, has the *Royal Victorian* which sails from Seattle to Ogden Point, Victoria in 4½ hours. A car and driver costs $55.

The ferry MV *Coho*, operated by Black Ball Transport (☎ 386-2202), 430 Belleville St, is much cheaper. It sails between the Inner Harbour and Port Angeles just across the Juan de Fuca Strait. It costs US$6.50 per person or US$26 with a car. It's a 1½-hour trip, and there are four a day in each direction during the summer months. From Victoria the ferry leaves at 6.20 and 10.30 am and 3 and 7.30 pm.

Victoria Express (☎ 361-9144) also goes to Port Angeles. The journey time is one hour and the return fare is $20. The *Victoria Star*, operated by Victoria Cruises (☎ 1-800-443-4552) who are based in Bellingham, Washington goes there once a day. The foot passenger-only ferry leaves from Wharf St down from Bastion Square and the one-way fare is US$42.

Lastly, Washington State Ferries (☎ 656-1531; ☎ 381-1551 in Victoria), 2499 Ocean Ave in Sidney, has a ferry service from Swartz Bay through the San Juan Islands to Anacortes on the Washington mainland. One way it costs US$7 or US$36 with a car. It's a very scenic trip and you can have stopovers on the islands (see San Juan Islands later for more details).

Getting Around

The Airport PBM Transport (☎ 475-2010), operates the airport bus to Victoria International Airport from any of 60 downtown area hotels. It leaves every half hour from downtown and the airport for the 25-km trip and costs $13.

City bus No 70 passes within 1.5 km of the airport, while a taxi to the airport from the downtown area costs about $30 to $38.

Bus For local transit information call Busline (☎ 382-6161) or get a copy of BC Transit's guide from the Travel Infocentre listing bus routes and fares. The city buses cover a wide area and run quite frequently: every 10 to 30 minutes. The normal one-way fare is $1.50; it's $2.25 if you wish to travel out to suburbs such as Callwood or Sidney. Have the exact change ready. You can get an all-day pass for $4 for as many rides as you want, starting as early as you like. These all-day passes are not sold on buses but are available from various outlets around town such as convenience stores.

Bus No 70 goes to the ferry terminal in Swartz Bay; bus No 2 goes to Oak Bay. The Oak Bay Explorer double-decker bus costs just $1 and takes a 90-minute run between the Empress Hotel and Oak Bay. You can stay on or get off along the way.

Car For rentals, shop around as prices can vary. One of the cheapest places is ADA Rent A Used Car (☎ 474-3455), 892 Goldstream Ave, which rents older cars by the day from $9.95 to $19.95 depending on the car's age; add 10 cents per km and $7 to $9 insurance for both. Another is Rent-A-Wreck (☎ 384-5343), 2634 Douglas St, where you can rent a car from $25 a day plus 10 cents per km and $8 optional insurance.

All major companies and more are represented in and around the downtown area. Three on Douglas St are:

Avis
 843 Douglas St (☎ 386-8468)
Budget
 757 Douglas St (☎ 388-5525)
Tilden
 767 Douglas St (☎ 381-1115)

Budget offers a daily rate of $40 with unlimited km plus $12 insurance. Avis has a daily rate of $50 with unlimited km plus $12.95 insurance.

Taxi Two of several companies are Victoria Taxi (☎ 383-7111) and Blue Bird Cabs (☎ 384-1155). You can also hire three-wheeled bicycle taxis called pedicabs – a more leisurely way of getting around.

Bicycle Downtown you can hire bikes from Harbour Scooters (☎ 384-2133), 843 Douglas St, adjacent to the Avis car-rental office. They cost $5 per hour or $19 for 24 hours; you must also pay $2 insurance. Bikes are also available at Sports Rent, (☎ 385-7368), 611 Discovery St and at the HI Hostel.

Ferry Victoria Harbour Ferry runs an enjoyable, albeit short, ferry trip of about half an hour return from Inner Harbour to Songhees Park (in front of the Ocean Pointe Hotel), Fisherman's Wharf and Westbay Marina. The boat takes just a dozen people per trip and costs $2.50 one-way.

AROUND VICTORIA
Western Shore
West of Victoria, Hwy 14 takes you from the city's manicured parks and gardens to the pristine wilderness of the west coast. The highway runs through Sooke then along the coast overlooking the Juan de Fuca Strait to Port Renfrew at the southern end of the West Coast Trail (see Pacific Rim National Park later for details). There are parks and beaches along the way for walking, beachcombing and picnicking.

Before you reach Sooke follow the signs from Milnes Landing to the **Sooke Potholes** where you can go swimming, picnicking and hiking. Sooke's Travel Infocentre (☎ 642-6351) and local museum are housed in the same building at 2070 Phillip's Rd. Victoria's bus network extends to Sooke: take bus No 50 to the Western Exchange then change to No 61.

Further along Hwy 14, the windswept **French Beach** and **China Beach** provincial parks have swimming, camping and walking trails.

At **Port Renfrew**, often the destination for a day trip from town, the main attraction is Botanical Beach, a sandstone shelf, which at low tide is dotted with tidal pools containing all manner of small marine life: starfish, anemones, etc. To return to Victoria without retracing your tracks, take the logging road across the island to Lake Cowichan, from where better roads connect with Duncan and Hwy 19. (See Getting Around under Duncan for more information on the logging roads.) For those without transport, the West Coast Trail Connector (☎ 475-3010), 767 Audley St, (also listed under PBM Transport) runs buses from Victoria to Port Renfrew twice a day. Use it for an interesting day trip to the west coast beaches along the Juan de Fuca Strait or to begin the hiking trail to Bamfield. (See under West Coast Trail for more information.)

San Juan Islands (USA)
Lying east off the coast of Victoria are the San Juan Islands, just beyond the US border, making them a part of Washington state. The big three of the grouping, San Juan Island, Orcas Island and Lopez Island, form a rough circle about halfway between Vancouver Island and the US mainland.

Washington State Ferries connects Swartz Bay in Sidney with Anacortes on the Washington mainland via the islands, making it a very scenic route between these ports. Stops are made at Orcas, Shaw, Lopez and San Juan. The ferries take cars, bicycles and kayaks and from Anacortes buses connect with Seattle. For information about buses contact Gray Line (☎ 206-624-5077) at the Greyhound Bus Depot on the corner of 8th Ave and Stewart St in Seattle.

The islands are good for cycling around and hitchhiking is accepted. The ferries sell a good road map indicating the topography, and there are numerous campgrounds and guesthouses on the principal islands. Note that you must pass through customs. Also, foot passengers may travel free between the main islands in either direction.

Southern Gulf Islands

Lying north of Victoria, off Sidney really, at the northern end of the Saanich Peninsula, this string of nearly 200 islands is squeezed between the mainland and southern Vancouver Island. The ferry from Tsawwassen edges between a handful of them on its route into Sidney.

With a few important exceptions, most are small and nearly all of them virtually uninhabited, but this island-littered channel is a

boater's dream. Vessels of all descriptions cruise in and out of bays, harbours and marinas much of the year. The fishing is varied and excellent: several species of prized salmon can be caught in season. BC Ferries connects with some of the larger islands, so you don't need your own boat to visit them. The fare from Tsawwassen is $8; from Swartz Bay and between the islands it's $4.50 return. Before heading to the islands check at the Travel Infocentre in Victoria about activities, accommodation and transport. Pick up a copy of the free newspaper *The Gulf Islander* which also has details of these.

Due to the mild climate, abundant flora & fauna, relative isolation and natural beauty, the islands are one of Canada's escapist-dream destinations. Indeed, many of the inhabitants are retired people, artists or counter-culture types of one sort or another. In fact, some of the 'farmers' are taking their new product to Amsterdam where they compete in contests, much the way brewers compete for international medals.

The loon, which appears on the $1 coin, has a distinctive call which is heard across the country

There are cycling routes on the islands: contact the Bicycling Association of BC for details.

Salt Spring Island Salt Spring Island is the largest island in both size (29 km by 14 km) and population; its usual population of over 8500 swells to three times that size in summer. Artists, entertainers and crafts people have chosen to live here. As a consequence, there are craft fairs and art galleries with national reputations. The island has a long, interesting Native Indian history followed by settlement not by White people but by pioneering US Blacks. Seeking escape from prejudice and social tensions, a small group of settlers formed a community at Vesuvius Bay. Unfortunately, the Native Indians didn't care for them any more than they cared for the British in the area. Still, the Blacks stuck it out, began farms and set up schools. Later, immigrants came from Britain and Ireland.

Ganges, not far from the Long Harbour landing, is the principal village. It has the most accommodation and has a summer arts & crafts fair, a few tourist-oriented shops and a Saturday morning market. Artists welcome visitors to their studios – the Travel Infocentre (☎ 537-5252), 121 Lower Ganges Rd, has a list. **Mouat Provincial Park** is nearby and has 15 camp sites.

South of Ganges, **Mt Maxwell Provincial Park** offers excellent views, fishing and picnic areas. In **Ruckle Provincial Park**, a former homestead 10 km east of Fulford Harbour ferry terminal, you can enjoy hiking through forest and along the shoreline, plus fishing and wilderness camping.

Places to Stay At HI *Cusheon Creek Hostel* (☎ 537-4149), 640 Ocean Lake Rd, you can sleep either in a dorm or in a Native Indian teepee. The cost is $13 for members, $16 for nonmembers. The hostel is a short walk from the lake or ocean beach. There are quite a few B&Bs, some of which will have someone pick you up at the ferry terminal. Scattered around the island are resorts – usually with cottages for rent and maybe with some camping, a beach, and boat rentals. The cottages range in price from about $70 per double. Near the ferry terminals there are also a few motels with rooms for about $50/60.

Getting There & Away There are three ferry terminals: Long Harbour serves Vancouver, Swartz Bay, the other Southern Gulf Islands and the US mainland; Fulford Harbour and Vesuvius Bay are for ferries plying back and forth to Vancouver Island: the former to Swartz Bay, the latter to Crofton.

Getting Around Salt Spring Island Bus (☎ 537-2311) runs between Ganges and the ferry terminals. Cycling is possible but this is a fair-sized island and the terrain is hilly.

North & South Pender Islands Together these two islands, joined by a small bridge across the narrow channel that separates them, have nearly 1600 people. There are art & craft studios to visit and a golf course. For beaches, try **Hamilton** in Browning Harbour on North Pender and **Mortimer Spit** on South Pender (just after crossing the bridge). You might see some of the more-or-less tame deer around the islands. You can hike and camp at **Prior Centennial Provincial Park** on North Pender, close to **Medicine Beach** at Bedwell Harbour. On South Pender there are good views from the summit of the 260-metre **Mt Norman**.

Places to Stay Accommodation is mainly in B&Bs and cottages. If you want to splurge you can try the heritage farmhouse *Corbett House* (☎ 629-6305), in Corbett Rd, one km from the ferry terminal. It has rooms for $70/85 including breakfast.

Saturna Island At Saturna Point by the ferry terminal in Lyall Harbour there's a store and pub. **Winter Cove Marine Park** has a good sandy beach from where you can go swimming, fishing, boating and hiking. At the top of **Mt Warburton Pike** is a wildlife reserve with feral goats and fine views. There are also good views of the Washington Mountains from the road on the island's leeward side. Just north of Saturna Island is **Cabbage Island Marine Park**, with swimming, fishing and wilderness camping.

Places to Stay Accommodation is mostly in B&Bs. *Breezy Bay B&B* (☎ 539-2937), on a farm less than two km from the ferry terminal, has doubles for $65 including breakfast.

Mayne Island The ferry between Tsawwassen and Swartz Bay squeezes through Active Pass, which separates Mayne and Galiano islands. Village Bay, on the southern side of Mayne Island, is the ferry terminal, although there are docking facilities for boaters at other points. There are some late 19th-century buildings at **Miners Bay**, including the museum, which was formerly the jail. There are only a few places to stay, mostly B&Bs, so it's best to book ahead.

Galiano Island Galiano is a good island to visit. Despite its relatively large size, it has only 900 residents stretched along its long, narrow land mass. About 75% of the island is forest and bush. There's a Travel Infocentre (☎ 539-2233) at the ferry terminal in Sturdies Bay. Again, local artists and artisans invite visitors to their studios.

You can hike almost the length of the east coast and climb either **Mt Sutil** (323 metres) or **Mt Galiano** (342 metres), from both of which you can see the Olympic Mountains about 90 km away. If you're willing to tackle the hills, you can go cycling, while Porlia Pass and Active Pass are popular places for diving and fishing. The coast is lined with cliffs and small bays, and canoeing along the western shoreline is possible in the calmer waters. On the north-eastern tip of the island is the rugged **Dionisio Point Provincial Park** with swimming, fishing, hiking and wilderness camping.

Places to Stay You can camp at *Montague Harbour Marine Park* and around the island there are B&Bs and several places with cottage rentals. *Sutil Lodge* (☎ 539-2930) dates from the 1920s and is on the beach at Montague Harbour. It has singles/doubles from $50/65 and offers free use of canoes.

From Sturdies Bay there are two ferries daily to Tsawwassen and Swartz Bay.

DUNCAN & COWICHAN VALLEY

About 60 km north of Victoria along the Trans Canada Hwy is the small town of Duncan. It marks the beginning of the Cowichan Valley running westward and containing large Lake Cowichan. This is the land of the Cowichan people, who comprise BC's largest Native Indian group. Despite some problems they still maintain aspects of their unique culture.

A good day trip from Victoria, for those with wheels, is to head up to Chemainus, back to Duncan, then over to Lake Cowichan, across to Port Renfrew and down the west coast back to town. It's a lot of driving but if you're in no hurry and can stop a lot it makes an interesting, full day.

The Travel Infocentre (☎ 746-4636) in Duncan, on the corner of the Trans Canada Hwy and Coronation St, is open daily from 9 am to 5 pm. In Lake Cowichan township the Travel Infocentre (☎ 749-4324) is open Sunday to Thursday from 9 am to 5 pm, and Friday and Saturday from 8.30 am to 8 pm.

There really isn't much to see in Duncan (although the old part of town is worth a look round) or the township of Lake Cowichan, but the valley and lake are good for camping, hiking, swimming, fishing and canoeing. The turn-off for Lake Cowichan is about four km north of Duncan, left (east) of the Trans Canada Hwy; from the turn-off the lake is another 22 km.

Since 1985, Duncan, the 'City of Totems', has developed a project with the Cowichans to have totem poles carved and displayed in the town area. There are now more than 20 examples of this west coast art form.

Duncan is also home to the 'world's largest hockey stick'.

Native Heritage Centre

Coming to Duncan from the south along the highway take the first turn left after crossing the bridge, into Cowichan Way. The centre

(☎ 746-8119), 200 Cowichan Way, is 150 metres along on the left. It has exhibits of Cowichan craftwork and carvings which you can see being made. There's a gift shop and restaurant serving Native Indian foods. The admission price of $6.50 includes a 20-minute movie about the centre and Cowichan People. In summer, it's open daily from 9.30 am to 5.30 pm.

Cowichan Valley Museum

Located in the train station on Canada Ave, this locally oriented museum (☎ 746-6612) is open in summer Monday to Saturday from 11 am to 4 pm.

BC Forest Museum

This is about three km north of Duncan, offering on its 40 hectares both indoor and outdoor features. There's a stand of original forest of Douglas firs, 55 metres tall, that were present before Captain Cook arrived in 1778. Included in the price is a ride around the site in a small steam train. You can visit a bird sanctuary or view a replica of an old logging camp and logging equipment. There are also indoor displays and movies of old logging operations. The museum (☎ 748-9389) is open daily in summer from 9.30 am to 6 pm and admission is $7.

Industrial Tours

The valley is a logging centre worked by several companies, some of which offer free mill tours on summer weekdays. Two are MacMillan Bloedel at the Chemainus Mill (☎ 246-3221) and Fletcher Challenge at the Crofton Pulp & Paper Mill (☎ 246-6391).

Activities

There are many hiking trails around Cowichan River and Lake Cowichan. One is the **Cowichan River Footpath**. It's about 18 km long with a good variety of scenery along the way. You can do it in a day or camp enroute. The path goes to Skutz Falls; from there you can head back to Duncan or keep going up the river. Maps of the trail are available at sporting stores. The lake gets warm enough

to swim in. You can also go fishing and canoeing in the lake and river.

Places to Stay & Eat

Lakeview Park Municipal Campground (☎ 749-3350) is on the southern shore of Lake Cowichan about three km west of the town. It has showers, toilets and free firewood. They charge $15 a car, less without one. Further west along the lake there is a government-operated campground at *Gordon Bay Provincial Park* with 130 sites for trailers and tents. The fee is $14.50. For more remote camping, some of the forestry companies have set up unsupervised sites mainly between Lake Cowichan and the west coast of Vancouver Island. The Travel Infocentres or the logging companies have more information on these.

There are plenty of hotels and motels, especially along the Trans Canada Hwy in Duncan and in the small townships along the river and lake. One of the cheapest is *Duncan Motel* (☎ 748-2177), 2552 Alexander St, Duncan; it has singles/doubles from $38/42 and some with kitchens.

In Duncan most of the eating places are along the Trans Canada Hwy but there are a few small places in the old part of town. *Good Rock Café*, is a 1950s-style diner on the corner of Government and Jubilee Sts, complete with juke box (and old 45s hanging from the ceiling). It's good for breakfasts and has Friday night East Indian buffets. Also, nearby at 195 Kenneth St is the *Arbutus Café*.

Getting There & Away

Island Coach Line buses travel between Duncan and Victoria for $9 including tax, one way. The 70-minute train trip on the E&N Railiner costs $11 including tax; there is one a day in each direction.

Getting Around

The area around Lake Cowichan is full of logging roads, some of which you can use, though they're often rough; for some advice and rules, ask at the Travel Infocentres. The well-used logging road from Lake Cowichan to Port Renfrew is gravelled and in good shape; with a basic map, you shouldn't have any difficulty. The detailed maps showing all the logging roads look like a dog's breakfast so are more difficult to follow.

Hitching here and all over the island is common and accepted.

CARMANAH PACIFIC PROVINCIAL PARK

Also reached by logging road from Lake Cowichan is this majestic wilderness park adjacent to the West Coast Trail formed after years of bitter fighting over logging rights. The park protects a rich rainforest containing some of the world's tallest trees including a giant sitka spruce 95 metres high. There are some basic tent sites, drinking water, about five km of marked trails and an information office. Trails extend beyond the park north into the Carmanah Valley with wilderness camping. The rough trails can often be very muddy. The road from Lake Cowichan takes 2½ hours and watch for trucks! Along the way is Nitinaht Lake, the 'confused sea', renowned for windsurfing and another road leading to the Ditidaht First Nation visitor centre. It offers tours around the region. The Infocentre in Duncan has some information on the park (see the Organised Tours section under Victoria for trips to Carmanah).

DUNCAN TO NANAIMO
Crofton

About 16 km north of Duncan on Hwy 1A is the small town of Crofton, from where you can catch ferries to Vesuvius Bay in the north of Salt Spring Island (see Southern Gulf Islands in the Around Victoria section earlier).

Chemainus

Chemainus, 10 km north of Crofton, had a novel and interesting way of putting itself on the tourist map. In 1983 the town sawmill shut down, and to counter the inevitable slow death, a tremendously successful concept was nursed to fruition: murals. An artist was commissioned to paint a large outdoor mural relating to the town's history. People took

notice, more murals were painted and now there are over 30 of them. A bustling and prosperous community developed and the sawmill re-opened.

The brightly painted Chemainus Theatre has been restored and is the most striking building in town. There are now lots of craft shops and restaurants, all making a short visit a worthwhile proposition. The Travel Infocentre (☎ 246-3944) is in an old railway carriage on Mill St.

Off the coast of Chemainus are **Thetis** and **Kuper islands**. Kuper Island is a Native Indian reserve for which you need permission from the chief to visit.

The ferries for these islands leave from Oak St and the ticket office is opposite the Harbourside Café; the fare is $3.50 and $9.75 for a car. The ferry to each island takes about 30 minutes from Chemainus. Thetis Island is primarily geared to boaters and has two marinas. There is a pub, however, at Quinn's Marina: turn left when you get off the ferry then left again into Harbour Drive where you see the anchor sign. There's one restaurant, the Pump House, which you can see to the left as the ferry pulls in. At Pilkey Point there are sandstone formations along the beach.

Ladysmith

Ladysmith, a small town about 26 km north of Duncan, on the Trans Canada Hwy, sits on the 49th Parallel which on the mainland divides Canada from the USA. Originally built as a coal-shipping port by the industrialist James Dunsmuir, he named it after the South African town of the same name when the latter was rescued in 1901 from the Boers by the British during the Boer War.

The Travel Infocentre (☎ 245-8544) and the **Black Nugget Museum**, in Gatacre Ave, are in the same building, constructed in 1896 as a hotel. Many of the turn-of-the-century buildings have been restored. The warmest sea waters north of San Francisco are said to flow at **Transfer Beach Park**; it's right in town and you can camp there. About 13 km north of town, a 15-minute drive off the highway, on Yellow Point Rd (follow the signs), pub aficionados will find the *Crow & Gate*, the oldest British-style pub in the province. It's very authentic looking and the setting is peaceful.

Petroglyph Provincial Park

About three km south of Nanaimo on the Trans Canada Hwy, this small green park features some ancient Native Indian carvings in sandstone. Most of them are now barely visible having been overgrow with moss and plants. As well as the original petroglyphs there are castings from which you can make rubbings.

NANAIMO

Nanaimo is Vancouver Island's second major city, with a rapidly increasing population now over 70,000. It is one of the fastest growing cities in the country. Long considered drab and still bad-mouthed by residents of Victoria, Nanaimo gets an unfair rap. It's got a diverse cross section of people, a busy little downtown and a major people-oriented waterfront redevelopment.

A number of Native Indian bands once shared the area, which was called Sne-Ny-Mos, a Salish word meaning 'meeting place'. Coal was discovered in 1852 and for the next 100 years coal mining was the main industry in the town. Coal has declined in importance, but the city is now the centre of a forest-products industry as well as being a major deep-sea fishing port and a terminal for BC Ferries. Tourism continues to gain importance and the city has become a retirement centre as well.

Nanaimo is the jumping-off point for Gabriola and Newcastle islands, but there are a few points of interest in town as well as some in the immediate vicinity. During research a new branch of the Island Hwy from Victoria was under construction. This will permit motorists to bypass downtown Nanaimo on the way north.

Orientation & Information

Nanaimo, about 110 km north of Victoria, is a convenient stopover and a departure point

to Vancouver, the islands just off Nanaimo Harbour and points up island.

The entire waterfront area off Front St along the harbour has been redone with a seaside walkway, docks, shops, restaurants, coffee bars and pubs.

Behind the harbour lies the central core. Most of the restaurants and shops are in Commercial and Chapel Sts and Terminal Ave, which run more or less parallel to the harbour. To the south, Nicol St, the southern extension of Terminal Ave, leads to the Trans Canada Hwy. To the north, Terminal Ave forks: the right fork becomes Stewart Ave and leads to the BC Ferries terminal in Departure Bay; the left fork becomes Hwy 19, which heads north up-island to Courtney, Campbell River and Port Hardy. Sealand Market at the Departure Bay terminal has a couple of restaurants, a pub, tourist-oriented shops and the Oceanarium, a commercial attraction featuring underwater viewing of sea creatures.

The Travel Infocentre (☎ 754-8474), 266 Bryden St, just north of the downtown area at the corner of the Island Highway, has a walking guide of the town's historic area around the harbour. Many of the original buildings have been destroyed and are now marked only by plaques. If you're interested in seeing the ones that are left, get a copy of *Step Into History*, a booklet giving a walking tour of Nanaimo's historic buildings. Throughout the summer there is an information office open daily located in the Bastion historical site on the waterfront.

The Old City Quarter, a small section of downtown around Bastion, Fitzwilliam, Selby and Wesley Sts is being rejuvenated. The main post office is located at, but outside, the Harbour Park Shopping Centre which is at the corner of Front St and Terminal Ave. It's open Monday to Friday from 8.30 am to 5 pm. Nanaimo Regional General Hospital (☎ 754-2121) is at 1200 Dufferin Crescent, north-west of the downtown area. The bus station is north of the town centre behind the Tally Ho Island Inn at 1 Terminal Ave, while the train station is west at 321 Selby Rd.

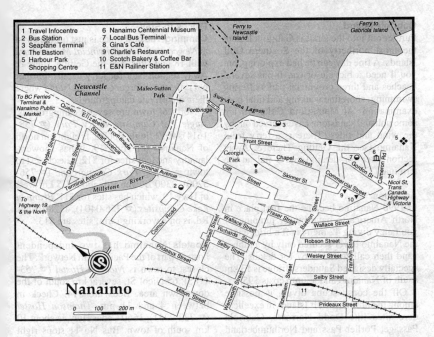

1 Travel Infocentre
2 Bus Station
3 Seaplane Terminal
4 The Bastion
5 Harbour Park
  Shopping Centre
6 Nanaimo Centennial Museum
7 Local Bus Terminal
8 Gina's Café
9 Charlie's Restaurant
10 Scotch Bakery & Coffee Bar
11 E&N Railiner Station

Ferry to Newcastle Island

Ferry to Gabriola Island

Newcastle Channel

To BC Ferries Terminal & Nanaimo Public Market

Mafeo-Sutton Park

Footbridge

Swy-A-Lana Lagoon

Queen Elizabeth Promenade

Stewart Avenue

Bryden Street

Davies Street

Terminal Avenue

Terminal Avenue

Millstone River

To Highway 19 & the North

Cornox Road

Prideaux Street

Campbell Street

Richards Street

Selby Street

Milton Street

Wentworth Street

Nanaimo

0   100   200 m

Front Street

Georgia Park

Chapel Street

Cliff Street

Skinner St

Fraser Street

Wallace Street

Robson Street

Wesley Street

Selby Street

Fitzwilliam Street

Franklyn Street

Bastion Street

Commercial Street

Gordon St

Cameron Rd

Prideaux Street

Wallace Street

To Nicol St, Trans Canada Highway & Victoria

Nanaimo Centennial Museum

The small museum (☎ 753-1821), at 100 Cameron Rd, displays items of significance in the growth of Nanaimo. Included are Native Indian, Hudson's Bay Company and coal-mining artefacts. It's open Monday to Friday from 9 am to 6 pm, and Saturday and Sunday from 10 am to 6 pm. Admission is $2.

Down the steps is Fisherman's Wharf where seafood can be bought.

The Bastion

The Bastion, in Front St, on the corner of Bastion St, is the highlight of Nanaimo's old buildings. Built by the Hudson's Bay Company in 1853 for protection from Native Indians, it was never used but for the odd firing of a cannon to quell a disturbance. It's now a museum and tourist office and is open daily from 9 to 11.30 am and from noon to 5 pm. Admission is free. From Wednesday to Sunday at noon the cannons are fired over the water.

Parks

There are quite a few parks in and around Nanaimo. The waterfront promenade, which takes in a number of the downtown ones, begins at the seaplane terminal and heads north to **Georgia Park**, where there are a few totem poles, a display of Native Indian canoes including a large war canoe and a fine view of Nanaimo Harbour. It then continues to Swy-A-Lana Lagoon (good for children to splash in) and **Mafeo-Sutton Park**, from where ferries leave to Newcastle Island.

Newcastle Island Provincial Marine Park

Just offshore of the downtown area is Newcastle Island, which offers cycling, hiking and beaches. It's also a good place for a picnic or overnight camping. Cars are not allowed. The island was once dotted with mine shafts and sandstone quarries but later became a quiet resort. In summer a small ferry travels between the island and the mainland every hour.

BRITISH COLUMBIA

Gabriola Island

Further out into the strait is Gabriola Island, the most northerly of the Southern Gulf Islands. A fine day can be had exploring, but you'll need a bicycle or car. It has several beaches and three provincial parks offering swimming, shoreline walking and tidal pool examination. At **Malaspina Galleries** are some unusual sandstone caves carved out by the wind and tides. There is a ferry from Nanaimo (see the Getting There & Away section later for details) and a pub at the terminal.

Activities

In 1990 Nanaimo became the first place in North America to have bungy jumping. If you fancy diving 42 metres off a bridge into the Nanaimo River secured only by a rubber band then call ☎ 753-5867 for details. The specially designed Saunders Bridge is 13 km south of Nanaimo and a jump costs $95.

Off the coast, scuba diving is possible among the northern Gulf Islands in excellent dive sites like Dodd Narrows, Gabriola Passage, Porlier Pass and Northumberland Channel. Three nearby spots where you can go hiking or canoeing are **Nanaimo Lakes**, **Nanaimo River** and **Green Mountain**. Hikes from **Colliery Dam Park** lead to Harewood and Overton lakes. Kayaks can be rented at the Kayak Shack beside the Sealand Market.

Nanaimo also has three good spots for bird-watching: **Buttertubs Marsh Sanctuary**, **Morrell Sanctuary** (take Comox Rd west off Terminal Ave to both) and **Piper's Lagoon Park** off Hammond Bay north of the city.

Festivals

The top annual event is the Nanaimo Bathtub Race to Vancouver, held each mid-July as part of the Marine Festival. Hundreds of fibreglass tubs start out, about 100 sinking in the first five minutes.

Through June and July the Nanaimo Festival presents both classic and modern plays at the Malaspina College south of town. For information call ☎ 754-7587.

Places to Stay

Camping The best place is just off the coast at *Newcastle Island Provincial Marine Park* with 18 tent sites. See the Getting There & Away section later for ferry details. Further out is the much larger *Gabriola Island* where there are private campgrounds.

North of town are several campgrounds. *Jingle Pot Campsite & RV Park* (☎ 758-1614), 4012 Jingle Pot Rd, is eight km north of Nanaimo off Hwy 19. It has showers, laundry and tent sites for $12. The closest to town is *Beban Park Campground* (☎ 756-5200), 2300 Bowen Rd, about 1.5 km west of Hwy 19, which has sites for $11. *Brannen Lake Campsites* (☎ 756-0404), 4228 Briggs Rd, is on a working farm; sites are $13.

Hostels Nanaimo has two independent hostels, part of the Pacific Rim Network. The closest to town is *Nicol St Hostel* (☎ 753-1188), 65 Nicol St, several km south of the downtown area. Beds are $14. Check in between 4 and 11 pm. *Thomson Hostel* (☎ 722-2251), 1660 Cedar Hwy, is about 10 km south of town. Bus No 11 stops right outside. It offers use of the kitchen and canoes and charges $12 per night; or you can camp on the lawn for $5 per person. The congenial owner will pick up travellers at the bus station in the evening at 6 pm, and will take them back there at 9.30 am.

B&Bs There are quite a few of these in town. The Travel Infocentre has a photo binder of many. Rates drop by about $5 per person outside June-September; otherwise singles/doubles start from $35/$45. A central one is *Marge & Ted's* (☎ 754-3514) at 1580 Brierly Hill, near the Departure Bay ferry.

Motels Many of the motels are on the highway north and south of the city. One of the cheapest, six blocks south of Nanaimo, is *Big 7 Economy Motel* (☎ 754-2328), 736 Nicol St, which offers singles/doubles for $35/42 and has a restaurant. Two blocks further north the *Diplomat Motel* (☎ 753-3261), 333 Nicol St, has rooms from $37/42.

In northern Nanaimo, 950 North Terminal

Ave close to the Departure Bay ferry terminal, is the *Colonial Motel* (☎ 754-4415). Rooms cost from $39/45. Similar and close by, is the *Bluebird Motel* (☎ 753-4151) at 955 North Terminal Ave where rooms cost $44/52, and there's a 24-hour restaurant next door.

Places to Eat
A stroll along Commercial St from the corner of Terminal Ave will turn up a number of places. The *Scotch Bakery & Coffee Bar*, 87 Commercial St, has good cakes priced from around $1 including Nanaimo bars, a classic Canadian sweet known across the country. On the same side and up the hill is *Charlie's Restaurant*, a large spacious restaurant with sandwiches priced from $5.25, including fries or salad, and burgers from $4.50.

For lunch or dinner, *Gina's Café*, perched at 47 Skinner St is recommended for its Mexican food, atmosphere and view. Lunch costs are about $6, dinner under $10 with beer extra.

Another fine place for an evening meal is the pleasantly casual *Dinghy Dock Floating Pub* at the waterfront over on Protection Island, an eight-minute trip from downtown on a small ferryboat. Seafood and various barbeque meals are offered from about $10. The outdoor patio has views across the harbour to Nanaimo and after dinner you can stroll the small, quiet residential island. Get the ferry from the docks at the south end of Government Wharf across from the museum.

Nanaimo's numerous pubs, some along the waterfront, others near the BC Ferry terminal at the Public Market have the usual fare. Stewart Ave also has numerous restaurants including the *Bluenose Chowder House* near the BC ferry terminal at 1340 Stewart for seafoods and $4 chowders.

Things to Buy
Hill's Indian Crafts, 20 Commercial St, sells the famous Cowichan sweaters.

Getting There & Away
Bus & Train Island Coach Lines (☎ 753-4371) connects Nanaimo with points north

and south; the one-way fare to Victoria is $16.25. The station is at 1 Terminal Ave north of the centre near Comox Rd. The E&N Railiner passes through once a day in each direction; the one-way fare to Victoria is $19. There's no ticket office at the station (part of the station building is now used as a meeting place for local Alcoholics Anonymous) which is at 321 Selby St; ring ☎ 1-800-561-8630 for information. Tickets can be purchased from the conductor.

Ferry The 39-km ferry trip to Horseshoe Bay takes about 1½ hours. There are about 12 to 15 services in each direction daily, depending on the season. Tickets are $6.50 per person, and $25 for a vehicle on weekdays, $2 more on weekends. The ferry between Nanaimo and Tsawwassen, the *Mid-Island Express*, goes four times a day in each direction and takes two hours and is the same price. The terminal is in Departure Bay, at the northern end of Stewart Ave. A new ferry terminal is being built south of town at Duke Point to handle the Tsawwassen ferries.

Getting Around
Bus For information about local buses call ☎ 390-4531 or get a transit guide at the tourist office. All buses pass through the Gordon Exchange at the corner of Front and Gordon Sts. Bus No 2 goes to the Stewart Ave ferry terminal.

Ferry Ferries to Newcastle Island leave from Mafeo-Sutton Park and cost $4 return. It's the same price to Protection Island. The ferry to Gabriola Island leaves from near the Harbour Square Shopping Centre and takes cars for $10, but only charges $3.50 if you're walking and bikes are free. After 2 pm you're stuck on the island until the next morning when the ferry returns. The ferry trip takes about 20 minutes.

PARKSVILLE & QUALICUM BEACH
These towns and the coast towards Comox are known for the long stretches of beach. Though still not fabulous, the beach at Parksville is busier, wider and sandier than at other

places and you can stop by the road, tone up the tan and have a quick swim in the nippy water. From Nanaimo the highway is slow and congested and stays this way to Campbell River. The new Island Hwy being constructed will improve the situation. There is camping at **Rathtrevor Beach Provincial Park**, three km south-east of Parksville.

PARKSVILLE TO PORT ALBERNI

South of Parksville is Hwy 4, the road to Port Alberni and the west coast. You can also connect with Hwy 4 from Qualicum Beach via Hwy 4A. At Coombs check out the goats grazing on the roof of the general store! From Parksville to Port Alberni is some very fine scenery, with several provincial parks where you can stop a while.

Englishman River Falls Provincial Park, 13 km south-west of Parksville at the end of Errington Rd, is a pleasant side trip with its 30-minute walking trail through the woods past waterfalls and emerald pools. There is also swimming and camping. **Little Qualicum Falls Provincial Park** is another good park with hiking, fishing and camping. Both areas are heavily forested and scenic. South-west of here, **Mt Arrowsmith** has skiing in winter, hiking trails in summer.

Cathedral Grove (MacMillan Provincial Park) right by the road at the western end of Cameron Lake is a must half-hour stop. Regarded by Native Indians as a sacred place, it is a grove of virgin forest with huge Douglas firs and red cedars some dating back 800 years. A series of trails lead through the delicate, ancient ecosystem of towering trees. It does get busy, so please respect the sign asking you not to touch the trees or plants.

PORT ALBERNI

Halfway across the island is this town (population 19,000) built on forestry and fishing. Over 300 commercial fishing boats work out of the area, most catching salmon. At Harbour Quay, at the bottom of Argyle St, there's an observation tower, the Forestry Visitor Centre (☎ 724-7890), open daily

from 10 am to 8 pm and some restaurants. Visitors can tour both the paper mill and the sawmill, inquire at the forestry centre.

Hikers can reach Della Falls (see the Strathcona Provincial Park section later for details) by an alternative route: canoeing the length of Great Central Lake from Port Alberni and taking the trail up from there.

At **Stamp Falls Provincial Park**, nine km north of Port Alberni, salmon can sometimes be seen jumping on their way up the river and there are petroglyphs at nearby **Sproat Lake**.

Perhaps the most noteworthy features of Port Alberni are the MVs *Lady Rose* and *Frances Barkley*, which sail out of Harbour Quay to the west coast of the island. They're operated by Alberni Marine Transportation (☎ 723-8313). The freighters, which take mail and cargo as well as passengers, ply between Kildonan on Alberni Inlet, Bamfield at the end of the West Coast Trail, the Broken Islands and Ucluelet. Those planning to canoe or kayak around the Broken Islands can take their boats on board. The ferry company is one place that rents canoes and kayaks.

Fares to Bamfield are $18 one way, to Ucluelet $20. One-day return trips allow passengers some free time at Bamfield and Ucluelet for exploring. On Sunday during the summer a longer stay in Bamfield is possible.

The freighters depart Port Alberni for Bamfield on Tuesday, Thursday and Saturday all year, and for Ucluelet and the Broken Islands on Monday, Wednesday and Friday from 1 June to 30 September. In midsummer there are Sunday cruises to Bamfield only. Regardless of the weather, take a sweater and/or raincoat.

Aside from motels there is the *Port Alberni International Hostel* (☎ 723-2484) at 4908 Burde St.

Island Coach Lines (☎ 723-6924), 4541 Margaret St, runs twice daily to Tofino and Ucluelet. Western Bus Lines (☎ 723-3341), 4521 10th Ave, has one bus Monday and Friday to Bamfield for $17. It also picks passengers up at the main Island Coach Lines bus station.

PACIFIC RIM NATIONAL PARK

Of the many parks in the area, this is the granddaddy! A rough, rugged, inhospitable yet beautiful coastal area, the park is a long, thin strip of land divided into three distinct sections. Each is separated by land and water and is reached by a different route.

Whale-watching trips can be a highlight of a visit to the west coast. From mid-February to June Pacific grey whales migrate up the coast from Mexico to the Arctic Ocean; the peak time to catch them heading north is mid-April. In late fall they head back south. Other attractions are the rainforest and undeveloped beach. With the forests of huge cedar and fir meeting the edge of the beach, and the huge waves rolling in off the Pacific, it really does feel like you are standing at the far edge of the continent.

Long Beach

The most northerly third of the park is Long Beach. It is the easiest to get to and is closest to all services. Hwy 4 leads from Port Alberni through the magnificent scenery (some heavily logged areas notwithstanding) of the Mackenzie Ranges at the southern

edge of Clayoquot (pronounced clak-wot) Sound into this section of the park. Long Beach is exactly that – about 20 km of wide, log-strewn surf and windswept, sandy beach. At other parts, the waves pound into a craggy, rocky shoreline.

In summer there are interpretive programmes and guided walks run by the Wickaninnish Centre next to the beach. At each end of Long Beach is a small fishing and tourist village – Tofino in the north, Ucluelet in the south.

There are eight short hiking trails in the park; the Park Information Office (☎ 726-4212) will have a description of them. The South Beach Trail leads to an area good for watching, and hearing, the huge waves. Half Moon Bay Trail leads to a calm, sandy bay. Radar Hill is good for views and has trails leading down to some small, secluded beaches. The Rainforest and Schooner Cove trails are good, accessible forest walks. Another activity is looking for and maybe watching some of the local marine life. Seals, sea lions and porpoises are common, killer and Pacific grey whales a possibility depending on the time of year. Good viewing spots

---

Clayoquot Sound and Old-Growth Forests

Clayoquot (pronounced 'clak-wot') Sound on Vancouver Island's west coast has become a symbol for the continuing struggle between the forestry industry and those who seek to preserve Canada's old-growth forests.

The Clayoquot Sound region, about 200 km north-west of Victoria, contains fjords, islands, mountains and forests with trees as old as 1000 years and as high as 75 metres. The valuable timber has long been sought by the forestry industry. Enviromentalists argue that old trees are removed carelessly and that a regenerated forest will not support the same biodiversity or even the same number of forestry jobs.

The debate built for at least a decade, with frequent bitter confrontations between the two sides. In 1993 the BC government bought $50 million worth of shares in the forestry giant MacMillan Bloedel and became the company's biggest shareholder. The government legislated to allow logging by that company in some parts of Clayoquot Sound but still the fight continued and development was put on hold. In 1995, after a major scientific report concluded that wide-scale logging would permanently damage the forest's ecosystem, a victory of sorts was declared by environmentalists. There is to be some logging, but far less than what was originally called for and it is to be tightly regulated.

The conflict has polarised residents of the two communities of Tofino and Ucluelet where some depend on tourism for jobs, others on logging. The issue is further complicated by the land claims of the region's 3000 Native Indians. They're not necessarily opposed to logging, but say they deserve a larger voice in the decision-making process.

Also in 1995, the Stein Valley of the south-western BC mainland was protected, adding to the impressive list of parks and protected areas established by the BC government, which now has the best environmental record in the country. ∎

BRITISH COLUMBIA

are Schooner Cove, Quistis Point, Radar Hill with its telescope, and Combers Beach near Sea Lion Rocks. Note that you must pay for parking everywhere.

Hundreds of thousands of geese and ducks fly overhead in spring and fall. Also, the pools left behind by the tides are often filled with interesting life forms: starfish, anemones, sponges, fish, snails and many other small creatures.

Long Beach reputedly has the best surfing in BC. Note that the weather is generally poor here. Most days are cold, windy and rainy. A warm, sunny day about a km or so from the coast can disappear into mist and fog at Long Beach. A sweater or raincoat is protection not only against the weather but also against the mosquitoes. The water, too, is cold – those doing any water sports should use wetsuits or drysuits. Surf boards can be rented but ask about etiquette as there have been run-ins between locals and visitors over which waves are whose.

Places to Stay There is one place to camp in the park itself, *Green Point Campground* (☎ 726-4245, 1-800-689-9025). It has washrooms with hot water and flush toilets and costs $18. It's generally full in summer: arrive early in the morning to get a place or have reservations made by calling the above number. A tip is that they have a few walk-in sites that are often vacant even at the end of the day when the 'No Vacancy' sign is up. They're not far from parking, cost less and are good sites near the water.

Tofino

At the northern end of Long Beach, just outside the park boundary, is the village of Tofino, the centre of the coast's tourism and one of the major destinations of Vancouver Island. Once a simple fishing village, the winter population of about 1200 swells to at least twice that through the summer. It's a busy, resort-like place with a bit of an undercurrent of tension resulting from the friction between environmentalists and those involved in the resource industries. All in all

it makes an interesting town for a few days of activities. The Travel Infocentre (☎ 725-3414), 380 Campbell St, is open daily from 9 am to 7.30 pm. The Friends of Clayoquot Sound (☎ 725-4218) have an office at 331 Neill St. The Forest Information Centre (☎ 725-3295), 316 Main St, is open from 10 am to 6 pm.

Things to See & Do The Whale Centre, 411 Campbell St, has a small museum and whale exhibit. The **Eagle Aerie Gallery** on Campbell St, houses the paintings and carvings of Roy Henry Vickers, an internationally established Native Indian artist based in Tofino.

Whale watching, fishing and rainforest trips can be arranged in town. For around $40 several companies offer boat trips to see Pacific gray whales. Best time is March to May when they migrate through the area, but many linger through the summer. Clayoquot Whaler will take you out and also fill you in on the history and Native Indian culture of the area. For information and tickets call Clayoquot Sound Charters (☎ 725-2888, 1-800-665-WHALES), 320 Main St. The Whale Centre (☎ 725-2132), 411 Campbell St will also take you to see the whales and other wildlife. Matt's Tours, operated and run by Matt, a Native Indian, has two-hour whale trips departing the docks at 2nd and Main Sts. Remote Passages (☎ 725-3330), 585 Campbell St, uses rubber zodiacs, a good way to get close.

A good trip is to **Hot Springs Cove** where a 20-minute hike will lead you to the hot springs (the only ones on Vancouver Island) overlooking the ocean. There are several pools, which become progressively cooler down the hillside to the sea. You can hire a boat or seaplane to the cove: contact Remote Passages or the Whale Centre. Overnight camping is possible.

Highly recommended is a trip to **Meares Island**, a 15-minute cruise past the Harbour Islands. This is a magical place of virgin rainforest with trees of mind-boggling age and stature: one is over 1000 years old and nearly 19 metres in diameter. Species include cedar, yew and varieties of spruce.

To organise a trip call Dutch before 10 am or evenings at ☎ 725-3793. His small boat, *Salty Dog* goes several times a day for $15 return from the dock at the foot of Fourth St. Make arrangements with him for how long you want to stay. Weigh West Marine Resort (☎ 725-3277), 634 Campbell St, also offers the same deal but they can't match Dutch for character.

There are several rugged but well-marked trails on the island; the basic loop takes about 2½ hours. Before going on to the island find out about the condition of the trails; except for the boardwalked area at the beginning, mud can be a problem.

Tofino Sea Kayaking Co (☎ 725-4222), also at 320 Main St, offers paddling tours to the nearby islands from $50 for four hours.

For fishing, try Springtime Charters (☎ 725-2351), 586 Campbell St.

Tofino Airlines (☎ 725-4454) has scenic flights of the islands and whales for $122 for 20 minutes for three people. The seaplanes leave from the wharf at the bottom of 1st St.

Places to Stay Tofino is very often booked out in summer, so don't get caught looking after dark or you'll be on the park bench – if it's not taken. There are several private campgrounds south of town but they are not cheap. On Mackenzie Beach *Bella Pacifica Resort & Campground* (☎ 725-3400) has full facilities and good beach sites from $20. Much smaller but also about three km to town, *Mackenzie Beach Resort* (☎ 725-3439) also charges from $20. *Crystal Beach Resort* (☎ 725-4213), 1165 Cedarwood Place, has sites from $18. It also has housekeeping log cottages from $110. There is cheaper tent camping on Indian Island off Grice Bay, south of Tofino. It's run by Matt who also provides whale trips. Find him around the dock at 2nd and Main Sts.

Several other places offer housekeeping cottages for rent, and there are quite a few B&Bs at about $70 double. In town *Backpackers' Hostel* (☎ 725-2288), 241 Campbell St, has room for 18 people in dorm beds for $15 and double rooms for $30 with lower off-season rates. It's pretty basic and

cramped but it fills a need and books out. There are two other hostel-style places located on nearby islands. The closest, within view of town, is *L'Auberge on the Island* with room in the house for $19 or camping for $15. You must use the marine telephone operator to contact them. Call ☎ 0, ask the marine operator for channel 24 Tofino, and then ask for Sea Slip N111658. A call costs about $3. Alternatively try the comfortable, quiet *Vargas Island Inn and Hostel* (☎ 725-3309). Here lodge rooms begin at $60 including meals but hostel accommodation is offered at $40. Both also include transportation, which is a 20-minute boat ride from town. Cabins and camping are offered at another island retreat, *Dream Isle*, ☎ 0, channel 24 Tofino, Dream Isle 2, N11483.

Cheapest of the motels is *Dolphin Motel* (☎ 725-3377), 1190 Pacific Rim Hwy three km south of Tofino, with singles/doubles from $45/50.

Places to Eat The *Common Loaf Bake Shop*, 180 1st St, is recommended. It has just a few tables but a large selection of excellent, delicious homemade muffins, cookies, breads and cakes. In the morning try the still-warm cinnamon buns. The shop is open daily from 8 am to 9.30 pm. The *Alley Way Café* tucked in the yard behind the corner of 1st St and Campbell St has a range of all-day breakfasts, Mexican-style dishes and various vegetarian meals all under $8. It's open to 9 pm every day. *Organic Matters*, on Campbell St near 4th St, sells organic food and has vegetarian soup and salad lunches for $5.50. Other restaurants such as the cosy *Schooner's*, 331 Campbell St, stress seafood.

Entertainment The pub downstairs in Maquinna Lodge is the only place in town for a beer and is a real happening place on Friday and Saturday nights with a DJ and lots of dancing.

Ucluelet
Ucluelet (the name is a Nootka word meaning 'people with a safe landing place'), with a

population of around 1700, is not as attractive as Tofino and is nowhere near the visitor mecca. It's more a town for the locals working in fishing and logging. The Travel Infocentre (☎ 726-4641), 227 Main St, is open daily in summer from 9 am to 6 pm.

You might like to walk to the lighthouse at **Amphitrite Point**, at the foot of Peninsula Rd, or take one of the trails at **Terrace Beach** north of town. Big Beach is a quiet, rocky bit of shoreline with tidal pools. Subtidal Adventures, on the right as you head into town just after Ucluelet Campground, is an outfit offering trips to see Pacific grey whales, from $36 for two hours, in March and April only. It also runs tours around the Broken Group Islands, will drop off people wishing to camp on an island and has scuba-diving cruises. Majestic West Coast Wilderness Adventures (☎ 726-2868) offers one and four-day kayaking trips starting at $40 for 2½ hours.

Places to Stay *Ucluelet Campground* (☎ 726-4355), 260 Seaplane Base Rd overlooking the harbour, with hot showers and flush toilets, has sites from $15. There are several motels, mostly on Peninsula Rd, and a couple of simple cheaper hotels. *Ucluelet Hotel* (☎ 726-4324), 250 Main St, has doubles without bath at $30. Near Long Beach, at 1755 Peninsula Rd the *Pacific Rim Motel* (☎ 726-7728) has rooms for $60/65.

Broken Group Islands
The middle section of Pacific Rim National Park, called the Broken Group Islands, is made up of about 100 islands at the entrance to **Barkley Sound**, famous for its variety of rockfish.

This area is popular with canoeists, is good for wildlife and offers some of the best scuba diving in Canada. You can view wrecks in shallow waters and the abundant marine life found around all the islands. The waters can be dangerous and you should prepare for a trip using *Marine Chart 3670*, available from the Canadian Hydrographic Service, Chart Sales, Institute of Ocean Sciences, 9860 Saanich Rd, PO Box 6000, Sidney V8L 4B2.

The only way to reach this section is by boat from Bamfield, Ucluelet or Port Alberni. There are some primitive campgrounds on the islands.

West Coast Trail
The third and most southerly section of the park is called the West Coast Trail, one of Canada's best known and toughest hiking paths. It's a 77-km stretch between Port Renfrew and Bamfield. Either end can be reached by road, but to reach one from the other you've got to walk – and that's a challenge along this rugged, often rain-soaked trail. It is *not* for novices although some people walk for just a day or two at the north end. To protect the environment and to keep hiker traffic to manageable limits, a quota system restricts the number of hikers using the trail. Only 52 people are permitted to begin the trail each day, 26 in each direction. Of those, six in each direction are on a first-come, first-served basis, the others have all been prebooked. Prebooking costs $85, the trail fee without the reservation is $60. You may well not get a place by turning up at the trailhead and so should put your name on the waiting list, however, you may have to wait several days. For an information package and reservation registration call ☎ 1-800-663-6000 from Canada or the USA or write to the Pacific Rim National Park Reserve, Box 280, Ucluelet, BC, V0R 3A0. Reservations are taken after 1 March for the upcoming summer, and in the first day July is pretty well booked out. The main season is from 1 May to 30 September. You can go two weeks earlier and later at half price but these times are not recommended as the weather can be even more brutal. July and August are the driest and best months.

The trail is clogged with trees, and the camping areas are wherever you can find them. Passing cliffs, beaches and rainforests, the trail takes between five and eight days to travel. You've got to take all your food. The southernmost part is the most rough and difficult, but you get to see some spectacular scenery and a chance to test your stamina. Some people prefer to do this last when the pack is lighter and the legs stronger, others want to get it out of the way and then 'cruise' to the other end. Near the centre of the trail you pass close to the old growth Carmanah Valley. There are two small ferries to take along the way, totalling $15, which are operated by Native Indians. The trail was historically used as a life-saving route for shipwreck survivors and you should carry tide charts. **Bamfield**, the village at the northern head of the West Coast Trail, has a Marine Biological Station, a life-saving station and not much else. The West Coast Trail Information Centre (☎ 728-3234) is five km south-east of the village on **Pachena Bay**.

There are only a few places to stay including two campgrounds. The nearest is eight km east of Bamfield and is run by the Ohiaht people. The other is 20 km north of Bamfield. *Sea Beam Resort* (☎ 728-3286) has singles/doubles for $20/40 and camping for $18.

Bamfield can be reached by boat from Ucluelet and Port Alberni; the one-way fare on the MV *Lady Rose* or *Frances Barkley* from Port Alberni is $18. There is also 100 km of gravel road from Port Alberni. Western Bus Lines (☎ 728-3491, 723-3341 in Port Alberni) operates the Pachena Bay Express, which connects Pachena Bay and Bamfield with Port Alberni on Monday and Friday. From Victoria, West Coast Trail Express (☎ 380-0580) runs a daily 11-person shuttle van to Bamfield and Pachena Bay for $48. To save hikers a lot of logistical hassles there is a boat service, West Coast Express Charters (☎ 647-5409) which links Bamfield to Port Renfrew three times a week. The Pacheenaht Indian Band (☎ 647-5521) runs a similar service but by road.

At the southern end of the trail is **Port Renfrew**, which can be reached by dirt road from Lake Cowichan or by the mainly paved Hwy 14 along the coast from Victoria. PBM Transport (☎ 475-2010) runs buses between Victoria and Port Renfrew. There is a seasonal trail information centre (☎ 647-5434) in the village. To reach the start of the trail

you must charter a boat to take you across the narrow San Juan River. Because of the difficult terrain, getting out of the bay here is, well, let's say, one of the less enjoyable segments of the trail northbound. You can camp along the beach in Port Renfrew or there is a hotel with a pub and a couple of B&Bs. There is also a small store, but supplies are limited. (See also the Around Victoria section earlier for details.)

HORNE LAKE PROVINCIAL PARK
Back on the east coast, north of Qualicum Beach, 16 km off Hwy 19, spelunking (caving) enthusiasts can explore the limestone caves here. A visit is recommended for anyone. There are three undeveloped but explorable caves and tours of varying lengths and difficulty occur daily in July and August, and at weekends in June and September. They range from inexpensive half-hour introductions to challenging five-hour $60 trips with full equipment and training in Riverbend Cave, the most spectacular, with a total of 383 metres of mapped passages. Don't drink much at breakfast because there is no going to the toilet until you're back in daylight. Alternatively, equipment can be rented to explore the lesser two caves, Main and Lower Main independently. Bring some very warm clothing and a good pair of shoes. For reservations call ☎ 248-7829. The park also has a good campground on the lake. The road to the park is an active logging road, so be careful of the trucks.

DENMAN & HORNBY ISLANDS
Further up the east coast are two lesser known Gulf Islands – Denman and Hornby. There's good bird-watching on Hornby Island. The ferry for Denman Island leaves from Buckley Bay, about 20 km south of Courtenay, and takes 10 minutes. For Hornby Island you take another ferry from Gravely Bay on Denman Island. The fare for each is $3 per person, or $8.50 with a car.

Each island has provincial parks, hiking, swimming, fishing, scuba diving and beaches, but only **Fillongley Provincial Park** on Denman Island allows camping. There are several private campgrounds and quite a few guesthouses and B&Bs.

COURTENAY & COMOX

Basically commercial centres for the local farming, logging and fishing industries, these two towns, with a collective population of 25,000, are also important supply hubs for Mt Washington, 32-km west of Courtenay, and Forbidden Plateau just outside Strathcona Provincial Park (see that section later), two major summer and winter recreation areas. Courtenay is the larger of these two essentially joined towns. The Travel Infocentre (☎ 334-3234), 2040 Cliffe Ave, in Courtenay serves both towns and is open daily from 8 am to 8 pm.

In Courtenay there is a small museum (☎ 334-3234), 360 Cliffe Ave, and not far out is the Puntledge River Fish Hatchery which farms salmon. At the Canadian Air Force base in Comox an international air show takes place each August in even-numbered years.

There is good hiking in the area, from afternoon walks to some overnight climbs. **Miracle Beach Provincial Park** (☎ 755-2483), north of Comox, has hiking trails, a campground and a long, sandy beach. **Comox Glacier** is a good two-day hike, as is **Mt Albert Edward** in the Forbidden Plateau area, which offers excellent views. Ask at the Travel Infocentre for more information. You must register if you're going on an overnighter.

A good circular tour is to take the ferry from Tsawwassen to Vancouver Island, travel up the island to Courtenay, go back across to the mainland by ferry from Little River near Comox to Powell River, and then travel down to Vancouver along the Sunshine Coast.

Places to Stay

Six km out of Courtenay, at 4787 Lake Trail Rd is the *North Comox Lake Mini-Hostel* (☎ 338-1914), which charges $12. Meals are available and someone can pick you up at the bus or train station. It's open all year and in summer there is extra sleeping space in a teepee.

There are at least two dozen B&Bs in the area with prices generally $35 to $45 for singles and $45 to $65 for doubles. In both towns you'll find numerous motels, and near Comox are several places renting cottages by the beach. One of the cheapest motels is *Economy Inn* (☎ 334-4491), 2605 Cliffe Ave (the name of the highway through town) in Courtenay. It has a pool and sauna and singles/doubles from $45/50.

CAMPBELL RIVER

Campbell River (population 27,000) is a major centre for salmon fishing, and marks the beginning of the northern part of the island. It is also the main departure point for Strathcona Provincial Park. The Travel Infocentre (☎ 287-4636), 1235 Shoppers Row, is open daily from 10 am to 8 pm. In the same building is the Campbell River Museum, open daily from 10 am to 4 pm.

There isn't much to see or do in town itself. Most visitors come here to fish for one or more of the five salmon species. But there is now another option. Campbell River Snorkel Tours offers fascinating guided river trips to watch the migrating salmon. Get details at the tourist office. Off the coast in **Discovery Passage**, scuba diving is excellent at such dive sites as Row & Be Damned, Whisky Point, Copper Cliffs and Steep Island. On **Quadra Island** just offshore you can see marine and birdlife or the ancient petroglyphs of the Kwakiutl people at Cape Mudge in the south. Some petroglyphs are in the Kwakiutl Museum along with tribal costumes, ceremonial masks and potlatch artefacts. The island also has hiking trails including one up Chinese Mountain. **Cortes Island**, east of Quadra Island, has plenty of deserted beaches and lots of wildlife. It's about an hour and two ferries from Campbell River.

Places to Stay

North and west of Campbell River there are government-run campgrounds in *Elk Falls Provincial Park*, on Hwy 28, in *Loveland Bay Provincial Park*, at Campbell Lake, and *Morton Lake Provincial Park*, 16 km from the Hwy 19 turn-off. Sites are $9.50, $7 and $8 respectively. There are also several private campgrounds. RV parks and numerous motels line the highway south of the downtown area. For B&Bs contact the Travel Infocentre.

On Quadra Island there is a backpackers' hostel, *Travellers Rural Retreat* (☎ 287-9232) at Quathisaski Cove. Call ahead. Quiet Cortes Island has the *Amigo's Hostel* (☎ 935-6403) on Manzanita Rd about a 20-minute drive from the ferry, rides can be arranged. Cost is $15. The hosts can tell you how to spend some time around the laid-back, off-the-track island. Don't linger too long in the hot tub. There are several B&Bs and a restaurant on the island too.

Entertainment

For some down-home country & western music visit the Quinsam Hotel, on the highway north of downtown.

Getting There & Around

Island Coach Lines (☎ 287-7151), on the corner of 13th Ave and Cedar St, runs one bus north daily to Port Hardy ($41 one way) and four buses south to Victoria. For information about local buses call ☎ 287-RIDE.

Ferries leave regularly from Discovery Crescent across from Tyee Plaza for Quathiaski Cove on Quadra Island; the return fare is $3. Another ferry departs Heriot Bay on Quadra Island for Whaletown on Cortes Island; the return fare is $4. Ask about the van service to Cortes four times a week from the Island Coach Lines depot.

NORTH OF CAMPBELL RIVER

Travelling north of Campbell River, Hwy 19 heads inland and much of the urbanisation that characterises the eastern coastline to the south disappears. It's a less-populated, less-visited, rugged area with lots of good opportunities for outdoor activities. Aside from Strathcona and Cape Scott parks, the Telegraph Cove – Port McNeil area is of most interest with its whale watching and Indian sites. Many of the travellers you meet

will be heading north to Port Hardy to catch the ferry to Prince Rupert.

STRATHCONA PROVINCIAL PARK

This is the largest park (☎ 755-2483) on the island and is basically a wilderness area. To simplify, the three main areas of interest each have different access points. Campbell River acts as the main one with Hwy 28 between Campbell River and Gold River cutting across the most developed portion of the park providing access to campgrounds and some well-marked trails. The Mt Washington area, just out of the park, and Forbidden Plateau are reached by different roads out of Courtenay.

At **Forbidden Plateau**, to the east of the park, are a series of high-altitude hiking trails, as well as trout fishing in the lakes on the plateau. In winter it's a major ski area, the island's original. In summer, the ski lift runs Wednesday to Sunday from 11 am to 6 pm to give hikers a head start into the alpine areas. A ticket is $8 return. At **Mt Washington**, it's much the same thing. Here the lift operates summer weekends only and is $10. The Paradise Meadows hike leading to the plateau is popular. This major ski resort has five lifts and 41 major marked runs, plus 35 km of cross-country ski trails.

In the Buttle Lake district, two well-known hikes are the **Elk River Trail** and the **Flower Ridge Trail**. Both lead to very fine alpine scenery. Like other developed trails, these two are suitable for all age groups. This area also has a number of short trails and nature walks. Other less-developed trails demand more preparation and lead to remote areas.

In the south of the park the **Della Falls Trail**, for example, is a tough two or three-day walk but is great for scenery and ends at the highest falls (440 metres) in North America. You need a good map. Other fine walks are those in the **Beauty Lake** area and one crossing the **Big Interior Massif** up to Nine Peaks. From the highest peaks, such as Golden Hinde (at 2200 metres the highest on the island), Colonel Foster and others in the 650-metre range, you can see the ocean to the west and Georgia Strait to the east. One thing you won't have to look at is a grizzly bear: there aren't any on Vancouver Island.

Places to Stay

The park has two serviced *campgrounds* with running water and toilets. Buttle Lake (north) near the entrance to the park is the nicer, the other is at Ralph River, at the southern end of the lake on its eastern shore. Camp sites are $12 and $9.50 respectively. Wilderness camping is free.

Strathcona Park Lodge (☎ 286-8206), a resort outside the park on Upper Campbell Lake, has a range of accommodation. You can camp near the beach for $15 with the use of facilities. Camping equipment can also be rented. Alternatively, you can bed down in hostel-style rooms for $15 with use of a communal kitchen. There are also lakefront cottages and apartments priced from $60 to $125. Van transportation from Campbell River can be arranged.

You can rent canoes, kayaks and bicycles, or go rock climbing, windsurfing, hiking, sailing and swimming. Or you can take organised day trips if you wish. The lodge has an education centre which offers courses in various outdoor activities.

GOLD RIVER

In the centre of the island, west of Strathcona Provincial Park, Gold River, accessed by Hwy 28, is the last stop on surfaced roads. The little town is a caving capital and is the headquarters of BC's Speleological Association. Visitors can join spelunking trips to **Upana Caves** and also to **Quatsino Cave**, the deepest vertical cave in North America. Kayakers can try their luck on the white-water section of the river known as the **Big Drop**. For more information, ask at the Travel Infocentre (☎ 283-2418) in Village Square Plaza.

Summer cruises go to **Friendly Cove**, where Captain Cook first met the west coast Native Indians in 1778. The working freighter, *Uchuk III* (☎ 283-2325), a converted WWII mine-sweeper, makes year-round trips to some of the remote villages

and settlements in **Nootka Sound** and **Kyuquot Sound**. Passengers can go on a choice of two one-day trips or on an overnight trip.

VALLEY OF 1000 FACES

Worth a visit is the Valley of 1000 Faces west off Hwy 19 at Sayward Junction, north of Campbell River. Along this woodland trail are over 1400 figures painted on slabs of cedar, the work of a Dutch-born artist, Hetty Frederickson. The natural wood grain is used as a base for the image and the slabs are then nailed to trees. Facial portraits, with their wide variety, are best. It's open daily 15 May to 1 September from 10 am to 5 pm and admission is $3 to the trail and gallery.

Nearby, **Sayward** is a logging port, and there are whale-watching tours from the terminal.

TELEGRAPH COVE

East off Hwy 19, about eight km south of Port McNeill, this small community is one of the best of the west coast's so-called boardwalk villages – villages in which most of the buildings are built over the water on wooden pilings. Formerly a sawmill village, it's got good fishing, but its main attraction is **killer whales**. Johnston Straight between Sayward and Alert Bay is one of the very best places in Canada to see them and this is the closest departure point to where the whales are generally found. The boat tour to Robson Bight, an ecological reserve south of Telegraph Cove is recommended. The tour, run by Stubbs Island Charters (☎ 928-3185/17, 1-800-665-3066 in BC), might seem a bit pricey at $60, but you are out for five hours and it includes lunch. It's a good idea to book ahead and take warm clothing. Trips run from June to October. It's about a five-hour drive to Nanaimo. Other good trips operate from Port McNeill. All use hydrophones so the whales can be heard as well as seen.

PORT McNEILL

Here you can go scuba diving, book fishing charters or go on killer-whale tours. Port McNeill is also the departure point for Cor-

Killer Whales

Using sonar to track the fish, sixteen pods of killer whales (each pod containing about 20 members) come to Johnstone Strait in summer to feed on the migrating salmon. In Robson Bight, along one of its beaches, many of the whales go to swim, rubbing their sides and stomachs on the pebbles and rocks that have been smoothed and rounded by the action of the water. No-one knows quite why they do this, but the whales obviously get a lot of pleasure from it and maybe that's reason enough. Killer whales can also be seen from boat tours out of Victoria.

The Johnstone Strait killer whales feature in David Attenborough's documentary, *Wolves of the Sea*. ■

morant and Malcolm islands. The regional offices of three major logging companies help sustain this town of over 2700. The Travel Infocentre (☎ 956-3131) is next to the ferry terminal. There are several campgrounds, including one near the terminal, and hotels for spending the night.

Sea Orca Expeditions (☎ 1-800-668-6722) offers three-hour whale trips in Zodiacs (recommended) or longer, more expensive sailing trips. Either way dress warmly.

Ferries (taking 45 minutes and costing $4 return) run to **Alert Bay** on five-km-long Cormorant Island, a blend of old fishing settlement and Indian culture. The Nimpkish Reserve is here. The U'Mista Cultural Centre show examples of Kwakiutl art, mainly masks, and the ceremonial Kwakiutl Bighouse can be seen. Like some other places in BC, Alert Bay claims to have the world's tallest totem pole, here measuring in at 52 metres. There are also a few minor historical sites including the Alert Bay Museum. Gator Gardens Ecological Park, with its giant cedars, mosses and wildlife is also worth a look. *Pacific Hostelry* (☎ 974-2026) in Alert Bay is an associate-HI hostel, open year round and with room for only 12 people, so call ahead. It costs $13 for members, $15 for nonmembers. There are also two modest hotels and a campground.

PORT HARDY

This small town at the northern end of Vancouver Island is best known as the departure point for the ferry trip aboard the *Queen of the North* through the famed Inside Passage to Prince Rupert. The terminal is three km south of town across Hardy Bay at Bear Cove, which is one of two sites where evidence of the earliest human occupation of the central and northern coastal areas of BC – around 8000 to 10,000 years ago – was found. The other site is Nanamu, now a canning town on the eastern shore of Fitzhugh Sound.

The Travel Infocentre (☎ 949-7622), open daily in the summer from 9 am to 8 pm, is at 7250 Market St and there's a laundromat up the hill on the same side.

There's little in the town itself except a small museum at 1110 Market St, open Monday to Saturday from 10 am to 5 pm, but the area around Port Hardy has good salmon fishing and scuba diving. North Island Diving & Water Sports (☎ 949-2664), on the corner of Market and Hastings Sts, rents and sells equipment and runs courses. You can also rent canoes and kayaks at the end of the jetty.

Places to Stay

In and around town there are campgrounds, hotels, motels and about 20 B&Bs. Several of the campgrounds are near the ferry terminal. One of the closest campgrounds is *Wildwoods Campsite* (☎ 949-6753) on the ferry terminal road with sites for $11. Others are *Sunny Sanctuary Campground* (☎ 949-8111), 8080 Goodspeed Rd, and *Quatse River Campground* (☎ 949-2395), 5050 Hardy Bay Rd.

Kay's B&B (☎ 949-6776) at 7605 Camarvon Rd is close to town and costs $30/50. One of the cheaper hotel options is the *North Shore Inn* (☎ 949-8500) 7370 Market St, across Hardy Bay from the ferry terminal, with rooms from $63.

Remember that the town fills up the night before a ferry is due to depart so it's worth booking ahead.

Getting There & Away

Island Coach Lines (☎ 949-7532), on the corner of Market and Hastings Sts, has one bus a day to Victoria for $78. North Island Transportation, operating out of the same office, runs a shuttle bus to/from the ferry terminal for $5 one way. The bus will pick you up and drop you off wherever you're staying.

Ferry – The Inside Passage BC Ferries run the 15-hour, 440-km trip along the coast, around islands and past some of the province's best scenery. The ferry leaves every second day at 7.30 am (check in by 6.30 am, if you have already booked a place) and arrives in Prince Rupert at 10.30 pm. (In winter the ferry leaves once a week.)

There's a short stop at Bella Bella, about a third of the way up, which is mostly for the locals but also to drop off kayakers. The one-way fare per person is $100, $205 for a car and $340 for campers up to 20 feet long (about six metres). Outside the summer peak period (late May to the end of September) the fares are less.

If you're taking a vehicle in summer you should reserve well in advance. Call the office in Vancouver or Victoria. Both are open seven days. However, it's possible to go standby and if you do you should put your name on the waiting list as early as possible and be at the ferry terminal by 5.30 am at the latest on the day of departure. Binoculars are useful as you're often close to land and the wildlife viewing is good: the possibilities include bald eagles, porpoises, sea lions, and humpback and killer whales.

Once in Prince Rupert you can: continue on Alaska State Ferries further north to Juneau and Skagway; catch BC Ferries to the Queen Charlotte Islands; or go by land into the BC interior and up to the Yukon and Alaska.

CAPE SCOTT PROVINCIAL PARK

About 60 km west of Port Hardy over an active logging gravel road, this remote park offers those wishing to get away challenging hiking, wilderness camping and exploring along pristine beaches. Most accessible is the undisturbed expanse of sandy beach at San Josef Bay under an hour's walk along a well-maintained trail.

Beyond this, things get serious. The eight-hour 24-km slog to wild Cape Scott, an old Danish settlement at the park's far end, weeds out the Sunday strollers. Just submit totally to the 'goddess of mud' and rewards will come to you. Nels Bight beach at six hours and with camping is one of them. Wildlife is abundant.

Note that the west coast of this northern tip of the island is known for strong winds, high tides and heavy rain. You'll need to take all supplies and equipment if you're camping. Also, it's suggested water be purified. Be careful of trucks on the drive in and stay well to the right.

South-Western British Columbia

The heavily populated area immediately surrounding Vancouver is known as the Lower Mainland. Most people see the region as something to get through on the way to somewhere else. We won't quibble with this, but there are a few places to break up the trip and once into the Fraser Canyon, BC's legendary topography takes over.

At the small town of Hope, 150 km from Vancouver, the road east splits. The Trans Canada Hwy follows the Goldrush Trail (the route the old wagon trail took to the Cariboo gold rush) north up the Fraser River Valley towards Cache Creek. As the road follows the river, which winds and twists through the canyon, there are many points of interest and viewing areas. The further north you go, the drier the land becomes and the fewer trees

there are, until around Cache Creek the landscape resembles that of a cowboy movie.

North-east of Hope the Coquihalla Hwy heads to Kamloops. It's a wide, straight express route with a $10 toll. Service stations are few, so leave with a full tank. The scenery along the way is pleasant and there are plenty of places to stop and view it. Further west, between Chilliwack and Vancouver, the road is uninterestingly flat and straight; it's more or less an expressway right into the city. There's no point trying to hitch along this stretch, as it's illegal for cars to stop.

The Crowsnest Hwy (Hwy 3) east of Hope heads first southward through Manning Provincial Park and then into the Okanagan Valley – the dry, beautiful fruit-growing region of BC. The green hills of the Hope area fade to brown as the road heads towards Osoyoos.

HOPE

There's not much in Hope itself but it's a good access point for the Fraser River Canyon and southern BC. Several lakes and more than a dozen provincial parks are close by. If you have a bit of time, the **Othello Tunnels** 15 minutes by car from Hope, is worth the trip. Situated in the Coquihalla Canyon Recreation Area and running alongside the river of the same name, a series of tunnels were cut for a railway line between 1911 and 1919. It's an interesting hour stroll along the gorge and unique enough to have been used in several movies including *Rambo* and *Yellow Dog – The Journey Home*.

South-east of town, a 15-minute drive on the Crowsnest Hwy, are the remains of the infamous 'Hope slide': in 1965 four people were killed when a small earthquake caused part of a mountain to crumble.

The Travel Infocentre (☎ 869-2021), 919 Water Ave near the river, is a good place from which to collect information. There's plenty of camping in the area and both long and short hiking trails. Motels can be found on the Old Princeton to Hope Rd as well as downtown, with singles or doubles starting from $40. The cafeteria occupies most of the

South-Western British Columbia

Greyhound Bus Depot (☎ 869-5522), at 833 3rd Ave on the corner of Fort St. A bus leaves daily for Yale and Lytton at 9:15 am; the one-way fare (before tax) to Lytton is $14, to Vancouver $17.50.

FRASER RIVER CANYON

One of the province's principal rivers, the swift flowing historic Fraser, pours out of central BC into the ocean at Vancouver. The Thompson River, a major tributary, joins it at Lytton. A trip along Highway 1 by the steep-sided canyon offers some of the more impressive scenery of the province.

There are several provincial parks along the canyon. **Emory Creek Provincial Park**, just north of Hope, has camping, fishing and hiking. A good picnic stop is **Alexander Bridge Provincial Park** one km north of Spuzzum. The open grate suspension bridge, built in 1926, spans the Fraser River and is free to cross.

Whitewater rafting down the Fraser and its tributaries' fast-flowing rapids is popular and a number of companies offer trips. Fraser Rafting Expeditions (☎ 863-2336), in **Yale**, 32 km north of Hope, has river trips from one-day ($90) to six-days long; food is provided. Kumsheen (☎ 1-800-663-6667), in **Lytton**, the 'rafting capital of Canada' does trips of from three hours ($72) to three days ($329). Several other companies do similar trips. The motorised rafts allow more time for watching the ever-changing scenery, the paddle rafts where you have to work are more exciting but either way you'll get soaked.

About 25 km north of Yale is the **Hell's Gate Airtram**, a widely advertised cable-car system that goes down to the rushing Fraser River daily. Look it over before buying the hype and $8.50 ticket.

Lytton is a pleasant town sitting where the clear Thompson waters meet the cloudy Fraser River. Northward the road to Cache Creek goes through almost badland terrain. There's camping at Skihist and Goldpan provincial parks. North off Highway 12 is the wonderfully diverse **Stein Valley**, the last major unlogged valley in south-western BC and declared a provincial park in late 1995.

MANNING PROVINCIAL PARK

This 66,000-hectare park in the Cascade Mountains, close to the border with the USA, is about a two-hour drive east from Vancouver: take the Trans Canada Hwy to Hope then follow the Crowsnest Hwy south-east. The park is noted for wildlife which includes more than 206 species of birds plus mammal species such as marmots, black bear, mule deer and coyote. In the summer there's swimming, fishing, canoeing, hiking and wilderness camping. In the winter there's downhill and cross-country skiing (with nearly 80 km of trails), and snowmobiling. The **Pacific Crest Hiking Trail** begins in this park and goes south all the way to Mexico. See you, good luck!

The park has four fully serviced *campgrounds* with sites for $9.50 and $15.50 or at *Manning Park Resort*, on the highway, you could try one of the cabins which start at $65/70 a single/double.

KAMLOOPS

Sitting at the point where the North Thompson, South Thompson and Thompson rivers meet, Kamloops has always been a service and transport crossroads. In fact the town was once called 'Kahmoloops', a Shuswap word meaning 'meeting of waters'. The Trans Canada Hwy cuts east-west through town; the Yellowhead Hwy (Hwy 5) heads north, Hwy 5A heads south and the Coquihalla Hwy heads south-west to Vancouver. With this strategic location, the city has grown rapidly since the late 1960s and is the major service and industrial centre in the district.

The city is not all business, though. It is surrounded by some 200 lakes, making it a good watersports area. The dry, rolling hills make interesting scenery and excellent ranching territory. Summers can be extremely hot with temperatures of 40°C.

Kamloops, with a population of over 72,000, is spread over a very wide area. There are many motels, restaurants and other services in both directions along the Trans Canada Hwy. The core itself is quiet, clean and pleasant.

Kamloops

0   250   500 m

To Via Rail Station,
Secwepemc Native
Heritage Park,
Paul Lake, Tod Mountain,
Jasper & Edmonton

To Motels,
Kamloops
Wildlife Park,
& Calgary

Yellowhead Highway

Yellowhead Bridge

South Thompson River

North Thompson River

Thompson River

Overlander Bridge

Red Bridge

Mt Paul Way

Athabasca Street

River Street

Lorne Street

Lansdowne Street

Victoria Street

Seymour Street

St Paul Street

Battle Street

Nicola Street

Columbia Street

Pine Street

Douglas Street

Fraser Street

Glenfair Drive

Riverside Park

1st Avenue
2nd Avenue
3rd Avenue
6th Avenue
7th Avenue
8th Avenue
9th Avenue
10th Avenue
11th Avenue
12th Avenue

Trans Canada Highway

1 97

1

Pemberton Terrace

Greenstone Terrace

Grandview Terrace

McGill Road

Arrowstone Drive

Summit Drive

Notre Dame Drive

West Columbia Street

To Knutsford Brookside RV Park,
Lac Le Jeune, Williams Lake & Hwy 5A

To Travel
Infocentre

PLACES TO STAY

1 Silver Sage Tent
  & Trailer Park
4 Plaza Hotel
5 HI Old Courthouse Hostel
9 Bambi Motel
11 Sagebrush Motel

PLACES TO EAT

2 Barb's Pie Place
3 Zone Organic Market
  & Restaurant

OTHER

6 Kamloops Museum
  & Art Gallery
7 Main Post Office
8 Laundromat
10 Royal Inland Hospital
12 Greyhound Bus Depot

BRITISH COLUMBIA

Vancouver lies 356 km to the south-west, Calgary 619 km to the east.

Orientation & Information

Train tracks separate the Thompson River's edge from the downtown area. Next to the tracks, running east-west, is Lansdowne St, one of the main streets. The other principal streets are Victoria and Seymour, both parallel to and south of Lansdowne. The Trans Canada Hwy is several blocks further south. On the north-western corner of the city, along Lorne St, is Riverside Park, a pleasant spot for picnicking and swimming. The North Thompson River meets the Thompson River across from the park's shoreline. Some great sunsets can be seen over the Overlander Bridge from this point.

The Travel Infocentre (☎ 374-3377; 1-800-667-0143 within BC) is at 1290 West Trans Canada Highway, south-west of downtown. It's open daily from 8 am to 8 pm in summer. The main post office (☎ 374-2444), 301 Seymour St near the corner of 3rd Ave, is open Monday to Friday from 8.30 am to 5 pm. The Royal Inland Hospital (☎ 374-5111) is at 311 Columbia St. There's a laundromat on Seymour St, between 4th and 5th Aves.

Things to See & Do

The **Kamloops Museum & Art Gallery** (☎ 828-3576) are in the same building at 207 Seymour St on the corner of 2nd Ave. On display are pioneer implements and Salish tools and ornaments. It's open Monday to Friday from 9 am to 8 pm, weekend afternoons and admission is by donation.

The **Secwepemc Native Heritage Park** (☎ 828-9801), 355 Yellowhead Hwy north of the centre, is the most interesting site in town. With a large outdoor area, including re-created traditional winter and summer houses, and an indoor museum the park outlines the history and the culture of the European-named Shuswap People.

It's open Monday to Friday from 9 am to 5 pm and Saturday noon to 5 pm. Entry is $5 and guided tours around the 2000-year-old site are offered and recommended. Archaeo-

logical work is on-going and the park continues to develop. Ask about the date of the annual Pow Wow. There is also a gift shop. Unfortunately, there is no city bus to the park.

The **Kamloops Wildlife Park** (☎ 573-3242) is 18 km east on the Trans Canada Hwy. Open year round (from 8 am to 8 pm in summer, to 5 pm the rest of the year), it has many animals found in Canada's west as well as camels, jaguars, monkeys and other animals from foreign lands. Admission is $6.

You can fish for salmon, trout and steelhead; as a general rule, the bigger the lake, the bigger the trout. **Adams River** is said to have very large sockeye salmon. There is even a Kamloops trout. The lakes and rivers also provide plenty of opportunities for swimming and water sports.

In winter there's downhill and cross-country skiing. **Tod Mountain**, 53 km north-east of Kamloops, off the Yellowhead Hwy, is the best spot for downhill, with many long, dry, powder-snow runs and a large chalet. It also has 24 km of cross-country trails. Call ☎ 578-7232 for snow information. Better cross-country skiing can be found at **Lac Le Jeune**, 25 km south of town.

Places to Stay

Camping *Silver Sage Tent & Trailer Park* (☎ 828-2077), north-east over the river at 771 East Athabasca St, is nothing special but is quiet and there are views across the river to downtown which is walkable. It has sites from $14 and a laundromat and showers. *Knutsford Brookside RV Park* (☎ 372-5380) is 12 km south-west of town, on Hwy 5A (the Kamloops to Princeton Hwy), about six km south off the Trans Canada Hwy. All facilities are available, including showers and a laundromat; a site for two people costs from $12.

You can also camp in two nearby provincial parks. *Paul Lake Provincial Park*, 24 km north-east of Kamloops, has sites for $9.50, as does *Lac Le Jeune Provincial Park*, 37 km south-west of town. Check in before 11 pm.

Hostel The spacious HI *Old Courthouse Hostel* (☎ 828-7991), 7 West Seymour St on the corner of 1st Ave, is in a beautiful old building close to downtown. It has a kitchen, laundry, TV room, lounge and dining room (the latter two contain some of the original courthouse furnishings) and a very good noticeboard. The office is open from 7 am to 1 pm and from 4 to 11 pm. The 78 beds, $14 for members, $19 for nonmembers are usually all taken in summer. From the Greyhound Bus Depot take local bus No 3 to the corner of Seymour St and 3rd Ave, then walk two blocks west.

The YM-YWCA (☎ 372-7725), at 400 Battle St, has no rooms but does offer showers ($1.50) to travellers.

B&Bs The Travel Infocentre has a sheet listing B&Bs in and around Kamloops. You could also try the Canada-West Okanagan B&B Registry (☎ 1-800-561-3223), which provides a reservation service with singles/doubles from $40/65.

Two central and inexpensive ones are *Joyce's B&B* (☎ 374-1417), 49 West Nicola St, which has rooms for $38/45 and *7th Abe B&B* (☎ 374-1099), 770 7th Ave with rooms for $30/45.

Hotels & Motels The central *Plaza Hotel* (☎ 372-7121), 405 Victoria St, is basic but cheap with bathless singles/doubles at just $20/27. There's a cafe and bar downstairs.

There are two main areas for motels: in Columbia St, west of the downtown area, and on the Trans Canada Hwy, east of town. *Monte Vista* (☎ 372-3033), 2349 Trans Canada Hwy, is an old motel with rooms for $35/38. There are no telephones in the rooms but it serves free coffee. *Kamloops Thrift Inn* (☎ 374-2488), at No 2459 Trans Canada Hwy, has a heated swimming pool and rooms for $40/42. Rooms have air-con and colour TV. Motels in Columbia St are pricier. One of the cheapest is the *Sagebrush Motel* (☎ 372-3151), 660 West Columbia St, which has rooms from $45/50 and some housekeeping units.

Another reasonably priced place is *Bambi Motel* (☎ 372-7626), 1084 Battle St, which runs east-west just south of the downtown core. Rooms cost from $38/44.

Places to Eat
Along and around Victoria St there are numerous places for a meal or just coffee. The *Plaza Café* in the Plaza Hotel serves good breakfasts and has soup, sandwich and dessert lunch specials for $5.50. It's open from 6 am to 3 pm.

The *Zone Organic Market & Restaurant* at 446 Victoria, with the outdoor tables, is both a store and an eatery serving a range of tasty international and vegetarian dishes. There is often live music at night too.

Barb's Pie Place at 222 Victoria St also has tables outside and serves breakfasts and snacks for $4 and delicious fruit pies for $3.

Getting There & Away
Bus The Greyhound Bus Depot (☎ 374-1212), 725 Notre Dame Drive south-west of the downtown area off West Columbia St, has a cafeteria and left-luggage lockers. There are regular buses daily to Vancouver, Calgary, Jasper, Edmonton, Prince George, Prince Rupert and Penticton. Some sample fares (including tax) are: Jasper, $47; Calgary, $74; Vancouver, $42; and Prince George, $61.

Train The VIA Rail station (☎ 1-800-561-8630) is 11 km north of town off the Yellowhead Hwy and is only open 30 minutes prior to departures. There are three trips weekly either east to Jasper or south to Vancouver. For Prince George you must transfer in Jasper. Call for the current schedule.

The privately operated *Rocky Mountaineer* tour train stops here overnight on its various trips. (See the Getting There & Away section in Vancouver for details).

Hitching Hitching is not allowed within the city limits.

Getting Around
For information about local bus routes call Kamloops Transit Service (☎ 376-1216). A one-way fare is $1 and a day pass costs $2.50. For a taxi call Yellow Cabs (☎ 374-3333).

WELLS GRAY PROVINCIAL PARK

In the Cariboo Mountains about halfway between Kamloops and Jasper, off the Yellowhead Hwy (Hwy 5), is this huge, undeveloped, and relatively little-visited, 520,000-hectare wilderness park. In **Clearwater**, the Travel Infocentre (☎ 674-2646), on the corner of the Yellowhead Hwy and Clearwater Valley Rd, has lots of useful information and maps on the park.

You can hike along more than 20 trails of varying lengths, go mountain biking, canoeing on the lakes and rivers, whitewater rafting on Clearwater River, mountain climbing, downhill or cross-country skiing, and horse riding. Canoeing often provides the only access to hiking trails and only experienced, fully equipped mountaineers should attempt climbing or venture onto the snowfields and glaciers. Wildlife is plentiful. Of the many scenic waterfalls in the park **Helmcken Falls**, where the Murtle River plunges 137 metres, is the most spectacular.

Places to Stay

Wells Gray has four designated *campgrounds* (Dawson Falls, Clearwater Lake, Falls Creek and Mahood Lake) with sites costing $9.50, plus plenty of wilderness camping along the shores of the larger lakes.

Getting There & Away

There are three access points to the park. From Clearwater to the south, the Clearwater Valley Rd enters the park at Hemp Creek; from Blue River a 24-km gravel road and 2.5-km track lead to Murtle Lake in the south-east; and from 100 Mile House off Hwy 97 it's 88 km on paved road to Mahood Lake in the south-west.

MT ROBSON PROVINCIAL PARK

Skirting the Fraser River, the Yellowhead Hwy and VIA Rail line run along the valley of this 217,000-hectare park which adjoins Alberta's Jasper National Park. At the western end of the park, Mt Robson (3954 metres) is the highest point in the Canadian Rockies and, when the clouds are not hugging it, is visible from the highway. At the base of the mountain the visitor centre has information on the park and runs interpretive programmes during the summer. Like Wells Gray, the park offers the full range of activities as well as many picnic areas and lookout points. In August and September you can see salmon spawning on the river at Rearguard Falls.

Adjoining the western end of the park is the tiny **Mt Terry Fox Provincial Park**, named after the runner who lost a leg to cancer, then attempted to run across the country to raise money for cancer research.

Places to Stay

Mt Robson Provincial Park has three *campgrounds*: two are near the visitor centre at Robson Meadows and Robson River with sites for $14.50; the third is at Lucerne on the southern shore of the Yellowhead Lake 10 km west of the Alberta border, with sites for $9.50. There is also wilderness camping in the park and commercial facilities at its western edge.

KAMLOOPS TO WILLIAMS LAKE

West of Kamloops, the Trans Canada Hwy heads to **Cache Creek**, north of which Hwy 97 (the Cariboo Hwy) follows the Goldrush Trail to Barkerville east of Quesnel. The dry, scrub-covered hills around the cross roads of Cache Creek give way to endless forest as you head north from Clinton. From 100 Mile House (named after the roadhouse located at this distance from the start of the original Cariboo Wagon Rd) you can travel to Mahood Lake in Wells Gray Provincial Park.

Unattractive **Williams Lake** is a transport and primary industry centre best known for the Williams Lake Stampede which takes place at the beginning of July. It's BC's answer to the Calgary Stampede and is a wild time lasting four days. It includes athletics and other sports as well as the rodeo. Accommodation prices go up a little while it's on.

North of Williams Lake is **McLeese Lake**, a small lakeside resort with log cabins. Bighorn sheep can be seen along Highway 20 west towards huge, undeveloped Tweedsmuir Provincial Park.

Okanagan Valley

The Okanagan, a beautiful and unique area of Canada, is a series of valleys running about 180 km north-south in south-central BC. To the east are the Monashee Mountains, to the west the Cascade Mountains. The valleys were carved out by glaciers and are linked by a series of lakes, the largest of which is Okanagan Lake. The varied and interesting landscape makes the entire region very scenic.

The northern end is gentle green farmland that climbs to woods of evergreens. The further south you get, the drier the terrain becomes. Near Osoyoos, close to the US border, cactuses grow on desert slopes that get only 250 mm of rain a year. And everywhere are rolling, scrubby hills, narrow blue lakes and clear sky.

The Okanagan is a significant retirement centre. This, in some measure, is responsible for the large growth of the area's major towns which are increasingly popular with seniors from not only BC but also from across the prairies and as far as Ontario. The entire region is also a vacation mecca for those searching for some hot summer sun which is so unreliable in the mountains or on the coast. Through July and August expect all types of accommodation to be tight.

Okanagan Lake is said to contain a monster similar to that of Loch Ness but known as Ogopogo. The Native Indians first reported it and would offer the creature sacrificial animals before venturing on the lake. Though sightings occur occasionally, no-one has yet photographed it.

For a detailed description of outdoor recreational activities in the valley pick up a copy of *Okanagan Country* ($14.95) by Murphy Shewchuk, available in bookshops and some newsagents.

Fruit Orchards & Vineyards

The hot, dry summers attract many visitors, but the climate, in combination with the fertile soil and heavy irrigation, has made the region the country's top fruit-growing area as well. There are about 100 sq km of orchards in the Okanagan.

During April and May the entire valley is enlivened with blossoms from thousands of fruit trees. In late summer and autumn the orchards drip with delicious fresh fruit. Stands dotting the roads sell the best and cheapest produce in Canada. Grapes, grown on 12 sq km of vineyards, are the last fruit of the summer to ripen. So-called agri-tourism with visits to farms, orchards and wineries has become very popular.

Work There's work fruit picking; it's hard and the pay isn't great, but you don't always need a work permit and you'll meet lots of young people. Arrive early and shop around. Quebecers in particular, both male and female, come in numbers as much for the adventure as the money. The approximate harvest times are:

Harvest Times	Fruit
25 June-25 July	cherries
15 July-10 August	apricots
20 July-10 September	peaches
20 August-1 September	pears
28 August-30 September	tomatoes
1 August-20 October	apples
1 September-20 September	prunes
9 September-18 October	grapes

Remember there are overlaps and other produce to fill in the gaps. The season starts first around Osoyoos, where the weather is warmer. The Agricultural Employment Services has a number of offices in and around the Okanagan Valley which are divided into north and south regions.

North
    Kelowna (head office) – 1517 Water St
    (☎ 860-8384)
    Vernon (and Armstrong) – 9 3100 35th St
    (☎ 542-9565)
South
    Penticton (head office) – 212 Main St
    (☎ 493-3727)
    Creston – 139 10th Ave North (☎ 428-9455)
    Grand Forks – 102 7337 2nd St (☎ 442-3035)
    Keremeos – 710 7th St (☎ 499-5341)
    Oliver – 9939 350th Ave (☎ 498-4496)
    Osoyoos – 8523 76th Ave (☎ 495-6925)

To Kamloops

To Sicamous
& Revelstoke

97B 97A

MONASHEE

Mabel
Lake

Shuswap River

Enderby

Armstrong

Westwold

97

97

Spallumsheen

Mt
Tuktakamin
1771m

Swan Lake

Silver Star
Park

Vernon

Lumby

6

Coldstream

To Upper
& Lower
Arrow Lakes

Okanagan
Valley

0   20   40 km

Killiney
Beach

Mt
Tahaetkun
2039m

Okanagan
Lake

Kalamalka
Lake

MOUNTAINS

To Merritt

Wood Lake

Stalwell Lake

97

Postill Lake

INTERIOR

Kelowna

Big White
Mountain
2317m

97C

Westbank

PLATEAU

Peachland

97

Okanagan
Mountain
Provincial
Park

Beaverdell

33

To Princeton &
Cascade Mountains

Naramata

Summerland

Mt Lookout
2063m

Penticton

Apex
Mountain
Recreation
Area

Skaha Lake

3A

Okanagan Falls

To Princeton,
Manning Provincial
Park, Hope &
Vancouver

Hedley

Crowsnest
Highway

Dominion Radio
Astrophysical
Observatory

Pocket

Vaseux Lake

Mount
Baldy
2301m

Westbridge

To Castlegar,
Nelson &
Kootenay
Lake

Keremeos

Cawston

Similkameen
River

97

Oliver

Desert

Anarchist
Mountain
Pass 1234m

Crowsnest Highway

3

Cathedral
Provincial
Park

Osoyoos

Osoyoos Lake

W A S H I N G T O N
(USA)

OSOYOOS & AROUND

Osoyoos is a big resort in a small town. It sits at the edge of dark-blue Lake Osoyoos in an area of stark, dry rolling hills at the southern end of the Okanagan Valley. The skies are sunny and the waters warm.

In 1975, in cooperation with the provincial government, the locals adopted a theme to beautify the town. Because of the climate, topography and agriculture, a Spanish motif was chosen and some businesses and houses maintain this look. With its hot, dry weather, the Osoyoos region produces the earliest and most varied fruit and vegetable crops in Canada. Look for roadside stands selling cherries, apricots, peaches, apples and other fruit. There are also many vineyards in the area.

On the eastern side of the lake lies a small desert, known as a 'pocket desert', which runs about 50 km northward to Skaha Lake and is about 20 km across at its widest point.

Averaging less than 200 mm of rain a year, the area has much specialised flora & fauna, including the calliope hummingbird (the smallest bird in Canada), rattlesnakes, painted turtles, numerous species of mice and coyotes and various cactuses, desert brushes and grasses. The area is actually an extension of the northern Mexican desert and the life found here is remarkably similar to that at the 600 metres level in the Mexican portion.

In a province where all the superlatives describing scenery work overtime the stretch between Osoyoos and Penticton on a clear day has to rank as one of the more deserving. And it's not too shabby leading west out of town toward the Okanagan Highlands either.

Orientation & Information

Osoyoos is at the crossroads of Hwy 97 heading north to Penticton (past several provincial parks where you can camp) and the Crowsnest Hwy running east to the Kootenay region and west to Hope.

The US border, cutting through Lake Osoyoos, is just five km to the south.

The Travel Infocentre (☎ 495-7142) is slightly north-west of town, on the corner where the Crowsnest Hwy branches off westward from Hwy 97, next to the Husky service station. The office of the Agricultural Employment Services, 8523 Main St, is open Monday to Friday from 7 am to 3.30 pm. The Greyhound Bus Depot (☎ 495-7252) is in the Petro-Canada service station on the Crowsnest Hwy east of downtown.

Note that in 1995 many of the city street names were changed from numbers to words eg, 91st St became Heron Lane, so you may hear both.

Things to See & Do

The climate makes **Lake Osoyoos** the warmest in the country. That together with the sandy beaches means great swimming.

The small **Osoyoos Museum** (☎ 495-6723), at the bottom of Main St by the lake, has displays on natural history, the Inkameep people, orchards and irrigation. It's open daily between June and October from 10 am to 4 pm and admission is $3.

Less than a km east of downtown, over the bridge, is **Dutch Windmill** (☎ 495-7318), a replica of one built in Holland in 1816. In summer you can tour the windmill, see grain being ground and buy the delicious bread and cakes baked there.

The **pocket desert**, off Black Sage Rd, is on the Inkameep people's reserve but you can visit by first asking permission from their office there. If you follow Black Sage Rd north from there to Oliver you'll pass several **wineries**. From Oliver, rough Camp McKinney Rd goes east to the **Mt Baldy** ski area (☎ 498-2262) which has cross-country trails and 11 downhill runs with a vertical drop of 420 metres. East of Osoyoos, on the Crowsnest Hwy, the **Anarchist Mountain Lookout** at 700 metres, offers a superb view of the town, valley, desert, lake and US border. You need a car or a ride to reach it.

West of town eight-km on the south side of Highway 3 look for the **spotted lake**, a weird natural phenomenon. Further west is **Cathedral Provincial Park**, a 33-sq-km mountain wilderness area characterised by unusual rock formations. Mule deer, mountain goat and California bighorn sheep may be seen. It's accessed by a gravel road off the

Crowsnest Hwy three km west of Keremeos. Surrounded by orchards **Keremeos** is most noted for its fruit and wines. Fruit stands dot the highway as it passes through the town and valley.

Places to Stay
Camping *Haynes Point Provincial Park* (☎ 494-0321) jutting into the lake two km south of downtown has the most sought after sites. In fact, short of using a shot gun you're not likely to get in until next year. You can call about the early morning number system but it's not really worth the trouble for the $14.50 spots.

A good alternative and where there are usually some spaces is *Inkameep Campground* (☎ 495-7279) on the Indian Reserve four-km west of town at 45th St. Tenting is $15. There are RV sites as well as a beach.

More developed *Cabana Beach Campground* (☎ 495-7705), 2231 East Lakeshore Drive, on Rural Route 1, three km south-east of town, has small cabins, as well as tent and trailer space. Two people tenting costs from $16 to $22. There are a couple of simpler campgrounds south of town along Highway 97 toward the US border.

Motels Aside from the pricey central beach-side motels along motel row on Main St, there are others along the Crowsnest Hwy east of the downtown area over the bridge, and some along Bartlett Place (89th St). *Boundary Motel* (☎ 495-6050) is on Rural Route 2, which leads to the US border, and rooms cost $35/39 plus tax.

Places to Eat
The *Oysoyoos Burger House*, 6910 Main St (62nd Ave) has cheap soups, sandwiches and burgers. The *Green Apple* beside the bus station on Highway 3 east is open daily for everything from schnitzel to seafood and various barbeque items.

PENTICTON
Penticton, the southernmost of the three Okanagan sister cities, sits directly between Okanagan Lake and Skaha Lake which are connected by the Okanagan River. The sun shines for an average of 600 hours in July and August – about 10 hours a day – and that's more than it shines in Honolulu! It's not surprising, then, that the number-one industry is tourism.

To the Salish, Pen-Tak-Tin means 'place to stay forever', an idea that many White people took to heart. Between 1975 and 1985 the population rose from 13,000 to 25,000 and is now over 30,000. Penticton became a townsite in 1892, when several nearby mine claims were being developed. The Canadian Pacific Railway made it a freight terminal and fruit companies started buying up land in early 1900. The industries grew and by the 1930s Penticton's location and climate was gaining a reputation. It soon became a vacation destination. The downtown core is undergoing something of a revival, particularly along the small Front St.

There is not a lot to do here, but this land of peaches and beaches is a good spot in which to cool your heels for a day or two.

Orientation
The downtown area lies just south of Okanagan Lake. Most of the land alongside the lake is park. Lakeshore Drive runs west beside it from the downtown area to Riverside Drive and Hwy 97. The main street is Main St, running north-south; at the southern end it continues straight on to South Main St, and to the right it forks off to become Skaha Lake Rd, which then turns into Hwy 97.

The downtown area extends for about 10 blocks southward from the lake. Martin St to the west and parallel to Main St is also important. Traffic on Main St is one way northbound, while on Martin St from Westminster Ave it's one way southbound. Running west-east, Westminster, Nanaimo and Wade Aves are the principal thoroughfares. Most of the restaurants and bars are in this area. This central area is small and easy to get around.

Information
The Travel Infocentre (☎ 492-4103), in the Jubilee Pavilion of the Chamber of Commerce

at 185 Lakeshore Drive, is open Monday to Friday from 9 am to 5 pm, weekends from 10 am to 4 pm. There's another on the corner of Westminster and Eckhardt Aves and one on Hwy 97 south of town. There is a postal outlet at Plaza Card & Gift shop, 1301 Main St. The Toronto Dominion Bank, on the corner of Nanaimo Ave and Martin St, is open on Saturday from 9.30 to 4 pm. Penticton Regional Hospital (☎ 492-4000) is south of downtown at 550 Carmi Ave. The Bookshop on Main St has a huge collection of second-hand books.

Things to See & Do

Close to the downtown area, **Okanagan Beach** is about 1300 metres long. It's sandy and the water temperature is about 22°C. You can visit the SS *Sicamous*, an old stern-wheeler, which sits dry-docked at the western end of the beach. This section of the Okanagan Lake has some of the best wind-surfing conditions in the Okanagan Valley. California Connection (☎ 490-78444) rents windsurfing boards and cata- marans from $12 and $25 per hour.

Parasail Penticton (☎ 492-2242) offers rides on both lakes: you start on the beach and a speedboat pulls you up 50 metres into the air. It costs $40 for a 10-minute ride, but people say the feeling and the views are worth the money. At the southern end of town **Skaha Beach** is about 1.5 km long and has sand, trees and picnic areas and there's windsurfing here too.

Coyote Cruises (☎ 492-2211) at 215 Riverside Drive rents inner tubes that you can float on all the way down to Skaha Lake. It takes nearly two hours and then they'll bus you back, all for $8.

The **Penticton Museum** (☎ 490-2452), at the library complex, 785 Main St, is an excellent small-town museum. Displays are varied, well-presented and pleasingly eclectic. Admission is by donation and it's closed Sunday.

Of the many area **wineries**, Hillside Cellars (☎ 493-4424), 1350 Naramata Rd north-east of downtown is the closest. As always there are free tours and taste samples.

On 2.25 sq km of dry land overlooking Skaha Lake, the **Okanagan Game Farm** (☎ 497-5405) has about 650 animals of 130 species, including Canadian and foreign animals. It's eight km south of Penticton, on Hwy 97, and is open all year from 8 am to dusk. Admission is $9, or $7 for students.

North of Skaha Lake you'll find adults' and children's waterslides at **Wonderful Waterworld** (☎ 493-8121), at 225 Yorkton Ave. It's open in summer from 10 am to 8 pm daily.

Festivals

The city's premier event is the Peach Festival, a week-long event that has taken place around the beginning of August since 1948. There are sports activities, novelty events, music and dance, nightly entertainment, and a major parade held on Saturday. The week following the festival is the Annual British Columbia Square Dance Jamboree. It goes on for six nights from 8 to 11 pm, and about 3500 dancers take part. There's an enormous dance floor in Kings Park. There are also street dances, dances held at both lakes – in the water! – pancake breakfasts and other activities.

At the end of August athletes are put through their paces in the Ironman Canada Triathlon. In early October for 11 days the Okanagan Wine Festival, centred in Penticton, takes place throughout the valley.

Places to Stay

Camping There are many tent and trailer parks, especially south of town, around Skaha Lake. Many are just off Hwy 97. Most are about $15 to $22 for two people in a tent. This is in no way wilderness camping, but is a cheap place to stay. The beach closes at midnight and stays that way until 6 am. If you try to sleep on the beach you'll probably be rudely awakened by the police.

Hostel The excellent HI *Penticton Hostel* (☎ 492-3992), 464 Ellis St, is right downtown just south of the Greyhound Bus Depot. Facilities include private rooms, kitchen, laundry, patio, bike rental and discounts in town. It also has details about finding fruit-picking work. The office is open daily from 7 am to 12.30 pm, and from 4 pm to midnight. Rates in a dorm are $14/18.50 for members/nonmembers.

B&Bs The Travel Infocentre has a list of local B&Bs. One that's been going a long time is *Apex Mountain Guest Ranch* (☎ 492-2454) in Green Mountain Rd, 22 km west of Penticton. Rooms cost $45. It's near the ski resort and offers horseback riding and hiking. Close to downtown, *Budget B&B* (☎ 492-6743), 230 Farrell St, is open all year and has reasonable rates at $35/50.

Hotels There aren't many hotels in Penticton and they're not cheap. *Three Gables Hotel* (☎ 492-3933), 353 Main St, is the most reasonable one, with rooms from $45/52. It's in the centre of town, three blocks south of Okanagan Lake, and has a good pub downstairs.

Motels Penticton is chock full of motels with Lakeshore Drive/Riverside Drive and South Main St/Skaha Lake Rd being the two main areas. *Club Paradise Motel* (☎ 493-8400), 1000 Lakeshore Drive, is a motel fronting Okanagan Lake. It has free coffee and air-con with singles and doubles costing from $50 to $70. Also fronting the lake but closer to the downtown area is the more expensive *Slumber Lodge Penticton* (☎ 492-4008), 274 Lakeshore Drive, where rooms start at $60/70.

At the southern end of town *Holiday House Motel* (☎ 492-8422), 3355 Skaha Lake Rd, has rooms from $49/55. *Valley Star Motel* (☎ 492-7205), at 3455 Skaha Lake Rd, has rooms from $50/55. Both have air-con and are close to Skaha Lake Beach.

Places to Eat
Nearly all the downtown restaurants are on or near Main St, and the revival of the downtown core has brought an increase in choice. Many of the chain-store restaurants are also on Main St but south of Duncan Ave.

The *Elite*, 340 Main St (the restaurant with

the 1950s Las Vegas-type sign outside) serves standard fare. Eggs with hash browns and toast cost $4.50 and it has lunch-time specials for $4. *Kay Ess* on Whyte Ave just east of Main St is recommended. It's small, comfortable and serves cheap home-made Mexican dishes. More upmarket, the very attractive *Tumbleweed Grill*, 314 Main St near the corner of Nanaimo Ave, serves Mexican as well as Spanish food. For coffee try the *Java Shop* at 445 Main. There are several restaurants along the waterfront of Okanagan Lake including the *Wild Goose Café* at 274 Lakeshore Drive which is good for salads ($5), and *Saba's* next door for pastas ($10).

Entertainment
Tiffany's, 535 Main St, is the rock-music place in town, bringing in bands from Vancouver. There's usually a cover charge of around $5. *Chaparal's*, 218 Martin St near the corner of Westminster Ave, has country music and dancing. A quieter spot is the large pub-like bar in the *Three Gables Hotel*.

Getting There & Away
The Greyhound Bus Depot (☎ 493-4101), 307 Ellis St on the corner of Nanaimo Ave one block east of Main St, is open daily from 6 am to 5 pm and has a cafeteria and left-luggage lockers. Buses depart daily for Vancouver ($41), Kelowna ($9.50), Vernon ($15) and Kamloops ($28). The fares include tax.

Getting Around
For local bus information contact Penticton Transit (☎ 492-5602), or visit the Travel Infocentre and pick up a copy of the leaflet *Penticton Rider's Guide*, which lists routes and fares. The one-way fare is $1.25 and a day pass is $3. The lake-to-lake shuttle bus runs along both waterfronts back and forth every day until 7.30 pm. Also, bus No 202 from the corner of Wade Ave and Martin St goes down South Main St to Skaha Lake. There are no buses on Sunday or holidays, except for the summer lake shuttle.

AROUND PENTICTON
Dominion Radio Astrophysical Observatory

Seen many of these lately? The observatory (☎ 490-4355), about 20 km south-west of Penticton, contains radio telescopes that receive radio waves from the Milky Way and other galaxies. The waves are then amplified and analysed to provide information that conventional equipment cannot. You can see the equipment, hear a recorded explanation and visit the interpretive centre. Call for details on the changing events, star-gazing, and tours. The observatory is on White Lake Rd, about a 15-minute drive from the first turn south of Kaledan Junction on Hwy 97.

Vaseaux Wildlife Centre

Just south of Okanagan Falls watch for the small sign at the north end of Vaseaux Lake. There is excellent bird-watching here as well as bighorn sheep and the northern Pacific rattlesnake.

Summerland

Summerland is a small lakeside resort town north of Penticton. From **Giant's Head Mountain**, an extinct volcano south of the downtown area, there are great views of Okanagan Lake. In town there are some fine 19th-century heritage buildings.

Summerland Trout Hatchery You can tour the hatchery (☎ 494-3346), 13405 Lakeshore Drive, from 8.30 to 11.30 am and from 1.30 to 4.30 pm all year for free. This is one of three BC hatcheries used to stock lakes; here they concentrate on rainbow, eastern brook and kokanee trout.

Agricultural Research Station This centre, 11 km north of Penticton on Hwy 97, was designed for the study of fruit trees, their growth, diseases and production. There is an ornamental garden displaying a variety of plants and trees, as well as picnic grounds. Tours are available, in the summer only, at 1 pm Monday to Friday but the grounds are open from 7.30 to 8.30 pm, to 5.30 pm the rest of the year.

Apex Mountain Ski Resort

For skiing enthusiasts, Apex Mountain Ski Resort (☎ 292-8222), 37 km west of Penticton, off Green Mountain Rd, has more than 40 downhill runs which cater for all levels of ability, plus cross-country trails.

KELOWNA

Kelowna sits halfway down Okanagan Lake, midway between Vernon and Penticton encircled by the rounded, scrubby hills typical of the valley. Closer to town they become greener, with terraced orchards lining their slopes and, unusually, the greenest area is the town itself, with its many parks and gardens. Beneath skies that are almost always clear, sandy beaches rim the dark blue water of the lake.

The city's name is a Salish word meaning 'grizzly bear'. A number of oblate missionaries arrived in 1858. One of them, Father Pandosy, established a mission and planted the area's first apple trees. He has become Canada's lesser known equivalent of the USA's Johnny Appleseed. It was the success of his work that led to the first full-scale planting of apples in 1890.

In 1892 the townsite of Kelowna was drawn up and today with 87,000 people, it is the Okanagan's major city. As the hub of Canada's largest fruit-growing district and with important lumber and wine industries, it is a valuable economic centre.

There are nearly 2000 hours of sunshine here each year. Summer days are usually dry and hot, the nights pleasantly cool and winters are not harsh. The combination of excellent weather and the lake makes Kelowna not only an ideal agricultural area but a very popular tourist destination. The numbers of visitors lend the town a distinct resort feel.

Orientation

The large City Park on the lake's edge forms the western boundary of town. Starting from the big white modern sculpture 'Sails' and the model of Ogopogo, the mythical lake monster, at the edge of City Park, Bernard Ave runs east and is the city's main drag.

PLACES TO STAY

9 Willow Inn Hotel
11 Royal Anne Hotel
13 SameSun International Hostel
21 Prestige Inn
24 Backpackers Hostel

PLACES TO EAT

10 Sai-Gon
12 Divino's Café
14 Christopher's
15 Casa Margaritas
16 Lunch Box
17 Jana's Delicatessan
18 Lena's Pancake & Omelet House

OTHER

1 Kelowna Mail Processing Plant
2 Calona Wines
3 Seaplane Terminal
4 Rose's Waterfront Pub
5 Kelowna Marina
6 Mosaic Books
7 National Exhibition Centre
8 Fintry Queen
19 Towne Centre Mall
20 Ted's Paperbacks & Comics
22 Travel Infocentre
23 Kelowna General Hospital

Gordon Street

Gaston Avenue

Clement Avenue

Coronation Avenue

Cawston Avenue

Wilson Avenue

Fuller Avenue

Stockwell Avenue

Martin Avenue

Lawson Avenue

Bernard Avenue

Lawrence Avenue

Leon Avenue

Harvey Avenue (Highway 97)

Saucier Avenue

Dehart Avenue

Rowcliffe Avenue

Sutherland Avenue

Beach Avenue

Park Avenue

Burne Avenue

Cadder Avenue

Cadder Avenue

Glenwood Avenue

Glenwood Avenue

Royal Avenue

Strathcona Avenue

Strathcona Park

Guisachan Avenue

Christleton Avenue

Birch Avenue

Cameron Park

Francis Avenue

Water Street

Haynes Avenue

Smith Avenue

Doyle Avenue

Queensway Avenue

St Paul Street

Bertram Street

Richter Street

Ethel Street

Abbott Street

Pandosy Street

Ellis Street

Lake Avenue

Okanagan Lake Floating Bridge

City Park

Okanagan Lake

To Westbank
& Penticton

To Motels,
Greyhound Bus Depot,
Airport, Winfield
Bear Creek
Provincial Park,
Big White
Mountain &
Vernon

To Lakeshore Rd, Father Pandosy
Settlement & Okanagan Mountain
Provincial Park

Kelowna

0   125   250 m

Other important thoroughfares are Water, Pandosy and Ellis Sts, all running north-south. South of town Pandosy St becomes Lakeshore Rd. Hwy 97, called Harvey Ave in town, is the southern edge of the downtown area; it heads westward over the bridge towards Penticton.

Eastward, along roughly a 15-km stretch, Harvey Ave is an ugly, sprawling commercial strip lined with service stations, junk-food restaurants and motels.

At the northern end of Pandosy St, where it meets Queensway Ave, is the town clock tower, standing in a fountain that marks the civic centre. Beside the fountain, surrounded by flowers, is the museum and art gallery contained within the National Exhibition Centre.

There are an amazing 65 parks in the city area, including seven with beaches along the shore of the lake. Several other parks are south-west of town, on the other side of the bridge.

Information

The Travel Infocentre (☎ 861-1515), 544 Harvey Ave (Hwy 97), near the corner of Ellis St, is open Monday to Friday from 9 am to 5 pm, weekends from 10 am to 4 pm. Another is on the western side of the lake, near Okanagan Lake Bridge, and there's a third on Hwy 97, about 10 km north of town, near the airport. Both of these only operate between May and September.

Most of the banks are on Bernard Ave, between Water and Ellis Sts.

If you're having mail delivered to Kelowna pick it up from the Kelowna Mail Processing Plant (☎ 762-2118), 530 Gaston Ave north of downtown. However, for other postal services go to one of the retail outlets around town; there's one in the Towne Centre Mall on Bernard Ave.

Mosaic Books (☎ 763-4418), 1420 St Paul St, sells maps (including topographic ones), atlases, travel and activity guides and has a section on Native Indian history and culture. Ted's Paperbacks & Comics ☎ 763-1258), 269 Leon Ave one block up from City Park, is a used-book store.

Kelowna General Hospital (☎ 862-4000) is south of Harvey Ave, at 2268 Pandosy St, on the corner of Royal Ave.

City Park & Promenade

The central downtown park is excellent, with sandy beaches, lots of shade trees, and water just slightly cooler than the summer air at 23°C. There are flower gardens and tennis courts and with the view across the lake, it's no wonder would-be fruit pickers are sitting around picking only guitars.

The beach runs from the marina to **Okanagan Lake Bridge** west of City Park. This is Canada's longest floating bridge; it's supported by 12 pontoons and has a lift span in the middle so boats up to 18 metres high can pass through.

From Bernard Ave, the lakeside promenade extends north past the marina, lock and artificial lagoon to a condominium complex, a blend of Canadian and Spanish architectural styles. The promenade is good for a stroll or jog in the evenings.

Fintry Queen

At the foot of Bernard Ave, behind the model of Ogopogo, the old ferry boat *Fintry Queen* (☎ 763-2780) is moored in the lake. Now converted into a restaurant, it also provides lake cruises. The two-hour cruise alone costs $9. Lunch only is $11, dinner only is $18.50.

National Exhibition Centre

Housing the **Kelowna Centennial Museum** (☎ 763-2417) and **Kelowna Art Gallery** (☎ 762-2226), this is part of the civic centre complex, at 470 Queensway Ave, on the corner of Pandosy St. The museum features a reconstructed Salish underground winter home. Other exhibits include models of some of the town's first buildings and stores, stocked with goods and relics. The art gallery has a small permanent collection, mainly of the works of BC artists, plus regularly changing displays. Admission to both is free. The centre is open from 10 am to 5 pm Monday to Saturday (Tuesday to Saturday in winter).

Father Pandosy Settlement

This is the major historic site in the area. On the spot where this oblate priest set up his mission in 1859 are some of the original buildings. The church, school, barn, one house and a few sheds from what was the first White settlement in the Okanagan have been restored.

The site is small, well out of the centre and there's not a lot to see, but it's free. To get there, go south along Lakeshore Rd, then east on Casorso Rd to Benvoulin Rd. It's open from 8 am to sundown.

Beaches

As well as the beach in town, there are several beaches south of Okanagan Lake Bridge along Lakeshore Rd. You could walk this far. Some of the campgrounds along the lake also have beaches.

Activities

There is excellent hiking around town with over a dozen places to explore. Well worth asking about is the **Kettle Valley Railway Trail**, an eight-km loop around the Myra Canyon through tunnels, over old trestles and with great views. Access to it is by rough logging road or try cycling. Vintage Tours (764-7223) offers trips or ask at SameSun hostel. The 10.5-sq-km **Okanagan Mountain Provincial Park**, south of Kelowna off Lakeshore Rd, is a popular spot for hikers and horse riders. Many of the trails date from the days of the fur trade.

Fishing is possible on Okanagan Lake and many of the 200 lakes near Kelowna. From Kelowna Marina you can take fishing trips or cruises. Windsurfers leave from the old seaplane terminal near the corner of Water St and Cawston Ave.

About 8.5 km north-west of Kelowna, **Bear Creek Provincial Park** also has windsurfing as well as fishing, swimming, hiking and wilderness camping. For skiers there's **Big White Mountain** (☎ 765-3101), 55 km east of Kelowna, off Hwy 33. It's covered in deep dry powder and is the highest ski area in the province. South-east of town, in Westbank, off Hwy 97, there's

Crystal Mountain (☎ 768-5189), which has night skiing.

Ask about agri-tours of orchards and juice plants.

Wine & Whisky Tours Wine tours are one attraction you might not want to miss. Most of BC's wineries are in the Okanagan. From Kelowna southwards, there are 12 sq km of vineyards. Several vintners in and near Kelowna offer tours and free samples.

Calona Wines (☎ 762-9144), 1125 Richter St, right in Kelowna, is BC's largest producer and was the first in the Okanagan: it started in 1932. In Westbank, about 13 km south-west of Kelowna, is Mission Hill Winery (☎ 768-7611). It's on Rural Route 1, in Mission Hill Rd, off Boucherie Rd, and has tours, tastings and sales. Cedarcreek Estate Winery (☎ 764-8866), 5445 Lakeshore Rd, has won international awards for its wine.

Hiram Walker Okanagan Distillery (☎ 763-4922), 8999 Jim Bailey Rd, Winfield, north of Kelowna, produces Canadian Club whisky and has free tours and tastings Monday to Friday.

Places to Stay

In common with the rest of the Okanagan Valley, accommodation here can be difficult to find in summer; book ahead or arrive early in the day.

Camping Camping is the cheapest way to stay in the area, though you'll be a fair way from town. The best place is *Bear Creek Provincial Park* (☎ 494-6500), nine-km west of Kelowna near Summerland, where a site is $15.50.

There are numerous privately owned places around Kelowna, especially in Westbank and south along Lakeshore Rd. The grounds are usually crowded and the sites close together. To get to Westbank, head west along Hwy 97 over Okanagan Lake Bridge then turn off at Boucherie Rd. Follow this for quite a while and you'll hit the so-called resort area. This area is quite far from town – you'll need a car. Sites cost between $15 and $25.

About six km south of the city is *Tiny Town Tent & Trailer Park* (☎ 762-6302), 3327 Lakeshore Rd. It's on the beach and has showers and bike rentals; sites are $15. Also on the beach, further south, is *Hiawatha RV Park* (☎ 861-4837), 3787 Lakeshore Rd. It's open from mid-May to mid-September and has tent sites for two people at $23.

Hostels Kelowna has a good, new, much-needed hostel, *SameSun International Hostel* (☎ 763-9800), centrally located at 730 Bernard Ave. Associated with HI, it has 40 beds at $15 members and $19.50 non-members, all facilities and rents bikes. From the bus station catch the No 10 to Richter St. The office is closed between 11 am and 5 pm. Reservations are recommended.

The *Backpackers Hostel* (☎ 763-6024) is on the corner of Christleton Ave at 2343 Pandosy St just south of the general hospital – a short walk from the beach. It costs $10 for a dormitory bed or $30 for a private double room and has a kitchen, TV room and parking. Guests are a not always harmonious mix of budget travellers, fruit-pickers and social service cases. From downtown, 1.5 km away, catch the Mission bus along Pandosy St.

B&Bs Contact Okanagan B&B Association (☎ 764-2124), PO Box 5135, Station A, Kelowna, V1Y 8T9, for information about staying in B&Bs, or ask at the Travel Info-centre. Prices begin at $30/40 single/double but most are $15 more.

Hotels There are no cheap hotels in Kelowna. Downtown, the *Willow Inn Hotel* (☎ 762-2122), 235 Queensway Ave, on the corner of Abbott St, is right by City Park and the lake and is quite good value. Singles/doubles cost from $55/65 with breakfast included. It has a restaurant and basement bar, the latter featuring female strippers.

Close by and more upmarket is *Prestige Inn* (☎ 860-7900), 1675 Abbott St, which has a pool and air-con rooms priced from

$89/99. *Royal Anne Hotel* (☎ 860-7200), 348 Bernard Ave, has similar facilities but with rates from $60/70.

Motels Most of the motels are along Hwy 97, north of the downtown area. There are some good choices not far past the Hwy 33 junction. *Western Budget Motel* (☎ 763-2484), 2679 Hwy 97 North, is the cheapest, with singles/doubles priced from $39 a room but it's more than that in peak season. The *Town & Country Motel* (☎ 860-7121), 2629 Hwy 97 North near the junction with Hwy 33, has rooms from $45/48 with air-con and TV. It also has a pool and sauna.

Closer in, *Ponderosa Motel* (☎ 860-2218), 1864 Hwy 97 North, is reasonable, with rooms including kitchen priced from $45/54.

Places to Eat
Many of the eateries are in Bernard Ave. *Lena's Pancake & Omelet House* at No 533 is open every day and has all types of pancakes and omelettes from $4.75, and cheaper breakfast specials. Next door, *Jana's Delicatessen* sells European sausages and cheeses and serves soup-and-sandwich lunches for $4. At the *Lunch Box*, near the corner of Ellis St, you can sit outside with their excellent salads for $3, sandwiches for $4.50 or pies such as chicken and asparagus for $3.50

Still in Bernard Ave, between Water and Mills Sts, there's a couple in the middle-range price bracket. *Casa Margaritas* serves Mexican food; tacos at lunch go for $5.50, dinners are priced from $10 to $15. The Vietnamese *Sai-Gon* has spring rolls for $5.55 and main meals from $8. At *Earl's* you can eat on the roof, from where you get a good view of the lake. The restaurant serves sandwiches and burgers from $5.50 and is licensed.

East along Bernard Ave, on the corner of Bertram St, and a little more upmarket is *Divino's Café*, which serves delicious Italian food. Pasta dishes are priced from $10 to $14. The food is good and the restaurant offers a range of local wines.

BRITISH COLUMBIA

If you're after something a little more spicy then try *Shalimar's*, 538 Leon Ave, an East Indian restaurant. More expensive *Christopher's* at 242 Lawrence St is the best place for steak or seafood. If you need a fast-food fix head for Harvey Ave south and east of downtown where you'll find all the regular outlets.

Entertainment

The Sunshine Theatre Company (☎ 763-4025) puts on a range of productions during the summer at the *Kelowna Community Theatre*, on the corner of Water St and Doyle Ave. Every summer Sunday afternoon there are free music concerts in City Park.

The Royal Anne Hotel, though an expensive place to stay, contains a popular pub-type bar, *Sergeant O'Flaherty's*. It's frequented by all types: visitors, workers and locals and entry is from the rear of the hotel in Queensway Ave. Lively *Rose's Waterfront Pub*, off Water St, is good for a beer and view of the promenade and lake.

Getting There & Away

Air The airport is about 20 km north of town, on Hwy 97. Air Canada and Canadian Airlines have daily flights to and from Vancouver, Calgary and Edmonton; the regular one-way fares (including tax) are $204, $266 and $392 respectively. Regional airlines link the city to smaller cities around BC.

Bus The Greyhound Bus Depot (☎ 860-3835) is north of the downtown area, at 2366 Leckie Rd, off Hwy 97. To get there, take city bus No 110 from the corner of Bernard Ave and Ellis St. It goes back and forth roughly every half hour from 6.30 am to 9.30 pm. The station is open from 6.30 am to 10.30 pm daily, and the ticket office from 7 am to 7 pm.

Daily there are four buses to Penticton; five to Vancouver and Vernon; and two to Osoyoos, Kamloops, Prince George, Prince Rupert, Dawson Creek, Revelstoke and Calgary. Some sample one-way fares (including tax) are Calgary $72, Prince George $80, Prince Rupert $159, and Vancouver $46.

Hitching If you're hitching south, walk over Okanagan Lake Bridge and start there; northbound on Hwy 97, begin west of the commercial strip.

Getting Around

The Airport The Kelowna Airporter bus (☎ 862-2455), shuttles between town and the airport Sunday to Friday. It takes about 20 minutes and is available for each incoming flight. The one-way fare is $6 and the bus stops at the larger hotels as well as at other places on request. The one-way fare in a taxi is about $25.

Bus For information about local buses call Kelowna Transit Systems (☎ 860-8121) or pick up a copy of *Kelowna Regional Rider's Guide* from the Travel Infocentre; there are three zones and the one-way fare in the central zone is $1. A day pass for all three zones costs $3.50.

Car Kelowna has all the major rental companies.

Budget
    1130 Leathhead Rd (☎ 765-2299)
Rent-a-Wreck
    2702 Hwy 97 North (☎ 763-6632)
Thrifty Car Rentals
    1980 Springfield Rd (☎ 765-2800)

Both Budget and Thrifty rent cars from $44 per day, with 100-km free then 15 cents per subsequent km, less on weekends. They all offer free pick-ups and drop-offs.

Taxi Kelowna has several taxi companies; try Kelowna Cabs (☎ 762-4444/2222).

VERNON & AROUND

Vernon, the most northerly of the Okanagan's 'Big Three', lies in a scenic valley encircled by three lakes: the Okanagan, Kalamalka and Swan. The town developed because of its location. First there were the fur traders, then the gold prospectors streaming up the valley to the Cariboo district. Later, cattle was brought in, and in

1891 the railway made it. But it was in 1908, with the introduction of large-scale irrigation, that the town took on an importance that was more than transitory. Soon the area was covered in orchards and farms.

Vernon's population of 31,000 is surprisingly cosmopolitan, with good numbers of Germans, Chinese and Native Indians. The Native Indians have a reserve to the west of town. Vernon itself doesn't have many attractions but accommodation is cheaper than in Kelowna or Penticton.

Orientation
Surrounded by rolling hills, downtown Vernon is a clean, neat, quiet place. Main St, also called 30th Ave, is lined with trees and benches. To the north of 30th Ave, 32nd Ave is an important thoroughfare, as is 25th Ave to the south. At 25th Ave, Hwy 6 leading south-east to Nelson and Nakusp, meets Hwy 97, which runs north-south, becoming 32nd St in Vernon and bisecting the city. On 32nd St, north of 30th Ave, is a commercial strip with service stations, motels and fast-food outlets. The other major north-south street is 27th St, which eventually joins Hwy 97 north of town.

On 27th St is the provincial courthouse, the city's most impressive structure. All the downtown sights are within easy walking distance of each other.

Information
The Travel Infocentre (☎ 542-1415) is about five km north of town on Hwy 97 (on the south-bound side) near the south-eastern shore of Swan Lake, so it's a bit of a hike to get to if you don't have your own transport. It's open Monday to Friday from 9.30 am to 4.30 pm. Another Travel Infocentre is only 2.5 km south of the downtown area, on Hwy 97, towards Kelowna, near the army camp. It operates from May to September. If all you need is a map and visitor's guide to Vernon, get them from the Chamber of Commerce (☎ 545-0771), downtown at 3700 33rd St.

The main post office (☎ 545-8239), 3101 32nd Ave, on the corner of 31st St opposite the civic centre, is open Monday to Friday from 8.30 am to 5 pm.

Bookland (☎ 545-1885), 3401 30th Ave, between 33rd and 34th Sts, has topographical maps of the region plus travel guides and books on activities in the Okanagan and BC.

The Vernon Jubilee Hospital (☎ 545-2211) is at 2101 32nd St.

Polson Park
Polson Park, off 25th Ave and next to 32nd St, is very pleasant, with lots of flowers and shade and the small Vernon Creek running through it. If it's hot this is a good rest spot. The Japanese and Chinese influence is evident in the gardens and open cabana-like structures dotting the park, at one end of which is a floral clock.

Provincial Courthouse
Built entirely of local granite, the courthouse (☎ 549-5422) sits majestically at the eastern end of the downtown area, on the corner of 30th Ave and 27th St. In front of it across the road is a rather bizarre garden with a waterfall over a log platform which is supported by concrete sculptures.

Greater Vernon Museum & Archives
This museum (☎ 542-3142) is in the civic centre, on the corner of 32nd Ave and 31st St, behind the glockenspiel-like clock tower. On display are historical artefacts from the area, including old carriages and clothes. It has a good antique telephone collection and lots of photos of the area and the locals. It's open from 10 am to 5 pm and entry is free (closed Sunday). There's an art gallery, too.

O'Keefe Historic Ranch
Twelve km north of Vernon, this old ranch (☎ 542-7868), on Hwy 97, was founded and lived on by the O'Keefe family from 1867 to 1977. Most of the buildings and artefacts were the property of this family. Among other things you'll see the original log cabin, a general store and St Ann's, the oldest Roman Catholic church in the province. The ranch is open daily, spring to autumn, from 9 am to 5 pm. Admission is $5.

Beaches & Cruises

On blue-green Kalamalka Lake, about four km south of town, is **Kalamalka Beach** with a campground nearby. To get there take Kalamalka Rd south off Hwy 6. There's also **Kin Beach** on Okanagan Lake, which is about seven km west of downtown. Head west along 25th Ave which becomes Okanagan Landing Rd, then turn right onto Tronson Rd which leads to the beach. It has a campground as well. Cruise Okanagan (☎ 549-1669) runs popular boat trips around the lake.

Provincial Parks

The 8.9-sq-km **Kalamalka Lake Provincial Park**, south of town and on the eastern side of Kalamalka Lake, provides swimming, fishing, hiking and picnic areas. **Ellison Provincial Park**, 25 km south-west of Vernon on Okanagan Lake, is the only freshwater marine park in Western Canada. Scuba diving is a popular activity here.

Silver Star Provincial Park is 22 km north-east of Vernon. Take 48th Ave off Hwy 97. The park offers good walking in summer, with views possible all the way west to the Coast Mountains. In winter it has 50 km of cross-country skiing on **Silver Star Mountain** and downhill ski runs plus trails for snowmobiles. In Lumby, **Mabel Lake Provincial Park**, 76 km north-east, off Hwy 6, has beaches, swimming, and fishing.

Places to Stay

Vernon has a wide range of campgrounds, B&Bs, hotels and, especially, motels. Downtown accommodation is cheaper here than in Kelowna and Penticton, but camping is the only real option for budget travellers since there are no hostels.

Camping By far the best campground is *Ellison Provincial Park* (☎ 494-0321), but it has only 54 campsites and is often full, so call ahead. A site costs $12.

There are lots of privately owned campgrounds, some close to town at Okanagan and Kalamalka lakes. These, too, get crowded. One of the closest campgrounds to town is *Swan Lake RV Park* (☎ 545-2300), 7255 Old Kamloops Rd, five km north of Vernon, which has tent sites from $10 plus tax. Head west along 43rd Ave then turn right (north) onto Old Kamloops Rd. Two km south of town *Dutch's Tent & Trailer Court* (☎ 545-1023), 15408 Kalamalka Rd, has sites from $15 for two people.

B&Bs Vernon has lots of B&Bs many located on the surrounding hills. For information contact the Travel Infocentre or Okanagan High Country B&B (☎ 542-4593), Rural Route 8, Site 10, Comp 12, which has singles/doubles priced from $35/40. Close to downtown at 3101 Pleasant Valley Rd, is *Tuck Inn* (☎ 545-3252), a large, white Victorian house with doubles for $65 including full breakfast. Nearby at 4008 Pleasant Valley is the *Pleasant Valley B&B* (☎ 545-9504), at $55 double.

Hotels The *National Hotel* (☎ 545-0731), 2922 30th Ave on the corner of 30th St, is a reasonably kept downtown hotel with the usual working-class bar downstairs. Single rooms without/with bath cost $23/27. Rooms include TV and air-con; a sauna is available and there's an old-style barber shop downstairs. The reliable *Travelodge* (☎ 545-2161), downtown at 3000 28th Ave, is a notch up and fairly priced at $50/60. Further north, *Coast Vernon Lodge* (☎ 545-3385), 3914 32nd St on the corner of 39th Ave, is more expensive. Singles/doubles cost from $70/75. The hotel has an indoor tropical garden, disco and nightclub.

Motels There are many, many motels in and around Vernon especially along 32nd St (Hwy 97). The *Polson Park Motel* (☎ 549-2231), 3201 24th Ave, on the corner of 32nd St and opposite the park, is central and good value. It offers free coffee, a heated pool, air-con and TV movies for $40/50 singles/doubles and a kitchen is $5 extra. Also close to town is *Schell Motel* (☎ 545-1351), 2810 35th St, on the corner of 30th Ave with a heated pool, sauna, TV, and air-con. Rooms cost $42/50, or $8 extra with a kitchen.

Places to Eat

For a small town, Vernon has lots of eateries – particularly little coffee shops and sandwich places. It seems to keep the quality up and the prices reasonable.

Downstairs at 3313 30th Ave, near the corner of 34th St, is *Jackie's Coffee Shop*, popular with the locals and good for breakfast. In the same vein, the cafeteria in the *Greyhound Bus Depot* has sandwiches for $4 and lunch specials for $5. It's basic but clean with some Ukrainian dishes.

Recommended is the *Internet Café* in the Red Dog bookstore, 3306A 32nd Ave. It has good cheap meals and is wired to the world via computers. *Sunseed* at 2919 30th Ave is a vegetarian/health food cafe which charges by the gram. Opposite the bus station is pub-like *Paddington Station*, 2921 31st Ave, which has halibut & chips for $7.50 and salads for $3.50.

Boa Thong, 3210 30th Ave, is a Thai restaurant with starters for $6 and main dishes from $7.50. For a splurge, try *Kelly O'Bryan's*, 2905 29th St, near 30th Ave, which serves pasta, seafood, beef and vegetarian dishes. Fettucini costs from $12. The restaurant has subdued lighting, stained-glass windows and an Irish theme.

Entertainment

The *Wildhouse Saloon*, on the corner of 30th Ave and 29th St next to Kelly O'Bryan's, features live country or country rock nightly Wednesday to Saturday from 8 pm to 2 am. On the corner of 30th St and 30th Ave, *Cloud 9* has rock music. *Nite Magic*, 2900 29th Ave, varies from karaoke to comedy to wet T-shirts.

Getting There & Away

The Greyhound Bus Depot (☎ 545-0527), is on the corner of 31st Ave and 30th St. The ticket office is open from 5.30 am to 9 pm, but it closes between 1 and 2 pm and between 4 and 5 pm. Buses depart regularly for Vancouver, Kelowna, Penticton, Calgary, Jasper and Prince George. Some sample fares, including tax, are Vancouver $49, Calgary $67 and Prince George $74.

Getting Around

For information about local buses contact KIA Transit (☎ 545-7221), 4210 24th Ave, or get a copy of the leaflet *Vernon Regional Rider's Guide*, which gives details of fares and routes, from the Travel Infocentre. The one-way fare is $1 and a day pass costs $2.50. For Kalamalka Lake catch bus No 1 south on 33rd St; for Okanagan Lake take bus No 7 west on 30th Ave.

For a taxi, try City Cabs (☎ 549-2227).

NORTH OF VERNON

At Sicamous there's a major highway junction where Hwy 97A meets the Trans Canada Hwy. From there the Trans Canada Hwy heads east past Shuswap Lake to Salmon Arm and Kamloops; west the highway goes to Revelstoke then through Mt Revelstoke, Glacier and Yoho national parks to Lake Louise in Alberta.

The Shuswap Region

The district around **Shuswap** and **Mara** lakes is picturesque, with green, wooded hills and farms. The grazing cattle and lush, cultivated land make a pleasant change of scenery no matter which direction you're coming from. There are many provincial parks in the region, three with camping: Shuswap Lake, Herald and Yard Creek.

Salmon Arm, at the northern end of the Okanagan Valley on the southern tip of one of Shuswap Lake's 'arms', is mainly a resort town, although timber and fruit-growing are also important. If you're here in October head north to Adams River in **Roderick Haig-Brown Provincial Park** where you'll see between 25,000 and 2½ million sockeye salmon migrating upriver to spawn. Haig-Brown, a Canadian naturalist and angler, has many books in print.

One way to explore the Shuswap and Mara lakes is by houseboat, which can be hired from **Sicamous**, the self-styled 'houseboat capital of Canada'. You can also rent them from Salmon Arm.

The *Squilax General Store and Hostel* (☎ 675-2977) about 10 km east of Chase on Shuswap Lake makes a rural hub for exploring the area. In summer remember to duck your head under the bats at the storefront. Rates are $12.50.

South-Eastern British Columbia

The south-eastern part of BC is dominated by the Rocky, Selkirk, Purcell, Monashee, and Columbia mountain ranges. National and provincial parks found throughout the area preserve and make accessible much of the varied terrain. Wedged between the parallel mountain chains is an incredibly scenic series of lakes, rivers and thinly populated valleys.

The Purcell Mountain region below Golden, west from the Rockies and including Kimberley is known as the East Kootenays. The West Kootenays run in and around the Selkirk Mountains west of Creston to Grand Forks and include Nelson, Nakusp and the Kootenay, Slocan and Arrow lakes. This, in particular, is a gorgeous area of mountains and valleys generally overlooked by visitors and definitely worth considering for a few days' exploration. But it's all an outstanding region for outdoor activities: camping, hiking and climbing in summer, and some of North America's best skiing in winter.

The south-eastern corner of BC is on Mountain Standard Time, while most of the rest of the province is on Pacific Standard Time, a difference of an hour.

REVELSTOKE & AROUND

This small town with a population of around 8000, on the Trans Canada Hwy, 70 km east of Sicamous, is picturesque, with quiet residential streets lined with neat wooden houses and tidy gardens. It's surrounded by mountains (not often seen) at the western edge of Mt Revelstoke National Park and is about halfway between the Okanagan Valley and the Rocky Mountains. Revelstoke is also a busy railway centre.

The main street is 1st St and MacKenzie is the major cross street. Grizzly Plaza, between MacKenzie and Orton Aves, is a pedestrian precinct. The Travel Infocentre (☎ 837-5345) is in the Chamber of Commerce, on the corner of 1st St and Campbell Ave. The main post office on 3rd St near the corner of Campbell Ave, is open Monday to Friday from 8.30 am to 5 pm. For information about Mt Revelstoke and Glacier national parks contact Parks Canada (☎ 837-7500), on the corner of Boyle Ave and 3rd St; it's open Monday to Friday from 8 am to 4.30 pm.

Most of the things to see are not in the town itself but around the Revelstoke area, so you'll need transport.

Revelstoke Museum
Revelstoke Museum (☎ 837-3067), on the corner of 1st St and Boyle Ave, open Monday to Saturday from 10 am to 5 pm, is worth a few minutes. Admission is by donation. It holds a permanent collection of furniture plus odds and ends of historical interest from the area including mining, logging and railway artefacts. The art gallery upstairs has changing exhibits.

Railway Museum
The new railway museum (☎ 837-6060) in a beautiful building downtown on Victoria Road has a couple of steam locomotives and displays on railroad history.

Mt Revelstoke National Park
This is a relatively small national park, just east of Revelstoke, in the Selkirk Mountains which are known for jagged, rugged peaks and steep valleys. The view of these from Mount Revelstoke is excellent. Access is along the 26-km Summit Rd (1.5 km east of Revelstoke, off the Trans Canada Hwy) which leads through cedars, alpine meadows and near-tundra to Balsam Lake within 1.5 km of the peak. From here walk or take a shuttle bus to the top.

There are some good hiking trails from the summit, with backcountry camping permitted. No other camping is allowed. The park

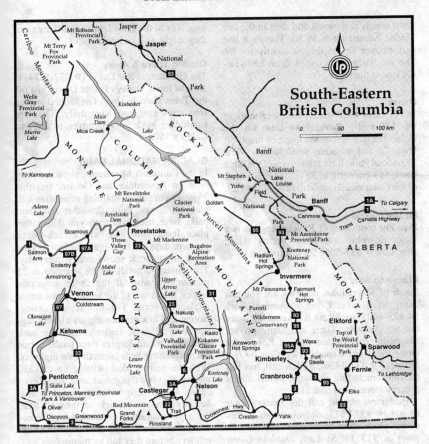

South-Eastern British Columbia

0   50   100 km

gets busy in the summer and there has been some environmental damage from visitors leaving the designated trails; the affected areas are being rehabilitated by the Canadian Parks Service. There's good skiing in the very long winters. Much of the summer is rainy.

Canyon Hot Springs

These springs (☎ 837-2420) are a great spot for a quick visit, 35 km east along the Trans Canada Hwy between Revelstoke and Glacier national parks. The site consists of a hot pool (40°C) and a larger, cooler swim-ming pool. The site is open from 9 am to 9 pm and early in the morning you can have the place to yourself. Admission is $4.50 and that includes a locker and shower; a day pass is $6.50. You can rent a bathing suit and towel for $2.50 each.

Three Valley Gap

On the Trans Canada Hwy, 19 km west of Revelstoke, is this re-creation of a pioneer community (☎ 837-2109). It has more than 20 buildings including a saloon, an old hotel, a barber shop a blacksmith's and a theatre. Nearby is the site of Three Valley, a mining

BRITISH COLUMBIA

town which blossomed and died in the late 1880s. Admission is $6.50. There's a live performance in the theatre nightly for $9. The site has a motel too, with an 850-year-old tree at the front.

Dams

BC Hydro (☎ 837-6211) runs free tours of the 175-metre **Revelstoke Dam** on the Columbia River, four km north of town, off Hwy 23 and adjacent to Columbia View Provincial Park. It also runs tours of the **Mica Dam**, 149 km north of Revelstoke, in a bend of the Columbia River, at the end of Hwy 23.

Mt Mackenzie

Five km south-east of Revelstoke, this is a major downhill and cross-country skiing area. Call ☎ 837-5268 for information.

Places to Stay

South of Revelstoke, on Hwy 23, you can camp at *Blanket Creek Provincial Park* (☎ 825-4421) for $9.50. It has running water but no showers. There are many private campgrounds east and west of Revelstoke along the Trans Canada Hwy. *Canyon Hot Springs* (☎ 837-2420), 35 km east, has full facilities including showers, toilets and a grocery store. Sites cost $15.

Budgeters should call the *Smokey Bear Hostel* (☎ 837-9573), for directions to this casual place close to outdoor activities. In town at 313 1st St East, *Daniel's Guest House* (☎ 837-5530) is a 100-year-old three-storey house with dorm rooms at $14 and private rooms available as well.

Piano Keep (☎ 837-2120), 815 Mackenzie Ave, is a 1905 heritage home B&B at $65/$75. Vern Enyedy, the owner, collects pianos from all over the world (now numbering over 40) and keeps them all in working order.

The *R Motel* (☎ 837-2164), at 1500 First St in town is the most modest place with singles/doubles $38/40. There are many other places, mostly motels, along the highway. If the day is getting on or it's wet, consider staying here, or in Golden, as it's a

long way to the Lake Louise-Banff area and they might well be booked up.

Getting There & Away

The Greyhound Bus Depot (☎ 837-5874) is west of town, at 1899 Fraser Drive, just off the Trans Canada Hwy. Greyhound makes four trips east and west daily. The fare (including tax) to Vancouver is $61, to Calgary $50.

GLACIER NATIONAL PARK

In the Columbia Mountains, about halfway between Revelstoke and Golden, lies this 1350-sq-km park containing more than 420 glaciers. If you think the other mountain parks have been wet then you'll like this place. It only rains here twice a week – once for three days and then again for four. It's the same in winter; it snows nearly every day. The annual snowfall can be as much as 23 metres. Because of the sheer mountain slopes, this is one of the world's most active avalanche areas. For this reason skiing, caving and mountaineering are closely regulated; you must register with the park warden. Around Rogers Pass you'll notice the many snowsheds protecting the highway. With the narrow road twisting up to 1330 metres, this is a dangerous area, sometimes called Death Strip – an unexpected avalanche can wipe a car right off the road. Still, the area is carefully controlled, and sometimes snows are brought tumbling down with artillery before they fall by themselves.

At the east side of the park is the dividing line between Pacific Standard and Mountain Standard time zones.

At Rogers Pass there's an information centre, open daily from 8 am to 8 pm in summer, and a park-warden office (☎ 837-6274 for both), open 24 hours a day. The centre has films on the park and in the summer organises guided walks. There's a 24-hour cafeteria and a service station next door.

Not far from here are the park's only two campgrounds: at *Illecillewaet River* and *Loop Brook*; both have running water and flush toilets.

GOLDEN

As you travel along the Trans Canada Hwy from Alberta, this town of 3800 people is the first of any size in BC. It's also at the junction with Hwy 95 which connects the town with Radium Hot Springs and Invermere to the south. Despite what the tourist brochures say and what its name might suggest, Golden is not much more than a commercial strip of motels, fast-food restaurants and service stations although there is an older downtown area off the highway. Golden is the town to which workers in the area come for a bite to eat and a booze-up – something you might want to do yourself if you've been a while in the backcountry.

The Travel Infocentre (☎ 344-7125), 500 10th Ave, is open daily from 9 am to 7 pm in summer, weekdays in winter. This and the centre of town are two km south of the highway. *Golden Municipal Campground* (☎ 344-5412), 1407 South 9th St, has most facilities including showers (but no laundry) and sites costing $8 to $12.

Golden is the centre for whitewater rafting trips on the turbulent Kicking Horse River. These trips are among the roughest with lots of class-three and four rapids. Wet'n'Wild (☎ 1-800-668-9119) with exciting half ($45) and full day trips is recommended.

Wildlife-observing float tours of the major Columbia Valley wetlands are offered by Kinbasket Adventures (☎ 344-6012).

Heli-Skiing & Hiking

South of Golden, in the Purcell Mountains, is the world's centre for helicopter skiing – in districts such as the Gothics, Caribous and, perhaps best known, the Bugaboos. The latter is a region of 1500 sq km of rugged, remote mountains accessible only by helicopter during the winter months. This dangerous, thrilling sport attracts rich visitors from around the world each winter and spring. The Bugaboos has been a favourite area for two decades.

The skiing is superb but a portion of the appeal is the danger. Avalanches are not uncommon, tumbling snows claim lives on a regular, though not frequent, basis – just often enough to give the run down that extra kick.

Canadian Mountain Holidays (CMH) (☎ (403) 762-7100; 1-800-661-0252), 217 Bear St, Banff, Alberta T0L 0C0, is one of the oldest, most established operators providing visitors with transportation, comfortable lodges and helicopter lifts to pristine mountain tops with spectacular scenery and fine powder snows. ABC Wilderness Adventures (☎ 344-2639), PO Box 1829, Golden, offers a similar service. A week-long ski holiday can cost $5000.

During the summer months you can visit some of the lodges and enjoy hiking. The five-hour walk from the parking lot to Cobalt Lake is good. Both companies offer helihiking but some visitors find all the noise an irritant. Mountaineers, too, come from around the world to test their skills on the sheer rock faces and granite pinnacles in Bugaboo Glacier Provincial Park ('The Bugs').

YOHO NATIONAL PARK

Yoho National Park in the BC Rockies, adjacent to the Alberta border and Banff National Park to the east and Kootenay National Park to the south, offers mountain peaks, river valleys, glacial lakes and beautiful meadows – a bit of everything. A number of excellent day activities can be enjoyed. Yoho is not as busy as Banff and has campground vacancies when Banff is full. A possible drawback is the often wet or cloudy days. Still, Yoho is more accessible and the weather better (not saying much) than at Glacier. The name is a Cree word expressing astonishment or wonder. The rushing Kicking Horse River flows through the park.

Field

Very small Field, lying in the middle of the park, is the first town in BC as you head west along the Trans-Canada Hwy (which follows the Kicking Horse River). Many of its buildings date from the early days of the railways.

The park information centre and warden

office (☎ 343-6324 for both) are open from 8 am to 8 pm in summer, to 4.30 pm the rest of the year. BC Tourism and Alberta Tourism both have desks here and there is a post office in town.

The Siding General Store, open daily, is a good place to get supplies, including alcohol, if you're going to stay in the park. It's cheaper than the store near Takakkaw Falls and there's a pleasant little cafe with home-made food. Still, you're better off getting groceries in Golden or Banff.

Lake O'Hara

Nestled high in the mountains this somewhat exclusive beauty spot more than lives up to its exalted reputation. It's definitely worth the sizeable hassle to reach for the excellent series of walking trails in what is in effect a miniaturisation of the Rockies. Compact wooded hillsides, alpine meadows, snow-covered passes, mountain vistas and glaciers are all concentrated around the stunning lake. Day and half-day hikes, most fairly rigorous, make it all accessible. A simple day trip is well worthwhile, but overnighting makes hiking more trails possible. The very fine Opabin Plateau circuit trail offers a bit of everything. A basic trail pamphlet and snacks are available at the lake. See the following headings for more details.

Hiking & Other Activities

Near Field is the turn-off for **Takakkaw Falls** – at 254 metres, one of the highest waterfalls in Canada. In the Yoho Valley the trail from Takakkaw Falls to **Twin Falls** makes a good day hike. The trail is mostly flat, with views of lots of rapids and waterfalls.

The beautiful green **Emerald Lake** has a flat circular walking trail with other trails radiating from it and the water in the lake is warm enough in late summer for a quick swim.

The **Burgess Shale World Heritage Site** protects the amazing Cambrian age fossil beds on Mt Stephen and Mt Field. These 530 million-year-old fossils preserve the remains of marine creatures you'd swear were from a distant planet.

Also east of Field by the highway are the famous **spiral tunnels**, the feats of engineering that enable the Canadian Pacific trains to navigate the challenging Kicking Horse Pass.

Places to Stay

Yoho has five campgrounds. Only the *Kicking Horse River* campground at $15 has showers. This makes it the most popular. *Chancellor Peak* ($10) has the river and good views. Other campgrounds are the very wooded *Hoodoo Creek* ($12) and *Takakkaw*

Burgess Shale

The Burgess Shale fossil site, near Field in Yoho National Park, BC, was discovered accidentally in 1909 by Charles D Walcott from the Smithsonian Institute, Washington DC, when he was out horse riding. The Cambrian-age fossil beds on Mt Field and Mt Stephen contain the fossilised remains of marine animals that lived around 530 million years ago. The site is remarkable for its number, variety and detailed preservation of fossils of soft-bodied creatures such as worms and sponges, and of hard-bodied creatures (with their soft-body parts) such as molluscs.

One major reason for their preservation was their burial in deep water where the oxygen level, and therefore the rate of organic decay, was low. In recognition of its importance to our understanding of evolution, Burgess Shale was declared a UN World Heritage Site.

Faced with the dilemma of preserving the site while allowing visitors the chance to see and learn about it, Yoho National Park restricts the amount of public access. Visitors can go on rigorous guided walks (which must be booked in advance and are limited to 15 people) with two organisations. Call Canadian Wilderness Tours (☎(604) 343-6470) or Yoho-Burgess Shale Research Foundation (☎1-800-343-3006) for rates and schedules.

If you don't get onto a guided walk or don't fancy the long, steep hike to Mt Field or Mt Stephen there are exhibitions on Burgess Shale in the park information centre near Field, at the Kicking Horse River campground, and at the Lake Louise Visitor Information Centre in Banff National Park, Alberta. ∎

Falls ($10). Note that you can have a swim at the pond beside the Field information office.

Field has several B&B's and an inn. The HI *Whiskey Jack Hostel* (☎ (403) 762-4122), just before the Takakkaw Falls campground, is open mid-June to October and has 27 beds. Nearby and recommended are the pleasantly rustic, *Cathedral Mountain Chalets* (☎ 343-6442), at the base of Cathedral Mountain from $50 single or double. There's a cafe here.

For camping at Lake O'Hara, reservations (☎ (604) 343-6433) for the $10 sites are required and are taken one month in advance. Reservations are offered from 8 am to 4 pm. These are sold out every day, 30 days in advance, by early morning as are the reservations for the bus to the lake. However, there is one way around this system. Each day five places on the bus and five places in the campground are held for first-come, first-served visitors for the following day. In order to get one of these places you must wait in line to sign in at the park information office in Field. The office opens at 9 am, be there at 7 am (with a thermos of coffee) and you'll bag a spot. Note the washrooms in the information building are open 24 hours and are heated.

There is a maximum camping stay of four days, you must treat drinking water, and cooking fires are only permitted at kitchen shelters. Day trippers, take water. Be well prepared for rain. The Lake O'Hara Lodge with a long list of regulars is very expensive and generally booked 10 months in advance.

Getting There & Around

The Greyhound bus stops at Field. For Lake O'Hara you can hike the 12.8 km in along the Cataract Brook Trail, or take the bus operated by the lodge, but you need transport to get to the bus stop. To book a seat on the bus see the information in the preceding Places to Stay section. Alternatively, show up at the bus stop and try for a standby place. A return ticket is $11. Ask at the park office for directions to the bus departure point.

KOOTENAY NATIONAL PARK

Kootenay National Park is solely in BC but is adjacent to Banff National Park and runs south from Yoho National Park. Hwy 93 (the Banff-Windermere Parkway) runs down the centre and is really the only road in the park. From the northern entrance at Vermillion Pass to Radium Hot Springs at the park's southern end there are campgrounds, points of interest, hiking trails and views of the valley along the Kootenay River.

Kootenay has a more moderate climate than the other Rocky Mountain parks and in the southern regions especially, summers can be hot and dry. It's the only national park in Canada to contain both glaciers and cactuses.

The Vermillion Pass Information Centre (no phone), eight km south of the pass, is open between June and September, Monday to Thursday from 9 am to 4 pm, and Friday to Sunday from 8 am to 6 pm. The West Gate Information Centre (☎ 347-9505), at the southern entrance, is open daily from 9 am to 9 pm June to early September, then weekends only till early October.

Stop at **Marble Canyon** for the 30-minute walk – it is a real adrenalin-rush. The trail follows the rushing Tokumm Creek, crisscrossing it frequently on small wooden bridges with longer and longer drops below as you head up to the waterfall. Two km further south there is a short, easy trail through forest to ochre pools known as the **Paint Pots**. For years, first the Kootenay people and then European settlers collected this orange and red-coloured earth to use as a colouring agent.

The four-hour Stanley Glacier Trail is the park classic. You can also try whitewater canoeing or rafting on the Kootenay River, or mountain biking in the Golden Triangle.

At the southern edge of the park where Hwy 93 joins Hwy 95, is **Radium Hot Springs**, with an odd blend of new and old, garish and tasteful architecture. Drop in to see shocking-haired Rolf Heer, a Swiss, known as the Woodcarver of Radium. His central place is impossible to miss. The hot springs, two km north of the town, are always worth a visit, though they can be busy in summer when they're open daily from 9 am to 9 pm. Admission is $4.

Places to Stay
The *Marble Canyon Campground*, across the road from the information centre, is good, but basic with no electricity or showers; it does have toilets and cold running water. *McLeod Meadows Campground*, in the park's south, is similar. *Redstreak Campground*, near the West Gate Information Centre, is fully serviced including showers. All sites are $12 and are less busy than Banff. If you're looking for a roof over your head, Radium Hot Springs has lots of motels, many in alpine style.

MT ASSINIBOINE PROVINCIAL PARK
Between Kootenay and Banff national parks is this lesser-known, 39-sq-km provincial park, part of the Rockies World Heritage designated area. The craggy summits of Mt Assiniboine (3618 metres), often referred to as Canada's Matterhorn, and its near neighbours are a magnet for climbers. The park also offers hiking and all the usual activities.

Access is by foot. From Hwy 93 two hiking trails start from near the highway at Vermillion Crossing in Kootenay National Park. From Banff National Park in Alberta a gravel road takes you close to the park through the ski resort of Sunshine Village. Another road leads from Spray Reservoir south of Canmore to the trailhead near Shark Mountain. The trails all meet at Lake Magog where there is the park headquarters, a campground, some cabins and the commercially operated Mt Assiniboine Lodge (☎ (403) 678-2883 in Banff). There's wilderness camping in other parts of the park.

RADIUM HOT SPRINGS TO CRANBROOK
South from Radium Hot Springs, Hwy 93/95 follows the Columbia River between the Purcell and Rocky mountains until the road splits shortly before Wasa. From there Hwy 95 heads south-west to Kimberley and Cranbrook, while Hwy 93 goes south-east to Fort Steele.

Invermere, 14 km south of Radium, is a small, local resort town, on the shores of Windermere Lake. The Travel Infocentre (☎ 342-6316), on the corner of 5A St and 7th Ave, is open daily May to September. **Mt Panorama**, in the Purcell Mountains 18 km south-west of Invermere, is BC's second world-class ski resort (after Whistler/Blackcomb). Mt Panorama has a spectacular setting and almost two-thirds of the downhill runs are ranked intermediate. **Fairmont Hot Springs** is another resort town mainly for residents with the hot springs as its focus. A single swim costs $5. It gets very crowded on weekends and public holidays and caters to families. At Skookumchuck, shortly before Wasa, a gravel road provides access eastward to **Top of the World Provincial Park**, where there are hiking trails and wilderness camping.

At 1117 metres, **Kimberley** is the highest city in Canada and the best place to stop for sustenance in the East Kootenays. Before 1973, Kimberley looked like what it is – a small mountain mining town – but was revamped to look like a Bavarian alpine village. Most of the downtown section, the Platzl, was transformed and with enough detail to make it interesting. The world's largest functioning **cuckoo clock** and several good restaurants are in this area. Accommodation can also be found here or around the outskirts. A restored mining train tootles 2.5 km around town. The Julyfest in Kimberley is a week of dancing, parades and lots of beer.

To the north-west, **Purcell Wilderness Conservancy** has hiking trails, fishing and wilderness camping; access is by a gravel road off Hwy 95A. In winter the skiing on nearby **North Star Mountain** is excellent.

The heritage park of **Fort Steele**, 20 km south-east of Wasa on Hwy 93, is a re-creation of an East Kootenay town in the late 1800s. Fort Steele was the first Northwest Mounted Police (later to become the RCMP) outpost in Western Canada and arose as a commercial, social and administrative centre when major silver and lead discoveries were made in 1892. It was named after Sam Steele who was the first commander of the fort. He and the police fort here eased tensions between settlers and Native Indians. Its fortunes turned when, in 1898, the BC Southern Railway bypassed it in favour of Cranbrook. Fort Steele has more than 60 restored and reconstructed homes and buildings. The Fort is open daily from 9.30 am to 8 pm and admission is $6.

CRANBROOK & AROUND

Sitting at the base of the Rocky Mountains, Cranbrook, with a population of 17,000, is about 30 km south-east of Kimberley, on the Crowsnest Hwy. The Travel Infocentre (☎ 426-5914), 2279 Cranbrook St North, is open year round. There's not a lot to see in the town itself, but it is located where you can enjoy many outdoor activities on the nearby lakes and mountains. The municipal campground with full facilities is central at 14th Ave and 1st St south, but you'll find much more pleasant surroundings (without showers) at **Jim Smith Lake** and **Moyie Lake** provincial parks south-west of town. Many motels line the highway at the northern end of town, and there are a few hotels downtown.

Fernie, sitting between the high peaks of Sisters Mountain and Mount Fernie, had a devastating fire in 1908 which resulted in a brick and stone building code. These fine turn-of-the-century buildings give the town an appearance unique in the East Kootenays.

Down near the US border, **Creston** is the centre of a green, fruit-growing district. Just off Canyon, the main street, at 11th Ave, take a look at the murals depicting the region's character. West of town along the highway, the wetlands of the Creston Valley Wildlife Centre are excellent for birding. Further out is the Kootenay Pass Summit with a provincial park and campground. Grizzlies and caribou frequent the area.

NELSON & AROUND

Nelson, 43 km north-west of Castlegar, at the junction of Hwy 6 and Hwy 3A, is beautifully situated on the shore of Kootenay Lake surrounded by the Selkirk Mountains. The very picturesque town, nestled in the hillside, with over 350 carefully preserved and restored turn-of-the-century buildings, is the perfect base for exploring the region. Its friendly, laid-back character and location make it the heart of the Kootenays. The large, active artists' colony adds a cultural and alternative flavour which helped induce Steve Martin to shoot his 1986 film *Roxanne* here.

Baker and Vernon Sts are the two main downtown thoroughfares. Baker St has many shops and restaurants, while Vernon St has government buildings including city hall, the courthouse and the post office. In summer the Travel Infocentre (☎ 352-3433), 225 Hall St, is open Monday to Friday from 8.30 am to 7 pm, Saturday and Sunday from 10 am to 6 pm; it closes on weekends the rest of the year. The post office, 514 Vernon St, is open Monday to Friday from 9 am to 4.30 pm. The Greyhound Bus Depot (☎ 352-3939), 1112 Lakeside Drive, is in the Chacko Mika Mall.

In town there's a walking trail through **Lakeside Park**, or, using the *Heritage Walking Tour* leaflet from the Travel Infocentre, you can take a look around the town's historical buildings. From the top of **Gyro Park** there are good views. **Streetcar No 23**, one of the town's originals, has been restored and now follows a track beside the lake from the bridge near Lakeside Park to the wharf at the bottom of Hall St.

Excellent outdoor possibilities abound. Practically in town is the climb to **Pulpit Rock** affording fine views. There is swimming, hiking, fishing and camping at **Kokanee Creek Provincial Park** north of town, and an **old growth forest** off the Kokanee Creek Road. A free ferry runs between Balfour and Kootenay Bay across scenic Kootenay Lake and the road then travels south along the lake. At **Ainsworth Hot Springs** on Hwy 31 not only is there the usual pool to soak in but also hot-water-filled caves. Good exploratory tours are offered at

BRITISH COLUMBIA

Cody Caves four km further north. Hiking and backcountry camping is superb in lake-filled **Kokanee Glacier Provincial Park**. The two-hour hike to Kokanee Lake is wonderful and can be continued to the glacier. Get all maps and information beforehand, facilities are non-existent. In quiet, attractive **Kaslo** with many Victorian-style buildings visit the old sternwheeler SS *Moyie* on Kootenay Lake and ask the locals how to find nearby Fletcher's Falls. These secluded, impressive falls are just a short drive or walk off the main road. Near Silverton, Sandon is a mining **ghost town**. In **New Denver** is a memorial centre which commemorates the displacement of thousands of Japanese-Canadians who were moved to internment camps in the area during WWII.

In winter the attraction of this area is skiing. You can go downhill at **Morning Mountain**, north-west of town, off Hwy 3A; or at **Whitewater Ski Area**, 19 km south-east, off Hwy 6. The latter also has well developed cross-country skiing; for wilderness skiing head for Kokanee Glacier.

Places to Stay & Eat

In Nelson, convenient camping is available at *City Tourist Park* (☎ 352-9031), downtown at the corner of High and Willow Sts. The central *Dancing Bear* (☎ 352-7573), 171 Baker St, is an associate-HI hostel that was completely and very thoughtfully renovated in 1995 under new owners. It's comfortable, immaculate and offers kitchen and laundry facilities. It makes a good base for spending a few days walking and exploring this superbly scenic, under-visited region. Prices are $17/20 members/non-members and there are family rooms and doubles.

For B&Bs ask at the Travel Infocentre or contact Lake City B&B Registry (☎ 352-5253), which has rooms starting at $35/55. There are many motels along the highway at the northern end of town, and some hotels downtown. One of cheapest is the *Lord Nelson Hotel* (☎ 352-7211), 616 Vernon St, with singles/doubles from $55/65. Rooms

are clean and have TVs and telephones and there's a bar and coffee shop.

For breakfast don't miss *Mimi's*, 702 Vernon St, and their Belgian waffles or omelettes. The *Book Garden* on the corner of Josephine St and Victoria St is a comfortable cafe. *Rosy's*, on the highway on the east side of town, is a cappuccino bar with food and a laundromat.

NAKUSP & AROUND

Quiet Nakusp, sitting on Upper Arrow Lake, is the main town in the valley south of Revelstoke, east of the Okanagan Valley. The dry, picturesque valley follows a chain of lakes between the Monashee and Selkirk mountain ranges. This is a very attractive portion of the province which benefits from not having the high profile and hence major attention of some of the better-known districts.

In town are a couple of good little cafes on Broadway St and a campground. The *Selkirk Inn* (☎ 265-3666) on 6th Ave is a moderate place for spending the night at $40/45. About 12 km north-east of Nakusp, off Hwy 23, are the tranquil **Nakusp Hot Springs** set in the mountains and complete with classical music. They're open daily year round and have a cramped campground with full facilities including showers for $12. Ask at the tourist office about trails to undeveloped hot springs in the woods. Arrow Lakes Bus Lines runs between Vernon and Nakusp three times a week in each direction stopping at the Kuskanax Lodge in town.

South-west of Nakusp, Hwy 6 heads to Vernon in the Okanagan Valley, going over the 1189-metre Monashee Pass. Near Vernon, the road goes through beautiful country scenery of small farms and wooded hills. There are campgrounds and a few small provincial parks along this route.

South-east of Nakusp, Hwy 6 heads to Castlegar and Nelson, through the Slocan Valley past rugged **Valhalla Provincial Park** with hiking trails and wilderness camping mainly accessed by boat; canoes can be rented. **Slocan Lake** provides excellent canoeing and the Slocan River, from the town of Slocan south to the Kootenay River, has Grade 3 rapids in its upper sections for the whitewater canoeist and less-demanding water further down. *Valhalla Lodge & Tipi Retreat* (☎ 365-3226) at Slocan Lake has teepees for rent at $98 for two people for two nights including a boat trip to the site, a canoe, communal kitchen and a sauna.

North, Highway 23 runs along pretty Upper Arrow Lake to the free ferry at Galena Bay to connect with Revelstoke.

CASTLEGAR

Castlegar, a sprawling town with a population of 7000, sits on the Kootenay River at the southern end of Lower Arrow Lake, at the junction of the Crowsnest Hwy and Hwy 22. Recent development has robbed the town of any charm or character it may once have had; stop instead in Nelson where the more limited growth has been achieved with a sense of environmental harmony and history. The Travel Infocentre (☎ 365-6313), 1995 6th Ave, corner of 20th St is open year round. The post office (☎ 365-7237) is at 1011 4th St, and the Greyhound Bus Depot (☎ 365-7744) is at 365 Columbia Ave.

This is an area where many members of the Russian Christian pacifist sect, the Doukhobors, settled at the beginning of the 1900s. Borscht is available at every restaurant. The reconstructed **Doukhobor village** on the east side of the Columbia River off Highway 3 is little more than a couple of buildings and the small museum can be given a miss. Next door there is a restaurant serving Doukhobor specialities.

Seventeen km north-west of Castlegar, on Lower Arrow Lake, is 2.25-sq-km **Syringa Creek Provincial Park**, open from April to October. It has hiking, fishing, swimming, sailing and beaches. The campground is open May to October with sites for $13.

TRAIL & AROUND

Trail is an industrial town 27 km south-west of Castlegar, at the junction of the Crowsnest Hwy and Hwy 3A. It's home to Cominco, the world's largest smelter of silver, zinc and lead, whose enormous mishmash of buildings dominate the skyline. Those, together with the houses squeezed along the cliffs by the Columbia River, give the town a strikingly different character.

The Travel Infocentre (☎ 368-3144), 843 Rossland Ave, is open year round. The post office (☎ 364-2585), is located at 805 Spokane St and the Greyhound Bus Depot (☎ 368-8400), right downtown, is at 1355 Bay St.

There are free tours of the **Cominco smelter** which can be booked through the Travel Infocentre, and the museum on Victoria St by the bridge provides background. The many Italian migrants who came here at the end of the 1800s to work in the mines have left their mark and their descendants in Trail.

There are several provincial parks close by. Try **Nancy Greene Provincial Park**, south-west; or **Champion Lakes Provincial Park**, north-west of Trail, off Hwy 23. Both have hiking, swimming, fishing and campsites. Nancy Greene, a former Canadian Olympic medal winner, remains one of the country's best-known ski heroes. Off Hwy 3B, about 10 km north-west of Trail, is the **Red Mountain Ski Resort** (☎ 362-7384 in Rossland) which has 30 downhill runs with a vertical drop of 850 metres, and cross-country trails.

South-west, the once ore-rich mines of **Rossland** that fed Trail can be seen. There is a small mining museum, gold-mine tours in the ancient volcano, a tearoom and the tourist office in town.

Further west, the lovely **Christina Lake** is a good place to stay for a day or two, especially if you are camping, and the nearby small town of **Grand Forks** is known for borscht and sunshine. Russian food is offered through the area and campgrounds and motels can be easily found along the highway. The road running along the US border cuts through rich farmland and then rises into the Okanagan Highlands before descending through the hills of Bridesville into Osoyoos.

BRITISH COLUMBIA

North-Eastern British Columbia

North-Eastern BC is a largely undeveloped, sparsely populated region dominated by the Rocky Mountains to the west and south, and by the Interior Plain to the north and east.

Two major highways connect this region with other parts of the country: east-west the Yellowhead Hwy (Hwy 16) runs between the Alberta border and Prince Rupert in the Pacific north-west; Hwy 97 connects the south of the province with Dawson Creek where it becomes part of the Alaska Hwy and heads north-west toward the Yukon. The two highways meet at Prince George, the largest town in the region. Hwy 29 connects the major settlements circling Dawson Creek. The VIA Rail line follows the Yellowhead Hwy.

Like the south-eastern corner of the province, the area around Dawson Creek is on Mountain Standard Time.

PRINCE GEORGE

Prince George was established as Fort George by Simon Fraser for the North West Company in 1807. Now known as 'The Gateway to the North', it is not an interesting or attractive town but does serve as a useful crossroads point. BC Rail and VIA Rail meet here, as do the Fraser and Nechako rivers, the Yellowhead Hwy (Hwy 16) and Hwy 97.

The town of 73,000 people sprawls over a large area. To serve the through traffic there are dozens of motels and several hotels. Pulp & paper is an important industry. The university, with a specialty in Native Indian affairs, has helped to diversify the city. Prices tend to be high in this area, especially for food.

Orientation & Information

Hwy 97 from Cache Creek cuts through the centre of town on its way north to Dawson Creek and the Alaska Hwy. Hwy 97 between Cache Creek and Prince George is also known as the Cariboo Hwy and is part of the Goldrush Trail, which begins north of Hope.

The Yellowhead Hwy (Hwy 16) runs east-west through town: westward is the long, winding route to Prince Rupert on the coast; eastward, it goes through Jasper to Edmonton. From Prince George, it's 377 km to Jasper, 734 km to Prince Rupert and 781 km to Vancouver.

The downtown area is small, with little character. The main roads running east-west are 2nd, 3rd and 4th Aves, parallel to the train tracks. The main north-south thoroughfare is Victoria St, which also forms part of the Yellowhead Hwy; Patricia Blvd, which becomes 15th Ave, is also a major street.

The Travel Infocentre (☎ 562-3700), 1198 Victoria St, on the corner of Patricia Blvd, is open Monday to Friday 8.30 to 6 pm. A second infocentre (☎ 563-5493) sits four km south of downtown on the corner of Hwy 97 and the Yellowhead Hwy and operates daily during summer. The hours here are 9 am to 8 pm. The main post office (☎ 561-5184), 1323 5th Ave, on the corner of Quebec St, is open Monday to Friday from 8.30 am to 5 pm.

Mosquito Books (☎ 563-6495), 1209 5th Ave on the corner of Dominion St, has a good selection of travel guides and maps. There's a laundromat on George St near the corner of 2nd Ave.

Things to See & Do

The **Fort George Regional Museum** (☎ 562-1612), in Fort George Park, south-east of the downtown area, on the corner of 20th Ave and Queensway was renovated and expanded in 1995. It's still a small museum and takes about a half an hour to see. Best is the section on the pioneers and European settlement and development. There are a few Carrier, Cree and Kwakiutl artefacts and a hands-on section geared to kids. Unless you're a real buff it probably isn't worth the $3 given some of the other museums around the province. The museum open daily from 9 am to 5 pm.

There are many parks in Prince George. One close to the downtown area is **Cottonwood Island Nature Park**, north between the railway tracks and the river. **Northwood**

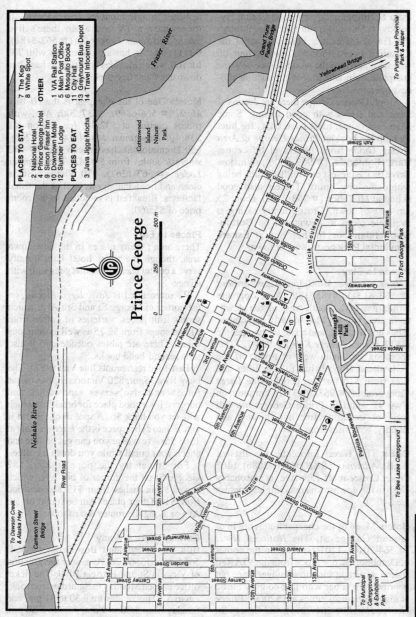

Prince George

PLACES TO STAY
2 National Hotel
4 Prince George Hotel
9 Simon Fraser Inn
10 Downtown Motel
12 Slumber Lodge

PLACES TO EAT
3 Java Jigga Mocha
7 The Keg
8 White Spot

OTHER
1 VIA Rail Station
5 Main Post Office
6 Mosquito Books
11 City Hall
13 Greyhound Bus Depot
14 Travel Infocentre

0   250   500 m

Fraser River

Cottonwood
Island
Nature Park

Grand Trunk Pacific Bridge

Yellowhead Bridge

To Purden Lake Provincial Park & Jasper

Nechako River

Cameron Street Bridge

To Dawson Creek & Alaska Hwy

River Road

Connaught Hill Park

Queensway

Patricia Boulevard

To Fort George Park

To Bee Lazee Campground

To Municipal Campground & Exhibition Park

BRITISH COLUMBIA

Pulp & Timber and Northwood Central Plywoods (☎ 562-3700) run free tours through the Travel Infocentre. Also ask about the Canadian Forest Products all-day tour on which you go into the woods to see how the complete pulp and timber production process operates.

Around Prince George there are dozens of lakes and rivers with good fishing. Some have camp sites; most have boats for hire. Pick up the booklet *Prince George & Area Hiking Guide* from the Travel Infocentre. **Hart Highlands** (☎ 962-8006), Winslow Drive, is the closest downhill ski area being within the city limits. There's also good skiing at **Mt Tabor** (☎ 963-7542), about 25 km east of town. Cross-country skiing is available close to downtown on **Cottonwood Island** or further out at **Eskers Provincial Park** north-west of town.

Places to Stay

Prince George Municipal Campground (☎ 563-8131), 4188 18th Ave, opposite Exhibition Park, south-west of the downtown area, is open May to early September. It has hot showers, and a site for two people is $12. *Prince George KOA* (☎ 964-7272) is about six km south-west of town, off the Yellowhead Hwy. It has full facilities and sites from $16 for two people. *Bee Lazee Campground* (☎ 963-7623), 15 km south on Hwy 97 south of Prince George, has full facilities including free hot showers and laundry, with sites from $12.

B&Bs The Travel Infocentre has lists of B&Bs. *Adrienne's B&B* (☎ 561-2086), 1467 Fraser Crescent off 15th Ave, is reasonably close to the downtown area. Singles/doubles are $40/50.

Hotels Many of the cheaper hotels are in or around George St. The *National Hotel* (☎ 564-7010), 1201 1st Ave, on the corner of Dominion St, one block from the VIA Rail station, is alright for a low-budget place but is principally a bar with live country music at night. Singles/doubles are $20/30. *Prince George Hotel* (☎ 564-7211), 487 George St,

is better. Singles/doubles cost $36/39; all rooms have a TV and again there's live music. The *Simon Fraser Inn* (☎ 562-3181), 600 Quebec St, has air-con rooms with TV for $60, which includes breakfast. It has a bar downstairs and free parking.

Motels One of the cheapest is the *Hi-Way Motel* (☎ 564-6869), 1737 20th Ave, with rooms starting at $32/36; for air-con it's $38/40. *Downtown Motel* (☎ 563-9241), 650 Dominion St, has air-con and TV and singles/doubles from $40/42. The *Slumber Lodge* (☎ 563-1267), 910 Victoria St, is clean and has a laundry as well as the usual facilities. Breakfast is included in the room price of $55/60.

Places to Eat

There aren't many places in the downtown area, though the older hotel bars usually serve a decent cheap meal that goes well with a beer.

Recommended is *Java Jigga Mocha*, on the corner of George St and 3rd Ave, which serves fruit juices, varieties of coffee from $1 and soups from $2.75 as well as delicious cakes. There are tables outside and it also sells second-hand books.

Fast-food restaurants line Victoria St. The busy *White Spot*, 820 Victoria St, has pastas for $8 and also serves sandwiches and burgers. It's a good place for breakfast which will set you back $6. A spot to check out if you're into cyberspace is the *Internet Café* at 1363 5th Ave where you can get on line and check your email while you down a coffee.

For dinner try the popular *Keg*, 582 George St on the corner of 6th Ave, which serves steak dishes from $17 and seafood from $18. Other places can be found on 5th Ave or along the routes out of town.

Getting There & Away

Bus The Greyhound Bus Depot (☎ 564-5454) is at 1566 12th Ave, near the junction of Victoria St and Patricia Blvd. The ticket office is open Monday to Saturday from 5.30 am to 5.30 pm, and from 8.30 to 11 pm, and Sunday from 5.30 to 9 am, 3.30 to 5.30 pm, and 8.30 to 11 pm. The station has a cafeteria and left-luggage lockers. Buses to Jasper and Edmonton leave at 6 am and 10 pm; those to Vancouver leave at 6.30 and 10.15 am, 5 and 10.45 pm; to Prince Rupert at 7.45 am and 10.15 pm. Some one-way fares (including tax) are Vancouver $86, Jasper $45, and Prince Rupert $83.

Train The VIA Rail station (☎ 564-5233, 1-800-561-8630), 1300 1st Ave near the top of Quebec St, is open Wednesday, Friday and Sunday from 7 pm to 3 am, and Tuesday from 7 pm to 1 am; it's closed Monday, Thursday and Saturday. There are three trains a week west to Prince Rupert and another three a week east to Jasper and Edmonton. The one-way fare (including tax) to Prince Rupert is $82, to Jasper $63 and to Edmonton $149. Remember that you must overnight it in Jasper and then make a connection onward. The BC Rail station (☎ 561-4033) is south-east of town, over the Fraser River, at Terminal Blvd, off Hwy 97. The train goes daily at 7.15 am south to Vancouver, following the historic Cariboo Trail through Quesnel, an old mining town, to Lillooet and North Vancouver. The one-way fare to Vancouver is $171 and includes three meals. There is no transportation-only ticket.

Hitching Hitching is not allowed within the city limits. It's OK to hitch between Prince George and Prince Rupert, although the weather is unpredictable. There are plenty of places to camp along the way, but many campgrounds close after Labour Day (the first weekend in September).

Getting Around
Contact Prince George Transit (☎ 563-0011), 1041 Great St, open Monday to Friday from 8 am to 4.30 pm, for information about local buses; or get the leaflet *Prince George Rider's Guide* from the Travel Infocentre. A one-way fare in the central zone is $1.25.

PRINCE GEORGE TO SMITHERS
From Prince George the Yellowhead Hwy (Hwy 16) heads west to Smithers, Terrace and Prince Rupert, from where most people pick up ferries either south to Vancouver Island and Washington state or north to Alaska. The road travels through a corridor of forest interspersed with lakes, rivers and farmland. (See also the Prince Rupert to New Hazelton section later for details.)

The first settlement of any real size is **Vanderhoof**, mainly a service centre for the area and most noted for its annual international airshow held the fourth weekend in July. East of here, Hwy 27 heads 66 km north to **Fort St James National Historic Site**, a former Hudson's Bay Company trading post on the south-eastern shore of Stuart Lake. The nearby provincial parks at Paarens Beach and Sowchea Bay have camp sites (no showers).

The other towns along the highway have the usual run of campgrounds and motels. Burns Lake is the centre of the lakes district, a canoeing and recreation area. You can get a taste of the wilderness by heading north to **Babine Lake**. There are hiking trails in **Red Bluff Provincial Park**.

Smithers, in the pretty Bulkley Valley, is another centre for outdoor activity. There's hiking, climbing and skiing on Hudson Bay Mt, 24 km south of the junction with the Yellowhead Hwy, and whitewater rafting and canoeing on the Bulkley River. The Travel Infocentre (☎ 847-9854), 1425 Main St, has the details. Motels line the highway. If the weather is good the road toward Terrace provides spectacular scenery.

PRINCE GEORGE TO DAWSON CREEK
As you travel north from Prince George the mountains and forests give way to gentle rolling hills and farmland, until near Dawson Creek the landscape resembles more the prairies of Alberta. For the first 150 km the road passes **Summit**, **Bear** and **MacLeod** lakes with provincial parks and camping along the way. North of MacLeod Lake, Hwy 39 heads north to Mackenzie which sits on the southern shores of the immense

Williston Lake. Nearby there is skiing at **Powder King Ski Resort** (☎ 997-6323) on Azu Mountain.

From **Chetwynd** you can take Hwy 29 north past Hudson's Hope (a 20-minute drive from the eastern arm of Williston Lake) to join the Alaska Hwy north of Fort St John.

DAWSON CREEK

Dawson Creek, a city of 11,000 people, 412 km north of Prince George on Hwy 97, is most notable as the starting point – 'Mile 0' – for the Alaska or Alcan (short for Alaska-Canada) Hwy. The Alaska Hwy from Dawson Creek goes via Watson Lake and Whitehorse in the Yukon all the way to Fairbanks in Alaska. The Dawson Creek Travel Infocentre (☎ 782-9595), 900 Alaska Ave, can give you the details. It's open daily in summer from 8 am to 8 pm; in winter Monday to Friday from 9 am to 5 pm. The best place to eat is the *Alaska Café & Pub*, 10209 10th St downtown near the 'Mile 0' marker. Pasta dishes start at $5.50. It also has accommodation (☎ 782-2625) from $36/42. One traveller has recommended the *Dawson Creek Bakery*, 1019 102nd Ave, for its donuts and coffee.

DAWSON CREEK TO THE YUKON

Heading north-west from Dawson Creek, the landscape again changes as the prairies are left behind and the Alaska Hwy crosses the Peace River on its way into the foothills of the Rocky Mountains. Except for Fort St John and Fort Nelson, most of the towns on the highway usually have little more than one or two service stations, campgrounds or lodgings.

Fort St John's main function is as a service centre for the oil and gas industries and the surrounding farms. The Travel Infocentre (☎ 785-6037) and the Fort St John-North Peace Museum are together at 9323 100th St, the town's main street. **Fort Nelson** has one museum at the western end of town, and shops, restaurants and motels strung out along the highway. At **Mile 244** (393 km from Dawson Creek), past Fort Nelson, the

Liard Hwy (Hwy 77) heads north to the Northwest Territories.

At **Stone Mountain Provincial Park** there are hiking trails with wilderness camping and a campground with sites for $9.50. The moose in the park can often be seen eating nonchalantly by the side of the road. The 'stone mountain' in question is Mt St Paul (2127 metres).

Muncho Lake Provincial Park has several lodging and camping areas plus wild-life (mainly goats), swimming in the emerald-green lake, and hiking trails. 'Muncho' means 'big lake' in the Tagish language and at 12 km long it's one of the largest natural lakes in the Rockies. This park is part of the northernmost section of the Rockies which, ending at Liard River 60 km north-west, do not continue northward into the Yukon and Alaska. The mountains which do extend northward, the Mackenzies, are geologically different.

SOUTH OF PRINCE GEORGE

South of Prince George, Hwy 97 follows the Goldrush Trail through the northern reaches of the goldrush district known as Cariboo country.

Quesnel

Quesnel's setting at the confluence of the Fraser and Quesnel rivers, and the carefully cultivated flowers in the streets can't disguise the fact that this is first and foremost a logging town. The pulp mills dominate the townscape and the smells coming from them permeate the air. The observation tower at the east end of town looks over the most concentrated industrial area for wood products in North America. However, it's worth stopping at the Travel Infocentre (☎ 992-8716), 703 Carson Ave, to get the lowdown on the area's main attractions: the Alexander Mackenzie Trail and the gold rush trail to Barkerville Historic Park and Bowron Lake Provincial Park.

Barkerville Historic Park

This restored goldrush town is 89 km east of Quesnel at the end of Hwy 26.

@@@@@@@@@@@@@@@@@@@@@@@@@@@@@@@@@@@@@@@

Cariboo Trail
Between 1858 and 1861 the Cariboo Trail, now Hwy 97, was pushed north from Kamloops to Quesnel. It was lined with hastily built towns and gold prospectors came from around the world. In 1862, a Cornishman, Billy Barker, hit the jackpot, making $1000 in the first two days of his claim. Soon Barkerville sprang up, to become the largest city west of Chicago and north of San Francisco. The big boom was instrumental in British Columbia's becoming a crown colony in 1858. ∎

@@@@@@@@@@@@@@@@@@@@@@@@@@@@@@@@@@@@@@@

Today, you can see Barkerville as it was, with its general store, hotel, shops and, of course, saloon. In the Theatre Royal, dancing shows are staged in the manner the miners once whistled at. There is also a museum that gives some of the background story and displays artefacts. It's open daily in summer from 8 am to 8 pm. Try your luck panning for gold at the site and maybe you'll have a town named after you. Admission to the park, good for two days, is $5.50.

There are two campgrounds with sites for $12, and facilities include showers. Or you could stay at Wells, eight km west of Barkerville, which has a commercial campground and several motels. There's no bus to Barkerville so you'll have to hitch if you don't have a car.

Bowron Lake Provincial Park
There is an excellent circular canoe route in Bowron Lake Provincial Park, near Barkerville. A number of lakes, separated by rapids and portages, form a connecting route around the perimeter of the park. The 116-km route takes an average of seven days to complete, no more than 50 individuals are allowed to start the route each day and canoeists must register at the park registration centre before heading out. Mountains in and around the park are about 2000 metres high. Access to the park is along a gravel road that leaves Hwy 26 just before you get to Barkerville. There are tent sites for $9.50. Attractive, *Becker's Lodge* (☎ 992-8864), made from logs, has rooms, a restaurant, camping and canoe rentals.

Alexander Mackenzie Trail
Heading north-west from Quesnel, this refurbished route follows ancient trails from the Fraser River west to Bella Coola, on the Pacific Ocean. Mackenzie made the first recorded crossing of continental North America here in 1793 in his search for a supply route to the Pacific Ocean. His graffiti can still be seen carved in a rock near Bella Coola. This 420-km trail winds its way through forest and mountains and is a tough 16-day walk. At least one food drop is required. You can do some of the more accessible segments for a few days: for example, the section through the southern end of Tweedsmuir Provincial Park and day hikes from Quesnal. For detailed trail guides contact Alexander Mackenzie Trail Association, PO Box 425, Station A, Kelowna, V1Y 7P1.

Pacific North-West

North-west BC is a huge, little-developed, scarcely populated region whose remoteness is one of its main attractions. This largely inaccessible area is one of the last true wilderness regions of North America. Various Native peoples have long inhabited the area and to this day they make up a considerable percentage of the permanent residents. The land is dominated by forest, several mountain ranges, and scores of lakes and swift rivers. The Yellowhead Hwy (Hwy 16) runs east to Prince George; the mostly gravel Cassiar Hwy heads north to the Yukon.

PRINCE RUPERT
After Vancouver, Rupert, as it's called, is the largest city on the BC coast. Originally built

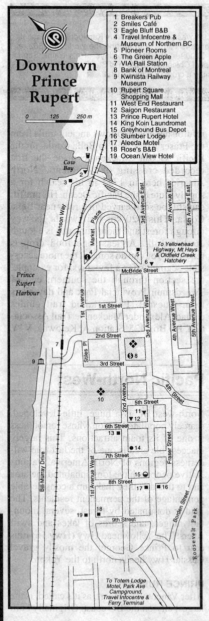

Downtown Prince Rupert

0   125   250 m

1 Breakers Pub
2 Smiles Café
3 Eagle Bluff B&B
4 Travel Infocentre & Museum of Northern BC
5 Pioneer Rooms
6 The Green Apple
7 VIA Rail Station
8 Bank of Montreal
9 Kwinista Railway Museum
10 Rupert Square Shopping Mall
11 West End Restaurant
12 Saigon Restaurant
13 Prince Rupert Hotel
14 King Koin Laundromat
15 Greyhound Bus Depot
16 Slumber Lodge
17 Aleeda Motel
18 Rose's B&B
19 Ocean View Hotel

Cow Bay

Manson Way

Market Place

3rd Avenue East
4th Avenue East
5th Avenue East

To Yellowhead Highway, Mt Hays & Oldfield Creek Hatchery

McBride Street

Prince Rupert Harbour

1st Avenue

1st Street

Stiles Pl

2nd Street

3rd Street

2nd Avenue

3rd Avenue West
4th Avenue West
5th Avenue West

4th Street

5th Street

2nd Ave

6th Street

Fraser Street

7th Street

Bill Murray Drive

1st Avenue West

8th Street

9th Street

Borden Street

Roosevelt Park

To Totem Lodge Motel, Park Ave Campground, Travel Infocentre & Ferry Terminal

in the early 1900s as the western terminal of the Grand Trunk Pacific Railway, it's now the fishing centre for the Pacific north-west, but its port also handles timber, minerals and grain. Once known as the world's halibut capital, it has adopted a new title, the 'City of Rainbows', which is one way of saying that it rains a lot. The area has one of the highest precipitation rates in all of Canada. Despite this, the town's setting can look magnificent and when it's not raining, misty, foggy or under heavy cloud, you'll appreciate it. Surrounded by mountains, sitting at the mouth of the Skeena River, looking out at the fjord-like coastline, the area is ruggedly beautiful.

Prince Rupert is a good starting point for trips to Alaska and the Queen Charlotte Islands. Many people, mainly young, arrive here in summer looking for work; and this town with around 17,000 inhabitants fills its needs quickly. Remember, too, that with the influx of tourists, accommodation in July and August can be difficult to find.

Orientation & Information

Prince Rupert is on Kaien Island and is connected to the mainland by a bridge. The Yellowhead Hwy passes right through the downtown area, becoming McBride St then 2nd Ave which, along with 3rd Ave, forms the downtown core. McBride St divides the city between east and west. The ferry terminal is in Fairview Bay, three km south-west of the centre of town.

The Travel Infocentre (☎ 624-5637), open daily 9 am to 9 pm in summer, and Monday to Saturday 10 am to 5 pm in winter, is beside the Courthouse at the corner of McBride St and 1st Ave East. There's another one at Park Ave Campground, which is south of town, about one km from the ferry terminal. It's open till midnight on nights when the ferry arrives/departs.

The Bank of Montreal (☎ 624-9191), 180-309 2nd Ave West, only charges $2 for cashing as many travellers' cheques as you wish. The post office (☎ 627-3085) is in the Rupert Square Shopping Mall on 2nd Ave West. It's on the second floor at the back of one of the shops – you'll have to ask. If you need a laundry try King Koin laundromat with a small coffee bar at 745 2nd Ave West on the corner of 7th St. The general hospital (☎ 624-2171) is south-west of the downtown area, in Roosevelt Park.

Things to See & Do
The **Museum of Northern BC** (☎ 624-3207) at time of writing was beside the downtown Travel Infocentre at McBride and 1st Ave but is slated to move across the street. It contains a good collection of Tsimshian art and craftwork, including masks, carvings and beadwork. It also has an art gallery, books for sale and a room showing films on a TV screen of the history of the area. It's open Monday to Saturday 9 am to 8 pm, and Sunday 9 am to 5 pm through the summer. Hours are reduced in winter when it's closed Sunday. Admission is free. The museum also organises daily boat tours to archaeological sites in the harbour and visits two villages. Cost is $20 which includes an introductory slide show. Don't miss the cedar shed behind the museum where Native Indian carvers and artisans work at any given time on totems, masks, drums or jewellery in wood, argillite or gold.

Totems can be seen all around town. Many of them are replicas of very well known traditional works. The tourist office offers free guided heritage **walking tours** around town.

Seashore Charters (☎ 624-5645) offers whale-watching trips, various tours and also rents bicycles. It has a ticket booth beside the museum. The **Kwinitsa Railway Museum** from 1911, is opposite the VIA Rail station on the waterfront.

A number of **hiking trails** can be found in and around town. One goes up 732-metre **Mt Hays** situated just south of the ferry terminals. On a clear day you can see local islands, the Queen Charlotte Islands and even Alaska. Beginning at a parking lot on the Yellowhead Hwy, three km south of town just past the industrial park, trails lead to **Mt Oldfield**, **Tall Trees** (leading to old cedars) and **Butze Rapids**. The rapids walk is a flat four km loop to Grassy Bay, the others are more demanding. The Infocentre has details on these and others.

Along Wantage Rd (take the turning after the civic centre), you can visit the **Oldfield Creek Hatchery** (☎ 624-6733) a small salmon hatchery. It's open daily in summer from 8 am to 4 pm and there are tours.

About 20 km south of Prince Rupert, **North Pacific Cannery Village Museum** (☎ 628-3538) at 1889 Skeena Drive in the town of Port Edward, gives a history of fishing and canning along the Skeena River. It's open in summer daily from 10 am to 7 pm and admission is $5. This designated historic site was the coast's first cannery village. Try not to say 'something smells fishy around here'.

About 16 km east of town **Diana Lake** and **Prudhomme Lake** are two provincial parks where you can picnic, swim, fish, hike or take out a canoe.

Canada's first **grizzly bear preserve**, the remote, rugged Khutzeymateen Valley, is 80 km north along the coast. Two to 10-day eco-tours by boat or plane and kayak are available from Rupert.

Places to Stay
Camping You can camp beside the lake at *Prudhomme Lake Provincial Park* (☎ 847-7320), open April to November, for $9.50. *Park Ave Campground* (☎ 624-5861), near the ferry terminal, has 87 sites, hot showers, laundry and flush toilets. A tent site for two people costs $9; in summer on ferry nights it's best to book ahead.

B&Bs There are several B&Bs in Prince Rupert. One with a good location is *Eagle Bluff B&B* (☎ 627-4955), 100 Cow Bay Rd down by the marina. It has five rooms beginning at $45/50 for a single/double with shared bath, going up to a suite for $70 which can accommodate six people. Also central is *Rose's B&B* (☎ 624-5539), the pink place at 943 1st Ave West, with rooms for $40/50. Rose speaks French and provides free bicycles. There are also kitchen facilities.

BRITISH COLUMBIA

Hotels The cheapest place in town is *Pioneer Rooms* (☎ 624-2334), 167 3rd Ave East, and is the nearest thing in Prince Rupert to a travellers' hostel. It's an excellent and immaculate central place with a range of prices. A single with a curtain door is $15, a lockable wooden door $25. There are also double and twin rooms, the latter being the most expensive at $35. Bathrooms are shared. There's a cooking area/common room just inside the door and you're free to use the barbecue and back yard and even pick the salmonberries. The basic but friendly *Ocean View Hotel* (☎ 624-6259/9950), opposite Rose's B&B at 950 1st Ave West, has rooms for $30/35. The shower and toilet are shared. *Prince Rupert Hotel* (☎ 624-6711), on the corner of 2nd Ave and 6th St, has air-con rooms for $66/76, a licensed restaurant and free parking.

Motels *Aleeda Motel* (☎ 627-1367), 900 3rd Ave West, has rooms for $50/60 with free parking underneath. The *Slumber Lodge*, close by at 909 3rd Ave West, offers free breakfasts in its price of $60. *Totem Lodge Motel* (☎ 624-6761), 1335 Park Ave, is good but because it's close to the ferry terminal gets booked out early, and rooms cost $65.

Places to Eat
West End Restaurant, 610 3rd Ave West, opens at 8 am and is one of several restaurants in the same street offering Chinese as well as Western food. Cereal is $2 and omelettes cost from $4.50. *Charlie's* in the Prince Rupert Hotel, opens at 6 am and has continental breakfasts for $3.65.

With fishing a major local industry it's not surprising to find seafood on just about every menu. Salmon and halibut are headliners. Top billing goes to the storied *Smiles Café*, 113 George Hills Way, on the waterfront at Cow Bay. It serves a variety of fresh ocean fare but steaks and sandwiches, too. Lunch prices on the seafood are a couple of dollars less than at dinner and there are daily specials. A salmon dinner goes for $15. Flip over the placemat for a look at the 1945 menu when a hamburger could be had for 25 cents.

It's open daily and serves breakfast from 10 am.

For fish & chips try the *Green Apple*, 310 McBride St, on the corner of 3rd Ave East. The *Saigon Restaurant*, on the corner of 2nd Ave and 6th St, adds a Vietnamese choice in town. Most dishes are about $7.50 and there are some vegetarian meals.

Two good neighbourhood pubs worth trying for a meal and a beer are *Breakers*, a busy place with a patio close to Smiles Café, and *Solly's*, at 2209 Seal Cove Rd, about four km north of the downtown area. Solly's is out by the float plane base and tends to serve primarily local people.

Overlooking the water and docks the *Cow Bay Café* on Cow Bay Rd serves coffees and desserts and a range of wines.

Cheap food can be found at many places in the Rupert Mall.

Getting There & Away
Air Air BC (☎ 624-4554), 112 6th St, is near the Prince Rupert Hotel. Canadian Airlines (☎ 624-9181) is at 200-500 2nd Ave. With Air BC the standard one-way fare to Vancouver, including tax, is $350.

Bus The Greyhound Bus Depot (☎ 624-5090), in 3rd Ave between 7th and 8th Sts, is open Monday to Friday from 8.30 am to 12.30 pm, and 3 to 8 pm, and weekends and holidays from 9 am to 1.15 pm, and 6 to 8 pm. It has left-luggage lockers. Buses head east twice a day, at 11.15 am and 8 pm, buses arrive in Prince Rupert at 9.40 am and 6.30 pm. The fare, including tax, to Prince George is $82, while to Vancouver it's $165.

Train The VIA Rail station (☎ 1-800-561-8630) is at 1150 Station St, by the harbour. The office is open Monday, Thursday and Saturday from 1 to 4.30 pm and Tuesday, Friday and Sunday from 9 am to 12.30 pm. The inbound train arrives Monday, Thursday and Saturday at 3.40 pm; the outbound one leaves Tuesday, Friday and Sunday at 11.30 am. The standard, one-way fare to Prince George is $83, but if you book seven days in advance you can get a 40% reduction.

Ferry From Prince Rupert, Alaska State Ferries head north through the Alaskan Panhandle. First stop is Ketchikan, but you can go north past Wrangell, Petersburg and Juneau to Skagway, where the Klondike Hwy comes south from Whitehorse in the Yukon. Various commercial cruise lines do the route as well, but they're all costly. The ferry systems are much cheaper and you'll see pretty much the same things.

Alaska State Ferries (☎ 627-1744), also called Alaska Marine Hwy, has its office – open from 7 am to 2 pm (or later if there's a delay in loading the ferry) – at the ferry terminal. The one-way fare to Skagway is $124 and $286 for a car. Meals and berths are extra. If you're travelling by car or RV you should book well ahead. You can go standby of course but you may not get on; if that happens your name goes on the waiting list for the next boat. If you do get on they warn you that local (that is Alaskan) traffic has precedence and they may put you off ('bump you') temporarily at one of the stops along the way.

The route between the Alaskan Panhandle and Washington state is known as the Inside Passage. It's a long, expensive trip but offers beautiful scenery past many bays, inlets, islands and small Native Indian settlements. It's not uncommon to see seals, herds of sea lions or pods of killer whales. You can take just part of the trip rather than the whole voyage.

BC Ferries (☎ 624-9627) run the MV *Queen of the North* and MV *Queen of Prince Rupert* between Rupert and Vancouver Island. Reservations are a good idea, especially if you're taking a vehicle. (See the Getting There & Away section under Port Hardy for more details.)

If you're coming from Port Hardy and you intend to continue north to Alaska by ferry then you should remember that the schedules of BC Ferries and Alaska State Ferries do not coincide and that you will have to spend at least one night in Prince Rupert.

BC Ferries also operates between Prince Rupert and Skidegate in the Queen Charlotte Islands; there are daily sailings five days a week in each direction through July and August then service drops in frequency. The one-way fare is $24 and $85 for a car.

Getting Around
For information about the local buses contact Prince Rupert Transit (☎ 624-3343), 225 2nd Ave West. The one-way fare on buses is $1 and a day pass costs $2.50.

There is limited service to Fairview Bay and the ferry terminals about three km from the centre. Call for details. Rupert's city buses do connect with buses in Port Edward at no additional charge.

QUEEN CHARLOTTE ISLANDS
The Queen Charlotte Islands, sometimes known as the Canadian Galapagos, are an archipelago of some 154 islands lying 80 km off the BC coast and about 50 km from the southern tip of Alaska. As the only part of Canada that escaped the last Ice Age, the islands are rich in flora & fauna markedly different from those of the mainland. Essentially still a wilderness area, the Queen Charlottes are warmed by an ocean current from Japan and hit with 127 cm of rain annually. All these factors combine to create a landscape of 1000-year-old spruce and cedar rainforests, abundant animal life and waters teeming with marine life.

The islands have been inhabited continuously for 10,000 years and are the traditional homeland of the Haida nation, generally acknowledged as the prime culture in the country at the time of the arrival of Europeans. The arts of the Haida people – notably their totem poles and carvings in argillite (a black, glass-like stone) – are world renowned. They were also fearsome warriors who dominated the west coast.

Today the Haida are still proud, defiant people. In the 1980s they led an internationally publicised fight to preserve the islands from further logging. A bitter debate raged, but finally the federal government decided to save South Moresby and create South Moresby Gwaii Haanas National Park. Logging still goes on of course in other parts of the Queen Charlottes.

The islands' relative remoteness coupled with the lure of the land and Native Indian culture has put the Charlottes on the travellers' map. In conjunction, a number of new hostels and services have sprung up to meet the needs of the intrepid.

Getting There & Away

The ferry from Prince Rupert to Skidegate, the MV *Queen of Prince Rupert*, sails daily but Tuesday taking 6½ hours and costing $22 and $83 for a car. Some crossings are day trips and some overnight. Another ferry goes between Skidegate and Alliford Bay on Moresby Island; the return fare is $3 and $8.50 for a car.

Graham Island

About 80% of the population lives on Graham Island, the only island with any real road system. The principal towns are **Skidegate** and **Queen Charlotte City**, on the south-eastern shore, and **Masset**, on the northern shore. The Travel Infocentre (☎ 559-4742) in Queen Charlotte town is open year round and has lots of information on the islands.

Near the ferry terminal in Skidegate is the **Queen Charlotte Islands Museum** (☎ 559-4643) with good displays on the area's history, including an excellent collection of Haida works. The Yellowhead Hwy heads 110 km north from Queen Charlotte past Tlell and Port Clements (famous for its golden spruce tree on the banks of the Yakoun River) to Masset, where you can go birdwatching at the **Delkatla Wildlife Sanctuary**, off Tow Rd, north of town.

The north-eastern corner of the island is taken up by **Naikoon Provincial Park** which

---

Totem Poles

Totem is an Ojibway word meaning 'guardian spirit' or 'mark of my family'. The word refers to an object, plant, animal or natural occurrence – or its representation – believed to have some connection with a tribe, clan or family group. Originally, totem poles were house corner posts and beams with designs of these totems carved on them. Eventually the totem poles came to signify the chief's prestige which was often emphasised by the poles' height and detail.

Totem-pole carving reached its peak in the second half of the 19th century when Native Indians were able to use the metal tools bartered from Europeans. The practice of building totem poles was most common among Native Indians along the Pacific north-west coast.

Anthony Island in the Queen Charlotte Islands has the largest, original group of totem poles in the world. Until 1994, the world's tallest totem pole, at 52.7 metres, stood in Alert Bay on Cormorant Island off Vancouver Island's north-east coast.

In August of 1994 a taller one was raised in Victoria for the opening of the Commonwealth Games. Made from a 250-year-old red cedar from the Nimpkish Valley on Vancouver Island, the 54.8-metre totem pole was given the name Spirit of Lekwammen (Lekwammen means 'land of the winds') and symbolises the speed of the athletes. The totem pole is divided into eight sections and each section was designed and carved by a different coastal Native Indian nation. The carvers from Alert Bay created the top section. ■

Potlatch

The potlatch (a Chinook jargon word derived from the Nootka word *patschmatl* meaning 'to give' or 'gift') was a feast or ceremony common among the Native Indians of the Pacific north-west coast, especially the Kwakiutl. Its main purpose was to validate the status of the chief or clan, although individuals also used it to try to enhance their social ranking. The potlatch involved the public exchange of gifts and destruction of property in a competitive display of affluence. A significant social event such as a wedding or funeral was used as an occasion for a potlatch.

The potlatch was prohibited by the federal government in 1884, when the Kwakiutl, at the cost of their own impoverishment, used it to shame and humble their former enemies. However, the practice continued in secret; the ban was lifted in 1951 and small-scale potlatches again take place.

Nowadays the word is often used to mean a 'spree' or 'raucous party'. ■

has hiking, swimming and wilderness camping; most of the park's 60-km coastline is sandy beach. Scuba diving and ocean kayaking are other popular activities.

There are several commercial campgrounds on the island, and one at *Naikoon Provincial Park*, which has two campgrounds with sites for $9.50. They have toilets, water and firewood and are open all year.

Queen Charlotte City has *Spruce Point Lodge & Hostel* (☎ 559-8234) with kayak rentals and boat tours. It's at 609 6th St. At Tlell is *H'ltunwa Kaitza* (☎ 557-4664), 40 km from the ferry dock. This is a hostel and guesthouse with camping, dorm beds at $10 with your own sleeping bag, and private rooms from $25. Call for directions, however, it's close to the beach on Hecate Strait. It's also known as Cacilia's B&B.

In Massett there is the Naikoon Park Motel & Hostel (☎ 626-5187) at 15 Tow Hill Rd. There are other hostels, some offering work-for-stay deals. The towns also have their share of B&Bs, lodges and motels but it's wise to book ahead in summer.

Moresby Island

Most of Moresby and its neighbouring islands are accessible only by plane, boat or foot. **Sandspit**, a mainly logging town on the north coast, is the island's only permanent settlement. The Canada Parks office (☎ 637-5362), on Beach Rd, can give you information on **South Moresby Gwaii Haanas National Park**. There's free camping

on the beach in Sandspit and a couple of B&Bs and hotels.

Tiny Anthony Island, near the southern end of the chain, is part of the park. It protects an old Haida village, **Ninstints**, called the most impressive coastal Native Indian site in the Pacific north-west. It is both a National Historic Site and UN World Heritage Site. There are 32 totem poles and remains of 10 longhouses. Sea kayaks can be used to explore around this and other park shorelines.

PRINCE RUPERT TO NEW HAZELTON

Prince Rupert sits near the mouth of the **Skeena River** and east out of town the Yellowhead Hwy (Hwy 16) follows the river, with some magnificent scenery of lakes, forests and mountains, and camping in provincial parks along the way. There are rest areas where you can stop for a while and take it all in.

Terrace, 147 km east of Prince Rupert, sitting in a valley surrounded by mountains, is a logging, service and transport centre. Hwy 16 becomes Keith Ave through town. The Travel Infocentre (☎ 635-4689/2063), 4511 Keith Ave, just south and east of downtown, is open daily in summer from 9 am to 8 pm and has lots of information on the region. The Greyhound Bus Depot (☎ 635-7676) is nearby at 4620 Keith Ave.

In **Kitimat**, south of Terrace, at the end of Hwy 37, there are free tours of the Alcan Aluminium Smelter and the Eurocan Pulp & Paper Mill. At **Nisga'a Memorial Lava Bed**

Provincial Park, north of Terrace, you can go fishing or hiking, but there's no camping.

The Hazelton area is the centre of some interesting **Native Indian sites**. West of town there are totems at Kitwanga and further north the **Kitwanga National Historic Site** which marks the location of the country's only Indian fort. North of the restored pioneer-like Hazelton, is **K'san**, one of the province's most significant Native Indian attractions. The recreated village of the Gitksan people features longhouses, a museum, various outbuildings and totem poles. You can wander the site for free but the guided tours by natives with entrance to the longhouses are very informative. On Friday night in summer, traditional dance performances are offered at additional cost. East of town stop at **Moricetown Canyon** in the Bulkley Valley where local Native Indians may be seen fishing this traditional salmon river.

CASSIAR HWY

Between Terrace and New Hazelton, the Yellowhead Hwy's northern tributary, Hwy 37, goes to Meziadin Junction and Stewart. The part of Hwy 37 extending north from Meziadin Junction is known as the Cassiar Hwy (also called the Stewart-Cassiar Hwy) and meets the Alaska Hwy in the Yukon.

The Cassiar is a mostly gravel road and passes through some beautiful countryside at places like Spatsizi Plateau Wilderness Park and **Dease Lake**. The highway is about 750 km long and there aren't many service stations along the way, so if you're driving, make sure the vehicle is in good working condition and take spare parts and extra gasoline. Flying gravel can crack the windscreen or headlights and dust can severely restrict your vision so treat approaching vehicles with caution, especially logging trucks.

Stewart & Hyder

From Meziadin Junction it's 67 km west to Stewart on the Alaskan border. On the way you pass **Bear Glacier**, 49 km from Stewart; there's a rest area where you can view the glacier. From Stewart the road goes straight through to Hyder in Alaska: there are no immigration or customs, and Hyder accepts Canadian money except in the post office. At **Fish Creek**, about three km past Hyder, between late July and September you can see salmon swimming upstream to spawn and bears coming to feed on them.

In Stewart, *Stewart Lions Campground* (☎ 636-2537) on 8th Ave has sites for $10. There are only two motels and one hotel, all with similar prices; book for all three at the *King Edward Hotel* (☎ 636-2244), on 5th Ave. Singles/doubles cost from $55/65.

Seaport Limousine Service (☎ 636-2622), PO Box 217, Stewart, operates a bus to Terrace. There's one a day in each direction Monday to Friday; the trip takes four hours and costs $28.

Spatsizi Plateau Wilderness Park

In this vast wilderness which includes the Spatsizi Uplands, the Stikine Plateau and the headwaters of the Stikine River, you can hike, canoe, raft or go horse riding. In the park, Gladys Lake Ecological Reserve is home to Stone's sheep, mountain goats, moose, grizzly and black bears, caribou and wolves.

Mt Edziza Provincial Park

This park has a volcanic landscape featuring lava flows, cinder cones and fields and an extinct shield volcano. It's accessed by gravel road from Dease Lake to Telegraph Creek and has hiking trails and wilderness camping.

Stikine River

The Stikine River, which cuts through the glacier-capped Coast Mountains to Alaska and the Pacific Ocean, is one of the best rivers for wilderness whitewater canoeing. In the upper reaches some rapids are deadly Grade V. The section west of the Cassiar Hwy as far as Telegraph Creek is considered unnavigable and you must pre-arrange to be picked up when you reach the Pacific Ocean.

Top: Museum of Anthropology, University of British Columbia, Vancouver
Left: The Steam Clock, Gastown, Vancouver, British Columbia
Right: Musicians performing on Inner Harbour with the Parliament Buildings in the background, Victoria, British Columbia

TOM SMALLMAN

MARK LIGHTBODY

Top: Kamloops and surrounding hills, British Columbia
Bottom: The Takakkaw Falls in Yoho National Park are, at 254 meters, one of the highest in the country and crash into a mist in a totally undeveloped mountain setting. Trails lead right up beside it into the spray.

ATLIN

This small, remote town in the north-western corner of the province is reached by road via the Yukon. Take Hwy 7 south off the Alaska Hwy; from the junction of the two highways it's 60 km to the town. It sits at the edge of Atlin Lake, which is surrounded by the huge icefields and glaciers of the Northern Coast Mountains. Atlin Provincial Park is to the south.

The Yukon & Northwest Territories

HIGHLIGHTS

- Hike along historic gold-rush routes such as the Chilkoot Trail
- Canoe down the country's major rivers such as the Mackenzie
- Visit Dawson City, a preserved pioneer outpost
- See the glaciers, mountains and wildlife in Kluane National Park
- Try whitewater rafting on the spectacular South Nahanni River
- Explore the Native Indian communities and outposts on the Arctic Ocean
- Be amazed by the summer's unending daylight and by the aurora borealis, which is best seen in the spring or autumn
- Look at the world's largest bison herd at the Mackenzie Bison Sanctuary

Yukon Territory
Area: 483,450 sq km
Population: 31,500
Territorial Capital: Whitehorse

Northwest Territories
Area: 3,426,320 sq km
Population: 64,000
Territorial Capital: Yellowknife

Canada's northern territories make up a vast tract of land stretching from the northern boundaries of the provinces to within 800 km of the North Pole and from the Atlantic Ocean to the Pacific Ocean. A third ocean, the Arctic, links Alaska and Greenland across the many islands of the far north.

For the most part, this land of the midnight sun is as reputation has it: a barren, treeless tundra that's nearly always frozen. But it is definitely not all this way. There are mountains and forests, abundant wildlife and, even if the season is short, warm summer days with 20 hours of light.

In general, the development of the far north has occurred where conditions are most hospitable and the land is most varied and scenic. Fortunately, these areas are the most accessible and tourism increases each year.

The designation of the Yukon and Northwest as territories rather than provinces is a political one. Because they have relatively small populations, the territories have not been given full status in parliament.

Yukon Territory

Some say God was tired when He made it;
Some say it's a fine land to shun;
Maybe; but there's some as would trade it
For no land on Earth – and I'm one.
  From *The Spell of the Yukon* by Robert Service

The Yukon is a triangular slice of northern Canada wedged between the Northwest Territories and Alaska. To the south is British Columbia; the north is bounded by the Beaufort Sea in the Arctic Ocean. It's a sub-Arctic region about one-third the size of Alaska. Mountain ranges, including some that continue from the Rockies, almost entirely cover the Yukon.

For the visitor, the Yukon offers many outdoor activities – camping, hiking, climbing, canoeing and fishing – amidst a scenic wilderness of mountains, forests, lakes and rivers. US currency is accepted at many hotels and retail outlets, but the exchange rate can vary quite a bit. Other than in Whitehorse and Dawson food is pricey. At Inuvik, for example, costs are nearly three times higher, so take supplies with you. Alaska is cheaper than anywhere in the Yukon.

Poet Robert Service and writer Jack London both lived and worked in the Yukon. Their words are highly respected and often recited throughout the territory.

History

In the 1840s Robert Campbell, a Hudson's Bay Company explorer, was the first European to travel the district. Fur traders, prospectors and whalers followed him. In 1870 the area became part of the region known as the Northwest Territories. But it was in 1896 that the biggest changes began. Gold was found in a tributary of the Klondike River near what became Dawson City and all hell broke loose. The ensuing gold rush attracted hopefuls from around the world. The population boomed to around 38,000 – quite a bit higher than today's – and transport routes were opened up. Towns grew overnight to support the rough-and-

ready wealth-seekers, but it was the suppliers and entertainers, rather than the prospectors, who raked in most of the money.

In 1898 the Yukon became a separate territory with Dawson City the capital, but the city declined as the gold ran out. The construction of the Alaska Hwy in 1942 opened up the territory to development. In 1953 Whitehorse became the capital, for it had the railway and the Alaska Hwy. It now acts as the main distribution and transport centre of the Yukon.

Climate

Summers, spanning June, July and August are short but warm, even hot. Many places are open from May to September. Outside of these months visitors are few. Winters are long, dark and cold. The mountains to the west act as a barrier meaning low precipitation all year.

Economy

The most important industry is mining with gold, lead and zinc the big three. The economy and population ebb and flow along with mine openings and closings dictated by world markets. Tourism is the second-biggest moneymaker followed by fishing, forestry and furs. Whitehorse is a government centre.

Population & People

Most of the population lives in towns, about two-thirds in the Whitehorse region. The bulk of the rest live in and around mining camps. Many people come for the jobs, spend a year or two and then head back down south. The young and recent immigrants make up a lot of this group. The Dene (pronounced 'de-NAY' and meaning 'person'), the collective name for the various Yukon Native Indian groups, are by far the majority in the smaller communities. They and the Inuit are the original inhabitants and together remain a significant portion of the population.

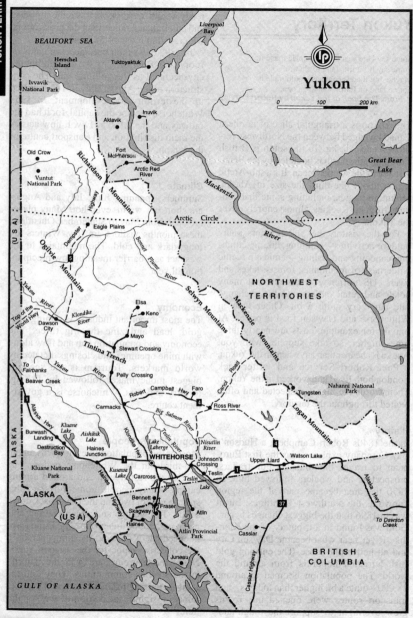

BEAUFORT SEA

Liverpool
Bay

Herschel
Island

Tuktoyaktuk

Ivvavik
National Park

Aklavik

Inuvik

Old Crow

Fort
McPherson

Arctic Red
River

**Great Bear
Lake**

Vuntut
National Park

Richardson Mountains

Mackenzie

River

Arctic Circle

Eagle Plains

Dempster Highway

Ogilvie Mountains

Bonnet Plume River

Selwyn Mountains

Yukon

0   100   200 km

**NORTHWEST
TERRITORIES**

Yukon River

Top of the
World Hwy

Klondike River

Elsa

Keno

Dawson
City

Mayo

Stewart Crossing

Tintina Trench

To
Fairbanks

Yukon River

Pelly Crossing

Mackenzie Mountains

Canol Road

Nahanni National
Park

Beaver Creek

Robert Campbell Hwy

Faro

Ross River

Tungsten

Logan Mountains

**ALASKA
(USA)**

Carmacks

Big Salmon River

Burwash
Landing

Kluane
Lake

Aishihik
Lake

Klondike Hwy

Lake
Laberge

Teslin River

Nisutlin
River

Destruction
Bay

Haines
Junction

WHITEHORSE

Johnson's
Crossing

Upper Liard

Watson Lake

Kluane National
Park

Kusawa
Lake

Carcross

Teslin

Teslin
Lake

Alaska Hwy

ALASKA

Haines
Highway

Bennett

Fraser

Skagway

Haines

Atlin

Juneau

Atlin Provincial
Park

Cassiar

37

To Dawson
Creek

**BRITISH
COLUMBIA**

GULF OF ALASKA

Cassiar Highway

Information

Territorial Symbols The official Yukon flower is the fireweed.

Tourist Offices The Yukon has six main tourist offices, called Visitor Reception Centres (VRCs): these are at Beaver Creek, Carcross, Dawson City, Haines Junction, Watson Lake and Whitehorse. They're all open from mid-May to mid-September. As well as information and maps on the territory, each has exhibits and laser-disc TV displays. They even broadcast their own combined radio service, CKYN Yukon Gold (FM 96.1), for visitors. Tourism Yukon (☎ 667-5340), PO Box 2703, Whitehorse Y1A 2C6, sends out free information on the territory. Particularly useful is its free brochure *Canada's Yukon*, published annually, which has information on activities, events, accommodation and travel.

Telephone The area code for the territory is the same as Alberta's – 403.

Time The Yukon is on Pacific Standard Time.

Tax There is no territorial sales tax in the Yukon.

Health Warning If you're drinking water from lakes or streams boil it for at least 10 minutes. The lakes and streams may contain the intestinal parasite *Giardia lamblia* which causes giardiasis. If you're going to be outdoors take insect repellent.

Activities

The Yukon VRCs can supply you with general descriptions and specific information on hiking, canoeing, rockhounding, gold prospecting, climbing, skiing, fishing and various adventure tours. There are outfitters and tour companies to cover all these activities. You don't need an organised trip and don't need to be wealthy to enjoy camping, hiking or canoeing in the Yukon.

Hiking The most well-known trail is the Chilkoot Trail but Kluane National Park also has excellent hiking from short and easy to long and demanding. The Tombstone Mountain area north of Dawson is also good. The North Fork Pass is called the classic hike of the region. Also above the treeline in alpine terrain is the MacMillan Pass at the NWT border accessible by the north Canol Rd from Ross River. Great hiking can also be found in the Firth River area of Ivvavik National Park but this is accessible only by air and has no services. There is also some walking around Faro and Keno.

Canoeing Canoeists have the whole gamut of choice, from easy float trips down the fast-flowing waters of the Yukon River and its tributaries to challenging whitewater rivers. Among the many options are the following trips.

Gentle float trips down the Yukon from Whitehorse for a few hours or 16 days all the way to Dawson are popular. Many people start or end at Carmacks, the halfway point, making an eight-day trip. Boat rental and return charges for such an eight-day one-way trip are about $200 and transport to the beginning can be arranged.

A fine scenic trip suitable for those without a lot of experience is the eight days down the Teslin River from Johnson's Crossing to Carmacks. The Big Salmon River in this same area has a longer run into Carmacks. The Nisutlin River offers beginners a good five-day trip into Teslin Village. It runs along the Canol Rd north of Johnson's Crossing.

A three-day excursion on the Takhini River from Kusawa Lake west of Whitehorse has some whitewater and some lake paddling. Among the more challenging is the canoe trip down the remote but renowned Bonnet Plume River in the north-east. This two-week voyage covering hundreds of km is the most popular trip in the northern Yukon. Parts of the Tatshenshini River can be canoed too.

For all trips, seek out local advice before dipping the canoe in the water.

Kayaking & Whitewater Rafting The Alsek and Tatshenshini rivers are ranked among the best and wildest in North America. They're found in BC, south of Kluane accessible only from Haines Junction. Trips can be booked in Whitehorse. Other major areas are the Lapie (near Ross River) and Takhini rivers.

Accommodation

The Yukon government's series of campgrounds is good, with many along the highways; most have drinking water. There are also numerous private grounds which offer hook-ups, showers and laundry facilities; some of these campgrounds are geared strictly to the large recreational vehicle (RV) market. Many visitors tour the north in rented RVs which means transport and a place to stay as well. There are hostels in Whitehorse, Dawson City and Beaver Creek as well as B&Bs across the Yukon. Towns all have hotels and motels although prices are higher than in southern Canada.

Getting Around

The major towns in the Yukon are connected by air and bus (see the Getting There & Away sections for Whitehorse and Dawson City for details). Buses run to several centres in Alaska and to Kluane National Park.

Road Driving your own vehicle is the best way to get around, and there are car and RV rental outlets in Whitehorse.

The road system in the Yukon is fairly extensive, if rough. Remember that most roads are gravel. The main highways in the Yukon are the Klondike, the Dempster and the Alaska. Most of the Alaska and Klondike highways are paved but not necessarily smooth and some parts may be gravel or muck especially where the never-ending maintenance is taking place. The Yukon VRCs have information on the highways, what there is to see from them and road conditions. Roads connect most southern towns. To the north the unsealed Dempster Hwy connects Dawson City with Inuvik in the Northwest Territories (see the Dempster Hwy section later).

A good circular trip is to travel the Klondike Hwy from Whitehorse to Dawson City, then take the Top of the World Hwy to the Alaska border. From the border, take the Taylor Hwy south to Tetlin Junction in Alaska and then follow the Alaska Hwy north-west to Fairbanks. On the way back take the Alaska Hwy south-east past Beaver Creek, Kluane National Park and Haines Junction to Whitehorse.

There are campgrounds along most of the highway routes. Keep your headlights on at all times.

Gasoline Gasoline prices along the highways are pretty outrageous so it's worth filling up at cheaper places even if you don't need to. It's a good idea always to have some spare too. Generally, along the main routes, there's a service station every 50 km, but in some areas there may be no competition for 150 km or more. Prices are lower in the main towns than they are out on the stretches, but they can vary considerably for no apparent reason.

Three places where gasoline is not so expensive are Dawson Creek in British Columbia, Whitehorse and Dawson City. Gasoline is very expensive in Inuvik.

WHITEHORSE

Whitehorse, on the banks of the Yukon River, is by far the largest town in the territory. In fact its official city limits cover 421 sq km, making it one of the largest urban-designated areas in Canada. Despite this, the central core is quite small and the total population is only around 24,000.

The town sits on the Alaska Hwy about halfway between Dawson Creek in British Columbia, where the highway starts, and Fairbanks in Alaska. Despite its growth, Whitehorse still has something of a frontier feel about it although the people are condescendingly known as 'southerners' by those living in the more northerly areas of the territory. There are significant numbers of German, Chinese and French Canadian people in town.

Orientation

Whitehorse stretches for several km along the banks of the Yukon River. The Alaska Hwy passes through the city although it bypasses the city centre which is reached by South Access Rd or Two-Mile Hill Rd. Downtown is designed on a grid system and is easy to walk around. The downtown core is between 1st and 6th Aves and Hanson and Strickland Sts. The main traffic routes through downtown are 2nd and 4th Aves.

Information

Tourist Offices The VRC (☎ 667-2915), with information on the Yukon, is south-west of town and off the Alaska Hwy, close to Whitehorse Airport and the Yukon Transportation Museum. It's open May to September daily from 8 am to 8 pm. The building itself is interesting architecturally and caused some local controversy because of its modern design and the fact that the architect was from Vancouver, not the Yukon. The City Information Centre (☎ 667-7545) is housed in the TC Richards Building at 302 Steele St on the corner of 3rd Ave. It's open May to September daily from 8 am to 8 pm; October to April, Monday to Friday from 9 am to 5 pm. A new, large tourism building with offices and information centre is being planned for downtown on 2nd Ave across the street from the Yukon government building. Incorporating wood planking and logs, it is to have an historic appearance.

There's also a Parks Canada information office (☎ 667-4511, 668-3398) next to the SS *Klondike*, on the banks of the Yukon River south of downtown.

Several banks are on the corner of Main St and 2nd Ave.

Post The main post office is downstairs at Shoppers Drug Mart, on the corner of 3rd Ave and Main St. It's open Monday to Friday from 8 am to 6 pm, and Saturday from 9 am to 5 pm. There's another post office in the Qwanlin Mall.

Bookshops & Maps Mac's Fireweed Books, at 203 Main St, sells a good selection of books on the history, geography and wildlife of the Yukon plus a section on Native Indian culture of the region. Topographical maps of the Yukon are available at several places in Whitehorse including a government office in the Elizah Smith Building, the green and sandstone monstrosity at the corner of Main St and 3rd Ave. The Geoscience Information and Sales Office (☎ 667-3204) is open Monday to Friday. The mailing address is: Geoscience Information and Sales Office, Exploration and Geological Services Division, Mining Recorder Office, Room 102, 300 Main St, Whitehorse Y1A 2B5.

You can also get maps at Jim's Toy & Gift (☎ 667-2606), 208 Main St, Whitehorse Y1A 2A9 . If planning ahead, they are also available from Canada Map Office (☎ (613) 952-7000), 615 Booth St, Ottawa, Ontario K1A 0E9. Indicate the correct coordinates for the area or get their order information sheet first.

Medical Services Whitehorse General Hospital (☎ 667-8700) is at the end of Hospital Rd on the eastern side of the river. To get there, take Robert Campbell Bridge from the southern end of 2nd Ave, go over the river onto Lewes Blvd and then turn left.

Things to See

In the town itself there isn't much to see, and what there is can be done in a day. For a view of the city, river and mountains beyond, there's a steep footpath at the western end of Hanson St.

SS Klondike The SS *Klondike* (☎ 667-4511) was one of the last and largest sternwheel riverboats used on the Yukon River. Built in 1929, it made its last run upriver in 1955. Now restored as a museum and drydocked near the junction of South Access Rd and 2nd Ave, it's open daily 9 am to 7 pm from mid-May to mid-September. Admission is $3 and includes a guided tour.

MacBride Museum This museum (☎ 667-2709), on the corner of 1st Ave and Wood St,

YUKON TERRITORY

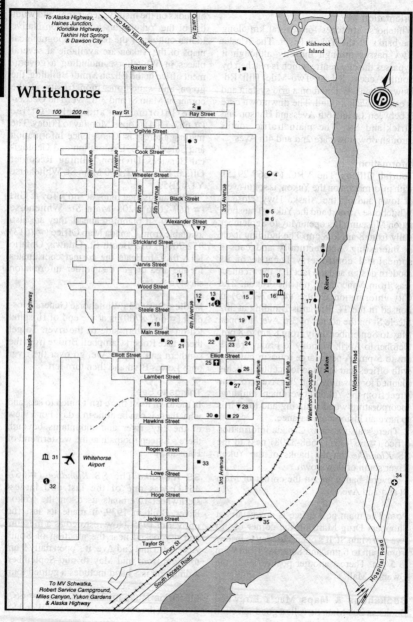

Whitehorse

To Alaska Highway,
Haines Junction,
Klondike Highway,
Takhini Hot Springs
& Dawson City

Two Mile Hill Road

Quartz Rd

Kishwoot Island

Baxter St

Ray St

Ray Street

Ogilvie Street

Cook Street

Wheeler Street

Black Street

Alexander Street

Strickland Street

Jarvis Street

Wood Street

Steele Street

Main Street

Elliott Street

Elliott Street

Lambert Street

Hanson Street

Hawkins Street

Rogers Street

Lowe Street

Hoge Street

Jeckell Street

Taylor St

Drury St

Whitehorse Airport

8th Avenue

7th Avenue

6th Avenue

5th Avenue

3rd Avenue

4th Avenue

2nd Avenue

1st Avenue

3rd Avenue

Alaska Highway

Waterfront Footpath

Yukon River

Wickstrom Road

Hospital Road

South Access Road

0   100   200 m

To MV Schwatka,
Robert Service Campground,
Miles Canyon, Yukon Gardens
& Alaska Highway

PLACES TO STAY		11	Tung Lock	17	MV *Youcon Kat*
		12	No Pop Sandwich	22	Hougen Centre
1	Sourdough City RV		Shop	23	Main Post Office
	Park	18	Sam 'n' Andy's	24	Mac's Fireweed
2	Family Hotel	19	Talisman Café		Books
6	Roadhouse Inn	28	The Deli	25	Old Log Church
9	Regina Hotel				Museum
10	98 Hotel	**OTHER**		26	Log Skyscrapers
15	Westmark			27	Klondyke Medical
	Whitehorse Hotel	3	Qwanlin Mall		Building
20	Gold Rush Inn	4	Greyhound Bus Depot	30	Yukon Conservation
21	Town & Mountain	5	Bikes & Boards		Society
	Hotel	8	Kanoe People	31	Yukon Transportation
29	Hawkins House B&B	13	Yukon Historical &		Museum
33	High Country Inn		Museums	32	Visitor Reception
			Association		Centre
PLACES TO EAT		14	City Information	34	Whitehorse General
			Centre		Hospital
7	Alpine Bakery	16	MacBride Museum	35	SS *Klondike*

is in a log cabin with a turf roof. It contains a collection of materials from the indigenous cultures, the fur trade, gold-rush days and the construction of the Alaska Hwy. It also has displays of Yukon wildlife. It's open daily 10 am to 6 pm from mid-May to the end of September and admission is $3.50.

Old Log Church Museum The church (☎ 668-2555), on the corner of Elliot St and 3rd Ave, was built by the town's first priest in 1900. Known as the only wooden cathedral in the world, it is also the oldest building in town. Inside are artefacts from early churches around the territory. It's open early June to the end of August, Monday to Saturday from 9 am to 6 pm, and Sunday from noon to 4 pm. Admission is $2.50. Sunday services at 10.30 am are mostly for the Native Indians and include hymns in the Gwich'in language.

'Log Skyscrapers' Look for these small two and three-storey wooden cabins on Lambert St between 2nd and 3rd Aves. One is used as the office of the local member for federal parliament.

Yukon Transportation Museum The transportation museum (☎ 668-4792), east of town at Whitehorse Airport, features the history of transport in the territory. Displays

range from snowshoes to stage coaches. It's open daily July to the end of August from 10 am to 7 pm. Entry is $3.

Yukon Gardens The Yukon Gardens (☎ 668-7972) are on South Access Rd close to the Alaska Hwy, about three km southwest of town. The gardens, covering almost nine hectares, have large displays of wild plants and flowers that can only be found in the north, plus vegetables and fruit trees. The gardens are open daily mid-May to mid-September from 9 am to 9 pm. Admission is $5.

Yukon Wildlife Preserve The preserve (☎ 668-3992) is about 25 km north-west of town, off the Klondike Hwy on the Takhini Hot Springs Rd. A fine selection of northern animals such as elk, caribou, Dall sheep, moose, mountain goats, muskox and others can be seen on the rolling 280-hectare spread. With grasslands, cliffs and wet areas the animals are in a natural setting and yet can often be observed at close range. The sanctuary was set up in 1965 for breeding and research purposes.

Call Sabrina for details about the best time to visit. A van takes visitors around the site very inexpensively. The preserve can be visited as part of a Gray Line bus tour from Whitehorse for $24.

Takhini Hot Springs Down the road about five km from the wildlife preserve in a quiet wooded area are the hot springs (☎ 633-2706). Together with the preserve, a visit here makes a fine day. You can rent bathing suits and towels for 50 cents each. The springs are open daily all year, from 8 am to 10 pm. Admission is $4. There is a B&B nearby and camping at the site.

Activities
Bicycles can be rented at Bikes & Boards (☎ 667-6501), 2155 2nd Ave. For a good walk close to the centre, **Bert Law Park** is on a small island next to the Robert Service Campground and is connected by an old military bridge. A winding footpath leads around the natural wooded area. Around Whitehorse you can go hiking and cycling, particularly at **Mt McIntyre Recreation Centre**, and at **Grey Mountain** east of town and **Miles Canyon** south of town. All along the **Ibex River Valley** is good for cycling. The hiking trails become cross-country ski trails in winter.

Sportslodge (☎ 668-6848), in the Hougen Centre on Main St, offers kayaking and canoeing courses from beginners to advanced on Chadburn Lake and the Yukon and Wheaton rivers. A beginner's course starts at $80 for one day. A range of short or long-duration canoe adventures can begin in and around Whitehorse. Several companies rent canoes, offer guided tours or help do-it-yourselfers put their trips together with rentals, advice and transportation. Kanoe People (☎ 668-4899), at the corner of 1st Ave and Strickland St but right at the river's edge, can arrange any type of trip. Prospect Yukon (☎ 667-4837), 3123 3rd Ave and Up North (☎ 667-7905) on the river opposite the MacBride Museum offer similar services. At the latter, German is spoken.

Organised Tours
The Yukon Historical & Museums Association (☎ 667-4704) at Donnenworth House, 3126 3rd Ave between Wood and Steele Sts, conducts guided walking tours daily of the downtown area for $2.

The Yukon Conservation Society (☎ 668-5678), 302 Hawkins St, offers free nature walks in the area on weekdays during July and August.

Gray Line Yukon (☎ 668-3225), in the Westmark Whitehorse Hotel, has several tours. The four-hour, grand city tour takes you around the city and out to the Yukon Wildlife Preserve for $24. From early June to mid-September another tour combines this with a boat cruise across Schwatka Lake and up the Yukon River for $39. Tickets for the two-hour tour can also be purchased at the hotel or the dock, a five-minute drive south.

The MV *Youcon Kat* (☎ 668-2927) does two 2½-hour trips daily on the Yukon River for $17. This small, open-air boat leaves from opposite the MacBride Museum.

If you'd like to do something more adventurous then there are plenty of opportunities. Atlas Tours (☎ 668-3161), in the Westmark Whitehorse Hotel, can take you on a six-hour, frothy rafting trip of the Blanchard and Tatshenshini rivers for $100. Cloudberry Adventures (☎ 668-7711) offers combined course and trips from four days and longer.

Prospect Yukon offers guided wilderness canoe trips starting at $99 for one day and going up to 18 days. For related information see the previous Activities section.

Places to Stay
Camping *Robert Service Campground* (☎ 668-3721) is one km south of town on South Access Rd. It's open late May to early September and has toilets, showers and firepits. The campground is closed between midnight and 7 am. A tent site, of which there are 40, costs $8. *Sourdough City RV Park* (☎ 668-7938), at the northern end of 2nd Ave, past the Greyhound Bus Depot, has a laundry and free showers. It's mainly for RVs but you can put up a tent on the patches of grass behind the office for $10. *Pioneer RV Park* (☎ 668-5944), eight km south of Whitehorse on the Alaska Hwy, has drinking water, laundry and showers. Tent sites are $8.

You can camp at *Takhini Hot Springs* (☎ 633-2706), about 30 km north-west of town off the Klondike Hwy, for $8 (plus $2 for power), and walk to the hot springs. South of Whitehorse there is a *Yukon-government campground* at Wolf Creek (16 km) and one at Marsh Lake (50 km); sites cost $8.

Hostels The *Roadhouse Inn* (☎ 667-2594), 2163 2nd Ave, has hostel rooms with bunks and shared washrooms for $20 a person. Singles/doubles are $50/55 at this central place with a bar. The *High Country Inn* (☎ 667-4471), at 4051 4th Ave, despite its upgrading and new management still keeps a few rooms for hostellers. This is high living at basement prices! The twin rooms cost $22.50 a bed and the hotel has laundry facilities and a restaurant.

B&Bs The City Information Centre keeps brochures of B&Bs in and around Whitehorse. *Barb's B&B* (☎ 667-4104), 64 Boswell Crescent, south of downtown on the eastern side of the river, has two rooms with private bathroom. A single/double costs $60/65 and includes a complimentary evening snack. *International House B&B* (☎ 633-5490), 17 14th Ave in Porter Creek, north of downtown, has the same facilities and prices.

Central is the deluxe Victorian-style *Hawkin's House* (☎ 668-7638), 303 Hawkins St, with four distinct rooms each with private bath and balcony at $110 double. A full breakfast is provided.

Hotels & Motels *98 Hotel* (☎ 667-2641), 110 Wood St, is basic but central and cheap, with a single room for $35 with shared bath, or others for $45 with bathroom. It is best known for its bar.

The well-kept *Family Hotel* (☎ 668-5558), 314 Ray St, charges $60/65 with private bathroom and TV. There's a laundrette and 24-hour restaurant attached.

The good-value *High Country Inn* (☎ 667-4471), 4051 4th Ave, has a range of rooms as well as a restaurant, bar and free shuttle service to the airport. Singles/doubles start at $50/75 and there are family suites with kitchens. The central *Regina Hotel* (☎ 667-4243), 102 Wood St, has a licensed

restaurant and heated underground parking. All rooms have private baths, and cost from $60/70. In the same class is the *Town & Mountain Hotel* (☎ 668-7644), 401 Main St, with 30 rooms, from $60/65 depending on time of year and amount of traffic. There's a licensed restaurant and a piano bar. The central *Stratford Motel* (☎ 667-4243), at 401 Jarvis St, is good with rooms from $59 and some with kitchenettes. Weekly rates are available.

The top hotel in town is the *Westmark Whitehorse Hotel* (☎ 668-4700), on the corner of 2nd Ave and Wood St, which has 181 rooms at $145 single or double, and is home to the Frantic Follies revue.

Places to Eat
The popular *Talisman Café*, 2112 2nd Ave, between Steele and Main Sts is comfortable and good for any meal. Breakfast can be had for about $6. Lunch and dinner fare ranges from pseudo Middle Eastern to Mexican and vegetarian and there are good salads. Lunch will set you back $6 to $8, dinner about $10. This is also a fine place for an afternoon cappuccino.

The *No Pop Sandwich Shop*, 312 Steele St, is a long-time favourite with residents. Tasty sandwiches with interesting names like Beltch, Roman or Tel Aviv cost around $4.25; vegetarian burgers are $4.50. It has a patio out back.

The Deli, 203 Hanson St, is cheap at around $3 to $5 for light meals of soups, salads or homemade sausages. A variety of cold meats and cheeses is available to take out. It's closed on Sunday.

Busy *Sam 'n' Andy's*, 506 Main St, specialises in Mexican food and you can have a beer with your meal in the garden out front. Nachos cost $7.50 and main dishes are from $7.50 to $17.

Of the several Chinese restaurants *Tung Lok* at 404 Wood St, open every day but for dinner only on weekends, is recommended. Seafood is emphasised but there is a wide selection. Vegetables and other ingredients are expensive in town meaning higher prices for Chinese food. Dishes start at $7.95.

Most of the hotels have restaurants or dining rooms. The *Alpine Bakery* on Alexander St at 4th Ave has great bread. *Food For Thought* at 307 Wood St is a health food store.

Entertainment

Strictly for the tourists is The Frantic Follies, an 1890s-style revue with comedy skits, dancing girls and the poetry of Robert Service. The show is held nightly in the *Westmark Whitehorse Hotel* through the summer and tickets cost $18. In the same vein is the Canteen Show, a recreation of a 1940s US army show, at the Best Western Gold Rush Inn, 411 Main St. *Robert Service Campground* has regular poetry readings.

If you want a taste of what the locals do for entertainment head for the *Saloon* at the Roadhouse Inn where country & western musicians play most nights.

Things to Buy

Northern Images at 311 Jarvis St sells crafts made by the Inuit and Native Indians. Murdoch's Gem Shop at 207 Main St with a variety of unusual items is also very interesting to browse through.

Getting There & Away

Air Whitehorse Airport is east of town off the Alaska Hwy. All major airline flights into Whitehorse go through Vancouver. The standard one-way fare with Canadian Airlines (☎ 668-3535) from Vancouver is $555. Booking flights from another city straight through is much cheaper than booking one to Vancouver and then another on to Whitehorse.

Air North (☎ 668-2228) connects Whitehorse with Dawson City and Old Crow, and the Alaskan towns of Fairbanks, Anchorage and Juneau. The standard one-way fare to Dawson City is $195. They offer a three-week travel pass good for all the above stops. Alkan Air (☎ 668-2107, 1-800-661-0432) goes to places within the Yukon and to Inuvik in the Northwest Territories; the standard return fare to Inuvik is $780 plus tax but there are weekend excursion return rates of $507 plus tax.

Bus The Greyhound Bus Depot (☎ 667-2223/2772), 2191 2nd Ave, is open Monday from 8 am to 5.30 pm, Tuesday to Friday from 5 am to 5.30 pm, Saturday from 5 am to noon, and Sunday from 5 to 9 am. Greyhound buses leave every day but Sunday to Edmonton and Vancouver; the one-way fare to Edmonton is $227, to Vancouver $293. Cheaper tickets are available if you book seven days in advance.

Norline Coaches (☎ 668-3355) runs three times a week (twice a week in winter) to Dawson City from the Greyhound Bus Depot for $73 (including tax) one way.

Gray Line of Alaska (☎ 668-3225, 1-800-544-2206) operates Alaskon Express buses to Skagway, Tok, Anchorage, Fairbanks and Haines in Alaska and other communities along the way. The one-way fare to Fairbanks is $206, to Anchorage $245. Some journeys involve an overnight stop so you'll need to add on the cost of accommodation.

Alaska Direct Busline (☎ 668-4833, 1-800-780-6652) also has buses to Skagway, Anchorage and Fairbanks and points in between such as Haines Junction. The bus goes by Kluane making stops such as Beaver Creek. Buses meet in Tok, Alaska coming from each direction three times a week. The bus to Skagway is a daily and can be picked up in Haines Junction. The Whitehorse office and station is at the Regina Hotel.

Train There is a privately owned, 177-km, narrow-gauge railway line called the White Pass & Yukon Route (WP&YR) that together with a bus connection can be used to link Whitehorse with Skagway, Alaska. It's a very scenic trip as it winds through the mountains and over rough terrain. It has an interesting historical angle, too: the line opened in 1900 to feed the gold rush. Later, the train relied heavily on fees raised from transporting ore from mines, but with the fall in world metal prices the line was closed from 1982 until 1988.

Today it travels from Skagway over White Pass Summit through Fraser in northern British Columbia (Canadian customs) and on to Lake Bennett. You can go just to the summit and return, all the way and return, or travel one way. Hikers of the Chilkoot Trail can get on board at Bennet Lake. Buses connect with the train at Fraser for the trip into Whitehorse.

To use it for transportation between Skagway and Whitehorse, the train departs daily from Skagway at 12.40 pm and the connecting bus arrives in Whitehorse at 6 pm; from Whitehorse the bus leaves at 8.15 am, and the train arrives in Skagway at noon. The one-way fare is US$95 (about $125 Canadian). From Skagway the summit-return trip is three hours and the Lake Bennett return is 5½ hours.

For information and bookings contact Whitehorse Travel (☎ 668-5599) in the Klondyke Medical & Dental Building on the corner of 3rd Ave and Lambert St; or Atlas Tours (☎ 668-3161) in the Westmark Whitehorse Mall. Reservations should be made well in advance.

Car Whitehorse is connected with Watson Lake in the east and Haines Junction and Beaver Creek in the west by the Alaska Hwy. The Klondike Hwy (Hwy 2) heads south to Carcross then to Skagway in Alaska; north of Whitehorse it connects the city with Stewart Crossing and Dawson City.

Cars can be rented from the following rental companies:

Budget
    4178 4th Ave (☎ 667-6200, 1-800-268-8900)
Klondike Rentals
    25 MacDonald Rd (☎ 668-2200,
    1-800-268-8900)
Rent-A-Wreck
    Whitehorse Shell Centre (☎ 668-7554)
Tilden
    9030 Quartz Road (☎ 668-6872)

The daily rate with Tilden starts from $30 on weekends with the first 200 km free and 14 cents for each subsequent km. Rent-A-Wreck has vans and Klondike has a range of campers.

Getting Around

Bus Whitehorse Transit (☎ 668-8381), operates buses Monday to Saturday; there are no buses on Sunday or public holidays. The one-way fare is $1.25 but a day pass for $3 allows unlimited travel. If you're going to the airport take the Hillcrest bus from Qwanlin Mall. For schedules and routes, get a copy of the city bus guide from the City Information Centre.

Taxi Among the local cab companies is Yellow Cab (☎ 668-4811). A trip from the airport into town is about $10.

ALASKA HIGHWAY

The Alaska Hwy (also called the Alcan Hwy), the main road in the Yukon, is about 2400 km long and starts in Dawson Creek, British Columbia. It enters the Yukon in the south-east and passes through Watson Lake, Whitehorse, Haines Junction and Beaver Creek en route to Fairbanks, Alaska. A joint project between the USA and Canada, it was built in 1942 as part of the war effort and was originally known as the Alaska-Canada Military Hwy. Now, each summer, it's very busy (some even say clogged) with visitors, mainly driving RVs. At times there are 10 of these homes-on-wheels for every car or truck. Services for gasoline, food and lodging occur at regular intervals along the highway.

The highway is nearly all paved except for a few stretches where road construction is taking place. On these stretches the biggest problems are dust and flying stones from other vehicles: slow down and keep well to the right. Potholes, too, can be a problem. A spare tyre, fan belt and hose are recommended. Many people attach a bug-and-gravel screen or headlamp covers.

Hitching on the highway is good but be prepared for the occasional long wait – it's a good idea to carry a tent, some food, water and warm clothing. And don't consider hitching outside of the short summer season.

Watson Lake

Originally named after Frank Watson, a British trapper, and now billed as the 'Gateway to the Yukon', Watson Lake is the first town in the territory as you head north-west on the Alaska Hwy from British Columbia. The town stretches out along the highway. The VRC (☎ 536-7469), at the junction of the Alaska and Robert Campbell highways, has an excellent video show on the history of the territory and the Alaska Hwy. The centre is open mid-May to mid-September daily from 8 am to 8 pm.

The town is most famous for its **Signpost Forest** just outside the VRC. The original signpost of 'Danville, Illinois' was put up in 1942 by the homesick Carl Lindlay, a US soldier working on the construction of the Alaska Hwy. Other people added their own signs and now there are over 22,000 and you can have your own sign made on the spot.

Twenty-six km west of Watson Lake is the junction with the Cassiar Hwy which heads south into British Columbia.

Teslin

Teslin, on the Nisutlin River about 280 km west of Watson Lake, began as a trading post in 1903 set up to serve the Tlingit people. The **George Johnston Museum** (☎ 390-2550) has photographs, displays and artefacts on the Tlingit people and from the gold-rush

---

The Alaska Highway

The construction in 1942 of the Alaska Hwy is one of the major engineering feats of the 20th century. Canada and the USA had originally agreed to build an all-weather highway to Fairbanks from the south as early as 1930, but nothing serious was done about it until WWII. Japan's attack on Pearl Harbor, then its bombing of Dutch Harbor in the Aleutians and occupation of the Aleutian islands of Attu and Kiska increased Alaska's strategic importance. Japan's military successes gave it near military control of the Pacific and made a full-scale invasion of North America's west coast seem likely. The US army was told to prepare for the highway's construction a month before Canada's prime minister, WL Mackenzie King, signed the agreement granting the USA permission to do so.

The route chosen for the highway followed a series of existing airfields – Fort St John, Fort Nelson, Watson Lake and Whitehorse – known as the Northwest Staging Route. This route was used by US pilots as part of the lend-lease programme to ferry aircraft north to Fairbanks where the aircraft were then picked up by Soviet crews who flew them to Siberia.

Thousands of US soldiers and Canadians, including Native Indians, built the gravel 2450-km highway between Dawson Creek in British Columbia and Fairbanks in Alaska. They began work on 9 March 1942 and completed it before falling temperatures (in what was to be one of the worst winters in recorded history) could halt the work. Conditions were harsh: sheets of ice rammed the timber pilings; floods during the spring thaw tore down bridges; bogs swallowed trucks, tractors and other heavy machinery; in the cold months the road crews suffered frostbite while in the summer they were preyed on by mosquitoes, blackflies and other biting insects.

In spite of these hardships the single-lane pioneer road was completed at the remarkable average rate of 12 km a day, the road crews meeting, a little over eight months after construction began, at Contact Creek close to the British Columbia and Yukon border. The highway cost US$135 million to construct.

The Alaska Hwy was officially opened on 20 November at Soldiers' Summit (Mile 1061) overlooking Kluane Lake in the south-west corner of the Yukon. Five US soldiers and eight Royal Canadian Mounted Police constables all dressed in uniform lined up facing a red, white and blue ribbon stretched across the road. The ribbon was cut by Ian MacKenzie, a member of Canada's federal parliament, and EL Bartlett, a US congressman. The following year the Canadian Public Roads Authority made it an all-weather road.

Several reasons were put forward to explain why the original road had so many curves and slopes. One is that they were constructed deliberately to prevent Japanese pilots from landing their aircraft. But it's more likely, with speed so essential and with the bulldozers right behind them, that surveyors didn't have time to pick the best route.

In April 1946 the Canadian part of the road (1965 km) was officially handed over to Canada. In the meantime private contractors, under the control of the Public Roads Authority, were busy widening, gravelling and straightening the highway; levelling its steep grades; and replacing temporary bridges

days. It's open May to September daily from 10 am to 8 pm, and admission is $2.50. There's canoeing and camping at nearby Teslin Lake.

Johnson's Crossing & Canol Rd

About 53 km north of Teslin, is Johnson's Crossing at the junction of the Alaska Hwy and Canol Rd. During WWII, the US army built the Canol pipeline at the same time as the Alaska Hwy, to pump oil from Norman Wells in the Northwest Territories to Whitehorse. The only services on Canol Rd are in Ross River at the intersection with the Robert Campbell Hwy. The road ends near the Northwest Territories' border; to go any

further you have to hike the Canol Heritage Trail (see the Northwest Territories section later).

Haines Junction

Haines Junction, just outside Kluane National Park, is reached by the Alaska Hwy from Whitehorse or by the Haines Hwy (Hwy 3, also called Haines Rd) from Haines in Alaska. The VRC (☎ 634-2345), on Logan St, is in the Kluane National Park headquarters building. They have all manner of information about the park including an audiovisual display, and organise guided walks into the park. It's open mid-May to mid-September daily from 9 am to 9 pm.

---

with permanent steel ones. In 1949 the Alaska Hwy was opened to full-time civilian travel. For the first time year-round overland travel to Alaska from the south of the continent was possible. The completion of the highway opened the north-west to exploitation of its natural resources, changed settlement patterns and altered the Native Indian way of life forever.

The name of the highway has gone through several incarnations. In its time it has been called the Alaskan International Hwy, the Alaska Military Hwy and the Alcan (short for Alaska-Canadian) Hwy. More irreverently, in the early days it was also known as the Oil Can Hwy and the Road to Tokyo. Officially, it is now called the Alaska Hwy but many people still affectionately refer to it simply as the Alcan.

The Alaska Hwy begins at the 'Mile 0' cairn in Dawson Creek in north-eastern British Columbia. It then heads north-west through Whitehorse the capital of the Yukon to Fairbanks in Alaska. Actually the highway officially ends at Delta Junction (Mile 1422) about 155 km south-east of Fairbanks (Mile 1523). Between the two you follow the Richardson Hwy which comes north from Valdez in Prince William Sound.

Milepost signs were set up in the 1940s to help drivers calculate how far they had travelled along the road. Since then improvements, including the straightening of the road, mean that its length has been shortened and the mileposts can't be used literally. On the Canadian side the distance markers are in kms. Mileposts are still much in evidence in Alaska, and communities on both sides of the border still use the original mileposts for postal addresses and as reference points.

Until the mid 1970s conditions along the highway were extremely difficult. Traffic had to face loose gravel (which could puncture gasoline tanks or crack windscreens and headlights), dust stirred up by other vehicles, and sparsely strung-out services. Travellers also had to take plentiful supplies of food, clothing, gasoline and spare parts for their vehicle. The highway is now almost completely surfaced except for stretches where road crews are doing maintenance work on potholes and frost heaves (raised sections of bitumen caused by water freezing below the road), and there are services every 50 km or so. Millions of dollars are spent annually maintaining and upgrading the road.

Although it's possible to travel the highway year round most visitors go between May and September when the weather is warmer and road conditions less hazardous. All the attractions, services and accommodation are open then too. During this time the traffic noticeably increases, particularly the number of RVs. In winter the number of vehicles dwindles and the road is left mostly to logging, oil and mining trucks, other commercial traffic and to military transports transferring personnel between postings.

As you travel the highway you see some magnificent scenery. North-west from Dawson Creek you pass through flat, rich, agricultural land growing, cereal and canola (a hybrid of rapeseed). Toward Fort Nelson then beyond to Watson Lake and Whitehorse in the Yukon the scenery gives way to coniferous forests, tundra, lakes, icefields and mountains as you cross the Rocky, Cassiar and Coast mountain ranges. Between Whitehorse and Fairbanks the highway skirts the St Elias, Wrangell and Alaska mountain ranges. From the road you can catch sight of wildlife including black and grizzly bears, coyotes, moose, eagles and, if you're lucky, snowy owls. ■

There's also a smaller visitor cabin (☎ 841-5161) at Sheep Mountain north-west of town in the park.

Haines Junction, big on the map, tiny in three dimensions, has a post office, service stations, two campgrounds, several motels and lodges and a B&B. The *Village Bakery & Deli*, opposite the VRC, is a good place to eat and keeps the same hours as the centre in summer. The *Mountain View Motor Inn* is busy every morning for the good, cheap breakfasts and has rooms at $65/75. Next door is the Kluane Park Adventure Centre (☎ 633-5470) with organised raft trips, heli-hiking, trail rides as well as bike and canoe rentals. Flights over and into the park can also be arranged in town.

Kluane National Park

This rugged but accessible wilderness UN World Heritage Site covers 22,015 sq km in the extreme south-western corner of the Yukon adjacent to Alaska's Wrangell-St Elias National Park. Kluane means 'many fish' and is pronounced 'klu-AH-nee'.

The park consists primarily of the still growing St Elias Mountains and the world's **largest nonpolar icefields**, remnants of the last Ice Age. Two-thirds of the park is glacier. Interspersed there are valleys, glacial lakes, alpine forest, meadows and tundra.

The Kluane Ranges averaging 2500 metres are seen along the western edge of the highway. In behind, hidden, are the icefields and, largely blocked from view, the towering Icefield Ranges with 5950 metre **Mt Logan**, Canada's highest mountain and 5488 metre **Mt St Elias**, the second highest. Glimpses of the interior peaks can be had at the km 1622 viewpoint on the way into the park from Whitehorse and from around the Donjek River bridge.

A green belt area in and around the Kluane Ranges is where most of the animals and vegetation live.

Turquoise **Kluane Lake** is the Yukon's largest. A short worthwhile side trip can be gained by taking the fork to the east as the road approaches the south end of the lake. A few minutes drive takes you to the almost

disappeared **Silver City** where you can poke around by the edge of the lake among the ruins and remains of a trading post and Northwest Mounted Police barracks.

The park scenery makes for excellent hiking either along marked trails or less defined routes. There are about a dozen in each category, some following old mining roads, others traditional Native Indian paths. They range from about an hour in length to 10 days or so. The leaflet *Hiking in Kluane National Park* has a map and lists the trails with distances and starting points. Detailed trail guides are available after registering for a backcountry permit. You can buy topographical maps at the VRC or at Madley's store in Haines Junction.

One of the more popular trails is the 30-km trek to **Kaskawulsh Glacier** – one of the few that can be reached by foot. You can overnight at the end of this difficult-class trail and spend the next day climbing Observation Hill for a look over the glacier before returning the next day. Another is the easier hike to **St Elias Lake** with or without camping the night. Hikers should take precautions to avoid attack from bears (for details see Dangers & Annoyances in the Facts for the Visitor chapter) and inquire about the plastic food containers available at the information offices.

Fishing is good and wildlife abounds. Most noteworthy are the thousands of Dall sheep which can be seen on **Sheep Mountain** even from the road in April, May and September. In summer they go over the top and down the other side. There are also moose, grizzly bears, a small herd of caribou and 150 varieties of birds, among them rare peregrine falcon and eagles.

Famous amongst mountaineers, the internationally renowned Icefield Ranges provide excellent climbing.

The only campground technically within the park is at Kathleen Lake, 24 km south of Haines Junction off the Haines Hwy. It's open from mid-June to mid-September and costs $8 for an unserviced site. There are a couple of other campgrounds just outside the park on the highway, one at Kluane Lake.

They are seldom full. Of course, you can try backcountry tenting along overnight trails but you will need a permit. There is also commercial accommodation at Kathleen Lake.

Winters are long and harsh while summers are short; generally temperatures are comfortable from mid-June to mid-September, which makes that the best time to visit.

Soldiers' Summit
Near the Sheep Mountain Visitor Centre, from the parking lot off the highway, a path leads up to Soldiers' Summit, site of the official opening of the Alaska Hwy, on 20 November 1942. From the site there are good views overlooking Kluane Lake.

Destruction Bay
This small village of about 50 people sits on the shore of Kluane Lake about 108 km north of Haines Junction. Like Burwash Landing and Beaver Creek, it started off as a camp and supply depot during the construction of the Alaska Hwy. It was given its present name after a storm tore through the camp. You can go boating or fishing on the lake and the village has a service station, campground and motel.

Burwash Landing
Sixteen km north of Destruction Bay, Burwash Landing is most noted for the **Kluane Museum** (☎ 841-5561), and its very good animal exhibits. There are also displays on natural history and the Southern Tutchone people or Dan as they call themselves (they are part of the family of Dene, or Athapaskan peoples). The museum is open mid-May to early September daily from 9 am to 9 pm and admission is $3. The church and school of the early mission can be visited and there is also a gasoline station and store.

Beaver Creek
Beaver Creek, Canada's westernmost town, is on the Alaska Hwy 457 km north-west of Whitehorse close to the Alaska border. The VRC (☎ 862-7321), open mid-May to mid-September daily from 9 am to 9 pm, has

information on the Yukon and Alaska. The Canadian customs checkpoint is just north of the town; the US customs checkpoint is about 30 km further west. The border here is open 24 hours. *The Beaver Creek Hostel & Campground* (☎ 862-7903) has low-cost accommodation.

Tatshenshini-Alsek Wilderness Provincial Park (British Columbia)
Tucked along the southern Yukon border west of Hwy 3 this remote and rugged park is also part of the regional World Heritage designation. Together with Kluane and the adjacent national parks of Alaska it makes up one of the world's largest protected areas. The park can be viewed and some trails along abandoned roads accessed along Hwy 3 south of Haines Junction to Klukwan, Alaska. The Kluane Park office in Haines Junction should have some information and a rough map.

Services are nil but whitewater rafting trips down the Grade III and IV rapids of the 'Tat' are run through the Kluane Park Adventure Centre daily in summer. See under Haines Junction for details. Other outfitters run longer kayak and rafting trips down both rivers. These trips should be booked well in advance. Half the daily permits are issued to private parties but there is a waiting list of several years for these. The standard float trip down the Tat is six days after putting in at Dalton Post. Whatever your plans get the information package available through the Kluane National Park Office, BC Parks, or the Glacier Bay National Park information office, Gustavus, Alaska.

ATLIN (British Columbia)
The small, remote town of Atlin, 182 km south-east of Whitehorse in British Columbia, is reached by road via the Yukon – take Hwy 7 south off the Alaska Hwy. The scenery is great, with forests in Atlin Provincial Park and snowcapped mountains around Atlin Lake. (See also the British Columbia chapter.)

ROBERT CAMPBELL HIGHWAY

From Watson Lake, this gravel road is an alternative route north to Dawson City meeting the Klondike Hwy near Carmacks. Named after Robert Campbell, a 19th-century explorer and trader employed by the Hudson's Bay Company, it is a scenic and less-travelled road with few services. **Ross River**, 362 km from Watson Lake at the junction with the Canol Rd, is home to the Kaska people and supply centre for the local mining industry. It has a campground and a couple of motels. There's also a small government campground 13 km further west at Lapie Canyon. Little used Canol Rd goes to the NWT border and the beginning of the lengthy **Canol Heritage Hiking Trail** (see under NWT for more information) in one direction and to Johnson's Crossing in the other. Remnants of its construction can still be seen.

Faro, 10 km off the Robert Campbell Hwy on the Pelly River, was created in 1968 to support the huge (largest in the Yukon) copper, lead and zinc mine in the Anvil Mountains. Since then the mine has opened and closed several times depending on the world markets. Contact Curragh Resources (☎ 994-2600) for details on mine tours. There are motels, a campground nearby and some walking trails around town. Sheep Trail is an eight-km return trip, others lead to a waterfall or Mount Mye. Wildlife is abundant particularly Fannin (Dall) sheep. The road between Faro and the Klondike Hwy, and even down to Whitehorse, can be busy with trucks from the mine.

KLONDIKE HIGHWAY

The 716-km Klondike Hwy from Skagway in Alaska, through the north-western corner of British Columbia to Whitehorse and Dawson City, more or less traces the trail some 40,000 gold seekers took in 1898. The highway, open year round, is paved most of the way but there are some long stretches of gravel where construction is taking place. Watch for flying stones when the Faro mine is operating and truck traffic is heavy. Smoke

and forest fires may be encountered through the summer but the road is rarely closed.

Skagway (Alaska)

Skagway is at the southern end of the Klondike Hwy, which heads north through Whitehorse to Dawson City. The drive between Skagway and Whitehorse takes about three hours, passing lakes, mountains and meadows. A narrow-gauge railway line over White Pass, called the White Pass & Yukon Route (WP&YR), which was completed in 1900, can also be used (with a bus connection) to travel between the towns. (For more information on the train, see the Whitehorse Getting There & Away section.)

Skagway is the northern terminal for ferries and cruise ships plying the continental west coast. Beginning in San Francisco, Bellingham (Washington state), Vancouver, Vancouver Island and Prince Rupert, these ships edge along the coastline to Skagway. For details of ferries going south contact Alaska State Ferries (☎ 907-983-2229; 907-465-3941 in Juneau). The Alaska State Ferries company is commonly referred to as the Alaska Marine Hwy.

BC Ferries handles most of the traffic south of Prince Rupert along the Inside Passage (see the Getting There & Away sections of Prince Rupert and Port Hardy in the British Columbia chapter for more information).

Chilkoot Trail & National Historic Site

Skagway was the landing point for many in the gold-rush days. From there began the long, slow, arduous and sometimes deadly haul to the Klondike gold area near Dawson City. One of the old routes, the Chilkoot Trail over the Chilkoot Pass, is used today by hikers. For information packages on the trail contact the National Park Service Visitor Center (☎ (907) 983-2921), on the corner of Broadway St and 2nd Ave in Skagway; or the Parks Canada information office (☎ 667-4511, 668-3398), 300 Main St in Whitehorse. Before starting the hike you have to clear Canadian customs which you can do by calling ☎ 821-4111.

The well-marked, 53-km trail begins near Dyea, 13 km north-west of Skagway, then heads north-eastwards following the Taiya River to Bennett in British Columbia, and takes three to five days to hike. You must be in good physical condition to attempt it and come well equipped. Weather conditions are unpredictable: take a few layers of clothes and be ready to constantly peel them off then pile them back on again.

The most strenuous part of the trail is the hike up to Chilkoot Pass. Along the trail you can see hardware, tools and supplies dumped by the gold seekers. At several places there are wooden shacks where you can put up for the night, but these may be full. There are also 10 designated campgrounds.

At the northern end you can either catch a boat from Lake Bennett to Carcross from where you can catch a bus to Whitehorse; or you can head to the Klondike Hwy and hitch or take the bus to Whitehorse or Skagway.

For more information on the trail see Lonely Planet's *Alaska – a travel survival kit*.

Carcross

Carcross, 74 km south-east of Whitehorse, is the first settlement you reach when coming to the Yukon from Skagway on the Klondike Hwy. The site was once a major seasonal hunting camp of the Tagish people and the town's name is an abbreviation of Caribou Crossing – so called because caribou herds used to cross the narrow strip of land between Bennett and Lares lakes. The VRC (☎ 821-4431) is in the former WP&YR train station, next to the old sternwheeler SS *Tutshi*. The centre is open mid-May to mid-September daily from 9 am to 9 pm. Young Tlingit dancers perform by the centre.

Two km north of town, **Carcross Desert**, the world's smallest, is the exposed sandy bed of a glacial lake that retreated after the last Ice Age. Strong winds allow little vegetation to grow.

Whitehorse to Carmacks

North of Whitehorse between the Takhini Hot Springs Rd and Carmacks the land is dry and scrubby though there are some farms with cattle and horses. The road skirts several lakes where you can go swimming, boating and fishing. The largest is lovely **Lake Laberge** with a beach, 40 km north of Whitehorse, followed by **Fox Lake**, 24 km further north, and **Twin Lakes**, 23 km south of Carmacks. Each has a campground with shelters and pump water. Near Carmacks the mountains become lower, rounded hills and the land more forested. On the way to Dawson keep an eye out at service stations for the cinnamon buns the size of a bear cub.

Carmacks

Sitting on the banks of the Yukon River, Carmacks was once a fuelling station for riverboats and a stopover on the overland trail from Whitehorse to Dawson City. It's now a small community of around 400 people with a service station, campground, hotel, motel and other services. Originally known as Tantalus, the name was changed to Carmacks to honour George Washington Carmack who, along with two Native Indians, Skookum Jim and Tagish Charley, discovered gold at Bonanza Creek near Dawson City in 1896 and sparked off the Klondike gold rush.

Just south of town is a short walking trail. It goes through the woods to an area where you can search for gems and then beyond over the stream into a boggy meadow. North of town about two km, by the bridge, another trail leads to Coal Mine Lake where you can swim and fish. North of town about 20 km, stop at the **Five Finger Recreation Site** where stairs (a hell of a lot of stairs) lead to a path overlooking some rocky outcrops in the Yukon River which caused no end of trouble for the early river boats.

Stewart Crossing

Stewart Crossing, once a supply centre between Dawson City and Whitehorse, sits at the junction of the Klondike Hwy and the Silver Trail (Hwy 11). A small kiosk beside the road has information on the trail, another route taken by prospectors but this time in search of silver. Canoeists can put in here for the very good, five-day **float trip** down the

Stewart River to the Yukon River and on down to Dawson. Though you travel through wilderness, and wildlife is commonly seen, it is a trip suitable for the inexperienced. Canoeists should organise and outfit in Whitehorse or Dawson City (see under Activities in those city sections).

The Silver Trail
The Silver Trail heads north-eastward to three old, small mining and fur-trading towns: Mayo, Elsa and Keno City. The road is paved as far as Mayo. There are some good accessible outdoor possibilities in the area as well as campgrounds and other lodgings although there are no services in Elsa. Mayo is the starting point for a popular canoe trip to Dawson City via the Mayo, Stewart and Yukon rivers. Beyond Mayo 26 km is **Mount Haldane** with a six-km trail to the top and superb views. Round trip with an hour at the top takes about six hours. **Keno Hill** in Keno City (pop 50), with its signposts and distances to cities all over the world, offers good views of the mountains and valleys. There are hiking and driving trails in the vicinity, ranging from two km to 20 km long, providing access to old mining areas and alpine meadows. Also from Keno is a circular canoe route beginning at McQuesten Lake.

Tintina Trench
Tintina Trench can be seen from a lookout 60 km south of Dawson City. The trench is one of the Yukon's most important geological features and extends in a straight line for hundreds of km across the territory and into Alaska. The sides of the valley reveal visible evidence of plate tectonics.

DAWSON CITY
Dawson City, a compact town with a population of about 2000, at the confluence of the Yukon and Klondike rivers just 240 km south of the Arctic Circle, became the heart of the gold rush. Once known as 'the Paris of the North', it had deluxe hotels and restaurants, plush river steamers and stores stocking luxury items cherished by the world's wealthy. Today it is the most interesting of the Yukon towns, with many attractions remaining from its fleeting but vibrant fling with world fame and infamy. Many of the original buildings are still standing and Parks Canada is involved in restoring or preserving those considered historically significant. Regulations ensure that new buildings are built in sympathy with the old. Aside from being a unique and fun place there is a lot to see and although small, a two or three-day visit is not a bad idea.

As many as 100 companies, employing 500 people, are still mining for gold in the region around Dawson City. In 1992 gold to the value of $33 million was found. One entrepreneur once offered to pay compensation for the complete removal of the town and the inconvenience it would cause, mine the land beneath it, then replace the town just as it was. The residents refused.

Orientation & Information
Dawson City is small enough to walk around in a few hours. The Klondike Hwy leads into Front St (also called 1st Ave) beside the Yukon River.

On the corner of Front and King Sts is the good VRC (☎ 993-5566), housed in a large wooden building. It's open daily from mid-May to mid-September between 9 am and 9 pm. Staff are dressed in turn-of-the-century costumes. Worth a look are the Klondike-era films on mining, the gold rush and other subjects shown continually in the centre. Many of the town's attractions are National Historic Sites for which there is a fee. Combination tickets are sold here which offer a good reduced rate.

Opposite the VRC is the Northwest Territories Visitor Centre (☎ 993-56167), open daily June to August from 9 am to 9 pm, which has maps and information on the territories and Dempster Hwy.

The main post office (☎ 993-5342), on 5th Ave between Princess and Harper Sts, is open Monday to Friday from 8.30 am to 5.30 pm. If you're having any mail delivered, this is where you pick it up. The original post office still operates and is on the corner of King St and 3rd Ave. It's open from noon to 6 pm every day during the summer.

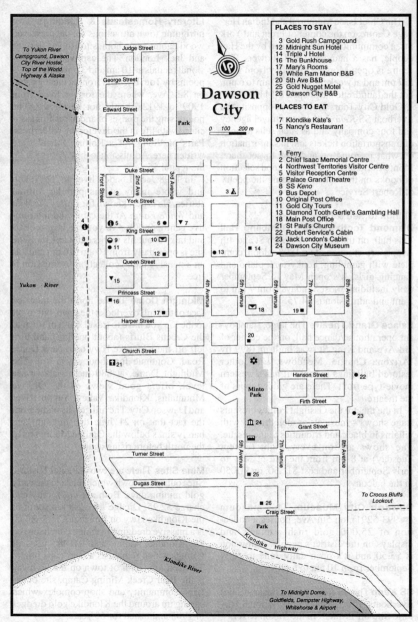

PLACES TO STAY

3 Gold Rush Campground
12 Midnight Sun Hotel
14 Triple J Hotel
16 The Bunkhouse
17 Mary's Rooms
19 White Ram Manor B&B
20 5th Ave B&B
25 Gold Nugget Motel
26 Dawson City B&B

PLACES TO EAT

7 Klondike Kate's
15 Nancy's Restaurant

OTHER

1 Ferry
2 Chief Isaac Memorial Centre
4 Northwest Territories Visitor Centre
5 Visitor Reception Centre
6 Palace Grand Theatre
8 SS Keno
9 Bus Depot
10 Original Post Office
11 Gold City Tours
13 Diamond Tooth Gertie's Gambling Hall
18 Main Post Office
21 St Paul's Church
22 Robert Service's Cabin
23 Jack London's Cabin
24 Dawson City Museum

The Chief Isaac Memorial and Indian Heritage Centre, on the corner of Front and York Sts, a community centre operated by the Han people, has a laundrette and showers. The centre is open Monday to Friday from 9 am to 7 pm and at weekends from 10 am to 6 pm, but the laundrette stays open till 11 pm.

Gold City Tours on Front St opposite the riverboat SS *Keno* is the town travel agency and tour company and as such sells a range of transportation tickets and has information on what is going on and how to get there. Monte Carlo on Front St has a good selection of books on the Yukon including the poetry of Robert Service.

Things to See & Do
Diamond Tooth Gertie's Gambling Hall
This hall, on the corner of Queen St and 4th Ave, is a re-creation of an 1898 saloon, complete with gambling, honky-tonk piano and dancing girls. It's open May to September daily including most Sundays from 7 pm to 2 am and admission is $4.75.

Palace Grand Theatre The large, flamboyant opera house/dance hall, on the corner of 3rd Ave and King St, was built in 1899 by 'Arizona Charlie' Meadows. Like other restored buildings in town, it has a western movie-type front. There are guided tours of the theatre.

In the theatre the Gaslight Follies presents stage shows – musicals or melodramas with villains in black and Mounties to the rescue. The shows are on every night (except Tuesday) at 8 pm from the end of May to early September and cost $11.50, or $13.50 in the balcony.

Dawson City Museum The museum (☎ 993-5291), on 5th Ave, houses a collection of 25,000 gold rush artefacts and displays on the district's people. Admission is $3.50 and it's open daily June to early September from 10 am to 6 pm.

SS *Keno* The SS *Keno*, one of the area's last riverboats, is on display as a National Historic Site off Front St in the Yukon River.

Literary Homesteads & Readings Two intriguing town attractions are the preserved wood cabins once homes to Robert Service and Jack London. The captivating professional recitals at 10 am and 3 pm of Service's poems by Tom Byrne in front of the log cabin on 8th Ave, where the former lived from 1909 to 1912, should not be missed. The poems sing the praises of and hardships associated with life in the developing wilderness. Parts of 'Songs of a Rolling Stone' were written here. Admission to the cabin is $2.25, the recital $5.

In 1898 Jack London lived in the Yukon and wrote many of his popular animal stories. He is best known for *Call of the Wild* and *White Fang*. At the cabin and interpretive centre on 8th Ave you can hear recitals and talks about his works daily at 1 pm. The site is open daily from 10 am to 6 pm and has an extensive photo collection. Admission is free.

Midnight Dome To the north the quarried face of this hill overlooks the town, but to get to the top you have to travel south of town to the Crocus Bluffs (about one km) and turn left off the Klondike Hwy onto New Dome Road. Continue for about seven km. The Midnight Dome, at 880 metres above sea level, offers good views of the Ogilvie Mountains, Klondike Valley, Yukon River and Dawson City. The hill gets its name from the fact that on 21 June the midnight sun barely sinks below the Ogilvie Mountains to the north before rising again.

Mine Sites There are two National Historic Sites outside of town which relate to the early gold mining days. Both are open daily and charge $2.25. Dredge #4, 12.3 km south of the Klondike Hwy on Bonanza Creek Road, is a massive dredging machine which tore up the Klondike Valley and left the piles of tailings which remain as a landscape blight. Thirteen km south of town on the highway is the Bear Creek Mining Camp, site of the large community and shop complex which sprang up around the Klondike gold dredges in 1905 and lasted for 60 years.

Gold Panning You can try panning for gold in nearby creeks. This can be done at the GuggieVille RV Park (☎ 993-5008) about two km south of town on Bonanza Creek Rd or at the Dawson City RV Park & Campground (☎ 993-5142). It costs about $6 and you're almost guaranteed to find some gold. If you want to go as part of a tour contact Gold City Tours (see Organised Tours). Alternatively, you can go by car to one of the historic mining sites. Many other claims in the area are private, so pick your spot carefully. People have been killed for less!

Organised Tours The VRC has walking tours of the city four times daily. Gold City Tours (☎ 993-5175) on Front St opposite the SS *Keno*, has two bus tours. One includes a city tour and trip to the Bonanza Creek gold mine site where you can do some panning. The other, which runs at night, goes up Midnight Dome.

River Klondike Rafting (☎ 993-6973) has 2½-hour trips down the Yukon River. The *Cleo Maria*, (☎ 993-5705) a rough-hewn rivercraft, does river drifting twice a day with a stop at a nearby farm.

Gray Line operates the *Yukon Queen* which cruises down river to Eagle, Alaska and back in four to five hours. There is one trip daily throughout the summer. Standby tickets are a possibility (see Activities).

Activities Dawson Trading Post (☎ 993-5316) rents out canoes and offers wilderness camping trips. One of the main do-it-yourself canoe float trips goes from Dawson three days downstream to Eagle City, Alaska. This trip is good for inexperienced canoeists. Ask about returning with the *Yukon Queen* tour boat, they'll take canoes. Also popular is to float north down the Klondike River for a few hours (putting in at Rock Creek 20 km south of town) or a full day (putting in at Dempster Corner) right back into the centre of Dawson.

Bicycles can be rented on Front St. At Crocus Bluff there is a short nature and interpretive trail leading to a viewing platform overlooking the Klondike River. To reach it

by foot follow King St into Old Dome Rd uphill behind town. The trail is by the cemetery and can also be reached by car from New Dome Rd.

Festivals
Events to look for include the Midnight Dome Race and the three-day Dawson City Music Festival in late July. In mid-August, there's Discovery Days, a three-day event commemorating the discovery of gold in the Klondike in 1896, featuring parades, music, dances and canoe races. In early September is the three-km Great Klondike International Outhouse Race (on wheels) – four people propel the outhouse through town while one sits on the seat.

Places to Stay
The growing competition to supply accommodation for Dawson City's visitors has kept prices stable. Accommodation fills up in July and August so booking early, especially for B&Bs, may be worthwhile.

Camping *Yukon River Campground* on the western side of the river has toilets, drinking water and shaded sites for $8. It's about 250 metres up the road to the right after you get off the ferry. You can also pitch a tent at the hostel – see the next section. In between the two is so-called tent city, a squatters area where people, some semi-permanently, have devised all manner of cheap housing. The city doesn't like it and is talking of closing it all down but has turned a blind eye because many of the residents are summer workers who have nowhere else to live. In town, *Gold Rush Campground* (☎ 993-5247), on the corner of York St and 5th Ave, is for RVs only and has sites for $10 or $15 with electricity.

Hostel Dieter Reinmuth runs the excellent HI-affiliated *Dawson City River Hostel* (☎ 993-6823) across the river from town and up the hill from the ferry terminal. It operates between mid-May and early September, has cabins for two to four people, spaces for tents and a cooking area. It's best described as rustic fun(k). There's no electricity and you have to pay cash. It's $8 for a tent and $13/15 members/nonmembers for a cabin bed. Bicycles and canoes are for rent.

B&Bs The VRC keeps a folder listing the B&Bs in the Dawson City area.

White Ram Manor B&B (☎ 993-5772), the pink house on the corner of Harper St and 7th Ave, is a friendly, easy going place with a laundry, kitchen and hot tub to ease those aching muscles. They'll also pick you up from the airport. Singles/doubles cost $70/80 with shared bath. *Dawson City B&B* (☎ 993-5649), 451 Craig St at the southern end of town, charges $69/79; lunch, dinner and transport to and from the airport can also be provided. Another worth trying is the cheaper *5th Ave B&B* (☎ 993-5941) near the museum. There are kitchen facilities and the one room which is smaller than the others is particularly good value. *Bonanza House B&B* (☎ 993-5772) by Minto Park at the corner of 7th Ave and Grant St has doubles for $75.

Hotels & Motels One of the cheapest places

to stay is *Mary's Rooms* (☎ 993-6013), on the corner of Harper St and 3rd Ave, which has basic singles/doubles with a communal bathroom for $39/45. It doesn't accept credit cards. Nor does the *Gold Nugget Motel* (☎ 993-5445), on the corner of Dugas St and 5th Ave, which is comparably low brow but cheap with doubles for $46.

A better option is *The Bunkhouse* (☎ 993-6164), the frontier-styled place on Princess St near the corner of Front St. Opened in 1993 it has clean rooms for $45/50 or $75/80 with private bathroom. Its season is from May to September.

More upmarket is the *Midnight Sun Hotel* (☎ 993-5495), on the corner of Queen St and 3rd Ave. It has a licensed restaurant, a bar and singles/doubles for $88/98. The *Triple J Hotel* (☎ 993-5323), on the corner of Queen St and 5th Ave, occupies the whole block and has motel rooms for $85 or log cabins (with kitchenettes). There are several other motels in this price range.

Places to Eat

Klondike Kate's, next to the motel of the same name on the corner of King St and 3rd Ave, does very good breakfast specials for $5 with unlimited coffee. They also serve reasonably priced lunches and dinners including pittas, salads and cappuccinos inside or on the patio.

There are several places along Front St. *River West* in the Chief Isaac Memorial Centre is a good place for a coffee and a cheap bagel or sandwich ($4.50) and to catch up on some post cards. It also sells muffins, sweets and other health foods. *Nancy's Restaurant* has outdoor tables and reasonably priced soups, salads, sandwiches and pastries from $4 to $7. It's open daily May to September from 6 am to 9 pm.

The *China Village* restaurant in the Midnight Sun Hotel has an all-you-can-eat, lunch-time buffet for $10.

You can have all the barbecue salmon you can eat with vegetables and salad aboard the *Pleasure Island Restaurant* paddlewheeler as it cruises the river. Call ☎ 993-5842 for information.

Inukshuks are human-like figures made of rock

The Han First Nation regularly puts on salmon barbecues for $20 which include an arts & crafts display. For details ask at the Chief Isaac Centre on Front St.

Many of the hotels have their own dining rooms for steak, seafood or pastas.

Getting There & Away

Air There is an airport 19 km east of town off the Klondike Hwy, with daily flights to Whitehorse and twice-weekly flights to Inuvik in the Northwest Territories. One way to Whitehorse with Air North (☎ 993-5110) is $227 including tax. The flight to Inuvik with Alkan Airways (☎ 993-5440) costs $290 one way or $560 return. The flights are on Monday and Thursday; the return leg to Dawson City is on the following day. For tickets and transport to the airport contact Gold City Tours.

Bus From the bus station on the corner of Front and King Sts, Gold City Tours (☎ 993-5175) has two vans a week for the 12-hour ride to Inuvik. The Arctic Tour Company (☎ 979-4100 in Inuvik) has three buses a week in each direction for $198 one way plus tax.

Norline Coaches (☎ 993-6010) runs buses to Inuvik, Fairbanks and Whitehorse. There are three buses a week to Whitehorse; the one-way fare is $73 (including tax). The office is at the Gas Shack at the Chevron gasoline station.

Car Three highways connect Dawson City with the rest of the continent: the Top of the World Hwy (Hwy 9) to Alaska; the Dempster Hwy to the Northwest Territories; and the Klondike Hwy to the southern Yukon. (See the relevant sections for details.)

DEMPSTER HIGHWAY

The Dempster Hwy (Hwy 5 in the Yukon, Hwy 8 in the Northwest Territories) starts 40 km south-east of Dawson City off the Klondike Hwy. It heads north over the Ogilvie and Richardson mountains beyond the Arctic Circle and down to Inuvik in the Northwest Territories near the shores of the Beaufort Sea.

The highway is named after Corporal Dempster of the Royal Northwest Mounted Police. In the winter of 1910-11, one of the coldest on record, four officers en route to Dawson City lost their way amid the Ogilvie Mountains. Dempster was sent to search for the lost patrol and he found them frozen to death near Fort McPherson, a little over 40 km from where they had begun their journey.

The highway, opened in 1979, makes road travel along the full length of North America possible. Inuvik is a long way from Dawson City – along 741 km of gravel road – but the scenery is beautiful: mountains, valleys, rivers and vast open tundra. The highway is open all year but the best time to travel is between June and September when the ferries over the Peel and Mackenzie rivers are able to operate. In winter ice forms a natural bridge over the rivers.

Accommodation and vehicle services along the route are few (at Eagle Plains in the Yukon and Fort McPherson and Arctic Red River in the Northwest Territories) so go well prepared and carry extra gasoline. The Yukon government has three basic campgrounds – at Tombstone Mountain (also called Campbell Mountain), Engineer Creek and Rock River; and there's a Northwest Territories' government campground three km south of Fort McPherson. For maps and information on road conditions ask at the Northwest Territories Visitor Centre (☎ 993-5175) in Dawson City.

TOP OF THE WORLD HIGHWAY

At the northern end of Front St in Dawson City a free ferry crosses the Yukon River to the start of the scenic Top of the World Hwy (Hwy 9). The five-minute ferry taking about half-a-dozen vehicles runs 24 hours. Open only in summer, the gravel road extends 108 km to the Alaska border. The small customs & immigration checkpoint is open between June and mid-September daily from 9 am to 10 pm; you can't cross outside these times. From the border, the Taylor Hwy runs south through Alaska to meet the Alaska Hwy at Tetlin Junction.

VUNTUT NATIONAL PARK

Vuntut, a Gwitch'in word meaning 'old crow flats', was declared a national park in 1993. It is south of the village of Old Crow, the most northerly settlement in the Yukon. Each spring a porcupine caribou herd of 200,000 still follows its migration route north across the plain to calving grounds near the Beaufort Sea. In Canada these calving grounds are protected within Ivvavik National Park, but the grounds extend into Alaska where there is lobbying by oil companies to open them up for exploration.

With its many lakes and ponds, Vuntut National Park is visited by around 500,000 waterbirds each autumn. Archaeological sites contain fossils of ancient animals such as the mammoth, plus evidence of early human occupation.

The only access to the 4400-sq-km park (about two-thirds the size of Prince Edward Island) is by aeroplane or on foot.

IVVAVIK NATIONAL PARK

Formerly the Northern Yukon National Park, Ivvavik, situated along the Beaufort Sea and adjoining Alaska, covers 10,170 sq km. The park is dominated by the British Mountains and its vegetation is mainly tundra. It's on the migration route of the porcupine caribou (see the previous section) and is also a major waterfowl habitat. Its facilities are minimal and, though there's no road access, flights on one of the small regional airlines will get you there.

Off the coast is **Herschel Island**, the Yukon's first territorial park. A former whaling station, it is rich in bird and other wildlife.

Northwest Territories

Stretching 3200 km from the Yukon in the west to Greenland in the east, the Northwest Territories cover an enormous area, about a third of Canada. The territories have a population density of around one person per 60 sq km. That's a lot of breathing room. Nearly half the region is north of the Arctic Circle and includes many islands in the Arctic Ocean.

The territories are divided into three districts: Mackenzie, Franklin and Keewatin. The District of Mackenzie in the west is the only one accessible by road and is the most developed, containing the territories' largest towns of Yellowknife, the capital, and Inuvik. The District of Franklin to the north and east includes the huge islands of Baffin and Ellesmere. The District of Keewatin is bordered in the south by the provinces of Manitoba and eastern Saskatchewan and in the east by Hudson Bay.

Mining has long been and continues to be a major source of income and impetus to development. In the early 1990s large scale industrial diamond exploration began. At the time of writing North America's first diamond mine, owned by Broken Hill Pty Ltd (BHP), the huge Australian mining concern, was about to be built around Lac de Gras 300 km north of Yellowknife.

Given, however, the ever fluctuating fortunes in natural resources, the territories are relying more each year on tourism as a money earner. Increased accessibility, together with the lure of pristine wilderness, means a continuing rise in the number of visitors to the territories. Other sources of income include fish, fur and handicrafts.

History

The earliest known inhabitants of the Northwest Territories, the Dene, or Athapaskans, came to the region from Asia somewhere between 10,000 and 40,000 years ago. The Inuit are thought to have arrived between 4000 and 8000 years ago.

The Vikings were the first Europeans to see the Northwest Territories, arriving in about 1000 AD. Later the search began for the legendary Northwest Passage – a sea passage from the Atlantic Ocean to the Pacific Ocean and the shortest route to China and its riches. Canada was thought of as merely a stopping-off point on the way to Asia. From 1524, British, French and Dutch adventurers all joined the search for a water-

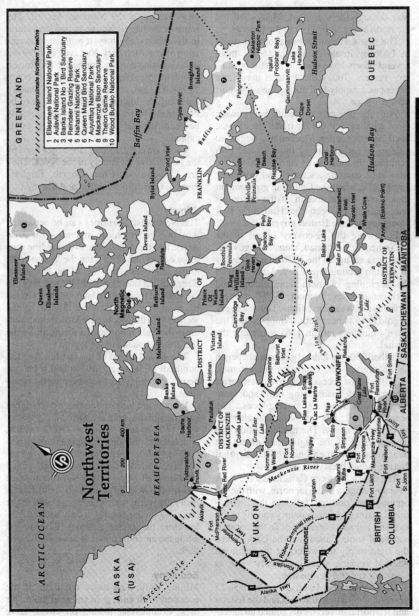

NORTHWEST TERRITORIES

Northwest Territories

0   200   400 km

ARCTIC OCEAN

BEAUFORT SEA

GREENLAND

Baffin Bay

Hudson Strait

QUEBEC

Hudson Bay

Approximate Northern Treeline

1 Ellesmere Island National Park
2 Aulavik National Park
3 Banks Island No 1 Bird Sanctuary
4 Reindeer Grazing Reserve
5 Nahanni National Park
6 Queen Maud Bird Sanctuary
7 Auyuittuq National Park
8 Mackenzie Bison Sanctuary
9 Thelon Game Reserve
10 Wood Buffalo National Park

Ellesmere Island

Queen Elizabeth Islands

North Magnetic Pole

Devon Island

Bylot Island

Pond Inlet

Clyde River

Broughton Island

Kekerton Historic Park

Pangnirtung

Iqaluit (Frobisher Bay)

Lake Harbour

Qaummaarvit

Cape Dorset

Bathurst Island

Melville Island

Resolute

Prince of Wales Island

King William Island

Boothia Peninsula

FRANKLIN

Baffin Island

DISTRICT OF FRANKLIN

Banks Island

Victoria Island

Holman

Cambridge Bay

Gjoa Haven

Spence Bay

Pelly Bay

Igloolik

Hall Beach

Melville Peninsula

Repulse Bay

Coral Harbour

Sachs Harbour

Paulatuk

Coppermine

Bathurst Inlet

The Back River

Chesterfield Inlet

Rankin Inlet

Baker Lake

Baker Lake

Whale Cove

Arviat (Eskimo Point)

Dubawnt Lake

DISTRICT OF KEEWATIN

MANITOBA

SASKATCHEWAN

DISTRICT OF MACKENZIE

Colville Lake

Great Bear Lake

Rae Lakes

Snare Lakes

Lac la Martre

Rae

Edzo

YELLOWKNIFE

Great Slave Lake

Reliance

The Thelon River

Fort Resolution

Fort Smith

ALBERTA

Tuktoyaktuk

Inuvik

Arctic Red River

Fort McPherson

Aklavik

Norman Wells

Fort Norman

Wrigley

Fort Simpson

Fort Providence

Hay River

Enterprise

Mackenzie River

Nahanni Butte

Fort Liard

Tungsten

Fort Nelson

Fort St John

BRITISH COLUMBIA

YUKON

WHITEHORSE

ALASKA (USA)

Arctic Circle

Dempster HWY

Klondike HWY

Robert Campbell HWY

Mackenzie HWY

Alaska HWY

way through the continent. Many died but the north was mapped out in the process.

The first successful navigation was made in 1906 by Roald Amundsen. Since then, several others have done it, mostly in military vessels. Today the route is used little except as a supply line during the very short summer thaw.

With the prospect of wealth being made from whaling and the fur trade, Europeans, such as Alexander Mackenzie, began to explore in earnest during the 18th and 19th centuries. In their wake came missionaries who built churches, schools and hospitals. Until 1870, when the Canadian government took over, administration of the territories was shared between the Hudson's Bay Company and the British government.

Following the discovery of oil in the 1920s near Fort Norman, a territorial government was set up. In the 1930s the discovery of radium around Great Bear Lake marked the beginning of more rapid change and 20th-century development. WWII brought airfields and weather stations. The discovery of gold in 1934 near Yellowknife swelled the town's numbers and in 1967 it became the capital.

In the 1950s the federal government began health, welfare and education programmes. The 1960s saw accessibility to the territories increase, with roads being built and more airplanes connecting more places. The search for oil, gas and minerals changed some areas rapidly. The modernisation and development of the region has meant the near-total disappearance of traditional Native Indian lifestyle.

The debate between Canada and the USA over sovereignty of the far north, with the US arguing that portions fall into the international realm so no one country can lay claim to them, remains unresolved. To the consternation of some Canadians, the USA claims the right to ply the waters of the far north without seeking what opponents view as Canada's rightful permission.

On 12 November 1992, after more than 15 years of negotiation, the Inuit and the federal and territorial governments signed an agreement known as the Nunavut Accord. The result of the largest Native Indian land claim in the country's history, it promises the creation of a new territory, Nunavut, in 1999 out of the existing eastern Northwest Territories. Nunavut, meaning 'our land', will cover 219,000 sq km, about one-fifth of Canada's land surface. Iqaluit, Baffin Island, is to be its capital. The western section will probably be renamed and keep Yellowknife as its capital.

There are eight official languages used by the Legislative Assembly of the NWT. They are Chipewayan, Cree, Dogrib, English, French, Gwich'in, Inuktitut and Slavey.

Climate

The Northwest Territories can be separated into two geographical regions – the sub-Arctic and the Arctic. The dividing line runs more or less obliquely from the Yukon coast to the south-eastern corner of the District of Keewatin on the shores of Hudson Bay. To the south of this line the land is characterised by short coniferous forests which spread westward to the Mackenzie Mountains straddling the Yukon border. To the north lie the flat, treeless plains of the tundra.

The glacial action of the last Ice Age left hundreds of lakes and rivers and a permanently frozen layer of subsoil called permafrost.

Winters are long and extremely cold, but summers in the south are surprisingly warm, with temperatures reaching 30°C, which, coupled with the long daylight hours (due to high latitude), makes travelling very pleasant. The climate is dry, the average annual rain/snowfall being less than 30 cm. Most visitors travel in July and August but June is generally warm, too, with breezes and fewer bugs. By the beginning of July around Yellowknife, the sun sets at about 12.30 am and while the air cools down, it never really gets dark.

Economy

Mining is far and away the base of the economy with zinc, gold and lead the major ores. Commercial fishing on Great Slave

🕸🕸🕸🕸🕸🕸🕸🕸🕸🕸🕸🕸🕸🕸🕸🕸🕸🕸🕸🕸🕸🕸🕸🕸🕸🕸🕸🕸🕸🕸🕸🕸🕸🕸🕸🕸🕸

Northwest Passage

Soon after 1492 it became clear that Columbus had landed on a 'new' continent and had not discovered a westerly route to Asia. Others then began the search for a waterway to the Orient sailing around the Americas. The southern route was successfully navigated by Ferdinand Magellan in 1521, but the northern route – the Northwest Passage – was to take a good deal longer.

Many famous explorers – including Sir Martin Frobisher, Sir Francis Drake, Henry Hudson and Captain James Cook – tried but failed. The most tragic failure was in 1845 when Sir John Franklin, along with 128 crew members, disappeared somewhere among the islands of the Arctic.

The first successful navigation of the Northwest Passage came early this century when the Norwegian explorer, Roald Amundsen, completed a three-year (1903-1906), east-west voyage in a converted fishing boat, the *Gjöa*.

In 1942, the *St Roch*, a Royal Canadian Mounted Police schooner under the command of Sargeant Henry Lawson, became the first ship to navigate the Northwest Passage from west to east. It then became the first ship to do the crossing from east to west in one season. The *St Roch* is now on display in the Vancouver Maritime Museum. In 1960 the US submarine *Seadragon* was the first to do it under water.

In 1988 a New York-based cruise ship became the first tourist vessel to navigate the Northwest Passage, from Newfoundland to Alaska. The 40-day history-making trip cost each passenger a tidy $20,000. ■

🕸🕸🕸🕸🕸🕸🕸🕸🕸🕸🕸🕸🕸🕸🕸🕸🕸🕸🕸🕸🕸🕸🕸🕸🕸🕸🕸🕸🕸🕸🕸🕸🕸🕸🕸🕸🕸

Lake is also important. Hunting and trapping is still critical to many daily lives and arts & crafts is a major income generator. Tourism's significance increases steadily.

Population & People

Around Mackenzie River and Great Slave Lake the people call themselves the Dene, or Athapaskans. Together with the Inuit, who live mainly along the northern coast and on the Arctic islands, they are the original northern peoples. The word Inuit refers in general to an Eskimo in Canada, as opposed to the Eskimo of Asia or the Aleutian Islands (Alaska). The term Eskimo is not appreciated by the Inuit and is being used less and less. The term Inuit simply means 'people'. Roughly a third of people speak Inktitut.

The Inuit number about 23,000 and the Dene 10,000; the rest are mainly Métis (of mixed race, 45000) and non-Native 25,000.

About half the population of the NWT is under the age of 25 in stark contrast to the aging population of Canada as a whole.

Information

Territorial Symbols The territorial tree is the jack pine and the official floral emblem is the mountain avens, a member of the rose family. A logo featuring the polar bear appears on many government publications and all vehicle licence plates are shaped like one. The gyrfalcon, the largest of the falcon species, is the territorial bird.

Tourist Offices For information on all parts of the territories contact Northwest Territories Tourism (☎ 1-800-661-0788). The mailing address is NWT Tourism Information, Box 2107 (EX), Yellowknife, NT, Canada X1A 2P6. The good, free booklet *Explorers' Guide* is published annually and contains much useful information.

The Department of Economic Development & Tourism (☎ 873-7200) in Yellowknife oversees tourism operations.

The territories have been divided into eight different travel zones each with a regional (sometimes remote) office. Should you require specialised information from one of them, their addresses may be obtained from the main office listed above.

Roadside Visitor Information Centres can be found in Yellowknife, Fort Providence, Enterprise, Hay River, Fort Smith and Inuvik. There's also one on the Yukon border (Dempster Hwy) and one on the Alberta border (Mackenzie Hwy at the 60th parallel), both of which are open from May to September. In addition, there is Wood Buffalo

National Park Visitor Centre in Fort Smith and Nahanni National Park Visitor Centre in Fort Simpson.

Telephone The telephone code for places within the District of Mackenzie is the same as that for Alberta and the Yukon – 403. In Franklin and Keewatin it's 819.

Time The Northwest Territories cover four time zones. From west to east these are Mountain, Central, Eastern and Atlantic standard time. When it's noon in Yellowknife it's 2 pm in Iqaluit at the eastern end of Baffin Island.

Tax There is no territorial sales tax.

Activities

For a lot of visitors, a trip to the Northwest Territories means canoeing, fishing, hiking and camping in the national and territorial parks during the short summer season. For others it's to observe the wildlife or even to rock and ice climb. These activities permit the visitor to see the area's uniqueness and rugged beauty. There is every manner of package tour and all-inclusive guided trip for visitors to pursue these outdoor activities, but – in the District of Mackenzie at least – many things can also be done on your own, which is much cheaper.

National & Territorial Parks The Northwest Territories have five national parks. Auyuittuq National Park is on Baffin Island to the east. Ellesmere Island National Park is on the north of Ellesmere Island, just across Robeson Channel from north-western Greenland. Nahanni National Park is in the Mackenzie Mountains in the far south-west. On the north of Banks Island, Aulavik National Park is the newest of the territories' national parks. Wood Buffalo National Park, south of Great Slave Lake, is the only one accessible by road.

There are three historic parks: Kekerten Island and Qaummaarviit, both off the east coast of Baffin Island; and Northwest Passage at Gjoa Haven on King William Island.

There are also more than 30 parks run by the territorial government for recreation, and a number of wildlife sanctuaries. The territorial parks have had much upgrading in recent years and improvements and expansion continue as tourism increases. Most parks and their campgrounds are open from mid-May to mid-September. Campgrounds tend to be small, simple and cheap often with no attendant. Except at a few there is rarely a problem getting a place.

Survival in the north is hard for any form of life, but despite the harsh conditions there is a greater variety than commonly imagined. The parks are a good place to observe some of it. A range of mammals and birds can be seen including bears, bison, caribou snowy owls and ptarmigans. Whales, walruses and seals can be seen along the northern coastlines and in the waters around the northern islands in summer.

The Northwest Territories has more than 800 plant species, from the mosses, lichens, ferns and grasses of the Arctic tundra to the spruce, larch and white-birch trees of the sub-Arctic region.

Accommodation

Yellowknife is the only place with much choice and includes a number of fine B&Bs. Motels or hotels can be found in all towns of any size and territorial campgrounds (generally small and basic) are conveniently situated along the highways and at town sites. Reservations are rarely necessary.

Independent Travel

Increasing numbers of travellers are visiting the territories and more of them without a prebooked excursion. Facilities and small, modest tour or outfitting businesses are slowly increasing with them. The only area for this, though, is the region located around Great Slave Lake and the BC border. The territory's only road network and public ground transportation is here. See under Bus later for travel details.

Bus services cover most towns although a vehicle (brought or rented) offers the flexibility required to see much of this land. Independent budget travel here necessitates some good quality camping equipment. Campgrounds can generally be found within walking distance of the centre of most towns. Getting into the wilderness for the most part means having or renting a canoe. Hiking is restricted by several factors. The bush can be very dense and there are the three B's to contend with: bugs, bears and bison. Old trails are few as this has not been a traditional means of travel and tourism is young enough here that new trails have not been developed in great numbers. This is changing, though, especially around Yellowknife.

There are four main areas which can be explored independently. The area around Yellowknife offers a number of cheap, short possibilities. Some of these can be done by bus, by boat, on foot or with small commercial tours. With a car, the Ingraham Trail can be explored in anywhere from a day to several weeks. Along this road leading east of town are several walking trails. A more in-depth look can be had by using one or more of the established canoe routes. They range from simple day trips to much longer excursions and vary in difficulty from easy tracks suitable for novices to more demanding routes. Most of them are on lakes (flat water) rather than rivers, so rapids and currents are not an issue.

The second area to investigate is the Mackenzie River for canoe and boat trips. These can be done from several places but the primary one is Fort Simpson where canoes can be rented. Some people spend weeks going with the current all the way to the Beaufort Sea. The Mackenzie can be entered at other points such as Fort Providence where some long-distance paddlers begin. Short trips are also possible and the information offices can help with suggestions. This area is not for the inexperienced. The waters are swift and there are absolutely no designated camp sites. But one-day and longer moderately priced boat trips are offered to several places from Fort Simpson.

The third area is Nahanni National Park. Although most of the trips here are highly organised, pre-arranged and expensive, it can be done. An aeroplane or helicopter can be hired to reach the park where there is camping and hiking. Headquarters for excursions is Fort Simpson.

The fourth area is Wood Buffalo National Park where there are both novice and advanced hiking trails and a range of canoe routes. There are outfitters in Fort Smith who will rent equipment or organise various camping adventures into the park.

Of course there are also the roads to be explored, all of which have territorial camping parks and sight-seeing points of note. A circuit combining parts of Alberta and British Columbia can be driven in the south-western corner. The Mackenzie Hwy from the Alberta border to Fort Providence, with its many waterfalls, is of special interest. Also, anywhere in the NWT is never far from the wild.

NORTHWEST TERRITORIES

Organised Tours

Well organised package tours have long been the principal means of seeing some aspect of the NWT. Some of the simpler tour possibilities have been outlined above. For many, the best or only way to see the more inaccessible parts of the Northwest Territories, especially the districts of Franklin and Keewatin, is on an organised tour. These can be either general or highly specialised trips. Dog-sled trips, caribou-photography excursions and wilderness fishing are all possible. These are, however, usually quite expensive. The Explorers' Guide has lists of companies, their addresses and the types of tours they offer. For further information contact the Department of Economic Development & Tourism in Yellowknife.

Getting There & Around

Air Canadian Airlines flies from Edmonton, Winnipeg and Montreal to Yellowknife. The one-way, no advance notice fare between Edmonton and Yellowknife is $470 including tax. Canadian North (☎ 873-5533 in Yellowknife), a division of Canadian Airlines, flies to destinations within the Northwest Territories such as Hay River and to Quebec and northern Manitoba. Air Canada flies from Edmonton and Calgary to Yellowknife, with connecting flights on NWT Air (☎ 920-2500, 1-800-661-0789) to Inuvik, Cambridge Bay, Fort Simpson and Coppermine. NWT Air also flies between Winnipeg and Rankin Inlet, and between Yellowknife and Iqaluit. Note that, unfortunately, there is no major airline which flies between Yellowknife and Whitehorse. Any flight you may find for this is big dollars.

From Whitehorse, Alkan Air (☎ 668-2107 in Whitehorse) has flights four times a week to Inuvik. First Air (☎ 873-6884 in Yellowknife, 1-800-267-1247), flies from Ottawa and Montreal to Yellowknife, Pangnirtung, Broughton Island, Rankin Inlet and other destinations. They also have a flight from Iqualuit to Greenland. Air Inuit (☎ (514) 636-9445 in Dorval, Quebec) connects northern Quebec with communities in the District of Keewatin including Cape Dorset and Baffin Island.

About 10 small companies have scheduled flights between points within the territories. Many more operate on a charter basis, using floats (on lakes) or wheels to land in summer, and skis in winter. The Explorers' Guide lists many of these companies under each region.

Bus Greyhound Bus Lines has a service every day but Saturday from Edmonton in Alberta, to Hay River for $122 one way. There's a long stop in Peace River.

Connections for points around the NWT are made with Frontier Coachlines. The main office (☎ 873-4892), is at 328 Old Airport Rd, Yellowknife. It goes north from Hay River and Enterprise and continues via Fort Providence and Edzo to Yellowknife. Fares and schedules are available through Greyhound Bus Lines. The one-way fare between Edmonton and Yellowknife is $176 and the bus arrives in town at 10.50 pm. If you're coming from Edmonton and you don't want to go to Hay River you can change buses in Enterprise. Note that Frontier only runs Monday to Friday.

Frontier also runs buses from Hay River to Fort Smith. Weekdays there is one a day in each direction from Yellowknife and Fort Smith to Hay River, but no through bus; you must make a stopover in Hay River. Hay River to Yellowknife is $60, Fort Smith to Yellowknife $91. These prices include tax.

There is no bus service to the Fort Simpson/Nahanni area. Buses do run from Dawson City, Yukon to Inuvik.

Car Only the District of Mackenzie in the west, north of Alberta, is accessible by car, and most of the highways are gravel. The Mackenzie Hwy north from Edmonton is almost completely paved as far as the junction with Hwy 3 north of Enterprise. A combination of paved and gravel roads connect Hay River, Wood Buffalo National Park, Yellowknife and Fort Simpson. The Mackenzie Hwy is the name for the section

DEANNA SWANEY

MARK LIGHTBODY

Top: Kluane National Park in the autumn, Yukon
Bottom: The RCMP are on hand to celebrate Canada's birthday, Dawson City, Yukon

TOM SMALLMAN

W LYNCH

Top: Float-plane base, Latham Island, Yellowknife, Northwest Territories
Bottom: Lowell Glacier, Kluane National Park, Yukon

linking northern Alberta with Fort Simpson and Fort Smith.

The Liard Hwy, which heads north off the Alaska Hwy near Fort Nelson, is also gravel and links northern British Columbia with Fort Liard in the Northwest Territories. It then goes on to meet the Mackenzie Hwy (Hwy 1) south of Fort Simpson. From there the Mackenzie Hwy heads eastward to Enterprise.

The first part of the road from Fort Providence north to Yellowknife runs along the edge of the Mackenzie Bison Sanctuary and it's not uncommon to see bison on the road. Sandhill cranes and ptarmigans from the bird world are also fairly common. The ponds you'll notice by the side of the road are due to holes dug for sand and gravel needed for the road's construction.

In the northern part of the District of Mackenzie, the Dempster Hwy connects the Yukon with Inuvik. This route passes through excellent mountain scenery much of the way to the Mackenzie River Delta, nipping into a portion of the huge Reindeer Grazing Reserve before ending up at Inuvik.

There are vehicle-rental outlets in Hay River, Fort Smith, Yellowknife, Norman Wells, Inuvik, Tuktoyaktuk and Iqaluit.

For information about conditions and ferry crossings on the Dempster Hwy the numbers to call are ☎ 1-800-661-0752 toll free or ☎ 979-2678 (Inuvik). For other highways call ☎ 1-800-661-0750 or ☎ 874-2208 (Hay River). For information about ferries call ☎ 1-800-661-0751 or within Yellowknife ring ☎ 873-7799. Road work is ongoing during the short summer and can mean delays and slow-going through the mushy, dampened areas being graded.

Warning During a six-week period in the late autumn and early spring, when river freeze-ups and ice break-ups occur, ferries cannot run over the rivers. Therefore there is no road access or bus service for this period. This includes to Yellowknife.

Precautions There can be long distances between service stations so take extra gaso-line, spare parts, water and food with you. Because most of the roads in the Northwest Territories are not paved it's a good idea to protect your lights and windscreen with coverings. Some people also guard the gasoline tank. Rental agencies may ask for extra insurance fees or may not insure against cracked windows. Forest fires sometimes interrupt road travel but you will be advised enroute.

Campers should bring an axe. Most campgrounds supply wood – in the form of unsplit logs. You could freeze to death looking at a pile of it!

DISTRICT OF MACKENZIE

The District of Mackenzie is the most accessible area, being the only district with any roads, and is where most visitors go. It borders the Yukon in the west and Alberta in the south. This is the only area of the territories with a forestry business, and it has most of the fishing as well.

The Mackenzie Mountains, with peaks of 2700 metres, straddle the Yukon border. The Mackenzie River, the longest waterway in Canada, runs north-west along the Mackenzie Valley from Great Slave Lake to the Beaufort Sea in the Arctic Ocean. Most of the population lives around Great Slave Lake and Great Bear Lake, which has many mines. The two national parks in the District of Mackenzie are Nahanni in the south-west, and Wood Buffalo, which spreads south across the Alberta border.

The District of Mackenzie has fairly warm, dry summers with an average temperature of 13°C.

RV or tent camping is really the only way to see this part of the country at a reasonable price. Long-distance travelling, and food and accommodation in the towns are expensive with a capital E. To keep costs down you'll have to work at it, which means going without some comforts and conveniences.

Both camping and canoeing are possible along the district's highway system. Several communities rent boats or canoes. From roadside campgrounds, trips can be taken around the lakes, and away from the roads you can pick your own camping spot. It is not hard to have a lake to yourself; inquire at one of the Visitor Information Centres for more information. Remember that the water is cold enough to kill you in 15 minutes, so keep close to shore in a canoe.

Along the highway system the fee for a site at a government campground is $10. Campgrounds have firewood and are open from 15 May to 15 September. Don't forget to bring insect repellent.

Yellowknife

Rising out of the wilderness in a region once occupied by the Slavey people, the city gets its name from the copper-bladed knives they used. Although gold was first found here in 1898 by Klondike-bound prospectors, it wasn't until the discovery of richer veins first in 1934 and again in 1945 that Europeans were attracted to the area in large numbers.

Yellowknife has a population of around 16,000 and is by far the largest town in the territories, of which it is the capital (at least until 1999). A modern, fast-growing settlement on the northern shores of Great Slave Lake, 341 km from Fort Smith by road, Yellowknife is essentially a government town. It also acts as the commercial and service centre for the region and people from all over Canada now live and work here. Visitors use Yellowknife as a base for camping and fishing trips as well as for exploring the rocky landscape and nearby lakes.

Orientation Yellowknife sits on the northern shores of Great Slave Lake and is connected with the south by the Mackenzie Hwy. The city is divided into the new (south) and old (north) parts of town, which are connected by Franklin Ave (50th Ave), the main thoroughfare. The new part of town has the shops, businesses, services and hotels. Hilly, residential Old Town wedged between Back Bay and Yellowknife Bay is far more interesting to stroll with its history, variety of housing, float-plane base and views. Coming from the south into the city, the highway leads you past the airport, along 48th St and into Franklin Ave.

Frame Lake, about the size of central Yellowknife, lies along downtown's western edge. The 5.6 km walking trail around it is a popular jogging spot and pleasant evening stroll. It goes past the Heritage Centre and Legislative Assembly on to the western side of Jack Lake and out to Hwy 3 by Fred Henne Park.

Information The Visitor Information Centre (☎ 873-3131) is at 4807 49th St near the Prince of Wales Northern Heritage Centre. There is a wealth of information here; the staff is knowledgeable and helpful and there are some good displays and printed matter to look over. Also climb aboard the bush plane elevator. You can get maps, canoe routes and a guide to settlements across the territories, and also special fishing, canoeing and motoring guides. The centre is open daily from 8 am to 8 pm. Also here is the Northern Frontier Visitors Association which covers the region around Yellowknife.

The main post office, on the corner of Franklin Ave and 49th St, is open Monday to Friday from 9 am to 5.30 pm. The Bank of Montreal in the Centre Square Mall is open on Saturday from 10 am to 3 pm. The Book Cellar, in Panda II Mall, has a good selection of books on Native people's culture and history of the Northwest Territories.

Topographical maps are available in Yellowknife at the Map Sales Office (☎ 920-8299), 5013 51st St across from Canadian Tire. The office is open for sales in the summer Monday to Friday from 8.30 to 11.30 am and 12.30 to 4.30 pm. Maps in Yellowknife are in short supply, so getting one beforehand is not a bad idea if you need one with a very small scale for canoeing.

The Canada Map Office (☎ (613) 952-7000), 615 Booth St, Ottawa, Ontario K1A 0E9, has all types of detailed maps of the territories, including small-scale topographical ones. The office will send you an index and you'll have to pick the map numbers you need from that.

The Arctic Laundromat is at 4310 Franklin Ave.

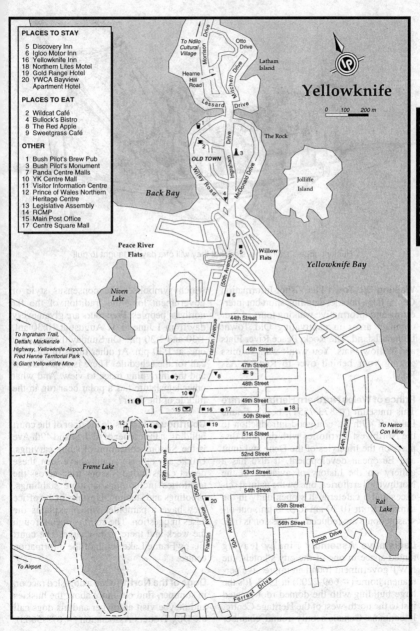

PLACES TO STAY

5 Discovery Inn
6 Igloo Motor Inn
16 Yellowknife Inn
18 Northern Lites Motel
19 Gold Range Hotel
20 YWCA Bayview
Apartment Hotel

PLACES TO EAT

2 Wildcat Café
4 Bullock's Bistro
8 The Red Apple
9 Sweetgrass Café

OTHER

1 Bush Pilot's Brew Pub
3 Bush Pilot's Monument
7 Panda Centre Malls
10 YK Centre Mall
11 Visitor Information Centre
12 Prince of Wales Northern
Heritage Centre
13 Legislative Assembly
14 RCMP
15 Main Post Office
17 Centre Square Mall

Yellowknife

0   100   200 m

NORTHWEST TERRITORIES

Husky puppies sitting in a sled that they will one day be taught to pull

Walking Old Town The Visitor Information Centre has a booklet detailing short but interesting and informative walking tours of four compact areas in captivating Old Town: Latham Island, The Rock, Peace River Flats and Willow Flats. You won't want to miss getting your behind over to Ragged Ass Road.

Prince of Wales Northern Heritage Centre This museum (☎ 873-7551), beside Frame Lake off 49th St, is a good introduction to the Northwest Territories with diorama displays on the lifestyles of the Dene and Inuit and European development. It also has a gallery on the history of aviation in the Northwest Territories, one on the natural sciences and a cafeteria. It's open daily in the summer from 10.30 am to 5.30 pm; out-of-season hours are reduced. Admission is free.

Legislative Assembly Finally leaving rented space in one of the city's hotels, the NWT government found an impressive permanent home (☎ 669-2200) in 1993. It's the large building with the domed roof located just to the north-west of the Heritage Centre. It contains Canada's only round chamber which symbolises the consensus style of government long the tradition of the far northern peoples. Free tours are given every day from 1 June to 31 August at 10:30 am, 1:30 and 3:30 pm. On Sunday there is only one, at 1:30 pm. At other times of the year call for the schedule. There is some fine art and the intriguing mace to view. And what other legislature has a polar bear rug in the middle of the floor?

Courthouse Just inside the door of the court building at the corner of 49th St and 49th Ave is the Sissons collection of stone carvings. Unlike any others you may have seen, these depict cases Judge Sissons tried across the territories including soapstone stabbings, shootings and stealing. Upstairs in the office they have a pamphlet which explains the cases in question. The court is open through the week and there is no charge. The court sits by Frame Lake south of the information centre.

Dogs of the North To see a dog-sled race or, in summer, find out more about the huskies and maybe visit an owner and his dogs call the Dog Trotters Association (☎ 873-5603).

A breeder in town, William Carpenter, has an on-going project in the south-western end of town which has successfully preserved the *kingmik*, a rare Inuit dog.

Bush Pilot's Monument For a good view of the town walk north up Franklin Ave to the Bush Pilot's Monument in Old Town. You can see over the lake and the town's odd assortment of architecture.

Ndilo Village At the northern end of Latham Island, Ndilo (pronounced 'di-lo' and meaning 'end of the road') is the Dogrib Dene aboriginal community of Yellowknife. You're welcome to stroll and often the older men like to chat and can tell you about the old days and ways. On my last visit Richard Edjericon (☎ 873-9830) was setting up some cultural events allowing visitors the chance to see such traditional activities as tanning hides and preparing food. Visitors may also get the chance to have a go at making traditional crafts. Also try the Ndilo Band Office at ☎ 873-8951 for more information.

Dettah This is a small Dogrib Dene village south-east of town across Yellowknife Bay where you can get a look at the traditional way of life of these people. There is nothing particular or striking to see but you can wander around and talk to people and may see some interesting handiwork. You will

also hear the commonly used Dogrib language. There are no tourist facilities. To reach the village, hire a boat or take the 11 km road off the Ingraham Trail north-east of Yellowknife.

Fred Henne Territorial Park In Fred Henne Territorial Park (☎ 920-2472), off the Mackenzie Hwy opposite the airport, there is sandy **Long Lake Beach** and the four-km long **Prospector's Trail**. The excellent walk leads over rocky outcrops, through some bush and around muskeg and by a lake – a real little microcosm of the far north topography. Get the map from the park office and get well oriented because it's not hard to lose the path. Regular, free talks and tours are offered explaining the ecology and geology of the region. Call for details. There is also a campground.

Aurora Borealis From December to April a major attraction is the fabulous northern lights which hold a special fascination for the Japanese. A viewing platform has been set-up 50 km east of town for tours and the chilly, midnight observations.

Organised Tours There is a vast range of short and long tours offered in and around Yellowknife. Among them are walking tours, boat trips, kayak adventures, photography safaris, fishing expeditions and more.

Aurora Borealis

The aurora borealis can be seen from the Yukon, the Northwest Territories and in the far north of the provinces. The best time to see it is around March and April and from late August to late October. It appears in many forms – pillars, streaks, wisps, haloes of vibrating light and sometimes looks like the rippling folds of a curtain. Most often, the aurora borealis glows faintly green or pale rose, but during periods of extreme activity it can flare into bright yellows and crimsons.

The aurora borealis is commonly known as the northern lights, while in the southern hemisphere the phenomenon is known as the aurora australis or southern lights.

The visible aurora is created by solar winds (streams of charged particles from the sun) flowing through the earth's magnetic field in the polar regions. These winds are drawn earthward where the particles collide with electrons and ions in the ionosphere about 160 km above the earth. This collision releases the energy which creates the visible aurora.

The Inuit and other groups attach a spiritual significance to the aurora. Some consider it to be a gift from the dead to light the long polar nights, while others believe it to be a storehouse of events past and future. ■

Raven Tours (☎ 873-4776) offers a variety of options. They have a basic three-hour bus tour of the city and nearby gold mine for $20. A four-hour van trip goes down the Ingraham Trail to Cameron Falls for $30. There are fly-in fishing trips, flights to the barrenlands to view the caribou and other choices.

Author and ecologist Jamie Bastedo of Cygnus Ecotours (☎ 873-4782) leads six recommended nature walks. The two-hour Niven Lake trip features Yellowknife birdlife and a beaver colony and costs $28. The ever-present Canadian Shield, among the world's oldest rock, is discussed. Longer back-country hikes are also offered.

For those with some (minimal) experience, Above & Below Sports (☎ 669-9222) has midnight and Yellowknife shoreline kayak paddles for $45. Those with better skills can consider the multi-day trips.

The Whitlock Family (☎ 873-2489, 1-800-661-0894), offer sailings aboard the MS *Norwetta* cruise ship. There are regular evening cruises on Great Slave Lake for $14 or costly 10 to 12-day voyages up the Mackenzie River to Inuvik in the $2500 range.

Great Slave Sledging Company (☎ 920-4542), has dog-team expeditions for one week to two months. These would be great trips, travelling some traditional routes and seeing wildlife, but they're very costly.

Activities Several outfitters here rent canoes and/or kayaks. Above & Below Sports (☎ 669-9222) at 4100 Franklin Ave has both by the hour or week. Canoes are $25 for 12 hours, the kayaks are more expensive. They also offer kayaking courses.

Canoes can be rented at Eagle Point Rentals (☎ 873-1683) right by the Yellowknife River Bridge on Highway 4 leading out of town. From here you can paddle along the river independently or join in one of the evening nature tours. There are numerous birds and animals to see from this natural area close to town. Across the street from the dock is a picnic area.

The Sportsman (☎ 873-2911), 5118 50th St, rent canoes by the day ($30) and camping supplies.

For the hardy there is swimming at the beach in Fred Henne Park.

Festivals There are various festivals and events held periodically through the year. The Visitor Information Centre will have an up-to-date list of activities planned.

The Caribou Carnival is an annual festival held in late March each year, with parades, concerts, skits and contests like igloo building. The main event of the carnival is the Canadian Championship Dog Derby, a three-day dog-sled race about 240 km long. Folk on the Rocks is a three-day folk concert with musicians from all over the country and the USA. It takes place at Long Lake on the second or third weekend in July. Performances include traditional Inuit throat singers and Dene dancers.

Places to Stay Accommodation and food are expensive in Yellowknife. The cheapest way to live is to buy food at the supermarket in the YK Centre Mall and stay at one of the campgrounds.

The closest campground to town is at *Fred Henne Territorial Park* (☎ 920-2472) which has full facilities including showers and toilets. A site costs $10. If you're arriving by bus ask the driver to drop you off at the entrance. Downtown is easily walkable in under 30 minutes using the trail around Frame Lake. For those with transport, you can also camp at *Prelude Lake Park* or *Reid Lake Park* along the Ingraham Trail for $10; both have toilet and washing facilities.

The *YWCA Bayview Apartment Hotel* (☎ 920-2777), 5004 54th St on the corner of Franklin Ave, takes in both sexes and has 70 rooms that can be rented by the night, week or month. Singles/doubles with kitchenettes cost $75/85. There's dormitory accommodation for $20 a night but it's geared to residents of NWT staying on a long-term basis, not travellers – and it's usually full. Try booking ahead if you want a dorm bed (as the bus from the south arrives about 11 pm).

The Visitor Information Centre has a list of B&Bs, most of which are in the appealing Old Town and they're less money than the hotels. Very good value is *Barb Bromley's* (☎ 873-4786), 31 Morrison Drive overlooking Back Bay. She's been in town a long time and knows it well and charges $50/60. The Old Town's restaurants are just a short stroll away. Nearby the *Pilot's Rest* (☎ 873-3702) up the hill at 3505 Ingraham Trail near the Bush Pilot's Memorial is recommended. It's comfortable, and offers fine views for $50/60. *Eric & Eva's* (☎ 873-5779), 114 Knutsen Ave south of downtown, has rooms for $60/70. The prices for these places includes tax. They are open all year but don't have a lot of space, so it's a good idea to phone before going.

In the hotel category, *Gold Range Hotel* (☎ 873-4441), 5010 50th St, is one of the cheapest at $65/75. It has a bar downstairs which can get a bit noisy and a cafe for basic food at good prices. The *Northern Lites Motel* (☎ 873-6023), on the corner of 50th St and 51st Ave, has rooms for $89/99. *Igloo Motor Inn* (☎ 873-8511), 4115 Franklin Ave half way between downtown and the Old Town, is a friendly place and charges $94/99. At the *Discovery Inn* (☎ 873-4151), 4701 Franklin Ave, rooms are $105/120. *Yellowknife Inn* (☎ 873-2601), on Franklin Ave between 49th and 50th Sts, is the largest hotel in town. Rooms with all the amenities cost $130 single or double.

Places to Eat The eateries in Yellowknife are also a bit pricey, but there are some relative bargains. For the best and cheapest breakfast in town head to *The Diner* on 50th St near Franklin Ave beside the Gold Range Hotel. A full breakfast with unlimited coffee is $5. They also offer value lunch and dinner specials. At the *A&W* on the corner of Franklin Ave and 49th St you can get a hamburger, salad and root beer for just over $5. *Ryan's Family Restaurant*, on the main floor of Panda II Mall, has standard lunches for about $7 but also pastas for a little more. The *Red Apple*, on the corner of Franklin Ave and 47th St, serves Western and Chinese food and has a bar. Sandwiches cost from $4.50 and chop suey $7.50.

For a treat head for the *Wildcat Café* on the corner of Wiley Rd and Doombos Lane in the Old Town. Set in a log cabin reminiscent of Yellowknife's early days, the Wildcat is the territory's best known restaurant. It serves all three meals everyday and on Sunday has a brunch. Lunch, for example fish and rice, costs about $7; dinners such as caribou bourguignon are around $20. It's very popular, particularly in the evening.

Bullock's Bistro at 4 Lessard Drive, in Old Town right by the float-plane base, is a fine, friendly place specialising in fresh fish including char and Great Slave cod. There is also caribou on the menu. Prices range from $8 to $17 but portions are large. It's open six days from 10 am to 9 pm, and Sunday noon to 6 pm. The outside deck is a bonus.

More upmarket is the colourful *Sweetgrass Café* at 5022 47th St with a hip, internationally flavoured menu prepared with care.

Entertainment There are a number of pubs on and around Franklin Ave, most offering live music. If you want to taste some locally brewed beer and aren't too demanding, check out the casual *Bush Pilot's Brew Pub*, 3502 Wiley Rd in the Old Town, more or less opposite the Wildcat Café. You get a free basket of peanuts with your drink and you just throw the shells on the floor.

Things to Buy Yellowknife is the distribution centre and major retailer of craft items from around the territories. Of course, prices are lower in more remote areas but also higher in southern Canada. Whether artistic or purely functional, the goods are not cheap but are authentic and usually well made. Northern Images in YK Centre Mall has various Dene and Inuit works. The North West Company at 5005 Bryson Drive in Old Town, also with an assortment of goods including a wide selection of pelts, is fun to browse around.

Getting There & Away Long-distance buses leave from outside the Yellowknife Inn. Bus tickets for other parts of Northwest Territories and south can be bought from the shop in the lobby, which is the agent for Frontier Coachlines. See also the introductory Getting There & Around section.

Getting Around With strong legs and some time, anywhere in town is walkable. Arctic Frontier (☎ 873-4437/8) runs a city wide bus service which connects the airport, southern suburbs, central downtown and northern old town all the way to Latham Island. It travels along Franklin Ave in the middle portion. The one-way fare is $2 and it doesn't run at night.

The two local taxi companies are City Cab (☎ 873-4444) and Gold Cabs (☎ 873-8888). A cab to the airport is $7 to $10. The city bus will also get you to the airport but it's very slow and doesn't go early in the morning. Avis, Budget and Tilden car-rental companies have representatives in Yellowknife. One of the cheapest though, is Rent a Relic (☎ 873-3400), on the corner of 41st St and Franklin Ave, which has vehicles starting

Native Indians wearing goat wool blankets

from $29 a day. In summer, reserving before arrival is suggested. Bicycles can be rented at Sports Traders on 48th St at the corner of 49th Ave.

Around Yellowknife

The **Ingraham Trail** (Hwy 4) just north of the city is the best and quickest get-away in the Northwest Territories. Starting from the junction with the Mackenzie Hwy, the easily accessible 50-km or so route reveals superb, hilly, rocky Canadian Shield topography dotted with lakes. There are great views and opportunities for good fishing, hiking, canoeing, camping and picnicking. It's best with a car but cycling is possible and several companies from town offer excursions to highlights along the trail. The information centre has a series of pamphlets on the area canoe routes. They range from easy one-day paddles to more challenging five-day civilisation escapes. There are five hiking trails along or near the Ingraham Trail all of them under five km. Aside from those, there is the Martin Lake Trail near Vee Lake and the Bighill Lake Trail near Madeline Lake.

The road is more or less paved to Prelude Lake but in good shape all the way to the end at Tibbit Lake which can be reached in just under an hour.

At **Prelude Lake**, 30 km east of Yellowknife, there is camping, a beach and a 1½-hour-long nature trail. This is a busy weekend, family-oriented spot. Further east watch for the **Cameron Falls** trailhead. The path leads over classic shield terrain to the falls. Nearby at **Bailey Bridge**, which spans Cameron River, there is a small waterfall where the local people swim, though these waters ain't Miami Beach. You can also canoe in the river.

At **Reid Lake**, 60 km from Yellowknife, you can camp, swim or canoe. The Reid Lake campground is busy on weekends otherwise it's very quiet – this is, after all, one of the more remote campgrounds in the country. There's a good beach and walking trail and some fine camp sites on the ridge. Ask for site No 22.

The road ends at **Tibbett Lake**, which is said to be excellent for fishing and is also the start of some fine canoe routes including one to **Pensive Lake**.

Alberta Border to Yellowknife

The first stretch of the Mackenzie Hwy follows the Hay River which flows north into Great Slave Lake. At the border with Alberta, the Visitor Information Centre is open daily in summer from 8 am to 8 pm. As well as road and travel information it has a display of arts & crafts and free coffee. Nearby is a campground with a kitchen shelter and running water. The area between the border and Fort Providence provides the visitor with a good introduction to the uncluttered, wildness of the territories. There are some good stops along the way with campgrounds and walking trails.

About 72 km north of the border is **Twin Falls Gorge Territorial Park**. Here 33-metre Alexandra Falls, named after Princess Alexandra of Britain, is not to be missed. A short trail leads to a platform overlooking the high and wide falls. Nearby, stairs lead down to the water and rocky ledges by the lip of the falls. A further two km north is the parking lot for the smaller, but still impressive, Louise Falls where there is overnight camping. A 45-minute walking trail along the Hay River gorge links the two falls and is a very pleasant hike especially beginning at Louise and heading toward thunderous Alexandra. Just a few km further north is **Escarpment Creek**, a good picnic place with views of the gorge.

Enterprise, with a population of about 60, is the first settlement in the Northwest Territories that you come to. There's a small information office in the Esso service station, a store and a motel. From Enterprise the Mackenzie Hwy is paved most of the way as far as the junction with Hwy 3 which leads to the Mackenzie River ferry at Fort Providence. This portion of the road is also called the Waterfall Route. (North-east out of Enterprise, Hwy 2 takes you to Hay River.)

North of Enterprise is the picnic site of **McNallie Creek Falls** with a waterfall tumbling into a water-worn bowl of rock. About nine km north the **Hart Lake Fire Tower** provides views as far as Great Slave Lake.

Near the village of Kakisa (no services) is **Lady Evelyn Falls** with a walking path to views and the river right beneath the falls. There is good fishing and a very fine campground with tall trees presided over by the roar of the falls. A site is $10 and it's usually full on weekends.

The Mackenzie River ferry, the MV *Merv Hardie* operates well into winter until the ice-bridge is thick enough to carry large trucks. It runs daily between 6 am and midnight, takes about 10 minutes to cross and is free.

Fort Providence, a Slavey community of 700, lies on the banks of the Mackenzie River, 312 km south of Yellowknife. The site was settled in 1861 when a Roman Catholic mission was established, followed soon after by a Hudson's Bay Company trading post. In town there are benches atop the 10-metre cliffs overlooking the river. Past the beautiful wooden church the road leads to the dock. From here you can walk along the shore of the inlet to a small beach and picnic area. The road continues past the large rock to the town cemetery.

The fishing is very good and pike, walleye and maybe grayling can be caught from shore.

About two km before town is a good campground by the river; it has pit toilets and drinking water. Also on the outskirts *Big River Motel* (☎ 699-4301) has a service station, reasonably priced restaurant, general store and rooms from $60. Closer to town, the larger *Snowshoe Inn* (☎ 699-3511) charges $80/100 a single/double. Many of the rooms are booked by anglers. The bar in town is a friendly place. The bus station is at the Snowshoe Inn.

North out of Fort Providence, Hwy 3 follows the western boundary of the **Mackenzie Bison Sanctuary** for nearly 100 km. The sanctuary holds the largest herd of free-ranging pure wood bison in the world, some of which can occasionally be seen by the side of the road. Hiking is not recommended as there are no trails, it's easy to get lost and the bison can be dangerous. From here it's a long haul to the North Arm of Great Slave Lake and the next place to stop.

The dusty but wide and straight road passes through treed and hilly terrain into the twin Dogrib communities of **Rae** and **Edzo**. There is no reason to stop at Edzo although there is a campground just south of town. In Rae there is a gasoline station and basic variety store. Notice the Native Indian street names and the women in their distinctive long dark-blue skirts and colourful kerchiefs. Northwards to Yellowknife you see the rounded, copper-coloured rock outcrops that form part of the Canadian Shield. The road is slow, winding and pretty rough.

Hay River

The town of Hay River, with a population of 3200, sits on the southern shore of Great Slave Lake, 38 km north of Enterprise. This is the heart of Big River Country which encompasses the area and communities by the Mackenzie, Hay and Slave rivers and Great Slave Lake.

With two distinct districts, Hay River tends to sprawl over a wide area. The old town which was badly flooded in the early 1960s is at the north end on Vale Island. The campground and the Métis West Channel fishing village are here. The newer section of town on higher ground is to the south and will be seen first on arrival by road. Most of the services are here including the Visitor Information Centre (☎ 874-3180) on the corner of Mackenzie Hwy and McBryan Drive as well as the modern residential streets. The bus station is between the two areas of town by the bridge over the West Channel.

There are a few things to see around this small but busy town. It's a major distribution centre where barges load up for trips to settlements along the Mackenzie River and up to the Arctic coast. There is a significant commercial fishery here including packing and shipping, primarily of whitefish and lake trout. The broad sandy beach is attractive and you can fish in the surf. A nature trail winds along the Hay River. The Dene Reserve

village of about 260 people, across the river from Old Town, can be visited. There is a Visitor Resource Centre and crafts are available. A series of cultural and sporting events are put on through the summer.

Places to Stay The *Hay River Campground* on Vale Island near the old part of town has sites for $10; facilities include hot showers and a barbecue area. The beach is here and yes, you can swim. There are several hotels and motels and a B&B in town. *Cedar Rest Motel* (☎ 874-37632) is near the bus station and has rooms from $40. *Migrator Motel* (☎ 874-6792) is also close to the bus station and has rooms with kitchenettes for $60/65.

Places To Eat There is a surprising amount of choice here and most of the hotels have dining rooms. The *Boardroom Restaurant* offers caribou, muskox, buffalo and char. Near Old Town is the *New Spring* for Chinese.

Getting There & Away As well as the bus (see Getting There & Around, Northwest Territories earlier) several airlines service Hay River: Canadian North (☎ 874-2434) flies to Inuvik, Yellowknife and points south; Buffalo Airways (☎ 874-3333) flies to Yellowknife; Air Providence (☎ 699-3551 in Fort Providence) connects with Fort Providence; and Ptarmigan Airways (☎ 873-4461 in Yellowknife) flies to Yellowknife, Fort Simpson and other communities on Great Slave Lake.

Fort Smith

This town of 2500 sits astride the Alberta border at Mile 0 of the Northwest Territories highway system. It was once a fur-trading post in the north-western network of depots.

There is a general information centre and one for Wood Buffalo National Park. Also central are the bus station, a museum and the trail to the Rapids of the Drowned. Fort Smith Mission Historic Park is the site of the old Catholic mission. A pelican nesting viewpoint is south of town. The main street is McDougall Rd running right angles to King and Conbear Sts.

There is a campground at Queen Elizabeth Park on the banks of Slave River close to town on the west side. At Liz's Corner Store, 376 Cedar Ave, is the *Fort Smith International Hostel* (☎ 872-3097). Canoes can be rented here. Also in town, the *Pinecrest Hotel* (☎ 872-2320) is quite reasonable, at $50/55 for single/doubles without bath. *Pelican Rapids Inn* (☎ 872-2789) has rooms with kitchenettes for $75.

Nearby is the entrance to Wood Buffalo National Park, for which the town acts as a supply centre. Get your food in town: there is nowhere to buy it in the park.

Wood Buffalo National Park

The road from Hay River travels into this UN World Heritage National Park and then forks splitting off for Fort Smith and Peace Point. Before the turn is Little Buffalo River Falls. The road south from Fort Smith to Fort Chipewyan is not open in summer. For details on the park see the Alberta chapter.

West of Great Slave Lake

At the junction of Hwy 3 south of Fort Providence, Hwy 1, the Mackenzie Hwy, continues west to Fort Simpson and beyond. The gravel road parallels the winding Mackenzie River. At about two-thirds of the way to Fort Simpson stop at **Sambeh Deh Falls** with waterfalls, a gorge and campground.

The 1800-km **Mackenzie River** is Canada's longest river and the 13th longest in the world. The river has been travelled by Native people for thousands of years. Although its present official name honours the Scotsman, Alexander Mackenzie, who canoed and mapped the river in 1789, it is known locally as Deh Cho which simply means 'big river'. It's an important transport route, linking Fort Providence on Great Slave Lake with Inuvik and the Beaufort Sea in the north. Because of the extreme cold, however, it is only navigable for about four months of the year.

There is a ferry to take across the Liard River south of Fort Simpson on Hwy 1 and another one across the Mackenzie at Ndulee Crossing north of Fort Simpson.

Fort Simpson

About 360 km west of Yellowknife, Fort Simpson sits at the confluence of the Liard and Mackenzie rivers. The population of 1200 is mostly Dene with some Métis and non-Native people. This is the major town of the Deh Cho region. With its tour operators and charter airlines, it is also the main park access point for Nahanni, 145 km west of Fort Simpson. The town has a park information office, campground, one hotel with a restaurant and a motel with kitchenettes. It is also the centre for canoe trips along the Mackenzie River and area. There is another campground south of town at the Liard River crossing.

From Fort Simpson the road continues (2½ hours) north to the small Dene community of Wrigley overlooking the Mackenzie River. Hunting, trapping and fishing remain the basis of this mainly log-cabin village. Winter roads connect Norman Wells.

Independent travellers and those with budgets insufficient for Nahanni National Park trips might consider contacting the North Nahanni Naturalist Lodge (☎ 695-2116). Only canoes ply the South Nahanni so for boating, longer trips and flights are required and these cost thousands of dollars. Here, the lodge uses power boats. Run by a Dene husband and wife team, the lodge offers five very interesting trips ranging from three hours to overnight. One goes north along the Mackenzie 32 km to the lesser known **North Nahanni River** which runs through the Mackenzie Mountains. There are plans to build a lodge on Cli Lake from where longer trips up the North Nahanni will be possible. A five-hour trip covering a lot of territory through national park-like scenery along the North Nahanni and the isolated Tetcela Rivers costs $150. There are also boat trips to the Dene outposts of Wrigley and Jean Marie which is otherwise inaccessible in summer. Stops are made along the way at houses, old cabins and hunting camp sites. Trips start at the Ndulee Ferry Crossing on the Mackenzie Hwy 78 km north of Fort Simpson. Wildlife such as bears or moose can sometimes be seen.

Liard Highway (Hwy 7)

From south of Fort Simpson the Liard branches west off the Mackenzie Hwy along the Liard River valley for Nahanni Butte and Fort Liard. The Mackenzie Mountains can be seen to the west. The road then travels south into British Columbia to Fort Nelson making a circle through BC, the NWT and Alberta possible. From Fort Nelson in BC the Alaska Hwy goes northward. Across from Nahanni Butte is Blackstone Territorial Park with information, hiking trails, camping and views of the Liard River. Many trips from the national park end here.

Nahanni National Park

This magnificent wilderness park in the south-western corner of the District of Mackenzie, close to the Yukon border, is one of the major draws of the NWT and attracts visitors from around the world. Nahanni National Park protects a superb portion of the Mackenzie Mountains and the turbulent South Nahanni River with its spectacular canyons. It is visited mainly by canoeists wishing to challenge the white waters (considered amongst the best on the continent) of this renowned 322-km Canadian Heritage River. The park has been designated as a UN World Heritage Site because of its dramatic, pristine nature.

Other highlights include the waterfalls, particularly **Virginia Falls**, which at 96 metres is about twice the height of Niagara Falls, and also the sulphur hot springs at **Rabbitkettle** and **Wildmint**. The park also has abundant wildlife and good hiking and photographic opportunities.

With no road access, the park is not cheap to get to. The only way to reach it is by aeroplane or helicopter, usually as part of a tour although you can do your own self-guided trip.

There are basically two types of visits. The first is on the water. Six-day to three-week canoe or rubber-raft trips eastward take in many of the parks main sites. Four companies offer similar tours geared to a range of ages and abilities including beginners. Adventurers with intermediate paddling

skills can do the river on their own. The 'classic' average trip is 14 days with nine days paddling and five days for hiking and delays. Of course, you could get flown in and canoe back for just a day or two. All canoeists and rafters end up at Blackstone Territorial Park on the Liard River.

The second type of visit is a fly-over sightseeing tour with or without a landing to allow hiking. These trips range from a simple 30-minute flight to a couple of days for some more serious hiking. The basic here is the one-day hike around Victoria Falls. All visitors on a self-guided trip must register with the park office. For camping, there are seven primitive areas set aside with tables as well as fireplaces. There are park offices for information in Fort Simpson (☎ 695-2310), Nahanni National Park, PO Box 348, Fort Simpson, NT X0E 0N0 and at Blackstone Territorial Park.

Organised Tours The park information offices can offer advice and details on short one or two-day trips or the longer tours. Either way, most leave from Fort Simpson. For short park tours and on-your-own river trips see the following Getting There & Away section.

The long, guided canoe and raft trips offered by four operators are excellent but expensive. Prices and nature of the excursions are similar. Different times of the season offer different advantages so ask for details to best match your interests. All of these operators have offices here but trips should be pre-booked, preferably months in advance. You have to get yourself to Fort Simpson. Raft trips are more relaxing, provide more time to enjoy the scenery and are suitable for all ages. The canoe trips are best for people with some basic experience although you needn't be an advanced whitewater paddler.

Whitewolf Adventure Expeditions (☎ (604) 944-5500, 1-800-661-6659), 41 1355 Citadel Drive, Port Coquitlam, British Columbia V3C 5X6, offers several trips ranging from eight to 21-day excursions. The eight-day raft tour is $2200, the 12-day canoe trip $2650 and the full-length tour is $3670. Tax is extra. Black Feather Wilderness Adventures (☎ (613) 722-9717, 1-800-574-8375), 1960 Scott St, Ottawa, Ontario K1Z 8L8, has a similar line-up.

Also try contacting Nahanni River Adventures out of Whitehorse and Nahanni Wilderness Adventures in Alberta. Their addresses and those of other related area businesses can be found in the Nahanni-Ram section of the *Explorers' Guide*.

Getting There & Away There is no road access but the Liard Hwy, which connects Fort Liard with Fort Simpson, follows the eastern side of the Liard River. It passes within 30 km of Nahanni Butte and offers access to the river at Blackstone Territorial Park. Perhaps one day a bridge will make Nahanni more accessible and considerably cheaper.

From Fort Simpson, Fort Liard, Fort Nelson (in British Columbia) or from Watson Lake (in the Yukon), you can fly in by charter plane. Most companies are based in Fort Simpson. Basic half-hour look-see flights are $200 for up to four passengers. Flights into the depths of the park to Moose Ponds with all gear and canoe are in the range of $1650 for two people.

Blackstone Aviation (☎ 695-2111) with a variety of options flies in from Lindberg Landing, near Blackstone Territorial Park. Their float plane can take three passengers with gear or two with gear and canoe. Using a different plane (with wheels) which can take four passengers, a flight to Virginia Falls with a 90-minute stop is $612.

Deh Cho Air (☎ 770-4103) in Fort Liard will fly you in to the falls for $150 per person with four people and can leave you for a couple of days. Wolverine Air (☎ 695-2263) has a couple of half-day and longer trips. Simpson Air/Nahanni Mountain Lodge (☎ 695-2505) in Fort Simpson offer various packages.

For hiking, helicopters can offer more choices. Great Slave Helicopters (☎ 695-2669) have a number of options, and, along

with Wolverine Air and South Nahanni Airways (☎ 695-2007), have begun to offer trips into more remote destinations in the southern Mackenzie Mountains with its spectacular physical features including countless caves, jagged peaks, Scimitar Canyon and tundra-lined Hole-in-the-Wall Valley. On an eight-hour adventure, for $400 if the plane is full, visitors can journey 600 km to the Cirque of the Unclimbables with a stop on a glacier. Helicopters taking up to five passengers make cave exploration in the fascinating karst topography of the Nahanni and Ram Plateaux possible and no special equipment or skills are required.

Blackstone Aviation, Deh Cho Air, Simpson Air and all major tour operators rent boats and equipment.

Fort Liard

At this largely traditional town of 500 there is a two-storey log building erected by Roman Catholic missionaries in 1921. Among the Dene crafts here the birch bark baskets made by women and adorned with porcupine quills are noteworthy.

Norman Wells

On the northern shore of the Mackenzie River halfway between Fort Simpson and Inuvik, this town of 800 has long been (and remains) an oil town. There's a campground in town and several hotels. Air service is available from Edmonton, Yellowknife and Inuvik. Canadian Airlines (☎ 587-2361) has an office here and Great Bear Aviation (☎ 1-800-661-0719) flies to Yellowknife.

Of more interest is the **Canol Heritage Trail**, a hiking trail designated a National Historic Site which leads 372 km south-west to the Yukon border. From there, a road leads to Ross River and the Yukon highway system. Originally intended as an oil-supply route to Whitehorse during WWII, the trail has the remains of army camps and abandoned equipment, as well as peaks, canyons, barrens and lots of wildlife. There are no facilities along this trail.

Inuvik

Inuvik, with a population of 3500, is the territories' second largest town, although it was only founded as late as 1955 as a supply centre. It lies on the East Channel of the Mackenzie River about 90 km south of the Arctic coast. For nearly two months each year, from the end of May, it has 24 hours of daylight every day. The population is roughly divided between Inuit, Dene and non-Native people. Note that the first snow falls sometime around the end of August. Crafts, including locally made parkas, are for sale. The Visitor Information Centre is on Mackenzie Rd, Inuvik's main thoroughfare.

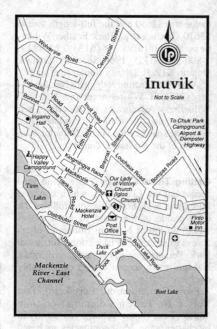

Inuvik

Not to Scale

Things to See & Do The two main attractions in town are the igloo-shaped **Our Lady of Victory Church** and **Ingamo Hall**, a three-storey community centre built of logs. There are several short walking trails beginning from Loucheux Rd. Walking, bus, boat and wildlife-viewing tours are available. The Arctic Tour Company (☎ 979-4100), 181 Mackenzie Rd, offers a 1½-hour bus tour of the town and surrounding tundra for $23. (See also Around Inuvik later.)

Festivals The Arctic Northern Games, the biggest northern games of their kind, are often held in Inuvik in July, but the location and dates change, so ask where and when somewhere further south. The games feature traditional Dene and Inuit sports, contests, dancing, music, crafts and the 'Good Woman' contest, during which women display various household skills such as animal skinning.

Delta Daze is a smaller celebration held on Thanksgiving weekend (October) before the long winter sets in.

Places to Stay Chuk Park Campground, about 3.5 km before town on the Dempster Hwy, is open from June to October and provides hot showers and firewood; the office is open 24 hours a day for the duration. The Dene operate the campground, charge $10 a site and put on various activities. The campground has a good view of the delta and the

breeze keeps the mosquitoes down a bit. In town, Happy Valley Campground has similar facilities and also charges $10 a site.

Hillside B&B (☎ 979-2662), 68 Reliance St, close to the centre and with good mountain views has two rooms at single/double $75/85. In town try Robertson's B&B (☎ 979-3111), 41 Mackenzie Rd, which has laundry and kitchen facilities and rents out bikes and canoes. Both are open year round but you should book ahead in summer.

There are three hotels in Inuvik, all charging about the same price. Cheapest is the Mackenzie Hotel (☎ 979-2861), which has rooms from $110. Finto Motel Inn (☎ 979-2647), on the corner of Mackenzie Rd and Marine Bypass, has singles/doubles for $115/125.

Places to Eat Inuvik doesn't offer a lot of choice. If you're driving, consider bringing in your food (especially from Alaska) and you'll save a few dollars. The Roost, a sand-

⊕⊕⊕⊕⊕⊕⊕⊕⊕⊕⊕⊕⊕⊕⊕⊕

Longest Word
The following is the longest word in the language of the Inuvialuktun Inuit (are you ready?):
Tuktusiuriagatigitqingnapinngitkyptinnga.
It means,'You'll never go caribou hunting with me again'. So there. ■

⊕⊕⊕⊕⊕⊕⊕⊕⊕⊕⊕⊕⊕⊕⊕⊕

wich and burger take-out, is one of the cheapest in town. The hotels have restaurants but the meals aren't cheap. On the menu at the *Green Briar Restaurant* in the Mackenzie Hotel is muskox stew, something rarely seen down south.

Getting There & Around There are scheduled air services from Edmonton, Yellowknife and Whitehorse. (See also the introductory Getting There & Around section.) Aklak Air (☎ 979-3777) flies to places within the region including Tuktoyaktuk, Aklavik and Fort MacPherson. Arctic Wings & Rotors (☎ 979-2220) flies to Aklavik and Tuktoyaktuk. Williams Aero (☎ 587-2243 in Norman Wells) connects Inuvik with Norman Wells. These airlines also offer charter services.

Several companies run buses along the Dempster Hwy between Dawson City and Inuvik. Arctic Tour Company (☎ 979-4100) has three buses a week in each direction; Gold City Tours (☎ 993-5175 in Dawson City) has two a week. The Arctic Tour Company charges $198 one way plus tax. Norline Coaches (☎ 668-3355 in Whitehorse) runs buses from Whitehorse.

Around Inuvik
Inuvik lies in the **Mackenzie Delta** which, covering an area of over 12,000 sq km, is the largest river delta in Canada and one of the world's great wildlife regions. It's home to many fur-bearing animals, and hundreds of species of bird use it for summer nesting.

A number of companies offer a variety of trips on the Mackenzie River. Arctic Tour Company (☎ 979-4100) has two-hour cruises along the East Channel of the river and delta for $30. It also has four-hour, midnight-sun cruises through the delta to Tuktoyaktuk for $130. Midnight Express Tours (☎ 979-2104) offers similar cruises. Western Arctic Nature Tours (☎ 979-3300), next to the igloo church, specialises in ecotourism and has trips to Tuktoyaktuk to view beluga whales and to Herschel Island in the Yukon to watch birds and other wildlife. Small planes connect the more remote communities of the Arctic.

Tuktoyaktuk
About 137 km north-east of Inuvik in Kugmallit Bay on the Arctic coast is Tuktoyaktuk, commonly known as Tuk. Originally the home of the whale-hunting Karngmalit or Mackenzie Inuit, it's a land base for some of the Beaufort Sea oil and gas explorations. Pods of beluga whales can be seen in July and August. In the land around Tuk are *pingos* – huge mounds made of earth and ice caused by frost heaves.

Aklavik
Aklavik, 113 km north of the Arctic Circle and about 50 km west of Inuvik, is home to the Inavaluit and the Gwich'in who, over the centuries, have traded and sometimes fought each other in this region. Aklavik was for a time the administrative centre for the area, but serious flooding and erosion prompted the federal government to move in the 1950s to a new site at Inuvik. The Mad Trapper Jamboree, held at Easter, keeps alive the memory of Albert Johnson, the Mad Trapper of Rat River. He murdered other trappers for their gold fillings, but was finally gunned down in a shoot-out at Eagle River in 1932 by the Mounties, after he'd killed one of their officers.

Paulatuk
This small Karngmalit community is on the Arctic coast at the southern end of Darnley Bay near the mouth of the Hornaday River, about 400 km east of Inuvik. The town's name means 'soot of coal' and one of the main local attractions are the **Smoking Hills**,

NORTHWEST TERRITORIES

which contain smouldering sulphide-rich slate and seams of coal. It's also possible to see caribou, muskox and polar bears in the surrounding lands.

Banks Island

Lying in the Arctic Ocean to the north of Paulatuk, Banks Island may have been inhabited for nearly 3500 years. **Sachs Harbour**, a small Inavaluit community, is the only settlement on the island. Wildlife is abundant and the island has two bird sanctuaries where you can see flocks of snowgeese and sea birds in the summer. In **Aulavik National Park**, on the north of the island, most visitors canoe or raft the Thomsen River. But there is also the world's largest concentration of muskox, badlands, tundra and archaeological sites. Fly-in visits are possible though there are no facilities at all.

Victoria Island

The site of **Cambridge Bay**, in the southeast of the island, was a traditional meeting place of the Inuit who came here for the excellent fishing. Explorers in search of the Northwest Passage often took shelter here and you can see the remains of Roald Amundsen's schooner *Maud*, on the beach in the harbour.

Today Cambridge Bay is a transport and service centre for communities along the Arctic coast. From the town you can hike to **Mt Pelly** to view the birds and other wildlife.

DISTRICT OF FRANKLIN

The District of Franklin is the most northerly and has many islands, including Baffin Island, one of the world's largest, which contains Auyuittuq National Park. Ellesmere Island National Park consists of the northern section of Ellesmere Island way up at the peak of the Canadian Arctic, not far from Greenland's north-western edge. Not one tree grows in the entire District of Franklin but many flowers bloom during the short summer. The northern regions are almost completely uninhabited. There is the odd weather station, military installation or biological research centre.

Access to the district is by boat or plane.

Baffin Island

Iqaluit This town, formerly called Frobisher Bay, is on the east coast of Baffin Island in the eastern section of the territories. In 1984 the town voted to change the name back to Iqaluit (pronounced 'ee-KAL-oo-it'), its original Inuit name meaning 'the place of fish'. It was established in 1942 as a US Air Force base and is now a fairly large settlement of 2600. In 1999 it will become the capital of Nunavut. Iqaluit is the first stop on the fly-in trip to Auyuittuq National Park. There is not much to see or do here but a variety of side trips is possible and there are a number of hiking trails marked by inukshuks (human-like figures made of rocks), which take you past archaeological sites and out into the tundra. Most people coming here stop off as part of a package tour enroute to somewhere else.

Places to Stay Accommodation is costly. *By-The-Sea Accommodations* (☎ 979-0219) in Apex, five km from town has B&B rooms

---

🏵🏵🏵🏵🏵🏵🏵🏵🏵🏵🏵🏵🏵🏵🏵🏵🏵🏵🏵🏵🏵🏵🏵🏵🏵🏵🏵🏵🏵🏵🏵🏵🏵🏵

The North Pole

The North Pole, the imaginary point at the northern tip of the Earth's axis and about 800 km north of Ellesmere Island, lies in neutral territory – an area of permanently frozen water without national jurisdiction. However, the Magnetic North Pole, the direction to which a compass needle points at an angle to true north, is in Canada. Although it wanders around from year to year, the Magnetic North Pole is currently just north of Bathurst Island west of Cornwallis Island at about 100° longitude. In 1966 it was south of the island, in 1979 it was on the island and now it is just beyond the northern end of the island. ■

🏵🏵🏵🏵🏵🏵🏵🏵🏵🏵🏵🏵🏵🏵🏵🏵🏵🏵🏵🏵🏵🏵🏵🏵🏵🏵🏵🏵🏵🏵🏵🏵🏵🏵

at single/double $95/120. There are kitchen and laundry facilities. The *Toonoonik Hotel* (☎ 979-6733) charges $125/145 and there is a dining room. Even more expensive is the *Navigator Inn* (☎ 979-6201) with restaurant and bar.

There is a *campground* as well.

Getting There & Away Canadian Airlines (☎ 979-6470) has an office in Iqaluit. Once a week in the summer, First Air (☎ 979-5810) flies from here to Nuuk, the capital of Greenland. It also has scheduled air services from Montreal, Ottawa, Yellowknife and Edmonton.

Auyuittuq National Park Covering an area of 21,470 sq km, this is Canada's third largest national park and one of the world's few national parks north of the Arctic Circle. Pronounced 'ah-you-EE-tuk', the word means 'the land that never melts'. Most of the park is a beautiful, pristine wilderness consisting of mountains, valleys, fjords and meadows. Most visitors go for the hiking along 96-km **Pangnirtung Pass** – between late June and early September when it's free of snow. Cross-country skiing in the spring and climbing are also good. Being north of the Arctic Circle the park has 24 hours of daylight each day from May to the end of July, although the weather is unpredictable and temperatures remain low.

Many tour companies offer trips in the park – see the Northwest Territories *Explorers' Guide*.

Places to Stay There are two primitive *campgrounds* in the park: at Overlord and Summit Lake. There are also seven emergency shelters along the Pangnirtung Pass. Hikers should be physically fit as the trail is considered hard going. Most visitors spend four to seven days. For more information on the park, contact the Superintendent (☎ 473-8828), Auyuittuq National Park, Pangnirtung, NWT, X0A 0R0.

Getting There & Away The problem with the place is getting there – it's expensive.

The gray, or timber, wolf lives in packs of several to two dozen and is thought to mate for life

First you must fly from one of the major cities to Iqaluit, which is nearly 300 km from the park. Canadian Airlines and First Air fly to Iqaluit from where you have to catch another flight to Pangnirtung near the southern edge of the park or to Broughton Island, at the eastern edge. First Air flies from Iqaluit to both places and from either point you walk or go by canoe (after the ice breaks up in July) into the park.

Pangnirtung Pang, as it's often referred to, is a town with about 1100 residents, beautifully set alongside a fjord amidst mountains at the entrance to Auyuittuq National Park. It lies at the southern end of Pangnirtung Pass 40 km south of the Arctic Circle and acts as the jumping-off point for park visitors. No alcohol is permitted in the town: this is one of numerous northern communities that have voted themselves 'dry' to help alleviate alcohol-related problems. First Air has daily flights to Iqaluit.

Things to See & Do Two walking trails begin in town. One, following the Duval River, takes about three hours. The other, following the Ikuvik River uphill, offers a fine view of the fjord and takes about six hours. Good boots are recommended for both trails.

About 50 km south of town is the **Kekerten National Historic Park**, an old whaling station. A trail leads around parts of the island past the remains of the 19th-century houses, tools and graves. An interpretive centre provides background information. The park is about two hours by boat from Pangnirtung.

Places to Stay There's camping at the *Pisuktinu-Tungavik* campground or you can stay at the *Auyuittuq Lodge* (☎ 473-8955) for $125; the lodge also has a dining room.

Things to Buy The town has a reputation for its woven tapestries which can be seen and purchased at several shops or at the Inuit Co-op in town. Most of the tapestries are pictorial, depicting scenes from the tradi-

tional lifestyle of the region. Prices range from the high hundreds to several thousand dollars. Less costly items such as sweaters, scarves and the popular crocheted Pang hats are also available.

Cape Dorset At Cape Dorset, on the southwest coast of Baffin Island, the remains of an ancient Inuit civilisation which existed between 1000 BC and 1100 AD, were first found. Nowadays it is most noted as a centre for contemporary Inuit art. It's also a good place from which to go hiking, or bird watching in the **Dewey Soper Bird Sanctuary**.

Bylot Island

Off the north-east of Baffin Island in Lancaster Sound, is this island bird sanctuary, a summer nesting ground for snow geese and home to other birds like murres and kittiwakes. The waters around the island are also rich in marine life. Access is by boat from Pond Inlet.

Ellesmere Island

Ellesmere Island National Park This national park, way up at the northern tip of Ellesmere Island at the top of the world, is for wealthy wilderness seekers only. Visitors camp and walk. It features **Cape Columbia**, the northernmost point of North America, **Mt Barbeau**, one of the highest peaks on the eastern side of the continent, **Lake Hazen** and numerous glaciers. Around the park are thermal oases where plants and animals are able to survive despite the harsh climate.

DISTRICT OF KEEWATIN

To the west, the District of Keewatin consists of a vast, rocky, barren plateau, part of the Canadian Shield, with only 4800 people; to the east its official boundaries incorporate much of Hudson Bay and James Bay. Most of the Inuit population lives in this district, in settlements along the western shores of Hudson Bay. As well as English, the main language of the area is Inuktitut which means 'language of the people' and is written in a series of symbols.

Farley Mowat's *Never Cry Wolf* tells the

story of a man who lived among the wolves in Keewatin; another, *People of the Deer*, tells of the hardship inflicted on the Padlirmiut Inuit as a result of the change in migration patterns of the caribou in the 1940s and 1950s.

Accommodation is available in all the communities, but it is expensive and you'll need to book ahead. Calm Air (☎ 645-2746) has scheduled flights to Rankin Inlet from Churchill in Manitoba and serves other communities in the district. NWT Air connects Rankin Inlet with Yellowknife and Iqaluit.

Arviat

Arviat, formerly called Eskimo Point, is Keewatin's most southerly settlement. This was originally the site of a summer camp used by several groups of Inuit who lived along the western coast of Hudson Bay and on the mainland tundra. The Hudson's Bay Company established a trading post here in the 1920s and the community now has a population of about 1100. People still make a living from fishing, hunting and trapping.

From Arviat you can arrange a trip south to **McConnell River Bird Sanctuary** where, from June onwards, about 400,000 snow geese nest, together with snowy owls, Arctic terns, falcons and others.

Rankin Inlet

Founded in 1955 as a mining centre, Rankin Inlet, with a population of about 1500, is Keewatin's largest community and the government and transport centre for the district. From here you can go fishing in the bay or in the many rivers and lakes. In Hudson Bay, about 50 km from Rankin Inlet, is **Marble Island**, a graveyard for James Knight and his crew who were seeking the Northwest Passage in the 18th century. Some 19th-century whaling ships are there too. You can also hike to the **Ijiraliq Archaeological Site**, at the mouth of the Meliadine River, and explore the 15th-century underground houses of the Thule Inuit.

Baker Lake

Geographically, Baker Lake lies at the centre of Canada. It's good for fishing and is the departure point for canoe or raft trips on the Dubawnt, Kazan and Hanbury-Thelon rivers. From Baker Lake you can arrange a visit west to **Thelon Game Sanctuary**, founded in 1927 by the federal government to save the then-endangered musk ox, and where many indigenous animals are now protected. Baker Lake is also noted for its Inuit artwork.

Repulse Bay

Sitting on the Arctic Circle at the southern end of Melville Peninsula, Repulse Bay is a natural harbour. For centuries whaling ships set off from here. You can go whale-watching to see beluga or narwhal whales (August is the best time) or take a boat out fishing.

Glossary

Acadians – The first settlers from France who lived in Nova Scotia.

Atlantic Provinces – This refers to Newfoundland, Nova Scotia, Prince Edward Island and New Brunswick. See Maritime Provinces entry later.

aurora borealis – Also called the northern lights, they are charged particles from the sun which are trapped in the earth's magnetic field. They appear as other-worldly coloured, waving beams.

badlands – A dry, barren, arid region of unusual, irregular features of erosion and prehistoric fossils. In Canada, this region is mostly found in southern Alberta.

bakeapple – Also called the golden bakeapple and a speciality of Newfoundland, it's a type of berry which is often used for jam or pies.

beaver fever (giardiasis) – The bacteria which causes this disease is found in many freshwater streams and lakes. It affects the digestive tract and can be avoided by boiling drinking water.

boîtes à chanson – Generally cheap, casual and relaxed folk clubs, popular in Quebec.

boondoggle – A futile or unnecessary project or work.

boreal – Refers to the Canadian north and its character, as in the boreal forest, the boreal wind, etc.

Bluenose II – A well-known, widely travelled replica of Canada's famous sailing vessel.

brew pub – A pub that brews and sells its own beer.

cabin fever – A traditional term still used to indicate a stir-crazy, frustrated state of mind due to being cooped up indoors over the long northern winter. By extension, it's used to denote the same feelings due to being forced to remain in the house, cottage, or tent for a period of time because of inclement weather or bad health.

calèche – Horse-drawn carriages which can be taken around parts of Montreal and Quebec City.

Canadian Shield – Also known as the Precambrian or Laurentian Shield, it is a plateau of rock that was formed 2.5 billion years ago and covers much of the northern region of the country.

ceilidh – Pronounced 'KAY-lee'; a Gaelic word meaning an informal gathering for song, dance and story. It is sometimes known as a house party; especially popular in Prince Edward Island.

clearcut – This is an area where loggers have cut every tree, large and small, leaving nothing standing.

coulees – Gulches, usually dry.

Cowichan – The name of a Native Indian people originally from the Lake Cowichan area on Vancouver Island (BC); also the name given to the hand-knitted, 100% wool sweaters they produce.

dome car – The two-levelled, glass-topped observation car of a train.

Doukhobours – A Russian Christian pacifist sect, some of whom settled in Canada during the 19th century.

First Nations – A term used to denote Canada's aboriginal peoples. It can be used instead of Native Indians or Native people.

flowerpots – Unusual rock formations, these irregular geological forms are created by erosion effects of waves. Examples can be seen at Tobermory in Ontario and at The Rocks in New Brunswick.

fruit leather – A blend of fruit purees dried into thin sheets and pressed together. It's great for backpacking and hiking.

gasoline – Petrol, known as gasoline or simply gas (gaz in Quebec). Almost all gasoline in Canada is termed unleaded and comes in regular and more costly higher-octane versions.

Haligonians – Residents of Halifax, Nova Scotia.

hoodoos – Fantastically shaped pillars of sandstone rock formed by erosion found in badland regions mainly in southern Alberta.

igloo – The traditional Inuit houses made from blocks of ice.

information chalets – Tourist information booths found in Newfoundland.

Innu – Another name for the Montagnais and Naskapi peoples.

inukshuk – Inuit preferred to trap caribou in water where they could be hunted from a kayak. For this reason they built stone figures called 'inukshuks', next to lakes to direct the animals into the water.

Inside Passage – The sea route from the Alaskan Panhandle to Washington state that runs between the coast of mainland British Columbia and the chain of islands off the coast.

interior camping – This refers to usually lone, individual sites accessible only by foot or canoe. When found in provincial or national parks, pre-registering with park authorities is required for your own safety.

Liveyers – European descendants who lived in small villages along the Strait of Belle Isle in Labrador.

Lotto 649 – The country's most popular, highest-paying lottery.

Loyalists – They were residents of America who maintained their allegiance to Britain during the American Revolution and fled to Canada.

mall – A shopping centre, usually enclosed and containing a range of retail stores. The larger ones generally include a number of low-cost fast-food places at which to eat.

Maritime Provinces – Also known as the Maritimes, this refers to the three provinces: New Brunswick, Nova Scotia and Prince Edward Island.

Mennonites – A religious Utopian group originating in Europe who are mostly found in the Kitchener-Waterloo region of southern Ontario.

Métis – Canadians of French and Native Indian stock.

Mounties – Royal Canadian Mounted Police (RCMP)

mukluks – Moccasins or boots made from sealskin and often trimmed with fur; usually made by Inuit people.

muskeg – Undrained boggy land most often found in northern Canada.

Naskapi – A group of Native Indians, also called the Innu. They are found in north-eastern Quebec.

Newfie – A term applying to residents of Newfoundland, or 'The Rock' as it is sometimes known.

no-see-um – Any of various tiny biting insects which are difficult to see and which can annoy travellers when out in the woods or along some beaches. No-see-um netting, a very fine mesh screen on a tent, is designed to keep the insects out.

Ogopogo – A monster, similar to the Loch Ness monster, thought to reside within the waters of Okanagan Lake (BC). It has never been photographed.

outports – Small, isolated coastal villages of Newfoundland, connected with the rest of the province by boat.

permafrost – Permanently frozen subsoil that covers the far north of Canada.

portage – The process of transporting boats and supplies overland between navigable waterways. It can also refer to the overland route used for such a purpose.

petroglyphs – Ancient paintings or carvings on rock.

potlatch – A competitive ceremonial activity among some Native people, usually those found along the coast of BC, which traditionally involved a lavish distribution of gifts and destruction of property to emphasise the wealth and status of the chief or clan. It now refers to a wild party or revel.

public/separate schools – The two basic school systems. Both are free and essentially the same but the latter is designed for Catholics and offers more religious education.

pysankas – Ukrainian term for painted Easter eggs.

qiviut – The wool of the musk ox that was traditionally woven into garments by some Inuit groups in the far north.

Québecois – The local tongue of Quebec where the vast majority of the population is French; also known as *joual*. The term also refers to the residents of Quebec although it is only applied to the French, not English Quebeckers.

rock hounds – Rock collectors.

rubby – A derelict alcoholic who is often homeless. The term comes from rubbing alcohol which is often mixed with cheap wine for drinking.

RV – Recreational vehicle (usually a motorhome).

screech – A particularly strong rum once available only in Newfoundland, but now widely available across Canada, but in diluted form.

sourdough – Refers to a person who has completed one year's residency in northern Canada.

spelunking – The exploration and study of caves.

steamies – Hot dogs in Quebec which get their name from the way they are cooked.

sub-compact cars – These are the smallest cars available either for purchase or rent. They are smaller than compacts, which are one size down from standard cars.

sugar-making moon – A former Native Indian term for the spring date when the maple tree's sap begins to run.

sugar shack – The place where the collected maple sap is distilled in large kettles and boiled as part of the production of maple syrup.

taiga – The coniferous forests extending across much of subarctic North America and Eurasia.

trailer – In Canada, as well as in the USA, this refers to a caravan or a mobile home (house trailer). It can also refer to the type of vehicle used for transporting goods.

trap line – A marked area along which a trapper will set traps to catch fur-bearing animals.

tundra – The vast, treeless Arctic plains, north of the treeline and with a perpetually frozen subsoil.

voyageur – A boatman employed by one of the early fur-trading companies. He could also fill the function of a woodsman, guide, trapper or explorer.

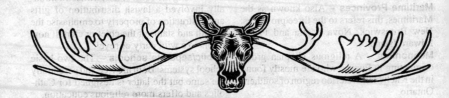

Index

MAPS

951

LONELY PLANET JOURNEYS

FULL CIRCLE: A South American Journey by Luis Sepúlveda (translated by Chris Andrews)
Full Circle invites us to accompany Chilean writer Luis Sepúlveda on 'a journey without a fixed itinerary'. Extravagant characters and extraordinary situations are memorably evoked: gauchos organising a tournament of lies, a scheming heiress on the lookout for a husband, a pilot with a corpse on board his plane . . . Part autobiography, part travel memoir, *Full Circle* brings us the distinctive voice of one of South America's most compelling writers.

THE GATES OF DAMASCUS by Lieve Joris (translated by Sam Garrett)
This best-selling book is a beautifully drawn portrait of contemporary Syria. Through her intimate contact with local people, Lieve Joris explores women's lives and family relationships – the hidden world that lies behind the gates of Damascus.

IN RAJASTHAN by Royina Grewal
Indian travel writer Royina Grewal takes us behind the exotic facade of this fabled destination: here is an insider's perceptive account of India's most colourful state. *In Rajasthan* discusses folk music and architecture, feudal traditions and regional cuisine . . . Most of all, it focuses on people – from maharajahs to itinerant snake charmers – to convey the excitement and challenges of a region in transition.

ISLANDS IN THE CLOUDS: Travels in the Highlands of New Guinea by Isabella Tree
This is the fascinating account of a journey to the remote and beautiful Highlands of Papua New Guinea and Irian Jaya. The author travels with a PNG Highlander who introduces her to his intriguing and complex world. *Islands in the Clouds* is a thoughtful, moving book, full of insights into a region that is rarely noticed by the rest of the world.

KINGDOM OF THE FILM STARS: Journey into Jordan by Annie Caulfield
With honesty and humour, Annie Caulfield writes of travelling in Jordan and falling in love with a Bedouin. Her book offers fascinating insights into the country and unpicks some of the tight-woven Western myths about the Arab world within the intimate framework of a compelling love story.

LOST JAPAN by Alex Kerr
Lost Japan draws on the author's personal experiences of Japan over a period of 30 years. Alex Kerr takes his readers on a backstage tour: friendships with Kabuki actors, buying and selling art, studying calligraphy, exploring rarely visited temples and shrines . . . The Japanese edition of this book was awarded the 1994 Shincho Gakugei Literature Prize for the best work of non-fiction.

SEAN & DAVID'S LONG DRIVE by Sean Condon
Sean and David are young townies who have rarely strayed beyond city limits. One day, for no good reason, they set out to discover their homeland, and what follows is a wildly entertaining adventure that covers half of Australia. Sean Condon has written a hilarious, offbeat road book that mixes sharp insights with deadpan humour and outright lies.

SHOPPING FOR BUDDHAS by Jeff Greenwald
Shopping for Buddhas is Jeff Greenwald's story of his obsessive search for the perfect Buddha statue. In the backstreets of Kathmandu, he discovers more than he bargained for . . . and his souvenir-hunting turns into an ironic metaphor for the clash between spiritual riches and material greed. Politics, religion and serious shopping collide in this witty account of an enlightening visit to Nepal.

LONELY PLANET TRAVEL ATLASES

Lonely Planet has long been famous for the number and quality of its guidebook maps. Now we've gone one step further and in conjunction with Steinhart Katzir Publishers produced a handy companion series: Lonely Planet travel atlases – maps of a country produced in book form.

Unlike other maps, which look good but lead travellers astray, our travel atlases have been researched on the road by Lonely Planet's experienced team of writers. All details are carefully checked to ensure the atlas corresponds with the equivalent Lonely Planet guidebook.

The handy atlas format means no holes, wrinkles, torn sections or constant folding and unfolding. These atlases can survive long periods on the road, unlike cumbersome fold-out maps. The comprehensive index ensures easy reference.

- full-colour throughout
- maps researched and checked by Lonely Planet authors
- place names correspond with Lonely Planet guidebooks
  – no confusing spelling differences
- legend and travelling information in English, French, German, Japanese and Spanish
- size: 230 x 160 mm

Available now:
Chile & Easter Island; Egypt; India & Bangladesh; Israel & the Palestinian Territories; Jordan, Syria & Lebanon; Laos; Thailand; Vietnam; Zimbabwe, Botswana & Namibia

LONELY PLANET TV SERIES & VIDEOS

Lonely Planet travel guides have been brought to life on television screens around the world. Like our guides, the programmes are based on the joy of independent travel, and look honestly at some of the most exciting, picturesque and frustrating places in the world. Each show is presented by one of three travellers from Australia, England or the USA and combines an innovative mixture of video, Super-8 film, atmospheric soundscapes and original music.

Videos of each episode – containing additional footage not shown on television – are available from good book and video shops, but the availability of individual videos varies with regional screening schedules.

Video destinations include: Alaska; Australia (Southeast); Brazil; Ecuador & the Galápagos Islands; Indonesia; Israel & the Sinai Desert; Japan; La Ruta Maya (Yucatán, Guatemala & Belize); Morocco; North India (Varanasi to the Himalaya); Pacific Islands; Vietnam; Zimbabwe, Botswana & Namibia.

Coming soon: The Arctic (Norway & Finland); Baja California; Chile & Easter Island; China (Southeast); Costa Rica; East Africa (Tanzania & Zanzibar); Great Barrier Reef (Australia); Jamaica; Papua New Guinea; the Rockies (USA); Syria & Jordan; Turkey.

The Lonely Planet TV series is produced by:
Pilot Productions
Duke of Sussex Studios
44 Uxbridge St
London W8 7TG UK

Lonely Planet videos are distributed by:
IVN Communications Inc
2246 Camino Ramon
California 94583, USA

107 Power Road, Chiswick
London W4 5PL UK

Music from the TV series is available on CD & cassette.
For ordering information contact your nearest Lonely Planet office.

PLANET TALK

Lonely Planet's FREE quarterly newsletter

We love hearing from you and think you'd like to hear from us.

*When...*is the right time to see reindeer in Finland?
*Where...*can you hear the best palm-wine music in Ghana?
*How...*do you get from Asunción to Areguá by steam train?
*What...*is the best way to see India?

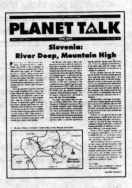

For the answer to these and many other questions read PLANET TALK.

Every issue is packed with up-to-date travel news and advice including:

* a letter from Lonely Planet co-founders Tony and Maureen Wheeler
* go behind the scenes on the road with a Lonely Planet author
* feature article on an important and topical travel issue
* a selection of recent letters from travellers
* details on forthcoming Lonely Planet promotions
* complete list of Lonely Planet products

To join our mailing list contact any Lonely Planet office.

Also available: Lonely Planet T-shirts. 100% heavyweight cotton.

LONELY PLANET ONLINE

Get the latest travel information before you leave or while you're on the road

Whether you've just begun planning your next trip, or you're chasing down specific info on currency regulations or visa requirements, check out the Lonely Planet World Wide Web site for up-to-the-minute travel information.

As well as travel profiles of your favourite destinations (including interactive maps and full-colour photos), you'll find current reports from our army of researchers and other travellers, updates on health and visas, travel advisories, and the ecological and political issues you need to be aware of as you travel.

There's an online travellers' forum (the Thorn Tree) where you can share your experiences of life on the road, meet travel companions and ask other travellers for their recommendations and advice. We also have plenty of links to other Web sites useful to independent travellers.

With tens of thousands of visitors a month, the Lonely Planet Web site is one of the most popular on the Internet and has won a number of awards including GNN's Best of the Net travel award.

http://www.lonelyplanet.com

LONELY PLANET PRODUCTS

Lonely Planet is known worldwide for publishing practical, reliable and no-nonsense travel information in our guides and on our web site. The Lonely Planet list covers just about every accessible part of the world. Currently there are eight series: *travel guides, shoestring guides, walking guides, city guides, phrasebooks, audio packs, travel atlases* and *Journeys* – a unique collection of travellers' tales.

EUROPE

Austria • Baltic States & Kaliningrad • Baltic States phrasebook • Britain • Central Europe on a shoestring • Central Europe phrasebook • Czech & Slovak Republics • Denmark • Dublin city guide • Eastern Europe on a shoestring • Eastern Europe phrasebook • Finland • France • Greece • Greek phrasebook • Hungary • Iceland, Greenland & the Faroe Islands • Ireland • Italy • Mediterranean Europe on a shoestring • Mediterranean Europe phrasebook • Paris city guide • Poland • Prague city guide • Russia, Ukraine & Belarus • Russian phrasebook • Scandinavian & Baltic Europe on a shoestring • Scandinavian Europe phrasebook • Slovenia • St Petersburg city guide • Switzerland • Trekking in Greece • Trekking in Spain • Ukrainian phrasebook • Vienna city guide • Walking in Switzerland • Western Europe on a shoestring • Western Europe phrasebook

NORTH AMERICA

Alaska • Backpacking in Alaska • Baja California • California & Nevada • Canada • Florida • Hawaii • Honolulu city guide • Los Angeles city guide • Mexico • Miami city guide • New England • New Orleans city guide • Pacific Northwest USA • Rocky Mountain States • San Francisco city guide • Southwest USA • USA phrasebook

CENTRAL AMERICA & THE CARIBBEAN

Central America on a shoestring • Costa Rica • Cuba • Eastern Caribbean • Guatemala, Belize & Yucatán: La Ruta Maya • Jamaica

SOUTH AMERICA

Argentina, Uruguay & Paraguay • Bolivia • Brazil • Brazilian phrasebook • Buenos Aires city guide • Chile & Easter Island • Chile & Easter Island travel atlas • Colombia • Ecuador & the Galápagos Islands • Latin American Spanish phrasebook • Peru • Quechua phrasebook • Rio de Janeiro city guide • South America on a shoestring • Trekking in the Patagonian Andes • Venezuela

Travel Literature: Full Circle: A South American Journey

ANTARCTICA

Antarctica

ISLANDS OF THE INDIAN OCEAN

Madagascar & Comoros • Maldives & Islands of the East Indian Ocean • Mauritius, Réunion & Seychelles

AFRICA

Arabic (Moroccan) phrasebook • Africa on a shoestring • Cape Town city guide • Central Africa • East Africa • Egypt • Egypt travel atlas • Ethiopian (Amharic) phrasebook • Kenya • Morocco • North Africa • South Africa, Lesotho & Swaziland • Swahili phrasebook • Trekking in East Africa • West Africa • Zimbabwe, Botswana & Namibia • Zimbabwe, Botswana & Namibia travel atlas

ALSO AVAILABLE:

Travel with Children • Traveller's Tales